The Age of Interconnection

JONATHAN SPERBER

The Age of Interconnection
A Global History of the Second Half of the Twentieth Century

OXFORD
UNIVERSITY PRESS

Oxford University Press is a department of the University of Oxford. It furthers the University's objective of excellence in research, scholarship, and education by publishing worldwide. Oxford is a registered trade mark of Oxford University Press in the UK and certain other countries.

Published in the United States of America by Oxford University Press
198 Madison Avenue, New York, NY 10016, United States of America.

© Jonathan Sperber 2023

All rights reserved. No part of this publication may be reproduced, stored in a retrieval system, or transmitted, in any form or by any means, without the prior permission in writing of Oxford University Press, or as expressly permitted by law, by license, or under terms agreed with the appropriate reproduction rights organization. Inquiries concerning reproduction outside the scope of the above should be sent to the Rights Department, Oxford University Press, at the address above.

You must not circulate this work in any other form
and you must impose this same condition on any acquirer.

Library of Congress Control Number: 2022937044

ISBN 978–0–19–091895–8

DOI: 10.1093/oso/9780190918958.001.0001

1 3 5 7 9 8 6 4 2
Printed by Lakeside Book Company, United States of America

CONTENTS

List of Figures   vii
List of Tables   ix
List of Maps   xi
Acknowledgments   xiii

Introduction   1

Part 1: The Material World   9
CHAPTER 1   Nature   11
CHAPTER 2   Disease   41
CHAPTER 3   Technologies   82

Part 2: Interactions   127
CHAPTER 4   Markets   129
CHAPTER 5   Migrations   168
CHAPTER 6   The Powers   206

Part 3: Varieties of the Social   295
CHAPTER 7   Societies   297
CHAPTER 8   Labor   357

CHAPTER 9	Leisure 400	
CHAPTER 10	Consumers 436	

Part 4: Dreams and Nightmares 475

CHAPTER 11	Beliefs 477
CHAPTER 12	Mass Murder 530
CHAPTER 13	Utopias 572

Aftermath 626

Conclusions 641

Notes 655

Select Bibliography 737

Index 755

LIST OF FIGURES

1.1	Average Yearly CO_2 Emissions, 1950–2010, by Decade	34
1.2	Atmospheric Carbon Dioxide Content, 1959–2014	35
2.1	Spread of Malaria, Worldwide, in the Last Third of the Twentieth Century	54
2.2	Worldwide Cigarette Consumption in the Twentieth Century	61
2.3	Mortality Rate for Non-Infectious Diseases in the US, 1950–2000	62
2.4	Overweight and Obese Adults (Ages 20–74) in the US, 1960s–1990s	66
2.5	Average Yearly Percentage Change in Infectious Disease Mortality in the US, 1900–1995	73
3.1	Global Energy Production, 1949–2000	84
3.2	World Auto Production, 1950–1998	97
3.3	Passenger Kilometers Flown Yearly, Worldwide, 1950–2000	98
3.4	Global Average Crop Yields, 1961–2000	108
4.1	Growth of International Financial Transactions, 1973–1998	145
4.2	Foreign Investments, Worldwide, 1914–2000	146
4.3	Yearly Change in the Global Product, 1951–2001	164
5.1	Immigration to Three Major Trans-Pacific Destinations, 1950–1999	196
5.2	Immigrant Proportion of US Population, 1860–2010	203
5.3	Immigration into Sweden, 1950–2016	204
7.1	Natural Population Increase Worldwide, 1950–2000	310
7.2a	Total Fertility Rates Worldwide, 1950–2000	311
7.2b	Life Expectancy at Birth, 1950–2000	312
7.3	Youth and Age in the World, 1950–2000	313

7.4	Women of Peak Reproductive Age (25–29) in the Labor Force, 1950–1990	344
7.5	Women College Graduates per 100 Men College Graduates, Age 25 and Older	347
7.6	Illegitimate Births in Five Countries, c. 1970 to c. 2010	350
8.1	Union Membership in Five Countries during the Twentieth Century	379
8.2	Strikes in Wealthier Countries during the Second Half of the Twentieth Century	384
8.3	Strikes in Poorer Countries, 1950s–1980s	385
9.1	International Tourist Arrivals, 1950–2015	432
10.1	Growth in Number of Air Passengers Worldwide, 1950–2000	457
10.2	Growth in Number of US Air Passengers, 1950–2000	458
11.1	The Fate of Progress in the Second Half of the Twentieth Century	490
C.1	The Exponential Function, $y = e^x$	642

LIST OF TABLES

2.1	Global Obesity 2008: Percent Over-20 Population Obese	67
3.1	Crossing the Threshold of Automobilization, 1950–2000	92
9.1	Reaching 200–250 TV Sets per 1,000 Inhabitants	411
10.1	TVs and Telephones (in Millions) Worldwide, 1960–1990	460
13.1	The Economic Fate of Post-Communist Eastern Europe	623

LIST OF MAPS

	The World in 1945	xv
	The World in 2001	xv
	Colonial Empires in 1945	xvi
	Colonial Empires in 2001	xvi
6.1	Countries under Communist Rule, 1945–2000	213
6.2	Germany, 1949–1990	230
6.3	Revolutionary Nonaligned Countries of the 1970s and 1980s	246

ACKNOWLEDGMENTS

IN THE COURSE OF writing a very long book, I have received a lot of advice and encouragement. What follows is a small selection from a larger universe.

Material from this book was presented at the University of Chicago, Carnegie-Mellon University, and as the 2021 Gerald Feldman Memorial Lecture at the German Historical Institute in Washington, DC. Invitations for these opportunities were extended by Jan Goldstein, John Boyer, Donna Harsch, Simone Lässig, and Kenneth Ledford. My thanks to them and to the participants in the events for their many questions and observations. I am indebted to my colleagues in the department of history at the University of Missouri, who made unusually helpful suggestions, generously deployed their specialized knowledge, and saved me from evident blunders: Merve Fejzula, Gerrit Frank, Victor McFarland, Jay Sexton, Robert Smale, Steven Watts, and Dominic Meng-Hsuang Yang. I am particularly obligated to Catherine Rymph and John Wigger, who provided cogent criticisms of my approaches and findings; read portions of the manuscript; and, above all, listened patiently as I rambled on about my overly ambitious aspirations. Any remaining mistakes are, of course, to be attributed to me and not to them. Tim Bent of Oxford University Press demonstrated his considerable editorial skills in his work on the manuscript I submitted. As this book was going to press I received the sad news of the death of my agent, John Wright. I remember him not just for his actions on behalf of his clients but also for his dedication to the literary genre of serious nonfiction.

The writing was completed in the shadow of the COVID-19 pandemic, a particularly unpleasant example of an interconnected world. I dedicate this book to the healthcare personnel, scientists, and public health workers who have battled the pandemic, often against considerable resistance and in difficult circumstances.

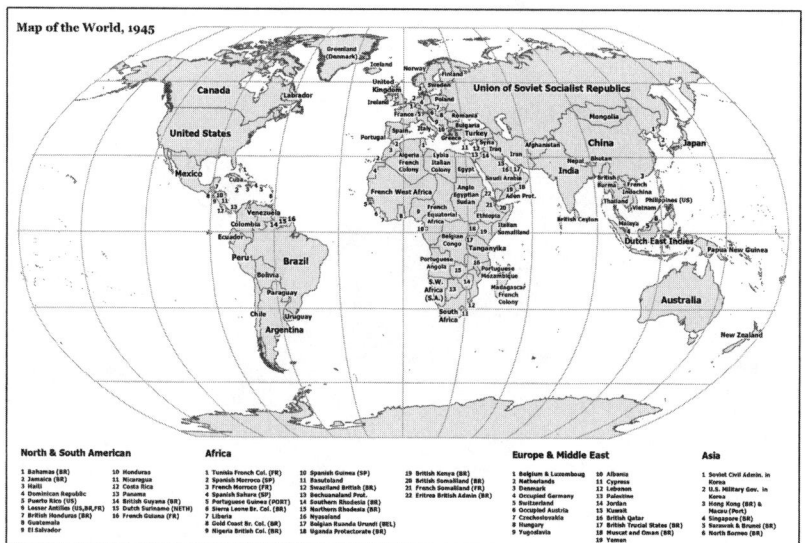

The World in 1945

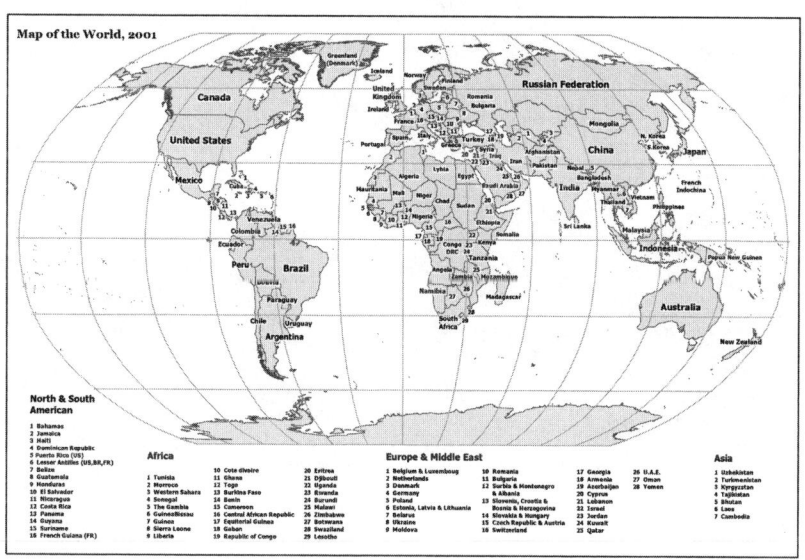

The World in 2001

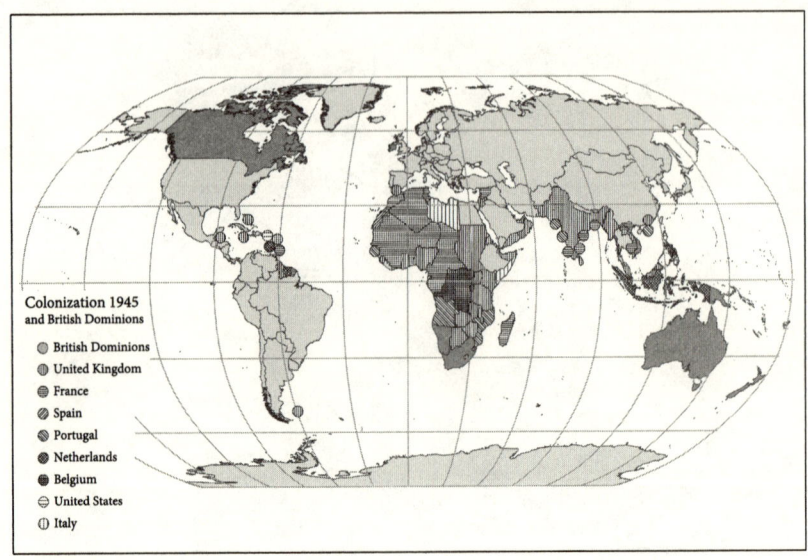

Colonial Empires in 1945

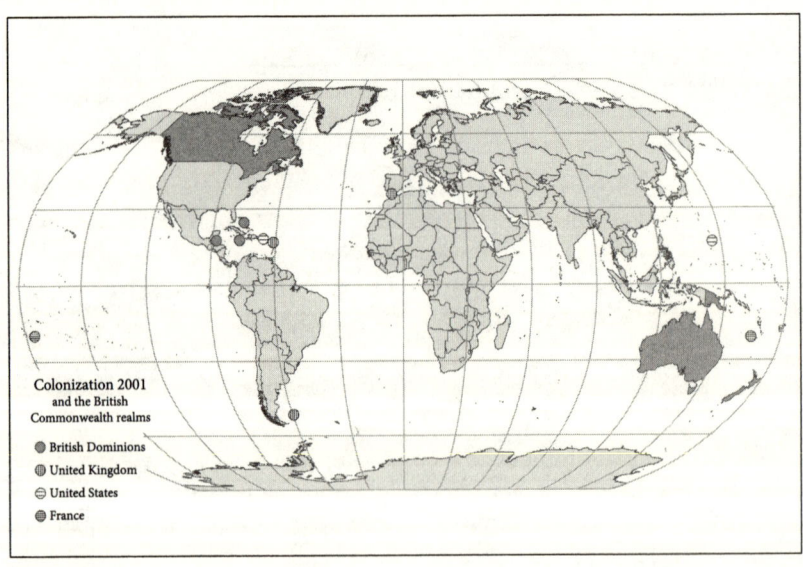

Colonial Empires in 2001

| Introduction

Now, in the third decade of the twenty-first century, it is time to perceive the years 1945–2001 as a period of human history separate and distinct from the present, in some ways rather distant from it, yet also at the origins of our contemporary condition. There is good reason to do so, since those fifty-five years between the end of the Second World War and the onset of the new millennium were a period of varied, enormous, and far-reaching transformations, from human relations with nature, to interactions of the Great Powers; from the structures of production and exchange of goods and services to the structures of religious faith. These were all changes that occurred on an increasingly global scale.

Overestimating the changes of the years between 1945 and 2001 would be difficult. Emerging from the most destructive war in human history, the world experienced a quarter century of unparalleled economic growth, along with unprecedented growth in population and in human exploitation of the biosphere—only to be followed by a period of economic crisis and then unsettling global economic, demographic, and environmental realignments. The entire five decades were an era of scientific and technological advances, eliminating deadly diseases that had killed hundreds of millions of people, uncovering the secrets of life and of the origins of the universe, expanding agricultural productivity, computing power, and worldwide communications in ways previously unimagined and even unimaginable.

Most of the second half of the twentieth century was an age of global political confrontations, when humanity teetered on the brink of extinction in a thermonuclear conflagration, while millions of combatants and civilians died in proxy conflicts across the world, and millions more through mass murder. Colonial empires covering most of the globe were dismantled, in both peaceful and violent fashion. The centuries-old worldwide domination of European countries and their former settler colonies was called into question. The all-encompassing combat that was the Cold War came to an unexpectedly peaceful end, as heavily policed authoritarian regimes suddenly collapsed before a handful of demonstrators. Hopes that the end of this global confrontation also marked the end of all major dissonances and political conflicts around the world were disappointed, most dramatically in 2001, and more gradually over the following decades.

The question for a history of the second half of the twentieth century is how to understand the nature of these transformations and to offer a narrative of their development. One answer comes from journalists and pundits who overuse phrases like "globalization," "the world is flat," or the "singularity," all implying unprecedented and worldwide changes. Their work tends to lack historical context, flattens out the past, and fails to make distinctions between the past—even the recent past—and the present. Historians, tracing change over time, attempt to provide a systematic account of the origins and shaping of the contemporary world, global in a double sense: worldwide and also encompassing central realms of human existence. Yet so much of global history focuses on a distant past. Responding to the contemporary realities of globalization with, for example, lovingly drawn portraits of the silk route, or of the crisis of twelfth-century monarchies, is to investigate a time when global connections were sparse, change slow and hesitant, opportunities for global comparisons few and far between, and links to the present hard to find.

Increasingly, historians have been studying the half century following the Second World War, particularly as these decades draw farther away from us, but have struggled to find a coherent framework. Overviews of the period often present a picture of one thing tumbling after another, unconnected. There were crises in Berlin, Cuba, Southeast Asia, Lebanon, Afghanistan. The Cold War arrived and then was over when a wall fell. Computers, lasers, genetic engineering, nuclear power, nuclear weapons, rockets, jet aircraft, the Internet—these are characterized as a jumble of science and technology. Women and minorities achieved greater equality and there were lots of protests and demonstrations. Former colonies became independent. The global economy changed—and it had to do with the European Union, oil price shocks, the International Monetary Fund, deregulation and privatization, cell phones, the rise of East Asia, and McDonald's. This way of proceeding produces little better than a collection of old headlines and grand statements.

There are global histories that have offered more. A prime example is the account of the nineteenth century by the German historian Jürgen Osterhammel.[1] His work, characterized by an analytical and thematic approach to the past, through which long-known events or prominent figures reduced to cliches appear in a new and unfamiliar light, has been both a model and an inspiration. A central feature of his book is the representation of the nineteenth century as distant and alien, while simultaneously tracing features within it that have led up to the present.

Applying this approach to the recent past requires an understanding of the second half of the twentieth century as involving two different versions of connection, geographic and temporal, or if one wants to be fancy about it, synchronic and diachronic. The first, synchronic version concerns global connections: tracing the worldwide occurrence and global intertwining of political, diplomatic and military, economic, social and demographic, and intellectual, cultural, and artistic trends. The second half of the twentieth century is an extraordinarily rich period for this sort of investigation. Politics and diplomacy then played out in a global arena—and, at times, threatened to destroy the entire world. Humans have been transforming their natural environment since their days as hunter-gatherers, but from the 1950s onward environmental impacts moved steadily from locally to globally perceptible. Commerce and finance were practiced on a global scale—not an entirely unprecedented development, but to an unprecedented extent. The globalization of industrial production, beginning in the 1970s, and gathering momentum ever since, was something quite new. Enhanced and accelerated global communications networks encouraged worldwide interconnections of political mass movements, scientific and technological research, habits of consumption, popular culture, and religious practice.

In quite another respect, the years between 1945 and 2001 were an era of connection, temporally, or diachronically, between their predecessor, the Age of Total War, 1914–1945/50 and their successor, the initial decades of the twenty-first century, our current condition. A history of the second half of the twentieth century requires portraying the shaping force of the age of total war on the decades after 1945—and not just in the immediate postwar era but extending down to the very end of the century. In some ways, as this book will show, the Second World War really only ended in 1990. It is not enough, though, to emphasize the shaping power of the age of total war, or even to observe that its shaping power began to wane by the final decades of the old millennium. A complete history of the years between 1945 and 2001 also needs to understand the emergence of political, social, economic, demographic, and cultural developments, particularly in the last third of the twentieth century, which moved in new directions, established new structures, broke with the past, and set the stage for today's world.

Imagining the Era

To give meaning to the generalizations I have already made, consider the following features of the second half of the twentieth century, every one of which will appear in much greater detail in the course of this book:

1. The rate of global economic and population growth over the years 1950–73 was greater than at any previous time in human history—and at any subsequent time, as well.
2. In 1950, the United States was the only country in the world with at least 250 privately owned automobiles per thousand people, having just reached that point. By 2000, there were twenty-four countries worldwide at or above this level of automobile ownership, though none in Africa or Latin America, and just one in Asia. The United States had by then reached eight hundred automobiles per thousand inhabitants.
3. In the five years after the end of the Second World War, one person in thirteen in the world was a refugee.
4. About one-tenth as many people were killed in wars of the second half of the twentieth century as during the two World Wars. Nonetheless from 1950 to 1989 the threat of a nuclear exchange that could wipe out all life on earth was a constant presence and on at least three separate occasions seemingly imminent.
5. The decolonization of Asia and Africa, occurring in three large bursts, the first in 1945–1950, the second in 1960–1965, and the third in 1970–1975, saw the end of the largest colonial empires in human history.
6. While there were very widespread expectations that the onset of space travel would lead to a new stage of human existence, characterized by the colonization of the solar system, except for a few Apollo missions to the moon, human presence in space has been limited to low earth orbit. Robotic spacecraft, on the other hand, have explored the entire solar system, rolled around on the surface of Mars, and surrounded the earth with an impressive network of telecommunications and GPS location satellites.
7. As late as 1960, atmospheric CO_2 levels were little above their preindustrial values, but by 2000 were more than 40 percent higher.
8. By 2000, there were more women university students than men in all parts of the world, except for African and Islamic countries. The latter were also the only places in the world where the birth rate was well above population-replacement levels.
9. In 1960, the vast majority of commercial passenger aircraft were propeller planes; by 1970, they were overwhelmingly jets.
10. The combination of the introduction of antibiotics, the widespread use of DDT, and the implementation of mass vaccination campaigns reduced infectious disease so drastically in the quarter century after 1945 that its eventual elimination seemed certain. But between 1980 and 2000 infectious disease made a comeback, and in certain instances—especially AIDS, tuberculosis, and malaria in Africa—had

reached hitherto unknown levels. This was all before the COVID-19 pandemic of the early 2020s, ongoing as this book was reaching completion.
11. In 1995, there were only sixteen million users of the Internet, less than one-half of 1 percent of the world's population. Five years later, that figure had soared to 361 million, a jump of over twenty-two-fold in half a decade, one of many examples of exponential growth rates in the second half of the twentieth century.

The question is how all these remarkable features of the years 1945–2001—birth rates, technology, gender equality—can be understood as part of a broader historical process, and not merely as a succession of disconnected headlines. In other words, how can the structures and trends behind the headlines, underlying the events, large and small, of the age be illuminated? The answer to this question comes in two parts: first establish a chronology and second, set out broad elements of thematic development. Both appear in every chapter of the book.

To help with the chronology, the years 1945 to 2001 can be divided into three distinct and separate eras. The first runs from the end of the Second World War and its immediate aftermath, 1945/50, until the mid-1960s. In this Postwar Era, political conflicts, leaders and aspirations, the interactions between the Great (and not so Great) Powers, social and demographic structures, crucial technologies, economic institutions and trends, even human relations with the biosphere, were all heavily influenced by the preceding age of Total War, which extended from 1914 through 1945/50. There followed an Age of Upheaval in the 1960s and 1970s, when the structures and institutions of the postwar era were attacked, dissolved of their own accord, or suddenly and unexpectedly collapsed. During the third historical period, the last two decades of the millennium, the Late-Millennium Era, one might say, new structures and institutions, setting the stage for our current condition, made their appearance.

The second unifying idea of this work is that the second half of the twentieth century was, as the title of the book states, an age of interconnection, one in which economic, political, cultural, demographic, and informational relations spanned the world, integrating far-flung continents and countries of very different levels of economic development, social structures, and political systems. A crucial point is that the process of expanding interconnection was not uniform, linear, continuous, or unidirectional. Periods of rapid growth alternated with ones in which connections grew more slowly, or even declined. Advances of interconnection in one area of human existence might bring with them rejections of it in others: the globalization of manufacturing, the labor market, and communications in the last two decades of the twentieth century, for instance, resulted at least as much in the growth of nationalism and religious intolerance, as they did of cosmopolitanism and multiculturalism.

In articulating these two structuring principles—dividing this half century into three distinct historical eras and the uneven rise of global interconnection—the book has a primarily thematic orientation. Each of its four parts approaches the years 1945 to 2001 from a different direction. In Part 1, "The Material World," the emphasis is on the relationship of humanity to the physical and biological environment—human impact on the biosphere, the spread and decline of diseases (which is a form of human impact on the biosphere, taking place inside the human organism), or the ways science and technology changed human use of the physical world. Part 2, "Interactions," follows the very uneven creation and development of global networks, and their consequences, from economic structures and economic growth, to relations between the Powers, great and small, to the paths people took in crossing borders, continents, and oceans. Part 3, "Varieties of the Social," considers human interaction in a different vein, the many facets of society, from structures of class, gender, and generation, to labor relations, tourism, and consumerism, all portrayed in their development across five decades, their forms of global interaction, and in their different expressions around the world. The fourth and final part of the book, "Dreams and Nightmares," turns the focus to beliefs and aspirations, and their—often extreme—consequences, including the worldwide vicissitudes of the belief in God or of the belief in the idea of progress, the three waves of worldwide utopian aspirations, each connected to the upheavals of one of the fateful years of the era—1945, 1968, and 1989—or the repeated and varied instances of mass murder in the second half of the twentieth century.

Individual events and trends reappear in different ways across these four sections. To take an example of one of the better-known events of the era, at the time more than a little traumatic, the oil price shocks of the 1970s, the book's first section discusses their influence on understandings of human relations to the natural world, as well as their role in promoting large-scale changes in automotive engineering. The same price shocks are investigated in the second section as part of a broader set of changes leading to a profound structural transformation of the global economy, playing a large role in the development of the Cold War and in the relations between the world's wealthier and the world's poorer countries, as well as redirecting global flows of migration. The price shocks and the inflation and slowdown in economic growth they helped bring about affected both labor strife and consumer choice, topics of Part 3. The way rising oil prices reinforced, in both a material and spiritual sense, forms of integralist religion, in Christianity and Islam, are considered in the book's fourth section. Repeatedly following this procedure, re-envisaging well-known (and more obscure) events in multiple contexts produces a multifaceted portrayal of a central era in recent history.

Writing history on a worldwide scale is always a challenge. No book can deal with every single issue and every single sovereign state. Information is not available to an equal extent for every continent—to say nothing of every country—and every writer, definitely including myself, has specialized knowledge and limited linguistic abilities. If this book does not mention, or mentions insufficiently, any reader's favorite country or particular interest, please accept my apologies in advance.

A combination of the availability of information and authors' capability of accessing it all too often results in a "global history" comprised mainly of the North Atlantic world, North America, and Western Europe, sometimes also including a few other affluent lands, such as Japan and Australia. This global history often envisages developments occurring first in wealthy countries, with the rest of the world engaged in "catch-up." Though sometimes accurate, this approach is both fundamentally antithetical to an understanding of history as global process and increasingly inappropriate to comprehending the world of the late twentieth and early twenty-first century, in which there has been a shift from the Atlantic to the Pacific.

Attempting to cover the entire world across a period of over five decades is ambitious chronologically as well as geographically. I have lived through most of the century's second half, and on occasion add my own memories to the story, though I of course do not use my experiences as the sole basis for this book's basic assertions. Those will stand on their own. Still, personal experience can sometimes be part of a broader process of bringing irony, humor, and human scale to a global story.

PART I

The Material World

1 | Nature

WORKERS CLEAR-CUTTING FORESTS IN Brazil, Indonesia, and Oregon; rapid population growth in Rwanda pushing farmers into cultivating ever-steeper slopes and more easily eroded soil; massive DDT (dichloro-diphenyl-trichloroethane, a synthetic insecticide) applications in the United States, Italy, India, and Africa, killing the mosquitoes that carry malaria but also birds and fish; the air irritating, choking, and even fatal for the ill, elderly, and newborn, from sulfur dioxide and particulates in London, ozone in Los Angeles or sulfur dioxide, particulates and ozone in Jakarta, Delhi, and Shanghai; volunteers in Santa Barbara and Brittany desperately trying to wash spilled oil from seabirds; the Aral Sea pumped dry to irrigate cotton crops in Soviet Central Asia; the Cuyahoga River in Cleveland catching fire; salmon and flounder living in the Rhine River, for the first time in decades; refineries producing gasoline without tetraethyl lead: all these scenes from the second half of the twentieth century testify to the most basic feature of those five decades: human interaction with nature.

Of course, humans had been interacting with nature—procuring food and raw materials, depositing wastes, changing the landscape, transforming, reducing, or eradicating other species, serving as hosts to bacteria and viruses and facilitating their spread—since their days as Stone Age hunters and gatherers. There had been phases of acceleration and intensification of interactions, such as the invention of agriculture in the "Neolithic Revolution," some twelve thousand years ago. In more recent centuries, the beginnings of more rapid global population growth around 1700; the large-scale burning of coal with the onset of the Industrial Revolution during the first half of the nineteenth century; and the development and increasingly widespread manufacture of artificial fertilizers, synthetics, and petroleum products, as well as the large-scale generation of electricity, in the Second

Industrial Revolution beginning c. 1890, marked important waypoints in human relations with the biosphere.

But the second half of the twentieth century was an era of a new quality of human influence on the natural world, stimulating a new level of awareness of that influence and its consequences for humanity, as well as for all other species residing on the earth, and, in view of these consequences, quite unprecedented and steadily more controversial efforts to limit, regulate, and direct that influence. At the beginning of the new millennium, Paul Crutzen, a Nobel Prize-winning chemist, gave all these changes a name—the "anthropocene," suggesting a new era, in which human population and human economic and technological activity had become the dominant force shaping the global environment.[1]

Sometimes, the increase in the intensity of the interaction of humanity with nature appears as a straight linear pattern, a steady increase from 1945 to 2000. But breaking down this interaction, by considering its regional modalities across the globe; the similarities and differences with past historical eras; the effects of economic, demographic, and technological change; or efforts to respond to the interaction, at local, regional, national, and international levels, reveal a more complex picture. A postwar era in which taking the natural environment for granted was the norm gave way to a period of rethinking and actual changes during the Age of Upheaval in the 1960s and 1970s, followed by the Late Millennium Era in which new relations between humanity and nature formed—relations whose consequences often defied appropriate responses.

Taking Nature for Granted in the Postwar World

In the quarter century following the Second World War, human relations with the biosphere followed a pattern set in the first half of the twentieth century—perceiving the natural environment as an adaptable and inexhaustible resource, to be exploited and managed. Electric power and home heating (in colder climates), came from burning coal, with the resulting train of particulates and sulfur dioxide in the atmosphere. Automobiles added lead and nitrogen oxides, the latter broken down into ozone. Farmers, carrying out both large-scale, mechanized agriculture and smaller-scale cultivation, with human and occasional animal power, acted as if soil reserves were unlimited, in spite of paying occasional lip service to conservation measures, such as contour plowing. At least in the regions of mechanized agriculture, farmers also added steadily larger amounts of nitrates to the soil.

What was true of farming extended to other forms of exploitation. Fishermen and whalers harvested as though the sea's living resources were without end. Industrial wastes, including mercury and heavy metals, were dumped into streams and rivers or emitted into the atmosphere; industrial workers had little if any protection from toxic chemicals in the workplace, such as lead or vinyl chlorides. Large-scale construction projects, for instance, the channeling and canalization of France's Rhône River, in order to generate hydroelectric power, were carried out in an impressively rapid and dynamic fashion, but without any particular consideration of the effects of this hydraulic engineering on the inhabitants of riverside villages, to say nothing of fish and wildlife.[2]

In this treatment of natural surroundings, there were some distinctly new elements, products of the technological changes stemming from the Second World War. One example was the introduction of radioactivity into the environment as the result of nuclear chain reactions. Later in the century, the consequences of using nuclear power to generate electricity would stand at the center of environmental interest, but until the 1970s there were virtually no atomic power plants. Rather, it was nuclear warfare, more precisely, the preparation for it, that was the major environmental consequence of atomic fission. Building nuclear weapons was environmentally toxic. At the two major sites of the production of weaponized plutonium, Maiak, near Ozersk, in the Russian Urals; and Hanford, near Richland in Washington State, administrators and site workers demonstrated a distinctly cavalier attitude toward massively radioactive substances. No sooner had the Ozersk plant started production in 1948 than plutonium was bubbling through its ventilation system. Spills of radioactive substances occurred everywhere, and workers generally ignored the (few and totally unenforced) safety guidelines. Between 1949 and 1951, 7.8 million cubic yards of toxic and radioactive chemicals were dumped into the Techa River on the eastern flank of the Urals. At the end of that two-year period, Soviet scientists found villagers in the vicinity were receiving a lifetime's dose of radiation in a mere week. The unsuspecting villagers were hustled away without warning, while all their possessions were burned and their livestock shot. The culmination of lax practices toward radioactivity came in 1957, when an underground storage tank holding radioactive waste exploded, blowing its 160-ton cement cap into the air, producing a cloud of radioactive gas a half mile high, and showering the vicinity with radioactive particles.

While there was nothing quite so extreme in Hanford, millions of gallons of radioactive waste were dumped in the Columbia River and buried in the vicinity; construction workers who were not plant employees were never monitored for exposure. Since the end of the Cold War, the problems facing the site's decontamination—seventeen hundred pounds of plutonium-239 amid fifty-three million gallons of waste being just one small part—have proven well-nigh unresolvable. Nobody is even attempting to resolve the much-larger issues of radioactive pollution in Ozersk.[3]

Horrific as these instances of radioactive contamination are, they were both strongly localized in the vicinity of the plutonium plants. Exploding atomic weapons in the name of attempted mutual intimidation known as nuclear testing, spread radioactive debris—"fallout," contemporaries called it—across the entire northern hemisphere and parts of the southern half of the globe. Sometimes, the results were immediate and undeniable, as happened to the crew of the Japanese fishing boat the *Lucky Dragon*, who were sprayed with fallout from a US hydrogen bomb test in the Pacific in 1954. Amazingly, only one of the *Lucky Dragon* crew members, the radioman Aikichi Kuboyama died, and it is not clear that radioactivity killed him.

Compared to the other forms of human action, the environmental impact of radioactivity in the 1950s and 1960s was modest.[4] Noticeably greater effects on the natural environment during the postwar era came from another technological innovation of the Second World War, organochloride insecticides, the most famous of which was DDT. Along with their more toxic cousin compounds, the organophosphates, these chemicals were used around the entire world against insects causing diseases and, especially, damaging crops. The routine broadside aerial dissemination of such insecticides—in 1958, one hundred million acres in the United States, one-sixth of all cultivated land—as well as special campaigns, such as the efforts of the US Department of Agriculture in 1957–59 to wipe out the gypsy moth and the fire ant by intensive aerial spraying of DDT, suggest the extent to which concerns about the biosphere were neither pronounced nor widespread at the time.[5]

As a result of their novelty, both radioactive fallout and organochlorides would open the way to considering more broadly the effects of human action on the environment. Nonetheless the actual environmental effect of these new departures paled in comparison with older forms of technology: the murderous effects of sulfur and coal dust, such as the great killing London coal fog of 1952, or a similar event a decade later in the Ruhr Basin, center of Germany's heavy industry; the accumulation of atmospheric ozone from automobile exhaust, for which Los Angeles with its smog had become the poster child; and the steady declines of wildlife in and around the great rivers of industrialized countries and their estuaries as a result of toxic industrial discharges and nitrate-laden agricultural runoff. The danger was less from the new substances being introduced into the environment than the quantity of older ones. In contrast to the first half of the twentieth century, in which population growth had been slowed by two world wars and severe economic crises, population growth in the postwar years was the fastest in human history. Not only were people populating the earth at an unprecedented pace, they were producing and consuming at a rate never seen before. During that same postwar period economic growth, worldwide, was the fastest it has ever been.[6]

This combination of population and economic growth meant that older methods of dealing with environmental impacts, above all, dilution and dissipation—tall smokestacks scattering emissions over a wider area and greater volume of air, or dumping waste products in rivers and oceans, dissolving in large masses of water—lost their previous (admittedly limited) effectiveness, because the amount of toxic emissions and discharges had grown beyond the capability of the air and water to dilute and to absorb them. A simple variant on this theme was in the realm of sewage disposal. Most suburban and rural areas of the United States used septic tanks. Although less effective than sewer systems and waste treatment plants, septic tanks worked so long as their number remained small and dispersed in areas of low population density. But the postwar construction boom—result of both population and economic growth—more than tripled the number of units built between 1945 and 1960, reaching over fourteen million in that latter year, deployed in subdivisions of as large as eight thousand homes, overwhelmed the system, polluting groundwater and rivers, and bringing sewage back to the surface.[7]

As this example suggests, in the postwar decades the combination of economic and population growth weighed most heavily on the environment in those countries where industry was most developed and consumer goods manufactured and consumed to the greatest extent: North America, Western Europe, Japan, Australia, and, in smaller measure, the lands of the Eastern Bloc. Economically less-developed countries in Asia, Africa, or Latin America primarily experienced environmental impacts when they were drawn into the networks of wealthier countries as suppliers of raw materials: intensive banana cultivation for the US market in Central America, for instance, using large amounts of artificial fertilizer and pesticides. Soviet authorities cultivated cotton extensively in Central Asia, the economically least-developed portion of the USSR, using immense amounts of fertilizer and pesticides, as well as large amounts of irrigated water. The upshot was polluted soil, toxic drinking water, and a dried out, heavily salinated, Aral Sea.[8]

A striking variation on this trend took place in China under communist rule. In its economic development plans, the government of Mao Zedong understood the natural world as completely subject to human shaping. The 1958 "Wipe Out the Four Pests" campaign was aimed at killing sparrows that were eating the grain supply. The entire population, including schoolchildren, was mobilized to kill sparrows, destroy their nests, and even to bang on pots constantly, so the birds got no rest and died from sheer exhaustion. The campaign did succeed in eliminating sparrows, who aside from grain consumed grain-eating insects, which multiplied, resulting in even greater crop losses.[9] These efforts and their consequences were fundamentally akin to the use of insecticides in economically more-developed countries that killed beneficial as well as harmful insects and insects' avian predators, producing a similar boomerang effect.

Whether caused by DDT or schoolchildren, the results suggest a common attitude toward the natural environment in the postwar decades across different socioeconomic and political systems, and the battle lines of the Cold War.

Contemporaries did occasionally express concerns about relations between humans and the natural environment. Throughout the 1950s, farmers and other locals in the Black Forest in the south of West Germany fought to preserve the great gorge in the Wutach River, which runs from the Danube into the Rhine, against efforts to dam the gorge for hydroelectric power. This dispute, which had been simmering since the 1920s, and went on for an entire decade, ultimately ended in a victory for the locals against the electric utility company planning to build the dam. In the state of Lower Saxony, residents fought to preserve the Knechtsand wetlands, where the Weser River flowed into the North Sea, from plans of the RAF to use it as a bombing range—a dispute that combined nationalist feelings with concern for the well-being of seabirds and crab fishermen. Of course, against these instances should be set a much larger number of failures—for instance, efforts to prevent high-voltage power lines from being strung in the Bavarian countryside, or the vain protests of the inhabitants of the villages of Bollène and Donzère that hydraulic work on the Rhône River to build the Donzère-Mondragon electric power plant caused their wells to dry up, their farmland to sink, and their houses and barns to collapse. Action could be ineffective, as was the 1958 prohibition of the interior use of lead paint by the New York City municipal government, which the city's Health Department found was blithely ignored for years.[10]

These kinds of actions had been occurring sporadically since the early twentieth century, when old-fashioned naturalists engaged in cataloging nature and biologists fighting for the preservation of wild animal species, particularly birds, joined forces with outdoor enthusiasts for untamed nature. In relatively lightly populated countries, such as the United States and the USSR, they succeeded in setting aside areas as wilderness—national parks in the United States, *zapovedniki* or nature preserves in the USSR. The numbers of these activists were very small (seven thousand members of the Sierra Club in 1950, for example) and their influence and campaigns in the postwar decades probably less than around 1900, and their previous accomplishments under attack, as, happened in the USSR, when the Soviet government in 1951 cut the size of its *zapovedniki* by 90 percent.[11]

Most of these early environmentalists shared the idea first proposed in 1797 by the English economist Thomas Malthus—that human population growth invariably outstripped food supply. Malthus himself was not an environmentalist or even a proto-environmentalist but proponents of his ideas in the second half of the twentieth century interpreted his theories in these terms. The American naturalists, Fairfield Osborn and William Vogt, whose 1948 books *Our Plundered Planet* and *The Road to Survival*, were both bestsellers (*The Road to Survival* was even serialized in *Reader's Digest*) and translated into thirteen and nine languages respectively, put this quite forthrightly. "The tide of the earth's population is rising," asserted Osborn, "and the reservoir of the earth's living resources is falling." His counterpart, Vogt, stated that "Where human populations are so large that available land cannot decently support them, man's destructive methods of exploitation mushroom like the atomic cloud over Hiroshima." Attributing the Second World War to "overpopulated" countries such as Germany, England, and Japan lacking agricultural land to feed themselves, both saw the postwar world as short of natural resources—particularly farmland—to supply its growing population. Efforts to provide these resources would only further degrade the natural environment and, ultimately, exacerbate the problem.[12]

Such rewritings of Malthusian ideas extended well beyond the English-speaking world. Roger Heim, director of the French Natural History Museum, in his 1952 book, *Destruction and Protection of Nature*, articulated similar ideas, as did the Swedish plant breeder Georg Borgstrom, whose 1965 book *The Hungry Planet* was a bestseller and appeared in six different languages. Julian Huxley, the first head of one of the major UN agencies, UNESCO, was an enthusiastic Malthusian and saw his international work as being directed, above all, at dealing with overpopulation.[13] Malthus's ideas about population and food supply, sometimes taken simply in that way, sometimes expanded to include a broader consideration of the natural resources and the natural environment, would provide a long-lasting framework for the development of new attitudes toward the biosphere.

RETHINKING NATURE IN THE AGE OF UPHEAVAL

By the time Borgstrom's *Hungry Planet* appeared in 1965, these new attitudes were already beginning to make their appearance. The decades of the 1960s and 1970s were in this respect, as in so many others, a period of upheaval and transformation. Public interest in environmental questions skyrocketed; new groups dedicated to dealing with human interactions with the environment appeared and expanded in size and scope; government ministries or agencies devoted to the issue were created across the globe, along with legislation protecting the natural environment. The combination of pressure from civil society, bureaucratic resources, and legal tools produced measurable changes in behavior and in the natural world—a rather remarkable development. Although the versions of Malthusian ideas prevalent in the postwar era continued to be important, there also developed new conceptions of humanity and nature that helped to guide aspirations and actions.

One sign of change was organizational development. In 1960, there were six major environmental organizations in the United States, all but one founded before 1945, with a total of 123,000 members. At the end of the decade, these groups' membership had grown sevenfold to 819,000, and by 1983, they and five additional groups, all founded around 1970, counted almost two million dues-paying adherents. Although the growth of environmental organizations may have begun in the United States, it was far from an American peculiarity. Membership in the eight most important British environmental organizations grew eightfold between 1971 and 1992, from about five hundred thousand to four million. In 1999, a team of intrepid sociologists and political scientists distributed a questionnaire in fifty-six different countries and found that more than one inhabitant in twenty was a member of an environmental group, almost as many as were members of a political party. Proportions ranged from 45 percent in the Netherlands to just 0.2 percent in Turkey. The percentages tended to be highest in affluent countries of North America or Western Europe, although over 8 percent of the inhabitants of India, Vietnam, Uganda, the Philippines, and Venezuela claimed to belong to an environmental organization.[14]

Changes in the nature of groups devoted to environmental issues reflected new intellectual orientations. In 1960, over half of the membership in American environmental groups came from just two organizations, the Audubon Society, a group devoted to birds; and the Izaak Walton League, a wildlife preservation group founded by hunters. Just the names of the groups founded about a decade later—the Environmental Defense Fund, Natural Resources Defense Council, Greenpeace—reveal a more aggressive orientation, one that the older organizations quickly began to imitate. Earth Day, launched in 1970, emerged from an offhand suggestion by a US senatorial back-bencher, Gaylord Nelson of Wisconsin, and developed into a massive nationwide event—events, actually, with thirteen thousand across the United States; thirty-five thousand speakers; week-long television coverage; and millions of participants.[15]

Closely related was the global development of governmental administrations devoted to environmental issues. The world's first environment ministry was established in Sweden in 1967, followed by the Environmental Protection Agency in the United States three years later. The 1972 Stockholm Conference of UNESCO on the environment, with delegates from 114 countries, led to the creation of the United Nations Environmental Program, thus placing human-nature interactions on the world's agenda. Around the time of the Stockholm Conference there were about twenty environmental agencies or ministries in existence; a decade later there were 180. Of course, these governmental offices did not have much in the way of budgets, staff, or legal authority. Robert Poujade, named France's first Environment Minister in 1971, later entitled the memoirs of his time in the job, *The Ministry of the Impossible*.[16] Yet newly created bureaucracies soon received legal tools to use, whether the Clean Air and Clean Water Acts of 1970 and 1972 in the United States, the Japanese Basic Law on Pollution Control of 1967 and the Nature Conservation Law of 1972, as well as the South Korean Environmental Preservation Act of 1977, the Danish Environmental Protection Act of 1973 or the Organic Law on the Environment, promulgated in Venezuela in 1976—to give just a few examples.[17]

All this points to a change in the understanding and even the practice of the interaction between humanity and nature, taking place on a global scale, starting around 1965. "Environmentalism," was, in some ways, part of the political mass movements and cultural departures in what we call for convenience the "sixties." A good example of this connection was the creation in 1971 of the group Greenpeace, which would become a paradigmatic example of environmental activism. Its founders were left-wing US pacifists who had fled their native country out of disgust at its nuclear weapons and its wars in Southeast Asia, joined by a younger group of Canadians, including an ecologist, an enthusiast for *Gestalt* psychology, and someone who played the flute for whales, all of whom came together in Vancouver, the capital of the Canadian counterculture. Starting with a campaign to oppose American nuclear weapons testing in the Aleutian Islands, by sailing a ship into the vicinity of the test, the group expanded its high-publicity campaigns to include French nuclear testing, whaling, seal hunting, oil spills, and much more. Spreading down the western coast of North America and then to Western Europe over the course of the 1970s, the organization reached Latin America and Asia in the following decade, growing from a small, localized group to a worldwide network of activists.[18]

Protecting the environment often had a left-wing political coloration, environmental agencies inaugurated in the United Kingdom by the Labour government, and in West Germany as one of the many reforming efforts—from foreign policy to labor relations to women's rights—of the social democratic government of Willy Brandt. But eminently conservative governments did the same: Richard Nixon in the United States and George Pompidou in France, or the 1970 "Pollution Diet" in Japan, when the national legislature dominated by the conservative Liberal Democratic Party, passed fourteen pieces of environmental legislation—all measures that enjoyed broad support across the political spectrum. While opposition to environmentalism would become, at least in some countries, a signature of conservative politics, this was not the case in the Age of Upheaval.

Interest in protection of the natural environment gained traction from the impact of industrial accidents and disasters. Oil spills have been a classic example, including, in this initial phase of environmentalism, the Torrey Canyon tanker disaster off the coast of Brittany in 1967 or the Santa Barbara oil spill of 1969—the latter often seen, incorrectly, as the impetus for the founding of Greenpeace. Large and repeated spills from tanker accidents or offshore drilling problems have of course continued to the present. Along with them were the great chemical disasters, explosions, or other forms of massive emissions of toxic chemicals, beginning with Seveso, in Italy, 1976. Bhopal, in India, eight years later, was the greatest of them all, with the most loss of human life; Basel, in 1986, when a chemical warehouse fire led to heavily toxic discharge eliminating most living substances in the Rhine; or, perhaps less well known, the 1988 fire in the Protex chemical plant near Tours in France, that wiped out fish on a large stretch of the Loire. We could add to this list the great nuclear accidents, Three Mile Island (1979), Chernobyl (1986), and Fukushima (2011).[19]

Especially in the last third of the twentieth century, as media became global and ubiquitous, such disasters were motivating agents, stimulating political movements and legal initiatives. A whole school of sociology, following the idea of a "risk society," devised by the German social theorist Ulrich Beck, argues that these accidents are an inevitable result of the technology and economic exchanges of the late twentieth century.[20] A certain skepticism in regard to both the symbolic and the real effects of such immense accidents might be in order. The effects of accidents depend on their perception. A classic example was the burning of the Cuyahoga River in Cleveland in 1969, perceived both at the time, and in retrospect, as a major impetus for the passing of the Clean Water Act in the United States the three years later. Yet the river, or, more precisely, the oil and chemicals dumped into it, had burned in 1868, 1883, 1887, 1912, 1922, 1936, 1941, and 1952 (news images of the 1969 fire were actually from the much-larger conflagration of 1952) without leading to any similar effect. From the Second World War onward, the Chisso chemical company in Japan regularly dumped methyl mercury into Minimata Bay, contaminating the fish and shellfish there. First the cats and then the people in Minimata City developed symptoms from consuming the contaminated seafood—uncontrollable twitching, uncoordinated body movements, dementia. Children were born twisted and crippled. Throughout the 1950s, the Japanese response to this was to shun the inhabitants as polluted and to avoid them as potential spouses, fearing their ailments were hereditary. It was only in 1973, when a court judgment provided compensation for the victims, that the mercury emissions were ordered halted.[21]

An emphasis on the spectacular diverts attention from the far greater negative effects of the regular, procedural workings of technology and the economy. The death toll in Bhopal was somewhere between 2,500 (the Indian government's official figure), and 16,000 (according to activists). This was a horrific number of people to die from incompetence and negligence, but, compared to the 400,000 to 600,000 who died every single year in the second half of the twentieth century from the regular technological workings of furnaces, power plants, and automobiles; and the sulfur dioxide, lead, particulates, and nitrogen oxides they emitted, relatively modest.[22] What was true of effects was also true of the motivation for developing new environmental policies in the 1960s and 1970s: less the example of horrible accidents than the daily consequences of a quarter century of unprecedented population and economic growth.

In the 1960s and 1970s the relationship between the perceptible effects of human actions, and changing frames in which these actions were perceived, shaped the relationship between humans and their environment. Three books from the time, originating in either North America or Western Europe but all with global ramifications, reveal the nature of the transformation: Paul Ehrlich's *The Population Bomb*, Rachel Carson's *Silent Spring*, and the Club of Rome's *The Limits to Growth*.

An expert in population biology, Ehrlich's 1968 book became an immense bestseller, with over one million copies sold. His argument was a reiteration in more dramatic form of the points raised two decades before by Osborn and Vogt. Explaining how he had been inspired by a 1966 trip to India, where he had been horrified by the sight of New Delhi streets "alive with people," eating, washing, arguing, begging, herding animals, and defecating, Ehrlich concluded that humanity's numbers were too great. The catastrophic overpopulation Vogt and Osborn saw as looming had already arrived. "The battle to feed humanity is over. In the 1970's the world will undergo famines—hundreds of millions of people will starve to death . . ." Even attempting to deal with the situation had already produced massive environmental deterioration. Ehrlich was a member of the Earth Day organizing committee, whose events invariably emphasized the evils of overpopulation, and went on to a long career as an outspoken environmentalist.[23]

Ehrlich's mention of pesticides as one example of environmental deterioration resulting from overpopulation was an implicit reference to Rachel Carson's 1962 *Silent Spring*. By training a naturalist, former employee of the US Fish and Wildlife Service, and author of bestselling, lyrically written accounts of life in the sea, Carson was moved to pen her attack on indiscriminate use of insecticides by massive spraying campaigns against the fire ant and gypsy moth in the late 1950s. Two features of her work stand out. One was the emphasis on new, post-1945 features of interaction with the environment, explicitly linking nuclear fallout with chemical pesticides in their effect on all living organisms. The other was the concern with nonhuman nature. The main focus of her book was on the chemicals' impact on insects, fish and birds—as the very title of the book indicates, a world without birdcalls.

Carson elucidated the pragmatic arguments against the use of insecticides—that their application backfired by killing harmful insects' natural predators—and called for more modest and careful use of chemical insecticides as well as the development of biological methods of pest control.

A central and very effective feature of her book was her elegant and passionate opposition to organochlorides that endangered a wide variety of animal species. Taking a leaf from the page of the veteran English ecologist Charles Elton, whose 1958 work *The Ecology of Invasions* had emphasized the need for the "conservation of variety," or, as we would say today, biodiversity, Carson urged humanity not to disrupt the complex web of interactions between different species making up the natural world.[24]

Selling one hundred thousand copies in its first two months of publication, *Silent Spring* attracted immense press and media attention. Chemical manufacturers immediately and vehemently denounced Carson as a communist and hysterical woman. The book was quoted in a debate in the British House of Lords; it played a central role in energizing actions to limit or prohibit outright the use of DDT and other organochlorides across the world in the 1970s.[25]

Explicitly Malthusian themes were absent from *Silent Spring*, although Elton, whose work was one of Carson's intellectual inspirations, was very much a Malthusian; and Ehrlich, a half decade later, would integrate Carson's condemnation of chemical pesticides into his own Malthusian viewpoint. The third major environmental work, *Limits to Growth*, appearing in 1972, revived and expanded the Malthusian perspective. The book was commissioned by the Club of Rome, the brainchild of an eccentric Italian corporate manager, Aurelio Pecci, a one-time executive at both the auto-manufacturer Fiat and Olivetti (famous for its typewriters), who had grown increasingly interested in problems of global economic development and global economic inequities. Members of the club were mostly economists and statisticians who worked for UN agencies or the Organization for Economic Cooperation and Development, a different background from biologists and naturalists. In view of the interests and inclinations of the club's members, it was not too surprising that they commissioned a systems analyst, Jay Forrester at MIT, to produce their study of global trends.

Unlike the elegiac Carson or the angry Ehrlich, *Limits to Growth* was self-consciously analytical, filled with references to its computer projections, at a time when such devices were still unfamiliar and intimidating. Characterized by flow charts, graphs, tables, and the occasional equation, the work breathed scientificity. Its three main points each expanded on Malthus's observations. According to Malthus, food supply, especially farmland, was the decisive feature of the natural world that would be outstripped by population growth. In *Limits to Growth*, everything was being outstripped—not just grain and the farmland needed to grow it, but fish and seafood, water, and every kind of mineral and energy source imaginable. What was causing the outstripping of natural resources was not just population growth but its combination with economic growth. Humanity's demands on the natural environment were increasing exponentially.

The authors concluded that the natural world could not stand this ever-accelerating pace of growth. At some future point, natural resources would give way under the strain and collapse, bringing human civilization down with it. Although not a very appealing picture, it was an immensely compelling one. The book was translated into thirty different languages and sold over ten million copies worldwide.[26]

Part of the attraction of *The Limits to Growth* was the coincidence of its appearance with the first oil price shock of 1973 and the subsequent gasoline shortages, quickly followed by price spikes and then shortages of foodstuffs and a wide variety of minerals. The future, it seemed in the 1970s, had arrived: the collapse of natural resources under the weight of population and economic growth was already occurring, not just a possibility for the first half of the twenty-first century, as the charts and graphs of *Limits to Growth* implied. This interpretation raised to a much higher level the sense of unease about human interaction with the environment that had been a characteristic feature of the Era of Upheaval.[27]

Unexpected Complexities in the Late Millennium

One way to sum up the previous section would be to say that many in the 1970s viewed their moment as a race between disaster and developing the means to prevent it. The last two decades of the twentieth century would see the result. The crises that Paul Ehrlich or the Club of Rome foresaw did not happen: The Malthusian apocalypse so feared in the 1970s never came to pass. Hundreds of millions of Indians did not starve to death; supplies of raw materials and energy remained available and affordable—even petroleum products, whose accessibility seemed very seriously in question after the oil price shocks of 1973 and 1979. So perhaps the movements, agencies and institutions developed in the 1970s won the race. Or, maybe, the race was still ongoing and the winner remains unclear. Perhaps there was never any race in the first place; or there was a race but on a very different track from the one to which everyone was paying attention.

A BALANCE SHEET OF FEARS

There were two main reasons for this anticlimax. One was that exponential increases so highlighted and feared in the Club of Rome's report relented. Global economic growth fell back from the pace of the postwar decades, and never again reached that pace, down to the present day. Population growth slowed as well, albeit more so in economically advanced countries, containing a smaller portion of the world's population that nonetheless claimed a disproportionate share of its resources.

It was not just that these resources were in less demand; they were also being used much more efficiently. Always a weak link of Malthus's theory was the assumption that agricultural productivity grew slowly if at all. Even as Paul Ehrlich and many others were proclaiming that hundreds of millions were going to starve, the "Green Revolution"—the name for the extension of the high-productivity agriculture practiced in North America in the quarter century after the Second World War into Asia and Latin America—was making it possible to expand the amount of food available faster than the population was growing. High prices spurred the exploration of new sources of minerals and energy sources, and these sources were used more efficiently. In the United States, for example, energy density—the amount of energy needed to produce a dollar's worth of GDP, which had changed little between 1955 and 1973—fell about 20 percent in the last quarter of the century, reaching a lower level in 2000 than in 1950. There were similar trends in Great Britain, Canada, and Japan. In China, the corresponding movement started a bit later, around 1980. Nonetheless the fall by two-thirds in the last two decades of the twentieth century was the fastest decline in energy density—or, rise in energy efficiency—in human history.[28]

Unlike Malthus himself, proponents of offshoots of his theory in the second half of the twentieth century emphasized not just the inadequacy of natural resources to keep up with population growth, but the destructive effects of trying to do so. Yet the last two decades of the twentieth century were a period in which some of the worst consequences of the postwar era disregard of the natural environment were rectified and even reversed. The best example was the elimination of tetraethyl lead from gasoline. The single largest source of a toxic substance, whose health effects include heart disease and brain damage, especially in urban areas, leaded gasoline's use was first limited in Japan in 1971. Fifteen years later, Japan became the first country to ban it altogether. By 1990, gasoline lead consumption in OECD countries, the world's wealthiest and technologically most advanced, had declined by 78 percent from its 1970 levels. The first decade of the twenty-first century saw the further spread of the leaded gas ban, particularly in Asia and Africa, to the point that in 2011 there were just six countries left in the world—Afghanistan, Algeria, Iraq, Myanmar, North Korea, and Yemen—where leaded gasoline was still available. This reformulation of gasoline was part of a broader, if, admittedly not so drastic, decline in heavy metals emissions worldwide.[29]

A similar improvement in air quality came from the decline in emissions of sulfur dioxide. Yearly emissions fell, worldwide, about 20 percent, from 125 million metric tons in 1980 to 100 million in 2000. Not quite so pronounced a decline as that for lead in the atmosphere, nor so widespread, it was a significant change, in view of the lung diseases and deaths attributable to SO_2. On a similar scale was the improvement in water quality, particularly of streams and rivers, reflecting the building of sewage treatment plants. A whole series of international agreements among the countries bordering the Rhine River starting in the 1970s, led to substantial declines in salts, heavy metals, and halogens. Salmon, extinct in the river by the 1970s, have been successfully reintroduced in the Rhine and its tributaries, along with pike, pike-perch, catfish, and flounder.[30]

Even in the terms set during the 1960s—and, as will be seen, the Late Millennium Era introduced a whole new set of issues concerning human interaction with the natural world—not all measures were quite so successful. A particular problem was nitrogen oxides and the ozone they produced, largely the result of auto exhaust. The increasing use of catalytic converters and more efficient engines cut each car's emissions by an average of 90 percent between 1970 and 1990. Nonetheless, the growing number of automobiles offset the declining emissions per automobile. As a result, nitrogen oxide emissions across the world actually increased, by about 20 percent, in the last quarter of the twentieth century. There were examples of successful efforts against ozone. In New York City, the number of days during which ozone levels exceeded WHO health standards fell from 119 in 1980 to 9 in 1989. Circumstances were less favorable in Los Angeles, much more dependent on automobiles and facing an unfavorable topography, with mountains on three sides and ocean winds keeping in unhealthy air on the fourth. America's second-largest city experienced no reduction in ozone levels and ozone alert days remained over one hundred yearly in the twenty-first century.[31] Ozone is a particularly tenacious problem, but the issues stemming from attempts at its reduction can be generalized, namely that declines in environmental effect per capita or per unit of GDP are either limited or downright outweighed by the effects of population and economic growth. All those declines in country's energy density during the last quarter of the twentieth century have not meant that less energy was used. Quite the opposite, since GDP increased faster than energy efficiency did, energy use rose as well.[32]

Another way to look at the changes in human relations with the environment in the late twentieth century is to consider their occurrence in regions of differing levels of economic development or socioeconomic and political systems. The greatest disparity was between the western, more affluent, capitalist countries and the communist lands of the Eastern Bloc. Quite simply, none of the measures of pollution abatement occurring in the United States, Western Europe, Japan, or Australia were found in the East. Industrial facilities continued to pour out untreated heavy metals into the water and the air; pesticide use ran unchecked; the sulfur dioxide content of the air was steadily rising. By the 1980s, in the great steel manufacturing center of Magnitogorsk, children were being treated in medical clinics with blasts of oxygen, so they would have something tolerable to breathe; increasingly adults received this therapy as well. Water in the Elbe River, which was a dumping ground for the wastes from the manufacture of synthetics and fertilizers in both Czechoslovakia and East Germany, was undrinkable, unsuitable for washing, and toxic to swimmers, to say nothing of the few fish remaining in it being inedible; it was even too polluted to use for cooling. When I was in East Germany in 1988, primarily the cities of Halle and Merseburg, part of the country's most polluted region, it required no scientific apparatus to perceive the presence of toxic chemicals in the air. Perhaps the most striking example was that the sulfur dioxide in the atmosphere mixed with rain to form a dilute sulfuric acid that burned one's skin.[33]

What was particularly appalling about this state of affairs was that the link between expanding population and economic output on the one hand and impact on the natural world on the other, so characteristic of the postwar decades, had been broken. The Eastern Bloc countries produced far fewer goods than their Western counterparts but had much more pollution per unit of output. In the mid-1980s, the industrial output of the USSR was about half that of the United States, but its per capita emissions of toxic substances into the atmosphere, at 854 pounds, was almost the same as that of the United States, at 873 pounds. The comparison between East Germany, the westernmost edge of the Eastern Bloc, and West Germany, the eastern outpost of the west in Europe, was even more depressing. Although there were about seven times as many motor vehicles in the western state as in the east, per capita nitrogen oxide emissions were 27 percent lower in the west. Per capita sulfur dioxide emissions in the east were ten times what they were in the west; typical daily levels of sulfur dioxide in the most polluted regions of the east during the 1980s were up to twice as high as the highest, smog-alert levels found in the most industrialized regions of the west in the 1960s, before pollution control measures came into play.[34]

Measures of environmental protection in Western countries were implemented against the often very tenacious and embittered opposition of business interests: utility companies furious about restrictions on sulfur emissions; automobile manufacturers steadfastly resisting building engines that ran on unleaded gasoline; manufacturers rejecting health and safety protections for their workers from chemical emissions; developers refusing to accept limits on building on hillsides or wetlands, to mention just a few examples. Wedded to notions from the postwar decades of cost-free, infinitely absorbable natural surroundings, capitalists worked hard to preserve their profits by avoiding the costs of environmental protection. Environmentalists' outrage at this attitude could be cited at some length, but even more impressive is the testimony in the memoirs of the 1970s West German Interior Minister, Hans Dietrich Genscher, leader of the pro-business Free Democrats, that the "intransigence of industry lobbyists" was an "object lesson" in "environmental policy." These sorts of attitudes have led many twenty-first century environmentalists to see capitalism as the chief enemy of the environment.[35]

The environmental record of the Eastern Bloc countries, from the mid-1960s until their end in 1989–1991, shows that centrally planned economies, quite lacking private property and profit motives, can nonetheless be environmentally destructive—more so than their capitalist counterparts, all while producing far fewer consumer goods than them. Repulsion at the visible environmental destruction played a major role in the mass movements opposing communist rule in Europe during the years 1989–91, although the environmental improvements that followed the end of communism were due less to democratic government or new attitudes toward the environment than to the collapse of noncompetitive industries exposed to a world market. If there is no industrial production, there are no emissions of toxic gases from factories.

The years after 1970 also saw large-scale changes in the relationship between humans and the environment in the economically less-developed countries of Africa, Asia, and Latin America. Four elements predominated, all somewhat different from circumstances in either the wealthiest countries of the world, or the USSR and its allies in the Eastern Bloc. One is that growing industrialization, and a spread of consumer capitalism, particularly in Asia, brought together at one time what had been problems in the more affluent Western countries in separate periods. Worldwide declines in sulfur dioxide emissions are entirely attributable to Europe and North America, while these emissions rose in the rest of the world. Adding to high sulfur dioxide and particulate levels, from the burning of coal for power, cities such as Beijing, Bangkok, Mexico City, or Delhi acquired from the 1970s onward steadily higher levels of nitrogen oxides as automobile use became ever more common.[36]

A second element was the great expansion of worldwide economic interactions in the last three decades of the twentieth century, what generally goes under the heading of "globalization." Its effects were multifaceted and put particular stress on human interactions with the biosphere in Asia, Africa, and Latin America. Globalization meant both new economic departures, including the rise of industrial production in countries such as China, India, Thailand, South Korea, or Brazil, as well as the intensification of the previous role of African, Asian, and Latin American countries in supplying raw materials to Western Europe, North America, or Japan. The great tropical forests of the southern hemisphere, especially the Amazon Basin and in Southeast Asia—reservoirs of the globe's biodiversity—were the main victims. It was not so much that they were clear-cut to harvest exotic woods—although that certainly happened—as that they were eliminated in order to be replaced with palm oil plantations, coffee bushes, soybean fields, or cattle pastures, whose products were destined for export to more prosperous countries.

In September 1997, fires set in the forests of Borneo and Sumatra in Indonesia, to eliminate the indigenous vegetation for replacement with palm oil plantations, got out of control. There were 9.76 million hectares burned, equivalent to about half the land area of Great Britain, and plumes of smoke spread to Malaysia, Singapore, Brunei, southern Thailand, and the Philippines. Airplanes and ships collided in the gloom; the air pollution index in the Malaysian city of Kuching reached 800—at 250, people are supposed to refrain from working outdoors. Damages, estimated at over $4.4 billion, were greater than the Exxon Valdez oil spill and the chemical disaster at Bhopal put together. The spread and effects of the 1997 fires were particularly extreme because of the strong El Niño that year, but haze and smoke from the burning of tropical forests in Indonesia has become a regular annual occurrence.[37]

If economic change, whether in the form of industrialization or intensified international trade, led to increased pressure on the natural environment in much of Asia, Africa, and Latin America during the last quarter of the twentieth century, so did its opposite, economic stasis, particularly when combined with high rates of population growth. When there was no increased agricultural productivity, more people could only be fed by expanding farmland, at the cost of forest or grasslands, or by increasing cultivation on steep hillsides and other topographically questionable areas. Growing urban populations meant a greater market for large-scale woodcutting, intensifying deforestation. While these developments were common in parts of Central America and South Asia, they were perhaps most prevalent in East Africa, one of the very poorest areas in the entire world. In highland Ethiopia, where the effects of poverty and population increase were aggravated by war and political upheaval, farmers expanded cultivation into forestland. Lacking fertilizer and needing crops, they could not leave land fallow to restore its natural fertility. Forests and shrub land declined in size by 30 to 50 percent between c. 1960 and c. 1990.[38]

Finally, the environmentalist wave of the 1970s crested noticeably lower in less-developed countries. There was a strong tendency, part of a broader anti-imperialist attitude, to see the negative consequences of human interaction with the biosphere as both a problem brought on by economically developed countries, and one that they needed to solve, while poorer nations had other, more pressing, concerns. India's Prime Minister Indira Gandhi stated, at the 1972 Stockholm conference on the environment: "Are not poverty and need the greatest polluters?" A few months earlier, Brazil's UN Ambassador Miguel Ozório de Almeida told the General Assembly that it was outrageous for North Americans or Europeans to be concerned with deforestation of the Amazon, since it was not the responsibility of Brazil to deal with the excesses of the world's wealthy countries. He poured sarcasm on many of the themes of an emerging environmentalism, which he described as based on "para- or-pseudo-scientific extrapolation" of the "brain-washing kind": the melting ice-caps, exhaustion of oxygen, toxic pollution, overpopulation.[39]

The prevalence of these attitudes—and not just prime ministers and ambassadors held them—made for difficult relations between North American or West European environmentalists campaigning to save the Amazon rain forest or tigers in India, and the Brazilians or Indians who saw these campaigns as imperialist impositions.

There was plenty of environmental activism in Asia, Africa, or Latin America during the last three decades of the twentieth century. Much of it resembled the kind prevalent in Western Europe or North America during the 1950s—localized, particular, directed toward preservation of group interest against larger projects, whether they involved building a dam, dumping toxic wastes, or creating a wildlife preserve. Theoretically, such groups could have recourse to environmental legislation or environmental bureaucracies, but the influence of these laws and government officials at the local level varied widely.[40]

Two examples from Brazil show how different the interaction between local activists and the government could be. One concerns the city of Cubatão, located between São Paulo and the Atlantic Ocean. A major center of Brazilian industrialization, whose steel mills and petrochemical complexes, produced almost 60 percent of the country's fertilizer, 15 percent of its steel, and 14 percent of its gasoline, Cubatão was, also, immensely polluted. At the end of the 1970s, there was no sewer system, few houses with running water; mercury levels in the Santos estuary were twenty-five times the recommended maximum. High infant mortality and frequent birth defects gave the city and its vicinity the sobriquet the "Valley of Death." Inhabitants of slum neighborhoods formed their own group in 1980, "The Association of Victims of Pollution and Bad Living Conditions of Cubatão," a typical example of a locally oriented organization. Perhaps surprisingly, the local activists benefited from interest and support of both the national and the state governments, then still under military rule. Sewers were built, laws on toxic emissions were enforced, and conditions improved immensely.

The counterexample to this development is the immense Amazon rainforest, mostly, in Brazil, comprising about half of all the tropical forest in the entire world. There were certainly laws protecting the region's environment, beginning with the 1965 Forest Code, requiring that at least 50 percent and usually 80 percent of any land parcel in the Amazon remain unlogged. But large landowners, working closely with local politicians, ignored the law with impunity, clear-cutting the forest and replacing it with soybean fields and cattle pasture. Some of Brazil's national governments openly sympathized with the landowners, seeing the Amazon region as their country's national patrimony and a key to its future economic development. But even more pro-environmental national governments had difficulty exercising their authority against the alliance of local officials and landowners, who flouted the law with impunity. Lúcio Flávio Pinto, a crusading Brazilian journalist, stated in 2005 that "Criminality has turned Amazonia into an enormous green Sicily." As in Cubatão there developed local organizations defending their own interests against environmentally destructive actions, particularly the league of rubber tappers who wanted to preserve the forest and its rubber trees for their own livelihood. Their group's president, Chico Mendes, was murdered in 1989 by gunmen working for the landowners. Largely untouched until the 1970s, about a fifth of the Brazilian Amazon has been deforested since then—admittedly, not so great a proportion of the tropical forest as in Indonesia or Thailand, where even nominal governmental control over the actions of landowners and politicians is absent.[41]

EMERGING ISSUES

Looking at the consequences of changes in attitudes and practices toward the environment beginning in the 1960s and accelerating, as we've seen, the following decade, a pessimist might note their limitations: improvements primarily in economically advanced countries, and even there, some areas, such as nitrogen oxide levels, where progress was slow. A rosier view would take in the declines in emissions of substances with especially pernicious health consequences, such as sulfur dioxide, particulates, and heavy metals; restrictions on or prohibitions of organochlorides; improvements in conditions of rivers and lakes; greater efficiency in energy use; and noticeably less-toxic workplaces. These changes for the better were mostly in wealthier parts of the world, but the experience of Taiwan or South Korea showed that greater affluence led to increased concern about human relationship to the natural world, and the large number of environmental activists in India, Venezuela, or Brazil, suggested improving future prospects.

The problem with deciding whether the pessimists or the optimists are right is that in the last two decades of the twentieth century new forms of human impact on nature emerged. Their effects were global in scope and, potentially, at least, unprecedented in their consequences, making past criteria for evaluating the effects of human action on the natural world obsolete and also revealing the inefficacy of previous remedial measures. Two new environmental issues of the Late Millennium Era, destruction of the ozone layer and climate change from greenhouse gases, illuminate these developments.

A key feature distinguishing these new elements from past ones was a lack of perceptibility. Unlike Londoners choking on coal-dust-laden fog, the cats of Minimata staggering about, banging into walls and falling into the sea, rivers catching fire and smelling like chemical wastes, or the children of Magnitogorsk being given whiffs of oxygen, there were no consequences of the destruction of the ozone layer or the increase in heat-trapping gases that were immediately and evidently apparent to the human senses. Even more, the effects that did occur were not evidently attributable to their causes. Global warming appears as additional days with higher temperatures—but such days occur regularly each year and public opinion polling has found that stretches of hot weather increase the public's belief in the reality of climate change, while cold spells decrease it. In addition, there are many causes of warmer weather or related changes in precipitation preceding the increased presence of greenhouse gases in the atmosphere and continuing afterward as well. Natural processes, such as volcanic eruptions, affect atmospheric ozone, and while the rising amount of ultraviolet radiation from the sun reaching the earth's surface as a result of declining atmospheric ozone does cause skin cancer, plenty of skin cancers occur even with an intact ozone layer.

Another distinguishing feature of these new elements is their elimination of the geographic link between causes and effects. Consequences of the emissions of nitrogen oxides, the discharges of heavy metals, or the spraying of pesticides were greatest where they occurred. Sulfur dioxide emissions could be blown by winds across national boundaries, creating the cross-border problem of acid rain, and nitrates in fertilizer could be washed off farmland down rivers into oceans hundreds or even thousands of miles away. Even these effects were centered in particular regions—the ocean's so-called dead zones (technically areas of eutrophication and hypoxia) for instance, at the mouths of major rivers, caused by the concentration of nitrates.[42] By contrast, CO_2 emissions from a power plant in Guangzhou, a truck on an interstate in Illinois, or as a result of the clearing of tropical forest in the Amazon affect the climate across the entire globe. Action to deal with these new forms of human environmental impact would have to be on a worldwide scale.

The combination of lack of perceptibility and ambiguity of causation with the crossing of boundaries of nations, social systems, and levels of economic development made coming to terms with the consequences of emissions that damaged the ozone layer and increased the heat-trapping ability of the atmosphere extraordinarily difficult. Under these circumstances, it is striking how different the efforts to do so turned out. The prohibition on the production of chemicals damaging to the ozone layer begun with the Montreal Accords of 1988, has been eminently successful, and the ozone layer has already begun to recuperate. Similar attempts to limit the emissions of greenhouse gases, beginning with the Kyoto Protocol of 1997, have failed: greenhouse gas emissions and their concentration in the atmosphere have both risen at an accelerated pace.

The idea that human activities could influence global climate was first proposed in 1896 by Svente Arrhenius, a Swedish chemist, one of the first recipients of the Nobel Prize. Arrhenius's argument was that burning coal gave off carbon dioxide, a gas that absorbed infrared radiation, preventing it from streaming out into space and so gradually warming the earth's atmosphere and its surface. His hypothesis was widely debated, almost exclusively in scientific circles, during the first three-quarters of the twentieth century. Interest in it centered on efforts by geologists, physicists, and meteorologists to understand the development of earth's climate over the course of hundreds of thousands and millions of years, in particular the reason for the appearance and disappearance of the ice ages. As late as the 1970s, there were experts who thought that the interglacial period characteristic of the world's climate for the last twelve thousand years was coming to an end, and that the globe's future temperature trajectory was downward. However, even at this relatively early date, most scientists investigating the issue foresaw a warming future.[43]

A prime difficulty scientists faced was lack of data. People had been systematically recording temperatures since the nineteenth century, but in different ways and to very different extents in various parts of the world. (It was not necessarily the case that economically advanced regions of Europe and North America had better records than less-developed parts of the world, for nineteenth-century imperialists had sometimes kept good temperature records in their African or Asian colonial possessions.) Records had to be standardized and made compatible, gaps filled in, and new information systematically collected. The Cold War unintentionally helped: military weather stations to facilitate the use of airpower and observations of the atmosphere to detect hostile countries' nuclear testing both provided masses of new data. By the 1970s, satellites were beginning to add information about the condition of the earth's atmosphere, particularly its upper layers, much harder to study from the ground.

Going from data to analysis and projections required the elucidation of mathematical models of the earth's climate. The challenge to any model was that many factors needed to be considered—solar radiation, greenhouse gases, clouds, topography, bodies of water, movement of the air, just to mention a few. Because the equations in these models were nonlinear, they had no exact solutions, so approximate answers had to be calculated, a procedure involving thousand- or even million-fold iterations. This required increasing amounts of computing power to solve ever-more-complex equations with multiplying climatic variables. The steady expansion of computing capacity from the 1960s onward made these calculations possible.[44]

Investigations of atmospheric ozone followed a similar path to that of greenhouse gases. The initial discovery of the ozone layer in the stratosphere occurred in the 1920s, but detailed research had to wait for high-altitude flight and rocketry in the postwar era. The question of whether human action could affect atmospheric ozone first emerged in the wake of plans in the 1960s and 1970s to create large fleets of supersonic commercial aircraft. Those fleets, and their exhaust gases, potentially damaging to the ozone layer, never came into existence—not as a result of environmental concerns, but because supersonic aircraft were unprofitable. Hence scientific attention turned to a group of chemicals used as aerosols, refrigerants, and solvents—the chlorofluorocarbons, or CFCs. Much as was the case with greenhouse gases, ascertaining the presence and consequences of CFCs required developing a global network of observations and mathematical models of the gases' circulation in the atmosphere and chemical interaction with the ozone there.[45]

So by the last quarter of the twentieth century, a network of global observations, was in place—precisely as the greenhouse effect and damage to the ozone layer developed on a large scale. Although invented in the 1920s, chlorofluorocarbon use only became widespread in the 1960s, growing exponentially over the two subsequent decades. While humans had been pumping greenhouse gases into the atmosphere since the mid-nineteenth century, atmospheric CO_2 levels in the mid-1960s, at about 320 parts per million, were just 10 percent above their preindustrial average of 290 ppm, but were about to begin a rapid rise. The convergence of scientific analysis and physical reality meant that global warming and the decline of the ozone layer went from subjects of recondite scholarly debates to hot-button issues.[46]

Attempts to resolve both issues were characterized by similar tensions. Industry and business groups fiercely resisted any limitations, proclaiming the results would be economic disaster and asserting that the science behind the environmental effects was, at best, uncertain, at worst, fraudulent. Governments in the industrialized nations of North America, Western Europe, and Japan jockeyed for position, trying to ensure that any environmental measures would hurt the economies of their competitors more than their own. Governments and public opinion in the developing countries of Asia, Africa, and Latin America asserted that they bore no responsibility for environmental damage caused by wealthier countries and refused to be bound by any restrictions or limitations.

Nonetheless, at the Montreal Conference of 1987, the participating countries agreed to cut CFC emissions by 50 percent. In follow-up conferences, held regularly during the 1990s, additional countries, particularly India and China, joined the accords. Agreement was reached on the total elimination of CFCs; the timetable for this elimination was pushed up. Other products attacking the ozone layer, such as the pesticide and insecticide methyl bromide, were added to the list of chemicals to be eliminated. Initially, CFCs were replaced with hydrochlorofluorocarbons, which do about 1 percent as much damage to the ozone layer. After 2000, international agreements were drawn up to eliminate them as well. Emissions of gases attacking the ozone layer have declined by about 95 percent from the late 1980s to 2012; the concentration in the atmosphere of such gases has also come down between 17 and 31 percent at different latitudes and initial signs of recovery in atmospheric ozone began to appear in the second decade of the twenty-first century.[47]

It all seemed like an encouraging precedent for the task of limiting greenhouse gas emissions. Public concern about global warming and damage to the ozone layer rose in tandem, and polling data in North America and Western Europe from the late 1980s and early 1990s showed that there was widespread confusion of the two. The UN-sponsored Villach and Toronto Conferences of 1985 and 1987, respectively, and the 1988 UN decision to form an Intergovernmental Panel on Climate Change, the IPCC, reflected rising public interest in the issue. Following a series of international working group meetings, the 1992 UN Conference on the Environment and Development in Rio de Janeiro began the process of working out an international agreement on limiting the emissions of greenhouse gases, set down in the Kyoto Protocol of 1997. Just as was the case with the CFC agreements, follow-up meetings, particularly in Copenhagen in 2009 and Durban in 2011, would further enhance the process. The proposed procedure was very similar to that of the Montreal Protocol. North America, Europe, and Japan would begin reducing emissions, to be followed by Brazil, India, and China.[48]

None of this worked as planned. The US Senate almost unanimously rejected the Kyoto Protocol, so the United States never participated. Asian, African, and Latin American countries refused to adhere to it. The upshot appears in Figure 1.1.

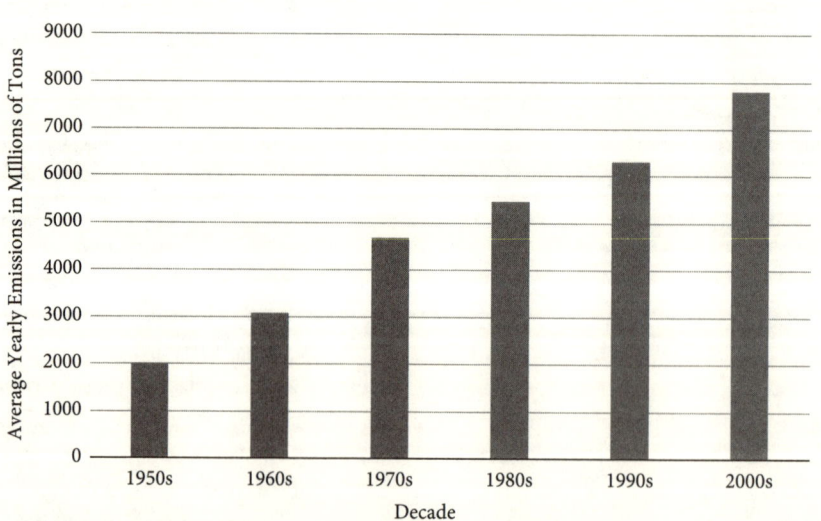

FIGURE 1.1 Average Yearly CO_2 Emissions, 1950–2010, by Decade

CO_2 emissions increased dramatically during the postwar period of rapid economic growth, with average yearly emissions rising by about 50 percent per decade in the 1960s and 1970s. Following the oil price shocks of the years 1973–79, and the gradual development of greater energy efficiency in industry, transportation, and residential and commercial structures, as well as declines in the rate of economic growth, emissions continued to increase, but at a noticeably slower pace, about 15 percent per decade in the 1980s and 1990s. After 2000, when the Kyoto Protocol was supposed to be fully in effect, not only did average yearly emissions ppm not decline, their rate of increase actually rose, yearly averages in the first decade of the new millennium, 24 percent above those of the 1990s. At the beginning of the millennium, there were modest declines in emissions from European countries, the chief supporters of the accords reached in Kyoto, although these were mostly the result of the collapse of industrial production in the former Eastern Bloc during the 1990s. US carbon emissions increased by about one-seventh in the twenty years following 1990. Nonetheless all these developments were simply dwarfed by the fourfold jump in CO_2 emissions occurring in China.[49] With all the greenhouse gases being pumped into the air, the carbon dioxide content of the atmosphere continued to rise more rapidly than ever. Figure 1.2 shows the yearly average CO_2 concentration at the peak of Mauna Loa in Hawaii (the best, continuously observed, data series).[50]

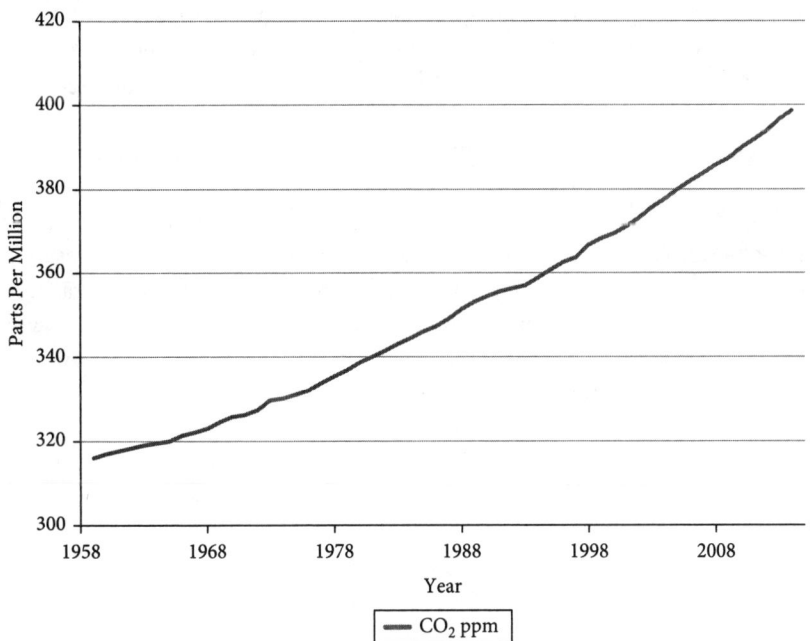

FIGURE 1.2 Atmospheric Carbon Dioxide Content, 1959–2014

How can we explain the astonishing difference in the outcome of similar procedures about similar issues brought up at about the same time—rapid declines in gases affecting the ozone layer, exponential increases in CO_2 levels? One answer is that the state of knowledge about the ozone layer was better than that about greenhouse gases and global climate; the famous ozone hole over the Antarctic, for instance, offered clear and compelling evidence of the effects of CFCs, making it easier to propose banning them. The trouble with this argument is that the dramatic announcement of the discovery of the Antarctic ozone hole in mid-September 1987 came two weeks after the conclusion of the Montreal negotiations. The ozone hole may have propelled the process begun in Montreal, though the connection between CFCs and the ozone hole was not immediately established.

There were ozone skeptics but far fewer than for global warming. "Climate skeptics," as they call themselves, or "global warming denialists" as their opponents designate them, have raised questions about growing carbon dioxide concentrations, increasing temperatures, and the links between the two: questions that had a certain plausibility, in view of the extremely complex forms of data collection, model-building, and mathematical analysis needed to understand climate change. These self-same objections—often coming from the very same people and the foundations at which they were employed—were raised against the data on CFC emissions but had been overcome.[51]

There has been, starting in the 1970s and continuing into the twenty-first century, massive and well-funded opposition to the idea of limiting greenhouse gas emissions from wealthy and very powerful fossil fuel companies. But eminently powerful and wealthy chemical firms, including DuPont, BASF, and Imperial Chemicals Industries, strongly opposed any restrictions on CFCs. They promoted scientific research raising questions about the connections between CFCs and the ozone layer and proposed, instead of taking any action to limit CFCs, extended studies of the matter—precisely the same tactics that fossil fuel companies have taken toward proposals to limit greenhouse gas emissions. Ironically, the IPCC itself and increasingly detailed studies of greenhouse gas emissions and global temperatures were the result of these delaying tactics.

A very similar point could be made about another chronic problem with the Kyoto Protocol and its sequels: the constant sparring between wealthier and developing countries. These disputes also occurred in the wake of the Montreal Accords. Limitations on CFC emissions originally excluded countries from Asia, Africa and Latin America, which joined the phase-out regime in the 1990s, only after wealthier countries agreed to compensate them. The compensation payments themselves have been a source of tension, as wealthier countries seek to limit their contributions and to administer them through the World Bank, while the developing countries want more funds and less oversight on how to spend them. Both sides have negotiated in bad faith about these compensation payments. Somehow, the elimination of production and consumption of chemicals damaging the ozone layer has continued unabated.

So what explains the difference between the ozone layer and climate change issues? One more plausible reason is that while the gases destroying the ozone layer had a wide variety of important industrial and consumer uses, from aerosol cans to air-conditioners to cleaning silicon chips used in microelectronics, their applications pale in comparison to those of greenhouse gas emissions. About two-thirds of such emissions come from burning fossil fuels, primarily to generate energy. Most of the rest result from agriculture, especially deforestation.[52] Food and energy are basics. It was and remains much harder to find substitutes.

This greater challenge certainly explains why there might have been slower progress on limiting greenhouse gas emissions than eliminating CFCs, but not why there has been movement in the other direction. The reason is the role played by the world's wealthiest and most powerful country, the United States, which was at the peak of its global influence in the 1990s, when crucial decisions about greenhouse gases and the ozone layer were being made. It was the US government and American public opinion that stood behind measures to eliminate production of gases damaging to the ozone layer. Aerosols containing CFCs were prohibited in 1978, and the United States was the first country to do so. The American government was the major driving force behind efforts to get an international agreement reducing CFCs and other ozone-depleting gases (with assistance from the Netherlands, Scandinavian countries, and Canada), even, surprisingly, during the administration of Ronald Reagan, known for its skepticism of and hostility toward environmentalism. Other industrial countries resisted American efforts. The Japanese environmental protection agency announced that ozone layer depletion was no problem, because Asians are immune from skin cancer. European governments denounced research on the effects of CFCs on the ozone layer as "U.S. science," and condemned American diplomats for "pandering to an environmentalist gallery." As for the government of USSR, for years it simply did not show up at international conferences on the ozone layer.[53]

With greenhouse gases, roles were almost entirely reversed. The United States has blocked attempts to draw up plans for limitations. Such actions reflect a broader intellectual and political trend of the 1990s; large swathes of public opinion refused to accept the reality of climate change occurring through greenhouse gas emissions, and acceptance of this idea and consequent opposition to any efforts to limit CO_2 emissions became a signature item of right-of-center politics. These anti-environmentalist attitudes and their connection with right-wing politics had not been the case in the 1960s and 1970s, and were also not the case in other parts of the world.[54]

One of the characteristic features of this opposition has been the conflation of anti-environmental attitudes with pro-capitalist ones. Particularly prominent American "climate skeptic" scientists included Frederick Seitz, one of the physicists who worked on the creation of the atomic bomb' and S. Fred Singer, a physicist and leading rocket scientist. They, and their fellow climate skeptics, were veteran Cold Warriors, who went from battling communists to battling environmentalists, whom they perceived as the latest enemies of capitalism. Opposing restrictions on greenhouse gas emissions was a way of promoting the virtues of individualism and creating a deregulated, privatized free market, a guiding ideal of the Late Millennium Era in the English-speaking world. When US Interior Secretary Donald Hodel attempted in 1987 to torpedo the Montreal Accords and CFC regulation by rejecting government controls on industry and calling for personal responsibility and individual initiative in dealing with increased ultraviolet radiation and subsequent cancer risks by wearing hats and sunglasses, and applying sunscreen, his assertions were met with a blast of public derision. What was unacceptable in the late 1980s would be normative a decade later.[55]

Whether policies to reduce greenhouse gas emissions really are anticapitalist remains debatable. One might think that developing wind and solar power, building electric smart grids, manufacturing fuel-efficient or electric cars, or simply installing insulation in residential and commercial structures offers manifold opportunities for entrepreneurs to make money. Nonetheless, the perceived connection between the two has been a powerful political force, especially when helped along with financial contributions from fossil fuel corporations and exploited by conservative politicians and media outlets, helping to prevent any action from being taken.

In the end, the two great worldwide instances of problematic human relationship to nature have left a very different heritage for the future. Damage to the ozone layer done by CFCs and other ozone-destroying chemicals will last until somewhere around 2070, but emissions have been drastically reduced and the ozone layer has begun to recuperate. Emissions of CO_2 and other greenhouse gases, by contrast, have risen and their atmospheric concentration continues to increase. Consequences for the global climate seem well established, although their magnitude and extent remain unclear. Generally, collecting more data and developing more sophisticated models to analyze it tends to exclude the possibility of extreme results. In the case of climate change, the opposite is true. The more information we gather and analyze, the more extreme the consequences appear.[56]

Three Avatars of Malthus

One way to analyze the human relationship to the biosphere across the entire Age of Interconnection is via the theories of Thomas Malthus and their revisions and extensions. Three versions of Malthus's ideas—we might call them $Malthus_1$, $Malthus_2$, and $Malthus_3$—seem relevant, each focusing on different elements in the relationships of humanity and nature, each having its heyday in one of the three distinct periods, characteristic of the years 1945–2000, and each appearing somewhat differently in the early years of the new millennium.

$Malthus_1$ is closest to the original concepts of the economist and moralist himself, namely—as discussed earlier—that human population tends to outstrip the food supply. This idea had its heyday in the postwar era. The widespread starvation of Malthusian fears has never come to pass, above all, because of increasing agricultural productivity. Whether growth in agricultural output can continue to keep up with population increases in the twenty-first century is an issue that agronomists and economists continue to debate.[57]

$Malthus_2$ expands upon and differentiates the arguments of $Malthus_1$ by adding economic growth to population growth and asserting that their combination tends to outstrip the availability of all natural resources, not just agricultural products. This idea flourished above all in the 1970s, articulated in the Club of Rome's report. Since the Club of Rome's doomsday was sometime in the middle decades of the twenty-first century, it may be that we are just not there yet. Nonetheless, it would be fair to say that the particularly hyperbolic version of $Malthus_2$ prevalent in the 1970s, a period of shortages, inflation, and oil price shocks, all perceived as consequences of excessive and unsustainable human demands on nature, seems less plausible. In part, this was because the exponential growth in population and the economy characteristic of the quarter century after 1945 and presupposed in the Club of Rome's report did not continue in the last quarter of the twentieth century. Just as $Malthus_1$ assumed that food could not be produced more productively, $Malthus_2$ assumed that resources could not be used more efficiently and that new resources could not be found or existing ones used in new ways. Even if, as environmentalists insist, the resources of the natural world are finite and limited, this does not imply they are so finite and so limited that there is no way for humans to stretch their use a long way into the future.[58]

Still more difficult to appraise is $Malthus_3$, which relates to climate change, the idea that the combination of population and economic growth places demands on the biosphere that are unsustainable, undermining the conditions necessary for economic and population growth. This was an idea that post-1945 Malthusians certainly considered, although it was generally subsidiary to their views on growth outstripping resources. Popular environmental movements had a lot to say about strains on the biosphere from technological change and economic and population growth, in the form of air and water pollution, oil, chemical and nuclear disasters, and threats to the survival of individual species and of biodiversity more generally. But the impetus of these movements, and of influential books that inspired them, like *Silent Spring*, was toward finding ways to end pollution or to ameliorate its effects rather than the relationship between production and pollution.

The emergence of globalized and non-sensuous forms of human impact on the biosphere gradually brought to the fore the problems of $Malthus_3$. One of the very first accounts outside of scientific circles of increasing atmospheric CO_2 came in *The Limits to Growth*. The book's 1972 prediction of the 2000 level of atmospheric carbon dioxide was very accurate—not too surprisingly, since greenhouse gases have grown at an exponential rate, as the Club of Rome assumed population and output would. But the report mentioned atmospheric carbon dioxide as one example of human overuse of natural resources among many.[59] Only in the Late Millennium Era did the problems posed by $Malthus_3$ became completely clear. $Malthus_3$ both encompassed and superseded $Malthus_2$ and $Malthus_1$. If the technology needed to grow enough crops to feed a rising global population was dependent on farm equipment powered by fossil fuels and large amounts of nitrates as fertilizers—both sources of greenhouse gases—the climate change generated by these greenhouse gases could make it impossible to continue growing the necessary food. If innovative uses of scarce natural resources depended on generous amounts of power—created by burning fossil fuels that emit the largest portion of greenhouse gases—then the climate change generated by these innovative uses could undermine the global economy in which natural resources are exploited and turned into useful goods and services. The challenges posed by $Malthus_2$ and $Malthus_1$ were by no means obsolete. It would still be necessary to grow food for the globe's rising population and to deploy the natural resources needed to keep the economy functioning. However, these would have to be accomplished while allowing the biosphere to retain the necessary conditions for human life to flourish on the earth.

The question posed in the Late Millennium Era about the human presence in the natural world—namely, could it continue in ways that would not degrade the biosphere so as to make that presence impossible—remains to be answered. Addressing it will require action across lines of geography, national sovereignty, economic development, and political systems. The contrast between the effort to limit the emissions of ozone-destroying and greenhouse gases suggests different answers.

2 | Disease

OUR RELATIONSHIP TO NATURE occurs as much within us as outside us. This internal version can be harder to perceive because it is individualized. The presence of toxin-emitting microorganisms, malignant cells, or arterial plaque in any one person might be the consequence of personal behavior, genetic makeup, or chance; but aggregate them across a country, continent, or the entire world over a period of decades and a different picture emerges. The increase or decline of disease in large groups of people is as much a result of their relation to nature as levels of CO_2 or nitrogen oxides in the atmosphere, or concentrations of nitrates at the mouths of rivers and forest cover in the tropics.

An Age of Antibiotics

The dominant form of illness at the start of the Age of Interconnection, and the chief source of mortality was infectious disease. There were the great killers: malaria, smallpox, and tuberculosis; waterborne maladies like dysentery, typhoid fever, and cholera; as well as syphilis and yaws—a predominantly tropical disease caused by a microorganism similar to the syphilis spirochete but spread by skin contact. A new (or perhaps just newly discovered) malady, polio, had emerged on a large scale in the 1920s. Pneumonia, meningitis, or staphylococcus and streptococcus infections could all result from a trivial illness or injury but have a fatal outcome.

It would be unfair to imagine that experts were helpless against these threats. As early as 1796 Edward Jenner had discovered that vaccination could prevent smallpox. Measures of environmental improvement, from draining swamps to eliminate mosquito habitat, to providing clean drinking water and adequate sewage, or better ventilated living spaces, to say nothing of rising standards of living enabling better nutrition and so a more active immune defense system, had reduced mortality from malaria, dysentery, or tuberculosis—at least in parts of the world. But once infectious diseases struck, physicians were largely helpless. In 1924, the sixteen-year-old son of US President Calvin Coolidge got a blister on his foot from an ill-fitting tennis shoe. It became infected, the bacteria reached his bloodstream, and he died in a few days.[1]

The possibilities for treatment were completely transformed between 1935 and 1955 by the discovery of a fundamentally new kind of drug, the antimicrobials. The very first example of these drugs, prontosil, part of the broader group known as the sulfonamides, was synthesized in the laboratories of the German chemical giant, IG Farben, which had a long history of seeking medical uses for synthetic dyestuffs. Following animal experiments and patent applications, the drug's effect on streptococcus bacteria—cause of rheumatic fever, scarlet fever, childbed fever, and septicemia—was made public in 1935 by the pathologist Gerhard Domagk, who had directed the research. He was awarded the Nobel Prize in medicine for his discovery, but the Nazi regime, smarting from the awarding of the Nobel Peace Prize to the pacifist Carl von Ossietzky, who was imprisoned in a concentration camp, prevented Domagk from traveling to Stockholm to accept it.

By 1945, there were twelve different sulfonamide drugs on the market. Prominent patients included another US president's son, Franklin D. Roosevelt Jr., in 1936—with a happier outcome than that of Calvin Coolidge Jr.—and Winston Churchill in 1943. Although representing the beginning of a new medical era, sulfonamides had distinct clinical limitations. They were only effective against a narrow range of bacteria and required very high doses, often with unpleasant side effects, to destroy disease-causing microorganisms. The drug that shaped the new era of antimicrobials would not have these drawbacks.

That drug was, of course, penicillin, and the story of its discovery has become legendary. In September 1928, British surgeon and bacteriological researcher Alexander Fleming, investigating the staphylococcus bacteria, found that one of the petri dishes in his lab at St. Mary's Hospital in London, had been contaminated by mold. About to throw it out, he observed that where the mold had grown, the bacteria had died. He eventually concluded that the mold, whose Latin name was *Penicillium notatum*, contained an antimicrobial agent, which he dubbed "penicillin." This would be the first antibiotic, an antimicrobial produced from a living organism. Contributing to the legendary character of its discovery was its serendipity. The contamination only occurred in the first place because the temperatures were unusually cool that summer. The mold spread because Fleming had left his petri dishes to go on vacation. On his return, he happened to notice the effect, which was very different from the organized and systematic chemical investigations producing the sulfonamides.

In the decade following Fleming's discovery, isolating the antibacterial agent proved difficult, and by 1939 researchers at Cambridge had only succeeded in producing minute quantities, useless for any actual medical care. The outbreak of the Second World War, an immense hothouse of technological progress, turned a scientific curiosity into a fundamentally new kind of medicine. There were obvious battlefield uses for an antimicrobial, if it could be produced in sufficient quantities. This was accomplished in the laboratories of the US Department of Agriculture in Peoria, Illinois, devoted to studying fermentation processes using food remnants. In the case of penicillin, the key to its large-scale manufacture was fermentation with the assistance of corn steep liquor, a byproduct of the manufacture of corn starch.

During the war, every combatant nation tried to produce penicillin. Experiments with its industrial production went on, not just in the United States and the United Kingdom, but in Germany, the USSR, Japan, and China, as well as in labs in France, the Netherlands, and Czechoslovakia under German occupation. The Anglo-American efforts were the only ones leading to large-scale production. The new drug's antimicrobial action decreased the death rate of soldiers with chest wounds by over two-thirds. German POWs ruefully noted that the sulfonamides their army physicians had at their disposal were much less effective against sepsis in wounds. Ads from the American drug company Schenley Laboratories showed a wounded soldier receiving an IV on the battlefield, with the caption, "Thanks to PENICILLIN . . . He Will Come Home!" The company did not publicize an equally important military use for the new drug: quickly curing soldiers with gonorrhea and syphilis and returning them to the battlefield.

Although not as decisive as radar or the atomic bomb, antibiotics helped the Allied powers ensure their victory. Following the war's end, penicillin manufacture was spread by the victorious powers and UN agencies across the world with a liberality difficult to imagine in today's regime of rigid intellectual property rights. Czechoslovakia, Austria, Italy, and Japan all became major centers of production. The origins of the new drug led to a search for other fungi, molds, and bacteria with an antimicrobial effect. The results were astonishing: some 250 new drugs in the second half of the twentieth century. Penicillin itself was part of a broader group called the β-lactam antibiotics. Following them were the aminoglycosides, whose best-known exemplar is streptomycin, introduced in 1946. They were succeeded, in the late 1940s and early 1950s, by the tetracyclines—so-called broad-spectrum antibiotics—and rifamycins. The macrolides, such as erythromycin, were developed in the 1950s, followed by the quinolones. The latter were the last major antibiotic family to be discovered, although in the 1980s new drugs were derived from these families, including azithromycin from the macrolides and ciproflaxin from the quinolones. For all these innovations, the first antibiotic remained the king. As late as the first decade of the twenty-first century, over half the outpatient antibiotic prescriptions written in Europe were for penicillin and its chemical derivatives.

The new "miracle drugs" changed everything. People at the brink of death from pneumonia, tuberculosis, or staph infections were cured almost overnight. Demand surged; in the United States alone, output of penicillin jumped sevenfold between 1948 and 1956. By 1980, global penicillin production had reached 17,000 metric tons, enough to treat every single person in the entire world. The new medicine spread quickly on a global scale, partly due to the campaign to eliminate yaws, launched during the 1950s by the World Health Organization, a branch of the newly founded United Nations. More than forty-three million people, especially in the tropical regions of southeast Asia and Africa, received doses of penicillin. At least one-and-a-half million Nigerians were injected with the drug, spreading awareness of the new medicine and encouraging popular belief in its widespread curative powers in Africa's most populous country.[2]

The use of penicillin heralded a new era of medicine and encouraged visions of an even more remarkable future. Consider this paean to the new drug issued in 1946 by George Bankoff, an English popular science writer and a prominent physician, "Soon young ladies will be able to buy their lipsticks impregnated with Penicillin. They still will have their lips made beautiful and inviting, but the danger of infection that every kiss potentially can transmit will be removed. Facial creams, mascaras, and, of course, all tooth-paste will be impregnated with Penicillin too, thus preserving teeth healthy and unblemished." It was a whole new world, according to Bankoff. "Penicillin given in sufficient dose to any would-be dictator, or any evil genius trying to discover more potent rockets or liquid air-bombs, will perhaps mellow their brain and subdue their evil desires."[3]

It is easy now to smile at this naivete, but human health really was improving, across the entire world, in the decades following the Second World War. The statisticians of the United Nations found that life expectancy at birth, for both sexes combined, increased by more than ten years in the postwar decades, from about forty-seven years in 1950–1955 to fifty-eight in the first half of the 1970s (or 1970–75). This increase spanned all continents and countries, though both larger and more rapid in the "less developed" countries than in the more developed ones, where life expectancy advanced by only six years, or 10 percent.[4] In other words, life expectancy rose faster and furthest where infectious diseases were the most prevalent, strongly suggesting that there was a close connection between the success in combating these diseases and the decline in mortality rates. Public health measures to provide clean drinking water and reduce sewage—as simple as systematically building latrines—played a major role, as did an increasing frequency of vaccinations. In the immediate postwar years, the invention of a vaccine for polio appeared to the public as a similar scientific miracle and its use spread from wealthier to poorer countries over the second half of the century. Less spectacular but more significant was vaccination against a far more prevalent disease with a very high fatality rate, diphtheria. A World Health Organization vaccination campaign starting in the 1980s reduced the incidence of this disease, particularly common in Africa and South Asia, by two orders of magnitude.[5]

The wonder drugs were understandably greeted with fervor, resulting in a distinctly indiscriminate use of antibiotics. Patients clamored for them even when suffering from viral illnesses, against which antimicrobials had no effect. In North America or Europe, they had to badger their doctors to gain access to these medicines, which were generally available over the counter in Africa or Latin America and in many Asian countries—sometimes legally, and if not, existing laws and regulations on prescription drugs were generally not enforced. Even when antibiotics were prescribed patients were likely to take their medicine erratically, skip doses, or not complete the entire prescribed course.

Not content with the very-considerable profits from introducing new antimicrobials, pharmaceutical firms rushed to market reformulations of existing drugs. When Dorsey Laboratories introduced "Tain," in the 1960s, a combination of the antibiotic triacetyl oleandomycin placed in a tablet along with aspirin, a decongestant, and an antihistamine, Heinz Eichenwald, chair of pediatrics at Texas Southwestern Medical Center, observed, "One might wonder why the manufacturer did not include vitamins, sex hormones, a contraceptive and corticosteroids to cover all other eventualities."[6] Combining corporate rush for profit with lack of controls, pharmaceutical corporations exported to poorer countries stocks of antibiotics not admitted for use in wealthier ones.

Contributing to the massive use of antibiotics were doctors themselves. Every bit as much influenced by the expansive possibilities of miracle drugs, and the very real effects they had, they overprescribed the new medicines, and took a more casual attitude toward antisepsis and sterile practice in hospitals, since antibiotics could easily deal with resulting infections. Physicians resisted any effort to control, or even to devise guidelines for, antibiotic use, setting their clinical experience against government or scholarly experts. In 1974, toward the end of the age of indiscriminate use of antibiotics, one Texas doctor pronounced "that the only thing being over-prescribed," was an "over-dose of government being rammed down the esophagus of the medical profession." His libertarian assertion had a point. The first countries to regulate strictly the use of antibiotics were communist Czechoslovakia and the social democratic Scandinavian lands.[7]

It would be fair to say that in the postwar era antibiotics were deployed much like pesticides. And like pesticides, the indiscriminate use of antimicrobials posed the danger of development of resistance. Antibiotics given for useless purposes, such as combating viral infections, or taken in inadequate doses, threatened to replace a population of bacteria susceptible to the drugs with one immune to its effect. An awareness of the problem of antibiotic-resistant bacteria began to affect the practice of medicine in the 1980s and 1990s and even to reach the general public via headlines about so-called superbugs. Yet knowledge of the potential for the development of bacterial resistance was present from the very beginning. Alexander Fleming's Nobel Prize acceptance speech in 1945 warned that "negligent use of penicillin" could change the nature of microbes, rendering the drug ineffective against them.[8]

Within a few years of using antibiotics, cases of resistance began to be reported. Max Finland, a Harvard Medical School professor, America's most prominent infectious disease expert in the 1950s, spent much of that decade warning of the dangers of developing resistance. First uses of antibiotics to treat tuberculosis in Kenya, Rwanda, Burundi, Sudan, Hong Kong, and southern India, during the 1950s and early 1960s, brought, surprisingly quickly, in their wake cases of the disease impervious to the standard antibiotics, Streptomycin and Isoniazid.[9] Yet the broad-based reality was that infectious diseases really were declining in the postwar era. In 1967, the US Surgeon General William H. Stewart was reported to have asserted, "It is time to close the book on infectious diseases and declare the war against pestilence won." It was a remark that would be quoted endlessly, for decades to come. Stewart, a physician worried about the potential for the development of resistance to antibiotics, never said such a thing. Believing he had made that statement reflected the conviction that antimicrobials had opened a new chapter in the history of the human relationship with nature.[10]

SMALLPOX, MALARIA, AND TUBERCULOSIS IN THE POSTWAR ERA

The stories of three great killers among infectious diseases—smallpox, malaria, and tuberculosis—in the quarter century following the Second World War explains the euphoria with which antibiotics were initially greeted. All three diseases had rampaged through the world in the first half of the twentieth century, each probably causing more deaths than both world wars put together. After 1945, they were in decline and the prospects for their permanent reduction or even eradication seemed bright. But the combination of their nature, the possibilities for new medical treatments, and the state of public health on a global scale would lead to very different results.

Smallpox cut a long and deep swath through human history. An example of the death it brought in its wake occurred when European explorers brought the virus to the Americas after 1492, infecting an indigenous population that had had no contact with the disease and so had built up no immunities. A Spanish friar described how the Aztecs, contracting smallpox, "died in heaps, like bedbugs."[11] Native American populations fell by 30 to 50 percent in a decade and up to 90 percent after a century, at least in part as a result of smallpox. Survival rates in other parts of the world, where there was a long history of exposure to the illness, were better, but those who escaped death had to tolerate a high fever, the possibility of blindness, and the deep scarring over the entire body, giving the disease its name.

Smallpox was also a disease for which an effective prophylaxis was developed: vaccination, the deliberate rubbing into the skin of material from the pustules of a similar but minor disease, cowpox. In today's medical language, the cowpox virus stimulated the body's immune defense system to attack the genetically similar smallpox virus. Of course, none of that was known in 1796, when the British physician Edward Jenner, observing that milkmaids who came into contact with cows seemed not to contract smallpox, began experimenting with vaccination. The procedure, adopted and made compulsory in much of Europe in the course of the nineteenth century, resulted in a sharp decline in the incidence of the disease.

In spite of vaccination, the disease remained vigorously present in Europe. Vaccination only worked for about ten years, leaving people in danger of a renewed infection; governments lacked the ability to enforce universal vaccination or met—particularly in English-speaking countries—with vehement opposition to the procedure. Opponents clamored against government interference in their lives or violation of their rights, and feared, among many other things, the introduction of foreign substances into their bodies. Even in European countries where vaccination was common, there were occasional waves of smallpox, such as the 1870–1871 epidemic that took a half million lives. Although the situation in Europe and the Americas gradually improved, the First World War temporarily disrupted public health measures, resulting in still more smallpox epidemics in central and eastern Europe, as well as in the United States, where popular opposition to vaccination was widespread.

Assessing the human toll in South America, Asia, or Africa, where vaccination programs were, at best, sporadic and the disease was endemic, is difficult. Official figures were worth little, as researchers in the 1950s found. They compared statistics on cases of smallpox in a given area with the number of individuals showing the characteristic pockmarking, finding that the actual prevalence of the disease was from eight to fifty times the official numbers. A plausible guess would be that smallpox claimed between one hundred and two hundred million victims—the exact number depends on the relative prevalence of the less fatal *variola minor* strain (as opposed to the more lethal *variola major*) during the first half of the twentieth century: many more than the eighty million who died in both world wars.[12]

A disease caused by a virus, smallpox proved impervious to antibiotics. But it was susceptible to the optimistic attitude about infectious disease in the postwar era. In 1958, the World Health Assembly, the meeting of national delegations to the World Health Organization, accepted a proposal for a campaign to eliminate smallpox globally. Full funding only became available in 1966, but the program accomplished its goals. The very last case of naturally occurring smallpox, contracted by a cook named Ali Maow Maalin, was recorded in the Somali harbor town of Merca on October 30, 1977.

Technology played a relatively minor role in the campaign, which profited from the development of a freeze-dried form of the smallpox vaccine, one that remained usable for a month without any need for refrigeration—particularly helpful in tropical countries. The other major technological "advance" was the creation of a bifurcated needle, a two-inch-long piece of stainless steel with two narrowly separated prongs at the end. The prongs could pick up the right amount of vaccine, holding it in place while they were used to scratch the skin, depositing the vaccine at just the appropriate depth.

The success of the campaign was in part a result of the suspension of Cold War rivalries and hostilities. The initial proposal was made by the Soviet delegate to the World Health Assembly, while the program itself was largely administered out of WHO headquarters in Geneva by a small team of Americans from the Centers for Disease Control. Geopolitically speaking, the campaign was resisted in parts of Africa and Asia, where local experts, staffing the regional directorates of the World Health Organization, tended to oppose it. One reason was that they regarded it as impossible to vaccinate everyone. But proponents had no intention of doing so. Rather, they relied on a combination of surveillance and vaccination. Local informants would let public health officials know of any cases of smallpox—and the distinct pockmarks the disease produced made it impossible to hide. Then a team of vaccinators would show up and immunize everyone who might have been exposed. The procedure worked like a charm, producing a maximum of results with distinctly limited resources.

The last human death from smallpox occurred a year after it was eliminated in 1977. Janet Parker, a medical photographer at the University of Birmingham, was infected by viruses that escaped from a research laboratory in the same building where she worked. Since its eradication in nature the smallpox virus has existed only in research labs, and in biological warfare laboratories in the United States and the USSR (and its successor state, the Russian Federation). A standard justification for the continued existence of this massive killer is that it remains useful for research purposes, should smallpox reoccur in nature or be deliberately spread. Given that the smallpox vaccine is not made from the smallpox virus, this seems dubious. More than anything else, the current state of affairs is the result of bureaucratic inertia and the institutional self-preservation of a military apparatus from the Cold War. It is a sad, if (still) minor coda to a remarkable public health accomplishment that overcame barriers of diplomatic suspicion and hostility.[13]

Malaria has as long and almost as deadly a history as smallpox. Its arrival in the New World in the blood of European colonists and the enslaved Africans they shipped to the Americas was yet another fatal import for Native Americans. Although today understood as a malady specific to the tropics, malaria was found worldwide well into the twentieth century, with outbreaks as far north as Siberia. According to one estimate, as many people died from malaria between 1900 and 1950 as from smallpox.[14]

Very much like smallpox, malaria was swept along in the post-1945 euphoria about eliminating infectious disease. In some ways, prospects of that seemed more favorable, because the Second World War had produced new chemicals that could both combat the disease and the environmental conditions in which it thrived. The World Health Organization's campaign to eradicate malaria began a decade before the one to eliminate smallpox and was better funded. The outcome, however, was less happy. Although mortality rates from the disease did decline in the second half of the century, the number of malaria cases continued to climb, particularly in Africa.

In part, this stemmed from the disease's biology. Malaria is the result of a protozoan—a large, single-celled organism with a complex life cycle. Carried by the many species of anopheles mosquito, the protozoan reaches humans when female mosquitoes feed on their blood. The sporozoite form of the protozoan roots and proliferates in the liver, where it is transformed into the merozoite form, bursting out in regular intervals to attack red blood cells. These attacks cause the recurring fever and deep chills that are characteristic features of the disease. Some of the protozoans are transformed into gametocytes, which are returned to the mosquito with another bite and reproduce, producing new sporozoites, ready to infect another person.

It is the parasite's presence in the blood cells that causes the damage. In the particularly malignant species of the protozoan, *Plasmodium falciparum*, up to half the body's red blood cells can be attacked, destroying the blood supply to the kidneys and the brain, and killing its victims. Small children and pregnant women are particularly vulnerable. *P. falciparum* requires persistent warmth to thrive, not reproducing if temperatures fall below 19° C, so cannot spread much beyond the tropics. The other major species, *Plasmodium vivax*, attacks fewer red blood cells and is less likely to bring about a fatal outcome. But its sporozoites can remain in the liver for years, allowing for a recurrence of the fever long after the infected person seems to have recovered from the disease. *P. vivax* is resistant to cold and the dominant form of malaria in temperate climates.

Humans have little natural opposition to malaria: it takes several recurrences before any immunity develops, and even then, it can be lost quickly. Repeated reinfections make the illness chronic; long-term victims suffer from anemia and distended spleens and are plagued by apathy and lack of energy. Lack of natural immunity has dogged efforts to develop an effective vaccine, which would have to stimulate immune responses to the many different forms the protozoan takes in the human body—a task as yet unaccomplished.

Climate, land use, and standards of living play a large role in the spread of malaria. In more moderate climates, unlike the tropics, it is a seasonal disease, since the mosquitoes that spread the parasite, are only present in warmer months. Changes to the land, particularly a result of farming practices that provide environments for the anopheles mosquito to breed—for most, although not all, species, this means pools of stagnant water—affect the prevalence of the disease. So do other factors, such as the use and location of farm animals, an alternative blood source for the mosquito; the quality of housing, providing greater or lesser barriers to the entrance of mosquitoes; and density of human settlement in areas where the mosquitoes breed.

There was a preindustrial and prescientific medicine for malaria. It had been known since the seventeenth century that the bark of the Peruvian cinchona tree was both a prophylaxis against and a treatment of the illness. The drug cannot penetrate the liver to kill the infection there but does destroy all other stages of the protozoan in the bloodstream. In the early nineteenth century, French chemists isolated the active element in the bark—quinine. The raw material was still in short supply, but later in the century efforts to establish cinchona plantations on the island of Java (then Dutch East Indies, today Indonesia) proved successful, greatly increasing the supply of quinine and reducing its price to one-seventh its early nineteenth-century levels. A popular way to ingest the bitter-tasting and nausea-inducing medicine was to dissolve it in sweetened "tonic" water. Drinking a gin and tonic reiterates the medical precautions the British took to rule a very malarial India.

Treating malaria was one thing, trying to roll it back where it was endemic another. As the progress of biology provided knowledge of the etiology of the illness and its insect disease vectors, treatment first became a possibility. Italy, where the disease was more prevalent than anywhere else in Europe or the Americas, became the global laboratory for anti-malaria programs. Starting before the First World War under the rule of the reform-minded prime minister Giovanni Giolitti, the government began an anti-malaria public health program that included handing out quinine to the general population, especially agricultural laborers very prone to malaria, educating them on why they should be taking this proverbially bitter medicine, and trying to overcome the opposition of large landowners and other vested interests. Malaria death rates in 1914 were about one-ninth their

1900 levels. The fascist dictatorship of Benito Mussolini followed up on these efforts in the 1930s, with the regime's public works program to drain the Pontine Marshes south of Rome, a center of disease-bearing mosquitoes for millennia. The results were a major propaganda victory for the dictator, who could tout the transformation of the malarial marshes into rich farmland, whose new settlers lived in sturdy brick houses with screens on their windows and were no longer subject to the dread disease. (Its ravages among the laborers who had actually drained the swamps were something *Il Duce* preferred to pass over in silence.[15])

There were similar developments in the malaria-ridden south of the United States, where programs to hand out quinine in the 1920s and the swamp-drainage and flood-control projects of the Tennessee Valley Authority of the 1930s (these even included arranging for pasturing cows near riverbanks to eliminate vegetation in which mosquitoes could breed) also helped decrease cases of malaria. The Brazilian government and the Rockefeller Foundation teamed up during the same decade to eliminate, successfully, disease-bearing anopheles mosquitoes inadvertently imported from Africa.

As had been the case with the development of antibiotics, the Second World War provided new technologies for the pursuit of these programs. One was the manufacture of new drugs, a priority for the Allied powers after the 1942 Japanese occupation of the Dutch East Indies cut off the world's supply of quinine. Stealing earlier research by IG Farben into the anti-malarial possibilities of its synthetic dyestuffs—efforts that were precursors to the invention of the sulfonamides—US laboratories produced large quantities of the anti-malarial drug atebrine. Its distribution to Allied troops provided yet another technological advantage in the Pacific War, fought on South Pacific islands, New Guinea, and Burma, where malaria was endemic. Atebrine has the unpleasant side effect of turning the user's skin yellow, and a substitute drug, once again from IG Farben, chloroquine, was deployed late in the war, chemically similar to atebrine, but without the side effects, it was highly effective against the malaria-causing protozoans.[16]

The second new chemical to emerge was the insecticide DDT. It was first tested and produced in 1939 by Geigy AG, a Swiss chemical company that in the great tradition of Swiss neutrality sold the product during the war to both sides. It was particularly appreciated in the United States, where the major prewar insecticide, pyrethrum, manufactured from chrysanthemum petals, had been imported from Japan. As with quinine, the outbreak of the Pacific War closed off supplies.[17]

So the war had produced a new drug against the malaria-causing protozoan and a new, long-lasting poison lethal to the disease's insect vector. Together, the chemicals seemed to offer the prospect of implementing, on a much larger scale and across the world, earlier anti-malarial public health initiatives. Italy became a laboratory here as well. The war had disrupted public health initiatives—most notoriously, when the Germans, furious at their Italian allies for switching sides in 1943, destroyed the dikes and pumping stations that had drained the Pontine Marshes—and malaria was once again rampant. The resurgent malaria was quickly combated. The most celebrated example was on the island of Sardinia, which had been known as hotbed of the disease, since the days of the ancient Roman Empire. A massive campaign of DDT spraying rendered the island malaria-free for the first time in millennia. Equally effective were insecticide-based actions against malaria carried out in Ceylon (today's Sri Lanka) and Venezuela.

Use of DDT to combat mosquitoes carrying malaria found broad support. Newly independent India joined in the spraying campaign with great vigor. Even Mohandas Gandhi, otherwise generally skeptical about modern science and medicine, and a strong opponent of smallpox vaccination (which he described as a "savage custom," "sacrilege," and "tantamount to partaking of beef") endorsed the use of DDT. His celebrated "reverence for life" did not extend to mosquitoes, and India's Jains, adherents of a religion opposed to taking the life of any species, were also willing to make an exception for those disease-bearing insects.[18] All these postwar experiences suggested that malaria could be eliminated through a public health program that would combine anti-malarial drugs and insecticides. Five to eight years of this program would suffice, epidemiologists thought, to end the parasite's existence. In 1955, the World Health Organization officially launched the Malaria Eradication Program. In malarial regions, chloroquine combined with table salt was handed out in large doses. House walls would be doused with DDT, the "indoor residual spray," so the long-lasting insecticide would keep mosquitoes out for months at a time. Following the Sardinian example, there would be large-scale spraying of marshy anopheles breeding grounds.

Although not officially cooperating, the People's Republic of China, at the time not a member of the United Nations (UN), and the USSR, still boycotting the UN over its position on the Korean War, launched their own massive anti-malaria campaigns, involving a similar mixture of spraying insecticide and handing out antimicrobials. Most countries participated in the UN program. Working closely with the WHO and its regional directorate, the Pan-American Sanitary Bureau, Mexico, for example, threw itself into the fight against the disease, hiring 2,700 field workers outfitted with hand sprayers and water-soluble DDT powder, who dispersed the insecticide in millions of houses yearly from 1957 to 1962. Public health workers took 6 million blood samples and handed out 11.2 million doses of anti-malarial drugs. Hundreds of trainees from other Latin American countries were educated by the Mexican anti-malaria staff. There were materials distributed to schoolteachers and lessons for schoolchildren about malaria, a comic book, posters, pamphlets, film shorts, radio, and TV spots, even a *corrido* or Mexican ballad, including the lines, "How beautiful is the spraying! / With DDT or dieldrin." The Archbishop of Mexico City asked the blessings of the Virgin of Guadeloupe on the attempt to eradicate malaria.

Not everything went entirely smoothly. In the tropical, southern part of the country, where the inhabitants did not speak Spanish, the spraying teams were regarded with profound suspicion. And there were practical problems: spray would not stick to the reed walls of commonly used housing, and many people slept outdoors in the warmer months, exposed to the mosquitoes. Moreover, repeated applications of DDT, some Indians complained, seemed to be having the opposite effect on other insects, increasing the number of bedbugs, who were becoming steadily more immune to the poison. Years before *Silent Spring* was published, one provincial physician became convinced of the effects of the DDT in killing wildlife and domestic animals, even poisoning people.

Still, the campaign in Mexico was deemed a success. The number of reported cases fell from 137/100,000 inhabitants in 1955 to 10/100,000 in 1960. In the later 1960s, the spraying came to an end—in part the result of funding difficulties—and by the 1980s, malaria had rebounded, with over 100,000 new cases reported most years, about the same number per capita as in the 1950s. It had become more prevalent than ever in the tropical southeast, the poorest part of Mexico, where, for climactic reasons, the more malignant *P. falciparum* was endemic.[19]

Mexico's experience was characteristic of the entire malaria eradication campaign. The disease was eliminated in a few countries, most prominently Taiwan—conveniently an island, where opportunities for reinfection from outside were more limited—as well as most of southern and eastern Europe, and greatly reduced in the more temperate or drier climactic zones of the Americas, Asia, and Africa. These were all areas where the dominant form of the disease was the less deadly *P. vivax*. In the tropics, by contrast, in parts of south and southeast Asia and Latin America, but especially in Africa, home to about 90 percent of all cases of malaria by the end of the century, the disease surged to unprecedented levels. Figure 2.1, drawn from World Health Organization statistics, gives the number of new cases, worldwide, every year from 1962 to 2000. The official figures, particularly for African countries, are incomplete, and involve a lot of undercounting, but the long-term increase shown is certainly correct.[20]

As with programs for ozone and greenhouse gases, the contrast between the outcomes of programs to eradicate smallpox and malaria could not be more glaring. Even though the latter had much greater resources, commitment on the part of the UN, and support from national public health agencies and officials, it not only failed to eradicate the disease, but seems to have made it more prevalent. One explanation, popular in conservative circles beginning in the 1990s, is that the failure of the program was the fault of environmentalists. They banned DDT, ending a successful effort to

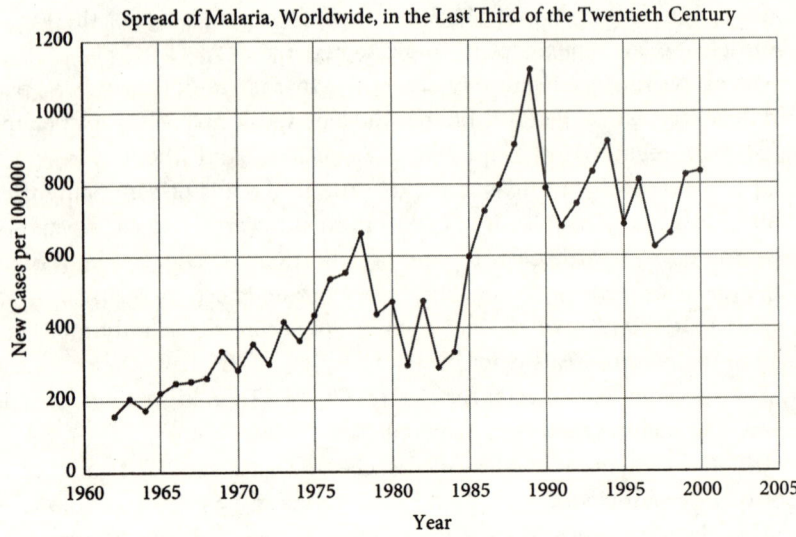

FIGURE 2.1 Spread of Malaria, Worldwide, in the Last Third of the Twentieth Century

eliminate mosquitoes, resulting in a resurgence of the insect-borne disease. One group accused Rachel Carson of being a bigger sponsor of genocide than Hitler.

The truth is less hyperbolic. The WHO's Malaria Eradication Program, which had been in decline since the mid-1960s, ended in 1969, three years before the United States outlawed DDT. Opposition to pesticides didn't bring the program to an end. The resurgence of Malthusian ideas did. Saving people from malaria only meant that they would eventually starve. Public health funds were redirected toward population control efforts.

More crucially, the assumption that continued DDT spraying would have wiped out mosquitoes contravenes Darwin's theory of natural selection (which, admittedly, many conservatives do not accept) and runs against the empirical evidence. By 1968, the WHO counted forty-five different species of anopheles mosquito that had developed a resistance to DDT. The only major country where DDT continued to be used on a broad scale was India, where health warnings about the insecticide were seen as examples of Western imperialism. Malaria had been almost eliminated in India during the 1960s, then jumped back to six million cases per year in the 1980s.

The originators of the WHO malaria eradication program, many of them veterans of 1930s anti-malaria campaigns, were well aware of the problem of resistance. They pressed to start the program as quickly as possible, before insects could develop resistance to DDT. Their whole plan to destroy the life cycle of the plasmodium protozoan through a few years of spraying was based precisely on the assumption that repeated use of the insecticide would induce insects' immunity. Their calculations were accurate enough in temperate regions, where mosquitoes were not quite so prevalent. These also tended to be relatively more affluent parts of the world in which there were better agricultural practices, sturdier and better-built housing, and more effective public health systems. In more tropical and also poorer countries, especially in Africa, but in parts of south and southeast Asia as well, plagued from the 1970s onward by economic decline and violent internal conflict, handing out chloroquine and spraying DDT would not suffice.[21] Malaria largely defeated the postwar era optimism about the use of new technology, new drugs, and new chemicals to combat infectious disease.

Efforts to fight tuberculosis in the postwar era did not have the global success of the anti-smallpox campaign, but did work out better than the anti-malaria program. A disease with a history every bit as long as that of smallpox or malaria, the name by which it was known well into the nineteenth century, "phthisis," was given to it by Greek physicians in classical antiquity. In more recent times, Napoleon Bonaparte's personal physician examined the emperor for signs of tuberculosis three times a week, tapping on his chest to listen to the resonance in his lung cavity. In 1883, the German biologist Robert Koch discovered the cause of the disease, the tuberculosis bacillus, *Mycobacterium tuberculosis*. The microorganism could and did infect different parts of the body—the skin, the abdomen, the spinal cord, and the brain, or the lymph nodes (also known as scrofula, or the "King's Evil," and supposedly cured by royal touch)—but its most common site of infection was the lungs.

This pulmonary tuberculosis, which spread by airborne contagion, as the sufferer coughed and spat up blood, gave the malady its distinctive social and economic profile, quite different from those of malaria or smallpox. Although broader statistics are lacking, and the WHO only began compiling global figures in 1995, tuberculosis seemed related to economic development, spreading in areas of densely packed and poorly ventilated housing and in dust-filled industrial facilities. A peculiarity of the illness was that humans could harbor the bacillus for decades, without developing any symptoms, as the body's immune defense system kept it at bay. Today, medical estimates are that merely 10 percent of people infected actually come down with the disease.[22]

Both these factors made tuberculosis an affliction of the urban poor, who could be infected at home or at work and lacked the necessary nutrition to activate the immune defense system to fight off the disease. Tuberculosis struck people from all social classes—but the poor were its prime targets. Statistics compiled in England and Germany at the end of the nineteenth and the beginning of the twentieth century showed that they were two to three times more likely to contract the disease than the wealthy and two to three times more likely to die from it, once they had contracted it.[23]

As standards of living improved, the likelihood that anyone would contract the disease declined. A model example was Great Britain, where the tuberculosis death rate fell from 400/100,000 in the 1830s, to 100/100,000 by the eve of the First World War and further to 50/100,000 by the 1930s. This mortality decline suggested that medical treatment and even public health measures had little to do with combating tuberculosis; it was all about standards of living. Statistics from Germany, Switzerland, and some American cities (nationwide US figures on tuberculosis mortality only date from 1950) show similar developments. But this was not a worldwide trend. Tuberculosis mortality rates were much higher in France than in the United Kingdom or Germany, at least twice their levels before 1914 and, as far as statistics could show, had declined relatively little from earlier decades. In Japan, tuberculosis mortality steadily rose over the course of the nineteenth century, to more than 200/100,000 in the initial decades of the twentieth century. It was still at this level during the 1930s. Victims of the disease were dismissed from their jobs. They and their families were shunned, regarded as impure, and carriers of hereditary defects. Although there was no such stigma attached to tuberculosis in Finland, the death rate from tuberculosis there was comparable to Japan's through the 1940s. Figures on tuberculosis mortality before 1950 in Asia, Africa, or Latin America are hard to come by, though in Brazil they ran about 150/100,000 from the early twentieth century through the 1940s.[24]

Even in countries with declining tuberculosis mortality, a patient who actually contracted the disease faced dismal prospects. In the early part of the twentieth century, a stay in a tuberculosis sanatorium, a specialized hospital for TB cases, became increasingly common. Treatment consisted largely of breathing fresh air and eating. Tuberculosis has a long literary history, culminating in the modernist classic, Thomas Mann's *The Magic Mountain*. His tuberculosis-ridden characters, luxuriating in an exclusive Swiss sanatorium, have love affairs, fight duels, and debate the future of Western civilization. Reality was very different. Most sanitarium patients were young and poor; their days were strictly regulated, less discussion about the fate of Western civilization and more about their own fate. Half of the patients of TB hospitals discharged as "improved" or "cured" died within five years.[25]

Medicine had little to offer in the way of treatment for tuberculosis, and efforts at prevention were also unavailing. There was the BCG vaccine, manufactured from attenuated tuberculosis bacilli, invented by two French biologists, Albert Camette and Camille Guérin in 1908. Its initial usage was overshadowed by a scandal in 1930, when children in the German city of Lübeck received vaccine doses contaminated with live bacilli. Seventy-two died. Such accidents aside, it is not entirely clear that the vaccine actually works.[26]

The appearance of antibiotics completely transformed the clinical situation. Streptomycin proved effective against tuberculosis and by 1946 there was a clamor for the drug, complete with desperate personal pleas to its inventor, the Ukrainian-born Jewish American Selman Waksman, bribes and black market dealing. An early recipient was George Orwell, who suffered a powerful allergic reaction and so could not continue the treatment, leading to his death in 1950. Systematic use soon made it clear that *Mycobacterium tuberculosis* possessed the ability to develop resistance to any one drug relatively quickly. Doctors responded with multi-drug therapy, exponentially more difficult for the development of resistance. Central to this form of treatment was isoniazid, yet another product of the labs of IG Farben, usually used in conjunction with para-aminosalicylic acid, or PAS, a close chemical relative of aspirin. By the end of the 1950s, this form of treatment of tuberculosis was well established; death rates from the disease quickly plummeted toward zero in Europe, Japan, and the Americas; sanitariums were closed, converted into hospitals for heart disease, or, as in Switzerland, turned into ski resorts.[27]

The question was whether the same approach that worked so well in wealthier countries would work in poorer ones. An answer came with the Madras (today's Chennai) clinical trials of 1956, sponsored by the World Health Organization, the Indian state of Tamil Nadu, and the British Medical Research Council. It compared multi-drug chemotherapy for TB sufferers on an outpatient basis with a combination of the chemotherapy and residence in a sanatorium. The outpatient therapy worked every bit as well.[28]

One final issue, particularly relevant for the treatment of tuberculosis worldwide, was the length of the therapy. The drugs prevalent in the 1950s had to be taken for two full years before the bacillus could be completely eliminated—a difficult treatment regimen to follow, especially for poorer people and inhabitants of poorer countries. The discovery of a new class of antibiotics by Italian researchers in the 1950s, the rifamycins, led to the introduction of rifampin in 1966—a much faster-acting anti-tuberculosis drug, with few side effects. Used in conjunction with isoniazid, it cut the treatment duration to six months, of which only the first two involved daily, intensive drug taking—"short course therapy," as it quickly came to be known.[29]

Of the three great infectious disease killers—smallpox, malaria, and tuberculosis—the fate of tuberculosis was the only one linked directly to the invention of antibiotics. Yet in the postwar era all three were the subject of organized campaigns of eradication. The results differed, ranging from total elimination of smallpox to a global decline in tuberculosis, to regionally limited successes against malaria. For decades after World War II, majority opinion interpreted the results as reflecting problems not with the science but with global reach and inadequate resources.

Tackling Noninfectious Diseases

In 1958, Sir John Charles, the UK's chief medical officer, noted that over the previous two decades tuberculosis deaths had declined from 26,000 yearly to 4,800, while deaths from lung cancer had risen in the same interval from 4,700 to 19,000. What he was describing has come to be known as the "epidemiological transition." This involved a shift in the nature of disease-caused mortality—from an era in which infectious diseases were the major cause of death and the deceased were disproportionately young, to one when noninfectious diseases—chiefly heart attacks, strokes, and cancer—dominated as causes of mortality, and their victims were mostly elderly.[30]

As physicians, at least in wealthier countries, increasingly turned their attention to noninfectious diseases, they found a fundamentally different etiological landscape. Infectious diseases had a definitive cause, a microorganism. Medical researchers talked about the "Koch postulates," for determining the cause of a disease, devised by the Robert Koch, the German biologist who had discovered the *Mycobacterium tuberculosis*. The microorganism that was the cause of the disease had to be present in all cases of it; it had to be possible to grow it outside the body of a disease victim, in a lab culture or a healthy animal; introducing that microorganism to a healthy animal would give it the disease.

Cancer and heart disease did not work that way. There was no definitive cause, and efforts to find one, like the search for a "cancer virus," came away with little or nothing. Instead of individual causes, there were "risk factors," including personal characteristics, behaviors, or environmental conditions. People exposed to these factors were more likely to contract the disease than those not subject to them. There could be and usually was a large gap in time—decades—between exposure to the risk factor and appearance of the illness. Even more importantly, these risk factors showed no effect at the level of the individual; they only became evident by studying large groups, in which a higher percentage of those exposed to the risk factor developed the disease or died from it than those not exposed. Since there were, potentially, many different risk factors, their separate effects needed to be disentangled, and their joint effects needed to be accumulated. Causes could only be approached statistically, rather than in a laboratory. During the first half of the twentieth century, significant statistical investigations of risk factors were mainly undertaken by life insurance companies, seeking data to set premiums for their policies. Even as late as the early 1950s the medical community had little knowledge of or experience in how to investigate, evaluate, or to understand the relationship between risk factors and disease.[31]

Beginning in the late 1950s new treatments started to proliferate, leaving the whole complex question of risk factors behind. This was particularly the case for heart disease, difficult to treat because until then there had been no way to operate on the heart itself, without stopping its circulation of blood to the lungs and the brain. Beginning with surgery carried out during the Second World War (here, as in so many other areas, a great impetus for innovation), physicians sought ways to operate on the heart. Early ideas included cooling off the patient drastically, dropping body temperatures by 15°F, to slow vital processes and allow time to do heart surgery. Another possibility was "cross-circulation," bringing a blood donor into the operating room, whose blood vessels were connected to a vein and artery of the patient undergoing surgery. One skeptic noted this created the possibility of an operation with a 200 percent mortality rate. The perfection of the heart-lung machine in the 1960s made this kind of surgery closer to routine: a coronary bypass to circumvent clogged arteries, likely to produce a heart attack, or the insertion of a cardiac pacemaker to regulate an irregular and life-threatening heartbeat. The height of these procedures was the first heart transplant carried out by the South African cardiac surgeon Christian Barnard in 1967.[32]

Surgical treatment for cancer, by contrast, had already had what might be called its heroic surgical period in the first half of the twentieth century, when doctors excised tumors and ever-larger portions of surrounding tissue, to ensure that every last cancer cell was gone from the body. The signature operation of the 1920s and 1930s was the radical mastectomy, in which surgeons dealt with breast cancer, the most common kind of cancer affecting women, by cutting out the breast, neighboring muscles, lymph nodes, parts of the chest cavity, and even some ribs. This procedure assumed that tumors spread from one site in the body to the next, but because microscopic, undetectable metastases could have already reached distant parts of the body via the bloodstream or the lymphatic system before any surgery, these drastic measures accomplished little to nothing.

In the 1950s, physicians began experimenting with a new approach, using drugs that seemed to have a particularly large effect on tumorous cells—chemotherapy—which could be used to attack these cells everywhere in the body. In the following decade, the procedure came into its own, and became increasingly widespread, as a result of multi-drug therapy, using different anti-cancer medications simultaneously. Multi-drug therapy was the pharmacological equivalent of the heroic surgery of earlier decades, since the drugs, which also destroyed healthy, noncancerous cells, were given at the maximum dosage the patient's body could withstand, bringing the patient to the brink of death.[33]

Physicians in the pre-antimicrobial era had used similarly extreme treatments to combat infectious diseases, such as the artificial pneumothorax—collapse of a lung—for tuberculosis. Rather more effective had been prophylaxis: administering vaccines, building clean and well-ventilated living spaces and workplaces, providing clean drinking water, draining swamps where the anopheles mosquito lived, and general improvements in the standard of living, including higher protein diets to activate the immune defense system. Such prophylactic options for noninfectious diseases were more challenging, because they involved first statistically ascertaining risk factors and then developing ways to deal with them that could be proven—once again, statistically—to have an effect.

One example was the use of drugs to reduce blood pressure—a clearly proven risk factor for both cardiovascular and cerebrovascular diseases. The first blood pressure drug was marketed in 1958 and their use had become steadily more prevalent by the 1970s. Other risk factors were either more debatable—such as whether fat or cholesterol intake increased the risk of heart disease—or more difficult to gauge, like the connection between lack of physical activity and heart disease, or between income and mortality rates. At least the risk from blood pressure was uncomplicated. While there were evident risk factors for some very specialized kinds of cancer, like the connection between exposure to asbestos and mesothelioma, risk factors for some of the most common forms of the disease, including breast, prostate, and colon cancer, were hard to ascertain.[34]

More precisely, there was one very evident risk factor, but dealing with it showed the difficulties of prophylaxis of noninfectious diseases. This was tobacco consumption, cigarette smoking in particular. Recent estimates are that smoking increases the chance of developing cancer twenty-two-fold—far more than any other risk factor. Eating processed meats increases cancer risk 1.3 times, exposure to high levels of sulfur dioxide 1.4 times, drinking 30–60 grams of alcohol per day, 3.2 times, and breathing in fine particulates perhaps as much as 5.2 times.[35] Smoking does not just increase the risk for lung cancer, but for other lung ailments, a whole series of cancers and for cardiovascular and cerebrovascular diseases as well. Across the entire second half of the twentieth century, in the affluent countries of Western Europe, North America, Japan, and Australia plus the lands of the Eastern Bloc, the USSR and its allies, almost one-fifth of men's deaths—50 million out of 260 million—were the result of smoking.[36]

Americans associate the link between cigarettes and lung cancer with the 1964 Surgeon General's report, which brought the matter to widespread public attention in the United States. But this connection had already been known for decades. The first national anti-smoking campaign occurred in Nazi Germany, which also promoted its opposition to alcohol, as well as recommendations to eat less meat and more organic fruits and vegetables, whole grains, and soybeans. Statistical studies during the 1950s solidified the connection between cigarettes and lung cancer. In the seven years before the Surgeon General's report, the British Medical Research Council and the Royal Council of Physicians, public health authorities in the Netherlands (a hotbed of smokers) and Norway, as well as the World Health Organization, had all publicly warned of the tumor-inducing consequences of cigarettes.[37]

Public health measures to reduce smoking ran into ferocious resistance from vested interests, whether tobacco and cigarette corporations, as in the United States, or government monopolies, as in Japan. Their decades-long war on tobacco regulation was every bit as tenacious and multifaceted as fossil fuel producers' opposition to measures against global warming—and, in systematically attempting to cast doubt on statistical relationships, set a precedent. As with opposition to global warming, however, corporate skullduggery was not the whole story. Cigarettes were a feature of rising global standards of living in the twentieth century, as Figure 2.2 shows.

While tobacco consumption fell in Western Europe and North America during the last quarter of the twentieth century, the rise in East Asia compensated for it. Cigarette consumption peaked in the 1990s at over 5.5 trillion per year—roughly 900 cigarettes for every single man, woman, and child across the globe, or close to one pack per person per week. With infectious diseases in the pre-antimicrobial era, prosperity reduced both the prevalence of disease and its mortality. When it came to cigarette consumption, prosperity has had the exact opposite effect.[38]

If we consider the combined effects of prophylaxis and various forms of treatment on the most prevalent forms of noninfectious disease starting after the Second World War, a pattern emerges. Figure 2.3 shows mortality rates from cancer, heart disease, and strokes (or, speaking medically, neoplasms, cardiovascular, and cerebrovascular disease) in the United States, between 1950 and 2000.

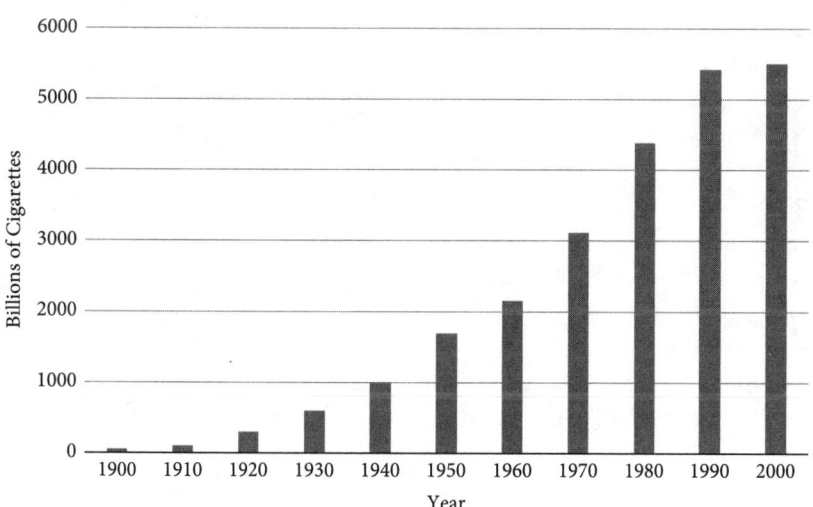

FIGURE 2.2 Worldwide Cigarette Consumption in the Twentieth Century

Source: WHO Tobacco Atlas, 2004, http://www.who.int/tobacco/en/atlas8.pdf, accessed July 7, 2016.

While death rates from strokes declined by about two-thirds, and from heart disease by about half, cancer death rates changed relatively little. The combination of new treatments and declining exposures to risk factors made arterial disease less lethal, while with cancer advances in chemotherapy, or screening and early detection at best kept pace with the exposure to risk.[39]

What accounts for this discrepancy? One answer is that other improvements indirectly lessened the risk of arterial disease. Rheumatic fever, caused by the streptococcus bacteria, was a common childhood disease in the pre-antibiotic era, leaving behind a damaged heart liable to future heart attacks. The illness could be treated with antibiotics. Although physicians initially neglected their use, they became more attentive to treatment possibilities and by the 1980s rheumatic fever had disappeared. Another reason was the gradual decrease in the number of low birth weight babies—a reflection of both rising standards of living and improved prenatal care. Low weights at birth were directly connected to high blood pressure in middle and old age. Along with relatively simple medical treatments, particularly drugs for blood pressure reduction, all of these changes were responsible for the decline. Drastic surgical interventions, like heart transplants, although very exciting individual stories, have had relatively little effect.[40]

The death rate for most common kinds of cancers (breast, colon, prostate) remained essentially the same from 1950 to 2000. Mortality from lung cancer

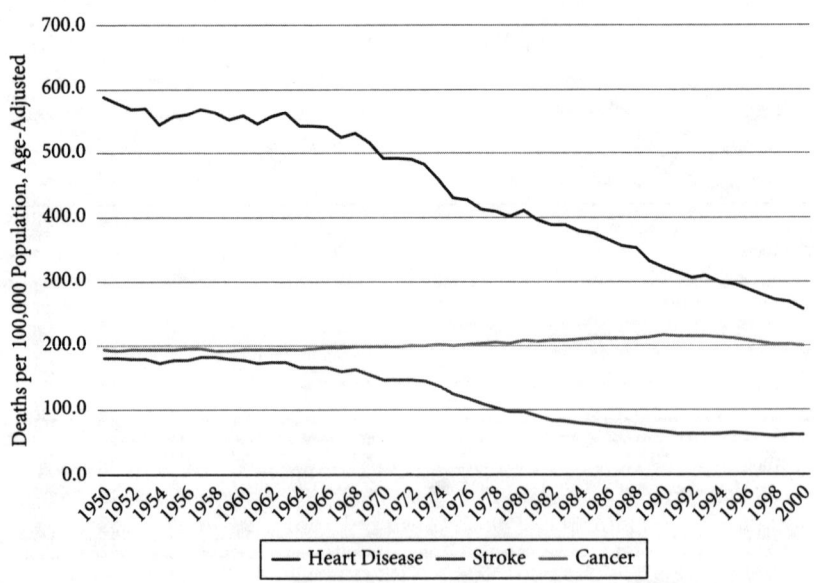

FIGURE 2.3 Mortality Rate for Non-Infectious Diseases in the US, 1950–2000

Source: CDC reports at http://www.cdc.gov/nchs/nvss/mortality/hist293.htm and https://www.cdc.gov/nchs/data/nvsr/nvsr50/nvsr50_15.pdf, both accessed July 8, 2016.

grew throughout most of the period, following, with about a two-decade lag, increases in cigarette smoking. Deaths from lung cancer were always much higher for men than for women, because men were more likely to smoke. As smoking became more common for women, their mortality rates from lung cancer began to increase, while those for men stabilized and declined a bit. This was balanced out by a decline in the frequency of and mortality from stomach cancer—a common illness in the early twentieth century.[41]

While mortality rates from heart disease have consistently varied considerably among wealthier countries, cancer mortality rates have always been much closer. In the United States, as in most affluent countries, there was a decline in cardiovascular and cerebrovascular death rates over the second half of the twentieth century; cancer death rates, on the other hand, rose slightly.[42] As is often the case, reliable statistical information from poorer countries is less available; this is especially true for historical data series. Data from 2000 onward shows that cancer mortality rates are noticeably lower in poorer countries than wealthier ones—by as much as a half. However, as cigarette smoking becomes more prevalent in poorer countries, the map of cancer mortality will take on a quite different appearance. Since these mortality statistics are age-adjusted, the differences are not just the result of the higher birth rates and younger populations.

One might expect a similar pattern for heart disease—higher mortality rate in affluent countries, lower in less affluent—but the reality is almost the exact opposite. Age-adjusted death rates from cardiovascular disease are generally three to four times higher in Africa, South and East Asia (and higher still in the countries of the former Eastern Bloc) than they are in North America, Western Europe, Australia, or Japan. As a result, cardiovascular diseases have now become the most common cause of mortality worldwide, accounting for 12 million deaths in 1990, and 15.6 million in 2010, about twice as many as were caused by cancer. Although the statistical evidence is thin, the second half of the twentieth century saw cardiovascular mortality rates moving in opposite directions in different parts of the world: very high in more affluent countries in 1950, and declining steadily after the 1960s; beginning much lower in poorer countries and rising. The crossover of death rates occurred sometime in the first decade of the twenty-first century.[43]

Hence the immense research effort and large sums of money that have gone into combating noninfectious diseases have yielded relatively little in the way of results, certainly when compared with most infectious diseases. This observation is reflected in life expectancy, at birth which rose 6.5 years in the world's economically most developed countries between 1950 and 1975 but only increased by 3.5 years between 1975 and 2000, peaking at 74.73. For less-developed countries, where infectious disease remained a significant source of mortality, the rise in life expectancy was greater, but followed the same pattern, growing by thirteen years between 1950 and 1975, but by less than nine in the last quarter of the twentieth century, peaking at 63.68 in 2000.[44]

In some respects, the period 1975 to 2000 was to noninfectious diseases what the pre-antimicrobial era had been for infectious ones. Mortality rates from strokes or heart disease declined, as had been the case with tuberculosis, smallpox, or malaria earlier in the century. Again, this was mainly because changing social and economic conditions and public health measures made disease less likely to occur. The persistence of cancer mortality rates through the 1990s seems the exception, but the modest fall in cancer mortality after 2000, following declining cigarette consumption, suggests a potentially similar story. Very much like the case with infectious diseases, medical intervention against noninfectious diseases has accomplished relatively little. It remains to be seen if biomedical research can develop fundamentally new forms of therapy on a par with antimicrobials.

This analogy between infectious diseases and noninfectious ones in the first and second half of the twentieth century breaks down in two ways. One is that the decline in infectious diseases seems to have been worldwide—if greater in affluent countries. By contrast, only wealthier countries saw mortality from cardiovascular and cerebrovascular illness decline; if anything, they became more common in poorer countries. The other is that the impact of social and economic development on disease has varied. Growing prosperity created conditions that decreased infectious disease mortality. Occasionally, this has also been true for noninfectious diseases, as was the case with the relationship between the decline in low birth weight and mortality rates from heart disease. But more generally, the impact of prosperity on noninfectious diseases, from cigarette smoking to higher-calorie diets to lack of physical movement in everyday life, has been to introduce new risk factors rather than to eliminate existing ones.

***RISK FACTORS IN THE LATE TWENTIETH CENTURY: THE GLOBAL OBESITY EPIDEMIC

As life insurance companies began their statistical studies in the 1920s, one of their salient discoveries, besides the dangers of smoking, was that their overweight clients seemed to die at a higher rate and at a younger age than their thinner counterparts. Differences in mortality from heart disease were particularly pronounced. This finding, which has since been confirmed many times over, was the beginning of the recognition of what has come to be known as the global obesity epidemic.[45] An epidemic it may be, but one very different from, say, smallpox. Ascertaining the nature, causes, and extent of obesity has proven difficult, because of the sparseness of reliable information and disputes over what obesity is. Still, following the modest thread of information tells us a lot about the nature of disease after the era of antimicrobials.

Problems begin with the most common measure of obesity, one that became standard after 1985—the body mass index (BMI), found by dividing a person's weight, in kilograms, by the person's height, in meters, squared. A BMI of 22 to 25 is usually taken as showing normal weight; 25 to 30, first signs of overweight; above 30, obesity; and over 35 (to say nothing of over 40) morbid obesity. Use of this measure has incited considerable controversy. Many assert that though overweight, they are perfectly healthy. There are also heavy smokers who live into their nineties. Critics have pointed out that very muscular individuals, such as bodybuilders, have a high BMI. Risk factors only show their effect statistically, when aggregated across groups. More seriously, it could be argued that the BMI misses other signs, such as the presence of body fat, which is a risk factor, particularly for cardiovascular disease. BMI does not measure stomach fat—or, put medically, abdominal adiposity—and some individuals with a lower BMI have a larger amount of stomach fat. However, just about every individual with a high BMI has a lot of stomach fat, so use of BMI offers a good approximation of a major risk factor.[46]

Determining the point at which BMI becomes a health risk is more challenging. The conventional cutoff point for obesity is a BMI of 25, though some studies have suggested that mortality rates are lowest for individuals with slightly higher BMIs, in the 26–28 range, and that individuals with low BMIs, under 22, say, have noticeably higher mortality rates—sometimes as high as those who are severely obese. Many of the low-BMI individuals studied were either heavy smokers, or suffering from cancer, AIDS, and other wasting diseases. This is particularly the case when age is taken into account, since the mortality risk for low-BMI individuals increases strongly with age—and given that people tend to get heavier as they get older, it is likely that a steadily greater proportion of the low-BMI group among the middle-aged and elderly are individuals with a fatal disease.[47] There is no disagreement over the fact that a BMI exceeding 30 is a risk factor—increasing mortality rates by 50 to 100 percent. One estimate done in 1991 revealed that between 250,000 and 350,000 deaths in the United States, 12 to 16 percent of all deaths in that year, were due to obesity—a result that certainly justifies the description of obesity as an "epidemic."[48]

How global is this epidemic? In countries for which there is some long-term information—more precisely, records, usually relating to military service, which can be turned into long-term information—such as France, England, and the United States, evidence suggests that the average BMI has been increasing for the last 300 years.[49] Through the early part of the twentieth century, rising BMIs were signs of a larger, better nourished, and healthier population, with lower mortality rates and growing life expectancies. At one point this changed, and, in particular, the proportion of the population with a BMI over 25 or 30 began to rise. Why is not quite so easy to ascertain. National figures are only available for the United States and the United Kingdom, starting in the 1960s. Figure 2.4 shows the proportion of the US adult population, ages 20 to 74, that was overweight or obese at different points in the last four decades of the twentieth century.[50]

Even as early as the 1960s, almost half of American adults had a BMI over 25. The proportion of the moderately overweight changed little in the course of the next thirty-five years, but the percentage who were obese, whose weight was a large health risk, almost doubled in that time, going from 13 to 23 percent.

By the beginning of the twenty-first century, the American situation was very largely reflected in the world's more affluent countries. There were many individual differences, with obesity rates particularly low in Japan and Denmark, and especially high in English-speaking lands, but overall obesity was on the rise and had been for decades.[51] But was this development truly global? The first broad worldwide statistics of the World Health Organization only date from 2008; the results, shown in Table 2.1, show the global contours of obesity.

The extent of obesity in the early 2000s was very clearly related to a country's standard of living. In poor and very poor lands, where malnutrition was a large and persistent problem, say Bangladesh, India, Burkina Faso, or Niger, there were fewer fat people. The transition to "upper middle-income

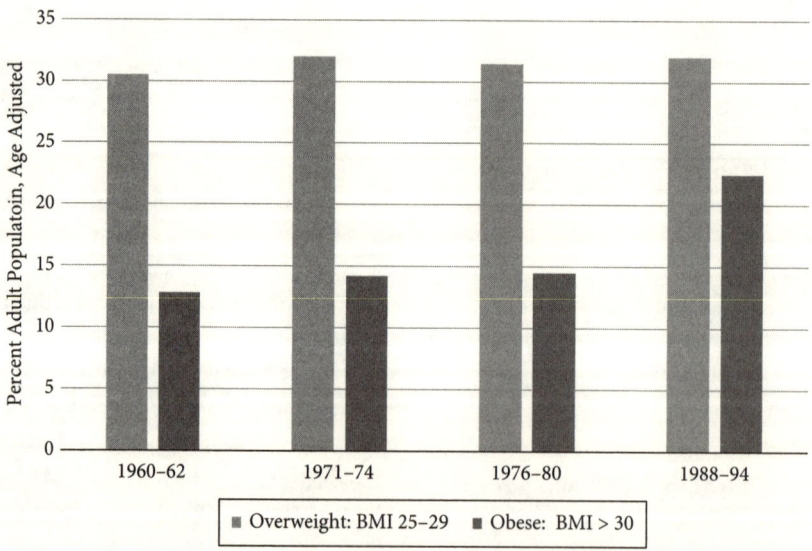

FIGURE 2.4 Overweight and Obese Adults (Ages 20–74) in the US, 1960s–1990s

TABLE 2.1 Global Obesity 2008: Percent Over-20 Population Obese

Country by World Bank Income Group	Men (%)	Women (%)
Low	2.6	5.1
Lower Middle	4.7	8.4
Upper Middle	19.5	28.9
High	21.8	21.6
World	10.0	14.0

Source: WHO, "World Health Statistics, 2011," 113, http://www.who.int/gho/publications/world_he alth_statistics/en/, accessed July 15, 2016.

countries" (per capita incomes between $4,000 and $12,000 US per year in 2015 dollars), places such as China, Mexico, or the lands of the former Eastern Bloc, marked the turning point. Obesity became truly a global epidemic. As larger portions of the world's population crossed that line, particularly in East Asia, the obesity epidemic spread.

The transition also occurred in the social situation of obesity. Among women in particular, it was linked to social class and income groups. (For men, class and income distinctions made relatively little difference.) In very poor countries, the wealthiest quarter of the population were the most likely to be obese; the poor were very thin. By contrast, starting in those "upper middle-income countries," and moving into more affluent ones, obesity was most common among the poor and less prevalent in the top percentiles of the population.

The key question is whether as countries became more prosperous and obesity became more widespread, its prevalence moved down the social scale—and if so, when this happened. In Brazil, from the mid-1970s to the late 1990s, obesity rates overall more than doubled, increasing for both sexes and all income groups. In 1975, the rich were generally fatter than the poor. This continued to be the case among men for the next quarter century. For women living in urban areas, the relationship between wealth and obesity was reversed: obesity was now most common among the poor—14 percent of the bottom quarter income group—than among the more affluent, just 9 percent of adult women in the top quarter. In the countryside, the older pattern of the wealthy being heavier continued to prevail. Unfortunately, there is no way of knowing whether this was the case in other countries, and whether this shift had some relationship to the epidemiological transition.[52]

Obesity is called an epidemic because it represents an important mortality risk factor. By the early 2000s it had reached most places outside of sub-Saharan Africa and South Asia. What exactly might have caused it? Although there have been a number of suggestions—including the replacement of sugar with corn sweetener or changes in the microbiomes of digestive tracts—the simplest and most cogent explanation involves the development of individuals' energy balance: the consumption of more calories in food than are expended in physical activity. Merely fifty extra calories a day adds about five pounds of weight in a year. The list of suspects is well known, including high-sugar-content soft drinks, pizza, french fries, and fast food, accompanied by declines in fruit and vegetable consumption. This was all part of a trend toward diets with a greater proportion of sugar, fats, and carbohydrates, containing more calories per gram than other foods. The global spread of these food from the 1970s onward helped cause rising obesity.

The explanation for declining physical activity is less obvious. Tracking individuals' daily physical exertion, which has been done in the United States, the United Kingdom, China, Brazil, and India, at different points between 1960 and 2010, has shown a common trend. In their free time, people are more active. However, this increase in activity has been outweighed, about three to one, by declines in physical activity in other areas of life. This explains the seemingly paradoxical result that the rise in obesity has paralleled the rise in the popularity of physical fitness—workouts at the gym cannot compensate for the declining numbers of jobs involving manual labor without assistance of machines, the expanded use of labor-saving devices in households, and the rise in travel by car. The relative importance of eating more and exercising less in rising BMIs remains in dispute, but there can be no doubt about the result of the combination.[53]

The global obesity epidemic is very much a feature of the Era of the Epidemiological Transition, occurring primarily in the second half of the twentieth century, the time period that is the subject of this book. In the earlier Age of Infectious Diseases, rising BMIs signaled a more active immune defense system, more able to ward off infections. Where noninfectious diseases became prevalent after the Second World War, the very same trend became a risk factor for heart disease, diabetes, and even some forms of cancer. In other words, the epidemiological transition was a social transition, as obesity became a condition more prevalent among the poor than the rich.

That said, in the world's wealthier countries, as obesity went up, mortality rates from heart disease went down. The effects of the decline in those other risk factors—rheumatic fever or low birth weights—and perhaps from improved treatments, such as blood pressure medication, outweighed the consequences of increasing weight. It is also the case that in poorer countries, where strenuous physical activity in everyday life remains the rule for most people, and where fast food is scarce and unaffordable, making obesity correspondingly rare, other risk factors make cardiac mortality rates higher than in places where obesity is more prevalent. None of these facts refute the steady trend toward increasing obesity across large portions of the world and the increase in mortality that it causes.

Infectious Disease Strikes Back

At the beginning of the 1980s, as the old millennium was nearing its end, physicians in Los Angeles, San Francisco, and New York began to observe a strange phenomenon: growing numbers of young men dying from a rare form of pneumonia, *Pneumocystis carinii*, or an even rarer form of cancer, Karposi's sarcoma, both previously seen only in the very elderly, whose immune defense systems had declined. As the number of cases increased, and the examples of a collapsing immune defense system became more varied and widespread—fungal infections, rashes and sores over the entire body, uncontrollable diarrhea, wasting, dementia—medical researchers were increasingly convinced that the cause of these many symptoms was a previously unknown microorganism. Identified in 1985, after a very unseemly spat between French and American biomedical researchers over who had made the actual discovery, it was quickly dubbed the human immunodeficiency virus or HIV; the disease it caused was named acquired immunodeficiency syndrome, or AIDS.

It would be difficult to underestimate the panic and sheer terror the new disease produced. Medical personnel refused to touch, much less to treat, patients who might have had the disease. Airlines refused to fly HIV positive passengers. The German Automobile Club added polyvinyl chloride gloves to the accident emergency kits sent to its members, so they would not be exposed to potentially infectious blood. Parents withdrew their children from school on finding out that one of the classmates was HIV positive, demonstrating with placards stating, "Our children want grades, not AIDS." While that last example comes from the United States, similar attitudes proliferated globally.[54]

Part of the fear arose from the fact that infectious disease had seemed obsolete, or at worst restricted to the poorest parts of the world. Another element was the connection of the disease with sexuality, particularly gay sexuality that remained, at the onset of the epidemic, for a majority of the world's population, a repugnant and immoral practice. There was another, distinctly globalized, element of the panic about AIDS—its status as an alien disease. In North America, much was made of "patient zero," the flight attendant Gaetan Dugas, whose globetrotting gay sex "lifestyle" had ostensibly brought AIDS into the continent. For Europeans of the early 1980s, AIDS was the "American disease"; in Brazil and other South American countries it was a "North American" infection. The xenophobic response to AIDS was strongest in Japan. Gay bathhouses starting banning foreigners, a practice that began to spread to ordinary public bathhouses, a long-term element of Japanese culture. In 1987, the men's magazine *Shukan Playboy* warned its readers about dating "women who like soul and frequent discos where blacks hang out."[55]

The physiological history of AIDS does show its pattern as a globalizing illness. Like malaria, it stemmed from Africa, which has always been the home and center of the disease, with by far the most cases. Both genetic markers and medical records suggest that the human immunodeficiency virus was an offshoot of a similar microorganism that infects chimpanzees of western equatorial Africa; at some point, around 1930, the virus crossed the species barrier and first infected humans. Such infections remained very rare until the 1960s, when they spread very rapidly in Kinshasa, capital of the newly independent Congo, probably the result of both prostitution and inadequately sterilized needles for vaccinations and administration of antibiotics. The disease became steadily more prevalent in Africa throughout the 1970s, but in view of the long incubation period between infection with the virus and the appearance of symptoms, frequently a full decade, it did not make much of an appearance. Early cases were generally mistaken for malaria or tuberculosis.

The United Nations provided assistance to the newly independent Congo; the largest group of UN aid workers were from Haiti. Their sexual relations with the local population brought the disease to the Western Hemisphere. In the 1970s, Haiti acquired a reputation in European and American gay circles as a party island and sexual contacts there moved HIV north. A substantial portion of the supply of blood plasma in Europe and North America during that decade was purchased from donors in poor countries, such as Haiti, so that recipients of blood transfusions, especially hemophiliacs, became another group in which the disease could spread. Between 1990 and 2010, AIDS spread to the former communist countries of Europe and Asia, typically through IV drug use, and in South Asia, where a large proportion of sex workers were infected.[56]

By the second half of the 1980s, AIDS etiology had been well-established. The disease was the product of a retrovirus that used RNA to produce DNA, the opposite of the way most biological reproduction occurs. The HIV virus, as its name indicates, attacks the human immune defense system, turning the T4 cells, which play a crucial role in suppressing foreign organisms, into factories that produce more of the virus. As the number of functioning T4 cells decline, and the immune system weakens, the patient's body finds it more and more difficult to fight off infectious agents or tumors.

Antimicrobials had been persistently useless for the treatment of viral diseases, but immunization had been successful at preventing them. Just a few years before AIDS reached the headlines, for example, smallpox had been completely eliminated. Unfortunately, trying to activate the body's immune defense system against a virus that preyed on it, proved more difficult than rubbing cowpox virus under the skin to thwart smallpox. In spite of intensive research efforts, a successful vaccine against AIDS has yet to be invented.

The question emerging in the world's wealthier countries was what public health measures to take against an untreatable viral disease, spreading mainly through sexual relations, although also via the sharing of needles by intravenous drug users. One model followed practices developed decades earlier for treating other sexually transmissible infectious diseases: widespread screening for the infection, contact tracing, and even, if necessary, compulsory hospitalization. The other approach was based on the postwar experiences with noninfectious diseases. It focused on decreasing risk factors by encouraging the avoidance of behavior that would spread the disease. There were disagreements about exactly how to go about this, generally more related to political and moral opinions than to medical and biological ones: condom use vs. abstinence, distributing sterile needles to drug users vs. preventing them from injecting drugs in the first place.

The dispute took on a political edge. Proponents of the infectious disease approach tended to be conservatives and adherents of orthodox religion, who wondered why sodomites' civil rights should take precedence over public health. Prominent politicians who took such an approach, included two aggressive, second-rank conservative leaders: US Senator Jesse Helms of North Carolina; and Bavarian government minister, Peter Gauweiler. By contrast, gay activists, mobilizing around the disease, generally finding support on the left wing of the political spectrum, strongly opposed compulsory measures. After the invention of a blood test for the virus in 1985 made contact tracing possible, one Minneapolis activist denounced it, stating, "The road to the gas chambers began with lists in Weimar Germany." When it came to policy, the risk-factors approach almost always triumphed. Ironically, the chief exceptions, employing the infectious diseases model, came mostly from progressive countries. Sweden was the only western European country to insist on compulsory contact tracing for individuals testing positive for HIV. (Admittedly, the conservative government of Bavaria followed a similar policy.) The very peak of the infectious diseases model was in Cuba, where testing was compulsory, contact tracing was pervasive, and HIV positive individuals were detained, indefinitely, in hospitals. Devout anticommunists passed over in silence the similarities of Cuban practice to their own preferences; admirers of revolutionary Cuba and its healthcare system were reluctant to discuss its treatment of AIDS victims, while denouncing similar proposals in their own countries.[57]

AIDS was the headliner for the recurrence of infectious disease during the 1980s, but behind the scenes physicians were observing another, disquieting phenomenon—the declining effectiveness of antimicrobials. As seen earlier in this chapter, fears about microorganisms developing resistance had accompanied antibiotics, almost from the moment of their first use, and reports of resistance started as early as the 1950s. A 1969 editorial in the *New England Journal of Medicine* even made an explicit connection between the rise of insect resistance from indiscriminate use of DDT, and the development of drug-resistant microorganisms from similarly careless use of antimicrobials. Yet the steady progression of new antibiotics after 1945 seemed to resolve the problem: there was always a new drug to treat bacteria resistant to an old one. Therefore, the 1980s marked a turning point. At the start of the decade an international conference of clinicians and microbiologists in Santo Domingo culminated in a "Statement Regarding Worldwide Antibiotic Misuse." The issue was promptly taken up by the World Health Organization.[58]

In the two decades that followed, antibiotic resistance became an increasingly serious problem for treating all manner of bacterial diseases, from cholera to gonorrhea. Chloroquine, the extraordinarily effective anti-malarial drug, began to lose its effect on the malaria plasmodium, an important factor in the resurgence of that disease in the 1990s. However, two versions of antibiotic resistance that appeared in Late Millenium Era stand out. One was the re-emergence of tuberculosis, a disease eliminated in wealthier countries, and seemingly on the way out in poorer ones. This was a result of the appearance of strains of the *mycobacterium tuberculosis* that were impervious to the standard treatment with rifampin and isoniazid—so-called multi-drug-resistant tuberculosis. By 2000, the efficacy of even the more unusual and expensive antibiotics was declining, heralding the emergence of extreme drug-resistant tuberculosis. The other version of antibiotic resistance was the increasing presence of untreatable staphylococcus and streptococcus bacteria, particularly MRSA—or methicillin-resistant staphylococcus aureus. These antibiotic-resistant bacteria were primarily found in hospital environments, on patients who had undergone surgery or had had catheters or IVs inserted. But the distinct possibility existed that they might spread beyond hospitals into the general public, reverting to the state of affairs that existed when Calvin Coolidge Jr. died from an infected blister six decades earlier.[59]

INFECTIOUS DISEASE APOCALYPSE?

By the last decade of the millennium there arose a fundamental question about the public health meaning of the AIDS epidemic and the presence of antibiotic-resistant bacteria. Were they localized exceptions? If so, then it was likely that they were temporary setbacks to the decline in infectious disease that had been underway on a global scale at least since the twentieth century started, and much less of a public health concern than smoking or obesity. Or were these infectious diseases signs of a new and pernicious relationship to the biosphere within the human organism? Would the side effects of postwar globalization, microorganisms piggybacking on the increasing movement and interconnection of human beings, bring the new diseases out of their geographical and sociological niches into a much wider population, perhaps even reversing the epidemiological transition and returning humanity to the Era of Infectious Disease? Experiences of the early twenty-first century suggest that the worst fears of an infectious disease apocalypse during the Age of Interconnection were exaggerated, in large part because microbes would prove to be less globalized than people, but there were enough sobering counterexamples to make those fears seem plausible enough, even in retrospect—and certainly following the COVID-19 pandemic of the early 2020s.

There is no question that a number of indicators at the end of the millennium pointed toward an unsettling infectious disease future. Figure 2.5 shows the annual average percentage change in death rates from infectious disease in the United States across the twentieth century.

The figure shows the period of the introduction of antimicrobials in the pre- and postwar years, saw a very rapid decline—a plummeting—of the death rate from infectious disease. In both the preceding and subsequent decades, death rates also declined, but at a more modest pace. Then, starting in 1980, the situation turned around: AIDS and antibiotic-resistant bacteria caused the infectious disease death rate to increase—and at a vigorous pace, almost 5 percent per year. Of course, that increase could not outweigh three-quarters of a century of decline: the US infectious disease mortality rate in 1995, for example, of 63/100,000, if about twice that of 1980, was

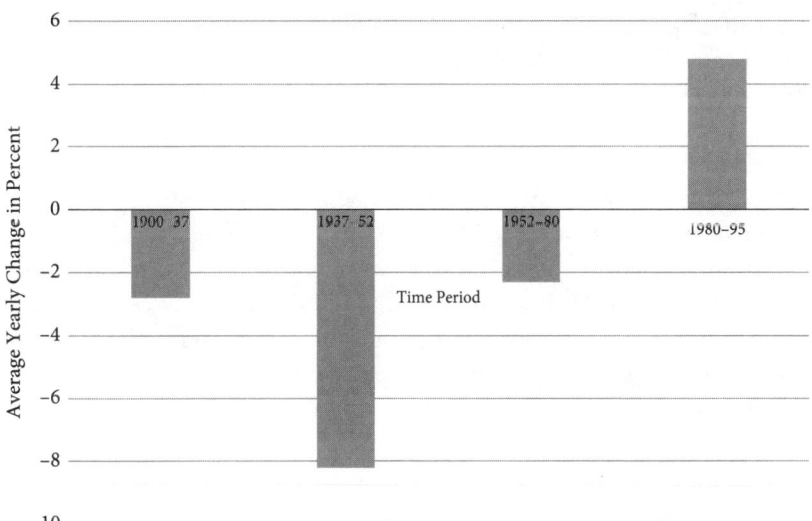

FIGURE 2.5 Average Yearly Percentage Change in Infectious Disease Mortality in the US, 1900–1995

Source: Gregory Armstrong, Laura Conn, and Robert Pinner, "Trends in Infectious Disease Mortality in the United States during the 20th Century," *Journal of the American Medical Association* 281 (1999): 61–66.

still less than one-twelfth of 797/100,000 in 1900. Nor was the epidemiological transition in doubt, since in the 1990s about four times as many people died from heart disease and three times as many from cancer as from infections. For all that, the turnaround—a marker of the full flowering of the Age of Interconnection—was a potentially worrying reversal of a very long-term trend.

There was plenty of blame to go around for the growth in antibiotic-resistant bacteria, though the most flagrant examples of the problem were in the poorer countries, where antibiotics were widely available without a prescription. Indian Ayurvedic healers, generally opponents of Western medicine, nonetheless also handed out penicillin to their patients. Inadequate dosage versions of antibiotics circulated, as did counterfeit pills with no medical value whatsoever. Ironically, those fraudulent pills did less damage: useless for curing illness, they also did not spur on the development of resistant bacteria. Inadequate dosage antibiotics were worse since both failed to treat illness and also helped bring forth antibiotic-resistant microorganisms.

Even when proper antibiotics and medically appropriate treatment were available, they were, all too often, difficult to administer. Could impoverished patients in Port au Prince, Lima, or Lusaka (say nothing of patients in rural areas), lacking access to reliable transportation, facing daily challenges of unemployment, lack of money for basic necessities, or caring for children, make their way across a large urban center, on a regular recurring basis, for months at time, in order to receive the entire necessary course of antibiotics? Compounding the problem were the economic difficulties experienced by African and Latin American countries in the 1980s, and 1990s, sometimes called the "lost decades," when funding for public health declined, and patients were increasingly expected to pick up part of the costs of drugs themselves.[60]

Multiple drug-resistant tuberculosis reached New York City at the beginning of the 1990s. The bacillus strains had come from abroad and a disproportionate number of the sufferers were immigrants. Mowing down a large portion of New Yorkers suffering from HIV and, so, weakened immune systems (fatality rates hit 80 percent), but also killing some of the medical personnel tending to them, the epidemic was eventually contained, albeit at the cost of about $1 billion. Of course, given that the outbreak occurred in the world's media capital, it was very well reported. It was also an object lesson in the possibilities for infectious disease in an age of international circulation of people and microbes.[61]

The statistics on life expectancy at birth reflected this resurgence of infectious disease in the 1990s. In two regions of the world, life expectancy actually declined. From the 1960s onward in the USSR, life expectancies at birth had changed little, moving up and down between about 61 and 63 for men, and 71 and 73 for women—already not a good sign, in a world of generally rising life expectancies. In the decade that followed the end of the communist regime in 1989–1991, they moved downward, reaching 58.9 for men, with a lesser decline for women. The other region of declining life expectancies was southern and eastern Africa. In Botswana, Lesotho, South Africa, Zimbabwe, Malawi, or Zambia, life expectancies at birth fell between 5 and 15 years, an astonishingly large drop, bringing them to the upper forties or low fifties, about where they had been in the 1960s. In these African countries antibiotic-resistant bacteria and AIDS were simply out of control. It was unclear at the time whether developments in the former Eastern Bloc and regions of Africa were exceptions to the broader trend of improving health, or the vanguard of a worldwide downward spiral. The global statistics were far from reassuring. The rises in life expectancy that had been typical for the postwar decades slowed to a crawl at the end of the millennium. Worldwide, female life expectancy at birth just grew 1.7 years from 1990 to 2000, ending at 69.8; for men, the increase was even smaller—1.4 years, concluding at 62.5.[62]

The worst, in fact, did not happen. One reason was the development of medications that proved effective against viral infections—an area where previous efforts had come up empty. Just as soon as HIV was identified, doctors began experimenting with various drugs, and it quickly turned out that AZT, a drug developed twenty-five years previously as a treatment for leukemia (at which it failed) could limit the reproduction of the virus. It took almost a decade to get the treatment right, but from 1995 onward, the use of a multi-drug approach, combining AZT with protease inhibitors, drastically reduced the presence of the virus in the body. Multi-drug treatments, following the model used on cancerous tumors, or for that matter, tuberculosis, did not actually cure the disease, since the human immunodeficiency virus remained in the body, albeit at very low levels, and would resume its growth if the treatments were stopped. The side effects were many and unpleasant; the combination drug regimen was expensive and difficult to follow, but it did have the potential to transform AIDS from invariably fatal to a chronic and relatively stable illness.

These treatments changed the lives of AIDS patients, at least those who could afford the drugs. As was the case with cancer or heart disease, the real progress in treating AIDS lay less in medical treatment than in the reduction of risk factors. In the United States, even by the mid-1980s, as the mortality toll was steadily rising, the incidence of new infections was decreasing; when the multi-drug treatment came out in 1995, the actual population of HIV-infected individuals was already in decline. The use of condoms, coupled with abstinence from sexual practices likely to spread the infection, had done its work. There were similar developments among IV drug users, although progress there was not quite so quick, and their sexual partners became a potential new group of victims. The story of AIDS in the United States was basically repeated in Europe, the former Eastern Bloc, and Asia. A relatively small group bore the main burden of the disease—gay men in the Americas and northern Europe, IV drug users in southern Europe and the former communist countries, and prostitutes in south and southeast Asia. But the development of behaviors to avoid spreading the infection, whether encouraged by government policy, the actions of volunteers and NGOs, or just the self-interest of members of the affected groups, prevented AIDS from spilling over into the general population. Probably the closest call came in Thailand, where there was a large and thriving sex industry catering to wealthy tourists from Europe and Japan. In the early 1990s, about 15 percent of all women in Thailand had worked as prostitutes at one point in their lives, and a conservative estimate was that one in seven prostitutes (actual figures may have been much higher) was HIV positive. But even there, an aggressive campaign promoting condom use limited the spread of the infection. World Health Organization statistics from 2005 gave the proportion of adults between the ages of 15 and 49 in Thailand who were HIV positive as 1.5 percent—two to five times the rate in most other countries of the world.[63]

There was one very large and tragic exception to this state of affairs, namely Africa. At first, it did not seem that way. In 1985, as the cause of the new disease was being discovered, the director of the World Health Organization, Halfdan Mahler, a Danish physician with a fierce commitment to social justice and a strong believer in its intimate connection to public health, dismissed AIDS as a disease of the wealthy: "AIDS is not spreading like a brush fire in Africa. It is malaria and other diseases that are killing millions of children everyday," he wrote. African statesmen generally agreed, asserting that if the disease existed in Africa, degenerate Americans and Europeans had brought it there, and the idea that it had originated in Africa was racist and imperialist. As one official put it, "AIDS is primarily a disease of homosexuals and there is no homosexual in Botswana."[64]

AIDS was, however, spreading like a "brush fire" in Africa, as became painfully clear by the 1990s. The WHO changed its policy, but by then the epidemic had reached unprecedented levels. In Africa the disease did not remain confined to relatively small sociological niches. It reached the entire adult population, and, transmitted through breastfeeding, from HIV positive mothers to children as well. The WHO's 2004 statistics showed that one African in fourteen between the ages of 15 and 49 was HIV positive, ten to twenty times the rate in other continents of the world. The problem was most concentrated in southern Africa, nine countries from Zambia to South Africa, with 2 percent of the world's population and 30 percent of its AIDS cases. There may have been no homosexuals in Botswana, but by 2000 more than one adult in four there was HIV positive—the highest proportion of any country in the world.[65]

The reasons for this striking discrepancy between Africa and other parts of the world remain murky. One factor is that in Africa the virus was easily transmitted from women to men, a very rare development elsewhere, probably attributable to the presence of other sexually transmitted diseases, which created open genital sores. The question of whether distinct sexual practices contributed to the spread of AIDS in Africa is also in dispute. Africans neither engage in sexual relations unusually early nor do they have more sexual partners than people elsewhere in the world. There was certainly nothing like the practice of having 500 to 1,000 sexual partners a year, which spread AIDS among gay men in northern Europe and North America. In southern Africa men and women often have long-term sexual relationships with more than one partner, which facilitates the spread of sexually transmitted diseases. The colonial heritage of migrant labor in mining has helped the disease cross national borders, and miners and long-distance truck drivers were vectors of infection. Infection rates have been much lower in predominantly Islamic countries of western Africa, in part because of the practice of circumcision, which seems to impede the passage of the virus between women and men. Moreover, restrictions on women's independence and their sexuality in Islamic countries have prevented them from spreading the disease as in the southern portion of the continent.[66]

The turn of the millennium was a public health low point for AIDS in Africa. The disease seemed out of control; young adults were struck down; by 2004, there were twelve million AIDS orphans, children under the age of 15, who had lost at least one parent to it. Multi-drug antiretroviral treatments were reducing the severity of AIDS in more affluent countries but too expensive for a poor continent. Somewhat surprisingly, the situation began to improve over the subsequent decade. Antiretrovirals became more affordable, largely because Brazilian and Indian manufacturers pirated them from pharmaceutical firms in Europe and North America. Also, AIDS activists in and out of Africa pressed the pharmaceutical manufacturers very hard on this point. In some African countries, Uganda and Senegal being the two most prominent, sexual practices gradually became more careful, following government and NGO initiatives. By 2010, the proportion of adults in Africa who were HIV positive had come down, to under 5 percent—still very high, and conditions in southern Africa, the center of the epidemic had only improved very modestly.[67]

According to the best estimates of the World Health Organization, in the twenty-five years after 1990, some 32.2 million people in the entire world died from AIDS-related causes. This is a tragically high number, but it is also about equal to the global death toll from heart disease in two years. AIDS is a scary disease, which has been and continues to be a major public health disaster in Africa, especially in the southern end of that continent, but elsewhere it has never gone beyond small and shrinking sociological niches to infect large portions of the general population or threaten to reverse the epidemiological transition.[68]

Another feature of the 1990s that received overblown media coverage, were "superbugs"—antibiotic-resistant bacteria showing up in scratches and blisters or emerging after a cold, athlete's foot, or pneumonia, with a fatal outcome. Infections from antimicrobial resistant staphylococcus and streptococcus bacteria have remained overwhelmingly nosocomial, as doctors say, meaning restricted to healthcare facilities. There, people with weakened immune systems—the elderly, patients having just undergone surgery, or needing catheters and IVs—are in the greatest danger of infection. Looking at this issue on a global scale, there are familiar distinctions: poor countries, with less control over use of antibiotics and less-than-optimal possibilities for strict infection-control procedures in hospitals, have noticeably higher rates of resistant germs. Unlike the case with AIDS, this is not the whole story. Neighboring countries have had very different bacterial populations. One study of hospitals in the EU dating from 2000 showed that the percentage of staphylococcus bacteria resistant to methicillin, MRSA, was 0.6 percent in the Netherlands, but 23.6 percent in neighboring Belgium and 13.8 percent in nearby Germany. In a very similar study, carried out in 2004, 80 percent of such bacteria in Peruvian hospitals were methicillin resistant but just 36 percent in neighboring Bolivia, 42.5 percent in Argentina, but 80 percent in Chile. There are similar discrepancies from country to country in Asia as well. These figures suggest that bacteria lag humans in mobility, not just not less globalized, but also having greater difficulty crossing national borders. More plausibly, differences in infection-control procedures and the prescribing of antibiotics have eliminated the potentially globalizing effects of these bacteria.[69]

Antibiotic-resistant tuberculosis was yet another frightening prospect during the 1990s. In the world's affluent countries, the threat it posed was eliminated by DOTS—daily observed treatment, short course. Patients receiving antibiotics for tuberculosis were required to take their daily dose in front of a public health official, to make sure that they did the entire drug regimen to eliminate every trace of the *Mycobacterium tuberculosis*. If the old standards, isoniazid and rifampcin, no longer worked, other, more expensive antibiotics, the "second-line drugs," could take their place. In poor countries of Africa, South Asia, and parts of Latin America, the lack of public health infrastructure and the money to pay for the second-line drugs meant elimination was impossible.

What made the situation with drug-resistant tuberculosis much worse was its intersection with AIDS. The presence in humans of the *Mycobacterium tuberculosis* is all too common. One WHO estimate is that a third of the entire world's population is infected with the bacillus. A functioning immune system can keep the bacillus in check, but as the AIDS virus systematically destroys the body's defenses the bacillus gains the upper hand. People with AIDS are very likely to develop all the symptoms of tuberculosis, and where

AIDS spreads tuberculosis goes along with it. In eastern and southern Africa, the worldwide epicenter of AIDS, as the disease expanded between 1980 and 2000, tuberculosis rates increased as much as sixfold. Both AIDS and tuberculosis, even most cases of drug-resistant tuberculosis, are treatable with multi-drug therapy. It was and is hard enough to keep people on one multi-drug treatment. AIDS and tuberculosis together require two.[70] The global fate of tuberculosis at the beginning of the twenty-first century was not just entwined with that of AIDS, it also largely followed the same lines of geography and economic inequality.

Looking back over the Age of Interconnection, three distinct eras of disease appear, three periods of the biosphere inside the human organism. The first was the postwar decades, the age of antimicrobials. Like so many other aspects of the years 1945 to 1965, this was a period profoundly influenced by the age of total war, in this case, by the development of antimicrobials, a feature of the Second World War. The postwar era was also a period in which the biosphere inside the human body was treated like its counterpart outside the body: indiscriminately bombarded with antibiotics, just as crops were being sprayed with DDT. The two even interacted in the postwar efforts to eliminate malaria and were embodied in the WHO's abortive campaign in the 1950s and 1960s to wipe out the disease worldwide, by a combination of DDT and chloroquine. The anti-malaria campaign did not achieve its global goals. Nonetheless, it was part of a broader effort at pushing back infectious diseases, most effective in the wealthiest countries of the world, but enjoying successes against some diseases everywhere.

The 1960s and 1970s were a period in which a lot of the effort in biomedical research and the avant-garde of medical treatment turned to noninfectious maladies, particularly cancer and heart disease. Tens of billions were spent in advanced research; remarkable new pharmaceuticals manufactured and complex and difficult medical procedures, like open-heart surgery, developed and practiced everywhere more widely. All this occurred, again, in the world's wealthier countries, while attention to still unvanquished infectious diseases, particularly malaria, declined. But the large efforts against noninfectious diseases produced small results: changes in risk factors, particularly matters like rheumatic fever, low birth weights, obesity and, especially, cigarette smoking had a much larger effect on mortality rates than all the expensive medical treatments.

Both the development of new medical technologies and the increasing public health attention to risk factors continued into the twenty-first century, though, as we've seen, the last two decades of the twentieth were overshadowed by the threatening return of infectious disease. The late 1980s and early 1990s was an era in which fears of drastic changes in both the external and the internal environment, in changing global climate and changing global viruses and bacteria, were steadily more widespread. Fears about the former proved more justified, in part because vigorous public health measures helped curtail dangers from the latter, while international efforts to curb global warming were, as explained in the previous chapter, depressing failures. The 1990s pause in life expectancy came to an end in the subsequent decade: worldwide, life expectancy at birth for men increased by 3.2 years and for women by 3.5. The 1990s era decline in life expectancy in the former Eastern Bloc was reversed, and countries regained previous highpoints or exceeded them. There was no such favorable trend in the AIDS- and tuberculosis-ravaged lands in southern Africa.[71]

The epidemiological transition that is a key feature of the Age of Interconnection was not reversed, but continued, reaching countries in Asia and Latin America. Worldwide, obesity was a far greater cause of mortality than AIDS or tuberculosis. By the first decade of the twenty-first century, it would be fair to say that illnesses, far from spreading across the world, were becoming de-globalized, with infectious diseases concentrated and very largely isolated in Africa, and, to a much lesser extent, poorer countries in South Asia and Latin America, in the form of scary outbreaks of viral diseases such as Ebola, but primarily in the less dramatic and less lethal but more prevalent AIDS, malaria, and tuberculosis, while the rest of the world suffered greater health risks from quaffing too many soft drinks and smoking too many cigarettes.

At least this was the case until the COVID-19 pandemic beginning in 2020 raised the possibility that the de-globalization of infectious disease was coming to an end, the epidemiological transition will be reversed and the global infectious disease apocalypse feared in the 1990s will really come to pass. The pandemic is certainly globalized, although its extent worldwide is no greater than diseases of the first half of the twentieth century including tuberculosis, malaria, smallpox, or the Spanish flu pandemic of 1918, to say nothing—going farther back in human history—of cholera and bubonic plague. Disease spreads across the world much more rapidly than such pandemics in past times, as a result of the much higher speeds of travel and a greater proportion of the world's population traveling over long distances.

Initial epidemiological data suggests that the corona virus is most likely to be fatal among the elderly and people with preexisting medical conditions, including high blood pressure and type 2 diabetes, which is to say precisely the sort of issues resulting from increased life expectancy and from risk factors for degenerative diseases, linked to the obesity epidemic that is also a hallmark of the latter decades of the Age of Interconnection. What remains to be seen is if COVID-19 will be, as Halfdan Mahler said of AIDS, a disease of the wealthy, or, in this case, of wealthier and more middle-income countries, given the initial spread of the pandemic in China, Iran, western Europe, and the United States. Since the virus seems much more lethal in the elderly and mild or even asymptomatic among the young, this would imply that poorer countries, with higher birth rates, and a younger population, would be less affected. Of course, it is also possible that the pandemic will reach the world's poorer countries later, and that the death toll from a virus spreading primarily among people in close proximity and affecting individuals with a weakened immune system will be much greater in large, very crowded cities, such as Delhi or Lagos, and among the immunocompromised, suffering from AIDS and malaria or lodging the tuberculosis bacillus. Mortality from the disease has not yet been well diagnosed, hence final judgment will have to wait until mortality statistics are available worldwide, and the "excess mortality" of the initial years of the 2020s, the higher death rates of those years compared to previous ones, can be ascertained, both around the world and in specific countries and regions.[72]

Will COVID-19 confirm the worst fears of a re-emergence of infectious disease, or ultimately defeated by a vaccine and/or deployment of antiviral drugs? Reaffirm the split in the world between wealthier countries suffering from degenerative diseases often related to obesity and poorer ones where infections continue to rule, or herald of a globalized resurgence of infectious disease? It is possible that the determinant of the severity of the pandemic will not be levels of economic development or preexisting risk factors but the capability of governments to devise and enforce public health policies in response to a pandemic, the willingness of politicians and policy makers to implement them, and the public to support them. At the moment of this writing (Fall 2021), it is unclear how COVID-19 will develop and what it will imply for potential future pandemics. As with other elements of the human relationship to the biosphere, the outcome remains uncertain.

3 | Technologies

MOST POPULAR AND JOURNALISTIC accounts view the Age of Interconnection as the Age of Technological Wonders. Profound scientific discoveries and brilliant engineering innovations combined, producing jet aircraft streaking through the sky; satellites circling the earth; men walking on the moon; and robotic spacecraft driving on the surface of Mars and exploring the furthest reaches of the solar system. There are machines that can think—or come close to it—and new sources of cheap and abundant energy, developed during this period, are a few years away. Electronics were miniaturized almost to the vanishing point. Genetic engineering produced new pharmaceuticals vanquishing stubborn diseases and new crops that promised to bring hunger to an end.

Of course, not all observers of these innovations struck such an optimistic note. There are darker versions as well, in which technological innovations were limited to North America and Western Europe and denied to the impoverished masses of Africa, Asia, and South America. These new technologies were less wonders than nightmares, bringing government surveillance, human alienation, economic inequality, and environmental degradation in their wake. Yet, gloomy or upbeat, they all assert that the decades between 1945 and 2001 were when technology was unleashed.[1]

This view might be accurate if one looked at the entire period from a great distance—say, from somewhere outside the orbit of Mars. Closer examination reveals a different story. Most of the innovations were actually products of the Age of Total War, as were notions of how they would be applied. The introduction and implementation of these technologies show more complex and less consistent patterns: long periods in which their use remained largely unchanged; big visions and large dreams confronting the intractable realities of economics, political choices, and—still more intractable—the laws of physics; momentous unintended consequences, very different from the original visions.

Four forms of technology shaped the fifty-five years following the end of the Second World War: energy extraction and production, transportation, agricultural productivity, and electronics. Although the development and global reach of each of these technologies has its own unique features, the very broadest outlines of the story might run as follows. In the twenty-five years immediately following 1945, technological innovations spurred by the war spread out from North America to Western Europe and other more affluent regions—Japan, Australia, even parts of the Eastern Bloc—bringing dreams of great promise. By the 1970s the geographic spread and progress of these technologies had slowed or even halted; the great expectations associated with them faded. In some areas of technology, nothing changed, but then the last two decades of the twentieth century ushered in a new period of technological innovations, particularly in unexpected uses for existing technologies.

Energy

In 1945 the world was coal-fired. This might seem a perverse observation, since that year marked the end of a war whose outcome was determined by the use of petroleum products to power fighter and bomber aircraft, submarines and aircraft carriers, tanks and self-propelled artillery, and, above all, to move infantry swiftly and decisively, leaving horse-drawn armies outmaneuvered, surrounded, and defeated. But all those gasoline- and diesel-powered engines of war were built in the factories of Detroit, Sheffield, Bochum, Magnitogorsk, or Osaka, whose machines ran on electricity generated by burning coal.

The newly founded United Nations, following in the footsteps of its League of Nations predecessor, began surveying global energy use, a task it continues to perform down to the present day. In the very first survey of 1949, UN statisticians found that coal accounted for 64 percent of all the world's commercially generated energy. Except for a few smaller countries with a lot of oil—Venezuela or Saudi Arabia, for instance—coal was the dominant commercial source of energy in every region of the world, whatever its phase of economic development.[2] The energy story of the postwar decades was the relative decline of coal and the rise of petroleum. To some extent, petroleum products replaced coal in heating and electrical power generation, but it was, above all, their rising use in automobiles and aircraft that made the difference.

Figure 3.1 shows the UN's statistics of energy production across the Age of Interconnection. During the second half of the twentieth century, the UN distinguished four major sources of energy: coal, petroleum products, natural

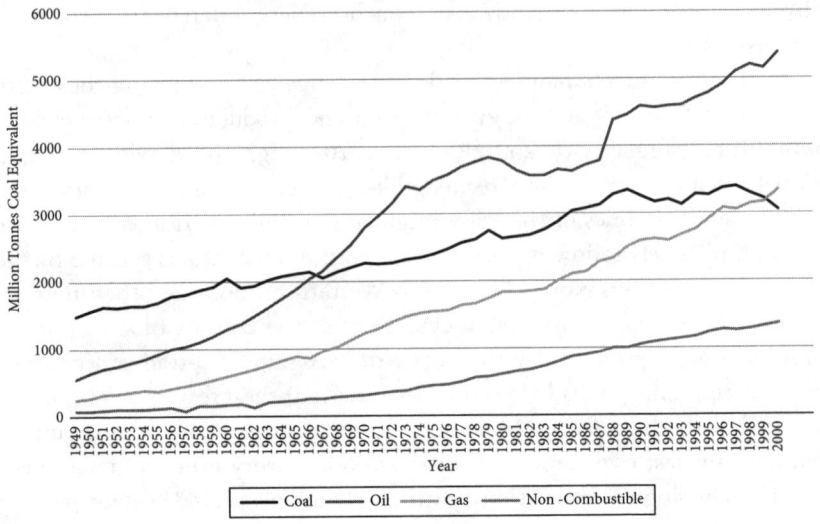

FIGURE 3.1 Global Energy Production, 1949–2000

gas, and non-combustibly generated electricity—at first, hydroelectric power, later nuclear, and still later geothermal and renewables. The figures only cover commercial production, and those four sources of energy, so leaving out, for instance, African and Asian peasants burning animal dung as fuel, or North American homeowners heating their houses with wood (as I did between 1985 and 1994). While non-commercial energy sources were certainly not negligible—UN experts estimated that they made up about one-fifth of global energy use in 1949—they represented, over time, a steadily declining portion of the world's energy palette.[3]

The first year that coal no longer accounted for a majority of global energy production was 1962; five years later, oil surpassed it and has remained the largest through to the end of the millennium. It was not that coal use declined; quite the opposite, it grew steadily in the postwar years. The world's production of petroleum products increased exponentially, rising at an increasing pace from year to year. The oil rush was global. Coal's chief stronghold was the Eastern Bloc, where it remained the largest source of energy through the 1970s, though even there the use of petroleum for energy grew twice as fast as coal.

Yet if petroleum dominated the postwar era, the energy dream of those years was nuclear power. Humans would fly to the moon in atomic-powered spaceships; the atom would power automobiles, locomotives, and airplanes, as well as surface ships and submarines—expansive expectations articulated, among other places in the United States, the USSR, Western and Eastern Europe, India, Japan, and Ghana during the 1950s. Nuclear power, Japan's illustrated weekly magazine, *Asahi Gurafu* informed its readers, would even prevent sashimi from spoiling. A popular manga comic, *Testuwa Atom* about a nuclear-powered robot, was a Japanese bestseller from 1951 to 1968; it became the first Japanese animated cartoon.

In this nuclear future, energy would be available in enormous abundance. In 1954 Lewis L. Strauss, the chairman of the US Atomic Energy Commission, maintained that atomic energy would be too cheap to meter, and he was hardly alone in his optimism. Homi Bhabha, an Indian physicist, the central figure of India's post-1945 nuclear research and development effort, asserted just two weeks after the bombing of Hiroshima and Nagasaki, that as a result of atomic energy, "Limitless quantities of power would be available at a cost so low that for all practical purposes it would be free. Every need of humanity could be supplied." Anatoli Alexandrov, the physicist who was director of the Kurchatov Institute, the USSR's main center of nuclear research, predicted that atomic energy would make it simple and easy to build roads and cities in Siberia, expand agriculture there, and even transform its climate into the subtropical version prevalent around the Black Sea.[4]

There were legitimate triumphs of atomic navigation: the voyage of the nuclear-powered submarine U.S.S. *Nautilus* under the North Pole in 1958; or the maiden voyage of the USSR's atomic-powered icebreaker *Lenin* the following year. The efforts of both Cold War rivals to create nuclear-powered air- and spacecraft quite literally did not get off the ground, however, since the weight of the nuclear reactor and the shielding needed from its radioactivity made the craft too heavy to fly—an inconvenient fact nuclear physicists had been pointing out for years.[5] Not getting off the ground might be the best way to describe the realities of nuclear power in the 1950s and 1960s. Individual reactors were built. The very first in the world was the facility at Obninsk in Russia, which started sending power through the electric grid on June 26, 1954. The next atomic power plant in the USSR only appeared a full decade later—a pace of building characteristic of all the countries that tried their hand at nuclear power during the postwar era, including the United States, the United Kingdom, France, West Germany, Italy, Canada, and Japan. In 1970, nuclear energy accounted for all of 1.4 percent of the world's total electric generating capacity.[6]

The difficulties of constructing a nuclear reactor that could consistently produce electric power over a long period of time proved to be far greater than expected, a state of affairs reflected in the serious accidents that plagued the first nuclear power plants—Chalk River in Canada (1952), Windscale in England (1957), and St. Laurent in France (1969).[7] All involved problems with controlling the chain reaction, making them precursors of the major nuclear accidents that followed—Three Mile Island, Chernobyl, and Fukushima. Contemporaries were aware of this problem, as can be seen in the testimony of Henry Young, vice president of the Liberty Mutual Insurance Company before the US Congress in 1957: "Even if insurance could be found, there is a serious question whether the amount of damage to persons and property would be worth the possible benefit accruing from atomic development."[8]

Young's point about catastrophe, as might be expected from an insurance executive, was couched in economic terms. In an age of cheap petroleum, nuclear power was not competitive with fossil fuels; businesses showed a corresponding reluctance to invest in very capital-intensive nuclear reactors. Even in France, a country where the development of atomic energy was a prestige-driven national priority, there was a backhanded recognition of this fact. A decade later, explicit recognition brought to an end any aspirations to a large nuclear power program in India, another country where nuclear power was a matter of national prestige. Kwame Nkrumah, the anti-imperialist and pan-Africanist president of Ghana, the first sub-Saharan nation to wrest its independence from British colonial rule, promoted a nuclear power program for his country, as part of his program of attaining for Africans equity with their former imperialist overlords. "No country has a monopoly on ability," he stated, in regard to scientific expertise in general, and nuclear physics, in particular. The reactor building and the water-cooling tanks for it were built on the outskirts of Accra, and the government of the USSR pledged to put a reactor in them. However, following the coup that overthrew Nkrumah in 1966 and the pro-Western government that replaced him, the structures remained empty, and continue to be so down to the present. Lacking employment in their native country, the Ghanaian physicists and engineers whose advanced education Nkrumah's regime had eagerly supported, mostly ended up in universities, research facilities, or power plants in Western Europe and the United States.[9]

As these examples suggest, nuclear power projects of the 1960s emerged from a desire for national prestige or, more importantly, as adjuncts to the development of atomic weapons. Proponents of atomic power liked to distinguish its peaceful uses from its military applications. Nkrumah, for instance, was as vigorous an opponent of the testing of atomic weapons (fallout from French bomb tests in the Sahara found its way to Ghana) and proponent of worldwide disarmament as he was a supporter of atomic power. Utopian expectations of nuclear power in the postwar era were invariably described as a positive use of atomic energy, contrasted to the disturbingly negative one of nuclear warfare. In reality, civilian and military uses of atomic energy were inextricably linked, for the ordinary running of a nuclear reactor produces large amounts of plutonium, an element admirably suited to the production of nuclear weapons.[10]

In terms of actual energy use, as opposed to future expectations, the postwar decades were an age of petroleum, which the oil price shocks of 1973 and 1979 brought to a jarring conclusion. As Figure 3.1 shows, global oil production fell after 1979, not reaching that year's level again until 1988. While petroleum use expanded in the 1990s, it did so at a much slower pace than in the postwar years; its increase was linear rather than exponential. But if the era of cheap and abundant oil was over, what would replace it?

The oil price shocks and oil shortages were, or at least seemed to be, monumental events, so there was a natural tendency to envisage the new energy era as involving equally monumental changes in energy technology. One possibility posed at the time was a back-to-the-future initiative, reviving a technological process from the Age of Total War—the transformation of coal into gasoline. It had worked during the Second World War, providing Nazi Germany with most of the petroleum it needed: over 90 percent of its aircraft fuel, and 57 percent of all its gasoline. However, a technology successful in wartime proved dubious in peacetime. Coal gasification was fine when no one cared about its costs, but too expensive for the bottom-line realities of a peacetime economy. The only country where the process was attempted was South Africa, whose apartheid regime had been cut off from regular sources of oil by international boycotts and so had its own version of an emergency situation.[11]

As impractical as coal gasification may have been, it had one distinct virtue, namely that it forced people to seek a substitute for petroleum's single most important use, which was in transportation. Finding alternatives for electric power generation could only replace a relatively small portion of oil consumed.

One possibility was solar energy. It produced no emissions, something strongly appealing to growing environmentalist sentiment. But solar energy had broader appeal than just to the energy counterculture. It was always available—a key point in a world jolted by oil embargoes. "No one can ever embargo the sun," President Jimmy Carter stated in 1979. His administration offered moral support and substantial subsidies; it seemed to be riding on a wave of wide public approval. "Solar energy has captured the public imagination," announced Carter's energy secretary, James Schlesinger, a conservative, pro-free market economist, former head of the Central Intelligence Agency and one-time secretary of defense. If Schlesinger, the very opposite of a tree-hugger, could endorse solar energy, who could be against it? Certainly not business; by 1980, there were a thousand companies in the Solar Energy Industries Association, including some of America's largest corporations. Japan's Ministry of International Trade (MITI) launched a large-scale program to mobilize the country's growing electronics industry to produce solar cells.

Yet it was all over within a few years. Environmentalists like to blame the pro-hydrocarbon, anti-environmentalist policies of the conservative government of President Ronald Reagan, starting in 1981. His administration's 1986 dismantling of the solar water heater his predecessor had installed on the White House roof rankled environmentalists for decades. But blaming one country's policy makers does not explain why solar power had no particular success anywhere else in the world for the rest of the twentieth century. The promise of solar power was greater than the reality: it would take decades before the conversion of sunlight into electricity could be done in an even remotely effective fashion.[12]

Adherents of nuclear power had been promising great things for decade, and the disorienting and frightening jump in oil prices gave them their chance to take nuclear energy programs already underway in the 1960s—for prestige and weapons purposes—and expand them into a true alternative to petroleum. The 1970s in particular were the nuclear decade. Nuclear power plants' share of the world's total electrical generating capacity jumped fivefold, from just 1.4 percent in 1970 to 7.0 percent ten years later. This rapid escalation slowed dramatically over the following twenty years, with atomic power making up 11.9 percent of electrical generating capacity in 1990, and actually declining as a proportion of total capacity to 10.9 percent at the beginning of the new millennium.[13] The combination of overhype and the exposure of some downsides of this form of energy generation, downsides that its proponents had been unwilling to emphasize or even acknowledge, led to this result.

With the seeming shortages of petroleum in the 1970s, atomic power's promise of unlimited energy came to the fore. The fissionable isotope U-235, which provides the nuclear reaction in an atomic pile, makes up just a relatively small proportion of the uranium fuel rods: over 90 percent of these rods' content consists of the non-fissionable U-238. But the neutrons given off by U-235 are absorbed by the U-238, turning it into plutonium, which is itself fissionable and can be used to start its own nuclear reactions. So atomic power plants, it seems, can create their own fuel, making them a virtually inexhaustible energy supply. A particularly enthusiastically greeted variant on this idea was the "fast-breeder reactor"—the "fast" referring to the speed of the neutrons emitted by the fissionable U-235—which could turn even more U-238 into plutonium. All that would be needed was a little "recycling"—a clever appropriation of an environmentalist phrase—to convert the spent fuel rods into plutonium fuel for still more atomic power.

As usual, the devil is in the details, only much more so than usual in the case of nuclear recycling. The recycling process, involving work with both highly toxic and highly radioactive used fuel rods, proved to be both technologically difficult and intolerably expensive. It was actually cheaper to mine uranium ore, refine it, separate out the fissionable U-235 (so-called uranium enrichment), and make new fuel rods than to use the recycled plutonium fuel. The fast breeder was a still more complicated technological project and even less successful. Only one such reactor ever got out of the experimental phase—the French Super Phoenix, which was run between 1986 and 1996, but only in operation for six months in those ten years. It was constantly in need of repair. This was probably a good thing, because of the additional fissionable material they were producing fast breeders were in danger of going out of control and producing a massive nuclear meltdown. Such an accident came within a hair's breadth of happening at one of the very first such facilities, the Enrico Fermi nuclear reactor in Monroe Michigan, thirty miles from Detroit, in October 1966. Although it may have been an exaggeration to say that "we almost lost Detroit," as one journalist put it in a book about the event, the chain reaction did get out of control, fuel rods did melt, engineers desperately worked twenty-four hours a day for a month to prevent a major catastrophe.[14]

It is against this background of poorly working processes and near accidents that the major problems of large-scale use of nuclear power emerged. If "recycling" used fuel rods proved impractical, what was to be done with them? Elaborate schemes were drawn up to bury this "nuclear waste" in large underground repositories. These would have to be extremely secure from human intrusion or environmental influences, since the fuel rods would deliver a lethal dose of radiation to anyone who got near them for the next ten thousand years. If this were not enough, there were two major and globally publicized nuclear power accidents involving large-scale meltdowns of the atomic piles. These were of course at Three Mile Island in Pennsylvania in 1979, and Chernobyl in Ukraine in 1986. Together, they were the coup de grace to an atomic future.

Proponents of nuclear power still blame the anti-nuclear mass movements inspired by Three Mile Island. They assert that the opposition of people living near sites of central waste repositories (so-called NIMBYs) made those impossible. Accidents, they say, which occur in all kinds of power plants, killed no one at Three Mile Island. The same cannot be maintained of Chernobyl, but nuclear power fans point to the inferior, backward technology used there, concluding that the mega-accidents were no reason to terminate nuclear power. Apprehensions about having a nuclear waste site in one's backyard that would need to be guarded for a longer time than the entire previous extent of human civilization, do not seem entirely unjustified. The spectacular meltdowns in Pennsylvania and Ukraine occurred against a backdrop of smaller accidents caught just in time and much-promised but unsuccessful efforts at nuclear recycling. Fears may have played a big part in the decline of nuclear energy, but cool cost and efficiency calculations of insurance and utility companies—calculations that were already being made in the days of wondrous nuclear expectations in the 1950s—played the decisive role. Countries such as France, which continued and expanded their use of nuclear power for generating electricity, did so by borrowing and spending on an immense scale. By the mid-1980s, *Electricité de France*, the state-owned power company responsible for the atomic power program, was the third-largest borrower in the US bond market after Ford and General Motors. A quarter of all utility payments went to debt service and the company could only remain solvent with very large government subsidies.[15]

There was another option for atomic power, namely nuclear fusion, the forcing together of hydrogen atoms, rather than the splitting of uranium ones. Fuel would be cheap, derivable from seawater; radioactive waste from the fusion reaction would be minimal (proponents tended to avoid mentioning that the containment vessel in which the reaction would take place, would be bombarded with neutrons and become radioactive), so that all the promises of fission, which had proven so disappointing, could actually be fulfilled. Scientists across the world had been working on nuclear fusion since the 1950s, initially with very high hopes, but quickly found one intractable problem. The difficulty with nuclear fission was keeping the chain reaction controlled. With fusion the problem was starting the reaction in the first place, pressing together hydrogen atoms that strongly repel each other due to electromagnetic force. One could do so by exploding an atomic bomb around them—this produced in turn the hydrogen bomb, an uncontrolled fusion reaction good for destroying all life on earth, bad for generating energy—or, via the force of gravity from the enormous mass of the sun, not a method too helpful on a terrestrial scale. The preferred procedure for "controlled fusion" has been to place the hydrogen in extremely powerful magnetic fields that force the atoms together. After sixty years of increasingly elaborate experimentation, with different forms and shapes of magnetic fields—a chief favorite has been fields in the shape of a figure eight—physicists have still not gotten controlled fusion to work. For a brief moment in 1989, the claim of two researchers at the University of Utah that they had achieved "cold fusion," the merging of hydrogen atoms without the need for high pressure, high temperature, and immense amounts of energy, created a stir: the great dreams of atomic energy might yet be realized. Or perhaps not, because other scientists were unable to replicate these results. Although cold fusion still has its adherents, most physicists are of the opinion that there is no such a thing, just poorly calibrated instruments and inexact measurements.[16]

So in other words, there was no scientific alternative to the drama of the oil price shocks and the end of the era of petroleum and its exponentially growing consumption. The energy story of the last two decades of the twentieth century was simpler: as Figure 3.1 shows, less oil (or at least a more slowly increasing rate of consumption of oil) and more natural gas, to the point that by 2000 it was in second place, globally, as an energy source, outpacing coal. But gas is still a fossil fuel, so that the world's energy future remained dependent on the remains of creatures that had lived one hundred million years in the past; hydrocarbons were a seemingly inescapable energy destiny. Twenty-first-century efforts to expand the use of renewable sources of energy, particularly solar and wind power, have had to start from a very low baseline.[17]

There was one feature of the newer energy regime that actually worked against the trend of globalization in the last decades of the twentieth century. Unlike oil, which went overland by pipelines and could be easily pumped onto tankers at seaports and shipped all over the world, natural gas's transportation ended oceanside. In theory, gas could be liquefied in special port facilities and shipped via equally specialized LNG tankers, but this is a procedure requiring very large capital investments for the equipment and involving substantial risks, since an accident can lead to a devastating explosion. The rise of natural gas meant that energy markets became less globalized, more regional—a movement counteracting and contradicting the broader lessons of the Age of Interconnection. The classic example has been the export of Siberian natural gas to central and western Europe. Beginning in the 1970s, it quickly became more appealing to utilities and industrial users in West Germany, Italy, or France, than LNG imports from Algeria. With the growing importance of natural gas, the trade has continuously expanded since the 1970s, surviving both the Cold War, its end, the disruptions emerging from the end of the USSR, continuing and expanding down to the present day.[18]

Transportation

In 1953, *Cruzeiro*, very roughly the *Time* magazine of Brazil, commented that "Brazilians in general are divided into two classes: those who *have* a car and those who *want* a car."[19] It was not just Brazilians who fell into those two classes, but the entire human race. The Age of Interconnection was the Age of the Automobile. It reshaped space and time, transformed society, absorbed ever greater amounts of petroleum, and became the most important consumer durable. The car was also the chrome-trimmed embodiment of dreams of personal freedom and roaring speed, as well as those dreams' nightmare opposite of jammed traffic and choking smog. But, as the writer of *Cruzeiro* saw at the beginning of the era, the automobile's place was precisely in its duality, in the difference between the aspiration toward an auto and the possession of an auto, and not just for individuals, but for entire nations and regions of the world.

At what point is it possible to describe a society as automobilized? The dividing line is always arbitrary. Still, a good place to draw it would be at 250 automobiles (most, although not all, statistics exclude taxis and other commercially used autos) per 1,000 inhabitants, a point at which a majority of households are in possession of their own private car. Before 1945, no country in the world had reached that point, although the United States had come closest, at 225/1,000 in 1941. Table 3.1 lists the countries that crossed the line after 1945 and the year in which they did so.

TABLE 3.1 Crossing the Threshold of Automobilization, 1950–2000

Country	Year	Country	Year
USA	1950	Austria	1977
Canada	1963	Belgium	1979
New Zealand	1964	Finland	1980
Australia	1965	Spain	1986
Sweden	1967	Japan	1989
France	1970	Kuwait	1990
West Germany	1972	Portugal	1990
Switzerland	1973	Czech Republic	1993
Italy	1974	Greece	1998
Denmark	1975	Poland	2000
UK, Netherlands, Norway	1976		

Sources: Calculated from Brian R. Mitchell, *International Historical Statistics: The Americas 1750–2005*, 6th ed., Tables A1 and F6; ibid., *International Historical Statistics: Africa, Asia & Oceania 1750–2005*, 5th ed. (Basingstoke: Palgrave Macmillan, 2007), Tables A1 and F5; ibid., *International Historical Statistics: Europe 1750–2005*, 6th ed. (Basingstoke: Palgrave Macmillan, 2007), Tables A1 and F6.

The table shows a progression and geographic expansion in the postwar decades and then a great deceleration in the last twenty years of the century. Leading the expansion were the one-time settler colonies of the British Empire, the United States, Canada, Australia, and New Zealand, prosperous and sparsely populated countries, where cars were unusually helpful for getting around. The 1970s was the decade of the automobilization of western Europe. Since then, however, very few countries have been able to cross the threshold: a few poorer stragglers in southern and eastern Europe in the 1980s and 1990s, and two countries at a surprisingly late date—Japan in 1989 and Kuwait the following year. (Saudi Arabia was probably earlier, but its pre-1990 statistics on auto ownership are incomplete and unreliable.)

The former Soviet Union offers an interesting case. In the 1930s party leaders and ordinary citizens of the USSR had been fascinated by automobiles. They were great admirers of the prototypical early twentieth-century capitalist Henry Ford and envisaged a motorized future for a fully communist Soviet Union. Auto rallies held, involving adventurous trips across the state's immense Eurasian landmass, lacking much in the way of paved roads, were heavily promoted by the government and followed by giant crowds of fascinated spectators. But the countries of the Eastern Bloc could not match their west European counterparts in producing or procuring this hotly desired consumer durable following the Second World War. Soviet citizens certainly wanted cars, as the two million members of the All-Union Voluntary Society of Auto Enthusiasts (founded 1972) and its very popular magazine, *Behind the Wheel*, testified. Trying to get people to work on the Baikal-Amur mainline railway, being constructed in Siberia during the 1970s and 1980s, the government offered volunteers willing to sign up for a three-year labor commitment vouchers that were good for the purchase of a new car.[20]

None of the vouchers were ever honored. Privately owned automobiles never had the necessary priority in communist regimes. Even harder to find than cars were, spare parts (when parking, motorists took their windshield wipers and side view mirrors with them, to prevent them from being stolen), repair shops, or just gasoline. Soviet planners understood the 250/1000 automobilization threshold, but the country never even reached a rate of 100/100,000, with, private auto ownership in the USSR at only 45/1,000 in 1985. Ownership rates were twice that in the USSR's most affluent Baltic Republics, and even higher in the furthest western stretches of the Eastern Bloc, reaching a peak of 224/1,000 in the German Democratic Republic in 1989—matching US levels of auto ownership in 1941. Of course, that was the year that the communist German state dissolved, a process beginning when tens of thousands of its citizens drove their cars to Hungary and crossed over to the West at the newly opened border with Austria, leaving behind their autos—the *Trabant* with its plastic body, and heavily-polluting two-cycle engine, used elsewhere for chainsaws and edge-trimmers.

The story of the Eastern Bloc parallels that of Latin America, Africa, and large stretches of Asia. The dreams certainly persisted. Brazil's utopian new capital city Brasilia was inaugurated at the end of the 1950s with a "Caravan of National Integration," in which columns of Brazilian-made autos left Porto Alegre, Rio de Janeiro, Cuiabá, and Belem for the national capital. Arriving, they found broad boulevards, no sidewalks, and a garage parking place for every single apartment.[21] But in most places the reality was more modest. At the beginning of the twenty-first century, in Argentina, Mexico, and Brazil, the most heavily automobilized of the Latin American countries—and the latter two with a substantial domestic auto industry—auto ownership rates were only 146, 113, and 87 per 1,000, respectively. (Argentina's auto ownership rate was about the same as that of the post-Soviet Russian Federation at the time.) There were just about 93 private autos per 1,000 South Africans, but a more typical figure for that continent would be Nigeria's 4.2/1,000. At the beginning of the new millennium, a few Asian countries were on the verge of mass auto ownership, with South Korea, Israel, Taiwan, and Malaysia all between 190 and 240 privately owned cars per thousand inhabitants. Private car ownership in the world's two most populous countries, China and India, stood at 7 and 6 per 1000, respectively. A rule of thumb was that about 10 percent of the vast population of the two Asian giants in the year 2000 was "middle class," able to aspire to amenities common in more affluent parts of the world. If we imagine those 10 percent as making up their own separate countries, their auto ownership rates at 60 or 70/1,000 would have been below South Africa's and in line with those of Turkey or Venezuela.

There are certainly lots of reasons for the progress, or lack of it, when it comes to "automobilization": slower in more densely than in more lightly populated countries, or, related, where there are different policies about public transportation and private auto ownership. Both of these reasons help explain why the United States, Canada, and New Zealand became car societies relatively early; and why the Netherlands, West Germany, and Japan did so relatively late. But more than anything else, the spread of auto ownership reflected the growth of income and the global patterns of the world economy: mass affluence moving from North America to Western Europe in the booming quarter century after 1950, and then, with the dramatic slowdown in global economic growth following the disruptive beginnings of globalization in the 1970s (discussed in detail in the next chapter), contracting, except in some of the East Asian countries that defied the global trend in the final decades of the century.[22] These economic changes and worldwide shifts, evident as they are in the consumption of automobiles, are even more apparent in their production and engineering.

The postwar decades were the era of the large American car, with its massive stretches of chrome and giant tailfins. Though now viewed by many in the rosy glow of nostalgia, they left quite a bit to be desired: largely based on 1930s technology (the big innovation of the 1950s, automatic transmission, had first been introduced in 1938), not very durable and prone to frequent breakdowns, spewing toxic exhaust and sporting fuel consumption of fifteen miles per gallon, about half that of Henry Ford's Model T. These vehicles dominated the auto picture globally. In 1950 about 85 percent of all autos were manufactured in North America and ten years later still over half were. Even in the United States, such cars were not universally acclaimed, as became clear in the auto "buyers' strike" in the wake of the 1958 recession. Detroit responded with the compact car, which quickly gained market share in the early 1960s. However, the American Motors Ramblers, Ford Fairlanes, and Plymouth Valiants of the era were just shrunken versions of their larger counterparts, containing most of the latter's failings. (I say this as someone who still has nostalgic memories of learning to drive on a 1964 Dodge Dart.) By the end of the 1960s, large cars had re-conquered at least the American auto market.[23]

The main alternative to the large American car in the postwar era was the celebrated Volkswagen Beetle. A classic product of the Age of Total War, the "people's car" was invented by Austrian engineer Ferdinand Porsche in car-crazy Nazi Germany at the behest of its *Führer*, who wanted a cheap and simple auto that could be purchased en masse to create a motorized society, a development in which he had a keen interest. The Second World War, a matter in which the dictator was even more keenly interested, intervened, leaving in the lurch the 270,000 Germans who had been making installment payments on the car. (Unlike American installment payments, or German ones for that matter, purchasers of the Nazis' VW had to finish their three years of installments before they could take delivery.) Production resumed in 1949 and reached 369,000 yearly by 1961. Rugged, and durable, outfitted with a simple and fuel-efficient air-cooled engine, cleverly marketed at home and abroad, the "Bug" was an immense global success. Even after production and sales ceased in Europe and North America between 1977 and 1984, *Volkswagen do Bresil and Volkswagen de Mexico* continued to build and sell the *vochito*, as it was called in Mexico, until 2003.[24]

But for all its miniature charm and frugal virtues, the Beetle was a technological dead end. Its underpowered, thirty-nine-horsepower engine may have burned gasoline efficiently, but its emissions were considerable. The engine was rear-mounted, which did not make the vehicle the safest place to be in a crash. These problems could be remedied, but only by making the car more expensive and much less cute.

The true alternative to the large US cars of the 1950s was a vehicle quite forgotten today, except among some old-car enthusiasts, coming from a country better known for its post-1945 industrial disasters—the Morris Mini of British Motors. (This is not to be confused with today's Mini, produced by BMW, which has little in common with the original but the name.) Debuting in 1959, the car was the first widely sold vehicle with front-wheel drive, a transversely mounted inline engine, and independent suspensions. It proved immensely popular and by 1965, total production had reached one million units, a figure it took the VW Bug ten years to attain.[25]

After the rapid expansion of the postwar decades, when total auto production worldwide almost tripled from 8.2 million units in 1950 to 22.3 million twenty years later, the figure just barely doubled over the subsequent thirty years, reaching 45 million units by 1998.[26] By the end of the century, cars had become quite different vehicles, as a result of two fundamental challenges to automotive engineering, both with roots in the 1970s: the price of fuel and the demand for reduced emissions. Solving these two challenges simultaneously was particularly difficult, since the engineering measures needed for one goal generally obstructed the other.

The secret of automotive engineering in the late twentieth century was adapting the innovations of the Morris Mini to resolve these contradictory challenges. Ultimately, doing so would require deployment of electronics— the computer-regulated mixture of oxygen and gasoline in automobile engines and the replacement of carburetors with fuel injectors. Successful manufacture of fuel-efficient, durable, low-emissions vehicles became a signature of East Asian countries, first Japan and later South Korea. At the end of the 1990s, both Honda and Toyota extended this use of electronics by manufacturing the first hybrid cars, in which the computer-controlled assistance of an electric motor made it possible to use an unusually small and thus fuel-efficient internal combustion engine to drive a vehicle.

In the 1980s, Communist regimes took a shot at making fuel-efficient vehicles, although the results, such as the East German Trabant, or the Russian Lada, the Zastava or Yugo from Yugoslavia, and the Polski Fiat—the latter three all, basically, the same car, manufactured on license from Fiat—were not terribly satisfactory, lacking both electronics and emission controls. At its end, the USSR produced, with one-tenth the number of cars and one-half the truck traffic of the United States, two-thirds as much toxic vehicle emissions.[27]

Not that the United States had done that well: American manufacturers floundered during the 1970s and 1980s, conspicuously falling short of their newly energized Japanese competitors in producing fuel-efficient, reliable and durable cars. If Japanese competition was undermining US auto manufacturing in the small car/low price point segment, the Germans were rapidly conquering the global luxury car market, a development that appears linguistically in changing designations for wealthy consumers in poorer countries: from the *cadilaquenos* of 1950s Brazil to the *Wabenzi*, the tribe of Mercedes owners, of Kenya, Nigeria, and South Africa, by the end of the century.[28] It is hard to think of anything more characteristic of the end of the postwar era and the Age of Upheaval following them than the crisis and decline of US auto manufacturing: once globally dominant, by 1980 it was fighting for survival. It was only able to save itself and to enjoy a modest renaissance in the last decade of the twentieth century by finding ways to sell light trucks to consumers, in place of cars. At the same time that Japanese manufacturers were using fuel injection and computer-controlled engines to build hybrids and other highly fuel-efficient cars, their American counterparts were using the same technology to produce very large vehicles, with mediocre fuel consumption.[29] Figure 3.2 shows the resulting global realignments in automobile production: the sharp fall of North American manufacturers from their global dominance in the 1950s and their modest revival in the last decade of the millennium, along with the rise of auto manufacturing in Western Europe and, with about a decade's delay, in East Asia.

Another major feature of the postwar transportation technology is connected to the rise of air travel. The crucial element in this ascent was the introduction of a classic piece of technology—again from the Age of Total War—jet aircraft engines. Invented in Nazi Germany, the Third Reich's jet fighters never got off the ground due to pervasive fuel shortages. However, they emerged as combat aircraft just a few years later, during the Korean War of 1950–53. Unlike motor vehicles, where civilian and military uses were not very closely related (few lessons could be applied from building

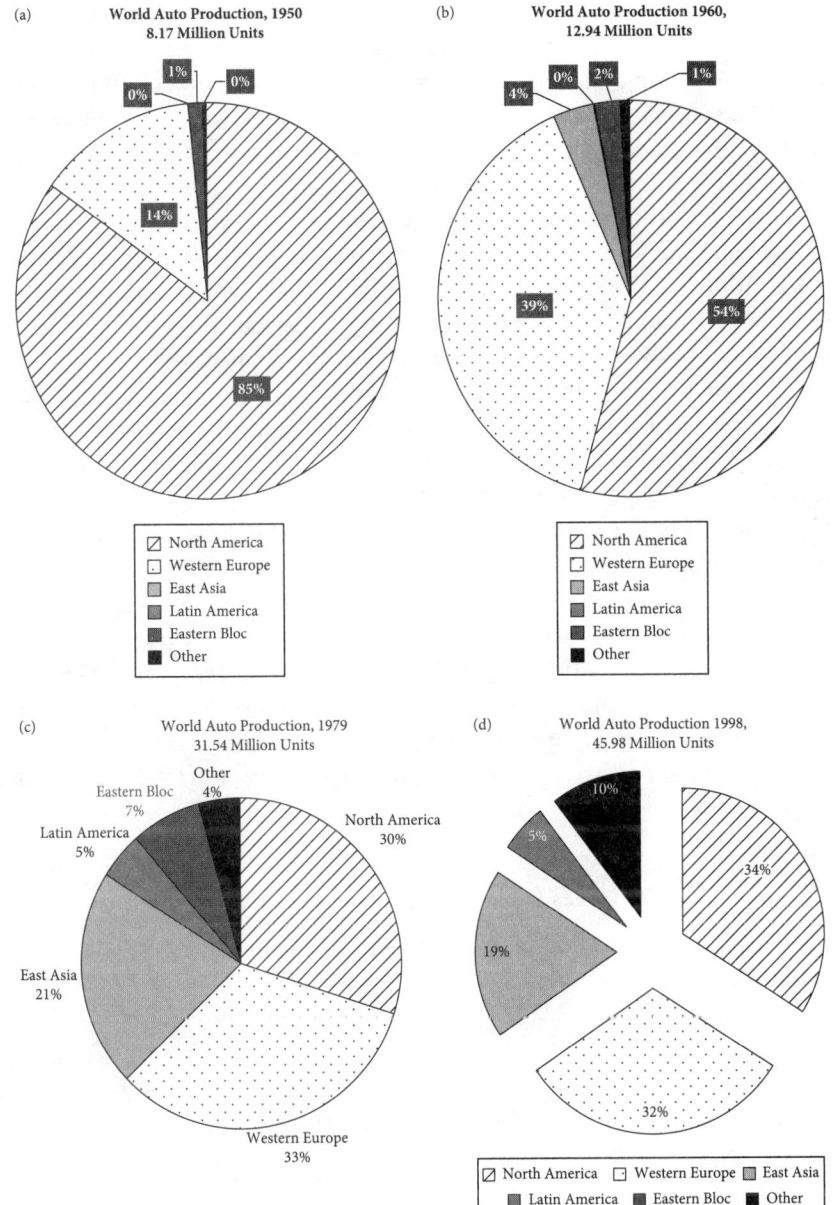

FIGURE 3.2 World Auto Production, 1950–1998

tanks to building front-wheel drive cars, or vice versa), in aviation the same manufacturers of military airplanes built civilian ones and the technology first employed in combat aircraft made its way to civil airliners.

For jets, it took about a decade. In 1957, according to the statistics of the International Civil Aviation Organization, there were only twelve jets among the world's commercial airline fleet of some 4,600 planes. By 1963, there were 872 jets in regular airline service and, at the end of the decade, 3,499, decisively outnumbering the 2,190 piston-engine (i.e., propeller) planes in use.[30] The jet era really began in the 1960s, with an acceleration in pace of air travel, as Figure 3.3 shows, settling into a steady pattern of linear increase across the rest of the century—showing no slowdown in the 1970s and 1980s, as was the case with petroleum use or the spread of automobiles. By 2000, there were 1.6 billion passengers on commercial airlines, about a fourth of the world's entire population. By then, the number of air passengers exceeded the number of personal automobiles owned, by margins ranging from 9:1 in Kenya and 7:1 in China, to 2–3:1 in countries as diverse as the United States, France, India, Japan, and Brazil.[31]

The very first commercial jetliner was manufactured in Great Britain—the de Havilland Comet, which went into service in 1952. No sooner was this first jet flying then it was grounded, because design flaws caused cracks to appear in the fuselage, so that pressurized air from the cabin could explode the plane in midair, as happened twice in quick succession. American aviation firms, adopting their military transport and jet refueling planes to civilian use, manufactured more reliable jet aircraft five to ten years after the pioneering British venture. The Americans—Boeing, McDonnel Douglas, and Lockheed—seemed likely to monopolize global passenger jet production outside the Eastern Bloc until British, French, and West German manufacturers pooled their assets in the 1970s, creating the Airbus firm,

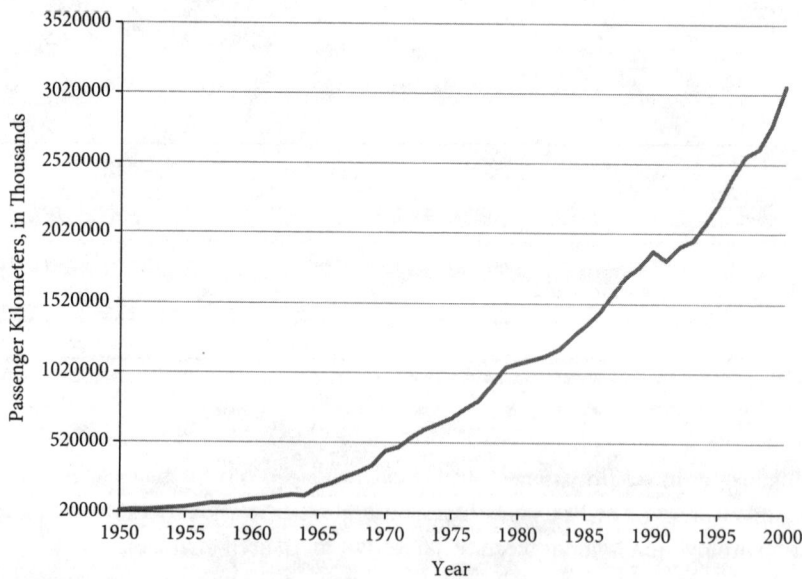

FIGURE 3.3 Passenger Kilometers Flown Yearly, Worldwide, 1950–2000

and, with very generous subsides of the European Economic Community (the chief executive of Airbus admitted in 1990 that the enterprise had never shown an operating profit in the previous twenty years), began turning out Airbus planes from factories in Toulouse and Hamburg. The collapse of the USSR confirmed this Euro-American duopoly in the manufacture of large, commercial jet aircraft, a state of affairs quite different from that in auto manufacturing.[32]

The very name of the European product reveals a change in the nature of aviation, from exciting, exotic, elite (and risky, of course) to functional and prosaic and depressingly common. From the 1960s onward, jet airlines did get larger, could fly steadily longer distances without needing to refuel, utilized ever more sophisticated electronics for navigation, communications and, ultimately, steering the plane itself—in this respect, paralleling similar developments in automobiles. These new aviation technologies, along with the development of a worldwide network of air traffic control systems, made flying much safer. Fatalities per 100 million aircraft miles of US air carriers went from 44 in 1960 to 1.2 in 2000.[33] But commercial jets, unlike military ones, traveled no faster in in the year 2000 than they had thirty years earlier. Other developments, in airport security, route realignment following the deregulation wave of the 1980s and 1990s, and air traffic congestion, resulted in flying being generally slower in the technologically sophisticated maturity of the jet age than in its more primitive youth.

In the heady days of the 1960s—the peak of post-1945 prosperity—commercial jets had seemed as if they were launching an age of aviation acceleration. A Franco-British consortium, Boeing in the United States, and the USSR's aviation industry were all working on supersonic transports, passenger jets that could fly two and three times the speed of sound, making possible an Atlantic crossing in just three hours. Like so many aspirations of those years, the promise of high-speed, high-tech flight withered and died. Sonic booms generated when these planes broke the sound barrier—and their size made the boom much louder and more overwhelming than one produced by a small fighter jet—generated intolerable noise, broke windows, and created havoc, as an initial test series over Oklahoma City demonstrated. The planes could only be deployed on overseas routes, where the noise would reverberate over the (relatively) uninhabited ocean. Supersonic flight required large amounts of fuel, making such planes unattractive to profit-making commercial airlines, even before the rapid increases in jet-fuel prices during the oil price shocks of the 1970s.

Boeing aircraft abandoned its efforts when US government subsidies were cut off in 1971. The Franco-British consortium persisted, and did create the Concorde, which began commercial service in 1976. A Soviet SST, the TU-144, quickly dubbed the "Concordski," for its suspicious similarities to the West European aircraft, a result of industrial espionage, crashed at the 1973

Paris air show. Fourteen Concordes were built, with seven each going to Air France and British Airways. Underbooked and very heavily subsidized, they struggled on until 2003. Twelve units of the competing Soviet model were constructed, but the TU–144 was taken out of service in 1984 as uneconomical, showing that in this instance communist bureaucrats could calculate the costs and benefits of supersonic flight rather more precisely than their capitalist counterparts in Western Europe.[34]

This Age of Interconnection pattern—technology developed in the age of Total War, rapid increases and great expectations in the postwar decades, giving way to routine disillusion and not entirely expected uses—appears much more dramatically in jet propulsion's raucous cousin rocketry, and aviation's dream-filled counterpart, space travel. Their modern history goes back to the initial decades of the twentieth century, when, in Europe, North America, and Japan, groups of enthusiasts, generally young men with a background in engineering or physical science, began to form clubs, such as the Nippon Rocket Society, tinker with small rockets, and read futuristic literature about travel into outer space—known in Russia, as *astronomocheskii roman*, in England as "scientific romance," and, following the coining of Hugo Gernsbach, the US engineer and pulp fiction mogul, "science fiction." For a technology that would be totally dependent on government support and financing, the initial history of rocketry was one of private groups of enthusiasts—even in Stalin's USSR, where everything was run by the state.[35]

In the 1930s, there was only one government in the whole world that offered space travel enthusiasts support and encouragement, Hitler's Third Reich. The upshot of this endorsement during the Second World War was the V-2, the first ballistic missile, a frightening weapon, although in many ways not a terribly effective one (more people died manufacturing it than were killed by it), but whose design and liquid fuel propulsion system remain the basis of rocketry down to the present day.[36] Both the rockets and the engineers who designed them were hastily scooped up by US and Soviet forces following their conquest of Germany in 1945. These kidnappings and expropriations were one of the very first signs of the Cold War. And it was the Cold War that provided one of the decisive contexts for rocketry in the quarter century after 1945, particularly the potential use of long-range missiles as delivery systems for nuclear weapons.[37]

As was the case with atomic power, in the postwar era rocketry was a source of fears of annihilation but also of dreams of the future. First advanced by the leading figures of the early twentieth-century rocketry enthusiasts—the Russian Konstantin Tsiolkovsky, the American Robert Goddard, and the German Hermann Oberth—the dream of human exploration and colonization of outer space moved out of its prewar niche in pulp fiction and among a few enthusiastic engineers, to conquer a large public audience in the 1950s. Americans watched the settlement of Mars on Walt Disney's TV broadcasts, or read all-cap headlines in the March 22, 1952 issue of *Colliers* magazine, "Man Will Conquer Space Soon!" Their Soviet counterparts were not far behind.[38]

The role of space travel as a postwar dream of the future was close to that of atomic energy, as can be seen in how the two were merged in governmental administration. The newly founded Indian Space Research Organization was placed in 1961 under the purview of the Department of Atomic Energy. During the previous decade, France had created a government Ministry of Atomic and Space Affairs.[39] This bureaucratic congruence was not a result of similar technologies, for nuclear power and rocketry have little in common, but a function of their position as similar emblems of a scientific future and national prestige.

Dreams of space travel seemed on the verge of becoming reality between 1957 and 1969, framed at one end by the launching of the first satellite, and at the other by the landing of astronauts on the moon. From the very beginning, the entire era was dominated by competition between the United States and the USSR. Both countries had begun programs to place satellites in orbit in the mid-1950s, largely as spinoffs of their military research into ballistic missiles. Scientists' agreement that the period from mid-1957 to mid-1958 should be the International Geophysical Year, devoted to the study of the earth and its place in the cosmos—ironically, designed to foster cooperation across the boundaries of the Cold War—became the incentive for governments of both countries to place a satellite in orbit, as part of their ongoing competition. The launch date of Sputnik, October 4, 1957, had, in fact, been pushed up by the Soviet government, to forestall what it feared would be a US first step. As part of this public relations offensive, Soviet technicians polished the satellite to a high gloss, so that once in orbit, it would catch the rays of the sun and be visible to the naked eye.

Sputnik's visibility proclaimed the scientific superiority of communist countries, first to begin to realize the dream of space flight, but also potentially first in utilizing rocketry for nuclear warheads and outer space for military purposes. "The moon," US Air Force Brigadier General Homer Boushey stated in the wake of Sputnik's launch, "represents the age-old military advantage of the high ground." The humiliating failures of the initial US efforts to compete—the Vanguard missile that was supposed to send a satellite into orbit blew up on the launch pad—only completed the Eastern Bloc's triumph. Soviet success in placing the first human in orbit—the cosmonaut Yuri Gargarin on April 12, 1961, almost a year ahead of his American counterpart John Glenn—built on initial rocketry victories. The USSR promptly sent the first man into space on worldwide publicity tours. His appearances in India were particularly impressive. Over a million people turned out in Calcutta (today's Kolkata) to cheer him on. He complained that he was so busy with his public appearances that he had no time to see an elephant.[40]

The American Cold War response to Sputnik would have to wait for the arrival of the administration of John F. Kennedy in 1961. Exploiting the resources available at the very height of post-1945 prosperity (and deploying fiscal policies to maximize that prosperity by accelerating economic growth), he set out to meet the twofold Sputnik challenge—rocketry as nuclear nightmare and rocketry as dream of space exploration—by deploying a massive arsenal of intercontinental ballistic missiles and by committing the United States to land an astronaut on the moon within a decade.

In 1961, the USSR, in view of its repeated space triumphs, had seemed more than capable of meeting the US challenge. Soviet engineers, following Gargarin's flight, had drawn up an immensely ambitious program of space exploration for the following decade, beginning with placing space stations in orbit, and using them to launch a manned mission to Mars, passing the moon by. But the Soviet Union lacked the resources to pursue both full-scale military and civilian rocketry programs; the former always had priority. In particular, Soviet efforts at building giant rocket boosters, needed for a lunar landing, were late and underfunded. There were various desperate schemes to use available, underpowered rockets—assembling the lunar lander in earth orbit, or cutting down the number of cosmonauts who would land on the moon to save weight. The N1 rocket booster, the largest and most powerful ever built, was rushed into production during the 1960s without adequate testing, and repeatedly blew up on the launching pad or in its initial moments of ascent. It never flew successfully.[41]

The US effort, spearheaded by the German engineers who had learned rocketry on the V-2, and involving a massive ramping up of its technology, resulted in the eminently functional Saturn V booster—the largest successful launch vehicle in human history. The US lunar program reached its climax on July 20, 1969, when Apollo 11 touched down on the Sea of Tranquility. The relatively new medium of television sent images of the realization of a great twentieth-century futuristic dream worldwide.

Video of Apollo 11's landing was played in the front window of the United States Information Agency Office in Kolkata, on closed-circuit TV, because regular television broadcasts had not yet begun in India. Bengal was the most anti-American part of the country. Crowds in Kolkata had given Soviet cosmonaut Yuri Gargarin a hero's welcome at the beginning of the decade, and usually gathered at the USIA office to hold demonstrations. In this case, instead of smashing windows, spectators gathered to stare through them, in fascination, at the images of the lunar landing. It was a striking example of the global appeal of the dream of colonizing space, transcending Cold War divisions and distinctions between economically and scientifically advanced and developing countries.[42]

Even more striking was that the dream vanished almost from the moment of its realization. After three more Apollo missions, the United States focused its manned space efforts on a new launch vehicle, the space shuttle, designed to place both humans and satellites in earth orbit. It did neither very well. Never able to match the American development of very powerful booster rockets needed for the voyage to the moon, the USSR centered its space efforts on low-earth orbit, with the construction of a series of space stations, beginning in 1971. Since Apollo, humans have never ventured beyond this low-earth orbit.

Not unlike the adherents of nuclear power, supporters of space travel were frustrated with developments in the closing decades of the century, and have been inclined to blame human failings—a failure of will and a lack of desire, budget-cutting, problematic design choices. None of these explanations are entirely wrong. The more difficult economic conditions that followed the end of the postwar era of rapid economic growth, did make space travel more expensive and politically more contentious. There were problematic decisions, such as equipping the space shuttle with delta wings, so that it could be used for military purposes, rather than swept-back jet aircraft wings, meaning the shuttle could not land on a regular runway.[43] But the problems with space travel went deeper. It was less economic conditions and human decisions that shattered the original dreams of space travel and colonization of the solar system than the laws of physics, and discoveries in biology and astronomy.

The main problem with getting anything into space is the initial step: climbing earth's "gravity well" and reaching earth orbit. Each ton of fuel the Apollo 11 lunar lander needed to leave the moon's surface and rendezvous with the command module required 2.5 tons of fuel to bring that ton of fuel from earth orbit to the moon, and 1,544 tons of fuel to get that ton of fuel from the surface of the earth into earth orbit. One could imagine dealing with this problem by building ever-more-powerful rockets to lift from the earth, carrying ever more fuel. Increasing fuel is a partially self-defeating measure, since the rocket then needs to lift the mass of the additional fuel—and this without even considering the extra weight required for fuel tanks, pumps, and propulsion chambers. This problem, known since the beginning of the dream of space flight, can be precisely calculated according to the so-called Tsiolkovsky Equation, devised by Konstantin Tsiolkovsky in 1903. The increase in a rocket's final velocity is not proportional to the amount of fuel added but to its natural logarithm, so that increasing fuel mass ten times just increases velocity 2.3 times; increasing fuel mass one-hundred-fold, 4.6 times. Using different fuels, whose combination produces a greater explosive power from the same weight of fuel, increases velocity of the rocket they power. Even today, though, some rockets continue to use the oxygen and kerosene mixture of the V-2, and the very best alternative fuels, which are very difficult to handle, since they involve using highly corrosive fluorine gas, only produce a final velocity about 1.33 times greater.[44]

This direct result of workings of gravity explains why 1950s fears of weapons in space were totally unfounded. For the amount of fuel needed to lift a warhead into orbit or to the moon and then to bring it back to earth (unlike bombs that can simply be dropped from airplanes, weapons in outer space need to be powered to reach their targets on the ground), as the Apollo example of fuel consumption suggests, one could fire thousands of warheads directly from the earth. As the president of the California Institute of Technology pointed out six months after Sputnik, "Why transport a hydrogen warhead together with all men and equipment 240,000 miles to the moon, just to shoot it 240,000 miles back to earth, when the target is only 5000 miles away in the first place?" The 1967 treaty between the United States and the USSR renouncing stationing nuclear weapons in space was less a victory for disarmament than for Newton's laws of motion.[45]

The difficulty in leaving earth's gravity well is particularly pronounced for manned space flight, since the life support systems for human passengers add significant weight to a spacecraft, requiring more fuel, which, as the Tsiolkovsky Equation shows, decreases efficiency. To take a simple example, the weight of the oxygen, water, and food needed to support one astronaut on a three-year mission to Mars and back is 3.837 metric tons, more mass than all but the very largest unmanned communications and surveillance satellite placed in earth orbit.[46] (This observation makes using the manned space shuttle to launch satellites appear particularly bizarre.) Once in space, humans face an environment far more hostile than the early twentieth-century dreamers and their post-1945 epigones had conceived. They had imagined that weightlessness—technically, micro-gravity—would be beneficial, prolonging life and even helping to treat heart conditions.[47] Reality was just the opposite; muscles and cardiac health steadily deteriorated without gravity's pull, so that long-term stays in space left humans debilitated. Extreme, potentially lethal, bursts of radiation from the sun and, especially, from distant stars in the form of cosmic rays, pulse through space at irregular and unpredictable intervals. Astronauts in low-earth orbit are protected from them by earth's magnetic field, but further out there is no natural shield.[48]

Finally, one of the results of space exploration was the discovery that there is nowhere to go. As late as 1963, astronomers thought that Venus's climate, shrouded from direct observation by a dense cloud layer, was warm and damp, like Earth's in the Cambrian era, five hundred million years ago. Robotic space probes found, instead, that temperature on the planet's surface was about 800° Fahrenheit and the clouds shielding it from view were made of sulfuric acid. Mars had always seemed to be the best prospect for earth-like conditions, but the Viking landers in 1976 found no life, little atmosphere, subzero temperatures, and no surface water—an immense disappointment to the celebrity astronomer Carl Sagan, leading public face of Mars exploration. Sagan consoled himself by suggesting that Mars had once been warmer and wetter, only one hundred thousand years ago; most scientists thought that it had been more like a billion years.[49]

Exploration of outer space continued, producing remarkable results, whether detailed images of Saturn's rings, the Voyager spacecraft's epic journey from its launch in 1977 to interstellar space, thirty-five years later (the Voyager's total launch mass of 815 kilos was less than one-quarter the mass of supplies that would be consumed by one astronaut on a mission to Mars), or rovers sending back images of the surface of Mars, as they drove around the planet. But these were all the results of robotic spacecraft, with humans watching from Earth. Even there, technological progress was slow and halting. Advances in computing and electronics were not matched by those in propulsion: after the Viking probes reached Mars in 1976 the next powered landing on the red planet (as opposed to parachute descent and bouncing around on the surface) would not be for another thirty-seven years. NASA's "faster, better, cheaper" initiative of the 1990s attempted to make a virtue of this slow pace of progress by using less expensive, quickly devised, and largely untested technology, smaller missions dedicated to just one objective and lighter spacecraft with fewer instruments—an approach that would be way too risky for rockets with human passengers but might work for robotic spacecraft. Results were distinctly mixed. While some efforts of this initiative, such as the Genesis Mission, which measured particles emitted by the sun, or the Lunar Prospector, were eminently successful, in 1999 NASA lost five robotic spacecraft in one year, including two on missions to Mars.[50]

Unlike aviation, the last decades of the twentieth century were not just more of the same for rocketry and exploration of outer space. Instead, uses of space were reoriented, from exploratory and outward-looking, to directed at earth itself. The uses were not new and had been developing since the placing of the first satellites into earth orbit, but they came into their own in the decades after 1980. Satellites were employed for international television and telephone communication, although that use that became noticeably less important with the laying of transoceanic fiber-optic cable in the 1990s. Weather satellites provided precise images of the development of storms, becoming familiar features of TV news broadcasts (in Japan, for instance, by the mid-1980s, from the *Hiniawari* weather satellite) and enabled meteorologists to triple the time range of their forecasts, while increasing their accuracy.

Space did turn out to have military uses, not for weapons but for photoreconnaissance. After an initial period in the 1960s of film cameras and Rube Goldberg-like devices for recovering their images, including airplanes with flying hooks intercepting parachuting canisters, the development of electronic imaging made it possible for satellites to photograph ballistic missile launches and launch sites, troop concentrations, movement of armored columns, and a plethora of matters of military significance. The first satellite with an electronic camera was launched by the United States in 1976, and satellite electronic surveillance became standard in the last two decades of the twentieth century. Developing in parallel with photoreconnaissance was satellite navigation, using signals sent from satellites to determine precisely the location of aircraft, naval vessels, and the targets of missiles with nuclear warheads. Even before the system became fully operational for military purposes (a large number of satellites were required, and budget cuts in the late 1970s and early 1980s temporarily put the whole idea on hold), it developed important civilian applications in surveying. The Gulf War of 1991 saw the first military use of the newly developed Global Positioning System or GPS—in splashy and spectacular fashion for guiding missiles and bombs to their targets, so-called smart bombs. Actually, the vast majority of bombs used in that war were of the old-fashioned, stupid variety; GPS was much more effective in helping troops of the United States and its allies to determine their precise position in the desert in the midst of a sandstorm. Throughout the 1990s, civilian uses of GPS expanded, guiding aircraft or maritime traffic, even precisely regulating application of fertilizer in large fields. In the initial decade of the twenty-first century, cell phone apps that depend on signals sent from satellites brought the new technology to a global consumer mass market. All these earth-oriented uses are a very far cry from placing a colony on Mars, but the former that have turned out to be the main use of rocketry and space travel rather than the latter.[51]

In the age of the space race, rocketry and space travel were a US-Soviet duopoly. The leading role of the United States and the post-Soviet Russian Federation has continued into the twenty-first century. However, the last two decades of the twentieth century saw the gradual expansion of the circle of space travel. The European Space Agency, founded in 1975, rather like Airbus, as a cooperative venture of national space programs, sent up its first satellite on the Ariane rocket in 1979. Of course, for all its considerable contributions to robotic planetary exploration, the ESA's budget is an order of magnitude below that of the United States, and its efforts correspondingly less. In 1970, both Japan and China launched satellites into orbit. Their rocket technologies stemmed from the Second World War, Japan's from its own rocket research during the conflict, China's from V-2's the USSR had delivered in the 1950s. India followed with its own satellite, launched by an indigenously developed rocket in 1980 (previous Indian satellites had been launched with Russian vehicles). In the last two decades of the century, these three Asian countries sent a modest, if growing number of satellites into space, a development culminating in the first non-Western manned space flight in 2003, the Chinese *Shenzhou* 5 mission that placed astronauts, or *taikonauts*, as the Chinese call them, into earth orbit. Less prestigious, but certainly more significant, have been the launching of satellite navigation systems by Russia, the EU, China, and India.[52]

The spread of rocketry in the final two decades of the twentieth century put mastery of this technology somewhere between the Euro-American duopoly on commercial aircraft and the much wider global reach of automobile manufacturing. Yet this expansion of the number of countries with space programs, and the extent of these programs themselves, seems very modest compared to the fading of the dreams of outer space in the final decades of the Age of Interconnection.[53]

Agriculture

Compared with landing on Mars, photographing Saturn's rings, producing power too cheap to meter, or turning Siberia's climate subtropical, improving the per-acre yields of wheat, corn, or rice, may not seem quite so exotic or entrancing. But in view of the tripling of the earth's human population between 1950 and 2000, the improvements in agricultural productivity were the single most important technological development of the entire post-1945 era. Without them, it would have been an Age of Starvation rather than one of overall rising standards of living. Global statistics of crop yields, produced by the UN's Food and Agriculture Organization, only begin in 1961, but they paint a very clear picture for the last four decades of the twentieth century [see Figure 3.4]. The world's three major grain crops, corn or maize, rice, and wheat, all show the same pattern of steady increase, with per-hectare output of wheat tripling and maize and rice doubling.[54] The technology behind this remarkable result is one of the great but little-known stories of the twentieth century.

Humans had been trying to breed crops and animals since they began practicing agriculture some 12,000 years ago, but the really crucial advances in the technology of agricultural production occurred in the first half of the twentieth century.[55] Central to the plant-breeding enterprise was the confluence of three strands of biology: natural selection, genetics, and heredity and population mathematics. Their combination made up what biologists call the "modern synthesis." When applied to crop breeding this synthesis guided the process of crossing different varieties of plants, in the hope of producing greater yield or resistance to parasites and diseases.

Although the knowledge basis was well-established by the decades between the world wars, the need for more productive plant varieties might not have seemed particularly pressing. Agricultural output had expanded enormously in earlier decades and even without these scientific techniques there hardly seemed to be a food shortage. Quite the opposite. During the Great Depression, farm prices were so low that farmers found it impossible to

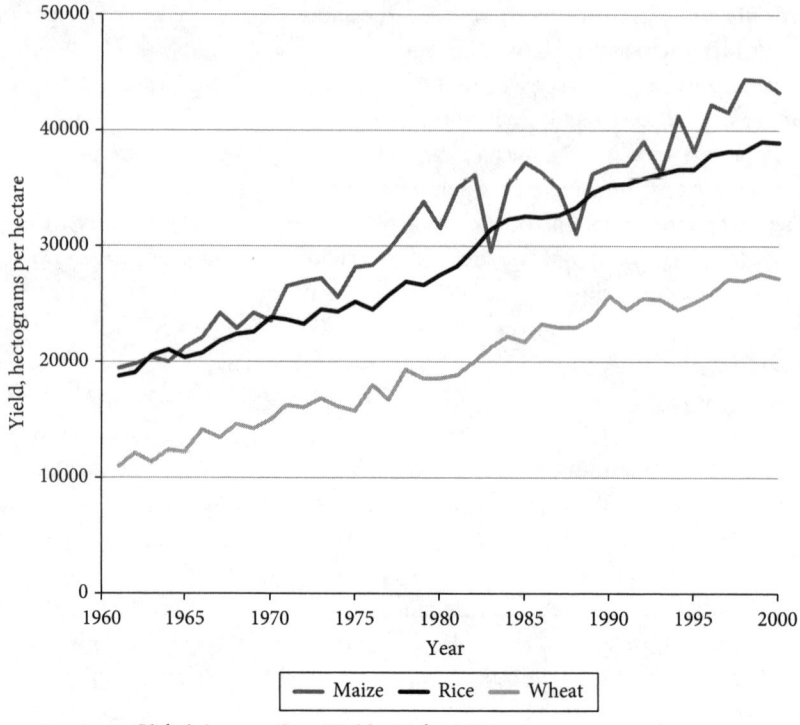

FIGURE 3.4 Global Average Crop Yields, 1961–2000

make a living and governments were busy destroying agricultural surpluses to raise prices. However, a large part of that output growth came from putting new areas under the plow—on the order of a billion acres, primarily in North America, Argentina, and Australia—and not from increasing yields. According to the statistics of the US Department of Agriculture, per-acre yields on corn in the 1930s (though a decade of poor weather) were actually 9 percent lower than they had been in the 1870s. More crop was produced but twice as much land was being used to raise it.[56]

This began to change precisely at a time when it seemed least needed. During the low-price and crop-surplus years of the late 1920s and 1930s, agronomists' research into crop breeding were first commercialized and made widely available. In 1926, Henry A. Wallace, an Iowa journalist, entrepreneur, and politician, founded the Pioneer Hi-Bred Corn Company, which sold high-yielding hybrid corn seeds to farmers. As is the nature of hybrid corn varieties, these seeds did not breed true. Seed derived from corn plants grown from hybrid seeds, when planted in turn, did not have the same desirable properties as the original hybrids. So farmers had to purchase seed anew every year from a seed company. Some would denounce this practice as a particularly evil example of unrestrained American capitalism and imperialism.

Yet the man who did more than anyone else to introduce hybrid corn, and the need for farmers to purchase their seed every year, was the Iowa-born Henry A. Wallace, who served as vice president during FDR's third term and one of the most progressive politicians of his day.[57]

Farmers took on the burden of purchasing seed with considerable rapidity: less than 0.5 percent of US corn acreage was planted in hybrid seeds in 1934, but 59 percent—a hundred times greater—a decade later. The reason is quite simple. The new seeds increased yields immensely. Already 40 percent higher in the 1940s than the 1930s, US per-acre corn yields were twice the 1930s average by the 1950s and triple that a decade later. Unlike the case with energy or jet aircraft, there was no stagnation of agricultural technology in the last decades of the century. US corn yields in the 1990s had reached four-and-one-half times their 1930s levels. In short, from the 1930s to the 1990s, total production of corn in the United States had grown by 330 percent, while the amount of land planted in corn had declined by 15 percent. The post-1940 pattern of much more corn grown on less land was a complete turnabout from the sixty years running from the 1870s to the 1930s, when yields had fallen but acreage had drastically increased.[58]

This was an enormous technological advance that made its way almost silently—certainly, without any of the great expectations attached to nuclear power or space travel—in the same period. If there were any futuristic expectations connected to food in those decades, they took the form of envisaging a future in which people would be eating algae or having an all-chemical diet. More prevalent than expectations of food abundance were fears of widespread starvation, as population outstripped food supply.[59]

The new techniques of crop breeding spread to other staple crops, particularly wheat and rice. The crucial element for those crops was the cultivation of dwarf varieties that produced large seed heads on short stalks. These were generally more productive than other varieties, particularly when cultivated with liberal amounts of fertilizer and water from irrigation. Varieties with larger stalks grew even more when they received additional doses of nitrogen, phosphorus, and water, but much of the growth was concentrated in the stalk, eventually leading the plant to fall over—what crop breeders call "lodging"—ruining the seed head for harvesting. Dwarf varieties, by contrast, continue to stand up straight and produce a larger seed head, expanding the portion of the plant that humans can eat. Cultivation of these dwarf varieties was a global enterprise. The dwarf Japanese variety Norin 10, for example, which provided the basis for high-yielding wheat in the 1950s when crossed with American varieties, itself stemmed from a cross Japanese agronomists had made in the 1930s between indigenous wheat, Mediterranean varieties, and Russian wheat brought to Japan from the United States.[60]

Breeding and agricultural use of high-yield crop varieties began, rather like the automobilization of society, in the United States during the 1950s, and spread out through more affluent countries. What followed was fundamentally different, however, as these new agricultural technologies quickly developed on a global scale in the 1960s and 1970s. More than anyone else, this development is associated with another Iowan, the crop-breeder Norman Borlaug, who directed a project of the Rockefeller Foundation to bring high-yielding varieties of wheat to Mexico. In what can only be described as a frenzied plant-breeding program, cutting in half the time for development of varieties by making two crosses a year, Borlaug and his team developed a whole series of high-yielding wheat strains that were quickly brought into widespread production, especially on the irrigated plains of northern Mexico. From a large wheat importer, by the 1960s Mexico became a major exporter; wheat yields there increased ninefold in the second half of the twentieth century.

This was accomplishment enough, but what made Borlaug as famous as any agronomist could ever be, and brought him the 1970 Nobel Peace Prize (his acceptance speech warned of the dangers of population outstripping food supply), was taking his hybrid grain to South Asia in 1965. The trip turned out to be epic, involving border delays and then delays in the Los Angeles port because of the Watts Riots, which had just erupted.[61] The imported wheat grew very well in South Asia, and wheat yields in both Indian and Pakistan doubled over the next thirty-five years. Both countries went from severe food shortages and large food imports to self-sufficiency in grain—an immense accomplishment, and the exact opposite of what contemporaries expected. In a speech in 1968, William Gaud, director of the US Agency for International Development, talked about what had happened in India and Pakistan as "a green revolution."[62]

Gaud's phrase was immediately capitalized, becoming the "Green Revolution." Its original meaning was not environmental but a product of the Cold War—contrasting a green to a red, communist, revolution. With a lag of some ten to fifteen years, basic features of selecting for yield and disease resistance spread from corn and wheat to rice, the world's largest grain crop, in the wake of breeding programs in the Philippines and China. Already prevalent in western Europe and North America, the new varieties spread throughout Latin America, South, Southeast, and East Asia. Their impact was smaller in Africa, which had a very different palette of staple crops from the rest of the world, and the lack of improvements in agricultural productivity contributed considerably to what is sometimes referred to as that continent's "lost decades" in the 1980s and 1990s. Breeding for higher yields of cassava, millet, or varieties of beans, African staples, only began in the 1990s.

The great exception to the global use of high-yield varieties was in the former Soviet Unions and the countries of the Eastern Bloc. One could ascribe this to the problems central planning had with agriculture in general, or to the move from extensive to intensive economic growth. Nikita Khrushchev's late-1950s initiative, the "Virgin Lands" project, planting corn on previously uncultivated land, was much like what had happened the United States in the nineteenth century—producing more crops by expanding the area under cultivation—rather than growing more on less soil. This might seem odd, given that on the whole the enterprise of breeding high-yield crops actually fit the strength of central planning—the ability to pour resources into one limited area, which produced massive weapons arsenals and an array of Olympic gold medalists. There was just such a program in China in the 1960s and 1970s, the period of the Cultural Revolution. The government started an intensive nationwide search for a strain of rice with the right characteristics to assist plant geneticist Yuan Lonping in his efforts to breed hybrid rice. After the strain was found, thirty thousand people were sent to work on Hainin Island to hand-pollinate the rice crop under Yuan's direction.

More than anything else, what undid the possibilities for crop breeding and increased productivity in agriculture of the USSR and its eastern European subordinates, was the rejection of one of the central tenets of the biologists' modern synthesis—Gregor Mendel's theories of genetics and heredity. Under the direction of Trofim Lysenko, an undistinguished agronomist but a highly skilled political operator, who convinced both Stalin and Khrushchev that Mendelian theories of heredity were anti-Marxist and politically reactionary, biologists and crop breeders holding scientific views were arrested, sent to Siberia, or shot. A whole field of scientific endeavor was destroyed, permanently damaging agriculture.[63]

The Green Revolution has come in for criticism from advocates of a red revolution—particularly activists who perceive the redress of forms of social inequality as far more important than technological progress and who assert that high-yield crops actually increase inequity. High-yield crops are denounced as forms of American imperialism, taking away poor peasants' right to their own seeds and to their own traditional practices of cultivation, placing them in the hands of multinational corporations. High-yield varieties' need for large doses of fertilizer and ample irrigation means that only (relatively) affluent farmers can afford to plant them, undermining the prospects of smallholders, tenant farmers and landless laborers, thus worsening poverty.

It is not just the red versus the green in the Green Revolution, but the transformation in the meaning of green since 1968 that has led to opposition. High yield became the object of increasing environmental criticism. The worldwide use of a few high-yield varieties, as opposed to the past cultivation of many landraces (crop varieties prevalent in a particular climatic and topographic zone), eliminates genetic diversity and threatens the risk of devastating crop failure, should an insect or micro-organism be particularly effective against one of these few varieties. The fertilizer, irrigation water, and pesticides these crops need to obtain their high yield are unsustainable: they drain water tables, drain subsurface reservoirs, cause salinization of the soil and indiscriminately destroy insect and plant life.[64]

None of these criticisms is unfounded, but, unlike similar sorts of attacks on the use of nuclear energy (often made by the same critics, or at least coming from the same social circles and intellectual backgrounds), they seem, ultimately, misguided. Seeing high-yield crops as imperialism, as wealthy capitalists suppressing the knowledge and crops of the world's poor, doesn't reflect the reality of their origins. From Norman Borlaug working closely with Mexican agronomists and *campesinos* to develop his high-yield wheat varieties, to the Indian agronomist Monkombu Sambasivan Swaminathan, who was a central figure in the breeding and cultivation of high-yield wheat varieties in South Asia, to the Pan African Bean Research Alliance, founded in 1996, and developing 245 new bean varieties in the subsequent decade, crop breeding has always been a global enterprise. Of all the crucial technologies of the Age of Interconnection, it is the one that has spread and been practiced most widely, across continents, levels of economic development, education, and social structure. Large multinational chemical firms have certainly profited from providing fertilizer and herbicides for the crops grown in the Green Revolution, but the driving force behind the new crops came from foundations, and government- and university-sponsored researchers, who were, if anything, critics of such firms.[65]

It is true that cultivating high-yield varieties favored farmers with larger landholdings—in places like India and Bangladesh, this meant possessing on the order of five to ten acres—who were the first to plant the new varieties. Farmers in Iowa had gone through similar experiences (as had farmers in Mexico) a generation earlier, although, of course, US farms were a couple of orders of magnitude larger than their Indian counterparts. In both North America and South Asia, smaller farmers did eventually adopt new, high-yield grain varieties, although it is hard to deny that the benefits of the Green Revolution only reached the landless poor of South Asia indirectly, through non-farm employment or development of niche occupations, such as keeping a dairy cow or two.[66] To use a phrase developed in a very different context, it was an example of trickle-down economics—not a particularly encouraging result. However, the economic situation of the landless poor in Asia before the Green Revolution had been even less encouraging.

Environmentalist complaints that the victorious progress of high-yield varieties was leading to a decline in biodiversity was all too frequently validated. Norman Borlaug's cross-breeding wheat in northern and southern latitudes of Mexico resulted in varieties not at all sensitive to the amount of daylight, making them suitable for use in a wide variety of regions, and so driving out varieties adapted to local conditions, especially in South Asia. The southern corn leaf blight, affecting American agriculture in the 1970s, emerged because all the hybrid varieties being cultivated contained a gene making them susceptible to the fungus. The introduction of high-yield rice varieties in the Philippines led to the disappearance of, literally, thousands of other varieties between the mid-1960s and the mid-1980s. There were counter-trends: the varieties of wheat grown in the United States tripled between 1919 and 1984, with similar developments in Europe (fruit varieties increased to a much greater extent). Moreover, one high-yield seed, the product of the crossing of a dozen different varieties, contains within itself a good deal of genetic diversity.[67]

Still, these examples of greater diversity do seem more like exceptions to a broader trend. Other green criticisms of high-yield crops were also cogent. Nitrate runoff from excessive fertilizer use was polluting waters, causing algae blooms that suffocate aquatic life. Pumping ever more groundwater for irrigation was bringing to the surface chemical salts that degraded the soil and destroyed its natural fertility.

Nonetheless, considering the steady growth of the world's population, it is unclear just what alternatives there were, or are, to high-yield agriculture. Although critics like to point to individual farmers who can achieve great yields with organic methods, such as crop rotation or "green fertilizers" (i.e., nitrogen-fixing crops, like pulses or alfalfa), none of these go beyond individual instances, perhaps the result of unusually favorable soils or microclimates. There does exist a systematic body of evidence—produced by the Broadbalk experiments at the Rothamsted British agricultural research station— that involve a comparison of different methods of growing winter wheat, which has been ongoing in one form or another since the 1850s. Results from the last quarter of the twentieth century show that returns for irrigated, fertilized, high-yield varieties are nine times greater than what can be achieved without any such aids. Organic wheat farming using animal manures and crop rotation does a good deal better than "traditional" methods, but its yields are about 60 percent of its fully technological counterpart.[68]

Finally, it is fair to note that Green Revolution and "traditional" agriculture are not contradictory forms of farming; they can be effectively combined. Since the 1980s, plant breeders have been working with landraces to develop locally optimized varieties. Chemical fertilizers and manure are more efficient when used together, as are crop rotations, green manures, and agricultural chemicals when used in combination. More precise and effective use of chemical fertilizers and optimal combination of their contents, such as increased phosphorus and potassium, with decreases in nitrogen, can improve yields and reduce nitrate pollution runoff at the same time.[69]

If crop breeding's global spread in the 1960s and 1970s made it different from other forms of technology, it, too, went through an era of new developments in the last two decades of the twentieth century, developments that proved hugely controversial. These developments were a product of a revolutionary advance in biological science during the early 1950s: the discovery of the chemical basis of heredity, the structure and functioning of the DNA molecule. It was a short step from science to technology, from understanding how DNA regulates the formation of proteins to altering the DNA so that it produces the desired proteins. This recombinant DNA, the transfer of genes from one organism to another, began in earnest in the 1970s. Its first, and for some twenty years its primary, use was in manufacturing pharmaceuticals. Recombinant DNA seemed appropriate for plant breeding, and as early as the 1960s scientists had begun experimenting with gene transfer in plants. The technological difficulties were considerable, and it was only toward the end of the 1980s, after two decades of experimentation, that effective techniques were developed.[70] Even then, it was another decade before genetically modified seeds entered agricultural practice, starting around 1996 and reaching almost one hundred million acres planted in such crops by the beginning of the new millennium.

This was truly a precursor to the twenty-first century, for the acreage in transgenic plants had quadrupled by 2010. Two genetic modifications were far and away the most prevalent: one enabled plants to withstand high doses of the herbicide glyphosate (better known by its trade name Roundup™); the other was the ability to express a protein, BT, present in bacteria, that was a potent insecticide. The steadily increasing use of genetically modified crops, and the controversy they touched off worldwide, reveal both the continuities with the plant-breeding initiatives, but also the new circumstances created by genetic modifications.

Opposition to genetically modified organisms, or GMOs for short, naturally echoed the hostility to the agriculture of the Green Revolution. Genetically altered plants, critics thundered, subordinated farmers to multinational capitalists and their lust for profit, preventing farmers from reusing their own seeds; such deeply and profoundly unnatural plants contained grave dangers to the environment and to human health. These sentiments have been most influential in Europe, where GMOs, although not officially prohibited, have been excluded, by a combination of import bans and impossibly strict safety standards. They are rarely used in Africa. By contrast, the Americas have emerged as a stronghold of GMO crops, and they have been increasingly used in East and South Asia.

To most biologists, agronomists, and plant breeders, what is striking about GMO crops is not their novelty but their similarity to the broader enterprise of plant breeding that preceded them. The point has been to transfer specific genes responsible for favorable characteristics into plants that can be grown on a large scale. Agronomists have not been content just to seek out genes in existing landraces, but created entirely new genes by bombarding seeds with x-rays or gamma rays, and looking for desirable characteristics— durability, size of the crop—in the resulting mutations. They have doused plants with the alkaloid colchicine, a toxic, carcinogenic chemical and potent insecticide, which doubles the number of a plant's chromosomes and restores fertility to otherwise sterile hybrids. Agronomists have crossed very distant species, such as rice and grasses; the resulting embryos are not capable of surviving in the plant, so they are grown in a culture medium steeped in stimulative chemicals. All the plants resulting from these very unnatural interventions are then repeatedly "backcrossed" with existing varieties, until most genetic differences have been eliminated and only the desired characteristics are retained. None of these methods have met with any public opposition and, in fact, grain varieties bred in these ways, such as "golden barley" and triticale, a crossing of wheat and rye, are popular products in natural food stores, sold as non-GMO and totally organic. Such plant-breeding all occurs within existing species, or at least related ones. Recombinant DNA techniques, do, admittedly, transfer genetic material from totally unrelated species. Nonetheless the study of organisms' genomes has revealed that a large proportion of their naturally occurring DNA comes from other, often quite distant species.

While GMOs seem more like an extension of earlier plant breeding, the context in which they arise is quite different. Unlike the crops of the Green Revolution, developed by scientists working for nonprofit institutions, and made freely available for worldwide use, GMO technology reached the stage of practical application during the Late Millennium Era of privatization and a globalized, deregulated capitalism (more details on the economics of these decades in the next chapter). A very small number of multinational corporations, exploiting the research results of their own scientists and those from publicly funded institutions (which themselves have been privatized or required to act more like profit-seeking corporations), have monopolized most GMO technology. Farmers were forced to purchase hybrid corn seed every year due to the genetic characteristics of hybrid corn. The fact that farmers are still required to purchase GMO seeds yearly has no similar basis. Instead, it reflects claims to property rights.[71] The close connections between such firms' economic interests and the genetic modification they have introduced—glyphosate manufacturers breeding plants that can withstand ever-higher doses of it—rather than, for instance, developing plants that can flourish in saline soils or conditions of near-drought, understandably raises suspicions. Admittedly, the two most common genetic modifications—glyphosate resistance and expressing the insecticidal BT protein—are the easiest to do, involving characteristics controlled by a single gene, while other desirable properties, like flourishing in saline soils, are controlled by multiple genes and are much harder to develop.[72]

GMO crops developed in the late twentieth century set the stage for those of the twenty-first, but what was new about their direction was much less in their technology, which was largely a continuation, perhaps with other means, of the enterprise of breeding high-yield varieties. Rather, the discontinuity occurred in the social and economic context of their origination, production, and global spread. GMO crops have also shown a continuity in the public perception of agricultural technology. Rarely the object of broad public recognition or the subject of grand aspirations, plant breeding has been more closely associated with fears—ranging from overpopulation to environmental destruction. It is a strange fate for a technology that has been one of the great triumphs of the Age of Interconnection and a key to the survival and flourishing of humanity.

Microelectronics

The building of power plants generating electricity, the creation of large-scale grids to distribute this electricity, and the manufacture of devices using this newly available electric current—these were among the great stories of the late nineteenth century. So great was the impact of the new electrical economy that, along with the similar expansion of chemical manufacturing, it has become known as the "Second Industrial Revolution." One feature of this new technology was a device that controlled electric circuits, switching them on and off, allowing electric current to flow only in one direction, and generating and amplifying electromagnetic waves. It consisted of a glass tube with the air pumped out of it and wires placed at either end: the vacuum diode, later modified to include a third, grid-shaped wire in the middle, making the vacuum triode, or, in its generic popular name, the vacuum tube. By the 1920s, the technology associated with such tubes had acquired a new name: electronics.[73]

The vacuum tube was one of the twentieth century's greatest technological feats, central to radio, television, radar, and X-ray machines, all devices invented and used to a greater or lesser degree before and during the Second World War. Vacuum tube manufacturing continued throughout the second half of the twentieth century; one version, the cathode ray tube, was used to generate television images. Although replaced with newer technologies in economically more advanced countries discarded, picture-tube TV sets shipped to Africa and reconditioned by craftsmen there remain in operation to the present day.

For all the virtues of the vacuum tube, its weaknesses were also apparent. Fragile and easily broken, susceptible to losing their vacuum, the tubes needed time to warm up before they functioned and required a relatively large amount of electrical energy. Utilizing the new science of quantum mechanics, the physicist Walter Schottky, employed at Siemens, Germany's leading manufacturer of electrical equipment, published a paper in 1938 confirming what engineers had suspected: that the right combination of solid substances could create the same effects as vacuum tubes, or, in other words, that "semiconductors" and "solid-state" circuits were possible. Research into the possibilities for semiconductors was actually already underway even before Schottky's paper was published, among other places in the research division of the Western Electric Company, the manufacturing subsidiary of the American Telegraph and Telephone Company—or, as the establishment was known, Bell Labs. Hired in 1936, after the lifting of a long hiring freeze following the onset of the Great Depression in 1929, one of the researchers there was the young physicist William Shockley, who began studying potential solid-state circuits.

This research was terminated by the Second World War, but wartime development of radar revealed the material needed to create semiconductors: almost completely pure samples of the metal germanium, containing just the right kind of impurities. Some of these impurities produced a negative charge ("n-type") and others a positive one ("p-type"). Placing the two together, the "p-n junction," current would flow from the n- to the p-type. After the war research on semiconductors resumed at Bell Labs, with the first successful device produced in 1947. Although Shockley would later receive the Nobel Prize for this invention, it was actually built by two of his coworkers, John Bardeen and Walter Brittain. Their version was a clumsy device, with a spring-held, gold-leafed polystyrene wedge suspended over and just barely touching p- and n-type materials sitting on a metal slab. Their nominal supervisor, Shockley, quickly realized that the whole thing could be simplified, eliminating the wedge, the springs and the base, by creating a three-layered slab with a p-type center, surrounded by two n-type surface layers. A committee of scientists and engineers at Bell Labs dubbed the new device a "trans-resistor," or "transistor," which was duly presented to the world at a press conference on June 30, 1948.

It would be difficult to underestimate the protean character of the invention. Not just solid-state circuits, but lasers, LCDs and LEDs, solar power cells, fiber-optic cables, and digital cameras are all offshoots of the transistor. Yet, at first, nobody was quite sure what to do with it. Even significant technological innovations, such as making these semiconductors out of silicon instead of germanium—cheaper and much more readily available but requiring more complex methods to introduce the right degree of impurities—did not change the state of affairs. AT&T, the patent owner, actually decided in 1952 to license the transistor to all comers for the modest sum of $25,000, even offering seminars in how to make and to deploy the device. Such a decision was both a measure of its relatively low priority and the immense difference (to be discussed in the next chapter) between the post-1945 world of regulated capitalism and the wildly competitive age that was to follow: when businesses hold on to patents fiercely and conduct savage litigation about them.

One of the licensees was a small Japanese firm, Tokyo Tsushin Kogyo—Tokyo Telecommunications Technology. Utilizing cheap labor and copying the ideas of an American competitor, Texas Instruments, the firm began manufacturing small, battery-powered portable radios that utilized effectively the compact size and low power requirements of solid-state circuits. To sell their device in the Americas and Europe, they changed their name to the Latin *Sonus*, or "sound," and became Sony. While this was the beginning of one of the world's great multinationals, among whose accomplishments was the last major innovation in vacuum tubes (the Trinitron TV picture tube, producing the best color picture), the firm's initial product was a tinny-sounding radio. Through the early 1960s, most transistors were used by the armed forces, in radio and radar, since their sturdy nature and low power needs made them much preferable to vacuum tubes on the battlefield.

What made transistors into a transformational technology was their marriage with another device, the mechanical calculator. Used extensively in the Second World War for codebreaking and for calculating artillery and bomb trajectories, the calculator was turned into a larger-scale electronic calculating device by wartime research projects. The first result, the Electronic Numerical Integrator and Computer, or ENIAC, for short, built between 1944 and 1946 at the University of Pennsylvania, could perform up to five thousand additions and subtractions per second. It was quite literally a giant brain, weighing over sixty thousand pounds and containing more than seventeen thousand vacuum triodes. Unfortunately, after a few seconds of operation, one of the tubes would blow, making the device useless. Replacing these tubes with solid-state circuits made the computer possible, the first all solid-state prototype produced in 1954.

From that point onward computers began being manufactured and used in science, commerce, government, and the military. Over the course of the 1960s and 1970s their use spread, in a familiar pattern, from the United States to other economically advanced countries, although computer manufacturing remained, for all intents and purposes, a US monopoly until the 1980s. It was logical that manufacturers of piston-engine planes would build jet aircraft, another emerging technology of the same era, but computers lacked such pre-1945 precedents, so it was unclear who would build them. A plausible choice was one of the industrial giants of the first half of the twentieth century, RCA, the Radio Corporation of America. Its top management understood very well that a focus on manufacturing radios would be a bad decision and that it should move into the manufacture of new products. This it did, producing devices for radar, telecommunications, and above all, television. RCA became a pioneer of color television, and not just as a manufacturer of TV sets but as a key supplier of basic components for other producers. The firm also built computers in the 1950s, but they were a small part of its product palette, and RCA's efforts to move into the field on a large scale during the following decade were a dismal failure, taking investment capital and research resources away from its successful consumer electronics business. In the 1970s it attempted to diversify into a random assortment of other businesses, from paper manufacture to frozen foods, to carpets, to auto rentals. These effectively destroyed RCA, and its remnants were taken over by General Electric in 1986.

Rather, computers were built by a very different kind of enterprise, a manufacturer of office equipment—typewriters, punched-card readers, and tabulators. Although certainly a substantial corporation, International Business Machines, IBM for short, was much smaller than RCA and had no particular expertise in electronics, coming from the mechanical calculator side of the technological marriage producing computers. IBM began manufacturing computers in the early 1950s, initially for military use (its first computer was called the 701 Defense Calculator) and then, in 1954, the 650, the "computing Model T," as the firm's president, Thomas J. Watson, Jr., later put it.[74] For thirty years it was overwhelmingly dominant in global computer manufacturing.

In the postwar era, computers were often perceived as a futuristic technological marvel, about to become reality, perhaps not on a scale with space travel or nuclear power but still impressive enough. These giant electronic "brains" would think more deeply, more complexly, and more rapidly than their human counterparts. They would be at the heart of a "third industrial revolution," a "cybernetics" revolution, a "scientific-technical revolution"—that last phrase, a favorite of the Eastern Bloc. (These phrases were all precursors of one that became common in the 1990s, the "information economy.") Computers were used for complex scientific calculations, in, for instance, nuclear physics and nuclear weapons development, but by the 1960s it had become clear that their most common use was for business bookkeeping or tracking inventory and transactions—very useful functions but more mundane than futuristic. Alongside the dream of expanded leisure was the nightmare scenario of unemployment—computers taking our jobs—though in fact there was little opposition to the use of computers out of fear of technological employment, with the exception of India, where, in the 1960s and 1970s clerks and their unions physically blocked their installation. When physicists at the Saha Institute of Nuclear Technology at Calcutta University proposed to use a computer, they published an open letter in local newspapers, promising that the machine would be used exclusively for physics calculations and never for administrative purposes. The computer was installed in October 1971, three years after it was purchased, under armed police guard, and during university vacation, when few people were around.[75]

The gap between postwar great expectations and prosaic realities, a familiar pattern with different forms of technology, appeared in computers as well, described in 1987 by the Nobel-Prize-winning economist Robert Solow, as the "productivity paradox." If computers were such a revolutionary innovation, why did their increasingly widespread use in North America, Europe, and to some extent, the Eastern Bloc during the 1970s and 1980s, coincide with a period when economic productivity was stagnant, or, at best barely rising, a state of affairs very different from the largely computerless two decades that preceded them? Computers were "everywhere," Solow said, "but in the productivity statistics."

Economists debated this at some length. Some supported Solow's assertion, albeit for different reasons; others suggested that without computers things would have been worse; others argued that the computer sector was too small a part of the economy to make much of a difference in overall productivity; and still others stated that it was all a measurement problem, with existing statistics poorly adapted to measuring computers' impacts.[76] Whichever version of the explanation of the "productivity paradox" one endorses, the phrase encapsulates a common experience of the 1970s and 1980s: that computers seemed to make things less rather than more efficient. I was a student in Germany during the mid-1970s, and when I was enrolled at the rather old-fashioned University of Münster, a clerk took my documents, wrote out the relevant information longhand on a card, stamped it, and handed me my student ID. The following year, I enrolled at the newer and self-consciously modern University of Düsseldorf, where a clerk took my documents and told me it would take a week for the computer to issue a student ID.[77]

While it may still be an open question just how productive the first two decades of widespread computer use were, there is no doubt that the second two decades saw the beginning of a fundamental transformation in the use of microelectronic devices, leading directly to contemporary conditions. This transformation came in two elements, miniaturization and connection. Each did arise out of earlier developments but came to fruition at different points between 1980 and 2000.

Miniaturization is often formulated in terms of "Moore's Law," the observation made in 1965 by Gordon Moore, one of the founders of the semiconductor manufacturer Intel, that every year twice as many circuits could be placed on the same silicon semiconductor as previously. The doubling actually occurred about once every eighteen months, but the point remained: more and more calculating capacity could be crammed into diminishing space. The 1971 invention of the microprocessor—a silicon chip containing circuitry for reading input, processing that input, and outputting the results—was one expression of Moore's Law. Industrial applications of such microprocessors, for instance in fuel injection, so that autos could be both more fuel efficient and generate less emissions simultaneously, placed them in small spaces. All this was a long way from the 1950s giant electronic brains, filling a whole room, or even the 1960s mainframe computers the size of a refrigerator.

Miniaturization meant devices that fit on a desktop, or by the 1990s, into a briefcase. The work such personal computers did was generally not solving complex mathematical equations (although they could do those too) but replacing typewriters, keeping lists, calculating interest rates, or retouching photographs. The triumphant march of such "personal computers"—or PCs— through North America, Western Europe, Japan, and other affluent countries—and very much not through the lands of the Eastern Bloc, one of many signs that they were losing the Cold War—was enabled by the development of a new operating system, the graphical user interface. Replacing the "command line interface"—arcane combinations of symbols that users previously were required to type in, and impossible for most people to master— this graphic interface used a "mouse" to click on little on-screen images. Here was the decisive breakthrough in turning computers into widely used consumer durables. Moore's Law enabled this development, since deploying graphics in this way requires much greater computing capacity.

As computers became miniaturized and "personal," the locus of their manufacturing began to shift. Although the first personal computers were brought out by the dominant mainframe manufacturer IBM, and then by other American firms, during the 1980s the manufacturing of computer chips began to move to East Asia, and, in the following decade the building of personal computers themselves, following the pattern seen in other branches of industry, of first Japan, then South Korea, Hong Kong, Singapore and Taiwan, and, finally, China. In the 1960s one US firm, IBM, had, all by itself 80 percent of the world computer market. By 1985, US share of global computer production had dropped to just over half, Europe and East Asian countries having about a quarter each. By 2000, the United States accounted for a third of computer production, Europe under a fifth, and East Asia, 47 percent. The East Asian triumph in semiconductors and computers was not quite so complete as in consumer electronics, but the movement of the center of gravity of technology and production of microelectronics from North America to East Asia was yet another sign of the growing global influence of that part of the world.[78]

The second major form of transformation in the use of computers involved tying them together, yet another example of an Age of Interconnection. Such "networks" began with the initial manufacture of computers in the 1950s. The first network went into operation in 1958 and was related, like so much semiconductor technology, to potential nuclear warfare, linking the images from the radar stations of North American Air Defense. By then, work on two major business networking projects was already underway, one for airline reservations—the SABRE system—and one for tracking banking transactions. Both were immense enterprises, taking a decade to set up and profoundly shaped the development of software and the practice of computer programming. The former went live in 1965 and remains, in heavily modified form, active today. The latter, the ERMA (Electronic Recording Machine Accounting) system, deployed in 1962 with a festive celebration hosted by a politically ambitious actor, Ronald Reagan, was limited to the Bank of America, and was the precursor to later interbank networks, generally working on a national level, the Automated Clearing Houses, and the SWIFT network for international financial transactions, which began operations in 1977.[79]

These early networks linked large, "mainframe" computers together; as miniaturization brought computing to ever more users, the question became how they could be networked, and to what purpose. There were two major networking projects in the Late Millennium Era. Begun with very different premises and for different reasons, they met quite different fates. The first one to become available, organized, and designed for consumer use, never exceeded a limited number of applications and a national niche. Another, designed for totally different purposes, encompassed, in ways never initially envisaged, the entire globe.

France was the first country to move to a completely digital switching system for its national telephone network. Building on that accomplishment, *France Télécom*, the national telephone company, launched a national videotext network, Minitel, in 1982, when personal computers were still devices in the hands of a few hobbyists. The telephone company distributed the distinctive, small, beige-colored Minitel terminals for free to households, so that by 2000 two-thirds of all French households and one-third of all businesses had the device. Users could connect to government databases, check their bank balances, get stock-market quotes, purchase train tickets, buy consumer goods from catalog retailers, or, via *Minitel Rose*, engage in erotic chats with *femmes fatales*, some of whom were actually male, freelance journalists, trying to earn a living. About twenty-five thousand private businesses, the "Minitel mafia," had a presence on the network. Users paid for connections by the minute, although different connections came at different rates—government information much cheaper than pornography—with all billing done by the telephone company that then funneled the funds to the relevant firms. It was an immensely popular system, but it was centralized, inflexible, text-based, and incapable of allowing individual household users to create their own content or to interact with each other. In spite of the government's best efforts, it was never adopted on a large scale outside of France.[80]

The other networking project, ARPANET, was begun by the US Defense Department in the 1960s and activated in 1971. It was intended to connect American computer resources, so that they could function in case of a nuclear war. Crucial to the new project was "packet switching"—the decentralization of the exchange of information. Previous information transmission, in telephone networks (and utilized in Minitel), was centralized. Individual users sent a message to a central switching station that then sent the signal containing the message to another user, either directly, or via another central switching station. This sort of centralized connection was obviously vulnerable to atomic attack. The scientists and engineers of ARPANET devised a system by which information could proceed from one user to another via any number of paths. Their software stripped a message into small digital pieces. Each individual piece contained a "header" with information about the message to which it belonged, its sender, and its goal, enabling all the different pieces to take different routes and to converge on their destination, where they would be brought together.[81]

The new networking system worked well. However, without a nuclear war, it also seemed to lack an immediate purpose. ARPANET's organizers proposed to use the network to enable remote use of computing facilities. In, say, India, such a network would have been immensely useful for the scientists at the Saha Institute of Nuclear Technology. Before they got their own computer, they had to journey over one thousand miles on the train from Kolkata to Bombay (Mumbai), clutching a bag containing all their punched cards, to use the computer at the Tata Institute.[82] But ARPANET connected US universities, all of which had their own computing facilities—and considerable bureaucratic resistance to letting them be accessed remotely. Graduate students, the chief users of the network, began realizing it had another possible use, namely to exchange messages, with each other, much faster and more cheaply, especially over long distances, than could be done with the post or telephone. They called it "electronic mail," or "e-mail," and a long-running, although possibly apocryphal, story has it that the main use of the new form of communication was to score drugs.

Whether true or not, the graduate students had discovered what would be the crucial use of computers, namely for communications. If the computer itself was the offspring of a marriage of the transistor and the electric calculator, its twenty-first-century descendants were the progeny of a second marriage, between smaller computing devices—desktops, laptops, after 2000 tablets and smartphones—and telecommunications networks. With the danger of nuclear war waning and privatization policies waxing, ARPANET went, through a series of gradual steps, from a government-controlled, limited-access military project to a privately run and publicly accessible one. It came to have a new name, dating from the basic communications software devised for ARPANET in 1973, the "Internet Protocol." By the late 1980s and early 1990s, the Internet really was a network of computer networks, including government-run networks set up primarily for academic research, on every continent of the world except Africa, and small networks of hobbyists and computer enthusiasts in the United States. Some two thousand computers were connected to the Internet in 1985, and 159,000 by the end of the decade—a rapid, indeed exponential, growth rate, but still representing a tiny proportion of the world's computing resources, to say nothing of its population.

Two more features were needed to bring the Internet as we now know it into existence. One was the development of a network of fiber-optic cable that could carry the large amount of information traffic needed for a globally functioning Internet, beyond the capacity of copper telephone wires. The fiber was laid in the 1990s. The second feature was the development of a graphical user interface for accessing the network, done by a group of scientists using the computer network at CERN, the European particle accelerator in Switzerland. Under the direction of Tim Berners-Lee and Robert Cailliau, the CERN team developed hypertext software, allowing users to click on text and images, taking them to files on computers in the network. This was the Hypertext Transfer Protocol, or "http" for short, and Berners-Lee thought its use would create a "world wide web" of information.[83]

The Web as a global communications network came very late in the twentieth century. In 1995, there were sixteen million Internet users, less than one-half of 1 percent of the world's entire population, mostly affluent and well-educated individuals in wealthy countries of North America, Western Europe, and East Asia. Computer use was by no means synonymous with Internet access. According to the US Census Bureau, there were computers in about thirty-seven million households in 1997, about 37 percent of all households, but only half of them had a connection to the Internet. By the end of 2000, there were about 361 million users of the World Wide Web, a twenty-two-fold increase. Computer use had become much closer to synonymous with web access. In 2000, for the first time a majority of US households owned a computer, and 80 percent of them were connected to the Web.[84]

Those last years of the twentieth century saw a feverish tech boom, as established businesses and aspiring entrepreneurs rushed to realize value from the new medium of communication. Large amounts of fiber-optic cable were laid, including transoceanic connections, bringing to mind a previous connection of the world with telegraph cables in the nineteenth century. Routers, modems, and switching devices were produced in a complex manufacturing network stretching across the Pacific Ocean. Internet Service Providers offered endless deals to entice computer owners into going online. All manner of firms were founded to develop web sites and use them for sales. First private investors and then initial public offerings, or IPOs, of stock gleefully offered financing, leading to a frenzy of stock speculation. There was full employment and more for programmers and coders, demand for their work only enhanced by the "Y2K" problem, the revision of older software to encompass dates once the millennium had turned.

Much of the activity was based, economically, on air—heady stock valuations for business with little or no income, such as pets.com, Webvan, iVillage, Razorfish, or—and this one happily never got the investors in the first place—funerals.com, a site that would "put the fun back in funerals."[85] The bubble burst in 2000 and the crash of tech stocks took down entire stock markets in Europe and North America, leading to the recession of 2001. Yet for all the vapor, securities fraud and overhyped promises, the era also contained the seeds of a high-tech future—global networks of fiber-optic cable or the founding in 1998 of an obscure tech startup with a bizarre name, Google. If the promised microelectronic future failed to arrive in the 1990s, it was at least in part a result of technological factors, the very slow connection speeds modems of the era delivered, making access to a graphically designed web painfully tedious. A few more hardware and software improvements, a few more turns of Moore's Law and the offspring of the second microelectronics marriage would emerge.

It is always a bit of a shock to realize just how recent today's digitized world of telecommunications is. Yet microelectronics represents a characteristic, if extreme, example of broader technological developments. In some forms of technology—by no means all—the Late Millennium Era marked a break from the devices, the deployments and the dreams of the Age of Total War that had dominated the postwar decades and made the 1970s into a period of disillusionment. Some of the subsequent changes—the gradual shift from one hydrocarbon to another, oil to natural gas, as a main energy source, or the use of microprocessors to make internal combustion engines simultaneously more efficient and less polluting—were the very opposite of dramatic. Others, such as the reorientation of uses of outer space, were immensely useful but meant breaking with long-term and deeply held aspirations. Initial plantings of GM crops were often portrayed as a dramatic, and pernicious, break with the past. A more careful look, however, shows substantial elements of continuity. Like GM crops, the development of microelectronics into a mass consumer digital communications technology came very late, in the last five years of the Age of Interconnection, but for all the overblown hype of the time, it created both the vision and the potential reality of a new era that is unfolding, on a global scale, all around us.

PART 2

Interactions

4 | Markets

IN JULY 1944, OVER seven hundred delegates from forty-five different countries as well as various international organizations met, as a prominent participant, the celebrated economist John Maynard Keynes, stated, "every minute of our waking hours . . . for . . . four weeks." To avoid the stifling summer heat, the conference was convened in the New Hampshire town of Bretton Woods, in a resort hotel conveniently available because it had been closed for the duration of the Second World War. It was not an ideal setting, however. Its public rooms were small, and their mediocre acoustics made it hard for the delegates to hear one other.

This might have been just as well, because members of the US and British delegations were suspicious of one another's intentions. One of the leading Americans present, Dean Acheson, openly accused Keynes, the fast-talking head of the British delegation, of inserting his views into the proceedings: "when anybody says section 15-C he knows what it is. Nobody else in the room knows. So before you have an opportunity to turn to Section 15-C and see what he is talking about, he says, 'I hear no objection to that,' and it is passed. Well, everybody is trying to find 15-C. He then says, we are talking about Section 26-D." Keynes retorted that the Americans were hiding their plans for global economic domination in a dense cloud of legal verbiage, all too characteristic of "this lawyer-ridden country." In the end, the Americans did get their way.[1]

For all their differences, the delegates were united in a common endeavor: creating an international financial architecture that would promote recovery from the disaster of total war, facilitate international trade and financial transactions, and ensure a postwar era of growing prosperity. Keynes remembered all too well a previous effort at postwar economic reconstruction, following 1919, which had earned his bitter and eminently justified criticism. The two decades after that first total war had been ones of false starts, abortive prosperity, repeated economic and financial crises, misaligned currencies, and complex and deeply restrictive international financial regimes, like bilateral clearing agreements. None of it had facilitated global commerce or economic growth and much of it had aided the Third Reich to prepare for a new war. Although Keynes did not have his way at the conference, a policy defeat but also a personal defeat for a man who did not suffer fools gladly (and who had a rather expansive definition of fools), the Bretton Woods delegates did create new international financial institutions, organizing a system that preserved fixed exchange rates, linked to the US dollar and to gold, which made international trade foreseeable, provided financing for trade imbalances, and allowed the possibility of realigning currency values if circumstances required.

Out of the chaos of the Second World War emerged two dominant systems of economic organization. These two versions of economic organization would underpin the global economy for over twenty years. Under their aegis, economic growth would proceed at a remarkable pace across different economic systems and levels of development.

One of these two systems was the communist economy of state ownership and centralized planning. Devised and implemented before 1939 in the USSR, its results had included both mass starvation and an enormous increase in industrial output during the 1930s and the Second World War. That war's outcomes, which included the Red Army's control of Eastern Europe and the communist conquest of power in China, brought the system to a third of humanity.

In retrospect, one does have to marvel at the very idea of planning an entire economy, especially one so technologically advanced with so many complex interconnections. The basic method used was that of "material balances," the weighing of inputs and outputs. Take, for instance, the production of steel, a favorite commodity in communist countries, reflecting both the metal's central position in mid-twentieth-century industry, and its use for armaments. The plan would lay down the amount of steel to be produced. From there, the inputs would be calculated: the amount of coal and iron ore needed to produce the steel, as well as the machinery needed for this process. The outputs would be calculated as well: steel being exported, used for industrial machinery, for rails, for construction, and for many other purposes. But there was what is called feedback: the coal or machinery used as inputs for steel production required some of the steel, which was an output. Then there were those interconnections: plans for industrial machinery required certain amounts of steel, as did plans for construction, so that the outputs of one part of the plan were the inputs of other parts.

Deriving a material balance of one commodity ending up involving all the other commodities, which made the planning immensely complicated. The yearly industrial supply and distribution plan of the USSR's central planning board, *Gosplan*, ran to seventy volumes, twelve thousand pages dealing with thirty thousand commodities. Contributing to this was the lengthy process of formulation, as *Gosplan* took the broader dictates of the Communist Party, converted them into a draft plan, sent it for comments to managers of industrial facilities, and then revised the plan following their replies. Even after it was all put in final form, the plan for industrial output did not encompass agriculture, labor, services, education, and a host of other central elements in any modern economy.[2]

These plans required endless calculation, and in the 1950s the most common calculating device used in the USSR was the abacus. By the 1960s, Soviet planners, followed by counterparts in many countries of the Eastern Bloc, were contemplating the use of the mathematical tools of linear programming and optimization theory, and the deployment of computers for the calculations. Communist Party leadership and top figures of the planning bureaucracy took an interest, founding the Central Economic Mathematical Institute of the Academy of Sciences, known by its Russian acronym as TSEMI. The chief inventor and advocate of such procedures, the mathematician Leonid V. Kantorovich, received the Nobel Prize in economics in 1975, the only citizen of an Eastern Bloc country ever to do so. However, the methods he and his adherents in TSEMI proposed ran into increasing bureaucratic opposition and never got beyond a few pilot projects.[3]

As a result of this process, and the incremental changes that the plan brought from year to year, there was a constant temptation to break through the web of complex feedback and interconnections, and their tedious calculation, with a few bold strokes. Centrally planned economies seem to have been particularly subject to this temptation toward the end of the 1950s. In part, it was the effect of Sputnik, whose success seemed to promise that the communist regime of central planning could accomplish great things. The persistent competition with Western countries in the Cold War gave an additional impetus, and initiatives of the period were characteristically aimed at overtaking the West economically, just as Sputnik had seemed to do technologically.

Some of the initiatives, such as Soviet leader Nikita Khrushchev's "Virgin Lands" program, designed to raise grain output by planting millions of hectares in Kazakhstan and Siberia in corn—areas generally too dry for the corn to flourish—were more accounting failures than anything else: the return on the investment was lower than what could have been achieved with another use of these resources. Mao Zedong's effort to avoid the tedious planning of material balances and complex interconnections of different industrial products, by drastically expanding the output of steel, known as the "Great Leap Forward" of 1958, was a disaster on a cosmic scale. It was not just that his plan, involving massive increases in steel output by setting up backyard furnaces, was fantastic. The resources in labor and material taken from agriculture to attempt it led to widespread crop failure and massive starvation. China's GDP fell by 20 percent in five years; between twenty and thirty million people, possibly more, died.[4]

The Chinese economic disaster remained unique in the two postwar decades. But this exception nonetheless reveals a central feature of the communist system of economic planning. Ironically, for a self-proclaimed internationalist political system, planning was done within the framework of individual nation-states. There was no overall economic plan for the entire Eastern Bloc. In spite of the creation of COMECON, which was supposed to be a general system of economic exchange among the communist countries, most of their trade was on a bilateral basis. Communist countries bargained hard with each other: at times, too hard. In the last years of Stalin's rule, the ministers of foreign trade of Czechoslovakia and Bulgaria were executed for trying to obtain a too-favorable result in their countries' negotiations with the USSR. Some fifteen years later, in 1965, the East German minister of economics committed suicide after he had been caught buying raw materials from the USSR, turning them into finished products and then, instead of returning them to the Soviet Union, selling those products to capitalist countries.[5]

Globally counterpoised to this centrally administered and government-owned economic regime was the capitalist market economy. One might expect to find the word "free" between "capitalist" and "market," and Cold War propaganda emanating from Western countries certainly had a lot to say about freedom. But the market economy of the postwar era was not exactly free; it was administered and tightly regulated.

Just consider a few examples from the United States. Telephone rates were set by the Federal Communications Commission, which also distributed licenses to radio and television broadcasters, setting distinct conditions, such as providing different points of view on controversial issues (the "equal time" provision); rates for moving freight by rail or truck were set by the Interstate Commerce Commission. The Civil Aeronautics Board assigned routes for passenger air travel and set airfares. The Federal Reserve Board, through its "Regulation Q," determined what interest rates banks could pay depositors. State and local governments' "fair-trade laws" allowed manufacturers to set binding retail prices for their products. Agricultural marketing boards fixed prices and determined output for most fruits and vegetables grown in California; the oddly named Texas Railroad Commission set prices and petroleum output for the state's most important commodity and the central source of energy in the post-1945 world. All this in a country with vigorous and long-standing libertarian and laissez-faire traditions.[6]

In Western Europe or Japan, some of this regulation was unnecessary, but mainly that was because the state owned and administered the railroads, airlines, telecommunications, and broadcast facilities. There were plenty of regulations on retail, such as West German department stores' limitation to two store-wide sales per year (a relic of the Nazi regime), although similar limitations were in force elsewhere as well. The 1953 Japanese anti-monopoly law, a singularly misnamed piece of legislation, allowed industrial enterprises to fix the retail prices of their own products. To run one's own crafts business in West Germany—mostly construction trades, but hairdressing, auto repair, and tailoring, as well—one had to have permission of the relevant craftsman's guild and become a member of it. This rule, what the Germans call *der große Befähigungsnachweis*, had been a long-term desire of master craftsmen, rejected by the governments of Bismarck and the Kaiser and introduced by the Nazis, then abolished by the occupying powers after the war and triumphantly reinstated in 1953.[7]

Financial transactions were enmeshed in a particularly thorny thicket of regulations. The distinction between commercial and investment banks, set up by the Glass-Steagall Act of 1933 was one of many US peculiarities; elsewhere, the model of the universal bank, combining commercial credit and investment financing, was more common. But pretty much everywhere in the Western world, very sharp distinctions were made between savings and commercial banks. The former—under private ownership in English-speaking countries, run by the post office in Japan, by both the post office and consumers' cooperatives in West Germany—were designed to funnel the funds of small savers into the housing market. The latter, by contrast, were designed for commercial services, ranging from individual checking accounts (very far from universal) to funding business payroll and inventory. An elaborate system of fixed commissions and trading restrictions governed individuals' access to stock markets. Participation was not widespread in any event. In 1952, less than one household in ten in the world's wealthiest and most capitalist country owned stock shares. Probably the strangest form of connections with equity markets was the UK arrangement of brokers and those called jobbers. The former dealt with the public, but could not purchase stock directly; it was the latter, the jobbers, who traded stock, but could only sell to the investing public via brokers.[8]

The market in labor was yet another realm of regulation. Few countries went quite so far as the Netherlands, where collective-bargaining agreements required approval from the Board of Government Mediators, which also issued guidelines for wage increases. But the two postwar decades were a global golden age of trade unionism, in which substantial proportions of the labor force were organized. Anything resembling global statistics of trade union membership date only from the 1970s, but they show membership rates in the economically advanced countries of Western Europe, North America, Japan, Australia, and New Zealand ranging from two-thirds of the labor force (these highs in the Scandinavian countries) to figures in the 20 to 30 percent range—the United States and Switzerland, which might be expected, but also France, a bit of a surprise. Union densities were lower in Asia and Latin America, with wild fluctuations (just 5 percent of the labor force in Paraguay; 33 percent in Bolivia) but in larger countries, such as India, Brazil and Mexico, membership rates ranged from 15 to 20 percent. The prevalence of unions and collective bargaining agreements cordoned off at least part of the labor market as a regulated space. But beyond membership statistics were the plethora of government mediation and arbitration services, labor relations courts, and a whole host of administrative arrangements shaping the labor market.[9]

All these are examples of individual nations regulating their domestic markets. But the post-1945 decades were a period of expanding international trade, commerce, and communication; these also attracted a large degree of regulation and administration. There was a well-known way to administer and restrict international trade, one which had been in use for over a century—namely, protective tariffs. Expelling foreign competitors from a domestic market, or at least making their products more expensive was a simple task and had been gaining steadily in popularity worldwide from the 1870s through the Great Depression. Maybe it had been a little too effective and popular, since a prevalent post-1945 diagnosis held such hindrances of international trade to have been a major cause of the Depression and of its severity and duration. The result was a series of postwar negotiations steadily lowering tariff rates, the most famous of which was the "Kennedy Round" of the 1960s, named after the eponymous president, which brought tariffs in economically advanced Western countries to their lowest level since the 1850s.

These negotiations had an umbrella designation, the General Agreement on Trade and Tariffs—GATT—whose very name is revealing. It was an agreement rather than an organization, a series of ad hoc meetings, rather than a permanent international agency. Just such an agency, an International Trade Organization, had been a subject of extensive diplomacy in the 1940s; protectionist impulses in the United States, Western Europe, and Latin America, foiled its creation.[10] The new regime of lowered tariffs by no means prevented what economists like to call "non-tariff barriers," forms, sometimes subtle and sometimes overt, of regulating trade. A champion of such measures during the 1950s was Japan, which created its consumer electronics industry by refusing to import electronics from American firms and insisting that the new technologies they developed be licensed to Japanese producers, like Sony. The following decade the same thing would happen with computer technology.[11]

Tariffs and trade restrictions pitted individual nations against each other, but they could still collaborate in the administration of international economic relations. The International Air Transport Association, founded at a global conference in Havana, right at the end of the Second World War (there had been a precursor organization, dating from 1919, and terminated by the war) parceled out international air routes and set the fares on these routes. Since so many airlines were government-owned, the IATA's deliberations had distinct similarities to diplomatic conferences. There was an outlaw airline— *Loftleiðir*, or Icelandic, as it was known to the rest of the world. Its management refused to join the IATA, which meant its planes could only fly to and from their native country. Undaunted, the airline charged much lower fares, and flew passengers in turboprops, designed to transport airfreight, from New York City to Luxemburg via Reykjavik—legally speaking, two flights, each connecting with Iceland. The airline became a favorite of young people willing to put up with an endless, droning trip for a bargain price. Pilots and flight attendants referred to these flights as the "hippie express." *Loftleiðir*'s quasi-black-market evasion of international air transport regulations only underscored their dominant character; the "hippie express" was the free-market exception that proved the rule of regulation.[12]

The most prominent example of regulated international trade was oil. Global oil prices were set in complex negotiations between international companies and national governments, resulting in long-term contractual agreements. Through the late 1970s, over 90 percent of all oil traded was via such long-term fixed price accords. The US government set import quotas, ensuring that the vast majority of the petroleum marketed there came from domestic producers. Lacking US oil reserves, other economically advanced countries, such as France, Italy, and Japan, developed their own set of regulations and government-sponsored enterprises, with the intent of securing supplies and reducing prices, rather than subsidizing domestic producers. These measures also shaped the global petroleum market. It is common to think of OPEC, the international cartel of oil exporting countries, as having created fixed and administered prices, ending the age of free markets. But the truth is just the opposite. OPEC emerged in the 1960s as a rejection of the regulated oil market. The cartel was formed by the governments of Venezuela, Saudi Arabia, and Kuwait, which believed that the existing arrangement guaranteed at their expense oil companies too large a share of the profits.[13]

Even greater restrictions applied to financial transactions. The Bretton Woods system set up fixed exchange rates for the currencies of all participant nations. Each of these was linked to the US dollar, which, in turn, was linked to gold at the rate of $35 per ounce. Dollars were as good as gold, and could be used to settle trade balances between individual countries. The system created two new international financial institutions—the International Monetary Fund, which offered short-term credits to finance temporary trade imbalances between countries; and the International Bank for Reconstruction and Development, better known by its informal name, the World Bank, which provided long-term loans for the purposes mentioned in its name.[14]

At the conference, John Maynard Keynes, although favorably disposed to the new international banks, opposed plans for the central role of the US dollar and wanted to see accounts between different countries settled with a special, newly created international currency, the "bancor." Keynes's antagonist was the head of the American delegation, Harry Dexter White, whose agenda was to promote the American currency as the medium of global trade and finance, eliminating any possible influence of the British pound sterling, which had previously played that role. The dominant economic and military standing of the United States at the end of Second World War meant that the Americans would, as we've seen, win out. White's triumph illustrates the emergence of the Cold War out of the Second World War. Not only was he head of the Treasury's Office of Economic Research, he was also a secret agent of the USSR. At Bretton Woods, at least, he did the Soviets no favors. The system he shaped functioned well in the first two postwar decades, far better than the period after the First World War, ensuring that the economic crises of the interwar decades would not be repeated. The Bretton Woods system helped capitalism flourish and so provided a major boost to the Western powers. Stalin should have had better agents.

In part, the Bretton Woods system worked so well because the financial transactions it was regulating were not all that common. Until the end of the 1950s, most Western currencies were not freely convertible; they could only be exchanged for foreign ones with government permission. Controlling international currency movements in this way was a complex business. The Exchange Control division of the Bank of England, for example, counted 1,600 employees in 1950, a quarter of the bank's entire staff.[15] Private international lending was more the exception than the rule. The US dollar, as the linchpin of global capitalist finance, was freely convertible and tradable for gold at the fixed rate, but most countries were happy with dollars—indeed, for a decade after 1945, there was a dollar shortage—so that dollar-gold convertibility was effective because there was little interest in actually exchanging dollars for gold.

Were there any alternatives to these two dominant economic systems? The decades after the Second World War were, after all, the age of a Third World and a Third Way, as will be seen in Chapter 6. To a great extent, the answer to this question would have to be no. Economically less-developed countries in Asia, Africa, and Latin America, many of them under colonial rule until the 1960s, were integrated into the regulated capitalist market system as providers of raw materials. It was precisely this feature of less-developed economies that led to the one major variant economic system in the two decades after 1945, "Import Substitution Industrialization," or ISI. The chief intellectual proponent of this idea, at least in its early form, was the Argentine economist Raúl Prebisch, head of the UN Economic Commission on Latin America. In a 1949 essay, "The Economic Development of Latin America and its Principal Problems," or, as it quickly became known, the "Havana Manifesto," Prebisch asserted that over the long run prices of raw materials in international trade tended to fall relative to prices of manufactured goods, giving countries that had been the first to industrialize a fundamental advantage. The essay was based on his experience at the Argentine Central Bank during the Great Depression. As he put it, in a speech in 1949, "The forced march of the first countries in the Industrial Revolution has created an economic firmament with a sun composed of the developed economies at the center, around which the peripheral countries rotate in their disorganized orbits."[16]

Proponents of ISI set out to move the orbits in this economic solar system by urging governments of less-developed countries to reject free trade and to encourage the manufacture of industrial products rather than importing them. Such measures were adopted, in quite different ways, by the governments of three of the most prominent of the less-developed countries—Argentina, Brazil, and India. During the course of the 1960s they would be joined by other developing nations, including Turkey, Egypt, and Indonesia. ISI policies included heavy taxation and strong limitations on—or even outright prohibitions of—the import of crucial industrial goods—steel, for instance, a good these countries sought to produce themselves. Domestic manufacturers of such goods would receive subsidies and tax breaks, as well as licenses to import raw materials and machinery needed to ramp up their production.[17]

Adherents of free trade and free markets were horrified by the ISI policy. Jacob Viner, an American economist and one of the founders of the libertarian Chicago School of Economics (best known for the extreme free-market views of its leading figure, Milton Friedman), began lecturing in Brazil, shortly after the promulgation of the Havana Manifesto. He pronounced ISI an anathema based on "malignant fantasies, distorted historical conjecture and simplistic hypotheses."[18] ISI was denounced as communism, a viewpoint that became even more pronounced toward the end of the of the twentieth century, when its policies were dismantled, across the globe. Jagdish Baghwati, an Indian economist, outdid Viner in his rhetoric, condemning India's ISI policies in a 1993 book as "a bureaucratic, control-infested straitjacket that would stifle economic initiatives and hinder development," characterized by "the iron fist of controls over the private sector, the spreading stain of inefficient public enterprises and an inward-looking trade and investment strategy," based on "quasi-Marxist models," of "defunct socialist doctrines."[19]

It is difficult to square these attacks on ISI with its originator. A dour, strait-laced central banker with a taste for large American cars and blue pin-striped suits, Prebisch was, like most central bankers, a great admirer of private property and a profound enemy of price increases. He denounced the egalitarian, redistributive, and inflationary policies of the post-1945 Argentine government of Juan Peron—ISI but the wrong kind. Prebisch supported the Bretton Woods system and wanted Argentina to join the IMF, leading Peron and his followers to accuse him of being a cats-paw for British and American international financiers. They quite literally drove him out of the country, which is how he came to direct the UN's Latin American economic commission, with its headquarters in Santiago de Chile.

ISI's socialist reputation stems mainly from Indian's post-independence prime minister, Jawaharlal Nehru. Both a proponent of ISI and a self-described socialist, Nehru created a state economic planning commission to implement his ideas for import substitution and designed them around a series of five-year plans, a term with a distinct communist resonance. Yet neither the forms of property ownership in ISI, nor the planning system, nor its intellectual lineage had much to do with communism. The whole idea was an updated version of public policy practiced in nineteenth-century France, Germany, and the United States, when politicians and businessmen of those eminently capitalist countries, making ample use of tariffs, subsidies, and import restrictions, strove to reduce the importance of raw materials exports and industrial imports for their economy. They did this by building up their domestic industries in competition with the dominant manufacturing power, Great Britain.

ISI was distinctly capitalist. The manufacturing firms producing the import substitutes were privately owned. Nehru's followers in the Congress Party who took his socialist rhetoric seriously and advocated government ownership of the largest manufacturing firms involved in the import substitution initiative were quickly sent to the political sidelines. Businessmen made deals with government agencies to gain the coveted import licenses and to exploit a de facto monopoly. Nehru's planning commission had no power to do any real planning; individual government agencies and ministries made their own ad hoc arrangements with favored businessmen.[20] For all the occasional socialist rhetoric attached to it, in other words, ISI was really a variant on the regulated, administered capitalist economic system of the postwar era.

Regardless of what economic system was in use or what it was called, the ultimate results were successful. As we've seen, economic growth in the postwar decades occurred at the very fastest rate in human history, and one not seen since. Until 1973, the output of all the goods and services of the entire world grew at an annual rate of almost 5 percent (4.90 percent), a blistering pace. The population of the world also increased at the fastest rate ever seen, once again, before or since, yet even the per capita rate of economic growth was a vigorous 2.92 percent per year. And this growth rate was widely shared. Communist and capitalist economies both grew briskly, as did countries with an industrial economy, those that were primarily raw materials producers, and those attempting to go from one to another via ISI. One of the poorest regions of the world, the colonies and new nations of Africa, had the lowest rate of economic growth, but this rate was still

4.43 percent per year (2.00 percent per capita), which at almost any other time would be seen as astonishingly high.[21]

Of course, these figures are approximations, based on adding up the data series of every individual country, not all of them reliable. Still the basic trend is clear: the postwar decades were a period of unprecedented rapid increases in economic output that was distributed across the world. The data on the distribution of the growing income within each country is somewhat scantier, but suggests that every sector of the population and every income groups benefited.[22]

There have been a number of names for the prosperity of the period, but *das Wirtschaftswunder*, "the economic miracle," which emerged in West Germany during the 1950s, is most fitting. Since then there have been the "Asian miracle," the "Korean miracle," the "Indonesian miracle," the "Chinese miracle," the "Brazilian miracle," the "Mexican miracle," and many others—really, anywhere and anytime there has been a period of sustained, rapid economic growth. We shouldn't let this numb us to the original use: after a catastrophically destructive world war, itself preceded by a long period of stagnation or slow growth, punctuated with repeated economic disasters, there was a sudden, gigantic and unexpected surge of prosperity.

This usage of the word goes along with a common economists' explanation of the period of rapid economic growth. They assume that there is a long-term average rate of economic expansion, a "trend line," and the vigorous growth of the decades after the Second World War were about reverting to the trend, after prewar stagnation and wartime damage. It is true that countries devastated by the Second World War, such as the USSR, West Germany, and China, had their very fastest rates of growth in the 1950s (in China's case at least until the disaster of the Great Leap Forward), rather than in the 1960s, as was true in much of the rest of the world, including Japan another country severely damaged by the war. It is not really clear, though, if such a long-term average rate of economic growth represented by a trend line actually exists or remains the same over time.

If returning to the trend line does not offer an entirely convincing explanation of postwar expansion, it does suggest that it was related to developments in the Age of Total War. In those decades, as we've seen, basic scientific and technological advances—in steel manufacturing, in the production of chemicals, electrical equipment, and motor vehicles, in the creation of electric power grids, in the invention of broadcasting, in pharmaceuticals and agricultural chemicals—and the industrial infrastructure needed for them were all put in place. These investments finally paid off after the war, with the help of economic institutions that made it possible for all these innovations to be translated into global economic growth.

Two other major elements were crucial in facilitating this growth. The widespread availability of petroleum and the belief that the biosphere as an unlimited and seemingly cost-free resource. There was no need—better put, little understanding of the need—for emission controls, pollution regulations, lead-free gasoline, protection against radiation or environmental restrictions on land use. In reality, these uses of the biosphere were not cost-free.

From Initial Dysfunctions to Global Upheaval

While the 1950s were for some countries the most prosperous decade, the 1960s saw the fastest economic growth, and the greatest and most dynamic increases in prosperity. Yet precisely as prosperity was reaching its peak, elements of dysfunction were beginning to appear in both communist and capitalist economic regimes, precursors of the turbulence and chaos that would ensue.

Problems for communist regimes came from trying to improve their system. From Stalin's industrialization plans of the 1930s through postwar reconstruction, these regimes had increased output by increasing input, using their planning system to add more labor and more raw materials to the sector whose production they wanted to expand. This procedure could produce disaster, as was the case in the Great Famine of the USSR or the Great Leap Forward in China, or it could be relatively benign. Still, as early as the end of the 1950s, economic planners and party leaders began to understand, however vaguely, that the process was reaching its limits. Future economic expansion would come from producing more output from the same input by using that input more efficiently and more productively via improved economic organization and more advanced technology. Economists describe this transition as the move from "extensive" to "intensive" economic growth. Cybernetics—what we would today call IT—became a hot topic in the Eastern Bloc; individual countries devised plans for technology-based economic growth. East Germany's leaders, for instance, decided in 1958 on a "Chemistry Program" an attempt to use this high-tech economic sector (a German specialty going back well into the nineteenth century) as the key to a dynamic future, even to overtaking their capitalist rivals on the other side of the Iron Curtain in West Germany.[23]

It remained to be seen if output of such high-tech industries could be expanded the same way that, for example, steel had been. Increasing efficiency across the entire economy was noticeably more difficult: it meant comparing the worth of different forms of output, assigning prices for goods and services that were not just arbitrary. These prices could be assigned by decentralization, by letting managers of individual firms set them and creating, in effect, a market. Such was the idea of the Soviet economist Evsei Liberman and his Czech counterpart Otto Šik, using linear programming.

The idea proved to have one very distinct problem. Whenever it was implemented, it turned out that basic consumer goods were very underpriced and in an efficiently run economy they would be much more expensive. Experiments with realigning prices this way led to the single largest antigovernment disturbance in the postwar USSR. Following food price increases in May 1962, workers in the industrial city of Novocherkassk went on strike by the thousands. They blocked railroad tracks, marched from their factories on the outskirts into the city center, attacked and smashed up the municipal Communist Party headquarters, and stormed police stations, seeking to liberate prisoners. Four members of the Presidium (the former Politburo) were rushed to the scene, but proved unable to resolve the situation peacefully. Soldiers and armed units of the Interior Ministry opened fire on the demonstrators. The cobblestones of Lenin Square, where they had been gathered, were covered with blood, and agents of the KGB hustled away corpses. The Square was asphalted over to remove signs of the conflict, which was kept secret until 1989. Similar strikes and riots occurred in Temirtau, Murom, Alexandrov, and other cities. Technocratic economic efficiency resulted in the massive disruption of public order, a price that communist regimes were unwilling to pay.[24]

Initial problems in the capitalist West had no such violent repercussions. They emerged in the arena of international exchange, as might be expected in an economic system characterized by large international transactions. During the 1950s, certain countries would experience a negative balance of payments, more money flowing out of the country than entering it. This payments imbalance could emerge from capital flows, or from higher costs for raw materials. However, the most common reason was what should have been a good development—one country's economy growing more rapidly than those of its trading partners, so that it imported more than it exported. If this imbalance kept up even for a relatively short time, like a year or two, the affected country would face the prospect of expending all its reserves—whether of precious metals or US dollars—to settle accounts. The most common reaction was to raise taxes, cut spending, and increase interest rates, thus slowing economic growth and so decreasing imports. Another option would be to borrow the money to cover the balance of payments deficit. Because there was little international lending in the postwar decades, and most currencies were not freely convertible, that meant going to the IMF, which would usually help with the condition that the country adopt precisely those fiscal and monetary policies slowing down economic growth.

This problem was dubbed "stop and go" in postwar Great Britain, meaning alternating periods of faster and slower economic growth (given the way the situation developed, it should really have been called "go and stop"). In the United Kingdom, these occurrences were a reminder of the country's fall from its former global dominance, and also signified the termination of the pound sterling as the central currency for international commerce and finance. Episodes of "stop and go" also occurred in France, in Italy in 1963–64, and even in future export powerhouses Germany and Japan. The very last instance of this problem also occurred in a future world export leader, China, as Deng Xiaoping's procapitalist reforms in the 1980s ramped up economic growth to levels noticeably higher than China's trading partners, while continuing legacies of communist economic policies kept the country out of international financial markets.[25]

The Chinese government followed the advice of technocrat Chen Yun and curtailed imports by cutting economic growth. This action was a late reaffirmation of what France and Great Britain had done earlier, stemming from currency crises that were the result of their last imperial adventures, in Vietnam, Algeria, and Egypt. The compounding of trade issues, military expenditures, and international currency flows brought stop and go from a problem with potential solutions to a systemic breakdown. This occurred when it reached the United States, stemming from the cost of stationing a half million American troops in Western Europe. Balance of payment problems became more prominent in the following decade as American economic growth accelerated, producing, by the end of the 1960s, in classic stop-and-go fashion, actual balance of trade deficits—a sharp break from the long history of US trade surpluses. Maintaining a large military establishment in Europe during the decade of the 1960s while fighting a hugely expensive war in Vietnam accelerated the dollar outflow and worsened the situation. European restrictions on American exports, further exacerbated balance-of-payments issues.

These chronic deficits, draining American gold supplies, threatened the fixed connection between the dollar and gold that had been set up at Bretton Woods. The 1960s were a decade of expedients to deal with the problem. Selected currencies—West German and Dutch especially —were revalued upward against the dollar in 1961 and again in 1969. "Currency swaps," short-term loan agreements between central banks, were instituted, as was the "gold pool," in which the governments of the United States and seven west European countries agreed to intervene to maintain the $35 per-ounce price of gold. "Burden-sharing" agreements committed Western European countries, the Germans in particular, to help bear the cost of American military stationed abroad. The US government instituted an "interest equalization tax" in 1964, taxing foreign investments more heavily than domestic ones. A publicity campaign extolling American vacation spots was intended to discourage US citizens from taking vacations abroad. Still, chronic balance of payments deficits produced unrepatriated dollars, billions of them, which fueled the "eurodollar" market—that is, bank loans made between and within European countries, denominated in US dollars. The size of the

Eurodollar market soared from $7 billion in 1963 to $57 billion by the end of 1970.[26]

In 1971, Richard Nixon's Treasury Secretary John Connally complained to a German government official that their counterparts in France had informed a "major American manufacturer" that unless he built a plant there he would not have access to the French market. Yet at the same time, France constantly protested about US foreign investments.[27] The conditions under which the international trading system had been created in 1945, namely US global industrial and economic supremacy, and the centrality of US dollars, no longer existed. This was precisely because the Bretton Woods system had worked so well. Recovery from the Second World War in Western Europe and Japan, unlike what had happened after the First World War, undermined the system of regulated capitalism.

John Connally's observation served as an obituary for the Bretton Woods system. Five weeks earlier, the US government announced that it would no longer trade its gold supplies for dollars at the rate set in 1944. Supposedly, this was a temporary measure, until new agreements concerning exchange rates, the dollar, and gold could be negotiated. In Japan, the so-called *Nikkuson Shokku*, the "Nixon shock," was not interpreted as provisional.[28] The "float" of the dollar marked the end of an era, inaugurating a period of disorienting economic turbulence. The most famous example was of course the "oil price shocks," bringing in their wake shortages of gasoline, redistributing wealth on a global scale. It was not just petroleum products that surged in price: the 1970s was the decade of "galloping" inflation, with periods of annual price increases ranging from double digits to over 25 percent in Western Europe, North America, and Japan, and well into the triple digits in Africa and Latin America. At times, the world seemed to be upside down, as sheiks, North African dictators, and Islamic revolutionaries, brandishing their petroleum—as well as Kalashnikovs—suddenly seemed able to intimidate and confound their former colonial overlords and Cold War patrons.

Long-established features of individuals' lives, like regular deposits in savings accounts, went from prudent and considered to senseless and harmful. It was an age of "stagflation," the phrase a coinage of the decade, denoting the coincidence of recession and inflation, something economists had previously regarded as impossible. People who lived through that era will not forget it, but an exclusive focus on the shock and the unprecedented, ignores both its more profound origins and fundamental consequences. All these disruptions were symptoms of broader changes that would terminate the postwar regulated capitalism, begin to undermine its socialist counterpart and create a globalized market, stretching its tendrils into commerce, finance, and industrial production, in a way that had never been seen before.

DISRUPTIONS IN THE 1970S

These disruptions took four main forms, two of which are well-known; a third is more obscure; and the fourth is an example of a seemingly small matter, with momentous consequences. The development of a system of floating currencies, the oil price shocks, the increasing integration of the countries of the communist Eastern Bloc into the fast-changing global system of capitalist finance and international exchange, and the rise of the shipping container—all features of the decade of the 1970s—took on myriad forms and brought a host of both expected and unexpected results. All together, they killed regulated capitalism and centralized economic planning and laid the groundwork for ever-more globalized interconnections in commerce, finance, and industrial production.

Floating the US dollar was the first of many experiments with market deregulation and privatization that would come at an accelerating pace in the Late Millennium Era. Previously promoted by free-market guru Milton Friedman and implemented by his disciple George Shultz in his term as US Treasury Secretary under Richard Nixon (he would later be Ronald Reagan's Treasury Secretary as well), floating currencies were presented by their proponents as a simple, painless, market-based solution to the balance-of-payments problems: no need for gold pools, currency swaps, capital controls, or any of the increasingly Rube Goldberg-like mechanisms required to fix the values of different countries' currencies against each other. Constant market interactions would value and revalue currencies, based on a nation's balance-of-payments and inflation rates. By changing terms of trade and profitability of investments, this ongoing revaluation would restore equilibrium.

The market certainly worked its magic, though sometimes in ways that its proponents and propagandists had not expected. Returns from exports or international investments fluctuated, since they were denominated in a currency whose value could change—drastically. Businesses could purchase currency futures to guarantee their returns against these fluctuations, but such trades required what is today called a counterparty, someone to take the other side: in short, a speculator. This observation is not a moralistic condemnation of speculation; productive business interests require speculators. Speculation begets speculation. The amount of foreign currency traded increased exponentially, as Figure 4.1 shows.

By 1998 it had grown almost one hundredfold in the course of the previous twenty-five years, reaching the astonishing figure of $1.3 trillion *per day*, so that within a couple of months, the sums traded in foreign exchange would exceed the value of the entire product of the world economy in a year.[29]

A lot of that money tended to stay where it was sent. In other words, foreign investments increased along with foreign currency trading. The variety of such investments was considerable—short- and long-term, loans, portfolio

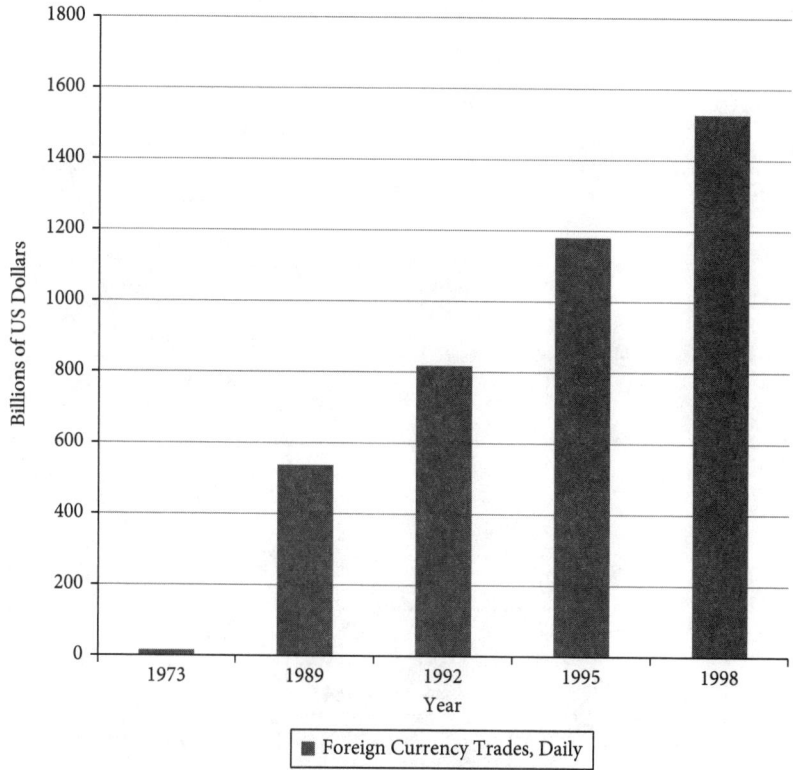

FIGURE 4.1 Growth of International Financial Transactions, 1973–1998

investments, and direct investments—and difficult to track on a global scale. Thanks to the detailed research of the economist Maurice Obstfeld, we do have some approximations, graphed in Figure 4.2.[30]

The exponential growth in investments shown on the chart involves figures in nominal dollars, adjusted neither for inflation, nor for the growth of total economic output. Even taking these into account, however, total foreign investments, increased 9.5 times between 1960 and 2000.

This global flood of capital, a direct result of the introduction of flexible exchange rates, did resolve, as pro-free-market theorists stated it would, the problems of the Bretton Woods System. What these theorists did not predict was that it created new kinds of crises. Since foreign currency trading required speculation, as noted, it offered the opportunity for failure on a scale large enough to bring down financial institutions. Within a year of the introduction of the floating dollar in 1971, both the Herstatt Bank in Cologne and the Franklin National Bank in New York had collapsed because of bad choices. In 1995, Baring's Bank, one of Great Britain's most venerable financial institutions, personal bankers to Her Majesty the Queen, went out of business because of the questionable transactions of just one junior

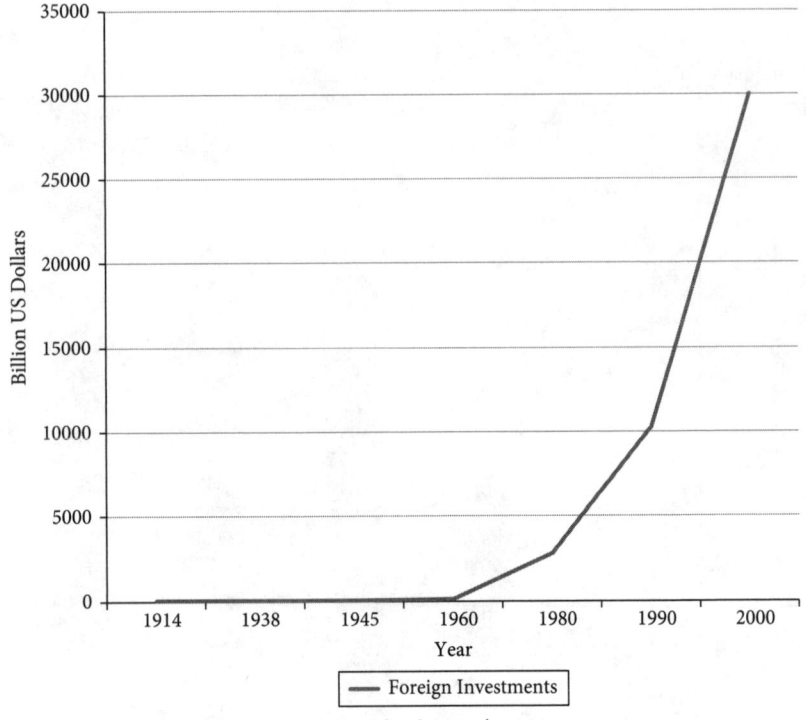

FIGURE 4.2 Foreign Investments, Worldwide, 1914–2000

management figure, who lost his all his bank's capital speculating in the Japanese stock market. Just three years later, the hedge fund Long Term Capital Management collapsed after making a complex series of highly risky trades in the financial instruments of different countries, nearly taking the global financial system down with it.[31]

Unleashed financial markets and flexible exchange rates did eliminate the problem of "stop and go" that had plagued the postwar decades, since both international borrowing to finance the balance of payments deficit and market realignments of currency to eliminate the deficit were now possible. However, the combination of large-scale borrowing and free currency exchange created a new kind of balance-of-payments problem, described by a phrase coined in Argentina, where it first came to the fore at the end of the 1970s: *la bicicleta financiera*. Foreign loans to a country with a balance-of-trade or balance-of-payments deficit tended to increase the value of that country's currency (because foreign lending meant selling the creditor's currency to purchase financial obligations in the debtor's currency), in turn making imports cheaper and exports more expensive, thus increasing the deficit, requiring still more lending, leading to a further appreciation of the debtor's currency. This financial cycle went around and around, until foreign creditors became alarmed at the possibility of losing their investments and withdrew their funds, leading to a credit crunch and wild inflation spikes, typically followed by a severe recession.[32] Such new, free-market balance of payments crises were repeated often during the Late Millennium Era, most prominently in the so-called Great East Asian financial crisis of 1997–98.

Magnifying the impact of a global capital market were the "oil price shocks" of 1973 and 1979. These were a sign of the end of the postwar era expansion. Energy was no longer cheap, as the 40 percent jump in US gas prices at the pump during the fall of 1973 testified. There ensued panic gasoline buying, gasoline rationing, or the West German government's introduction of "Auto-free Sundays," when the Autobahns stood empty. Shortages and panic spread beyond the petroleum environment, like the great toilet-paper shortage that gripped Japan in the autumn of 1973 as oil prices soared.[33] (Contemporary toilet-paper panics, in the wake of the COVID-19 pandemic, show in their way how the oil price shock was perceived as an existential threat.) A gigantic global realignment was apparently underway, as wealth drained out of prosperous, industrially advanced countries and went off to formerly marginal petroleum exporters. Abu Dhabi and Kuwait appeared to eclipse Great Britain, Japan, or France in economic influence. Political power did not, as Chairman Mao suggested, come out of the barrel of a gun, but out of an oil barrel: OPEC's punishment of Western countries for supporting the wrong side in the 1973 Arab-Israeli War by refusing to sell oil to them, or the Islamic revolutionary government of Iran launching its anti-Western offensive in 1979 while successfully agitating for the second increase in global oil prices. As one contemporary bestseller put it, it was the end of the "auto-industrial age." (The work even appeared as an early audiobook, so drivers could contemplate a future in which they would not be driving, while it was still possible to do so.[34])

In this fanfare of despair, economists asserted there was no crisis but a simple demonstration of the relationship of supply and demand. Rising oil prices meant that demand was outstripping supply. They would provide an incentive for consumers to use oil more efficiently, and for producers to find new petroleum reserves. Reducing demand and increasing supply would bring oil prices back down. And this is exactly what happened following the oil price shocks: cars, in particular, became more fuel efficient; for power generation and home heating, oil was replaced by other hydrocarbons, particularly natural gas; above all, new sources of oil were discovered—the two big examples were the offshore North Sea Oil and the oil fields of Alaska's North Slope—and brought onto the market. By the mid- to late 1990s, global petroleum prices were back to their 1960s levels. All of this was done, largely if not exclusively, through market forces (automobile manufacturers in the United States, did have to be dragged, kicking and screaming, into building more fuel-efficient vehicles) and didn't entail fundamental economic or technological transformations.[35] Individual vehicles powered by internal combustion engines remained central to transportation and petroleum continued to be a dominant energy source. Dreams of renewable solar energy or massive coal gasification remained just that.

The true impact of the oil price shocks was their role in spurring the growth of a deregulated global market economy. It was no coincidence that the jump in oil prices coincided with the introduction of floating exchange rates. Petroleum was priced, internationally, in dollars, so as the dollar was floated and declined in value, a rise in oil prices, given the increasing demand for energy in the boom years of worldwide feverish economic growth, was inevitable. OPEC rejected the system of long-term fixed contracts between petroleum suppliers and consumers. Why have such contracts when you could just constantly raise the price of oil? If OPEC got the process started of treating oil as a commodity with constantly fluctuating prices in a constantly changing global oil market, the next step came from a rather more obscure source—a minor commodities exchange in New York, specializing in trades on the price of, as it happens, Maine potatoes. In 1983, the Nymex introduced a new financial product for trading: oil price futures. Very quickly, trading in such futures, intimately linked to deals on oil for immediate delivery, the so-called spot market, completed the transformation of the market in the world's largest energy commodity from regulated to fluctuating.[36]

The increase in oil prices terminated other features of the post-1945 petroleum market, such as US restrictions on oil imports, or limitations on the rise in the price of domestic fossil fuels. But an even larger role in the end of the world of regulated capitalism was played by inflation. Prices were already rising in the boom years of the late 1960s and early 1970s, but the oil price shocks caused inflationary trends to ripple through the global economy. Regulated interest rates, typical of the financial sector, particularly of savings banks, led to circumstances in which the rate of inflation was higher than the rate of interest so that saving money meant losing it. The next logical step to take was to deregulate interest rates and, following them, other elements of banking.[37]

Inflation also undermined other forms of regulation. Characteristic of post-1945 regulation, especially of transportation and shipping costs but also of agricultural commodities, retail sales, or financial products, was passing cost increases on to consumers. When such increases were modest, there was no problem with the procedure; when costs began rising at yearly double-digit rates, the regulations were increasingly seen as an economic problem, rather than an economic solution. The inflationary surge was particularly prevalent in less-developed countries, and decisively undermined the system of Raúl Prebisch's Import Substitution Industrialization, which had run on both cheap energy and passing along price increases to consumers. In the postwar decades, these features were obscured by a broadly growing prosperity. But, as this prosperity vanished in the 1970s, ISI increasingly appeared as a practice by which government favorites were protected from the difficult conditions created by inflation. Both Indira Gandhi's India and Anwar Sadat's Egypt became theaters of this perceived corruption.[38]

Ultimately, inflation would be vanquished in the 1980s by government policies of austerity—very high interest rates and budget slashing—diminishing demand and causing the worldwide recession of 1982, the steepest global economic decline in the entire Age of Interconnection. By then, however, regulated capitalism had fallen victim to the inflationary surge, although its adherents would fight a rear-guard battle, lasting into the twenty-first century.

One final feature of the surge in petroleum prices was the transfer of wealth from consumers to producers. At the time, there were some wild estimates of its extent. In 1975, the World Bank thought that OPEC would accumulate a surplus of $1.2 trillion within a decade. Actual numbers were more modest. One estimate puts the current accounts surplus for OPEC countries from 1974 to 1978 at about $177 billion; another puts this surplus for all oil-exporting countries between 1974 and 1987 at $487 billion. Both are on the order of $35 billion per year, something like 0.75 percent of the world's GDP at the time.[39]

The situation was different for oil exporters with more people and less petroleum: countries such as Venezuela, Iran, Algeria, Libya, Nigeria, or Indonesia. A comparison of the latter two is particularly revealing. In 1970, Nigeria's per capita GDP was a little over $1,200 (in 1990 purchasing power parity terms); Indonesia's a little under. But both countries had substantial petroleum reserves and the oil price shocks flooded them with money. By the mid-1970s, oil accounted for as much as 90 percent of export proceeds and 80 percent of all government revenues. Nigeria became the global poster child for misuse of this oil money, much of which made its way straight into Swiss bank accounts. "Capital flight" has been estimated at $63 billion between 1970 and 1996. But even the effort to use the oil money productively led to disaster. Construction boomed as a result of the oil bonanza, and officials from the Ministry of Defense and their cronies brought sixteen million tons of cement into the country, far beyond needs or even harbor capacity in Lagos. In 1975, a "cement armada" consisting of hundreds of vessels, sat in the harbor, the bulk cement in their hulls slowly hardening.

Corruption was no less prevalent in Indonesia, where much of the oil wealth made its way to business cronies, largely ethnic Chinese, of President Suharto. At least they invested it more productively. The country's fossil-fuel exports diversified away from crude oil to refined products and liquefied natural gas; both agriculture and industrial production grew steadily. By contrast, Nigeria remained completely dependent on crude oil exports. The one form of economic diversification was to become a hub for the smuggling of cocaine from Latin America to Europe. By 2000, Indonesia's per capita GDP was about two-and-a-half times 1970 levels; the proportion of the population living in poverty had fallen by half (to about 20 percent); infant mortality rates were just one-quarter of what they had been. Nigeria's per capita GDP remained the same; infant mortality rates had declined a bit, but remained over three times what they were in Indonesia. Twenty-eight percent of Nigeria's population was estimated to be living in poverty in 1980. The figure had reached over 70 percent by 2000.[40]

African countries were widely regarded as prime examples of economic mismanagement. Great Britain and Norway were seen as the opposite. Both countries benefited immensely from the discovery of oil in the North Sea yet made very different use of that oil. The government of Margaret Thatcher sold off state-owned shares of British Petroleum, and encouraged private investors to pump out as much oil as quickly as they could, so that the bulk of Britain's North Sea oil was sold during the low-price years of the later 1980s and 1990s. Tax revenues from the oil exports were used to fund tax cuts on upper-income groups. The Norwegian government coordinated its private oil contractors, via a state-owned holding company, *Statoil*. Oil export revenues paid for larger publicly owned shares of oil exploration firms and a public investment fund whose assets eventually exceeded $800 billion, revenues from which would remain as a lasting benefit for years.[41]

The transfer of wealth connected to the explosion of petroleum prices in the 1970s had a profound impact on the debit side—meaning income and assets draining away from countries that were net petroleum consumers. Painful as the price was for wealthy countries—and they paid it in the form of both rampant inflation and much slower rates of economic growth—it pales in comparison to what the less-developed nations, especially in Latin America and Africa, had to endure. Their economic martyrdom took a very distinct form, yet another example of the role of the oil price shocks in creating a globalized economy. Their bills for oil imports reached into the hundreds of billions of dollars—the rise in oil prices alone accounted for $80 billion. Before the 1970s, there would have been no way to finance such expenditures, but the deregulation and liberalization of global capital markets made it possible.

Between 1974 and 1980 alone, these poorer net oil importers borrowed $200 billion, mostly from banks in Europe or North America. They received much of the funds for these loans from the oil exporters of OPEC, at least $150 billion in the same time period.[42] Contemporaries referred to these transactions as the "recycling" of "petrodollars." The very phrase echoed environmentalist rhetoric but there was nothing altruistic about it, since the bankers "recycling" OPECs oil proceeds were expecting to be repaid with interest. In fact, they were as desperate to lend the money their oil-rich customers were placing with them as Argentina or Ghana were to borrow it. Journalistic accounts portrayed inexperienced young bankers, pushing crushing loans on a greedy and corrupt clientele. The truth is that nobody at the time had experience in large-scale private international lending, which had not been done to any great extent since the 1920s.[43]

The upshot was inevitable: the loans could not be repaid. In the subsequent "restructuring" the lending financial institutions took a hit, but the greatest damage was done to the debtor nations. Both in direct negotiations with creditors and in bailouts of the International Monetary Fund, whose "structural adjustment programs" were required in thirty different African countries, the debtors were forced to cut back drastically on public expenditures, especially for public health, education, and social welfare, and raise taxes and interest rates, as part of a broader policy of economic austerity. The consequences had another designation, much less cheery than "recycling": the "lost decade," referring to the fact that the output of the economies of most Latin American countries in the 1980s was no higher, and sometimes somewhat lower, at the end of the decade than at the beginning. Conditions improved in Latin America after 1990, but for most African countries, the duration of the lost decade was doubled, with any noticeable economic growth only beginning in the new millennium.[44]

The oil price shocks had been good for the USSR and Romania, Eastern Bloc countries with petroleum products available for export. They were not so good for other bloc countries that were net petroleum importers. The *Druzhba* [friendship] oil pipeline, built in the 1960s to carry Soviet oil to its East European allies, seemed a lot less friendly when the USSR began selling its oil to Western countries at world market prices, rather than to its satellites at low, fixed prices. However, the changes in the global oil market were a small—and, in retrospect, not the most important—part of the growing global interconnections of communist countries during the 1970s and 1980s. The accession to the global economy for the USSR and its subordinates in Eastern Europe (the Chinese were much more cautious in this respect) came via the global expansion of finance. Eastern Bloc regimes began borrowing money from Western banks.

As we've seen, efforts at improving economic efficiency and productivity during the 1960s had not worked in the Eastern bloc, or at least led to unpalatable consequences. Centralized economic planning systems were not up to the challenge of providing an increasing palette of consumer goods—not just the basics of food, clothing, and shelter, hard enough as it was to get them in adequate quantities and quality, but consumer electronics, household appliances, and automobiles—while simultaneously expanding military production to compete with and even defeat the United States in the Cold War. Western currency meant the possibility of importing Western consumer goods. The amounts borrowed were actually quite modest, compared with the petrodollars being "recycled" in Africa and Latin America—roughly $50 billion by the end of the 1970s. But repaying the loans proved very difficult, because the bankers had to be reimbursed in Western currencies—dollars, D-Marks, British pounds, Swiss francs, and the like. Obtaining these required exports to Western countries and the communist countries had little, except petroleum products or natural gas, that Westerners wanted. With declining energy prices in the 1980s, even the export of fossil fuels became less lucrative. The burden of hard currency debt mounted steadily, reaching 250 percent of yearly hard currency earnings by the 1980s.[45]

Communist countries engaged in increasingly frenzied efforts to pay off the debt. The government of Romania ordered all thermostats in the country turned down to 50° F in the winter, in order to save oil for export. Romania at least had petroleum; the German Democratic Republic, generally seen as the economically most advanced country of the Eastern Bloc, did not. Its government appointed a special commissioner for "commercial coordination," Alexander Schalck-Golodkowski, an agent of the *Stasi*, the secret police, to comb the country for artworks, valuable literary manuscripts, and anything else that could be sold for Western currency. After the end of communism, Schalck-Goldokowski, used the experiences and connections he had developed in his position to become an international trade consultant.[46] Both Romania and East Germany developed the practice of selling people for hard currency. They would allow the emigration of imprisoned political dissidents in the GDR, and of ethnic minorities, mostly Jews and Germans, in Romania, to Western countries in return for payments of $25,000 per person. The government of Poland did not try such exotic measures. It attempted to save on Western currency by raising the price of (frequently imported) foodstuffs, leading to riots and anti-regime demonstrations in 1976 and 1980. The latter culminated in the formation of the Solidarity trade union movement, a foreshadowing of the end of communism.

The one thing the communist regimes did not attempt to do was to default on their obligations, as desperate Latin American countries contemplated in the 1980s, via their largely unsuccessful efforts to form a debtors' cartel, and as Argentina would finally do with very considerable success in 2002. For all their denunciation of capitalism, Eastern Bloc governments obediently followed bourgeois norms in paying off their debts—maybe more so than some of the bourgeoisie. This represented a decisive step toward a genuinely global market, one that integrated the one-third of humanity not living in countries with market economies. In the Age of Total War, the USSR had been quite outside the capitalist order of the rest of the globe, as became especially evident during the Great Depression, when the Soviet economy grew rapidly (admittedly at immense human cost), while the rest of the world struggled to overcome the post-1929 economic crisis. But even in the post-1945 decades, communist countries had few economic ties to the rest of the world. The rapid development of international financial transactions following 1970 brought them into global market connections for the first time, while simultaneously laying the groundwork for their transformation into market economies.

One more major contribution to the creation of a global market in the decades of the 1960s and 1970s, yet one little known and seemingly insignificant, was the shipping container—basically a large box. Early versions were made of steel, twenty feet long, eight feet high, and eight wide. Cargo could be loaded onto it at a warehouse, shipped by truck or rail, placed by crane directly on a ship, carried overseas, and then unloaded, reversing the same sequence of transportation, until it reached its destination. Experiments in containerized shipping were first conducted in the 1950s; international agreement on standard container sizes was reached in the following decade. In the 1970s, these containers became the standard means of shipping; harbor facilities around the world were rebuilt for them, and something like one thousand new specialized ships were built, increasing the world's total container cargo capacity to ten million tons, by 1980.[47]

The container made moving freight over long distances faster, simpler, and cheaper. It obviated the need to offload items one-by-one going intermodal (i.e., from one form of transportation to another), as well as long stays of freight on the docks, as longshoremen working by hand, or with simple machines, fit individual items together into the hold of a freighter to maximize cargo capacity, or unloaded freight, one item at a time (while often making off with desirable cargoes, like bottles of whiskey). From start to finish, the freight stayed in its container.

Containers transformed globalized manufacturing. They also changed the nature of multinational enterprise, which had existed since the nineteenth century. Until the 1960s, there were two basic forms. One was natural resource firms, such as Royal Dutch Shell, the United Fruit Company, or the Rio Tinto mining firm. Then there were manufacturers like Siemens, the Ford Motor Company, British American Tobacco, or the Singer Sewing Machine Company, which set up production facilities in foreign countries for the purpose of serving those countries' markets—not exporting. As late as 1968, 89 percent of the industrial output of US-owned multinationals (which accounted, at the time, for about half the world's direct foreign investment) was sold in the country where its production occurred—and most of the remaining 11 percent came from the sale in the United States of cars made in the Canadian suburbs of Detroit.[48]

Containerization made it possible to take advantage of low labor costs, cheaper raw materials, or less stringent environmental regulations. A company could manufacture in one country and sell in another. Containerization also enabled the division of different phases of manufacturing between countries. A good example is the Barbie doll. By the mid-1990s, the nylon used for Barbie's hair came from Japan, the plastics of her body from Taiwan, the pigments with which her plastic body was painted from the United States, while her cotton clothing was manufactured in China. The parts were all assembled in Chinese factories using US-made molds, and Japanese and European machines, before being shipped to customers around the world. Computers, consumer electronics, motor vehicles—their manufacture followed the same lines as Barbie's. The result was that by 2000, multinational enterprises accounted for two-thirds of the world's merchandise and service exports. Forty percent of all international commerce involved "intra-firm trade," that is, divisions of the same multinational in different countries selling to one another.[49]

Global financial and commercial interactions, or globalized investment, increased to an unprecedented extent in the last three decades of the twentieth century. The globalization of industrial production, however, was something fundamentally new. Its progress appears from a simple if somewhat obscure statistic: the ratio of merchandise trade to merchandise value added—the latter referring to the difference in price between the components of an industrial product and the product itself. As late as 1970, this ratio was in the vicinity of 15–30 percent, which, for most large advanced industrial countries, was not fundamentally different from where it had been in at the start of the First World War, or even earlier. In the United Kingdom, the ratio was higher than elsewhere, 41 percent, but that was much lower than the 76 percent it had been in 1913. The state of affairs changed fundamentally. In France, between 1970 and 1990, the ratio doubled from 26 percent to 54 percent. For the United States, during the same period, the figures went from 14 percent to 36 percent. Similar increases occurred in Germany, Italy, Canada, Sweden, Denmark, and Great Britain—eloquent statistical testimony to the spread of the manufacturing process around the world. One major industrial country was an exception to the trend, namely Japan: the ratio of trade to value added went from 16 percent to 19 percent. In this respect, as in so many others, the island kingdom went its own way in the world.[50]

DEREGULATION AND REREGULATION IN A GLOBALLY INTERCONNECTED ECONOMY

The Late Millennium Era marked the vast expansion of earlier trends toward a worldwide, deregulated market. These were the years in which deregulation and privatization accelerated, containerization of shipping and the globalization of the manufacturing process that accompanied it scored new triumphs, and when the volume and pace of international financial transactions rose and became steadily more complex and nontransparent, with the rise of derivatives trading. The market-oriented "Washington consensus"—as it was called by its coiner, the economist John Williamson— dominated economic policymaking. Yet nothing more characterized the triumph of the global market than the end of its chief alternative, the communist system of publicly owned, centrally planned production. Already modified in a more capitalist direction, and partially integrated into a global capitalism in the 1980s, the communist economic systems came to a complete end in the following decade, with the exception of North Korea (Cuba remained stuck in the 1980s process of partial market orientation and integration), making a globalized capitalism truly global for the first time since 1914. Primarily as a result of this development, the 1990s were a decade of worldwide free-market enthusiasm and unleashed global markets.

A paradoxical feature of the situation was that the seeming triumph of a globalized, deregulated capitalist market was underpinned by a countertrend toward re-regulation. In fact, four years after the *Nikkuson Shokku* the first meeting of the G-7 took place (in 1975, and actually a G-6, since Canada only came on board the following year). The world's most affluent capitalist countries gathered to develop policies to counteract the effects of market liberalization. Although the fixed exchange rates of the Bretton Woods era never reappeared, the European Currency Union and the European Monetary Union attempted to limit exchange-rate fluctuations among the currencies of members of the EEC and later EU, leading, ultimately, to the creation of the single currency, the euro. A number of countries, particularly in Latin America and Asia, tried to fix their currencies to the US dollar. But the most remarkable example of re-regulation was the growth and success of the East Asian economic model, with its close government-industry cooperation, its distinct restrictions on international financial transactions, and its multifarious forms of restrictions and export subsidies.

The East Asian economic model is a particularly interesting example of what happened at the end of the Age of Interconnection, since these countries had by far the highest economic growth in that period. Unlike its communist counterpart, it was not designed as a challenge to free-market capitalism, nor as a model with universal validity. Rather, it developed and thrived in a symbiotic (some critics would have said parasitic) relationship with countries that pursued a deregulated and privatized capitalism. This interrelationship between deregulation and reregulation was characteristic of the global economy at the time. Buoyed up by the collapse of communist regimes, proponents of deregulation and free markets in the 1990s overlooked the essential role that reregulation played in global capitalism.

A few simple facts can give an idea about the extent of global markets in the last decade of the millennium. In 1990, the world's twenty largest shipping container ports handled some 34.5 million containers; by 2003, the number of containers moving through those ports had increased to 144.7 million. This rapid growth testified both to the expansion of global trade and to the ever-greater strides in the globalization of industrial production, which containerization had made feasible. The Bank for International Settlements, the global clearing house for central banks, estimated that in 1995, the first year for which figures were collected, $880 billion worth of financial derivatives were traded daily, worldwide; by 2001, the figure had grown to $1.39 trillion every single business day.[51]

Although the deregulation of international financial transactions had been well under way since the beginning of the 1980s, the following decade saw a number of administrative landmarks of deregulation, including the North American Free Trade Agreement of 1994 and the Maastricht Accords of 1992, which transformed the European Economic Community, or Common Market, into the European Union. What characterized both NAFTA and the EU was not just their free trade element, since trade in North America and in Europe was already pretty free, but their abolition of boundaries to cross-border investment and finance. The EU immediately hastened to eliminate restrictions on derivatives trading. In the United States, the 1999 Gramm-Leach-Billey Act repealed the Glass-Steagall Act of 1932, a classic piece of the age of regulated capitalism, that had prevented mergers and joint activity of different kinds of financial institutions. Not content with merely dismantling past regulations and leaving the interconnections of banks, insurance companies, brokerage houses, and investment banks to the forces of the market, Gramm-Leach-Billey contained provisions prohibiting any future regulation of financial derivatives, testament to the widespread—and, in hindsight rather questionable—belief in the virtues of unleashed, unregulated market mechanisms.[52]

Margaret Thatcher, the British prime minister and public policy face of the trend toward globalized and deregulated markets, coined the celebrated acronym, TINA—"there is no alternative." During Thatcher's tenure in the 1980s, plenty of alternatives were being advocated. By the following decade, however, this was no longer the case. One obvious reason was the end of communism on a global scale: although politically concentrated in the years 1989–91, it had been happening in one form or another since the early 1980s. It might seem that the end of communism led to the global expansion of markets, but the reverse is true: the spread of markets led to the end of communism.

The two main communist nations, China and the USSR, had both begun introducing markets, market-based pricing, and forms of private ownership in the 1980s, In China, it had started under the energetic leadership of Deng Xiaoping; in the Soviet Union, following 1986, under the rule of Mikhail Gorbachev. These ideas spread throughout the countries of the Eastern Bloc, at times with the willing cooperation of the local Communist Party leadership, as was the case in, for instance, Hungary or Vietnam, and at times very much against local leaders' wishes, in East Germany or Czechoslovakia. Capitalism developed under communism from the top down, reflecting the frustrations of party leaders with a system of economic planning that could barely guarantee the basic necessities of food, clothing, and shelter, and that faced immense difficulties in providing more advanced consumer goods, particularly the iconic consumer durable, the automobile. The old system also groaned under the burden of the increasingly technologically complex and resource-heavy demands of armaments production in the late phases of the Cold War.

Introducing private ownership and market-determined pricing and production into an economy centrally planned around public ownership was a high-wire act—indeed, a double high-wire act. First, it required coordinating two fundamentally different economic systems within one country, having administered prices coexisting with market prices, a setup ripe for problematic practices—like buying goods at low, administered prices and then selling them at much higher market prices. This would not only do nothing to increase output and efficiency; it positively decreases and destroys them. The second was introducing market ideas to a country where rejecting them had been the central tenet of the political system for decades.

The outcome was fundamentally different in Europe and Asia. In the USSR and its satellite states, the effort was a disastrous failure: the more reform that was initiated, the worse the economy got and the less legitimacy the whole communist system possessed, until it collapsed in 1989–91. The lesson that post-communist policy makers drew from this experience was that the introduction of market elements into the communist system failed because it had happened too slowly. Post-communist regimes introduced "shock therapy"—privatizing all property, setting prices loose, and deregulating all international financial transactions, and doing it all at once—which often led to wild inflation, the transfer of formerly publicly owned resources into a few, private pockets, and massive declines in output, standards of living and even life expectancy.[53]

By contrast, the gradual introduction of market elements, such as was the case in China and Vietnam, proved much more successful. There were periods of crises and hesitations, but the upshot of the reforms was the initiation of a period of increasingly rapid economic growth and rising standards of living. For all this capitalism, the governments continued to call themselves "communist" and the Party maintained its hold on political power. Yet in the context of the global forward march of markets in the 1990s, the communist label seemed little more than lip service.[54]

In 1990, the economist John Williamson's "Washington Consensus" had become the basis of policy recommendations for economic growth. Williamson had a list of ten, but there were three key features: deregulation, privatization, and opening to international capital flows. Derived from the experiences of the World Bank and the International Monetary fund in Latin America during its "lost decade" of the 1980s, the Washington Consensus became the dominant viewpoint on economics, worldwide, at the end of the Age of Interconnection.[55]

From its very beginnings in the 1970s, deregulation called forth reregulation—new forms of government intervention that functioned only in the context of unleashed markets and played a crucial role in making them work. Such reregulation occurred at the international, regional, and national levels. At the international level, the most significant was the G-7 (the actual number of countries involved has varied from 5 to 20), the annual meetings of the leaders of the countries with the world's largest economies, preceded and supplemented by additional meetings of these countries' respective ministers of finance. Cynics see these gatherings as little more than politicians' photo ops, but on at least two occasions their actions revealed that the deregulated and floating currencies of the post-1971 world did not result in the automatic adjustments their proponents claimed.

At the Bonn summit of 1978, for example, the assembled governmental leaders reached an agreement about how to improve economic growth in the entire non-communist world, which had been lagging since the global recession of 1974–75, while not accelerating inflation. The plan involved the world's three largest capitalist economies: the governments of Germany and Japan would provide an economic stimulus, via tax cuts and spending increases; the US government would commit to deregulating domestic oil prices, which, it was hoped, would encourage more oil production, decrease imports, and lessen demand pressures on global petroleum prices. The plan was designed to rebalance global trade, decreasing the German and Japanese export surplus while spurring on US exports—a readjustment that floating exchange rates were supposed to bring automatically and until then had not. It was a good example of an arrangement involving unpleasant concessions on all sides—Germany and Japan taking on more inflation risk and accepting more imports, the US agreeing to the higher gasoline prices via deregulation. The plan's effects were largely swamped by the second oil price shock of the following year.[56]

If intervention in and management of supposedly market-driven currency values was one of the themes of the 1978 agreement, they were central to the Plaza Accords, implemented in 1985. Just as the Bretton Woods system had been threatened by the coming of "stop and go" to the United States, the new world of floating currencies was endangered when *la bicicleta financeria* reached the United States in the first half of the 1980s. The combination of very high interest rates and large government deficits, typical of financial and monetary policy during the first administration of US President Ronald Reagan, brought foreign assets flowing to the United States, raising the value of the dollar after its plunge in the 1970s, making US exports more expensive and imports cheaper. As a result, the trade deficit increased, requiring more foreign funds to finance it, raising still further the value of the dollar.

The cycle was going around and around, only this time in the world's largest economy rather than in Argentina. By mid-1985, the dollar was about three-quarters of the way back to the value against other currencies it had enjoyed in the Bretton Woods days. But the world had changed. Major American manufacturers of steel, machinery, autos, electronics, and virtually every other industrial product were in a rage over their difficulties competing in US and world markets, as the highly valued dollar made their goods too expensive; the possibility loomed of a violent reversal of currency values, an explosive dollar collapse. The finance ministers and central bank heads of the United States, France, Germany, Japan, and the United Kingdom (so five of the G-7), meeting at the Plaza Hotel in New York, reached an agreement to avert this possibility: the four non-US countries would sell some of their stores of dollars in the international currency markets. The measure did help bring the value of the dollar down by about 50 percent, improving the US balance of trade and banning the danger of a dollar collapse. However, it led to the concomitant rise in the value of the Japanese yen, and the flood of capital streaming into Japan helped create the real estate bubble that inflated over Japan in the second half of the 1980s. Among the bubble's more peculiar features was that at one point the value of the land in the city of Tokyo was greater than the entire value of all the assets in the United States. The inflow of money also promoted dubious financial speculations and questionable deals involving close ties between financial institutions and the *yakuza*, Japanese crime syndicates.[57]

If efforts of the G-7 to manage and to regulate the new world of global financial markets were sporadic and, at best, partially successful, the governments of Western Europe put a good deal more work in their efforts, with more long-lasting results. As soon as the dollar had been floated and the Bretton Woods system brought to an end, they sought to align their currencies with each other in a stable, or largely stable arrangement. European currencies might fluctuate greatly in value against the dollar or the yen, but they would not change much against each other. Cynics might say this was done largely to ensure predictability of the farm-subsidy payments that made up such a large portion of the budget of the common market. A less-jaundiced assertion would be that the creation of stable exchange rates was understood as a necessary part of expanding trade and investment across national boundaries. In other words, that deregulation and market liberalization required reregulation.

Stabilizing exchange rates in a world of larger and more open capital flows proved difficult. Speculators poured money into the low-inflation countries of northern Europe and took it out of the high-inflation countries of the south of the continent, constantly bringing exchange rates out of alignment. As a result, there were a series of different arrangements: the "snake" of 1971–78; the European Monetary System (EMS) of 1978–92; and the European

Monetary Union, leading to the creation of the single currency, the euro, in 1992–2002. The breakup of the EMS, connected to the fiscal turbulence resulting from Germany's unification in 1990, was particularly spectacular. The Swedish government at one point tried to defend the *krona* by raising overnight interest rates to 500 percent; the speculator George Soros made over $1 billion selling short the British pound. As a result of these monetary experiences, neither Sweden nor the United Kingdom were willing to join in the euro.[58]

By far the most important and most successful example of reregulation both opposed to and yet dependent on a globalized, deregulated capitalism was that of Export-Led Industrialization, or ELI. Clausewitz famously described war as the continuation of politics by other means. ELI was the continuation of ISI by other means. It was a new and different version of the attempt of economically less-developed states in Latin America and Asia to use government shaping of the market to compete with and catch up to the wealthier countries in Europe and North America.[59] And this different way was, on the face of it, odd, almost perverse. Proponents of ISI, as I've noted, wanted less-developed countries to increase their manufacturing capacity, producing more consumer goods for their citizens, or, initially, more producers' goods, like steel, which could be used to make more consumers' goods. The citizens would consume more and would be more prosperous. By contrast, in ELI, less-developed countries were to increase their manufacturing capacity not for the purpose of domestic consumption, but to export their manufactured goods to wealthy countries.

As with ISI, ELI involved large-scale government intervention in the economy. Among the measures used were tax subsidies and subsidized loans to exporters; setting exchange rates at low levels to encourage exports; import subsidies for raw materials; direction of savings and investments to favored industries; discrimination against, or outright prohibition of imports that might compete with favored industrial sectors; rejection of investments from foreign multilaterals or equity investments from foreign interests; and direction of foreign investment toward loans to domestic industries, or making foreign investments dependent on the licensing of advanced technologies. None of this was exactly in line with the unregulated market trend sweeping the globe, but it differed from ISI in one key respect, namely its export orientation. Under ISI, protected manufacturers had a captive domestic market, with no particular incentive to improve the quality of their products. In ELI, while manufacturers were protected from foreign competition, they had to sell their wares in the markets of economically advanced countries, whose consumers had lots of options, forcing exporters to compete furiously on both price and quality.

The model example of ELI was South Korea. In 1960, it was one of the poorest countries in the world, with a per capita GDP below that of

Somalia.⁶⁰ Still recovering from the devastation of the Korean War, South Korea could not enjoy the long-term benefits of investment in mining and manufacturing that had occurred under Japanese colonial rule in the Age of Total War, for those had been in the northern part of the country, governed after 1945 by the communists. South Korean ISI policies had led to little, aside from increasing the wealth of the *chaebol*, clan-based major businesses.

The situation changed in 1961, with the coup d'état that brought to power army general Park Chung Hee. A communist sympathizer in the immediate aftermath of the Second World War, General Park began his rule by arresting the leaders of the *chaebol* and putting the head of Samsung on trial. He therefore might not have seemed like the ideal individual to develop a new version of capitalism. Yet he and his advisers, working closely with South Korean's top businessmen, did just that. Their deployment of the policy tools of ELI to encourage industrialization moved the country up the technology and skills ladder from textiles in the 1960s, to steel and shipbuilding the following decade, and then on to motor vehicles, consumer electronics, and computers. Economic growth rates between the early 1960s and the mid-1990s averaged 9 percent yearly, an astonishing figure to maintain for over three decades. By 2000, per capita GDP was twelve times its 1960 levels. The one-time poorhouse now ranked with the world's affluent countries.⁶¹

The breakneck pace of economic growth, characterized by a sustained and unusually high level of capital investment, all carefully nurtured by ELI policies, led to periodic crises. One of them, which took place in 1979, culminated in President Park's assassination, but his successors continued his policies. Another, in 1997, caused by a combination of excess capacity and high levels of foreign debt, led to bankruptcies of major corporations and difficulties in meeting foreign currency obligations. Yet corporate mergers and restructurings, generally sponsored by government officials, and currency devaluations to boost exports, resolved these crises and resumed the rapid pace of economic growth.

South Korea's ELI policies were widely emulated throughout the region—in Taiwan, Malaysia, Indonesia, Thailand, and China. ELI became the East Asian model of economic development. It is often asserted it began with the region's wealthiest nation, Japan. While certainly true that in the aftermath of the Second World War Japan first utilized some of the economic development tools of ELI, including close cooperation between large corporate enterprises and the government, or strong restrictions on imports and foreign investments, there is one crucial difference. Unlike South Korea and its imitators, whose rapid economic growth was the result of exports, Japan's equally fast economic growth was largely due to the domestic market. Exports were 10 percent of GDP or less, half the level of West European countries, and much closer to those of the United States. When Japan became a global export powerhouse in the 1970s and 1980s, its days of yearly GDP increase in the 9–10 percent range were long over.[62]

The East Asian model proved immensely successful in economically troubled times when other versions of the organization of the economy have faltered. Its success, however, occurred precisely because it was an exception to the global trend of liberalized and deregulated markets. Its export-oriented development strategy worked because other countries would accept East Asian exports. Had these countries followed the East Asian strategy of discouraging imports, restricting capital flows, and decreasing the value of their currencies to promote exports, no one would have seen rapid economic growth. This interaction of deregulation and reregulation was characteristic of the closing decades of the Age of Interconnection.

The Global Economy at the End of the Millennium

By the 1990s, the process of reregulation had reached the point that there had developed something resembling a second Bretton Woods, though a more informal and partial version. Unlike its predecessor, however, it encompassed the entire world, including the former communist countries of Europe and Asia.[63] The original Bretton Woods had featured currencies at fixed exchange rates; in this second Bretton Woods, some but not all currencies were fixed. East Asian governments, as well as those of Latin American countries, such as Argentina, maintained a fixed exchange rate against the US dollar. The EU countries maintained a fixed exchange rate against each other, allowing their currencies to float, jointly, in financial transactions with the rest of the world. The original Bretton Woods system had been anchored by a fixed relationship of the dollar to a commodity, gold at $35 per ounce. In the second, the dollar was linked to an entirely different commodity, namely oil, and at a price that fluctuated between about $20 and $40 per barrel.

Government officials, economists, journalists, and consultants who articulated and formulated the euphoria of unregulated and privatized markets overlooked the extent to which these informal versions of reregulation underpinned the deregulated markets of the 1990s. Three global economic crises of that decade and the responses to them only confirmed the distorted perceptions of free-market enthusiasts. These crises, the Mexican of 1994–95, the East Asian of 1997–98, and the Russian of 1998, were all examples, on a much larger scale, of *la bicicleta financeria*. Capital, primarily in the form of short-term loans, poured into these countries, raising the value of their currencies, making imports cheaper and exports more expensive, so worsening their balance of trade, requiring more loans and raising the value of their currency once more. In the most severe of these crises, the East Asian, the effect of the *bicicleta* was exacerbated by the policy of tying a country's currency to the US dollar. As the latter appreciated in the 1990s, the Thai *baht*, the South Korean *won* and the Malaysian *ringgit* appreciated as well, accelerating the growing capital inflow. The situation could continue merrily for years—eight, in the case of East Asia—with seeming prosperity. Imported goods were cheaper; more and more people could buy more and more consumer goods. Then it came to an end. On July 2, 1997, panicked lenders, including large, money-center banks and mutual funds, abruptly refused to roll over their short-term loans, causing a sudden decline in currency values, the danger of defaults and a deep, powerful recession.[64]

This row of crises had a further financial repercussion, the collapse of the hedge fund Long Term Capital Management—a true signal of the era. Investing on a global scale in Russian bonds, German and British stocks, Japanese stock futures, US interest rate swaps, and Brazilian options, the fund's financial choices reflected the decades of liberalization of international capital markets. The firm made its investments primarily through derivatives, newly invented financial instruments that were totally unregulated; these investments were heavily leveraged, 95 percent financed with borrowed money (unlike conventional banks, hedge funds' leverage was also unregulated), meaning even small declines in the investments' value would wipe the firm out. Guided by theories about optimizing investment portfolios devised by partners in the firm, the Nobel Prize-winning economists Myron Scholes and Robert Merton, which asserted that the broad diversification of their investments would prevent serious losses, the fund was run by libertarian bankers and traders committed to the ideals of unleashed markets.

The 1998 Russian financial crisis, caused when the government defaulted on its bonds, resulted in a global wave of panic selling. Markets across the world moved in unison, a result of their interconnection in a unified network of global finance, which negated any value of diversification and eliminated Long Term Capital Management's $2 billion of capital within a few weeks. That was hardly a large sum for international banking as a whole but as a result of the firm's very large leverage, it was the basis for over $1 trillion in derivatives positions, whose unwinding raised the specter of freezing up global financial markets entirely. All this required a consortium of Wall Street banks mobilized, against the will of their top management, by the Federal Reserve Board to rescue the fund and to avoid a possible collapse of global finance.[65]

This row of financial crises demonstrated the problems inherent in the deregulation and globalization of markets, and the inadequacy of the reregulation measures of the Second Bretton Woods system to contain them. But the policy responses to the crises were taken from the playbook of the Washington Consensus and involved still greater liberalization and opening of markets. The IMF bailed out East Asian economies, while requiring them to introduce austerity programs, and to open their economies to even greater capital flows from foreign countries. The Long-Term Capital Management disaster only made central bankers, politicians, and government officials more determined to deregulate derivatives. Global capital markets did survive the turmoil of the mid to late 1990s, as well as the stock exchange crashes of 2000–2001, the bursting of the so-called tech bubble. The euphoric trust in the power of unleashed markets, survived into the next century, at least until the global financial crisis of 2008 showed what lessons had not been learned.

Looking back at the entire quarter century, from the end of postwar prosperity in 1973—those oil shocks—to the beginning of a new millennium, one can only be struck by the global deceleration of economic growth. Figure 4.3, based on the calculations of the late Angus Maddison, the OECD chief economist, shows yearly changes in the global product, the world's GDP as it were, every year between 1951 and 2001, both the annual real change, and the per capita change, so taking population increase into account.[66]

Not surprisingly, there were lots of year-to-year fluctuations in the economic growth rate. Nonetheless the dividing line of 1973–74 is stark, with a sharp deceleration of economic growth after that. Per capita growth rates followed exactly the same pattern so that the slowing rate of population increase did not make up for decline in the rate of economic growth. Overall,

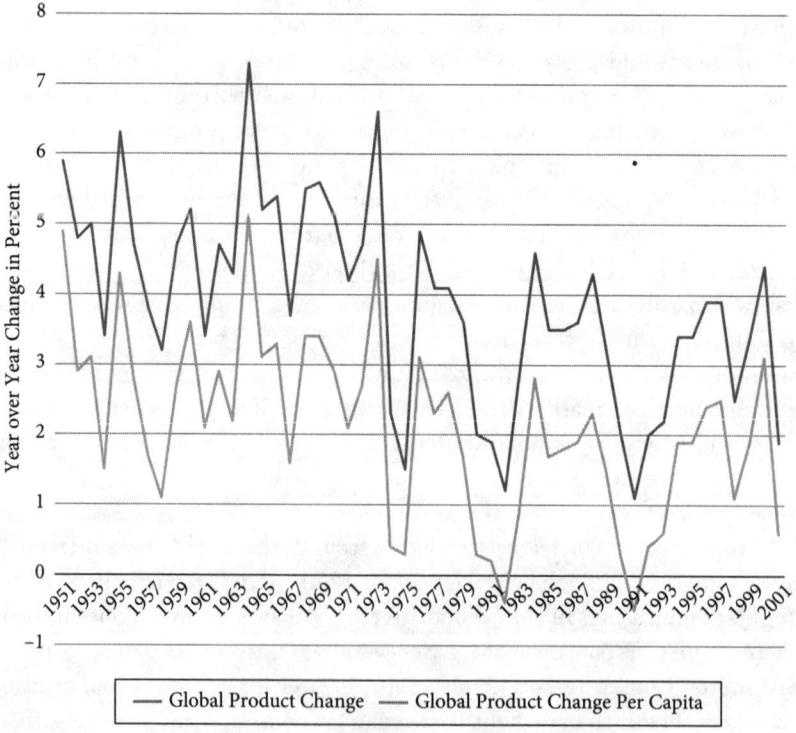

FIGURE 4.3 Yearly Change in the Global Product, 1951–2001

the annual per capita GDP growth rate of the entire world between 1973 and 2001 was less than one-half of its 1950–73 value, falling from 2.92 percent per year, to 1.41 percent. The economic outlook had not been unrelievedly bleak. Periods of slower economic growth alternated with better economic performance, but the overall result was very distinctly inferior to the quarter century after the Second World War. To be sure, even this decelerated rate of growth was noticeably higher than in the Age of Total War, 1913–50, but just a few fractions of a percentage point above what had been in achieved in that age's more peaceful predecessor 1870–1913.

The postwar years had been a period of economic expansion, worldwide, but Maddison's calculations show that pronounced regional differences in rates of economic growth appeared following 1973–74. Per capita GDP in Africa grew at the meager pace of 0.19 percent per year between 1973 and 2001, while in the USSR and its successor states, per capita GDP actually fell by almost 1 percent per year, making this close of the century an Age of Impoverishment, a transition from a stagnant communist economy to a collapsing post-communist one. Developments in Latin America were only more modestly favorable, average yearly growth rates in the same period only a third of the postwar. The wealthiest parts of the world—Western Europe, North America, Australia, Japan—continued to experience economic growth but at rates that were noticeably slower, between about one-quarter and three-quarters of the postwar period. It was only in Asia that economic growth accelerated, the annual per capita GDP growth rate doubling in both India and China: the latter's figure of 5.32 percent per year (Maddison's figures tend to downplay the extent of economic growth; other estimates are higher), was the best among major countries. Another way to put it would be to note that the economic output of China and India was a little under 8 percent of the global total in 1973 but almost 19 percent, by 2001. The end of the twentieth century was the age of Asia, especially East Asia.[67]

Since India and China alone accounted for almost 40 percent of the world's population, their rapid economic growth had a quite unexpected result—a lessening of inequality between countries, reversing a trend to a steadily more favorable position of the world's wealthier nations, which had been ongoing at least since 1800. This development may have been cold comfort to citizens of African and Latin American countries, whose economic experiences in the 1990s were generally less favorable (to some extent this would change in the new millennium) but it was nonetheless a profound transformation, closely connected to another long-term upheaval of this period, the transition from a world economy centered on the Atlantic Ocean to one centered on the Pacific.

Yet the decline in economic inequality between countries went along with an increase in inequality within countries. Very much unlike the postwar era, when the benefits of rapid economic growth were distributed in a fairly egalitarian way, the rewards of the generally slower economic growth of the post-1973 years went primarily to the wealthiest 10 percent of the population. Owners of capital, disproportionately located among the affluent, generally did better than wage earners. Income and wealth inequality increased steadily. Strongest in the English-speaking countries, and in post-communist regimes, but present globally this development is probably best illuminated by the data-filled analyses of the French economist Thomas Piketty. He was far from the first person to point it out, and others, following him, have elaborated on his analysis.[68]

This profound, worldwide change in the pace and beneficiaries of economic growth is one of the most crucial developments of the Age of Interconnection. There are three areas where an explanation might be sought. One is in the end of cheap and easy use of the biosphere and natural resources. Following the oil price shocks, energy became much more expensive; the cost of environmental mitigation and controlling the harmful effects of industry on the environment, which began about the same time as the oil price shocks, took their toll as well. This element certainly explains the way that the post-1945 boom came to a sudden end after 1973, but not the long-term decline in economic growth, as economic reorganization and the progress in the efficiency of energy use have made these problems less of an economic bottleneck.

Another element was the waning effect of the leading sectors of the post-1945 economy: chemicals, electrical equipment, steel, and, especially, motor vehicles. On the rise since the very beginning of the century, they reached the limits of their contribution to the acceleration of economic growth in affluent countries by the 1970s, and made relatively little headway elsewhere in the world, especially in Latin America and Africa, whose economies were crippled by the Lost Decade. One might wonder why new leading sectors did not emerge to produce an additional surge of economic growth. There were certainly plenty of new technologies available—microelectronics, biotechnology, and nanotechnology, for instance.

The connection between globalization and the unleashing of markets to declining inequality between countries and increasing inequality within countries is perhaps no surprise. Container-driven possibilities for globalizing industrial production meant formerly good-paying industrial jobs could move to lower-wage countries, while the increasing profits from these cost reductions accrued to the owners of capital. The end of communism brought large amounts of labor onto the world market, but little capital, changing the supply-and-demand relationship between labor and capital to the benefit of the latter. In post-communist countries that enjoyed an economically successful 1990s with a broadly rising standard of living, particularly China and Vietnam, as well as those for whom that decade was a disaster—the former USSR, and other Eastern Bloc lands, such as Romania—the privatization of public assets and economic possibilities into the hands of a smaller group of entrepreneurs, often dubbed the "oligarchs" (in some countries difficult to differentiate from gangsters) increased inequality. Deregulated and globalized financial markets tended to divert corporate profits to financial firms and to increase capital income and salaries of generally (very) well-paid bankers.[69]

The slowing economic growth rate, though, seems more mysterious, especially given economists' assertions that deregulating markets should increase efficiency and lead to more and faster economic growth. Economists might maintain that without deregulation economic expansion in the last quarter of the century would have been even more meager than it was. The fate of the communist alternative to the market economy, the system of centralized economic planning via material balances, which proved unsustainable and collapsed in the decade of the 1980s, would support such an assertion. East Asian countries—capitalist market economies, but in which business and government carefully regulated markets—were the only ones to defy the trend toward slower economic growth; their businesses gained ever-greater shares of global markets, at the expense of their more laissez-faire-oriented competitors in Europe and North America.

It does seem futile to yearn, as some do, for the postwar period of heavily regulated capitalism. It proved unable to master the many economic challenges, from global trade imbalances, to disruptive financial flows, to the drastic increase in energy prices, that characterized the Era of Upheaval in the 1960s and 1970s. Whether the widespread belief that the system of deregulated and globalized markets was an improvement on its postwar predecessor was correct is another question. The role of various forms of informal reregulation in supporting this deregulated globalized economy might suggest one answer, as might the financial crises of 1994, 1997, and 1998, all of them precursors of the biggest of them all, the crisis of 2008.

5 | Migrations

REFUGEES FROM CIVIL WAR in the Middle East and central Asia have been storming into Europe by the millions in the last decade. Enterprising or just desperate, inhabitants of poorer countries in Africa, Asia, or Latin America have been trying their luck moving, whether legally or illegally, to wealthier lands in the Persian Gulf, Western Europe, or North America. Their remittances crisscross the globe, both through formal banking systems and informal currency-transfer agents. Increasingly, more countries, and not just prosperous ones, find they have whole communities of immigrants in their midst, many with profoundly different cultural and religious practices. The migrants' presence has led to unsettling transformations in social structures and labor markets. Real and imagined fears have become hot-button political issues. Many candidates for public office demand that legal and physical barriers be constructed to keep foreigners out, and that those already arrived be sent back home as soon as possible. Mass migrations are unquestionably a constitutive element of our world.

But the nature of these migrations—what drives them—remains profoundly in question. Are they examples of unprecedented globalization, as technological changes allow people, goods, and information to move ever more freely around the globe, making borders of sovereign states irrelevant, or, at least, extremely porous? Or is this all nothing new? People have been moving around, over considerable distances, as long as *homo sapiens* have existed. In fact, international migration reached high levels in the three decades preceding the First World War. They were, by some measures, even higher than they are today. Moreover, as a proportion of the world's population, migration has changed little since 1970.

The answer is neither and both. To put it differently, migration has changed dramatically and repeatedly over the past 150 years, both the absolute numbers of migrants and the percentages they make up of the population in their countries of immigration, as well as their origins and destinations. Much else has also changed: the territories they traverse; their intent in migrating; their plans and abilities to return to their original homes; the work they do, or don't do; their age and gender; their reasons for moving; and whether their movement was voluntary or coerced. This is to say nothing of changes in the individual countries' laws governing and international agreements regulating their departure and arrival. Economic and demographic trends certainly played a large role influencing migration, as did legal changes, particularly the extent to which racist attitudes were enshrined in laws and their enforcement over the course of the twentieth century.

However, the single most important factor determining the nature of migration in the modern world was the nature of the Age of Total War. The world wars disrupted pre-1914 migration practices and habits and reduced greatly the number of migrants, while creating a whole new category of people moving around—the refugee. By the 1950s, the circumstances created in the Age of Total War had come to seem familiar, even something of a natural state of affairs. As with so many other things, developments of the 1960s and 1970s disrupted previous practices and assumptions, and created new migration patterns, setting the stage for the twenty-first century.

Moving About: The Great Wave and The First Era of Globalization

The period between 1820 and 1920 was the Age of the Great trans-Atlantic Migration. Some forty-five million people were involved, three-quarters of whom went from Europe to the United States, with the rest going primarily to Canada, Brazil, and Argentina. This immense population movement was not evenly spread out across the century; the majority of the migrants arrived in the latter part of that one-hundred-year period. Many have dubbed the migratory highpoint of the years 1880 to 1914 the Era of "First Globalization."[1] This era is particularly well-known to Americans, most of whom are descendants of migrants reaching the United States after its Civil War, and has become a constantly evoked and displayed part of the nation's history and self-perception. But from a global perspective, trans-Atlantic migrations were not the whole story of the Age of the First Globalization, and not even the main part of that story.

Because today, trans-Pacific migrations are very large, one might wonder about their extent during the First Globalization. The Pacific did not become an arena of economic and population interchange comparable to its

Atlantic counterpart until fairly recently. Trans-Pacific migrations during the nineteenth century were on the order of 4 percent of trans-Atlantic ones. Partly this is because popular opposition in North America and Australia to Chinese immigration, for example, drastically restricted or totally eliminated immigration from Asian countries in general, and China in particular.[2] But even before the beginning of the Era of the First Globalization, and before there were any legal restrictions, the number of immigrants from China in the United States or Australia were only 5–10 percent of those from Europe. Migrants from China and India found more of a welcome in some Caribbean islands and in a few South American countries, including Peru and Chile, although largely because they were restricted to the dirtiest and most unpleasant jobs, like harvesting sugar cane, or gathering guano to be used as fertilizer, while working on labor contracts that were little short of slavery. The big Asian population movements ran instead across the Bay of Bengal and the South China Sea, bringing tens of millions of laborers to work on plantations and in mines of the British colonies of Malaya and Ceylon, and the Dutch East Indies, today's Indonesia, and in numbers comparable to the great trans-Atlantic migrations. The Indians were almost entirely laborers. Chinese migrants included brokers and agents—groups that organized these migrations in the first place—money-changers, merchants and shopkeepers, who developed into an ethnic Chinese capitalist class, an important influence in Thailand, the Philippines, and pre-communist Vietnam, and became, and remain, central to the economies of Malaysia, Singapore, and Indonesia.[3]

To understand the total picture of people moving over large distances during the First Globalization, we need to drop an obsession with crossing bodies of water and state borders. Particularly in Europe, poorer countries on the south and the east of the continent—the Austro-Hungarian and Czarist Empires, Romania, Spain, Portugal and Italy—which sent the most people across the Atlantic between 1880 and 1914, also sent millions of laborers to wealthier countries in Europe, to toil on the docks in Marseilles, the steelworks of Lorraine, or the coal mines of Germany's Ruhr Basin. By 1914, about 40 percent of the mineworkers four hundred thousand workers and probably a majority of those who worked underground, were Polish-speaking: most were German citizens from the far eastern end of the German Empire, one thousand miles from the coal fields; others were from the Austro-Hungarian and Russian Empires.[4]

Overland migration with a different impetus involved agricultural cultivation. The late nineteenth and early twentieth centuries saw large-scale expansion of grain output, yet with little in the way of increased per-acre crop yields. It was therefore only possible by bringing new lands into production. The settling of the western two-thirds of the United States and Canada, or the grain-growing and cattle-raising interior of Argentina were examples. However, by far the largest movement of this kind in the world was from central China into the northeastern region of Manchuria. For this overland migration, largely within the same country (although the hold of the imperial Chinese government and its post-1911 republican successor on Manchuria was pretty tenuous), figures are vague, but the total number of migrants may have been somewhere around thirty million.[5]

During the First Globalization/Great Wave, tens of millions of people were on the move, at a pace unimaginable before, but there was another very distinct feature of this pre-1914 mass migration: most of it was temporary and reversible. Between 1890 and 1920, for example, 12.6 million people moved from India and China to countries of Southeast Asia; 11.9 million came back. Exact numbers on the Chinese who migrated to Manchuria are sparser, but they suggest that 40 to 50 percent of them returned. Americans view trans-Atlantic migrations as a permanent commitment to life in a new world and an affirmation of their nation and its freedoms, but the statistics—admittedly not too complete—tell a very different story. Argentina has the best, and from 1857 to 1914, people leaving Argentina amounted to 43 percent of those arriving from foreign countries. Brazil only kept figures between 1899 and 1912, but these show emigrants were 66 percent of immigrants. US statistics are sparser still, only beginning in 1908, but from then through 1914 emigrants were about 53 percent of immigrants.[6]

Permanent settlement was the exception in international migration before the First World War. More common was that immigrants stayed a few years, usually toiling in unpleasant conditions, perhaps sending back remittances, and then returned home. Migrants moved over increasingly long distances and seasonally. There were the "swallows," the same name given to Chinese laborers who left Shandong Province to work on the harvest in Manchuria, returning home in the winter, and the Sicilians who came to Argentina to work on the wheat harvest in the summer of the Southern Hemisphere and returned in its winter, summer in their native land, to work on the harvest there. Slovaks who came to the United States between 1880 and 1914 to mine coal in Pennsylvania during the winter, the period of peak demand for coal, and returned home in the summer to do farm work, when demand for coal slacked off, followed the same pattern, with the seasons reversed.[7]

The age and sex of pre-1914 migrants reflected this migration patterns. Emigrants from Asian countries were almost exclusively single young men, at a stage of their lives when their physical strength was maximized and personal ties and responsibilities minimized. (The very few women who emigrated were typically either recruited or coerced into providing sexual services to these men.) There were more women among trans-Atlantic migrants, and more people coming in family groups: about half of the Europeans moving to Brazil and Canada were women. But for the United States and Argentina, the two largest New World destinations during this prewar period, between 60 and 70 percent of the immigrants were men, the proportion of males actually increasing toward 1914.[8]

This entire system of global migrations, built up across the nineteenth century, and reaching its peak in the years before the First World War, collapsed completely as a result of the war and the political, social, and economic upheavals it provoked. Obviously, the fighting itself made movement within Europe impossible, while the largest group of potential migrants was in the army. The war prevented others in the central and eastern regions of the continent from reaching seaports, and rendered trans-Atlantic travel expensive and dangerous. But the Armistice did not bring a restoration of prewar conditions. New legal measures and an increasingly hostile attitude toward immigrants ensured that previous migration patterns would not resume. The breakup of the great inland European empires such as Austria-Hungary into smaller nation-states made for more borders to cross and the postwar states were much less willing to allow this, requiring passports and visas, as had largely not been the case before 1914. Immediately after the war, the US government enacted a series of temporary immigration restrictions, culminating in the Johnson-Reed Act of 1924, which both limited the total number of immigrants from Europe, and, through its system of national quotas, ensured that migrants from the eastern and southern regions of that continent, who had, as we've seen, made up the bulk of immigration in the four previous decades, would be unable to reach the United States. Immigration dropped off drastically and the proportion of Americans born in a foreign country declined steadily for the next forty-five years. Other New World destinations did not take up the slack—particularly in view of the widespread unemployment and economic decline following the Great Depression in 1929—so that the age of the great trans-Atlantic migrations was at an end. There was one brief and curious revival in the 1950s, when 330,000 people, mostly from Italy, moved to Venezuela between 1950 and 1958, as exploitation of oil reserves brought an economic boom. The overthrow of that country's military government in the latter year brought a more anti-immigration regime to power, terminating this exceptional interlude.[9]

The immediate effects of the First World War and its aftermath were less pronounced in East and South Asia, which saw little fighting and no breakup of large empires. Migration rates were even higher in the 1920s than before 1914. With the onset of the Great Depression, and the associated collapse in demand for and prices of the products of plantations and mines, new migrations ceased. Previous migrants to Southeast Asia returned to India and China, especially after riots by indigenous workers, attacking immigrant competition. The decline in migration was very long-lasting; Asian migration rates would only exceed their 1920s levels in the 1990s.[10]

If the postwar years saw the termination of the previous migration patterns, and began a decades-long great decline in migration rates, they also marked the beginning of a new form of mass movement across international borders and within individual countries—coerced, not voluntary, generally one-way and not reversible, and affecting people of all ages and sexes, not simply concentrated among young men. This was the movement of refugees—people fleeing war, civil war, political, ethnic, racial, or religious persecution. Refugees appeared from the very beginning of the First World War. Some 75,000, for instance, poured into the Austro-Hungarian imperial capital of Vienna in the war's first months, as the Russians overran the Habsburgs' eastern province of Galicia. One hundred and forty thousand Serbs fled Austro-Hungarian armies advancing into their country; about 240,000 Armenians took refuge in Russia from the authorities of the Ottoman Empire, who were trying to kill them, with the enthusiastic assistance of the Turkish population. Probably the most people displaced were in Russia itself. By 1917, there may have been as many as seven million civilians uprooted by the war. The war's end brought new streams of refugees fleeing the Russian Civil War, 1.6 million, scattered from Shanghai to Paris. Following the 1919–22 war between Greece and Turkey, brought on by Greek efforts to seize portions of the former Ottoman Empire, another 1.6 million became refugees, a quarter of them Muslims expelled from Greece and the rest Orthodox Christians deported from Turkey, these deportations partially organized and definitely legitimated by the peace settlement ending the war.[11]

As these examples suggest, the first massive movements of refugees in the Age of Total War were located primarily in Central and Eastern Europe, and in the neighboring regions of the Near East, where territory had changed hands frequently, as compared to the much more static trench warfare on the Western Front, and where the postwar upheavals, resulting from the destruction of the defeated powers—the German, Austro-Hungarian, Russian, and Ottoman Empires—were much greater than anywhere else in the world.

Refugees generated by the Second World War and its aftermath would be some fifty to one hundred times those from 1914–18, and would be found all over Eurasia. That war, particularly as it was fought on the Eastern Front in Europe, was one in which the murder, enslavement, and expulsion of civilians was a central war aim. Nazi plans for a racial reorganization of the European continent, emphasizing mass murder, also featured deportations of Poles and resettling of ethnic Germans by the millions. The defeat of the Third Reich in 1945 created massive upheaval. There were the "displaced persons" or DPs, concentration camp survivors (the best known but by far the smallest group of DPs); slave laborers deported, mostly from Eastern Europe, to work in German war industry; POWs from Poland and the USSR—those who survived their captivity, anyway—and former collaborators with the German occupiers, especially from Ukraine and the Baltic lands, who had fled the post-1943 advances of the Red Army, along with the *Wehrmacht*. There were probably as many Soviet citizens displaced within the USSR—who had fled the German invasion, been evacuated by the authorities, or deported as potentially disloyal—as there were outside the Soviet Union's territories.

The defeat of the Third Reich created refugees, but so did the victory of its opponents. Twelve to fourteen million ethnic Germans were expelled, mostly from Czechoslovakia and pre-1939 Poland, as well as the additional territories in Eastern Germany granted the Poles by the war's victorious powers at their 1945 Yalta Conference. There were also smaller groups of Germans expelled from Hungary, Yugoslavia, and Romania. These expulsions, as the victorious powers proclaimed in their Potsdam Conference of 1945, were to proceed in "orderly and humane" fashion. They were anything but, characterized by wild panicky flight, internment before expulsion, assault, rape, and murder. Arriving in a defeated and devastated rump Germany, where the occupying powers were having a hard time feeding the indigenous inhabitants, who were not particularly friendly toward the refugees, the survivors of the mass expulsion (as many as two million may have died on the way) faced, to put it mildly, an uncertain future. There were "smaller" expulsions related to the war's outcome—although only smaller when compared to the expulsion of the Germans: Poles from those parts of eastern Ukraine that had been in pre-1939 Poland, but were annexed by the USSR; Hungarians from Transylvania; and Italians from Dalmatia, previously ruled by Mussolini's fascist Italy, after 1945 part of Yugoslavia. All in all, there may have been as many as sixty million refugees and displaced persons in Europe, including all of the USSR, in the summer of 1945.[12]

Chaotic as the situation was in Europe, it was worse in Asia. About 5.7 million Japanese civilians, who had settled in the Japanese empire in Korea, Manchuria, or the South Pacific, had to return to the Japanese islands following the destruction of that empire at war's end, often in violent and chaotic conditions, not unlike those surrounding the expulsion of the Germans from Eastern Europe. The number of Japanese refugees created by the rise and fall of the Japanese Empire pales in comparison to what that empire had wrought in China. By 1945, China had been at war with Japan which had occupied the eastern two-thirds of the country, for fourteen years. The Chinese government and its armed forces had retreated to the southwest, followed by countless civilians, who fled from the invaders, and their habit of murdering civilians, as they showed in 1937 in Nanjing. Measures the government took to stop the invasion, like the destruction of the dikes on the Yellow River in 1938, which caused disastrous flooding killing hundreds of thousands of people and submerging immense amounts of farmland, also produced countless refugees. Estimates of the number of people forced from their homes in China range as high as ninety million.[13]

Far from terminating the creation of refugees, the end of the war led to still more, a result of the war's undermining of European colonial empires.

The world's greatest empire, Britain's, shrank, as its colonial subjects demanded independence and the mother country, bankrupted by its wartime expenditures, could no longer afford to garrison and rule a restive population. While much of the empire survived into the 1960s, the 1947 decolonization of India and Palestine resulted in millions more refugees. This was a consequence of partition, the division of one colonial territory into sovereign states. Partition was supposed to be a way to avoid conflict, by separating mutually hostile groups, Moslems and Hindus or Sikhs, or Arabs and Jews, who, placed together in a sovereign self-governing state—as opposed to a colony governed by a foreign, imperial power—would have fought a civil war. The realities of partition showed the fallacy of the approach. The new lines did not actually separate the two hostile groups. Sir Cyril Radcliffe, the British official who devised the borders between the future India and Pakistan, had never been to South Asia before. He knew little about the area, which has earned him more than his share of opprobrium, including a savage condemnation by W. H. Auden, in his poem "Partition": "Shut up in a lonely mansion, with police night and day/ Patrolling the gardens to keep the assassins away,/ He got down to work, to the task of settling the fate Of millions." Using out-of-date maps and faulty census returns, Radcliffe and his line divided a continent, "for better or worse," and then he returned to England, "where he could quickly forget/The case, as a good lawyer must."[14]

Radcliffe may not have had much prior knowledge or experience of the region, but he did consult closely with leading politicians from the Congress Party, future rulers of India, and the Muslim League, future rulers of Pakistan. Both heavily influenced his decisions and were happy to let him take the blame for their outcome. But no matter how knowledgeable, no one could have drawn up dividing lines cleanly separating Muslims from Hindus and Sikhs, especially in the two partitioned provinces of Punjab and Bengal.

Although supposedly designed to separate hostile groups, the partition plans made explicit the assumption that they would not accomplish this. In the 1947 UN partition plan for Palestine, almost half the population of the "Jewish" state was to be Arabs. As many as one hundred million Muslims would remain in post-partition India and, in fact, the leaders of the new, Muslim state of Pakistan wanted them there, because they did not believe that their country had the economic capacity to absorb them. On a somewhat lesser scale, this was true of India as well. Its political leaders expected that the ten million Hindus living in the eastern portion of the province of Bengal would continue to reside there after it had become part of Pakistan.

Partition plans were a mass of contradictory expectations: peoples so hostile to each other that they needed to be placed in separate states, except that the states would not actually separate them. It is no surprise that the effects of partition were the opposite of what was intended. The rumor of it alone led to panic and orchestrated violence. In India, the massacres in Punjab were systematically organized by politicians, with the connivance of police and government officials. Often spearheaded by veterans of the Second World War, rioters robbed, sexually assaulted, and killed members of the future minority (Hindus in areas destined for Pakistan; Muslims in those assigned to India), rendering them homeless and forcing them to flee (sometimes after an intermezzo in a refugee or internment camp), and then attacked trains filled with refugees or immense walking columns of them. The years 1946–48 saw massacres throughout the Indian subcontinent, starting with the "Great Calcutta Killing" of 1946, and continuing through Bihar, Bengal, the Punjab, Delhi, and Sindh, among other places. The upshot was that in 1947 alone there were fifteen million refugees, about two-thirds from Punjab—with millions more following, especially in Bengal, during the early 1950s. These made up the largest and most violent coerced migration in human history, exceeding even the very large-scale expulsions of ethnic Germans from Eastern Europe, occurring at the same time.[15]

At least in South Asia, there was partial agreement between the leaders of the future partitioned states about their borders—excluding of course, disputed territory, such as Kashmir. In Palestine, the Arabs rejected the UN partition plan, and while the Jews formally accepted it, they planned to undermine it. Instead of partition, there was a war, in which each side expelled members of the other group in the territory it seized. While both sides went into the first Arab-Israeli war with intentions of expelling enemy civilians, the war ended with a clear Israeli victory, so it was Arabs who lost their homes. Three-quarters of a million Arabs were expelled or fled after their defeat, the *nakba*, or catastrophe, as the Palestinians now refer to it.[16]

Taking together, during the years 1945–50, all these refugees in Europe and Asia. along with a few other examples, like those fleeing the communist victory in the Chinese Civil War, gives a number on the order of 175 million people, about one person in thirteen on the planet. To be displaced, wrote the American aid worker Kathryn Hulme, after working with refugees in postwar Germany, had "become the accustomed ailment of the century."[17]

For most of those displaced following the end of the Second World War, their condition was not permanent. The tens of millions who had fled the war in China and the USSR, as well as most of the displaced persons in Western Europe, were able to make their way back home. There remained, the so-called last million, who could or would not return: Jews in DP camps in Germany and Austria who had no interest in being repatriated to Eastern Europe, where anti-Semitism had raged so fiercely, and other Eastern Europeans who would not go back to countries now under the control of communist regimes. By the early 1950s, however, most of these were resettled, outside of Europe—in the United States (which made a partial exception to its post-1924 hostility to immigrants for the refugees), Canada, Australia, and, for the Jews, Israel.[18]

But for thirty to thirty-five million people, there was no returning. The expelled Germans, contrary to what politicians told them for three decades after their expulsion, would not be going back to their one-time homes in Eastern and East-Central Europe. Theoretically, it was possible for refugees who were expelled or fled during the partition of India to return, and some tried to do so. All too often they found that their property had been seized and was under government administration, while their former dwellings were now occupied by refugees who had gone in the opposite direction. If anything, public policy, especially in India (far more Muslims wanted to return to India than Hindus or Sikhs to Pakistan), ran in the direction of creating more refugees. It was not just "evacuees" whose property could be placed in public custodianship, but, as the government described them, "intended evacuees," that is, Muslims regarded by the local authorities with suspicion. Individual Muslims who visited family members in Pakistan could be designated Pakistani citizens and refused re-entry into India. It was a vicious circle. If they wanted to dispute this decision in Indian courts, they needed to return to India, which would only be possible with the proper papers—namely, a passport issued by Pakistan—which was proof that they were no longer Indian citizens.[19]

Of all the victims of war and civil war between 1945 and 1950, the Palestinian Arabs have become the global symbol of the refugee condition. After the breakdown of the Lausanne peace talks between Israel and the Arab states in 1949—and one of the main reasons for the talks' failure was the Arab insistence on a return of all the refugees, as against Israeli willingness to take back one-seventh of them—the Palestinians have been permanently excluded from what was their homeland. Much like the situation in South Asia, their property has been seized and administered by the Israeli government (Israel developed a similar category to India's intended evacuees as well) and their dwellings occupied by other refugees—at first, displaced persons from Europe, but then, and in much larger numbers, Jews from Arab countries, whose property had been seized and whose departure from Yemen, Syria, Egypt, Iraq, Algeria, or Morocco was, to a greater or lesser extent, not entirely voluntary.[20]

Unlike the Germans expelled from Eastern Europe or the Muslims, Hindus and Sikhs of South Asia, the Palestinians became refugees without any refuge, since most of the Arab countries to which they fled, with the primary exception of Jordan, refused to recognize them as citizens and have been reluctant to integrate them. Seven decades later, the original refugees are mostly deceased, though today there are six times as many descendants, whose lives remain suspended in legal limbo. Palestinian themselves frequently rejected the designation as refugees; they were "returnees," who would soon be going back to their homes, or, increasingly, those of their ancestors.

One expression of their plight was what happened in Lebanon during the 1970s. Because of its own precarious balance among different religious groups, Lebanon had been the least welcoming of Arab countries toward the Palestinians, insisting that they live exclusively in UN-sponsored refugee camps, and even prohibiting the buildings in those camps from having zinc roofs, because that would have been a sign of permanent residence. In the political upheavals following the 1967 Arab-Israeli war, the Lebanese government permitted armed PLO units to administer the camp and to use them as bases for guerilla action against Israel—and, as it turned out, to intervene in Lebanese politics. Liberated and their commitment to return reaffirmed, the refugees ironically celebrated by building concrete houses, adding second stories to existing structures and topping them with zinc roofs—in other words, by accepting the permanence of their status as refugees and exiles.[21]

The number of refugees created in the five years following the Second World War exceeded the entire number of international migrants in the years 1880–1914. But these two massive population movements were deeply and fundamentally different. Obviously, refugees moved due to the use of force and threat of violence. Pre-1914 migrants generally did not face this sort of coercion, moving to improve prospects for themselves or, more commonly, their families. Unlike the peacetime migrants, a large majority of whom were single young men, wartime refugees represented a cross section of the expelled population. In fact, women, children, and the elderly were more likely to end up as refugees, since in many cases (China, the expelled Germans) young and often middle-aged men were in the army, POWs, or dead. Most migrants before 1914 were temporary sojourners, returning to the places of departure. While this was possible for some, maybe even most, of the post-1945 refugees, for tens of millions of them their flight was a one-way journey. Unlike pre-1914 migrants, who lived in a world of permeable borders without required documentation, the post-1945 refugees faced legal barriers to settlement, difficult to overcome, and long sojourns of quasi-internment in refugee camps. They were forced to leave but found it very difficult to arrive.

Particularly in a world in which migration had been in decline, the refugees stood out. They became the subject of international action. The newly created United Nations soon had a High Commission on Refugees, the UNHCR, founded in 1950, although it was preceded by other agencies—the International Refugee Organization, the United Nations Relief and Rehabilitation Agency, or the League of Nations High Commissioner for Refugees (who was just one individual, without any organization or staff to support him), the latter two predating the UN itself. The UNHCR has dealt with refugee problems ever since, expanding its ambit from Europe into Asia and Africa, often hampered in its activities by the way great power politics impinges on the UN. One exception to its rule is, again, the Palestinians, province of a separate UN agency, the United Nations Rehabilitation and Works Agency for Palestinian Refugees in the Middle East, or UNRWA. The UNHCR would act according to the 1951 Refugee Convention, which defined refugees as people outside their native country because of "well-founded" fear of persecution for their race, religion, nationality, membership in a social group, or political opinion. The Convention established the principle of *non-refoulement*, recognizing refugees could not be sent back to the countries from which they were fleeing.[22]

In the half century following its founding, the UNHCR has had plenty to do. Large waves of refugees have followed the armed conflicts of the Cold War—in Korea, 1950–53; the Chinese government's suppression of rebellion in Tibet; anti-communist uprisings in 1950s Eastern Europe; decades of flight from the communist government of Cuba; the exodus of millions of "boat people," following the communist victories in South Vietnam and Cambodia in 1975; refugees fleeing the civil wars in Central America during the 1980s—in that latter case it was mostly US-backed anti-communist groups, who were creating the refugees, rather than the communists—and in the wake of the Soviet intervention in Afghanistan during that same decade. For a while, the Afghanistan conflict made Iran, of all places, the country harboring the most refugees in the world. Ironically, if the Cold War created refugees, so did its end: hundreds of thousands fleeing the civil war in the former Yugoslavia; millions of ethnic Russians who had resided in the non-Russian republics of the USSR, returning, often not entirely voluntarily, to Russia following the collapse of the Soviet Union. The end of the communist regime in Afghanistan led to decades of civil war and new foreign interventions, from Pakistan, Arab Islamists, and the United States and its allies, generating still more refugees, whose numbers have only expanded following the victory of the Taliban in 2021.

Ethnic and religious conflicts, sometimes interacting with the Cold War, sometimes not, have been another major generator of refugees. Millions of Bengalis fled East Pakistan at the beginning of the 1970s, following the Pakistani government's violent suppression of the movement for autonomy or independence there, but were able to return, relatively quickly, when the secessionist cause triumphed, with Indian military assistance, producing an independent Bangladesh. The Rohingyas, a Muslim minority group living in Burma (Myanmar), have not been so lucky; with broad popular support (something it did not enjoy on other issues), the long-term Burmese military dictatorship has been rejecting their claim to citizenship, claiming that they are Bengali immigrants, and forcing them to leave the country. The expulsion of Asians from Uganda in 1972 by the government of Idi Amin, then newly come to power via a military coup, was a boost to his regime's popularity. There was the additional element of the elimination of members of an ethnically and racially alien middleman minority, and the seizure of their property. In the last two decades of the twentieth century, Africa became the global center of the refugee condition. Millions fled war and civil war in Ethiopia and Somalia; civil war and rebellion in South Sudan and Darfur; large-scale ethnic violence and mass murder in Rwanda and Burundi; and the civil war in Congo, which followed in the mid-1990s directly on the events in Rwanda. While today most of these refugee issues continue to plague Africa, millions more refugees have fled the Middle East, in the wake of the 2003 US invasion of Iraq and the civil war in Syria, following the Arab Spring of 2011.[23]

This is a disheartening picture to an observer, to say nothing of how Somalis, who have been living for decades in refugee camps in Kenya, feel about their situation. It certainly seems to confirm Kathryn Hulme's statement that refugees are "the accustomed ailment of the century." Yet the spectacle of the continued suffering of refugees, and the wars, civil wars, and blatant violations of elementary human rights that create them, should not blind us to the fact that the number of refugees has declined dramatically since the chaos in the aftermath of the Second World War. In the decade of the 1990s, a period of upheaval in the aftermath of the Cold War, there were about one-quarter as many refugees; instead of one person in thirteen being a refugee, somewhat less than one in a hundred were. Horrible as the plight of refugees has been and still is, they were not the group at the center of migration during the second half of the twentieth century, as they had been in the Age of Total War. Developments had created entirely new migration patterns and entirely new volumes of migration.

Recasting Migration in the Age of Upheaval

The new definition of refugees created by the 1951 Refugee Convention solidified their status as the most common kind of global migrant. In regard to other forms of international migration, the subsequent decade saw the continuation and sometimes the enhancement of the interwar era of legal barriers and restrictions. The xenophobic communist regimes that came to power in much of Eurasia, exactly at the same time that the postwar number of refugees reached its global peak, were very reluctant to allow their citizens to leave—and certainly not in order to travel to foreign, capitalist powers. This made legal departure from China and Eastern Europe, two of the major sources of earlier emigration, impossible. The one place where people could depart the Eastern Bloc during the 1950s was communist East Germany. About two and three-quarters million of its residents left for West Germany between 1949 and 1961—although, at least as far as West Germany was concerned, this was not technically migration, since the West German government did not recognize East Germany as a separate, foreign country.

Diplomatic nonrecognition aside, the building of the Berlin Wall in 1961 brought that possibility to an end.[24]

Even had these new communist regimes been willing to allow them to leave, emigrants would have had a hard time finding destinations. The major trans-Atlantic goal, the United States, continued its post-1924 course of drastic reduction of immigration. There were even reinforced efforts to root out immigrants already present. A prominent example was "Operation Wetback," the 1954 mass deportation of tens of thousands of Mexican citizens, living in the southwestern United States. Less well-known were efforts to deport Chinese Americans begun in the 1950s and even continuing into the following decade. From 1904 until the Second World War, all Chinese immigration into the United States had been barred, and although this absolute prohibition was lifted in 1943, as a gesture to a wartime ally, the immigration quota created then was absurdly tiny. Both before and after 1943, there were some limited exceptions to the ban on immigration for the immediate relatives of Chinese residents in the United States. It was an open secret that many of the beneficiaries of these exceptions were not actual direct relatives, but more distant family members, or people from the same village—"paper sons," they were called. The lack of any official registration of vital events—marriages and births—in China made this evasion of the law much easier. During the 1950s, the Immigration and Naturalization Service launched an investigation of the practice, claiming that it was being used to smuggle communist spies into the United States, gaining, with this accusation, the enthusiastic support of the strongly anti-communist FBI. Because a large majority of Americans of Chinese descent, and especially those admitted following the loosening of the immigration procedures during the Second World War, were anti-communists and supporters of the *Guomindang*, the Chinese communists' nationalist enemies, the whole justification was a thinly veiled pretext for reinforcing past practices of racial exclusion. In the end it was revealed that twenty-two thousand Chinese had come to the country illegally—an impressive number, since there were only some two hundred thousand Americans of Chinese descent living in the United States at the time. The program was only terminated in 1966.[25]

Against this backdrop of continuation and even reinforcement of the migration patterns (or lack of them) of the Age of Total War, some new tendencies did make a very modest appearance in the 1950s. The most important was intra-imperial migration, the movement of dark-skinned colonial subjects to their European mother countries. A reason this could occur was that the politicians and civil servants running the world's two largest colonial empires, the British and the French, were trying to ensure their survival in a world of mounting anti-imperialist sentiment, which they planned to do by bringing colonies and mother countries together in some kind of federation, one key feature of which would be freedom of movement within it.[26]

The "New Commonwealth" (i.e., colonies with a nonwhite population) immigrants to Great Britain stood out, in some ways, because even after the Second World War the United Kingdom continued its long history as a country of net emigration, one with more emigrants than immigrants each year, a state of affairs that would only end in the 1990s. Prominent among these immigrants were West Indians, initially recruited by London Transport to work on the city's buses and the tube, perhaps because the Britons who had previously taken those sorts of jobs had left for Australia. By 1958, there were eight thousand West Indians employed by London Transport. The Jamaican ticket taker had become the public face of mass transit, and the core of a West Indian community that attracted the hostility of young, white working-class Londoners. The upshot was the Notting Hill race riots of 1958, when "Teddy Boys"—we might say today teenage gang members, wearing their gang colors, in this case black and white, early twentieth-century Edwardian outfits—attacked West Indians living in that north London neighborhood.

Although those riots were precursors to racialized clashes between native-born inhabitants and immigrant groups, the number of the New Commonwealth immigrants in this early period was not huge. There were 218,000 in the United Kingdom in 1950, their number growing to 541,000 in 1961, an increase of 330,000, which was about the same as net immigration from Ireland—a very old supplier of labor to Great Britain—at around the same time. Adding to the Irish, the 82,000 "European Volunteer Workers" recruited from Eastern European DPs in Great Britain's "Westward Ho!" labor supply program in the aftermath of the Second World War, makes it clear that while newer groups of migrants of African or Asian descent may have been more visible in 1950s London, they were still outnumbered by migrants from more familiar European sources.[27]

Because of its long-term low birth rate, France had been a net importer of labor since the late nineteenth century. This continued after the Second World War and included French colonial subjects—or citizens of the *Union Française* as they were officially called—from North and West Africa. While Algerians among these migrants did clash with the police, and often very violently, particularly in the course of the Algerian rebellion against French colonial rule from 1956 to 1962, Notting Hill-style race riots were not a feature of French life. This allowed French intellectuals to assert that, unlike circumstances in Anglo-Saxon countries, their one and indivisible republic knew no racial differences. The future would undermine this assertion, but through the 1960s the actual number of such immigrants was relatively small. In Paris, center of migration in France, there were 13,500 sub-Saharan Africans in 1946 and only 15,200 in 1962. A rise in birth rates after the Second World War made immigration seem less necessary for the labor market, and most immigrants who did arrive came from southern European countries—Italy, Spain, and, especially, Portugal.[28] Ironically, British and

French colonial subjects would only start moving in larger numbers to Britain and France after their countries had gained independence, so that they were no longer colonial subjects and the rules on migration were rather stricter than they had been in the 1950s.

Overall, the new elements of migration in the 1950s were very much outweighed by continuities with circumstances in the Age of Total War. For that reason, the changes in migration patterns, practices, and regulations in the Age of Upheaval in the 1960s and 1970s were particularly upsetting and unsettling. They were also irreversible; after they occurred there would be no return to the world of limited and restricted migration, although there would be those who would call for it.

One central reason for the upheaval in global migration patterns was the development of the labor market. In view of the rapid postwar economic growth, there had been a very substantial and steadily rising demand for labor in the more affluent regions and countries of Northern Europe. Through the 1950s, this demand had been supplied primarily by wartime refugees and migrants from rural areas (as the number of farms and farmers steadily shrank with the increasing mechanization of agriculture), or through long-term arrangements with neighboring countries—between Ireland and Great Britain, for instance, or Finland and Sweden. By the early 1960s, these sources were running out, unemployment rates were tending toward zero, and an actual labor shortage was growing, not seen since before 1914. The shortage was particularly acute at the lower end of the workforce: in industry, especially coal mining, steelmaking, auto manufacturing, or metallurgy; and in construction and in some service-sector branches, particularly restaurants and hotels.

The response was to recruit labor from farther afield. In the organized and state-regulated world of post-1945 capitalism, this recruitment was frequently arranged by the government, such as the West German Federal Employment Agency, which recruited migrant workers or *Gastarbeiter* ("guest workers"), and the French National Office of Immigration and similar agencies in the Benelux countries. Some large businesses did their own recruiting. Renault, the French auto manufacturer, was known for hiring Africans to work in its factories in the Paris metropolitan area. As the 1960s progressed, individual migrants began to try their luck, coming on tourist visas, finding work, and counting on the authorities to tolerate them, or even to legalize their situation retrospectively. By the early 1970s, as many as 80 percent of migrants to France were arriving in this way and meeting with surprisingly little resistance, a demonstration of the considerable difference between that era and the early twenty-first century.

The main direction of this labor migration was from the Mediterranean Basin to countries of Northern Europe. Migrants came from Portugal, Spain, Southern Italy, Greece, and Croatia, from Algeria and Morocco, and from

Turkey. The migrants moved to Northern Italy, France, Germany, Austria, Switzerland, and the Benelux and Scandinavian countries. This was a largely unprecedented route and pattern. The recent refugees from civil war in Syria and Iraq who have been streaming into Europe are following migration routes first set out and organized in the 1960s.[29]

This recent wave of refugees has included a substantial number of sub-Saharan Africans or South Asians either pretending to be refugees or just joining the large refugee movements, and sub-Saharan and South Asian participation was also a development typical of what we might call the Great Trans-Mediterranean Migration of the 1960s. Paradoxically, as I've noted, sub-Saharan and South Asian migration, usually involving former colonial subjects moving to their former mother countries, occurred after the colonies had gained their independence, and the free movement of the colonial era was replaced with considerably greater restrictions. For example, from 1964 onward, the residents of the former French colonies in West Africa, such as Senegal, Côte d'Ivoire, or Mali could only settle permanently in France if they had a labor contract arranged by a French business and the National Office of Immigration. Almost none of them had one, especially as the Immigration Office had no actual representatives south of the Sahara. West Africans could come to France with a tourist visa, if they provided a destination address. On their arrival at Orly Airport, south of Paris, they were met by customs officials who interrogated them, questioned their documents, and sent a high proportion of them back to Africa. Yet in spite of this treatment, the number of sub-Saharan Africans in France grew from fifteen thousand in the 1950s to forty thousand in the following decade. By the mid-1970s, according to official statistics (almost certainly an undercount), there were some 81,000 sub-Saharan Africans living in France, plus another 120,000 people of African descent who were citizens from the former colonies turned "overseas departments" in the West Indies.[30]

Not having quite the same rapid rate of economic growth or labor shortage as continental European countries, Great Britain had not been one of the receiving countries of the Trans-Mediterranean Migration, but as noted it did become the destination of former colonial subjects. The British government issued increasingly strict restrictions on their entry into the country, with a greater focus on Asians than Africans. The 1962 Commonwealth Immigration Act, while preserving the right of citizens of the predominantly white former colonies, Canada, Australia, and New Zealand, to move to Great Britain, stripped that right from people of the "New Commonwealth" countries—that is, citizens of the newly independent, predominantly nonwhite colonies in Africa and Asia. And yet, somehow, in spite of this very evident attempt to eliminate immigration, reinforced with additional legislation in 1968, the number of people of "New Commonwealth" origin in the United Kingdom went from 541,000 in 1961 to 1.2 million ten years later.[31]

A few simple figures will give an idea of the suddenness and size of this migratory surge. In 1950, in seven northern European countries, there were about 5 million foreigners resident (not including colonial subjects). A decade later, the number was 6.875 million; by 1974, it had reached 13 million. By the mid-1970s, as a proportion of the population, immigrants ranged from a low of 2 percent in the Netherlands to 16 percent in Switzerland. But this statistic considerably underestimates the role of the 1960s immigrants, in the labor force—twice as great a proportion as in the population. In 1973, immigrants made up a remarkable 30 percent of the labor force in Switzerland, 10 percent in France, and 12 percent in West Germany. That latter figure had increased almost eightfold in thirteen years, since migrants were just 1.5 percent of the West German labor force in 1960.[32] The year 1973 was the very highpoint of the Great Trans-Mediterranean Migration. The first oil price-shock of that year, and the subsequent worldwide recession, marked the end of the long postwar- boom and with it, the need for additional labor. The fifteen-year period of large-scale labor recruitment, which had already come in for considerable criticism in the early 1970s, was terminated; northern European countries closed their borders to new migrants and began seeking ways to send back home the ones already present.

However, the same surge in oil prices that brought to an end the buoyant economic growth in Europe and with it the need for migrant labor to fill jobs, particularly at the low end of the labor market, created a great demand for labor in the lightly populated, oil-rich countries between the Persian Gulf and the Red Sea. These countries already had attracted a number of postwar migrants, mostly from the Arab world: Palestinians, as particularly excluded refugees, and inhabitants of poorer countries, such as Egypt or Yemen. In the 1970s, the migrant labor force exploded, from 660,000 at the beginning of the decade to six million by the end—slightly less than half the number of Trans-Mediterranean Migrants of the previous decade, but in countries whose populations were one-tenth or less than those of Northern Europe. Migrant laborers came to make up to 80 percent of the entire labor force of countries such as Kuwait, the United Arab Emirates, or Oman. Unfortunately, the government of Saudi Arabia, the largest and most influential of Gulf oil countries, either did not collect such statistics or has not released them, but there, as in the smaller Gulf states, immigrants were omnipresent in higher-end administrative and engineering positions, on construction sites or working in schools, hospitals, hotels, air- and seaports.

Not only were there more migrant laborers in the Gulf oil countries during the 1970s, they came, increasingly, from very different parts of the world, particularly South Asian countries, Pakistan, India, and Bangladesh. By 1980, these constituted a third of the migrant workers in the Persian Gulf region. A celebrated example is the south Indian state of Kerala, whose inhabitants make up about 3 percent of India's population, but between one-third and one-half of all the Indians working in the Persian Gulf region. The Muslim minority in Kerala was particularly well represented among these labor migrants, but Hindus and Christians—the latter a substantial minority in Kerala—were streaming to the oil lands by the tens of thousands as well. At the beginning of the 1980s, Christian pastors had taken to saying that many of their flock were neglecting the Heavenly Kingdom in favor of the Gulf Kingdoms.[33]

Most were men under the age of twenty-five. The migrations across the Mediterranean to Northern Europe and across the Indian Ocean to the oil states were strongly reminiscent of a nineteenth-century world in that respect. The migrants were mainly male, and their stays were generally short term and characterized by substantial fluctuations. Between 1966 and 1972, for instance, 2.89 million foreigners, mostly from Mediterranean countries, moved to West Germany to work, but over those same seven years, 1.85 million left the country. Returnees were 64 percent of arrivals—a return rate reminiscent of pre-1914 transatlantic migrants.[34]

Both sensibilities and political circumstances changed in the intervening six decades and treatment of the Trans-Mediterranean Migrants in Northern Europe came in for sharp criticism. They were exploited and mistreated by their employers and landlords, forced to work at the worst jobs for the lowest pay and live in barracks, slum housing or even cardboard shacks, the so-called *bidonvilles* on the outskirts of Paris. Migrants were the victims of constant harassment by the authorities and repeated racist insults by the media, and a hostile general public—an attitude summed up in the phrase invented in German speaking Switzerland, *Überfremdung*, difficult to translate into English, perhaps best rendered as "swamped by foreigners." None of these assertions is false, but the Trans-Mediterranean Migrants were also covered by labor-protection laws and eligible for social welfare benefits; trade unions accepted and even recruited them as members and they were paid according to collective bargaining contracts, admittedly, generally at lower levels of the wage scales. If they had residence permits, which some did not, they were legally entitled to remain in their country of migration and change jobs at will—a legal point sometimes not mentioned to them by employers and local government officials.

Labor migrants in the countries of the Persian Gulf enjoyed no such entitlements. Their passports were confiscated; they could be expelled on a moment's notice, particularly, as was often the case, if they had smuggled themselves into the area, by pretending to be pilgrims on the *Hajj* to Mecca, but going on to work illegally. Often recruited by labor brokers, or brought in by smugglers, they owed to whomever had arranged their trip extortionary sums and could not change jobs until they had repaid their debts. Unions were nonexistent, and to the extent that labor-protection legislation and social welfare systems existed in the Gulf states, or were in the process of formation, they were reserved for the small citizen minority of the labor force.³⁵

As this comparison shows, while economic developments created the need for migrants streaming across the Mediterranean Sea and the Indian Ocean, legal regulations and cultural attitudes were crucial for their reception in the countries of immigration. The other major changes in migration during the 1960s and 1970s were almost entirely the result of political and cultural changes, generally not driven by economic issues such as labor shortages. The results of this were not immediately apparent, but would fundamentally transform population movements around and across the Pacific.

Both new legal regulations and cultural attitudes were encapsulated in legislation passed in the three major destination lands of trans-Pacific migration, the United States, Canada, and Australia during the 1960s and 1970s. After a long period of welcoming migration in the nineteenth century, all three countries had taken measures to limit and restrict immigration—we've seen the 1924 American Johnson-Reed Act. Frankly racist motivations were of course at the center of these decisions, which excluded Asians and Southern and Eastern Europeans. To the extent that immigration was to be allowed at all, as in Australia under its so-called white Australia policy, it was to come from Northern Europe, especially the British Isles. By the 1950s, Australia was running out of Anglo-Saxons and had to settle, somewhat reluctantly, for immigrants from Eastern and Southern Europe. Like the United States, they were still dead set against Asians.

Three legal measures—the 1965 revision to US immigration law known as the Hart-Cellar Act; the 1976 Canadian Immigration Act; and the 1973 declaration of the new Labour Party government, rejecting a "white Australia" policy, completely transformed the regulatory basis of immigration. In place of preference given to individuals of a specific national or racial origin, immigrants were to be admitted on the basis of universally applicable criteria: job skills and financial assets, but also family relationship to residents. This immigration system has undergone smaller changes and amendments but remains the basis for the regulation of immigration to these three countries to the present day.

What impelled these legal measures? Unlike in Northern Europe and the Persian Gulf oil states, these momentous changes in migration were not driven by economic considerations. There was no labor shortage, no zero unemployment rate. Rather, they were the result of profound changes in mentalities. They repealed past race-based restrictions, aimed primarily at Asians, but at Eastern and Southern Europeans as well, a distinct repudiation of racism, the result of new attitudes developing since 1945 and especially in the decade of the 1960s. The new legal measures are best understood as symbolic gestures, a rejection of past attitudes. There was no expectation that they would lead to dramatic changes either in the number of immigrants or in their places of origin, since the widespread assumption was that the era of large-scale, uncoerced trans-oceanic population movements had come to an end in the 1920s and would never resume.[36]

A New Global Migration Order in the Late Millennium

The last two decades of the millennium would show just how incorrect these expectations were. Labor migration to the oil countries of the Middle East both expanded and was increasingly dominated by people traveling ever longer distances to reach them. While the great trans-Mediterranean migrations of the 1960s to Northern Europe never resumed, the number of people from the Mediterranean Basin, Africa, and Asia living in northern European countries steadily increased, developing into large ethnic enclaves, often at odds with the indigenous population. Countries with a long history of net emigration, including Italy, Spain, Portugal, and Great Britain, saw, for the first time in modern history, their migration balances reverse, becoming home to steadily growing numbers of immigrants, in spite of a thicket of formal and informal measures to keep them out. Migration across the Pacific Ocean and the Caribbean Sea, made possible by the legal changes of the 1960s and 1970s, attained unprecedented heights. Distinctions between involuntary refugees, forced to flee by threats and coercion, and voluntary migrants, seeking to improve their lot in the world, became blurred. Although there has been some dispute about the global numbers of migrants, there is no doubt that their cultural impact has risen and that their economic influence, through the remittances they send home, has become steadily a larger and more considerable part of the global economy.

NORTHERN EUROPE: FROM LABOR MIGRANT, TO WHAT EXACTLY?

I remember a conversation in a Munich tavern at the beginning of 1988, during which my interlocutor, by no means a racist or bigot, began a statement with, "Those *Gastarbeiter*, or whatever you call them nowadays . . ." His remark pointed to a social transformation that had occurred throughout Northern Europe. Those "guest workers" were temporary migrant, whose presence in the labor market was to be determined by economic conditions, which was very much the way migration had proceeded before the First World War, and was also the way it had worked in the 1960s. It ebbed and flowed, depending on economic circumstances. There was a large outflux of migrant labor from Germany during its 1967 recession, for instance; a half million left, against 178,000 arriving. Yet, although the labor recruitment programs had been terminated, preventing new workers from arriving, or at least making their arrival illegal, and the job market had been persistently less buoyant for a decade and a half, those guests had not left. They were now permanent residents—still culturally distinct, certainly not German, but something else entirely.

Geographers have a phrase for what happened: "demographic normalization." In the 1960s, the migrants were as we've seen predominantly younger men, either single or working in foreign countries while their families stayed home. By the 1980s, they had been joined by their family members, or had married women from their native countries, brought them to Northern Europe and had children with them there. This development was an unintended result of the post-1973 legal situation. Recruitment of migrant laborers had been terminated, so that any migrant who returned to his native country—previously a common practice—would not be able, at least legally, to come back to Northern Europe, a region, which, in spite of the oil price shocks and the worldwide recessions of 1974 and 1982, was still more prosperous than the Mediterranean Basin. But if no longer recruiting new workers, northern European countries were not expelling the old ones; migrants possessing residence permits could stay, indefinitely, and bring their family members to join them. This is exactly what they did. It was the halfway policies of the European countries receiving migrants—to put it more diplomatically, their increasing respect for human rights—that made this situation possible.

While in most European countries, there was a decline in foreign-born populations following 1973, Sweden, which had the most liberal regulations on bringing in families and dependents, was an exception. By the end of the decade and through the 1980s more foreigners were entering northern European countries than leaving them. By 1989 the total foreign-born population of those countries was higher than its 1973 levels: generally, modest increases of 10–15 percent, so much less than in the 1960s, although in the Netherlands the number of resident foreigners grew by half between 1975 and 1989.[37]

There was a transition from a group of immigrants mostly young, single, and male to a more even balance of ages, sexes, and marital status. During the 1960s and 1970s, Migrants to Northern Europe had been workers: they were much more likely to be in the labor force than the locals. By the end of the century, this situation was reversed. Economic growth had slowed; many jobs for unskilled workers had vanished. This was a development particularly hard on foreign migrants, who generally had less education and difficulties speaking the local language. Migrants were more likely to be unemployed. In 1990s France, their unemployment rates ranged from 20 to 24 percent, twice that of native-born French people. By 2000, this discrepancy existed in every single European country: foreigners or the foreign-born had unemployment rates that ranged up to more than twice as high as native-born inhabitants. Foreigners were not just more likely to be unemployed; they were usually less likely to be in the labor force at all.[38] The image of the migrant had shifted from bus ticket taker, street sweeper, assembly line worker, construction laborer, or hotel housekeeper, to welfare recipient, drug dealer, street vendor—generally of stolen or counterfeit goods—or purse-snatcher.

As migrant communities consolidated, they came to live in very distinct neighborhoods: for instance, West Berlin's Turkish quarter, Kreuzberg, a corner of the city with old tenements that had survived Second World War bombing, right up against the Berlin Wall; or northern Paris suburbs like St. Denis, whose 1960s-era public housing came to be inhabited by immigrants from Algeria or Mali. Whole cities became increasingly characterized by their migrant population, such as the one-time English textile town of Bradford, now commonly called "Bradfordistan." It was a distinct irony of historical development that job seekers and their descendants should be increasingly clustered in declining industrial cities, whose steel, textile, and shipbuilding plants or coal mines had closed down, where few jobs were to be found: the Rust Belt cities of Northern France, Walloonia in Belgium, or Germany's Ruhr Basin; the dying textile towns and ports of the English Midlands or Yorkshire, the Swedish port city of Malmö.

The combination of a bad public image, ghettoization, and declining connections to the labor force was both toxic and self-reinforcing. Already under-skilled and so having difficulties in the job market, migrants and, even more, their descendants found that assumptions about them made them targets for the police, and hampered their efforts to upgrade their skills or to look for employment. Discrimination against migrants in the workplace was open and blatant. All these problems were exacerbated by one particular feature of most migrant populations, namely their religion. Muslims, who made up a majority of the immigrant population just about everywhere in Europe, attracted greater hostility from the indigenous inhabitants than non-Muslim migrants. This was apparent in the experiences of South Asian Hindus and Sikhs versus South Asian Muslims in the United Kingdom, between Turks and Spaniards, Greeks, Italians or Croatians in Germany, or between North and West Africans and Portuguese in France. Islamism, combining strict Muslim piety with religiously based political radicalism, on the rise during the 1990s, found recruits among Muslim migrants to Northern Europe, for whom being a holy warrior was a welcome alternative to being a scapegoat. This is very much *not* to say that all, or even most, immigrants or most Islamic immigrants in Northern Europe were unemployed, unskilled, petty criminals, or *jihadis*, but it is to note the changes in an immigrant population that had turned a group of mostly temporary migrant laborers into a permanent population within a quarter century.[39]

MIGRANTS IN THE GULF KINGDOMS AT THE END OF THE MILLENNIUM

This transformation did not occur in the Persian Gulf, mainly because the governments there would not allow it to. Migrants have remained what they were in the 1970s: relatively short-term sojourners, without political or workplace rights. Their numbers have fluctuated with oil prices, although showing a long-term upward trend. The proportion of South Asians among the migrants has risen gradually over time, while that of Arabs has declined.[40]

There was one particular moment when the otherwise gradual switch from Arab to Asian migrant workers in the Gulf Kingdoms jumped, and that was as a result of the 1990 Iraqi invasion of Kuwait. Following the elimination of the Iraqi occupation, after Iraq's defeat in the Gulf War, the government of Kuwait proceeded to expel all the Palestinians residing in Kuwait. About four hundred thousand people were forced to leave, the vast majority for Jordan, and most of the rest to the Israeli-occupied West Bank and Gaza. The restored Kuwaiti authorities, strongly supported by the indigenous Kuwaitis and their militia groups, accused the Palestinians of having collaborated with the Iraqi occupiers. While some Palestinians in Kuwait may have cooperated with the invading Iraqis, far more fled the invasion. Kuwaiti Palestinians were taking the blame for the excessive enthusiasm shown for Saddam Hussein by Palestinians in the Occupied Territories, Jordan, Egypt, and Syria. There was a similar story with citizens of Yemen, one of the few countries to endorse Saddam's aggression. Yemeni citizens working in Saudi Arabia, Kuwait and other Gulf countries—as many as eight hundred thousand—were also expelled.

The expelled Arabs were replaced by fresh labor from Asia, and not just from Pakistan, India, and Bangladesh. Hundreds of thousands of workers were recruited in Indonesia and the Philippines. There were a growing number of women among them—a new element, when compared to the 1970s—working as domestic servants and providers of sexual services.[41]

At about the same time as the expulsions from the Gulf countries, a quite similar development occurred in a very different Middle Eastern country, Israel, resulting in yet another setback for the unfortunate Palestinians. Following the Israeli conquest of the Gaza Strip and the West Bank of the Jordan River in the 1967 Arab-Israeli War, the Palestinian inhabitants of those regions had gradually been integrated into the Israeli labor market, so that by the end of the 1980s they made up about one worker in twelve of the Israeli labor force, generally at its menial end, as with the trans-Mediterranean migrants in Northern Europe or the South Asians in the Gulf. Then the *Intifada*, the 1990s Palestinian uprising against the Israeli occupation, stemming from the same political motives that led Palestinians to endorse Saddam Hussein's invasion of Kuwait, caused a change in Israeli labor market policy (not unlike that of postwar Kuwait). The change was subtler, since there was no expulsion, no dramatic turnabout as had been the case in the Gulf States, but over the course of the decade, about half the Palestinians working in Israel were replaced with migrants from far overseas, especially Thailand, the Philippines, and Romania. With the failure of the Israeli—Palestinian negotiations in 1999–2000 and the *Intifada*, the Palestinians ended up with the worst of all worlds: no state of their own and no jobs in Israel, or in the oil lands of the Persian Gulf.[42]

This change illustrates the accelerated pace of globalization at the end of the millennium. Long-distance labor migration was very definitely not new, but it had once tended to reflect the drying-up of more localized pools of labor. By the 1990s, labor was recruited from thousands of miles away, not because there was a lack of local migrants, but because these migrants were regarded as culturally alien and politically dangerous. Similarly hostile perceptions of migrants certainly were prevalent in Northern Europe, or in the United States, Australia, and Canada, but for a number of reasons—greater political stability, the more pervasive rule of law, and the often-tortuous path of legal and bureaucratic procedures—they did not translate into the same sort of mass expulsions as happened in the Middle East.

ACROSS THE PACIFIC, CARIBBEAN, AND THE SONORAN DESERT

The generally unintended and unexpected consequences of the changes in immigration law, starting with the US Hart-Cellar Immigration Act of 1965 and culminating with the Canadian immigration law of 1976, reverberated ever more strongly in the Americas and in countries bordering the Pacific Ocean. In the Late Millennium Era, these regions experienced a transformation in migration patterns, and social structures affected by them, that can only be called revolutionary.

One of the more peculiar features of the earlier restrictive immigration regime in the United States was its isolationist intensity. Laws prohibited not merely some but all Asian immigration into the United States, and the quota system reduced legal migration from Southern and Eastern Europe to the merest trickle. The Immigration and Naturalization Service, customs officials, and the border patrol were all focused on keeping out racially undesirable immigrants coming across the Atlantic or the Pacific. But there were no quotas at all on immigration from any of the countries of the Western Hemisphere. The two-thousand-mile-long US-Mexican land border was, at best, very lightly patrolled. The result was a largely free flow of labor from Northern Mexico to neighboring areas in Texas, New Mexico, Arizona, and California, although groups of Mexican workers found their way as far north as Chicago. The legal status of these workers was indistinct: some legally recognized immigrants, some in temporary workers' programs—the so-called *braceros*—some with no legal basis to work or to reside in the United States. Regardless of their legal status, most labor migrants from Mexico did not settle permanently. They moved back and forth across the border, not unlike the case with most migrants in the Age of Mass Migration up to the First World War. During and after the Second World War, this overland migration from Central America was joined by a trans-Caribbean pathway that brought sugar-cane pickers from Jamaica to Florida, and unskilled labor from Puerto Rico or the Dominican Republic to northeastern US cities, such as Philadelphia and New York. These migrations, as well, were two-way movements.[43]

US public policy responses to migrants from Central America and the Caribbean were very mixed: encouraging in periods of low unemployment, such as the 1920s and, especially, the Second World War; roundups and deportations when jobs were scarce, such as during the Great Depression. Operation Wetback, the large-scale deportation of hundreds of thousands of Mexican laborers during the 1950s, which were prosperous years, might seem like an exception to this rule, but many of those deported returned to the United States almost immediately, with the open support of their employers, particularly big farmers, who needed their labor for the harvest.[44]

Just counting legal migrants, those from the Western Hemisphere made up as much as 40–50 percent of all immigrants to the United States through the two postwar decades. If there were reliable figures on all migrants, including those crossing the border illegally, that percentage would almost certainly have been higher.[45] The 1965 Immigration Act changed this situation in two ways. By giving priority in immigration to relatives of US citizens and permanent residents, it encouraged migrants to stay in the United States, to become permanent residents and citizens, so that they could bring in family members. Yet the law also created a yearly immigration quota—120,000 persons—for the countries of the Western Hemisphere, a restriction on legal immigration. By changing the past condition of legal ambiguity, the Immigration Act was both an inducement to immigration and a restriction of immigration. Above all, it was an invitation to cross the border illegally.

This was precisely what happened in the years that followed. Initially, migrants from Mexico continued to act as they had earlier in the century, moving back and forth between the United States and their homeland. As migrants' numbers increased, very visibly and at a time of rising unemployment, there was growing sentiment for "securing the border," and deporting "illegals." Politicians and the mass media, particularly although not exclusively those of a right-wing orientation, picked up on these sentiments and the border was made more "secure," by increasing the number of people patrolling it and putting up actual physical barriers, like the walls installed in the vicinity of San Diego begun in 1988 and steadily expanded over the following twenty years. This policy of exclusion, not unlike the one adopted in Northern Europe a few years previously, had the paradoxical result of increasing the number of Mexicans who became permanent, illegal residents of the United States. As it became more difficult to cross the border, labor migrants who had previously moved back and forth were far more likely to stay; as border regions of the US Southwest were more heavily patrolled, illegal migrants spread out across the country. And since the US-Mexican border is very long, passing through rough, lightly populated terrain, all the measures taken to secure it are ineffective. Instead, a human smuggling industry emerged, and professional smugglers known as coyotes brought people across the border. By the 1980s, migrants from Mexico were being joined by refugees from civil war in Central America, the communist regime in Cuba, and political upheaval in Haiti—although it was difficult to tell with these hundreds of thousands of refugees just how many really met the 1951 Refugee Convention's criteria of a "well-founded fear of persecution," and how many were joining Mexicans in seeking work. The result was that the number of immigrants living illegally in the United States went from 3.3 million at the beginning of the 1980s, to 8.4 million twenty years later.[46]

While Central Americans were pouring into the United States, a similarly large stream of migration across the Pacific Ocean was developing, bringing people from East, South, and Southeast Asia to North America and Australia. A basic precondition was the same removal of legal barriers to Asian immigration, which occurred in the United States, Canada, and Australia starting in 1965. There were also developments in Asia itself that encouraged emigration. The rapidly growing numbers of Filipinos in the United States were reminiscent of the British and French experience with former colonial subjects, who began to move to the one-time mother country after their native lands had gained independence from it. The victory of the communists in the Southeast Asian war led to a stream of refugees from Vietnam and Cambodia. Later, when the communist regimes developed a less hostile attitude toward the capitalist world, these resettled refugees, using the family reunification provisions of the Immigration Act, could then bring in family members.

However, the single most important development in terms of migration from and within Asia was the end of the Maoist regime in China, starting with the Great Helmsman's death in 1976. Gradually, key elements of Mao's rule, including rigid (and at times somewhat crazed) central planning and xenophobic hostility toward much of the world gave way to a very high-growth-rate economy, containing substantial market elements and a willingness to engage with foreign countries, particularly the United States. These changes unleashed an unprecedented wave of population movements. Peasants from the poorer provinces of central China moved in staggering numbers—perhaps as many as 150 million—to the booming cities of the coasts, to labor on construction sites and in factories. These migrants often came from the same regions that had sent so many laborers to Manchuria fifty to one hundred years earlier, and there were indeed many similarities, including seasonal population movements and return migration. The sheer number of migrants at the end of the century put the previous movement to Manchuria at its start in the shade. Unlike those earlier migrants, who were exclusively young men, these later internal migrants included large numbers of women, working as domestic servants and, especially, toiling in factories making consumer electronics, textiles, shoes, toys and a wide variety of other products of light manufacturing, while their male counterparts did construction work.

The same processes unleashing internal migration also produced a large rise in emigration. Some of it involved educated young people going abroad to study at universities in North America and deciding, for political or career-related reasons, not to return home. But most were migrants from the coastal regions of Southern China, doing what they had been doing for centuries— moving overseas. Now they were heading eastward across the Pacific to North America, or southward to Australia and New Zealand. Admittedly, compared to the population movements within China, the numbers of overseas migrants were relatively small, at most 10 percent of the internal migration, but to their destination countries their numbers seemed considerable.[47]

The priority granted family members in the new immigration regulations in the United States, Canada, and Australia certainly helped stimulate migration from Asia, just as they had from Central America to the United States. Skilled immigrants—particularly in Canada and Australia, less so in the United States—were given priority and this favored Asians, since migrants from there, quite unlike their Latin American counterparts, tended to be disproportionately well-educated and were far more likely to have managerial or professional occupations. In a study done in 2004, forty years after the less restrictive policies were in place, almost half of Asian-born Americans held such jobs, as against less than one-eighth of US residents born in Latin America.[48]

As was the case with Central Americans, not all immigration from Asia followed proper legal channels. Of course, crossing an ocean border was more difficult than entering a country overland. There were stories about Chinese immigrants hiding in cargo holds of freighters. The most common method of illegal entry, however, was more prosaic: arriving on a tourist visa and simply not going back. This sort of migration had a distinct class component, mainly involving the less-educated population of coastal Southern China.[49]

Figure 5.1 summarizes the results of all these changes, giving the number of legally registered immigrants per decade in the three major trans-Pacific destinations—the United States, Canada, and Australia. These figures leave

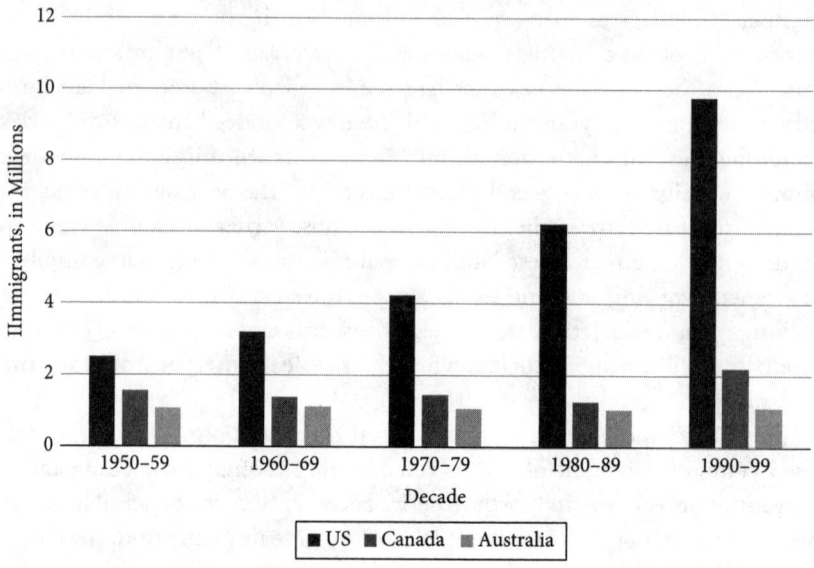

FIGURE 5.1 Immigration to Three Major Trans-Pacific Destinations, 1950–1999

out illegal immigrants and do not take into account people leaving as well as arriving.

The increase in immigrants to the United States is particularly striking, starting in the 1970s and accelerating. The number of immigrants in the 1990s, 9.78 million, set a new record. In Canada, immigration doubled, also reaching an all-time high. Immigration to Australia would increase after 2000, when the number of migrants jumped about 2.5 times.[50] Altogether, during this three-decade-long period, something like twenty-eight million immigrants were registered as moving; if we add to them the eight million or so illegal immigrants living in the United States, this adds up to about the same number of people who moved to the Americas at the high point of the great Trans-Atlantic Migrations at the start of the century.

But the late-century movements were precisely not trans-Atlantic. At the time of the 1965 Immigration Act, roughly a third of immigrants to the United States came from Europe, while only one-seventh came from Asia. By the new millennium, the proportions were reversed. Since the total number of immigrants had grown fourfold, there were actually more Europeans coming to the United States at the end of the old millennium than in the 1960s, but by then they were very heavily outnumbered by new arrivals from Asian countries.[51] About half of all immigrants to the United States during the second half of the twentieth century came from countries in the Americas. Although the number of migrants to Canada and Australia did not show the same immense growth as was the case with the United States, the changes in their national origins were pronounced. At the beginning of the 1960s, 90 percent of Canada's immigrants came from Europe; after the millennium, just 11 percent. Most non-European migrants came from the Asia-Pacific region, especially China, India, the Philippines, and Pakistan. Through the 1960s, "white Australia" was very white, with just 4 percent of immigrants from Asian countries in 1968; by 2007 immigrants from Asia outnumbered Europeans about 2 to 1.[52] There was one feature of these trans-Pacific, trans-Caribbean, and trans-Sonoran migrations that made them quite different from former trans-Mediterranean migrants. Their unemployment rates were very close to or only slightly above those of the native-born population. Migrants to North America or Australia—to say nothing of Chinese peasants moving to coastal industrial cities—had come to work and were generally successful in finding employment.[53]

By the end of the twentieth century, trans-Atlantic migrations had given way to trans-Pacific ones; population movements within Asia now favored the coastal, urban, and industrial regions of China, rather than Manchuria or Southeast Asia. The total number of migrants was at least as great as in the decades before the First World War, in many areas larger, although not always as a proportion of the population.

MIGRATION FRENZY

By the end of the 1990s, the world seemed to be in a migration frenzy. People streamed from Asia and Latin America across the Pacific, the Caribbean, and the Sonoran Desert into North America, both following proper legal procedures and ignoring them, at an ever-faster pace and in ever greater numbers. The oil countries of the Persian Gulf recruited more migrant laborers and from ever farther away. The end of communism in Eurasia meant millions of Russians returning to their native land from areas in Europe and Asia that had become independent countries—some of which, as a result of the history of the USSR, rather hostile to Russians. As noted, the end of Mao-style communism in China led to internal migrations on a scale never before seen in human history. Northern European countries, still adjusting to the fact that their one-time transitory, migrant laborers from the Mediterranean Basin were now permanent ethnic minorities, faced a wave of refugees, and immigrants posing as them, from the civil war in the former Yugoslavia and, increasingly, from the Middle East and Africa. Countries such as the United Kingdom, Spain, Portugal, and Italy, which had been, for centuries, lands of emigration—of people leaving for other places—became receivers of millions of immigrants from some of the former communist countries of Eastern Europe as well as from Latin America, Asia, and Africa. Immigrants to the lands of the Iberian Peninsula were coming from those countries' former colonies, not unlike circumstances in

England, France, or the United States, in the postwar years. Added to all these longer-distance population movements were more regionalized ones, of workers from poorer countries to their more affluent neighbors: among others, from Mali and Senegal to Côte d'Ivoire, from Burma and Indonesia to Thailand, Malaysia or Singapore, from the Philippines to Hong Kong or Singapore, from Paraguay and Bolivia to Argentina or Brazil, from Haiti to the Dominican Republic, from Syria to Lebanon, and from New Zealand to Australia. Some of these migrations had been going on for decades, even centuries; some had only become border crossing as the result of specific political changes, such the transformation of the colonies of French West Africa into independent, separate, sovereign states, making workers from Mali or Senegal on the plantations of the Ivory Coast international migrants. Still others, like the tens of thousands of Filipinas working as domestic servants in the two major Southeast Asian cities, came later. While it is difficult to provide long-term figures for them, it does appear that these sorts of migrations were also involving more people and taking place at a more rapid rate. None of this came to an end in 2000; the migration frenzy continued into the new millennium, at least until the global economic crisis of 2008, and often beyond it.[54]

The effect on the global financial system was considerable. These masses of migrants were moving rivers of money around the world. Total remittances tripled, going from some $40 billion in 1988 to $120 billion in 2000. Generally, and not surprisingly, this money flowed from wealthier countries to poorer ones, amounting to three times official foreign aid. Migrants did not make much use of banks, so the exact extent of remittances is difficult to ascertain. Their funds mostly traveled by a number of informal routes: carried by hand, or sent through the mail, handled by "ethnic stores," immigrant small businessmen, who had connections in both countries—probably the most common way—or via the *hawala* system, a casually organized network of currency transfer agents, which after 9/11 developed a reputation for helping to finance terrorism. For a much steeper fee, between 8 and 12 percent, migrants could send their remittances with greater security via currency exchange firms, such as Western Union. The world's leading money transfer business, with 170,000 agents worldwide, handling about a quarter of the total global remittance traffic, the company had successfully made the transition from an obsolete technology, the telegraph, to a newer one, electronic funds transfer, providing services to a steadily growing population of migrants.[55]

There was, and remains, one exception to this global trend, a country that has resolutely refused to go along with the rest of the world on immigration. In this respect, as so many others, Japan charts its own, very distinct path.

During the years of the great mass migration leading up to the First World War, Japan was a country of emigration. Japanese departed their native islands for trans-Pacific destinations in the Americas, until exclusionary legislation kept Japanese out. For two decades after 1925, emigrants changed destinations, to areas in Japan's short-lived Asian and Pacific Empire and, more briefly, after the Second World War to South America, especially Brazil—altogether, perhaps three-quarters of a million people. By the mid-1950s, the era of emigration had come to an end and was followed by an age in which few people moved to or from Japan. In 2000, there were approximately 1.5 million foreigners resident in Japan, barely over 1 percent of Japan's inhabitants, a fraction that of the affluent countries of Western Europe and even smaller than that of the classic emigrant destinations, Canada, the United States, and Australia. Of that 1 percent in Japan, about half were the so-called "old-comers," in Japanese *ōrudokamā*, primarily Koreans, former Japanese colonial subjects, many of whom had been brought to Japan during the Second World War as slave laborers, as well as their descendants who had not become Japanese citizens. Labor needs in the rapidly expanding postwar Japanese economy were largely met by members of the rural population, not unlike the case in Northern Europe, although this phase of economic development continued in Japan for far longer.

By the 1980s, rural sources of labor were drying up and labor shortages were developing, especially in the era of the so-called bubble economy late in the decade. Even then, nothing much happened. The number of people legally entering Japan for employment purposes, did rise, from the low twenty thousands in the middle of the 1970s to about one hundred thousand by the end of the century—a derisory number in a country of 124 million. As many as three-quarters of these migrants were, according to official records, "entertainers," which is to say sex-workers, primarily from the Philippines, often brought into the country by the *Yakuza*, Japanese organized-crime syndicates, frequently via Filipino middle-men (or -women), to work as "hostesses," masseuses, strippers, and prostitutes.

While these entertainers may have been meeting some labor needs, they were not much help with the "three-k" jobs, *kitani*, *kitsuis*, and *kiken*—in English, the three "d's," dirty demanding, and dangerous—in construction and with small industrial firms that did not offer the generous pay, benefits, employment guarantees, and good working conditions prevalent in Japan's large conglomerates. There were ways around official immigration restrictions, like bringing in "trainees"—almost fifty thousand yearly—conveniently exempt from minimum wage and labor-protection legislation. A quarter-million foreigners at the time had arrived on tourist visas and overstayed. They were mostly from poorer countries in South and East Asia, including China, Indonesia, South Korea, Thailand, Bangladesh, and the Philippines, as well as, somewhat oddly, Iran. Regular gatherings of Iranians at Ueno and Yoyogi Parks in Tokyo at the beginning of the 1990s, looking for work as day laborers, gathering for conversation and recreation on Sundays, generated an enormous panic. Japanese citizens expressed fears of being raped, robbed, or murdered by these foreigners; sensational reports appeared in the press and on TV news; and right-wing nationalist groups attacked the gatherings. Eventually, the police intervened, officially to protect the parks' azalea bushes in danger of being trampled by Iranians. This was part of a broader pattern in which the police searched, for, rounded up, arrested and detained illegal immigrants—a practice hardly unknown in other countries, although generally pursued with more vigor and less attention to legal niceties in Japan than elsewhere, especially in view of the very small numbers of foreigners actually present in the country.[56]

Among the more recent migrants, the *nyūkamā* or "newcomers," the only ones explicitly recruited and welcomed into Japan were the *nikkeijin*—Japanese who had emigrated to South America, especially to Brazil, and their descendants. In a country reluctant to embrace immigration, they seemed like an ideal choice—not immigrants but natives returning home. Hardly any were resident in Japan in the middle of the 1980s, for example, but there were a quarter-million of them by 2000. Most were temporary sojourners, who would move back and forth between Japan and Brazil. Some, though, began sending for their families and settling in for a longer stay.[57]

The whole program was based on a fundamental misunderstanding: the *nikkeijin* may have looked like Japanese—for the *mestiço* minority among them, at least partly Japanese—but they were culturally Brazilian. Their Japanese-language abilities tended to be modest at best. Even worse was their behavior outside of work: wearing casual clothing, even when at the bank or post office, talking loudly in Portuguese, and sauntering down the street in groups, rather than moving Japanese-style, which is to say individually, briskly, and with a distinct destination in mind. Some found these groups every bit as frightening as Iranians. Their more relaxed attitude seemed to rule at the workplace as well. Japanese foreman, team leaders, and ordinary workers were frustrated with their seemingly native coworkers, who were not willing to put in the same effort, or at least the show of it. (It did not help that many of the migrants were from educated or propertied backgrounds in Brazil, as was typical of Brazilians of Japanese descent, forced, by the economic difficulties Brazil faced during its so-called lost decades, to work as unskilled manual labor in Japan.) Far from being Japanese, the returners from South America were just another kind of *gaijin*, or foreigner. As one official at the Ministry of Labor told the Japanese American anthropologist Takeyuki Tsuda: "But those who actually came were not the type we expected . . . If we had known so many *nikkejin* would come, we would not have allowed them to freely enter Japan."[58]

None of this is entirely surprising in a country where stores, bathhouses, bars, and hotels were at the time plastered with signs refusing accommodation to foreigners, and whose TV, press, pulp literature, and the National

Police Agency constantly reminded the public about the dangers of foreign criminals. Japanese self-understanding as a racially, ethnically, and culturally homogeneous society distinct and separate from the outside world has been a constant feature. This self-understanding does not mean that Japan was culturally isolationist. Quite the opposite, it coexists with products of foreign culture, like the great popularity of the distinctly American sport, baseball, in Japan, and its greatest star, the slugger Oh Sadaharu (with 868 career home runs) who was half Chinese, his father coming from Taiwan; or the many entertainers and athletes of Korean descent. Accepting large numbers of foreigners, who look and, even more, talk and act differently, seems to be more than the Japanese self-understanding can bear.[59]

Japan's labor shortages and recruitment of foreign labor were reminiscent of similar circumstances in Northern Europe. Brazilian immigrants to the United States, moving there at about the same time and for the same reasons as Brazilians in Japan, faced similar issues of adaptation to a different culture and developed similar feelings of nationalist self-assertion as a result. Popular fears and sensationalist media, in addition to legal measures restricting immigration and law enforcement efforts to round up and deport illegal aliens, are hardly a Japanese specialty.

What is distinct is the very different outcome of attitudes and policies in Japan—a country, fearing for its identity, refusing to accept large, or even modest numbers of immigrants. The most pronounced example concerns caregivers for the elderly. In Europe and in the classic emigration destinations in North America and the South Seas, this is an occupation, that has been taken up by an ever-increasing number of immigrants. Due to its low birth rate, Japan has one of the world's highest proportions of the elderly in the population; by the mid-twenty-first century, demographers project that close to three-eighths of its inhabitants will be over sixty-five. Under these circumstances, one might expect to see more immigrants. This is very largely not the case. A few nurses from the Philippines and Indonesia have been admitted, but mainly for a year or two at a time and are then sent home. Instead, public policy is moving in the direction of designing robots to care for the infirmed elderly.[60] If nothing else, this illuminates Japan's grim determination to prevent aliens from threatening its ethnic identity.

This idea of Japan as an exception to the worldwide rule of mass migration depends on the idea that other countries were experiencing an unprecedented mass migration at the end of the century. Not everyone agrees with this assertion. Skeptics point out that in the year 1900 approximately 3 percent of the world's population were international migrants, which is about the same proportion as in 2000. According to UN statistics, international migrants went from 2.6 percent of the global population in 1960, a year of purportedly low migration rates, to 3.3 percent fifty-five years later, at a time of supposedly much higher migration. In absolute numbers, this was a large increase, from

79 to 250 million people. However, since the world's population has grown from 3 to 7.3 billion in the interval, migrants continue to make up a very small proportion of the world population, and one that has grown only very modestly.[61] It all seems far from a flood of migrants or a frenzy of migration.

All these statistics ultimately stem from the estimates provided by the United Nations, in particular the Population Division of the Department of Economic and Social Affairs and the International Organization for Migration. These, in turn, derive, as is usually the case with UN statistics, from the figures collected by the UN from individual countries' own statistical services. And here the problem emerges, for these statistics, unlike many of the others the UN collects, have limitations.[62] One is that they only cover international migration, people moving permanently—or, at least for longer periods of time—between sovereign states. Great internal migrations, like the 150 million Chinese laborers who have moved from economically stagnant rural areas of the interior to rapidly growing coastal industrial cities, are not included.

The figures presented by the UN generally do not include migrants not officially recorded by national governments, "undocumented" or "illegal" migrants.[63] Exactly how many there are is unknown. Estimates for the United States, deriving from the difference between the census figures on the foreign-born and records on the number of green cards handed out, are, by global standards, pretty good, but even there very substantial discrepancies are possible. The sociologist and historian Xiaojian Zhao has argued that the census bureau count of 115,000 Chinese residing illegally in the United States in 2000, was only one-seventh the actual number—and this all in a country with relatively reliable record keeping, good opportunities for cross-checking different data sources, and a liberal migration policy. In Japan, with good records and strict immigration policies, there were at least as many people each year overstaying their tourist visas, as there were migrants legally admitted to work. In Thailand, a country whose rapid economic growth in the fifteen years before the Asian financial crisis of 1997 made it an ever more popular destination for migrants, without much government ability to regulate or control immigration, at least a million and a half of the migrants were undocumented; by 2005, in spite of amnesties and better registration procedures, probably over a third of all immigrants, 800,000 people, remained in that condition.[64]

While the exact number of illegal immigrants is unknown, it seems very likely to have been increasing, both absolutely and as a proportion of all immigrants—definitely above the First Age of Mass Migration, when there were few legal barriers to migration, and almost certainly over the quarter century following the Second World War. The transition from migrants as mostly male itinerant laborers to migrants as permanent settlers, with families and children—who may, or may not be citizens, depending on the laws in the country of immigration—has meant that in Europe and in the classic countries of immigration, the presence of migrants has increased well beyond the measure of the number of foreign-born residents, since the children of immigrants grow up in and are part of the immigrant community. While migrants may not have been any greater a proportion of the population in 2000 than in 1900, because of the fall of birth rates in most of the world during the twentieth century, migration had become a much larger proportion of the population increase. In the last few years, deaths outnumbered births in Europe, and it was only migration that prevented an actual population decline. Birth rates were higher in North America, but almost half—to be exact, 42 percent—of the total population increase in those years came from migration. This growing demographic weight of migration in the world's wealthier countries was a trend that had been unknown in the post-1945 decades.[65]

Two charts, each representing migration in a different country, demonstrate the increasing influence of migration on population, beginning in the 1970s. Figure 5.2 shows the proportion of the population of the United States, which, for over a century, has been the world's premier migration destination, who were immigrants.[66]

From the 1860 to 1920, immigrants made up 13–14 percent of the US population. The 1924 Johnson-Reed Act changed that situation and resulted in a four-decades-long decline in immigration. The ethnic makeup of America stabilized, and with it, class structure, closely related in America to ethnicity. By 1970, only about 5 percent of Americans were immigrants. By then, the Immigration Act of 1965 had already changed conditions, and

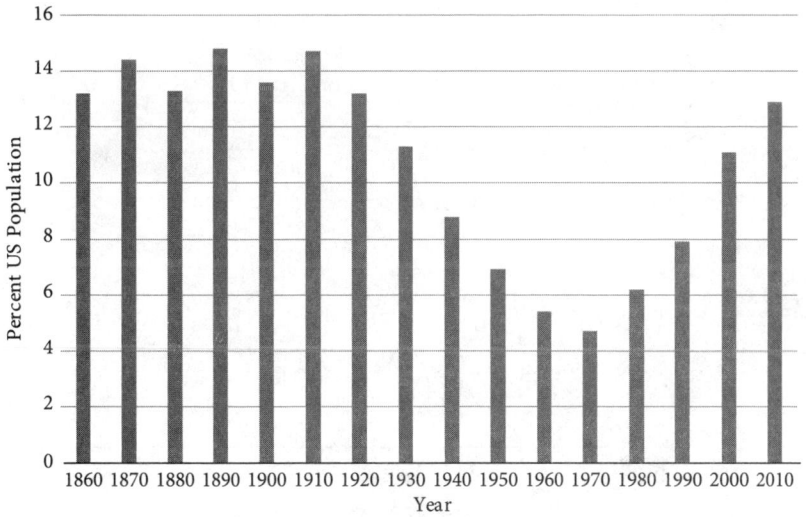

FIGURE 5.2 Immigrant Proportion of US Population, 1860–2010

over the subsequent four decades the number of immigrants reached new highs, so that by the early twenty-first century the proportion of the US population that were immigrants had returned to the levels of the years of the Great Migration. This flood of migrants alone was alarming to the native-born population. But the new immigrants came from very different regions than their trans-Atlantic predecessors—from Central America and Asia, with growing numbers from Africa and South America—making their presence more striking.

The second chart, Figure 5.3, pertains to Sweden, which had been a land of large-scale net emigration during the phase of the Age of Migration. The figures don't give the proportion of immigrants in the population, what demographers call the "stock" of immigrants, but the number of immigrants accepted into Sweden each year, the "flow" of immigrants, from 1950 to 2016.[67]

Sweden's condition as both a prosperous northern European country, and one with a generous policy about accepting refugees, is apparent. We see the wave of trans-Mediterranean migration to Northern Europe, reaching a highpoint in the early 1970s, the fall-off over the following decade followed by a renewed wave of immigration, mixing political refugees with more economically motivated immigrants, first from the former communist countries of Eastern Europe, peaking in the early 1990s at levels higher than had ever been seen before and then, after 2000, from Africa and the Middle East, growing to about four times the typical post-1950 figure.

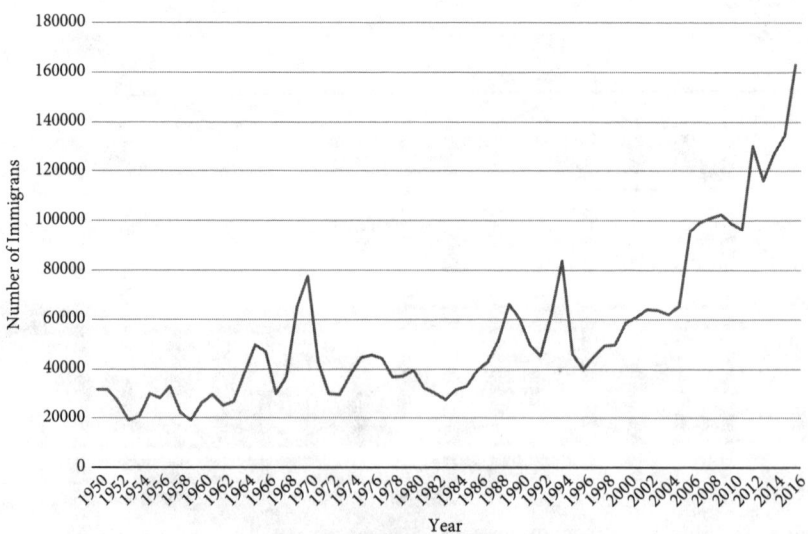

FIGURE 5.3 Immigration into Sweden, 1950–2016

Both these charts reflect a larger global reality. Following the end of the Great Migration in 1925/30, there was a pause of forty to fifty years in which migration became unusual, and exceptional—the result of war, civil war, or persecution, the refugee condition. But the 1960s and 1970s changed that, beginning a new wave of global migration—a wave that surged forward, especially in the 1990s, and has continued to rise into the twenty-first century. Encompassing far more people than the First Wave and a noticeably larger proportion of the world's population (to say nothing of the intervening period of lower migration rates), this new wave had a number of very distinct features. They involve new pathways of migration, replacing the formerly dominant routes across the Atlantic, the Bay of Bengal, and the South China Sea, with new ones across the Pacific, the Caribbean, the Mediterranean, the Indian Ocean, and the Red Sea, resulting in groups of migrants from new ethnic groups and national origins.

Because this new migration wave is occurring in a world of fortified boundaries, legal restrictions on crossing them, and increasingly elaborate paperwork in order to do so—quite unlike circumstances in the First Wave—the previous pattern of travel and return, has been replaced by a combination of more permanent change of country of residence and a steadily growing gray zone of illegal, semi-legal and quasi-legal international population movements. Along with the expansion of this realm of illegality and quasi-legality has gone a blurring of the distinction between refugee and migrant, which had once seemed so clear. Finally, declining birth rates have made the social and demographic impact on countries of immigration more pronounced than ever before.

In all these ways, long-distance population movements, across the borders of sovereign states and within them, temporary and permanent, became a defining feature of the Age of Interconnection and a shaping feature of the decades ahead.

6 | The Powers

THE AGE OF INTERCONNECTION began with the atomic bombing of Hiroshima and Nagasaki and ended with the terrorist assault on "Ground Zero" (a nuclear reference), the Twin Towers of the World Trade Center in New York. Between the era's bookends lay five decades of sporadic warfare, coming in a wide variety of forms and with an equally wide variety of combatants. The two most powerful states, the United States and the USSR, were directly involved in large-scale conflicts in Korea, Vietnam, and Afghanistan. There were five wars between the Arabs and the Israelis—in 1947, 1956, 1967, 1973, and 1982—and intervals between open war featured almost uninterrupted guerilla struggles, terrorist attacks, troop incursions, and air strikes. Anti-colonial uprisings escalated into warfare and civil war in Vietnam, Indonesia, Algeria, Angola, and Mozambique. The two large successor states of the British Empire in South Asia, India and Pakistan, went to war in 1947, 1965, 1971, and 1991. The Persian Gulf was the site of two wars: a protracted one between Iran and Iraq, lasting most of the 1980s; and a briefer sequel, pitting Iraq against most of the world, in 1991. Ethiopia and Somalia fought a war in the Horn of Africa from 1977 to 1978. To all these we can add two civil wars, in Yemen during the 1960s, in Nigeria between 1967 and 1970, and a combination civil war, ethnic cleansing, mass murder, proxy wars, and open interstate warfare in central Africa, particularly but not exclusively Rwanda and the Democratic Republic of the Congo, in the last five years of the century.

Yet all these conflicts—and the paragraph above offers a list that is far from complete—were overshadowed by the threat of a Third World War fought with nuclear or thermonuclear weapons. Its consequences would have ranged from, at best, hundreds of millions dead and a decades-long setback for human civilization, to, at worst, the extinction of all life on the planet. For about thirty-five years, this apocalyptic prospect was like a mushroom cloud hanging over international relations. Atomic arsenals multiplied in size one thousand-fold, while the individual weapons became fifty to one hundred times as powerful as the bombs that destroyed Nagasaki and Hiroshima in 1945. Delivery systems went from slow, easily trackable, propeller aircraft to supersonic, individually targeted, multiple-warhead ballistic missiles, counting fifteen to thirty minutes between launch and impact. The number of countries possessing atomic weapons rose but the number with the technological capacity to build these weapons was much larger. War plans, even for small-scale conflicts, included firing off atomic weapons; aggressive if peaceful diplomatic maneuvers, standard practice of powerful states since the end of the Napoleonic Wars, bore the risk of escalating to crisis level and from there to a proliferation of nuclear strikes; a false or falsely interpreted reading on a radar screen could have led to nuclear war by mistake—and was, in retrospect, the most likely way such a war could have occurred.

There is an alternative, diametrically opposed understanding of international relations in the second half of the twentieth century, first proposed by the historian John Gaddis. Far from being a period of wars, cold or otherwise, the post-1945 decades were the age of a "long peace."[1] Unlike the first half of the twentieth century, when the great powers squared off against each other in two devastating and all-encompassing wars—conflicts that coined the phrase Total War—the United States and the USSR, to say nothing of other nuclear-armed powers, including the United Kingdom, France, or China, consistently avoided such confrontations. The combination of continuity, statesmen remembering the Age of Total War and determined not to repeat it; and reluctance to unleash or to suffer the unprecedented destructive power of nuclear weapons, combined to produce an arena of international relations in which conflicts were more likely to be resolved through negotiations. There were lots of wars, but they were limited in scope and destructive power.

There is something to say for Gaddis's argument. Great power confrontations did not lead to a Third World War even more apocalyptic than the first two, which already ranked high on the apocalypse scale. The Cold War reached a very unexpectedly peaceful conclusion between 1989 and 1991. European colonial empires, the largest in human history—and even those of the smaller European nations, such as Portugal, the Netherlands, or Belgium were impressively large—were dismantled, sometimes with violence, more often in peaceful fashion. Total war deaths were one-tenth of the eighty million victims of the two world wars. In North America, Europe, and northern Asia, the post-1945 decades were much less haunted by armed conflicts than the preceding thirty years of the Age of Total War. The same cannot be said of the Middle East, southern Asia, Central America, or Africa, where much of the warfare of the years between 1945 and 2001 was concentrated, but the global picture of a strong contrast to the years 1914 to 1945 remains.

This added up to a distinct element of the Age of Interconnection: one of constant war and threat of more disastrous war, yet one in which war was either limited or avoided. Reconciling this paradox requires understanding that international relations in the years 1945 to 2001 were characterized by two structured conflicts playing out in both violent and peaceful fashion. One of these conflicts is obvious, the Cold War, pitting against each other two power blocs, two political and socioeconomic systems; two, as contemporaries said, "superpowers" (although "super" as their power was, they required allies and subordinates).[2] The other conflict is harder to grasp. A favored designation in the post-1945 decades was "anti-colonialism" or "anti-imperialism," although the struggle continued long after colonial empires had come to an end and imperialism was no longer so obvious. In recent decades, one term for it was the "North-South conflict," but this is problematic. India, China, the Middle East, and substantial portions of Africa and Latin America, purportedly part of the South, are in the Northern Hemisphere. The "global South" is mostly ocean.

A preferable, if perhaps a little ponderous, name, placing this clash in the broader context of world history, is the Global Realignment Struggle. At some point between 1550 and 1800—different historians give very different years—European countries along with their settler colonies became the most powerful and wealthy in the world, dominating and exploiting other regions of the world. The latter's riposte to that control swung into high gear after the Second World War, and has continued well past the end of colonial empires into the Postcolonial and Post-Imperial ages. Changing form, interacting with the Cold War, but continuing after its termination, this Global Realignment Struggle remains a structuring principle of international relations down to the present day.

Thinking about the Cold War

The defining feature of the Cold War, so apparent when it was ongoing that it seemed as if it would be a permanent feature of international relations, was that it was not merely a clash between powers, motivated by self-interest and raison d'état, but a broader struggle of opposed ideologies, political, and socioeconomic systems, even ways of life—two opposed visions of the world. The totalizing nature of the conflict created a force field that drew in other social and political struggles. Politicians on either side accused their rivals of being dupes or even agents of the enemy (a practice known in the United States, as McCarthyism, after its most determined proponent). Strife involving labor relations, racial conflicts, clashes between different tribal groups, even anxieties about changing gender roles—they were all attributed to the machinations of the Cold War.[3]

This was not totally unprecedented. The wars of the French Revolution and Napoleon had also been ideologically charged conflicts, during which a wide variety of struggles with an even wider variety of causes, from Haiti to Ireland to Poland, had become intertwined with the armed confrontations between France, at least purporting to represent new principles of political and social organization, and the other powers of Europe, claiming to represent the old regime. Both world wars, especially the second, had distinct elements of a struggle between opposing political systems and very different ways of life. During the early years of the Cold War the conflicting parties both understood and portrayed the struggle as a reprise of the Second World War. But conflict during the Cold War took other forms.

A nuclear confrontation remained, albeit menacingly, in the background, emerging three times as a palpable possibility: during the Korean War of 1950–53, during the crisis years 1958–62, and again, during the war scare of the early to mid-1980s. Both major Cold War protagonists were only too happy to wage proxy wars, enlisting client states or insurgent movements to fight on their behalf. Sometimes, as was the case in both southwestern and northeastern Africa during the 1970s and 1980s, each superpower had its own proxy or proxies fighting for it. The Soviets proved better at using proxies, only deploying their troops in brief, one-sided actions to retain the loyalty of their subordinate states in Eastern Europe. In Korea and Vietnam, the Soviets let their Asian allies do the fighting, costing these allies millions of lives and their territory devastated by American aerial bombardment. Over one hundred thousand American soldiers died in both wars combined, the United States spent hundreds of billions of dollars—two orders of magnitude more than Soviet expenditures on weapons and supplies for the communist forces—and, in the latter conflict, suffered a disastrous decline in its strategic and diplomatic position, to say nothing of its reputation.

The USSR spoiled its good proxy wars record by sending troops into Afghanistan in 1979. At the time, the intervention was seen as evidence of a Soviet bid for global supremacy in the wake of the US defeat in Vietnam, a daring thrust toward the Persian Gulf and its oil fields. Evidence that has become available following the end of the USSR has revealed almost the exact opposite: a hastily made and ill-considered decision, taken largely out of fear of appearing weak by abandoning a communist ally, and regretted almost from the moment it was taken.[4] Although not really at Vietnam levels— Soviet troop commitments in Afghanistan were about one-fifth the US ones in Vietnam, and combat deaths about one-fourth—the United States did try to turn the tables, and the Islamic warriors it supported with money and weapons made the ensuing conflict very difficult for the Soviets. There were unintended consequences, unpleasantly perceptible on September 11,

2001—"blowback," as it was put at the time. These occurred because the conflict in Afghanistan, like the other proxy wars, were arenas in which the Cold War intersected with the other major confrontation of international relations, the Global Realignment Struggle.

What was perhaps most interesting about the Cold War and what most distinguished it from the ideologically laden conflicts of the era of the French Revolution or the Age of Total War was that on the whole it did not involve actual warfare, or even diplomatic confrontations. Rather, it was fought in the realm of culture, sports, leisure, and consumer goods. There was a highbrow version of this conflict: Soviet ballet dancers Rudolf Nureyev and Mikhail Baryshnikov defecting—that is, acting like soldiers changing sides in wartime—to the West; the CIA funding *Encounter* magazine, a venue for erudite, left-of-center intellectuals; French philosophers, such as Jean-Paul Sartre and Maurice Merleau-Ponty, publicly propounding elaborate justifications for Stalin's policies; Pablo Picasso depicting US troops murdering women and children in Korea, or devising the dove that would be the symbol of the World Peace Council, an organization that called US nuclear weapons "warlike" and Soviet ones "peaceful." The real action lay in which countries from the competing power blocs could field the best soccer teams or win the most Olympic gold medals. Who could produce and distribute more luxurious kitchens or automobiles and televisions? Whose fashion lines were the most desirable, who dominated pop music, who produced the best movies and TV shows, spreading the sounds and images across the world, through radio and television broadcasts and, later, via cassettes and videotapes?[5] In the end, soft power proved to be the decisive arena of Cold War confrontation.

The Cold War, like the Second World War out of which it emerged, was a global conflict, yet its geographic focus expanded and contracted. At its beginning was the falling out among the anti-German coalition—and it took the horrors of the Nazi regime to impel three such different entities, the British Empire, the Soviet Union, and the United States, to ally against it—over the future of the European continent. As appropriate, the Cold War was first centered in Berlin. The airlift of 1948–49 was the first tangible manifestation of a new kind of conflict. During the (now-forgotten) Berlin Crisis of 1958–61, when President Kennedy mobilized the Army Reserves, nuclear war was a very real possibility. There were lots of Cold War confrontations outside of Europe in the postwar era and throughout them all—even in the Korean War or the Cuban Missile Crisis—Berlin remained a locus of strategic planning.

This Eurocentric confrontation gave way during the Age of Upheaval to a very different kind of Cold War. The supposedly temporary post-1945 division of the continent was seemingly rendered permanent by a series of diplomatic initiatives promoted by the governments of the Federal Republic of Germany (then West Germany) and the United States, culminating in the 1975 Helsinki Conference on Security and Cooperation and Europe. Contemporaries talked of détente, of an *Ostpolitik*, a West German foreign policy initiative aimed at improving relations with the communist lands of Eastern Europe. What happened instead was a movement toward Latin America, Asia, and Africa. The Vietnam War of 1965–1975—actually, the Southeast Asian War, since the war was fought in Laos and Cambodia, as well—is the best example. But there were civil wars in Central America and Southern Africa, with the two superpowers backing different parties. There was a conflict between a pro-Soviet Ethiopia and a pro-US Somalia in the Horn of Africa; or the overthrow, in 1973, of Salvador Allende's left-wing government in Chile—a prime example of political and social conflicts being sucked into a Cold War vortex. Capping the era was the Soviet intervention in Afghanistan.[6]

Many of these conflicts staggered on into the 1980s, but in that decade the final major arena of the Cold War was once again in Europe. The introduction of medium-range nuclear missiles that could reach western Europe from the USSR and vice versa was a last upward spiral of the nuclear arms race, once more bringing fears of an apocalyptic global war to the fore, sparking massive popular protests and taking relations between the two superpowers to their lowest ebb in two decades. The USSR's new leader, Mikhail Gorbachev, coming to power in 1985, launched a whole series of foreign policy initiatives around the globe aimed at creating a new basis for international relations—his "new thinking."[7] But it was in Europe that the fate of his initiatives was decided. The Cold War ended where it began, in Berlin, on the night of November 9, 1989, with the opening of the Berlin Wall—as contemporaries instantly recognized. From central Europe, around the world, and back to central Europe: this was the path of the Cold War.

If the Cold War was actually a war, a zero-sum game conflict, then its outcome was never really in doubt. Throughout the four decades of contention, the United States maintained a distinct military superiority in air and naval forces, which it could use to good effect, such as in the 1962 Cuban Missile Crisis. Its edge in nuclear weapons and their delivery systems meant that through the early 1960s, it could probably have won a nuclear war—admittedly, at a terrible cost. After an extensive and ruinously expensive arms buildup, the USSR reached parity in nuclear weapons with the United States in the 1970s, a state of affairs that promised little in the way of advantages.[8] (The same observation is true of the Warsaw Pact's edge in tanks and troops over NATO in Europe.) The United States, along with its wealthier allies in Western Europe and the Pacific, was persistently more affluent than the USSR and its Eastern Bloc subordinates, far better able to afford an extensive military establishment while simultaneously producing an ever-larger and ever-broader array of consumer goods. The advantage in cultural, athletic, and consumer goods competition was still greater. Eastern Bloc athletes, lavishly subsidized, carefully trained and heavily dosed with performance-enhancing drugs, could gain an edge in Olympic competition, but when it came to just about everything else Western superiority was manifest. Visitors from Eastern Bloc countries to the West were overwhelmed by the sheer variety and the immense amount of consumer goods. In 1971, future Soviet leader Mikhail Gorbachev, along with his wife, Raisa, a sociologist, got to visit Italy, rent a car, and drive around the country. After several days of taking notes, Raisa asked, as Gorbachev later recalled, "Misha, why do we live worse than they do?"[9]

This retrospective observation is at odds with the waves of Cold War panic that swept through the United States and other Western countries at regular intervals between the late 1940s and the mid-1980s. Whether the source of it was paranoia, misperception, manipulation by politicians seeking to stoke fears to gain office, self-interest of a Cold War military and civilian bureaucracy, or the economic special interests profiting from permanent mobilization—what President Eisenhower, in a celebrated phrase, dubbed the "military-industrial complex"—is another issue.[10] It was due to all of those things, but there were also other factors at play. One is that while the USSR may have been in a chronically weaker position, its leaders more often than not played their bad hand with considerable skill—imposing their rule in Eastern and Central Europe after 1945, in spite of their country having been devastated by the German invasion, exploiting the Global Realignment Struggle to their advantage, with very modest expenditure of their own resources, particularly, as noted earlier, via proxy struggles, letting the United States use its own immense resources to self-destructive ends, as happened in Southeast Asia. Contrasting the Soviets' skillful use of an inferior position was Americans' clumsy and inefficient deployment of their military and economic superiority, with some exceptions, such as the Marshall Plan. It would not be entirely unfair to say that the West in general and the United States in particular, triumphed in the Cold War in spite of its diplomatic and military policies, rather than because of them.

Another way to understand Western Cold War anxieties is to look at Map 6.1, showing the countries that could be counted as communist, with centrally planned, non-market economies and one-party political systems, over the years 1945 to 2000.

What becomes clear is the expansion of communist regimes in the wake of the Second World War. While communist regimes gained no further ground in Europe, additional communist governments began appearing: the first in Cuba, of course, although Asia and Africa, would prove more hospitable to communist regimes than Latin America. Also apparent was that in the postwar decades, communist regimes expanded—no country, having come under communist rule ever changed back. By 1980, the long-term trend might have seemed favorable to the communist side in the Cold War.

THE POWERS | 213

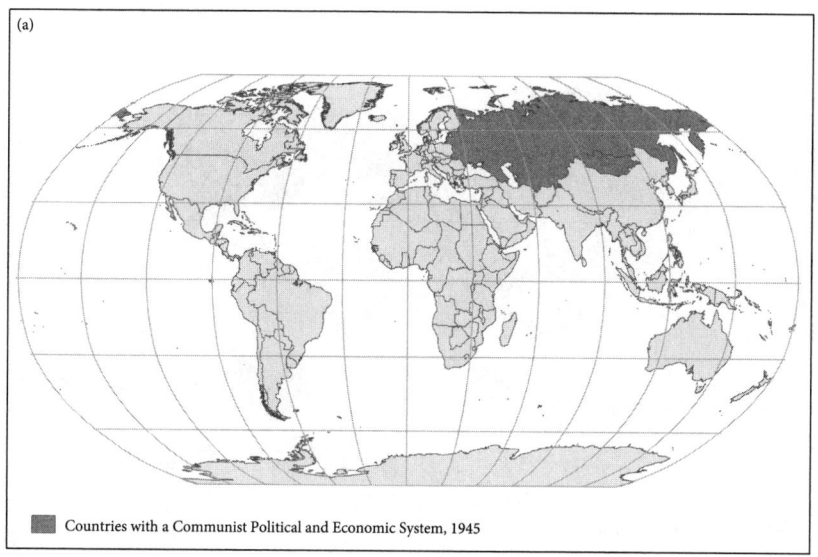

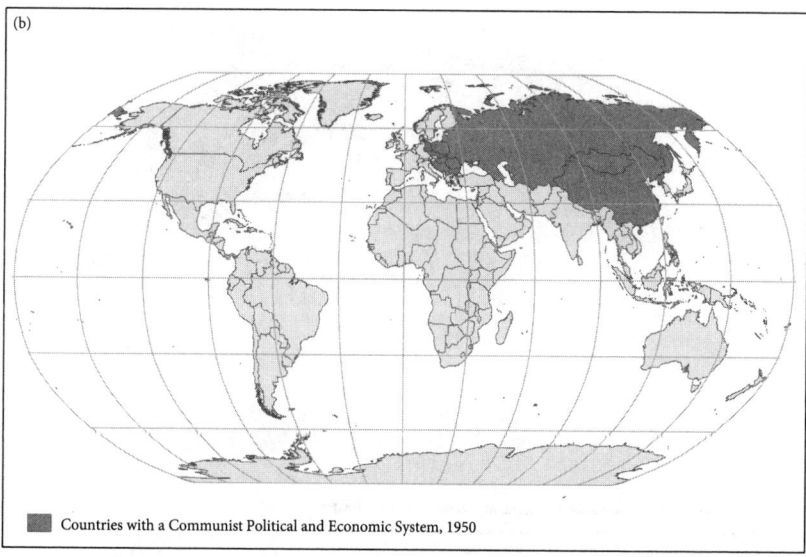

MAP 6.1 Countries under Communist Rule, 1945–2000

214 | INTERACTIONS

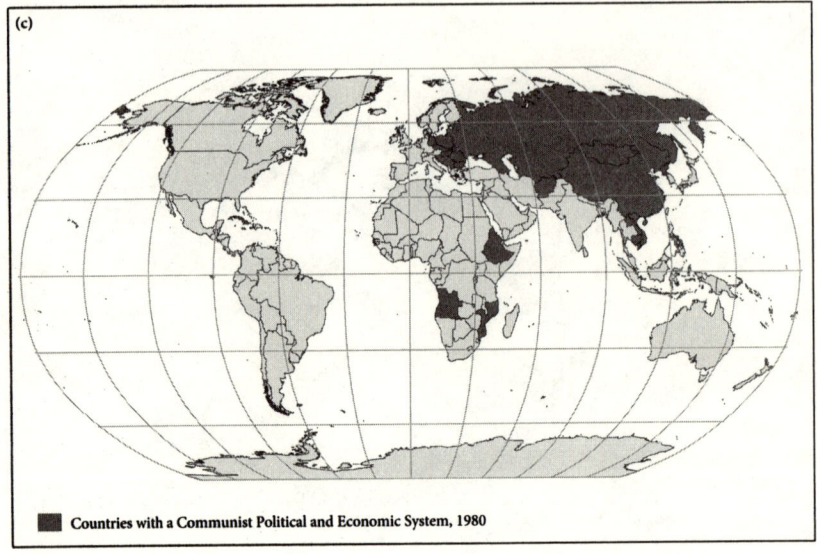

Countries with a Communist Political and Economic System, 1980

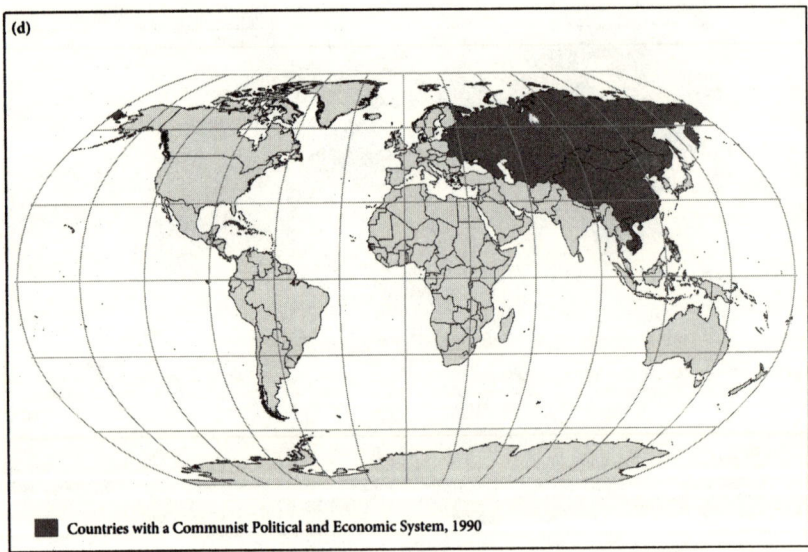

Countries with a Communist Political and Economic System, 1990

MAP 6.1 Continued

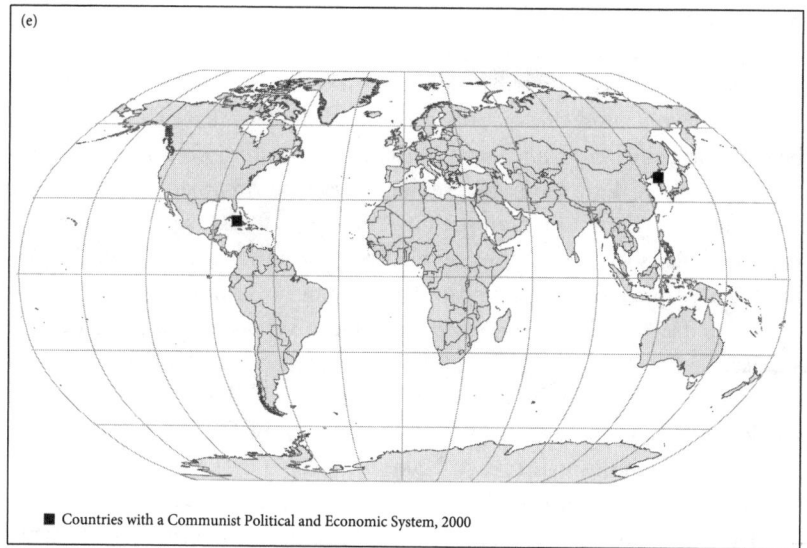

■ Countries with a Communist Political and Economic System, 2000

MAP 6.1 Continued

Later maps show a very different picture—the sudden and total termination of communist regimes in the last two decades of the century, leaving just a few remnants at the beginning of the new millennium. In 1980, however, this was a prospect nobody even imagined; a continuing expansion of communist regimes in Asia and Africa seemed much more plausible.

DUAL NATIONS IN THE COLD WAR

One of the strangest features of the Cold War oppositions was that certain nations consisted of both: the Federal Republic of Germany (West Germany) and the German Democratic Republic (East Germany); the People's Republic of China (Communist China) and the Republic of China (Nationalist China); the People's Democratic Republic of Korea (North Korea) and the Republic of Korea (South Korea); the Democratic Republic of Vietnam (North Vietnam) and the Republic of Vietnam (South Vietnam). The geographical designations are misleading. Officially and rhetorically, each side claimed to represent the entire nation, while denouncing the other as the tool of a foreign power. This played out quite differently in each of the four nations, but all of them show how the Cold War emerged from the Age of Total War.

In the Yalta and Potsdam Conferences of 1945, the Allies—the USSR, Great Britain, and the United States, agreed that defeated Germany would be divided up into zones of occupation, one for each of these powers plus France (largely by courtesy), and that the central administration would be located in Berlin, ultimately leading up to the creation of a new German national government that would sign a peace treaty ending the war. Yet within a few years the decision to treat defeated Germany as one country led to the creation of two states, one on the territory of the Soviet zone of occupation, the other in the occupation zones of the three Western powers. Berlin, now in the middle of East Germany, remained jointly occupied but any notion of the creation of a single national government, one that would sign a peace treaty had vanished. The Allies blamed each other for this outcome, a position loyally upheld by their respective German governments, each of which presented itself as the true conservator of the values of the nation and its policies.[11]

In this competition, West Germany had by far the more advantageous position. With almost four times the population of East Germany, an even greater edge in industrial capacity, and a much more popular major ally, it had an evidently more acceptable form of government. The contrast with East Germany was painfully revealed on June 17, 1953, when the government of the German Diplomatic Republic (GDR) was overthrown by worker strikes and demonstrations and only saved by the intervention of the Red Army. Unlike the citizens of other communist countries, East Germans could leave for a Western world of civil liberties and rapidly growing consumer bounty yet still technically be in their native land. Through the 1950s hundreds of thousands did each year. To counter this, East Germany had only one card to play and played it for all it was worth: its status as an "anti-fascist" regime, a government, economy, and society, run by one-time opponents of the Nazis, many of whom had spent the years 1933–45 in prison, concentration camps, or exile. East German officials highlighted the contrast between them and a West German *Bundeswehr* commanded by former *Wehrmacht* generals, a business community of one-time Krupp and IG Farben executives who had been central to the Nazi military-industrial-genocidal complex; and a head of government, Konrad Adenauer, himself with impeccable anti-Nazi credentials, but whose chief of staff, and close political confidant, Hans Globke, wrote the definitive commentary on the 1935 Nuremberg laws. This contrast between war histories would be typical of all the dual nations.[12]

The government of West Germany nonetheless pressed its advantage, trying to isolate, delegitimize, and undermine its East German rival. It refused to enter into diplomatic relations with any country recognizing the East German government and to prevent any delegation from that government to be recognized at any international gathering. Although at times in a precarious position, the communist regime did not collapse. By building a barrier around the French, British, and American sectors of Berlin in 1961, which it dubbed the "anti-fascist protective rampart," it created a symbol of the Cold War, one that cut off any possibility of leaving the country and ensuring its continued existence.

The East German regime fought hard against the efforts of its West German counterpart to isolate it in two ways. One was seeking relations with the newly independent countries of Africa and Asia, offering generous economic assistance, while emphasizing its profoundly anti-imperialist credentials. The other was in sports. In spite of West German efforts to assert that it represented the real Germany in international sports competition, East German teams had gained recognition as independent from the West, by 1957 in thirty-five different athletic disciplines. West German diplomats desperately tried to prevent the East German yachting team from having their picture taken with the British royal consort Prince Philip, or watched in frustration as the Crown Prince of Japan observed the East German wrestling team marching into the arena behind their national flag at a competition in Tokyo. The West was able to maintain a unified German Olympic team through 1964, but only at the price of having it compete behind the Olympic rather than a German flag, and using Beethoven's Ode to Joy at medal ceremonies instead of the national anthem.[13]

The center-left government that came to power in West Germany in 1969 changed course and decided that its goals could be better achieved by entente with the East than opposition to it. With its new *Ostpolitik*, or Eastern policy, it de facto recognized the GDR Republic, dropped opposition to its appearance in international organizations, and pressed for greater personal and media contacts between the two Germanys. The communist leadership of the GDR responded by trying to isolate their country still further, insisting that it was a separate nation, and so renouncing any nationalist aspirations to uniting the two German states. By the 1980s, this seemed like a permanent state of affairs. Yet via their televisions, East Germans were closely tuned in to life in West Germany. The East German government remained fixated on its Western counterpart, and communist leader Erich Honecker's great triumph came on his 1987 visit to West Germany, when he received the full honors due a sovereign head of state—"Erich's coronation," as East Berlin wits put it. When the communist regime in East Germany came to an end in 1989, the old claim that West Germany was Germany suddenly and unexpectedly came true. The two Germanys were not reunited; rather, the East agreed to join the West on the latter's terms.[14]

If in Germany the western state was the dominant power, the circumstances in China were just the opposite. There, the communists had the upper hand following their victory in the civil war of 1947–49, when they forced their nationalist opponents to flee to the island of Taiwan. The official communist description of this victory was and remains "liberation" from imperialist powers who had pushed China around for a century, and from a dictatorial Chinese regime that had never fought the Japanese occupier during the Second World War, and whose continued existence was dependent on the support of the imperialist United States. Actually, both the nationalists and the communists had spent the Second World War jockeying for position in China while the armed forces of other countries, including the United States and the Indian colonial troops of the British Empire, defeated Japan.

The nationalist government of Jiang Jieshi (or Chiang Kai-Shek, as he was known in an older transliteration) denounced the communists as agents of a foreign power, the USSR, and continued to proclaim its desire to "return to the mainland." With the support of the United States, which refused to recognize "Red China," the nationalist government in Taiwan was able to retain the Chinese seat on the UN Security Council and to pose internationally as the legitimate representative of the nation. This was not a position shared by US allies, such as Great Britain, which had an ambassador in Beijing, to say nothing of newly independent countries in Asia and Africa. The International Olympic Committee, in contrast to its attitude toward divided Germany, recognized the Beijing government as the Chinese one. Painful confrontations were avoided when Beijing refused to send athletes to the Olympic Games, preferring the 1963 Games of the New Emerging Forces, a short-lived Third World athletic festival.

American diplomats understood how unrealistic their position was, but it was politically impossible in the heated Cold War atmosphere of the 1950s, or during the Southeast Asian conflict of the following decade, to do anything about it. Richard Nixon and his National Security Adviser Henry Kissinger quite suddenly changed policy in 1971–72. This happened at the same time as the West German *Ostpolitik* and stemmed from the same impulse: to create a more realistic political strategy. The People's Republic became the official China, taking up the seat on the UN Security Council in 1971.[15] Yet though it has lost most of its international diplomatic recognition, the regime in Taiwan has retained its independent existence for five decades. As what exactly is not clear. A majority of its inhabitants would like their country to proclaim itself an independent, non-Chinese nation-state, which would sit very poorly with the government of China, which lays claim to all "national" territory. In the Late-Millennium Era, following the pro-capitalist economic reforms of Deng Xiaoping, China and Taiwan have become economically intertwined. China's development into an authoritarian one-party state with rapid capitalist economic growth, following the East Asian model of export-led development, was largely an imitation of what had happened in Taiwan, two decades earlier—an unexpected version of the return to the mainland.

Although Korea is geographically close to China, its own version of a dual nation seems closer to Germany's. This is perhaps not entirely surprisingly, since Korea and Germany have a long history of cultural and economic ties. Just as with Germany, the original plan for Korea called for a temporary occupation regime, a "Trusteeship," to be jointly administered by the United States and the USSR, with each power having its own zone of occupation, divided at the thirty-eighth parallel. And, as in Germany, it took a few years for this plan of joint administration to turn into two states on opposite sides of the Cold War. In fact, the creation of the Koreas in November 1948 preceded their German counterparts by about half a year.

The situation in Korea was more fluid than in Germany, above all because the pro-Western regime faced large-scale opposition from communists within its borders, leading to a repeated history of uprisings, violent suppression by US forces, and their South Korean subordinates (unlike in Germany, the United States rather than the Soviets appeared as the more oppressive occupier) and border clashes with the North between 1948 and 1950. In that latter year, after having secured support from both the Russians and the Chinese, the communist government proceeded to send its army south across the thirty-eighth parallel, to unite the Korean peninsula by force. (This decision promptly unleased a panic in West Germany that East Germany was about to follow the North Korean example.) The subsequent war, characterized by first American and then Chinese intervention, ended with a military reaffirmation of the division line between the two states at the thirty-eighth parallel, each state claiming to be the authentic representative of the nation—thus ending up in the same place as the two German states, but through a far bloodier process. As in Germany, the communist government made much of its past during the Age of Total War, proclaiming itself the regime of opponents of the Japanese imperialists who had ruled the country before 1945, exaggerating the resistance deeds of communist leader Kim Il-Sung in doing so.

If turning a guerilla commander who spent most of the Second World War in the Soviet Union into a national hero was a distortion, the implicit contrast between a communist regime led by opponents of the pre-1945 Japanese imperialists, and a Western country, whose cultural, financial, and administrative elites had worked closely with the Japanese occupiers, and whose police and army were largely composed of veterans of the Japanese imperial forces, remained stark. South Korea's first president, Sygman Rhee, had impeccably nationalist and anti-Japanese credentials. His successor, and founder of modern South Korea, Park Chung Hee, however, had been an officer in the Japanese Army during the Second World War, and once in power surrounded himself, with his classmates from the military academy the Japanese had established for their puppet regime in Manchuria.

One feature in particular distinguished Korea from all the other dual countries. For a long time, it remained unclear which of the two governments had the upper hand. Both Koreas were devastated by the war, but most of the industry—built up by the Japanese imperialists before 1945—was in the North: 80 percent of Korea's industry and 90 percent of its electric power-generating capacity. Each Korea received considerable assistance from wealthier powers on opposite sides of the Cold War. Delegations from East Germany to North Korea competed with those from

West Germany in South Korea. Into the early 1970s, the per capita North Korean GDP was equal to or greater than that of South Korea. The rapid industrialization of South Korea, based on the East Asian model of state-controlled export-led development, broke the stalemate and gave South Korea its edge—by 1990, a per capita GDP about nine times that of its communist rival—both in the international arena and in the intra-Korean competition to represent the nation. As the Second World War faded into the past, so did the economy of North Korea, which tried to keep up by proclaiming its solidarity with anti-imperialist movements in Asia, Africa, and Latin America. For all the revolutionary sympathies the North's diplomacy evoked, the choice between communist slogans and economic prosperity became particularly clear. When North Korea called for a boycott of the 1988 Olympic Games in Seoul, it was ignored by its one-time African and Asian allies, deciding the outcome of the diplomatic competition to represent the nation.[16]

In one of the many examples of how the effects of the events of 1989 played out differently in Europe and Asia, the North Korean communist regime was able to sustain itself, unlike its counterpart in East Germany. If anything, the government of North Korea has become more Stalinist and totalitarian over the years, moving in the opposite direction of just about every other communist regime. It continues to maintain its claim to represent the Korean nation, and denounces the South Korean government as a tool of foreign imperialists. This makes the situation seem like an odd remnant of the Cold War, almost comic—or it would be, were it not for the hundreds of thousands of North Koreans who died in the 1990s famine, and the fact that a pariah regime is armed with nuclear weapons.

Unlike the case with Germany, China, or Korea, the two regimes in Vietnam did not originate immediately as a consequence of the Second World War. Instead, they emerged from the communist-led uprising against French colonial power that began in 1945 and ran on for almost a decade—until the French forces suffered a decisive defeat at Dienbienphu in 1954. At the subsequent Geneva Conference, the triumphant Vietnamese communists let the USSR talk them into a provisional administrative division of the country, Korean-style, at the seventeenth parallel. This was supposed to be a temporary state of affairs, soon to be followed by elections to create a national government. The elections were never held and the temporary administrative division turned into a permanent partition, with two governments—one communist and one Western-oriented, each claiming to represent the nation. In Germany, the communist regime had balked at the idea of national elections; in Vietnam, it was the anti-communist South, and its US ally and patron, that would not go along.

In the clash over representing the nation, the communist North held all the trump cards. Vietnamese communists could claim the heritage of Second

World War anti-fascism, leading resistance to the Japanese occupiers, with whom the French colonial regime had largely collaborated. They could don the nationalist mantle as well, as leaders of the struggle for independence from colonial rule—a claim buttressed by executing Vietnamese anti-imperialists with different ideological positions. The first president of South Vietnam, Ngo Dinh Diem, rather like his Korean counterpart Sygman Rhee, had strong credentials as both a nationalist and an anti-communist, but was also a devout Catholic, that is, to say adherent of a minority religion brought to Southeast Asia by the French imperialists. Developing his own, eccentric political theory, one based on the French Catholic philosopher Emanuel Mounier, and surrounding himself with the six hundred thousand Catholic refugees from communist rule in the north of the country, the new ruler became a hero to Catholics in the United States. But in doing so he alienated the majority Buddhist population in southern Vietnam, as well as the highly popular (and well-armed) members of the Cao Dai and Loa Lao religious sects, both offshoots of Buddhism.[17]

The communist leaders of North Vietnam responded to this situation in ways reminiscent of the North Koreans a decade earlier: by going to war. Combining guerilla actions by supporters in the south, reinforced by adherents of the Cao Dai and Loa Lao sects, many of whom renounced their anti-communism out of hostility toward the autocratic Catholic ruler, Diem, with assaults of regular army units across the eighteenth parallel, the communists worked toward their goal with great determination. They rejected suggestions from the USSR, which bankrolled their war effort, and supported it with arms and ammunition, for a negotiated settlement. There would be no repeat of 1954, when they saw victory snatched from their hands by diplomacy. Massive American airpower and the commitment of a half-million US troops after 1965 temporarily stopped the communists, but spread a swath of destruction through Vietnam, Laos, and Cambodia. Following the withdrawal of American combat troops in the early 1970s, one final offensive in 1975 caused the government of South Vietnam—whose armed forces, in terms of numbers of soldiers and weaponry were in no way inferior to those of the North—to collapse. Vietnam was the one example of a Cold War national dualism decided by military victory, although the price, in money, lives, and environmental destruction, was high indeed.[18]

The dual nations were a Cold War in miniature, played out in the contention for control and legitimacy of a national territory, as well as in terms of superpower proxy wars. The communists' strong suit in the conflict was military—whether in claiming legitimacy from the anti-fascist struggle, or from victory in civil war, as was the case in China, Korea (before American intervention), and Vietnam. Vigorous economic growth and the provision of a bounty of consumer goods was the chief riposte of the Western regimes. One might wonder about the attractions of freedom—more precisely, multiparty competition, civil liberties, and the rule of law—for the cause of the states aligned with the West. These political conditions were certainly present in West Germany, in spite of its Nazi past. In Taiwan and South Korea, they gained traction only from the 1980s onward, and in South Vietnam feebly at best.

Realigning the Globe

If the Cold War had clearly demarcated antagonists, with clashing visions and ways of life, elaborate military alliances, such as NATO and the Warsaw Pact; and formal diplomatic agreements, such as the Test Ban Treaty, the START talks, or the Helsinki Conference on Security and Cooperation in Europe, the Global Realignment Struggle was more amorphous. The protagonists of realignment were a shifting mixture of governments—some just liberated from colonial rule, others with a centuries-long history of independence—and popular insurgent movements, whose forms of institutional cohesion, such as the nonaligned movement, or the UN's so-called Group of 77, were loosely knit at best. The currents of ideas motivating them varied, and included socialism, liberalism, nationalism, populism, and Islamism. Those ideas changed over time.[19] Unlike the clear and enduring alignments of the Cold War, a number of countries altered their position in the realignment struggle. Others never fit into it very well, including Japan, South Korea, and the Arab Petrostates. As for the protagonists of the other side, the affluent and powerful nations of Western Europe, North America, and the South Seas, their leaders frequently denied that they represented a side in a struggle, or even that a struggle existed in the first place, since admitting that struggle's existence would have cast them and their past and present position in the world in distinctly negative terms.

Nonetheless, a few clear themes emerged that ran through the Age of Interconnection. One was the idea of self-determination: at first, independence from colonial rule, but gradually resistance to the forces of economic globalization, emerging from the wealthier and powerful countries, and expressed through the institutions founded in Bretton Woods, the International Monetary Fund, and the World Bank. Self-determination was a collective right, adhering to peoples and nations, not to individuals. Governments in Africa or Asia understood the exercise of a collective right of self-determination as requiring the repression of individuals' human rights, or as the suppression of self-determination rights for minority peoples within the "national" territory. Julius Nyerere of Tanzania made this point when criticizing the Nigerian government's suppression of the independence movement of the Biafrans in the southeastern part of the country in 1968: "we will soon be tolerating fascism in Africa as long as it is practiced by African governments against African peoples."[20]

If the worldwide economic institutions developed at the end of the Age of Total War became a rampart to be stormed in the name of realigning the globe, another institution developed at the same time, and largely by the same people, became a crucial means to do this: the United Nations. Although founded on a wave of utopian aspirations generated by the Second World War, the UN very quickly became a front in the Cold War confrontation between the United States and the USSR. And even during its idealistic beginning, the UN was very far from being a voice against imperialism or colonialism. If anything, imperial powers, such as France and, especially, Great Britain, saw the new international organization as a means to maintain their empire rather than dismantle it, a point of view held by one of the leading early statesmen of the UN, the South African Prime Minister Jan Smuts. There were anti-imperialist voices at the time, particularly the government of newly independent India, but they were unable to use the organization to accomplish much. With the wave of decolonization in the 1960s, the UN, particularly the General Assembly, where each member state has one vote, became increasingly dominated by the voices of the countries seeking a redistribution of economic resources and political power. In doing so, they gave the UN an actual, independent political purpose, separate from the interests of the great powers.[21]

A major—perhaps *the* major—theme of the Global Realignment Struggle was that it was racial conflict. In his 1903 book, *The Souls of Black Folk*, the African American sociologist and political activist W. E. B. DuBois stated, in an oft-cited phrase: "The problem of the twentieth century is the problem of the color-line—the relation of the darker to the lighter races of men in Asia and Africa, in America and the islands of the sea."[22] In retrospect, the color line was not behind either world war or the Cold War. Nor has it been central to the post–Cold War world. But as a description of the Age of Upheaval in the 1960s and 1970s, the conjunction of the struggles of members of dark-skinned nations in Africa, Asia, or Latin America against wealthier and whiter countries in Europe, North America, or the Pacific, as well as the struggles of dark-skinned citizens of those whiter nations—it rings true.

The nightmare of the Western powers was the potential interconnection of a racially inflected Global Realignment Struggle with the Cold War, bringing together the Eastern Bloc with the countries of Africa, Asia, and Latin America, against a common enemy. As Sir Hugh Foot, Lord Caradon, a leading British diplomat, put it in 1966: "For long past I have feared a division of the world on racial issues with all the Africans and all the Asians and the Russians (and the Communist Chinese too) on one side and the Western powers on the other . . ."[23] Within a few years it appeared that Lord

Caradon's fears might actually come true, in the form of an alliance between the nonaligned countries and the USSR. Combined with the immensely destabilizing effects of the 1973 Oil Shock, which seemed to be leading to a global economic realignment, and the US military debacle in Southeast Asia, it created an atmosphere of fear and gloom in Western nations, confident self-assertion on the part of the USSR, deep concern in a communist China locked into a rivalry with the USSR, and jubilation among at least some leaders of African and Asian countries and their left-wing sympathizers in Western Europe and North America. All of these reactions would turn out to have been misplaced: the tentative alliance between Eastern Bloc and the nonaligned powers of Asia, Africa, and Latin America proved harmful to both sides; it was the Western countries that dealt best with the economic realignments coming with the surge of globalization in the 1970s and 1980s, while the result of these new trends were damaging, even destructive, to the economies of the Eastern Bloc and African and Latin American countries. Moreover, the rise of Islamism, beginning with the Iranian Revolution of 1979, would transform the Global Realignment Struggle and international relations more generally in ways no one could have imagined.

CREATING THE THIRD WORLD

If there is one well-known phrase characterizing the proponents of Global Realignment, it is the "Third World." It became a form of racial self-representation, denoting those outside the circle of Europeans and their descendants, and an assertion of the need to redress relations of inequality and exploitation.[24]

Yet the expression was coined by the French demographer Alfred Sauvy, who used it in an essay entitled, "Three Worlds, One Planet," appearing in the August 1952 issue of the intellectual newsweekly, *Le Nouvel Observateur*.[25] Writing during the postwar euphoria about antibiotics and insecticides, Sauvy noted that the application of DDT had destroyed malaria in Ceylon and Algeria, resulting in a situation where "these countries have our death rates of 1914 and our birth rates of the eighteenth century." Very much in the style of Malthusian worries about rising population prevalent in the decades after 1945, Sauvy feared a demographic catastrophe, leading to social and political upheaval, which he saw as already underway in political disputes and uprisings in North Africa, mostly against European colonial rule. The results of these upheavals would mark a new, non-European stage of the Cold War, one in which, "underdeveloped countries of a feudal nature can move much more easily into a communist regime than a capitalist democratic one." He called on the Western powers to redirect their economic resources from arms production to aid for the Third World. Finishing with a reference to one of the famous manifestoes of the French Revolution of 1789, *What is the Third Estate?* of the Abbé Sièyes, Sauvy asserted, "For, in the end, this Third World, unknown, exploited, scorned, as was the Third Estate, wants, just like it, to be something."

Sauvy's piece established the four main characteristics of the Third World: it was part of neither Cold War bloc (designations of these blocs as the "First World" and the "Second World came later and were not part of Sauvy's essay). Third World countries were poor, or, as was said in the postwar era, "underdeveloped"; and they were located in Asia and Africa. (Latin America was not part of the original description and would only be joined to the Third World in the 1960s.) Finally, just as members of the Third Estate were the overwhelming majority of France's inhabitants in 1789, the peoples of the Third World represented the majority of the global population. But Sauvy saw this Third World as the object of assistance from the wealthier countries acting out of enlightened self-interest. The Third World was not, in his understanding, a political subject, much less involved in a Global Realignment Struggle.

Sauvy's ideas were adopted by French leftists, who rejected both the capitalist West and the Stalinist Eastern Bloc and sought for a revolutionary "Third Way." They identified this Third Way with the Third World and saw its impoverished inhabitants as new revolutionary subjects, replacing the older, Marxist revolutionary subjects, the working class, which seemed, in wealthier countries during the era of post-1945 prosperity, to have become too affluent for the revolutionary role Marx and his followers had ascribed to them. This notion was transferred to the Third World itself, via those French intellectuals, who sympathized with and took part in the Algerian revolt against French colonial rule, above all by the psychoanalyst Franz Fanon— very much a French intellectual, if of African descent—whose anti-imperialist manifesto, *The Wretched of the Earth*, evoked the impoverished masses of the Third World as the bearers of a new revolution. Post-revolutionary Algeria did become a center of the nonaligned movement, also hosting Third World enthusiasts from all around the world, including former Black Panther leader Eldridge Cleaver.

Another 1960s supporter of the Global Realignment Struggle was Fidel Castro's revolutionary Cuba, whose 1967 Tricontinental Congress made Latin America the third continent of the Third World. The Cubans strongly promoted the very idea that Sauvy had feared in 1952—that Third World countries could gain backing in their struggle from the Soviet Union. This notion of the Third World as a collective revolutionary subject, reached its high point during the 1970s.

After that, rapid economic growth in East Asia made it clear that the onetime Third World was no longer a homogeneous collection of impoverished countries: South Korea or Taiwan might have more in common with the

United States or France than with Nepal or Burkina Faso. Following the end of the Eastern Bloc in 1989–91, the so-called Second World came to an end, removing a fundamental element of the Third World's existence—as well as the Cold War competition that Third World countries had used toward their ends. The Third World may be gone, but the Global Realignment Struggle through which it came into existence continues, albeit under rather different auspices, to this day.[26]

In the Wake of Total War: International Relations, 1945–1962

The Second World War had left a trail of death and devastation across the entire Eurasian landmass, from the Atlantic coast of France to Manchuria.[27] Three world powers remained. The USSR, which had suffered immense destruction and twenty-five to thirty million deaths had nevertheless gained control of a substantial territory, from Pyongyang to Khorasan in northern Iran to Lviv, Riga, and Magdeburg. The British Empire had survived its greatest challenge, defeating European and Asian antagonists who had tried to destroy it, but was, for all intents and purposes, bankrupt. Finally, the United States: essentially unbloodied in the war, possessing an overwhelming naval and air superiority, and most of the world's industrial production. But global politics was new to the United States, whose past international relations had been primarily with the countries of the Western Hemisphere. It had a new president, a one-time senatorial back-bencher who knew where all the bodies were buried in Jackson County, Missouri, politics, but, by his own admission, had little knowledge of world affairs.

Within a half decade, these one-time allies had not just fallen out but clashed in a broad, ideologically charged conflict that seemed likely to lead to a new and even more destructive world war. As early as 1945, there was already mutual distrust and jockeying for position in a future war—perhaps more than anything else, suggested by the way that the former allies went through newly conquered Germany, rounding up every nuclear physicist and aeronautical and rocketry engineer they could find, as well as carrying off both the blueprints for the V-2 medium-range ballistic missile, and the remaining stockpile of these missiles. Yet there were other examples of policy that complicated the picture. One was the end of British colonial rule in Palestine, pitting Soviet and American support for the creation of a Jewish state there against British hostility toward it. Another was the civil war between the nationalists or *Guomindang* and the communists in China. The Soviets turned over to the Chinese communists military supplies they had captured from the Japanese in Manchuria (at least those materials they did not seize and take back to the USSR) and the United States airlifted Nationalist troops from their bases in the southwestern Sichuan Province to the crucial Manchurian civil war front in the Chinese northeast. However, these acts of assistance were not part of a broader policy of support—quite the opposite. Far from betting on a communist victory, the Soviets signed agreements with the Nationalist government and continued to recognize it diplomatically until days before its flight to Taiwan. Stalin openly snubbed communist leader Mao Zedong, a slight that would gall the future Great Helmsman for the rest of his life. American civilian and military policy makers, fed up with the corruption and incompetence of the *Guomindang* government, and frustrated by its inability to combat the Japanese during the war, had sponsored negotiations between it and the communists, even brokering a truce in the war between them in 1946, when the Nationalists seemed to have the upper hand.[28]

Generals, it is said, are always preparing for the last war, and the Cold War developed out of a similar conjunction: the governments of the United States and the USSR trying to plan for the postwar world by means of lessons learned during the war. These plans might not have been incompatible, but the way they were implemented created a dynamic of escalating mutual suspicion that became the Cold War. For Stalin and his Kremlin subordinates the great lesson of the war was the need for military security. The trauma of the German invasion of 1941 and the ensuing near-destruction of the communist regime meant that its leaders were determined to surround their country with a ring of sympathetic and friendly governments—a sphere of influence, as diplomats say. In the White House and at State Department headquarters in Foggy Bottom, by contrast, the lesson was that the prewar regime of closed trading blocs and hostile Great Powers was a fertile ground for war. A peaceful world would be one of open markets and global commerce—plans for which were already in the works since the Bretton Woods Conference in 1944—and collaborating powers, with the United Nations and its Security Council as a venue for that cooperation.[29]

Perhaps these postwar visions could have been reconciled through, for instance, countries that recognized Russian security interests while being part of a global regime of open markets, like Finland, or, later, Austria. Perhaps American aspirations for an open postwar world could have been realized by navigating between the USSR and the British Empire, two realms whose leaders were both skeptical of a world without trading blocs, an idea that had seemed tempting to FDR before his death. Postwar realities turned out quite differently. In particular, the USSR's leaders increasingly understood a friendly neighboring government to be one modeled on the Soviet Union—a one-party state with a centrally planned economy, led by communists long resident in Moscow. In some neighboring areas, such as the Czech territories, or in those portions of northern Iran with a majority of ethnic Azeris, these plans enjoyed a certain amount of indigenous support. Elsewhere, in Poland, Hungary, Slovakia, or Romania, for instance, Soviet security plans meant coerced regime change, suppression of civil liberties, and the imprisonment or execution of opposition politicians—a state of affairs prevalent in those countries by 1947–48. At the same time, American policy was moving in the direction of implementing its plans for an open postwar world with the assistance of the British Empire against the USSR, rather than in cooperation with it.[30]

Conflict was already preprogrammed into these decisions, but the postwar period had made them appear more sinister. The creation of a ring of communist regimes on the western borders of the USSR appeared as the opening move in a bid for global domination, as the Nazis had just tried, an action of "red fascists," to mention a popular designation of communists in the late 1940s. As Truman said, following the communist coup in Czechoslovakia in February 1948, the United States found itself in "exactly the same situation with which Britain and France were faced in 1938–39 with Hitler." Early post-1945 US foreign policy initiatives included protests against the creation of communist regimes in Eastern Europe, or more concrete efforts to replace a bankrupt British Empire in the Mediterranean—demanding Soviet troops vacate Iran (which they did), supporting Turkey against Soviet claims for free naval passage through the Dardanelles or assisting a right-wing Greek government against Second World War resistance fighters turned communist insurgents. (Those latter two were known as the Truman Doctrine.) These appeared to Stalin and other leading Soviet figures, including foreign minister Vyacheslav Molotov or chief ideologist Andrei Zhdanov, as evidence that sinister, reactionary, proto-fascist forces had gained control of US foreign policy and were leading it in an anti-Soviet direction reminiscent of the plans of the Western "imperialists" during the 1920s and 1930s, or even those pursued by the Third Reich. To Stalin, Churchill and his American supporters, bore "a striking resemblance to Hitler and his friends," but were more dangerous, since their plans were backed up with nuclear weapons not available to the *Führer*. In public, communists described US policy makers as "American Nazi imperialists," "fascist reptiles," and "guided by the idea of race superiority and negation of progress inherited from Nazism." By 1947, these mutually reinforcing suspicions had a name—originally invented by George Orwell but brought into common usage by the American journalist and pundit Walter Lippmann—the "Cold War." The term, initially rejected by the Soviets, would always remain a primarily Western designation.[31]

The legacies of the Second World War in the early stages of the Cold War point to the very center of the conflict. In other words, not to Greece, Turkey, Iran, China, or even Poland, but to that war's main defeated power, Germany. The United States and the USSR were putting their increasingly opposed policies for the postwar world to work in the very same country that they were jointly occupying. In these circumstances, it was no surprise that the different zones of occupation moved steadily apart, and that conferences of foreign ministers of the victorious powers could not agree on the creation of a German government with which to sign a peace treaty. As of 1949, there were two separate German governments, and the old national capital, Berlin, located in the midst of the eastern, communist state, jointly occupied by the four Allies until the conclusion of a peace treaty ending the war—which of course could not happen because there was no German government to sign it. This state of affairs, portrayed in Map 6.2, continued for the next four decades. The Cold War was a never-concluded Second World War.

The creation of two separate and opposed German states in 1948–49 coincided with two aggressive, Europe-focused, US initiatives: the Marshall Plan, aid for postwar economic recovery in Western Europe, within the framework created by the Bretton Woods agreements of 1944; and the North Atlantic Treaty Organization, or NATO, a military alliance between the United States and most of the Marshall Plan recipients. Both initiatives pretended not to be related to the hostilities between East and West—NATO, because regional security pacts were allowed under the UN charter, so the military alliance could be presented as a supplement to the UN, rather than a rejection of its founding assumption of postwar cooperation among the victors. Marshall Plan assistance was offered to the USSR and other Eastern Bloc governments, who turned it down, ostensibly because of the requirement that recipient countries draw up a plan, explaining what they would do with the aid, creating the odd spectacle of communist regimes denouncing economic planning. Both initiatives were part of a policy to construct a US-led power bloc. As these initiatives, unquestionably the two most successful of postwar US foreign policy, were under way, the USSR exploded its own nuclear weapon in 1949, underlining the potentially disastrous consequences of hostilities escalating into a global armed conflict.[32]

The Korean War seemed to offer just such a possibility. It was less the war in Korea itself. Stalin would only agree to support North Korean Kim Il Sung's proposal for an invasion of the southern half of the peninsula if no Soviet troops were involved. Newly communist China was another matter; under Soviet pressure, the Chinese agreed to back their communist Korean allies. Committed to fighting in Korea to the last Chinese soldier, Stalin hoped that the war would tie down American forces, enabling him to make his move in Europe. It is unclear just how far Stalin was prepared to go, but the fact that he was readying a large-scale purge of top communist leaders in the USSR was a disquieting sign. Stalin and other top Soviet leaders had regarded the last great purge they had carried out, from 1936 to 1938, as having been crucial to their victory in the Second World War by brutally clearing away disloyal elements. This perspective was delusional. The purges had eliminated almost the entire Soviet officer corps and many of the government's most loyal supporters, while sowing fear and mistrust across the country, leading to a near collapse of the communist regime during the

MAP 6.2 Germany, 1949–1990

initial months of the 1941 German invasion. Regardless, Stalin's plans for a new purge suggested the possibility of a new world war.[33]

This first of three post-1945 occasions for a Third World War never came to pass. Hundreds of thousands of American soldiers were tied down in the conflict in Korea, but US economic superiority meant that it could simultaneously increase the number of troops stationed in Western Europe tenfold, expand and modernize its air and naval forces, and build up its nuclear arsenal (testing, in 1953, the first hydrogen bomb). Stalin never had the opportunity for his thrust toward Western Europe, although at the time of his death in 1953 he was having Soviet generals draw up plans for an invasion of Alaska. Truman's refusal to use nuclear weapons in Korea or China—against the advice of the commander of the Western forces in the Korean War, General Douglas McArthur, prevented another possibility for the outbreak of a new world war.[34]

Stalin's death helped end the war in Korea on the basis of the status quo ante. There were hopes, particularly articulated by the very elderly Winston Churchill in his last years as the UK's prime minister, that Stalin's passing from the scene meant the possibility of negotiating an end to the division of Europe, the signature element of postwar tension. The post-Stalin leadership of the USSR, particularly, Lavrenty Beria, head of the secret police, did incline to exploring such possibilities. But the response to attempts at de-Stalinization—uprisings in East Germany in 1953, and Poland and Hungary in 1956—combined with a noticeable unwillingness on the part of Eisenhower's new Republican administration in Washington to negotiate, meant that the status quo ante continued. If anything, it was reinforced by the rearmament of the two German states in 1955–56, and the creation of the Warsaw Pact, an anti-NATO Eastern Bloc military alliance. The chief change in strategy of the new governments in the United States and the USSR was an attempt to limit military spending by cutting back infantry and conventional weaponry, and placing ever more emphasis on the use of nuclear weapons in a potential conflict, a doctrine known in American policy circles as "massive retaliation." These plans meant that the next major confrontation would bring the globe the closest it would ever come to a thermonuclear Third World War.[35]

The post-1945 decade also marked a new phase in the Global Realignment Struggle, a direct result of the undermining of European colonial empires in Africa and Asia by the war. The Japanese conquest of British, French, and Dutch realms in South and Southeast Asia had made it all too clear that European dominance was at an end, and the imperial Japanese government's assertion that it represented dark-skinned peoples in their war with Europeans included support for independence movements in the Dutch East Indies and in India. The European powers' defense of their colonial empires was carried out almost entirely by colonial troops. Indian soldiers very largely were the British war effort in South Asia, and Charles de Gaulle's "Free French" consisted of a thin stratum of European officers commanding Arab and African soldiers from the French colonies. If the colonial subjects had to defend themselves in wartime, many asked, what need did they have of a colonial ruler?

The response of Europe's imperial powers in the postwar era was to insist on the reassertion of their colonial rule. The British Empire, the world's largest, did retract, terminating its rule in the Indian subcontinent and Palestine—leading, as we've seen, to mass violence, war, ethnic cleansing, and hundreds of thousands or millions of refugees. But there were no plans at all to abandon other parts of the empire. The European rulers of the French, Dutch, Portuguese, and Belgian empires were equally unwilling to make such large concessions. Violently and brutally suppressing pro-independence demonstrations in Algeria and Madagascar, for example, the French set out to regain the colonial possessions they had lost to the Japanese in Southeast Asia, as the Dutch did for territories in the East Indies. There was little dissent in the European metropoles on this point, aside from some muted disagreement from communists. One astonishing fact is that underground resistance movements during the Second World War supported the retention of colonial empires. One might think that those who had risked their freedom and their lives resisting foreign domination, would have had some sympathy with colonial subjects.[36]

Rulers of the largest colonial empires did make some post-1945 gestures in the direction of self-determination for their colonial subjects. The British considered expanding the Commonwealth, previously a club of the empire's self-governing, white settler colonies, to include their Asian and African subjects. Of course, this expansion would only occur when those subjects were ready to run their own local affairs—perhaps in a generation, and even then, the armed forces and foreign policy would remain in British hands. Across the Channel, there were more ambitious schemes for the creation of a "French Union," a federated global France of one hundred million citizens, in which former colonial subjects would elect representatives to sit in the Chamber of Deputies in Paris. Although noticeably more egalitarian, and certainly more elaborate than British plans to expand the Commonwealth, there was a strong element of denial in these aspirations, as contemporaries understood very well. Swiss journalist Herbert Luethy asked in a widely read 1953 book, whether the French Union meant that "sovereignty over the French homeland is one day to be shared with sixty million Africans and Asians possessing equal rights and whether three-fifths of the seats in the Paris Parliament of the one and indivisible republic are one day to be evacuated to make room for them."[37]

Interestingly, imperial resistance to decolonization intersected relatively little with growing East-West tensions, given the Eurocentric nature of that conflict in its early phases. The end of the British Empire in South Asia involved as we've seen violent confrontations between Hindus and Muslims, and while there were certainly communists in India, particularly in Bengal and Kerala, their influence on events was modest, at best. Communist insurgencies did exist in other parts of Britain's South Asian empire, in Burma and Malaya, although in both cases the insurgents were concentrated almost exclusively in ethnic minorities—the Karens in Burma and the Chinese in Malaya—so that the uprisings were at least as much national and racial antagonisms as they were Marxist revolutions. In Palestine, the situation crossed lines, with the United States and the USSR both supporting the creation of a Jewish state, against British opposition.

During the Second World War, American policy makers—and FDR in particular—had become increasingly skeptical of European colonial empires; this attitude was retained in the early postwar era, as long as European-oriented concerns did not overrule them, as could be seen in the post-1945 French and Dutch efforts to reconquer their Asian colonies. The United States opposed the Dutch counterinsurgency efforts in their East Indian colony, fearing they detracted from a Dutch economic recovery under the Marshall Plan and Dutch military commitments to Western European defense in NATO. By contrast, American policy makers were reluctant to oppose French attempts to reconquer their colonies in Southeast Asia, out of fear it would lead France to reject NATO membership, so the United States increasingly financed France's anti-colonial conflict. The anti-imperialist insurgents in French Indochina were led by communists, while in the Dutch colony nationalist and Islamist opponents of Dutch colonial rule slaughtered thousands of communist insurgents. These two developments helped orient US policy. But the reluctance with which the United States came to support the French counterinsurgency policy, and the State Department's frank admission that the communist leader Ho Chi Minh was the hero of Vietnamese nationalists made it clear that conditions in Europe were the chief determinant of US policy toward colonial empires in the decade after the 1945.[38]

Anglo-American covert operations leading to the overthrow of the nationalist government of Mohammed Mossadeq in Iran in 1953, and the CIA-sponsored coup against the reforming administration of Jacobo Arbenz in Guatemala the following year, were both partly justified as terminating governments that were not exactly communist but susceptible to Soviet subversion. Actual communist influence was modest at best, and there was more than a whiff of early twentieth-century Gunboat Diplomacy in both cases, deposing regimes that wanted to nationalize the petroleum fields of the Anglo-Iranian Oil Company (today's BP) and the banana plantations of the United Fruit Company, respectively.[39]

By contrast, one of the great social revolutions of twentieth-century Latin America, the 1952 uprising in Bolivia, leading to the nationalization of the tin mines and the division of the *haciendas* among landless Andean laborers, did not provoke America; the United States not only recognized the revolutionary regime but offered it economic assistance. Part of the reason for this decision was the skilled lobbying of the long-term Bolivian ambassador to the United States, Victor Andrade, who cultivated his connections with Washington insiders, playing golf with Eisenhower, and entertaining journalists, politicians, and businessmen at the embassy with lots of alcohol, and even his personal performance of Ayamara-language folk songs. It also helped that the radical elements of the Bolivian revolution were Trotskyists—that is, anti-Soviet communists. Still, this detached attitude of US policy makers toward what we might call a Third World revolution, is yet another indication of the modest connections between the post-1945 upheavals of the Global Realignment Struggles and the early Cold War.[40]

Two developments in the mid-1950s brought the Age of Imperial Reassertion to an abrupt end. One was largely symbolic—the 1955 Asian-African conference, held in Bandung, Indonesia. Delegates from twenty-eight countries roundly condemned colonialism and exulted, as their host, Indonesia's president Sukarno, veteran leader of his nation's struggle against imperialism and colonial rule, praised this "first international conference of colored peoples in the history of mankind." This framing of the Global Realignment Struggle as a racial conflict, endorsed by a gathering of representatives of sovereign states, was widely reported. It was not quite yet the Third World, since Latin America countries were neither invited nor represented at this Asian-African conference.

Behind the rhetoric of racial solidarity at Bandung, tensions peeped out. The delegates were divided between a group of Cold War "neutralists," led by India's Jawaharlal Nehru, Egypt's Gamal 'Abd al-Nasir, and Indonesia's Sukarno; communists, very ably represented by China's Zhou Enlai, who impressed the conference as the nonwhite face of the Eastern Bloc; and a pro-Western group, including representatives of Turkey, Iran, Lebanon, and the Philippines. The latter embarrassed everyone by introducing a resolution denouncing Soviet rule in Eastern Europe as equivalent to colonialism. The neutralists at Bandung were able to head off any public discussion of this issue. Five years later, however, when the Philippine representative at the UN repeated the assertion, Soviet leader Nikita Khrushchev, in a celebrated incident, responded by taking off his shoe and banging it on the table.[41]

The first Asian–African Conference was also the last; it created no organization to implement its ideas and resolutions. But its anti-colonial sentiments found expression the following year, 1956, during the Suez Crisis. Following years of growing tensions, Egyptian President al-Nasir nationalized the canal. France, whose citizens were the majority stockholders and Great Britain, the former colonial power in Egypt, set out to regain control of the waterway and overthrow al-Nasir. They devised an elaborate scheme, involving an Israeli invasion of the Sinai Peninsula, which would provoke a Franco-British armed intervention, ostensibly as a peacekeeping measure, keeping apart the Egyptian and Israeli forces, but also seizing control of the Canal and undermining Nasir's rule. For France, this would have the additional advantage of striking at a government supporting the insurgents in its Algerian colony.

British military and diplomats, generally supportive of Arab regimes and strongly anti-Israel, as well as still smarting at the latter's war of independence directed against them a decade previously, were reluctant to take part. The Israeli invasion went well, but the British especially had trouble mobilizing their forces for intervention, so the Israelis and Egyptians agreed to a UN-brokered cease fire. This happened before the British and French were ready to move, thus undermining the ostensible reason for landing their forces in the first place—which they did anyway. The USSR threatened to fire nuclear missiles at them: a bluff, as contemporaries were aware, but a very successful propaganda move in the wake of the Bandung Conference. More important were the actions of the United States. Outraged at not having been informed in advance, and fearful that the intervention would move Arab countries into the Soviet orbit, Eisenhower roundly condemned the intervention and called for a withdrawal of the Israelis, French, and British. This was more than just rhetoric; the United States refused to support Britain financially when speculators attacked the pound, creating a balance-of-payments crisis. The combined—although uncoordinated and indeed opposed—actions of the United States and the USSR did force a withdrawal of the invaders. Al-Nasir had triumphed over the imperialists—including over Israel, which the Bandung conferees, at the request of the Arab delegates, had denounced as an imperialist and colonial state.[42]

The Suez Crisis marked the triumph of the subordinate countries in the initial round of the Global Realignment Struggle. British Prime Minister Harold MacMillan, who came to power after Anthony Eden's humiliation in the Suez Crisis, recognized the situation in an often-quoted speech about the "wind of change" blowing in Africa. The wind was gale force and in the decade after 1956 the French, British, and Belgian colonial empires were completely dismantled. In 1960, the year of the "wind of change" speech, twenty-eight separate countries, mostly in Africa, gained their independence. Only Portugal would stubbornly cling to its colonial realm until 1974.[43]

This wave of decolonization, by far the most extensive dismantling of the largest empires in the history of humanity, went relatively smoothly and peacefully. Two large exceptions during the 1950s were in Kenya and Algeria, where European settlers staunchly opposed the granting of independence. The upshot was anti-colonial uprisings met with vicious counterinsurgency campaigns counting tens, perhaps hundreds of thousands of victims. Part of what made the process of decolonization in those two countries so violent and bloody was that the fighting was not just an anti-colonial uprising, but involved a civil war that overlapped with but was not identical to the struggle for national liberation. Later examples of violence resulting from decolonization, in the Congo and Southeast Asia during the 1960s and in the former

Portuguese African colonies during the 1970s and 1980s, contained this element of internecine war as well.[44]

As the wave of decolonization was peaking, the stabilization of the situation in Europe was coming to an end, resulting in a period of crisis when the world came the closest it ever has to a nuclear war. The crisis was centered yet again around the status of Germany, whose division still kept it from signing a peace treaty to end the Second World War. Khrushchev, who had emerged from the post-Stalin leadership struggles as the dominant figure in the USSR, launched his offensive against the West in 1958, the year after Sputnik, alongside his aggressive initiative to boost economic growth with his "Virgin Lands" program. Khrushchev took aim at the three Western sectors of Berlin, by threatening to sign a peace treaty with the communist government of East Germany, which would have left those three sectors completely surrounded by a now sovereign and hostile state. The point was to use the position of the one-time capital city to drive a wedge between the United States and its European allies, and between West Germany and its military protectors in NATO.

This was an audacious, if still peaceful, diplomatic maneuver. What could be more peaceful than signing a peace treaty? But the proposed peace treaty would have made the Western powers' access to their sectors of Berlin only possible by an invasion of East German territory, leading to a war, and the possible use of nuclear weapons. From 1958 to 1961, the tension steadily ratcheted up. In August of that latter year, Khrushchev opted for a provisional solution, taking up a suggestion of the communist leadership of East Germany, and constructing a wall around Berlin's Western sectors. The Berlin Wall become a symbol—in some ways *the* symbol—of the Cold War, but its construction had not been the aim of Soviet policy. Indeed Khrushchev and his advisers had long been frustrated by their East German allies' insistence on building a wall—demonstrating, they thought, that the German communists could not grasp the big picture.[45]

Warsaw Pact planning for a war over Berlin continued, even after the building of the Wall. The *Buria* (the Russian word for "tempest") war games held in the fall of 1961 outlined a nuclear/conventional weapons offensive, including such features as the Polish army occupying the West German city of Hamburg, after it had been struck with a hydrogen bomb. This idea of a swift offensive, bringing Eastern Bloc troops to the English Channel within a couple of weeks, would remain a staple of Warsaw Pact strategic planning for the next quarter-century.[46]

The flaw with these plans of the Polish army seizing Hamburg and marching along the north European plain into Denmark (another part of the war games) while the Russians closed in on Paris, was not taking into account a massive US nuclear response. Since the Americans had, at the time, seventeen times as many nuclear or thermonuclear warheads as the USSR, and effective means to deliver them (the Soviets' ICBM had just blown up on the launch pad in testing), it would be a devastating counterstroke. Khrushchev's resolution was to station medium-range Soviet missiles in Cuba, just outside the United States.

It is tempting to understand this act and the Cuban Missile Crisis of October 1962 it initiated as marking a new phase in East-West hostilities, shifting away from Europe toward the emerging Third World. Fidel Castro certainly saw it this way, imagining that the Soviet missiles were stationed there to defend his country, the first to adopt a communist government and to affiliate with the Eastern Bloc since the end of the Second World War. Although defending a new ally against attack was certainly one of the Soviet rulers' concerns, the Cuban Missile Crisis, like the Korean War before it, was an extra-European confrontation in which Berlin in particular played a central role. With missiles now stationed just a few minutes flight time from the United States, the Soviets could resume their aggressive attitude in Berlin, and try to reshape the post-1945 settlement in Europe without having to fear a massive American nuclear response.[47]

The discovery of the missiles, most of which were still not yet operational, by American spy aircraft led to the dramatic conclusion of the crisis, and marked the moment when humanity came the closest it ever has to a nuclear war. Rejecting his military advisers' suggestion of air strikes or an amphibious invasion, Kennedy made use of American naval superiority, and ordered a blockade of the Caribbean island. (Following diplomatic niceties, the action was called a "quarantine," since a blockade would have been an act of war.) In retrospect, both US and Soviet leaders showed restraint during the crisis. An American invasion would have been met with a Soviet nuclear response from the missiles in Cuba. Lacking the forces to oppose the US blockade, the Soviet response could only have been nuclear in nature, perhaps firing off rockets against the United States in a preemptive nuclear strike, as Castro, in an act of anti-imperialist bravado and extreme stupidity, recommended to Khrushchev. At the time, though, such restraint was far from evident to the general public and was very difficult to maintain. For ten days in October 1962, the prospect of a thermonuclear apocalypse was very close and very real.[48]

In the end, Khrushchev relented and agreed to withdraw Soviet missiles from Cuba, to Castro's immense disappointment, in return for secret US pledges not to invade the island and to eliminate US medium-range nuclear missiles stationed on the Soviet border in Turkey. Both sides had made concessions, but the Soviet effort to upset the postwar settlement in Europe had failed and the USSR had emerged as the loser in the diplomatic confrontation—one reason Khrushchev's colleagues in the Kremlin removed him from power two years later. In a broader sense, the missile crisis marked the end of the initial phase of the Cold War, centering on the condition of Europe.

A World in Upheaval: International Relations during the 1960s and 1970s

The shape of international relations changed sharply and drastically after the Cuban Missile Crisis. The Cold War and the Global Realignment Conflict continued but were transformed: their nature, the forms of alliance and associations underlying them, their interrelationship, and the proxies involved.

One major change was the weakening of the connections between the superpower leaders of the two Cold War blocs and their allies. For the Western powers, the main example was the relationship between France and the United States. French president Charles de Gaulle began steering a more independent course in international relations. The French nuclear weapons program had begun before his accession to office in 1958, but he extolled the *force de frappe*—a nuclear strike force controlled and targeted independently of the United States, or of any other country. De Gaulle followed this up by withdrawing French armed forces from the NATO command structure, if still maintaining nominal membership. Increasingly, he rejected American foreign policy initiatives, particularly the US war in Southeast Asia, making clear his sympathies for the Vietnamese opponents of the United States. All this diplomatic activity was aimed at the creation of a bloc of European countries led by France that could mediate between the United States and the USSR, in doing so overcoming the division of the European continent, creating, in de Gaulle's oft-quoted phrase, "one Europe between the Atlantic and the Urals."

This ambitious project was the climax of the career of one of the last leading figures of the Second World War still on the political stage. It was ultimately unsuccessful. The European bloc never came into existence, because other West European countries, forced to choose between France and the United States, chose the latter. The Soviets had little interest in de Gaulle's ambition to dissolve the power blocs in Europe; insofar as they were interested in any negotiations with any Western Europeans, it was with the Germans. De Gaulle's opposition to the US war in Southeast Asia, stemming in part from genuine sympathies for the Vietnamese, in part from a desire to take revenge on the United States for opposing the French military effort to retain its Algerian colony during the 1950s, was widely shared in Western Europe, if perhaps not all the motives behind it. That did not translate into assent to the idea of a French-led mediating bloc. American policy makers found de Gaulle frustrating, a frustration that leaked out into the general public. De Gaulle's policy initiatives were more an excuse than a cause. The broader reasons for the tensions between the United States and its European allies lay in the Bretton Woods system, especially the balance-of-payments problem presaging the collapse of the international financial architecture.[49]

For all the tensions between the United States and its European allies during the 1960s—tensions not reflected in US relations with extra-European allies, such as Australia, Japan, or South Korea—they pale when compared to the chaos within the Eastern Bloc. In particular, the two largest and most powerful countries of that bloc, the USSR and the People's Republic of China, had a falling out, although "falling out" is perhaps a mild way to describe a transition from close and trusted postwar allies to bitter enemies on the brink of war.[50]

In the background were old issues, particularly Stalin's snubbing of Mao and the Soviet leader's reluctance to support a communist revolution in China. But under Khrushchev the Soviet Union launched a massive assistance program for its largest ally. Between 1954 and 1959, 7 percent of the Soviet Union's national income went to economic aid for China; thousands of technical experts and advisers from the USSR and other Eastern European countries traveled there to assist in the construction and running of industrial facilities and modern infrastructure. The collaboration went beyond economic assistance. The USSR began to turn over to the Chinese information on the production of nuclear weapons and their delivery systems as well as some of the necessary material. During the uprisings of the fall of 1956 in Poland and Hungary that threatened Soviet domination of Eastern Europe, top Chinese leaders traveled to Moscow to offer their advice and assistance—gratefully received in the Kremlin, less for the actual suggestions as for the show of solidarity involved.

In part, these close connections may have backfired. All the economic and technological assistance underscored what could only seem like China's backwardness. Some Eastern European advisers, who rode around in rickshaws and acted in ways that were an unpleasant reminder of former Western imperialists, reinforced feelings of resentment. The Soviets' problems during 1956 inspired Chinese leaders, especially Mao, never known for his modesty, to think that China, rather than the USSR, possessed the Marxist knowledge needed to lead the Eastern Bloc.

This question of what was the right kind of Marxist knowledge was a central element of the split. Khrushchev, in his famed "secret speech" at the 1956 Soviet Communist Party Congress, had condemned Stalin for his policies of indiscriminate killing in the name of communist revolution, arguing for a more moderate and measured approach, both to internal governance and to external relations. The Chinese vigorously rejected this. It was not so much in defense of Stalin, for although Stalin fans across the world would rally to China, the Chinese party leaders remembered all too well Stalin's contempt for them. Rather, they denounced the Soviets as "revisionists," taking up a phrase early twentieth-century Marxist revolutionaries had deployed to condemn labor movement advocates of gradualism and reform. China would stand for an aggressive revolutionary attitude.

More than anywhere else, this militant revolution would occur in the nascent Third World. As Mao stated in a 1963 speech, there "two hundred million people in Africa, two hundred million in Latin America, more than a billion in Asia, and the revolutionary peoples of the world—they are all our friends." Part of this revolutionary friendship was the racial solidarity proclaimed at Bandung. Mao told a delegation from Guinea, a newly independent African country that had departed French rule on bad terms, "we are both of a colored race."[51]

The target was the capitalist nations of Western Europe and, especially the United States. Mao had no doubts about how to bring about the triumph of the right kind of Marxist knowledge: a global nuclear war that would destroy imperialism. There would doubtless be collateral damage, but, as he told the Soviet ambassador, "Chinese history provides much support for the fact that even a significant loss of population does not necessarily mean the destruction of the nation." The numerical superiority of the Third World would ensure communist victory in an atomic war: "The whole world has 2 billion 700 million people, possibly it will lose a third; or even more possibly it will lose half . . . but there will be another half; the imperialists will be hit completely, [and] the whole world will become socialist . . ."[52] The Chinese condemned the Soviets for backing down during the Cuban Missile Crisis, and betraying a non-Western revolutionary country; like Castro, Mao favored a thermonuclear war in the name of Third World revolution.

Later in the 1960s, both the USSR and China offered support to North Vietnam in its war with the United States. As noted, however, the Soviets kept pressing their allies to negotiate with the Americans, while China preferred to fight to the last Vietnamese soldier—reiterating Stalin's attitude toward China during the Korean War fifteen years previously.[53] At least in Vietnam, China and the USSR were on the same side. When Mao launched the Cultural Revolution, Sino-Soviet relations moved into a phase of open hostility, in spite of the efforts of the post-Khrushchev Soviet leadership to repair damage to them. In 1966 and 1967 "Red Guards," government-sponsored youthful revolutionaries, laid siege to the USSR's embassy in Beijing, hundreds of thousands of them surrounding the building, blocking it from the outside world, and screaming threats at the terrified diplomats inside. The Red Guards wanted to break in and take the Soviet officials hostage, anticipating what youthful revolutionaries would do to American diplomats in Iran a decade later. Unlike the Ayatollah Khomeini, however, Chinese premier Zhou Enlai talked the youthful insurgents out of their plans, but not before they had mistaken a group of East German diplomats for Russians, seized them, and almost beaten them to death. By 1969, Soviet and Chinese troops were exchanging fire across the Ussuri River, the border between the two countries, and war seemed a possibility. The USSR even inquired of the United States if it would condone a Soviet air strike, possibly a nuclear one, on Chinese nuclear facilities.[54]

The two communist regimes pulled back from the brink, but their diplomatic break could never be repaired. By the early 1970s, the Chinese government was involved in talks with the United States—an odd action for a regime that had relentlessly condemned the Soviets for a conciliatory attitude toward the leading capitalist-imperialist nation in the world. US-Chinese cooperation would grow steadily closer over the following two decades. As US fortunes reached their nadir following Vietnam, Chinese support helped assure that these fortunes did not sink even lower. This Sino-American rapprochement makes it clear that the USSR's difficulties with its one-time ally were far greater than any differences the United States suffered with France.

Another major feature of the changing Cold War was that it was a period of successfully concluded negotiations—the only such period, save right before the collapse of the Soviet Union. In short order, the United States and the USSR signed treaties banning above-ground tests of nuclear weapons, prohibiting the stationing of atomic weapons in space, attempting to limit the spread of nuclear weapons and, culminating the series of nuclear agreements, in the 1972 Strategic Arms Limitation Talks, rejecting the building of missile defense systems that might have tempted either side to launch a first strike. These agreements, which remain in force to this day, have shaped the worldwide nuclear weapons regime, and helped prevent the actual use of nuclear weapons. They contrast not just the inability to reach any such accords before 1963, but a long history of failed disarmament talks in the twentieth century.[55]

Nuclear weapons were one focus of this era of negotiations; Europe was another. Between 1969 and 1972, the government of West Germany agreed with the USSR, Poland, and Czechoslovakia to recognize the results of the Second World War, and the governments of the two Germanys agreed to recognize each other (de jure, as far as the East Germans were concerned, de facto was the official opinion in West Germany), paving the way for their admission to the UN, and recognition of separate sports teams. The former Allies agreed to regulate the status of West Berlin, whose condition had brought the world to the brink of thermonuclear war just a few years previously, and, in particular, to guarantee access to West Berlin from West Germany, across the territory of the German Democratic Republic. At the same time this treaty was being concluded, preparations for a much broader accord were in the works. The negotiations culminated in 1975 at the Helsinki Conference on Security and Cooperation in Europe that brought together members of the two opposing military alliances, as well as the European neutrals.

Three major points were involved in the Helsinki negotiations. One involved a ratification of the results of the Second World War, the *Ostpolitik*, or Eastern policy of the new center-left government in West Germany coming to office in 1969, an attempt to improve relations with the Eastern Bloc, began with the treaties recognizing the territorial losses and the national division as a consequence of the aggression of the Third Reich. West German Chancellor Willy Brandt made this point in a far more effective way than could be articulated in any diplomatic language in December 1970. On a state visit to Warsaw, to sign the West German-Polish Treaty (in which the Federal Republic renounced the "lost eastern territories," the lands to the east of the Oder and Neisse Rivers transferred to Poland at the Yalta and Potsdam Conferences of 1945), he took the occasion of a photo op at the memorial to the 1943 uprising of the Jews of the Warsaw Ghetto against the Nazis to sink to his knees in contrition. A determined opponent of the Nazis and a refugee from Nazi Germany, Brandt was the last German who needed to show contrition, but his willingness to do so, and to have the photo and video images of his act broadcast around the world, underscored his government's renunciation of his country's Nazi past—and earned him the Nobel Peace Prize.

The Four Power accord on access to Berlin, guaranteeing the position of the three Western powers in their sectors of the city, was also a ratification of the results of the Yalta and Potsdam Conferences—a result the USSR had tried to revise a decade earlier, even at the risk of a thermonuclear war. Also ratified were the sections of the so-called first basket of the Helsinki Accords, which rejected measures aimed at changing the post-1945 boundaries in Europe. As we've seen, the Second World War had not legally ended, because there was no German government that could sign a peace treaty doing so. The Helsinki Conference was a replacement, a de facto end to the war.[56]

A second major point about these negotiations over Europe was the reduced role played by the United States. Richard Nixon had regarded the West Germans' negotiations with the Eastern Bloc with suspicion. Admittedly, he regarded almost everything and everyone with suspicion, but Henry Kissinger was also suspicious, fearing the West German talks with the Eastern Bloc would undermine the NATO alliance. In the end, the United States came around and supported the initiatives of the Federal Republic, participating in the Helsinki Conference.

The third and decisive element of that conference was the so-called third basket, in which the treaty parties pledged to support human rights in their domestic policies, endorse national self-determination, and agree to further human contacts between the two Cold War blocs. This emerged from proposals of nine Western European countries, all members of the European

Community, predecessor to today's European Union. American diplomats regarded the whole initiative as useless and irrelevant.[57]

Kissinger's skepticism about human rights aside, this entire Era of Negotiation seemed to mark a new phase in the Cold War, one of reduced tensions and more peaceful policies, an age, as contemporaries said, of "détente." This perception was, to a great extent, an illusion. To understand why, we need to consider another, perhaps less well-known, phrase from the diplomacy of the era, used frequently by Kissinger and Nixon—"linkage." "Linkage" was the idea that the negotiations on nuclear weapons or on conditions in Europe were part of a global shift in Cold War policy, and could be deployed to that effect—an American agreement to an arms control treaty, for instance, in return for Soviet pressure on the North Vietnamese to accept US terms. If they didn't use the phrase, Soviet diplomats had similar expectations from these negotiations. So did the non-superpowers. Salvador Allende, the president of Chile, told the visiting president of Bowling Green State University in the fall of 1971 that surely the American government would negotiate over its differences with his regime's left-wing policies, since it was sitting down to discuss its far greater differences with the USSR or China.[58]

Allende's fate, overthrown and killed in a right-wing military coup, with at least tacit US support, a year and a half later in September 1973, shows the problem with "linkage." No one was willing to link. Détente, such as it was, was limited to conditions in Europe. The unprecedented burst of negotiations culminating in Helsinki did not decrease Cold War tensions. Instead, it shifted them—from a European center of the superpower competition, toward Latin America, Africa, and Asia. As a result, the Cold War became intertwined with the Global Realignment Struggle, changing the nature of both conflicts.

REALIGNING THE COLD WAR

Even before the negotiations on the interrelated questions of nuclear weapons and the post-1945 European settlement were underway, the United States and the USSR were beginning to compete in Asia and Africa. An initial version of this competition, in the wake of the 1955 Bandung Conference, was the attempt to develop better relations with Cold War neutrals. Soviet foreign policy under Khrushchev pioneered this, breaking with Stalin's lack of interest in (and indeed contempt for) non-Europeans. The United States was slower to follow, with Eisenhower's Secretary of State, John Foster Dulles, denouncing the very idea of neutralism as immoral in the Cold War conflict between (Western) good and (Eastern) evil, but Eisenhower's successor Kennedy and his foreign policy team showed a more flexible attitude.

This new orientation proved awkward for both superpowers. The USSR developed close relations with the al-Nasir's Egyptian government and with the Ba'ath Party regimes in Syria and Iraq, led by authoritarian nationalists who were busy arresting or shooting members of their respective countries' communist parties. The Soviets also worked hard to be on good terms with India, the leading neutral country, although tensions between India and the USSR's most powerful communist ally, China, were escalating, leading to a border war in 1962. The Soviet Union's refusal to take sides only reaffirmed the Chinese dismissal of Russian revisionism. American attempts to court neutrals faced similar dilemmas: being on good terms with countries that proclaimed themselves socialist and anti-capitalist, regularly attacked US foreign and domestic policy, particularly on issues of race, and were at odds with American allies such as Israel—(in the case of Egypt) Pakistan (in the case of India), Great Britain, and its former colony Malaya (in the case of Indonesia).[59]

These rather hesitant steps toward an extra-European focus were transformed by rapid changes in the Global Realignment Struggle, as that struggle moved from the demand for liberation from European colonial empires to a broader confrontation over the shape of economic and political relations. This shift occurred in different locations around the world, including the Middle East and Central and Southern Africa. However, it was most dramatic, concentrated and consequential as the result of two revolutions: in Cuba and Vietnam.[60]

The Cuban revolution of 1958 went quickly skidding from nationalist and vaguely leftist, as had been the case with the two other major twentieth-century Latin American revolutions, the Mexican of 1910 and the Bolivian of 1952, to explicitly communist and pro-Soviet. It was therefore the very first instance of the expansion of the Eastern Bloc beyond Eurasia in the aftermath of the Second World War. Openly challenging the United States from its doorstep, handily surviving an inept American-backed attempt to overthrow it in 1961, the Cuban government set itself up as a model of a new kind of communist revolution—youthful, dynamic, sexy, and rather nonwhite—one that it would attempt to bring to large parts of the world.[61]

No one symbolized this more than Castro's close companion, Che Guevara. Although Guevara became a cult figure, whose image figured prominently at New Left demonstrations, and on rock album covers and college dormitory walls around the world, his actual efforts to spread Cuban style revolution were hardly threatening. His first attempt, in the newly independent Congo in 1965, was dismissed by Egypt's al-Nasir, who compared Guevara to Tarzan: "a white man coming among black men, leading them and protecting them." The second, in Bolivia, a couple of years later, was less abortive but equally unavailing. The plan was to bring in a group of armed guerilla insurgents to mountainous terrain, like Castro's in Cuba's Sierra Nevadas, to incite Bolivia's landless Andean *campesinos* to fight the army, leading to a revolutionary outcome. The problem was that Bolivia's peasants already owned land, a result of their revolution in 1952, and tended to see the army as the guarantor of the post-revolutionary property settlement. They therefore had little sympathy with the insurgents. Guevara's expedition ended with his capture by the Bolivian military. Against the wishes of the CIA, who wanted the anti-American revolutionary alive, Bolivian soldiers executed (and martyred) him.[62]

More consequential for the spread of revolution than Guevara's Quixotic episodes was the Cuban-sponsored intellectual reorientation of the Global Realignment Struggle. The 1967 Tricontinental Congress in Havana, which featured public sessions proclaiming solidarity with anti-imperialist struggles the world over, particularly in Vietnam, brought Latin America into the Third World, as it had not been a decade earlier at Bandung. This endowed that Third World with a much harder, revolutionary edge. The successor to Bandung, the Non-Aligned Movement, was also given a distinct twist by Cuban participation. The first Non-Aligned Conference had been held 1961 in Belgrade and was attended by representatives of countries who were nonaligned—that is, they rejected the leadership of both the United States and the USSR. Cuba, by contrast, vigorously asserted that the USSR was the "natural ally" of the nonaligned states, and, by the late 1970s, had gathered around it a group of "Third World-ist" countries that endorsed such a point of view: among others, in the Middle East and North Africa, Algeria, Syria, Iraq, Libya, and South Yemen, along with the PLO, in sub-Saharan Africa, Ghana, Guinea, Guinea-Bissau, Angola, Mozambique, Tanzania, Benin, and Ethiopia; and in Asia, North Korea, and Vietnam—whose presence at a nonaligned conference shows where nonalignment was going. The global presence of the pro-Soviet non-aligned is shown in Map 6.3.[63]

Cuba was the tip of the revolutionary spear, sending weapons and fighters to support insurgent or potentially insurgent regimes. Salvador Allende's Chile was well stocked with Cuban weapons and military advisers, who were deeply disappointed that the embattled president did not take their advice to respond to the coup against him by retreating to the working-class suburbs of Santiago and launching a civil war with the weapons they provided. Perhaps remembering a similar civil war from his youth, in Spain, and its terrible consequences, Allende chose to remain in the presidential palace and die there. The Cubans were more successful in Africa than in Latin America, battling South African soldiers for control of the former Portuguese colony of Angola, and sending doctors, soldiers, and secret police advisers to the pro-communist military government of Ethiopia.[64]

By itself, Cuba was more a pinprick than a spear thrust to American interests. What made Cuban revolutionary intervention so effective was the American response to the Vietnamese revolution and its global consequences.

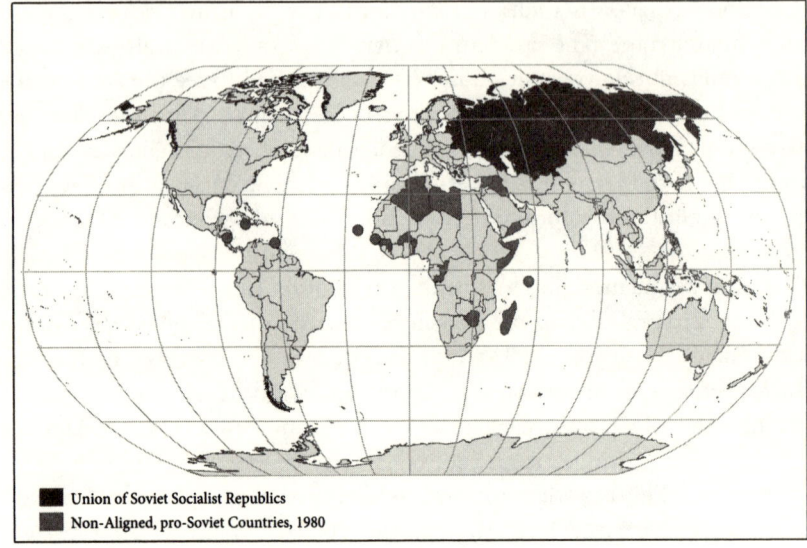

MAP 6.3 Revolutionary Nonaligned Countries of the 1970s and 1980s

Post-1945 American policy went through three stages. The first was supporting French colonial rule—rather reluctantly, more for France's position in Europe, then at the center of the Cold War, than endorsing its Southeast Asian empire. Following the French defeat at Dienbienphu in 1954, the collapse of French opposition to the Vietnamese Revolution, and the partition of the country following the Geneva Conference of that year, the United States threw its support behind the anti-communist Vietnamese nationalist Ngo Dinh Diem, who was unable to consolidate support among even anti-communist Vietnamese—largely, as we've seen, a result of his pronounced Catholicism, which alienated the majority adhering to Buddhism and Buddhist sects.

From 1965 to 1973, there was a direct US military intervention. One large part of it was counterinsurgency warfare, trying to root out guerillas who blended in with the civilian population. Counterinsurgency involved "strategic hamlets"—deporting villagers from their homes and moving into guarded enclosures that would keep them away from the Vietcong guerillas—generous applications of the defoliant Agent Orange and of napalm, "free-fire zones," declaring anyone not leaving a region to be an enemy combatant, and repeated killings of civilians, whom angry and overwhelmed American soldiers assumed were really underground combatants. The My Lai massacre of 1968 was only the most famous of these incidents. These were methods taken from some of the most brutal instances of colonial warfare, such as the French campaign against insurgents in Algeria. Whatever their military effectiveness, they were profoundly destructive to America's position in the world. The damage they did to Vietnamese and their natural environment remains apparent down to the present.[65]

But the Southeast Asian conflict was not just and not even primarily counterinsurgency warfare. It was a reprise of the Age of Total War, fought on the part of the United States with a massive conscript army and very liberal use of airpower in support of ground operations. Contrary to common assumptions at the time (and in some circles down to the present), this was a war that the Vietnamese communists wanted to fight. While the public faces of the communist and nationalist war against the United States were the grandfatherly anti-colonial revolutionary veteran Ho Chi Minh, and General Vo Nguyen Giap, the master of guerilla warfare and victor over the French, actual policy in North Vietnam was set by the party leader Le Duan, a former clerk in the French colonial railways and experienced communist bureaucrat, who opposed Giap's ideas and at one point contemplated arresting him. Le Duan opted for a strategy of invasion of North Vietnamese Army forces, complemented by guerilla uprisings, not unlike what the North Koreans had done in 1950. He ordered repeated assaults of this nature—in 1964, 1968 (known as the Tet Offensive), 1972, and 1975. The last attack, after American troops and, especially, airpower, had departed was finally successful.[66]

It is not hard to understand why the Vietnamese communists fought this war, how they could mobilize a large portion of the population behind them, or even how the war in Vietnam could become a central element in the Global Realignment Struggle. The more difficult question, already posed at the time and still discussed today, is why American policy makers were so misguided, as was already evident to contemporaries. The main justification, still repeated by apologists for US policy five decades later, was the "domino theory," the idea that while Vietnam itself was not important to the Cold War or the global position of the United States and its allies, a communist victory there would lead to other and larger victories throughout Asia and the Pacific rim.

There was something to this theory, less involving Vietnam, but Southeast Asia's most populous and most powerful country, Indonesia. During the first half of the 1960s, President Sukarno, under the influence of a very large and influential communist movement, had been veering away from the neutralist course he had advocated at Bandung in 1955 toward a confrontation with Western powers, especially over neighboring Malaysia, recently independent of British rule and containing a large piece of territory that he wished to incorporate into Indonesia. This policy, *konfrontasi*, Sukarno called it, was, by the mid-1960s, reaching the brink of war, in which an Indonesian victory and annexation of Malaysia really would have had a domino effect. Before it could come to that, Indonesia's leftist overreached themselves, when communist army officers attempted a military coup in 1965. Their nationalist and Islamist opponents responded by turning on the communists and slaughtering them—killing somewhere between five hundred thousand and one million people, one of the great mass murders of the second half of the twentieth century. The real threat of falling dominoes had thus been eliminated in precisely the year that the massive American troop buildup and rising air assaults in Vietnam began.[67]

Another explanation for US policy focuses on domestic politics, on the fear of appearing weak, of being vulnerable to political opponents' charges of surrendering a country to the communists.[68] As an all-encompassing ideological struggle, the Cold War did make such charges possible and plausible and politicians'—in this case, Lyndon Johnson's—fears of them understandable. But the doggedly self-destructive persistence of American policy over the course of eight years and two very different presidents from opposing political parties, strongly endorsed by most politicians, and public opinion (despite a small if growing, antiwar minority) suggests other motives were involved. Perhaps it was applying the lessons of the initial phase of the Cold War, the Eurocentric confrontation between two united power blocs, to a different era. The global struggle against colonialism and the postcolonial dominant position of European countries and their settler offshoots like the United States gave the Vietnamese cause a base of support, at home and abroad, which Stalin and his minions could never have enjoyed in Europe. Unlike the case in Korea, Berlin was not being defended in Vietnam, and America's European allies showed little inclination to support the United States in Southeast Asia, unlike in Northeast Asia fifteen years previously. The Vietnam War coincided with the growing hostility between the USSR and People's China, which should have strengthened the American position. As a result of American policy in Southeast Asia treating the Eastern Bloc as a monolith, even when the two communist countries were on the brink of war, however, had the opposite effect.[69]

As support for the conflict from both America's economic and political elites and the general public began to leak away in the late 1960s, Richard Nixon sought to find a way to bring the war to an end without conceding defeat. The strategies employed were a mixture of policies from the Age of Total War and the early decades of the Cold War, along with a recognition of the changing face of global politics. Reaffirmation of previous policies was most apparent in the greatly expanded use of air power, with massive bombing raids on North Vietnam as well as supply lines—the "Ho Chi Minh trail"—and military positions in neighboring countries, the most drastic example being the large-scale US aerial and infantry assault on Cambodia in the spring of 1970. But Nixon and Kissinger also understood that an exclusive orientation toward the early phase of the Cold War would be unsatisfactory. They began to withdraw US ground troops, and then terminated the draft, a recognition of the end of the era of massive and modestly trained conscript armies. They hoped to use negotiations with the USSR over nuclear weapons and conditions in Europe, to weaken Soviet support for the Vietnamese communists—"linkage" in its purest form—and to exploit the Sino-Soviet split for the same purpose. None of these strategies had much of an effect—other than spreading still more death and destruction across Southeast Asia, without reaching any intended goals. The collapse of the Nixon administration's political support, due to the Watergate affair of 1973, eliminated any chance of success.

The ultimate failure of US policies in Southeast Asia marked a dual defeat, in both the Global Realignment Struggle and in the Cold War. Che Guevara's cry, "One, two, many Vietnams," was no more realistic than his quixotic revolutionary adventures. However, to both statesmen and insurgents from the newly decolonized countries of Africa and Asia, and to Latin Americans seeking to get out from under the thumb of their domineering neighbor to the north, the triumph of the Vietnamese over the Americans was a sign of the declining position of Europe's greatest settler offshoot, and an incentive to work still more at changing the global balance of power. There would be global restructuring, using these countries' majority in the UN General Assembly to create a "New International Economic Order" and a "New International Information Order." As noted earlier, the oil price shocks of the 1970s and the explosion of raw materials prices more generally during the first half of that decade would give the demands for a new international economic order more weight. Insurgent movements against remaining colonies and postcolonial settler regimes in Southern Africa would be another, more violent arena of action, as would be the conflict between Arabs and Israelis, combining partisan warfare with new, terrorist tactics, which could reverberate worldwide on TV screens. Still other arenas of political action would appear in the region bounded by Somalia and Ethiopia on the west, and Pakistan and Afghanistan on the east.

The American defeat in Southeast Asia was also a triumph for the Eastern Bloc. Khrushchev had as noted already broken with his predecessor's indifference to insurgent movements among nonwhite people. Khrushchev's successors, the troika of party leader Leonid Brezhnev, Prime Minister Alexi Kosygin, and Minister of Foreign Affairs Andrei Gromyko (Brezhnev, often described in the West as a domineering leader on the model of Stalin or Khrushchev, was inexperienced in foreign affairs and always needed advice and approval), went all in on support of anti-American wars and insurrections outside Europe, abandoning Khrushchev's hesitations and thoughts about linkage. The victory of their proxy forces in Vietnam, at a modest cost to the USSR itself, convinced them to expand their arena of operations, supporting insurgent movements and left-wing governments in Africa. This close connection between the Global Realignment Struggle and Soviet foreign policy initiatives outside of Europe convinced the USSR's leadership, that, as

Karen Brutents, a leading figure in the international division of the USSR's Communist Party—an organization through which many of the Soviets' Third World initiatives were deployed—observed in retrospect, "the world was turning in our direction."[70]

The New International Economic Order, proposed and approved without opposition by the UN General Assembly, during a special session at the beginning of 1974, exemplified the era's initiatives in the Global Realignment Conflict. It called for national sovereignty over raw materials, allowed for nationalization of foreign firms, the international setting of raw materials prices and their indexation to the prices of manufactured goods, debt relief for poorer countries, and a redistribution of national influence in the Bretton Woods international financial institutions. The proposal was put forward by Algeria's revolutionary leader Henri Boumédiène, a veteran of the 1950s struggle for independence from France, and a star of the 1973 conference of nonaligned states held in Algiers. Algiers was a leading supporter of Third World revolutionary initiatives, and host to fleeing American racial insurgents, like Black Panther leader Eldridge Cleaver, and the proposal presented itself as a continuation of the anti-colonial struggle. UN General Assembly resolutions were and are more declarations of intent than enforceable decisions. This time the proposal was flanked by very real actions. Governments in Latin America, the Middle East Asia, and Africa expropriated the property of dozens of Western corporations—sixty-eight in all—including some very high profile oil and mining companies—as opposed to just six in 1960. The 1973 oil shock engineered by OPEC, behind which Boumédiène's Algeria was a driving force, aimed both to raise raw materials prices and also to punish Western nations for supporting Israel in its wars with the Arabs—an increasingly central cause for the nonaligned countries.[71]

The New International Economic Order was an initiative of the nonaligned countries, in which the Eastern Bloc played no particular role. This was not the case in two major armed struggles of the late 1960s and 1970s. One was the Arab-Israeli conflict. Through the 1950s, this had broken the bounds of Cold War alignments, with the United States and the USSR supporting the creation of an Israeli state in 1947–48 and both opposing the Israeli invasion of during the 1956 Suez Crisis. But in the Arab-Israeli wars of 1967 and 1973, the superpowers were lined up very closely with their respective Middle East proxies, providing them with intelligence, weapons, and munitions. In the period between the wars, there were twenty thousand Soviet soldiers stationed in Egypt, manning anti-aircraft weapons, and flying combat patrols against the Israelis. The fraught character of the 1973 Yom Kippur War, the only one of the Arab-Israeli conflicts in which the latter came close to defeat, and the intense and hasty military resupply efforts of the United States and the USSR briefly raised the specter of a superpower clash, perhaps a nuclear one, emerging out of a conflict in the Global Realignment

Struggle. Occurring in a period of détente, very different from the crisis years 1958–62, or the period of renewed Cold War tensions in the first half of the 1980s, the specter of a world war emerging from Middle Eastern conflicts proved ephemeral. It largely occurred in the first place, because during the crisis the leaders of the two superpowers were unable to provide firm policy guidance, Brezhnev because of his addiction to sleeping pills, Nixon because he was dead drunk.[72]

The Camp David peace accords of 1978 were only possible after Egyptian president Anwar Sadat had repudiated his country's close connections with the USSR and realigned with the United States. US allies in the Arab world were at least willing not to advocate openly military action against Israel. By contrast, the "rejectionist" regimes, Iraq and Syria, favoring a renewed anti-imperialist war, were closely aligned with the Soviet Union. The growing official hostility toward the Jewish population of the USSR, roundly denounced as "Zionists," was, seen in this context, a gesture of anti-imperialist solidarity on the part of the Soviet regime. That regime and its European subordinate states—the East Germans played a particularly prominent role—were strong supporters of the PLO, providing it with funds, weapons, military training, and diplomatic support. Although the rise of Islamism, following the Iranian Revolution of 1979, would introduce new elements into this political alignment, it remained largely intact until the end of the USSR.

Frustrated by the inability of the Arab states to oust the Israelis through conventional warfare, and buoyed by the endorsement of the nonaligned states, the UN's General Assembly, and the Eastern Bloc, the PLO made increasing use of a form of asymmetrical warfare that had played a central role in the Algerian rebellion against French colonial rule—namely, terrorism, attacks on civilians, whose very presence as colonialists was, implicitly, an act of war. (Whether this logic applied to the Jewish population of Israel, most of whom by the 1970s were refugees from Arab countries and their descendants, is another matter, but the PLO and its many sympathizers—in the nonaligned powers, the Eastern Bloc, and among leftists and anti-imperialists in Western Europe, North America, and the Pacific—certainly thought it did.) Ranging from spectacular events, like the kidnapping and killing of Israeli athletes at the 1972 Munich Olympics, or the hijacking of an El Al airliner to Entebbe in Uganda four years later, to more small-scale and localized shootings and bombings, this terrorist offensive became the face of the anti-imperialist-Eastern Bloc alliance in the Middle East throughout the 1970s.[73]

Equally characteristic of this alliance were the struggles in southern and southeast Africa. These were both anti-colonial, directed against the government of Portugal, which had refused to join the post-1956 wave of decolonization and was clinging to its colonial possessions, Angola, Mozambique, and Guinea-Bissau; and postcolonial, directed against the independent but white minority-ruled regimes in Rhodesia and South Africa. What linked them together was the military coup launched in 1974 by Portuguese colonial troops against the metropolitan government. Strains of anti-colonial warfare had led to another military coup, the overthrow of the government of the French Fourth Republic in 1958 by soldiers in Algeria, which had brought Charles de Gaulle to power. That coup had been designed to reinforce the French empire in North Africa, although de Gaulle would ultimately double-cross his military supporters and agree to Algerian independence, while the Portuguese military had the opposite intent: to end the war and allow the colonies their independence.

Paradoxically, it was the end of colonial rule that led to the greatest expansion of warfare in the former Portuguese empire, as different African opposition and insurgent groups contended for power in the newly independent countries. The opposition and rivalries between the groups were based on their largely ethnic and tribal bases of support. In Angola, the largest and wealthiest (oil) of the former Portuguese colonial possessions, where the conflicts were most violent and intense, the three major contenders for power each had different ethnic constituencies: the MPLA [Popular Movement for the Liberation of Angola] drawing its support from the Ambundu people, as well as from mixed-race inhabitants of urban areas, who looked down on Africans; the FNLA [National Front for the Liberation of Angola]from the Bakonogo; and UNITA [National Union for the Total Independence of Angola] from the Ovimbundu. In characteristic Cold War fashion, these hostilities and rivalries were drawn into the broader struggle between the power blocs, as the United States and the USSR, as well as their allies and proxies, Zaire and Cuba, supplied chosen groups with funds, weapons, and, eventually, troops. The situation was even more complicated through the involvement of China and its proxy, North Korea, and because the white minority government of South Africa intervened, sending its own troops into Angola and Mozambique. In the ensuing war, the MPLA, with extensive Soviet support and large Cuban troop contingents, triumphed over its rivals that were being supported openly by South Africa, and in covert operations by the United States and China. Just as it had done in the Middle East, the Eastern Bloc had allied itself with the end to colonial rule and the ongoing cause of opposition to postcolonial but alien settler regimes.[74]

During the 1970s, as the USSR's influence expanded across the world, that of the United States declined. American governments followed two, quite different strategies to deal with the new global situation. Nixon and his successor Gerald Ford, who continued to work closely with Nixon's foreign policy *eminence grise* Kissinger, pursued a policy of détente with the USSR, seeking to stabilize the situation in Europe, and limit the expansion of nuclear weapons. The "opening" to China would be an additional attempt to restrain the USSR. In Asia, Africa, and Latin America, direct US military involvement would be scaled back, following the Vietnam fiasco, and the emphasis would be placed on covert operations and, especially, on locally influential US allies exerting their influence—this was the so-called Nixon doctrine. After the failure of US covert operations to prevent the election of Salvador Allende in Chile, the Nixon administration outsourced much of its effort to undermine the Allende government to the very anti-communist military dictatorship of Brazil, an idea that proved successful. Deploying the apartheid but anti-communist South African government as the pro-US regional power in South Africa made sense in American domestic politics, coming from a president whose "southern strategy" involving appealing to white voters angry with the demands of African Americans, which to many seemed like the North American version of the Global Realignment conflict. It also placed the United States in an alliance with a regime whose policies were rejected not just by the nonaligned countries and the Eastern Bloc, but by most of America's European allies as well, paving the way for the defeat of the pro-US proxy forces in the former Portuguese colonies. Choosing the Shah of Iran as America's main regional ally in the Persian Gulf region appeared to be a sensible move in the first half of the 1970s, but the Iranian Revolution at the end of the decade would reveal its true cost. In 1971 the rebellion of the Bengalis of Eastern Pakistan against the dictatorial rule of the western part of the country led to the creation of an independent Bangladesh. The Nixon administration misinterpreted it as an attempt by nonaligned India in conjunction with the USSR to destroy Pakistan, another proxy regional power, and sent aircraft carriers steaming into the Indian Ocean to ward off a nonexistent threat.[75]

Jimmy Carter, elected US president in 1976, had his own views about the new global situation. He would re-emphasize that American idealism, ultimately stemming from the presidency of Woodrow Wilson during and after the First World War, which had gotten lost in the Vietnam War and the deeply cynical and Machiavellian *Realpolitik* characteristic of Nixon and Kissinger. Carter's signature issue was an emphasis on human rights in international relations, a timely rejection of the open contempt Nixon had shown for civil liberties. In practice, this human rights orientation, proved politically problematic. The USSR's leaders, who thought that Richard Nixon's forced resignation in 1974 stemmed primarily from opposition to his pro-détente foreign policy rather than to domestic politics, interpreted Carter's evocation of human rights issues, particularly the demand that the Jewish population of the USSR be allowed to emigrate, as an attack. They described it to their East German allies, as "a demagogic and provocative campaign," aimed at destroying détente—which was indeed the aim of some of its proponents.[76]

What differentiated Carter from anti-détente American conservatives, however, was his insistence that human rights transcended Cold War alliances.

Unfortunately for Carter's initiatives, many non-communist countries evidently in violation of human rights, including Brazil and the other military dictatorships in Latin America's "Southern Cone," apartheid South Africa, the Shah's Iran, Pakistan, and Indonesia, were also crucial pro-American regional powers. Carter found himself whipsawed between criticism that his emphasis on human rights was undermining America's already weak post-Vietnam global position and the contrary assertion that he was pulling his critical punches on governments blatantly violating human rights out of Cold War concerns. Neither Nixon's nor Carter's approach to the upheavals in international relations were able to stem the decline in America's global influence.[77]

AT THE END OF A DECADE

Two developments at the end of the 1970s reflected all the upheaval. Looked at in retrospect, they were the initial signs of the fundamental reorientation of international relations that would occur in the subsequent Late-Millennium Era. One was the Iranian Revolution of 1979, overthrowing the authoritarian and monarchical rule of the Shah, and replacing it with the world's very first Islamist revolutionary regime. America's close ally and chosen regional partner, complete with all the high-tech weaponry the United States had lavished on the Shah's armed forces, had been replaced with a very strongly anti-American revolutionary government, brought to power by insurgent crowds of, literally, millions, chanting "Death to America!" In the binary logic of the Cold War, a decline of American power could only mean an expansion of Soviet influence, in an oil-rich part of the world, at a time of soaring petroleum prices and gasoline shortages. Some Soviet diplomats and intelligence operatives shared this viewpoint, seeing the reign of the Ayatollah Khomeini as the prelude to a seizure of power by the Tudeh Party, the Iranian communists. Others feared that the new republic's clerical leaders, who had largely supported the CIA in its 1953 coup against the nationalist Mossadeq, would end up back on an anti-communist, pro-American course.[78]

Both viewpoints were fundamentally wrong. It was not just that the Iranian revolutionaries despised both the United States and the USSR, the "great Satan" and the "little Satan" in their parlance. Rather, they saw themselves as representing a new leadership and new orientation in the Global Realignment Struggle. A 1985 statement of Hezbollah, the "Party of Allah," the Lebanese Shiite armed revolutionary movement that had been formed, financed, and directed by the Iranian government, called upon "the disinherited throughout the world to constitute an international front that unites all liberation movements . . . only Islam is fit to embody the idea of resistance against tyranny . . ."[79]

Lebanon was a laboratory of this Islamist anti-imperialism. The 1982 Israeli invasion of that country was aimed at the old Palestinian resistance movement, the secular, leftist nonaligned/Eastern Bloc-oriented PLO, and drove its leading cadres out of the country. Hezbollah quickly took over the leadership of the anti-Israeli forces in Lebanon, ultimately forcing the invaders to evacuate the country, succeeding where the PLO had failed. Western intervention in Lebanon was foiled by Shi'ite militants blowing up the barracks of US Marines and French paratroopers in Beirut. These suicide bombings were an Islamist expansion of the tactics of terrorism, already employed by Algerian and Palestinian anti-imperialists. Hezbollah and its Iranian backers carried out such bombings, not just in Lebanon, but as far off as a Jewish community center in Buenos Aires. Westerners in the region were kidnapped and held hostage. The most famous example was the 1979 invasion of the US embassy in Teheran and the holding of American diplomats hostage, but dozens of Westerners, especially Americans or citizens of France, the former colonial power, were abducted, snatched from hijacked airliners, or just killed on the spot.[80]

Because the Iranians and their Lebanese allies were Shi'ites, adherents of a geographically limited minority confession within Islam, the broader implications of the rise of Islamism remained less evident for much of the 1980s. But Islamism was gaining strength among the majority Sunni confession in that decade and the creation of Islamist regimes during the 1990s in Sudan and Afghanistan, and the adoption of Islamist policies by, among others, the governments of Iraq, Pakistan, and Egypt, would begin to make apparent the fundamental transformation of the Global Realignment Struggle begun in the Iranian Revolution.

A second arena of tension and confrontation was the Euromissiles controversy. Since the humiliation of the Cuban Missile Crisis in 1962, the government of the USSR had been committed to a buildup of its strategic nuclear forces to reach the level of the United States, a goal pursued simultaneously with the nuclear arms control agreements of the 1960s and 1970s. As part of this arms buildup, the USSR began deploying in 1976 medium-range ballistic missiles known in the West as the SS-20s. These could not reach the United States, but could take out targets in Western Europe. Their deployment sparked fears among the Western Europeans that the USSR could fire off these missiles against them but that the Americans would be afraid to retaliate, because the Soviets would respond with a counter-blow against the United States itself. West Germany's Helmut Schmidt demanded that the United States respond by deploying its own medium-range nuclear missiles in Europe.[81]

Both the fear and the proposed response seem now difficult to comprehend. If the USSR attacked Western European targets with nuclear weapons and the United States responded with its own missile barrage, what did it matter whether these missiles were launched from Ramstein Air Force Base near Kaiserslautern in Germany, or from Ellsworth Air Force Base near Rapid City, South Dakota? Either way, they would have struck Soviet targets, leading to retaliation against the United States. There were nonetheless strong personal antagonisms between the two leading Western figures in this issue, Schmidt and Carter, reflecting as well the declining position of the United States in the world and an increasing lack of trust in America on the part of its allies. Setbacks in Asia or Africa were felt in Europe. After fifteen years of stability and détente, Europe became once again a cockpit of the Cold War. In returning the conflict to Europe, the USSR was moving to an arena that was less favorable to it, however, since it was one where the additional force of the Global Realignment Struggle could not be deployed. Little more than a decade after the beginning of the Euromissiles controversy, the USSR's position in world affairs would begin to collapse, in large part as a result of developments in Europe.

International Relations Transformed during the Late Millennium

For all its human rights rhetoric, the Carter administration had sought to maintain its predecessors' policies of détente in Europe and in disarmament negotiations, including a new round of Strategic Arms Limitations Talks, the proposed "SALT II" treaty. This policy was fast being replaced by a more confrontational attitude toward the end of Carter's term. Reasons for this change included the Euromissiles, the Iranian Revolution, and at the end of 1979, the Soviet intervention in Afghanistan.[82] Circumstances in that mountainous Central Asian country were typical of another version of the intersection between the Cold War and the Global Realignment Struggle, one quite different from Palestine or Southern Africa but reflected in both Afghanistan and the less well-known but very similar developments in Ethiopia.

In Afghanistan, as in Ethiopia, a long-term ruling dynasty, supported by powerful landlords/clan leaders and a religious establishment (Coptic Christian in Ethiopia, Islamic in Afghanistan), had been overthrown in a military coup in 1978 and 1974, respectively by a group of young army officers and intellectuals, who thought of themselves as Marxist revolutionaries. These revolutionaries wanted to end capitalism and replace it with socialism but Afghanistan and Ethiopia, especially their remote regions, were very far from capitalism, and arguably, had not even reached the stage of feudalism, which Marxist theory describes as the social formation before capitalism. In Third World politics, worldwide revolutionary initiatives counted for more than the actual political and socioeconomic conditions of the respective countries, so that the new rulers began turning their countries into communist regimes. After some initial reluctance, the Soviets went all in on these revolutionary enterprises in both countries, sending thousands of advisers, and bringing in thousands more from Cuba or East Germany, and offering billions of dollars in foreign aid. These were by far the largest examples of Soviet support for revolution, dwarfing assistance to the Palestinians, the anti-colonialist insurgents and anti-apartheid underground in Southern Africa, or the leftist governments in Chile and Nicaragua.

Not surprisingly, these revolutionary campaigns met with vehement opposition, compounded by issues of ethnic identity—the Somali minority in Ethiopia, the Pashtuns residing in both Afghanistan and Pakistan. The new regimes responded with extreme violence and repression, eventually hundreds of thousands of deaths. In the tradition of Stalinism, it was not just their enemies that the regime leaders killed but factional losers within their own system. While the *Derg*, the revolutionary military dictatorship of Ethiopia, was able to stumble on, the combination of especially violent factional struggles in Afghanistan with an anti-regime uprising in the city of Herat, inspired by the Islamic Revolution in nearby Iran, triggered Soviet intervention.[83]

In its last year, the Carter administration responded by moving forward with the stationing of medium-range Pershing rockets in Western Europe and offering clandestine support to anti-communist insurgents in Afghanistan. A "new Cold War" seemed to be underway, symbolized by the US boycott of the 1980 Moscow Olympic Games. Both in retrospect at and at the time there were questions about how effective such a boycott would be in changing the USSR's foreign policy, but diplomatic effect was not the point. The boycott was a sign of broader competition, going beyond diplomatic and military matters. In practice, the decision generated broad American popular support, and equally broad skepticism among America's allies in Europe and its one-time settler colonies. Teams from the United Kingdom and Australia competed. By contrast, a number of Asian lands, including Indonesia, Japan, and China—the latter at the time often supporting American policies more vigorously than America's allies—endorsed the boycott.[84]

The election victories of the Tories in the United Kingdom in 1979 and the Republicans in the United States in 1980, brought to power two new leaders, Margaret Thatcher and Ronald Reagan, who were at first controversial and later iconic figures of the New Cold War. Their prominence reflects its function as a vortex, sweeping up into it domestic political conflicts and social, economic, and cultural changes. While the earlier Cold War had always been a clash between capitalism and communism, between markets and private property on the one hand, and planning and collective ownership on the other, the capitalism of the period had been a carefully regulated one, with a large degree of government intervention and public ownership.

Reagan and Thatcher came to office on a platform of deregulation, privatization, and dominance of the market—their fervent advocacy of it differentiated them from other prominent conservatives, such as West German Chancellor Helmut Kohl or Japanese Prime Minister Yasuhiro Nakasone. In doing so, they gave the confrontation a much sharper edge.

Even more edged were the Anglo-American leaders' understanding of the Cold War as a war. They vigorously expanded their militaries—all branches of the armed forces, and both conventional and nuclear weapons. The efforts of the Regan administration to create a defense against nuclear missiles, the "Strategic Defense Initiative," or "Star Wars" program as it was known, undermined one of the most important features of the age of détente and of negotiations on nuclear weapons—the rejection of anti-missile systems, because they might tempt the possessor of them to launch a first strike. There was a lot of talk about war, especially nuclear war: fighting it, surviving it, winning it. Characterizing this attitude was the remark Deputy Undersecretary of Defense Thomas K. Jones made to journalist Robert Scheer in 1981. All it took to survive a nuclear attack, Jones opined, was to dig a hole in the ground and cover it with a door. "If there are enough shovels in the ground, everyone's going to make it."[85]

With all that talk about war, it seemed inevitable that there would be one. And, in fact, a year after Jones's confident assertion, one broke out. Somewhat peculiarly, it was against Argentina rather than the USSR, and, even more peculiarly, not about grand issues of freedom or global domination but the possession of the Falkland Islands.[86]

Fortunately, the Falklands War, with its distinctly comic-opera character, was the only one the United States and the United Kingdom fought in the first half of the 1980s. For the third time during the Cold War, there loomed the very real possibility of a thermonuclear confrontation between the USSR and the Western powers. The Soviets became convinced the United States and its allies were aiming at a decisive nuclear first strike. Contemporaries pointed out that the Strategic Defense Initiative would make it possible for the United States to launch an attack without having to fear decisive retaliation. At the time, there were many on both sides who seriously doubted whether such a system could actually work. Their doubts were entirely justified. Even today, after four decades of enormous advances in electronics, computers, radar, and software, anti-missile systems are extremely far from reliable.

A far more realistic prospect was using newly developed computerized targeting systems—what are now called "smart" weapons—to launch a precision attack on command centers, a "decapitating strike," making organized retaliation impossible. Although the medium-range ballistic missiles the United States was stationing in Europe in response to the Soviet SS-20s did not have that sort of targeting capability, their deployment, and other

NATO plans added to suspicions. These plans (promptly passed on to the Soviets via the East Germans' excellent intelligence service) called for precision strikes at command-and-control centers far to the east, in response to a Warsaw Pact invasion of Western Europe. It was not only the Soviets who feared a decapitating first strike; Petra Kelly, the West German pacifist leader and one of the founders of the German Green Party, made just such an argument about the goals of American and NATO military planning, as I heard her say in 1986.[87]

In the early morning hours of September 26, 1983, the duty officer at the Okos early-warning radar station in Moscow, Lieutenant Colonel Stanislav Petrov, received information from Soviet satellite radar that five US ICBMs were incoming. Instead of, as he was supposed to, reporting the strike to the Soviet High Command, which would have almost certainly led to a missile launch and a thermonuclear war, Petrov decided to wait, suspecting an equipment malfunction, since any American attack would have involved more than just five missiles. He was right; Soviet satellites had picked up the sun reflecting off clouds and their computer system had misinterpreted the glow as missile exhaust.[88] It was not the first time such a misidentification had occurred—in 1960, US early-warning radar had confused the moon with Soviet ICBMs—but it happened at a time of heightened tensions, when an attack seemed like a very real possibility. That day was the closet humanity has come to thermonuclear war; Colonel Petrov, though a minor player in the larger drama, was truly a hero of human survival.

The martial attitude of the early 1980s—arms buildup; open belligerence by the governments of Ronald Reagan and Margaret Thatcher, at least tacitly supported by China; intransigent response from the Eastern Bloc—was not limited to dancing on the edge of a thermonuclear holocaust. There was a continuation and expansion of the proxy wars of the 1970s. While potentially less destructive than an exchange of missiles, they ended up killing a lot more people. US policy in Southern Africa combined a realignment with the white-dominated apartheid regime in South Africa and reiterated clandestine support for guerilla movements in Angola. The 1980s saw the opening of a new front in proxy wars, this time in Central America. The Soviets and their Cuban allies helped revolutionary insurgencies against US-supported military regimes in Guatemala and El Salvador. In neighboring Nicaragua, the situation was reversed, with the Soviets and Cubans aiding the Sandanista government in Nicaragua, while the United States provided clandestine support to the *Contra* rebels, a mixture of disillusioned revolutionaries, holdovers from the corrupt and dictatorial Somoza regime the Sandanistas had overthrown, and disaffected ethnic minorities, like the English-speaking Moskito Indians on Nicaragua's Atlantic Coast. Such minority ethnic groups, doubtful about their future in a democratically run independent polity dominated by a hostile majority, had long been a thorn in the side of anti-imperialists in the Global Realignment Struggle. Other examples were the Berbers, who supported the French in Algeria, or the Vietnamese Montagnards and Laotian Hmong, whose militias fought with the United States during the war in Southeast Asia.

Characterized by extreme brutality, and slaughter of civilian populations, the African and Latin American proxy wars, ended along geopolitical lines. At the battle of Cuito Canevale, fought in Angola between September 1987 and March 1988, the largest military engagement in Africa since the Second World War, Cuban forces and their MPLA allies decisively defeated the South Africans and UNITA. There were no such major engagements in Central America, but the outcome of many smaller confrontations were peace agreements, according to which the left-wing insurgents laid down their arms and the revolutionary government left office, in return for which US allies agreed not to murder them—a result very much as US policy makers desired.

These were the last struggles of the Third World phase of the Cold War; two other major conflicts of the first half of the 1980s went in rather different directions, suggesting the future course of international relations.[89] One was the war between Iraq and Iran that ran from 1980 to 1988. The conflict was largely about leadership in the Global Realignment Struggle, pitting Saddam Hussein, a leader of the pro-Soviet wing of the nonaligned states, against the new revolutionary Islamic regime in Iran. Saddam Hussein's war aims, which did not initially even include—though widely thought at the time—the seizure of oil-rich regions of Iran, were based on the assumption of a short, decisive campaign, leading to the collapse of the revolutionary regime. Victorious Iraq would then be catapulted to a leading position in the nonaligned movement more generally, and in the war of the Arab states against Israel, in particular. The decision to invade a larger neighbor—Iran had about three times Iraq's thirteen million inhabitants and about twice its GDP—was a gamble, but in view of the chaotic conditions in Iran following the overthrow of the Shah and the disaffection of large portions of the Iranian armed forces officer corps from the new regime, it seemed like a reasonable risk to take. The combination of inept Iraqi military leadership and unexpectedly stiff Iranian resistance, especially from the *Pasdaran*, the Islamic militia, led to the failure of the Iraqi invasion, which began in September 1980. Iranian forces counterattacked, seeking to destroy the godless Iraqi regime and replace it with a Shi'ite-Islamist one. From spring 1982 onward, the Iraqi government was, literally, fighting for its life.

Both sides in the war claimed to be aligned with the oppressed masses of the Third World, denouncing their opponent as an agent of the chief imperialist, the United States. This was an understandable attitude on the part of Iran, less so on the part of Iraq. In the fall of 1980 pro-regime Iraqi students in New York carried large banners, showing the Ayatollah Khomeini as a puppet, with Uncle Sam pulling the strings. This was at the very same time that Iranian students, with the full backing of the Islamist government, were holding US diplomats in Tehran hostage. Some Iraqi leaders really believed that Khomeini was an American agent.[90] Realities of military and diplomatic support diverged from anti-imperialist representations. After some initial hesitation, both the USSR and the United States, along with their respective European allies, came to the support of the Iraqis, providing them with weapons and satellite intelligence. The revolutionary Islamists in Iran, having alienated most of the world's powers, found things more difficult. The country's prime minister, Abu al-Hasa Bani-Sadr, recognized that "our words and our slogans satisfy no one but us." Iran received some clandestine assistance from China, and even more from North Korea, whose combat engineers played a major role in the 1985 Iranian offensive in the Fao marshes near Basra. Since Iran was fighting the war with the armaments of the Shah's army, a one-time US ally, it badly needed spare parts and ammunition for its American weapons, which it procured through clandestine channels, from Switzerland, South Korea, Israel, and, in the wake of the "Iran-Contra Affair" (the clandestine sale of replacement parts to Iran, with the proceeds being used to support the Nicaraguan Contras, violating a legal prohibition on such funding) even from the United States itself, in spite of the American government's generally pro-Iraqi stance.

Fighting was characterized by atrocities. Iraq made generous use of nerve gas, accounting for about 20 percent of Iranian fatalities (as well as using these weapons on Kurdish rebels and Kurdish civilians in Iraq itself), and also launched indiscriminate missile attacks against Iranian cities. The Iranians specialized in human wave attacks, First-World-War style mass infantry assaults on the dug-in Iraqis. Their attacks were spearheaded by unarmed fourteen-year-old boys, sent into battle with keys hung around their necks, which would open the gates of the kingdom of heaven after their imminent demise. In the end, both sides exhausted themselves and in the summer of 1988 agreed to a peace on the basis of the status quo ante.[91]

From the 1960s onward, the Global Realignment Struggle had been closely connected to the Cold War. In the Iran-Iraq war, these connections were broken. The United States and the USSR were on the same side of a conflict—not totally unprecedented, since they had both, as noted, supported Israeli independence and both opposed the Anglo-French-Israeli invasion of Suez in 1956; they had also both supported the Nigerian central authorities against the Biafran secessionists in the civil war of 1967–70 However, the Iran-Iraq war was a much bigger event, and the United States and the USSR were generally on very bad terms during its first half. Iran, unable to ally with either Cold War superpower, received military support from North Korea and South Korea, and from Syria and Israel, Cold War antagonists and mortal enemies. This disconnection occurred even though the conflict, begun in the wake of the second oil price shock in 1979, was fought in the middle of the world's largest source of oil, and included attacks on oil tankers and port facilities. The Iran-Iraq war, which, in view of the future conflicts emanating from it, could be named, more accurately, the First Gulf War, was a sign of the end of the Cold War, almost a decade before it actually ended.

The contemporaneous Soviet intervention in Afghanistan, was a similar sign of disconnection between the two major forms of conflict in the post-1945 world. At the time, it appeared to be another proxy war, with the United States backing anti-communist insurgents, as the Reagan administration had done in both Southern Africa and in Central America. There was even a rumor, still today neither confirmed nor denied, that the government of Margaret Thatcher was training Afghan insurgents in mountain warfare in the Scottish Highlands. Unlike the proxy wars of the era, however, Soviet forces were directly involved, and the conflict, at least as seen in Washington, took on distinct lines of payback for Vietnam. If so, it seemed to be one that worked even better for the United States, for in Afghanistan China was on its side, training anti-Russian fighters in its western province of Xinjiang, arming and funding them, and sending Uighur (Chinese Muslim) volunteers. Soviet counterinsurgency tactics, like the Americans in Vietnam, told heavily on civilians, difficult to distinguish from the insurgents. Some five million refugees fled into neighboring Pakistan and Iran. Insurgents recruited from them and mixed in with them, making the Pakistani city of Peshawar their headquarters. From there they attacked Soviet troops—even launching attacks in Soviet Central Asia—and then slipped back across the border with Pakistan, out of reach of the Russians. This was much like the Vietcong "sanctuaries" in Laos or Cambodia, or the way that war materiel could travel, free from American interdiction, out of the USSR and China into North Vietnam. The war in Southeast Asia had been both a guerilla struggle and a more conventional conflict; the Afghani *mujahedeen*, or holy warriors, conducted a guerilla campaign, although occasionally with more sophisticated weapons, particularly the shoulder-launched Stinger missiles provided by the United States, which enabled the Islamic fighters to bring down Soviet helicopter gunships.

A crucial difference between Vietnam and Afghanistan is that in Southeast Asia, the Russians and the Chinese had been supporting fellow communists, whose basic political outlook, for all the individual differences and details, agreed with theirs. By contrast, the Islamist fighters the United States and China were supporting in Afghanistan, had different conceptions of the world. For much of the Cold War, Islamists had been aligned with the West: in Iran in 1953; in the 1950s British counterinsurgency campaign against communists in their Malayan colony, in their part in the 1965 massacre of communists in Indonesia; and in the government of Pakistan, more generally. Perhaps the most relevant example was the 1960s Egyptian intervention in Yemen in support of a leftist and pro-Soviet regime against Islamic tribal fighters, who enjoyed Saudi and, somewhat more ambivalently, Western support. That conflict is often known as "Nasir's Vietnam."[92]

In the 1980s, Islamism, in its Shi'ite and Sunni variants, was increasingly making the claim that it should take the lead in the Global Realignment Struggle, which meant not just rejecting the existing alliance between many of the nonaligned states and the Eastern Bloc, but hostility toward any of the world's secular or non-Islamic powers, whether aligned with the USSR, the United States, China, or India. The war in Afghanistan was just the first step in a broader program of global Islamic revolution, especially endorsed by the "Arabs," the volunteers from the Gulf States and other Islamic countries. Later, the best known of these would be the scion of a wealthy Saudi family, Osama bin Laden, but at the time it was Abdullah Azzam. A one-time secular Palestinian nationalist, Azzam had moved toward Islamism after the Arabs' defeat in the 1967 war with Israel, receiving a doctorate in Islamic religious law from the Al-Azhar University in Cairo. He formulated the Islamists' doctrine of *jihad*, proclaiming it every Muslim's duty to take part, either under arms or financially, in a war against the godless powers dominating the world. Azzam lived his own doctrine, directing the distribution of charitable funds to Afghan refugees from the Persian Gulf oil states and founding the "Bureau of Services to the *Mujahedeen*," recruiting, training, and dispatching holy warriors. In a 1988 sermon, preached at the feast of *Eid al-Kabir*—the second of Islam's holy festivals—he stated that being in Afghanistan was, "the accomplishment of *jihad* and of our devotion to the struggle." He added that this did not mean it had "forgotten Palestine," which was still at the core of "our feelings and our faith." In a similar way, the leading Egyptian Islamist in Peshawar, Ayman al-Zawahiri, had told confidants in 1980, at the very beginning of the war with the Soviets, that the real enemy—the so-called far enemy— was the United States.[93]

American intelligence officials were vaguely aware that their goals and those of their Islamist allies were different, retaining a certain skepticism about them—especially as compared to a naïve enthusiasm conservative American politicians and publicists expressed for the Islamic warriors, whom they fundamentally misunderstood as anti-communist freedom fighters. The US policy of funneling its aid through the Pakistani and Saudi governments, with their strong ties to Islamists, ensured that the most pious of the fighters would get the bulk of the money and weapons, and that their political crusade would not end with the USSR. The Afghan war marked a premature post-Cold War alignment.[94]

The militant Anglo-American policy of the New Cold War, at its high point in the first half of the 1980s, and its personification in the persons of Margaret Thatcher and Ronald Reagan, remains profoundly controversial four decades later. For many, Thatcher and Reagan were heroic leaders, who came to power at a time of weakness and decline, when Soviet and Cuban soldiers, KGB agents, Islamist, and secular leftist terrorists had the Western powers in general and the United States in particular on the defensive. Their defense of freedom, rhetoric backed up by forceful diplomacy, a powerful arms buildup, and aid to freedom fighters around the world, turned the tide. (Proponents of this view tend not to note that US policy, under Carter, whom they despise as a weakling, was already turning in this direction.) Pro-Soviet regimes in Latin America, Africa, and Asia collapsed, and the USSR itself, unable to bear the economic burdens of an arms race, was forced to sue for peace, before itself passing into history.

Detractors argue that the arms buildup and saber-rattling nearly led to a thermonuclear nightmare that could easily have destroyed all life on earth and prolonged the Cold War by preventing more sensible Soviet leadership from coming to power. Widespread demonstrations against nuclear weapons in both North America and Western Europe during the early 1980s underscore this judgment. (Reagan's defenders regard these mass movements as sponsored and manipulated by the Russians.)[95] The "freedom fighters" who enjoyed American support were merely thugs and religious fanatics. Far from conducting a coherent foreign policy, Reagan was an out-of-touch leader (which no one would ever say about Margaret Thatcher), possibly suffering from senile dementia, influenced by his wife's astrologer, surrounded by feuding factions, whose members advocated and carried out very different and sometimes diametrically opposed policies.

As always, there are points that can be made on both sides. The anti-Soviet activists the United States supported in, say, Poland, during the 1980s—Solidarity—seem in retrospect pretty admirable, while their anti-communist counterparts in Angola, Afghanistan, or Nicaragua far less so. Moving beyond these partisan, polemical, and clashing opinions requires seeing the distance between perceptions of global conflicts then and now. To contemporaries, the Eastern Bloc along with its nonaligned allies really did seem to be pressing forward on all fronts, while the United States and its allies were increasingly in retreat. Some of this perception stemmed from biased sources, like the so-called Team B that concluded in 1976 that the USSR was expanding its nuclear and conventional weapons, and on track to fight and win a nuclear war. Team B's conclusions played a large role in Reagan's administration, but their findings were the antithesis of empirical reality. Some of the individuals associated with the exercise, such as Richard Perle and Paul Wolfowitz, would play a key role in leading the United States into a war in Iraq a quarter-century later, based on equally dubious assertions. Yet fears of Soviet global predominance could be found far outside the US. Chinese leader Deng Xiaoping, returning to power after the Cultural Revolution, at the same time that Team B was doing its studies, was also deeply concerned about Soviet prospects for world domination. Deng advocated a policy of *yi tiaoxian*, "a single line," uniting countries in the same latitude in the northern hemisphere, China, Japan, the United States, and Northern Europe, against the USSR. That Deng—a cool, pragmatic realist, so unlike his predecessor, Mao Zedong, the ideologue and revolutionary fantasist—should support such an anti-Soviet alliance, says a lot about the state of international relations at the time.[96]

Viewed from the twenty-first century, both Eastern advance and Western retreat seem like an illusion. The USSR had expanded considerably its nuclear arsenal in the 1960s and 1970s, in an economically destructive effort, well before the immense American responses during the subsequent decade. Yet all that buildup had brought the Soviets no actual military or diplomatic advantages. While the USSR did seem to have acquired an impressive number of nonaligned allies, they were, as Dimitrii Volksii, a disillusioned foreign affairs commentator, observed at the end of the 1980s, more a burden than an asset. The "national-patriotic forces" supported by the Soviet Union started to behave like "feudal or even prefeudal princes," and their countries' "tired and indignant people had finally lost patience and overthrown their rulers."[97]

Problems with America's position in the world attributed to Soviet aggression actually had rather different causes. One was the economic upheaval caused by transition from the Bretton Woods world of regulated capitalism to the globalized, privatized, and deregulated Late-Millennium Era. Reagan and Thatcher's economic policies may have helped deal with these problems (or not), but the massive arms buildup and covert operations did not. Another major problem was the growing self-assertion caused by the Global Realignment Struggle. The rise of Islamism was a crucial element of this development and ignored by those who interpreted it through a Cold War lens and in doing so missing its significance.

We can see now that the strength of the Eastern Bloc at the end of the 1970s was largely illusory, or, at the very least, built on crumbling foundations, helping explain that bloc's astonishingly rapid collapse in 1989. Whether or not the US policies contributed to that collapse, the fundamental weaknesses of the USSR and its allies, both in Europe and in the nonaligned countries, were the main cause. What followed in the subsequent decade, the period from 11/9 to 9/11—the fall of the Berlin Wall on November 9, 1989, to the terrorist attack on the Twin Towers of September 11, 2001—stemmed, to a great extent, from developments that were largely overlooked in the drama of the end of the Cold War.

THE END OF THE COLD WAR AND ITS RAMIFICATIONS, 1985–2001

The main reason for the end of the Cold War was the decision of the leaders of the two largest communist states to introduce reforms. In doing so, they were demolishing a central element of the Cold War—its character as a confrontation of two fundamentally opposed socioeconomic systems. The West was not victorious over communism; the end of communism led to its triumph. Crucial to this was how differently the process played out between European communist states, including the Eurasian USSR, and Asian ones: in the former, with immense political upheavals and regime change, including the termination of the Soviet Union itself; in the latter, under the control, if shaky at times, of the existing regimes. These differences showed how the Cold War itself was closely tied to the outcome of the Second World War—and how that connection remains the case.

Mikhail Gorbachev's rise to power in 1985 was a sign of a new departure. Young and vigorous, a contrast to his elderly and incapacitated predecessors, Brezhnev, Andropov, and Chernenko, his program of domestic reforms, *perestroika*, (economic) restructuring and *glasnost* (social and political) openness, was flanked by an effort to reshape Soviet foreign policy, dubbed "new thinking" by Gorbachev and his foreign policy expert Eduard Shevardnadze. The basis of it was to end or at least scale back the nuclear arms race with the United States; reduce tensions between the Cold War blocs in Europe—Gorbachev talked about "a common European home"; draw down expensive commitments to friendly regimes and insurgent movements in Asia, Africa, and Latin America; and, last, to promote better relations with rival communist great power China. Within a few years, Gorbachev had achieved all these goals. However, the way he achieved them undermined his reform plans, his own position, and, ultimately, the existence of the country he led.

Gorbachev's foreign policy difficulties had three main causes. One was the failure of his economic reforms. Trying to replace central planning with market incentives, and government ownership with private property produced inflation, shortages, increasing economic chaos and a declining GDP rather than an increased availability of consumer goods, which citizens of the USSR, and all communist countries, had come to expect—a central Cold War competition that the Eastern Bloc was losing. A debate remains whether the reforms were too aggressive or not aggressive enough. Either way, their failure undermined and delegitimized the government's foreign policy initiatives, to which they were connected.[98]

The second reason was the response of the USSR's Cold War adversaries to its new initiatives. Margaret Thatcher seemed interested in Gorbachev's ideas, making her celebrated remark, "I like Mr. Gorbachev. We can do business together." American policy makers showed much less flexibility. They stonewalled his initiatives, refusing to compromise on any element of arms reduction negotiations. In the end, Gorbachev got his agreements, but only on American terms: scuttling all his medium-range nuclear missiles, in return for the far fewer American ones installed in Europe; accepting America's missile defense program; and making large cuts in Warsaw Pact conventional forces. After Reagan and his advisers had agreed to the "zero option"—the elimination of both blocs' medium-range missiles in Europe—Reagan's successor, George H. W. Bush, promptly began a program of installing new, short-range nuclear missiles in Europe. US policy treated Gorbachev as little different from Stalin, a rival to be defeated and humiliated rather than an adversary with whom it would be possible to cooperate (in Thatcher's phrase, "do business with"). Only after the Soviet regime had received fatal blows in 1989–90, did US policy shift in the direction of trying to support and endorse Gorbachev, but by that time it was too late.[99]

This brings up the third and most important reason for the failure of Gorbachev's initiatives: developments within the Eastern Bloc itself. In those parts of Eastern Europe that had come under communist rule after 1945, repeated instances of opposition to this imposed regime had been a feature of political life. The Helsinki Accords, with their "third basket" guarantees of human rights, provided an impetus to political opposition; the threat of nuclear war in the early 1980s became a reason for political protest as much in the East as well as the West. The 1980 strikes in the Polish city of Gdansk, leading to the formation of the Solidarity trade union movement, which quickly grew to encompass close to ten million members and was recognized by the Polish communist government as a bargaining partner, posed a particular threat. But with Soviet forces heavily engaged in Afghanistan and Ethiopia, and a nuclear and conventional arms buildup threatening economic stability, "The quota of interventions abroad has been exhausted," as then-KGB Chairman Yuri Andropov put it. The USSR had to rely on the Polish communists to deal with the oppositional mass movement, on the brink of becoming an anti-communist shadow government, which they did, by declaring martial law in December 1981.[100]

In many ways, Solidarity was an exception. Compared to the uprisings of 1953 and 1956, or the mass protests of 1968 and 1970, opposition movements in most Eastern Bloc countries had just a small circle of supporters and a limited political resonance. But Gorbachev's reform efforts in the years after 1985 unintentionally empowered them. Members of small and beleaguered opposition groups could and did state that they stood for his ideas; hard-line governments in East Germany, Czechoslovakia, Romania, and Bulgaria, to say nothing of anti-reform party leaders in the USSR itself, were in the awkward position of opposing the stated policy of the leader of the movement they had spent their lives serving.

This conjunction came to a head in 1989, leading to a wave of revolutions, comparable to the other canonical revolutionary years of modern European history—1789, 1848, and 1917. In the wake of these uprisings, the Cold War was terminated. The events began in 1988, with a new wave of strikes and anti-regime demonstrations in Poland, to which the embattled communist government responded by negotiating with Solidarity (still officially illegal). As a result of these negotiations, competitive multiparty elections were held in Poland the following year, the first in Eastern Europe since 1946. Solidarity candidates scored an overwhelming victory, leading to the creation of a coalition government, with Solidarity's Lech Walesa as prime minister and the Communist Party leader General Jaruzelski as president. This was followed in short order by the communist government in Hungary announcing, on its own initiative, without any oppositional mass movement, that it would hold multiparty elections and would open the border with Austria—or "tear down the iron curtain," as the phrase went at the time. These were quite unprecedented developments; in the past, anything even remotely similar, had brought Soviet military intervention, but Gorbachev perceived them as endorsement of his own reform plans, and, far from opposing them, embraced them.

Tens of thousands of citizens of East Germany took advantage of the new situation in Hungary to flee to West Germany via Hungary and Austria in the summer of 1989. Efforts of the East German government, whose hardcore Stalinist leaders were strong opponents of Gorbachev's policies, to keep its citizens out of other Eastern Bloc countries, incited anti-regime demonstrations, in the course of which dissidents suddenly emerged as leaders of immense crowds. The demonstrators sang, alternately, "We Shall Overcome," anthem of the US civil rights movement and the "Internationale," anthem of world communism. They chanted "Gorby! Gorby!," presenting themselves as the proponents of a true communism, rather than the regime that had taken that role for the past four decades. The East German communists, more hard line, more determined, more efficient than the Poles had been with Solidarity, no longer had the nerve to act similarly.

These different outcomes were, above all, the result of a different Soviet leadership: determined to preserve the status quo in 1981, equally determined to carry out reforms eight years later. Instead of shooting or arresting the opposition, the East German government offered it one concession after another, including, finally, one on the issue that had set off the crisis—the freedom to travel outside the Eastern Bloc. This decision explained in an impromptu answer to a question by an Italian journalist at a hastily called press conference in East Berlin on the afternoon of November 9, 1989—by an East German party official having no experience with press conferences—led the public to believe that the Berlin Wall would be opened. Crowds showed up at that Wall that very evening. Once again, rather than try to repress them, the authorities let them through.

The images of these crowds of people climbing and dancing on the Wall broadcast by TV around the world, made it clear to anyone watching that the Cold War, which had begun in that very spot in Berlin, the boundary between the Soviet and British occupation sectors, had returned to its origin to die. And die it did. Within a few months, similar mass movements had brought communist regimes in Czechoslovakia, Romania (rather more violently there; a distinct exception to the generally peaceful character of the events), and Bulgaria to an end. With the end of the communist government, the reason for the existence of an East Germany separate from West Germany had also been terminated, and the free and competitive multiparty elections that took place there in March 1990 would make this clear.[101]

This was Helmut Kohl's moment. Dismissed as a provincial politician, overshadowed for most of the decade by his flashier and more aggressive counterparts, Reagan and Thatcher, Kohl was determined to find a way to create, peacefully, a post-Cold War European state system. He was assisted in this endeavor by George H. W. Bush, another right-of-center statesman, who had also spent most of the 1980s overshadowed. Along with his foreign policy expert, James Baker, Bush rejected their previous skepticism about the possibility of changes in the Eastern Bloc and supported Kohl in his search for a new Europe. The solution they found was not entirely evident, the "two plus four talks," negotiations between the leaders of the two German states and the victorious powers of the Second World War. Although all the participants in those talks denied it, they were essentially participating in a peace conference, ending the Second World War. They terminated the military occupation of German territory, agreed to the merger of the two German states into a fully sovereign one, and recognized the territorial changes of the Yalta and Potsdam Conferences that had transferred the eastern territories of the German *Reich* to Poland. The united Germany, going by the name and with the constitution of the old West Germany, the Federal Republic, would continue to be a member of NATO—this was yet another point Gorbachev conceded in negotiations—although the possibility of an informal guarantee was floated that NATO troops would not be stationed in former Warsaw Pact territories, or, at least, in the former East Germany. The newly united Federal Republic would pay the USSR war reparations, some $40 billion, ostensibly to meet the costs of withdrawing Soviet troops from East Germany (although for that price all the three hundred thousand Soviet soldiers stationed there could have bought first-class airline tickets with almost all the money left over). The Cold War and the Second World War ended at the same time—as was only appropriate, since the first had emerged from the inability of the victorious Allies to find a peace settlement ratifying the outcome of the second.

The outcome of the two plus four talks rendered obsolete the 1975 Helsinki Conference on Peace and Security in Europe, which had ratified the division of the continent in general and defeated Germany in particular into opposing Cold War blocs. The dissolution of the postwar orientation had become apparent. The United States had enthusiastically supported Chancellor Kohl's efforts to unite the two German states, and Gorbachev had made no serious efforts to stop them. By contrast, President François Mitterrand had, as the French say, put a *bonne mine au mauvais jeu*—a cheerful face on a bad situation—and reluctantly gone along. Margaret Thatcher and her closest advisers had vehemently denounced the entire development and openly expressed fears of a revival of German domination of Europe.[102]

These fears, widespread at the time, were quickly disproven, for united Germany has been anything but a militarist, aggressive, or racist dictatorship. But the revolutionary events were more than the USSR could withstand. The oppositional mass movements of 1989 occurred in those areas of Eastern Europe that had come under communist control at the end of the Second World War, including parts of the Soviet Union: the Baltic states, as well as the western portions of Ukraine and Belarus. They were joined by regions of longer-standing, pre-Soviet opposition to Russian rule, especially in the Caucasus. An increasingly weakened Soviet system, whose economic reforms had backfired badly, and whose foreign policy had ended in humiliation, could no longer suppress this opposition. The decision of the largest non-Russian Soviet republic, the Ukraine, to secede from the USSR, spurred on a last desperate effort on the part of army officers and leaders of the security services to reverse the trend. Their August 1991 coup, in the course of which a number of its leaders were either in the hospital or a drunken stupor, was an embarrassing failure, sealing the fate of the USSR and its last leader.

What were the effects on the rest of the world? In 1989 small groups of dissidents had emerged as the leaders of mass demonstrations all across communist Eurasia, from Magdeburg to Beijing. The events in China had distinct similarities to what occurred in Eastern Europe, down to the enthusiasm for Mikhail Gorbachev. During his state visit to China in May 1989, official protocol was disrupted when a crowd of two hundred thousand spontaneously gathered in Beijing, cheering the Soviet leader and holding up placards reading, "We Salute the Ambassador of Democracy."[103] The outcome of these demonstrations, however, was fundamentally different in Asia. The Chinese government brought in the army to open fire on demonstrators in Tiananmen Square, killing large numbers of them, probably thousands. Reform-minded officials, like the General Secretary of the Chinese Communist Party, Zhao Ziyang, were arrested.

Demonstrators elsewhere in the fall of 1989 were uneasily aware of the Chinese precedent of repression; the East German government and party leadership in particular had praised the way their Chinese comrades had made short work of "counterrevolutionaries" and called for a "Beijing solution" to political dissent in their own country. Nonetheless their aggressive and militant language stood in contrast to their passive and concession-oriented response to antigovernment demonstrations. It was this regime response that made the difference between Europe and Asia. While the demonstrators in Tiananmen Square were a small group in a large country, the same was true almost everywhere in the Eastern Bloc (with perhaps the exception of Estonia). Even the largest demonstrations involved a small minority of the population. The demonstrations in China, which included blue-collar workers as well as students, were not limited to Beijing, but occurred in Shanghai, Harbin, Nanjin, Chengdu, and other cities as well. Gorbachev's economic reforms were rapidly failing in 1989 and delegitimizing both reforming and hard-line communist regimes. If not in such severe difficulties, China was suffering from slowing rates of economic growth and rapidly rising inflation. However, the Chinese Communist Party (CCP) leadership, untouched by a decade of failed military interventions and subsequent humiliating diplomatic concessions, lacking the USSR's array of satellite states whose destabilization was reflected back into the Soviet Union, was still sure it could maintain control of the situation.[104]

When the East German communists talked of a "Beijing solution," they meant both the violent suppression of dissidents and an end to Gorbachev's market-oriented economic initiatives. It was an open question whether the end to political dissent in China also meant an end to the reintroduction of capitalism in Asia's giant communist realm. The answer would become clear with Deng Xiaoping's "southern tour" two years later. Eighty-seven years old and suffering from Parkinson's disease, Deng traveled through the emerging industrial and market centers of Coastal Southern China, urging a continuation and expansion of the economic reforms he had initiated. The Fourteenth Congress of the CCP (in October of 1992) endorsed this idea and marked the triumph of the pro-capitalist wing of the party leadership.[105] The transition from communism to capitalism in China had shaken but not overthrown authoritarian rule; that same transition had destroyed every single government in the Eastern Bloc. If the Cold War ended with the defeat of the USSR and its allies, it also ended with China on the path to becoming a twenty-first-century superpower.

All of this fundamentally transformed the Global Realignment Struggle, which had become so deeply intertwined with it over the years. The nonaligned countries and insurgencies that were allied with the USSR had to rethink their policies when their superpower patron no longer existed. One rather more heartening example of this development was the end of the apartheid regime in South Africa. The white minority government's sole justification for its existence by the end of the 1980s was its role as an anticommunist bulwark. The opposition to white domination in South Africa itself was organized primarily by the African National Congress, which was led by communists and generously supported by the USSR. Civil wars in the former Portuguese colonies of Southern Africa had resulted in the triumph of pro-Moscow regimes.

Although there had been tentative gestures toward change in South Africa in the second half of the 1980s—back-channel conversations between the South African government and the ANC, or proposals for a new constitution, allowing for representation of the nonwhite population, while maintaining a dominant role for whites—the decisive step away from this state of affairs came with mass movements in the Eastern Bloc in 1989. South African president F.W. de Klerk, a hard-line supporter of apartheid, explained that the fall of the Berlin Wall "was as if God had taken a hand—a new turn in world history." "We had to seize the opportunity." "Seizing the opportunity" meant that in February 1990, the government released veteran communist and African National Congress Leader Nelson Mandela from twenty-seven years in jail, and legalized both the ANC and the South African Communist Party. Four years of difficult negotiations led to the 1994 universal suffrage elections, which brought the African National Congress to power, terminated the apartheid regime, and made Mandela South Africa's president. If the leaders of the apartheid regime saw the post-1989 handwriting on the wall, the same was true of its opponents. With the end of the USSR Nelson Mandela renounced his previous communist inclinations, becoming president of a distinctly capitalist post-apartheid South Africa, a regime that allowed the formerly dominant white minority to retain all its property.[106]

Mandela's choices have come in for criticism in left-wing circles, although the extent of his remarkable statesmanship in leading a peaceful transition to a post-apartheid regime can best be appreciated by considering what happened in Congo, one of sub-Saharan Africa's three most populous countries (Nigeria and South Africa being the other two). Congo's independence from Belgium in 1960 had led straight into a civil war, in which the anti-imperialist prime minister Patrice Lumumba was overthrown and murdered by his domestic enemies, working closely with the former Belgian colonial power and the CIA. Lumumba became a worldwide anti-imperialist martyr, but the Congo's ruler emerging from this conflict, Joseph Mobutu, who renamed himself Mobutu Sese Seko, and his country Zaire, proved a very reliable ally of the Western powers during the Cold War. Mobutu was also a military dictator whose reign was, even by African standards, dictatorial, violent, corrupt, kleptocratic and economically disastrous. The end of the Cold War made him and his government as superfluous as apartheid South Africa.

The governments of a number of African countries, including neighboring Rwanda, Uganda, and Angola, as well as Ethiopia and Eritrea, many of whose leaders were pupils or protégés of the Pan-Africanist, anti-imperialist statesman Julius Nyerere of Tanzania, resolved to rid the continent of

Mobutu. They invaded in 1995. Lacking American support (the US government even tacitly endorsed the invasion), Mobutu's rule quickly collapsed, and the invaders installed as the country's new leader Laurent Kabila, a onetime close associate of Lumumba. Kabila quickly fell out with his patrons, who also fell out with each other, and in 1997 a new war erupted, pitting ethnic groups in Congo and neighboring Rwanda against each other, and African powers against each other as well. This conflict, sometimes referred to as "Africa's Great War," lasted five years, and was characterized by large-scale looting of Congo's natural resources, and the fighting forces regularly raping, robbing, and murdering Congo's long-suffering civilians. Nominally ending with Kabila's assassination in 2001 and a truce, which left Congo without a functioning government, conflict continued at a lower level. Between 1998 and 2007, total deaths from wartime violence and disease may have been as many as 7.5 million.[107]

Another sign of the transformation of the Global Realignment Struggle by the end of the Cold War was the result of the 1990 Iraqi invasion of Kuwait, prompted by Iraqi leader Saddam Hussein's desperate need for money following the long, expensive, and futile Gulf War with Iran. After an initial unopposed march into Kuwait, the Iraqis could have continued into a largely undefended Saudi Arabia, gaining control of most of the Persian Gulf's oil assets, and making the expulsion of Iraqi troops a very difficult and problematic affair. Saddam's caution, even in potentially favorable situations, a problem that had plagued the initial phase of the Iraqi war with Iran, held him back and gave the United States time to ship forces to the Middle East and to assemble an anti-Iraqi coalition. The ensuing second Gulf War, pitting Iraq against virtually the entire world, had a not-particularly-surprising outcome.

The Iraqi government and its socialist revolutionary Ba'ath Party had been one of the leaders of the pro-Soviet revolutionary wing of the nonaligned nations and had, in the past, counted on the support of the USSR. But Saddam's invasion occurred as the USSR was in a state of collapse, unable to provide anyone with assistance. The only ally the Iraqi dictator could gain was another pro-Soviet nonaligned group—an insurgent movement rather than a sovereign state, the PLO. Its support was not worth much against the might of the US military, supported by the rest of the world. In the end, the second Gulf War suggested that the conclusion of the Cold War had ended the Global Realignment Struggle as well. There would be, as President George H. W. Bush first put it, in a September 1990 speech before a joint session of Congress, a "new world order."[108]

Such a world order would be, as contemporaries liked to assert, "unipolar," unambiguously dominated by the United States, which had become, as French Foreign Minister Hubert Védrine stated in 1997, a "hyperpower."[109] What really seemed to determine some of the larger-scale conflicts of the 1990s was the extent of US involvement: intervention in the civil war raging in the former Yugoslavia; intense mediation efforts in the clash between Israelis and Palestinians, contrasted with a total unwillingness to step into the mass murders in Rwanda, and the Great African War in the Congo closely linked to it; or the embittered civil war in Afghanistan, following the withdrawal of Soviet forces. A similar dichotomy between intervention and abstention appears in the debates over US foreign policy.

Everyone involved agreed that the United States was the dominant power in the world; the question was how it would use this position. One point of view was that the United States should be restrained, limiting the extent and frequency of economic and diplomatic involvement or military intervention, and doing so only in multilateral fashion. The opposite was that the United States should be more aggressive in its interventions, deploying its hyperpower to create a truly new global order, not worrying too much about allies. Advocates of different policies cut across the usual political lines, but overall Bush and Clinton tended to the more cautious options. There were certainly left-of-center advocates of the use of US military power in support of human rights—making a successful argument in Bosnia and Kosovo, although not in Rwanda—but most proponents of using US power for global reshaping were on the right, former militant Cold Warriors from the Reagan administration, grouped in organizations such as the "Project for A New American Century." They would get their chance at the beginning of the twenty-first century, during the administration of George W. Bush, less cautious than his father.[110]

In retrospect, the fundamental assumption of both sides of the policy debate that the United States had achieved a new and unchallenged position in the world was profoundly incorrect. Rather, the favorable position of the United States during the 1990s was temporary. Its Cold War antagonist, the USSR, had vanished, and the Soviet Union's successor states, especially the Russian Federation that had inherited its thermonuclear arsenal, were in an enfeebled and chaotic condition. America's chief capitalist rivals, Japan and Germany, were both going through periods of economic difficulty and so less able to exert their influence. While the government of China had mastered the transition from a centrally planned economy, with a large degree of public ownership, to a more capitalist regime, without collapsing, as had been the case with the countries of the Eastern Bloc, it would take two decades of rapid economic growth before it would be in a position to offer a serious challenge the United States.

A serious challenge to the United States would emerge before then, out of the Global Realignment Struggle. The nonaligned revolutionary regimes and insurgent movements were left unfunded and disoriented by the disappearance of the USSR, which had provided them with weapons, economic assistance, and diplomatic support. But their disarray did not mean that the

Struggle had vanished, as was often assumed at the time. Rather, a new ideological revolutionary movement, came to the fore with the defunding and disarray of its rivals, Islamism, and it steadily gained ground and influence in the course of the final decade of the twentieth century.

Aside from Iran, there were few new Islamist regimes—only Sudan and the partial rule of the Taliban in Afghanistan. Islamists won decisive election victories in, Algeria in 1991 and 1992. The existing government, successor to the nationalist, anti-colonialist insurgents against the French, and the radical nonaligned regime of the 1970s and 1980s, responded with a military coup, leading to a violent civil war between it and the Islamic Salvation Front. Among the anti-Israeli insurgents in Palestine, the Islamist group Hamas gained ground steadily against the secular-nationalist Fatah. The largest influence of Islamism was the way that non-Islamist governments in predominantly Muslim countries, including Egypt, Pakistan, and Malaysia, made one concession after another, including the introduction of *sharia*, Islamic law, in the civil and criminal code, funding Islamist charities and mosques, and letting it be known that practices contrary to Islamic religion, whether it was consuming alcohol or women not wearing headscarves, were not to be tolerated. Even Saddam Hussein, whose Arab nationalist and conspicuously secularist Baathist regime had battled both Sunni and Shi'ite Islamists, moved in that direction to the point that Arab nationalist Ba'ath Party veterans began complaining that Baghdad was increasingly resembling Riyadh.[111]

Islamists viewed the end of communism as their triumph, accomplished by the holy war they had waged in Afghanistan. The confidence they had gained in this struggle against the godless communists inspired them to go on to confront their new enemies, "the Judeo-crusading alliance," as Osama bin Laden declared in his 1996 "Declaration of Jihad against the Americans Occupying the Land of the Two Holy Sanctuaries." This unholy alliance's troops were present in Saudi Arabia, perilously close to the Islamic holy places, and of course, it occupied Jerusalem. Bin Laden called for the ouster of American troops stationed in Saudi Arabia and denounced infidel aggression against the faithful around the world: "The blood of Muslims . . . is flowing in Palestine, Iraq, and Lebanon . . . not to mention the massacres in Tajikistan, Burma, Kashmir, Assam, the Philippines, Pattani, Ogaden, Somalia, Eritrea, Chechnya and Bosnia-Herzogovina, where Muslims have been the victims of atrocious acts of butchery."[112]

In bin Laden's mind all attacks on Muslims were attributed to the "Americans and their allies." America was behind the anti-Muslim post-Soviet regimes in Chechnya and Tajikistan; it was behind the Cold War neutralist Indian government in Kashmir and Assam, or its counterpart in Burma; it was behind ethnic and religious clashes in the Horn of Africa; and it was behind anti-Muslim persecution in the former Yugoslavia (although

American intervention in Bosnia and Kosovo ended the mass murder of Muslims by Serbian nationalists). This assertion was the flip side of the United States as a hyperpower: since it was globally dominant, it had to be responsible for massacres of Muslims around the world.

Islamists rejected all the previous and more secular, nationalist, and socialist ideologies of the Global Realignment Struggle, seeing them as another version of imperialist oppression. Osama bin Laden had no truck with Saddam Hussein, the secular Third World nationalist, even proposing to the Saudi government in 1990 that he and his adherents, fresh from their victorious struggle against the USSR in Afghanistan, should oust the invading Iraqis from Kuwait. It was bad enough that the Saudi regime rejected the Islamist offer, but then it allowed American troops to deploy close to the holy places and, even worse, to be stationed there after the conclusion of the second Gulf War.

Islamists from around the world flocked to bin Laden's organization, Al Qaeda. Its leader and base of operations would be located in a country with a sympathetic government: initially, Sudan, whose military government was strongly influenced by the Islamist leader Hasan al-Turabi. Forced to leave under American pressure in 1996, bin Laden returned to Afghanistan, scene of the Islamist triumph over the USSR, increasingly under the control of the Taliban, whose reign enjoyed at least the tacit support of the government of Pakistan, and, especially, its military intelligence, both of which were moving in steadily more Islamist directions. There, bin Laden and his chief lieutenants, particularly the Egyptian physician Ayman al-Zawahiri, a veteran of a decades-long struggle of Islamists with secular nationalists in his native country, took aim at the United States. Although the leaders of Al Qaeda had nothing good to say about the leftist radicals of the PLO or the Islamist Shi'ites of Hezbollah, they imitated their past tactics: bombings of the US embassies in Nairobi and Dar es Salaam in 1998—the date, August 7, was the eighth anniversary of the arrival of US troops in Saudi Arabia, thus, in Al Qaeda's view defiling the Islamic holy places during the run-up to the second Gulf War—and the attack on the American warship, the *USS Cole* in the port of Aden in October 2000. There followed the largest and most elaborate terrorist attack in human history, striking the centers of American military and financial power. The airliners hijacked by Al Qaeda militants—once again, imitating tactics of the PLO and Hezbollah—were flown into the Pentagon in Washington, and the World Trade Center in New York's financial district on September 11, 2001.[113]

The assault, which caught US intelligence and air defense totally unprepared, made it clear that the unipolar decade of international relations was over, and that the Global Realignment Struggle, far from having been eliminated by the end of the Cold War, would continue under very different ideological auspices. Indeed, the defeat of the USSR, discrediting the secular radical ideologies it advocated and ending its support for adherents of such ideologies in Asia, Africa, and Latin America, made possible the rise of the Islamists, who by 1990 were the chief rivals of the nationalists and socialists in the nonaligned world. Another way to put it would be to say that there was a direct line leading from the fall of the Berlin Wall to the fall of the Twin Towers, and with that latter event an end to the structure of international relations in the Age of Interconnection.

Society and Economy

Television on its march toward global domination. Japanese boys stare, fascinated, at a TV set in 1960.

Source: AKG Images.

China Shipping Line, Container Vessel docking in Hong Kong harbor, 2010. The introduction of the shipping container in the 1970s played a major role in both the globalization of industrial production and in the economic rise of China.

Source: AKG Images

Seventy-six Turks, working illegally in West Germany, being rounded up for deportation in 1970.

Turkish "Guest Workers" at the Düsseldorf airport, also 1970, waiting for a flight back home, probably for vacation. The migration of labor from the countries of the Mediterranean Basin to the lands of Northern Europe during the 1960s, marked the beginning of a new global migration regime, following decades of low migration rates during the age of total war.

Source (for both): AKG Images.

Tourists on the beach at beach at El Arenal, Palma de Mallorca, 1999. Mass tourism in the countries of the Mediterranean Basin was one of the characteristic features of the development of consumer society in Europe during the last third of the twentieth century.

Source: Getty images.

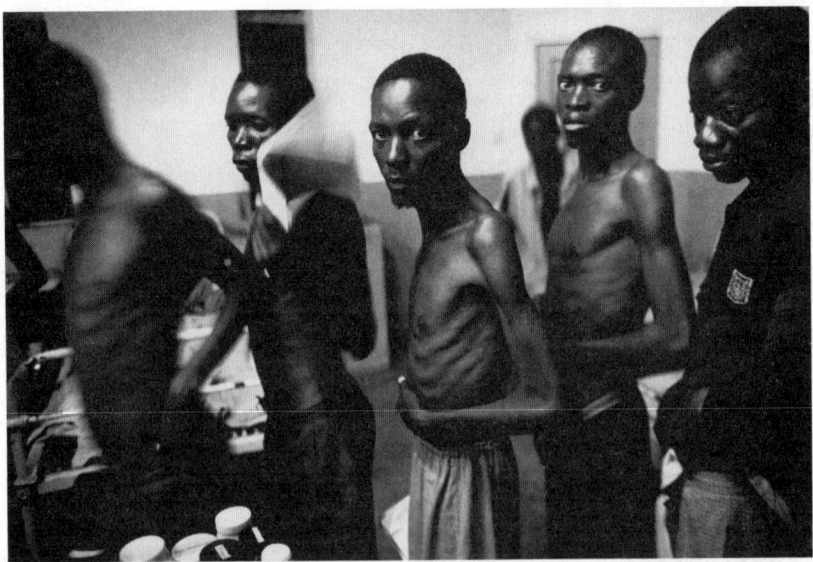

TB patients line up for medication in a Malawi hospital, 2000. The combination of HIV/AIDS weakening immune systems, and the spread of the *Mycobacterium tuberculosis*, which is particularly virulent, when the human immune system is weakened, led to tens of millions of deaths in Africa in the late twentieth and early twenty-first century. It may also have contributed to the belief that the world's wealthy and even modestly affluent countries were not in danger of a large-scale attack of infectious disease.

Source: Getty images.

Technology

One of the first computers, Remington Rand's UNIVAC, in 1951. The very large size of early computers fed dreams about giant brains that could perform unheard of calculations. The actual direction of microelectronics, toward ever smaller devices, performing more mundane tasks, was quite unexpected.

Source: AKG Images.

The astronaut Buzz Aldrin walks on the moon, during the Apollo 11 mission, July 1969. The lunar voyage of Apollo 11 seemed like the beginning of the realization of the twentieth-century dream of the human colonization of the solar system. Reality proved very different. Following the end of the Apollo program, humans have never left low earth orbit.

Source: NASA

The 1953 VW Beetle. A product of the age of total war, the main alternative to large, chrome-laden US cars during the 1950s, the "Bug" was, in the long run, an engineering dead end.

Source: AKG Images.

The Morris Mini, 1968. This now forgotten vehicle was the first mass-produced automobile with a transversely mounted front-wheel drive and independent suspensions. Most cars manufactured in the last quarter of the twentieth century used these features and were in some ways the Mini's descendants.

Source: AKG Images

The East German car, the Trabant, driving off the assembly line in Zwickau, 1958. The inability of communist regimes to produce either enough or good quality automobiles, one of the two great, hotly desired consumer durables of the second half of the twentieth century, played a large role in stirring up popular discontent and demonstrated the regimes' failure in their competition with the Western Powers in the Cold War.

Source: AKG Images.

The Nobel-prize winning biologist Norman Borlaug holds up sheaves of the high-yield, disease-resistant hybrid wheat he had developed. Although lacking the great resonance of space travel, computers or nuclear power, the hybridization of grains was, arguably, the single most important technological development of the second half of the twentieth century. The increase in crop yields it produced meant that even though the world's population tripled between 1950 and 2000, standards of living (overall) rose and people had (once again, overall) more to eat.

Source: Getty images

International Relations and their Conflicts

US Marines watch an atomic bomb test in the Nevada desert, 1953.

SS-4 intercontinental ballistic missiles, able to carry thermonuclear warheads, in the 1961 May Day parade on Red Square in Moscow.
The threat of an apocalyptic nuclear or thermonuclear confrontation hung over the world almost continuously, for most of the age of the Cold War.

Source (for both images): AKG Images.

A section of the Berlin Wall, at the corner of Bernauer Strasse and Schwedter Strasse, 1962, a year after the wall was built.

November 12, 1989. Following the opening of the Berlin Wall, crowds gather at Potsdamer Platz in Berlin.

The Berlin Wall was, of course, a symbol of the Cold War. Its location was a reminder that the Cold War began with a falling out of the victorious powers of the Second World War over the nature of postwar Europe. Its fall marked both the end of the Cold War and the final resolution of the outcome of the Second World War in Europe.

Source: (for both images) AKG Images.

This 1956 cartoon shows Egyptian president Gamal 'Abd al-Nasir nationalizing the Suez Canal. The Suez Canal controversy marked the beginning of the end of the efforts of French and British imperialists to retain most of their colonial empires, following the initial wave of decolonization in the wake of the Second World War.

Source: AKG Images.

Egypt's Gamal Abdul Nasser and India's Jawaharlal Nehru meet at the Afro-Asian Bandung Conference, 1955

Source: GettyImages50357888

Heroes of anti-imperialism and decolonization. In 1959, Sékou Touré, president of Guinea, the first sub-Saharan country to be free of French imperial rule, meets with Kwame Nkrumah, president of Ghana, first sub-Saharan country to be free of British imperialism.

Source: AKG Images

Mass Movements: Social, Political and Spiritual

May 1968, crowds of strikers and demonstrators at the Place de la République in Paris. The French "events of May [1968]" were a worldwide symbol of the social and political turbulence of the 1960s. The banner to the left, stating "Students and Workers in Solidarity," expressed more a hope than a reality, and pointed to the many ideological, political, and social cross-currents of this era of global utopian aspirations.

Source: AKG Images.

Italian feminists in 1975 demand the legalization of abortion. The feminist movement was both a consequence of the social and political upheavals of the 1960s and a reaction against them.

Source: AKG Images

Italian soccer fans wave the tri-color flag, following the victory of their national team over West Germany in the finals of the World Cup, 1982. A development already under way in the first half of the twentieth century, the ever-closer ties between sporting events and nationalist ceremonies were a characteristic feature of late twentieth-century nationalism.

Source: AKG Images.

Pentecostalists praying in late twentieth-century Nigeria. Both Pentecostalists and Africans were, by the 1990s, increasingly the global face of Christianity. The giant video screens have become very characteristic of this form of Christian worship.

Source: AKG Images.

Pope John Paul II, blessing the crowd of over 40,000, at a soccer stadium in Buenos Aires, 1987. Despite the pope's energy, determination, and personal charisma, he could never quite undo the damage done to the Roman Catholic Church, by the controversies emerging from the Second Vatican Council of 1962–1965.

Source: Reuters.

Beginnings and Endings

Castle Square in a destroyed and just liberated Warsaw, January 1945. At the end of the Second World War, large parts of Eurasia lay in ruins.

Source: AKG Images.

Post-Second World War "displaced persons" leave Munich in 1948, heading for France. In the years 1945–1950, about one person in thirteen in the entire world was a refugee.

Source: AKG Images.

February 1990, Nelson Mandela gives his first public speech, following his release from prison. The end of the Cold War, symbolized by the fall of the Berlin Wall in the midst of Europe, quickly produced ramifications around the world.

Source: AKG Images.

A demonstrator stands in front of tanks entering Tiananmen Square in Beijing, June 1989. Introduction of economic reforms and increasing elements of a market economy in the USSR and Eastern Europe, led to the mass demonstrations of 1989, which brought an end to communist rule. By contrast, the Communist Party in China was able to introduce even more extensive economic reforms, while suppressing anti-regime demonstrations, and maintaining political control of the country, thus setting China on the path to being a twenty-first-century superpower.

Source: Reuters.

Technicians sent by the International Tribunal for the former Yugoslavia search for human remains in Bosnia. The civil war in the former Yugoslavia was the scene of the first of a series of mass murders in the late twentieth and early twenty-first centuries, yet another reminder that the end of the Cold War had not eliminated either massive violations of human rights or brought violent conflict to an end.

Source: Reuters.

The terrorist attack on the World Trade Center, September 11, 2001, seen from behind the Brooklyn Bridge. This incident was just the most visible sign that post-Cold War utopian aspirations to a conflict-free world, characterized by unfettered market economies and a benevolent US hegemony, had reached their end.

Source: Reuters

PART 3

Varieties of the Social

7 | Societies

CLASSES, GENERATIONS, AND GENDERS are the building blocks of human society. Their shape, structure, and cohesion have manifestly been transformed during the Age of Interconnection. Just think of a characteristic development of its final two decades: former subsistence farmers crowding into global megacities—Shenzhen, Guangzhou, Mumbai, Jakarta, Bangkok, São Paulo, Cairo, Lagos—in some cases finding a job in new industrial centers, or maybe eking out a living as casual laborers and servants, or resorting to begging. At the same time that these metropolitan areas were growing, once-great industrial cities in the American Midwest, northern France, Belgium's Wallonia, Germany's Ruhr Basin, or the English Midlands and Yorkshire were shrinking, their businesses downsizing or going bankrupt, while the remaining inhabitants faced long-term unemployment or, at best, badly paid temporary work. This was a global development: Kolkata, once India's industrial center, or the copper-mining towns of Zambia were suffering the same fate.

From the 1950s onward, successive waves of young people have increasingly listened to the very same music and worn the same clothing throughout the world. They have also distanced themselves from their elders. These elders, as well, particularly the very aged among them, were rapidly growing in numbers and becoming a steadily greater proportion of the population in most parts of the world. In many countries, those over sixty began developing their own sense of generational identity and pioneering a new, post-labor phase of life, whose long-term implications, for both demographic developments and government finances, will reverberate throughout the twenty-first century.

The condition and status of women in the world changed dramatically in the second half of the twentieth century, probably more considerably and more drastically than at any other time in human history. Rights and legal position, paid employment, contraception, marital and family circumstances, education, participation in public life—these all were transformed and provoked strong reactions. Changes in women's lives were the most prominent element of still broader changes in gender norms, gender practices, and gender ideals and of new versions of families, or perhaps simply of their dissolution.

There is a pronounced tendency to perceive societal evolution and transformation in global terms as a process of diffusion from wealthier and more enlightened parts of the world—meaning Western Europe and North America—to poorer and more backward regions. The former supposedly represent the vanguard of progress; the latter are striving to catch up, and do so, or at least start to do so, at different points. This tendency, noticeable in many accounts of change on a global scale, is particularly pronounced in discussions of societies.

There are societal changes—the decline in birth rates, the shaping of class structures, or the increasing proportion of women among college and university students—that may actually have spread in this way: North to South, West to East. Ultimately, that model of social change, the diffusion of progress around the world, obscures more than it illuminates.[1] It is more helpful, if also more complicated (and so less suited to simplistic sloganizing), to perceive societal transformation as driven by economic and demographic trends, by cultural innovations, and by politics. All these occurred across the three eras of the second half of the twentieth century that I mentioned in the introduction—the Postwar Era, the Upheaval Era of the 1960s and 1970s, and the Late-Millennium Era—in an environment of increasing, if in unsteady and irregular fashion, global interconnection.

Social Classes

In the postwar era, there existed in Western Europe and North America a well-articulated structure of social classes that had been developing since the final decades of the nineteenth century, so for at least seventy-five years. This structure took the form of a hierarchy, arranged as a pyramid. At the top was an upper class of wealthy owners of large businesses and those firms' top management. Below them stood an upper-middle class of managers and professionals. There followed a substantial middle class of small proprietors and salaried employees. And, finally, as the largest and lowest group, the base of the pyramid, a working class, itself divided by levels of skill and steadiness of employment. There were many variations on this theme—most managers in the United Kingdom, for instance, were generally less well-educated and less highly ranked than their counterparts in North America or Continental

Europe; race, religion, or nationality played a large role in stratifying the working class—but overall this social order distinguished by occupation and forms of income. Typically understood according to ideas developed by the two nineteenth-century Teutonic social gurus, Karl Marx and Max Weber, this structure remains the way that people think about social structure.[2]

Communist regimes of the postwar era loudly proclaimed that they had abolished the hierarchy of social classes by abolishing private property. In reality, they had their own hierarchical pyramid of social classes, which had more in common with their capitalist rivals than they cared to admit. At the top were the politically vetted administrators and managers, the *Nomenklatura* or, in China, the cadres, who set policy, ran the government and economy, and filled the ranks of what might be called "middle managers." In the early years of the communist regimes, they were revolutionaries from modest backgrounds, but, as time went on, increasingly university educated and disproportionately the children of the ruling group. (Interestingly many became engineers, and a kind of love-hate relationship between communist governments and engineers has survived to this day in post-communist China.) Below the Nomenklatura/cadres were the "technical intelligentsia"— university-trained professionals. Below them were white-collar workers, a salaried middle class, and at the bottom were the industrial proletariat. One difference from capitalist countries was that the communist lower-middle class did not include many small proprietors.[3]

In one crucial respect social structures of communist countries differed sharply from those of their capitalist counterparts—the farmers. This was not a small matter, because in the postwar era, there were a lot of farmers in the world. While they were not the largest occupational group in the United States, Argentina, Great Britain, and much of northwestern Europe, they were largest everywhere else.[4]

In those capitalist countries in which they were the largest occupational group, such as France, Italy, or Japan, farmers fit into the broader social pyramid, mostly as small proprietors, but also as part of the working class. Agricultural laborers were at the very bottom of the social pyramid. In the United States, they were predominantly immigrants and members of racial and ethnic minorities, a trend that would intensify and spread over the subsequent decades. By contrast, in most communist countries, farmers were, numerically the largest group and the most downtrodden. They were peasants—badgered, threatened, propagandized, and harassed, until they agreed to cede their property and the autonomy of their labor to a collective. What this meant for their lives might be seen from one village in Romania, where the newly collectivized cows, being taken to pasture, would stop at the homes of their former owners and try to go back to them. Peasants' freedom to leave their village was limited, or taken away entirely, as was the case in China's *hukou* system of household registration, introduced in 1958, which tied farmers to their place of birth. Unlike urban workers, whose "iron rice bowl," as it was called, guaranteed a lifetime of employment at steady wages, Chinese farmers received their wages—or, often, just food—according to the "work points" their families had earned.

Communist regimes tried to justify the plight of peasants by creating rural scapegoats: former landlords and exploitative "large peasants" (owners of ten to twenty acres, or elderly widows, unable to farm their land, who hired workers to do so). These "large peasants" were burdened with crop delivery quotas, deliberately set to be impossible to meet, heavily taxed, exhibited, denounced, and humiliated at mass meetings; excluded from stores and taverns; shunned on the street, beaten and, occasionally, shot. (Though postwar communists' efforts at agricultural collectivization, having learned from Stalin's murderous destruction of the kulaks as a class, generally featured less in the way of mass killings.) The point was to get them to cede their property to the regimes' collective or state-owned farms, although sometimes, as was the case with the *chiaburs*, Romania's "large" farmers, the local communists directing collectivization would not let them join the collectives, since they were more useful outside as scapegoats and objects of derision. This status as enemies of the people was permanent, persisting after the expropriation of their property, and inherited by their children.[5]

By creating a class of scapegoats, the communists hoped to get the peasants to see themselves as part of the regime's social structure, as counterparts to and allies of industrial workers, ostensibly the social group at the heart of the communist system. For some, especially the landless and impoverished, or members of ethnic and religious minorities, this strategy was not without its effect. However, more broadly—insofar as it is possible to generalize about hundreds of millions of people across the Eurasian landmass—peasants retained a sense of distance from communist regimes, at least in their initial decades. One Romanian *chiabur* of the Hunedoara region, in the country's central plains, expressed this attitude in particularly combative fashion in 1953. Furious that the authorities would not let him sell his cow, insisting that he donate it to the collective farm instead, he screamed, "We toil only for the workers and nothing remains for us; everything is meant for the workers!"[6]

In much of the noncommunist world in Asia, Africa, and the poorer countries of Latin America there existed a class hierarchy very similar to that in Western Europe or North America. Whether it was the white-collar workers and professionals of Rio de Janeiro, the *empleados* (office, bank, and shop employees) of Lima, the millhands of Girangaon, the cotton textile manufacturing district of Bombay (today's Mumbai), the African teachers, ministers or attorneys of the British colony of Southern Rhodesia (today's Zimbabwe), this sector of the population was growing in numbers and in self-assertion.[7]

Yet very much like in communist countries, professionals, the white-collar middle class, and urban workers were considerably outnumbered by farmers who were part of an altogether different social structure. Rural areas in many noncommunist but non-Western parts of the mid-twentieth-century world remained a theater of seigneurialism, a form of social structure characterized by the domination of large landowners over a subject group of smallholders, sharecroppers, tenants, or laborers. Particularly blatant versions of seigneurialism, such as serfdom or slavery, still very much present in the nineteenth century, had mostly disappeared. But forms of coercion, intimidation, patronage, and protection were omnipresent, enforced by means ranging from benign—paying for weddings, being godparents, sponsoring festivities and celebrations, distributing alcohol—to insidious—moneylending and debt peonage—to openly oppressive—a private army of thugs and enforcers, or influence with the police and state administration for the same purpose, to keep people in line. As with the newly enacted *apartheid* policies in South Africa, seigneurialism could be couched in the language of racial discrimination, or as happened in India, could be facilitated by the persisting influence of caste, social standing determined at birth. Such forms of seigneurialism were by no means unknown in North America or Western Europe—think Sicily under the Mafia or the Jim Crow US South—but confined to poorer areas.[8]

A second form of rural social structure in non-Western, noncommunist countries, particularly prevalent in Africa and in parts of South Asia, was "tribalism." A more exact and less pejorative term would be a "lineage-based society," in which production and property ownership revolved around kinship relations, whether of descent, direct or indirect, or of marriage. Such societies often featured generational tension, pitting the young men against their elders, a contrast that tended to coincide with that between the propertyless and the propertied. In the postwar era, these societies were dissected by Western anthropologists who duly noted their many variations—affine versus lineal kinship, matrilineality or matrilocality versus patrilineality or patrilocality, for instance.[9]

These seigneurial and lineage-based agricultural societies were not hermetically sealed off from more recently developed forms of labor. Quite the opposite, people moved back and forth between them: the mining labor force in Southern Africa, for instance, or the Kikuyu tribesman in the Kenyan uplands, who worked as farm laborers for British colonial coffee growers (until the latter mechanized their operations and helped set off the Mau-Mau uprising against British imperial rule). Still even the lower classes in the modern social hierarchy of non-Western, noncommunist societies had a favored position, compared to most people in the seigneurially organized or kinship-based agricultural sectors. Efforts to encourage economic growth, by means of Import Substitution Industrialization, or imposition of a state trade monopoly on products of commercial agriculture only increased the disparity.[10]

In general, the postwar era social structures across the globe largely moved in the same direction. This was as we've seen an age of unprecedentedly rapid economic growth worldwide, rising urban and suburban populations, increasing numbers of people employed in industry and services, and shrinking proportions living in the countryside or employed in agriculture. The social hierarchy first created in the late nineteenth century was expanding rapidly. While it remained hierarchical, both the rapid economic growth of the postwar era and the broad distribution of its benefits meant that economic disparities were modestly mitigated. The postwar era was the age the rise of the middle class. That class has been rising since history was first recorded—but the difference now was not so much in the increase in numbers of a middle group within the social hierarchy as in a broader spread of prosperity and possibilities for acquiring consumer goods.[11]

Given this, it became possible to wonder if greater income equality between levels of the social pyramid was beginning to reverse, such as in the relationship between the lower middle and the working class. The argument that some blue-collar workers were living better than some of their white-collar counterparts go back to the early years of the twentieth century. Two Japanese socialists, Sakai Toshihiko and Morichika Unpei, wrote in 1907, "The living standards of policemen, prison guards and elementary school teachers are actually lower than those of the rickshaw pullers or longshoremen whom they so despise."[12]

Three developments of the postwar era and Era of Upheaval gave impetus to this trend. One was the gradual occupational shift, characteristic of wealthier countries, from industry to services, from blue-collar to white-collar occupations. This was, at least to a certain extent, a gendered transformation of the social hierarchy. Moving into the paid labor force in greater numbers, women were more likely to be found in salaried occupations, retail, or administrative work, turning formerly mid-level white-collar jobs into poorly paid and socially less esteemed "pink collar" work, moving it down the social pyramid, below male-dominated occupations featuring manual labor. Finally, there was a worldwide generational shift underway as Baby Boomers, a group better educated than its predecessors, began entering paid employment. The upshot was a rapidly increasing supply of labor for occupations in the middle- and upper-middle levels of the social hierarchy exceeding the demand for these positions. Educated young people competed with each other for jobs, drove down their own incomes, and made mid-level white collar and even some more upper-level professional occupations noticeably less lucrative.[13] Some asserted that it was no longer the working class—unionized, with steady employment at good wages, as was largely the case in Western Europe and North America—which composed Marx's group of the impoverished and exploited, but graduate students and young academics, whose meager stipends, low salaries, and uncertain future prospects made their lives far more precarious than those of auto- or steelworkers.[14]

There was some evidence for this. In the United States, on the eve of the Second World War, the average income of white, female college graduates had been higher than that of white men without college educations and disproportionately in blue-collar occupations. But in the postwar era that that gap had eroded and reversed to the point that in 1980, white women with a college education earned about $5,000 per year (in 1990 dollars) less than white men without one. Yet white-collar occupations continued to have a gender-specific income advantage over blue-collar ones—that is, as British studies showed, women in most white-collar jobs earned more than women engaging in manual labor, even if they generally earned less than men in blue-collar work. In the United States, throughout the 1970s, the economic advantage college-educated white men had over their peers without a college education declined—a decline most pronounced among recent graduates. Nonetheless even at that 1980 low point, white men who had gone to college still earned, on average, about $10,000 (again in 1990 dollars) more than their counterparts who had not.[15]

There was one major country in the world where the class position of educated young people changed dramatically for the worse during the 1970s, namely China in the late phase of Mao's communist rule. This was a result of the practice of *xiaxiang*, "going down to the country" developed in the aftermath of the Cultural Revolution. Between 1968 and 1980, the Chinese government and party leadership sent seventeen million educated young people (in China, an educated young person was someone who attended secondary school until the age of fifteen) from urban areas to the countryside, so they could be re-educated in revolutionary fashion by the peasants. They spent close to a decade doing unskilled labor for which they were unprepared, producing work of marginal value, and being greeted with open hostility and even violence. Following Mao's death in 1976, most were allowed to return to urban areas to try to resume their lives. Many of the young people could never get their lives back on track, although some like China's immensely powerful leader, Xi Jinping (who, admittedly, because of his political connections got to return home early), did manage to do so.[16]

TRANSFORMING CLASS STRUCTURE IN THE LATE-MILLENNIUM ERA

Xiaxiang stands out because it was an exception. Through the Upheaval Era, the hierarchical class structure based on occupation and income developed in the nineteenth century had preserved itself pretty well, surviving the sometimes-violent transitions from capitalism to communism and expanding its orbit into those parts of the world in which seigneurial and lineage-based agricultural societies existed. Economic and demographic developments of the last quarter of the twentieth century moved social structures, globally, in a new direction. It was not so much that the existing social hierarchy was reshaped, as that the entire hierarchy began to shift, a process continuing through the present day. Instead of being based on occupation and income, it was determined by relationship to an increasingly globalized market.

Three very large developments were the behind this shift. One was the globalization of production, at first industrial goods but with time also "services," such as answering phones in a call center or writing computer software. The second was migration, both across the borders of sovereign states and within them. The third, the largest and most decisive, was the end of communist economic systems across Eurasia, catapulting 1.5 billion people fully into the global market economy. What all these did was to take a class structure that was already becoming uniform in different regions of the globe and turn it into a global class structure.

At the peak of the new social hierarchy stood those who organized and shaped the global market, managers and owners of multinational firms, especially financial ones—the 1 percent, or, perhaps, the 0.1 percent, in the post-2008 financial collapse parlance. Those phrases refer not just to the wealth of those at the top but to their "too big to fail" invulnerability: they shaped global markets but bore no consequences for their shaping actions. These were many of the same people who had stood at the summit of the older social hierarchy, but now the businesses they ran operated on a global scale; their top management was increasingly recruited across national borders and showed less particular interest for the country in which their (sometimes nominal) headquarters was located. Their training had been increasingly globalized—think the rapidly growing number of Chinese students attending American and British universities starting in the 1990s—and they were more likely to reside in what sociologist Saskia Sassen has called "global cities." Career paths into this group increasingly ran through globalized occupations, like that of a management consultant.[17]

Below them in the new paradigm were a group whose members also enjoyed a number of protections from the pressures of the global market. These included people in professional occupations, whose licensing and educational requirements limited possibility for competition, especially from less-developed countries; unions also provided protection from competition; tenured civil servants; academics; or owners of and workers in businesses sheltered from foreign competition by legal restrictions, such as weapons manufacturing or security contractors.

The largest group in this new social hierarchy was composed of individuals, whether their income came from wages, salaries, or self-employment, who were not protected. Indeed, they were fully exposed to the blast of the forces of an increasingly globalized market in labor, goods, and services. They were workers whose jobs were outsourced, or who had to compete with material produced in countries with lower costs of living, and little or no labor or environmental protection legislation. Also in this group were people living in the formerly communist regimes of Eurasia, who no longer enjoyed employment or income guarantees and now had to find their way in an unfamiliar and increasingly difficult economic and legal environment. Or they were businessmen who faced competitors hiring cheap immigrant labor—or even cheaper labor from illegal immigrants.

A central feature of this new class structure was the growing numbers of people moving from the ranks of those protected from the world market to those subjected to it. These included former civil servants whose jobs were privatized, or, as happened throughout Africa, when salaries, benefits and positions were drastically cut back as a result of the austerity policies imposed by the World Bank. In China, they were "unit people" who had become "society people"—individuals who had previously enjoyed a guaranteed income and social welfare benefits through their state-owned workplace in a planned economy. Now they had to figure out how to earn a living on their own, often in precarious forms of self-employment, like street vending, while facing increasing competition in the labor market from migrants moving from rural to urban areas. Also in China and throughout the rural regions of formerly communist Eurasia, the one-time workers on collective farms were transformed back into agricultural entrepreneurs, sometimes—as was generally the case in Europe— getting their or their ancestors' former property back, and sometimes—as in China—just receiving a plot of land on a long-term lease from the government to farm on their own. In either case, the formerly despised and scapegoated "large peasants" and their descendants seemed to do noticeably better in the new situation than the families and descendants of previously landless laborers.[18]

At the same time that these developments were underway in Africa, or formerly communist Eurasia, large portions of the population of Western Europe and North America were also losing their protection from globalization. Once unionized industrial jobs disappeared, giving way to mechanization, or sent off to countries with lower labor costs. This was a process often understood, especially in the United States in regional terms. It resulted in the creation of "Rust Belts," areas where such jobs had previously been prevalent but disappeared overseas (or to Mexico), leaving behind a shrinking population with fewer favorable possibilities for work. Although the creation of Rust Belts might seem like a development specific to the wealthier countries of the world—the American Midwest, for example—the same forces of globalization led to the large-scale closure of textile mills in the Indian cities of

Mumbai and Ahmedabad, leaving workers in formerly secure and well-paid jobs trying to earn a living as street vendors and day laborers.[19]

At the same time that jobs were migrating from higher-wage to lower-wage countries, workers from those countries were migrating to higher-wage ones. Construction labor in the United States, which had offered secure, well-paying, unionized positions, was transformed in the Late-Millennium Era into an occupation dominated by non-union and increasingly immigrant labor, working at mediocre wages—or, to put it differently, from an occupation sheltered from global labor markets to one determined by them. In the Italian city of Prato, near Florence, the shift of manufacturing to low-wage countries and labor migration from them occurred simultaneously. Long a center of textile production, Prato's industry changed drastically in the 1990s, as Chinese migrant laborers moved there and began to work in textile and garment manufacturing firms owned by Chinese businessmen. Although arriving under tourist visas and having neither work nor residence permits, by 2008, there were forty-five thousand such Chinese workers toiling in 4,200 Chinese-owned firms, producing one million garments each year. They outnumbered the Italians still working in the field by over two to one. The former Italian textile workers who had lost their job to immigrant competition found new work, if at all, in temporary and precarious occupations; unemployment climbed as did business bankruptcies.[20]

The example of Prato shows how developments in poorer and wealthier countries, in the lands of the Cold War West, those of the former Eastern Bloc and the one-time non-aligned are all interconnected, a reflection of the creation of a truly global labor market. Whether in China, Africa, Guatemala, the United States, Japan, India, or the United Kingdom, individuals and families caught in the force fields of this labor market found themselves increasingly as casual labor—working as nominally independent contractors, in temporary positions (today they account for one-third of the entire Japanese labor force), lacking both government social welfare benefits tied to regular employment, and the non-wage benefits and perks of such employment. In South Gujarat, in Southwestern India, the decline in caste-based seigneurial relations in the countryside, occurring from the Upheaval Era onward, has led to an ever-growing number of migrant laborers, moving constantly to find work, in debt to their employers and dependent on labor contractors to find employment. The Gujarat laborers were no exception on the Indian sub-continent; even with the country's growing high-tech economy, most Indians were employed in this temporary way, and employment growth was largely in that area.

French sociologists began referring to people in temporary or seasonal occupations as the "precariat," and increasingly commentators have adopted the term to designate a new social class, trying to place it in the older hierarchy of class structure. Since members of the "precariat" can be self-employed, waged, or salaried, and working in a very wide variety of occupations, from agricultural labor to graphic design, it is difficult to fit them into a hierarchy based on occupation and forms of income—the old model, in other words. Rather than understanding it as a new social class it's more helpful to see its primary characteristic—temporary, poorly compensated work—as a constant possibility for members of the social group characterized by their submission to a globalized labor market.[21]

If a dominant trend in the Late-Millennium Era social structure has been the downward movement of people from being protected from the global labor market to being subject to it, there has also been a clear descent to the very bottom of the new social hierarchy: those shut out of that labor market entirely. These include the long-term unemployed, or people living more or less permanently from social welfare programs. Unemployment rates at the end of the millennium were over 10 percent in most EU countries, to say nothing of job droughts in formerly communist Eastern Europe. Nonetheless, these figures paled before unemployment rates in Africa of 25 percent or higher. Responsible for a shrinking portion of global production and global commerce (in mining and minerals, increasingly mechanized and needing much less labor than in the past), Africa has become the continent of the globally marginalized. One South African social researcher stated that if ten million people in his country suddenly dropped dead "the Johannesburg Stock Exchange wouldn't register so much as a ripple."[22]

By African standards, South Africa is a wealthy country, able to afford an unusually elaborate social welfare program which was sending benefits to almost half (44 percent) of all households. Yet even there, as in so much of the rest of the under developed world, the global lowest class was finding other ways to earn a living, in what has been called the "urban informal sector," meaning street vending, casual labor, and little craft workshops, quickly popping up and just as quickly disappearing, frequently unlicensed, untaxed, and off the books. Into the twenty-first century, the market women of Guatemala City continued to defy the *supermercados*, subsidiaries of American corporations, and do most of the city's retail business—although the street vendors themselves were divided, between those of Spanish and those of Indian descent, between those who have a permit and a regular stall and those who were selling on the street without permits or fixed locations. The global epitome of this sort of marginal existence is undoubtedly the Indian city of Kolkata. There the economic consequences of the partition at the end of British colonial rule in 1948 played an important part in creating an immense urban informal sector.[23]

Although sometimes hailed by economists as seedbeds of entrepreneurial activity and economic development, growing global connections have limited possibilities for the informal sector rather than enhanced them. A good example was the "fitters," the auto mechanics of Kumasi, Ghana's second city. In the era of import substitution industrialization, permission to import both new cars and parts for existing ones were hard to obtain—circumstances exacerbated by the shortage of foreign exchange during the oil price shocks of the 1970s. Fitters rose to the challenge with innovation and ingenuity, using increasingly sophisticated machinery and procuring necessary materials via *kalabule*, the black market. They were at the center of an industrial park, with spinoffs into metallurgy and to other crafts and manufacturing, counting about forty-five thousand people employed there at the end of the 1980s. The trade liberalization program required by the World Bank made it possible to import both new cars and spare parts for old ones, largely bringing the economic growth associated with the informal center and its spinoffs to an end. Other clusters of informal manufacturing in Africa, like the shoe and garment producers of the west Nigerian city of Aba, have not led to the great successes predicted by economists.[24]

A hallmark of this global transformation is that there is no longer a clear demarcation separating those receiving government benefits from informal sector economic activity. Neither was there a clear separation of legal from illegal activity, nor a firm distinction between more peaceful forms of law violation—tax evasion, trading without licenses, working off the books—and more violent, particularly gang-related, ones. Gang activity, in turn, shaded over into various forms of organized crime. In an odd parody of globalization in legal forms of economic activity, organized crime, particularly the smuggling of drugs, labor, and women, became increasingly globalized after the Upheaval Era—like the shipping of cocaine from Colombia or Asia to Europe via West Africa, or the trade in women from the former communist countries in Eastern Europe to be sex workers (whether their participation was voluntary or coerced) in the western part of the continent, that was a prominent feature of the Late-Millennium Era, and which persists to this day. Street gangs, very localized groups, based on neighborhood turf, became increasingly involved with a globalized drug traffic. Shut out of legal forms of participation in a globalized economy, members of the new global lowest class became prominent—if generally low-ranking—participants in a global world of crime.[25]

If the old class structure had the shape of a pyramid, with the size of classes increasing as one moved downward through levels of affluence and prestige, the new class structure has taken the form of a lopsided diamond, whose top is very narrow, and whose bottom, although broader than the top, is smaller than the middle. Another way to say this is that the lowest class of the contemporary world, those excluded from the global market, or at least from its legitimate side, is a minority of the world's inhabitants. However, within individual countries, its members are disproportionately made up of religious, ethnic, or racial minorities, who are placed in the role. They are not the exploited, as had been the case in the old social structure, as excluded and ignored.

All the features of the emergent global class structure appear in Chicago journalist Richard Longworth's pithy description of his native city in a book published in 2008. At the top, were the "global citizens: hardworking, well-educated, well-paid, well-traveled." At the bottom were "the global have-nots, separated by class and education as much as by race from any of the benefits of a global economy." And between them were "the global servants." These were, Longworth argues, "immigrants, mostly Mexican, who perform the services—valet parking, gardening, dishwashing, dog-walking, busing in bistros, low-level construction—that the global citizens need.[26]

This description would fit London, Paris, Hamburg, Shanghai, Mumbai, São Paulo, or Johannesburg. It is also exaggerated and incomplete. It omits the unionized construction workers, still to be found in at least some of America's large cities, or the civil servants employed by the city of Chicago, Cook County, the state of Illinois, and the US federal government, all clinging to a position at least partly insulated from the forces of globalization. These caveats aside, Longworth's account captures the nature of an emergent globalized class structure.

Generations

Age groups are, at least in part, biological entities. Their numbers rise and fall with changes in birth and death rates. Over the course of the Age of Interconnection, these demographic movements changed to a greater extent than at any other time in human history, although unevenly around the world.

In the case of generations, biology is not—or not entirely—destiny. They are also cultural products, forms of collective perception and self-perception, understandings shaped by social policies—the changing scope of education, for instance, or the introduction and expansion of old-age pensions—as well as by economic developments, such as the globalization of different forms of consumption, from clothing to music. Demography creates the "containers" of generations and social, economic, or political developments and fill them with "cultural content." Sometimes, that content just fills up a small portion of the container; other times, it overflows the container's walls and spills over into other ones.

It all begins with changes in population. After an understandably slow increase in the Age of Total War, when the number of the earth's human inhabitants rose from 1.9 billion in 1900 to 2.5 billion in 1950, the second half of the century saw an unprecedented expansion: global population more than doubled in fifty years to about six billion. Figure 7.1 shows the progression of the natural population increase (births minus deaths). This

310 | VARIETIES OF THE SOCIAL

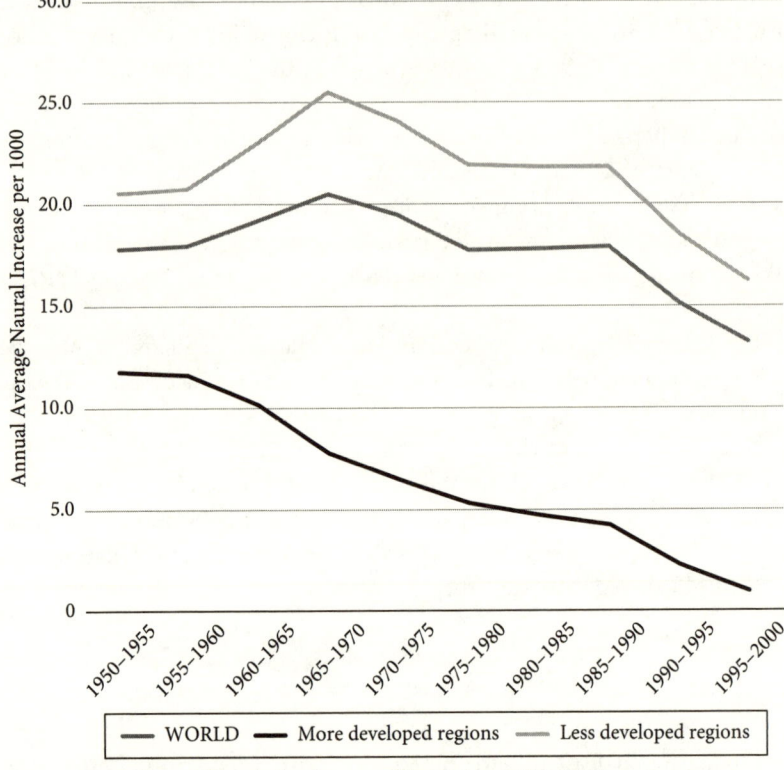

FIGURE 7.1 Natural Population Increase Worldwide, 1950–2000

chart is broken into three groups, following UN definitions: the entire world, the more-developed countries—North America, Europe, Japan, and Australasia—and the less-developed countries.[27]

The lines on the chart for the less-developed countries and the entire world move together closely, which is no big surprise, because most people live in these countries. They show very high and very rapid rates of natural population increase from 1950 until the Era of Upheaval, and then a decline in these rates of 40 to 50 percent in the Late-Millennium Era. By contrast, in the world's wealthier countries, the decline in natural rates of increase started by 1960, so about fifteen years earlier than in the rest of the world, and has been much steeper, to the point that by 2000 these lands are very close to zero natural population growth. Individual countries, all of which had been either part of the Second World War Axis Powers, or the communist Eastern Bloc—some, like Hungary and Romania, were in both—have gone beyond that threshold, into natural population decline. This connection between former fascist or communist regimes and declining populations remains largely unexplained.

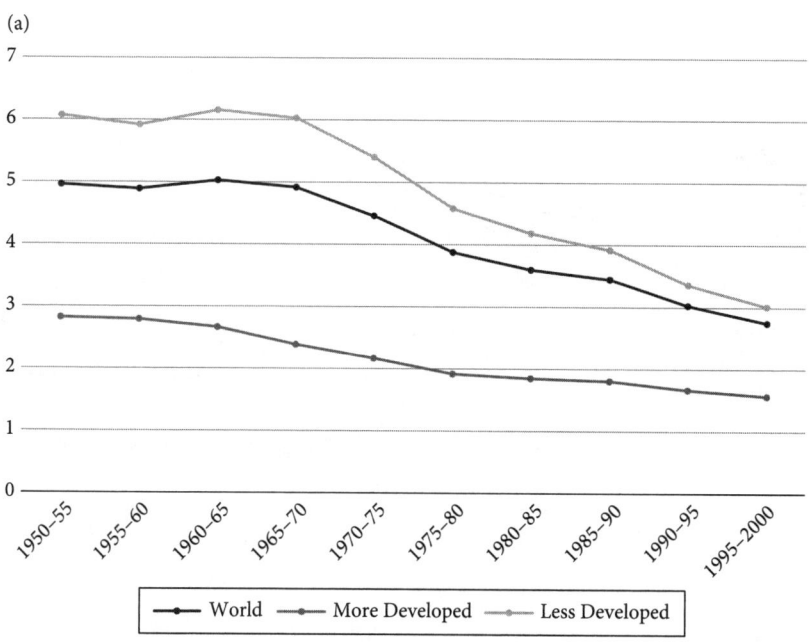

FIGURE 7.2a Total Fertility Rates Worldwide, 1950–2000

Natural population movements are naturally a function of both fertility and mortality, which are displayed in Figures 7.2a and 7.2b for the same groupings of the world as in Figure 7.1. These charts use the most complex and all-encompassing measures developed by demographers, both of which pay for their comprehensiveness and precision with a certain abstraction. Figure 7.2a shows the Total Fertility Rate, the number of children a woman entering her fertile years might expect to have during the fertile period of her life, ages 15 to 44, if her fertility in each year corresponded to the age-specific fertility rate in the year she reached sexual maturity. Figure 7.2b shows life expectancy at birth, a parallel measure, the average age someone born might expect to achieve if that person experienced the age-specific mortality rates existing in the year of that person's birth.

The story here is above all about trends in fertility. In the less-developed countries and the world as a whole, fertility remained very high throughout the 1950s and 1960s, averaging between five and six births for a woman, over the course of her fertile lifetime, and only starting to decline after 1970. By 2000, rates had about reached the point where the wealthier countries had been in 1950. The latter, starting from a noticeably lower level, also began experiencing a fertility decline—as noted, ten to fifteen years before the less-developed countries. By the second half of the 1970s, they had crossed the threshold of a Total Fertility Rate of 2.1, indicating, at current mortality levels, a decline in births below natural replacement.[28] By contrast, the

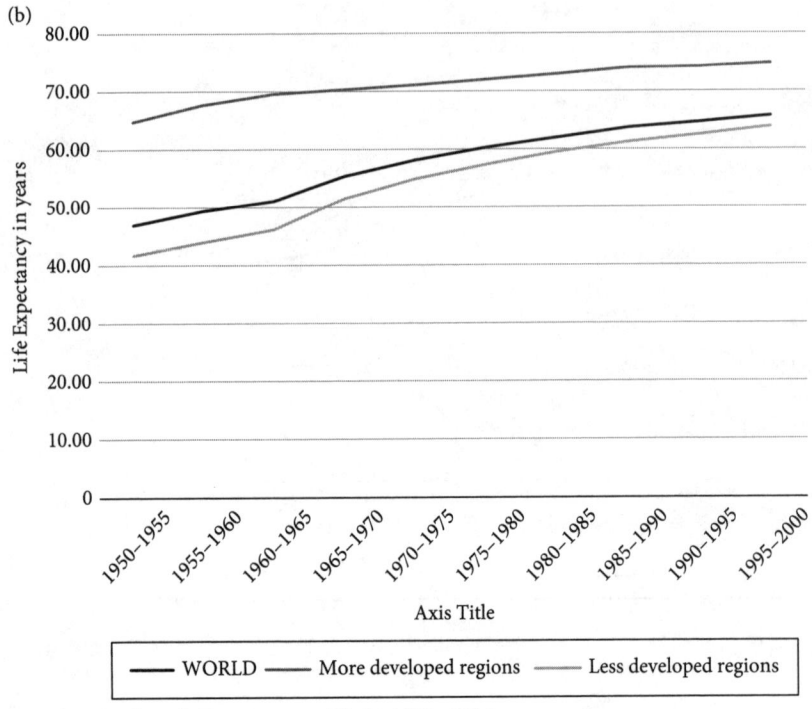

FIGURE 7.2b Life Expectancy at Birth, 1950–2000

movement of life expectancies looks somewhat steadier, a period of rapid increase in the postwar decades, a result of the introduction of antibiotics and large-scale immunization campaigns, unsurprisingly occurring a couple of decades later in the poorer countries than the wealthier ones, followed by a slower rate of increase and something closer to stagnation in the Late-Millennium Eras as infectious diseases, particularly AIDS, but also malaria and tuberculosis, became more and more prevalent, especially in Africa.

The rapid rise in the earth's population in the postwar era and beyond was a function of steadily high birth rates and declining death rates. From 1975 onward, birth rates began to move downward on a global scale, while increases in life expectancy occurred at a slower pace. The two demographic effects worked together to produce a twenty-five-year-long period of rapid population increase, and a subsequent quarter-century of slowing rates of population growth. Across the Age of Interconnection, declining fertility and declining mortality tended to balance each other out. The Total Fertility Rate fell, worldwide, about 45 percent between 1950 and 2000; life expectancy at birth rose, in that same period, roughly 40 percent.

One might expect that the persistently high birth rates of the postwar decades would lead to a population bulge of young people, while declining post-1975 fertility, coupled with steady life expectancies at birth, and rising life expectancies at advanced ages, would result in a growing number of the elderly. Figure 7.3, which provides the percentage of the population who were youths, ages fifteen to twenty-four, and the percentage who were seniors, sixty-plus, in both more- and less-developed countries, does not entirely fulfill these expectations.

More than anything else, this chart shows that global populations are like an oil tanker, only changing demographic direction slowly and gradually. For three decades, the proportion of young people in the total population did not change all that much, in either wealthier or poorer countries. In fact, the 1960s, which we think of as the very acme of youth and youth culture, marked a low point in the presence of young people in the population, below the percentages obtaining just a few years after the end of the Second World War. In the less-developed countries, youth as a percentage of the population didn't peak until the 1980s, and this percentage has been declining since then, across the globe.

The single largest change that appears in the chart is the steady growth in the number and percentage of the elderly among the population of the world's economically developed countries. Closing in on 20 percent of affluent countries' inhabitants by 2000—almost a quarter of the population, in several of these countries, most prominently Japan and Germany—people in advanced ages had reached a higher population share than in all of human history. Another way to formulate an understanding of these generationally

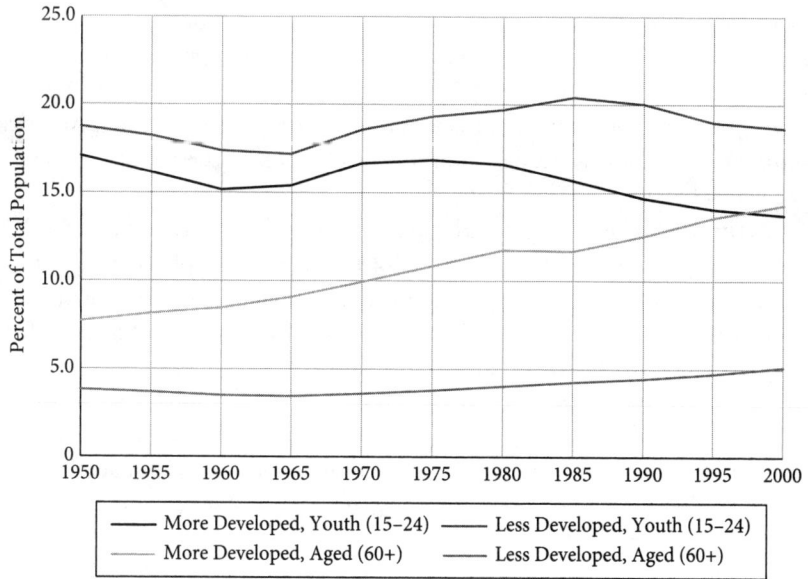

FIGURE 7.3 Youth and Age in the World, 1950–2000

based population changes would be to say that in the Age of Interconnection youth has been primarily a cultural category, one not always closely linked to demographic developments, while age has been primarily a demographic one, shaped primarily by changes in fertility and mortality.

MAKING YOUTH

Adolescents and young adults (the exact boundaries of these groups depended in part on the age of sexual maturity, which changed over time) have been around as long as there have been humans. Human societies have generally found ways, including rituals and organizations, to recognize them. Hence the question to ask is when did young people become "youth," a specific self-conscious, generational group. There were political approaches, such as Giuseppe Mazzini's 1830s secret society "Young Italy," which made "youth" (Mazzini seems to have had primarily university students in mind) central to the political project of nationalism. Both fascist and communist movements of the Age of Total War played with the idea of having a special appeal to youth and of representing a youthful point of view. Postwar anti-imperialist movements had a youthful face. Youth was not always celebrated. It could also appear less an ideal than a social pathology, articulated in the idea of "waywardness," of working-class young people, especially those living in large cities or industrial areas—and not just in Europe and the Americas, but in larger colonial African cities, such as Freetown in Sierra Leone—engaging in deviant behavior: for boys, belonging to gangs and engaging in petty or not-so-petty criminality; for girls, indiscriminate premarital sexuality. Responses to waywardness and teenage rebellion included special forms of social discipline or penal institutions for youthful offenders, and organizations, like the Boy Scouts, to steer youth away from these moral dangers. Beginning in the late nineteenth and early twentieth centuries in Europe and North America, some forms of these attitudes toward youth had made their way throughout the world by 1950.[29]

Attitudes about young people were not all that different from those of preceding years, yet another example of the persistence of conditions from the Age of Total War into the immediate postwar era. Fears about and campaigns against "JD"s (juvenile delinquents) in the United States; *stilyagi* in the USSR; *blousons noirs* in France; or "Teddy Boys," "mods," and "rockers" in the United Kingdom; *raggare* in Sweden; *naderumper* in Denmark; *teppisti* in Italy; *taizo zoku* in Japan; *gamberos* in Spain; *Halbstarken* in West Germany; *desmadrosos* in Mexico, with parallel developments in East Germany, Poland, Czechoslovakia, or Argentina, were very much part of a practice going back to the early years of the century. It was the Era of Upheavals that brought about large-scale changes.[30]

Two causes were central. One was the expansion of secondary and higher education. Because the UN statistics on education only begin in 1970, it is difficult to give a global picture, but the scattered figures available all show the same upward trend. The United States had always been a global leader in the extent of education, but the proportion of students in high school and college grew even substantially in the postwar era. In 1950, 83 percent of fourteen- to seventeen-year-olds were attending high school, a figure that reached 90 percent in 1959 and has been in the low to mid-nineties ever since. College and university students made up 14 percent of the American eighteen to twenty-four age group in 1950, 24 percent in 1961, and 40 percent in 1975. For Western European countries, the proportion of people in the twenty to twenty-four age group attending universities in 1960 ranged from a low of 3.6 percent in England and Wales, for example, to a high of 8.7 percent in France. Fifteen years later, the 1960s high was exceeded by the 1975 low—8.9 percent of the twenty to twenty-four age group in universities, once again in England and Wales—while the high was 22.9 percent in France, and the proportion was in double digits everywhere else. (Ireland, at 9.9 percent, required rounding up.) By the 1970s, the proportion of the population in communist Eastern Europe going to high school and college was similar to that of Western Europe; corresponding proportions in Japan were close to those in the United States. There had been similar increases in the proportion of the population attending secondary school in both Western and Eastern Europe.

In Argentina, admittedly the wealthiest of Latin American countries, the number of secondary school students quintupled between 1945 to 1970, from 201,000 to 985,000. In that latter year, 45 percent of the thirteen to eighteen age group was in school, a percentage exceeded among South American countries by Uruguay and Chile. Five percent of Argentine young people aged twenty to twenty-four were in universities in 1950, rising to 11 percent in 1960 and 20 percent in 1972, putting Argentina at the same point as the most education-friendly European countries. Starting from a lower level, university education expanded every bit as rapidly in Brazil and Mexico, rising in that latter country from 70,000 students in 1959 to 440,000 in 1974. Attendance at secondary schools, to say nothing of universities, was lower in South and East Asia and Africa than in Europe or the Americas, although in these countries as well, the proportion of the relevant age group attending high school was rising between 1960 and 1975, from close to zero to about 10 percent in sub-Saharan Africa, or from 20 to 40 percent in East Asia and the Pacific. At the beginning of the 1960s there were 545,000 secondary school pupils and 29,000 university students in Indonesia, Asia's third most-populous country; by the late 1980s, 10.9 million young Indonesians were enrolled in high schools and 1.66 million in universities. University College, Dar es Salaam, founded at the moment of Tanganyika's independence from colonial rule (the university was a long-term demand of the anti-imperialist movement there), began with fourteen students; a decade later, two thousand were enrolled in the renamed University of Dar es Salaam in renamed Tanzania.[31]

Although university students were, everywhere in the world, a minority, usually a modestly sized minority of their age group, in the period of vigorous educational expansion during the Era of Upheaval they were in the vanguard of an emergent youth culture. Their time was their own to an unusual extent. Growing numbers of university students living away from their parents were in a particularly favorable condition when it came to personal independence, especially in regard to sexuality, which would be an important element of youth culture and generational self-understanding.[32]

Even more important than education in the development of a youth culture was the prosperity of the post-1945 world and the subsequent emergence of common features of consumption. Employed young people, still living with their parents, no longer had to turn over their pay to them, as had been the practice in the past, but could keep a big chunk of it for themselves, to spend on items of their choosing. Postwar prosperity also made it possible to support steadily growing numbers of young people in secondary and higher education, receiving spending money directly from their parents or from government initiatives in support of education.

Young people had more income than in the past and their income was disposable, since they had not yet not yet married and started families and their costs for food and housing were being met. They could and did spend it on consumer goods, from mopeds to sports equipment, to personal grooming products to cameras, to portable radios, record players, and stereos. Mentioning consumer electronics in this connection is no coincidence, because they were a vehicle for one of the two forms of consumer consumption that was worldwide during the 1960s and 1970s and played a large role in shaping a youth culture and turning young people into a generation of youth: Rock & Roll and fashion. Both were distinctly Anglo-American. As one young French Rock fan, put it in 1966, England seemed "a kind of other world," a place where young people "can do pretty much what they want."[33]

The 1960s was the decade in which these two major forms of consumption spread across the world. West German radio stations stopped playing *Schlager*, German-language popular hits, and replaced them with American or British music. Even the French, who held on, much more fiercely, to their own language in popular music, began listening to British and American bands. Young women in Dar es Salaam began wearing miniskirts. Young people in Buenos Aires began appearing in blue jeans. By the early 1970s, young people in rural Chile were listening to *música international*—Jimmy Hendrix and the Beatles—on their radios and even watching it on TV, a new medium spreading rapidly among the rural lower classes, as a result of the efforts of the left-wing Popular Unity government of Salvador Allende to raise their standards of living. Supporting the efforts of a socialist government with close ties to Moscow and Havana was hardly what the capitalists responsible for the new youth culture, the record company executives of Los Angeles and the fashion designers of Carnaby Street, had in mind. They were primarily interested in opportunities to make money. Still, their efforts had unintended consequences, a cultural style that began with consumption of these commodities, but encouraged increasing doubts about the status quo, a "counterculture," as contemporaries said, and the anger and dismay this counterculture generated among adherents of the cultural status quo.[34]

You could call these adherents "conservatives," although supporting the status quo in the West and the Eastern Bloc had rather different political implications. Since both new fashions and popular music contained distinct elements of unleashed sexuality, which were taken up and amplified by the counterculture, it was no surprise that they ran into vehement opposition from supporters of revealed religions, for whom the restriction of sexuality in general, and that of young people in particular, was a central tenet of their faith. But enemies of an emergent youth culture were found in some unexpected places, such as the pan-Africanist, revolutionary, anti-imperialist government of Tanzania. Its Youth League launched a massive campaign of intimidation and arrest of young women in Dar es Salaam wearing miniskirts, accusing them of being immoral, publicly exhibiting their thighs, and tools of imperialist capitalism. Contemporary photographs show these transgressive young women in quite modest attire, pants suits and skirts ending just above the knee, which today would be right at home in investment banks and law firms. The Tanzanian government banned soul music, as yet another form of capitalist imperialism. It was an odd way to treat a cultural genre created by African Americans, especially from a government offering political refuge to African American radicals fleeing the United States and turning its university in Dar es Salaam into a global center of pan-African, anti-imperialist thought. The government of Idi Amin in Uganda, nominally anti-imperialist, although more kleptocratic than anything else, engaged in a similar crusade against women in pants and miniskirts.[35]

Not surprisingly, this sort of attack provoked a defiant response. A particularly articulate example came from Ole Grünbaum, a prominent Danish provo—that is, adherent of a group of hippie anarchists, common in northern European countries—who asserted in 1968 that eighteen-year-olds knew more about the Vietnam War than fifty-year-olds. Young people were "much better than educated than previous generations and more competent than ever in using their knowledge and ability to gain power." According to Grünbaum, the reason for this is that young people "can deal with wealth and modern life naturally . . . For the youth wealth is not a status symbol, but something they take for granted."[36] The statement is a succinct expression of the two major social developments that led to the creation of youth as self-conscious and distinct social group during the decades of the 1960s and 1970s: the spread of advanced education and the growth of postwar prosperity.

Painful as it is to admit, no one stays young forever, and members of Grünbaum's postwar generation are now populating old-age homes and cemeteries. But the social formations pioneered in the 1960s, of youth as a self-conscious group, marked off from other ages, has remained. The music may have transformed, from rhythm and blues to folk music to Motown to hip-hop, and the fashion expanded to include piercings and tattoos—but youth culture has become a permanent feature of global society, adopted in various forms by successive generations. This is because the two main conditions of the emergence of a self-conscious youth group—a large proportion in secondary and tertiary education, creating an interval between childhood and adult life, and a global culture of consumption—have not just endured but come to encompass more young people in every part of the world.[37]

RISE OF THE SENIORS

As with young people, the elderly have always been a biologically determined part of human society, those reaching an age of declining physical strength, sensory capabilities, and mental acuity. (As with youth, the point in life at which that occurs has changed over time.) Sentimental notions of the respected wisdom and dignity of the elderly to the contrary, old age has been throughout most of human history a period of unpleasant dependence, as individuals, increasingly unable to labor and to support themselves, have had to rely on family members, charity, or, for a lucky few, the property they had accumulated during their lifetime. Politicians in Europe and North America, beginning with Germany's Iron Chancellor, Otto von Bismarck, experimented with the idea of old-age pensions, publicly funded schemes to provide an income to the elderly, unable to work. The most generous of these early efforts, the UK's Pension Act of 1908, promised every citizen over seventy years of age and earning less than £26 per year, 5 shillings weekly, payable at the local post office. There are stories of grateful people in rural areas showering their postmistresses with apples and flowers from their gardens as thanks for the very modest funds they handed them each and every week. By the outbreak of the Second World War, such public-pension systems existed in fifteen European countries and, thanks to the New Deal, the United States. Their payouts were extremely small, amounting to just 15 percent of the average wage, so even in these countries for all too many of the elderly their choice in life remained the poorhouse or the kindness of their adult children.

In the prosperous postwar era, these programs became both steadily more common and increasingly generous. Countries in Western Europe, which had not possessed such pension systems before 1945, including Switzerland, Finland, Spain, and Portugal, brought them into being; European Eastern Bloc countries inaugurated them as well. In China, by contrast, public-pension schemes were limited to large, urban areas; in the countryside, where most of the population lived, the millennia-old expectation that the elderly would be supported by their sons and daughters-in-law remained, in spite of the drastic changes in property relations the communists introduced. Retirement plans spread beyond Europe and North America. They became very common in Latin America, introduced, among other countries, in Mexico, Brazil, Argentina, Venezuela, Uruguay, and Chile. Newly independent India began an—admittedly modest—retirement plan. A more considerable and more generous one, considered in relation to the country's economic output, was introduced, in Mauritius in 1958. Public pensions were installed by the 1970s in East Asian lands, including Japan, Taiwan, Malaysia, and South Korea and, to a lesser extent, in newly independent African countries. In 1994, the World Bank counted ninety-three different countries with some form of public retirement program—at least ones whose income and expenditures could be evaluated.

The programs were also considerably more generous than 5 shillings a week. Means testing generally went away (there were a few exceptions, such as Australia) to be replaced with benefits based on lifetime contributions, and three universal schemes, in Canada, Norway, and the aforementioned Mauritius, in which all recipients received the same yearly pension. Other innovations, such as the 1958 "dynamization" of old-age pensions in West Germany, through which pensions, rather than being permanently fixed, rose with the level of wages in the working population, or the indexing of American Social Security payments to inflation, done between 1972 and 1974, enabled the elderly to share in a country's broader prosperity. If old-age pensions had only accounted for 15 percent of average wages on the eve of the Second World War, by 1980 in those same countries, the proportion had tripled to 45 percent.[38]

It was the combination of these welfare benefits with declining birth rates and increasing life expectancy that turned the elderly into seniors or senior citizens: an independent, post-labor, post-child-rearing stage of life. The elderly were much less likely to work. According to the statistics of the International Labour Organization gathered in 1950, almost 25 percent of men over the age of sixty-five in the economically developed countries of the world were still in the labor force; by 1990, its statistics showed that figure had declined to under 10 percent. Poverty rates among the elderly dropped below those of the population as a whole in a number of European countries—especially Scandinavian ones, with unusually generous social welfare systems. If poverty rates of those over the age of sixty-five remained at or slightly above those of the population as a whole, which was a more typical state of affairs, this still marked a major change from a past era, when being old almost automatically meant being poor, especially as it went along with a decline in people in that age group gainfully employed.[39] As a result, by the Era of Upheaval, the elderly had become important players in a flourishing consumer capitalism. Tourism, a rapidly growing business in the postwar era, gained a large group of paying customers. An offshoot of tourism was "retirement communities," places where seniors could live and devote themselves to their new leisure existence, generally located in warm-weather touristic destinations, such as Arizona and Florida in the United States., or the Spanish island of Mallorca, increasingly overrun by elderly Britons and Germans. Because the combination of old-age pensions and rising life expectancy could postpone the deterioration of old age but not entirely negate biological inevitabilities, nursing and old-age homes became a new and somewhat macabre feature of economics and public life.[40]

The improvement in the condition and dignity of the elderly was one of the great triumphs of social welfare policy in the postwar era; it was very much a good thing. Combined with a declining birth rate and the post-1973 oil shock decline in rates of economic growth across most of the world, the question soon began to emerge if it was too much of a good thing. Could public pensions continue to function if the number of recipients, the elderly, steadily increased in relation to the number of people of working age, who were funding public-pension systems? More broadly, how would an economy function when a fifth or more of the entire population were out of the labor force? Even if these funding questions could be resolved—and the slow-growth economic environment made a resolution considerably more difficult—where would the labor come from to care for the growing number of the elderly who could no longer care for themselves in their activities of daily life? In some ways, it was less about actual conditions that led to these questions than projections of what they would mean by, say, the middle of the twenty-first century.[41]

Funding proved to be the less difficult problem to tackle, at least in wealthier countries with resources for it. The solution to a situation in which the expenses of old-age pension funds were threatening to exceed sources of revenue was to cut expenses and increase revenues. The value of pensions relative to average wages continued to increase after 1980, but at a much slower pace. In study done in 2017 of OECD countries (generally wealthier in Europe and North America, but also including some less well-off ones, such as Mexico and Turkey) old-age pensions were 53 percent of an average worker's wage, admittedly with an enormous variability, ranging from 97 percent in the Netherlands, to 26 percent in Mexico and 22 percent in the United Kingdom. Contrary to fears that grew up in the 1980s, financing, seemed surprisingly stable, at an average of 8.9 percent of GDP, projected to rise to 9.5 percent by the middle of the twenty-first century.[42]

The situation was noticeably less favorable in poorer countries, which were the particular victims of the unfavorable economic environment of during the Late-Millennium Era. The formerly communist countries of Eastern Europe had considerable difficulty maintaining their pension systems. As a result of their economic collapse in the 1990s, they faced a choice between very high tax rates, as much as 30 percent of payroll, or widespread poverty among the elderly, generally ending up with both. Two very different examples from Latin America demonstrate some of the problems of old-age pension systems in less-wealthy countries. In Venezuela, pensions were not adjusted for inflation, so that by 1992 they were one-fifth of their 1974 values. A different approach came from Chile, where the pro-capitalist military dictatorship of General Pinochet, coming to power after the coup against the leftist Popular Unity government in 1973, terminated the previous old-age pension plan and developed a new one. Instead of a defined-benefit plan, funded by contributions from younger people in employment, the new plan involved defined contributions, roughly 10 percent of wages and salaries that would be invested in individual accounts and available upon retirement. The plan was lauded by economists and the World Bank, who thought that competition among banks and other financial service providers would lead to high returns on investments and so offer future retirees more than they could hope for under a redistribution system, by which the younger, economically active population is taxed to pay for the retired elderly. Reality, as is so often the case, did not live up to economists' expectations. It turned out that financial service companies competed primarily on how high they could raise their fees; actual pensions were about half of what the system's designers had claimed they would be. Hundreds of thousands of furious retirees demonstrated in the streets of Santiago and across the country against the system in 2016 and 2017.[43]

The Chilean demonstrators were just part of a broader generational situation that today has left the world divided into two distinct groups. There were the areas of rapid natural population increase, with Total Fertility Rates, while perhaps not quite so high as they had been in the postwar decades, still above 4: Africa particularly, but also the Islamic countries of the Middle East and South Asia. And then there were the areas with TFRs either below the 2.1 natural replacement level or heading fast in that direction: Western Europe, the United States, Canada, Japan, Australia, and New Zealand, but also much of Latin America and, especially, East Asia, where birth rates and natural population increase had declined dramatically. The former were the countries of youth, the latter the lands of old age.[44]

It is easy to understand how rapid population growth was creating economic difficulties—eating up most of the expansion of the economy, keeping women's lives tied to reproduction. The lack of population growth also seemed to create economic difficulties, however: a disproportionate share of the elderly in the population meant both a decline in demand and a smaller proportion of adults in the labor force. One might expect an older population to be favorable to young people, since they would be able to obtain more favorable wages and better career prospects. Japan, the world's most elderly country, shows the exact opposite. There, an astonishingly high proportion of young people have been unable to find permanent jobs and wages that will enable them to be economically independent. The negative effects of slow economic growth resulting from a declining population seem to outweigh the positive effects of a shortage of young people. Fewer young people could afford to get married and to start families, leading to further population declines and a downward spiral.[45]

In some ways, population growth has become an economically addictive drug. Continued long enough, it loses its economically stimulative effects, as in Africa and other poorer countries with high fertility rates, but the results of demographic withdrawal, as can be seen in Japan, are unpleasant as well. Population change has interacted with economic development throughout human history, but it was in the Age of Interconnection that its opioid-like characteristics came to the fore, a consequence of an unprecedentedly rapid rate of natural population increase during the postwar era, and a subsequent unprecedentedly rapid decline in birth rates that began in different places during the Era of Upheaval. Particularly when combined with the worldwide slowdown in economic growth over the last quarter of the century and the increasing transformation in global class structures during that same period, future prospects for both young people and the elderly seem difficult and uncertain in the decades ahead.

Gender

Like generations, gender involves the interaction of the biological with the cultural: the way people understand the sexes and the actions that flow from those understandings. A helpful way to organize and categorize the interaction of gender is in terms of two groups of attitudes and behaviors: one encompassing reproduction, family, and sexuality; the other education, labor, and authority. The two groups are, of course, closely interrelated and this interrelationship leads to the creation of a gender "regime." Such regimes differ in different parts of the world, as a result of social structures, levels of economic development, cultural and religious practices, or politics and public policies. As a result, they have undergone large-scale changes: naturally, at varying paces and to varying extents, but with a very gradual, if partial, tendency toward the development of global uniformity.

As was the case with social classes, there existed in much of Europe and North America, as well as more affluent areas in the rest of the mid-century world, a gender regime that had been developing since the late nineteenth century. Although the Great Depression, the Second World War, and the postwar flood of refugees had temporarily disrupted that gender regime in some countries, it snapped back into place—indeed, was reinforced—by the early postwar era. Women's lives tended to be centered around family, household, and reproduction: men's around participation in the market, especially the market for labor. The word "tended" is important here; the gender regime was bipolar, dividing men and women, but not consigning them to mutually exclusive separate spheres. Women did generally engage in regular paid work—at least until they were married, at which point their participation came to an end, generally for reproduction-related reasons; if it resumed later, it was on an irregular basis. Boys and girls both received a basic elementary education; while secondary schools and universities were predominantly male, there was a significant minority of female pupils and students. Adult men and women often did socialize independently of each other, but the gradual growth of the ideal of "companionate marriage," a conjugal union in which both spouses spent a big chunk of their free time together, was slowly breaking down those barriers of social life.[46]

Politics was primarily, if not exclusively, a male realm. There were the occasional women parliamentarians and government ministers, such as Bertha Lutz, the first woman elected to parliament in Brazil, in 1932; Helene Weber, a German Catholic conservative, who sat in the Constituent Assembly that wrote the constitution of the Weimar Republic and, thirty years later, in the Parliamentary Council that wrote the constitution of the Federal Republic; or Frances Perkins, US Secretary of Labor from 1933 to 1945, and a major architect of the New Deal social welfare state. But they were lone female islands in a sea of men. At the end of the Second World War, only 2 percent of the members of democratically elected legislatures, worldwide, were women.[47]

The first half of the century did see the introduction of woman suffrage in most of the world. While there were a handful of exotic pre-World War One examples, New Zealand and Finland for instance, women gained the vote in two major, worldwide waves, following each of the two world wars: after the first, in the United States, the United Kingdom, and Canada (actually in 1917, during the war), as well as the nations of East-Central Europe, emerging from the defeated Tsarist, German, Austro-Hungarian, and Ottoman Empires, along with the largest Ottoman successor state, Turkey. With a decade's delay, a number of Latin American countries—Ecuador, Brazil, Uruguay, Bolivia, and El Salvador—enfranchised women. After the Second World War, woman suffrage followed in the other European nations, including France, Belgium, Italy, and Greece (Swiss men would hold out on woman suffrage until 1971);

the remaining Latin American countries (most prominently Argentina), Japan, and China, where the competing Nationalists and Communists both enfranchised women—although their respective dictatorial regimes made woman suffrage, or anybody else's for that matter, a hollow triumph. Woman suffrage came to India and Indonesia along with freedom from colonial rule. At least in some parts of India, contemporaries were deeply impressed with women's interest and participation in the first all-India elections of 1950. This South Asian combination of independence and votes for women would be repeated in the African, Middle Eastern, and Asian decolonization waves of the 1950s and 1960s, so that by the last quarter of the century women everywhere in the world could cast their ballots, aside from a few countries in the Arabian Peninsula. The enfranchisement of women was the single largest change in gender regimes during the Age of Total War and its extension into the postwar era.[48]

This modified bipolarity of the mid-century gender regime in education, occupations, and public life was echoed in the bedroom, the delivery room, and the family room. Reproduction occurred primarily in marriage. In Uruguay, a Latin American country with a population almost entirely of European descent and also with a good system of registering statistics, 1950 marked the low point of extramarital births—18 percent, as against 26 percent in 1900 and 48 percent in 2000. By Latin American and probably by broader standards, Uruguay's illegitimacy was high—in the United States, extramarital births made up just 5 percent of all births in 1950. However, the picture of the mid-century decades as an age of childbearing in wedlock prevailed across Europe and its former settler colonies. The UN's global statistics on this particular gender regime only begin around 1970, but they show that in every country in the entire world, illegitimacy rates then were lower—and generally much lower—than they are today.[49]

If there were so many in-wedlock births, it was because a lot of marrying was going on. At the beginning of the twentieth century, roughly half of all the women in the United States aged twenty to twenty-four were married; by 1950, 66 percent. The maximum point came in 1960: 70 percent. Referring to similar trends, Göran Therborn, the Swedish sociologist, describes the postwar era as the "Marriage Age," in the history of Western society, peaking in 1960, when the proportion of the population married was at its highest since the appearance of the very first records from which such figures can be derived, in the sixteenth through the eighteenth centuries.[50]

These statistics make it clear that sexuality and reproduction occurred primarily among married couples. It is not that there was no premarital sexuality. Quite the opposite—more people, women especially, were engaging in sexual relations before marriage in 1960 than at the beginning of the twentieth century, but these relations were generally a prelude to marriage. Of course, no statistics say anything about the way sex was experienced.

Such intimate matters are difficult to explore, as they leave relatively little behind in the way of written records; interviews, an important resource, are not always entirely reliable, since this is a topic about which people generally lie. There are a wide variety of attitudes toward and experiences of sexuality in the postwar era. However, two versions may have been common. One was expressed by a Chilean farmworker, reminiscing about her marital life in the 1950s. Sex, she stated, "is part of what a wife owes her husband even if it was something he enjoys much more than she." Another version, perhaps more common among the better educated, and often appearing in questions directed to institutional marriage advisers, was a husband understanding that his wife should enjoy sexual relations, but was unclear how that was achieved, or if he was capable of bringing it about. Women, at least decent proper ones, were expected not to know such things.[51]

Part of the reason for women's sexual reluctance was fear of pregnancy. Contraception in the 1950s was like tuberculosis before the Second World War. While increasing prosperity and improved public hygiene meant that fewer people suffered from the illness and mortality rates from the disease (in some countries at least) declined, there was little effective treatment for a person who had become consumptive. In a similar way, contraception had brought down birth rates in Europe and North America, and parts of Latin America as well. There were three leading methods. Only one was female-controlled, the diaphragm, which was messy and unpopular. As one British woman recalled, "you used to have to coat it with cream, and squeeze it to get it in, and often it used to just fly out of your hand, so after a few moments of chasing it round the bedroom all sexual desire had gone." Condoms enjoyed an immense growth in popularity after they had been handed out to soldiers during the war. Still, the old standby, withdrawal, was almost certainly the most widely used form of birth control, worldwide, until the 1960s. Just as there was no effective treatment for someone developing tuberculosis before antibiotics, none of these contraceptive methods, if overall reducing the frequency with which women had children, were reliable in preventing any individual pregnancy.[52]

Terminating an unwanted pregnancy was common, but also difficult and dangerous. The almost universal illegality of abortions—Japan was, in this respect, as in so many others, an exception—meant that the procedure would occur in unsanitary circumstances and with a good chance of harming a woman's health or even leading to her death. In France, where not just abortion but birth control was prohibited, there were something in the range of five hundred thousand to 1.2 million abortions per year during the 1950s; between ten thousand to fifty thousand had a fatal outcome for the women undergoing them. Chilean public health officials estimated that there were 140,000 abortions each year during the mid-1960s, one abortion for every two live births. One abortion in five resulted in the death of the woman seeking it.⁵³ These are devastating numbers.

Abortions, at least, were not an issue for people preferring members of their own sex as partners. Somewhat surprisingly, gender polarity tended to shape same-sex relations as well. People who practiced same-sex relations—it might be a bit anachronistic to refer to them as "gay"—tended to divide into two groups, one playing an active, masculine; the other a passive, feminine role. In Brazil, for instance, active men were called *homen* or *bofe*, passive ones, *bicha*, from the French word for "doe," *biche*. A *bicha* acted effeminately, might dress up as a woman, particularly during Carnival, when cross-dressing was publicly tolerated and had sexual relations exclusively with men; the *bofe* was masculine in appearance, often married, and had sexual relations with both women and men. This distinction, which was found across Europe and the Americas, from the late nineteenth century to the postwar era, applied inversely to women: it was the active woman, dressing and acting like a man, who stood out as different.

The marriage age was not a kind one for homosexuality. Public attitudes varied from the hard line, perceiving same-sex relations, particularly between men, as immoral, a threat to national security and a danger to society, needing to be snuffed out, to the therapeutic. In this viewpoint, same-sex relations were seen as a mental illness, to be cured with psychoanalytic therapy—or in Denmark and Norway, most violently, by means of castration. If anything, legal action against gay men was stepped up in the 1950s, the number of prosecutions in the United Kingdom increasing fivefold over that decade, with similar developments in the United States, Canada, or France. Paragraph 175 of the German Criminal Code, prohibiting sexual acts among men, was a piece of Nazi-era legislation enforced during the postwar era in both West and East Germany. Such legal measures were directed primarily against men. It took a while for the public to become aware that sexual relations between women were even possible and lesbianism tended to be perceived more as a curiosity to be tolerated (or, perhaps therapized) than as a threat to society. In a remarkable legal decision, very much typical of the era, the West German Supreme Court ruled in 1957 that it was constitutionally permissible to prohibit same-sex relations among men, but to allow them among women, because the former prosed a grave danger to the social order, while the latter, in view of natural female maternal instincts, did not.⁵⁴

Legal actions and prevailing opinions about same-sex relations were a particularly pronounced version of general social and legal disapproval of expressions of sexuality outside of marriage and reproduction. Censorship of theater, films, and the nascent medium of television, campaigns of church groups and law enforcement against pornographic literature—very widely interpreted—mounting even to book-burnings were par for the course. Abortion was outlawed; single mothers (admittedly at the time a relatively small group) were shamed; even contraceptive devices and birth control clinics were in a legal gray zone. As late as 1962, US customs agents seized diaphragms of women entering the country, on the grounds that the law only permitted medical personnel to import them. There were, of course, opponents of these views, who articulated dissident ideas about sexuality. Perhaps the most prominent was Alfred C. Kinsey, an Indiana University entomologist—his specialty was wasps—who turned to studying human sexual behavior (it says a great deal about the postwar era that its showcase researcher of human sexuality was an expert in insect behavior). His books on the topic, although very unscientific (the selection of subjects for questionnaires and interviews was distinctly non-random and so not representative of the entire population), revealed the frequency of nonmarital and non-heterosexual relations, became bestsellers, in spite of their wooden, academic style, and were quickly translated into a number of foreign languages. Yet for all the interest the books generated, they produced immense opposition as well, so much so that Kinsey's funder, the Rockefeller Foundation, pulled his grants and terminated his research.[55]

In the postwar era there was a distinctly different gender regime in much of Asia and Africa, as well as parts of Latin America, roughly the same areas as had kinship-based and seigneurial class systems. This, too, was a regime of gender bipolarity, although one expressed in very different ways.[56] The strong distinctions between female lives centered around the household and male ones around wage labor so typical of much of Europe and North America were much less present, because so much of the population was employed in small-scale farming, in which household work segued into production and wage labor was more of a sideline.

Gender dichotomies were expressed through lineage. A classic example was in China, where households were organized vertically, across generations, rather than horizontally, between marital partners. Sons owed their parents filial respect, which they expressed by bringing their wives into their parents' household to serve them. Marriages were arranged by parents to that end, at times with the future spouses still children. One version of such arranged marriages was for poor families to sell their female children as future brides. This arrangement made sons far more important than daughters; it was common in China to refer to daughters as "spilled water." Parents raised them, only to see them, as adults, go off into another household.[57]

As both these practices and attitudes suggest, there was a strong element of property transaction between two lineages in marriages. Taking a deep breath and overlooking countless particular, local customs, it is possible to see the world as divided into two different versions of these transactions. Typically found in East Asia and Africa, one generally goes under the name of bride-price, or bride-wealth, compensation the groom's family paid the bride's family—not the bride herself, of course—for loss of her labor to her new in-law's household. The other, the dowry, was a payment of the bride's family to the groom's a sort of advance on the bride's inheritance from her parents. Dowries were characteristic of Europe and its colonial offshoots, although by 1950, the prevalence of waged or salaried labor in the world's wealthier countries meant that dowries were not what they had been. They were becoming steadily more common in South Asia, increasingly replacing bride-wealth, a development continuing down to the present day.[58]

If experiences of sexuality in Europe and the Americas remain a realm of guesswork, only lightly influenced by scattered evidence, this is even more the case in Asia and Africa.[59] Four characteristic features of the gender regime in those parts of the world might provide some clues. One was the universality of marriage: well over 95 percent of women were married, and at a very young age, between fifteen and twenty, generally to men older than them. While the postwar era in Europe and the Americas may have been an age of marriage, this was nothing new in Asia or Africa. A second was the prevalence of arranged marriages, so that the newlywed couple had little or no opportunity to get to know each other before being married. A third was high birth rates; marriages with frequent bouts of childbearing, and little evidence of even the imperfect attempts at contraception typical of wealthier countries. If birth control was attempted, it was by periods of sexual abstention, prolonged breastfeeding, or simply infanticide. (There may have been some overlap in the practice of withdrawal.) Finally, there was the existence of polygamy and concubinage.[60]

All these together suggest that companionate marriages, perhaps still a minority in Europe and the Americas in 1950, were a rarity in Asia and Africa, limited to circles of urban, middle-class intellectuals, influenced by Western ideas.[61] Sexual pleasure, especially for women, would seem to have been, at best, very limited. Another point along those lines is the prevalence of practices that did real, physical harm to women.

It was girls, whose lives, as the Chinese said, would just be "spilled water," who bore the brunt of infanticide, whether in the form of the open murder of newborns, or a neglect of care of infants. Part of the reason for the universality of marriage among women was that, as a result of the killing of baby girls, they were in short supply. As a result, there was always a large bachelor population in China, typically from the poor, who were unable to find a wife. Less fatal, but disfiguring and often crippling, were the Chinese practice of foot-binding, done in primarily to girls from wealthier families and, especially, female genital mutilation, very widespread across all social groups in northern Africa and the Middle East, mostly, but not exclusively among Muslims.[62]

Just as the dichotomy between household-oriented women and workplace-oriented men was much less pronounced in Asia and Africa than in Europe and the Americas, so was the contrast between heterosexuality and homosexuality. Same-sex relations in Africa and Asia, particularly among men, were far from unknown. They often involved generational differences, particularly in Africa, where older men had relations with adolescents in initiation rites, or in the practice of "mine marriages," where married migrant mineworkers from the Tsonga people of southern Africa took younger coworkers as sexual and domestic partners, when away from their families. Cross-dressing men could even be one of a number of wives in a polygamist family, and were another feature of sexual life. The *bissu* of south Sulawesi, in today's Indonesia, were men who dressed as women, had sexual relations with other men, kept the royal regalia, and performed fertility rituals for members of the nobility. But none of these practices were distinct from heterosexual relations, nor were they criminalized—unless the colonial authorities decided to do so—or perceived as unnatural or immoral, except perhaps among converts to Christianity. This was very much unlike circumstances in Europe and the Americas where same-sex relations, particularly those between men were furtive and disguised; where people wanting to engage in those practices were, in the celebrated phrase, "in the closet," or, at best, confined themselves to closed-mouth subcultures.[63]

Gender regimes in mid-century Africa and Asia were distinctly patriarchal, characterized by overt and often physical domination of men over women. It is hard to argue that the gender regimes of Europe and the Americas at the time were not patriarchal; they were, but perhaps less blatantly and physically. This observation leads to one final question about gender regimes: Were they any alternatives, of a more feminist nature, opposed to patriarchy?

There had been since the late nineteenth century a number of women's groups, linked in the International Council of Women. Primarily active in Europe and the United States, there were also National Councils of Women in Uruguay, Argentina, and Peru, and the Women's India Association. (Admittedly, the latter had been founded by English women living in India or married to Indians, but quickly acquired ties to the nationalist movement against British imperial rule, including a prominent role for Uma Nehrau, cousin by marriage to the nationalist leader and independent India's first prime minister Jawaharlal Nehru.) A very late example was the Uganda Council of Women, formed in what was then a British colony in 1946–47 by educated British, Indian, and African women, who had been active in the Mother's Union, created by the Protestant Church. These associations focused their attention on what might be called "public uplift": improving public hygiene and workplace health, combating infant mortality, supporting new mothers, improving educational opportunities for women, campaigning against alcohol and prostitution. Sometimes the organizations, or some of their active members, took on explicitly questions of women's rights: suffrage, or equality with men in family and property law. A more overtly feminist orientation was particularly pronounced in English-speaking and Scandinavian countries, during the early part of the century. By 1950, this orientation, if still existing, was rather at a low ebb, generally not having moved much beyond the question of woman suffrage.[64]

Then there were the revolutionary regimes of communist Eurasia, officially pro-feminist, promising an upheaval in gender relations like the upheaval in class. And the communist regimes at least began their rule in feminist fashion, proclaiming equality of men and women in their constitutions, calling into existence large state-run women's associations, dramatically rejecting the past. This policy was most evident in China, where a 1950 marriage law abolished the "feudal marriage system," eliminating polygamy, concubinage, bride wealth, child marriage, and the selling of children as spouses. Marriage was to be based on the free decision of two adults; husbands and wives were proclaimed equal under the law; divorce was legalized and facilitated; children's rights were recognized and infanticide outlawed.[65]

And communists did, in some ways, carry out a revolution in gender relations, if perhaps not entirely as they expected. The onset of their rule raised both expectations and fears. The East German communists planned to revise the code of family law in 1954, to bring it in line with their constitutionally established equality of men and women. The rumor spread throughout the country that the new code would allow married men to stay at the home of their mistresses every day until 10 p.m. At about the same time in China, the government carried out a massive land reform, taking property from landlords and large farmers, and allocating it to poor peasants. Such poor peasants, in view of the surplus of adult men, were much more likely to be bachelors. Word spread that the government was planning to assign them women, to go along with the land. One woman, from a village in the vicinity of Shanghai, asked the authorities, "When we are assigned, is it okay if I not be assigned to a hunchback?"[66]

Communist political empowerment of women proved to be largely rhetorical. While there were plenty of women deputies to communist parliaments, these legislatures were just for show. Party central committees and other loci of political power were almost exclusively male. Particularly in the early years of communist rule, a few women were powerful communist politician, like the Romanian party leader Anna Pauker, or the East German Minister of Justice Hilde Benjamin, an Auschwitz survivor and militant Stalinist. It was more common for women at the top of the party pyramid to get there via their relations with men, like Elena Ceauçescu, wife of Nicolae Ceauçescu, the Romanian dictator; Margot Honecker, wife of East Germany's second and last leader, Erich Honecker; or, perhaps most notoriously, Jiang Qing, the leader of the "Gang of Four," the extreme leftists of 1970s China, the wife of Mao Zedong. Noncommunist feminists were not tolerated. When the Czech feminist leader Milada Horáková, president of the Council of

Czechoslovak Women, opposed the communist seizure of power in 1948, the regime responded by arresting her the following year, accusing her of being an imperialist spy, and executing her, following a show trial, in 1950.[67]

Since the late nineteenth century, Marxists had been proclaiming, beginning with Marx's close friend and chief disciple Friedrich Engels, that the key to the emancipation of women was liberation from the household through participation in wage labor. Communist regimes carried out this policy, a point that becomes apparent from the ILO's statistics on labor force participation rates for women of prime childbearing years, twenty-five to twenty-nine. The UN agency's systematic data collection began in 1950, at the onset of communist rule everywhere outside the USSR. Labor force participation rates of 60 percent and greater were typical of communist regimes—with only a few exceptions, including Czechoslovakia, Hungary, and East Germany, where they were in the 35 to 40 percent range, roughly similar to the highest rates of young women's labor force participation in the capitalist world, obtaining in the United States or northern Europe.[68] But during the 1950s, labor-force participation rates among women in communist lands rose steadily, reaching between 70 and 90 percent for the twenty-five to twenty-nine age group, while in capitalist countries, the rate was little changed, actually declining in some of them, including Denmark, Iceland, Norway, Ireland, Portugal, the Netherlands, and New Zealand. By 1960, the contrast between communist regimes in which a large majority of women, including mothers, were part of the labor force, and a capitalist world, where employment and maternity were, for most women, mutually exclusive, had reached an all-time high.[69]

It does seem that women in communist regimes, especially those doing new types of industrial labor, found it emancipating, although it is less clear that toiling on a collective farm brought the same psychic satisfaction. And for all that, communist workplaces continued to be distinctly gendered. Women may have become industrial workers, but much more in textile and garment production than in steel manufacture or coal mining; they consistently received lower pay than did men. The real catch in emancipating women from the household via paid labor was that household work remained to be done and it was women who did it—the famous "double burden" imposed on women in communist regimes. By the mid-1960s, employed married women in the USSR only had 57 percent of the free time that employed married men did; by contrast, in the arch-capitalist rival the United States, employed married women (to say nothing of married women who were not employed) had 80 percent of the free time enjoyed by their husbands. Speaking of leisure, there is nothing to suggest that the communist version of the emancipation of women did much to enhance female sexuality (or male sexuality, for that matter), and, in view of the restricted supply and poor quality of contraceptive devices—like most consumer goods—reason to think communist rule had a negative effect.[70]

It was in China that communist rule had the largest effect on gender regimes, although there, too, not in ways that the revolutionaries had anticipated. In the early 1950s, they held mass meetings to condemn former landlords, in which poor peasants would "speak bitterness" to denounce their oppressors. To everyone's surprise, the daughters-in-law of those poor peasants chimed in, bitterly denouncing the way they had been oppressed, not by capitalists, but by their mothers-in-law. Surprisingly large numbers of women in rural areas (rather fewer in big cities) filed for divorce, openly asserting that they saw no reason to live with their poor, worthless husbands and their tyrannical mothers-in-law.

While the communists certainly wanted to abolish "feudalism" in family life and make marriage a free relation between equals, they also envisaged the new marriages as stable ones, and intended to continue the millennia-old Chinese practice of sons expressing their filial obligations toward their parents. By legalizing divorce, redistributing rural property holdings and, later in the 1950s, seizing the peasants' property and putting it into state ownership, they were undermining their own goals. For the most part, Chinese parents could continue to count on their sons to support them in their old age, and their daughters-in-law to reside with them and to accept their authority. They could no longer choose their children's spouses or sell daughters, but arranged marriages, via acquaintances and matchmakers, became the norm. Communist rule had begun to undermine the gender regime in China; the reinstatement of capitalism during the Late-Millennium Era would not lead, as some feminists feared, to a return of that gender regime, but would undermine it still further.[71]

A GENDERED UPHEAVAL: THE 1960S AND 1970S

For all the communists' partial, half-hearted, and often primarily symbolic forays into questions of the social organization of gender, the postwar era was largely a period in which previously existing gender regimes continued, and were, if anything, reinforced, after the Great Depression, the Second World War, and the postwar chaos. Starting in the second half of the 1960s and expanding in the subsequent decade, the Era of Upheaval, existing gender regimes began to crumble. This development was something of a two-stage process. First, there was the "sexual revolution," a contemporary phrase referring to changes in sexual practices and attitudes, particularly about sexual relations outside of marriage. The "sexual revolution" was part of a broader change, associated with the rise of youth culture and the social and political radicalism of the era, the "Sixties," in common parlance.

Occurring at the same time was the development of new, more effective forms of contraception.

A second stage involved the rise of political movements devoted to transforming the gender regime, particularly for women's and gay rights. Occurring throughout the Era of Upheaval were major legal changes, both reflecting and encouraging these gender-based political movements. Rather like the rise of youth culture, these developments had a distinctly American face, although they touched all parts of the world in different ways. It is tempting to connect these developments, particularly those relating to women, to important social trends: the growing proportion of women attending colleges and universities, and the increasing number of women participating in the labor force at all points in their adult lives, including their childbearing years. On closer examination, this connection appears more tenuous. Feminist movements anticipated social trends more than were propelled by them; countries with the world's highest female labor force participation, the communist regimes of the Eastern Bloc, were not particular sites of upheavals in gender regimes.

Integral to promises of a sexual revolution and to any new gender regime were changes in the possibilities for contraception; these were closely linked to perhaps the most important pharmaceutical innovation of the postwar era, the birth control pill. Like so many technologies of the Age of Interconnection, it was a product of the Age of Total War and of initiatives occurring around the world. As early as the 1920s, biologists and pharmacists in Europe, inspired by the introduction of the hormone insulin to treat previously fatal diabetes, were working on the possibility of using hormones, especially the sex hormone progesterone, to suppress ovulation in women. A major problem was that the hormones could only be produced in very small quantities and at great expense. A Mexican firm, *Laboratorios Hormona*, and its successor company Syntex, whose chemists were largely European refugees from the Nazis, first found a way before and after the war, to synthesize hormones in large quantities and at reasonable costs from different varieties of the Mexican yam plant. These synthesized hormones provided the basis for the first birth control pill, which appeared on the market in 1957.

Originally marketing it as a means to regularize irregular menstrual cycles, the pharmaceutical manufacturers were only willing to admit that the pill could be used for birth control after a few years. When they did, it took off. In 1965 six million pills were manufactured. Two years later, that number had more than doubled. In 1968, one out of every three women between the ages of fifteen and forty-five in Australia and New Zealand was on the pill; in the United States it was one out of four, and in the United Kingdom one out of six. By 1973, two-thirds of all the married women in the United States had taken the pill at some point in their lives. The pill began as a birth-control practice in the Anglosphere; it later spread to Western and Northern Europe, reaching a high point in the Netherlands, where at least 40 percent of women of fertile age were taking the pill. Use was much less common in communist countries, where it was in short supply, and in Asia, Africa, and Latin America, where its considerable expense, opposition of Catholic and Muslim religious conservatives, and deep suspicions of the Western pharmaceutical firms manufacturing it (a particular issue in India), limited its possibilities. In some African countries, nationalists suspected the pill was designed to maintain European domination by reducing the number of Africans.

Use declined by the later 1970s. Fears that it increased the risk of cancer and stroke—fears that persist, in spite of decades of biomedical research showing no mortality danger—combined with uncomfortable side effects all helped reduce the popularity of the drug. Manufacturers developed versions of the pill with lower doses of hormones, which did reduce side effects but also increased risk of failure if a dose was forgotten. They were less effective on overweight women, an increasingly common circumstance.

Birth-control pills became a sort of gateway drug, leading to the widespread use of other forms of contraception. The global champion was sterilization, which, by the 1980s, had become the preferred method of contraception in the world's poorer countries and in the United States. Also popular in the poorer countries of the world was the IUD, which eliminated the need to take a pill on a daily basis.[72] The contraceptive experience of three Asian countries—India, China, and Japan—constituting a majority of the world's population practicing contraception, show new attitudes about birth control developing after the introduction of the birth control pill.

Sterilization as a birth control practice in India is closely connected with the "emergency," the two years of rule by Indira Gandhi between 1975 and 1977, when she assumed autocratic powers. A hallmark of that period was a campaign to reduce the birth rate by means of sterilization. A particular target of these policies were civil servants and teachers, who were told they would not receive salary or other benefits, or even be hired in the first place, if they had not submitted to the procedure. Government contractors were required to have their workers sterilized or lose their contracts. People were arrested and only released if they agreed to sterilization. Villagers were offered low-interest loans and free irrigation if they agreed to be sterilized. The government set up mobile sterilization camps to carry out the procedure across the country. Although villagers ran and hid when the sterilization units came, and Indian Muslims in particular, refused to cooperate, fearing it was all a plot to reduce their numbers, some ten million people were sterilized, before Gandhi was routed in the 1977 elections, partly as a result of her birth-control program.[73]

One element usually lacking in discussion of these controversial policies was their distinctly feminist coloring. Implemented by one of the very first female heads of government in the world in a strongly sexist country government controllers focused primarily on sterilizing men, fulfilling a feminist demand that men take responsibility for contraception. Many elements of the program, including the cash bonuses for sterilization, the pressure on government employees, and the mobile sterilization units, had been copied from previous efforts in the Indian state of Kerala, a stronghold of women's rights in an otherwise distinctly and oppressively patriarchal country.

If a coercion program was only temporarily effective in India, it achieved very different results in China. While the communist government had toyed with birth-control campaigns during the first three decades of its existence, Chairman Mao's insistence that a larger Chinese population meant a stronger communism—and more survivors of the thermonuclear war he expected to happen—limited their possibilities. The government's 1979 decision to implement a one-child per family policy, as part of its plans for dynamic economic growth, marked a sharp break with the chairman's world. The policy reached its coercive peak in 1983, when orders went out that all women with two or more children were to be sterilized and all with one child were to use IUDs. Women were literally dragged off to the hospital, tied down and aborted, sterilized, or had IUDs inserted, and sent back home. In that year, fourteen million abortions were carried out; over sixteen million women were sterilized; and close to eighteen million IUDs were inserted, measures that affected between 20 and 25 percent of women of childbearing age in the entire country. All these figures were multiples higher than in any previous year, making the compulsory nature of the campaign blatantly evident. After that point, the regime began to retreat. In rural areas, if the first child was a girl, couples were allowed to have a second. Rather than compulsory sterilization, couples were fined for having a second child (their villages would often put up the money to pay for the fines). The one-child policy was more strictly enforced in cities than in rural areas, where most Chinese lived.

In contrast to Indira Gandhi's efforts, Chinese contraceptive coercion was distinctly patriarchal, focused primarily on women: female sterilizations outnumbered male three and four to one—notable, considering that the process is more expensive and hazardous. Permission to have a second child if the first was a girl underscored the patriarchal nature of the government's population-reduction policy. While the communists had succeeded in eliminating the "feudal" practice of female infanticide, abortion of female fetuses became steadily more common in China, and the ratio of boys to girls born far exceeded the natural biological excess of boy over girl babies. In the end, the regime got its way. The Total Fertility Rate dropped drastically over the very short period (by demographic standards) of two decades; contraception use in China was among the highest of the countries of the world; younger people entering parenting age in the 1990s and beyond saw a two-child family as their ideal.[74]

Unlike China or India, Japan—at least after 1945—was not governed by a dictatorial regime. And by the time the birth control pill reached world markets in the 1960s, it was wealthy enough to afford it as a form of contraception. Yet its use was banned there until the very end of the millennium, ostensibly because of the health risks. Japan was one of the relatively few countries in the age of the postwar gender regimes, in which abortion was legal, a result of the "Eugenic Protection Law" of 1947. Abortion was the dominant method of birth control, and a lucrative one for the relatively small group among the country's gynecologists licensed to perform the procedure. Japanese midwives provided the chief contraceptive alternatives, selling condoms and diaphragms, often via the Japanese Family Planning Association, which also opposed the pill. Their influence ensured that worries about possible negative health effects of the birth control pill were taken more seriously. In 1964, Dr. Moriyama Yutaka, president of the Association of Obstetricians and Gynecologists, argued that taking the pill would cause women to develop masculine physical characteristics. As a result, the officials at the Ministry of Health and Welfare did a long and careful review of the pill's health effects—indeed so long and careful that it took more than thirty years. Approval was finally about to be granted in 1998, but at the last minute, fears arose that the hormones in the urine of women taking the pill would cause environmental damage. The fact that pregnant women have ten thousand times these hormones in their urine didn't seem to matter. Final approval did come in 1999, with the provisions that the pill was ineligible for health insurance coverage and that women taking it had to go in for a medical exam every three months, thus guaranteeing that even if legal it would not be used.[75]

Japan's unique contraceptive path might be seen as yet another example of how that island realm remains distinct from the rest of the world. With the lowest Total Fertility Rate of any major country in the world, its demographic history demonstrates that devices and pharmaceuticals are from determining sexuality and the outcomes of sexual practices.

This observation brings us to the second major element in changes to the gender regime during the Era of Upheaval, the sexual revolution. So much of it was a revolution in appearance and perception, a sharp break from the prevailing attitudes. Suddenly there was nudity in films and theater, to say nothing of a wide variety of printed representations of sex, ranging from literary classics to pornography and everything in between. Nakedness spread through high culture, from artistic "happenings" to topless cello performances. Popular music dropped the circumlocutions. Clothing was worn steadily tighter, emphasizing ever more the contours of the body; women's clothing, in particular, exposed noticeably more of it. Much of this was closely associated with an emergent youth culture discussed earlier and with the interrelated circles of the artistic avant-garde, but it reached beyond these to a broader public. In Europe, public nudism, long a niche practice, became steadily more prevalent and popular on beaches and in parks. Throughout the capitalist world, sexual references in advertising were omnipresent.[76]

Much of this was commercial noise, but the changes in appearance and perception appeared in more modest ways as well. In Catholic Ireland, where birth control was illegal, letters to the editor and advice columns of women's magazines during the 1950s dealt primarily with dating and relations of young women to their parents. In the following decade, the leading topic of these magazine rubrics, by contrast, was sexual relations. Even letters criticizing the Church's stance on birth control reached print. The increasing transparency of sex is reflected in the career of the German entrepreneur Beate Rotermund, who had spent the two postwar decades developing a mail-order firm that sent her customers condoms and marriage manuals, discretely concealed in plain brown paper wrappers. In the 1960s, Rotermund expanded her business, opening up retail sex shops that offered pornographic books and films, as well as sex toys. "Beate Uhse" stores (Uhse was the name of her first husband, killed in the war) spread across all of Western Europe during the 1960s and 1970s, becoming the largest business of its kind in the world.[77]

These examples raise the question of the relationship between perception and behavior and attitude. We might wonder whether the so-called sexual revolution was confined primarily to movies, advertising, rock music, and pornography, or reflected actual changes in sexual behavior or in the experience of sexuality, and whether it had an effect on gender norms. It also raises the question of whether they were limited to the affluent countries, or, like were movies or popular music, had a more global scope. The main question might be whether it played out primarily in cosmopolitan cities or more broadly.

Statistics on these intimate matters—very scattered and not always entirely reliable, as I've made clear—nonetheless do suggest significant changes. Not surprisingly, the United States is best documented. While between 1954 and 1963 slightly less than half (48 percent) of young people (fifteen or older) of both sexes had had premarital sexual relations by age twenty, a figure not that different from prewar years the percentage jumped to 65 percent between 1964 and 1973, the heart of the Era of Upheaval, when the sexual revolution was in full swing. It reached as high as 76 percent for the rest of the century.[78] Does an increase of about a third in the proportion of young people engaging in premarital sexual relations amount to a "revolution"? The changes in sexual behavior may have been less dramatic than those in its public representation. Still, the era did show the greatest changes in sexual behavior in the whole Age of Interconnection. And it was likely the case that these changes were particularly pronounced for women and reflected a different attitude toward premarital sex: not just a brief interlude leading up to marriage but a more prolonged period in life of sexual experimentation, multiple partners, and an expression of sexuality not tied to marriage—changes which have persisted until the present day. So perhaps "revolution" is not an entirely false description.

More difficult to ascertain is just how common the American experiences were across the world. Western and Northern Europe seem to have followed the American pattern of a large jump in the number of young people, especially women, having premarital sexual relations, a declining age of first sexual relations, and a growing number of sexual partners (Swedish women going from an average of 1.4 in 1967 to 4.6 in 1996) in the Upheaval Era, with a persistence of these trends in the Late-Millennium Era. In the 1990s, family planning experts began doing surveys of sexual behavior in Latin American, Asian, and African countries, mostly concerning contraceptive use and only going back to 1965. In the fundamentally different gender regimes prevailing in those countries, evidence of a sexual revolution seems pretty scanty, especially because most women were already married by their late teens and generally virgins at their wedding. There were some exceptions in parts of Africa and Latin America but even there, the proportion of young women engaging in premarital sexual relations seems to have increased slowly and gradually, so there was no sharp change, no revolution in sexuality. In large cities, like Buenos Aires, which had a European-style gender regime, there was something like a sexual revolution, but the same wasn't true of the countryside.[79]

If there was a sexual revolution outside of Europe and North America, it was in China. It wasn't in the realm of appearances. Young Chinese wore Mao jackets rather than jeans and miniskirts, and listened to "The East is Red," instead of the Rolling Stones. But the Cultural Revolution and the labor processes of collectivized agriculture brought together young men and women in an unprecedented way. The Chinese American anthropologist Yunxiang Yan, in his studies of family life, courtship, and individuality, has suggested that in this time young people, not just in large cities but in rural areas as well, began meeting, whether in campaigns of the Red Guards, or at the grain harvest, and choosing their future spouses themselves. It was a start to ending the many different forms of arranged marriage so common in China's past, including during the early years of the communist regime.[80]

Even at its most revolutionary, the sexual revolution, and the youth culture with which it is so closely associated, contained within it very pronounced elements of the existing gender regime. Women's lives remained tied to home and family, if perhaps with some counterculture alterations—breastfeeding, earth mothers, running organic households without chemical cleansers, rather than bottle-feeding, vacuum-cleaner-using, bleach-spraying suburban housewives. The sexual revolution, for all the potential liberation from the dour and puritanical atmosphere of the 1950s it upended, was distinctly male-oriented. It was about more women being more available to men in more ways than just one woman in marriage. The birth control pill played an important role, since it took away the excuse of fear of pregnancy women previously could use to refuse to have sexual relations. The sexual revolution was, above all, about gratifying men's needs. Women's might be too, but only if it could be done in the context of men concentrating on theirs.[81]

If the birth control pill and the sexual revolution reflected the initial stage of a change in gender regimes, the second stage was the development of a feminist movement. Some have tried very hard to trace connections between this "Second Wave" feminism and the women's associations and women's rights movements of the late nineteenth and early twentieth centuries. Others have not found their arguments convincing. By the 1950s, those latter groups were shrunken and vestigial, their members aging. Feminism in the developed countries emerged in the 1970s from two different venues. One was trade unions and left-of-center political parties. A famous example is Betty Friedan, author of the 1963 bestseller *The Feminine Mystique*, the first major feminist statement in post-1945 America, and chief mover in the 1966 founding of National Organization of Women (NOW), the pioneering Second Wave feminist group, influential not just in the United States, but in the entire world. Years earlier, Friedan had been active in the American Communist Party and a journalist for trade unions strongly influenced by it.[82] Western European social democratic, socialist, labor and—to a lesser extent—communist parties played a similar role. The other venue for incipient feminism was youth culture, the sexual revolution, and the political movements closely associated with them, the so-called New Left. Feminist groups emerging from this milieu, generally smaller, more localized and less formally organized, called for "women's liberation," making them, in contemporary jargon, the "women's libbers." They included, among many others, the New York Radical Feminists, the Chicago Women's Liberation Union, the *Rivolta Femminile*, or the *Mouvement de libération des femmes*.[83]

Feminists from the first venue—trade unions and leftist groups—are often described as liberal and from the second, the New Left—radical, but it might be more useful to see the first group as primarily opponents of the postwar era's gender regime and the second as opponents of the developments of the Era of Upheaval dissolving that regime. Opposing the postwar regime meant, above all, dismantling the legal barriers and prevalent attitudes that kept women tied to the household: discriminatory employment practices, inequities in family law, unequal educational opportunities, lack of access to birth control and child care. By contrast, women from the latter group were enraged at their second-class-citizen treatment in what was supposed to be an emancipatory movement. They complained of being ignored, of being sent to perform menial tasks—making coffee and typing—of being treated as sexual conquests. These came together in men shouting sexually derisive comments at women in political meetings.[84]

A characteristic feature of this feminism emerging from the New Left was its pronounced hostility toward the birth control pill. Feminists denounced it as a tool of capitalist pharmaceutical companies that both harmed women and allowed men to evade any responsibility for contraception, pointing out that it had been ruthlessly tested on unsuspecting and nonconsenting Third World women. Different editions of the American radical feminists' bestselling women's self-help book *Our Bodies Ourselves* took positions on the pill ranging from skeptical to downright hostile (limited acceptance of it only coming in the eighth edition of 2005). The Tokyo Women's center, *Ribu Shinjuku Sentā*, the leading Japanese feminist group in the 1970s, was strongly hostile to the birth control pill and insisted that the prominent feminist Enoki Misako, who was pro-pill, was actually a paid tool of pharmaceutical companies.

In retrospect, these charges were all dubious. Far from being advocates of the birth control pill, capitalist pharmaceutical companies had been reluctant to get involved in its development, fearing conservative, religious moralist opposition would hurt their brand image and sales. Research on the birth control pill had been funded by veteran American feminist and birth control crusader Margaret Sanger and her wealthy friend, the women's rights activist Katherine McCormick. Their primary goal was women's reproductive autonomy, and they would have found the charge that the birth control pill removed men's obligations unconvincing. After all, the diaphragm, a feminist contraceptive favorite, did not obligate men, either. It is true that some field tests of the pill had taken place in Puerto Rico, but also in many places in the United States. Far from being imposed without their consent, researchers found, women were volunteering to be involved in the testing, far more than these researchers could manage. The intensely hostile reactions of radical feminists to the birth control pill speaks less specifically to the pill itself and much more to the origins of their movement in a broader rejection of the sexual revolution.[85]

An important contingent among radical feminists were lesbians, and radical feminism provided the first instance of the large-scale public visibility of lesbianism. The intellectual and emotional pull of the radical feminist argument was in a lesbian direction, for if men were so abusive and exploitative why would women want to have intimate relations with them? The same forces that produced radical feminism also led to gay rights movements, producing groups such as the Revolutionary Homosexual Action Front in France, or Gay Liberation Fronts in English-speaking countries. Similar groups were founded in Argentina, Brazil, and Spain, a little later, following the waning of the dictatorial regimes in these countries. In the Eastern Bloc, they emerged only after 1989. Japan, a country where the postwar gender regime order proved very durable, only saw small and ineffectual gay rights groups developing at about the same time. By the 1990s, while Gay Pride parades in North America and Western Europe attracted hundreds of thousands of participants, they mustered a turnout of forty in Japan.

While the political style of gay rights movements was similar to that of radical feminists, its goals were closer to liberal feminists' opposition to the postwar gender order, and its persecution of and hostility toward homosexuality. Gay rights advocates and politicized gay men were also advocates of the sexual revolution, promoting its untrammeled expression of sexuality and its rejection of a sexuality limited only to married men and women. Accompanying these movements was a change in the gendered dimension of same-sex contacts—from a strongly dichotomized contrast between active, masculine individuals and passive, feminine, ones to same-sex relationships in which both partners were—well—the same. In Brazil, the contrast between *bofe* and *bicha*, while still enduring among the working class and in rural areas, was beginning to give way in the middle class of Rio de Janeiro and São Paulo to a new phrase, *entendido*, "those in the know," and referring to performing all sexual roles.[86]

Organized opposition to the postwar gender regime was very similar to the rapidly growing environmentalist movement in Europe and the Americas occurring at the same time. And, just as the "long" 1970s, running from around 1967 to around 1983, was a decade in which environmentalist legislation and environmental ministries and government agencies spread throughout the world, and became an issue taken up by the UN, the same was true of women's and gay rights. A small yet significant example of new initiatives was the legalization of divorce in Italy, passed by the parliament in 1969. Following intense pressure from the Vatican, there was a referendum on the question five years later, which, very much to everyone's surprise, ended in a resounding reaffirmation of legalized divorce. There were reforms of divorce laws in England, France, West Germany, and many US states. A related topic was family law; there was fairly widespread adoption of legislation that abolished the status of the husband as head of household, granted both parents equal rights in childrearing, household finances, and basic matters, like the couple's choice of residence. Somewhat less common was legislation prohibiting discrimination in education and employment. Such laws came to the United States early, in 1964. They were actually part of a ploy by opponents of the 1964 Civil Rights Act to sabotage it, by adding to its prohibition of discrimination by race, a prohibition of discrimination by sex. Unexpectedly, this did nothing to stop the law's passage. Similar legislation was passed in France, the United Kingdom, and West Germany.

Remaining restrictions on birth control were swept away, in France, in 1967. Seven years later, abortion was legalized there, following a manifesto composed by, among others, Simone de Beauvoir, Catherine Deneuve, and

Marguerite Duras, all admitting that they had had illegal abortions. By the end of the 1970s, abortion was legal pretty much everywhere in Western Europe, including Italy, except for Ireland. The 1973 US Supreme Court decision in *Roe v. Wade* legalizing abortion, which itself followed a wave of state laws that had already done so, was the American part of this international trend.[87]

All these examples of legal change come from the more affluent, capitalist countries and some of the wealthier enclaves of the rest of the world. Circumstances were different in the communist realms of Eurasia and the poor countries of Africa, South Asia, and much of Latin America. Communist regimes could argue that there was no need for any legal changes, for they had already accomplished the feminist goals of legal equality between men and women, and achieving women's workforce participation. Abortion had already been legalized in the USSR, Poland, Czechoslovakia, and Romania in the second half of the 1950s, in part a reflection of the lack of reliable birth-control devices. The sexual revolution in these places was a different story. At the beginning of the 1970s, the East German secret police reported, in a panic, that under the influence of the sexual revolution in West Germany, young women were coming to youth group meetings at the cultural center in Freiberg without wearing any panties. The East German government's policies of the time—legalization of homosexuality, relaxation of existing restrictions on abortion, and generally dropping the attitude that capitalism was sexually decadent—show its recognition that the sexual revolution was a reality.[88]

In South Asia and Africa, and in large parts of Latin America, where the postwar era's gender regime did not exist, and where the sexual revolution, was, at best, marginal, feminism—liberal or radical—appeared as distinctly alien. This became apparent when the UN took up the issue of women's rights, proposing to make 1975 "International Women's Year," during which a conference would be held in Mexico City to launch the International Women's Decade. This was when the communist countries of the Eastern Bloc and a steadily growing proportion of governments of the nonaligned nations were working closely together. At meetings in Hungary and East Berlin, the communist women's groups and their non-aligned allies prepared for Mexico City. As one Hungarian journalist explained their plans, feminism was a "luxury for the rich." The real problem facing women was imperialism. The Mexico City conference ended by condemning the Israeli occupation of the Gaza Strip and the West Bank, proclaiming imperialism and neocolonialism "the greatest obstacles to the full emancipation of and progress of developing countries and all the peoples concerned." The conference produced no statement about sexism or oppression of women, in spite of the efforts of the Western delegates. The Caribbean feminist Peggy Antrobus explained in her memoirs how she was misled at this conference into betraying her anti-imperialist credentials by working with the US delegation, who brought up issues of women's rights, since the anti-imperialists seemed to have forgotten about them.

The outcome was not unlike what had happened at the UN's 1972 Stockholm conference on the environment, at which Third World delegates insisted that economic development was the problem, not pollution. The follow-up UN conference on women, held in Copenhagen in 1980, took place in the wake of the Iranian revolution and revealed a new interaction between feminist demands and global politics. Women from Western countries condemned female genital mutilation and their Muslim counterparts rejected this as imperialist and Islamophobic.[89]

None of these UN conferences would seem to have promoted women's rights worldwide, yet women's rights activism in less-developed countries came primarily from these meetings. The Development Alternatives with Women for a New Era, or DAWN, the largest international feminist network of less-developed countries, was founded on the initiative of Antrobus at a meeting in Bangalore, to prepare for the 1985 UN Conference on Women in Nairobi. More generally, these conferences launched feminist groups in the world's poorer countries. A good example is the one founded at the University of Dar es Salaam in Tanzania, followed by associations of women's lawyers, journals, and legal aid clinic workers.

Women's and feminist groups in less-developed countries remain dependent on outside assistance. Of the twenty-six international organized women's networks existing in 2015, half had their headquarters in the United States. For example, the Women's Learning Partnership for Rights Development and Peace, founded in 2000 by Iranian-born feminist Mahnaz Afkham to organize women in majority-Muslim countries, has its headquarters in Bethesda, Maryland. In fact, only one of those twenty-six groups, the aforementioned DAWN, has headquarters outside Western Europe or North America. DAWN's founding occurred at a meeting funded by the Ford Foundation, and support from organizations like it is typical for women's groups in the less-developed world.[90]

AFTER THE UPHEAVAL: LATE-MILLENNIUM ERA GENDER REGIMES

The last two decades of the twentieth century witnessed the development of a globalized class structure and the expansion of a youth culture. During those same twenty years, the world became increasingly divided between demographic regimes of higher fertility and younger populations, and those with lower fertility, often below natural replacement levels, and a rapidly increasing number of the elderly. In part shaped by these developments, in part shaping them, gender regimes presented a complex picture. Common elements are the sexual revolution and responses (pro and con) to it; campaigns by feminists and gay rights activists; and changes in education and employment. The result was that while some trends did seem to go global, including a severing of the connection between marriage and childbearing, or the growth of women's education, others veered off in different directions. Gay sexuality took forms in Africa and India that had been seen a hundred years previously in Europe or the Americas; rejection or modification of lineage-based families; and aspirations toward companionate marriage grew in East Asia, while such marriages seemed to be on the wane in those parts of the world where they had originated. If there was a common theme in emerging gender regimes, it was a decline—sometimes drastic, sometimes very modest—in the polarity between masculine and feminine that had structured these regimes in the past.

One key trend was the gradual dissolution of the incompatibility between reproduction and gainful employment in women's lives. Figure 7.4, taken from the statistics of the ILO, gives the proportion of women of prime reproductive age, twenty-five to twenty-nine, gainfully employed between 1950 and 1990, for economically developed and less-developed countries.[91]

The ILO's figures show that the proportion in less-developed countries was already high in 1950, and changed relatively little during the years that followed. Circumstances for women in the wealthier countries followed a very different pattern. There was a very modest increase in the percentage of

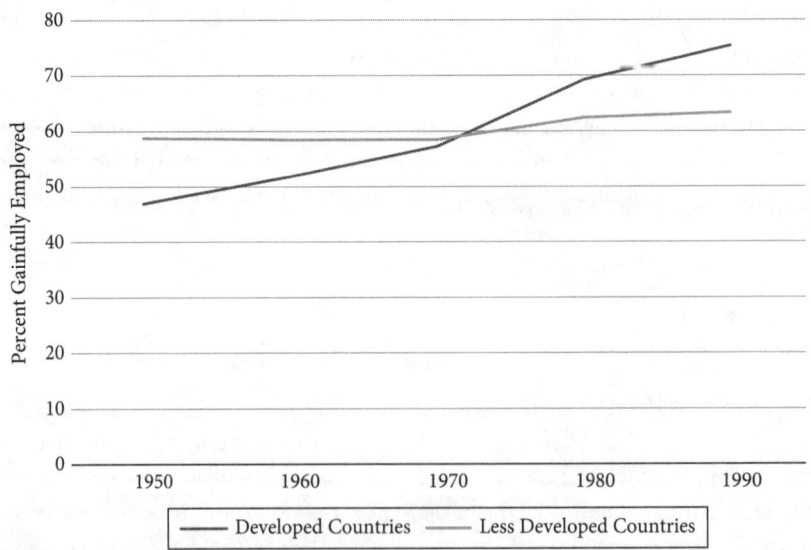

FIGURE 7.4 Women of Peak Reproductive Age (25–29) in the Labor Force, 1950–1990

women in their mid-to-late twenties working during the 1950s, a slightly larger growth during the 1960s, and then, what can only be called a takeoff of employment, passing rates in less-developed countries around 1975. This change was not a result of women having children later, since labor force participation rates for women in their thirties increased in precisely the same way. Differences between men's and women's employment histories did not vanish, as labor force participation rates of men in the second half of their twenties remained in the range of 95 to 97 percent. In a number of European countries, particularly the Netherlands and Norway, to a lesser extent in the United Kingdom, there was a strong tendency for women of childbearing age to work just part- rather than full-time.[92]

Some economically advanced countries had both lower women's labor force participation rates and very low birth rates—in particular, as noted, Japan and Germany. One does have to wonder what many adult women did there all day. Most likely, they kept house to exacting standards of order and cleanliness. But for all these caveats, the distinction between reproduction and employment, which had been so firmly part of women's lives in the wealthier parts of the world as late as the 1960s, had dissolved by the end of the millennium.

Closely related to women's greater labor force participation was their increasing use of education. One of the most striking features of social and gender change was the growing proportion of women in higher education. In the United States, where statistics are best, women comprised 32 percent of college students in 1950, a noticeably smaller proportion than the 42 percent they represented during the academic year 1929–30. By 1961, the figure had just reached 38 percent and, in 1971, was slightly below where it had been on the eve of the Depression. This state of affairs changed rapidly in the 1970s. By the end of the decade women were a majority of university and college students, and since then the proportion of students who are women has only continued to increase. Recent figures indicate that they comprise almost 60 percent of all college and university students.[93]

In Western European countries, women were about a fifth of college students in the 1950s, reaching a third by 1970, just under half in 1990 and just over half (52 percent) in 1995. The figures for communist regimes of Eastern Europe were almost identical to those in the United States between 1950 and 1990, so initially somewhat higher than in Western Europe, but converging with it by the end of the millennium. Probably the first country in the world where women were a majority of university students was the USSR—53 percent in 1950, in part a reflection of communist ideals, but also of the loss of so many young men during the Second World War. The proportion of women declined to under half in the 1960s and 1970s, returning to 1950 levels in 1990 and reaching 54 percent in post-Communist Russia in 1995, so also converging with the United States and European countries.[94]

In thirty developed countries, women were 46 percent of university students in 1985, a majority ten years later and 55 percent by 2005. Broader statistics collected by the UN show the end of the millennium as a period of rapid increase in women's presence in higher education worldwide. In the middle of the 1980s, there were thirty-four countries in the world, where women made up a majority of university students, as opposed to one hundred where the students were primarily men. A somewhat different count by UNESCO, the UN's educational, scientific and cultural organization, in 2000, indicated fifty countries in the world where a majority of students were women, as opposed to twenty-eight where they were men. A decade later, the same UNESCO statistics showed seventy-nine countries where most students were women and just twenty-three where they were men. Africa remained the bastion of predominantly male higher education, with women making up between 30 and 40 percent of university enrollments—although even there, their representation was on the increase. (African countries were also often lacking in the UNESCO statistics, which explains part of the difference with the 1985 figures.) South Asia was another part of the world where women remained a distinct minority of university students, even in the new millennium; in East Asia, women were either just above half, as in South Korea and Indonesia, or just below, as in China and Japan. In the rest of the world, with a few curious exceptions, such as Switzerland, women made up between 55 and 60 percent of all college and university students, even in places where one might not expect it, including Oman, the United Arab Emirates, and Saudi Arabia. Women students reached their highest proportions in the Caribbean—72 percent in Bermuda, 81 percent in Antigua.[95]

The broader social consequences of the growth of women's education can be seen in Figure 7.5, which gives the number of university-educated women for every one hundred university educated men in the adult (over twenty-five) population in eight different countries, located on five continents, between the 1950s and the early 2010s.[96] Because this figure encompasses the entire adult population, and so is the result of previous decades of access to higher education, it changes relatively slowly.

Between 1950 and 1970, men with university education considerably outnumbered women; in the United States and Bulgaria—two very different countries—the ratio of male-to-female college graduates in the general population actually increased. But as in so many ways during the Era of Upheaval, the 1970s marked a turning point: the ratio of women-to-men college graduates in the general population began to rise, everywhere in the world. In the United States, with its long history of higher education, and a relatively large percentage of the adult population who had gone to college, the rise was gradual; by contrast, in Zambia, where university study was new, it could occur very rapidly. By 2010, in four of the eight countries, there were more women with university degrees than men. A new gender bipolarity

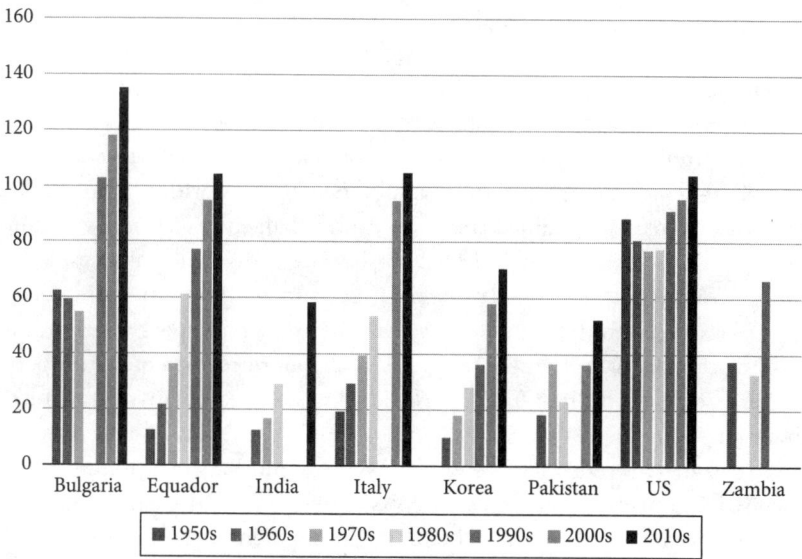

FIGURE 7.5 Women College Graduates per 100 Men College Graduates, Age 25 and Older

was in the process of developing, one where advanced education would be gendered female, a complete reversal of the situation that had existed for centuries.

Another element of gender realignment was what might be called the sexual counterrevolution. Begun by radical feminists, the cause was quickly taken up by religious conservatives, who focused their opposition on public representations of sexuality, extramarital sex, homosexuality, and birth control and abortion. In his 1968 anti-contraception encyclical *Humanae Vitae* Pope Paul VI anticipated radical feminist criticism of the sexual revolution, denouncing contraception as leading a man to reduce a woman "to a mere instrument of his desires."[97] These similarities aside, religious conservatives, quite unlike feminists, were interested in preserving postwar era gender regimes rather than undermining them. The HIV/AIDS epidemic of the 1980s, at least in part a result of unbridled sexuality, gave an additional impetus to the sexual counterrevolution and put gay rights activists on the defensive, forcing them to direct their energies into a campaign for medical treatment of an illness wreaking havoc in their communities.[98]

In the end, the counterrevolution had only limited effects. Married women with children continued moving into the labor force, and steadily more women, everywhere in the world, acquired an advanced education. The legalization of both birth control and abortion was generally not rolled back, although their further legalization, particularly in devoutly Catholic parts of South America and Islamic realms of the Middle East and South Asia, as well as in much of Africa, could be prevented. As a result, in 1990 there were an estimated 2.4 million illegal abortions in Brazil, as many as a million in Indonesia, and perhaps a quarter million in Kenya. At the 1994 UN conference on population and development, an alliance between the Vatican and delegates from Islamic countries led to a condemnation of abortion and birth control. Yet birth rates continued to fall in more of the world, and pre- and extramarital sexuality remained the norm rather than the exception. Although the evidence for this, as is usual for sexual desire and sexual practices, is very thin, it might be the case that, overall, both men and women are getting more pleasure out of sexual relations than they did in the postwar decades.[99]

Political changes seemed to provide a counterrevolutionary impetus. Islamist regimes in Iran during the 1980s and, especially, Afghanistan under the Taliban in the later 1990s, were murderously homophobic and tried to restrict women's life choices. While some Western feminists have defended Islamism, twisting themselves into ideological pretzels doing so, it represented the single most blatant and apparent rejection of both the sexual revolution as well as feminist and gay rights initiatives throughout the world.[100]

Another ominous sign was the end of nominally feminist communist regimes in Eurasia, and the rise of conservative, nationalist, sometimes religiously oriented political movements in the former Eastern Bloc, whose protagonists seemed to envisage a gendered future with strong similarities to conservative and fascist politics of the 1930s, in which women stayed at home having babies to increase the size of the nation. In Poland, nationalists in alliance with the Catholic Church succeeded in prohibiting abortion in 1993, one of the few examples of such a rollback, worldwide. In the formerly Soviet central Asian countries, nationalism and religious conservatism—in this case Islamism—have been, in contrast to Poland, more enemies than allies, but both have been hostile to women's rights. Yet, perhaps surprisingly, and certainly not what feminists (generally more worried by the end of communism than by the rise of Islamism) expected, women in the former Eastern Bloc countries continued to be active in the labor force, even in childbearing years, in fact are more likely to work full-time than their counterparts in Western Europe. Sociologists have found no evidence that men in Eastern Europe were any more reluctant to take on childrearing and housekeeping tasks than their counterparts in the West. For all the calls by governments for greater reproductive vitality, birth rates remained consistently low.[101]

Where have all these changes left gender regimes globally at the beginning of the new millennium? In the wealthier countries, the postwar era bipolar gender regime remains in a process of rapid dissolution, as can be seen in a number of areas, from women working outside the home and attending university, to the development of homosexual and lesbian identities not polarized into active/passive masculine/feminine dichotomies. Feminist organizations may lack the same membership or élan that they had in the 1970s, but many of the ideas they promoted have come to be accepted and implemented by the major political parties.¹⁰²

One way this is apparent is in the number of women who hold political office. The Inter-Parliamentary Union's figures show an increase from just 2 percent of parliamentarians who were women in 1945 worldwide to 11–12 percent in the last quarter of the twentieth century, rising to 19 percent by 2010. A different count for 2013 shows that Nordic countries were in a class by themselves, with women being 42 percent of parliamentarians, percentages in the mid-to-low twenties for the rest of Europe, the Americas, and Africa, and 19 percent in East Asia and Arab countries. A good example of enhanced participation of women in government was the process of writing a constitution for Uganda in the years, following the dictatorial rule of Idi Amin and Milton Obote. Women made up 18 percent of the delegates to the constituent assembly, and the resulting constitution included extensive guarantees of women's rights.

In the executive, only 21 of 195 countries in the world had women as a head of government or head of state in 2013; the proportion of government ministers who were women ranged between 15 and 30 percent throughout the world. It is, once again, in the Nordic countries, where women who are head of government are likely to be feminists; elsewhere, they were members of prominent political families—classic examples were Indira Gandhi in India and Benazir Bhutto in Pakistan—or not connected to, even downright hostile to feminist perspectives, as was the case for Golda Meir of Israel and, especially, the "Iron Lady," Margaret Thatcher, UK prime minister from 1979 to 1990.¹⁰³

As feminists point out, gender as a concept applies not just to the lives of women and ideals of femininity, but to the lives of men and ideals of masculinity as well. In many ways, the dissolution of the postwar era bipolar gender regime has left men in wealthier countries at the beginning of the twenty-first century disoriented and uncertain. It is not just that the ideal of the adult man, oriented toward the workplace, earning to support a wife and children, has faded, but that even the possibility of that has faded as well.¹⁰⁴ This has been a consequence of the relentless progress of economic globalization and the reshaping of class structure, placing steadily more people in the class of competitors in a globalized labor market and below that, in the class of the excluded and unemployable. Men in those classes are generally unable to support a family on their wages, assuming they have any. Since people without a higher education—disproportionately men—are particularly likely to populate those lower social classes, this only makes men's social position more precarious. This state of affairs is reflected in the decline of marriage and the breaking of the connection between marriage and childbearing. Since the 1970s, the proportion of children born out of wedlock has soared across most of the world. Figure 7.6 shows this development in five very different countries on five continents.[105]

It is not often that statistics are this consistent and unambiguous. Whether starting a somewhat higher level, as in Chile or Sweden, or a lower one, as in the Czech lands, illegitimacy rates have soared. The pattern of the countries in the chart is typical for Europe, the Americas, the Pacific, and Western Asia. As appears on the chart for Sweden, and is characteristic of Scandinavian countries more generally, this development reflects a growing preference among young people for cohabitation without marriage, or for only getting married after decades of cohabitation, rather than before. However, in most of the countries on the graph, and in most of the world it represents, the growth of single motherhood stems from the inability of a growing proportion of young men to earn enough to support a family. There are parts of the world, particularly in East and South Asia, where illegitimacy rates have remained very low. In Japan, a country where postwar era gender ideals have remained very strong, and women's labor force participation and women's attendance at universities have been at lower levels than in other wealthy countries, just under 1 percent of births were out of wedlock in 1970, rising only to 2 percent in 2010. The Japanese response to the growing number of young men unable to support a family—and remember, this a country where 30 percent of the labor force in 2010 was in temporary positions—has not been larger numbers of single mothers, but young people giving up on sexual relations altogether, as women increasingly refuse to engage in them with men unable to support them, and these men are more reluctant even to suggest such an activity to women. Quite a number have

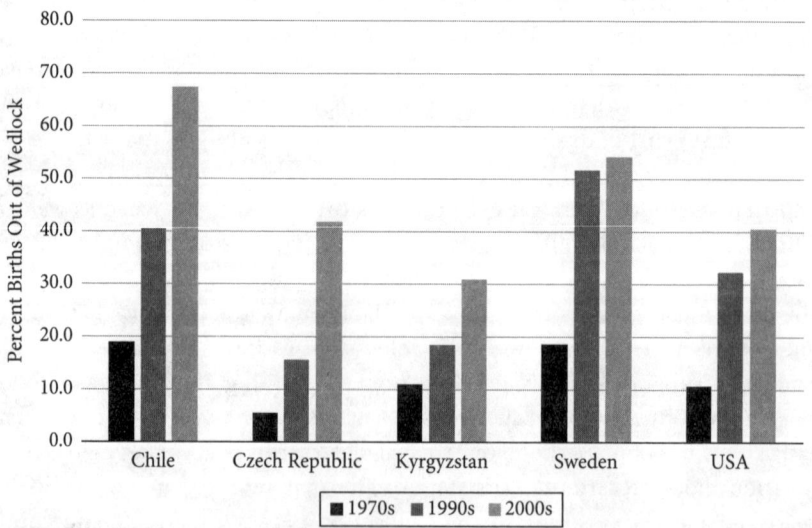

FIGURE 7.6 Illegitimate Births in Five Countries, c. 1970 to c. 2010

gone further, perhaps as many as one million according to a 2010 account, and become *hikkimori*, the socially withdrawn, who rarely leave the room in which they live and satisfy their erotic and romantic urges with *anime* and *manga* cartoon characters or video game figures.[106]

China is another East Asian country where births out of wedlock are very rare and where the government aggressively policed people's reproductive lives for decades. By the Late-Milliennium Era, the combination of decades of communist rule and of a post-1980 reversion to a capitalist market economy had led in the direction of the elimination of the lineage-based, patriarchal Chinese family. Young people, continuing more forcefully a trend beginning in the Maoist years of communist rule, insisted on choosing their own marriage partners and—this was a post-1980 novelty—refusing to live with the groom's parents, preferring, instead, to set up their own household as soon as possible. An important vehicle for this practice was the paying of bride wealth, as discussed, previously compensation paid by the groom's family to the bride for loss of her labor. By the 1990s in rural China, bride wealth had been transformed into a relatively large cash payment, and a newly coined word, *gangzhe*, to describe it, paid directly to the bride and under her control, which she could use to set up a household with her new husband, independent of her future in-laws. Paradoxically, the return to capitalism and an economic regime of private property had encouraged this trend, for the government had eliminated communist property relations in the countryside, distributing land parcels to individuals—but on long-term leases from the state, which could not be alienated. The groom's parents could no longer hold the promise of devolving their property to a son who would take care of them (more precisely, have his wife take care of them) in their old age. Instead, young people could use the bride wealth and their own individual shares of property distributed to them to set up their own households, and to live by themselves.

Young people in China were beginning to take up the ideal of a companionate marriage, in which spouses associate closely with each other, precisely as this ideal seemed to be increasingly unrealizable in the European cultural world where it began. This left the elderly, no longer able to rely on the care of their daughters-in-law in a difficult spot, a distinctly Chinese variant on the problematic position of different generations at the beginning of the twenty-first century. Older women whose lives followed the Chinese proverb, "A daughter-in-law must suffer to become a mother-in-law," discovered that the rules had changed, and their daughters-in-law were no longer willing to reside with them, take their orders and, ultimately, care for them, as they had done when they were newly married. The anthropologist Yunxiang Yan was present in 1990 at a family party in a north Chinese village, where a young woman loudly and publicly berated her father for having treated her mother so badly for decades. Some Chinese parents have begun to wonder if maybe daughters are no longer "spilled water," but a better bet on care in old age than sons. In Taiwan and Hong Kong, younger married women in more affluent families, university educated, and wanting to pursue their own careers, so no longer wishing to care for their elderly mothers-in-law, found another solution. They imported workers from the Philippines, yet another part of the turn-of-the-century migration frenzy, to care for them.[107]

In South Asia of the last few decades, the larger changes in gender regimes occurring further to the north and the east seem less apparent. Arranged marriages continue to be the rule, even among the educated and affluent urban upper-middle class, and, to a surprising extent, in the Indian and Pakistani diaspora, the many emigrants living in the United Kingdom, Canada, Australia, or the United States. Quite unlike their Chinese counterparts, mothers-in-law retained the upper hand in dealing with their sons' wives. As a contestant in the 1995 Miss India competition explained, to thunderous audience applause, "I'm for the joint family system [by which newlywed couples live with the groom's parents], because the joint family represents Indian culture; nowhere else in world have they got this system still."

As was the case in China, ideals of a companionate marriage, often of Western provenance, were promulgated in movies, women's magazines, and romance novels. Sometimes these were in opposition to ideas of lineage-based marriage, sometimes in odd conjunction with them, when the romantically linked young couple turn out to have been their parents' choice of spouses. A similar East Asian-South Asian comparison can be made about financial and property transactions occurring in marriage. Both bride wealth in China and dowries in India became larger and more prevalent during in the Late-Millennium Era. In China, bride wealth was refunctioned, turned as noted earlier from a transaction between families to compensate for the loss of a woman's labor, into a cash settlement, given to the bride for the purpose of setting up an independent household. By contrast, in India, dowries remained under the control of the husband's family; rather than facilitating a transition away from lineage-based families, as happened with bride wealth in China, the expansion of dowries reinforced such families. Particularly prevalent in urban areas, among the middle and upper-middle class social milieus where the distinctions of caste, so important to marriage and family in the countryside, were fading, dowries had become a way for groom's families to profit from their sons' marriage. Sensational news stories circulated of grooms' families murdering their daughters-in-law when their dowry was not large enough, or not paid promptly, or just to make way for a new, wealthier bride, bringing in a larger dowry. These were extreme cases. Still, they were part of a broader point, the way existing gender regimes in South Asia have adapted to the decline of previously important elements, such as the significance of caste, and the rise of newer ideals, like an interest in large-scale consumer goods, now to be financed via dowries.[108]

Gender regimes in the Late-Millenium-Era Africa showed a similar tenacity to those in South Asia. A very young age at first marriage, continuing high birth rates, prevalence, in some regions, of polygamy, persistence of lineage-based families—all these features of an earlier gender regime continued into the twenty-first century. In Africa, as well, aspirations toward companionate marriage existed—often described in Nigeria as "Christian" or "English" marriages, suggesting the origins of these ideas—but have not had a large impact on realities of relations between the sexes. Unlike the case in South Asia, there have been modest increases in out-of-wedlock births in some African countries, connected with tendencies toward slightly later ages of first marriage.[109]

One element of gender regimes that has been changing in both South Asia and Africa was same-sex relations. What has appeared, is an orientation similar to the earlier one in Europe and America—a distinction between "masculine" individuals taking an active role in sex and "feminine" ones taking a passive role, with the latter, the "flutes" (i.e., male performers of oral sex on other men) of Keralam, in southern India, being seen as the homosexuals. This passive, effeminate role, though, was strikingly inflected by global cultural contexts. As the anthropologist Mark Epprecht observed in his study of "queens," as they called themselves, in Zimbabwe, their effeminate behavior "was more reminiscent of Doris Day than any recognizable African femininity." Anthropologists have noted similarly globally inflected behavior about attitudes to what makes a man, or a woman, homosexual, in Mali, Nigeria, or the Philippines.[110]

Indonesia presents an interesting variant on this development. The *bissu*, cross-dressing men, having sex with other men, holding regalia and performing rituals for the aristocratic upper classes, were eliminated in the 1960s, when Islamists destroyed their regalia and either forced them to cease cross-dressing with death threats or killed them. By the Late-Millennium Era, men who are *gay* and women who are *lesbi*—terms reaching Indonesia sometime in the 1980s—have developed particular national versions on global patterns. *Lesbi* are divided into two groups, the *tomboi*, also called "hunters," and the *cewek*. The former wear masculine clothes, have short hair, go out at night by themselves, and also have considerable difficulty finding employment, in view of their appearance, while the latter dress, appear and act in very feminine fashion, but also generally get married to men and have children, which the *tomboi* absolutely refuse to do. Indonesian men who are *gay* do not show those sorts of binary distinctions, being, in that respect, rather more like Westerners. But they also expect to get married to women and have children with them, finding Western gay men's lack of interest in doing so rather peculiar. Gay organizations were founded late in Indonesia, and but focused their efforts on promoting social life among *gay* men. There were never more than a hundred people involved in gay rights activity at any one time.[111]

Although the language used to describe same-sex desire in Indonesia has certainly been globalized, the behavior of men and women engaged in same-sex relationship seems nationally distinct, or, at most, only very partially globalized. By contrast, homophobia has become distinctly more globally uniform. A well-known example in Africa are the Christian churches and politicians inspired by them who have called for strong legal measures against same-sex relations, sometimes even the death penalty, taking over ideas originally introduced by American Evangelical missionaries, whose ties to anti-gay politicians have been particularly close in Uganda. President Yahya Jammeh of Gambia's 2008 threat that he would behead all the homosexuals in his country, since their sinfulness could not be tolerated in an Islamic land, showed another global religion bringing homophobic attitudes to Africa.

There has been an additional, perhaps less well-known version of opposition to homosexuality, out of antiracist and anti-imperialist motives. In 1995, President Robert Mugabe of Zimbabwe declared homosexuality to be yet another imperialist imposition of Western countries on Africa. He was following in a long tradition of African anti-imperialist heroes, including Frantz Fanon and Cheikh anta Diop, who blamed imperialists for introducing this decadent practice into a victimized Africa, where it had previously been unknown. Leftist intellectuals in Keralam have insisted that "flutes" and men cruising for sexual partners in the capital city of Thiruvananthapuram are all examples of the pernicious influence of neoliberalism, which has placed materialist self-interest above solidarity and social progress. Ironically, these left-wing critics of same-sex activity are largely recapitulating the assertions of nineteenth-century European imperialists, who saw Africans as savages and Indians as backward, but felt that at least among them the pernicious, sinful, vice of same-sex relations, regrettably all-too-typical among civilized Europeans, was unknown.[112]

Hostility toward same-sex relations during recent decades in Africa has often taken on extremely violent forms, from assaults on gay men to the "corrective rape" of lesbians. These attacks against lesbians, which testify to a quite different form of homophobia than that than the version prevalent in postwar Europe and the Americas, which primarily focused on men, are part of a broader practice of sexual violence against women, particularly apparent in the African insurgencies and civil wars of the 1990s and 2000s, in the Congo, Liberia, Sierra Leone, Uganda, Nigeria, and Sudan. Both a result of patriarchal authority of the lineage-based gender order, and even more, the collapse of that order, with young men seeing no possibility of becoming a patriarch in their futures, this violence is an African version of the challenges to understandings and practices of manhood and masculinity developing as a result of the social, economic, and cultural changes of the final decades of the twentieth century.[113]

Talk about the great changes of the years 1945–2000, the Age of Interconnection, tends to focus on technology—rockets, antibiotics, TVs, computers—or on international relations—decolonization, the beginning and the end of the Cold War. The changes in the constituent elements of societies between the mid-decades of the twentieth century and the initial ones of the twenty-first seem at least as large-scale, and consequential, to say nothing of being equally global in scope. It is possible to extend this observation, to suggest that the second half of the twentieth century was an era of profound, deep-reaching social transformation, on a scale rarely seen before in human history, only to be compared to the changes wrought by the Industrial Revolution and, looking much farther back, by the introduction of agriculture during the Neolithic Revolution some twelve thousand years ago.

All things considered, it was the Era of Upheaval, the 1960s and '70s, that either marked the period of major transformations—in birth rates, attitudes about sexuality, women's educational and occupational aspirations, the emergence of youth culture—or the beginning of developments that would become fully apparent closer to the end of the century: particularly the initial phases of economic globalization and a new age of mass migration that would fundamentally transform class structures around the world. The moving forces were worldwide, but led, initially, to rather different consequences in different parts of the world: in the affluent, capitalist societies of Western Europe, North America, East Asia, and the Pacific, as well as the islands of this social order elsewhere, particularly Latin America; in the communist lands of the Eastern Bloc; and in the realm of lineage-based families and kinship- and seigneurial-based societies, mostly, although not exclusively, in Africa, Asia, and Latin America.

The end of the Cold War and the termination of communist societies and economies sped up changes already under way and gave a boost to the globalization of the building blocks of societies. Social structures have become increasingly aligned across the globe, as a result of the creation of a steadily more globalized labor market, certainly much more similar than they had been in 1950. When it came to generations, the world had been increasingly polarized into lands of age, with low-fertility rates and little or no natural population increase (sometimes even natural population decrease), a large proportion of the elderly, and lands of youth, in which birth rates, if a bit lower than in the 1950s, remained high; children, adolescents and young adults by far the largest portion of the population; and the elderly still relatively few and far between. It might be objected that there were already tendencies in that direction during the Age of Total War, and that the division of the world into high- and low-fertility regions was already present by the 1950s, although fertility rates, overall, were higher than several decades later. Perhaps. However, there were two very large changes that made the situation by the year 2000 exceptional and unprecedented. One was that low-fertility rates were not just characteristic of Europe (and to a lesser extent of its one-time settler colonies in the Americas and South Seas) but found in East Asia, as well—and so encompassed most of the world's population. High fertility regimes were primarily in Africa and the Middle East, with South Asia divided between lands on the high end of the low-fertility regime and on the lower-to-middle end of the high fertility one. The other unprecedented change is the steadily rising number of the elderly, reaching levels in low-fertility regions never before seen in human history.

Of all the three building blocks of society—classes, generations, and genders—it is gender regimes that present the most globally complex pattern of change. By the year 2000, it seemed that there was a close alignment between regions of large-scale change in gender regimes and those of low fertility, and less change in gender regime in areas of continuing higher fertility rates—which is really no surprise, since a central element of gender regimes is the role of reproduction in women's lives. There is another form of global division of gender regimes apparent: a separation not between regions but between the sexes. While women's lives have been changing along with understandings of manhood and womanhood, masculinity and femininity, this has been less the case for men, who have remained, to a surprising extent, stuck in postwar era roles and attitudes, as the broader social and economic environment has been rendering them increasingly obsolete.

8 | Labor

THE WOLOF PEOPLE OF West Africa relate the legend of the "hero of the fields," Baay Demba Waar Njay, from the sands of Kajoor, whose zeal in laboring, breaking the land with a harrow, defying even the heat of the midday sun in doing so, was so great he failed to notice that in his progress he had reached the sea and drowned. Demba Waar's toil was an inspiration to laborers and farmers, yet also carried within it an element of self-destruction.[1] This ambivalent attitude toward labor is not entirely dissimilar to the one in the book of Genesis, where the Lord labors creating the world for six days, then rests on the seventh, but also tells Adam, on expelling him from the Garden of Eden, that the punishment for his sin is to earn his bread by the sweat of his brow.

Labor remained both a blessing and curse in the second half of the twentieth century, as it had been throughout human history. But the process, hours, and organization of labor, as well as its links to social and political institutions were generally different in the Age of Interconnection than they had been, even in the relatively recent past and changed rapidly and dramatically over the course of its five decades and three eras, with ramifications reaching down to the present. Consider a few examples of labor from the era: autoworkers in Detroit, Osaka, or Wolfsburg straining to keep up with the pace of an ever-faster assembly line; women in Shenzhen or Taipei inserting components into a piece of electronics, with perhaps less physical effort than the autoworkers but with eye-straining speed; programmers sitting alone into the early hours, writing code; stevedores, from San Francisco to Le Havre to Mombasa, manfully wrestling crates into a ship's hold on twelve-hour shifts; shop clerks, or, as retail giant Walmart likes to call them, "associates" working for minimum wage; call-center phone operators and airline flight attendants, dealing as patiently as they can with abusive customers. The second half of the century saw gigantic strikes, like those of the dockers in Dakar and Mombasa in 1945 and across all of France in 1947 and 1968, which achieved their purpose. There were also labor defeats, especially the failed strikes of the US air traffic controllers, the textile workers of Bombay, and the coal miners in the United Kingdom, occurring in rapid succession during the 1980s. There were labor courts, workplace codetermination schemes, both real and fraudulent, and steady full-time employment at good wages, as well as temporary or contract work in wretched conditions of total insecurity.

Taking a step back from this welter of events, institutions, and practices, it is possible to ascertain three main interrelated issues determining the condition of labor across the world in these five decades. One involves control of the workplace and of conditions of employment, an area where labor's relatively strong position during the postwar era gave way to a very vigorous reassertion of the power of employers and managers. A second is the effect of the growing migration of labor and of capital on the condition of labor. Finally, there is the changing nature of labor, as physical strength and skill declined in importance, while patience and emotional empathy became more significant. As always, there are countless exceptions to these vast generalizations—national and regional peculiarities, or temporary reversals of trends—but overall, their appearance and resolution chart the course of the condition of labor during the Age of Interconnection.

Labor Ascendant

The Second World War ended in a blaze of labor self-assertion. New York City was, literally, paralyzed for a week at the end of September 1945 by a strike of elevator operators, the onset of a wave that would include, among many others, dockers, telegraph operators, teamsters, and tugboat crews. New York has always been its own distinct place in the United States—and, generally a stronghold of unionism, by American standards. Nevertheless in 1946, one American worker in ten went on strike, including steelworkers, electrical workers, railway workers (the autoworkers had already gone out in November 1945). There were general strikes in four US cities—Lancaster, Pennsylvania; Rochester, New York; Stamford, Connecticut; and, the largest and most dramatic, a strike in the gritty industrial and port center of Oakland, California where one hundred thousand workers walked off the job. Farther south in the Americas, the government of Argentine president Juan Perón was saved from a military coup in October 1945 by a nationwide general strike in support of him. In neighboring Brazil, a strike wave between 1945 and 1947 rocked the country's major urban and industrial centers, Rio de Janeiro and São Paulo. Mexico saw a record number of strikes during those years.[2]

In war-torn Europe and China, with their massive populations of refugees there was rather less to strike over, although 1947 was a year of large-scale and very violent and militant wave of strikes in France, with over two million workers off the job, a general strike and seizure of city hall in Marseilles, and clashes between striking miners and the police in the coal fields of northern France. In part a social conflict attracted into the force field of the nascent Cold War, as the French communists and the trade union federation they controlled, the CGT, tried to deploy the strikes against the anti-communist French government, much of the labor strife proceeded independently of communist leadership, and, in the case of the strike of the Renault autoworkers, in opposition to it. France was not unique. In Finland, the Netherlands, Belgium, and Denmark, more workdays were lost to strikes between 1945 and 1950 than in the entire Age of Interconnection. Łódź, Poland's industrial capital, which had suffered less wartime damage than most Polish cities, was the site of an astonishing five hundred strikes between 1945 and 1948, the most of any city in Poland and probably in all of Europe.

Labor's self-assertion took different forms in the postwar era. There was the totally unexpected outcome of the 1945 British general elections, in which voters turned Winston Churchill, the living embodiment of his country's victory in the Second World War, out of office, replacing him with a government that would implement social and economic policies to ensure an ascendancy of labor. Under the postwar Labour Party, strikes were at a historic low point, though trade union membership jumped from seven to thirteen million. In occupied Germany and Hungary, workers' factory committees sprang up at the end of the fighting, to revive production and take over management, especially as the latter was often closely associated with the Nazis and their allies. Everywhere in Continental Europe, workers streamed into trade unions in the postwar era.[3]

Another center of labor self-assertion was Africa. There were strikes throughout French West Africa right after the war, including a strike of dockworkers in the Atlantic port city of Dakar in December 1945 that quickly became a general strike. It was followed by a strike of railway workers in the French West African colonies. Lasting five months and involving seventeen thousand workers on four different railroad lines, it remains the longest strike in African history. The railway men were able to hold out so long and reach a compromise settlement because of the widespread public support they received. There were similar docker-led general strikes in Mombasa and Dar es Salaam, Indian Ocean port cities in British colonies on the other side of the continent; and a general strike, led by the railway men, in Nairobi. These were the largest strikes, but there were many others, including a 1950 general strike in Conakry, the chief city of French Guinea; and strikes by miners in Rhodesia (today's Zimbabwe) and South Africa; and strikes of railway workers in Sudan. In the West African British colony of the

Gold Coast, over forty-six thousand workers went on strike, led by the gold miners and railway workers, the latter prompting a 1950 general strike in the colony's capital city of Accra. Trade union organization and membership in the colony leaped forward, and unions in what would be renamed Ghana after its independence from British colonial rule, remain among the largest and most effective in contemporary Africa.[4]

In India and Indonesia, anti-colonial struggles—and, in the case of India, immense, violent clashes between Muslims and Hindus—tended to overshadow labor self-assertion. Even so, in Calcutta, then a major industrial center of newly independent India, there was a widespread wave of strikes in 1948–49, in which striking workers sometimes assaulted European foremen, managers, and engineers. Like those parts of Europe liberated from Axis rule, Japan experienced a dramatic surge in trade union membership after 1945, and the creation of factory committees. Australia had both a record number of strikes and a new Labour government. Similar to what had happened in France two years earlier, the Australian coal miners' strike of 1949 was sucked into the social force field of the Cold War, becoming a confrontation between a communist-led union and an anti-communist government.[5]

That strike was one of the last large-scale labor confrontations of the years immediately following the Second World War. Although there were certainly strikes in the 1950s, and sometimes quite large ones, like those of both Japanese and American steelworkers in 1959, the former lasting for 49 and the latter for 109 days, the turbulence of the first five postwar years was no longer present. But labor ascendancy did not end; it took on less conflictual forms. There was widespread collective bargaining, industry- or even nationwide in Western European countries, Australia and New Zealand; between unions and individual firms in India, the United Kingdom, the United States, and in the Americas more generally. The later postwar era was also a period of expanded labor influence in the workplace. In Continental Europe, this tended to occur in cooperative fashion, as elected works' councils or enterprise committees worked with management on hiring and firing, or the production process. In English-speaking countries, by contrast, a more antagonistic version of such influence prevailed through the "grievance system," in which union representatives promoted the interests of their members against an often-authoritarian management, aggressively championing their rights as set down in collective bargaining agreements.[6]

Both versions of labor influence were located primarily in the wealthier countries of the world. But labor's influence in South America and Africa was strong at that time as well. Import-substitution industrialization, encouragement of indigenous manufacturing, and protecting the domestic market from foreign competition, practiced in India, Brazil, and Argentina, gave workers in the protected industries a favorable position. The *Companhia Siderúrgica Nacional*, the Brazilian National Steel Company and its massive steelworks complex in Volta Redondo, an upland town on the rail line connecting Rio and São Paulo, was the veritable pride and joy of Brazil's ISI policies. It manufactured steel during the 1950s for the new national capital in Brasilia, the subways in the country's two largest cities, and many other prestige projects. In spite of the persistent hostility of the local political police, who regarded unions as by definition communistic—a hostility reinforced by the politics of the Cold War—the metalworkers' union acquired over the course of that decade a steadily more influential position in the steelworks. It won repeated wage increases—whose costs the firm, given its protected national market, could pass on to consumers—and established an organized pay scale, with career ladders and the principle of equal pay for equal work, thus weakening the power of management to discriminate among workers. The union's ascent culminated in 1962, when its president, Othon Reis Fernandes, was named the steelwork's director of social services.[7]

Part of the justification of the British and French governments for preserving their African colonial empires was the promotion of economic development. And their policies did lead to an expansion of ports, agriculture-related industries, such as mills transforming peanuts, the chief crop of Senegal, into oil and seedcakes, as well as employing growing numbers of Africans in the civil service and elementary education. This was a favorable environment for unions, and they scored a number of triumphs, such as getting the law on family allowances for workers in metropolitan France applied to the country's colonies in 1956. Although British and French policies to retain their African empires helped unions, these unions nonetheless played a major role in the growing movement for independence from colonial rule. The Gold Coast's unionists were strong anti-imperialists, one of the reasons that Ghana became the first sub-Saharan British colony to gain its independence in March 1957. The creation, also in 1957, of the General Union of the Workers of Black Africa, a federation incorporating the unions in French West Africa, breaking with the French trade union federations to which these individual unions had previously been affiliated, was an important step on the road to colonial independence. Sékou Touré, Guinean union leader—one of his accomplishments was directing the 1950 general strike in Conakry—and a major architect of the new African union federation, became the first president of Guinea, which, like Ghana and Great Britain, was the first French sub-Saharan African possession to be liberated from colonial rule.[8]

Ironically, the one place in the world where labor was neither ascendant nor even influential was in the ostensibly communist workers' states of the Eastern Bloc. Unions were very much present in those states, with a membership—often compulsory—making up a large portion of the workforce. Well-funded and possessing considerable assets, the communist unions ostensibly represented the interests of their members in the workplace.

Reality, as one report from the Donbas industrial region of eastern Ukraine noted, was very different: "In theory the workers enjoyed full rights to petition through their trade unions for redressing unfair treatment. In practice, workers were afraid to challenge them [their bosses] because they could only lose." If anything, especially during the period of intense reconstruction from the Second World War and preparation for a Third, unions represented the interests of management, campaigning for longer hours, more intensive labor, and lower wages—often in piecework, a mode of payment communists had always vigorously condemned when it was used by capitalists. It was nothing unusual, indeed, rather the rule, for local union officials to be firm managers as well. This is not to say that unions in the Eastern Bloc did nothing for their members. They arranged for vacations, cultural events at work, sometimes housing, healthcare and childcare. Instead of institutions of labor, they were institutions of leisure and consumerism, and crucial ones in societies where leisure time and consumer goods were in distinctly short supply.[9]

In what can only be called a Freudian return of the repressed, the power of labor in the postwar world, so carefully suppressed in the Eastern Bloc, reappeared at moments of systemic crisis. The uprisings of 1953 in East Germany; of 1956 in Poland and Hungary; the 1962 general strike in Novocherkassk; and the Polish uprisings of 1970, 1976, and 1980, were all centered on labor, with widespread strikes, insurgent strike committees, and marches of striking workers from industrial facilities on the outskirts of cities into town centers.

Labor's powerful position in the postwar era was, it needs to be emphasized, a historical novelty. Before 1945, there had certainly been very large strikes and moments of collective bargaining and organized labor influence at the workplace, but these had been mainly ephemeral, like the pre- and post-First World War strike waves, or retracted by changes in regime, as happened when the pro-labor government and constitution of the Weimar Republic in Germany were replaced by the fiercely anti-labor Nazis. Of all the countries in the pre-1945 world, only in Great Britain did unions hold anything even resembling a steady, long-term position of social and economic influence. There had been waves of strikes in the 1930s, and the ascendancy of pro-labor governments in many parts of the world—the New Deal in the United States and the Popular Front governments in France, Spain, Chile, or Mexico; the Saltsjöbaden agreement of 1938, which initiated national collective bargaining between the employers' association; and the trade union federation in Sweden, the first strikes of dockers and railway men in British and French colonial possessions. Nonetheless, these had been tentative and temporary, easily swept away by political turns to the right, or the domination of the Axis powers. Only after 1945 was labor's position reinforced and institutionalized—for a few decades, anyway.

Some have argued that the inability of labor to obtain all of the aspirations expressed in the immediate aftermath of the Second World War, marked the postwar era as one of labor's defeat. The Cold War—both within individual countries and, at the world level—split and hobbled the movement, they argue. The World Federation of Trade Unions, formed in 1945, was divided four years later, with the communists remaining in it, and the anti-communists walking out to form the International Confederation of Free Trade Unions. It is true that not all postwar labor aspirations were met: US businessmen and corporate managers rejected all European-style ideas about codetermination and insisted on their right to manage; West German workers had to be content with electing only half the members of the corporate boards of directors in coal and steel firms, while just getting to choose one-third of them in other corporations. In retrospect, however, these "defeats" look far from crushing. At least in the United States, where the Cold War split in the labor movement—and the expulsion of the communists from it—was particularly embittered, it is striking how many of their causes continued to be carried out by their opponents.[10]

A more relevant and, in retrospect, more worrisome weakness in labor's otherwise strong position were the limitations on union membership. The American South, characterized by racism, evangelical religion, and widespread support for laissez-faire, remained strongly anti-union; large-scale efforts at union organization in the postwar era were all failures. On a global scale, Asia was a region of weak unions and relatively feeble labor self-assertion. In spite of promising beginnings after 1945, unions in Japan increasingly developed in the direction of "enterprise unionism." They were based at individual firms, whose leaders rejected strikes and workers' self-assertion, preferring instead to be junior partners with corporate management in increasing firms' profitability and productivity. Cold War splits in the labor movement played a role in this development, although anti-communist unions in other countries did not adopt such an attitude. Trade unions in India, divided between two federations, one affiliated with the communists and one with the ruling Congress Party, remained weak, with relatively little influence. They were hampered by post-independence legislation that had imposed compulsory industrial conciliation and made strikes very difficult.[11]

Another limitation on labor self-assertion in India during the postwar era was the restriction of unions to the formal sector of the economy. Unions were confined to the realm of the regularly employed, leaving out the so-called informal sector, the self-employed—peasants, peddlers, street vendors—casual workers, and contract laborers, groups that represented the large majority of the labor force in South Asia. This was also true of African countries. With the onset of Import-Substitution Industrialization, and the economic development policies of French and British colonial rule, the formal sector of the economy was growing, and fairly rapidly. This was a state of affairs that

African unionists seem to have been more successful in exploiting than their Indian counterparts.[12]

Both of these circumstances, which might be called "geographic" and "sectoral" limitations on labor self-assertion could potentially be overcome by an expansion of unions. With hindsight, we know that the opposite happened: the limitations remained in place and became a wedge, undermining the position of labor where it had been stronger, all across the world. In an era of the institutional reinforcement of labor's social and political position, this was not a foregone conclusion; if anything, it seemed more likely that the Era of Upheaval would bring an expansion and further anchoring of labor's place in the world.

Labor Militant

And in many respects the later 1960s and 1970s were a period of labor's advance. There was a resurgence of militancy, bringing with it both gigantic strikes, shaking national political and social institutions, but also a level of strike activity that had never been seen before. Union membership grew, often reaching unprecedented levels; whole new categories of workers, particularly in the public sector, became involved in unionism. In a few countries, especially the social democracies of Northern Europe, new legal institutional bases for labor emerged. It would not be inaccurate to call the 1970s the high point of labor in the twentieth century.

Yet that decade was also one in which the foundations for the defeat of labor were laid. This defeat was partly self-inflicted, as a seemingly never-ending wave of strikes, seeking to keep up with inflation and under pressure of the 1973 Shock, began to provoke public hostility and anti-labor political countermeasures. Partly it was due to the beginnings of the globalization of manufacturing, and, more broadly, the increasing extent to which economic life crossed national boundaries, posing a growing dilemma for labor and the legal and social institutions that supported it, all organized on a national level. In the wealthier countries of the world, it would be primarily the Late-Millennium Era in which these trends would play out to the detriment of labor. But already in the 1970s, labor's defeat in Africa and South America, and continued marginalization in Asia were becoming apparent. The defeat of labor moved from the margins of the global economy to its center.

The most famous labor explosion of the era were the strikes in France in May 1968. The "events of May" began with a dispute between students at the University of Paris campus in the suburban town of Nanterre and the government but ended up with virtually the entire French labor force, public employees and private ones, blue- and white-collar, walking off the job—or actually not walking off, since strikers often occupied their workplaces.

Exact figures are unknown, because the officials in charge of compiling strike statistics were themselves on strike, but strikers numbered at least seven million, and may have been nine or ten. After between two and four weeks (depending on location and industry), the authorities did eventually regain control of the situation, but the French employers' association granted generous wage increases and in an indirect reaction President Charles de Gaulle stepped down the following year. Less well-known but equally consequential was the *Cordobazo*, the general strike in the Argentine industrial center of Córdoba occurring on May 29–30, 1969. As in France a year earlier, the strike was sparked by a confrontation between students at the university and the government. Taken up by militant unionists at the IKA-Renault auto works and the municipal power company, the strike sparked mass demonstrations, and had to be suppressed by the military. The *Cordobazo* was a major blow to the country's military dictatorship, starting Argentina on the path to the restoration of democracy and the triumphant return from in 1973 of the postwar pro-labor president Juan Perón, who had been overthrown and exiled by a military coup in 1955. (To the immense disappointment of his radical supporters, the elderly Perón, on returning to Argentina, proceeded to endorse anti-labor public policies.) Another example of a large labor insurgency was the British coal miners' strike in the winter of 1974. Aimed at the government's limitations on wage increases, an anti-inflation measure typical of the oil-price shock era, the month-long strike first forced the country on to a three-day week—oil shortages meant not enough oil available for electric power—and led to the electoral defeat of the anti-labor (and anti-Labour) Tory government of Edward Heath.[13]

These signature struggles were the crescendos of a rising movement of labor conflict. In 1968, there were five million working days lost to strikes in Great Britain; by 1972 the figure was close to twenty-four million, a level not seen since the general strike of 1926. Total yearly strike days peaked in the United States in 1970 at about sixty-five million, a noticeably higher level than the 1930s, usually taken as the acme of American labor militancy. Almost everywhere in Western Europe, strike activity was at a high point in the 1970s, about three times what it would be twenty years later. In Latin American countries, there was a similar pattern of expanded labor conflict, at least until military coups—Brazil 1964, Chile 1973, Argentina, 1976—established anti-labor dictatorships. Even in India, a country known for labor quiescence, there was a sharp increase in strikes and other forms of labor conflict after 1968, culminating in the 1974 all-India railway men's strike. Unprecedentedly large, shock waves from it ran through the entire country.[14]

Characteristic of labor strife in the Era of Upheaval was not just the sheer number of strikes and strikers but their issues and locations. The increase in strikes reflected a surge in rank-and-file militancy, producing what are known as wildcat strikes, often bypassing existing trade unions. All of

France's trade union leaders were completely taken aback by the strike wave of May 1968, and had to hustle to catch up with it and to turn it into a collective bargaining agreement. In the United Kingdom, strikes were mostly called by shop stewards, against the wishes or at least the advice of the leadership of the individual union or of the national union federation, the Trades Union Council. The two hundred thousand US postal workers who went out on strike in 1970, defying both federal law and their own union leaders, made up the largest wildcat strike in American history.

Although focusing on the classic issues of wages and hours, strikes of the era also turned on questions of control of the workplace, often in terms redolent of the broader social upheavals of the era. An important site of such disputes was auto manufacturing, a central economic focus, and the very epitome of industrial work at the time, known for its demanding, assembly line labor and its strict discipline. A particularly explosive mixture combined this discipline with assembly line workers who were members of different racial, national, ethnic, or regional groups from their foremen and supervisors. The early 1970s "revolutionary union movements" among African American autoworkers in Detroit, particularly strong in the Dodge/Chrysler plants there, and the repeated wildcat strikes of southern Italians toiling in the Fiat works in north Italian Turin, which initiated the celebrated 1969 "hot autumn" of labor unrest in Italy, were examples, as was the "Turks' strike," which pitted migrant workers against their German foremen at Europe's then-largest auto factory, the Cologne Ford works, in 1973. But it did not take ethnic or racial differences to spark wildcat strikes against an oppressive labor regime, as was seen in the GM plant in Lordstown, Ohio, where long-haired Vietnam veterans opposed a management that had sped up the assembly line from sixty to one hundred cars an hour. Even phlegmatic Swedish coal miners expressed similar sentiments in their 1969–70 strike (which set off a wave of wildcat strikes among Swedish metalworkers), demanding to be treated as "human beings," and not as "machines."[15]

Union memberships rose with labor militancy, reaching, as a percentage of the labor force high points by the 1970s in most Western European countries—and, in fact, around the world. This was not the case in the United States, where the peak was reached in the postwar era, but the Era of Upheaval saw the expansion of unions to previously unrepresented groups, even to the worst-off people in the labor force, agricultural workers. The farm workers' union proved ephemeral, but another development of the era, the growing interest of public sector workers in unionization, has proven more permanent. In 1968, for the first time, the proportion of public sector workers in the United States belonging to unions exceeded the proportion of private sector workers—a development that has persisted, down to the present.[16]

New pro-labor institutional accomplishments of the era include the implementation of the *scala mobile*, or automatic adjustment of wages to inflation, won in Italy in 1975, a result of labor militancy. Accompanying it was the merger of the three Italian trade union federations, communist, socialist, and Catholic, which had been split apart by the Cold War. The revision of West Germany's 1976 "co-determination law," led by the Social Democrats, gave employee representatives greater influence. Codetermination was expanded in Sweden at about the same time, and along similar lines.[17]

While there were an increasing number of strikes in West Germany during the 1970s, much of the decade's labor strife was the result of employers' aggressive use of lockouts, a measure directed as much against the pro-labor social democratic government there, as against militant workers.[18] Such an overtly anti-labor measure was still unusual in Western Europe and North America during the 1970s, but the same cannot be said of the rest of the world. Particularly compared to the earlier growing strength of labor, the second half of that decade and especially the following one were at best a disappointment, at worst a disaster.

If the late Colonial Era had been a good one for labor in Africa, the early years of independence offered a far less favorable environment for labor self-assertion and successful union action. During the 1950s, the European colonial powers, following their policies of economic development, had funded favorable collective bargaining agreements and work-related social welfare payments, particularly for workers in state-owned or state-run enterprises. The governments of the newly independent former colonies, which had come to power with the strong support of labor, then had to take over that funding. Without the resources of a Britain or France, they found this impossible. Virtually from the moment of independence, unions and the new African states came into conflict. As president of newly independent Guinea, Sékou Touré, trade unionist hero of the Guinean anti-imperialist struggle against French rule, quickly suppressed a teachers' strike in 1961, arresting its leaders, and brought all the unions in Guinea into a state-controlled federation that worked for "national" as opposed to labor interests. The same story was repeated throughout Africa, with the incorporation and taming of unions sometimes occurring relatively quickly, as in Ghana or the Côte d'Ivoire, sometimes after strikes confrontations, and military coups, as was the case in Benin, where the ruler subordinating the unions was Mathieu Kérékou, who had come to power in a 1972 coup, and then installed a Marxist-Leninist regime.

Benin was not alone among African in proclaiming itself socialist. Besides having a large state-owned economic sector, such regimes also introduced measures of codetermination, of the sort that were advancing in Europe during the 1970s—Algeria, Tanzania, Mozambique, Zambia, among others. African codeterminist labor regimes were characterized by a lack of codetermination, and by management's efforts to use both the codeterminist institutions and the state-run trade unions to campaign for more intensive work regimes and higher productivity. Their functions were becoming similar to those of unions in the Eastern Bloc, only the latter's ability to offer opportunities for leisure time activities, consumer goods, and housing were lacking in the much poorer African countries.[19]

Military dictatorships broke the power of labor in Brazil, Argentina, and Chile; indeed, breaking the power of labor was a major reason for the coups leading to the dictatorships in the first place. In Mexico, the most populous Latin American country not under military rule during the 1970s, the leading union federation, the *Confederación de Trabajadores de México*, was controlled by the dominant political party, not entirely unlike conditions in Africa, and was more a vehicle for state policy and the interests of politically well-connected businessmen than a labor representative. Smaller independent unions continued to exist in Mexico and to advocate for the interests of their members, particularly in auto manufacturing, a center of labor turbulence in the era.[20]

The 1970s were not an inspiring decade for labor in Asia, either. Trade unions in Indonesia, never very influential in the first place, were prohibited after the 1965 military coup and replaced with worker/employer syndicates, modeled on those in fascist Italy. Growing industrialization in the so-called four tigers of the region—South Korea, Taiwan, Singapore, and Hong Kong—was not accompanied by any growth in union organization, strikes, or workers' self-assertion. The already weak, marginalized, legally limited, and fragmented position of that small minority of workers in India represented by trade unions was fragmented still further in the 1970s. The two large national union federations, each affiliated with a political party, split into four federations in the 1970s, and ten by the end of the following decade. Indira Gandhi's period of authoritarian rule, the "emergency" of 1975–77, was not just marked by widespread compulsory sterilization, but the suspension of the right to strike, or to bargain collectively as well as by the institution of a wage freeze. Gandhi's political opponents, who ruled from 1977 to 1981, were no more pro-labor and tried, unsuccessfully, to pass a law prohibiting strikes in "essential" industries.

By far the largest union movement in Asia during the 1970s was in Japan, but Japanese unions were also committed to cooperating with management, on management's terms, in increasing labor productivity. Instead of strikes and labor unrest in Japanese auto manufacturing, unions supported "quality circles," small labor-management teams whose goal was to produce more rapidly and efficiently. The 1970s were the decade in which Japanese auto manufacturing became a global leader, reaching equality with the formally dominant North Americans and Western Europeans, and the Japanese economy generally managed that turbulent and difficult decade unexpectedly well. The transfer of the Japanese model of industrial relations to other countries, or, for that matter, its application within Japan itself, would not later prove so helpful for labor.[21]

Labor Defeated

If the omens for labor were mixed in the 1970s, they became abundantly clear in the following decade. A more unfavorable political environment, encouraging more aggressive action by owners and management against the institutions that had protected and empowered labor, dramatic large-scale conflicts ending in catastrophe for labor, and the increasing globalization of economic life and the transformation of social structures it entailed—all of these marked the onset of a period in which the gains of labor were rolled back. Only reinforced by the end of communism after 1989, the decline of labor that began in the 1980s has continued down to the present day.

THREE STRIKES

Three successive large-scale strikes—the US air traffic controllers in 1981, the Bombay textile workers in 1982–83, and the British coal miners, in 1984–85—each of which attracted widespread public interest, ended in the humiliating defeat of the strikers. For all the many differences between these three strikes, two major similarities stand out, one relating to the past and one to the future. The strikers were largely thinking in terms of the tactics and expectations from the age of labor militancy in the 1970s, which no longer produced the same results in a different economic and, especially, political, environment. If the strikes marked a break with the past, they also set the stage for other strike defeats, and, more broadly, for the weakening and downright elimination of those institutions and practices that had been so beneficial for labor since 1945.

The rapid expansion of commercial aviation after 1945, particularly following the widespread use of jet aircraft in the mid-1960s, made air traffic controllers an economically central occupation. This same development also made the job more stressful and difficult, as the controllers struggled to keep an ever-growing number of aircraft, flying at greater speeds, safe while operating on schedule—two difficult and sometimes contradictory occupational demands. These circumstances made questions of adequate staffing levels, length of shifts, and years of lifetime job service flash points of labor disputes (and remain so today, as the technology of air traffic control has barely kept up with the increase in air traffic).[22] In the United States, during the 1970s, two additional factors only worsened labor relations in air traffic control. One was that air traffic controllers were typically military veterans who had learned their trade while serving in the armed forces. As air traffic grew, and more controllers were hired, an increasing number of them were veterans of the Vietnam War. As a result of their experiences, they were suspicious of authority, influenced by the ideas of the 1960s counterculture, and generally hostile to the authoritarian management practices of the Federal Aviation Administration. The second factor was the rapidly increasing inflation of the 1970s, which led even well-compensated workers, like air traffic controllers, to press for large increases in pay.

To make their points, the air traffic controllers' union, the "Professional Air Traffic Controllers Organization," or PATCO, organized what are known as "work-to-rule" slowdowns, during which the controllers strictly enforced all the government's safety rules, so that flights were delayed getting off the ground or canceled, and planes already in the air had to circle for hours in a holding pattern before being cleared to land. At first, airline management, although officially opposed to this tactic, tacitly sympathized; some pilots, while flying in circles, got on the intercom and told their passengers—at the time, still disproportionately well-heeled business travelers—to write their congressmen in support of the union's demands. As the 1970s wore on, air traffic increased and controllers' incomes declined with inflation. As a result, the union became steadily more militant, adding sick-outs to its slowdowns, though never quite explicitly crossing the line into an outright strike, an illegal action for US government employees. Frustration with the largely hostile attitude of the supposedly pro-labor administration of President Jimmy Carter (who made offending his supporters a political specialty), PATCO endorsed Carter's Republican opponent in the 1980 presidential elections, Ronald Reagan.

PATCO's leaders expected this endorsement would lead to Reagan taking a more favorable attitude toward them. And he did. In the 1981 contract negotiations, the government team made a number of concessions, including a willingness to bargain about wages and hours, which was technically illegal with federal government employees. However, in a massive revolt of the rank and file, the union members angrily rejected the proposed contract and its concessions. Voting by a margin of 19–1 to authorize a strike, they insisted on their demands for a giant pay increase, starting with an across-the-board $10,000 (about $30,000 in today's money) salary boost and a four-day workweek, leading to a nationwide air traffic controllers' strike in the summer of 1981.

It turned into a disaster for the air traffic controllers. Making a 180-degree turnabout, the Reagan administration took a tough line, dismissing the strikers and announcing its intent to hire replacements for them. Although the non-striking minority of controllers, supervisors, hastily requisitioned military personnel, and speedily and superficially trained replacements were often stretched to the breaking point, air traffic continued without serious interruptions or accidents. Travelers and the general public bombarded their congressional representatives with letters and phone calls denouncing the lazy, greedy, entitled strikers. Neither other US unions (whose leaders felt the air traffic controllers had gotten what they deserved by supporting an anti-labor Republican for president), the airline pilots, nor other countries' air traffic controllers were willing to take action in support of the strikers. The strike failed and the strikers lost their jobs forever.[23]

The air traffic controllers' action was right out of the 1970s militant labor playbook: large demands, issues of workplace discipline, unrestrained and spontaneous action. But a decade of such militancy had left a void of public support and labor solidarity, making it possible for the employer to resist the union with impunity. Not only were the results of the strike the opposite of what militant actions had previously gained, they set a new pattern for the future. Taking their cue from the government's action against an illegal strike of public employees, American private employers responded to perfectly legal strikes by firing the strikers and hiring permanent replacements. This response to strikes had been a legal option since a 1938 Supreme Court decision on the topic; it had simply not been done—until it was. From that point onward, strikes backfired on American workers.[24]

The city of Mumbai—previously called Bombay—was the center of textile production in India, a country whose proportion of the output of cotton textiles, worldwide, had been rising since the late nineteenth century. Mumbai's large, integrated textile mills, combining all features of cotton manufacture—from spinning to weaving to dyeing and finishing, some utilizing the most modern textile machinery—were a key element in India's post-1945 import-substitution industrialization plans. They helped spark the development of other industries in the region, including the manufacture of chemicals and industrial machinery. After India's independence from colonial rule, labor relations in the large textile mills had been very closely state-regulated, nothing unusual in the postwar era. The Bombay Industrial Relations Act of 1946 had established the *Rashtriya Mill Mazdoor Sangh*, or RMMS, the textile workers' union affiliated with the nationalist Congress Party, as the sole legal representative of the workers in the city's textile mills. The workers themselves, many of whom supported unions affiliated with communists and socialists and who had taken part in large strikes in the late 1940s called by these unions and opposed by the RMMS (which generally showed little interest in labor conflict), were never polled about their own wishes in the matter.

Another part of government regulation was the "decasualization scheme" of 1950. Designed to phase out irregular and insecure employment relations, the scheme registered workers in the textile mills and divided them into two categories: the permanently employed and temporaries, the *badlis*, who were given work when it was available. As permanent positions opened up, *badlis* would be hired, although they required vetting by supervisors and union officials. It was no secret that the unionists often demanded bribes to transfer someone to a permanent position, a state of affairs that did nothing for the reputation of the RMMS.

The situation continued through the postwar era but began to change in the 1970s. One reason was growing labor militancy, spurred on in India, as elsewhere in the world, by the inflationary trends of that decade. There were wildcat strikes, outside the purview of the RMMS, and generally against it: one in 1971, over a meager yearly bonus, another in in 1973–74, over an agreement the RMMS had reached with the mill owners to end a weekly day off, when the mills were shut down, and replacing it with a system in which workers received one rotating day off per week. This latter strike featured demonstrations of workers in the streets and a mass of striking workers blockading the building of the *Vidhan Sabha*, the legislature of Maharashtra State in Mumbai. None of this succeeded in ending the new workweek arrangements. If workers were becoming more discontent with their situation, the mill owners were themselves facing increasing difficulty. Besides competition in world markets from cheaper Pakistani and higher-quality Chinese products, there was domestic competition as well, mainly from small workshops with power looms. (The rural handlooms, so praised by Mohandas Gandhi and still officially supported by government policy, did not actually produce much of anything.) These smaller workshops often wove yarn made from synthetics smuggled into the country and paid much lower wages. Workers were not represented by unions, who showed no particular interest in organizing them.

The bonus issue once again sparked strikes and demonstrations in October 1981; strikers marched in the streets to the house of Datta Samant, a Mumbai physician and Congress Party politician-turned union organizer, known for his leadership of militant and successful strikes in the region. When Samant declined to direct the strike, the workers occupied his house, refusing to leave until he agreed to lead them. Under his direction, the strikers called for large wage increases—300 rupees per month, the equivalent of about $360 US per year, a much smaller absolute number but about the same percentage increase as the US air traffic controllers had demanded—and that the *badlis*, who numbered about a quarter of the labor force, be taken on as permanent workers. All of Mumbai's textile workers, some 250,000 of them, defied their official union and joined the strike.

Lasting eighteen months, the Mumbai strike was the largest and longest in the history of India. Strikers occupied factories and marched repeatedly through the streets. Management and non-striking white-collar employees responded by sneaking in at night, to truck off finished product and even machinery. Many striking workers returned to their native villages, and Samant held massive pro-strike rallies in the countryside, bringing social turbulence with them. As the strike wore on, it turned increasingly violent. Strikers beat up and sometimes even murdered strikebreakers, while thugs hired by the official anti-strike union, working in close cooperation with the municipal police, did the same to strikers—on a much larger scale. Like their American counterparts, Indian employers dismissed the strikers and hired replacement workers; they farmed out work to the smaller weaving mills. Also like in the United States, the government—both the national government, once more led by Indira Gandhi, and the government of Maharashtra state—was quite openly on the side of the employers. Offers to "mediate" involved urging the workers to take their employers' terms. The authorities changed the law to cut workers and their families off from their disability benefits and public health insurance, to pressure them into returning to work. Other unions made occasional gestures of sympathy but offered no real support.

In the end, the strikers had to return to work. Unlike the air traffic controllers, some of the dismissed strikers were accepted back by their employers, but generally in a new employment category—as temporary workers, employed full time, but without any protection against being laid off. A number of the mills closed; their production shifted to the smaller workshops; the valuable urban real estate where the closed mills were located was sold to developers. Datta Samant continued his trade union organizing, until he was gunned down in 1997; the reasons for his assassination and those behind it remain unknown.[25]

The Mumbai textile workers, employed in a declining industry, one facing the end of import-substitution industrialization and the growing challenges of a global economy, were in a far weaker position than the air traffic controllers. But the common elements in their two epic strikes, the continuation of 1970s militancy in a politically more hostile environment, and the lack of sympathy and solidarity on the part of fellow unionists, denoted the onset of a new age for labor. The British coal miners' strike of 1984–85, although generally seen in the context of the US air traffic controllers, as part of the successes of the closely linked, militantly conservative governments of Ronald Reagan and Margaret Thatcher, revealed a number of serious differences from the strike of the air traffic controllers and some distinct similarities with that of the Mumbai textile workers. Like the textile workers, the miners were a trade in decline, as demand for coal fell in the postwar decades. In fact, the strike was not primarily about wages or hours, but about the government's plans to close a large number of the state-owned coal mines and lay off the miners who toiled there. Unlike the Reagan administration, which began its negotiations with a relatively benevolent attitude toward the air traffic controllers, Thatcher saw militant trade unionists as "the enemy within."

The British coal mines had been under government ownership since the end of the Second World War, and the Thatcher appointees who ran the

National Coal Board made no secret of their intent to close many pits, to discipline the workforce and, ultimately, to privatize the industry. Even before the nationwide strike officially began in March 1984, half the coal miners in Scotland were on strike over local disputes concerning these new management policies. For all the provocation, the decision of the National Union of Miners, and its communist President Arthur Scargill, to call a nationwide walkout helped them fall into the government's trap. The miners struck in the spring, at a time when demand for coal was at its lowest—unlike the air traffic controllers, who walked out at the height of the summer travel season, but like the Mumbai textile workers, who went out during a recession, when demand for textiles was low and manufacturers were sitting on full warehouses. Also very much unlike the air traffic controllers, who voted overwhelmingly to strike, or the textile workers, who walked out in defiance of their union leaders, the miners' union leadership called the strike without a members' ballot, specifically refusing to call for a strike vote. That same leadership showed little interest in mobilizing public support—Scargill's press secretary consistently refused to speak to the press—counting on mass picketing to shut down the coal pits and win the strike. Instead, the authorities utilized aggressive police tactics they had been preparing for years, broke the picket lines, arrested militants (over ten thousand criminal charges were filed in conjunction with the strike) and protected the minority of miners who continued to work. In this respect, the United Kingdom and its more recent former colony were very similar.

Changing the unemployment compensation law to deny benefits to strikers put them in a financial squeeze (again, not unlike India), when the strike dragged on for months. Negotiations between the miners and the government, mediated by the Trades Union Congress and the Labour Party—also like India—produced the possibility of a settlement that would have ended the strike on management's terms, but allowed the miners to save face, and, perhaps, their union. Scargill rejected this solution, which was even endorsed by the Communist Party, and continued the strike, until, after a year, the strikers had to admit defeat and return to work—unpunished, unlike the air traffic controllers, but most soon to be dismissed, as the government went about closing down or privatizing the coal mines. By 2000 coal mining had disappeared from the United Kingdom, and the one-time miners' villages were increasingly depopulated; the remaining inhabitants were un- or underemployed, while ever more of them were becoming addicted to heroin.

The labor tactics that had worked so well in the 1970s, during the 1974 strike that brought down the Tory government, or the 1972 national miners' strike, the first in the United Kingdom since 1926, when massed picketing, supported by tens of thousands of union members from other trades had won the day—an idea of Arthur Scargill, then a local union leader in Yorkshire, that had made his career. Scargill hoped to repeat that experience a decade later and bring down Thatcher's government as well. But public opinion, following the increasingly chaotic labor disputes of the 1970s, including the so-called winter of discontent of 1978–79, when the United Kingdom was beset by massive public employee's strikes, leaving mountains of garbage uncollected, had swung support away from labor militancy. As with the air traffic controllers, or the Mumbai textile workers, other unions would not call their members out in support of the striking miners. The miners' union itself refused to try to mobilize public opinion, and while the wives of the miners took over that task, and did succeed in gaining some support, especially from left-wing artists and intellectuals—who would soon come to see the use of coal as environmentally destructive—the miners' defenders remained a distinct minority. The beleaguered coal miners were dealt a bad hand—defending a declining, money-losing, environmentally questionable occupation. They played their bad hand poorly. The air traffic controllers had been in a favorable situation and threw it away with militant intransigence.

The miners' strike had a coda, two years later in the newspaper business. Rupert Murdoch, already on his way to being a right-wing global media tycoon, frustrated with the unionized typographers' opposition to the introduction of computerized typesetting—more precisely, to the typographers' insistence on being employed, after computers had made their skills obsolete—fired everyone who worked for his newspapers in their old, central London Fleet Street headquarters and moved their operations to a cordoned off and fortress-like center in Wapping, located in the south London docklands. The resulting printers' strike, which led to violent clashes with the police in the "Battle of Wapping" ended in a total defeat for labor.[26] Murdoch notwithstanding, the 1980s American management practice of firing strikers did not spread to the United Kingdom, but in both places public opinion turned ever more against unions, strikes became steadily fewer in number and extent, and union membership grew increasingly less common. All of these developments would eventually spread to Australia, making the Anglosphere (with the partial exception of Canada), a pioneer among wealthier countries in the Late-Millennium Era's defeat of labor.[27]

Whether defending positions in declining industries, as did the British miners and the Mumbai textile workers, or acting aggressively, in favorable circumstances, as was the case with the US air traffic controllers, the outcome of these three strikes revealed that the labor militancy of the 1970s would run into difficulties in a different political environment. In all three of these large strikes, union leaders, as well as rank-and-file workers, made serious errors in judgment and strategy. These errors were the result of using tactics that had once worked so well; in other words, from a lack of recognition that times had changed.

LABOR IN A DEREGULATED, GLOBALIZED ECONOMY

Not all large-scale strikes during the 1980s ended disastrously for labor, at least in the wealthier countries. The West German metalworkers, for instance, won their 1984 strike, and, with it, the key demand of the introduction of a thirty-five-hour workweek. If the Late-Millennium Era was a period of global decline of labor, individual strike defeats in particular countries were not the sole cause. At least as significant were the transformations of employment relations, reflecting the globalization of the economy and the change in the nature of class structure. These transformations fall into two groups: the casualization of labor—the replacement of regular, permanent employment by subcontracting, (nominal) independent contracting and temporary positions; and the changes in production resulting from the movement of capital and labor around the world.

Mark Holstrom, an English anthropologist studying the culture of factory work in India toward the end of the 1970s, noted, with incredulity and outrage: "In some factories, two workers stand side by side doing the same work, except that one is a regular worker earning two or three times as much as the other, a contract worker who cannot join a union, eat in the canteen or use the same lavatory."[28] For Holstrom, this practice of using outside contractors to cut labor costs was outrageous and immoral. He noted that one union leader called it "apartheid." It was a sign of the alien nature of labor relations in India, its poverty and lack of labor protection laws, or the ease employers had in evading them. It was simply unimaginable that something like that could be seen in Europe or North America.

Yet by 2000 it had become routine. Whole occupations, like long-haul truck drivers in the United States, had shifted from unionized and secure employment to self-employed independent contractors, resulting in declines in income, elimination of job benefits, and ever greater stress at work, as self-employed truckers, compensated by the mile, desperately strove to drive as far as possible, in as short a time as possible—safety laws and speed limits be damned. American trucking is a particularly interesting example, because there had been, even at the high point of union membership during the 1950s, a segment of trucking, hauling farm products, run by independent contractors, a non- and anti-union core from which contracting expanded to take over almost the entire occupation.[29]

At least as common was the coexistence of contract laborers and permanently employed workers. Sometimes, it was a question of outsourcing positions not directly related to business purposes—cleaning, food services, logistics, payroll, and IT—or sometimes, just as in India several decades earlier, more poorly paid contract laborers, working right alongside workers with job security. It is difficult to know how frequent these practices are, because governments have generally not collected relevant statistics, but some economists' estimates, taken from the United States and Germany, provide an idea. In the United States, these forms of work—workers employed by subcontracting companies or temporary agencies and independent contractors—first developed a significant presence in the 1980s, and, by the mid-1990s, were 10 percent of the labor force, a figure remaining about the same for a decade, and then jumping to 16 percent by 2015. In Germany, such forms of employment developed on a large scale about a decade later than in the United States. By 2008 people employed by subcontractors, temporary agencies, and as independent contractors in cleaning, security, and logistics operations alone, made up 8 percent of the entire labor force.[30]

Another increasingly prevalent way to evade the permanent employment arrangements typical of the high point of labor in the postwar era, and also pioneered in India, was to hire workers on a temporary basis. Young people were a favorite target of this practice. They worked alongside permanently employed and older coworkers. After 2000, young people in southern Europe or Japan were either unemployed or working in temporary position. Between half and two-thirds of the fifteen-to-twenty-four age group in Spain, Italy, and Portugal who were employed worked in temporary jobs. They were not so much jobs with no future guarantees as jobs with a guaranteed no future. Perhaps a less prevalent condition in other developed countries, there were still plenty of individuals in those countries, especially immigrants and members of ethnic and racial minorities, who bounced between unemployment and short-term jobs.[31]

An acknowledged impact of globalization in the Late-Millennium Era has been the transfer of work—at first in manufacturing, but, increasingly, in business services, from the wealthier countries of Europe and North America to lower-wage ones, particularly in Asia. The upshot was a decline in the number of positions offering steady, regular employment of the sort common in the postwar era, and their replacement with other, less secure forms of employment. Yet the movement from regular to irregular employment was not restricted to the world's wealthiest countries; it affected the world's poorest ones as well. In Africa, especially, but also in South Asia, regular employment was concentrated in the public sector, both public service and state-owned industrial enterprises, as well as in businesses protected by the measures of import-substitution industrialization. In 1980, about three-quarters of all regular employment in Africa was in the public sector. The World Bank's aforementioned structural adjustment programs, which called for opening up markets and cutting government expenditures, devastated these jobs. It was not just that laid-off workers streamed into the "informal sector," street marketing, and trading, casual labor, generally off the books, and illegal activities, but those still employed were no longer able to make ends meet, due to salary cuts, so they had to supplement their regular income with informal work as well. In Ghana—to take just one example—public employment went from 397,000 in 1985 to 156,000 just six years later. In that latter year, 80 percent of Ghana's workers were in the informal sector; fifteen years later, it was 85 percent.[32]

Of course, there were and are people who work off the books in the informal sector in the world's wealthy countries as well; in the United States, some estimates have put it at around 15 percent of the labor force by 2000. But the informal sector is much larger in poorer countries and the divisions between it and the formal sector infinitely greater. One particularly striking example comes from the production of perfume in Guinea (Conakry), an ongoing enterprise since the French colonial period, using as a raw material tree blossoms in the area. In the Late-Millennium Era, the perfume firm, nationalized in 1973 and re-privatized a decade later, had a total of forty-five regular employees, represented by a union and an enterprise committee. The regularly employed workers complained of low wages and poor health and safety conditions, but their union did nothing for them. For all the difficulties of the forty-five permanent workers, there were over five hundred contract workers—women who harvested tree blossoms for the perfume. They marked the trees on which they were working, by tying a handkerchief around them. Sometimes, more than one woman would claim a tree, there would be fights high up in the branches, and the loser would be pushed out of the tree. And all this for no money—the contract workers received a kilo of rice for every three kilos of jasmine and orange blossoms. Given the weight of flowers, one might well imagine how much work was involved. The trend away from regular employment in the direction of casualized labor was worldwide in the Late-Millennium Era, but its effects were much more brutal in the world's poorer countries.[33]

Political developments reinforced the trends working against labor. In particular, the end of communism in Eurasia created unparalleled opportunities for capital and labor mobility. The capital mobility was mostly to Asia, moving production jobs to low-wage sites in China, Thailand, and Vietnam. The labor mobility was particularly noticeable in Europe, due to a combination of the Maastricht Accords, ending any restrictions on migration within the EU, and the integration of the low-wage, formerly communist countries of Eastern Europe into the EU. Romanian workers, toiling on construction sites in Berlin, the capital of reunified Germany, were working for Romanian subcontractors, and could be paid according to Romanian labor laws, making them much cheaper than Germans. This particular example did come to an end, when the EU decided in its "Posted Workers Directive" of 1996 that workers were to be treated according to the labor legislation of the country in which they were employed, not that of the legal headquarters of their employer. Nonetheless, attempts to combine a continent-wide open labor market, with very different national labor and social welfare law, including suspiciously high numbers of migrants from Eastern Europe being independent contractors, were a constant feature of the European labor scene in the decades around 2000.[34]

Labor at the Beginning of the New Millennium

By 2000, the picture for labor was increasingly grim, worldwide. In the wealthy countries of the world, unions were hemorrhaging membership. Remaining members were aging—in Italy almost half were retired—and young people, so often working in temporary or part-time positions, either had no interest in joining unions or no opportunity to do so. (This pattern of aging union membership was not limited to wealthy countries but can be found worldwide.)[35] "Union density," the clumsy term used by sociologists and industrial relations experts to describe the proportion of the labor force who belong to unions, was very much in decline. Figure 8.1 shows this proportion in five affluent, or relatively affluent countries, on four continents, for much of the twentieth century.[36]

In Germany and the United States, for which figures go back over one hundred years, the proportion of the labor force unionized had, by the 2000, fallen back to the levels of the 1920s. These low levels were typical of the first decade of the millennium worldwide: statistics of the International Labour

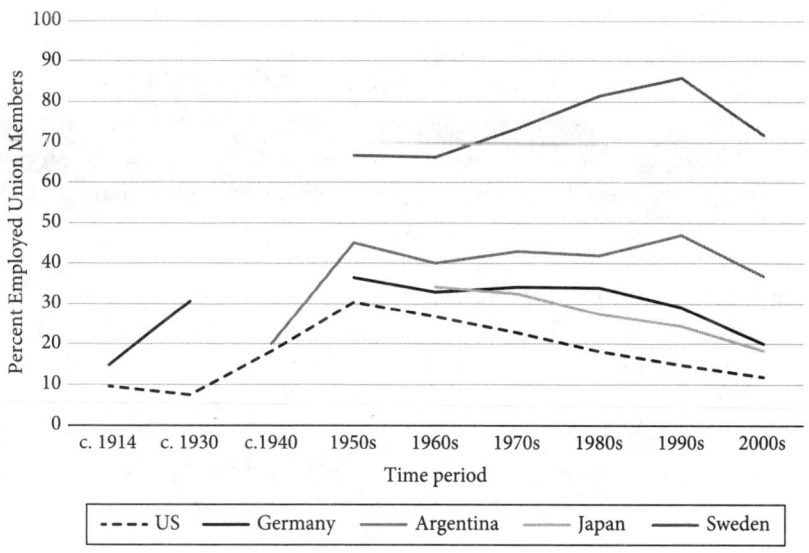

FIGURE 8.1 Union Membership in Five Countries during the Twentieth Century

Organization show that in 2000 there were just a handful of countries in which even a third of the labor force belonged to a union.[37]

In the world's wealthier countries, the chief strongholds of union organization were in those states that followed the "Ghent System," in which unemployment compensation, even if publicly funded, was administered by unions—Belgium, Denmark, Sweden, and Finland, the only countries in the entire world where a majority of the labor force was still unionized. (A bare majority of workers in Norway, a non-Ghent System country, were union members.) Even in the Ghent System countries, the position of unions was weakened by the development of non-union unions, in Denmark, organizations of the "Trade Union House," whose members had access to unemployment insurance, but which did no workplace representation or collective bargaining. The Swedish variant of this was for workers just to belong to the union unemployment insurance fund, but not to pay dues for union representation.

The one-time communist countries of Eurasia, ostensibly workers' states and in reality regimes of the subordination of labor, had experienced a violent social and economic discontinuity in the 1990s. It had only made labor's position there worse. Very much unlike earlier rebellions against communist rule in Eastern Europe, those of 1989 had not been centered on labor or involved strikes and workers' demonstrations. The Solidarity trade union had, of course, been the vehicle for the massive national opposition to communist rule in Poland in 1980. In the 1990s former Solidarity activists had seen their role as helping to implement a free market economy, and to improve productivity, to create capitalism, rather than to advocate for labor's position within capitalism. At least the Solidarity activists had a post-1989 goal; the leaders of the official communist trade unions had no idea of how to deal with the new capitalist circumstances, and the economic collapse of the post-communist states, accompanied by massive unemployment, left them without much in the way of power to do anything, had they even wanted to do. Union membership in the states of the former Eastern Bloc plummeted, dropping in Hungary, for instance, from 2.7 million in 1992 to 600,000 in 2003.

This was typical for most of Eastern Europe. Circumstances were somewhat different in Russia, Ukraine, and, to some extent, Romania, where the unions succeeded in maintaining control of the property they had accumulated during the communist years, and some of the leisure-time prospects, particularly vacations, that went with them. Membership rates remained higher in those countries, largely for the vacation prospects; unions could do little for their members' wages, employment security, or workplace conditions, in view of the extremely chaotic conditions and severe economic crises in the successor states to the USSR.[38]

China represented the other course out of communism in Eurasia—continuity of the political institutions of the communist regime, and a gradual and successful transition to private ownership and a market economy, in the context of rapid economic growth. One of the remaining institutions of the former communist economic and social system was the All-China Federation of Trade Unions (ACFTU), counting 175 million members in 2000, more unionists than in the rest of the world put together. Like unions in the former communist countries of Eastern Europe, the closure and privatization of state-owned enterprises had cost the ACFTU dearly in membership and revenues. But, unlike the case in Eastern Europe, it still had government authority on its side. One ramification of what happened comes from the firmly anti-labor Walmart stores, whose managers had no intention of allowing their "associates" in China to form unions, any more than in the United States. In 2004, the ACFTU, with the support of the government, compelled Walmart to recognize it. But, as the Nanjing ACFTU leader, Chen Siming, pointed out, "We trade union leaders will never organize the employees in launching a strike or asking for unreasonable benefits."[39]

Rather than representing workers' interests in an increasingly capitalist society, the Chinese union was continuing its communist role as an enhancer of productivity. Attitudes toward this kind of unionism varied by the nationality of foreign investor, since the government was reluctant to let the union operate in Chinese-owned businesses. Overseas Chinese and Taiwanese proved to be unrelentingly hostile to any kind of union, even a cooperative one. Already used to this kind of pro-management union at home, Japanese investors were delighted to use it in China, a viewpoint that their European and American counterparts generally shared. As one US executive stated, "It's nice to have a trade union that works with us rather than against us."[40]

For all its massive membership and the occasional support of the authoritarian Chinese government, the radius of the ACFTU's activities was restricted to the formal sector of the economy; the hundreds of millions of migrant laborers, living in booming Chinese industrial centers without legal permission, involved in construction (men) or light manufacturing (women) were outside its purview. These workers had to represent themselves, whether through occasional wildcat strikes, or associations based on their provincial place of origin—generally not very successfully.

This contrast between the formal and informal sector was even more the case for African trade unions, except that in Africa, where the formal sector was somewhere between 5 percent and 15 percent of the labor force, the problem this caused for unions was considerable. In Ghana, where unionism has a longer and more tenacious history than in most African countries, unions have tried to extend their activities to people in the informal sector, such as hairdressers, self-employed truckers, self-employed street vendors, or agricultural workers—including, in the latter group, beekeepers. There have been similar efforts at the organization of informal sector workers in India, particularly women. These efforts have met with, at best, modest success.[41]

In this less-than-cheery account of labor at the beginning of the new millennium, one might wonder whether there were any places in the world where the condition of labor was improving. Labor really did advance in two countries, where union organizing, and frequent and large-scale strikes were not just effective but a central part of a broader movement of social and political change. Brazil and South Africa have seen a continuation of 1970s labor militancy, and its expansion and incorporation into a network of social and political institutions that helped bring an end to a period of authoritarian and undemocratic rule.

The massive strikes of the São Paulo autoworkers in 1978, and of metalworkers in 1979, touched off a nationwide wave, in which about one Brazilian workers in eight was on strike. These could perhaps be seen as a late example of the labor militancy in the 1970s, but unlike most of the rest of the world, strikes in Brazil continued and expanded into the 1980s. Union membership increased fivefold, reaching twelve million by 1983, much of it in the newly formed and militant federation the *Central Única dos Trabalhadores*, which, by 1989, was able to lead a general strike that mobilized thirty-five million workers. The union and its aggressive campaigns were one of the many forces leading the military junta that had ruled since 1964 to return the country to civilian rule in 1985. The union sponsored and supported community groups in the slum neighborhoods of Brazil's largest cities, whose members demanded they receive the same public municipal services as in more affluent districts. It also sponsored the formation of a labor party, the *Partito del Trabalhadores*. Its most popular figure, the president of the metalworkers' union, Luiz Inácio Lula da Silva, would be elected Brazil's president in 2002.

South Africa's version of the labor militancy of the 1970s was the strike wave of 1973, centered around the city of Durban, involving over one hundred thousand strikers, mostly Africans, but supported by Indians and "coloured" (mixed race) workers. Emerging from this agitation was the 1985 Confederation of South African Trade Unions, or COSATU, which played an increasingly central role in the "United Democratic Front," the league of organizations opposed to apartheid rule. Unlike the case in Brazil, where labor actions stood in the forefront and community groups followed in its wake, in South Africa it was community-based actions, particularly the 1976 massive "Soweto uprising," the riots in the segregated suburbs of Johannesburg, which provided the impetus for labor. As with the election of Lula in Brazil, the upshot of the campaign was political transformation, the end of apartheid rule, and the election of anti-apartheid hero Nelson Mandela as president in 1994.[42]

The Brazilian and South African examples have not found much emulation in the world's poorer countries. Particularly in Africa, most unions have remained small and weak, not self-supporting, and, like women's groups there, dependent on financial assistance from NGOs, UN agencies, and the foreign aid of Scandinavian governments. As countries such as Tanzania and Zambia have transitioned from centrally planned economies with a lot of government ownership, to privatization and more market-oriented arrangements, the codetermination regimes of earlier decades have remained in place, though no more effective in the new circumstances than in the old ones. Workers' representatives are invited to meetings and given lots of preparatory documents, only written in English, which they mostly cannot read.

Transitions to democracy in other countries have done relatively little for labor. Unions and the strikes they called were important in the overthrow of authoritarian rule at the beginning of the 1990s in Benin and Mali, but the end of these governments didn't result so much in an expansion of unionism as the splitting of the union movement into smaller groups, each with steadily less influence. Transitions to democracy in East Asian countries, including South Korea and Indonesia, made it possible for unions to act independently, but these transitions were typically accompanied by severe economic crises, leading to recessions and large-scale unemployment, which made union action difficult. Japan's trade unions, long committed to cooperation with corporate management, as we've seen, found their strategy less than helpful after 1990, as Japanese firms sought to cut costs by cutting wages, decreasing the number of permanently hired workers, and replacing them with temporary hires. At the beginning of the twenty-first century, Asia has, in spite of its economic advances in the years following 1960, remained what it was previously: a global weak point of labor.[43]

In the world's wealthier countries, unions retain more members, greater assets and, in at least some of them, particularly Northern Europe, institutions of labor influence. There have been efforts at expanding union organization, begun in the United States, under the new AFL-CIO president John Sweeney in 1995, which were well-received and imitated in other English-speaking countries, as well as in Japan and Germany. Occasionally, there have been successes, such as the unionization of janitors in Los Angeles, which involved close connections between unions, organizations of immigrants, and middle-class sympathizers, particularly church groups. One of the very few successful, large-scale strikes in recent US history pitted the Teamsters Union against the United Parcel Service (UPS) in 1998. Besides the usual wage issues, the union focused on the changes in the job market, demanding that the company bring part-time and temporary workers into full-time, permanent positions. Very much unlike other strikes, this one was favorably received by the public, especially because of the gender dynamics involved. The largely male, uniformed UPS drivers regularly picked up and delivered packages to a mostly female clientele of secretaries, office managers, and executive assistants. The two groups enjoyed a good relationship. As Nan DeMars, a Minneapolis consultant to executive secretaries, said about UPS workers, "Here's a man I can count on—even if I can't count on any other men in my life."[44]

In the end, all these efforts have done relatively little to reverse the decline of labor. There are three major reasons for this state of affairs. One is the decline of strikes. Just how great an exception the UPS strike was is apparent from Figure 8.2, which presents figures on the number of strike days (workers on strike times days on strike) per one thousand waged and salaried workers in six wealthier countries: three from the English-speaking world (the United States, the United Kingdom, and Australia), one from the codeterminist labor regimes of Sweden; one from a southern European country of militant unionism, Italy; and one from a country characterized by strong management and cooperative unions, Japan.

In the United Kingdom, Australia, Spain, and Sweden, the peak of labor militancy occurred in the 1970s; in Japan and the United States, strikes were largest and most frequent in the 1950s. But the sharp decline in strike activity, in some cases to the point of extinction, during the Late-Millennium Era is apparent everywhere.[45]

While we might wonder whether things were proceeding differently in poorer countries, whether labor militancy was more pronounced there, it is very difficult to find reliable figures on the number of strike days per one thousand salaried or waged workers in South America, Africa, or Asia: both the numerator, the number of strikes and their duration; and the denominator,

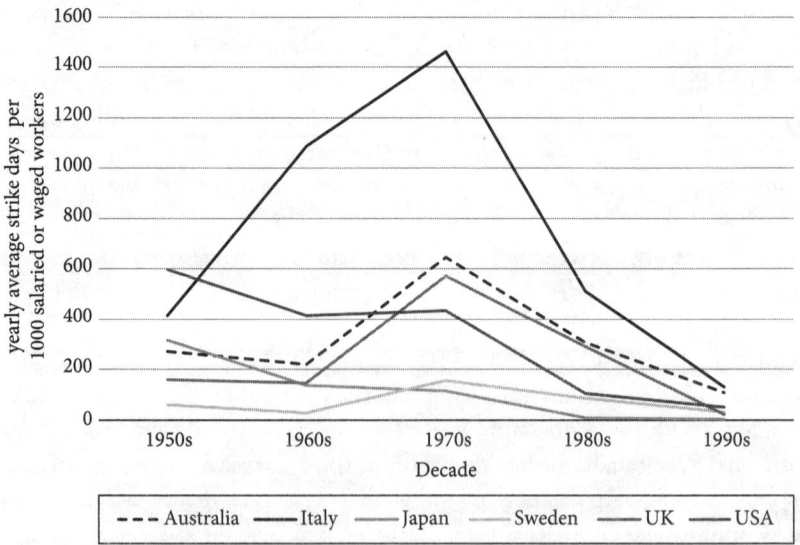

FIGURE 8.2 Strikes in Wealthier Countries during the Second Half of the Twentieth Century

the number of workers, were either not reported, reported inconsistently, or only available for a limited number of years. There were only three countries for which it was possible to devise even some very partial results, India, Ghana, and Kenya, which are shown in Figure 8.3.[46]

The absolute number of strike days per thousand was generally much higher in those countries than in the wealthier ones. However, this was primarily a reflection of the fact that most of the labor force in poor countries was in the informal sector, in marginal forms of self-employment, and hence the number of wage- and salary earners, the denominator in the fraction, was low. In the two African countries, strikes were very common in the late Colonial Era, a state of affairs continuing in Kenya into the first decade of independence, followed by a very steep decline in strike rates during the decades of the 1970s and 1980s. Strikes in India took a different path, with strike rates rising in the 1960s and especially the 1970s. Unfortunately, post-1980 Indian figures on the labor force are very different from earlier years, so no further calculation of strike rates is possible. There were still a lot of strikes in the early 1980s, especially as a result of the great Mumbai textile workers strike of 1982, but by the 1990s, the average number of strike days per year had fallen back to 1960s levels.

In 2004, the statisticians of the International Labour Organization tried to create a global index of strikes. Their figures, based on either partial or complete returns from forty different countries across four decades, weighted by countries' GDP, go from a yearly average of 317 in the 1960s (270, if one leaves out the events of May 1968 in France) to 297 in the 1970s, and then show a very sharp decline to 120 in the 1980s and just 54 in the 1990s.

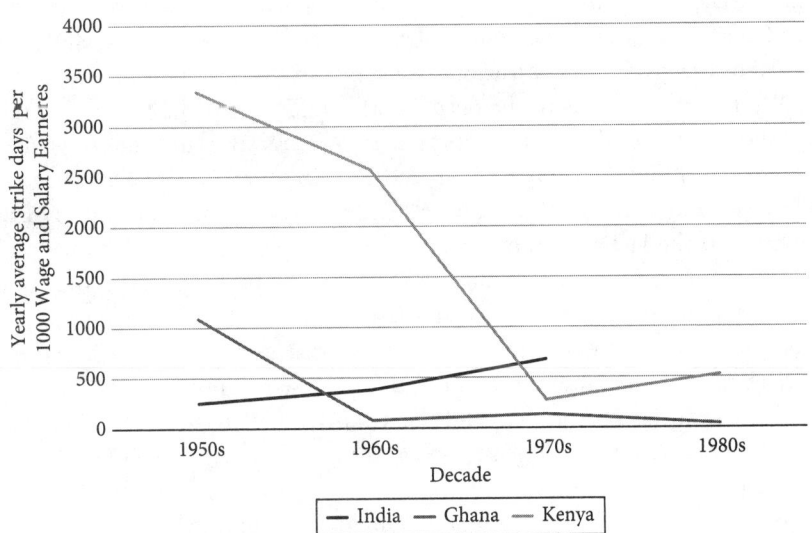

FIGURE 8.3 Strikes in Poorer Countries, 1950s–1980s

Despite the incompleteness and partial character of the statistics, it is difficult to doubt one universal result: strikes were frequent in the postwar and Upheaval eras. In some countries, the strike highpoint was the immediate postwar era; in others, the decades of the 1950s, 1960s, and—most commonly—the 1970s. In the Late-Millennium Era, the frequency of strikes has dropped, and dropped sharply, throughout the world—in wealthier and in poorer countries, on all continents, and in both the northern and southern hemispheres.[47]

A second reason for the decline of labor involves the increasing globalization of production. Unionized jobs can and are simply sent elsewhere, especially to Asia, the global black hole of labor, and have been for fifty years. It is no coincidence that the few successful efforts at trade union revival in Southern California were among truck drivers and deliverers, building maintenance workers, or (also in Los Angeles) construction carpenters—all forms of labor that cannot be sent to low-wage countries. It is also possible to bring low-wage workers to wealthier countries as a way of undermining unions, although one element of efforts at union revitalization has been attempts to connect with immigrants.

The third reason for labor's decline is the political environment. Even as the conservative political dominance of the 1980s gradually came to an end in the following decades, the center-left governments that replaced them in the United States, the United Kingdom, the Netherlands, and Germany, were all large disappointments for labor.[48] Left-of-center politicians have tended to accept the anti-labor policies initiated by conservatives in the 1980s, or just offered lip service to efforts to change it. They seem to have gone on to other issues—the environment, gender discrimination, and questions of individual rights—largely terminating the long-term close connection between organized labor and parties of the political left, a connection that made possible the pro-labor practices and institutions developed in the postwar era.

Expanding the focus to the entire world suggests that labor's difficulties are, above all, a result of the transformation of class structure resulting from the process of globalization. Unions, and pro-labor practices and institutions more generally, fit the class hierarchy developed in Europe and North America in the late nineteenth century and expanding all across the world by the 1960s. Unions were designed for and used by people working for a wage or salary, whether in manual, clerical, and even some technical and professional occupations, especially in the private sector. The new social hierarchy developing toward the end of the twentieth century was differently structured. Social position depended on individuals' relationship with the global labor market, making the previous understanding of labor's place in society obsolete.

Instead, "labor" has become a synonym for those protected from the effects of the world market. Probably the largest element is public employees, and, by 2000, unions were much, much more prevalent among them. In the former colonies of French West Africa, slightly over a third of public employees belonged to a union; a fifth in the organized private sector did; and in the informal sector, where the vast majority of the population worked, just one in fifty. Not just in Africa but everywhere in the world, a much higher proportion of public sector workers are unionized than private sector ones. The differences in union density are usually large. In 2000, the proportion of public sector workers unionized in the United States was four times than that of private sector workers (37 percent vs. 9 percent); it was eight times as great in Poland, six times as great in France, three times as great in Japan. Conditions in India were probably similar, but trade union statistics there are unreliable. In most countries, the gap in union density between the public and private sector was at least two to one; the exceptions were in the heavily unionized Nordic lands.[49] All this places labor in a fundamentally defensive position and encourages hostility on the part of those who lack unionized civil servants' protections from the global labor market and whose taxes fund public sector workers' salaries.

A related problem is that for almost a century, the trade unions, social welfare and workplace dispute legislation, and organizations were set up within individual sovereign states. As production became increasingly global, labor remained largely ensconced in its national borders. Solidarity between unions in different countries has been at most a rhetorical gesture. Even in the European Union, cooperation among unionists from different countries in European-wide enterprise councils is modest, at best. Particularly when there are decisions about which production site to close, the enterprise council representatives are more likely to favor closing a site in another country, than working together to preserve all locations. Of course, economic conditions in the different countries of the Europe Union are, on a global scale, relatively similar, making potential international cooperation easier. On issues such as the transfer of jobs from wealthy countries to poorer ones, the challenges of cooperation between labor in, say, the United States and India, or Germany and China are far bigger.[50] To put it simply, in the Late-Millennium Era, social structures changed, but labor and its representatives did not.

Four Workplaces

Illuminating the story of labor during the Age of Interconnection are those of four very different occupations, in four very different workplaces. Two are examples of manual labor: work on the docks and work on the assembly line in automobile manufacturing. The other two represent different kinds of work, though calling them "white collar," would be inaccurate, and rely on an archaic distinction. One involves airline flight attendants, whose work requires not just physical labor, but active interaction with customers. This is typical of a wide variety of service jobs, all of which feature a large proportion of women, in contrast to the largely male world of the assembly line and docks. The final occupation is computer programmer, characterized by the manipulation of symbols and information, and requiring an advanced education in science, mathematics, or related fields. All four of these occupations reflect the general picture of the development of labor presented in this chapter, but each in its own specific way.

To start on the waterfront, loading and unloading maritime cargo is a millennia-old occupation. (Technically, it consists of two occupations, that of longshoreman or docker, who handles the cargo on the pier or quay, and stevedore, who transfers the cargo in and out of the ship, though this distinction has blurred over time.) Working such a job requires great strength. This made the docks home to an all-male labor force and a macho atmosphere of power, violence, and heavy drinking. The dependence on human muscle power, and its cultural accompaniment went on much longer than one might think. As late as 1955 workers in the UK port of Hull, still unloaded grain by hand, picking the grain up with a large scoop and dumping it into canvas sacks.

Hull was, admittedly, rather backward by the standards of the time, and by 1955 there had seen a fair amount of mechanization of dock work. First steam-powered and then electric cranes helped to transfer cargo between ship and shore; electric and gasoline-powered carts made it easier to transport cargo once on land. Moving cargo from the ship's deck to its hold was facilitated by the electrification of winches. But increasing use of machinery did not mean less physical effort and less danger on the job. More powerful machinery meant larger cargo loads to stow in the hold or move off the docks in a shorter time. This meant greater dangers.

If a docker's job was dangerous and physically demanding, it was also precarious. Working on the docks was perhaps the ultimate example of casual labor, day to day. While dockers worked for a variety of employers, they invariably experienced the daily "shape up," in which they presented themselves at the docks and hoped to be picked for work. Typically, it was subcontractors, called *serangs* in the Indian Ocean port of Mombasa, who recruited a gang of laborers for a task. Being chosen for such a gang might involve paying a bribe to the subcontractor or belonging to the same ethnic or national group. In postwar New York, it was well known that the Irish dominated the Manhattan docks and the Italians those in Brooklyn. Generally residing in waterfront neighborhoods, so they could be at the daily shape up bright and early, dockworkers supplemented their meager and often erratic pay by pilfering. "Twenty quid a week and half the cargo," was how the dockers in Freemantle, Australia, described their pay. Shipments of whiskey, in particular, were unlikely to emerge unscathed. This small-scale appropriation easily shaded into more serious theft by gangsters, who were a strong presence on docks around the world.

From the late nineteenth century onward, dock workers had begun to organize and form unions. Their great demand was decasualization, the transformation of jobs into permanent positions with guaranteed pay. On the London docks, the first collective bargaining agreements involving decasualization were in the 1890s, but it was over seventy years before they became universal. The dockers of Hamburg, Germany's largest seaport, won decasualization agreements in 1919, as part of the labor upheavals following the First World War, only to lose them in the inflation crisis of 1923. Worldwide, it was in the postwar era, of labor's ascendancy, that dock work as precarious day labor came to an end. Dockworkers were split into two groups: those on the roster of permanent workers and could claim a daily wage, whether there was work for them or not; and those who were registered but only offered paid employment when it was available.

Decasualization proceeded in sometimes surprising sequences, earlier in Mombasa than in London, for instance. Perhaps the most turbulent and difficult example of decasualization was on the east and Gulf coast ports of the United States, where it involved the expulsion of the gangster-ridden leadership of the trade union, the International Longshoremen's Association, which had written casual labor into its collective bargaining agreements, as a way of intimidating and subordinating the union's members. (By contrast, the union representing West Coast dockworkers, the communist-dominated International Longshoremen and Warehouse Union, had strongly endorsed decasualization, and won it, following the great strike of 1934.) The course of decasualization was shown, admittedly with a good dose of melodrama, in one of the classics of American cinema, Elia Kazan's 1954 film *On the Waterfront*. Generally occurring with less conflict than in Hollywood's depiction, decasualization became the rule around the world.[51]

While there had certainly been mechanization of dock work in the postwar era, particularly the use of vacuum hoses to load and unload bulk cargoes of grain, or pipeline arrangements for oil tankers, an increasingly important form of cargo, brawny physical labor was still typical into the beginning of the 1970s. Then came the introduction of the shipping container, the metal box that could be moved intermodally. This transformed work on the docks beyond all recognition. In place of the eight eight-men gangs that loaded or unloaded an individual freighter, there was a UTR driver, whose vehicle moved the container on the pier, the crane operator, who ran the giant machine that transferred the containers from the pier to the container ship's hold and its deck, and two or three lashers, who secured the containers on deck.[52]

In the Late-Millennium Era, containerization spread around the world. The need for great strength in waterfront labor vanished, along with the skill and experience needed to stow cargo most efficiently in a ship's hold, and with them went most of the waterfront labor force. The twenty-five thousand men toiling on the docks in Liverpool during the 1950s, for instance, were reduced to just two thousand, by the end of the 1980s. In some wealthier countries, the redundant workers continued to receive a guaranteed wage. New York dockers had to report to the hiring hall every day, but could usually leave in a few hours, without working but with a day's pay. After that, some worked different jobs; others devoted themselves to caring for children or grandchildren, and even cooking for their families—a change from the macho culture of the docks. Margaret Thatcher eliminated these sorts of redundancy measures in the United Kingdom, leading 80 percent of the dockworkers to leave their occupation between 1989 and 1992. This was the Iron Lady's thanks to the dockers, who had refused to go on strike in support of the coal miners five years earlier and had unloaded imported coal. Poorer countries had no such measures; the surplus dockworkers in Mumbai fell into the ranks of the informal sector of the economy. In effect, the best that labor could hope for on the Late-Millennium Era waterfront was a managed retreat; efforts to resist the direction of dock work, such as the Liverpool dock strike of 1995–98, were resoundingly defeated.[53]

If dock work was a long-established occupation and form of labor, assembly line work in automobile manufacturing was a quintessential form of modernity in the twentieth century. The cinematic representation of assembly line work was Charlie Chaplin's 1936 film *Modern Times*—the title speaks for itself—that showed a human turned into a machine, and a badly malfunctioning one, by the need to keep up with the pace of labor set by an assembly line. Reality in automobile manufacturing was not so grotesque and definitely not so funny, but the rapid pace of work on the line, the tedium and physical strain of performing a single operation, and the resulting repetitive motion injuries, made the auto factory a difficult workplace. Unlike the gangs on the docks, who largely worked on their own, autoworkers faced strict labor discipline, authoritarian supervisors, and a workplace continuously reshaped by efficiency engineers. Although autoworkers' wages were often good—from the time Henry Ford started paying them an astonishing five dollars a day in 1914—and employment relatively steady (at least compared to dock work), the demanding working conditions made for high labor force turnover rates.[54]

Auto manufacturing was and remains divided into four main divisions (as usual, there are different variations on these, with different names): the machine shop, for producing the drive train; the press shop, which bends and stamps metal into auto body parts; paint and welding to turn those into auto bodies; and assembly, in which the engine and the passenger compartment are placed into the body. Most of the assembly work is unskilled, or, at least, required relatively little training. (There were exceptions, such as some of the welding.) The skilled workers who made the dies that stamped and bent metal into the auto body and maintained the production machinery were in a minority.[55]

There was nothing so transformative in auto manufacturing as the introduction of containers to dock work. Technological change maintained the basic structure of manufacturing with its four divisions, though gradually meant replacing humans with machines (primarily, robots) to do welding and painting. By contrast, the final step in the manufacturing process, assembly, which involves bodily contortion, workers crouching under lifted car bodies to fasten the undercarriage and the engine, or crawling inside car bodies, to put in the dashboard, was much better suited to human beings than to industrial robots. Probably the largest change in the labor of auto manufacturing was the introduction of a new version of labor relations, from the 1960s onward. This was the system of "quality circles," which purportedly replaced the mass production "Fordist" system of assembly line work, characterized by individual workers performing the same task, under hierarchical and authoritarian supervision, with groups of workers, supervisors, and management getting together to discuss ways to make production more efficient. As part of the discussion, workers within teams would trade off jobs, which would make assembly line labor both more varied and more productive, and, perhaps, not work on an assembly line at all.

The idea of quality circles began in 1950s Japan in the human relations departments of large corporations, who applied it to workers' wives, to encourage them to be more efficient and productive as homemakers. The proceeding was taken up by engineers, supervisors, and managers, and, by the 1970s, had come to include industrial workers. The rise of the Japanese auto industry in world markets was widely attributed to this new form of labor relations, and efforts were soon under way across the world to copy it.[56]

Quality circles have been the subject of debate among sociologists and industrial relations experts as to whether they are a genuinely new way of organizing labor relations in mass production industries in general, and auto manufacturing in particular, or whether they are largely a more sophisticated version of the existing state of affairs in mass production.[57] It is not clear if the increasing sales success of Japanese auto manufacturers was a result of a new systems of industrial relations, or of superior engineering, producing affordable vehicles that could decrease cars' emissions while simultaneously improving fuel efficiency. More broadly, the global spread of quality circles can best be seen as a response to industrial workers' militant strike actions and their rebellion against managerial discipline.

In the auto industry there were few dramatic examples of massive conflict, similar to the strikes of the air traffic controllers, the textile workers, and the coal miners. The one really drastic instance took place at the Fiat works in Turin, the center of Italian auto manufacturing. There, during the 1970s, labor indiscipline and rebellion against management authority had shaded over into violent acts by workers sympathizing with anarchist and terrorist groups: they sabotaged machinery, torched stocks of raw materials, and attacked union leaders, works council members, and even ordinary workers, who wanted to cooperate with management. Not only did militants blockade the factory, they occupied the streets around it, disrupting traffic in Turin and upsetting the city's inhabitants. In 1980, a large-scale strike against mass layoffs—some twenty-four thousand workers were to be dismissed—lasting several weeks, was decided when management, white-collar staff, and even some blue-collar production and maintenance workers, launched an enormous demonstration, some forty thousand strong, against the strike. The strikers returned to work the next day; the mass layoffs proceeded without interruption; and the firm's management regained control of the factory.[58]

More common than dramatic confrontation was the gradual reassertion of management control. The implementation of quality circles became a way to restore managerial prerogatives against militant labor rather than a way to introduce a new system of industrial relations. Many of the methods of purportedly improving efficiency proposed by members of one quality circle involved moving work to members of another quality circle. The crucial adaptation of quality circles to auto manufacturing—that anybody, even ordinary production workers, could stop the assembly line if there were production problems or defects—was generally not seen outside Japan. Stopping the line was a foreman's and management prerogative; workers who did so would be disciplined or dismissed. Some elements of production were taken off the assembly line and performed at non-moving workstations—such as the fitting of stamped and painted door frames with windows, controls, padding, and interior finish—but these had to be done at a rapid pace, so the finished product could be returned to the assembly line.

Finally, while quality circles fit well with the complacent, pro-management style of Japanese unionism, they fared less well in the antagonistic English-speaking or codeterminist European models of unionism. When Nissan—which went beyond most Japanese manufacturers in not even tolerating cooperative, pro-management unions—opened an auto plant in Melbourne in 1976, and summoned its militantly unionized Aussie workers to meetings to discuss improving productivity, the workers were convinced that all the talk about cooperation was just a pretext to get them to work harder. As for shifting jobs, they were reluctant to do that, because jobs to which they changed would be paid less. Never able to implement its vision of production, Nissan closed the plant in 1992. This experience shows why when opening plants in the United States or UK Nissan, exactly like other Japanese auto manufacturers, was very careful to insist on a non-union workforce and to choose economically depressed regions—rural areas of the

US South and Midwest, dying industrial cities of northern England—whose inhabitants were desperate for jobs and would work as directed.[59]

By 2000, growing mechanization of auto manufacturing and the expansion of the East Asian model of industrial relations in auto production had weakened the place of labor in auto manufacturing, its one-time stronghold. Union membership was in decline, and management, wielding the threat of transferring production to sites of cheap labor in Mexico, Eastern Europe, or Asia, was on the offensive. Yet both the Anglo-Saxon antagonistic and European codeterminist versions of industrial relations, and the unions that embodied them continued to exist. Labor's influence in codeterminist regimes was particularly apparent. In 2018, when most of the management of Volkswagen had discredited itself by its involvement in the diesel-emissions cheating scandal, it was the veteran metalworkers union representative and chair of VW's works council, Bernd Osterloh, who had emerged as the strong man in Europe's largest auto manufacturer.[60]

Talking of strong men makes the difference between flight attendants and dock or autoworkers clear: on the one hand, a predominantly male workplace, where the movement, shaping and construction of things was the main task; on the other, a predominantly female workplace, in which developing a rapport with customers was the central element. At the beginnings of commercial aviation during the 1930s, flight attendants were men, following the practice on railroads and passenger ships. Using women as flight attendants was a marketing novelty ploy, and the women first employed in that way before the Second World War—exclusively in the United States—were all registered nurses.

The occupation of flight attendant and its gender dynamics was a product of the postwar era, which saw the large-scale expansion of commercial aviation within an economic regime of highly regulated capitalism. Prices were fixed by national or international boards; outside the United States, airlines were typically government-owned monopolies. Without much in the way of price competition, airlines sought to gain passengers by providing in-flight amenities, and the amenity they offered was to staff each plane with a crew of attractive young women. Following in the wake of the pioneering nurses of the 1930s, these stewardesses would see to safety regulations, boarding, deplaning, stowing luggage, and directing an emergency evacuation. Nonetheless their chief and most time-consuming task was to interact with the passengers. They would serve them meals and liquor, but, still more important, be a smiling, cheerful presence, calming fears about flying, a new and scary way to travel. Elegantly dressed and carefully made up—a central and very closely monitored part of their job, complete with girdle and brassiere checks, as well as rules prohibiting hair-dyeing, then perceived as trashy—they encouraged the customers, very disproportionately affluent and male, to feel comfortable and appreciated, diverting them from the otherwise tedious and unpleasant experiences of air travel.

Stewardesses were young, chic, and glamorous; in the early 1950s, they were even compared to movie stars. They were a well-educated group. Half the stewardesses hired by the main US overseas airline of the era, Pan-American, had attended college, and 20 percent of them possessed a bachelor degree. They had to be single; marriage, to say nothing of motherhood, would end their career and airlines imposed an upper age limit—generally early thirties—after which they could no longer work. This occupational model was invented in the United States, and, like so much in the postwar era, spread from there around the world, with the result that men, who had dominated airline passenger service before 1945, were increasingly eliminated from the occupation. Canada and India hired American stewardesses to train their own employees in the right appearance, deportment, and attitude. Even the Soviets' communist airline *Aeroflot* adopted the American model. Although by contemporary standards a cesspool of sexism, veteran flight attendants themselves tended to look back on the 1950s as something of a golden age, when commercial flights, in slow-moving propeller-driven aircraft, still had relatively few passengers, leaving time for stewardesses to interact with them when the emotional and physical demands of the job were bearable and the work even enjoyable.

The introduction of jet aircraft in the 1960s transformed the occupation. The new planes meant more passengers and much shorter flight times. To deal with the need to serve more customers in less time, the meal cart was introduced on airplanes, replacing the previous practice of stewardesses bringing meal trays to passengers individually. While more efficient, the cart made it much more difficult to be gracious. As one stewardess put it in 1968, "To get the work done, you have to be short with the passengers." Another stated, "I just can't coddle 130 people at one time. But they all expect it and get downright rude when they don't get it." Airline deregulation, beginning in the United States at the end of the 1970s and spreading around the world in the two subsequent decades, magnified this state of affairs a thousand-fold. There were still more passengers, and, the previously dominant group of affluent business travelers were being swamped by *hoi polloi*, "discount people," or the "hairy armpit crowd," as flight attendants called them, who were unfamiliar with the social conventions of air travel. Adding to the pressure was the privatization of government-owned airlines and the rise of discount carriers, whose lower fares meant constant competitive demands for cost-cutting. In these circumstances, being elegant was increasingly a physically, and emotionally draining, performance.

During the postwar era of labor ascendancy, stewardesses had been unionized. (The exception in the United States was Delta Airlines, based in the virulently anti-labor South.) They had their own version of the Upheaval

Era labor militancy, which focused on the creation of autonomous unions, rather than affiliation with male-dominated airline pilots and transit workers' groups, as had previously been the case, and on eliminating the rules dismissing married or older stewardesses. Explicitly feminist ideas articulated in that era found, not too surprisingly, given the nature of the occupation, relatively little support among flight attendants—a phrase that generally replaced "stewardess." Instead, they made the argument that women over thirty or who were married could still be attractive. As a result, the occupation was gradually transformed from a brief, adventurous interlude in a young woman's life, traveling to exotic destinations, before settling into marriage and motherhood, into a long-term career, extending across marriage and family and well into middle age.[61]

As management on US-flag air carriers was pressured into eliminating this previous model, their European counterparts doing the same, Asian competitors took it up. Starting in 1972 with Singapore International Airlines, and going from there to Cathay Pacific, Thai International, Philippine Airlines, Malaysian Airlines, Air China and then, at the very end of the century, the Gulf airlines, particularly Emirates, management would only hire attractive, single young women as flight attendants, for relatively short periods of time. Playing on Western stereotypes, appealing to affluent, full-fare-paying, middle-aged, male business travelers, they became formidable competitors, especially on the booming trans-Pacific routes. It was yet another form of low-wage East Asian competition, for American or European businesses.[62]

By the Late-Millennium Era, flight attendants found themselves involved in labor conflicts, generally trying to defend their position against privatizing and cost-cutting corporate managers. The 1986 strike of TWA flight attendants was one of many in 1980s America to be defeated by the hiring of permanent replacements. Admittedly, the flight attendants were luckier than other strikers, because most of them did ultimately get their jobs back—only to lose them again in the airline's repeated bankruptcies and its absorption by American Airlines. By contrast, the 1993 strike of 3,500 flight attendants at Hong Kong-based Cathay Pacific Airlines, was a rare example of Asian labor activism and relatively successful labor activism at that. In 1997, flight attendants working for privatized British Airlines went on strike against cutbacks management proposed; their strike gained an unusual measure of international solidarity. Mechanics in the United States refused to service planes BA chartered to maintain service during the strike, and flight attendants from the United States and the Netherlands would not work on those planes. Ground crews in Zimbabwe and Malta blocked BA planes on the runway.[63]

If flight attendants have done a little better than many other occupations in defending their position during an era when trends were moving steadily in labor's disfavor, it is nonetheless the case that their workplace was irreversibly transformed in the Late-Millennium Era. It was not a fundamentally new technology that did so, as had been the case with the dockers, nor was it the combination of technological and organizational innovation, as occurred in auto factories. The labor of flight attendants was the same in 2000 as in 1965. Some elements of the job were modernized: girdle checks were out and women who were older, married, or mothers could continue to work, and by then made up a majority of flight attendants (creating other stresses). But the need to accommodate more people in in a shorter time, made it even less possible to demonstrate the emotional empathy required for the job. It was an issue increasingly faced by labor in other customer service positions, although being trapped in a giant metal tube at forty thousand feet amplified the difficulty.[64]

Dock work is a form of labor that goes back to antiquity; auto assembly began in the early twentieth century; and flight attendants largely after 1945. The work of coding and computer programming is basically an invention of the 1960s and the introduction of widespread computer use in business. The fundamental issue for employment in information technology was revealed at the very beginning of the occupation, in the course of the first large-scale networking projects of financial services and flight reservations. These and similar projects proved to be much more difficult than expected, experienced substantial delays and cost overruns, or failed entirely. The conclusion from this experience, drawn in the 1968 and 1969 NATO conferences on software engineering (the origins of that now-common phrase) in Garmisch-Partenkirchen and Rome was the idea of automating the writing of software. This aspiration has continued down to the present; current interest in AI, neural networks, and machine learning are the latest versions. Results have been less encouraging. As the saying goes, "Programmers have done a good job of automating everyone's work but their own."[65]

For such a high-tech branch of the labor force, the technology of programming has changed little in the Age of Interconnection. Programming languages have gone from FORTRAN and COBOL to C++ and Java, and programmers enter their code directly into a computer, rather than writing it out longhand on a spreadsheet (an actual gridded piece of paper, not the computer programs whose interfaces were designed to resemble it) having it typed up by a key-puncher, and the punch cards then placed in a reader by an operator. The problems of time, expense, and project difficulty or failure, however, have not abated. If anything, as the reach of IT has spread throughout the economy and into every crack and crevice of production, marketing, financing, and administration, these problems have grown more considerable.

Like the Internet, Google, GPS and so much of the contemporary IT world, major changes in the programming workplace were a product of the final decade of the twentieth century. These changes can be summed up very simply: if automation and technological innovation could not lower the cost of writing software, then it would be necessary to find a way to make the labor of writing software cheaper. An initial version of this aspiration was for businesses to outsource their IT operations to firms that specialized in information technology. The first major deal of this kind occurred in 1989, when Eastman Kodak contracted with IBM to run its entire computer operations. This form of outsourcing expanded rapidly in the subsequent decade, at first in the United States, but soon after in Europe and Japan. It has continued down to the present.[66]

Many of these outsourcing initiatives did not result in the large declines in labor costs that corporate managers were expecting, so the next step was not just outsourcing IT work but offshoring it to countries with cheap labor. Facilitated by the growth of the Internet and the development of a worldwide network of fiber-optic cables in the 1990s, this also began on a large scale in that decade, and has also continued down to the present, a major example of how the globalization of work has not been limited to production and manufacturing but expanded to include business services. The process has tended to follow linguistic lines, firms from wealthier countries looking to outsource their IT labor to countries where their language is spoken: from English-speaking countries to India, from Western Europe to Eastern Europe, and from Japan to northern China. Because this form of outsourcing began in the United States and has remained most common there—although EU countries and Japan have been rapidly catching up—this has made India the most important node of cheap IT labor.[67]

It is a matter of dispute just how successful and cost-effective this kind of outsourcing actually is. Top management generally has a far more favorable opinion of the costs saved by and the quality of the outsourced IT work than mid-level managers and IT experts who actually run the outsourcing projects. What is certainly the case is that outsourcing has not been the only way to revamp IT labor. Rather than sending IT work abroad, cheap immigrant labor has been brought to wealthier countries. In the United States, the H1-B visa program, instituted in 1990, supposedly for the purpose of redressing labor shortages, has been used for this purpose to considerable effect. Fifty-two percent of the recipients of such visas in 2001 worked in IT. While since the 1990s employers have periodically claimed that they cannot find anyone to do programming jobs, hence they must bring in additional labor from abroad, the reality seems somewhat different. As one tech CEO noted in 2000, "If you're willing to pay market rate, you can find people. The issue is if you're budget-constrained, you can't get the people you want." Repeated news stories of IT workers being laid off and told that they will only receive severance pay if they train H1-B visa holders replacing them reinforce the point that such visas are part of a broader search for cheap labor. It is the most experienced and best paid programmers who are the most affected by this practice. The IT director of a large law firm explained in 1998, "I'd love to have somebody with 20 years of experience, but unfortunately, I'm only paying for three or four." By the early twenty-first century, only one-fifth of individuals with computer science degrees were still working in their field twenty years after graduation, while half of engineers were doing so.[68]

Yet another way to cut the costs of IT work has been the use of temporary workers, contractors, and subcontractors. During the 1990s, the Microsoft Corporation, then the leading IT firm in the world, became famous for its use of contractors. Wearing their orange ID badges, and so distinguished from the blue-badge-wearing regularly employed workers at Microsoft's Redmond, Washington, corporate headquarters, contractors worked side by side with permanent employees, but without receiving the same pay or fringe benefits. Mark Holstrom's observation about conditions in Indian factories in the late 1970s, seen as strange and exceptional then—an outrageous peculiarity of an impoverished country—became a familiar US reality within a matter of two decades. In 2000, following an eight-year legal battle, Microsoft admitted that it treated the contractors not as temporary workers but as permanent employees and agreed to pay $97 million in back pay and benefits. Although the firm has been more cautious about fulfilling proper legal requirements since then, it has continued to employ contractors and to get workers from subcontractors—some two thousand of them in 2015. Those workers continue to wear their distinctive orange badge and to work alongside permanent workers. The size of the Microsoft Corporation and its public visibility make its employment practices particularly evident, but very far from atypical. In 1995, 13 percent of US IT workers were in temporary positions, independent contractors, or employed by subcontractors. Twenty years later, that figure had reached as high as 23 percent.[69]

Compared with dockers, autoworkers or flight attendants, computer programmers and code writers remain in a realm of high pay and autonomous labor. Their occupation has been relatively immune to the technological innovations that eliminated most of the dock labor force and made the labor conditions of autoworkers and flight attendants more difficult. But the economic forces reshaping labor at the end of the twentieth and the beginning of the twenty-first centuries, the globalization of production and services, and the casualization of labor, the move away from permanent employment, have affected programmers and code writers as well. Non-unionized (just 4 percent of IT workers in the United States were union members in 2015), and, given the prevalence of libertarian views in the occupation, unlikely to be interested in joining, programmers lack even the relatively feeble support unions can still provide, and remain at the mercy of market forces. In this respect, their situation is typical of labor in the Age of Interconnection, as the guarantees and bulwarks won by labor in its postwar era of ascendancy have been swept away in the rush of globalization at the end of the old millennium and the beginning of the new.

9 | Leisure

IF THE STORY OF labor in the Age of Interconnection is, ultimately, one of decline, its obverse, leisure, presents a very different picture—not just an increase in leisure time, but the introduction of distinctly new ways to fill nonwork hours. Reaching a conclusion about the extent and nature of leisure is trickier than it might seem at first, since leisure is a residual category, what remains of the day after paid labor, unpaid labor (household labor—cooking, cleaning, and childcare), and personal maintenance, in the form of eating, sleeping, and grooming, have been accounted for. In addition, there are large areas of overlap between each of the three forms of non-leisure activity and leisure itself. Studies done before the Second World War did not include childcare as labor, on the assumption that women just naturally enjoyed taking care of children. It seems clear that commuting, traveling from home to the workplace, while not paid, belongs with paid labor; the status of shopping—household, personal, or leisure—is more ambiguous.

Systematic studies of leisure—as opposed to casual observations, or the morally disapproving rumbles of pundits and philosophers—generally proceed from a very specific genre of social science research, the "time diary." Volunteers are asked to note precisely what they did during a given day or week, and how long they spent doing it. Although this kind of study began in the early twentieth century and has been carried out down to the present, only people in Europe, North America, and a few affluent countries elsewhere in the world have filled out these diaries. For most of Asia, Latin America, and Africa, accounts of leisure therefore remain more impressionistic.[1]

What the analysis of these documents shows is that the Age of Interconnection has been the age of leisure, a period of decline in both hours of paid labor and of unpaid work. While there had been some modest gains in leisure time earlier in the century, they were overshadowed by postwar years, leading to 2000, during which average leisure increased by about eight hours per week.[2] These results may come as a surprise to some readers, because they seem to go against two common impressions. One is that women have much less free time than men, because they have moved into the paid workforce without any lessening of their household obligations. The other is that the trend to more leisure has been reversed in the Late-Millennium Era, that people are working longer hours, commuting over greater distances, and taking less vacation. The impression is that life has become increasingly frenzied. Both impressions are basically wrong. A closer analysis of them reveals that people have more free time and are engaged in less labor. Yet while that seems like an unambiguously good thing, it proves to have some negative sides as well.

Since women across the globe do bear most of the burden of household labor, one common argument is that whatever makes such labor easier and potentially less time-consuming also makes it more exacting. Washing machines and vacuum cleaners make cleaning easier, quicker, and less physically demanding, but this just means that clothes get washed and floors, carpets, and rugs get cleaned more often and more extensively. Gas or electric stoves, refrigerators, and later, microwave ovens, reduce the time needed for buying and preparing food, but expectations of more elaborate meals result in more time put into cooking. Birth rates go down, but fewer children means that each child receives much greater and more time-consuming attention. Supporting this viewpoint are the findings of time diaries, which show that women in the United States were spending as much time—some fifty-six hours a week—doing unpaid household labor in the 1960s, as they had fifty years earlier. The large-scale movement of women into the paid labor force in the 1970s and 1980s shrank their leisure time still further.

The problem with this argument is that the initial studies done in years before the Second World War disproportionately involved upper middle-class women, a group that typically employed servants. During and after the Second World War, other and better employment opportunities opened up for domestic workers, so that work that had formerly been the paid employment of others now became the unpaid toil of these affluent and educated women. Estimates done by economist Valerie Ramey, who has taken into account the changing social composition of the keepers of time-study diaries, suggest that the weekly household labor of American women declined by four to six hours between 1900 and the mid-1960s from the upper to the lower '50s. This was followed by a steep drop, as much as nine hours per week, by 1975. American women's household labor has remained at that level, low-to-mid forty hours per week, ever since. That rapid change might be attributed to the growing numbers of women entering the labor force, though Ramey's figures show that the decline in household work was most pronounced (twelve hours) among women who were not employed outside the home. It was not a result of increasing use of labor-saving devices, since most American homes were already well-equipped with refrigerators, vacuum cleaners, and washing machines by the 1950s. Instead, this rapid and sudden decline in American women's household work—and there were parallel developments in Europe—was yet another feature of the Era of Upheaval, reflecting the spread of feminist aspirations.[3]

Another way to put this is to say that while both men and women in the world's wealthier countries experienced increases in leisure time, these were the result of increases in paid labor and decreases in unpaid labor, and these occurred in gender-specific ways. The time men spent each week doing paid labor went down, while the time they put into household work went up; for women, it was the other way around. The labor patterns of both sexes became closer, and the total number of hours of paid and unpaid work converged as well, although even today men continue to spend more time in paid labor and women more time in household work—the exact amounts differing from country to country.

The idea that people were working more and had less free time is another common notion not confirmed by the study of time diaries. Here as well, the misconception conceals two significant developments in the use of time. One is the growing divergence between the United States and all the other wealthy countries of the world. In the latter, the hours of paid labor have been in decline since the mid-1970s: both hours of work per week, and the number of weeks working per year have been decreasing. Nothing of the sort has happened in the United States. By 2000, Americans worked on average two to four weeks per year and two to five hours per week longer than their counterparts in other affluent lands. Hours of paid labor had been shorter in the United States than in the world's other wealthy countries between 1900 and 1950, and in the Era of Upheaval were roughly the same. As a result of the global realignments in class structure, and the particularly rapid and painful decline of the position and power of labor in the United States Americans found their leisure time lagging behind that enjoyed by inhabitants of peer countries at the end of the millennium. In Europe, Australia, and, increasingly, even Japan, thirty-five-hour workweeks, five weeks yearly paid vacation, and early retirement contrasted with an America of longer hours on the job, fewer and briefer vacations, and continued labor into the initial years of old age. It would be most accurate to say that the period brought more leisure for Americans but noticeably more leisure for inhabitants of other affluent countries.[4]

There is another way that the social distribution of leisure time changed in the Late-Millennium Era, reversing a decades-old trend, in this case within individual countries and not between them. Although reliable figures are only available from the 1960s, it seems likely that earlier educated men had shorter paid workweeks and more leisure time than their less-educated counterparts. This was not necessarily the case among women—though, of course, women were also much less likely to be in the labor force than men. (Figures for work and leisure by income are scanty and not entirely reliable, but they showed relatively little difference in the average paid workweek for men from different income groups, while poor women did more paid work than their affluent counterparts.) By the end of the century, this relationship had been completely reversed: education was associated with longer hours of paid labor and less leisure, both for men and women, while fewer hours of work and more leisure time were associated with lower levels of education: college graduates worked as high as 30 percent more hours on average than those who had not finished high school. In the Late-Millennium Era—statistics come from studies done between 1985 and 1999—people in the top quarter of the income distribution were working a lot more—between 30 and 70 percent more hours per week than the bottom income quarter. Between the 1960s and 2000, overall men's hours of employment had declined, and women's had increased, but the hours of employment of the educated and affluent had declined the least for men and increased the most for women, while poor and uneducated men were doing less paid work and their female counterparts were spending the same amount of time in paid employment. In other words, the decline in men's paid working hours was concentrated heavily in the lower classes of the population, while the increase in women's paid labor was concentrated in the upper classes.

The Late-Millennium Era was a period in which income inequality in the world's wealthiest countries increased dramatically. Economists sometimes like to suggest that instead of inequality increasing preferences in labor and leisure were changing: the affluent preferred longer working hours (or, at least, not much shorter ones) and higher incomes, while the poor preferred less paid work and more leisure. Only economists would say this. The poor had more leisure because they were unemployed or working part-time, a result of the transformations of global class structure and the growth of a lower class largely excluded from the global market economy.

One way to see the conviction that the Late-Millennium Era was an age of increasing labor is to look at the findings from the world's time-diaries expert, the British sociologist Jonathan Gershuny. Gershuny has analyzed the time spent at work during workdays between the 1960s and 2000. These show the development of the length of the average working day—not the number of weeks worked or the changes in work time produced by unemployment. The average paid working day declined from the 1960s into the 1970s, only to increase again. Admittedly, all the changes were very modest, just on the order of 5 percent, but revealed that by 2000 the average workday was getting longer. Outside the United States, the growth of vacations and public holidays more than compensated for the slight lengthening of the workday, while in an America—with fewer vacations and year-round labor—the change was more noticeable. While the best-educated and the most affluent had average workdays shorter than their poorer and less-educated counterparts in the 1960s, by 2000 they were generally working longer hours than them. Given that it is the experience of the educated and affluent that so often shapes public perceptions, their longer working day played a distinct role in the idea of a society having less leisure.[5]

In the end, leisure, like labor, appears as both blessing and curse. Overall, in the Age of Interconnection, the amount of free time increased. Since leisure is a residual, its rise was the result of developments in the realm of paid and unpaid labor; personal maintenance hours remained basically the same. Changes in household labor were clear: women's household burdens declined, the single largest change in the way the hours of the week were spent. Men put more time into household labor, and as a result the tasks involved in it were shared more equitably. The story with paid labor is more complex and ambiguous. Certainly, some developments seem positive. Overall, fewer hours each week were spent in paid labor, although men's working time went down while women's went up. However, the decrease in men's paid labor outweighed their increase in unpaid labor. And while women worked more paid hours, they worked increasingly fewer unpaid ones. In both cases, at least theoretically, leisure was always on the rise. It seems that the decrease in the paid workweek is actually a combination of unemployment and part-time labor for the less-educated and less-affluent, with steady or even sometimes rising hours of labor (as noted earlier) for the well-educated and well-to-do. There was a bifurcation of society into those with involuntarily too much time on their hands and those who feel harried and stressed by their jobs. Most of the decline in working hours came from the expansion of time off the job, in the form of vacations and holidays. Particularly in the United States, which went its own way in the late twentieth century by not reducing yearly labor time as in other affluent countries, the end of the millennium seemed like an era of intensified paid labor, with relatively little in the way of gains in leisure.

These observations of course all apply only to the world's wealthier countries. It is hard to know whether there were different trends in Asia, Africa, or much of Latin America. What figures—from the wealthier countries—show is that during the Age of Interconnection the poorer the country, the longer the hours men spent in paid labor and women spent in unpaid household labor, and the less leisure time they had. This suggests a world of greater toil and less free time outside of Europe, North America, Australia, or Japan, although it is certainly possible that in some of its more affluent regions—East Asia, parts of Latin America—leisure time may have been growing.

The Glowing Box

If we ask what people have done in their leisure time during the Age of Interconnection, the simple answer is that they watched TV. Once the box was in the house, there was no escaping. Between a third and a half of leisure hours were spent staring at it; increased TV viewing moved in lockstep with growing leisure time. While the usual caveats about those parts of the world lacking time diaries apply, anthropologists and communications scholars have observed the same rapid colonization of leisure time in Caracas, Hyderabad, Xian, and north Indian villages.[6] This equation between leisure and watching TV made the Age of Interconnection the era of television. The era's characteristics followed from the intersection of the development of broadcast technology and its rapid implementation with the desire of consumers to obtain and to use (even obsessively) devices to receive these broadcasts. This intersection evolved through the course of five decades, coming to affect most of the world. Over the decades, particularly the final ones of the millennium, broadcast technology and the economic, political, and social organization of broadcasting changed remarkably, as did the significance, meaning, and global interconnections of television viewing. What didn't change was the centrality of TV.

Television was the very opposite of a sudden development. Work on a device that could transmit moving images electrically dates back to the late nineteenth century, even before the invention of radio or motion pictures. Efforts moved into high gear in the 1920s, following the invention and widespread use of the vacuum diode. As a result, the number of people who can claim to have invented TV is large, and spread out over many countries. These include the Scotsman John Baird, the Japanese engineer Kanjiro Takayanagi, his French counterpart René Barthélémy, and the American teenage inventor Philo Farnsworth. By far the most colorful of this group was the German inventor Manfred von Ardenne—less for his work on TV than for his later career, which included running his own personal nuclear weapons program during the Nazi era and then becoming the most successful capitalist entrepreneur and the largest private employer in communist East Germany. If any one person can be regarded as television's inventor, however, it was the Russian-American engineer, Vladimir Zworykin, who constructed the first camera and receiver using cathode ray tubes to capture and to display images.[7]

Regular TV broadcasting began toward the end of the 1930s in Germany (the 1936 Berlin Olympic Games were the first sporting event to be televised, although the picture quality was poor), the United States, and the United Kingdom. The latter was by far the most advanced in this respect, with some twenty thousand TV sets receiving broadcasts on the eve of the Second World War. In a number of countries, including France, the USSR and Uruguay, there were initial experiments with TV transmission, if not yet any regular broadcasts. TV was clearly on its way, but the outbreak of the Second World War disrupted development. Broadcasting resumed in the immediate aftermath of the war, first in the United States, and then spread to the usual affluent suspects in Western Europe, Japan, and the South Seas during the 1950s. That decade also saw the beginning of broadcasting in the Eastern Bloc and in Latin America, where, somewhat unexpectedly, it was Cuba that took the lead in TV's introduction. After the 1958 revolution, large numbers of Cuba's television personnel fled the country, bringing their broadcasting expertise to Spanish-speaking audiences, from Los Angeles to Buenos Aires.[8]

No sooner were African countries free of colonial rule that they started TV broadcasting: among others, Zambia, Kenya, Burkina Faso, Ivory Coast, and Uganda by 1965; Zaire, Niger, Togo, Angola, Mozambique, and Djibouti, early in the following decade. Broadcasting also began in the Arab world in the 1960s. Although India, along with Pakistan and Indonesia, initiated TV broadcasts at that time, it was only on an experimental basis, with a very narrow range of educational programs, on the air for a few hours a day. Full-scale broadcasting in India started somewhat later, in 1976.[9]

This rapid adoption of the new medium, worldwide, is all the more impressive in view of the technological difficulties and the additional expense connected with it. Unlike radio waves, which can travel over long distances, making it relatively easy to broadcast to a wide audience, the very-high-frequency electromagnetic radiation used for TV broadcasts propagates only across line-of-sight, so an elaborate and expensive network of multiple television towers and connections via coaxial cable is necessary to broadcast over any substantial area. TV was a major prestige project, a sign of modernity and national self-assertion; governments and businesses were as obsessed with it as viewers. As the Upper House of the Japanese Diet announced in May 1951, "The world has already entered into the television age." The announcement called for the government to execute a specific plan to develop transmitting and receiving technologies. "It is necessary to plan for the fullness of the people's cultural lifestyle."[10]

The lifestyle features an obsession with television. Once broadcasting began and TV's became even a little affordable, consumers snapped them up. There was no hesitation about buying television sets on credit; even notoriously ultra-frugal German and Japanese consumers did so: in the late 1950s and early 1960s, slightly more than half the TVs in Germany and some three-quarters in Japan were purchased with borrowed money. In communist lands, state planners and consumers were in rare agreement about the desirability of TV sets. The result of this buying frenzy was that televisions achieved market saturation many times faster than other common consumer durables, including telephones, washing machines, refrigerators, vacuum cleaners, and automobiles. The only appliances snapped up at a comparable rate were ancillary devices, VCRs, and DVD players; and, a bit more modestly, the broadcast appliance of the first half of the twentieth century, radios. Computers and cell phones, which are fast turning into twenty-first-century broadcast receivers, have had a similar pace of market penetration.[11]

This consumer obsession predated the actual economic ability to purchase a set. Consider this example from 1953 in a Japan still devastated by the Second World War, and where a TV cost about as much as an automobile, a year's salary of a white-collar employee. One man recalled seeing . . .

> More than 20,000 people gathered in front of a street television to watch a live broadcast of a boxing title . . . trams were halted. Automobiles were unable to move. Taxi drivers abandoned their cars to watch the match. Spectators who had climbed trees to get a better view fell and were injured. In a neighborhood residence 20 people fell from a balcony which collapsed under the weight of house guests.[12]

This initial obsession seemed undeterred by the blurry image or the staticky sound. In the early years of TV broadcasting, these were aggravated by "snow" on the screen; vertical, horizontal and diagonal wavering of the picture; the need to clamber up onto the roof to adjust the aerial; or to pace around the living room with rabbit ear antennas, looking for a spot that would get any sound or image at all. And all this for picture and sound clearly inferior to a well-established alternative, namely cinema, an inferiority that remained very much the case until the advent of high-definition broadcasts half a century later. Yet people preferred the small screen at home (larger screens, difficult enough to manufacture if based on cathode ray tubes, would produce extremely blurry pictures) to the large one in cinemas and the establishment of TV everywhere was a major blow to the movies.

Part of the reason for fascination with television was precisely that television brought the world into the home. As one woman in New Zealand explained at the beginning of TV broadcasting in 1960, "It will be lovely, it'll be gorgeous. We won't have to go out; we can stay home and be entertained."[13] A more sophisticated account of the nature of the medium and its appeal comes from Jean d'Arcy, programming director of French television, 1952–59. Television's role "is to transmit the current moment and to give the spectator the ability to be present, by proxy, everywhere, simultaneously. Cinema is an art of recording, television an art of transmission."[14] To experience the current moment, present everywhere simultaneously, and to do so by proxy, is to be immersed in another reality, one that is transmitted to viewers in their own homes. Television is its own world, experienced in its immediacy, built from elements of personally experienced reality, and often confused with that reality, but fundamentally distinct from it—and, in view of television's domination of leisure time, a refuge from and an alternative to that experiential reality. Many facets of TV viewing, including the way it led (as noted) to the decline of cinema, and of (men's especially) socializing in bars and cafés, the particularly strong appeal it has for the elderly, shut-ins, and the unemployed, are examples of its replacement of the world of reality directly experienced or experienced indirectly via print, with a separate, transmitted reality.

From the very earliest days of TV broadcasting the question has been posed as to how leisure hours spent in television's transmitted reality would affect attitudes and behavior in experienced and lived reality. There has been no shortage of critics, decrying, among many other pernicious effects—TV's role in the decline of culture, the dissolution of social and familial ties, or the cheapening and distortion of political life. Accompanying these jeremiads and generally moving in synch with them has been a social science research program based on a model of replication: if viewers see lots of violence committed in TV shows they will be encouraged to commit violence in their own lives.[15]

The research model seems more than a little crude and moralistic, not really aligned with the feature of the medium as a transmitted reality. TV's effects are subtler, and the impact on individuals' lives, while very real, appears in more indirect fashion. A good example would be the immensely popular *telenovelas*, Latin American soap operas. The lead female characters of Brazilian *telenovelas* are always shown as childless, or with only one child. And there does seem to be a statistically ascertainable connection between the expanded viewing of the shows, and declining birth rates. It is not that the *telenovelas* discussed contraceptive methods or practices that were then imitated by their enthusiastic female viewers. Instead, the transmitted reality of smaller families came to seem real to them in their own lives.[16]

TV's influence on politics has moved along similar lines. Politicians used the mass media of the first half of the century—radio and film—to address the public directly, doing so in a form of rhetorical performance. Both the fascist dictators, Hitler and Mussolini, as well as their opponents, Churchill, Roosevelt, and de Gaulle, were all very effective at it (Stalin noticeably less so). Television has tended to work differently; it involves becoming part of viewers' reality, connecting with them personally. The aesthetics of the low-resolution, small screen, with its emphasis on facial close-ups, amplified this personal connection. When US Senator Joseph McCarthy was condemning countless politicians and government employees as communists and Russian spies during the 1950s, his enemies at CBS news put one of the senator's victims, Air Force Lieutenant Milo Radulovich, on camera, where he could tell his own story, and introduce his father, who professed his strongly anti-communist sentiments. Virtually overnight, there were eight thousand letters to CBS, running about 100 to 1 in favor of the sympathetic young lieutenant, transmitted into people's homes. Senator McCarthy demanded the right to reply but, on television came across as haranguing and bullying.[17]

Over the course of his three-decades-long political career, Charles de Gaulle discovered the distinct differences between broadcast media. His response to the giant wave of strikes pouring across France in May 1968, was to appear on French TV (whose news programs were quite blatantly manipulated to provide a pro-government account of events) and talk in his authoritarian, lecturing style, which only made matters worse. A week later, he issued a radio appeal, imitating his celebrated summons to the nation by radio from London to continue the war after being defeated by the Germans twenty-eight years previously. Unlike the failed TV speech, the radio oration sparked a dramatic political turnaround, ending in an electoral reaffirmation of his rule.[18]

In the countries of the Eastern Bloc, where the government consciously deployed TV for political purposes, the nature of the new medium as broadcast of sympathetic individuals into viewers' homes became especially apparent. Explicitly political programming—say news broadcasts where announcers read out reports about the overfulfillment of the plan, or clips of visiting African revolutionaries being greeted by members of the central committee—were unpopular and ineffective. By contrast, TV dramas showing a tough police detective foiling the plots of Western agents and communist reformers, or a sympathetic party activist carrying out agricultural collectivization, in spite of the problems it caused for his marriage, enjoyed a wide viewership and were the topic of discussion for weeks after each episode. The most successful creator of such TV shows, the Czech playwright Jaroslav Dietl, had been a supporter of the reform movement culminating in the Prague Spring of 1968, before returning to the Marxist-Leninist fold until his unexpected death in 1985. Although his shows were immensely popular, not just in Czechoslovakia, but across the Eastern Bloc (and even found an appreciative audience in Western Europe), party officials were perpetually suspicious of him. They kept insisting that he include in his scripts orations denouncing capitalism and praising communism. Their demands demonstrated that they, too, missed the point about the political uses of television.[19]

No one watches TV to hear a lecture or an oration—making the medium quite different from its predecessor, radio. The standards of rhetorical performance of the transmission media of the first half of the twentieth century were very much not those of the Age of Interconnection. Using television in a politically successful way meant making oneself a welcome part of the separate reality broadcast into viewers' homes.

A GLOBAL VILLAGE? TELEVISION AND GLOBAL INTERCONNECTION

Television plays a large role in theories of globalization, or, perhaps more accurately, globalization plays a large role in theories of television as mass medium. A famous example comes from the Canadian media theorist Marshall McLuhan, who pointed out that TV was a distinct medium, not just radio with pictures or movies at home—although the observations of Jean d'Arcy show that McLuhan was far from the only one or even the first to understand this. McLuhan asserted that television was creating a "global village," broadcast reality reviving ("by proxy," as Jean d'Arcy said) the face-to-face immediacy of past small communities on a worldwide scale, terminating an age in which the experience of distant places was mediated by print accounts, telegraphic communications, or even radio broadcasting. McLuhan's theories, put forth almost sixty years ago, at the beginning of the television era, have become an intellectual commonplace, even a cliché. There exists another version of TV as globalization—one that is sinister where McLuhan was idyllic, critical where he was affirmative. In this version, sound and images flow around the world via broadcasting, but they do so in just one direction, from the wealthy countries, particularly the United States, to the poorer ones. Everybody is watching *Friends* and the *Cosby Show*, or getting their news from CNN, so that the unidirectional flow of images and information becomes an element of domination, of cultural imperialism. Reformulated for the twenty-first century, one could say that while some formerly poor countries, such as China, can now stand up to the wealthier ones when it comes to finance or industrial production, in the realm of culture, especially popular culture, the United States remains dominant.[20]

Like any theory, these need to be put to an empirical test, and not just a static one, but one that charts changing circumstances across the three eras of the second half of the twentieth century. Looked at through the context of social and economic organization, as well as the technology of broadcasting, particularly in the Late-Millennium Era, the global spread of TV broadcasting and of TV sets, a rather different picture emerges. TV was not a global village, not a global anything, actually, until the very last decade of the twentieth century. While the flow of broadcast information was mostly one way, above all from the United States outward, this was, in part, an artifact of the economic and technological transformations in TV broadcasting. Television remained to a surprising extent a distinctly national medium, and there were also countercurrents of information coursing through the airwaves—and coaxial cables and satellite transmissions—of the world, moving in different directions, creating a more complex and multifaced picture of the world's chief leisure time occupation as an agent of global interconnection.

While TV broadcasting did spread rapidly around the globe in the postwar era, without TV sets to receive the broadcasts, there was no information that could be transmitted, globally or otherwise. The ideal measure of the possibilities for TV reception is the percentage of households owning a set. Unfortunately, that information is not available on a worldwide basis until the last few years, so we will have to settle for a replacement, much more widely available—the number of TV sets per thousand inhabitants. The usual cautions apply—for some countries the figures are for sets in operation, for others licenses to use TVs; figures include televisions used in businesses such as bars or cafes and not just homes—but comparing this measure with scattered information on the proportion of households with TV sets and the more systematic figures available after 2000, it would be fair to say that 200 to 250 TVs per 1,000 inhabitants corresponds roughly to at least three-quarters of households having their own televisions. Table 9.1 shows when different countries around the world reached that point.

Some elements of the story of the market penetration of TV sets are similar to the tale told in Table 3.1 about the other great consumer durable of the Age of Interconnection, the automobile. Both goods reached a large proportion of the population in the United States first, during the 1950s. The other former settler colonies of the British Empire and the countries of Western Europe followed in the 1960s and 1970s, usually a little earlier for TVs than cars—no great surprise, since the former, by the 1960s, were noticeably

TABLE 9.1 Reaching 200–250 TV Sets per 1,000 Inhabitants

Country	Year	Country	Year	Country	Year
US	1957	Belgium, Denmark, Finland, Switzerland	c. 1970	Argentina	1985
UK	1962	Netherlands	1971	China	1994
Canada	1964	France	1972	Cuba	1995
Sweden	1965	Bulgaria, Czechoslovakia, Poland, USSR	c. 1975	Mexico, Brazil, Chile, Uruguay	1997
West Germany	1968	Australia	1975	Egypt	1999
East Germany	1969	Kuwait	1980		
Japan	1970	Poland	1984		

Sources: Calculated from Brian R. Mitchell, *International Historical Statistics: The Americas 1750–2005*, 6th ed, Tables F10.; id., *International Historical Statistics: Africa, Asia & Oceania 1750-2005*, 5th ed. (Basingstoke: Palgrave Macmillan, 2007), F9; id., *International Historical Statistics: Europe 1750-2005*, 6th ed. (Basingstoke: Palgrave Macmillan, 2007) F10; Maddison, *The World Economy*, Tables C1–6; supplemented by Therborn, *European Modernity*, Tables 7.7–7.8

cheaper than the latter. At this point the story diverges. Communist regimes in Eastern Europe were unable to manufacture enough cars, but most of them could get TV sets into people's households (although complaints about the poor quality of the devices, as of most consumer goods, were a constant).[21] Also very much unlike automobiles, TVs became commonplace in much of the non-European world, starting in the mid-1980s. The second half of the 1990s saw the breakthrough of mass television viewing in China, North Africa, and the more affluent countries of Latin America.

Figures from the International Telecommunications Union on the proportion of households owning TVs between 2000 and 2015 confirm this picture and show how it has developed further in the initial years of the new millennium. By the latter date, in the countries of the Americas and the Caribbean, Europe, the Middle East and East Asia, over 90 percent of households owned a TV. In that same decade and a half, India went from having about a third of its households with a TV to just under a half; Indonesia's jump was even more dramatic. Sub-Saharan Africa remained, in this respect, as in so many others, in its own realm. Around 2000, only in South Africa did a majority of households have a TV; just one country had over one-third of households owning televisions, tiny Gambia. By 2015, the number had reached 80 percent in both. A few countries, including Senegal, Ghana, the Republic of the Congo, Nigeria, and Côte d'Ivoire, had struggled up to the point that the percentage of households with TV's was somewhere in the '40s, but in others, including Chad, Cameroons, the Central African Republic, the Democratic Republic of Congo (former Zaire) Niger, Malawi, and Mali, between one household in fifty and one in three had a TV set.[22]

In short, a majority of the world's population only had a TV in their homes by 2010 (the midpoint of the ITU figures). If TV had created a global village, it was one in which actual villagers were left out: the rural population in Latin America and China until the 1990s; in India, Bangladesh, Pakistan, and pretty much all of sub-Saharan Africa, people living in the countryside still did not have regular access to a television in the initial decades of the twenty-first century.

Another element in the global spread of television was the social and economic organization of broadcasting, particularly as it was combined with broadcasting technology. In the postwar era this organization generally followed along the same lines as radio. Private corporations dominated in most of the Americas; TV was state-run in the Eastern Bloc—no big surprise there—as well as in France, Italy, and most of Africa. In the United Kingdom and the Anglosphere outside the United States, the "BBC model" prevailed— a publicly funded but relatively autonomous broadcasting service; similar versions existed in West German and Scandinavian television. Yet these differences between public and private ownership, which usually coincided with distinctions between funding through advertising or through taxes and

TV set licenses, are easy to overstate. Different models coexisted: small private broadcasters in the United Kingdom or Canada, versus a large public network: the opposite in the United States. Japan also had coexisting public and private broadcasters.

More important, in this early era of television (which as noted continued in most of the world until the 1990s), viewers' choices were few. This was a consequence of the narrow band of the electromagnetic spectrum available for TV broadcasts, and the need to keep a clear separation between different broadcast frequencies to avoid interference. No more than six frequencies could be used in any one area, and three or fewer was typical, a state of affairs that continued until the Late-Millennium Era.[23] Early TV was also ephemeral; although videotape was invented in the 1950s, it did not come into wide use for another decade or longer. Except for kinescopes—movies made by focusing a motion picture camera on the TV screen—there was no way to record programs, which tended to be live representations—news, sports, and theater, or, especially, variety and vaudeville performances.

Regardless of the different forms of ownership, finance, and organization, TV was curated; viewers had to watch what they were given and had few options. Viewing was, inevitably, widely shared; it was a common experience. This sounds like McLuhan's "global village," only, in view of the limitations on broadcasting, the village was distinctly more national than global. Multinational ventures in broadcasting were unusual and modest in extent. American TV programs were exported, particularly with the growing use of videotape, but that, too, remained small in scale, hardly to be compared with global commercial success of US movies, which were of course more established.[24]

The TV program export trade expanded modestly in the 1970s and 1980s, mostly from the United States, followed, at some distance, by the BBC. Two American miniseries of the late 1970s, *Roots* and *Holocaust*, enjoyed a world market. Both presented, as might be expected from the nature and aesthetics of television, very personalized versions of immense historical tragedies—the trans-Atlantic slave trade and the "final solution to the Jewish question." In an unexpected version of television's transmitted reality influencing experiential reality, *Holocaust*—denounced by critics as kitschy and melodramatic—brought about a breakthrough in understanding and recognition of and willingness to take responsibility for the crimes of the Nazi era in West Germany, where it was widely watched. The show did what decades of more serious and intellectualized lectures, seminars, newspaper articles, movies, and politicians' speeches had not accomplished.[25]

The combination of economic and technological changes of the Late-Millennium Era increasingly globalized TV viewing. Television, like telecommunications more generally, was ground zero for the wave of privatization and deregulation that swept the world. This development took on different forms in different countries, including the rapid introduction of privately owned, commercial TV stations in France, Germany, or New Zealand; the repeal in the United States of the "fairness doctrine" (guaranteeing different political points of view airtime) and of antitrust limitations on media ownership; or the privatization of state-owned media in post-communist Eastern Europe.

Change due to deregulation and privatization interacted with two different innovative technological methods of overcoming the line-of-sight limitations on over-the-air broadcasting. One was to connect TV broadcast towers with coaxial cable so that the same program could be broadcast over a large area. Municipalities and later businesses in the United States began running these coaxial cables into individual homes during the 1950s and 1960s, creating "cable television." Initially, cable systems were built in areas where, for topographic reasons, over-the-air reception for individual households was poor or impossible. A second method involved sending satellites into orbit, which could receive TV transmissions and then beam them back across the globe. The first trial telecommunications satellite, Telstar, was launched in 1962. Initially, because satellites were few, their expense considerable, and their capacity limited, they were employed for the occasional big event, live broadcasts of the Olympic Games, for instance. The Tokyo games of 1964 were the first to be broadcast via satellite.

As satellite capacity grew and costs came down, American entrepreneurs realized that satellite and cable could be combined into a potent broadcast combination, a TV station sending its signal to a satellite, which could then relay it to cable systems across the country. Ted Turner, owner of an advertising agency, who turned an obscure Atlanta UHF TV channel, WTCG, into America's first "super-station," WTBS, in 1976 quickly followed this innovation with CNN, the 24-hour cable news channel. Just a year and a half afterward was televangelist Jim Bakker, who used the satellite-cable connection to broadcast his *PTL Club* throughout the United States—and soon to Latin America and East Asia as well. The *PTL Club* adapted the long tradition of American religious revivalism to the new medium, replacing fire-and-brimstone sermons with personalized chats with celebrity guests, creating a religious version of televised reality. Bakker's show was immensely successful and catapulted him into the ownership of a leisure-time religious empire, encompassing a TV network and vacation resorts, until it dissolved in a welter of sex and financial scandals in 1987.[26]

Both CNN and PTL were evidence of a more fundamental change in television: the combination of satellite broadcasting and cable connections eliminated the frequencies bottleneck that had limited to six or fewer the number of TV stations that could be received. This opened up a new world of "multi-channel television," tens or hundreds of stations that, freed from the need to appeal to a mass audience, could offer a range of increasingly specialized content. The introduction of the video cassette recorder in 1976, in widespread use by the following decade, made it easier for viewers to choose among this smorgasbord of content, by enabling them to watch programs at a different time from when they were broadcast, or even to watch one program while simultaneously recording another.[27] Further technological advances, in particular the improvement of satellite technology so that broadcasts could go directly from a satellite to an individual TV, without the need for a cable intermediary, and the introduction of a digitized signal, less subject to interference, making it possible to transmit more channels over the air, only amplified this state of affairs. First emerging in the United States during the 1980s, this broadcast technology, and the huge viewing choices it offered has been spreading across the globe ever since. Combining this technology with the deregulation and privatization of broadcasting had two major effects: a wave of mergers and acquisitions producing, for the first time, multinational TV enterprises; and a need for programming to fill up all the airtime on the many newly available channels.

The Late-Millennium Era was the period of an M&A frenzy in broadcasting. In 1980, there were fifty mergers and acquisitions of broadcast firms, with a total value of $1.3 billion—an impressive enough figure. At the M&A highpoint in 2000, the number of deals had jumped to 766, valued at $200 billion. The upshot was the giant international broadcast conglomerates, including the media empire of Rupert Murdoch, the Sky Channel satellite TV firm, Radio-Television Luxemburg, the German media firm Bertelsmann, the French Vivendi, TV Globo in Brazil, Televisa in Mexico, and, of course, veteran American media businesses, like the Walt Disney Corporation, and newer firms emerging from the satellite-cable nexus, such as Viacom and Comcast.[28]

As noted, a major issue these firms faced was how to fill up the hours on the rapidly expanding number of channels. American media companies were able to provide the necessary content. The United States had a well established television industry (stemming from Hollywood studios diversifying into television as cinema began to decline) and had a large-enough viewing population to amortize the costs of producing a TV show. This made it possible to offer shows for sale abroad at a reduced rate, generally a good deal more cheaply than it would have cost to produce a homegrown one. The issue of initial audience size was a chronic problem for small countries, even affluent small countries like New Zealand, trying to compete in the world market for TV broadcasts. By 2000 US TV export sales were running at about an annual rate of $6.5 billion, with Britain in second place at $1.3 billion, and France a distant third at $325 million.[29]

Although the flow of information did go primarily from a small number of wealthier and more populous countries outward, there were also alternative directions. Those aforementioned *Telenovelas* commanded $300 million in export sales in 2000—and not just within Latin America or to Spain and Portugal. The Latin American soap operas were widely shown in the former Eastern Bloc, especially popular in Hungary, but also broadcast in the Czech Republic, Slovakia, and Russia. Sales in Asia made up a third of export receipts. Chinese viewers flocked to the Latin soap operas, as did their counterparts in Indonesia, Malaysia, Vietnam, Singapore, and South Korea. Filipinos were so captivated by *Marimar*, a Mexican show launched in 1994 based on the life of a young woman of that name, that drivers abandoned their cars in the middle of the street to view it, and the government had to threaten to fire public employees caught watching during business hours.[30]

Telenovelas proved that TV exports crossed all sorts of barriers of language, culture, and geography, though this raises the question of what viewers were actually watching, or thought they were watching, and what was lost in the dubbing or translation. These problems are greatest with sitcoms, which, unlike crime, adventure, or romantic melodrama, translate poorly or oddly from one country to the next. Two that were widely exported, *Fresh Prince of Bel Air* and *Everybody Hates Chris*, perceived in America as abrasive commentary on race relations and on social class differences between whites and Blacks and within the African American community, were marketed abroad primarily to a youth audience as comic coming-of-age stories.[31]

The TV game show *Who Wants to Be a Millionaire?* originating in England in 1998, spread around the world; versions of it were broadcast in some eighty countries. It proved to be a giant hit in the Americas and India, but a failure in Japan, where flaunting one's wealth and abilities is bad form. The show was very successful in the Arab world; its host, the journalist George Kordashi, himself a Lebanese Christian, quizzed contestants about the Koran and about grievances of the Palestinians against their Israeli occupiers. A globally marketed product of a multinational corporation may be spread worldwide, but its consumption is shaped by culture—an observation not limited to TV shows.[32]

For all the talk about TV exports, multinational media firms, and one-way information flows, it is easy to underestimate the distinctly national character of television. The UN's Economic, Social, and Cultural Organization (UNESCO) sponsored a study of the transnationalization of viewing habits in five European and four Asian-Pacific countries in 1991–92. Based on TV-viewing diaries, like the time diaries used to investigate leisure, the results showed that in eight of the nine countries studied, nationally produced shows accounted for a majority of viewing time, as high as 90 percent—a particularly striking result, since UNESCO had long been sounding the alarm about one-way flows of information across the globe. It is also interesting that the two countries where domestic content was lowest, Australia at 46 percent,

Italy at 58 percent, were affluent. National content was higher in the Asian countries included in the study, making up 67 percent of viewing time in the Philippines, 91 percent in South Korea, and 92 percent in India.[33]

The UNESCO study was carried out in the early phases of the cable-satellite era, so that the expansion of channels in the 1990s, and the growth of private and multinational ownership of TV broadcasts would both have increased the proportion of foreign content available for viewing. There were also countervailing developments occurring, particularly after 2000, which was the highpoint of M&A. After that, the pace declined, and some of the media conglomerates created in the M&A frenzy of the 1990s, such as Vivendi-Universal, proved unprofitable and were broken up. And alternatives to US and European-based broadcasting began appearing on satellites and cable. The news offered by Al-Jazeera and RT (Russian state-controlled television), presented a rather different picture of the world than the one broadcast by CNN or the BBC.[34]

Since, by 2000, most people around the world have had access to TV broadcasts, it may be that TV has, in fact, turned the world into a global village. However, that village is not the harmonious face-to-face community that was Marshal McLuhan's model, but more lifelike, inhabited by feuding, hostile clans, individuals who never speak to each other, pronounced differences of religion, ethnicity or caste, property-owners strong-arming and exploiting the propertyless, and endless conflicts over local government and property boundaries. To put it a little differently, the regulatory, economic, and technological changes of the Late-Millennium Era have made TV viewing less of a community experience. In place of the curated, limited options, and shared viewership in which TV originated, they have created a multichannel world, less shared, more fragmented, and containing the potential for individual, self-curation of the TV experience. A cynic might retort that many of the channels are owned by the same few media conglomerates, that while viewers may have hundreds of channels at their disposal, they only actually watch a handful of them. In short, that nothing has really changed.[35]

The flow of sound and images has remained one way—from the broadcaster to the viewer—and the advent of interactive TV (except perhaps for shopping networks), predicted for decades, never came to pass. Also, the global information flow has been primarily from wealthier countries, especially the United States, outward, although with large national reservations and smaller flows in different directions. Still, the increasing possibilities for self-curation, especially when combined with recent technological developments, such as the use of digital video recorders, and the intersection of broadcast TV with the Internet, has the potential to change the nature of the reality broadcast into viewers' homes.

On Vacation

Television viewing and tourism are diametric opposites within the world of leisure. One is interwoven with everyday life; the other is a block of time, occurring at longer intervals, designed and experienced as an alternative to the quotidian. TV happens at home; tourism, by its very nature, requires traveling. Both involve experiencing the world. With television this is done by proxy as part of an alternate reality; with tourism, via direct physical experience of a different place.

If TV's progress through the world in the Age of Interconnection has been accompanied by a drumbeat of cultural criticism, it seems positively muted in comparison to the cacophony of denigration directed at tourists. Tourism is widely and loudly decried as an activity lacking in authenticity. Tourists go out into the world to experience different landscapes, peoples, and cultures, but their presence invariably transforms their ostensibly exotic destination—or, at least the parts of it they experience—into one whose inhabitants strive to make it like the tourists' original home. In doing so, they subvert the whole point of the experience of something different, raising the question of whether that was what the tourists actually wanted in the first place. Some people, often self-designated as "travelers," rather than "tourists," feeling the authenticity of previous destination has been spoiled, "overrun" by a mass of visitors, push on to less well-known, touristically undiscovered destinations. Of course, once purportedly more sophisticated travelers begin visiting a destination in larger numbers, tourists follow in their wake, so that the authentic destination is quickly transformed into precisely the inauthentic experiences travelers were fleeing.[36] An expansion of this criticism is that tourists do not even pretend to want an authentic experience of a different cultural world, but desire their own in another location: eating at British and German pubs or Norwegian restaurants in Mallorca, searching Paris for an American-style hamburger, going to Paris to visit Euro-Disney, shopping for local souvenirs, mostly made in low-wage countries in Asia, traveling in bus tours with their fellows, hermetically sealed off from the countries the bus occasionally stops to visit, demanding wealthy-country standards of accommodations and refreshment in much poorer ones.

Even more sinister is the accusation that tourists are fundamentally destructive. They tactlessly show contempt for the people, countries, and cultures they are visiting, and by their presence threaten indigenous cultures. This is globalization at its most pernicious. Exploiting poorer people's labor for their indulgent, inauthentic enjoyment, their presence is part of a transfer of wealth from local sources—usually understood as impoverished or marginalized—to grasping multinational enterprises. Tourists and the investment they encourage to cater to them plays no small role in environmental degradation.[37]

Two quotes articulate this global disdain. As one Hawaiian activist put it in the 1980s, "There are no innocent tourists." A decade earlier, the Greek Orthodox Church actually devised a prayer, "Lord Jesus Christ, Son of God, have mercy on the cities, the islands and the villages of this Orthodox Fatherland, as well as the holy monasteries which are scourged by the worldly touristic wave."[38] Repugnant and destructive—even to the point of calling for divine intervention against them: such are tourists.

They have their defenders. One viewpoint focuses on tourism as lucrative, a key to economic development, especially in poorer countries—a line persistently pursued by the UN's World Tourism Organization since its founding in 1976. Along with this goes the frequently maintained (if dubious) assertion that tourism is the world's leading industry. Even tourists have their advocates. Perhaps the authenticity they seek is less in the peoples, cultures, and landscapes they visit, than in the act of visiting itself. Or maybe the whole idea of "cultural authenticity" is dubious. All cultures are hybrids composed of different and widely varied influences; there is no reason to see any one as more authentic than any other. Visiting a replica of the Eifel Tower in Las Vegas is every bit as authentic an experience as seeing the original in Paris.[39]

Rather than staking out yet another position in this debate about the aesthetics and morality of tourism, it might be more helpful to trace its history across the Age of Interconnection. This was the time when tourism became a mass movement and spread around the world—more in terms of tourist destinations than in tourists' countries of origin. Previously elite practices, such as taking a cruise, became mass market pastimes. New forms of tourism, largely unknown before 1945— backpacking, bus tours, ecotourism, sex tourism, or trekking—became commonplace. Economic changes helped accelerate and expand tourism, most obviously, the spread of prosperity across Europe and North America in the postwar decades, as did technological innovations, particularly the introduction of commercial jet aircraft. The practice of vacations and the forms of tourism developed considerable differentiation, even between countries with similar societies and levels of economic development. Unlike TV, a leisure activity that grew rapidly and enjoyed great popularity across Cold War boundaries, tourism and vacations took very different forms on opposite sides of the Cold War divide. In this context of global expansion and diversification, the debates about tourism appear in a different light.

For all the precursors going back to ancient China or the Roman Empire, the seedbed of modern tourism lay in nineteenth-century Europe, when and where the actual expression "tourism" was coined. Two names, Thomas Cook and Karl Baedeker, suffice to make the point. The former was the pioneer of the travel agency and the guided tour; the latter, founder of the guidebook series. Both are institutions central to the practice of tourism. Although not quite so elite as the old regime "grand tour" of the European nobility, these early forms of tourism were very much restricted to the most affluent, those with the money, and, even more importantly, the leisure time, to travel and sightsee. This lasted down through the First World War.

The interwar years brought the first intimations of tourism as a mass movement. In the United States, the gradual expansion of automobile ownership, the construction of a national highway network—both still very modest by post-1945 standards—and the spread of paid vacations at work, made possible the prospect of a summer drive to a national park, staying at one of the newly constructed "motor hotels" along the way, or a more modest excursion to a country cabin, resort hotel, or bungalow colony. The Depression was a major setback to these initial steps toward mass tourism. By contrast, the idea of vacations and mass tourism in Europe was distinctly politicized and characteristic of the 1930s. Governments on the left, the French Popular Front, the social democratic regimes in Scandinavia, and even Stalin's USSR, all promoted the idea of a vacation, involving travel to a site far from everyday life, as part of a political project of improving the workers' lives and enhancing the power and influence of labor in society. The most effective politicization of vacations, though, was the work of the fascist governments in Italy and Germany. The former's National Afterwork Foundation and the latter's larger and better-known imitation, Strength through Joy, promoted vacations and tourism out of diametrically opposed political motives from those of their left-wing counterparts. These would compensate for destroying the power of labor and the institutions of the labor movement by supporting consumer expenditures and new and expanded uses of leisure. At least in 1930s Europe, all these initiatives across the political spectrum remained scattered, isolated, and only reached a relatively small minority of the population, gestures toward a touristic future rather than examples of a touristic reality. The only country in the pre-1945 world where vacations and tourism (of a sort) was anything like a mass phenomenon, was Great Britain, in which 40 percent of households were taking week-long holidays by 1938. This was not by coincidence, as it was the only country in the world where labor had a permanent presence and influence. To at least some observers the British vacation, a week at a cold and damp seaside resort, drinking warm beer and watching cheesy vaudeville, was modest tourism indeed.[40]

The only ones touring during the Second World War were occupying soldiers while off duty, but tourism resumed in the 1950s, to a great extent along the same lines as the interwar era, though greatly expanded in extent. The 1950s were the highpoint of the American automobile family vacation, of trips to national parks and patriotic monuments, or lengthier stays in rural hotels, cabins, or bungalows. US tourists streamed into Paris, as they had in the 1920s, in much greater numbers. They were still very heavily from educated and affluent backgrounds, and brought with them a sense of entitlement as representatives of the world's superpower.[41]

Within these lines of continuity there were some newer developments. The most significant was the rise of the inclusive, all-in-one vacation package. A pioneer was DER, the travel agency of the West German Federal Railways, which sold a combination train ticket and hotel accommodations with full pension in the Bavarian mountains for less than the cost of the train trip itself. These packages were particularly popular among single women, who could travel in a secure environment, with their fellow package tourists, and not worry about being harassed or eating at a restaurant alone. Bus tours and their disproportionately elderly clientele would soon follow. A more radical version of the all-in-one package was the vacation resort. The British entrepreneur Billy Butlin had started building "holiday camps" in the 1930s. Visitors to the facilities (usually gated) enjoyed accommodations, full board, sports, and other daytime diversions as well as nighttime entertainment. Butlin's empire reached its peak in the postwar era, when his holiday camps became the epitome of the family vacation; in 1948, one UK vacationer in twenty stayed at them. A still-more dramatic variant on the all-inclusive resort was *Club Méditerranée*. Founded in 1950 by the Franco-Belgian entrepreneur Gérard Blitz, whose family ran a mountain vacation resort in France's Haute-Savoie department, Club Med carried the all-in-one, get-away ideal to its extreme. Vacationers—themselves largely from the educated, professional, and managerial class—used no cash, dressed in swimsuits and sarongs, and lived out a romanticized South Seas existence on a stretch of beach in Spain or Southern France. Getting the vacationers into this enclosed fantasy world did require a certain amount of effort, and Club Med's *gentils organisateurs*—following in the footsteps of Billy Beutlin's "Redcoats," and the *Toomler* of similar all-inclusive resort hotels in New York's borscht belt—arranged a whirlwind of activities for this purpose.[42]

In the postwar era, tourism was an expanded and somewhat revised—less explicit politics, more all-in-one experiences—of the new touristic initiatives of the interwar years. The situation would change drastically, in the Era of Upheaval. One crucial reason was the introduction of commercial jet aircraft and their increasingly affordable airfares. Transatlantic air travel boomed; American tourists poured into Europe—and by the 1970s, there was a touristic flow going in the other direction as well. However, the main impact of air travel on tourism was in promoting somewhat shorter trips to beach destinations, from inland and northern Europe to the Mediterranean coast and from North America to the Caribbean. This was the age of the English and German colonization of the Spanish island of Mallorca, the years when the French government launched a massive effort to turn a 180 kilometer-long stretch of swampy coastline in Languedoc into a vacation wonderland, with hotels, condos, sport fishing, windsurfing, and the Mediterranean's largest nudist colony.[43]

Air travel, beach destinations, and package tours developed into an intimate relationship. In 1954, 15 percent of all West German vacationers, about one million of them, took a vacation outside the country's borders, mostly to neighboring Austria, although a few daring individuals ventured as far as Italy. By 1970, over half of vacationers, some ten million people, were vacationing in a foreign country; at the end of that decade, it was sixteen million, 61 percent of all vacationers. (These figures imply that the total number of vacationers had grown from 6.7 million in the mid-1950s to 26 million by the end of the 1970s.) Spain had become the most popular holiday destination, and the proportion of vacationers taking package tours, increasingly traveling to their destinations by air, had gone from 11 percent in 1961 to 26 percent in 1980 to 40 percent in 1988.[44]

Such rapid growth in the number of vacationers was impossible without crossing social boundaries. While the educated and affluent continued to be more likely to be tourists than the manual laborers or people from lower-income groups, and, especially, city dwellers more than countryfolk, these distinctions steadily declined over the course of the 1960s and 1970s. In affluent European countries, tourism became a more distinctly universal experience.[45]

Along with this expansion went the creation of new forms of tourism and new kinds of tourists. One version was tourists who strove to have a cheaper vacation—whether because they couldn't afford anything nicer or because of an interest in authenticity—on their own, rather than via a package tour. A major symbol and promoter of this kind of tourism was Arthur Frommer, an America GI, stationed in West Germany who used his time on leave to travel around the continent and write up a guide to traveling cheaply for soldiers. In 1957, he turned his ideas into a book *Europe on $5 a Day*, with its suggestions for cheaper hotels—rooms without a private bath, used by Europeans, but spurned by wealthier Americans—and budget restaurants. It became the bible of US bargain travelers in Europe, selling 150,000 copies per year in the 1960s. (This author had his own copy, in the second half of the 1970s, but by then inflation and decline in the value of the dollar had changed the title to *Europe on $35 a Day*.)[46]

A subgroup of the bargain travelers were the backpackers, young adults venturing to foreign countries on their own; if Americans in Europe, they were likely to have a copy of Frommer's book in their backpacks. A more adventurous group than bargain travelers, backpackers made their way to destinations well beyond Europe, appearing in large numbers on the beach in Goa, for instance, where their predilection for lounging about in the nude shocked the locals, mostly Christians, as Goa was one of the few parts of India with a large Christian population.[47]

Backpackers' presence in one of the most isolated countries in the world, Nepal, was a good indication of the changes in tourism at the height of postwar prosperity. During the 1950s, tourists first began coming to the Himalayan kingdom, staying at the appropriately named Royal Hotel in Kathmandu. Their ranks included the super-rich and celebrities, such as Alfred Krupp, John D. Rockefeller III, Ian Fleming, Ingrid Bergman, and Cary Grant. The typical tourist in Nepal was elderly and very well-to-do. This all changed at the end of the 1960s, as young people from Europe and North America began flocking to Kathmandu, sometimes arriving by air from India, but often traveling overland in rickety VW buses. Among them were counterculturalists seeking Buddhist spiritual enlightenment—an odd choice in the world's most Hindu country, probably the result of conflating Nepal with very Buddhist Tibet, then inaccessible under Chinese communist rule. They found, instead, a paradise of hashish. By the mid-1970s, the Nepalese capital was filled with youthful and very stoned tourists, staying in cheap lodging houses (a terrific business opportunity for entrepreneurial Nepalese), wandering the streets, or just lying in them, under chemical influence.[48]

Tourism and vacations in the countries of the Eastern Bloc underwent a similar process of expansion. The nature of tourism and vacations was fundamentally different in the communist world from its capitalist counterparts. The communist vacation was a form of industrial medicine and hygiene; its purpose was to restore individuals' minds and bodies, worn out from their labor, so that they could continue to be highly productive at work. Vacation spots and resorts were owned and administered by state-owned firms or by the official trade unions. Eligible workers did not book or pay for their holidays; they received a voucher, in the USSR a *putevka*, in East Germany a *Ferienscheck*, good for a stay at a medical facility, covering most of the costs.[49]

These facilities did tend to be located in vacation terrain: mountains and the seaside. During the 1950s, the Soviet leadership made a decision to use the Crimea, the portion of the country with the mildest climate, as a centralized location for medical rest and recuperation. The regime of hygienic rejuvenation promoted in the many clinics and rehabilitation centers built there included sunbathing, swimming, sports, games, singalongs, movies, and concerts, so the similarities with Billy Butlin's holiday camps or Club Med, were pronounced. The nature of the clientele also raised questions about just how medical stays at such facilities were. While it was manual laborers who were most in need of physical rest and rehabilitation, the people actually in attendance were disproportionately from professional and managerial, or at least administrative occupations. Their presence was especially pronounced in the Crimean seaside town of Sochi, which had the reputation, throughout the USSR, as the ideal spot for a vacation. Probably the height of the transformation of therapeutic into the recreational was at a rest home for pregnant women in the countryside near Moscow. By the 1960s, few of the guests seemed to be pregnant, and one day a man showed up, brandishing his *putevka*, demonstrating that his enterprise and trade union had attested to the medical necessity of his stay.[50]

If the actual purpose of communist vacations resembled those in Western Europe and North America, one element of the original ideal remained very pronounced and made such vacations very different from those in the West. These trips were assigned by workplaces and unions for purportedly medical purposes and went exclusively to individuals. Spouses were generally not included (which gave the vacation rest homes in the USSR the reputation of being a hotbed of extramarital sex) to say nothing of children, who were expected to attend summer camps of state youth groups, rather than travel with their parents. Whatever vacations in the Eastern Bloc might have been, they were not family vacations, and so in that respect very different from holidays and tourism in the world's capitalist nations.[51]

Inhabitants of the Eastern Bloc countries who wanted to have a touristic vacation with their families sometimes attempted to do so. They would often show up at the rest homes with spouses and children, demanding accommodations, explaining that their offspring were so small that could stay with them in their rooms. A related alternative was to ignore the entire system and try to travel to classic vacation destinations on one's own. This was easier in the Bloc countries than in the USSR. In the former, while hotels, spas and the entire tourist and vacation business had been brought into state ownership, remnants of capitalism remained, such as homeowners renting private rooms to vacationers. These capitalist remnants were lacking in the Soviet Union, so that private vacationers could overwhelm the few restaurants and public hotels available in Sochi and the Crimea more generally.

From the 1970s onward, government policy in the Eastern Bloc began to move away from the ideal of vacations and tourism as forms of the rejuvenation of labor power. Opportunities for family travel multiplied; more explicitly touristic versions of vacations developed; there was even the possibility of international travel, although typically just within the Eastern Bloc itself and not to Western countries. Vacations became far more common. In the USSR, there were a little under 4 million vacationers in the government-run health-oriented facilities in 1950, a number that had grown to 6.7 million in 1960, and 17 million in 1970. By 1980, there were 40 million such vacationers, reaching 50 million by 1986, the very last year of the communist economic system in the USSR. As a proportion of households, it was at least at the same order of magnitude as in Western Europe or North America. Like TV, vacations and holiday travel had become an expected part of Eastern Bloc life. The East German rock star Nina Hagen soared to fame in 1974 with a huge hit called "You Forgot the Color Film," in which the female protagonist berated her boyfriend for just bringing black-and-white film on their vacation trip to the Baltic Sea and ruining her memories of the vacation. Perhaps a criticism of drab everyday life in the GDR, and Hagen did leave for West Germany two years later, and enjoyed a long career as a punk-rocker, her song was also a recognition of the touristic practice of obsessive photography and the normality of travel vacations in the communist world.[52]

Neither vacations nor tourism in the Eastern Bloc ever reached Western levels. Low rates of automobile ownership made the driving vacation and auto tourism—long the American standard and increasingly common in Western Europe—a rare exception. There were shortages of vacation possibilities, especially for families, and a lot of negative comments about the poor quality of accommodations, food, and recreation, yet another variant on the chronic problems with the provision of consumer goods and the growing discontent about them typical of the last two decades of the Eastern Bloc. International travel for vacations, generally within the Eastern Bloc itself, was becoming more common in some communist countries, including Hungary, and Romania, although less so elsewhere in the Bloc. When the East German government sponsored cruises, some guests would jump overboard if their ocean liner got within swimming distance of a capitalist country; the crew was required to close the deck and lock all the passengers in an interior recreation room for that precarious portion of the passage. Later, the cruises just avoided capitalist shores altogether. Even trips to fellow communist countries were rare for citizens of the USSR. Only 630,000 people left the Soviet Union for any and all purposes in 1985, a modest figure when set against 50 million Soviet vacationers.[53]

Since one of the distinguishing features of tourism in the Late-Millennium Era was its increasing global scope, inhabitants of the Eastern Bloc were excluded from these new developments. One element of the globalization of tourism was its spread, like the case with automobiles, beyond Europe and North America to the economically rising countries of East Asia. Just as with cars, vacations abroad came late to Japan: 3.9 million Japanese traveled abroad in 1980, 9.7 million in 1989, and 17.8 million in 2000. By the end of the millennium, impressive numbers of tourists were traveling abroad from Singapore, Malaysia, Taiwan, and South Korea. This led to some embarrassing scenes in Thailand, when female backpackers from Singapore were mistaken for prostitutes, and Singaporeans and Malaysians treated like impoverished locals and kicked out of hotels and bars designed for tourists.[54]

These attitudes, besides demonstrating a fair dose of racism—albeit expressed by Asians against other Asians—also show the rapidity of the economic rise of East Asia, and the unfamiliarity with the idea of Asian prosperity. The largest and most dramatic example of this broader trend was the growth of the Chinese economy, though by 2000 this had not yet been translated into large-scale Chinese tourism. In part, this was a reflection of past attitudes, under Mao, when foreign travel by Chinese was largely prohibited, labor was the measure of life, and foreign tourism rejected, or just allowed in homeopathic doses from carefully selected foreign visitors with the right political orientation. Deng Xiaoping's great policy reorientation had changed the official attitude toward tourism, but it was a stage of consumer expenditure that China had very largely not reached in 2000. Beyond not possessing the funds, time for vacations was extremely limited. The new and upcoming thing was weekend trips for inhabitants of China's large cities, somewhat like the sort of tourism that Strength through Joy had promoted in Germany during the 1930s. As China's economic expansion roared on through the initial decades of the twenty-first century, possibilities for travel increased, and in 2016 the number of Chinese crossing their country's borders for foreign travel about equaled the number of Americans doing so coming from a country with one-fifth China's population. This is perhaps no surprise, since in 2015 about three-quarters of Chinese engaged in gainful economic activity had not had a paid vacation in the previous three years.[55]

The rise of mass tourism in East Asia was part of a broader global expansion of travel and vacations in the Late-Millennium Era, with the number of short-stay registered international arrivals (one very crude measure of tourism) growing by about two-and-a-half times, worldwide. The position of different parts of the globe in tourism changed relatively little over those years. Europe, which accounted for 64 percent of all short-term international arrivals in 1980, was still the destination of 57 percent of all arrivals at the beginning of the new millennium. France maintained its status as the number one tourist destination in the entire world, as it has down to the present day. The tiny Caribbean islands together continued to receive more tourists than all of South America, with the latter just pulling ahead by 2010. Declines in the proportion of tourist arrivals reaching North America and Europe corresponded to increases in tourists going to Asian, and, more modestly, African countries. But all these shifts in the relative position of tourist destinations pale in comparison to the sheer expansion in numbers of tourists around the globe.[56]

Greater numbers were just one part of the story of tourism by 2000. Another was the transformation of the package tours and all-in-one destinations that had been so key in the initial impetus toward vacations and tourism in the middle decades of the century. The growing accessibility of more distant places with commercial aircraft made destinations nearer by less attractive. The two largest of Billy Butlin's holiday camps, at Filey and Clacton, closed in 1983, as British vacationers increasingly preferred the warmer Mediterranean. A similar fate awaited New York's borscht belt hotels, or the rural resorts of northern Minnesota. All-in-one German railway packages dwindled, appealing, if at all, to a smaller group of less-adventurous elderly customers.

There were two very distinct replacements for these faded vacation destinations, one more prevalent in Europe, the other in North America. The European version was the touristic colonization of the entire Mediterranean Basin: going beyond its northern and western end in Spain and Italy, tourism moved east and south, to Greece, Cyprus, Yugoslavia/Croatia, Turkey, Tunisia, and Morocco. In contrast to the Butlin or Club Med ideal, in which the proprietor of the vacation resort chain organized the entire experience, in the Mediterranean the dominant, heavily capitalized travel agencies outsourced the actual vacation to contractors, in particular charter and discount airlines and individual hotel proprietors. Using their computerized booking systems, the travel agents guaranteed the airline operators full flights and the hotel owners fully booked establishments, using these guarantees to wring out discounts, which they could pass on to their customers. The weekly charter flights set the pace for the turnover of hotel guests and the tourist experience, more generally. That experience might seem more individualized than the 1950s predecessors, since there were no *gentils organisateurs* or Redcoats to guide vacationers' daily routines. The layout of the hotels with the daily competition for the best chairs and lounges near the pool or the ocean (often fought out between individuals of different nationalities) shaped these routines in a less overt way. Hotels' locations in a tourist zone, with restaurants and shopping designed for tourists, was another constraint, and departures from that zone usually occurred via local tour companies—yet another arm of the octopus of travel agencies' subcontractors—with their fixed destinations for different days of the week, hence one more way that the touristic itinerary was shaped within the weekly rhythms of arrival and departure.[57]

This sort of subtly enclosed experience was predominantly European and Mediterranean, but not exclusively so; Japanese tourists in Hawaii followed a similar pattern. As an enclosed environment, the Mediterranean tourist scene rather pales before another touristic innovation of the Late-Millennium Era, mostly, but not exclusively, North American: the mass market cruise ship. The one-time luxury or at least upmarket experience of the trans-Atlantic crossing, which persisted until the introduction of commercial jet aircraft, gave way to a journey around the Caribbean on ever-larger ocean liners, carrying two or three thousand passengers in whole self-referential worlds, with seemingly endless food and drink, sports, sunbathing, gambling, and professional evening entertainment—(and, unintentionally, the occasional virus spreading through the ship). There were largely ritual dockings on Caribbean islands, but most of the passengers, as anthropologists studying this new social phenomenon ascertained, rarely ventured more than a few blocks from the docks, shopping in the stores catering to cruise ship tourists. Within the common parameters of the cruise—and in this respect not entirely unlike the Mediterranean beach vacations—there was product differentiation between different cruise lines, often owned by the same holding company. Price was one form, but there were enterprises specializing in cruises for young singles, for families or for the elderly; and cruises for a wide variety of special interests, ranging from bridge players to opera aficionados.[58]

Changes in tourism were not just limited to openly or subtly self-enclosed touristic worlds. New forms of tourism also developed toward the end of the millennium. Three of the most prominent were sex tourism, ecotourism, and trekking. Although they might seem light-years apart in aims, objectives, and relations to the local population, there were a number of underlying commonalities, of which probably the most prominent is that they all involved tourists from affluent countries taking vacations in poorer ones, generally in Asia, the Caribbean, or South America. Sex tourism might seem one-sidedly exploitative and deeply sleazy and unhealthy, while trekking and especially ecotourism appear as high-minded and altruistic. On closer examination the one-sidedness of sex tourism and the altruism of the other forms seem less pronounced than at first glance.

Although the wish for sexual escapades has always been an important part of tourism—one might think of the decades-long appeal of Paris, the world's number one tourist destination, for its whores and strippers—contemporary forms of sex tourism date from the 1970s. They began when large Japanese businesses, which had long followed the practice of rewarding their most productive managerial and professional employees with visits to brothels, began sending these top performers on tours to South Korea for that purpose. Thailand quickly emerged as a destination, and these organized sex tourists were followed by individuals, at first from Japan, then from Europe, coming to Southeast Asia. Other centers of sex tourism began to develop, particularly in the Caribbean and the north Brazilian metropolis of Salvador de Bahia, which had emerged by 2000 as the global center of sex tourism.

It is hard to think of a leisure practice that has a worse reputation: middle-aged or elderly but affluent men exploiting children from poor countries. And that sort of child prostitution does occur, especially in Thailand. The dominant practices of sex tourism, however, move in a different direction. Far from being particularly affluent, the male tourists are often from their own country's more modest social strata. The Italian men streaming into Salvador de Bahia on cheap charter flights looking for sex have been dubbed by the locals *duristas*, a combination of the Portuguese *duro* or broke, and *turista*, tourist. African American men are another large clientele group among the sex tourists of the north Brazilian metropolis, enjoying a higher status than they can achieve in their native country. Most of the sex workers who service this clientele are adult women, making their own, very distinct choices about earning a living, and who see tourists as better-paying and usually better-behaved customers than locals. Connections with tourists open the possibility of foreign travel, accompanying tourists returning to their home countries. When the tourists do take their liaisons more seriously, and bring women from Asia, the Caribbean, or Brazil back to Canada, the Netherlands or Germany, the cohabitation in a wealthier country tends to work out badly, yet another reminder of the distinction between tourism as its own world of leisure and everyday life. As knowledge of these experiences has percolated back, some sex workers have embraced the idea of a temporary stay in a foreign country, doing their own version of tourism.[59]

The gender contours of sex tourism have also developed in some unexpected ways. If relationships between men from Europe and North America and women from Asia, the Caribbean, and South America remain the most common version, gay sex tourism is also a flourishing business. In the Late-Millennium Era there has been a rise in the number of women sex tourists, although the kinder and gentler phrase "romance tourism" has been coined for them. It emerged as an offshoot of gay sex tourism. Indigenous young men, "beach boys," as they were known in the Dominican Republic, who had engaged in sexual relations with paying male tourists during the 1970s and 1980s, found a growing number of women as clients in the final decade of the century. While other forms of sex tourism typically involved a fairly simple exchange of cash, the beach boys had to arrange to meet women, introduce themselves, take them to local attractions and to dinner and dancing before getting around to sexual connections. Rather more skill was needed: offering the right endearments in several languages, understanding appropriate target groups—generally older and heavier female tourists—abilities at socializing, conversing, and dancing, as well as in performing oral sex. Asking for money was another skill; unlike female sex workers, who generally engaged in a straightforward transaction of sex for cash, their male counterparts could never demand money, but would hint around about their need for supporting relatives, continuing their education, or starting a small business. In the Dominican Republic, young women who serviced male tourists were ashamed of their occupation and hid it from family members, but "beach boys" were proud of their skills. They had aspirations to use their liaisons with women tourists—very profitable, bringing in multiples of the average wage—to travel to foreign countries with their clients, although they too might face the disappointments of actually residing abroad.[60]

Sex tourism appears in many ways as a culmination of a number of trends. It was a product of globalization, of increasing human and economic interaction worldwide. The expansion of vacations and tourism on a global scale, which became available even to the less-affluent citizens of the world's wealthy countries in Europe and North America, brought the sexual fascination with an exotic, racial other from the realm of fantasy into that of reality, if one dominated by the instrumental use of emotions and intimacy. It was also a product of both the sexual revolution and the sexual counterrevolution, of the possibilities for same-sex sexual relations, for women to pursue their own sexual interests but also male frustrations with changing relations between the sexes in their native countries, leading them to seek alternatives in different kinds of societies.

If sex tourism represents the nadir of the reputation of tourism, never very high to begin with, ecotourism might seem like the best opportunity to improve the sullied image of this leisure activity. Developing since the 1990s, this involves, or purports to involve, a touristic experience of natural environments, particularly in Central America, Amazonian Latin America, and Africa, offering a maximum of nature and a minimum of socially and environmentally disruptive tourist infrastructure. Ecotourists, generally a more affluent group, seek out natural authenticity—the direct experience of wild nature, rather than a familiar built environment in a foreign country. Who could object to a tourism that is designed to preserve the environment, rather than to destroy it, providing jobs and income for indigenous people, while simultaneously funding conservation and nature protection measures? Unfortunately, the logic of tourism as transforming the exotic into the familiar applies, and applies particularly strongly, to nature as much as to human cultures. Ecotourism takes place in areas where nature is supposed to be cordoned off from detrimental human impact, in national parks, animal and nature preserves. The very presence of tourists in these areas leads to their deterioration, destroying the environment ecotourism is supposed to protect.[61]

Closely related to ecotourism is the practice of trekking, yet another newer version of tourism arising in the Late-Millennium Era. Generally younger and more energetic than ecotourists, trekkers would also experience nature directly, in their case by hiking through mountainous regions. As a form of tourism, trekking began in 1970s Nepal. The royal government, seeking income from tourists, and fed up with the hippies, who were, at best, a mediocre source of foreign exchange, banned marijuana cultivation and made life increasingly unpleasant for countercultural tourists from the world's wealthier countries. The oil price shocks of that decade and the broader decline in economic growth magnified the result of public policy and brought the era of countercultural backpacking tourism to an end.

Hiking through the Himalayas appeared as an alternative form of tourism, providing employment for tour guides and local agencies. Unlike the hippie tourists, who had come from Europe overland and stayed for long periods of time, the trekkers were wealthier, arrived by jet, and spent at most a few weeks hiking in the mountains, a combination that fit the leisure time practices of the affluent denizens of Europe and North America at the end of the millennium. The Nepalese royal government's anti-drug policies made the former hemp-growing regions into strongholds of the Maoist insurgency that would eventually end the monarchy, but trekking continued throughout the uprising, avoiding parts of the country where the insurgency was being waged.[62]

Inhabitants of other mountainous regions, particularly the Andes, sought to get in on the new development. In 1982, there were just two climbing parties in the *Ruta Normal* of Acongua in Argentina, that country's share of the South American highlands; ten years later, there were 2,600. A hotel was built at 14,000 feet, with private baths, helicopter landing pads, satellite TV, a restaurant and bottled oxygen, to accommodate trekkers. Increasingly, mountain hikers encountered debris and garbage from people who had previously taken the same route. As with ecotourism, trekking tends to deteriorate the natural conditions the trekkers themselves wished to experience.[63]

Tourism and Leisure at the Beginning of the New Millennium

If the Age of Interconnection was the age of television, it was also the age of vacations. Providing anything resembling exact figures about the extent of tourism or its total economic impact is difficult. Estimates and appraisals generally relate to travel or to hotel bookings, and it is a stretch, although a commonly performed one, to describe them as tourism. Even communist regimes, whose central planners kept close tabs on the economy, could not always tell how many people crossing borders or staying in hotels were tourists or vacationers. What is available are figures on short-term international arrivals, often called "tourist arrivals," although many of these travelers were on business trips, religious pilgrimages, visiting family, or evading immigration laws. In addition, over the entire second half of the century, the world's population tripled, and, as former colonial possessions became independent sovereign states, there were a lot more international borders that could be crossed. For all these reasons, figures on "international tourist arrivals" overstate the extent of tourism. However, they also understate it, since they do not include the hundreds of millions of tourists whose tourism takes place within their own country. Even acknowledging these problems and sources of uncertainty, Figure 9.1 shows the astonishing expansion of international arrivals, many of whom were tourists—53 percent of them in 2017, according to the estimates of the World Tourism Organization.[64]

Following a sixtyfold increase in short-term international arrivals, from 1950 to 2017, by that latter year these arrivals reached 1.2 billion, about one person in six in the entire world. Just half of these arrivals were tourists, but adding back individuals touring in their native countries and so not crossing any borders, it would be fair to conclude that somewhere between one human being in four and one in six was a tourist. Still the pastime of a relatively

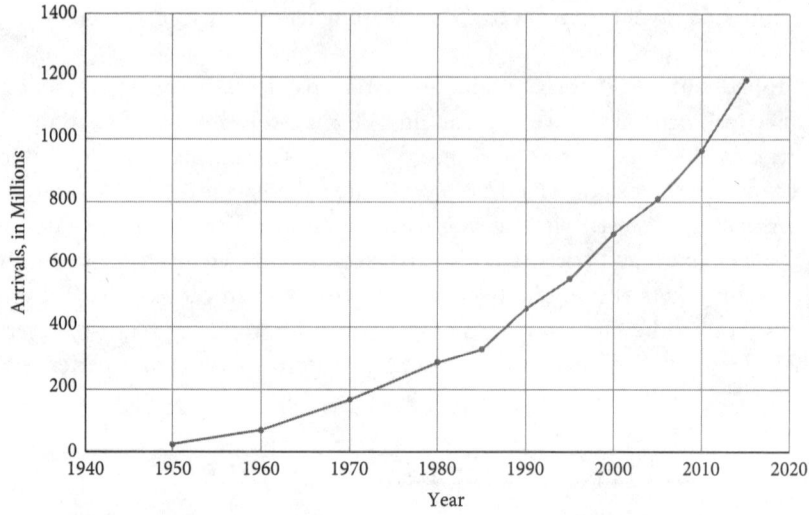

FIGURE 9.1 International Tourist Arrivals, 1950–2015

small elite group at mid-century, tourism that involved travel over longer distances had become, by the beginning of the new millennium, a mass and massive global leisure activity.

The ethical and aesthetic criticisms of tourism are best understood in the context of this expansion. Habitués of any tourist scene were perpetually being swamped by ever-growing numbers of newcomers, leading to the exploration of new venues, which, as the numbers of tourists continued to ratchet up at an accelerating pace, rapidly transitioned from insider experiences to sites of mass tourism. Crucial steps in this process were the jet-travel and backpacking explosions of the 1960s, as well as the other new forms of tourism, and its increasing global scope—whether in the form of tourists from East Asian countries, or the growing tourist arrivals outside of Europe and North America—in the Late-Millennium Era. By 2000, the entire world had been encompassed; the search for authenticity had led to a global tourist infrastructure.

If authenticity was out, what remained was stratification, which took two main forms. One was related to affluence. Travel and vacations were definitely not an area of leisure where the poor had more time than the rich. While in the wealthier parts of the world, tourism had become a practice for a substantial majority of the population, the upper classes were far more likely to take vacations, vacationed more often, and would do so more extensively and over longer distances, engaging in more elaborate forms of tourism. To take a couple of examples from the United States, in 2016, according to the Bureau of Labor Statistics, only about a third of people earning less than $25,000 per year had taken a vacation within the previous two years, while

85 percent of those making over $100,000 had done so. Not only do the affluent have more money for travel, they were far more likely to be employed in positions that included paid vacations. The vacations of the wealthy lasted longer and were more frequent than those of the less affluent. They also traveled farther. In 1999, only 3 percent of Americans flying overseas for leisure belonged to the census category of blue-collar workers, "laborers, craftsmen and operatives," while the most common occupations for people engaged in that sort of travel were "professional, managerial, and technical," followed by two groups, "students and retirees," most of whom were either aspiring to a professional, managerial, or technical career, or had already concluded one.[65]

These differences within countries were also present between countries. Considering the EU alone, and not differences between Europe and other, poorer continents, the proportion of the population engaging in tourism during 2015 ranged from 91 percent in Finland to 30 percent in Bulgaria, and more generally followed a gradient of wealth, with tourism and vacations being most common in the wealthiest countries of Western and Northern Europe, and least so in the poorer lands to the east and south. Many of those poorer southern countries, particularly in the Mediterranean Basin, were favored destinations of tourists from wealthier parts of Europe. However, this relationship—tourists from wealthier countries visiting poorer ones—very much did not hold on a global scale, contrary to what critics of tourism have frequently asserted. In the mid-1990s, according to the World Tourism Organization, about two-thirds of all international tourist arrivals were in the world's "advanced" economies, only a third in the "developing" ones ("advanced and developing," according to the categories of the World Bank). By 2016, the share of advanced economies had shrunk to 55 percent, but the expansion of the share was above all in East Asian countries that were developing fast; shares for the rest of the world, especially its poorest regions—in South Asia and sub-Saharan Africa—showed relatively little change. Since the number of tourist arrivals worldwide had doubled over the two decades following 1995, the number of tourists grew in all regions of the world, but the dominance of the wealthier countries, both as homes of tourists and as their vacation destinations, had remained.[66]

The second form of stratification relates to differences in the frequency and length of vacations. Here, the big development was that the United States moved in the opposite direction from other wealthier countries. Vacations shrank after 2000. After averaging some twenty days per year, average vacation time fell to sixteen by 2014. According to the surveys of the Gallup Organization, only 37 percent of Americans polled in 1954 had taken a vacation, or planned to. At the beginning of the 1990s, the figure had reached 59 percent, which put the United States at just about the EU average. Declining to 55 percent in 2002, by 2015, according to a different survey, only 44 percent of American adults had been on a vacation over the previous twelve months. To put this in perspective that is roughly the same proportion as in Croatia and Portugal, below the 61 percent EU average, and well below the percentage (as high as 80 percent) typical of the affluent countries of Western and Northern Europe.[67]

As a result of both business practices and legal requirements, Americans are taking fewer vacation days per year than their European, or Japanese, and Australian counterparts. And even when Americans had vacation days at their disposal, they were reluctant to take them, fearing that if they were away from work for a prolonged period, they might lose their jobs. Another way to put it would be to say that the defeat of labor worldwide, but especially severe in the United States, is reflected in this one particular version of leisure.[68]

If the Age of Interconnection was the age of leisure, and, even more so, of the two major and very different forms of leisure, TV viewing and tourism, there are at least three different ways to view the significance of this development—or, perhaps more accurately, one primary way, qualified by two caveats. These five decades were a time of increasing leisure, TV broadcasting (and television sets to receive the broadcasts), and international tourist arrivals. All these trends encompassed steadily larger portions of the planet and, overall, continue to this day—at least until the COVID-19 disruptions to international travel.

Yet these trends followed a distinctly regional gradient of affluence. North America came first, followed by Europe, along with Australia and New Zealand, and then East Asia, and the more affluent parts of Latin America, and, finally, the rest of the world. The leisure activity furthest along this gradient was TV viewing, which reached a majority of the globe's inhabitants by 2000. Tourism was another matter—involving the world's wealthy countries, both in origin and destination. Singaporean or Malaysian tourists in Thailand being taken for sex workers highlights the limited prospects for tourism among the world's poorer nations, and also the late accession of East Asian countries to this particular form of leisure.

In the age of the Cold War, the states of the Eastern Bloc—at least the USSR and Eastern European communist realms—seemed, in regard to leisure, closer to their affluent capitalist counterparts than to the world's poorer countries. This was perhaps most apparent in regard to television broadcasting and TV viewing, where the technological imperatives of over-the-air VHF broadcasting outweighed differences in television ownership and economic organization. Setting aside a time of the year for a journey to a distant site of recreation and experiences outside the everyday, were strikingly similar on both sides of the divide. The communist view of recreation as re-creation, as reinvigoration of workers' labor power, made for a different kind of vacation and touristic experience, but that changed during the Late-Millennium Era, when tendencies toward more Western styles of vacation and tourism grew.

Post-communist regimes, in both Europe and Asia, quickly picked up those Western styles.

It is the chronology of leisure that most brings into question or at least considerably modifies the simple picture of "more" and "further" about leisure. The postwar era, between 1945 and the early 1960s, were largely about increasing trends that had appeared in the Interwar Era: American auto vacations, European package tours, communist union-organized, health-related (or ostensibly health-related) spa trips, for instance. TV was then a new medium, and only reached a relatively small minority of households, even in most affluent countries. Total hours of leisure each week increased, but were still fairly close to where they had been before 1939.

The Era of Upheaval transformed leisure. For the first time, a majority of households in the world's affluent countries took annual vacations, and owned a TV set; women's leisure hours grew at a rapid pace; commercial jet aircraft expanded the realm of tourism and helped introduce new forms of tourism—the backpackers and budget tourists—part of a process of increasing differentiation of touristic experiences. A second set of transformations followed in the Late-Millennium Era: East Asian countries joining the leisure practices of the affluent world; a growing globalization of tourist experiences; even more differentiation of tourism, from the encompassing of the entire Mediterranean Basin with beachfront hotels, to sex tourism, ecotourism, and cruise vacations; and the transformation of TV viewing, through the cable-satellite nexus and the privatization and deregulation of broadcasting. Television, long hailed as an agent of globalization, seemed on its way to becoming such an agent, although the national context of TV remained strong after 2000.

The final decades of the century were also a period of new trends in leisure, including increases in the workday and workweek, and a growing differentiation, within the world's affluent countries, between a lower-class population of quotidian leisure and a more affluent, upper middle-class and wealthy population whose leisure was concentrated into short but frequent spurts of almost frenzied activities, distinctly separated from a work-saturated everyday life. Those unemployed or working part-time, parked in front of the TV set, with few opportunities for vacations and travel, contrasted with managers and professionals working longer hours and also taking more frequent and considerably more elaborate vacations, around the world. In the United States, where as noted vacation time declined, as did the proportion of the population taking vacations, this contrast was sharpest and most pronounced.

Were these American trends initial signs that the Age of Leisure was coming to an end? The decline in American vacations contrasts with their expansion in Europe and even in China. Still, the question of whether leisure and its most distinct forms and activities will continue its global advance remains open.

10 | Consumers

MORE THAN A CENTURY after Karl Marx and Friedrich Engels announced that the specter of communism was haunting Europe, another specter haunted not just Europe but the entire world: that of the consumer society. During the course of the Age of Interconnection the possibilities for the consumption of goods and services became overwhelming, expanding far beyond the necessities of subsistence. One could even say that consumption increasingly formed the basis of identity: people became what they purchased and how they used these purchases.

In the 1950s many welcomed this development. Consumption, they felt, was reflective of a new era of affluence, a welcome break from of the disasters of economic crisis and the catastrophe of total war. To them, it was a sign of health. Others decried it as ushering in a decline of frugality and a rise of debt, symptoms of a decadent lack of self-control. More than that, private wealth, they pointed out, coexisted with public poverty, and that the "bubble of affluence" in which Western consumers lived was generated by impoverishing other countries.[1] Much of this debate was carried out in the wealthier lands of the West in the 1950s, but by the following decade the authorities of the Eastern Bloc had decided that communism should be a consumer society. In the newly independent postcolonial regimes of Asia and Africa aspirations to consume were also widespread.

While the radical social movements of the Era of Upheaval in the 1960s and 1970s attacked consumerism and a consumer society, these movements and the youth culture so closely connected to them paradoxically promoted and diversified consumer aspirations, helping to spread them even farther into large parts of the world. The oil price shocks of the 1970s, and the global slowdown in economic growth that followed, put a brake on the expansion of consumer expenditures and dampened the euphoria. However, the

Late-Millennium Era was a time of the expansion of consumerism, not just into new categories of goods but increasingly into services. There was a rapid growth of globalized retailing, a different relationship between consumption and government regulations or government expenditures, and a new surge of consumer aspirations and consumption in East Asia.

The Age of Interconnection was the Age of Leisure. It was also the Age of the Consumer. Nonetheless, before proceeding to an investigation of the development and—uneven—global spread of consumerism it might be helpful to consider just what is meant by "consumer," "consumerism," or "consumer society," and how their post-1945 expansions and transformations fit into a longer global history. Probably the most important point is to distinguish "consumerism" from "consumption." The latter is a necessary and universal element of all human economies and societies. According to neoclassical economists, it is the goal and determining feature of all economic activity. What distinguishes consumerism from consumption are its four distinct features.

One is that goods and services are purchased and do not come from the consumer's own production. (The purchase does not necessarily have to be in a market, since consumers purchased goods and services under communist regimes.) A second feature of consumerism is a decline in the portion of consumption consisting of basic necessities, such as food, clothing, and shelter. There is a very helpful social science formulation of this point, Engel's law. Its formulator, Ernst Engel, today a forgotten figure, was a nineteenth-century social scientist, the pioneering director of the statistical bureau of the Prussian kingdom, whose empirical, fact-based approach to the world made him a constant thorn in the side of Germany's chancellor, Otto von Bismarck. His law states that the higher a household's income, the smaller the proportion of that income spent on food. Unlike so many social science "laws," this one seems to be mostly valid, whether taking a cross section of households with different incomes in a single country, comparing average households across different countries with different incomes, or evaluating changes in household consumption with changes in income over time.[2]

A third characteristic of consumerism is that purchasing behavior does not entirely accord with criteria of rational self-interest, but contains large elements of impulse, fashion, entertainment, pleasure, and diversion. This definition offends some economists, who believe that all purchasing behavior—in fact, all human behavior—is determined by rational self-interest. Conversely, there are social theorists who would assert that even in the most ostensibly rigorous economic decisions, corporate investment policies, or institutional financial transactions, for instance, rational self-interest is not the driving force. Of these two theoretical outlooks, the second seems more convincing, but they both carry explanations to extremes. A key to the relative importance of the rational and the emotional in consumerism is its development in tandem with advertising. The large role played by advertising in consumer purchases, and the fact—which only the most dogmatic of economists would dispute—that the motivations for purchasing advertisers seek to cultivate are not focused on self-interested rational calculation, is revealing. Closely related to this third characteristic is a fourth point—the intimate relationship in a consumer society between purchases and purchasers' identity, their self-understanding of their place in the world. This is not to say that consumption necessarily outweighs other factors shaping identity—nationality, race, religion, class, gender, generation, to name just a few—but that it plays an important role.

Throughout human history, there have always been people whose consumption has followed along the lines of these four characteristics, although generally a very small group, composed of monarchs and some of the preindustrial upper classes: nobility, aristocracy, gentry, or patricians. The expansion of the universe of consumers arguably started in the seventeenth and eighteenth centuries, when European empire-builders and commercial interests began to develop broader markets for the three bitter stimulants—chocolate, coffee, and tea as well as for the sugar needed to make those products palatable. The global expansion of economic activity in the nineteenth century created a background against which consumerism could flourish.[3]

A consumer society began to take shape in the years before the First World War, with the "second industrial revolution," the growth of the chemicals and electrical devices industries, whose goods would form the foundation for the consumerism we recognize today. This was also when department stores expanded, offering a new form of retailing in which spectacle, fantasy, and desire played an ever-larger role, and rational calculations faded into the background.

In the Interwar Era, consumerism began to take on a more distinct form. It was centered on a group of relatively expensive consumer durables, above all, the automobile, but including a range of electrical products, going from large purchases—refrigerators and washing machines—to radios, to vacuum cleaners, and telephones. (The latter was at least as much a service as a good, because its expense lay less in the device than in the charges for its connection to a communications network.) All these goods were the output of mass production, and for a large majority of the population, payment for them had to be spread out over time, involving some sort of credit, with the purchased item as collateral.

The name most associated with this expansion is Henry Ford (and, hence, "Fordism"). Inventor of the assembly line mass production of cars, and the employer who began paying his workers enough so that they could consider buying one, Ford was in some ways an icon of an early consumer society. In in other crucial respects this is misplaced. Ford rejected advertising, new auto models, different auto body colors, and the entire appeal to the emotions—all crucial features of consumerism—and this brought his enterprise to the brink of collapse. It also made the fortune of his corporate rival General Motors, a business quick to exploit these elements, including offering its own financing for the vehicles it sold, an idea Ford rejected.

The social, economic, technological, and cultural outlines of a consumer society existed in the Interwar Era, and while it was mainly begun in Europe and North America, there were signs of it globally. Santiago de Chile's wealthier inhabitants shopped in newly built department stores, purchased all sorts of electrical appliances, followed closely the latest developments in automobiles, and began to drive around in them. Even in China, a country mired in political chaos, social disorder and civil and foreign war during the first half of the twentieth century, consumer goods and aspirations toward their purchase made their appearance especially in the wealthier, southern coastal regions.[4]

Still, if there was anywhere consumerism reached beyond small groups of the affluent in the years after the First World War, then it was the United States. America was the exclusive home of a new form of retailing, the supermarket, which brought spectacle and desire to the very mundane business of purchasing food, turning consumption of basic necessities into consumerism. Even in the United States, there was a gap between the haves and have-nots, and an even larger gap existed between the United States and other wealthy countries. The gap became particularly apparent when Henry Ford decided to set up auto factories in a number of countries in Western Europe and wanted to find out how much workers there would need to be paid in order to have a standard of living roughly equivalent to those his own workers in Detroit enjoyed. He prodded the League of Nation's International Labour Organization (predecessor of today's UN-affiliated ILO) to carry out such a survey. It turned out that none of the European workers owned a car or much in the way of electrical devices—unlike half of Ford's US workforce—and would have to be paid two to four times the going wage rate to, aspire to this consumer cornucopia.[5]

The onset of the Depression in 1929 halted or at least greatly decelerated this movement everywhere. Like mass tourism, a later addendum to consumer society, consumerism was primarily an aspiration in the Interwar Era, one that would have to wait for the postwar era to be fulfilled. That era was also an age of an expansive and expanding state. Government expenditures after 1945 did decline from the high levels that they reached during the Second World War, but the share of the state in GDP remained elevated, a function of Cold War arms programs and, even more, of greatly expanded social welfare expenditures. It became commonplace in some circles to understand public spending and private consumption as antithetical, a viewpoint that became particularly pronounced during the deregulation and privatization of the Late-Millennium Era. In reality, the relationship between consumer-oriented private spending and state action was more complex and intertwined. Consumerism grew in the postwar era along with government regulation and social welfare spending; it was only following the 1970s economic crises that the relationship between the two changed. Even then, it was not so much that privatization and deregulation increased consumerism, or even that governments' share of GDP declined significantly, as that consumerism became increasingly globalized, escaping national government control.

Forging a Consumer Society

The Second World War did not immediately segue into a new world of consumerism. Quite the opposite, the lingering results of massive destruction and the numbers of refugees meant that consumerism was not at the forefront. The bread riots and subsistence disturbances in France from liberation to the early 1950s were more reminiscent of the age of Louis XVI and Marie Antoinette than harbingers of a consumer society. Even in the United States, the center of pre-1939 consumerism, untouched by the war and ending it with a far greater productive capacity than at the beginning, pent-up aspirations to the purchase of consumer goods competed with demands for a reinstatement of wartime price and rent controls. There were also demonstrations against higher food prices and consumer boycotts of expensive food.[6]

These issues faded and consumerism developed rapidly in 1950s America, complete with automobile ownership, suburbanization, shopping malls, supermarkets, homes filled with new furniture, and every electrical device, like TVs, mainly bought on the installment plan and driven by advertising. A nexus formed between different elements: shopping expeditions to the supermarket, large purchases that could only be carried off in an auto, and stored at home in a refrigerator, without which much of the food would have spoiled. Ancillary products, like Tupperware containers, were part of this universe of consumerism. Some groups, particularly racial minorities, remained on the margins of this cornucopia, yet African American demands for civil liberties and human rights were intimately connected to the aspiration to have an equitable part in this new world of consumption.[7]

Even in the world's other affluent countries, consumerism remained for much of the 1950s more an aspiration than a reality, perhaps available to a larger group than before 1939, but still leaving out most households. In Japan, consumerism was called the "bright life," a literal reference to higher wattage light bulbs, as well as to the idea of a household filled with electrical appliances. Pushed by both politicians and Japan's rapidly growing consumer electronics industry, reinforced by unprecedentedly noisy advertising campaigns, "bright life" was actually affordable only by a small minority of

Japanese households. Much was the same in 1950s France, where it was primarily the *cadres*, corporate managers, who could respond to the advertising, borrow money, and purchase consumer durables. Sometimes the advertising itself seemed like a mixed message. West German refrigerator manufacturers pitched their devices to housewives with phrases like, "You can save by buying in bulk."[8]

If consumerism remained more aspiration than reality in most of the world's wealthier countries, its prospects in less affluent countries were still more limited. In the USSR and the newly established communist regimes of the Eastern Bloc, economic planning was centered on rebuilding from wartime damage, promoting heavy industry, and preparing for a third world war. Wartime rationing and austerity continued well into the postwar era. Protests at the time did not invoke comparisons with Western countries. The strikers and antigovernment demonstrators of June 17, 1953, in East Germany were not demanding an end to rationing but more equitable rationing; rather than calling for a future of ever-greater consumption, they wanted the government to guarantee the same standards of living as in prewar years.[9]

Newly independent or newly self-assertive regimes in Africa, Asia, and Latin America were promoting import substitution industrialization rather than consumerism during the postwar era. In the long run, ISI was supposed to increase the supply of goods and create something resembling a consumer society. Initially, however, domestic industry would have to be built up, with priority going to steel and industrial machinery. By preventing the import of consumer goods from Europe and North America, high tariffs would protect domestic manufacturers—at consumers' expense. To reach a shiny future of consumerism, Indians and Brazilians would first have to endure shortages and restrictions.

One country in the southern hemisphere whose government tried to create a full-blown consumer society in the postwar era was Argentina under its charismatic president Juan Perón and his even more charismatic wife, Evita. Powered by the large export surpluses Argentina had run up during the Second World War, Perón proposed that all Argentines, not just the wealthy elites of Buenos Aires, should enjoy *la vida digna*, the dignified life—a concept not dissimilar to the "bright life" of a few years later—with widespread ownership of electrical devices, enjoyment of yearly vacations, and even, toward the very end of his turbulent decade-long reign, possession of a four-door sedan, the *justicialistia*, named after Perón's political party. Generous collective bargaining agreements and social welfare payments, neither one surprising under the authoritarian rule of a politician enjoying strong trade union support, would provide the popular purchasing power needed to enter the kingdom of consumerism. All this was to occur while Argentina continued to enjoy its long-standing position as a land of plenty, both food exporter and consumer of large amounts of farm products.

In some ways, Argentina's lower classes really did enjoy a dignified life. By 1950, nearly every household in the country owned a radio. While possession of more expensive electrical appliances was less widespread, their sales boomed, and the proportion of households owning them was at least as great as in Western European countries of the time. In what might be a rare example of a violation of Engel's law, meat consumption increased in parallel with the purchase of consumer durables, reaching an all-time world's record of 250 pounds per person in 1950. Unfortunately, the rapid rise in salaries and social welfare expenditures created a serious inflation problem, with price increases reaching 60 to 80 percent per year by the late 1940s. To maintain the supply of foodstuffs, the government restricted exports, leading to shortages of foreign exchange. Price controls were introduced, and Evita organized squads of housewives to go around from store to store, making sure that shopkeepers were selling at legal prices.

These practices produced both shortages and a black market. The indomitable Evita struck back. Her Eva Perón Foundation started its own chain of *proveeduria*, Peronist supermarkets, which sold groceries and household goods in large, well-lit, and enticing retail spaces, but at controlled prices. The global commodity boom following the outbreak of the Korean War improved the economic situation and made less painful the austerity program the government instituted to deal with the unintended effects of the dignified life, which enabled Perón to remain in power until 1955. The memory of the era, though, and its distinctly politicized—albeit in a uniquely Argentine way—promises of consumerism has remained an influential factor in Argentine politics ever since.[10]

Outside the United States, the 1960s—the start of the Era of Upheaval—marked the breakthrough of consumer society in the world's wealthier countries. In France, a quarter of all households owned TVs, refrigerators, or vacuum cleaners in 1960; eight years later, three-quarters had televisions and half the other two devices. This was the pattern for Western Europe (as for Japan), with wealthier countries in the north of the continent having reached a similar point a few years earlier; poorer countries in the south of the continent followed over the course of the 1970s. Automobiles succeeded electrical goods, with about a five- to ten-year lag. The growth of supermarkets and self-service foodstuff retailing more generally moved in sync with the purchase of refrigerators. Just as Engel's law would have it, the proportion of household income spent on food declined sharply in those years, in spite of the shopping in supermarkets to fill all those refrigerators. Tupperware accompanied this transition, as its sales and sales methods—parties given by housewife saleswomen for their fellow housewives—expanded internationally along with kitchen consumer durables. It was particularly popular in Japan where, by the mid-1960s, its per capita sales were running at twice US levels.[11]

Public policy in European communist countries began to move in the direction of consumerism as well, and household ownership of TVs, refrigerators and washing machines became widespread in the 1970s, at about roughly the same time as in southern Europe. Communist regimes outside Europe either rejected this whole policy direction—as was true in China under Mao, Cuba under Castro, and North Korea under Kim Il-Sung—or started from a much lower economic level and had to face almost constant war, as was the case in much of Asia and Africa. In those countries, achieving minimal subsistence was a success; consumerism was light years off.[12]

MYTHS AND REALITIES OF AN EMERGENT CONSUMER SOCIETY

To contemporaries of the postwar era, as well as to pundits and historians today, the emerging "consumer society" had four main features, each of which marked a distinct break with the past. Advertising and market research were everywhere; their presence encouraged or manipulated consumers into spending and purchasing. Second, this rush to purchase was encouraged still more by the massive expansion of consumer credit, delineating a transition, from a society of deferred gratification and rational calculation to one of debt and immediate fulfillment. Third, this private cornucopia was enabled by defunding public spending. Private and public expenditures were in conflict with each other. Fourth, these features were associated with Americanization. Born in the United States, the attitudes, institutions, and economic arrangements of consumer society spread outward from it in the postwar era, either by voluntary emulation or by imposition resulting from political calculation and economic power. All four of these features of the nature of consumer society are dubious, either openly false or at best half-truths. The actual story of the rise of consumer society and its destiny was more complicated.

Advertising as an industry and standard recourse for manufacturers of consumer goods began on a large scale in 1920s America. Not just limited to the key consumer durables, advertisers praised packaged foods, cosmetics, cleaning products, clothing, in fact virtually every consumer product offered for sale. Advertising's ubiquity showed the distinctly imperialist tendencies of consumer society—how the pleasures, fantasies, and identities of consumerism came to take over all forms of consumption, even those of basic necessities. In Europe and elsewhere, pre-1945 advertising remained largely limited to the reframing of the purchase of such modest necessities since the demand for more expensive consumer durables still did not exist on a mass scale.[13]

As this demand came into existence in the world's wealthier countries, especially in the 1960s, advertising expanded along with it. Advertisers in newly consumerist countries of Western Europe or Japan studied American advertising for its practices and techniques. But this post-1945 growth of advertising was not unrestrained. In the United States, for which figures on total advertising expenditures are available for most of the twentieth century, the amount of money spent on advertising, already running at some $2.5 billion annually in the 1920s, and, after declining during the Great Depression and the Second World War, soared upward in exponential fashion, going from $5.7 billion in 1950 to $248 billion in 2000. This sounds dramatic, but once inflation and the growth of the economy are taken into account, it turns out that the peak era for advertising expenditures was, in fact, the Roaring Twenties: the approximately 3 percent of US GDP spent on advertising per year was an all-time high. During the entirety of the second half of the twentieth century, yearly advertising expenditures have never even reached 2.5 percent of GDP.

The United States was and is the world's leader in advertising, with per capita expenditures reaching almost $250 per person in 1980. Even in West Germany, Japan, and France, per capita ad expenditures were just one-third of what they were in America. Australia, a country with many economic, historical, and cultural similarities to the United States, had among the highest advertising expenditures per person, as did, more surprisingly, Switzerland, Finland, and Sweden—none of them "Americanized" societies.[14]

While advertising has grown along with consumerism, it has not increased beyond all measure. In fact, by some measures, it has not increased at all. Of course, ads have changed venues and forms to fit those venues, going from predominantly print, to TV, to online. Advertising has certainly been part of the American way of life, but in other countries the presence of advertising and the degree of "Americanization" do not seem to be entirely related. This is even more true of another feature of the consumer-advertising nexus—market research. Although extensive in the United States in the postwar era, market research was actually a European product, and, somewhat surprisingly, a left-wing one. The first market researchers of the Interwar Era were social democrats. The pioneer investigator of the electronic mass media was Paul Lazarsfeld, an adherent of the Frankfurt School, the neo-Marxist critics of consumer culture. Lazarsfeld's Vienna research associate Ernst Dichter founded the Institute for Motivational Research in 1946 and become America's marketing guru and prominent cheerleader for a consumer society during the 1950s. Dichter's story is a characteristic one. American market research was founded by progressive Europeans who fled fascist and Nazi Europe for the United States and worked together with other Americans having strong connections to Europe, such as Arthur Charles Nielsen, founder of the TV ratings firm, the son of Danish immigrants who retained close ties to his parents' homeland.[15]

Common ideas about the geography of consumer society are further undermined by investigating credit. The standard take on consumerism locates it in a transition from saving to spending, from delayed to instantaneous gratification, and, above all, from cash to credit. Saying "charge it," paying "on time," using credit cards—these are all at the heart of a consumer society. Critics deplore the change in attitudes and periodically issue demands for austerity to rein in debt-based excesses, most recently after the global financial crisis of 2008. Connected to these Jeremiads are polemics against Americanization, where the extension of credit appears as the foisting of America's free-spending ways on inherently more frugal Northern Europeans or East Asians. Of all the (mis)understandings of consumerism, this one is the greatest.

The idea that there ever existed a cashed-based paradise of saving and renunciation is dubious. Credit was a regular feature of nineteenth-century consumer purchases in both Europe and North America well before a consumer society came into existence. Peddlers sold their goods on credit; shopkeepers and tavern owners let their customers run a tab. The civil courts were constantly dealing with purchasers defaulting, and declaring bankruptcy (when permitted by the legal system). The interplay of creditors and debtors—one seizing goods pledged as security against loans, and the other hiding their assets from them—was a popular spectator sport, taking up an immense proportion of court business.[16]

New forms of retailing closely associated with consumerism—department stores and supermarkets—rejected those earlier forms of credit and insisted on payment in cash. This practice proved a disaster in Italy, one of the then-poorer countries of Western Europe, where consumers clung firmly to the credit advanced them by butchers, bakers, or grocers. The first Italian supermarkets were, quite literally, an instance of Americanization, since they were founded by the International Basic Economy Corporation, a firm set up by the Rockefellers to spread the American gospel of consumerist retailing around the world. The opening of the proud flagship stores of *Supermarkets Italiani* in Florence and Milan in 1961 made clear the link between the rejection of credit and the consumerist institution of supermarkets. Italians from the lower and middle classes, expecting to run a tab at the store, stayed away; shoppers were primarily women from the upper echelons with the wherewithal to pay cash. They shopped wearing furs and bringing in their chauffeurs to carry out their purchases. As late as 1981, only 2 percent of Italians' food purchasing expenditures were made in supermarkets.[17]

What characterized consumerism was not simply borrowing, but different forms of borrowing for different purposes. Consumer durables required larger loans and a longer-term, fixed repayment schedule. In France, TVs were purchased by means of loans from specialized finance companies. CETELEM (*Crédit a l'équipement électromenager* or Credit for Outfitting Households with

Electric Devices), the largest, formed by a consortium of banks and consumer electronics manufacturers in 1953, funded the purchase of 3.3 million television sets in its first thirty years of existence, while also providing finance for other household electrical goods, and getting into auto loans in the 1960s. Across the Rhine in West Germany, it was savings banks and credit unions that pioneered funding the purchase of consumer durables, followed a bit later by the Federal Republic's commercial banks.[18]

These forms of credit were one-time financial transactions, tied to the purchase of something specific. By contrast, in the United Kingdom, the United States, and Japan, a different form of consumer credit dominated in the postwar era. Its pioneer was a British firm, the Provident Clothing and Supply Company, founded in the late nineteenth century. The Provident issued "checks" to its customers, coupons they could use to purchase goods at stores that had an arrangement with the firm. The customers then paid off the purchase price in installments, collected by a small army of agents who made weekly house calls. The firm profited from the interest on its advances, as well as from the fees it charged participating merchants. As the name suggests, the business was not originally oriented toward funding consumer durables, but more modest purchases by a working-class customer base. Its founder, Joshua Waddilove, a pious Methodist, hoped its business methods would keep working-class men from running a tab at pubs and spending the family's money on drink. After the Second World War, Provident began moving into bigger-ticket consumer goods (comparable businesses in continental European countries had not done so, opening the way to new kinds of financing for the nascent consumer society), spreading out payments over fifty or one hundred weekly installments, instead of the previous twenty. In 1951, Japan Credit Sales started a similar enterprise, distributing its "tickets" to consumers, who could then redeem them at participating stores. Playing a central role in financing consumer electronics in the 1950s and 1960s, the firm remains the largest finance company in Japan.

The American version of this form of credit was the department store charge card, which could be used for any purchase at the store issuing it. Begun in the 1920s, these store cards reached their high point in the postwar era. During the 1950s, one American household in two had a credit card issued by Sears, the nation's largest retailer. Tickets and checks, as well as department store cards, were all examples of revolving credit, since consumers did not need an additional transaction (including application, evaluation, and approval), to borrow again after paying off a loan—or, increasingly, even before paying off a loan—and could simply borrow more.[19]

Like advertising, however, it is too easy to overstate the influence of credit on the creation of a consumer society. In West Germany, for instance, the proportion of basic consumer durables purchased on credit during the 1960s—the breakthrough decade for these items—actually declined by about 20 to

30 percent compared with the previous decade.[20] The point can be made more broadly. The 1950s and 1960s, years of the establishment of a consumer society in the world's wealthier countries, were also high points of saving—whether measured as a percentage of GDP or as a percentage of disposable household income. In the United States, where as noted the data are best, the savings rate in those decades was over double what it had been during the 1920s, to say nothing of the years of the Great Depression. According to the World Bank's calculations, savings as a percent of GDP across the entire world reached a high point in 1972, the year before the oil shock, declining throughout the rest of the century. Saving and consumption grew together in the postwar era.[21]

As a proportion of GDP, credit increased substantially, according to one study of seventeen of the world's wealthier countries, doubling between 1950 and 2000, from about 50 to 100 percent of GDP. Most of that increase was the result of lending to private households, so one might suspect that consumer credits were responsible. In fact, three-quarters of the increase came from loans guaranteed by real estate—mortgages and similar forms of credit. These were different from consumer financing, because the property purchased was also an investment, which could, potentially, generate a considerable return (or, in some circumstances, with subprime loans, a considerable loss) something that generally did not follow from buying a TV, refrigerator, or automobile. Home ownership rates in these seventeen countries rose between 1950 and 2000 and was linked to the purchase of consumer durables. If there was clearly a relationship between consumerism and home ownership, there were also affluent consumer societies, such as those in Switzerland and West Germany, where most households were renters.[22]

As was the case with savings, government expenditures increased along with consumerism in the postwar era. The most extensive figures come from the United Kingdom. From 1850 to the First World War, government expenditures made up about 10 percent of GDP. After hitting 40 per cent of GDP during the Great War, the figure declined to 25 percent in the Interwar Era. Climbing to 70 percent during the Second World War, expenditures re-stabilized at around 40 percent of GDP during the three following decades. The United States followed a similar trajectory, albeit at lower levels. Government expenditures in the United States and the United Kingdom continue to take up a smaller percentage of the GDP than elsewhere in the world, but the higher levels of government spending in the postwar era were found everywhere.[23]

This parallel growth between consumer society and government spending shouldn't be surprising. Wages earned by members of the armed forces or workers in armaments production, and social welfare payments—the two main government expenditures—could both be turned into the purchase of consumer goods. As we've seen, the postwar era was an age of the triumph of labor: collective bargaining agreements with good wages and generous benefits also promoted consumer spending and made possible the widespread purchase of the big-ticket items that characterized the developing consumer society. A product of capitalism, later to be imitated by communist countries, consumerism was a product of the regulated capitalism of the era.

Challenges to and Expansion of Consumer Society

Like so many elements of the postwar world, consumerism and the affluent society came under challenge in the Era of Upheaval. Some of these challenges were dramatic: 1960s New Left activists rejecting consumer society as a particularly pernicious form of capitalism; hippies dropping out, leading a communal life without electricity or even money; a growing environmentalist movement that denounced consumerism for its destructive impact on nature, calling for a lifestyle with few or no consumer goods. Hard on the heels of this voluntary rejection of consumerism came the 1973 oil shock, stagflation, and global recessions of the 1970s and early 1980s. These seemed to foretell an end to the rapid economic growth and widespread prosperity of the postwar era, which had been the underpinning of the expansion and spread of a consumer society. If the dissidents of the New Left and the hippies and environmentalists who had accompanied and also succeeded them were proposing voluntary renunciation of consumerism, the economic difficulties suggested that consumerism's end would be compulsory. Ultimately, neither of these challenges seriously upset the consumer society that had developed in the world's wealthier countries. The real challenges to consumerism came from more unexpected sources—from consumers' movements and, more generally, from the question of the future of consumer aspirations.

One of the features of the New Left was its critical attitude toward affluence and consumerism. This was what made the New Left "new," in contrast to the left of social-democratic, communist, and labor parties, along with their affiliated trade unions, which had sought to create affluence for workers in the first place. Prominent New Left theorists like the founder of the *Situationists*, French writer Guy Debord, decried the "society of the spectacle" created by advertising and mass media. In his 1964 book *One Dimensional Man*, Frankfurt school philosopher and worldwide New Left guru Herbert Marcuse denounced the "one dimensional man" of affluent capitalist society, in which most were seduced by advertising into a psychopathology of obsessive accumulation of consumer goods while basic psychological human needs remained unfulfilled, a process Marcuse dubbed "repressive desublimation."[24]

These ideas struck a chord with New Left activists, who were outraged by the conjunction of consumerism in the world's wealthy countries, and the presence of poverty in what was then coming to be called the Third

World. In 1966, activists in West Berlin held demonstrations protesting the Vietnam War during the Christmas shopping season on the *Kurfürstendamm*, the city's main shopping street and a center of Western consumer culture in the midst of the Eastern Bloc. They followed it up with pamphlets calling for the burning of department stores, which some of their comrades in Frankfurt actually did, denouncing the "terror of consumerism." Arrested and put on trial, they presented their opposition to consumerism as part of resistance to the US war in Vietnam. Two of the arsonists, Gudrun Ensslin and Andreas Baader, would later become famous or infamous as leaders of the terrorist Red Army Group that kidnapped and assassinated prominent West German businessmen and government officials during the 1970s.[25]

Environmentalists of that decade used less violent means but were no less determined in their opposition to consumerism. Particularly in the wake of the publication of the Club of Rome study, *Limits to Growth*, with its warning of the impending exhaustion of natural resources, environmentalism took aim at consumer society. In an essay of 1972, the American poet and environmentalist Wendell Berry called on his countrymen to stop "contributing directly to the ruin of the planet," by driving fewer miles, consuming less, and taking up a "new kind of life—harder, more laborious, poorer in luxuries and gadgets, but also, I am certain, richer in meaning and more abundant in real pleasure."[26]

Whatever the effects on society and politics of the New Left and early environmentalism, their opposition to consumer society found little resonance. If anything, the youth culture so closely connected to these social and political movements expanded and diversified consumerism. Popular music expanded the demand for electronics, so central to consumerism, adding stereo speakers, amplifiers, receivers, turntables, and tape decks to radios and TVs. West German sociologists found that those living in communal housing had more TVs, stereos, washers and driers, and automobiles than conventional households. Scruffy dress, so typical of the era, expanded the realm of fashion—yet another example of consumerism turning the purchase of basic necessities into opportunities for pleasure and fantasy—beyond formal wear. Jeans, work shirts, and boots went from practical clothing designed for physical labor to fashion statements. These elements of consumer society, spread, via youth culture, across the world.[27]

As the USSR and its Eastern European allies increasingly promoted consumerism, there developed another version of this left-wing criticism, one that condemned the communists for trying to keep up with the capitalists instead of devising alternative, collectivist versions of the use of consumer goods: trying to build cars, instead of improving public transportation, providing women with refrigerators and new stoves to make shopping and cooking easier, instead of creating collective kitchens to liberate women from the oppression of preparing food. The French leftist André Gorz even condemned communist regimes for attempting to produce enough cameras for every household, instead of making them available collectively. After 1989, when the failure of the Eastern Bloc's efforts at promoting consumerism became apparent, this became self-criticism, though those articulating it were invariably intellectuals, professionals, or party and government officials—that is to say, members of the regime's privileged classes, who had the most and the best consumer goods. Workers in the Eastern Bloc, by contrast, had no such moral qualms. They believed that if there was anything authentic about communism it involved a consumer society available to all social classes.[28]

Probably the most effective opposition to consumer society came, paradoxically, from consumers' organizations and associations. Unlike New Leftists or environmentalists, consumer advocates did not wish to end or to restrict the purchase of consumer durables or other consumer goods. However, they did want to strip those purchases of fantasy, desire, and spontaneous gratification, and restore them to the realm of calculated, rational self-interest. Few consumer organizations were spoilsports, such as the Japanese consumer magazine, *Kurashi no techō* (*Handbook of Living*), which in 1955 informed the public that most households did not need washing machines. These households lacked enough clothing to wash, and the machines would ruin homespun fabrics. Three years later, it expressed skepticism about the value of refrigerators. Generally, however, consumers' groups and their publications tested an immense variety of consumer goods, evaluating their price, function, durability, and reliability, doing so by systematically comparing the products of different manufacturers. They denounced misleading advertising, and called for laws regulating advertising claims; ensuring that credit and contract terms were open, transparent, and understandable to consumers; and limiting or prohibiting the sale of hazardous items. Although consumers' groups never could bring consumer society to an end by eliminating pleasure and desire from consumer purchases—except perhaps among a small segment of their predominantly well-educated, upper middle-class membership—they did build an intellectual and legal bridgehead for calculations of economic self-interest. The historian Lizabeth Cohen, in her work on consumer society in post-1945 America, has counted no fewer than forty-four different federal government laws, administrative rulings, and new agencies created in the United States during the 1960s and 1970s in response to the demands of consumer groups. Similar consumer protection legislation was passed in the United Kingdom and Western Europe, all with the involvement of consumers' groups. The 1968 Consumer Basic Protection Law in Japan was still another example of this trend. In many ways, this wave of consumer-protective legislation seems similar to the legal initiatives protecting women's rights and liberating sexuality, or trying to implement environmental protection.[29]

The crucial role of the Era of Upheaval also appears in the history of the world consumer federation, the International Organization of Consumers' Unions. Founded in 1960, at a conference with representatives of fourteen countries, mostly from Western Europe and North America by 1970, another thirty-nine countries were associated or affiliated, mostly from Asia, Africa, and Latin America. In 2000, the renamed Consumers International held its sixteenth world congress in Durban, South Africa, attended by representatives of 115 countries.[30]

A different threat to consumer society emerged from the 1973 oil shock and the subsequent worldwide decline in economic growth rates. Consumerist spending retreated in years of particularly rapid inflation and recession, though, overall, in the world's affluent countries, such spending held up well—better, in fact, than other features of the economy.[31] Indeed, the expansion of consumer society to some of the less affluent nations of Western Europe continued apace in the 1970s. The question emerging in Europe, North America, Australia, and Japan during that decade was not so much the danger to consumer society as the nature of its continued expansion. The basic outlines of consumerism sketched in the 1920s—ownership of automobiles and household electrical and electronic goods, ubiquitous advertising, shopping in department stores and supermarkets—had been filled in. It was, of course, always possible to push for more—via a second car, or television; a second refrigerator, washing machine, or vacuum cleaner seemed less likely—or for improvements, replacing a black-and-white TV with a color version, a smaller car with a bigger one equipped with more features. Advertisers would do their best to present these as comparable to the dramatic changes that had been a consequence of the implementation of a consumer society, but for all their efforts the excitement of replacement was not the same as the initial acquisition.

In Africa, Latin America, and much of Asia, by contrast, the aspirations connected to the realm of consumerism had become increasingly pervasive—in part, as an unintended consequence of the spread of youth culture throughout the world. Had the global economic growth of the postwar era continued into the final quarter of the century, a consumer society might have begun to develop there as well. The oil shock and economic decline of the 1970s put an end to that prospect. For a few countries profiting from the rapid increase in oil prices, particularly the petrostates of the Arabian peninsula, the promises of consumerism became increasingly a reality. In most of Latin America and Africa, by contrast, the whipsawing of the spike in oil prices during the 1970s and their subsequent decline, and the institution of austerity policies produced that "lost decade" of the 1980s, which in Africa extended until the end of the millennium. The world seemed to be divided between countries where consumer society had reached fruition and lacked impetus for further development, and those in which it could not ever come into existence.

New Directions of Consumerism in the Late-Millennium Era

It is a tribute to the protean nature of consumerism that its seeming cul-de-sac in the 1970s gave way to a host of new developments in the Late Millennium, which continue to shape the nature of consumer society today. Four such changes seem particularly significant. One involved the interaction of consumer aspirations in the world's wealthiest countries with growing economic inequality. A second was the wave of privatization and deregulation characteristic of the era—themselves inspired, at least ostensibly, by the assertion that they would cut prices to consumers and increase their choices, thus reinforcing and expanding consumer society. There was also the expansion of consumerism into the realm of services, most apparent in travel and vacations, as discussed in the previous chapter, but also in areas such as restaurant dining and, especially, cell phones—a genuinely new device and new consumer practice of the very final decade of the twentieth century. Finally, and most significantly, was the increasing globalization of consumerism, breaking out of the North Atlantic nexus and reaching other parts of the world, particularly East Asia. Retailing took on a global tone, with the ubiquity of McDonald's fast-food restaurants or Carrefour supermarkets. The long-dominant, pioneering role of the United States in the development of consumer society wavered, as Americans spent the 1980s fascinated by Japanese products. And cell phones became objects of consumer desire in Europe a decade before the United States. Such a globalization of consumerism provoked fears, much as the growth of tourism had, that worldwide capitalist initiatives would submerge indigenous local cultures. Actual effects involved a wide variety of local uses of globally distributed consumer goods and services.

Fordism, with its mass production and assembly lines—the same goods for everybody—assumed a society in which forms of consumption would no longer be a marker of class status. Even in the Fordist Era, say from the 1920s through the 1970s, there were plenty of ways that consumption could be differentiated: one need only think of Ford's more successful rival, General Motors, which, as noted earlier, combined mass production with a differentiated product line, ranging from the plebian Chevrolet to the exclusive Cadillac. An important feature of market research as it was practiced in the 1950s was investigating different elements within a market and the possibilities for appealing to them. Yet, particularly in the postwar era, when rapid economic growth brought income gains to all segments of the population in the world's wealthy countries, and income inequality in those countries reached an all-time low point in human history, manufacturers and retailers tended to orient their business around the largest segment of a mass market—the middle.

As incomes began to drift apart in the Late-Millennium Era, and as acquisition of the central elements of consumer society—autos, household electrical goods, and electronics—became universal, the idea of aiming production and marketing to different segments of the population became more attractive.[32] One way this became apparent was in the decline of department stores, the temples of Fordist mass market consumerism. We generally think of this as a more recent development, in which these stores are squeezed between online retailers, luxury goods-oriented specialty shops, and low-end discount chains. In fact, this was a trend that began much earlier, well before desktop computers, to say nothing of the Internet. In the Federal Republic of Germany, department store sales rose about seventeen-fold between 1950 and their peak years 1974–1975. Taking inflation into account, these sales have declined, ever since. Department store share of total retail sales also reached its high point in the mid-1970s, at just under 11 percent and sank steadily to under 4 percent two decades later.[33]

In the United States, where income inequality was particularly pronounced, even maintaining central features of consumerism, much less expanding them, was becoming difficult for members of lower-income groups. It was at this juncture that new forms of credit came to the "rescue," retaining the possibilities of consumerism for the less-favored portion of the population. Above all others, there was the universal bank credit card.

Universal credit cards, not tied to particular businesses, came into existence in the United States in the postwar era. The initial versions, Diners Club and American Express, both of which required paying off the balance in full at the end of each month, were less a form of credit than a way for business travelers to avoid carrying around a lot of cash, a task more frequently accomplished with another American Express product, travelers' checks. In 1958, an upstart West Coast financial institution, the San Francisco-based Bank of America, issued the first bank credit card, guaranteeing its user a line of credit, neither limited to a particular business nor guaranteed by real property, as was a mortgage, nor secured by a consumer durable, as was the case with installment loans. Extending such unsecured credit was a risky practice, and in the first fifteen months of its credit card operation the bank ran up $15 million in losses. Universal bank credit cards gradually became more common in the 1960s and 1970s and were consolidated into two separate networks, Bankamericard (now Visa) and Master Charge. In view of the unsecured nature of the credit, banks were relatively cautious about handing the cards out, and users tended to be more affluent. In 1970, some 81 percent of households with an income over $25,000—quite a handsome sum at the time—had a bank credit card, as against under 20 percent of those with incomes beneath $3,000. The well-to-do were disproportionately "convenience users," who treated their bank cards as businessmen treated American

Express cards (there was probably a lot of overlap) and paid off the balance each month.

In the course of the 1970s bank credit cards were fundamentally transformed. Financial deregulation made it possible for banks to charge whatever interest rate they wanted on unpaid balances and the "spread," the difference between the interest rates banks paid to borrow money and the ones they charged their credit card customers, reached unheard of levels, between ten and fourteen percentage points, far higher than in any other forms of bank lending. Banks systematically marketed their cards to lower-income households less likely to pay off their balances, so that by the final decades of the country, something like two bank credit card users in three were keeping a—steadily growing—balance and paying annual interest rates on it of 15 to 30 percent.

This was a new form of credit, one nothing like the installment loans tied to individual purchases that had characterized the rise of consumer society. Credit cards could be and increasingly were used by lower- and middle-income households, not just to fund the purchase of big-ticket consumer durables or other large consumer expenditures like vacations, but to meet expenses during periods of unemployment or to deal with medical bills. In this respect, credit cards were not so much a facilitator of consumerism as a way to pay for basic necessities, almost falling back to a period before the rise of consumer society. This function of credit cards comes into sharper focus when considered alongside the rise of other forms of credit in the United States at the end of the millennium, aimed explicitly at subsistence spending among lower-income households: pawnshops, whose numbers went from 4,800 in 1985 to 14,000 in 2000; short-term unsecured loans, so-called payday loans; and short-term credits secured by title to the debtor's automobile, carrying yearly interest rates of from 300 to 1,000 percent.[34]

Rather than being the ultimate avatar of a consumer society, universal bank credit cards seem more like signs of that society's dissolution, as growing income inequality made it more difficult for poorer households to keep up with basic expenses, to say nothing of purchasing consumer durables. Outside the United States, credit cards have been most popular in the United Kingdom, another country with strong income disparities; in the course of the 1990s, the number of credit cards there went from twelve to thirty million. By contrast, in the somewhat more egalitarian lands of continental Europe, or Japan, credit cards have been noticeably less common. This was and is not because its citizens borrowed less than their British or American counterparts (counting mortgage loans, they often borrowed more as a percentage of GDP or of household income), but because they continued to use installment loans and other forms of secured consumer credit. Today, credit cards have become more common in countries enjoying rapid economic growth and a nascent consumerism, including Brazil, Malaysia, or China. In the latter, credit card users have charged as much per year as did their counterparts in France. In India, where economic growth and consumerism, while certainly underway, had not reached the levels attained in the countries named above, the use of universal bank credit cards remains uncommon and cash payments the rule; even people having plastic in their wallet tended not to take it out.[35]

The lifting of legal limitations on interest rates, which made possible the expansion of the credit card business in the United States, was just one very small piece of a much broader wave of deregulation and privatization, occurring around the world in the Late-Millennium Era. Proponents of these policies offered a myriad of arguments in their favor. Free to compete in the market under profit-seeking private ownership, firms would be more innovative, more efficient, more productive; society's total product would be distributed more equitably. Consumers would enjoy lower prices, as a result of competition, and a much greater variety of goods and services. These arguments and the deregulation and privatization they endorsed were part of a broader policy of rolling back the state: cutting taxes and government expenditures, especially for social welfare, reducing the state's share of GDP. This, too, would promote consumerism, by leaving more money in consumers' pockets.[36]

Offering an overall assessment of these arguments and the policies behind them around the entire world remains risky. At least some skepticism seems justified. In a number of countries—Egypt and Nigeria come to mind—privatization was a device by which public property could pass into the hands of politically well-connected families, a process that would play out on a very large scale in post-communist Eastern Europe. But privatization and deregulation were not just problematic in lands of barely functioning or failed states. Deregulating regulated monopolies—while simultaneously privatizing them, if they were in public ownership—resulted in deregulated monopolies. The classic example of this was the public-water utility in England. Private firms, now in control of water coming out of the tap and unafraid of competition, which would have required building an entire, enormous water-supply network, promptly more than doubled rates: a bonanza for stockholders and, especially, top management, although of relatively little use to consumers of a basic necessity. The nearly £100 their average yearly bills increased between 1985 and 1994 was money that could not be used for the goods and services of consumerism.[37]

It was in Margaret Thatcher's Great Britain, perhaps more than anywhere else in the world, that the idea of shrinking the footprint of the state through tax cuts, reduced public spending, deregulation, and privatization was turned into public policy. The economist Massimo Florio has attempted to analyze the consequences of these policies in a 2004 book. His conclusions suggest that the hopes associated with these policies remained unfulfilled. Government spending as a percentage of GDP largely stayed the same, although tax cuts made for larger budget deficits, a development seen in Ronald Reagan's America at about the same time. (Government spending as a percentage of GDP does not seem to have declined much of anywhere, except in the former communist countries after 1989.) Even social welfare spending, a particular target of Thatcher, changed relatively little, which is less surprising when one realizes that so much of that spending was for old-age pensions, which generally were not cut back. There is no evidence that the policies led to more rapid economic growth. Florio's analysis of privatization and deregulation is particularly sobering. He calculates the benefits to consumers at an average of about £30 per person per year. Shareholders—mostly upper-income individuals—who got to buy IPOs of privatized firms at well below market rates, walked away with billions of pounds. Management salaries in privatized firms went up about 250 percent, about fifty times the wage increase of non-management personnel, many of whom ended up, in any event, laid off. Florio concluded that the entire process was a form of income redistribution, from which the wealthiest 20 percent of Britain's population profited, while the poorest 20 percent became even more impoverished.[38]

Two forms of privatization and deregulation, in air travel and telecommunications, both among the first to be attempted, and occurring worldwide, produced substantial changes, which had a major impact on the consumption of services. Although the deregulation and privatization initiatives in air travel and telecommunications were very similar, they produced distinctly different results as a consequence of their interaction with technological change.

As we've seen, airline deregulation began in the United States at the end of the 1970s and spread across the world in the following two decades. Its advocates decried the heavily regulated system of air travel, with government bodies setting airfares, and allocating routes and landing slots, in order to guarantee existing carriers a return on their investment, while making it difficult or impossible for potential competitors to start up a business. Deregulation, and the privatization of publicly owned airlines would result in better, more frequent service and lower airfares. It would reinvigorate air service, whose growth, by the 1970s, seemed to have been slowing when compared with the postwar decades, and would also greatly expand the universe of air travelers. These assertions have remained a constant ever since, and were vigorously propounded at the fortieth anniversary of US air travel deregulation in 2018.[39]

The question is whether they are true. Figure 10.1 shows the average annual percentage rate of increase in the number of airline passengers around in the entire world, for each decade, from the 1950s through the 1990s.

Worldwide, the rates of increase of air traffic had slowed dramatically in the 1970s, especially in comparison to the previous decade, when commercial jet aircraft had taken over from piston-driven airplanes. However, the

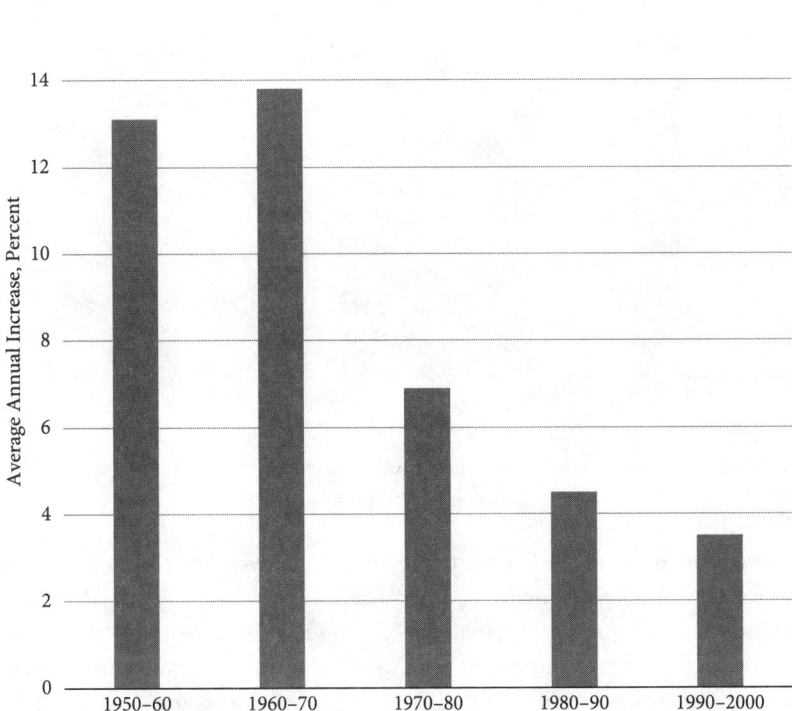

FIGURE 10.1 Growth in Number of Air Passengers Worldwide, 1950–2000

partially deregulated 1980s and the more pervasively deregulated 1990s saw no dramatic renewal in the growth of air travel; in fact, passenger growth rates declined still more.

Perhaps these figures are looking at too broad a canvas, a world where deregulation had only been gradually and partially introduced, even by the end of the millennium. Focusing in on the United States, in which had a very clear break in the nature of air travel right around 1980 should provide a clearer picture. Figure 10.2 does this.[40]

This more closely focused view does not alter the picture: air travel in the United States grew much more slowly after deregulation than in the booming 1950s and 1960s, and even the 1970s, when the declining pace of increase in commercial air travel had been an important justification of deregulation in the first place.

Then there is the question of airfares. As economic theorists would have it, deregulation introduced competition on certain routes, especially between large cities, which led to dramatic price declines. The problem is that airlines tried to make up for this by raising their fares on many other, less frequented routes. An early effort to calculate the gains to consumers from deregulation

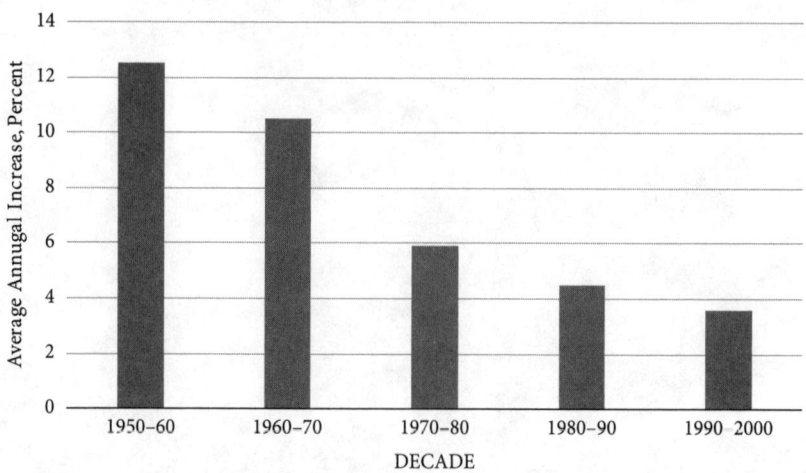

FIGURE 10.2 Growth in Number of US Air Passengers, 1950–2000

by two economists of the Brookings Institution, Steven Morrison and Clifford Winston, first carried out in 1986 and repeated in 1995, proceeded in ingenious fashion. Admitting that fare declines only modestly outpaced fare increases, they suggested that there were much greater consumer benefits from the increased number of flights, since passengers had to spend less time waiting around an airport for departure. Putting an hourly value on passengers' waiting time accounted for $6 billion of the $8 billion in the consumer benefits calculated by their initial study. However, they neglected to subtract the dollar value of time spent in the ever-more frequent flight delays, or in the longer flights needed to cover the same distance from departure to destination, as post-deregulation airlines moved away from direct flights toward a hub-and-spoke system.[41]

Airfares, overall, did decline, at least for domestic US flights between the onset of deregulation in 1978 and 2005. (There do not seem to be any comparable statistics for airfares on a global scale.) As with total passenger traffic, however, this overlooks the fact that airfares had declined every bit as much—actually, a little more—between 1950 and deregulation. In the pre-deregulation 1970s, airfares in the United States increased, which was another important impetus for deregulation, but this was a period of rapid inflation driven by the oil shock. Factoring this in—that is, taking into account the rise in the price level—airfares increased in the pre-deregulation 1970s less than the price level as a whole, so that real airfares were declining, despite the fact that airlines' costs were (and remain) heavily affected by the price of petroleum.[42]

The benefits of deregulation and privatization in air travel have been dubious, especially in light of the problems that have emerged from them.

Deregulation produced a burst of competition, as new firms entered the market, and established airlines went head to head with each other on heavily traveled routes. The upshot was a wave of airline bankruptcies, and, over a period of decades, the emergence of an oligopoly of a few dominant carriers. Deprived of favorable regulations and government support, privatized airlines have been competing with other carriers, such as Emirates, that enjoy state subsidies. A distinct feature of post-deregulation air travel has been the way that airlines have competed to make it maximally unpleasant for travelers, particularly their strategies for cramming ever more passengers into ever tighter spaces and ever more cramped seats. Quality has declined over time: what was typical for the early low-cost, low-amenity budget airlines in the 1980s, such as fees for checking luggage or for rebooking flights, have become the standard for regular, full-fare airlines today. As we've seen, this state of affairs has been maximally unpleasant for flight attendants and other airline employees.

One reason why the promise of deregulation remained at best only partially fulfilled involves the technological and physical constraints of air travel. The extent of airport runways and the capacity of air traffic control systems set limits to the number of airplanes that can take off and land in any given interval. This means that the possibilities for market entry are limited, making monopoly and oligopoly inherent to commercial air traffic. (Early theorists of deregulation asserted that actual competition was unnecessary, just its prospect would hold down fares—a prediction that has not been borne out.) Jet aircraft today are not fundamentally different from those of the 1970s; opportunities for cost-cutting and profit-enhancing innovations have been few, modest, and difficult to implement. Airplane manufacturers have improved fuel efficiency, for instance, but airlines need to use older, less efficient aircraft as long as possible to amortize their large purchasing and financing costs. As a result, maintaining profit margins has meant, more than anything else, putting as many passengers as possible on any one flight: planes that were half- or three-quarters full in the age of regulation, now fly at 90+ percent of capacity, with all the amenity issues this creates.

Air travel as a feature of consumerism is a recent development, stemming from the transition to jet passenger aircraft in the 1960s. Telephones are far older than passenger jets, but for most of the twentieth century they were the stepchild of consumer society. Like automobiles, they were an American specialty. In 1910, about two-thirds of the world's eleven million telephones were in the United States; forty years later, there were seventy-five million telephones worldwide, 60 percent of them in the United States. These figures include business use, and so are not exactly indicators of telephones as part of consumer society. As late as 1965, only one British household in five had a phone. Numbers of telephones grew, reaching 380 million by 1976, but even then, over half the world's population lived in countries where there was fewer than one telephone per hundred inhabitants.[43]

Automobiles, as discussed earlier, were also relatively limited in their global scope. However, they were a far more complex technology and far more expensive than the telephone. Another way to gauge the marginal position of telephones in consumer society is to compare their spread with that of TVs. Table 10.1 does that for selected countries around the world.

The figures are striking and unambiguous. Between 1960 and 1990, almost everywhere in the world, regardless of geographic location, economic system, or levels of income (and the selection of countries in Table 10.1 is fully representative of the broader picture) the number of TVs surpassed the number of telephones, though the former were and are considerably more expensive devices. The United States and Sweden, two countries that were global pioneers of telephony, seem like an exception to this trend, though the figures in Table 10.1 include all TV sets and all telephones, in households as well as in government and business. Telephones, in particular, are far more likely to be found outside the household, so these figures understate the ubiquity of televisions in these countries. Though there were sixty million more telephones than TV sets in the United States in 1990, more households had a TV than a phone, about 95 percent to 92 percent.[44]

From their origins in the early twentieth century, telephone networks were monopoly enterprises. The dense grid of copper wires, reaching across an entire country, and into vast numbers of households or businesses, connected by an intricate electromechanical switching system, could only work as one united enterprise. In most parts of the world, this was a state monopoly,

TABLE 10.1 TVs and Telephones (in Millions) Worldwide, 1960–1990

Country	1960		1970		1980		1990	
	Phones	TVs	Phones	TVs	Phones	TVs	Phones	TVs
Argentina	1.23	0.45	1.75	3.5	2.59	5.1	3.09	7.1
Mexico	0.52	0.65	1.51	2.99	5.02	7.5	5.36	12.35
US	74.34	46	120.22	60	180.42	80	153.45	92
Italy	3.96	2.12	9.37	9.72	19.28	13.31	32.04	15.07
Sweden	2.64	0.60	4.31	2.42	6.62	3.10	5.85	3.33
Poland	0.88	0.43	1.87	4.22	3.39	7.65	5.23	9.93
China	1.58	0.02	1.31	0.3	2.14	10	6.85	37
India	0.44	--	1.22	0.23	2.98	1.55	5.01	33
Nigeria	0.04	0.01	0.08	0.75	0.15	0.45	0.29	3.8
Senegal	0.02	--	0.03	0.04	0.04	0.042	0.04	0.27

Source: Brian R. Mitchell's collection of *International Historical Statistics* (as in Table 9.1), Tables F9–F10 in each volume.

typically run by the post office. In the Americas, the telephone network was under private ownership, but heavily regulated. Telephony in the United States was dominated by a monopoly enterprise, the American Telephone and Telegraph Company, "Ma Bell." It had a complex corporate structure, with a central firm administering service across local exchange networks, AT&T's "long lines" division, which handled "long distance" phone calls; its wholly and partially owned subsidiaries, which administered the local exchange networks (as well as some independent phone companies who had contractual arrangements with AT&T for long distance calls); a manufacturing subsidiary, Western Electric, which produced the necessary equipment; and a research arm, Bell Labs. The government regulation of American telephony was equally complex. Long distance service and the rates charged for it were under the jurisdiction of the federal government, through its Federal Communications Commission, while the local area service was under the purview of regulators from state governments. Arcane formulas determined the sharing of costs between local and long-distance service and the rates that could be charged for them.

In a number of countries, the monopoly telephone service was a source of complaint and aggravation. Just trying to get a telephone involved frustratingly lengthy bureaucratic procedures and there was a chronic backlog of orders for connection to the network. During the 1950s, there were three million subscribers to telephone service in the United Kingdom, and half a million on the waiting list for connections. These same issues dogged telephony in decolonized Asia and Africa, where the state monopoly had taken it over from colonial administrations. India was notorious for its delays in telephone connection. From independence to 1980, an average of two hundred thousand people were on the waiting list each year; by 1990, the waiting list had swelled to 1.9 million. Authorities responded to complaints about poor service by telling complainers to turn in their phones, as there were plenty of other people waiting for them. In much of Africa and Asia, particularly in rural areas, a telephone network simply did not exist.[45]

By contrast, the regulated monopoly in the United States had produced very large-scale service—and, as was also characteristic of airlines before deregulation, done so with falling prices. The real (inflation-adjusted) cost of monthly residential telephone service declined by about two-thirds from 1940 to 1980. Unlike most of the rest of the world, telephones in the United States were an established feature of consumer society. Bell Labs, whose funding came from the rates charged to telephone subscribers, was devoted to basic scientific research, and produced a number of major technological innovations, including the transistor, lasers, cell phone technology, and communications satellites. There were technological issues with the telephone network that gradually developed. Two prominent ones were the transition from electromechanical to electronic switching systems, and the wish, then entirely from business users, to connect new kinds of devices, such as computer modems, to the network, a wish treated with suspicion by AT&T's engineers.

Nonetheless, these were not the reasons that the monopoly enterprise was broken up and deregulated in the 1980s. Rather, they were a consequence of the efforts of individual entrepreneurs to engage in arbitrage: rates for long distance were set by regulators to subsidize the cost of individual access to the network, so if a competitor could offer long-distance service without the necessity of funding individual access, it could charge less. The first firm to attempt this, Microwave Communications Incorporated, or MCI, purported to be using new technology. It would set up a microwave link between two cities and customers would use their telephones to access this link. What the company actually wanted was to be granted access to the existing AT&T long-distance network, so that it could offer long-distance services at rates not involving a subsidy. After a lengthy legal and political battle, lasting most of the 1970s, MCI got its way and more. Aided by a favorable political climate, in which consumer groups understood the offensive against AT&T as part of the pro-rational-self-interest consumer legislation they were successfully promoting at the time, while pro-free-market economists, government officials, and jurists—usually the consumer groups' sworn enemies—saw the opportunity to prove that competition could work under all circumstances, even ones in which monopoly seemed inevitable. In 1982, AT&T was dissolved into several different firms. Keeping the company name was the deregulated long-distance service that would compete with other long-distance providers, which would have access to its network. The local area networks would be run by the former subsidiaries, now independent firms, the "baby Bells," which would continue to act as regulated monopolies, while the manufacturing subsidiary and the laboratory would also become independent businesses.[46]

This court decision launched a worldwide wave of telephony privatization and deregulation. Former monopolists would have to share access to their networks; publicly owned telephone networks would be sold off or reorganized as privately owned, profit-seeking corporations. Yet the unique physical telephone network remained; the new competitive firms wanted access to it rather than having to build a competing one. Why then, should a profit-seeking firm owning the telecommunications network offer to share it with its competitors, or to do so at rates that would enable these competitors to undercut it? The answer to this question is that the owners of the deregulated network would be compelled to do so by government regulators. Or, as the telecommunications historian Anton Huurdeman has pithily put it, "deregulation means reregulation." Monopoly would be replaced with competition, but firms' competition would be primarily for the political influence needed to get forms of de- and reregulation most favorable to them.[47]

What followed in the Late-Millennium Era was not unlike what occurred with air travel at the same time. A host of new competitors emerged, generally privately owned upstart firms, challenging the existing monopolist—whether still under government ownership or privatized. Perhaps the oddest version of this competition was in China, where China Telecom, owned by the Ministry of Communications, did market battle with the newly created China Unicom, owned by the state railways, and the Ministry of Electric Power. The competition between the two telephone companies was not always about price or service, but about each trying to convince the government and the Communist Party to prohibit or at least to limit drastically the activities of the other. The upshot of the competition was not unlike what happened with airfares, where post-deregulation longer flights became cheaper and shorter ones more expensive. With telephone companies, basic telecommunications services, including installation, connection, and access to the local network, became steadily more expensive, while the costs for long-distance calls from one local network to another, and internationally, declined. In the United Kingdom, between the mid-1980s and the end of the 1990s, the monthly residential base rate almost doubled; charges for connection to the network went up by as much as three-fourths. Local daytime calls became more expensive, but the cost of long distance and international dropped by more than a third. Economists' broader studies suggest that this pattern of realignment of costs was common around the world.[48]

The post-deregulation US experience is particularly interesting. The original idea had been that AT&T would compete in a deregulated market with other firms in providing long-distance services, while its former subsidiaries, now independent businesses, would have a regulated monopoly on local networks. However, the subsidiaries wanted to get into the long-distance business as well, and eventually convinced politicians and regulators to let them do so. As competition pressed on prices for long-distance services, the firms providing them ran into increasing financial difficulties, just as had happened with airlines. AT&T, whose engineers and managers were still living in the past world of regulation, increasingly had difficulty turning a profit. But MCI, which had begun the global wave of deregulation and was supposed to be used to the new, competitive environment, also did poorly. Renamed Worldcom, it hid its profit problems from investors by issuing fraudulent financial statements on a massive scale, until it collapsed in what was then the largest corporate bankruptcy in US history in 2002—one that would only be exceeded by the collapse of financial institutions in 2008. The former Bell Labs, transformed into the independent firm Lucent Technologies, no longer had access to its funding from network operations, and quickly went out of business, thus terminating what had been the most important center of engineering innovation in the second half of the twentieth century. By 2005, wired telecommunications in the United States was increasingly an oligopoly, in the hands of two of the former subsidiaries, Verizon and Southwestern Bell. The latter bought out AT&T and used its name.[49]

If deregulated telecommunications did not end up in quite the same dismal place as deregulated commercial air traffic, this was because during these years telecommunications underwent a technological revolution that would change telephone use beyond all recognition and also introduce a fundamentally new element into consumer society. Telephones became mobile, liberated from their fixed connection to a network of copper wires so that they could be used—at least in theory—wherever users carried them.

The idea of telephones connected by radio waves had been present since the end of the Second World War. The immense, bulky equipment needed to enable wireless telephony in the era of the vacuum tube—filling up the entire trunk of a car—simply made it impractical. Solid-state circuits reduced drastically the size of the apparatus, but nonetheless putting anything more than a handful of users on a switched system of wireless communication seemed technologically impossible. The crucial innovation, invented in the United States at Bell Labs and first implemented in 1979 in Japan, was to divide a network area into a series of cells, each with its own relay tower; as users moved, their signal, thanks to electronic, computerized switching, would move along with them from one cell to the next. By the end of the 1980s, there were ten million subscribers to cell phone service around the world, and the existing networks were reaching the limits of their capacity. Expansion into a mass medium required a second innovation, characteristic of the period, the digitalization of transmission, which, as would be the case with TV at about the same time, made possible an enormous increase in network capacity. In 2000, there were 740 million cell phone users around the world, an astonishing seventy-four-fold increase in the course of just a decade. Telephony, wired or wireless, had never seen anything like it. Growth in wireless telecommunications continued apace in the twenty-first century; by 2019, there were 4.68 billion cell phone users—over 60 percent of the world's population.[50]

Liberating users from the need to access an extensive, complex, and expensive copper wire network—or its fiber-optic successor, whose connection with individual users remains, at the very best, sporadic—cell phones made telephones into a feature of consumer society across the world for the very first time. The relatively modest expense of erecting a network of cell phone towers made it possible for the world's poorer countries to bypass the age of fixed wireline telephony entirely. Digital cell phones were not just portable versions of their landline predecessors. New features, such as Short Message Services, begun with digitalization in the 1990s, or Internet access, following Apple's introduction of the iPhone in 2007 and the subsequent mass of cheaper Chinese imitations, made cell phones into entirely new consumer devices. By the second decade of the twenty-first century, consumers in Shenzhen, Mumbai, and Lima could and did join their counterparts in Berlin, Los Angeles, and Tokyo in texting "LOL" and viewing pornography on their phones. Cell phones had broken out of the Europe-North America-Japan nexus of consumer society. Unlike previous features of that society, this new nexus had not begun in the United States. Of those 740 million cell phone subscribers worldwide in 2000, 39 percent were in Europe, 34 percent in the Asia-Pacific region, and just 16 percent in North America. Any American traveler in Western Europe during the 1990s could not help noticing the difference in cell phone usage. While in the United States, cell phones remained largely for business use ("car phones") or in the hands of affluent individuals, in Europe teenagers, migrant laborers, and even welfare recipients were walking around staring at their mobile devices, or chatting away on them.[51]

The whole legal and political process—as well as the painful disputes and debates about the deregulation and reregulation of telephony—was based on the existence of a complex network of copper wires and switching equipment, impossible or absurdly expensive to duplicate. Because they did not need to be connected to individual users (the celebrated "last mile" problem), cellular networks, smaller and cheaper, made all these issues and debates obsolete. There could be competing networks; costs for all telephone services, not just long-distance ones, declined. As digital cell phone use spread, reasons for the existence of fixed, wireline telephones, especially for households, seemed steadily harder to envision, and telecommunications companies increasingly shifted their efforts away from them to mobile phones, Internet access, and providing TV signals. These virtuous results occurred in most countries around the world; at least according to a 2011 study of the development of telephony in the EU, whether or not the relevant firms were in private or public ownership seems to have had little influence on these developments. Public policy promoting competition did lead to falling prices, but the effects of these policy changes paled before the consequences of the introduction of a fundamentally new technology.[52]

Telephony has always been a matter for individual sovereign states, and neither deregulation nor the onset of wireless phones changed that. There were great expectations in the 1990s for global telephone services, based on a network of satellites in low-earth orbit, but the sound quality was poor and the costs for both the phones and the service very high, so the market proved limited and the early satellite corporations, Iridium and GlobalStar, quickly went bankrupt. Global cell phones have remained a niche market, employed by the military, first responders, and maritime users. Phones connected to a service in one country generally worked in another, but users coming home from vacations or business trips discovered enormous "roaming fees," which could sometimes add up to more than the entire cost of their trip. There was no technological or business reason for these fees, which were yet another reflection of the problems involving deregulated monopolies and the crucial role of reregulation. After a protracted battle, the EU first limited these roaming fees among its member countries and finally prohibited them in 2017. Still, such fees remain prevalent elsewhere in the world. This is perhaps no surprise in the world of deregulated telephony which, began, after all, with efforts at rates arbitrage.[53]

THE GLOBALIZATION OF CONSUMER SOCIETY IN THE LATE MILLENNIUM

Cell phones were the first feature of consumer society not to be pioneered in the United States. Their rollout was part of a broader tendency toward the decentering and realignment of consumerism around the world in the final decades of the twentieth century. One simple measure of this trend are World Bank figures on the development of consumption expenditures between 1980 and 2000. They grew fastest, and by far, in Asia, rising in Japan, China, India, Malaysia, and Indonesia between 2.4 percent and 7.2 percent yearly (rates of growth also achieved in a few other countries, such as Turkey and Chile). In Western Europe, North America, and the South Seas, consumption expenditures managed 1 to 2 percent annual increases. In much of Latin America, consumption rates were flat, or increased by merely 1 percent or less per year, while in Africa these expenditures declined between 6.5 percent and 10 percent per year.[54] Of course these figures are just very crude indicators, since consumption encompasses basic necessities as well as the goods and services associated with a consumer society, and the calculations do not include the consumption of self-produced items. However, they provide at least an idea of global trends.

If there is any one story that characterizes the Late-Millennium Era and beyond it is the rise of the Chinese economy. As China has become wealthier consumption has increased and steadily moved in the direction of consumerism. In Mao's era, Chinese families longed for the "four big items"—sewing machines, watches, bicycles, and radios. These were modest consumer aspirations indeed. Most of these items were already prevalent in Europe and North America by the late nineteenth century, and only one of them, the radio, was part of the twentieth century's consumer durables. By the 1980s, attention was turning to the "six big items"—color TVs, refrigerators, cameras, electric fans, washing machines, and tape recorders, all goods typical of consumerism in the West. The 1990s brought a wider variety of consumer electronics, including computers and, especially, cell phones. And by 2009 China had become the world's largest market for automobiles. The proportion of the population owning cars remained low, compared to the world's wealthier countries, but the enthusiasm and vigor with which driving was taken up (and the sheer amount of auto bodywork that was the result) were yet another testimony of the progress of consumerism in East Asia. As had been the case in Europe and North America during the postwar era, this great leap forward of consumerism was not purchased at the expense of saving. Quite the opposite, between 1992 (the first year for which figures are available) and 2018, savings made up between 27 and 38 percent of disposable household income in China. This was a savings rate at least twice as high as that of any other country and, as far as is known, unique in the entire history of the world.[55]

The transition in China from a Maoist era, ranging from austerity to mass starvation, to decades of a steadily ramped-up consumerism has been both extraordinary and extraordinarily rapid. It has also been true across Asia. The Late Millennium saw expanding consumerism throughout the continent. Of course, the extent to which that consumerism has been shared within the population and the nature of the goods and services purchased have varied immensely between individual countries and within them. At the high end, there were Japanese tourists traveling in ever larger numbers across Europe, Asia, the South Pacific and North America, or affluent Malaysians who have developed a strong fondness for very high-powered Harley-Davidson motorcycles. In the middle was South Korea, where TVs, and household consumer electrical goods and electronics reached the same near-universal levels during the 1980s that they had in Western Europe two decades earlier; or Indian IT workers buying autos, furniture, and consumer electronics with installment loans, a state of affairs so unlike that of their parents, who had painfully saved up for such purchases over a period of years. More modest signs of consumerism were the growing numbers of Indian peasants with electricity and a refrigerator; and their Chinese counterparts with color TVs, exchanging text messages on their cell phones with their relatives, unskilled laborers in China's booming coastal regions. Bride price in China and dowries in India, became, increasingly deployed for the purchase of consumer durables.

Critiques of consumerism in Asia have appeared along with consumer society. "Frugality campaigns," carried out in South Korea by the government, the Central Bank, and the YMCA, decried the evils of a self-absorbed materialism and consumerism, and called for a more moral frugality—which usually meant that South Korean consumers should stop buying imported goods and purchase them from domestic manufacturers instead.[56]

If the rise of consumer society in China during the final decades of the millennium was typical of developments in most of Asia, the Asian pattern of surging consumerism was very much not typical of the rest of the world. Two regions, in particular, Eastern Europe and Africa, were Asia's consumption antipodes. Unlike the case in most parts of the globe, the World Bank was unable to gather statistics on consumption expenditures between 1980 and 2000 in the lands of the Eastern Bloc, the USSR and its allies in

Eastern Europe of the 1980s, and their post-communist successor states in the following decade. Even without statistics, the pattern of developments is very clear.

In the Era of Upheaval, the Eastern Bloc regimes broke with their past of heavy industry and preparations for war. Instead, the communist authorities put substantial resources into the manufacture and distribution of consumer durables and the promotion and expansion of consumer services, particularly vacations and tourism. Never able to match either the quantity or the quality of the goods and services available in wealthy capitalist countries, and even a number of the less wealthy ones—a state of affairs becoming slowly more apparent as contacts between the communist and capitalist worlds became more common and widespread—the effort sputtered and died in the midst of increasingly severe economic difficulties during the 1980s. Sometimes, as was the case particularly in Nicolae Ceaușescu's Romania, basic necessities were increasingly in short supply.

What made the situation in the Eastern Bloc seem unbearable was the way that consumer durables, or even more modest luxuries, such as gourmet foods and fashionable clothing, were available in the midst of shortages. Ruling elites had access to them, as had always been the case in communist regimes, but the new ways in which these goods became accessible beyond the elites only increased popular dissatisfaction with the regimes. Such consumer goods were on sale in special stores—Tuzex in Czechoslovakia, Corecom in Bulgaria, Pewex in Poland, Intershop in East Germany, Intertourist in Hungary, and Comturist in Romania—whose contents could only be purchased with "hard," Western currencies. As some of the names make clear, they were originally intended for capitalist tourists in Eastern Bloc countries, whose inhabitants were generally prohibited from even possessing bourgeois money, much less spending it.

With the deepening of the communist regimes' debt crisis in the 1980s, the need for Western currency caused the rulers to renounce their previous scruples and allow their citizens to acquire the formerly tainted monies and use them for shopping. The difficulty lay in how they could come into possession of Western currency. Exchanging their own communist currencies for it remained prohibited; there were largely no legal means to do so. This meant that black-market deals were the only possibility. In Czechoslovakia, a whole new occupation, the *wechslák*, or currency hustler, part of a growing underworld and underground economy, sprouted in the 1980s. The situation was most dire in the communist regime closest to capitalism, East Germany. Its government allowed its citizens to receive gifts of hard currency, West Germany's celebrated D-Mark, from relatives in the West. The more the D-Mark circulated in East Germany, the more it became required for any kind of transaction, especially those involving consumer durables. Since a prerequisite for having any kind of leadership position in the communist Germany was *not* having any contacts with West Germans, this meant that the regime's most loyal supporters had no access to hard currency and were therefore shut out of the best opportunities to take part in consumer society, a development profoundly undermining the last bastions of the regime's legitimacy.[57]

Although there were many motives for the mass movements against communist rule in Eurasia during the crucial years 1989–91—demands for basic civil liberties, the rule of law, governments stemming from free multiparty elections, opposition to the environmentally destructive consequences of economic policy, to name just a few—the desire for full participation in the consumer society so well established in Western Europe and North America (and rapidly on the rise in Asia) was the background to the massive discontent driving popular hostility to communist rule. Of course, the postcommunist regimes in most of Eastern Europe spent the 1990s in a state of uninterrupted economic crisis, hence aspirations to consumerism remained unfulfilled for another decade.

The setback to consumer aspirations was still more severe in Africa, and the opportunities to participate in consumer society still more limited, well past the Late-Millennium Era. There are, of course, cell phones, and fast-food chains. Eating in the latter, as opposed to consuming the products of street vendors, so key to the informal economy, is a sign of status and affluence. Consumer desires can take on forms of painful parody, particularly the wish for fashionable clothing, satisfied by vendors who peddle "dead white people's clothing"—secondhand clothing, originally donated to charity in Europe or North America, but sold by charities there to dealers who ship it to Africa. By some estimates, 70 percent of used clothing donated in this way ends up in Africa, with sales in the hundreds of millions of dollars per year. In the open-air markets of Lusaka, capital of Zambia, a country known as the fashion plate of Southern Africa, stands selling *salaula* (meaning in Bemba, the local language, something like "rummaging through a pile"), outnumber all others.[58]

If the Late-Millennium Era was a period of relative stagnation of consumerism in Western European and the Americas, rapid expansion in Asia, and deep crisis in Eastern Europe and Africa, and therefore transformative in extremely varied fashion in different parts of the world, it was simultaneously a phase of increasing globalization of consumerism. This was particularly evident in retail sales. It seemed as if the whole world was eating at the same fast-food restaurants, purchasing the same fashions, and the same brand name goods (or counterfeits of them), and shopping at the same supermarkets and "big box" stores. Celebration of this triumph of globalization was set against denunciation that were similar to attacks on television or tourism, of the way that such global capitalist enterprises were destroying local traditions and culture. Foodways were a flashpoint of this critique. "Slow food" movement advocates presented themselves as defenders of indigenous and healthy approaches to eating, and protestors raged against McDonald's. Proponents of "fair trade," the political movement demanding higher prices for raw materials from poorer countries, called on consumers to use their consumption expenditures, especially for more luxurious foodstuffs, such as gourmet coffees, to prop up small producers in the world's poorer countries, and to disrupt capitalist patterns of global trade, moving raw materials from those countries to the stores of the world's wealthy lands.

These observations corresponded to the realities of the Late-Millennium Era, a period of the growth of globalized retailing, of which fast-food restaurants were particularly prominent examples. While McDonald's began its expansion outside the United States and Canada in the 1970s, until the end of that decade it had only been in the world's wealthier countries, mostly in Western Europe. In 1979, the Golden Arches reached Brazil, within a few years the Philippines, Malaysia, Thailand, Mexico, Turkey, and South Korea; and in the 1990s, China, the former Eastern Bloc lands, Saudi Arabia, and South Africa. Large retailers that had limited their international expansion to what is sometimes called the "Triad Market"—the United States, Western Europe, and Japan—and not always successfully at that (the failure of Marks and Spencer's stores in Canada during the 1970s, for instance) but this began to change. The world's four largest multinational retail chains, the Dutch Ahold, the French Carrefour, the German Metro, and the American Walmart, expanded into eleven foreign countries during the 1980s and sixty-one during the 1990s.[59]

There was a spectacular element to some of this expansion, in part because it corresponded with the end of the Cold War and the collapse of communism. A McDonald's next to Tiananmen Square in Beijing and on Red Square in Moscow seemed a sign of a new era of the globalization of capitalist consumerism. However, the extent of globalized retail consumerism is easy to exaggerate. By 2008, only 30 of the world's 250 largest retailers had stores in China, and a mere 6 in India. Compared with manufacturing, retail globalization occurred on a very modest scale. In 2000, the world's ten-largest retail chains operated in an average of ten countries each; by contrast, the world's ten-largest pharmaceutical manufacturers were active in, on average, 137 countries and the ten-largest auto firms in forty-four. For all the spectacular multinationalism, retail remains (somewhat like television), dominated by businesses located in the same country as their customers.[60]

Even when retailers operate across the globe, their impact varies. Fast-food chains are a particularly good example of this. Their management tries to operate them the same way everywhere, at least in some respects—ignoring labor protection or union representation laws, for instance, and trying to get labor as cheaply as possible. Any attempt at uniformity does not hold when it comes to dealing with consumers. American fast-food chains that want to hustle their customers out the door as fast as possible have taken a very different approach in Asia, where their establishments have become places to linger: pupils after school, for instance, as a goal of family outings; or, in China, a place for women to dine, free from the macho atmosphere and heavy drinking that characterize the regular restaurant scene. And in Africa, as noted, eating at a fast-food chain—and local chains outnumber international ones—was a sign of affluence (this was, true in China as well, during the 1990s)—the opposite of circumstances in Europe or North America.[61]

Partially related to the fast-food business has been the global spread of particular cuisines in the Late-Millennium Era. Cuisines have spread via migration—Italian food to the Americas in the early twentieth century and to Northern Europe in the postwar era, or Chinese cuisine to the United States, a development that has continued down to the present on an accelerated scale. The number of Chinese restaurants in the United States rose from about 1,100 at the end of the Second World War, to almost ten times that in the 1970s, to as high forty thousand in 2007–8, more than all the branches of McDonald's, Kentucky Fried Chicken, and Burger King put together.[62]

A somewhat different development has been the expansion of cuisines without emigration. Mexican food spread in the United States through migrants from Mexico and cultural interchange in the US-Mexican borderlands, but it is immensely popular in Norway, where *Fredagstacoen* (Friday tacos) became a national pastime in the 1990s, spurred on by the World Cup being played in Mexico City. Another example is sushi, which stormed out of Japan across the world in the 1980s, a decade that established Japan in global consumer culture, from the Sony Walkman to fuel-efficient Hondas and Toyotas to *anime*. This was another early example of the erosion of the dominance of the United States in consumer culture.[63]

Norwegian tacos, typically homemade from US brands, contain ingredients familiar to inhabitants of North America—tortillas, cheese, salsa, lettuce—as well as others that are not, such as codfish. The penetration of Mexican food into Asia has been limited by widespread dislike of the taste of corn. In China, tortillas are made from rice flour. As consumed outside Japan, sushi has come to be characterized less by raw fish than by an odd variety of ingredients, including cream cheese in the United States, jellied meat, and pickled mushrooms in Russia, and tropical fruits in Brazil. One could denounce such dishes as a travesty of an authentic cuisine, or just see them as examples of cultural syncretism, as were the original "authentic" cuisines themselves. Mexican food, after all, came from combining ingredients native to the Americas, including corn, chili peppers, beans, and tomatoes, with others originally from Europe—cheese, wheat, pork, beef, and rice. Other authentic cuisines, including Italian regional specialties, such as Petruzian olive oil from the Teramo Hills, or Colonnata lard, or Oaxacan and Sonoran regional Mexican food, were ordinary food and ways of cooking in it, until they were taken up by merchandisers or restaurateurs and marketed as examples of regional resistance to homogeneous global food. The marketing was on a wide, at times global, scale, so that regional authenticity, far from being the opposite of globalized consumerism, appears as yet another product of it.[64]

This is all reminiscent of debates surrounding the authenticity of tourist experiences. A corollary is the fair trade movement, which began in the 1970s and rapidly expanded. In fair trade stores consumers in wealthy countries purchase tropical products—above all coffee but also, among others, cotton, oranges, and bananas—from producers in poorer ones at prices that offer the latter better economic opportunities. Fair trade consumerism is quite different in its goals and radius of action than consumer movements of an earlier period. They sought to return rational self-interest to the process of purchase and consumption in a consumer society in which they had had become permeated with emotionally laden impulses. Fair traders, by contrast, reject self-interest and voluntarily pay prices above the market rate. Previous consumer activism had usually taken place within individual sovereign states, or on the level of their federation, such as the European Union. Even while the International Organization of Consumers' Unions had become increasingly global, it remained a league of groups organized at the sovereign state level.

In these respects, fair trade and related forms of "ethical" consumerism—including not buying from firms that experiment on animals, engage in environmentally dubious practices, or exploit producers and workers in poorer countries—seem like ecotourism. Both seek to deploy participants in the consumer societies of wealthy countries to improve conditions in poorer ones. Ecotourism, as explained in the previous chapter, remains a dubious activity. This is not the case with fair trade practices. Nonetheless, fair trade sales, most common in wealthier countries in Northern Europe, affect a minuscule proportion of global transactions. In 2007, Swiss consumers, the world's champions of fair trade, spent, on average, about $27 per person on fair trade products; in the United Kingdom, the figure was the equivalent of $16 and in no other country as much as $14 and usually under $7. Fair trade advocates have certainly been on the side of the angels but share their ethereal nature.[65]

Yet for all their feeble impact, fair traders were a sign of how much the Late-Millennium Era marked a new departure for consumer society. The basic elements of that society, including the most desired consumer durables—the automobile and electrical or electronic goods—the basic business practices—advertising, department stores, supermarkets, installment credit—and the idea that consumption was a realm of emotions and desire, a signifier of identity, all gradually emerged in the first half of the twentieth century across the North Atlantic world, and were implemented to the greatest extent in the United States. In the postwar era all these elements were realized in that North Atlantic nexus, involving a large majority of those living there in a consumer society. A few other wealthier countries could be added to this group, such as Japan and Australia. There were partially successful attempts to join in this new world of consumerism elsewhere—Perón's Argentina after 1945, communist Eastern Europe in the 1960s and '70s—but for most people living in the world consumerism remained an aspiration or a spectacle of what more fortunate others were able to achieve. Somewhat surprisingly, the political, cultural, and economic changes that came about in the Era of Upheaval changed that picture relatively little.

It might be more accurate to say that the increasing globalization of production, the rise of income inequality within countries (though its decline among countries), or the development of new governmental policies of privatization and deregulation—that all these had longer-term effects helping to shape the new departures of consumerism, with effects reaching down to the present. Consumer society stagnated in the North Atlantic nexus where it began, or was, in some cases, propped up by new forms of credit that are confused with the installment credit regimes so instrumental to the rise of consumerism but actually rather different. In communist Eastern Europe, even that stagnation proved too much, and the agony of communism in the 1980s and the chaos of post-communism in the following decade were a disaster for all consumption, and that associated with consumer society in particular. By contrast, the Late-Millennium Era saw the breakthrough of a consumer society in Asia, most dramatically apparent in China, but evident in one way or another, in every single large country of the region, such as Japan, Malaysia, and South Korea, and more modestly in India and Indonesia.

While the wave of privatization and deregulation sweeping the world at that time was at least in part motivated by the wish to reinvigorate consumerism, its actual consequences for consumer society were modest. The great success of deregulation in telecommunications was less the result of a policy change than of a major technological innovation, the cell phone, which made telephony part of consumerism, and did so everywhere, even in places, such as rural Africa or India, previously excluded from consumer society. Contrary to what one might think, globalization came late to consumerism. For all the dramatic impact of opening McDonald's in Russia or Kentucky Fried Chicken in China, or for all the commitment and dedication of fair trade and ethical consumer activists, retail sales have lagged behind manufacturing in global scope. Fears of unrestrained consumer globalization trampling local cultures and local cuisines may make for good headlines, but those local cultures and cuisines are themselves a result of globalization, rather than its antithesis.

More broadly, it seems that the final two decades of the twentieth century were an arena of a series of interrelated social changes, stemming from the globalization of production and the rising tide of international migration.

The global spread of consumerism and its gradual expansion into services, the equally global decline of labor, the transformation of a class structure based on occupation and sources of income into one based primarily on placement in a global labor market, were all occurring simultaneously. They marked the beginning of a new era of society, one whose identity continues to unfold.

PART 4

Dreams and Nightmares

11 | Beliefs

THE REALM OF HUMAN belief is immense and varied. Attempting to explore that realm across five decades and the entire world might seem like an undertaking simultaneously audacious and futile. Even limiting the focus to those beliefs with a claim to worldwide acceptance would be to pursue an endless list. A whole book, not just a chapter, could be written about any one—astrology, vegetarianism, or anti-vaccinationism, for example—alone. Yet not attempting would be to eliminate a fundamental and intriguing part of the drama of the Age of Interconnection and to ignore basic motivations.

This chapter will focus on three objects of belief that played a large role in motivating political action and in providing social cohesion during the Age of Interconnection. Each had widespread, if immensely varied, acceptance, as well as considerable opposition and rejection, across the world. All predated 1945, but their pre-histories were very different, as were their global trajectories between 1945 and 2001, leaving each of them in a very different condition at the beginning of the twenty-first century. These three objects of belief are the idea of progress, the nation, and God.

Progress

While the idea of progress had a long genesis, going back to philosophers of classical antiquity, Daoist conceptions of human improvement, and the Judeo-Christian understanding of a linear rather than cyclical course of time, a broader conception of and belief in progress emerged from the Enlightenment, the eighteenth-century intellectual movement toward the use of science and reason to understand the natural and the human social world. For Enlightenment thinkers, progress was the development of human history in the direction of interrelated improvements. These included a greater scientific understanding of the physical and natural world; an increasing mastery of nature via technological utilization of scientific knowledge, a consequent improvement in human material condition; and finally a trend toward a better, more just, and more harmonious social and moral order. The nineteenth century was the great age of progress, during which belief in it spread around the world. New scientific discoveries, above all Charles Darwin's theory of natural selection, were interpreted—arguably, mostly misinterpreted—as further evidence of the existence of progress. Social theorists, from Herbert Spencer to August Comte to Karl Marx, developed elaborate schemes of human history as progressing through stages toward a steadily higher point. One might think that the Age of Total War would have dealt a blow to this belief in progress, and, to some extent it did, yet it proved surprisingly resilient. The preamble to the founding charter of the United Nations, signed in June 1945, announced one of the organization's goals was to "promote social progress." Reinforced by the rapid economic growth and remarkable healthcare advances of the postwar era, by the 1960s previous doubts about progress had been overcome and belief in it reigned supreme.[1]

Adlai Stevenson, the 1952 Democratic nominee for president of the United States, announced in a campaign speech that "progress is a basic law of life." A decade later, President Kennedy would dub his chief foreign policy initiative for Latin America the "Alliance for Progress." Turning to the other US political party, one of its prominent members, also scion of a celebrated family of American capitalists, New York State's governor Nelson Rockefeller, declared in 1963 that Americans "believe in . . . human progress, in the perfectibility of the individual human being and of the human society." It was not just American politicians who made these assertions. In France during the 1950s, the increase in sales and use of electric appliances was *progès ménager*, household progress. And, in fact, these appliances were part of the advertising slogan of one of the world's leading corporations, General Electric—"progress is our most important product." The motto, ubiquitous in America of the postwar era, was actually an abridged version of the introductory statement of a TV show sponsored by the firm: "In engineering, in research, in manufacturing skill, in the values that bring a better, more satisfying life, at General Electric, progress is our most important product." This statement, read out on the air by a B movie actor who would go on to bigger and better things, Ronald Reagan, was a concise expression of the ideal of progress.[2]

These affirmations of progress were made at the height of the Cold War, during which capitalist and communist countries posed sharply different visions of government, economy, and society. When it came to progress, though, the opposing sides were very much in agreement. Italy's communists, campaigning in 1946, tried to win over women, a group more inclined to the party's Christian Democratic opponents, by appealing to them to vote for the PCI "against reaction, for democracy, for liberty, for progress." In the USSR, Nikolai Bulganin, chairman of the Council of Ministers informed the Communist Party's Central Committee in 1955, that "the battle for technological progress is synonymous with the battle to build communist society." Reinforced by the USSR's success in sending a satellite into space, the role of this "scientific-technological revolution" for the development of communism, officially endorsed in the 1961 Communist Party program, grew steadily in importance, overshadowing concepts of class struggle—not just in the USSR itself but throughout the Eastern Bloc.[3]

Belief in progress was asserted by communists throughout the world. Mao Zedong's initiative to jump-start China's transition to scientific and technological modernity and rapid economic growth was, after all, designated the "Great Leap Forward." The progress envisaged extended beyond science, technology, and the economy, to human moral improvement. Emerging alongside of and in close conjunction would be a "new socialist man," altruistic, energetically and self-sacrificingly dedicated to the common good. Fidel Castro regarded the Darwinian, biological evolution of humanity as having ended in the Stone Age, but communism, he thought, would bring a resumption of human evolution, putting the new socialist man at a higher stage in the evolutionary progress of humanity.[4]

Indeed, communists saw themselves as the guardians of a belief in progress abandoned by their capitalist rivals, mired in the stagnation of their social and economic system. The USSR's English-language publishing house (incidentally, still very much in business today in Russia), bringing out the revolutionary texts of communism in the language of communism's chief rival, was named, appropriately, "Progress Publishers." In 1971, Leonid Brezhnev pointed out to his East German comrades the "sharp contrast between the confident advance of the socialist countries and their historical optimism on the one hand and the present state of the capitalist world on the other."[5]

Communists and capitalists also agreed on the need to bring progress to the rest of the world. This was a determining feature of the theory of modernization, central to the social sciences of the postwar era. Modernization theorists argued that European society and its overseas offshoots had gone from "traditional" conditions when progress was impossible or, at best, slow and hesitant, to "modernity," in which progress would take place at a very rapid rate. The transition from tradition to modernity involved changes in social and economic structures, and governmental and legal institutions, as well as in individuals' personalities and motivations. Modernization theory came in many variants, involving emphases on different crucial factors enabling conditions for progress to develop. One particularly famous example was MIT economist, and future architect of the Vietnam War, Walter

Rostow's *Stages of Economic Growth*. Published in 1960 the book classified human societies into different phases, with different capabilities for progress, culminating in the final stage of "high mass consumption," making the rapidly developing North Atlantic consumer society the culmination of the history of progress.[6]

Modernization theorists understood both the wealthier capitalist countries and their communist counterparts as exemplars of modernity, although they often described the communist regimes, like their earlier fascist counterparts, as negative versions of it. They perceived those portions of humanity soon to be dubbed the "Third World" as economically and socially "underdeveloped," needing the assistance of the modern ones, to achieve progress. The facilitation of progress was the original impetus for programs of foreign or development aid. The fourth point of Harry Truman's 1949 inaugural address, the beginning of such proposals, stated that the United States would "embark on a bold new program for making the benefits of our scientific advances and industrial progress available for the improvement and growth of the underdeveloped areas." Truman's proposals were brought forth in the context of the rapidly escalating Cold War and development assistance from both the Western and Eastern powers would be shaped by their global confrontation. But a belief in the desirability of bringing progress to underdeveloped peoples was shared by both adversaries. The Soviet dissident, nuclear physicist Andrei Sakharov, in his 1960s think piece *Progress, Coexistence and Intellectual Freedom*, even envisaged a future in which communist and Western countries would overcome their Cold War hostility by jointly bringing progress to the underdeveloped world.[7]

Today, such perspectives would be denounced as "Orientalist," as condescending if not racist. At the time, both leaders and ordinary citizens of Africa, Asia, and Latin America were also firm believers in the idea of progress and of the need for modernization. Such attitudes began in the nineteenth century. Indian intellectuals and other educated colonial subjects, especially in Bengal, then the think-tank of South Asia, accepted the assertion that their colonizers' cultural heritage had enabled them to make progress, and that Indians would do well to imitate them. Increasingly, they began to assert that India's own intellectual traditions were oriented toward progress. Sun Yat-Sen, leader of the 1911 revolution that overthrew the Qing Dynasty and founded the Chinese Republic, was the first person to use the phrase "development" in economic terms, as later modernization theorists would. Mustapha Kemal, "Ataturk," president of the Turkish Republic emerging from the core region of the Ottoman Empire, following its defeat in the First World War, was the pioneer user of the phrase "modernization" as the designation for his program to transform Turkey into a modern state, based on European institutions and intellectual models. He and his supporters endorsed the idea first propounded in India, that their nations' own past traditions were favorable for progress, but that, unlike Europe, they had strayed from this path and needed to return to it.[8]

In the postwar era, anti-imperialism and decolonization were intimately connected to belief in progress. While Mohandas Gandhi was a skeptic about progress and modern civilization, and his views on the future of an independent India were not modeled on European civilization, Jawaharlal Nehru, his right-hand man and dominant figure of post-independence India, had a very different take on the matter. Nehru's memoir and manifesto, *The Discovery of India*, written while imprisoned by the British in 1944, was one long paean to progress, linking it directly to the causes of anti-imperialism and national independence. Admitting that India's one-time progress had slowed in the past, that his native country had "remained rigid and immobile, while other parts of the world marched ahead," Nehru, the leader of the Congress Party, fiercely condemned foreign colonial rule as an "enforced stunting of India's growth and thus arresting of her progress." Other former British colonies that had obtained their independence, like the United States, had made "vast progress." As a result of colonial domination, "Political and economic progress has not only been directly prevented, but also made dependent on the agreement of reactionary groups and vested interests . . . thus putting formidable obstacles in the way of real change and progress." An independent India, he concluded, would be a regime of "national progress."[9]

During the 1950s, anti-imperialist African copper miners in the British colony of Northern Rhodesia, today's Zambia, sang *Calo cesu cileya pantanshi/ Na 'few bantu tuleya pantashi*, "Our country is going forward/And we the people too." Kwame Nkrumah, anti-imperialist president of Ghana, the first sub-Saharan country free of British colonial rule, told the US Council on Foreign Relations in 1958, "The hopes and ambitions of African people have been planted and brought to maturity by the impact of Western civilization . . . We cannot tell our people that material benefits and growth and modern progress are not for them." In Nkrumah's assessment, Africa had no choice. "We have to modernize."

Nkrumah was articulating a sentiment already widespread in African nationalist and pan-Africanist circles, propounded, among others, by Nkrumah's mentor, George Padmore, the journalist and activist from Trinidad. Nkrumah strove to bring modernization in independent Ghana from theory to reality, taking development aid from both Eastern and Western countries for a variety of projects, ultimately to include nuclear power plants. The largest of these projects was the Akosombo dam on the Volta River, which would generate electricity for industrial advancement, part of his plans for an "Africa drawing strength from modern science and technology." He even had a luxury hotel constructed overlooking the dam, so that official visitors could see Ghana engaging in progress. By the mid-1960s, seven hundred thousand people had been at the site.[10]

North of the Sahara, Egypt's president, Gamal 'Abd al-Nasir, read *Stages of Economic Growth* in 1965, when an Arabic translation of it was serialized in *al Ahram*, Cairo's leading newspaper. The nationalist Nasir was intrigued by Rostow's work and told William Polk of the US State Department that he would love to meet the author and discuss with him the application of his theories to Egypt's industrialization. This endorsement of modernization and progress was widely shared among Arab nationalists.[11]

Even the neo-Marxist radical critics of modernization, the so-called dependency theorists, shared the basic belief in progress. Unlike those who envisaged modernization as a global process, beginning first in the North Atlantic and gradually spreading across the world—as one country after another went from underdevelopment to developed, from tradition to modernity—the dependency theorists asserted that modernization meant the exploitation of poorer countries, thwarting their potential for economic development. These theorists nonetheless agreed that development, modernization, and progress were worthy goals, if proposing other methods, such as import substitution industrialization, to achieve them.[12] Left or right, east or west, north or south, in the postwar era belief in the idea of progress spanned ideological, geographic, and socioeconomic borders.

THREE MID-CENTURY CRITICS OF PROGRESS

Belief in progress has always had its critics. Proponents of religious orthodoxy, whether Roman Catholics in the mode of the nineteenth-century ultramontane pope Pius IX, strictly upholding doctrinal purity as it had been realized in the Middle Ages, or Hindus asserting the unshakable and unchangeable nature of the caste system, have rejected the notion of history as a process of improvement. There were more secular critics as well: the philosopher Arthur Schopenhauer, for instance, and his disciple Friedrich Wilhelm Nietzsche, who greatly expanded on his ideas and brought them to a much broader audience. After the First World War, Oswald Spengler's *Decline of the West* portrayed human civilization as cyclical, and currently on a downward slope. Like Schopenhauer, Spengler had a disciple who expanded on and popularized his ideas, the English philosopher-historian Arnold Toynbee, whose multivolume *A Study of History* employed a similarly cyclical structure.

The ideas of three mid-twentieth-century critics of progress both reflected the impact of the age of total war and also took up themes that would become far more widespread and influential in the Era of Upheaval and the Late Millennium. One critic was an Oxford don, a professor of Anglo-Saxon language and literature. His colleagues looked askance at him, because he never seemed to submit any of his scholarship (which everyone agreed was very impressive) for publication, but spent his time devising his own, ever-more elaborate private mythology. Combining a nineteenth-century Roman Catholicism along the lines of Pius IX, with elements of Nordic paganism, his mythical universe revolved around the consequences of the sin of pride, which was always connected to technological progress, investigation of nature, advocacy of political reform, and an unwillingness to accept and to enjoy the natural world as divine creation.

Before and during the Second World War, this mythology began to take more definite shape, in the form of an epic saga, which recounted the war as it should have been. He was not trying to write, he insisted, an allegory. He was appalled by the actual war, pitting his country against an evil, anti-Christian totalitarian regime he despised, but in alliance with a totalitarian, atheist USSR he hated as much as his country's enemy; and with a United States, whose soldiers listened to Boogie-Woogie music, thought England backward, and envisaged a future of global progress, introducing "American sanitation, morale-pep, feminism and mass production." The way the war was fought, especially its deployment of technological progress for destructive purposes in massive aerial assaults, culminating in the dropping of the atomic bomb, seemed to this retiring Oxford don, given his own aversion to technology and deeply traumatic experiences at the Battle of the Somme during the First World War, to be every bit as much a manifestation of evil as the actions of England's enemy had been.

Rather, his mythical war pitted a regime of scientific and technological progress, purported social and political reform, totalitarian rule and unchecked environmental destruction, against a motley coalition of nature lovers and (literal) tree-huggers, adherents of ancient wisdom—true knowledge always took the form of "lore," never newly derived ideas—medieval warriors, diminutively sized Edwardian Englishmen and their servants, along with proponents of the restoration of a traditional monarchy, whose claimant to the throne had distinct similarities to a biblical messiah. Always resisting the temptations of the sin of pride, their behavior guided, at crucial moments, by sentiments expressed in the Lord's Prayer, his unlikely protagonists miraculously carried the day. Their triumph was not just a military victory but a moral and ethical one as well, bringing a transcendent glimpse of divine presence to a mortal earth.[13]

At the same time that J. R. R. Tolkien was writing the *Lord of the Rings*, an Egyptian intellectual and government bureaucrat, an official in the Ministry of Education, was contemplating his country's relationship to its one-time colonial ruler. He observed that Egypt, along with many other countries of the "Orient," was being overwhelmed by a Western civilization "that is based on science, industry and materialism, operates with crazed speed and is without heart and conscience. Driven by invention and material advancement, it sets forth to destroy all that humanity has produced in the way of spiritual values, human creeds and noble traditions." This was progress, and it was achieved "at the expense of our psyches, morals, happiness and comfort... and wealth."[14]

At the end of the 1940s, Sayyid Qutb was sent by his government to the United States to investigate its educational system. Spending almost two years in America, traveling from New York City and Washington, DC, to Palo Alto and San Diego—via Greeley, Colorado—his experiences in the homeland of progress made him even more hostile to it. Writing down his impressions in 1951 following his return, he admitted America's technological progress was astonishing: "It has miraculously elevated life to levels that cannot be believed." But in the process Americans had "closed the windows to faith in religion, faith in art and faith in spiritual values," so their energies were "dissipated in sensual pleasure." Americans loved jazz, "the music that savage bushmen create to satisfy their primitive desires, and their desire for noise on the one hand, and the abundance of animal noises on the other." Qutb associated this primitive music with rampant and unchecked sensuality: American girls with their "round breasts, the full buttocks and... the shapely thighs," showing them off in public. Primitive sexuality was everywhere in American life, "the ties of thirsty bodies, burning passions and eye-popping sex that beckons through the limbs, and is embodied in motions and gestures." Even at church dances, Qutb noted in horror, sensuality held sway.[15]

Qutb's account was an attack on the unity of technological and moral improvement contained in the idea of progress, which led to the opposite—moral and religious regression. Another element of the decline of American civilization, its failure at the sociopolitical reform contained in the idea of progress, was its evident racism. Whites' treatment of Blacks, and particularly Muslims, was "worse than that of the Nazis." Qutb's own encounters with racism were actually mixed. He was turned away from a segregated movie house in Greeley, Colorado, but the president of the Colorado State College of Education posed for a publicity photograph with him, praising him as "a famous Egyptian author... and noted educator in his homeland."[16] Moreover, the same movie house that rejected him as an African American was ready to admit him when it was pointed out that he was an Egyptian.

On his return to Egypt, Qutb joined the Muslim Brotherhood, the Egyptian Islamist political movement, quickly rising within its ranks. Initially cooperating with the nationalist and anti-imperialist army officers who overthrew the pro-British Egyptian monarchy in 1952—Qutb himself was a close confidant and adviser of the officers' leaders, Mohammed Naguib, and Gamal 'Abd al-Nasir—the Brotherhood quickly came into conflict with the new military regime. Qutb was arrested the following year, along with many other Islamist leaders and spent almost the rest of his life in jail, until his execution in 1966. Qutb used his years in prison to organize secret

Islamist paramilitary cells, write commentaries on the Qur'an, and devise religious and political manifestos calling for a worldwide holy war or *jihad* of the Islamic faithful against their enemies. A crucial element of this struggle, he asserted in his last, great manifesto, *Ma'lim 'ala al-tariq*, usually rendered in English as *Milestones* or *Signposts*, was the decline of civilization because humanity was "devoid of these vital values for its healthy development and real progress." Even Western scholars, he argued, "realize that their civilization is unable to present healthy values for the guidance of mankind and does not possess anything to satisfy its own conscience."[17] Neither scientific and technological improvement nor economic prosperity automatically brought with them the necessary attributes, as adherents of progress suggested; only the global domination of Islam—and solely an Islam in its original purity, from the days of the Prophet—could create the moral realm needed to control technology and to make prosperity equitable.

Both Tolkien's and Qutb's skepticism about progress was grounded in their respective faiths, but the small band of postwar critics of progress also included outspoken atheists. The New York writer and literary critic Dwight Macdonald founded in 1944 a magazine he called *politics* (the lowercase letters were deliberate), designed for a niche readership: American radicals who rejected capitalism but found Stalin's USSR equally unattractive, despised fascism but were skeptical of their own country's participation in the Second World War. In the wake of that war, Macdonald published in his magazine an essay in left-wing rethinking, "The Root is Man," designed as a critique of Marxism, which became a wide-ranging, eloquent assault on progress.[18] Support of progress was, Macdonald stated, universal: prevalent among democratic capitalist nations such as the United States and the United Kingdom, and also among their totalitarian counterparts, like the just-defeated Nazi regime. The USSR was the world's leading adherent of progress, but radical opponents of Stalin's regime, such as the Trotskyists, with whom Macdonald had been politically affiliated, endorsed the idea of progress every bit as much. What these progressives had in common was the idea that "it can be easily shown that there has been enormous progress in science, and if scientific method can be applied to all of mankind's problems, then there is justification, almost a necessity for seeing a progressive pattern in man's history."

The Age of Total War, Macdonald averred, had completely refuted this optimistic view of human progress. The atomic bomb had not only vaporized Hiroshima but "the whole structure of Progressive assumptions." The consequences of progress were both destructive and violently oppressive. Not unlike Qutb, Macdonald saw scientific-technological and economic progress as encouraging retrogressive, oppressive irrationality.

To be truly radical, Macdonald asserted was to reject the nightmare of progress, which he, like adherents of modernization theory, identified with an emergent consumer society. People might conclude, "that they don't want electric iceboxes if the industrial system required to produce them also produces World War III."

Although Macdonald's Jeremiad might seem compelling today, his was a voice crying out in the wilderness. The very core of Macdonald's supporters and readers of *politics*, Bohemian leftist New York literati, meeting in Greenwich Village basements at public forums sponsored by his magazine to discuss his ideas, hooted him down and rejected his anti-scientific strictures and doubts about progress as dubious mysticism.[19] This marginalization was a fate he shared with his fellow critics of progress. Qutb was shut up in a jail cell, his writings unpublished, heavily censored, or immediately confiscated on publication by the Egyptian authorities, only available to a handful of secret conspirators. Tolkien struggled to complete his epic and to find a publisher willing to bring out such a lengthy work, complete with footnotes and appendices. The finished product had to appear in installments, because publishing it all at once was too costly. Reviews were decidedly mixed and for a decade after first publication in July 1954, his books were appreciated primarily by a small coterie of aesthetes and intellectuals. All three of the critics of progress would develop large audiences and gain influence, sometimes posthumously, in the Era of Upheaval, but in the postwar era they were rejected, isolated, and ignored.

PROGRESS UNDERMINED

The years I have been calling the Era of Upheaval, roughly from 1965 to 1980, were an unmitigated disaster for the belief in progress. Trends and events conspired to undermine individual elements of that belief—the benign nature of advances in scientific knowledge and the human domination of nature, for instance, or the possibility and desirability of an increasing expansion of human welfare. What's more, the idea of progress as unified movement, as simultaneous, interconnected advances in science, technology, the economy, society, and individual morality, came into question. What had just so recently seemed like common sense was increasingly perceived as foolish naivete.

As contemporaries observed, the long, postwar economic boom had become a central element of the belief in progress. The end of that era of prosperity—the oil shock, stagflation, declining rates of economic growth, and the "lost decades" of Africa and South America—brought "progress" into question. The rise of environmentalism was an even greater blow to it. Malthusian ideas about population growth inevitably outstripping food supply were fundamentally incompatible with a belief in progress, and those ideas were revived and renewed in the 1960s. In fact, those Malthusian ideas were expanded to include a broader understanding of the limitations on the possibilities of human use of natural resources, as exemplified in the ideas propounded by the Club of Rome's *Limits to Growth*. This made a belief in progress seem not just implausible but entirely untenable.

Closely related to this was a growing skepticism about the virtues of science and technology. Environmentalists saw advances in science and technology as producing the destruction rather than the mastery of nature. Increasingly, they linked them: aspiring to master nature inevitably resulted in its destruction and decreased rather than expanded prosperity. Technological advance itself became a source of disillusionment. Those central to the post-1945 belief in progress—atomic energy, space travel, and computing in particular—either failed to live up to hopes when they were utilized on a large scale, as was the case with nuclear power, or became increasingly prosaic and even annoying, the fate of both space travel and electronic data processing.[20]

One might call this the "Tolkien Moment," since many elements of science- and techno-skepticism reflected his ideas. His works were translated into some forty different languages, selling about 140 million copies, worldwide. It is, of course, impossible to know how many of his readers shared the author's doubts about progress—or even realized that he was expressing them. Still, one of the odder features of the immense popularity of this author is the way that a book written by a deeply conservative Roman Catholic became totemic to youth culture, something that bemused (and annoyed) the author himself in the final years of his life, especially when youthful enthusiasts from California took to phoning him without thinking about the time difference.

A particular casualty of the era was the social science underpinning of the postwar era's beliefs in progress, modernization theory, which was battered on all sides. Practical experiences were discouraging. Modernization theorists like Walter Rostow played a large role in promoting and advocating the disastrous US war in Southeast Asia, and war rationales were explicitly described in terms of modernization theory. America was engaged in the "forced draft modernization" of Vietnam, which would take South Vietnamese society out of the phase of transition from tradition to modernity, which modernization theorists understood as the most favorable moment for communist ideas. In practice, this meant terrorizing peasants by large-scale bombing, and forcibly relocating them into "strategic hamlets," in which they could be "modernized." Dwight Maconald's condemnation of the conjunction of progress and war was brought to reality. The modernization of African, Asian, and Latin American countries, which would bring them to Rostow's "high mass consumption stage" of progress, never quite seemed to happen. To the extent that high mass consumption did occur, it was largely the fortuitous conjunction of large oil supplies and high energy prices, not modernization.

As critics of modernization pointed out, the dichotomy between "tradition" and "modernity" was a dubious one. Aspects of "traditional" society, like strong extended families, were often quite helpful for "modern" developments, such as rapid economic growth. The broad expansion in public esteem of libertarian and free-market economists during the Late-Millennium Era was yet another blow to modernization theory, since these economists believed that human nature was always everywhere the same, characterized by the rational search for self-interest. Economic growth and mass-consumption societies came about by unleashing free markets, and allowing people to follow their self-interest, rather than creating individuals with the right, "modern," aspirations and psychological traits.[21]

Belief in an immutable human nature was a characteristic feature of theological orthodoxy, and this produced what could be called the "Sayyid Qutb Moment" for critics of modernization. Nasir's anti-imperialist regime of progress led neither to rapid economic growth nor economic equity, and certainly no mass-consumption society. Egypt's humiliating defeat by the Israelis in 1967 was another blow at its modernizing credentials. Anti-imperialist thought and action in Arab countries increasingly turned in different directions. For a while, it was toward the PLO and its policies of terrorism, carried out in close conjunction with the Cold War Eastern Bloc. By the 1980s, following the Iranian Revolution and the Soviet intervention in Afghanistan, Qutb's ideas, sponsored and empowered by Saudi petrodollars, about a strict Islam necessary to tame the scientific, technological, and economic momentum of progress acquired a steadily greater following.[22]

One might well ask whether by the Late-Millennium Era any belief in progress remained. Down to the mid-1980s, at least, the Eastern Bloc officially continued to be a bastion of that belief, and the doctrine of the linking of a communist future with the progress of the scientific-technological revolution. *Sotto voce*, occasional doubts were expressed about the validity of these beliefs, but, as was typical of the age of Leonid Brezhnev, the regimes plowed on, unchanging in their doctrines, undeterred by reality—at least until the nuclear accident at Chernobyl in 1986.[23]

Attitudes toward nuclear energy offer a particularly useful way to see changes in the political and intellectual locus of the belief in progress. During the 1950s, atomic energy was the very epitome of progress. Even the "ban-the-bomb" activists of that decade insisted on their support for peaceful nuclear power and the future of progress it promised. Opponents of peaceful nuclear power were found mainly among conservatives and traditionalists. Then things switched. By the 1970s, leftists, usually associated with environmentalist causes, emerged as the chief critics of nuclear power and the progress it would bring, often using the same critiques their conservative predecessors had made earlier, while conservatives rallied to the cause of atomic energy and the progress it would produce.[24]

Techno-optimism, the belief that technological progress would produce a future of abundance, while simultaneously resolving environmental and economic problems, remained a feature of conservative thought. It was particularly present among "futurologists," think-tank prognosticators, well into the 1980s. Interestingly, techno-optimism found a positive reception in the Eastern Bloc among futurologists, who even cooperated with their Western counterparts in the International Institute of Applied Systems Analysis, founded in 1972—yet another example of how the idea of progress was endorsed on both sides of the Cold War divide.[25]

Postwar conservatives had often been skeptical of progress, associating it with communism. Fred Schwarz, a pioneering Australian American anticommunist Protestant Evangelical, wrote sermons that accused communism of being a godless materialism with a faith in progress. This charge was not entirely wrong. Communists and their sympathizers throughout the Western world often used "progressive" as a euphemistic description of their programs and attitudes. At least some conservatives rallied to progress. In 1971, Ronald Reagan, who began his political career as we've seen explaining why progress was General Electric's most important product, denounced environmentalists as "doomsayers," "anti-technology," and "anti-industry," who ignored all progress in America since the 1930s. "Freedom and individual dignity," he said "are as important to us as the technology that made them possible . . . this is the brightest hope of men who seek a brighter tomorrow."[26]

Conservatives' late endorsement of the idea of progress differed from the classic belief in it, since they also generally asserted the existence of eternal moral and socioeconomic verities, not subject to progress, breaking the link between the progress of science, technology, and material well-being, on the one hand, and social and moral progress on the other. This point of view would be even more prevalent among late twentieth-century religious conservatives, such as the Protestant Evangelical proponents of the Gospel of Abundant Life (to be considered later in this chapter), who combined a belief in the advancement of both technology and individual well-being with an adamant assertion of biblical moral verities.

These invocations of a limited belief in the idea of progress cannot hide the basic fact that such invocations had become less and less common in the Late-Millennium Era. Evocations of progress as a public goal increasingly vanished from the pronouncements of politicians and government officials. In 1979, General Electric retired its affirmation of progress, deploying a new slogan, "We Bring Good Things to Life," a reference to a consumer society unlinked from any historical dynamic of forward movement.[27] It is possible to make these changes in the endorsement of progress quantifiable, thanks to Google's ngrams, which calculate the frequency with which any given word appears in the corpus of publications the giant Internet firm has digitized.

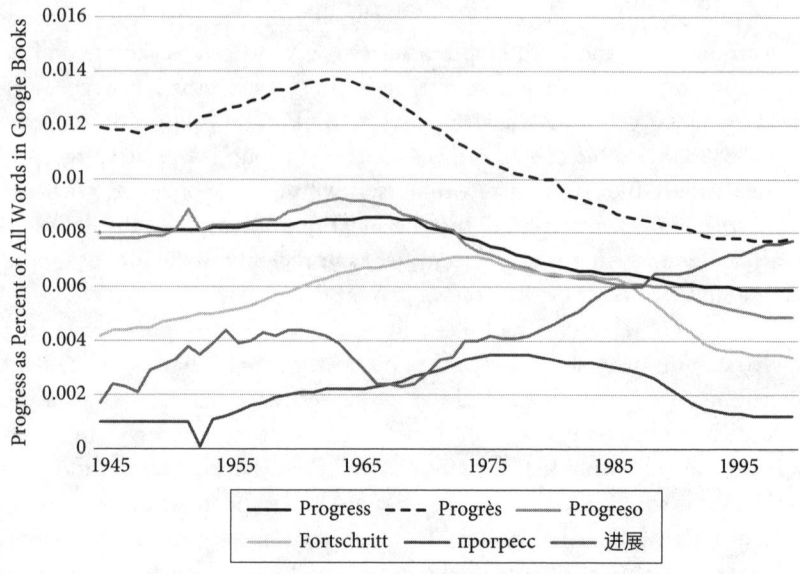

FIGURE 11.1 The Fate of Progress in the Second Half of the Twentieth Century

Figure 11.1 shows how often the word "progress" appeared during the Age of Interconnection in three global languages—English (progress), French (*progrès*) and Spanish (*progresa*); in German, spoken on both sides of the Cold War (*Fortschritt*); and in the two main languages of the communist world, Russian (ΠΡΟΓΡΕСС) and simplified character Chinese (进展).[28]

The chart is unusually clear. While there exist long-standing cultural differences in evocations of "progress," a word invoked most frequently in the Francophone world, the same general tendency appears almost everywhere: a steady rise from 1945 onward to high points in the 1960s or 1970s, followed by a rapid decline. "Progress" literally disappeared from view. This trajectory is common to all languages except Chinese. There, "progress's" rise was interrupted in the early 1960s, no doubt fallout from the disaster of the Great Leap Forward. But with the end of the reign of Mao, and the development of an aggressively capitalist regime, progress resumed its rise, almost overtaking French in the frequency of evocation by 2000. Since published works in China are under the government's (very) watchful eye, it is hard to know the extent to which the frequency of the evocation of progress reflects unofficial attitudes. Economic, scientific, and technological developments since 1980 in the world's most populous country would make a belief in progress plausible. However, in the increasing evocation of "progress" into the new millennium China is a very large but lonely presence in the world. Elsewhere, the belief in progress has been gradually fading away.

Nations

Another focus of human belief is the nation. Invoked under the heading of "nationalism," it takes the existence of human collectivities—geographically at least roughly contiguous, tied together by a number of features, among which the most frequently evoked are a common language, culture, historical experience, descent, or political and constitutional beliefs—and asserts that these nations should be the supreme object of individuals' loyalties. Such loyalties are both expressed and reaffirmed in a rich variety of ceremonies and cultural practices: displaying national flags and pledging devotion to them, collective singing of national anthems and other examples of national music, or military ceremonies. In the nationalist viewpoint, sovereignty is the expression of the nation, which should have the right to determine its own destiny—an idea that acquired during the First World War the designation, "national self-determination." The coining is usually attributed to US president Woodrow Wilson, although it was formulated and publicized by others, particularly his contemporary, British Prime Minister David Lloyd-George.[29]

Ever since historians and social scientists began investigating the origins and development of nationalism, rather than taking its existence for granted, two schools of thought on the topic have emerged. One sees nations as existing before they became the object of political loyalty and the locus of sovereignty in nationalism. Perhaps not all adherents of this view would go so far as the late historian Patrick Wormald, who described Stonehenge as the product of English nationalism, but their view of the long-term antecedents of the nation has given them the designation "primordialists." Opposing them are the "constructivists," who argue that the languages, traditions, or lines of descent that make up nations are largely an invention of nationalists. Far from being of remote origin, nations emerged in the late eighteenth-century age of democratic revolution, when the ideals of popular sovereignty produced collective political entities: nations composed of equal citizens. Just as the idea of progress was formed at this time, so was the idea of nations as subjects of belief and bearers of sovereignty, breaking with the previous belief that nations were the product of royal dynasties, particular religions, or bodies of the society of orders, composed of the privileged classes, such as the nobility. This fundamentally new understanding of the nation required inventing new bases of solidarity for a new political object and inventing forms of ceremony and cultural practices of political loyalty. Each viewpoint—primordialism and constructivism—has arguments in its favor, though constructivists have more.[30]

The big story of nations and nationalism has been their spread, to all strata of the population, and from the North Atlantic to the entire world.[31] Two instances of the spread of nationalism and its transformation of previous concepts of belonging, come from early twentieth-century Asia.

With its ancient civilization, China, might seem like the prime example of the "primordialist" thesis of the development of nationalism. In pre-1900 China, there was a long-term distinction between *xia*, followers of Chinese civilization; and *yi*, barbarians, especially the nomads living on the borders of the realm. But the latter could be transformed into the former, by adopting a sedentary, agricultural lifestyle, Chinese ritual behavior, morality, and the patrilineal system of surnames, either via coercive imperial policy, or through peaceful assimilation. Distinctly Chinese dynastic rulers, including the final, Qing, dynasty, were just such assimilated barbarians. But around 1900, leading up to the revolution of 1911, a new concept of Chinese collective identity began developing among intellectuals, expressed in a newly invented word, *minzu*, "people" or "nation," borrowed from the Japanese *minzoku*. Chinese nationalist intellectuals disagreed about whether the *minzu* was a biological entity, a group of common descent, or a cultural unity, as well as about whether it was a conglomerate of different races or just one. Nonetheless they all agreed that it was the basis of sovereignty and of the claims of a Chinese republic to the entire imperial territory of the former Qing Dynasty. Both the nationalist party, the *Guomindang* (whose name means, literally, "party of national citizenship") and their Chinese communist opponents shared this nationalist understanding. The one-time *yi* were redefined as *shaoshu minzu*, "minority nationals," sometimes understood as racially or culturally akin to the Chinese nation, sometimes not, who might be granted certain forms of autonomy by the government based on the Chinese nation or *minzu*, or who might be forcibly required to display their membership in and loyalty to a Chinese nation-state.[32]

Another example of the creation of nations by nationalists comes from the archipelago located between the South China Sea and the Indian and Pacific Oceans. Inhabited by peoples speaking many different languages, practicing different religions, and following very different cultural practices, it had been gradually conquered by the Dutch, between the sixteenth and the nineteenth centuries, to form the colony of the Netherlands East Indies. There was considerable indigenous resistance to the expansion of Dutch authority, by local monarchs and their subjects, along religious lines; the ruler of Aceh even sent a delegation to the Sultan in far-off Istanbul, asking him to help his fellow Muslims fighting the infidel invaders. In the 1920s, a group of young men, colonial subjects studying at Dutch universities, invented a new word to describe their entire archipelago, "Indonesia," which comes from the Greek "islands of India." The slogan they launched, "One fatherland, Indonesia; one *bangsa* [nation or race] *bangsa* Indonesia; one language, *Bahasa* Indonesia," became a nationalist rallying cry, ultimately resulting in the creation of an independent nation-state, one based precisely on the rejection of all long-developed cultural or linguistic traditions, or previous forms of resistance to Dutch imperialism.[33]

Contemporary Indian nationalists pursued a similar strategy. The efforts of Jawaharlal Nehru, secular leftist and proponent of the idea of progress, to present the modern Indian nation as a successor to the Hindu emperor Aśoka of the third century BC, and, in fact to place Aśokan symbols in the emblems and flag of an independent India, point in a similar direction. In fairness to Nehru and a tribute to his secularism, he was willing to include the sixteenth-century Muslim Mughal imperial dynasty in his gallery of predecessors. Nonetheless, all these efforts point to the way nationalists in Asia, as in the rest of the world, invented a nation with a purportedly long history.[34]

NATIONALISM CHALLENGED

By the early decades of the twentieth century, nationalism had become the increasingly accepted model of political identification; the collapse of multinational empires in the First World War had only intensified this state of affairs. Paradoxically, the Age of Total War, culminating the process of understanding nations and nationalism as the basic forms of political organization, also brought it into question. The battlefield slaughter in the name of the nation during the First World War; the extreme, racist version of the nation articulated in fascist regimes before and during the Second World War; and the mass murders they committed had caused belief in nationalism to waver, and other forms of political loyalty to challenge its priority.

The advances of communism, a declared enemy of nationalism, proclaiming the worldwide solidarity of the workers and the oppressed masses more generally as the acme of political loyalty, in the wake of both world wars, was one sign of these challenges. The USSR, the communist state emerging from the First World War, organized a "communist international," a single, worldwide political party, unlike its predecessor "socialist international," which had been an alliance of individual, national political parties—parties that had gone to war with each other in 1914. Members of the world communist movement were often denounced as and treated as traitors, as adherents of an enemy nation, for their allegiance to the USSR, but it would be fairer to say that they understood their loyalties as representing a new political principle, one going beyond nationalism. The governments of the communist states newly created in Eurasia between 1945 and 1949 continued this allegiance to the USSR as the center of a post-national form of political identity and loyalty. This attitude often took grotesque forms, like the cult of Stalin so prevalent among communist countries at the time, but this new bloc of states nonetheless represented a challenge to the authority of the nation. Opposition to the extension of communist rule in Eastern Europe was often expressed as nationalist hostility, and the new communist regimes dealt harshly with their opponents, imprisoning and executing nationalist politicians, such as the leader of Bulgaria's Agrarian Party, Nikola Petkov, or mounting counterinsurgency campaigns to suppress nationalist paramilitary and partisan groups in Poland, Ukraine, or Lithuania.[35]

A somewhat different challenge to the authority of nationalism was the enthusiasm for international federation and world government. Emerging about the same time as the global communist movement in the wake of the First World War, support for world government permeated various societal niches in the interwar era and peaked after the Second. Early public opinion polling found two people in three in the United Kingdom in favor of world government, and 80 percent of Americans endorsing their country's joining an international organization with the authority to police world peace. Although world federation enthusiasm was more pronounced and more common in the United States and the United Kingdom than in, for instance, Continental Europe, or the newly emergent communist regimes, there were some surprising exceptions. In France, the acts of a young American war veteran, Gray Davis, who renounced his American citizenship, proclaimed himself a world citizen, and attempted to harangue the UN General Assembly about his choice, attracted enormous sympathy, from intellectuals, such as André Gide, Jean-Paul Sartre, and Albert Camus, to some four hundred French municipalities, which proclaimed themselves *"mondialisé"*—global territory. Ranks of enthusiasts for global governance included Gandhi and Nehru, both of whom found the idea of an international federation a way to advance their campaign against imperialism. Perhaps not all world government enthusiasts shared the ideas of a prominent proponent of the time, the Anglo-Romanian journalist David Mitrany, who described nationalism as a form of mental illness. Still, support for global government was a clear rejection of nationalism's claim that the nation-state should be both the source of sovereignty and the highest form of political loyalty.[36]

Paradoxically, the collapse of these hopes of global identity and political legitimacy in view of the rapidly growing Cold War also worked against nationalism. Nations were left behind in the formation of two opposed power blocs. As the anti-fascist Italian priest Primo Mazzolari noted in 1949, his countrymen had become enthusiasts for "Slav or Eastern universalism, Anglo-Saxon or Western universalism." Italian nationalism, so vigorously promoted by the recent fascist government of Benito Mussolini, and opposed, in equally nationalist, if politically very different form, by the anti-fascist resistance movement of 1943–45, seemed to have vanished from the scene.[37]

Another version of postwar era political loyalties and identities transcending the nation was the idea of a European Union. Like enthusiasm for international federation, emerging as a serious political current after the First World War, European federalism, even advocacy of a United States of Europe, was much stronger after the Second. Unleashed nationalisms had left large parts of the continent in ruins. For supporters of a European Union, nation-states and the loyalties they evoked were both obsolete and a persistent danger to the continent.

Particularly strong advocates of a European Union were the newly created Christian Democratic political parties, endorsed by the Catholic Church. That church had been both critic and opponent of nationalism since its origin in the era of the French Revolution, and Catholic activists and politicians had been central to the initial expression of enthusiasm for a European federation in the 1920s. Conditions in postwar Europe were particularly favorable to this long-term skepticism about the virtues of nationalism. An example was the young Helmut Kohl, the future West German Chancellor who was instrumental in bringing about both the unification of the two German states after 1989, and also, at the time, jump-starting efforts at creating a closer European Union. As a teenaged Christian Democratic activist after the war, Kohl led a "Working Group European Reality," whose members, fellow youthful activists, tore down Franco-German border posts, an open rejection of nationalism. Christian Democratic pro-European, anti-nationalist enthusiasm was not limited to impetuous young people. At the 1954 conference of the MRP, the French Christian Democratic political party, one of its adult leaders, Étienne Bourne asserted, "We are the party of Europe. Europe is our form of refusing a return to the past."[38]

These ideas were not exhausted in rhetoric. In the early 1950s a series of actual initiatives and organizations moved in the direction of a European federation. In 1951, the European Coal and Steel Community was created, to organize heavy industry—this was an age of regulated capitalism—in six West European countries. The decision was followed by the signing of a treaty for a European Defense Community; a West European army; and, connected to it, a European Political Community, with a bicameral parliament consisting of a directly elected Chamber of Peoples; a Senate, chosen by national legislatures; and an executive council; court of justice; and council of ministers—in other words, an actual European government. There were certainly pragmatic reasons to support these initiatives, ones quite compatible with nationalism and nation-states. The new European institutions would promote economic growth and benefit nationally organized welfare states. A European army would be a response to US pressure on its allies to bear more of the burdens of the Cold War; it would also be a vehicle of French reluctance to see West German rearmament, so soon after the Nazi era. Yet for all these pragmatic and power-political motives, a post-national pan-European enthusiasm also played a major role. We see this proclaimed in the speech given to the first meeting of the coal and steel community by the French Christian Democratic politician and prominent civil servant Jean Monnet: "the United States of Europe have begun."[39]

While at least some Western Europeans were beginning to move toward a postwar form of transnational union, their colonial subjects were increasingly rejecting their rule. It seems self-evident that opposition to empire should take the form of demanding independent nation-states. The anti-colonial struggles of the late 1940s, leading to the independence of India, Pakistan, and Indonesia, certainly involved nationalist aspirations. But the division of former empires into individual nation-states was not foreordained. The leading political movement in France's African colonies during the 1950s, the *Rassemblement démocratique africaine*, extended across all of French West Africa, and was part of a broader current of anti-imperialism. It envisaged a post-imperial Africa organized politically in different ways than the European model of the nation-state.

The immediate postwar era was the high point of challenges to nationalism. There was, however, a more modest reprise of these challenges during the Era of Upheaval. Mass movements had an ambivalent relationship to nationalism, sometimes opposed, but also often carried along on a strong current of nationalist self-assertion—particularly true in Latin America, where political radicalism in Argentina was closely tied to the nationalist supporters of Peron; in South Asia, where this radicalism was integral to the creation of an independent Bangladesh; or in Eastern Europe, where political activism and nationalism ran together in the Prague Spring of 1968. In the United States, opposition to the war in Southeast Asia, particularly in its more radical variants, sometimes shaded over into open opposition to nationalism—burning the American flag, proclaiming solidarity with the national enemy. Solidarity with the North Vietnamese was a feature of radicalism around the world. African Americans sometimes denounced their nation and proclaimed that their highest political loyalty lay with a global community of Africans. In retrospect, a lot of these assertions, while making a large impression at the time, seem like posturing, the viewpoint of a minority, played up by the mass media and distinctly ephemeral. Nonetheless in the United States, a country with a long history of self-assertive and often un-self-reflective nationalist attitudes and practices, the era marked a high point of a critical perception of the nation.

Whether challenges to nationalism were stronger or weaker, widely supported or confined to narrower groups, in the end nationalism prevailed over all of them. The enthusiasm for European Union as a transnational form of political loyalty and identity definitely could not overcome it. When the treaty establishing the European Defense Community was brought before the French National Assembly in 1954, it was voted down by a large margin and the deputies followed up their no votes by standing and singing the Marseillaise. The European Political Community and transnational government went down with the European army. The Treaty of Rome in 1956 did establish the European Economic Community, or, as it was known in the English-speaking world, the "Common Market." However, this was very much an organization established and dominated by nation-states, far from the dreams of the postwar pan-European enthusiasts. The only borders the EEC tore down were those surrounding farm subsidies (which took up the vast majority of the organization's budget and most of its attention until the 1980s). Two years after the EEC was established, Charles de Gaulle, a very nationalist politician, came to power in France. His European vision was expressed in the slogan, "*Europe des patries*," a Europe of fatherlands, in which European unity was distinctly subordinated to the nation-state.[40]

About a decade after dreams of European unity had given way to the EEC, nationalism in communist regimes began to make the transition from enemy of the state to pillar of the state. The tensions between the USSR and China in the 1960s, leading by the end of that decade to the brink of war— and to actual wars between Vietnam and Cambodia and between China and Vietnam in the following decade–made it painfully clear that international communist solidarity had not been able to overcome nationalism. The war between Vietnam and Cambodia inspired Benedict Anderson, perhaps the most famous social science theorist of nationalism, to write his celebrated book on the topic, *Imagined Communities*.[41]

Many accounts, especially journalistic ones, of nationalism in communist regimes employ what might be called a "hydraulic model." The waters of nationalism are steadily rising, but prevented from flooding by the dams of the regimes' authoritarian policies. When these dams are weakened by diplomatic competition, as was the case in the Sino-Soviet split, in the Eastern European anti-communist uprisings of 1953, 1956, 1971, 1976, and 1980, and, following 1989, when the communist regimes collapsed across much of Eurasia, nationalism just comes flooding out. This is not entirely wrong. The Yugoslav authorities kept close tabs on incidents of "national chauvinism" in Bosnia-Herzegovina; between early 1960 and mid-1962, they counted 7,462 of them, ranging from curses and insults to assault and battery, in spite of the official communist insistence that Yugoslavia's nationalities all lived together in "brotherhood and unity." If the hostility between Serbs, Croats, and Muslims in Bosnia remained below the murderous levels it reached during the Second World War or in the 1990s, it was because the communist authorities still had the power to suppress it.[42]

The hydraulic model of nationalism under communist rule, like the primordialist theories of nationalism it resembles, remains dubious. Communist regimes transformed and encouraged nationalist ideas, whether intentionally or unintentionally. During the Cold War competition of the dual nations, communist regimes in Germany, China, Korea, and Vietnam had burnished their nationalist credentials. Emerging from a nationalist revolution, a communist Cuba permanently facing down the United States, the national enemy, was unthinkable without a strong component of nationalism. The Bolshevik notion of communism as internationalist solidarity of the oppressed via class struggle, faltering in the Era of Upheaval, no longer inspired even the beliefs of party loyalists. Communist governments therefore turned to the promotion of nationalism. In the USSR, the long-taboo idea of Russian nationalism, which potentially could undermine the multinational character of the Soviet Union, or even the communist state's very existence, came to enjoy increasing official favor. Works of fiction promoting the virtues of Russian peasants won the Gorky Prize, the USSR's highest literary honor, and were printed in very large editions. Russia's nineteenth-century Slavophiles, right-wing nationalists who promoted a connection between Russian nationalism, the Tsar, and the Orthodox Church, were historically rehabilitated. This was accompanied by denunciations of the way that the Asian population of the USSR was growing so much faster than its Slavic one, as well as attacks on the Jews. Citizen initiatives to restore Orthodox churches found official favor—in a distinctly atheistic government, generally hostile to unofficial initiatives.

While in the ruling circles of the Soviet Union, these policies were always disputed, in communist Romania, under the rule of its mercurial party leader, Nicolae Ceaușescu, there was no wavering in the promotion of nationalism. This was a sharp break from the policies of the Romanian communists in the post-1945 era, who had always emphasized their loyalty to the Soviet Union, even changing the official name of the country in 1953 from the Latin-derived *România*, to the more Slavic *Romînia*. From the mid-1960s on, the Romanian government often criticized Soviet foreign policy, such as the invasion and regime change in Czechoslovakia in 1968. It also insisted vigorously that communism and nationalism, far from being enemies, were compatible forms of political loyalties, and patronized various forms of Romanian national self-assertion—from the cult of Count Dracula, based on the medieval warrior, Vlad the Impaler, to the theory of "protochronism," which is based on the argument that all the major literary trends in modern Europe had first been practiced in Romania. All of this both encouraged and articulated hostility to Romania's communist allies, who had been pre-communist Romania's national enemies: Hungary, with whom there had been a long-running dispute over the territory of Transylvania (it was Magyars in Transylvania that Vlad the Impaler was said to have been impaling); and the USSR as the successor state to the Tsars, with whom Bessarabia, today's Moldova, had been another focus of long-term national antagonism.[43]

At least as important were the unintentional results of communist rule. The USSR had always opposed Ukrainian nationalism, and vigorously persecuted Ukrainian nationalists in the Western Ukrainian territories it had won after the Second World War. The largest city in this region was Lviv (Polish: Lwów), before 1939 inhabited primarily by Poles and Jews, with just a small Ukrainian minority. The Nazi occupiers had exterminated the Jews; after 1945, as part of the territorial realignments in East-Central Europe promoted by a victorious USSR, the Poles of the city, generally considered by the Soviets as anti-communist reactionaries, were expelled and deported to Poland. They were replaced by Ukrainians from rural areas, deported in turn from Poland, or moving from areas of Ukraine under pre-1939 Soviet rule. The Soviet government had, unintentionally, turned western Ukraine's largest city into a Ukrainian city, a capital of the Ukrainian nationalism the government understood, correctly, to be a threat to its existence.[44]

Around the same time that Europeanist dreams faded and communist regimes turned to nationalist ideas, European colonial empires, particularly in Africa, came to an end. The newly independent countries all took over the form of the nation-state, generally basing their territorial boundaries on those of the former colonies. Enthusiasm for an African or at least a West African federation faded, just as enthusiasm for European federation had done a decade previously. The historian Frederick Cooper who has studied this development intensively finds that previous plans of federation had been too closely linked to efforts of the French and the British to reorganize and to revive their empires. Nation-states appeared as the heirs of anti-imperialism; wider forms of political identity and loyalty, expressed in federalism, had become tainted with the heritage of colonial oppression.[45]

Part of the reinvigoration of nationalism was the development of new forms of expression and symbolism and new kinds of ceremonies. The close connection of nationalism and the military had been called into question by the Second World War. Even in the United States, a country without some of the painful legacies of the Second World War, the Vietnam War at least temporarily raised doubts about this link. The trend toward abolition of compulsory military service, occurring in the world's wealthier countries in reaction to the upheavals of the 1960s, eliminated an institution that had been central to nationalism, since its inception in the age of the French Revolution.[46]

One new possibility, probably most typical of the former Axis Powers, was to connect nationalism to pacifism. Although there were some examples of this attitude in Germany and Italy, it was by far strongest in Japan, where the phrase *hibaku nashonari-zumu*, "A-bomb nationalism," with its statement that Japan was "the only nation ever to have been atom-bombed," was reiterated by postwar prime ministers and politicians. The Hiroshima Peace Memorial was designed by the architect Tenge Kenzō, using the same plan he devised in 1942 for a nationalist war memorial, the "Commemorative Building Project for the Construction of Great East Asia." In view of the war's outcome, the latter memorial was never built, but its design was utilized for a new version of nationalism.[47]

Glorifying in defeat lacked the emotional appeal and the ceremonial edge that a nationalism connected to the military had provided, as repeated outbursts of more intransigent nationalism in postwar German and Japan would suggest. The 1950s and 1960s saw the emergence of new ceremonies of national identity and new forms of glorification of the nation's victories, in a—literally—different arena, namely via sports. As both large-scale spectator and participant pastime, sports emerged in the world's wealthier countries around 1900, reaching much of Asia and Latin America between the world wars. Characteristic features of modern sports (differing from the many forms of play and exercise that had been typical of humanity since its origins) included standardized rules and record keeping; organized clubs; formation of leagues and league competition, often in front of crowds of spectators numbering in the thousands or tens of thousands; and the delineation of a group of professional or semi-professional athletes. It also meant the growth of a large body of sports fans, cheering on the efforts of their clubs and teams.

The growth of sports was an early example of globalization, as competitions increasingly crossed the borders of individual states and international bodies emerged to regulate athletic competition, worldwide: the two best-known examples were the International Olympic Committee, founded in 1894; and the international soccer federation, FIFA, created ten years later. Globalization in this instance contributed to rather than diminished nationalism, as international competitions took the form of contests between national teams, so that fan loyalties could converge with nationalist ones. Groups of fans gathered in public spaces waiting for the telegraph to deliver the results of competitions, hoping their national team had won the day.

This combination of globalization and nationalism continued in the interwar era, generally not a good period for global interconnections. The first soccer World Cup, Montevideo in 1929, and the 1932 Los Angeles and 1936 Berlin Olympic Games were significant in this process. The modern Olympic medal ceremony, making athletes' success a national triumph, by raising the national flags of the medal winners and playing the national anthem of the gold medalist, debuted in Los Angeles. The organizers of the Los Angeles Olympics rejected the idea of live radio coverage of the competition, prompting NHK, the Japan Broadcasting Corporation, to send back home, via short-wave, re-creations of exciting events. In Berlin, four years later, extensive live radio was welcomed and supported, reaching three hundred million listeners across the world.[48]

The expansion on a global scale of first radio and then TV after the Second World War brought sports to the forefront of national identity. Great athletic moments, whether it was the West German national team winning the World Cup in 1954; the TV broadcast of the 1970 World Cup from Mexico City (the first in color and with slow motion replays); or the US men's hockey team defeating the Soviets at the Winter Olympics in 1980, became through electronic mediation, powerful affirmations of the nation. Fans watched the competition at home, but also in pubs and public spaces, waving flags and singing the national anthem. Particularly in soccer-mad Latin America, the idea of styles of play—Argentina's *la neustra*, Brazil's *futebol arte*, or Uruguay's *garra charrúa*—became both strategies for winning soccer matches and expressions of a nation's deepest identity.[49] Soccer articulates national identity more than any other sport—the World Cup is a global spectacle (1.5 billion TV viewers for the 2002 final between Brazil and Germany), rivaled only by the Olympic Games. Nonetheless a wide variety of other sports, from rugby or American football to field and ice hockey, to cricket, baseball and basketball, fill this role as well.

Beginning in the 1950s, sporting events have replaced military ceremonies as the site of national enthusiasm or national ceremonials—and national hostilities too, as soccer fans do battle with fans from other countries, sometimes with fatal consequences. This might be less the case in the United States, where military and flag ceremonies exalting the nation have remained a vigorous presence, but sporting events generally began with flag ceremonies and a rendition of the national anthem, along with military displays, such as fighter jet flyovers.[50]

PAN-ARABISM AND PAN-AFRICANISM

In 1971, just two years after coming to power in Libya, Muammar Qaddafi presented his vision of national destiny. The country would be key to the "unification of the Arab nation," by playing the role that Prussia had in Germany and the Piedmont in Italy.[51]

An eccentric dictator who came to a bad end, Qaddafi showed a keen historical understanding and a clear grasp of the politics of nationalism. It was not just about transforming realms based on dynastic loyalties into states based on national sovereignty, or destroying multinational empires by dividing them into nation-states, but about uniting individual states into one nation-state, encompassing an entire nationality. The classic nineteenth-century examples of this process were indeed the unifications of Italy and Germany. Convincing at least some of the inhabitants of the thirty-nine German and seven Italian states that they were members of the nation, and that their highest loyalty should be to an entity that did not yet exist was no simple task. Paradoxically, unification required one of those individual states to follow nationalists' policies—as Qaddafi noted, in nineteenth-century Italy, the Kingdom of Piedmont-Sardinia; in nineteenth-century Germany, the Kingdom of Prussia—to take the lead to accomplish those nationalist goals, which meant carrying them out in the context of the clashes between the Great Powers. Part of the vigorous reassertion of nationalism across the globe in the 1950s and 1960s was the idea of pursing such policies outside of Europe—uniting all of Arabia or Africa into one nation-state.

Pan-Arabism, the movement to encompass all Arabs in one nation-state, emerged as part of opposition to the imperialist rule of the Ottoman Empire, and, especially, of the European colonialists, who had already been encroaching on the Ottomans before 1914 and had taken over Arab territories following the First World War. Particularly influential among the growing ranks of the educated middle class, spurred on by the increasing Jewish presence in Palestine, encouraged by the clash of the Great Powers in the Second World War, Pan-Arabism took organizational form with the founding of the Ba'ath Party in Damascus in 1947. The party would organize in the entire Arab world with the slogan, "the Arab nation from the Atlantic Ocean to the Arabian Gulf." As was the case with postwar era anti-imperialism more generally, Arab nationalism was one of many political tendencies in the movement against European empires. Others included early forms of Islamism in the Muslim Brotherhood, supporters of communism, particularly influential in Iraq, or adherents of *al-Wataniya*, advocates of loyalty to existing dynasties, such as the House of Saud in Saudi Arabia, or the Hashemite rulers of Iraq and Jordan, but also to nonexistent realms like a "Greater Syria" that would include today's Syria, Lebanon, Israel, and Jordan.[52]

What brought Pan-Arabism from slogan and plan to potential realization was its adoption by a powerful Arab state, a role Libya, in spite of the pretensions of its ruler, could never fill. The overthrow in 1952 of the Egyptian monarchy, with its close ties to the British Empire, and its replacement by a nationalist military regime, led by Nasir, brought the most populous Arab country under the control of a Pan-Arabist regime. The *Sawt al-'Arab*, "Voice of the Arabs" radio station in Cairo, in rapid expansion, emerged as the world's sixth-largest radio service by 1960, well behind the BBC or the Voice of America, but far larger than any Arabic-language competitor. The Sawt al-'Arab proudly announced that it spoke for the Arabs, embracing their struggles, and expressing their unity, reminding its listeners—from Tunis to Amman—that the Egyptian government was "in the service of the Arab nation and its struggle against Western imperialism and its lackeys in the Arab world."[53]

Nasir's rejection of membership in the Baghdad Pact, organized by the British, his proclaimed Cold War neutrality, his participation in the 1955 Bandung Conference of African and Asian anti-imperialists, and, especially, his seizure of the Suez Canal, made him a hero to proponents of Arab national unity. When the Franco-British-Israeli invaders of Egypt were forced to withdraw in December 1956 under Soviet and American pressure, Arab nationalist jubilation knew no bounds. Iraqi Air Force officers visiting Morocco at the beginning of 1957 heard crowds chanting a variation on the Arab nationalist slogan: "From the rebellious Gulf/To the roaring ocean/At your service, 'Abd al-Nasir."

Following street demonstrations and general strikes, King Hussein of Jordan called parliamentary elections in October 1956; for the first time, political parties were allowed to campaign freely. The Jordanian National Movement, a coalition of Arab nationalist political parties, including the communists, but not the Islamists of the Moslem Brotherhood—who, there as elsewhere in the Arab world, generally opposed the nationalists—won an overwhelming victory. In neighboring Syria, politicians of the Ba'ath Party and army officers sympathetic to them went even further, bypassing the actual government and demanding the immediate unification of Egypt and Syria. Proclaimed at the beginning of 1958, the United Arab Republic was endorsed by near unanimity in plebiscites held in both countries. Culminating this series of pan-Arab triumphs, a May 1958 military coup in Iraq overthrew the pro-Western Hashemite monarchy. King Faisal II and his prime minister Nuri al-Sa'id, a veteran of the Arab revolt against Ottoman rule during the First World War, were shot and their bodies dragged through the streets of Baghdad. The newly proclaimed Iraqi Republic announced its support for Arab nationalism and sent a delegation to Cairo to negotiate joining the United Arab Republic. By the late 1950s, nationalism was everywhere in the Arab world. Even in Saudi Arabia, under the tight control of the royal dynasty, closely allied with Wahhabi Muslim clerics, support for Nasir and his Pan-Arab nationalism was by far the most important form of political opposition.[54]

In all these respects, Pan-Arabism appears as a pioneering example of the nationalist reaction to challenges to its political hegemony across the world. Its further history showed the difficulties of completing its political program. Overcoming the competitors to identification with the nation— dynastic loyalties, attachment to existing states, and religious affiliations— and subordinating state sovereignties in a world of Great Power politics proved far more difficult than they had seemed in the heady atmosphere of the Suez Crisis.

In April 1957, King Hussein, relying on pro-monarchical officers in the armed forces and Bedouin tribesmen loyal to him, carried out a coup (Pan-Arabists seem to have been planning their own coup against him), eliminating the power of the Arab nationalists in Jordan. A detachment of British royal marines would ensure that the monarch's rule held firm. Following a power struggle among the Iraqi revolutionaries, the pro-Nasir Arab nationalists were defeated; Iraq would not join the United Arab Republic, which had considerable difficult establishing its rule in Syria. For a while, it was the conservative anti-nationalist political forces that welcomed the unification with Egypt as a bulwark against the communists, while the nationalists of the Ba'ath Party rejected the Egyptian version of the Pan-Arab nationalism they espoused. When a military coup proclaimed Syria's independence after three years of being part of the United Arab Republic, opposition in Syria was nonexistent. Nasir himself refused to order a military intervention to preserve this first step on the way to Arab national unity. Afterward he would claim that he was always skeptical of the Syrian-Egyptian union and had been forced into it by popular nationalist demonstrations. The collapse of the UAR was also the beginning of the decline of the star of Nasir, the hero of Arab nationalism—a process completed by the long, difficult, expensive, and militarily unsuccessful Egyptian intervention in Yemen in support of a Pan-Arabist military coup there, and then the catastrophic defeat at the hands of the Israelis in 1967. Nasir's successor as Egyptian president, Anwar al-Sadat, renounced Pan-Arabist policies while attempting a reconciliation with the nationalists' rivals, the Islamists of the Muslim Brotherhood, as well as with the United States, which had generally supported opponents of Pan-Arabism. The Palestinian revolutionaries of Yassir Arafat's *Fatah* rejected Pan-Arabism as well, seeing their movement as part of a global Third World struggle against imperialism.

Pan-Arabism enjoyed a brief revival in the decade of the 1980s, when Saddam Hussein of Iraq attempted to become its champion. This was a dubious course. Iraq was not just much less populous and powerful than Egypt; its population included large numbers of Kurds, with their own nationalist cause, and Shi'ite Arabs, whose religious ties with their fellow Shi'a in Iran militated against a nationalist unification of all Arabs. Saddam's two invasions, of Iran in 1980 and Kuwait a decade later, were designed to make him the leader of Arab nationalism by glorious military victories, not unlike the way Bismarck had made Prussia the leader of German nationalism in the 1860s. Unlike the widespread nationalist jubilation throughout the Arab world for Nasir's struggle with the British in 1956, these wars brought, at most, a very limited nationalist echo, and both were military failures. Hussein could neither exploit Cold War rivalries in his war with Iran nor deal with the post-Cold War world and the powerful position of the United States following his incursion into Kuwait.[55]

By the late twentieth century, Pan-Arabism had become increasingly a relic of a past era. At a 1994 Pan-Arabist conference in Beirut, the gray-haired, stooped participants leaned on their canes and fiddled with their hearing aids. In the Arab Spring of 2011, a mass movement across the entire Arab world on a scale not seen since the heady days of 1956, calls for Arab national unity were nowhere to be heard.[56] Fifty years after it had taken root, the movement to unite all Arabs in one nation-state faltered, ultimately unable either to establish the nation as the primary focus of political identification and loyalty, or to master the power politics of absorbing individual sovereign states into a unified nation.

As the slogan of the Arab nation stretching from the ocean to the gulf suggests, Arabs live in a geographically contiguous area, at least potentially propitious to national unification. As a result of the slave trade in the Early Modern World, this was not the case with Africans, who came to live on both sides of the Atlantic. Pan-Africanism and even the idea of Africans as political subject, did not begin in Africa at all, but in the Caribbean. Nineteenth-century pioneers of Pan-Africanism, such as the author and politician Edward

Wilmot Blyden, whose 1872 newspaper *Negro*, was aimed at audiences on the African continent, the Caribbean and the United States, or the great Pan-Africanist of the early twentieth century, Marcus Garvey, were all from the Caribbean. (Louise Little, the mother of Malcolm X, the leading Pan-Africanist in the United States, came from Grenada.) Caribbean, activists especially the Trinidad native George Padmore, were crucial to postwar era Pan-Africanism, first articulated with the holding of a Pan-African Congress in Manchester in the fall of 1945. Attendees included future African anti-imperialist leaders, and advocates of Pan-Africanism, such as Jomo Kenyatta and Kwame Nkrumah, Africans who learned their Pan-Africanism from the Caribbean.[57]

The movement for independence from European colonial rule in 1950s Africa had strong Pan-Africanist overtones, but translating these sentiments into the realm of power politics, as occurred in the Arab lands at the same time, proved difficult. Individual leaders of newly independent African states, such as Tanzania's president Julius Nyerere, and especially Ghana's president Kwame Nkrumah, supported Pan-Africanist ideas. However, their regimes, unlike Nasir's Egypt, or even Hussein's Iraq, lacked the power to realize them. At the founding of the Organization of African Unity in 1963, Nkrumah pushed hard for devolving at least some sovereign authority onto the group but found no support from other African leaders. Renamed in 2001 the African Union, the organization has always been an association of nation-states, carefully guarding their sovereignty. Pan-Africanism has remained primarily a cultural aspiration, endorsed by intellectuals and artists on both sides of the Atlantic, finding expression in cultural and artistic festivals, such as the First World Festival of Negro Arts in Dakar in 1966; the Pan-African Cultural Festival of Algiers, three years later; the First Congress of African Writers in Dakar, 1976; or the Second World Black and African Festival of Arts and Culture in Nigeria, the following year. Nineteenth-century European nationalists had held similar kinds of congresses and festivals, as precursors to their political goals, but Pan-Africanism has largely not moved beyond the cultural realm in the direction of reaching the nationalist goal of creating a united nation-state.[58]

NATIONALISM IN THE LATE-MILLENNIUM ERA

Rather than seeing either Pan-Arabism or Pan-Africanism as failures for not reaching the goal of a united nation-state, it might be more appropriate to note how far each of these movements progressed, in spite of the considerable headwinds against them, generated by the world's Great Powers. In this respect, the careers of Pan-Africanism and Pan-Arabism were ultimately testimony to the appeal of nationalism. Around the world, in the Late-Millennium Era, nationalism went from strength to strength.

There was no greater testimony to this than the events of 1989–91 and the end of communism across Eurasia. Mass movements against communist rule were invariably a reassertion of national sovereignty, a reaffirmation of the doctrine of national self-determination, eight decades after its initial formulation—and in a part of the world for which the idea was originally conceived. There were the spectacular events of the anti-communist mass movements themselves: the demonstrators in Leipzig who went from chanting "we are the people" to "we are one people"; the "singing revolution" in Estonia, where rejection of Soviet rule took the form of the widespread choral singing of national anthems and national folksongs; the demonstrators in Bucharest waving tricolor Romanian flags, from which the communist insignia, the hammer and sickle, had been cut out, leaving the quintessential expression of nationalism. The end of communism in central Europe brought with it the unification of the two German states, the unexpected fulfillment of a nationalist goal that had come to seem like a vanished dream. The complementary process of the breakup of multinational realms into independent nation-states quickly followed on the end of communism: the smooth and peaceful division of Czechoslovakia into separate Czech and Slovak Republics; the less smooth and less peaceful division of the USSR—accomplished with relatively little violence in 1991, although setting the stage for future, much more violent nationalist confrontations in Chechnya and Eastern Ukraine; and the division of Yugoslavia, bringing in its wake civil war and mass murder.

The survival of genuinely and nominally communist regimes across the historical divide of 1989–91 was at least as much a testimony to the power of nationalism as the collapse of the other communist regimes. China, Vietnam, North Korea, Cuba, the communist regimes that persisted through the period of popular mass mobilization—and, in China's case violently suppressed anti-regime popular mobilization—were all countries where communism was closely associated with national self-determination, rather than, as was the case in most of Eastern Europe, foreign imposition. Nationalism enabled regimes to maintain legitimacy and popular support, as they began the transition away from a planned economy and collective ownership—China and Vietnam—or stuck stubbornly to those principles, in Cuba and North Korea.

Late twentieth-century nationalism often took more hard-edged forms. A prime example was India, where the Congress Party, emerging from the struggle against British imperialism for national self-determination, had consistently articulated its belief in a loyalty to India that transcended religious, linguistic, and ethnic differences. There had been a nationalist counter-current, understanding the Indian nation as integrally tied to the Hindu religion, and that only Hindus could be true Indians, organized in the nationalist organization, *Rashtriya Swayamsevak Sangh*, or RSS. One of its adherents had assassinated Mohandas Gandhi in January 1948, for his willingness to recognize Muslims as part of the Indian nation. But the RSS and the various political parties associated with it had always been a minority movement, and a relatively small one at that.

In the Late-Millennium Era, this less tolerant and more militant version of Indian nationalism came to the fore. Women's and youth groups promoting Hindu nationalism brought the idea out of the relatively narrow circles of the upper caste and educated upper middle-class adherents of the RSS. Campaigns, like the nationwide caravan of bricks to build a shrine to the god Ram on the site of the Babri Masjid mosque in Ayodhya (which the Muslims had supposedly usurped from the Hindus) in the north Indian state of Uttar Pradesh—the bricks wrapped in saffron cloth and paraded around in different localities for several days—attracted more than one hundred million spectators. The campaign culminated in a mass meeting and riot in December 1992, during which the mosque was demolished.

Enjoying considerable support from Indians in North America and the United Kingdom the militant Hindu nationalists created a new political party, the Bharatiya Janata Party, or BJP, which defeated Congress in both state and national elections in the 1990s, emerging as the dominant political party in India. One of the BJP's intellectuals, Jay Dubashi, placed the rise of an aggressively Hindu version of Indian nationalism in a global context, stating that "very same day the first brick of the Ram Shila foundation was being laid at Ayodhya, the Berliners were removing bricks from the Berlin Wall." History, he argued, had rejected Nehru's project of a secular nationalism in India just it had overthrown communism in Europe.[59]

There were two larger challenges to intransigent nationalism's hegemonic role in political identity and loyalty. One involved the idea of European unity. Starting in the 1980s and accelerating in the subsequent decade, enthusiasts for Europe began taking measures to transform the European Economic Community into a transnational body, culminating in the Maastricht Treaty of 1992, establishing a European Union, complete with a common currency. The end of the Cold War meant that such a union would be truly European-wide and not merely limited to Western Europe. As was the case with the original movement toward European unity at the end of the Second World War, there were pragmatic considerations—for example, the effort to revive economic growth, which had slowed considerably in the 1980s, by eliminating barriers to the free movement of goods, capital, and labor. There was also the appeal of reconciling other European countries to German national unification by constraining the new, larger, and potentially more powerful German state in pan-European institutions. But the European union included "European citizens," or "creating an ever-closer union among the peoples of Europe," phrases that were part of the project of writing and ratifying a European constitution.

Moving in the direction of a Europe that would supersede the nation-state proved to be traversing a bridge too far. Inhabitants and politicians of the countries of the former Eastern Bloc, who had just regained their national sovereignty from the transnational communist realm, proved unwilling to surrender it to another transnational project. Skepticism was strong in Western Europe as well, and when the project was put to the voters, in referenda held in Ireland, Denmark, the Netherlands, and France, they rejected it. The French and Dutch referenda in particular led to the scrapping of the project of a European constitution, and its replacement with the 2008 Lisbon Treaty, an agreement between sovereign states. Political scientists' analyses of the voting generally show that it was younger, educated, and more affluent voters who supported the idea of European unity, while older, less-well-off voters, fearful of both the economic competition of globalization and the cultural consequences of increasing migration from the Middle East and Africa, rejected it. If Hindu nationalists saw their triumph as part of a global trend, their European counterparts had endorsed an opposite meaning of nationalism as a refuge for those threatened by the trend toward increasing global interconnections. All these attitudes were demonstrated well before the Brexit referendum of 2016 showed them on an unprecedented scale.[60]

In some parts of Europe, the alternative to national loyalties was not transnational loyalties, but other kinds of national loyalties. Bretons in France, Basques and Catalans in Spain, the Irish and Scots of the United Kingdom, and Flemings in Belgium wanted to secede from the existing nation-state and create their own. Often described, in the fashion of primordialist theories of nationalist as the latest version of centuries-old antagonisms, most of these "regionalist" or secessionist movements took distinctly new turns, moving politically from right to left, as happened with both Basque and Breton nationalism—arguably the same was the case in Scotland—or falling into very different hands. Breton nationalists were led by native French speakers, former activists of the mass movements of 1968, who had moved to Brittany and transferred their insurgent enthusiasms from workers and students to the inhabitants of Western France, and were busy teaching native Breton speakers their authentic culture and language. The French nation-state was able to resist such regionalist and secessionist political movements fairly easily. Things were more difficult in Spain, the United Kingdom, or, especially, Belgium, where the differences between Flemish and French speakers had escalated by the 1990s to the point that all they had in common was rooting for the Belgian soccer team in the World Cup competition.[61]

A more effective and powerful Late-Millennium Era challenge to the hegemony of nationalism emerged from Islamism. Placing the *umma*, the global community of Muslims, above any national loyalty, and envisaging a future Islamic realm headed by a *khalif*, a righteous, pious ruler, Islamists denounced nationalism as un-Islamic—a viewpoint strongly shared by Sayid

Qutb and by Abu Ala Mawdudi, the leading Islamist thinker in South Asia. Prominent Islamists described the Pan-Arabist Ba'ath Party as "impious." By replacing Allah and His revelations as the basis of the state, popular sovereignty and national self-determination were "idolatrous"—a judgment quite similar to that of nineteenth-century European Christian conservatives.[62] Contrary to widespread opinions in the United States following the terrorist attacks of September 11, 2001, Islamists and Pan-Arabists had always been strongly opposed to each other. Muammar Qaddafi had attempted to combine the two, but his version of Islam was so peculiar and idiosyncratic that virtually all Moslem clergy and scholars regarded it as heretical.

Islamism in action, as seen during the war against the Soviets in Afghanistan during the 1980s, and in Al Qaeda, over the two subsequent decades, was a strongly multinational movement. This multinationalism reached its peak in the revolutionary rule of ISIS in Mosul and Raqqa between 2014 and 2018. *Mujahideen*, Islamic holy warriors, from Arab countries, Pakistan, West Africa, Indonesia, and Europe, including prominent rap musicians from Germany and the United Kingdom, rushed to join the Islamist regime, in an act of affirmation of an anti-nationalist political movement not seen since the journeys of communist revolutionaries from around the world to Bolshevik Moscow and Petrograd in 1918.[63]

The most powerful challenge to nationalism, Islamism has, like previous challengers, mobilized groups of adherents to its new principles of identification and loyalty. Yet it has ultimately also been unable to shake the dominant position of belief in the nation. In contrast to the decline of the idea of progress in the unfavorable conditions of the 1970s, nationalism was able to overcome the difficulties posed by the Age of Total War. Spreading around the world, making use of electronic mass media, sports, and global interconnections, nationalism has triumphed over its adversaries, reinforcing its position as the standard of political identity and loyalty. The nation has remained a core object of belief down to the present day.

God

If there is anything that deserves the term "primordialism," it would have to be religion, the belief in a supernatural deity or deities, and in a transcendent realm beyond material reality. As old as humanity itself, religion was also a pioneer of global interconnections. Long before the worldwide expansion of markets or of communications and transportation networks, religions with many adherents, including Christianity, Islam, and Buddhism, as well as smaller faiths, like Zoroastrianism and Judaism, linked coreligionists across state boundaries, continents, and oceans.

For all its venerable age, religion as a system of belief, group of practices, and ceremonies, guide to action and behavior, and form of organization has had to face particular challenges in the world since the Enlightenment. The rise of natural science and of secular scholarship, increasing scientific and technological control of nature; new forms of political frameworks for religion, involving an understanding of the public sphere as a realm of reduced or eliminated religious influence; and competing ideals of transcendent loyalties, especially the nation, but also radical regimes, from the Jacobins of the French Revolution to the communist realms of the twentieth century, to say nothing of the fascist idealization of a master race—all of these have undermined religion's place in the world. Sociologists have a word for this, "secularization." From the nineteenth-century classic sociological thinkers—Auguste Comte, Marx, Max Weber, Emile Durkheim—to the modernization theorists of the 1950s and 1960s, adherents of the idea maintain that in the modern world, religion, particularly in its organized forms, will be increasingly marginalized.

Not unlike the belief in progress, to which they are closely connected, theories of secularization have come in for rough treatment. Starting in the 1970s religious revival and renewal, particularly in Christianity and Islam, but in Hinduism, Judaism, and Buddhism as well, from Los Angeles to Peshawar, from Rio de Janeiro to Harare, occupied the public sphere, became strongly present in the mass media, and more influential in directing public policy. It was secularism that seemed to be marginalized and declining. The collapse of explicitly atheistic communist regimes in 1989 was apparently a final rejection of the power and validity of secularization. In the wake of these developments, prominent observers of the place of religion in public and private life, for instance, the sociologist of religion Peter Berger or the theologian Harvey Cox, went from being Sauls of secularization theory in the 1960s to Pauls of a reinvigorated transcendence three decades later.[64]

Considered on a global scale and across the Age of Interconnection, neither secularization nor its opposite seem to be a helpful way to understand the nature and extent of belief in God and the condition of the organized religions that embody this belief. As with the idea of progress and the nation, a more fruitful approach is to consider religion in the aftermath of the Second World War, which will involve a broader look at the development of religion. The Era of Upheaval dramatically altered this state of affairs, leading to very different circumstances at the end of the millennium—a particularly appropriate phrase for evaluating belief in God. Both the intensification and transformation of religious beliefs and practices and the rejection of them were upshots of this upheaval, both present worldwide but distributed differently among different confessions and in different parts of the world. Secularization and de-secularization were not so much opposites as complementary results of an enormous, worldwide, spiritual upheaval.

RELIGION IN THE POSTWAR ERA

There are two major features of the development of belief in God from the middle of the eighteenth to the middle of the twentieth centuries, one concerning theology and one concerning practice and belief. Speaking very broadly—and with apologies in advance to those who feel doctrinal subtleties are being unappreciated—theology fell into two large currents, perhaps best expressed by phrases characteristic of the Catholic Church c.1900—modernism and integralism. For adherents of the former, religious doctrine needed to be reconciled with the findings of science and scholarship, the progress of technology, and the new political environment emerging in the wake of the eighteenth-century age of democratic revolutions, with their promotion of nationalism, popular sovereignty, human rights, and a less explicitly faith-based public sphere. Supporters of integralism did not necessarily reject these new developments but did insist that they needed to be subordinated to divinely inspired truths articulated in religious doctrine and dogma. Both integralist and modernist tendencies could be found in all the major and minor world religions, with modernist ideas most influential among Protestants and Jews, weaker among Catholics, Orthodox, Muslims, Hindus, and Buddhists.

Modernist theology acquired a bad name in the Late-Millennium Era, decried as superficial, lacking spiritual commitment and, ultimately, conceding so much ground to secularism and non-belief that it has abandoned religion altogether. This is not an entirely fair judgment, and it might suffice to mention two earlier Protestant religious modernists. One was Dietrich Bonhoeffer, the anti-Nazi Protestant pastor, executed by the Third Reich at the very end of the Second World War, whose ideas of a religionless Christianity were influential for two controversial versions of late theological modernism, the "death of God" theologians of the 1960s and the proponents of what is called liberation theology in the following decade. The other was the leading spiritual figure of modern America, the Rev. Martin Luther King, Jr., a follower of the existentialist theology of Reinhold Niebuhr, and its recognition of the distinctly secular nature of the public sphere.[65]

Insistence upon the subordination of the modern world to religious truths took a very wide variety of theological forms. Two, one in Islam and one in Christianity, began in the mid-eighteenth century and were revised at the beginning of the twentieth. Although still relatively small at the end of the Second World War, they would develop a much greater importance, increasingly becoming the public face of religion by the final decades of the twentieth century. The Islamic version, Wahhabism, began with Muhammad Ibn 'Abd al-Wahhab, an eighteenth-century preacher and Muslim legal scholar from central Arabia, who emphasized the principle of *tawhid*, monotheism. He insisted that other forms of devotion, to saints and sacred shrines, for instance—very common in Islamic religious practice—were un-Islamic paganism, and that God's law, or *sharia*, should be the sole guiding light for individuals' lives and for social and political institutions. These doctrines were adopted by the tribal leader Muhammad ibn Saud, founder of the House of Saud, the ruling dynasty of Saudi Arabia, and "Wahhabism," adherence to the doctrines of Wahhab, has always had a distinctly Saudi context and feel.

In the initial decades of the twentieth century, Islamic theologians and legal scholars in Arab countries and in South Asia combined ideas of Wahhab with those of similar thinkers in Yemen, Syria, and Southern Asia. This combination became known as Salafism, from *al-Salaf*, "the ancestors," referring to a practice and belief ostensibly based on the ideas of the Prophet and his immediate followers, free of any intervening distorting or corrupting influences. Salafists added to the Wahhabist canon the rejection of the use of reason in theology and Islamic law, asserting that they needed to be based exclusively on the sacred texts, the Qur'an and the Hadith, the collection of Mohammed's sayings. There was often a strong messianic element in Salafism, a belief that a *Mahdi*, an Islamic messiah, would emerge to purge the world of evil and corruption. This was a distinctly integralist notion of religion, though Islamic modernists also called themselves Salafists, insisting that the pious ancestors had reconciled their faith with reason and science, and that it was time for Muslims to take up that practice again. By the 1960s, the integralist meaning of Salafism had become dominant.[66]

The Christian parallel to Wahhab, living at about the same time, was the British preacher John Wesley, and his theology of a personal, emotionally felt connection to God, mediated by Jesus and transforming the life of an individual—being, as would be said later, "born again." Dramatic preaching, in a revival meeting, would bring about this result, and a theology and practice of this kind—what would later be called Evangelicalism—spread widely in the English-speaking world during the nineteenth century. (There were similar, if less emotive, versions of this theology and religious practice among German and Scandinavian Protestants.) Like its Islamic counterpart, Evangelicalism often included a biblical literalism, an insistence on the divine truth of the Scriptures, and a rejection of the use of secular reason in their interpretation, and sometimes an apocalyptic view of the future as well. Similar to the movement from Wahhabism to Salafism—and also at about the same time—the early twentieth century saw a new development of Evangelical religion, Pentecostalism, which took the basic premises of the emotionally felt, personalized connection to God via Jesus and added to them speaking in tongues, faith healing, and emphasis on the idea that the Last Days, the end of the world, and the beginning of the biblical Apocalypse were at hand. Originating in Los Angeles, Pentecostalism spread rapidly throughout the world, reaching China, India, Mexico, South Africa, and Scandinavia within a few years.[67]

Both Evangelicals and Salafists claimed to be returning to original, pious practices, based exclusively on the sacred texts, which were self-evident and not in need of interpretation. Actually, they were both new ways of imagining and practicing religion, with their own distinct textual interpretations, and relatively little similarity to the medieval and ancient past they claimed to be reviving. Calling them Fundamentalists, for that reason, seems more than a little misleading. Although well established by the postwar era, these new religious movements remained relatively small and associated with marginalized groups—"backward" Bedouin tribesmen, or the American "Holy Rollers," a religion practiced by "hillbillies."

This observation brings up the question of the state of religious practice and belief around the world in the postwar era. One answer might be that they were very healthy. The proportion of Americans who belonged to a church was at an all-time high in the 1950s; proportions of Easter communicants, babies baptized, adolescents confirmed, and weddings celebrated in the Church of England during that decade were also at an all-time high. In European countries where belonging to a church was a formal, legal category, the vast majority of the population did so. Churchmen and theologians were a familiar presence in the press and the new mass media, Sunday school a regular part of children's lives. The end of the Second World War had coincided with a wave of religious renewal; full churches were a typical sight of the late 1940s and early 1950s.

The two-century-long confrontation with the ideas of the Enlightenment and the anti-clericalism brought forth by the French Revolution had left their effects. Particularly in Mediterranean Europe, there were pockets of strong resistance to the ideas of the Catholic Church, making them, as French churchmen had asserted during the Second World War, "missionary territories," whose inhabitants needed to be reconverted to Christianity. Of course, deeply pious regions, such as Western France, coexisted with these secularized ones. Secularism was associated with left-wing politics, and strongholds of the political left were often areas of religious hostility or indifference. A second pattern, rather more typical among Protestants, was a distancing from the church and religious practices: only occasional attendance at services, say at Christmas and Easter, but even there, religion denoted the milestones of a person's life—baptism, confirmation, marriage, burial. Parents might sleep in Sunday mornings, but children would be sent off to Sunday school. In effect, there was a contrast between regular churchgoers and only occasional ones, for whom religion continued to play a role at least at selected times in their lives.[68]

These observations pertain primarily to the predominantly Christian North Atlantic world; it is less easy to apply them elsewhere. Parts of Latin America, particularly Mexico and Argentina, fit the Mediterranean pattern of fierce anti-clericalism in some places and among some social groups battling with proponents of a strong Catholic piety. The first half of the twentieth century had been a period of vigorous missionary activity in Africa and Asia; the number of Christians in that former continent had grown from some ten million in around 1900 to almost two hundred million in 1970. With the onset of decolonization, independent African churches split off from colonial denominations and formerly European-dominated missionary churches were developing an indigenous clergy and lay leadership by the 1960s. If African animists were increasingly attracted by Christianity as well as Islam, missionaries had a harder row to hoe in China and India, making little headway against vigorous Hindu or Buddhist opposition, indigenous Islamic communities. and the widespread practice of ancestor worship. Perhaps 1 percent of the people living in the world's two largest countries had embraced Christian faiths.

It is even more difficult to make judgments about the religious practice of Islam, although it might have been the case that modernist forms of Muslim theology and secular lifestyles more generally were primarily prevalent among educated intellectuals in larger cities. This was not a numerically large group, but included the leaders of nationalist and anti-imperialist movements, so important in that era.[69]

One thing that can definitely be said about belief in God during the postwar era was that it was embedded in the great political confrontations of the time. Especially in its early phases, the Cold War was very much a war of religion. Communist regimes were expressly atheistic. It is true that the initial extreme hostility to religion in the USSR, with its League of the Militant Godless, had given way to a tolerance of the Orthodox Church during the Second World War, when there were no atheists in Soviet foxholes. Under Nikita Khrushchev, however, the regime's atheist offensive resumed. About half the churches in the country were closed. The space program, a venue for pro-regime propaganda in so many ways, became one for atheism as well, when cosmonauts were repeatedly cited mocking religion, stating that they saw no God in outer space.

The postwar era communist governments in Eurasia, learning from the difficulties of the Soviet experience, as was the case with agricultural collectivization, followed a less extreme course on atheism—not attempting to abolish religion outright, but to limit and marginalize it, while placing churches under government control. In China, the authorities denounced the Christian churches as agents of foreign imperialist powers, and demanded that they form "patriotic associations" without foreign ties, subordinating religion to the nation. It might seem ironic that a regime proudly proclaiming its place in a post-nationalist communist commonwealth should denigrate churches on nationalist grounds. Nonetheless, in doing so it was following in the footsteps of the original modern revolutionaries—those in post-1789 France, where the Civil Constitution of the Clergy in 1791 also attempted to subordinate the Catholic Church to the nation. As was the case in 1790s France, some Chinese churches did transform themselves into nationalist patriotic associations. Others, including the leading Pentecostalist church, split into pro- and anti-regime factions. Strong opponents of the regime, like Shanghai's pugnacious, integralist Catholic bishop, Ignatius Kung Pinmei, who asserted that freedom of religion meant maintaining ties to Rome, went to jail—a fate he shared with similarly minded churchmen, such as Hungary's Cardinal József Mindszenty.[70]

A somewhat peculiar variation on the contrast between religion and national loyalties came from Czechoslovakia, where the communist government rebuilt the chapel of Jan Hus, the Bohemian proto-Protestant who was burned at the stake for heresy in 1415. Rebuilding chapels was not typical of communist governments—quite the opposite—but doing so was a blow to the Catholic Church, the largest religious confession in Czechoslovakia, no friend of communism. It was an attempt by a communist government, like its Chinese counterpart, affirming its place in a transnational communist bloc, to embellish its nationalist credentials, since Hus had become a hero of Czech nationalists. The chapel remains a tourist attraction in Prague today.[71]

In predominantly Protestant East Germany, the communist government opened a new front in the war of religion, by concentrating on life-cycle ceremonies that had remained church monopolies, even among people who did not attend services regularly. Taking up a long-term practice of the German labor movement, it sponsored an atheist alternative to Protestant confirmation ceremonies, the "consecration of youth." Fourteen-year-olds swore allegiance to communism to the accompaniment of revolutionary songs and received the present of a book about the theory of evolution and a scientific view of the world.[72]

All these practices of sidelining and undermining religion that were characteristic of communist regimes in the 1950s and 1960s had a very wide variety of outcomes. A classic example of rejection of regime atheism and strong adherence to religion was in Poland, where the Catholic Church continued to run its own university throughout communist rule, quite independent of state control, the faithful attended Mass in large numbers, and only a handful of either clergy or laity were willing to work under the regime's auspices. One particularly celebrated instance of defiance came when the government built a steelworks and a whole residential neighborhood, *Nówa Huta*, in the city of Kraków. The new development was planned to bring the working class and a communist lifestyle to this non-industrial, bourgeois, conservative, and devout city, so that there were no plans for a parish church there—at least until the steelworkers demanded one, and forced the government to allow its construction.

Just to the west of pious Poland was East Germany, where the Protestant churches also took on the atheistic state, announcing that any young person who took part in the regime's consecration of youth could forget about a religious confirmation. Forced to choose between atheism and religion—and it should be emphasized, it was the church that was forcing the confrontation—young people and their parents chose godlessness, admittedly with some encouragement on the part of the government and the secret police. By the early 1960s, the state's ceremony had clearly prevailed, with over 80 percent of Protestant teenagers participating, and even 40 percent of East Germany's small Catholic minority.

Russia and the Orthodox Church stood somewhere in the middle. In urban areas, between 40 and 60 percent of children were baptized during the 1960s and 1970s (in the countryside, generally more)—a smaller proportion than in Western Europe, but not an overwhelming difference. The authorities forced parents to register baptisms officially. Even that measure, however, did not stop the practice. It was common to blame it all on the *babushka*, the elderly, devout grandmother, who had brought the infant to a priest, purportedly without the parents' knowledge. This was a convenient excuse, one that enabled even Communist Party officials to have their children baptized.[73]

The flip side of this Cold War confrontation was ostentatious piety among the Western adversaries of communism. It was during the 1950s, and specifically in order to issue a counter to godless communism, that "In God We Trust," was made the official US motto, replacing the previous, secular-nationalist *E pluribus unum*. The phrase "under God" was also added to the Pledge of Allegiance, breaking the rhythm of the secular nationalist phase, "one nation with liberty and justice for all." Ironically, the late nineteenth-century inventor of the pledge, Francis Bellamy, was a Protestant minister, but also a socialist whose affirmation was deemed inappropriate for a 1950s America locked in a struggle with a godless adversary.

Christian churches were generally not just supporters but passionate proponents of the anti-communist campaign, none more so than the Catholic Church. The climactic 1948 Italian elections, pitting devout Catholic Christian Democrats against the communists, was successfully fought by the former, to the accompaniment of no fewer than seventeen miraculous apparitions of the Virgin Mary calling on the faithful to reject the enemies of her Son, along with countless parades of sacred images of the Madonna. Pope Pius XII, known for his compromises with the Nazis, was an unbending adversary of communism, excommunicating all communist activists in 1949 and banning less-active adherents of communism from receiving the Sacraments. Protestants were not far behind in anti-communist zeal. Billy Graham, the leading figure in a new generation of American Evangelical revivalists, whose fiery sermons were televised, and who took his crusade around the world (preaching in England, where his audience included the Queen), stated that "communism is a religion that is inspired, directed, and motivated by the Devil himself, who has declared war against Almighty God." Graham went on to include trade unions, old-age pensions, and social welfare programs in his catalog of Satan's policies.[74]

Christians in the postwar era were not the only ones aligned against godless communism. Muslims were as well. Even the early Islamists of the Muslim Brotherhood, fiercely opposed to the allures of Western, capitalist countries and what they saw as their imperialist policies, had nothing good to say about the godless USSR. Wahhabi clerics in Saudi Arabia and other proponents of Salafism were of the same opinion. The most vehement and striking example of the anti-communist orientation of organized religions and their adherents came at the very end of the postwar era in 1965. In that year, an attempted communist coup in Indonesia led to savage retaliation, in which at least half a million people were slaughtered. Clergy and pious laypeople—in Indonesia that meant, above all, Muslims, but members of the Hindu and Christian minorities as well—were in the forefront of the anti-communist violence, working closely with the police and the armed forces, and justifying their actions as a holy war against the Satanic forces of communism.[75]

SPIRITUAL UPHEAVAL

As in so many other areas of social, political, and cultural life, the religious certainties of the postwar era came to an abrupt end in the decade of the 1960s. Throughout the world's wealthier countries—in Western Europe, North America, and the South Seas—church attendance plummeted; the faithful stayed away from communion; children stopped going to Sunday School (or their parents stopped making them go); fewer newly born children were baptized; fewer marriages were celebrated in church, and there were fewer religious funerals, although funerals were the life-cycle rite that remained with the churches the longest and to the greatest extent. Membership in church-sponsored associations dropped dramatically, and there were ever fewer people willing to become priests or pastors. Most of these changes were packed into the core of the Era of Upheaval, 1965 to 1975, with declines of as much as half. Numbers stabilized by the 1970s and 1980s, but more often the decline continued throughout the rest of the twentieth century, even reaching previously very devout countries, such as Ireland. By 1999, the European Values Study showed that of fifteen West European countries, only in three of them did a majority of the population attend church once a month or more. According to the same study, only a minority believed in sin, life after death, heaven or hell.[76]

Among these wealthy countries, it was usually the lands of the Anglosphere, which count as the most devout. In Canada, Australia, and New Zealand, census-takers regularly asked the population what their religion was, or to what church they belonged. In the United States and the United Kingdom, there were no similar census items, though various social science surveys posed the same question. In all these countries, through 1960, the number of people who responded to the question with "none" was zero, or so close as to be no matter. But after that the proportion began a steady rise, reaching in 2000 as much as 16 percent in Canada, Australia, and the United States, and as high as 35 percent in the United Kingdom and New Zealand. The rise has continued since then, with over a quarter of all Americans today describing themselves as having no religion.[77]

That these very large and seemingly irreversible changes were packed into a relatively small time period has attracted the attention of historians and social scientists. Some argue that the changes are attributed to affluence and consumerism, which provided alternative guides to life—expanding consumption rather than improving morality—and alternative forms of lifestyles—watching TV, rather than going to church. Yet during the postwar era affluence and piety went hand in hand, so something else must have been happening in the 1960s. And other things were happening: the sexual revolution struck directly at central elements of women's piety—and women had become crucial for organized religion in the Atlantic world—and the spread of new forms of spirituality.[78]

These are more plausible candidates for this wave of secularization, including changes within religion itself, particularly the modernist project of reconciling religion with the modern world, which accelerated during the 1960s, often with remarkable results. Since their founding, the Catholic religious orders, the Jesuits and the Dominicans, had always been at the center of the church militant, defying Protestants, aggressively missionizing heathens, denouncing the Enlightenment and the secular forms of politics introduced by the French Revolution, and modernist theologians who wanted to accommodate it. Yet in the 1960s the orders had brought forth such figures as the Jesuit priest and leading American antiwar and anti-imperialist activist, Daniel Berrigan, famed for destroying military draft records in opposition to the US war in Vietnam, or the Peruvian Dominican monk Gustavo Gutiérrez, a leading figure of liberation theology who interpreted participation in social revolution as contemporary Christianity, a viewpoint that the Jesuit order largely endorsed at its thirty-second General Congregation in 1975.[79]

A Protestant version of this attitude was a book by John Robinson, the Anglican bishop of Woolwich, called *Honest to God*, published in 1963. The book advocated dropping supernaturalism, and a theistic conception of God, while reorienting Christianity toward the amelioration of the secular world. It was a sensation, ultimately selling over one million copies, translated into seventeen foreign languages. Robinson's book was merely the opening salvo in a broader modernist barrage that would include what is sometimes called "Death of God Theology" and Protestant commitment to revolution, endorsed at the controversial 1968 Assembly of the World Council of Churches. The following year, that global league of Protestant churches set up a Program to Combat Racism, which included grants of substantial sums to armed anti-colonial liberation movements in South Africa.[80] Ironically, it was modernist religion itself—theologians, clergy, and laypeople following in the footsteps of Dietrich Bonhoeffer or Martin Luther King, Jr.—who played a large role in generating the wave of secularization that washed across the North Atlantic world during and after the Era of Upheaval.

Both religious modernism and the secularization it precipitated provoked a strong response on the part of more integralist religious movements, particularly Pentecostalism and Salafism. As noted, Pentecostalism and other forms of Evangelical Protestantism took off in 1970s America. Membership in denominations friendly to these ideas, skyrocketed, as did the "megachurches," giant, denominationally unaffiliated (but in doctrine and practice Pentecostal), Protestant churches, with thousands of members. Student activists of the Campus Crusade for Christ did battle with godless undergraduates, or those who followed "Satanic" Eastern spirituality, while politicized Evangelicals promoted ballot issues aimed at the sexual revolution—particularly on questions of homosexuality and abortion. Millions watched TV preachers, and the leading US bestseller of the decade was Hal Lindsey's *The Late Great Planet Earth*. Over ten million copies of the book—a counterpoint to *Honest to God*—were sold. The book told of an imminent apocalypse, reinterpreting the Book of Revelations in terms of the Cold War, as God, either by miracles or, more prosaically, with nuclear weapons, wiped out communist armies from the USSR and China invading Israel.[81]

The rise of Evangelicalism, especially its Pentecostal form, was a global phenomenon. Pentecostal churches gained tens of millions of adherents in Latin America, particularly in Brazil, Chile, Peru, and Guatemala, the very first time since the Reformation that Protestants succeeded in making converts among Catholics on a large scale. The same kind of churches rapidly increased their membership in Africa. South Korea has become another center of Evangelical Protestantism; the world's largest mega-church is the Yoido Full Gospel Church in Seoul. By 2000, it counted a congregation of over nine hundred thousand served by seven hundred full-time ministers, with fifty thousand neighborhood cells—prayer and Bible study groups.[82]

Parallel to the rise of Evangelical Christianity was that of Salafist Islam. If Evangelicalism was centered in the United States, but fanned out across the globe, Salafism followed a similar course of global expansion, starting in Saudi Arabia. The catalyst for this expansion was the flight of activists of the Muslim Brotherhood, persecuted by leftist, nationalist, secularist governments of Egypt or Syria, to Saudi Arabia—among these refugees, Sayyid Qutb's brother, Mohammed—where the government granted them central roles in the Saudi religious bureaucracy and institutions of higher education. Before this, Salafis had tended to be skeptical of the theological orthodoxy of the Islamists in the Muslim Brotherhood. Some even shaved their beards and wore Western clothing. Islamists had been critical of the Salafis' unwillingness to proselytize and to assert aggressively Islamic principles on a society-wide level. The Salafist upshot of the interaction between Muslim Brothers and Wahabbist theologians was a proselytizing Wahhabism, or an Islamism that hewed closely to the strict Wahhabist orthodoxy. Center of this new view was the Islamic University of Medina, which attracted by students from the entire Muslim world. As the Palestinian Islamist Shayk Ahmad, who studied there in the 1980s, observed, half of the students were from Pakistan or India. "They are the ones who created the madrasas from which the Taliban emerged."[83]

Both Evangelicalism and Salafism are integralist forms of religion, demanding the subordination of other forms of knowledge to doctrines they perceived as based on clear, self-interpreting, divinely inspired, and inerrant sacred writings. This attitude appeared in their relationship to the natural sciences, insisting that the basic tenets of biology, physics, astronomy, or geology—the theory of natural selection and the evolution of forms of life on earth, or the existence of the planet and the universe over a period of billions of years—contradicted scripture and were therefore false. This assertion could take the form of their own version of science, "proving" that godless theories and evidence for them were incorrect., Until his death in 1999, the Saudi Imam 'Abd al-'Aziz Ibn Bab, the country's most admired and venerated religious scholar, contended that the sun revolved around the earth, and that any Muslim who denied that was a heretic.[84]

Religious integralism was also hostile toward animist practices and customs. Quite in contrast to religious modernists, who felt obligated to uphold indigenous cultural traditions, Evangelical and Salafist preachers have no compunctions about denouncing ancestor worship, fetishes, calling on spirits, and other non-monotheistic objects and practices, as Satanic—an attitude that is particularly salient in Africa. In this way, these religions have become a weapon to criticize the older men who dominate a lineage-based society, making these faiths particularly attractive to women and younger men, the dominated groups in those societies.[85]

Statistics about religious affiliation, when they exist, are especially unreliable, so it is highly difficult to evaluate the extent of different forms of religion—whether (to take some examples) there are more Methodists, Lutherans and Episcopalians than Baptists or Pentecostalists, or more Sufis than Salafists, or more Reform or Conservative than Hasidic Jews. It is equally difficult to ascertain the trends in adherence to different forms of religion. However, what can be said is that integralists now dominate the public sphere, placing adherents of modernism on the defensive. One simple example would be how, in the United States, the word "Christian" has come to refer primarily to an Evangelical Protestant.[86]

This reflects broader socioeconomic, political, and cultural developments. Although often skeptical of the science that created modern media technology, Evangelicals and Salafists have made effective use of it, and to a greater extent than adherents of other forms of religion—from the American Pentecostal TV evangelist Jim Bakker pioneering the nationwide and then international distribution of TV broadcasts via satellite and cable, to Salafist clergy in Saudi Arabia putting their preaching on cassettes and selling them in video stores. Rising global interconnections were effective as well: Islamic preachers from South Asia or Northern Nigeria being educated in Salafist doctrines in Saudi Arabia; or Ezekiel Guti, the leading Pentecostal preacher in Southern Africa and founder of the immensely successful and popular church, the Zimbabwe Assemblies of God Africa, with its pan-African missionary affiliate, Forward in Faith Mission International, who was trained in Pentecostal theology and preaching at the Christ for the Nations Institute in Dallas. Saudi oil money helped fund both the preachers and the mosques and madrasas they started in their native lands; Texas oil money did the same for Guti. The global spread of integralist religions was another, rather unexpected, outcome of the 1973 shock.[87]

There is a certain temptation to see this very distinct form of globalization as manipulation—Saudi oil money, for instance, replacing a tolerant indigenous Islam with a *jihadi* version of the faith. In Latin America, both liberation theology Catholics and their politically and theologically conservative opponents could agree that the spread of Pentecostalism was a pernicious plot by Yankee imperialists. American money and training did help Guti in his meteoric rise, though he was just one of a galaxy of Pentecostalist preachers in Zimbabwe and Southern Africa more generally. The proselytizing and *jihadi* form of Salafism was not itself an exclusively Saudi product. It is certainly true that circumstances made for a wide spread of the message of Evangelicals and Salafists. The question might be why they found such a global resonance.[88]

There is no single, simple answer to that, certainly not one that would be valid anywhere in the world. But it is not impossible to grasp the contexts in which Late-Millennium Era versions of integralist religious flourished. One was a rejection of the cultural changes of the 1960s, including the sexual revolution, women's self-assertion, alternative forms of spirituality, far from the canons of the sacred texts, and, more broadly, secular and secularized approaches to society and to public life. The perception was that the adherents of religion itself, from churches and churchmen renouncing anticommunism, to Catholic priests advocating liberation theology, to Protestant thinkers talking about the death of God, seemed to be abandoning their sacred duties and positively encouraging the secular world. Among Muslims, the rejection of the secular nationalist ideas of a Nasir or a similarly secular left-wing radicalism, was an important part of the advance of Salafism.[89]

Both Salafism and Evangelicalism had a strong apocalyptic streak to them, and the circumstances of the decade that began with the 1973 oil shock and ended with the threat of an imminent nuclear war, had something of the apocalyptic about them, making the ideas associated with Evangelicalism and Salafism seem entirely plausible. The Salafists, who seized the Great Mosque in Mecca in 1979 (after practicing with semiautomatic weapons in the desert), did so to proclaim their leader Mohammed al-Qahtani as the *Mahdi*, the Islamic Messiah. They only carried a few days food with them, because they thought their actions would hasten the end of the world. Their action shook the Saudi monarchy to its very core and it took a two-week siege by Saudi military, with the clandestine assistance of French special forces, to root them out.[90]

In a less apocalyptic vein, integralist religion also seemed to fit well the trend toward privatization and suspicion of the role of the state in the Late-Millennium Era. Pious goals, religiously based charity, faith healing, funding through voluntarily granted tithes were all a part of religious life that emphasized individual effort and voluntary action while rejecting assistance from the state. The views of American "Christian Reconstructionists" who insisted that the gold standard was biblically mandated and that fractional reserve banking was godless, or that free markets and private charity were divinely sanctioned, while government regulation and the welfare state violated God's commandments, may have been extreme. Still, integralist religion's long-running skepticism about the government provided a backdrop to its growth in an era of government downsizing, especially when religious modernists had increasingly endorsed a welfare state.[91]

One particular version of this attitude was the Gospel of Abundant Life, popularly known, rather disparagingly, as the "prosperity Gospel." Developing among Evangelicals in 1950s America, this theological doctrine asserted that God wished his followers to live well, to enjoy good health and personal happiness, to live in ease and prosperity, to enjoy a bountiful harvest of consumer goods. American TV evangelists vigorously promoted this doctrine. The Gospel of Abundant Life was even more successful where the contrast between poverty and affluence was increasingly evident. Praying for wealth (or, more modestly, for a job), took Pentecostalism in Nigeria from a religion for small groups of the faithful in the 1970s, to the dominant form of Christianity in that country in the following decade—also an era when the wealth of the oil boom gave way to austerity and economic collapse. Nigeria was the poster child for the misappropriation of oil wealth; both Evangelicals and Salafists, in a country roughly half Christian and half Muslim, presented themselves as divinely inspired critics of a corruption involving godless, even purportedly Satanic practices. One could pray for one's own prosperity, admire preachers driving Mercedes as proof of their divine favor, while calling on God to curse those who had gained their wealth by impious means.[92]

We shouldn't of course dwell exclusively on the social, economic, or even political doctrines of integralist religion for its advance in the Late-Millennium Era. Rather, these doctrines were contained within a broader religious worldview, characterized by a personalized certainty of faith and a belief sure of its own divine inspiration, whether through a definitive interpretation of sacred texts, or a carefully structured experience of transcendence. This was a characteristic feature of the Hindu revival in India, or ultra-orthodox Judaism in Israel and the United States, or a Shi'ism of the sort reigning in Iran after the 1979 revolution. Nonetheless it was through Evangelical Christianity and Salafist Islam that it made its greatest impact on the world.

THE CATHOLIC CHURCH IN AN ERA OF UPHEAVAL

As the world's largest religion, with a billion adherents today, and humanity's oldest continuously existing institution—depending on how you consider it, between 1,000 and 1,500 years old—the Roman Catholic Church must find a place in any account of changes in religious practice and belief. Its story is a long and strange one: an attempt at religious renewal and revival gone oddly astray, arguably because it attempted both too much and too little, and was simultaneously too modernist and too integralist. Central to the story was the decision of Pope John XXIII, shortly after his election in 1958, to summon a council of the Church, a meeting of bishops and heads of the major (male) religious orders to Rome, the celebrated Second Vatican Council, which met from 1962 to 1965.

Already elderly when elected, Pope John was widely seen as a stopgap figure, following his predecessor, Pius XII, whose two-decades-long reign was characterized by conservative social and political attitudes, in particular a strong anti-communism, and a generally integralist approach to doctrine, especially in the final decade of his Pontificate, when prominent modernist theologians were prohibited from publishing and removed from positions teaching theology. It was a course that seemed successful and effective in the age of the high Cold War, when piety and godlessness stood opposed, when churches were full and the world's largest religion seemed to have braved the storms of the Age of Total War better than any other, as it had done so often through its millennia-long history. The Vatican prepared its council by sending out a questionnaire to the world's Catholic bishops, heads of the major religious orders, and universities with a papal charter, asking what issues they would like to see raised. The most common answers were the promulgation of a declaration denouncing communism, a condemnation of the moral failings of the modern world, and further doctrinal statements glorifying the position of the Virgin Mary—in other words, spiritual business as usual.

Yet almost from its festive opening session on October 11, 1962, in St. Peter's Basilica, the Council went in a very different direction. Guided by some of the very same modernist theologians who had been condemned by the Vatican in previous decades, the assembled bishops made a series of decisions that uprooted long-established religious practices, and seemingly well-settled doctrines. The main Catholic religious rite, the mass, was transformed. Not only was Latin replaced with the vernacular, but the priest celebrating the mass was to face the congregation rather than have his back turned. The church itself was redefined, as the "people of God," putting the laity alongside the clergy, while the authority of the bishops was strengthened, moving the pope in the direction of a first among equals rather than the assembled bishops' superior. Christian ecumenicism and outreach to Orthodox and Protestant churches was endorsed, without insisting, as had previously been the case, that the goal of such contacts was the subordination of these churches to the Vatican. All these measures went over surprisingly smoothly, with little disagreement. Even the two issues on which there was some controversy—rejecting the assertion that the Jews were responsible for the death of Jesus and endorsing freedom of religion as a fundamental human right, rather than a doctrine to be supported only when it helped the church—the margin in favor was on the order of 8 to 1.[93]

A widely used watchword of the Council was *aggiornamento*, "updating," reshaping doctrines and practices for the modern world. A less hierarchical church, a mass in a language people understood, would deepen and strengthen faith and popular involvement; with that, the Church would increase its influence in the world. For some Catholics, though, the changes in the Council did not go far enough. Abolition of clerical celibacy, for instance, or the declaration that radical action for social and political change was the true expression of Christian faith—whether in the form of Liberation Theology, with its Christian option for the poor and oppressed, or through "ecclesiastical communities," informal religious groups outside the official hierarchy, created by laypeople and clergy across Western Europe—seemed appropriate consequences of the decisions. Other Catholics reacted with dismay at the transformation of the religious ceremonies they had always known and associated with their faith, rejecting *aggiornamento*. They reasserted the integralist doctrines associated with Pius XII and his predecessors, reaching back to Pius IX and the decisions of the First Vatican Council of 1870. As Cardinal Michele Pellegrino, Archbishop of Turin, ruefully told an Italian journalist in 1968: "Some are firmly behind Vatican I; others have already arrived at Vatican III. There are only very few here who subscribe to the positions of Vatican II."[94]

Increasingly, many of the guiding spirits behind the theology of the Second Vatican Council, such as the German theology professor Joseph Ratzinger, began to regret the whole movement they had endorsed and supported. More than any other decision expressing this attitude was the 1968 Papal encyclical of Paul VI (who had succeeded John XXIII on the latter's death in 1963), *Humanae vitae*, condemning the use of birth control. Overruling theological advice, the pope, who had generally supported the reforming trend at the Second Vatican Council, re-emphasized authority and hierarchy. At least in Europe and North America, he found few willing to follow. In a confidential letter to the French episcopate, the theologian Marie-Dominique Chenu (who had gone from prohibited from teaching in the 1950s to a leading role at the Council) asserted that "Rome has lost, in a stroke, the authority it took sixteen centuries to construct." At the 1968 German Catholic Congress—an annual gathering of representatives of Germany's Catholic laity to express its support for the church, held since the mid-nineteenth century—the encyclical was put to a vote, and condemned by the delegates, three thousand to one hundred.[95]

The upshot of the combination of reform and reaction to reform was neither renewal of faith nor restoration of previous beliefs. Instead, church attendance declined, priests and nuns got married—not infrequently, to each other—and it became steadily more difficult to find people interested in a clerical vocation. In Latin America, the new initiatives of Liberation Theology had a disturbingly modest resonance. As the religious studies scholar Andrew Chestnut has noted, "the Catholic Church has chosen the poor, but the poor chose the Pentecostals."[96]

In his very long pontificate, lasting from 1978 to 2005, Karol Wojtyła, Pope John Paul II confronted these issues. Strongly anti-communist, as would be expected of a Catholic priest from Poland, in theological matters closely advised by Joseph Ratzinger (his successor, as Benedict XVI), he represented the conservative response to the Second Vatican Council: upholding clerical celibacy, denouncing birth control, disciplining adherents of Liberation Theology, and praising devotions to the Virgin Mary. A dynamic and charismatic figure, he carried his campaign across the entire world, following on a much larger scale his predecessor Paul VI, who had been the first pope in five hundred years to leave Italy voluntarily. (Several had been carried off by French armies.) His visits to his native Poland were political triumphs and played a large role in shaking the structure of communist rule in Eurasia. There were occasional successes in reversing the post-Vatican Two malaise, such as the 70 percent increase in the number of Catholic priests in Latin America in the Late-Millennium Eras. There were similar increases in Africa and Asia, making for a situation very different from circumstances in Europe or North America, and ending the long dependence on foreigners to fill the ranks of the clergy.

Nonetheless, the personal dedication of the pontiff could not resolve problems of alienation of lay Catholics, declining church attendance, and acceptance of the sacraments, to say nothing of the ever-more vigorous competition of Protestant Evangelicals in Latin America, Africa, or Asia.[97] The consequences of a partial reform and a partial retrenchment in the Era of Upheaval had been to introduce doubt and uncertainty into the heart of Catholic religious practice and theology, a poor combination in an era when successful and expanding religions exuded certainty and self-confidence.

Religious Belief at the End of the Old Millennium

At the beginning of the twenty-first century the world was increasingly divided between an Africa, Latin America, and Asia, where integralist religions were flourishing, and a Europe and its overseas offshoots, where a fading religious modernism confronted a growing detachment from religious practices and beliefs. Examples of this abounded. At the 1998 Lambeth Conference of the world's Anglican churches, a statement accepting of gay sexuality, supported by participants from the United Kingdom and North America, was defeated by the angry opposition of African and Asian bishops. Multinational social surveys find that a far greater proportion of the population in poorer countries assert that religion is important to them than in wealthier ones. A telling illustration of this state affairs comes from Germany in 2002. The League of German Protestant Churches invited pastors from Africa, Asia, and Latin America, to attend a symposium in the Wuppertal—a German region known for its long history of Evangelical Protestantism—on the ideas of the nineteenth-century atheist Ludwig Feuerbach. The German theologians wanted to discuss how Feuerbach's ideas about the sacrality of humanity could be integrated into contemporary theology. After the symposium, the invited pastors from Ghana, Nigeria, Sierra Leone, Ethiopia, Nepal, Vietnam, and Indonesia prayed, clapped, fell to their knees, and spoke in tongues for two hours, until, covered in sweat from their exertions, they pronounced, "In the name of Jesus we assert authority over Germany . . . We cleanse Germany from the spirits of Feuerbach, Marx and Freud, in the name of Jesus!"[98]

Are there exceptions to this global rule? Perhaps the United States would be one, and there is a whole sociological and historical genre of writings comparing pious America and godless Europe. Church attendance rates in the United States after 2000 do seem to be much higher than in Europe, perhaps twice as much, as, according to polling, 40 percent of Americans attended church each Sunday. Or claimed to attend church. A team of sociologists, led by C. Kirk Hadaway, has carefully evaluated these assertions, comparing actual with claimed church attendance. Their work has involved driving down back lanes and dirt roads to find every single church in Ashtabula County, Ohio, counting the number of people actually in churches or the number of cars in church parking lots on Sundays. They concluded that about twice as many Americans claim to attend church as actually do. Investigating this question by employing the same time diaries that were so effective for studying leisure has led to similar conclusions. The very fact that Americans find it necessary to lie to pollsters about their religious practice says something about the way piety appears as normative in America, compared to Europe. One is reminded of the saying that hypocrisy is the tribute vice pays to virtue, but perhaps another, less acerbic formulation would be to understand the early twenty-first-century United States as two countries: one following European practice, where secularization and a fading modernist religion hold sway; another more like Latin America or Africa, where Evangelical religion is powerful and influential. Both actual counts of church attendance and the evidence of time diaries would support such an interpretation. The two Americas might correspond, very roughly, to the coasts versus the South and Midwest, or cities versus the countryside, with suburbs somewhere in the middle.[99]

Another exception to this global distribution of belief might be post-communist Europe. The events of 1989 were, apparently, a victory of religion over an atheist regime. Solidarity, whose members and activists were so inspired by John Paul II, replaced the communist government in Poland. Demonstrators literally poured out of churches to confront the atheist East German regime; the close ties between the opposition and the church and the crucial role of the clergy in the events of the fall of 1989 earned the East German upheaval the sobriquet of the "Protestant Revolution."

In retrospect, however, the events of 1989 were a false dawn of religion in Eastern Europe. The Protestant Church and its clergy played a substantial role in opposition to communist rule and its overthrow in East Germany precisely because of its marginal position in society. Far from a religious revival, the transition from communism to capitalism in Eastern Germany and its unification with the West, only accelerated the pace of secularization: by 2008, just one-quarter of the inhabitants of the former German Democratic Republic described themselves as Christians, and only one in twenty-five attended church every week. In a particularly galling development, the communist regime's anti-confirmation ceremony, the "consecration of youth," continued after the end of communism; its popularity actually increased, while church confirmations languished. Along with the former East Germany, the post-communist Czech Republic, Hungary, Latvia, and Estonia were the most secularized and de-Christianized parts of the world by 2010. Already strongly devout in 1989, post-communist Poland retained its status as a pious Catholic land, and the Church was able to use its influence to outlaw abortion. Even in Poland, however, church attendance declined (albeit just by a bit) in the two decades following the end of communism.[100]

Were these developments, typical of the smaller countries of Eastern Europe, paralleled in post-communist Russia and China? The end of communism in the USSR certainly seemed to coincide with an explosion of piety. There were dramatic events, such as the decision of the St. Petersburg municipal authorities in 1990 to return the city's Museum of Atheism to the Orthodox Church, so it could once more be the Kazan Cathedral it had been before the Bolshevik Revolution. As a bonus, the relics of St. Seraphim, lost under communism, miraculously reappeared and were installed, with great ceremony, at the cathedral's reconsecration. In 1995, the Russian government decided to rebuild the Cathedral of Christ the Savior in Moscow, once Russia's largest church, demolished on Stalin's orders in 1931. Orthodox military chaplains returned to the armed forces, and Orthodox clergy regular blessed Russian weapons—with a particular emphasis on the nuclear missile force, the nuclear navy, and the space program. Between 1998 and 2016, Orthodox priests, and Orthodox parishes increased sixfold (both to about 36,000) and the number of Orthodox monasteries went from 22 to 926.

Cooperation between the authorities and the Orthodox Church intensified with the coming to power of Vladimir Putin in 2000. Personally devout, participating in pilgrimages to the Church of the Holy Sepulcher in Jerusalem and the monastery of Mount Athos in Greece, Putin knew how to cross himself properly in the Orthodox tradition (unlike the 1990s Russian politicians, who did it incorrectly), and was a regular worshipper at the Sretensky Monastery in Moscow, a favorite church of former KGB agents. Legislation against blasphemy and homosexuality demonstrated closer cooperation of church and state. Orthodox clergy, chapels, and religious ceremonies became regular events in the armed forces, and Russian pilots flying missions in Syria's civil war placed paper icons of the saints on their maps and target lists. Since 2007, space launches have been accompanied by holy water and banners of Christ and St. George—quite a reversal from the Soviet era, when the space program was central to the regime's atheist propaganda.

So religion was restored in public, but was it in private? Only 35 percent of Russians claimed to believe in God in 1990, but according to a study 71 percent did in 2008, suggesting a surge in piety. Of course, in that latter year, only 6 percent of Russians attended church weekly—putting church attendance in post-communist Russia at about the level of godless Eastern Germany—and just 9 percent had received Holy Communion. Perhaps it was all less piety motivating the Russian turn to Orthodoxy than a growing nationalism—since the two were always closely intertwined—and a conformity to an expected demonstration of religiosity—not entirely dissimilar to the United States.[101]

Very much unlike Russia, the government in post-communist China remains nominally communist and officially atheist. For that reason, increases in religious identification there from the 1980s onward, defying the state, seem more likely to reflect individuals' actual practices and beliefs. Older rites of ancestor worship and Buddhism have revived after the reign of Mao and the Cultural Revolution, when they were the object of violent attacks and official hostility. Perhaps the most interesting story has been the rapid upsurge in Christianity, from four million at the beginning of the communists' regime in 1949, to between twenty and one hundred million—figures on church membership in China are more imprecise than most religious statistics—in 2000. As has been the case elsewhere in Asia, Africa, or Latin America, many of the new Christians have been Pentecostals and Protestant Evangelicals, often gathered in small, unofficial congregations--so-called house churches Even the largest estimate of Christians would be just a small proportion of the 1.5 billion Chinese, and the government continues to keep a tight rein on the churches, still insisting that they be loyal to the nation and not have ties to foreign denominations. The future of religious belief, not unlike the future of belief in progress, in the world's most populous country remains unclear.[102]

Looking at the three large objects of belief, it is striking how they took their contemporary form in the eighteenth century. The nation and the idea of progress certainly did, and while of course belief in God predates the 1700s, two central forms of contemporary religion, Evangelical Protestantism and Salafist Islam, have their origins in that century. All three forms of belief weathered, and weathered fairly well, the political, social, economic, and cultural storms for 150 years, remaining, to a great extent, widespread certainties. The Age of Total War and the Era of Upheaval were both periods in which these certainties were put in question. While the latter period can hardly compare to the Age of Total War as a time of physical destruction the spiritual and intellectual fervor of the 1960s and 1970s was, overall (perhaps less so for nationalism than the other two objects of belief) far greater. Recovering or reinventing certainty about objects of belief proved extraordinarily difficult. Belief in progress never did recover; belief in God did, albeit only for religions that could loudly express certainty about their transcendent, divine inspiration. Modernist ideas about reconciling faith with reason, which involved living with doubt and uncertainty, have proven less attractive. As a result, the world today is increasingly divided between adherents of religious certainty, and secularists, who have abandoned organized religion, altogether. Of the three objects of belief, it is nationalism that has been most successful as a source of certainty, maintaining itself, enjoying widespread endorsement around the world, finding new forms of expression, and triumphing over its rivals—and, unfortunately, as the next chapter will show, sometimes becoming implicated in mass murder.

12 | Mass Murder

THE AGE OF INTERCONNECTION began in the shadow of mass murder. Nazi Germany in particular, but the Axis powers more generally, had accompanied their military campaigns with the slaughter of civilians, noncombatants, and prisoners of war. These killings were the culmination of a steadily mounting wave of mass murder during the Age of Total War: in the Balkans, the Ottoman Empire, and Stalin's USSR. Of course, mass murder was nothing new in human history. Great conquerors, such as Julius Caesar, who purportedly killed a million Gauls, Genghis Khan, or Tamerlane, left mountains of corpses in their wake—and one can only imagine what they could have done with machine guns or poison gas. The colonization of the Americas and Australia, and the European imperialist conquest of Africa had resulted in the deaths of large numbers of indigenous inhabitants, although the exact share of responsibility borne by brutal conditions of enslavement, outright killing, and disease varied considerably from case to case.[1]

The systematic nature of the mass murder perpetrated during the Second World War, and during the Age of Total War more generally, seemed to be something different, or at least had different consequences. After 1945, there were serious efforts made to hold perpetrators of these crimes responsible—a sharp contrast with the weak attempts to do so following the First World War. A new phrase, "genocide," was coined, to describe the extermination of whole groups of people, and the 1948 UN Genocide Convention put the world on record about it. Lessons had been learned, consequences drawn; humanity would put mass murder behind it. The Age of Total War was over.

Like so many aspirations emerging from the Second World War, this proved to be in vain. Genocide, in many ways a very problematic concept, quickly became more a political football, with charges hurled back and forth for propaganda effect, than an enforceable category of crime. Far from being banished, mass murder stalked through the second half of the twentieth century. Sometimes echoing the experiences of the Age of Total War, sometimes moving off in different directions, systematic and large-scale killing was a distinct feature of the era; its perpetrators could do so with little possibility of being stopped, and usually needed fear neither retribution nor being called to account.

Aftermath

As early as the beginning of 1942, when it seemed that the Axis powers might win the war, demands arose for postwar trials of the extraordinary crimes these powers had committed. The first governments to make such demands were the London governments-in-exile of European countries overrun by the Nazis, joined in their insistence by the Republic of China, itself an exile regime, having been driven by the Japanese from the Pacific coast to the city of Chongqing, eight hundred miles inland. By 1943, the United States, the United Kingdom, and the USSR had agreed on plans for trials, and they duly came to pass in the immediate postwar era.

The most famous, and the only one still widely remembered, was the International Military Tribunal at Nuremberg, which tried the twenty-four most prominent surviving leaders of the Third Reich. Its pendant was the International Military Tribunal for the Far East in Tokyo, which sat in judgment over the wartime leaders of Imperial Japan. The US military government held a series of group trials of Nazi elites, including generals, industrialists, diplomats, SS leaders, and concentration camp physicians. While the United States was the sole victorious powers to hold these large-scale trials of defeated Germans, the British joined it and both the nationalist and communist Chinese governments in placing Japanese defendants before national (in the British case imperial) military tribunals as well.

A long-forgotten element of this effort was the United Nations War Crimes Commission, set up in 1943 to facilitate and to coordinate the prosecution of Axis criminals in national courts around the world. These courts submitted cases to the Commission, which helped with the collection of evidence and with the identification and arrest of the accused. (One suspect was identified by a refugee from Nazi Germany serving in the US Army occupying Austria, Henry Kissinger, who came to have a different opinion about punishing mass murderers decades later.) It even sponsored an international conference in May 1945 of war crimes prosecutors. The Commission assisted in and sanctioned almost 8,200 cases of war crimes, involving about 22,000 defendants in Europe and Asia, including 151 cases of rape and forced prostitution. The Tokyo military tribunal's accounting of war crimes committed by Japan also encompassed many instances of rape. All this was five decades before the 1990s war in the former Yugoslavia, when it was often asserted that rape was treated for the first time as a war crime.[2]

This unprecedented mobilization of legal machinery has not left behind favorable memories. Paradoxically, it came to seem both too lenient and too severe. There were conspicuous omissions in the indictments, such as Japanese emperor Hirohito, an indication that, from the very beginning, politics prevailed over justice. Following the initial hearings of the major international military tribunals, the whole effort began to fade. The 1947 trial before a US military court of the top management of the German firm IG Farben—among other things manufacturer of the poison gas used at the Auschwitz concentration camp and chief beneficiary of the slave labor of the camp's inmates—pitted a team of inexperienced US government attorneys against Germany's top legal talent—whom the managers could afford to hire, even in the depths of the postwar economic disaster. Not surprisingly, the court rained down acquittals. Even that compared favorably with what happened within a few years. The United Nations War Crimes Commission, a body about which both British and American diplomats had been skeptical or downright hostile (the USSR simply refused to participate in it), was defunded in 1948 and its records remained secret until 2015. Trials were turned over to the new governments of the former Axis powers, who showed little interest in continuing them. As the Cold War intensified, the Western powers amnestied the individuals convicted by their tribunals; their communist rivals were more severe, but also increasingly used trials as a way to indict enemies of their newly created regimes, even if they had no actual connections to the original crimes.

Closely tied to this is the treatment of the survivors of the crimes of mass murder. It is well known that Holocaust survivors (primarily individuals who had fled to the USSR and spent the war in central Asia; many fewer inmates of concentration camps survived) were assaulted and murdered on their return to Poland or Slovakia. Attempts to reclaim their property or that of murdered relatives were met with outright official refusal or requests for death certificates, as though they were handed out in Treblinka to next of kin. Life insurance companies and Swiss bankers made similar demands of heirs trying to claim property. While starting in 1953, the government of West Germany did, reluctantly, agree to pay some very modest compensation to some victims of the Nazis, its Japanese counterpart certainly would not do so for Korean and Chinese "comfort women," forced into prostitution to service Japanese soldiers. Only in the 1990s, after most survivors were dead and their heirs scattered across the world, were the issues of compensation and restitution of lost property addressed to any extent.[3]

For all these examples of leniency, the post-1945 trials of mass murderers were also denounced as too strict. They were "victors' justice," indicting and convicting only citizens of the defeated nations, ignoring crimes committed by victorious countries: the Anglo-American firebombing of German and Japanese cities; the nuclear assaults on Hiroshima and Nagasaki; or the Soviets' 1940 mass murder of Polish POWs, the "Katyn Forest Massacre," as well as their large-scale killing of civilians and the rape of tens or even hundreds of thousands of German women. Dragged before military tribunals, whose judges and prosecutors were more interested in revenge than justice, tried with the use of juridical concepts devised from foreign systems of law, the accused were deprived of basic legal protections and had difficulty in mounting their own defense.

While it is difficult to see how accusations of excessive leniency and excessive severity could both be true, their coincidence reveals crucial features of the postwar trials. They represented an unprecedented effort, involving military and civilian, international and national, tribunals, far exceeding in scale any attempt to bring to justice mass murderers before then, to say nothing of recent attempts. Nonetheless, fundamental juridical issues arising during the trials dogged efforts to punish perpetrators of mass murder and related crimes, then and now. There remain four large, interrelated problems: ex post facto laws, punishment of regime criminality, individual responsibility, and state sovereignty.

The indictments of the two international military tribunals in Nuremberg and Tokyo concerned three groups of charges: war crimes, conspiracy to wage aggressive war, and crimes against humanity. The first, it could be argued, had become a part of international law, although there were plenty of disputes at the trials about whether the various treaties and international agreements on such matters as treatment of POWs or of civilians during wartime actually applied to the particular instances of the indictments, or had ever been ratified in the first place. By contrast, the other two charges were invented for the trials. Defense lawyers for the accused ex-Nazis liked to quote the Latin mottoes of ancient Roman law: *nullem crimen sine lege*, "there is no crime without a law"; and *nulle poena sine lege*, "there is no punishment without a law." The Romans had a point. At least in more recent years, prosecutors and judges can point to the Nuremberg and Tokyo precedents—although not all legal systems give precedents the central place they occupy in Anglo-Saxon Common Law—but in the 1940s this was not a possibility. New kinds of crimes, and the mass murders of the Age of Total War fit that description, required new kinds of law, whose retrospective application created feelings of unease at the time and ever since.

Criminal law is designed to punish individuals or groups who defy the legal rules set down by a government. Mass murder is typically implicitly or explicitly commanded, or at least sanctioned, by the government, so its punishment involves the condemnation not just of individuals but of an entire regime. This was possible after the Second World War because government authority in the defeated countries was in the hands of the victorious powers.

After an initial phase in which these powers held their own military tribunals or turned over accused individuals to third countries in which they had committed their crimes—Poland and China, for instance—they returned trials and punishment to the reconstituted governments of the defeated powers, whose state bureaucracies and judiciaries were staffed with individuals previously affiliated with the regimes that had initiated, organized, or encouraged these crimes. Little wonder that the prosecution of such crimes tapered off considerably.

Regime criminality and an organized system of killing raised the question of the role of individuals in the process of mass murder. Were the actual murderers, generally lower-ranking figures in the armed forces or security services, the culprits? They were, after all, subject to military or quasi-military discipline and expected to do what they were told. Or was it the leading figures who held command or official responsibility, set programs and guidelines for killing, and provided orders? Although the phrase, "I was just following orders" was coined later, some version of this argument was used by German defendants, often with the proviso that their own lives were in danger had they not done what they were told. And it was not just concentration camp guards or NCOs who used it, but high-ranking government officials and top corporate management as well. After all, they had all been living in a totalitarian dictatorship. By contrast, in the trials of Japanese war criminals, high-ranking commanding generals and government ministers used it to protest their innocence. They may have been theoretically responsible for the behavior of their subordinates, but they could not control what the latter did, purportedly without their approval. There were also those individuals and institutions, who neither issued nor carried out orders for mass murders, but whose assistance was essential to the program: the managers and workers of the German railway system, for instance, that transported victims to extermination camps.

These weighty concerns were all connected to the position of state sovereignty. The international military tribunals at least implicitly recognized sovereignty of the defeated powers. No Germans were convicted for measures taken by the former German government against German citizens on prewar German territory. There were not even any indictments of Japanese military and government officials for crimes committed in Taiwan or Korea, which had been annexed to Japan decades before the Second World War began. "Sovereignty" was not merely a juridical problem but a practical problem that led to juridical issues. Sovereign states committing mass murder could only be stopped and the perpetrators of such crimes held accountable by the actions of other sovereign states—generally, violent, military actions. Going to war, in other words. Even with the best of intentions, this warfare, especially mass, mechanized warfare, was going to involve large numbers of noncombatant victims, opening the only forces able to stop mass murder to the charge of committing such a crime themselves. By defeating, occupying, and then conducting trials in the defeated sovereign state, the victorious powers were, quite literally, engaged in imperialism, imposing their will, their legal systems, and their purported moral supremacy on a sovereign country.

This was not a topic limited to academic discussion. It was asserted by one of the judges at postwar trials, the Indian jurist Radhabinod Pal, who sat on the International Military Tribunal for the Far East, in Tokyo. Increasingly paying little attention to the court proceedings, or even attending them, Pal instead gathered his own evidence and then dissented—and at great length, since his dissents when published, went on for 1,235 pages—from every single verdict issued by the tribunal, voting to find all the accused not guilty. He offered a wide variety of reasons for his opinions. While admitting that Japanese armed forces occupying foreign countries had committed "devilish and fiendish" crimes, he asserted that the commanding Japanese military officers and civilian officials bore no responsibility for these actions of their subordinates. He maintained that Japan was not bound by international agreements on the treatment of POWs. More generally, he saw international law not as imposing on sovereign powers universally valid rules for conduct, but as a way for certain sovereign states to dominate others. This understanding appeared in his contention that Japan, far from being an aggressor, had been defending itself either against communism or from European and American imperialists, who had over the centuries committed "the detestable invasion of Asia," from the conquest of India to the bombing of Hiroshima and Nagasaki. It is a bit unclear how the Japanese invasion of a China governed by the fiercely anti-communist *Guomindang*—an invasion accompanied by many instances of mass murder, most prominently 1937 in Nanjing—was an example of a country defending itself against either Western imperialists or communists. However, empirical arguments were beside the point. Attempting to stop mass murder or to punish its perpetrators would invariably be imperialism, unless the forces doing so either had a blameless history or did so in morally impeccable ways (people making these arguments tend to have much higher moral standards for those trying to stop mass murder than for those actually committing it). If they had either, they would not have been in a position to stop a state from carrying out mass murder in the first place.

Pal did not convince his fellow judges or even contemporary antiimperialists. Prime Minister Jawaharlal Nehru of newly independent India rejected Pal's arguments and disassociated his government from them. These arguments did find a wide and very favorable reception in Japan, where Pal's 1952, 1953, and 1966 lecture tours were triumphal processions. During the last one, he was awarded the "First Order of Merit," by Emperor Hirohito for his contributions to world peace and justice. Versions of the arguments Pal made would appear again in debates over the prevention of mass murder or the punishment of its perpetrators in the decades that followed.[4]

The brief period during and after the Second World War, when these legal quandaries were revealed, was also a time in which attempts were made to resolve at least some them, particularly the issues of ex post facto law and of state sovereignty. The vehicle for these efforts was a new concept designed to grasp the enormity of the crimes of mass murder, genocide, coined by the Polish jurist Raphael Lemkin. A public prosecutor and enthusiast for international law during the interwar years, Lemkin participated in conferences designating international crimes, "offenses against the law of nations." These included a large number of offenses that by today's standards do not seem quite at the level of mass murder, such as counterfeiting, drug dealing, sex trafficking, and pornography. Terrorism and piracy, also to be condemned, might be closer to more serious crimes. Lemkin proposed to add to this list barbarity and vandalism.

Fleeing the Nazi invasion of his native country to the United States, Lemkin wrote a massive 1944 treatise *Axis Rule in Occupied Europe* that launched the concept of genocide. The work outlined a series of actions that constituted the cultural, moral, social, and physical destruction of ethnic, racial, national, or religious groups. Mass murder was one of these actions, which also included elimination of self-rule, economic exploitation, banning or discouraging use of native language and religion, taking measures to limit births, and to debase public morals by encouraging pornography and alcoholism.

Contrary to frequent retrospective interpretations, the idea of genocide was not a central feature of the postwar trials of mass murderers. When used at all it was in awkward ways—listed, for instance, in the Nuremberg indictments under "war crimes" rather than crimes against humanity. Lemkin himself lobbied vigorously for the inclusion of his concept in postwar trials and was frustrated by the refusal of them to create genuinely international law, in particular by the court's refusal to consider actions of the German government against German citizens as part of its remit. The significance of the concept was primarily its inspiration of the 1948 UN Genocide Convention, an attempt to create international law dealing with mass murder, in doing at least potentially resolving the issues of ex post facto law and state sovereignty that had bedeviled the postwar trials. In contrast to Lemkin's definition, and over his objections, the UN convention rejected "cultural offenses," defining genocide exclusively in physical terms: murder, causing severe bodily harm, creating conditions leading to physical destruction, preventing births, and kidnapping children.[5]

Both too narrow and too broad, genocide is a poor concept for the historical investigation of mass murder. It is too narrow because it excludes people victimized for reasons other than their race, nationality, or religion: systematic killing of political opponents, or the ruthless imposition of utopian policies of social and economic engineering, and their toll in human lives. These latter led to more deaths than any other form of mass murder in the Age of Interconnection. Historians, philosophers, and social scientists have tied themselves into intellectual knots, trying to cram particular instances of mass murder into the limited rubric of "genocide." In recent years, disputes about whether particular actions should be described as genocide, something which was not unusual in the International Tribunal for the Former Yugoslavia, did little to attribute responsibility or establish appropriate sanctions for murderous actions.[6]

Lemkin's original definition, and to a lesser extent the one used in the UN genocide convention, tars with the broad brush of mass murder activities that are not murderous. Would campaigns against female genital mutilation be an example of the suppression of national religions and cultures? What of monotheist religions' aggressive rejection of animist practices: a common practice in contemporary Africa, as was shown in the previous chapter? Some people would interpret the legalization of birth control or abortion as examples of the prevention of births. Are these instances of genocide or preparation for mass murder? When groups try to secede from a nation-state, and the national authorities take military action to prevent them, what could seem from one point of view as denial of self-rule, one of Lemkin's genocide criteria, might, from another, be seen as upholding national unity.

Taking mass murder as just that—mass murder—regardless of the reasons the victims were chosen, enables historical analysis, but leaves open the place of warfare. During the high point of mass murder in the Age of Total War, more people were killed in the normal process of warfare than in specific campaigns of mass murder. Had the nuclear or thermonuclear war the world's atomic powers were preparing for decades after 1949 actually occurred, then future historians—assuming there would have been any—would have regarded earlier genocides as mere bagatelles. As it was, a number of more recent wars led to hundreds of thousands or even millions of deaths: the US war in Southeast Asia, the Soviet war in Afghanistan, the failed war of secession of Biafra from Nigeria, and war of secession of East Pakistan from Pakistan to form Bangladesh. Many of the deaths were combatants, in what is still seen as the normal and legitimate process of war; others were noncombatant victims of military operations (sometimes euphemistically called "collateral damage"); still others the result of military actions taken without any particular regard for the possibility of noncombatant casualties; and some were part of a deliberate policy of killing civilians.

Mass murder often occurred in the context of warfare, although less so in the Age of Interconnection than in the Age of Total War; the armed forces were often agents of mass murder; and the killing of armed, organized, and designated opponents, members of enemy armies, could often blend into the indiscriminate murder of all opponents, or those perceived as such. Warfare does involve killing opponents who can defend themselves, unlike the slaughter of mostly defenseless noncombatants, and includes measures for opposing soldiers to surrender without being killed—even if these provisions are not always observed—different from systematic annihilation. In these respects, warfare ought to be distinguished from mass murder.

Mass Murder during the Cold War

Like so many other aspects of the world across the forty years between 1949 and 1989, it was the Cold War that provided a backdrop to the largest instances of mass murder. While governments on both sides of the divide bore responsibility for policies and practices leading to hundreds of thousands, even millions, of deaths, these were not mirror images. There was a distinct asymmetry in the nature of the policies leading to those catastrophic losses of life, as well as in their relationship to those of the Age of Total War. In post-1950 communist regimes, deaths followed above all from policies of relentless and inhuman social engineering, from attempts to create at high speed an idealized society and economy. Some communist regimes did murder their opponents, real and imagined, in substantial numbers, but the death toll from these political purges was less, sometimes substantially so, than from aspirations to a perfect quality of life. In these respects, communists, particularly in China and Cambodia, were following in the footsteps of Stalin's USSR during the 1930s. Mass killings carried out by the anti-communists of the West followed a different logic. They were above all about the elimination of political opponents: communists, other kinds of radical revolutionaries, and those purported to be so. Of course, anti-communists had been murdering communists in large numbers since the Bolshevik Revolution of 1917 and the ensuing civil war. What distinguished the Western anti-communist murders was that they occurred in peacetime, and on a scale not seen before.

Common to both communist and anti-communist violence was the role played by the government, in orchestrating and arranging the murder. Cold War mass murders were actions of a strong state, sometimes committing the murders itself, sometimes mobilizing social groups and political organizations to assist it, but basically in charge. Another common feature of the mass murder of the era was the almost absolute impunity of its perpetrators. If called to account, and most were not, it was only long after and in unsatisfactory ways.

UTOPIAS OF DEATH IN CHINA AND CAMBODIA

The greatest mass murder in the second half of the twentieth century, and, arguably, in all of human history, occurred in China between 1959 and 1961. A consequence of the "Great Leap Forward," a toxic mixture of failed economic planning, inhuman utopian aspirations, bizarre totalitarian rule, and the exaltation of human will above material reality, the mortality toll from overwork, disease, and starvation was compounded by large numbers of executions, emerging from a relentless refusal to admit mistakes. Not content with the disaster he had created, the person most responsible for the situation, China's communist leader Mao Zedong, launched yet another chaos-inducing utopian initiative, the "Great Proletarian Cultural Revolution," just a half-decade after the failure of the initial one. The death toll from this second round of utopian social engineering was far less than from the first round, but still enough to rank as one of the leading instances of mass murder in the age of the Cold War.

At heart, the Great Leap was a plan to accelerate economic growth, simultaneously increasing agricultural and industrial output. In retrospect, this aspiration was not inherently ridiculous, for China, as was true of most East Asian countries, would enjoy extended periods of rapid economic growth—double-digit increases in GDP over a decade or more—at later points. But the means Mao and his close advisers chose to bring about this desired result were, as China's knowledgeable planners, economists, engineers, and agronomists understood at the time, profoundly self-defeating.

The plan was for agricultural output to be increased both extensively and intensively, that is, by bringing new lands under cultivation and by increasing yields in existing arable. Marginal land, too dry or too steep, would be planted, and forested areas would be cleared for grain crops. Non-subsistence crops, such as tea or fruits and vegetables would be replaced with grain. Large scale irrigation works and dams would be required for this, and immense hydraulic public works were part of the effort. By planting rice seedlings close together, and by preparing fields with deep plowing, a suggestion of Soviet agronomists, agricultural output would soar.

The results were, unsurprisingly, a disaster. Too many seedlings planted together meant that none of them had enough nutriments to grow; deep plowing destroyed topsoil and rendered land infertile. Hastily constructed dams and improperly channeled irrigation works were downright counter-productive. In Henan Province, half the dams built collapsed within a decade; the giant showcase Banqio and Shimantan dams in that province failed catastrophically in 1975, resulting in deaths estimated to be as high as 230,000. Labor in the enormous public works was withdrawn from cultivating existing fields, so that crops rotted because there was no one to harvest them.

Central to plans for increasing industrial output was steel, the prime industrial product of the mid-century decades. Initial proposals to raise steel output from 5 to 5.8 million tons in one year—so 16 percent, a pretty impressive increase—were quickly junked in favor of doubling output and then raising it an additional five- or sixfold in the subsequent five years. Literally millions of "backyard steel-mills" were set up in rural areas across the country. The authorities ruthlessly seized woks, gates, bowls, iron rings on doors, iron window frames, and any other ferrous items they could find. Since there was not enough coal to fire the furnaces, wood was requisitioned everywhere—even coffins were burnt—and the steel drive was yet another blow to the forests. About 10 percent of China's forests were cut down in a three-month period in 1958. All this enormous effort produced was useless slag that "looked like bean curd residue," as one survivor remembered. The labor required for the steel drive was yet another input removed from growing crops.

These giant projects were both accompanied and made possible by equally utopian social engineering, focused on the large majority of Chinese then living in the countryside. Not only was all landed property collectivized, but personal property and living situations were as well. Houses were torn down, ostensibly because the walls were good fertilizer; household furnishings seized. Rural people would eat in collective canteens and be housed in barracks, with the sexes segregated (in addition, men were often dispatched to work large-scale industrial or public works projects far from their villages) and children separated from their parents. Sent out into the fields, military style, in work brigades, farmers were expected to toil twenty-eight days per month.

Anyone expressing opposition to these policies, whether an expert in Beijing casting doubt on viability of the proposals, or a villager using common sense, was denounced as a "right-wing deviationist," and "advocating bourgeois superstition." Imprisonment or "re-education through labor" would be the result. Worse, fear of being labeled a counterrevolutionary meant that the government officials in charge of this enterprise, at all levels, from the capital to the villages, gave unrealistic estimates of what could be and what was produced. A "wind of exaggeration," as contemporaries said, blew through the country, introducing the final act of the tragedy.

For if the official figures indicated large increases in production, especially of grains, then where were they? Counterrevolutionaries had to be hiding them, and party and state officials, backed by armed militiamen, searched farmers' homes, often tearing them down and destroying them, looking for the hidden grain. Individuals were tortured and executed. One particularly horrible punishment involved stripping people, hanging them up, dousing them in oil and setting them on fire—"lighting the celestial candle." This horrific style of execution was applied in the province of Sichuan, whose party leader, Li Jingquan, was a particularly ardent proponent of Mao's policies. But public humiliation, torture, and murder—either execution by firing squad, being beaten to death, or being turned away from the collectivized food supply—was a characteristic feature of the Great Leap, responsible for perhaps one death in ten.

Throughout the years of famine, agricultural exports continued unabated. What remained of food supplies was diverted to party and government officials. Decades later, survivors remembered how they tried to get by on very meager rations, while cadres stuffed themselves on sweet potatoes. The very foodstuff on which the cadres feasted, the humble sweet potato, in China typically fed to hogs, should give an idea of just how disastrous the Great Leap was. When government statisticians reported to Premier Zhou Enlai, no particular enthusiast for Mao's policies, although always careful never to oppose them directly, on the effects of the Great Leap on China's population, Zhou was so appalled that he ordered the report and all the supporting information immediately destroyed. Recent estimates, based on demographic analysis of preceding and subsequent census data, give a death toll from starvation, disease, exhaustion, and executions on the order of thirty to thirty-five million people.

Five years after the end of the Great Leap, when the economy had just barely recovered, came the Great Proletarian Cultural Revolution, calling first on university students, high school pupils and young people, and then on industrial workers, to attack the Communist Party and government bureaucracy. The resulting images of teachers, professors, doctors, scientists, public officials, and others being publicly humiliated, beaten, and sometimes murdered have long characterized this phase of Chinese history and remained a source of national trauma. Most of the deaths resulting from this upheaval came after its end, when the chaos it inspired became overwhelming and Mao sent in the army to restore order. The subsequent search for "counter-revolutionaries," who would be scapegoats for the chairman's policies, "Cleansing the Class Ranks," resulted in as many as eight hundred thousand executions, out of a total of perhaps 1.5 million people killed during the entire Cultural Revolution.[7]

Much of this is reminiscent of the USSR under Stalin's rule during the 1930s. There were initiatives aimed at rapid economic growth, Stalin's forced collectivization of agriculture and rapid industrialization, and Mao's Great Leap, each leading to the death of about one person in twenty in the entire country. These were followed a few years later by campaigns of politically oriented murders, Stalin's Great Purges and Mao's Cultural Revolution, which produced many fewer deaths but remained a dominant image of totalitarian rule, perhaps because the victims came disproportionately, although very far from exclusively, from the ranks of the educated and professional classes. Stalin's initiatives, for all their human costs, did at least lead to the establishment of heavy industry on a large scale, which played an important role in the USSR's victory in the Second World War; Mao's, efforts, by contrast, produced nothing but death.

These programs and their fatal consequences are often attributed to the ideas of Karl Marx, although if one is going to put the blame for them on the theories of a nineteenth-century German intellectual, then Nietzsche would be a more appropriate choice. Marx, after all, asserted the existence of a material reality independent of human ideas or actions; for Nietzsche, reality was decisively shaped by the ideas of influential people, their will to power. This understanding, already present in the Great Leap Forward, especially in its plans for enhanced agricultural productivity, emerged explicitly in the Cultural Revolution, when it was repeatedly asserted that the masses, armed with Mao Zedong's thought, could accomplish deeds scientists or technical experts evaluated as impossible—performing operations without anesthetics, or planting rubber trees in areas too far north for them to flourish. Material reality had a different opinion, as the death toll demonstrated.[8]

After his death, Mao's policies were repudiated by China's leaders, but they were very reluctant to admit it, since they were all implicated in his crimes. The great post-Mao statesman, Deng Xioaping, seeing what had happened in the USSR to Nikita Khrushchev, a former associate of Stalin's who had resolutely denounced his crimes, refused to follow that path. Mao remained and remains to this day a Chinese national hero.[9] In fact, authoritarian regimes in both China and Russia today have increasingly rehabilitated the image of both Stalin and Mao, allowing them to escape even posthumous condemnation of their murderous actions.

The four-year-long reign of the Khmer Rouge in Cambodia, from 1975 to 1979, was, in part, a highly intensified and expanded version of Mao's murderous campaigns, mixing perniciously utopian projects of large-scale social engineering with the murder of political opponents, but containing toxic elements of nationalism and racism as well. Occurring in a tiny southeast Asian country, lacking the Great Power impunity leaders of the USSR or China, the rule of the Cambodian communists was still a lesson in the difficulties of preventing mass murder, much less holding its perpetrators to account.

Coming to power in 1975, following the collapse of the pro-US Lon Nol government, the result of the enormous and indiscriminate US bombing campaign in Cambodia, designed to prevent the Vietnamese pro-communist forces from overthrowing the US-allied government of South Vietnam, the Khmer Rouge immediately took drastic measures. They evacuated the entire population of the capital city, Phnom Penh, some four hundred thousand people. Regime apologists asserted that the measure was to prevent a wartime food-shortage crisis, although sending most of the evacuees to the northwest of Cambodia, a region of chronic food deficits, would have been an odd response to such a crisis.

It quickly became evident that the Cambodian communists had something else in mind. Following in the wake of the Great Leap Forward, they abolished private property; instituted barracks-style, sex-segregated living; and separated children from their parents—doing so with much more gusto than in China. Money, banking, and commerce were all outlawed. Massive public works projects were instituted, for the purpose of vastly expanding the output of rice, by allowing it to be cultivated all-year round, and unrelenting agricultural labor was militarized. An integral part of the utopian program was the physical elimination of real and potential opponents. Tens of thousands of former soldiers and government officials of the Lon Nol regime were shot, and it was made painfully clear to the urban evacuees, the "new people," in the language of the Khmer Rouge, that their lives were worth little. "To spare you brings no benefits; to destroy you brings no loss." They could and would be killed at the slightest sign of noncooperation, to say nothing of resistance.

The Southeast Asian country's farmers, particularly those who had come under the rule of the communists in the course of their war against the pro-US Lon Nol regime, were designated the "base people," in the Khmer Rouge vocabulary. Having borne the brunt of the indiscriminate American air war, they at first rather enjoyed the spectacle of the former government's supporters, and city folk more generally, getting their comeuppance, being forced to work with their hands in intolerable conditions, punished or killed for the slightest infraction. As their property was confiscated and the practice of the Buddhist religion prohibited, peasants' initial approval of the new regime waned. But there was no way of opposing the Khmer Rouge's armed cadres, many of them teenagers or even preteens, uninhibitedly dedicated to the regime.

Something rather different from circumstances in China was the fierce nationalism of the Cambodian communists. While both the Great Leap Forward and the Cultural Revolution did not spare the ethnic minorities in China's western provinces, they were no more victimized by Mao's policy than the Han Chinese. The Khmer Rouge, by contrast, profoundly mistrusted the large, national minority groups—the Muslim Cham, the ethnic Chinese, and the ethnic Vietnamese—many of whom were executed out of hand, and who suffered proportionately much larger population losses than the ethnic Khmer. As the regime continued its policies, there were growing disputes among the party leadership, largely between those who were all in on the policy of creating a utopian communist regime, and those who were somewhat more reluctant. The militants got their way with large-scale purges. The notorious Tuol Sleng prison in an otherwise deserted Phnom Penh, where tens of thousands of inmates were tortured and killed, was largely filled with losers of the power struggles.

About two million people—a quarter of the entire country—died in the course of the Khmer Rouge's reign, roughly half from starvation, overwork, and disease; the other half from politically motivated killing, whose fortunate victims were shot, while the less fortunate ones were beaten to death or disemboweled, after suffering a wide variety of tortures. The regime was only brought to an end by a foreign power, as the victorious communists in Vietnam responded to repeated Khmer Rouge attacks on Vietnamese territory with an invasion of Cambodia and the imposition of the rule of pro-Vietnamese Cambodian communists.[10]

The similarities between the Great Leap Forward and the rule of the Khmer Rouge seem evident, including bizarre, self-defeating plans for the expansion of economic output, militarization of labor, enormous, public works projects, immediate abolition of all private property and destruction of family life, as well as the torture and murder of real and imagined opponents of the regime. The Khmer Rouge boasted that they would go much farther and faster in instituting a communist realm than the China had done during the Cultural Revolution.

The reign of the Khmer Rouge was not just a copy of the Great Leap Forward. Mao believed in rapid industrialization, envisaging communism as catching up with and surpassing the economically and technologically advanced capitalist countries. His backyard steel mills were part of an aspiration to overtake British steel output within five years. More generally, the assumptions underlying the Great Leap Forward seem like a variant—an extremely murderous variant—on the accepted attitudes of the idea of progress. While the Khmer Rouge certainly talked of a future of electrification and industrialization for Cambodia, in their policies such prospects faded before an exaltation of economic and technological primitivism. Cambodian communists proudly asserted that "we have no machines;" they denounced tractors as "iron buffaloes," and claimed that they did everything by "relying on the strength of our people."[11] Very much in the tradition of Stalin's plans for rapid industrialization, the main victims of Mao's policies were the peasants; in Cambodia, it was the "new people"—intellectuals, professionals, former inhabitants of the cities more generally.

Another striking feature of the reign of the Khmer Rouge was the international support it enjoyed and the impunity of its leaders. At the onset of its rule, left-wing, anti-imperialists, and determined opponents of the US war in Southeast Asia, accepted and defended the new regime's claims about its evacuation of the capital city and denounced early reports of the widespread killings as American anti-communist propaganda. This attitude is perhaps understandable for activists who had, with good reason, opposed American policy and the hundreds of thousands of deaths occurring in its wake, endorsing any force that would bring an end to intervention, and so were psychologically and ideologically unprepared to admit that opponents of US imperialism could be ruthless mass murderers. Morally deplorable as this attitude was, its effects were limited to certain sectors of public opinion. Far worse were the actions of Chinese and American policy makers in supporting the Khmer Rouge regime and continuing to recognize it as the legitimate government of Cambodia following its overthrow by Vietnamese forces. A move in the power politics of the Cold War, opposing the USSR and its ally Vietnam by supporting their opponent, the Khmer Rouge, this cynical policy traded limited gains in *Realpolitik* for the far greater moral degradation of endorsing a regime of mass murder and enhancing the human misery it instituted. One of the main architects of this policy was Henry Kissinger, who as a young man had helped round up war criminals and turned them over to the United Nations War Crimes Commission.

Punishing Cambodia's perpetrators was difficult. Khmer Rouge leader Pol Pot and his close followers held out, with open Chinese and tacit US support, in a small area near the Thai border until the leader's death in 1998. The Vietnamese-installed communist government consisted of one-time leading figures in the Khmer Rouge regime, before breaking with it. Even in the most favorable circumstances, holding trials of the Khmer Rouge leaders would have posed severe problems, since hardly any legally trained Cambodians had survived that regime. Finally, in 2006 a joint UN-Cambodian tribunal was instituted to try the remaining surviving leaders of the Khmer Rouge. Eleven years and $300 million later, three people had been convicted by the court; two other defendants died during the trial. Even in seemingly ideal circumstances—a small, weak country, the regime perpetrating the crimes overthrown—it proved almost impossible to bring to account those responsible for mass murder.[12]

ANTI-COMMUNISM AS MASS MURDER IN INDONESIA AND GUATEMALA

Capitalist regimes have also engaged in projects of utopian social engineering, leading to mass death. A prime example was the Great Famine in mid-nineteenth-century Ireland, a result of the doctrinaire imposition by the British government of a rigid free-market economy and an equally rigid rejection of any form of social welfare, even following massive crop failures and incipient mass starvation. In the Age of Interconnection, the most extreme of such capitalist initiatives—the Washington Consensus on economic and social policy in impoverished and indebted countries in Africa and Latin America, or the shock therapy recommended to post-communist regimes in Eastern Europe, both features of the 1990s—led to human suffering and economic setbacks. Nonetheless, they fell far short of the murderousness of the communist projects in Asia, or their 1930s Stalinist inspirations. Anticommunist and pro-capitalist regimes in the decades after 1950 engaged in mass murder as part of a program to eliminate potential communist opposition. The killings in Indonesia in 1965–1966 and in Guatemala in 1982–1983 are the two largest instances. Both occurred in countries in the midst of extreme political tension and social conflict.

During the early 1960s, Indonesia was a country on the brink of crisis, a result of both its foreign and domestic policies, arising out of the anti-imperialist plans of its president, Sukarno. A leader of the nonaligned movement and host of the 1955 Bandung Conference, Sukarno's anti-imperialism had taken on a particularly sharp edge, especially his policy of *Konfrontasi*, confrontation, with neighboring Malaysia, just released from British rule and, from Sukarno's point of view, a post-colonial stalking horse for Western imperialists. Engaging in low-level military conflict, and sponsoring guerilla fighters against the Malaysian government, Sukarno covered Indonesia with a web of military-led civil defense commands, to fight off the expected imperialist offensive.

In domestic policy, Sukarno had abolished elections and prorogued the parliament in 1957, instituting, as he put it, a "guided democracy." This was certainly authoritarian rule, but, unlike circumstances in totalitarian governments, competing political parties had not been outlawed, nor an official state party created. Indonesia's nationalist, Islamist, and communist parties continued to exist, very actively, in fact, although without elections they had no peaceful and legal way to measure their support. By the early 1960s, elections were not necessary to judge the rapidly growing strength of the Indonesian Communist Party, PKI. Counting some 3.5 million members, making it the largest non-ruling communist party in the world, through its affiliated farmers, workers, youth, and women's groups, the PKI had another twenty million followers. The party's policy of downplaying specifically communist goals and emphasizing anti-imperialism had made it a favorite of Sukarno, and spread its influence into the armed forces, particularly the air force—generally not where one would expect to find many communist sympathizers. A major success of the party's strategy was that Sukarno in the summer of 1965 took up the communists' idea of creating a people's army, a "fifth force," alongside the army, navy, air force, and police. The entire population would then be involved in the *Konfrontasi* with Malaysia and the imperialists.

Hostilities between the nationalists and Islamists, on the one hand, and the communists on the other, had always been strong. During the Indonesian war of independence against Dutch colonial rule, 1945–1949, the nationalist and Islamist armed units had taken a break from fighting the imperialist overlords to turn on their communist counterparts in 1948 and kill thirty thousand of them. Recovering from the independence-era setback, the growing strength and public influence of the communists in the first half of the 1960s seemed steadily more threatening to the Indonesia's other political forces, whose views were well represented in the army's officer corps. Sukarno's support for what sounded like a communist-dominated popular militia, a direct challenge to the regular armed forces, just ratcheted suspicions up higher.

By 1965 Indonesian communists and the opposing nationalists and Islamists, each with supporters in the armed forces, were watching each other with hostility and suspicion. But this state of affairs, typical of politics in the age of the Cold War, was not contained within national borders. The governments of the United States and China were both deeply involved in the Indonesian situation, which was part of the steadily escalating Cold War conflict in Southeast Asia. Indonesian Army officers were trained in the United States and absorbed America's intense Cold War anti-communism; Indonesian communist leaders, particularly the party chairman D. N. Aidit, were trained in China and frequently traveled there for political consultation.[13]

Still somewhat mysterious are the actions that led up to the massacre. In the early morning hours of October 1, 1965, a group of left-wing Indonesian army officers kidnapped six top army generals and proceeded to kill them. Troops sympathetic to these officers secured points in the capital city, Jakarta. Gathering at an air force base near the capital, the officers announced on the radio that they represented the "September 30 Movement" (the original plan had been to carry out the actions the previous day) whose actions were designed to stop a CIA-sponsored conspiracy of the generals to depose President Sukarno. Power would be taken from the government and placed in the hands of a new Revolutionary Council. Also present at the base were Sukarno, the pro-communist commander of the Indonesian air force, PKI leader Aidit, as well as a number of armed forces officers sympathetic to the communists and leaders of the communists' affiliated groups. This all seems very much like a communist-sponsored military coup, although very ineptly implemented, and quickly suppressed by the actions of anti-communist generals, led by Mohamed Suharto, commander of the army reserves, the most prominent army officer not to have been targeted by the conspirators.[14]

What followed was a massive reaction. Throughout Indonesia, mass meetings were held denouncing the communists and their ostensible plans to overthrow the beloved leader Sukarno. Anti-communist street demonstrations spilled over into mob violence, including the burning of national and regional PKI offices, and violent, sometimes murderous attacks. Soldiers, police, and armed militiamen began rounding up communists, imprisoning them in makeshift detention centers. Increasingly, instead of being imprisoned, the communists were simply killed. Some were shot or machine-gunned, but most were stabbed, beaten, and clubbed to death, or had their throats slit, the bodies thrown in rivers. Particularly in the central portions of the densely populated island of Java, whole villages, known for their communist sympathies, were attacked and their inhabitants killed. The total death toll remains unknown, although most estimates place it at between five hundred thousand and one million people, all within a six-month period, from October 1965 to March 1966. At least another million were arrested, although only about one in a thousand of them were brought to trial. The others were released, but officially marked for life as former communist sympathizers, a status shared by their children.

There can be little doubt that the killings were organized by the armed forces. Creating an anti-communist political front, the army also mobilized anti-communist paramilitary groups through the civil defense networks that President Sukarno had set up for his policy of *Konfrontasi*. The armed forces issued key propaganda charges that would reverberate throughout the massacre—that the six killed generals had been sexually mutilated by crazed communist women or that the communists were a godless threat to Islam. Soldiers, particularly of the commando unit, the RKPAD, carried out many murders.

Yet the assertion that the army was solely responsible for the killings or that all the participants in the murders did so on the command of the armed forces, seems exaggerated. Of the four hundred thousand Indonesian soldiers, a fair portion of whom (including their officers) were sympathetic to the communists, most were stationed on the border with Malaysia, as part of the policy of *Konfrontasi*. Available and committed troops did not suffice to hunt down communists all across Indonesia, a country of three thousand islands, spread out over three thousand miles, with, at the time, one hundred million inhabitants. The Australian historian Jess Melvin, in her study of the mass murder in the province of Aceh, on the island of Sumatra, is the most prominent proponent of the thesis that the army was responsible for the killings. Yet she admits that the killings were preceded by mass meetings with thousands or tens of thousands of participants, sponsored by the nationalist and Islamist political parties, their youth and women's groups, and even the *Pramuka*, the Indonesian Boy Scouts, fiercely condemning the communists, as well as mob attacks on communist party activists and party buildings. The issuing of a *fatwa* or Islamic judicial decision by the leading *ulema* of Aceh that communists were infidels who deserved death was another precursor to the killings.

As with other studies, her work shows that paramilitaries, particularly recruited from youth groups affiliated with the nationalist and Islamist parties, were active in the killings, whether in rounding and detaining the communists, who would then be murdered, or in killing outright the communists arrested by the armed forces As the *fatwa* in Aceh suggests, Islamist groups played a particularly large role in the killing, and cries of *Allahu Akhbar* as communists were murdered, resounded through the archipelago. This is a particularly drastic reminder of the fact that in the initial decades of the Cold War, Islamists and the Western powers shared a common anti-communism.

The army's anti-communist campaign unleashed long-standing antagonisms: the religiously based anti-communism of Indonesia's Muslims, but also of Hindus on the island of Bali and Catholics on the island of Flores. In central Java, owners of plantations, both private individuals and military officers (the army itself owned a large number of plantations) were involved in a long-standing conflict with the communists, who sponsored unions of plantation workers and demanded a redistribution of the land in the plantations to the landless and to small farmers. As a consequence of inflation and economic stagnation, both chronic since the mid-1950s, but particularly aggravated in 1964–65, these conflicts had become much stronger and the plantation owners eagerly exploited the opportunity to eliminate opponents who threatened their property. Attacks on Indonesia's ethnic Chinese minority—ostensibly for their pro-communist stance, although actually to loot their businesses—could only occur if the armed forces would permit them. These pogrom-like episodes make especially clear the conjunction of official planning and spontaneous popular violence.

What still remains obscure are the connections of the main Cold War Powers and their allies to the violence. Some historians, largely following the accusations of the September 30th Movement, assert that the Indonesian generals, in consultation with the CIA, were planning a military coup against the Sukarno government allied with the communists, followed by an attack on the PKI, and were just waiting for a pretext to carry it out. If so, it was a very badly planned coup, since the director of military intelligence General Parman, was completely unprotected, without even a bodyguard, and was one of the six generals kidnapped and murdered on October 1. While the generals directing the anti-communist violence wanted to eliminate the leadership of the PKI, they did not know who most of the provincial party leaders were. Once the killing was underway, the CIA helpfully provided a list of five thousand leading communists.

Similarly murky is the role of the Chinese government. What did Zhou Enlai mean when he told a group of ethnic Chinese from Indonesia at a banquet in Beijing on September 30, 1965, that "Indonesia will bring us a great present on our national day [October 1, the anniversary of the proclamation of the People's Republic in 1949]"? Rumors of consultations between the Chinese government and PKI leader Aidit about a potential coup parallel rumors about similar discussions between the CIA and Indonesian generals. Until records of intelligence agencies in both the United States and China are made available—and one probably should not hold one's breath while waiting—the exact role of the Cold War Powers in the origins and implementation of the mass murders will not be fully known.[15]

What is clear is the response to the mass violence on the part of the US government and its two main Cold War allies in the region, the United Kingdom and Australia. All three governments welcomed the anti-communist violence, and praised it in public statements and radio propaganda broadcasts. The governments provided assurances to the generals that they were not contemplating any military moves against Indonesia, so that soldiers stationed on the border with Malaysia as part of the policy of *Konfrontasi* could be safely withdrawn to assist in the anti-communist mass murders. The three governments sent few military supplies; those came, somewhat oddly, from Sweden. But in view of the very low-tech nature of so much of the killings, military aid was not a particularly crucial form of assistance. Although a handful of diplomats and journalists responded with horror, describing the killings as the worst mass murder since the Nazi era, the overwhelming response in the three Western powers directly involved and in the Cold War Western countries more generally, was indifference to or outright endorsement of the anti-communist campaign.

The anti-communist powers' endorsement of the mass murder was only reinforced by tepid condemnation coming from the communist regimes. While Eastern Bloc diplomats in Indonesia were privately appalled by the brutality of the attacks on communists, their governments, in view of the rapidly growing Sino-Soviet split, were unwilling to step up and defend publicly a communist party closely linked to China. Mao's response to the brutal murder of his Indonesian comrades was to write rueful poetry; both communist and capitalist governments competed for economic advantages and favorable trade deals with the new Indonesian regime. Indonesia's foreign minister, Adam Malik, deeply involved in the campaign of mass murder—he had, among other things, transmitted the CIA's list of communists to the generals—was elected president of the UN General Assembly for the year 1971 to 1972.

This outcome was yet another illustration of the impunity of mass murder. The generals leading the anti-communist campaign used it to seize power from an ailing President Sukarno, and they remained in power until 1998. The post-1965 regime rejected both Sukarno's anti-imperialism and his collectivist economic policies, largely supporting the Western powers in the Cold War, welcoming foreign investments and supporting a vigorous capitalism—albeit one in which close ties to the country's rulers and generous payments to them lubricated the market. The generals and their supporters made no secret of the mass murders with which their rule began and were quite proud of their suppression of communism. Post-1998, democratically elected governments have been reluctant to bring up the issue of the mass murders or to call those responsible to account. By 2010, the onetime perpetrators were elderly or deceased and there was little likelihood that they would ever be brought to justice.

The Indonesian killings were an integral part of a campaign to destroy an active communist movement, by no means the first example of such a campaign. Yet when compared with previous suppressions of powerful communist parties—in Italy, following the Fascist seizure of power in 1922; in Germany, when the Nazis came to power a decade later; in China, when the *Guomindang* broke with their one-time communist allies in 1927—the events in Indonesia were incomparably more violent. Fascist paramilitary groups, Italian blackshirts and German brownshirts, had murdered communists, with tacit approval of the authorities, or their open assistance, but the communist victims of the fascists numbered in the hundreds, at most the low thousands, not orders of magnitude more, as in Indonesia. The same limitation on the number of victims can be seen in the *Guomindang*'s 1927 repression of the Chinese communists, in what was then their stronghold, the city of Shanghai. Communist Party leaders in the 1920s and 1930s had been arrested and imprisoned—and incarceration in a Nazi concentration camp was no joke—but they had mostly not been murdered outright.[16]

This participation of civil society in anti-communist mass killings differentiates events in Indonesia from the other locus of anti-communist mass murders in the second half of the twentieth century. Repression of communists and other leftists in Cold War Latin America was fierce, especially after military coups in Brazil in 1964, Chile in 1973, and Argentina in 1976. The military regime emerging from that last coup carried out a systematic and secretive campaign of extermination of left-wing activists, resulting in as many as thirty thousand deaths. Yet harsh and cruel as all these were, they pale in comparison to the mass killings in the small Central American country of Guatemala, where the government's anti-communist campaign cost more lives than in all the rest of Latin America put together.[17]

Following the CIA-sponsored overthrow of Guatemala's leftist (although distinctly non-communist) president Jacobo Arbenz in 1954, opposition to the subsequent conservative regimes was relatively peaceful but continuous. At first, it was centered in the capital city and in the rural areas of the country's eastern lowlands, inhabited by *ladino*, people of primarily European descent. In the 1970s, supported by Cuba, and reinforced by Catholics radicalized in the wake of the Second Vatican Council through the ideas of Liberation Theology, the leftist element of the opposition changed its orientation. Rejecting the earlier, quasi-Marxist notion that Guatemala's native population was "backward" and unsuited for political mobilization, leftists concentrated their efforts on the western, mountainous regions, inhabited by the indigenous Mayans. The 1979 revolution in Nicaragua, which brought the radical Sandinistas to power, and the growing strength of liberation movements in nearby El Salvador that seemed by 1980 to be on the brink of seizing power, encouraged and strengthened armed opposition in Guatemala. Led by Marxist intellectuals of European descent, the insurgents gained increasing support among the Mayan people, often via enthusiasts for Liberation Theology and members of church-founded farmers' cooperatives.

When the left-wing political opposition was centered in the country's eastern provinces, the government, armed forces, and political conservatives of Guatemala's MLN Party had not hesitated to use large-scale violence against it. General Carlos Arana Osorio's 1967 counterinsurgency campaign, in the course of which eight thousand people, mostly noncombatants, were killed, earned him the nickname the "Butcher of Zacapa." The country's elites, mostly of European descent—like the left-wing leaders—looked down on the indigenous Mayans. They therefore felt even fewer compunctions about anti-communist violence when the opposition became centered in the western mountains. The presidency of General Romeo Lucas García, 1979 to 1982, was characterized by increasingly unrestrained attacks—not just targeting actual insurgents, but whole highland villages, raping women, locking families in their houses and burning them to death, and massacring children. The armed forces were responsible for most of the violence, but paramilitary death squads, organized and supplied with weapons by the army, and staffed in part with military personnel, were also active, particularly in the capital city.

In March 1982, the president was overthrown by a military coup led by General Efraim Ríos Montt. From a devout Catholic family—his brother was a bishop—he had previously been associated with the reforming Christian Democrats. In fact, in 1974 he had been the Christian Democrats' presidential candidate and apparently had won that election. His conservative opponent, however, was declared victor under suspicious circumstances. With this background, one might have expected Ríos Montt to have dialed back the violence of the anti-insurgent campaign. But in the interval the general had been "born again," becoming a member of the Church of the Word, a Pentecostal church. Like many others, the Church of the Word had started in Southern California, but achieved its greatest success outside the world's wealthy countries. By the time the general joined in 1977, most members and the church's leadership were from Guatemala, and the church was known as *Verbo*, from its Spanish name, *Iglesia Cristiana Verbo*.

Believing he had been chosen by God and giving weekly Sunday night speeches on TV, with his hand on the Bible, Ríos Montt set out to transform Guatemala into a land of piety, morality, and righteousness after he took over the government in 1982. God had punished Guatemala for its sins, but under the new regime the country would become one family, following God's will. Enemies of the new moral order would be eliminated. Insurgents were offered an amnesty if they surrendered. The highland Indians were given a choice of submitting to the government or being killed. Whatever their choice, about eighty thousand were killed in the first hundred days following the coup. Unlike the case with Ríos Montt's predecessor Lucas García, the violence was organized and systematic. Mountain communities who refused to renounce the guerillas were eliminated; razed to the ground; their inhabitants executed by firing squad, machetes, or being burned alive. Those who submitted to the authorities were enlisted in civil defense patrols and resettled in secure locations, invariably including a newly built Pentecostal church. The resettled Mayans received patriotic education and instruction in the Spanish language, which most spoke only haltingly, if at all. Rather than being treated as inferior, the Mayans would be incorporated into the divinely sanctioned Guatemalan national body.

Pentecostalism expanded rapidly. In October 1982, six months after the coup, three hundred thousand Pentecostals met in Guatemala City in a gigantic open-air meeting for song and prayer, as well as speeches by TV evangelists and the devout general. Guatemalan Pentecostals saw Ríos Montt's rule and their own rapid expansion as signs of the fulfillment of biblical prophecy and the imminence of the Second Coming. Though still a majority of Guatemalans, Catholics felt beleaguered; the papal visit of John Paul II in 1983, which included public pronouncements about the sanctity of human rights, was greeted by crowds in the hundreds of thousands, and had a rallying effect like his celebrated visit to communist Poland in 1979.

As counterinsurgency, Ríos Montt's campaign was immensely effective, eliminating the guerillas' base of support. Efforts by the insurgents to create a counterterror, assassinating members of the civil defense patrols, only weakened their position still further. Strange as it may sound, Ríos Montt's policies proved popular among the highlanders who were the victims of his campaign, precisely because the extreme violence was not indiscriminate, as in the past. Villages where the guerillas were not active were untouched; villages who submitted to the army were well-treated, so Mayans knew what they had to do to survive. The large number of Mayan soldiers among the troops carrying out the counterinsurgency campaign were proof of the general's popularity.

As a proportion of the population murdered, the killings in Guatemala were roughly as large as those in Indonesia—about 1 percent. In both countries, integralist religion was an important element of the anticommunist campaigns. These campaigns also featured an interplay between the armed forces and unofficial militias, although in Guatemala the armed forces seemed both more in control and responsible for a far larger proportion of the murders.

The killings were viewed differently in Western countries, a reflection of the changes in attitudes about the Cold War and human rights over the intervening time. The US government, for which the coup by Ríos Montt was unexpected, did not endorse his policies or provide him with weapons and other assistance. This was not a result of any particular sensitivity on the part of the fiercely anti-communist administration of Ronald Reagan. Strategic calculations were involved. Guatemala was less central to US policy makers, who saw Nicaragua and El Salvador as the crucial arenas of the struggle with Central America leftists. But the administration also understood that the opposition Democrats, who controlled one house of Congress, were unwilling to condone these massive killings in the name of anti-communism. In sharp contrast to Indonesia, the mass murder in Guatemala was the subject of debate and public condemnation in the United States and in Western Europe, a reflection of changing public attitudes. Church groups, formerly strongly anti-communist, were critical, aside from Evangelicals and Pentecostals, who stood with their coreligionists.

More broadly, some of the attitudes that had enabled Cold War-era mass murders were beginning to soften by the 1980s. Communist regimes were no longer engaged in projects of utopian social engineering with fatal outcomes, or carrying out the executions of perceived enemies that accompanied them. A willingness to place human rights above anti-communism had become more common in the Western world. Of course, these changes in opinion were cold comfort to the eighty thousand victims of political mass murder under the rule of Ríos Montt.

The pious general was overthrown in a military coup in October 1983, after seventeen months in office. The plotters denounced him for violating the separation of church and state, although a more likely motive was that Guatemala's conservative elites felt that Ríos Montt had performed admirably in destroying the insurgents, but that his eccentricities were scaring away foreign investors. He retained a powerful measure of public support; according to public opinion polls, he remained for years the most popular politician in Guatemala. However, the constitution adopted after his overthrow prohibited former perpetrators of a military coup from running for president.

He finally got the chance to campaign for the office in 2003, but in the interval commissions of inquiry, one sponsored by the government and one by the Archdiocese of Guatemala, had brought to light the facts about the mass murders. At an election rally in the highland village of Rabinal Baja Verapaz, the spectators hurled stones at him and cries of "*¡Culpable!*" His presidential campaign failed. In 2012, he was arrested and charged with genocide, the only head of state ever to be charged with such a crime in a national, as against an international tribunal. By then well into his eighties, the former general was convicted, had his conviction overturned on appeal, was retried and convicted but ruled too old and ill to serve a jail sentence. He died in 2018. This very modest effort to hold a perpetrator of mass murder responsible might be compared with the equally belated effort in Cambodia, although it was the judiciary of Guatemala that brought the charges all by itself, without need of UN intervention, a singular event in efforts to try mass murderers.[18]

Mass Murder at the End of the Millennium

The global upheavals of 1989–91, leading to the end of communist regimes and their potential for projects of utopian social engineering as well as the termination of the conflicts between communists and anti-communists, eliminated the basis of the mass murders of the Cold War. An era of worldwide peace and flourishing human rights seemed in the offing. Akin to the optimistic expectations prevalent at the end of the Second World War, the hopes circulating in the wake of the end of the Cold War quickly proved to be vain. There were two new instances of mass killings, one in the former Yugoslavia and the other in Rwanda.

Both followed different lines from their Cold War predecessors, and from those in the Age of Total War. Rather than the product of strong states, the millennial mass killings were the products of weak and feeble ones—"failed states." These were governments incapable of preserving public order so that privately organized and disorganized groups could engage in killing with little restriction. They lacked the functioning bureaucracy, police, or armed forces to carry out their policies, turning to armed bands and informal militias that showed no restraint. Arising less out of ideological confrontations, these killings emerged both from social conflicts and grievances as well as theories of racial, ethnic, and national difference. The latter became a fateful and fatal force. The end of the Cold War had opened new possibilities to prevent mass murders and to bring their perpetrators to justice. However, these new situations also brought to the fore the objections posed by Radhabinod Pal in Tokyo a half century earlier, discrediting international tribunals, tarring efforts to prevent mass murder with the brush of imperialism, and proving that the considerations of power politics and raison d'état, now freed from their Cold War straitjackets, could and did hamper responses to incipient or actual mass killings.

The killings in the former Yugoslavia during the 1990s were, in comparison to other mass murders, on a relatively modest scale. They attracted attention for two main reasons. The murders, along with the mass expulsions and rapes that accompanied them, were by far the largest episode of extreme violence in Europe since the Second World War. Precisely because the killings were occurring in Europe, they were not hidden; they took place in front of TV cameras, photographers, journalists, diplomats, and human rights observers.

All these atrocities occurred in the "former Yugoslavia," a phrase that gets to the heart of the matter—state collapse and the end of the one-time socialist and federal Yugoslav republic. In part, this collapse was structural and self-inflicted, the decision of long-term communist leader Josip Tito and his associates in the 1970s to decentralize power, moving authority from the central government to the individual federal republics. It was not the decentralization in and of itself that proved deadly, so much as its interaction with two other developments typical of communist Eurasia in the 1970s and 1980s. One was the waning of communism as a basis of political legitimacy and the increasing salience of nationalism that replaced it; the other was the deep economic crisis the communist world was experiencing, as part of the broader upheaval of the global economy begun in the 1970s. These all came together in 1989–91.[19]

As the Yugoslav economy declined, tensions rose among the federal republics. Inhabitants and policy makers of the industrialized northern ones—Croatia and Slovenia—perceived the economic planning of the Yugoslav federal system as siphoning off the wealth they created to the poorer southern republics. In those republics, Serbia, Montenegro, Bosnia, and Macedonia, opinion was that the central government's economic planning was degrading them to sources of labor and raw materials for the republics in the north, ensuring their permanently inferior condition. As decentralization preceded, the idea of secession, of the individual republics leaving Yugoslavia and becoming independent sovereign states, grew steadily more attractive.

As communism was collapsing across Eurasia, leading figures in the individual republics, especially Slobodan Milošević in Serbia, a veteran communist party bureaucrat, and his Croatian counterpart, Franjo Tudjman, a longtime dissident, began turning to nationalism as a way to rally support behind them. The nationalism they promoted was particularly toxic, drawing upon the trauma of Yugoslavia under German and Italian occupation during the Second World War. Tudjman and his supporters glorified the Croatian Ustaša government that under foreign occupation had murdered at least one hundred thousand Serbs, and consistently tried to deny or to minimize the atrocities. Milošević downplayed memories of the communist partisans of the Second World War, who had tried to rally Yugoslavia's nationalities against the foreign invaders, in favor of the Chetniks, the Serbian nationalist guerillas, who had regularly attacked other nationalities (and even, at times, collaborated with the Axis occupiers). Broadcast on the TV news, asserted in speeches, played up in every way possible, these traumatic memories were systematically re-emphasized.

There was nothing inevitable about this. The Second World War had left behind plenty of trauma and national hostilities in Central and Eastern Europe: between Germans on the one hand, and Czechs, Poles, and Russians on the other; between Poles and Ukrainians; or between Hungarians and Romanians. Yet somehow the events of 1989–91 did not exacerbate tensions between these nations, contrary to the expectations of journalists and political scientists. If anything, the end of the communist regimes in Western Eurasia vitiated the memories of the Second World War, decreasing old nationalist hostilities and facilitating closer ties between governments and ordinary citizens of once opposed nationalities. Another way to put it might be to say that by the 1990s reviving memories of the Second World War had become reactionary, in the original political meaning of the term: trying to revive and return to past circumstances, generally for nefarious reasons.

A common response was that the Balkans were different: national groups there had been killing each other for centuries or millennia; the breakup of Yugoslavia was the result of ancient tribal hatreds. Like the primordialist theories of nationhood on which it was based, this was a very dubious assertion. There had been centuries-long stretches of peace in the Balkans under the rule of the multinational Ottoman and Habsburg empires. Although the growth of nationalism in the nineteenth and twentieth centuries had led to violent clashes, particularly in the Age of Total War, these past experiences were not destiny. The southern federal republic of Macedonia had been the scene of large-scale expulsions and massacres during the runup to the First World War in the Balkan Wars of 1911–13, but the leading politicians there rejected exploiting memories of old killings after 1989 and determinately kept the peace between the republic's two main nationalities, the Albanians and the Macedonians.

There were as well politicians in Serbia and Croatia who refused to exploit nationalism as a way of procuring support in a post-communist world, emphasizing instead the promotion of democratic, multiparty politics and civil liberties, as well as the introduction of more market-based and, they hoped, more productive economies. Their supporters, strongest in larger cities, mounted very impressive demonstrations against Milošević in Belgrade. However, they were unable to prevail against the rising tide of nationalism. Indeed, the idea of the Balkans as a scene of ancient hatreds was promulgated by Milošević and his nationalist allies, with their obsession over the defeat of Serbian Prince Lazar by the forces of the Sultan at the Battle of the Field of Blackbirds in Kosovo in 1389. Drawing a line from that medieval conflict to the Second World War, Serb nationalists repeatedly insisted that their nation was facing the danger of genocide—a charge first made by nationalist intellectuals in the 1970s, reasserted in an official statement of the Serbian Academy of Sciences in 1986, and reiterated with ever greater force and frequency in the crisis years after 1989.

Czechoslovakia and the USSR were multinational communist states where nationalism became ever more politically salient after 1989, but their breakup occurred in largely peaceful fashion. The situation in Yugoslavia made this more difficult, because of the distribution of the Serbs, the largest nationality, among the federal states. The Serbian republic included two regions with large populations of other nationalities: the Vojvodina in the north, where many ethnic Hungarians lived; and Kosovo in the south, mostly inhabited by Albanians. In the Yugoslav governmental decentralization of the 1970s, both regions had been granted a substantial portion of autonomy. If many non-Serbs lived in Serbia, it was conversely the case that there were substantial Serb populations in other republics—in the Croatian regions of Krajina and Slavonia, and in large parts of Bosnia. Were Yugoslavia to be divided on national lines, violence seemed likely to emerge from the disjunction between the boundaries of the federal republics and the increasingly intransigent nationalism promoted by leading politicians of those republics.

While the post-Cold War world had made it possible for international action to forestall such violent conflicts the superpowers were not paying attention: the USSR was collapsing, and the US administration of George H. W. Bush, preoccupied with the Iraqi invasion of Kuwait, had little interest in resolving Balkan conflicts. Stepping in, the foreign minister of Luxemburg proudly proclaimed, "the hour of Europe," in which the individual nations of the continent, and the nascent European Union would peacefully preserve stability and human rights. Nonetheless, lacking both the capacity to enforce a settlement, and the willingness to do so, the Europeans' pacifist approach accomplished little. It even exacerbated the conflict.

There had already been clashes between Serb and Croatian nationalists in Krajina and Slavonia in 1990 and early 1991. The Croatian and Slovenian declarations of independence in June of that latter year were the signal for warfare on a larger scale. The government of Serbia, which retained control of the Yugoslav National Army, the JNA, opposed these decisions and took armed action against them. Subsequent clashes between the JNA, fully equipped with artillery, armor, and combat aircraft, and the ragtag Croatian and Slovenian militias, barely armed with some black-market weapons, should have been one-sided. Yet they were not. After ten days of half-hearted fighting, the JNA retreated from Slovenia, leaving it free to declare independence. In Croatia, the army found it painfully difficult to bring its massive superiority to bear. The two-month-long siege of the Slavonian city of Vukovar, in which a handful of defenders held off the well-equipped JNA forces, was one example. Another was the artillery assault on the ancient city of Dubrovnik on the Adriatic coast, a UNESCO World Heritage site (best known as the location of the exterior scenes of the city of King's Landing in the TV version of the fantasy series *Game of Thrones*). After weeks of bombardment, there were no efforts to seize the city from its 670 defenders, only 50 of whom were trained soldiers.

The JNA may have had the weaponry; it also had serious problems with soldiers, especially non-Serbs. Young men did not report for draft calls; soldiers did not return from leave; reservists ignored their mobilization notices. At the siege of Vukovar, a large group of recalled reservists dropped their weapons, sat down together, and began singing John Lennon's "Give

Peace a Chance." The Serbian government turned to informally organized nationalist militias, including the notorious Arkan Tigers, led by the gangster and black-marketeer Željko Ražnatović. He recruited heavily among fans of the Belgrade soccer clubs, Partizan and Red Star—a particularly horrifying example of the role of sports both in embodying nationalism and replacing military functions in the Late-Millennium Era. In the militia, the fans did not just curse out opposing teams or beat up other fans from enemy nations. The Tigers and similar groups engaged in expulsion, rape, and murder.[20]

Army and militias finally conquered Krajina and Slavonia, driving out hundreds of thousands of Croatians living there and in 1992 turned to Bosnia, a federal Yugoslav republic that had very reluctantly declared its independence. Serb forces intended to seize a large portion of Bosnia, annex it to Serbia, and drive out the Croat and Bosnian Muslims inhabitants living there. Between 1992 and 1995, militias ranged across Bosnia, imprisoning, torturing, and killing Croats and, especially, Bosnian Muslims, raping thousands, perhaps tens of thousands of women, destroying towns and villages. (It is true that on a few occasions, Croat and Bosnian troops acted against Serb civilians in similar fashion, but an overwhelming majority of the attacks on civilians were carried out by Serb militias.) The siege of the Bosnian capital city of Sarajevo, whose inhabitants, regardless of their particular ethnicity, generally rejected the Serb nationalists and supported the Bosnian government, was characterized by indiscriminate artillery attacks on civilians. Serb nationalists in Bosnia asserted that the Bosnian Muslims themselves had staged the attacks to gain international sympathy.

The Serb nationalists coined a phrase for their actions, *etničko ciscenje*, "ethnic cleansing," quickly taken up by journalists and applied worldwide, currently and retrospectively. The irony was that the cleansing the Serbs were carrying out was precisely not ethnic. Serbs, Croats, and Bosnian Muslims all speak the same language and share a wide variety of customs and practices. They are, of course, from different religions, but, like most inhabitants of former communist countries, not particularly devout: unlike the anticommunist murders, these were no religiously based killings. Rather, the "ethnic" differences were largely invented. This invention of ethnic and racial differences would characterize the mass murders at the end of the millennium.

While ethnic cleansing was taking place, the rest of the world was taking actions that made the situation worse. Having aided in provoking the war and subsequent atrocities with pressure to recognize Slovenian and Croatian independence, the European countries responded by offering up solutions involving some form of partition of Bosnia. This essentially recognized the results of the Serb nationalists' campaign. In any case the Serbs generally rejected these proposals. Some twenty negotiated ceasefires came and went.

The UN, whose General Secretary, Boutros Boutros-Ghali, described the events in the former Yugoslavia as a "rich man's war," one fought among

Europeans, diverting global attention from the world's poor, enforced an arms embargo, which meant that the Serbs, with access to the JNA's weapons, had a permanent military superiority over the Croats and Bosnians, who had to smuggle theirs in. Establishing an International Criminal Tribunal for the Former Yugoslavia in 1993 might be seen either as a positive step or as a pretext to avoid actually stopping any criminal actions. The role of UN peacekeepers would certainly support such an interpretation. Few in numbers and lightly armed, authorized to use their weapons only to defend themselves, they were seized by Serbian nationalist forces as hostages to prevent to any actions of which they disapproved, such as the occasional NATO air strikes to support Security Council resolutions. The UN also established so-called safe areas, cities in which Bosnian Muslims could gather, provided they laid down their arms. Since the UN peacekeepers stationed in these safe areas were only allowed to defend themselves and not the Bosnians living or taking refuge there, this was a nearly useless form of protection.

What happened following the seizure of the safe area of Srebenica by Bosnian Serb troops in July 1995, proves the point. While the Dutch peacekeepers were drinking champagne with officers of the Serb forces, an uncomfortable image that made its way around the world, the adult men in the city, numbering as many as eight thousand, were led away and shot. Other peacekeeping forces in the other safe areas of the Drina Valley, acted differently, defying their mandate. Welsh fusiliers in Goražde, fought off the Serbs, and even more badly outnumbered Ukrainians in Žepa, held them up until an agreement to evacuate the city was reached.

What finally resolved the war in Croatia and Bosnia was the reluctant intervention of the United States—the administration of President Bill Clinton overcame domestic opposition to being the world's policeman. Unlike the Europeans or the UN, the United States was willing and able to use military force to underscore its diplomatic initiatives. The Dayton Accords of November 1995, establishing Bosnia as a federation of two states, a Croatian-Muslim one and a Serb republic, de facto recognized the partition of the country established by ethnic cleansing. The Serb offensive in the Drina Valley, which included the massacre in Srebenica, was undertaken to obtain the most favorable position on the ground, in view of the impending peace agreement. Large numbers of Serbian troops and militiamen from Krajina and Slavonia had taken part in the offensive in the Drina Valley, leaving those areas undefended when the Croatian army, acting with tacit US approval, launched its offensive in the summer of 1995, reconquering the regions and driving out the Serb population.

Refugees in turn, the Serbs from Croatia, expecting a hero's welcome in Belgrade, were instead told that they needed to resettle in Kosovo, to reinforce the Serb position in that province. This was the final act of the Yugoslav drama. Largely inhabited by ethnic Albanians, Kosovo had been an autonomous region of Serbia since the 1970s. It had also launched Slobodan Milošević's career as Serb nationalist, when he revoked the province's autonomy in 1988 and proclaimed himself defender of the Serbs from the persecution of the ethnic Albanian communists who had run the province under its autonomy regime. This protection included firing all ethnic Albanians in public service and closing all Albanian-language educational institutions. Opposition to Serb persecution initially took the form of peaceful and passive resistance under the leadership of Ibrahim Rugova, often known as the "Albanian Gandhi." Under the impact of the war in Bosnia, and the lack of any effect of the peaceful policies, by the late 1990s more militant elements became organized into the Kosovo Liberation Army. The KLA was bankrolled by Albanians living in Europe and the United States. (The newly formed Al Qaeda had offered to support its fellow Muslims, an offer which the KLA leaders were sensible enough to reject.) Starting in 1998, open war broke out, a war characterized, as in Bosnia, by Serb attacks on noncombatants and efforts at ethnic cleansing—unlike in Bosnia, the Albanians really were a different ethnic group.

In contrast to Bosnia, Kosovo was part of Serbia, and the precedent of the post-1945 war crimes trials, that the international community would not hold sovereign governments accountable for acts against their own citizens, was very much in effect. No UN Security Council resolution was forthcoming. Both Russia, largely pro-Serb, and China, fearing international action concerning its own ethnic minorities, would not hear of it. Lengthy negotiations between NATO and the Serbs about sending in NATO peacekeepers failed, and in 1999 NATO launched a bombing campaign against Serb forces in Kosovo and in Serbia as well.

The Serb government responded by sending in paramilitaries to escalate the killing of Albanian civilians and redoubled efforts to expel Albanians, forcing hundreds of thousands to flee the province. As was already apparent in the Bosnian situation, though now on a much larger scale, the Serb position gained substantial support from pacifists and anti-imperialists all over the world, who saw the Serbs as victims of American imperialism, denounced the United States and NATO for acting without UN approval, and generally seemed much more worked up about attempts to stop the mass murder than the mass murder itself. In the end, however, the air campaign launched by NATO and the United States worked. Serb forces withdrew, and the returning Albanians drove out the Serb population—as well as the province's Romany (Gypsy) people. All sides of the conflicts in the former Yugoslavia had attacked the Romany.

The death toll is difficult to ascertain; recent analysis has reduced initial figures, although what remains is large enough. In Bosnia, perhaps one hundred thousand people died, almost 60 percent of them soldiers. The civilian deaths, almost forty thousand, were about 1 percent of Bosnia's population, roughly the same proportion as were killed in Indonesia or Guatemala. A majority were Bosnian Muslims, indeed about eight times as many of them as Serbs. Many of the Serb civilians killed were inhabitants of Sarajevo, killed by Serb nationalist artillery bombardments. There were perhaps ten thousand civilian deaths, almost all ethnic Albanians in Kosovo. Proponents of all sides in the civil wars killed civilians, raped women, and destroyed homes. Nonetheless it was the Serb nationalists who did by far most of the acts and were responsible for a very large majority of the victims. Hundreds of thousands of people were driven from their homes. At first, the Serbs did all the expulsions, driving out Croats in Krajina and Slavonia, Croats and Muslims in Bosnia, and Albanians in Kosovo. As the tide of battle turned, it was Serbs in Croatia and Kosovo who were expelled, as the populations they expelled returned; the only exception was in Bosnia, where Serb expulsions of Muslims and Croats were never reversed. In spite of clauses in peace agreements allowing or even encouraging refugees to return, they never have and almost certainly never will.

Some eighty leading figures in the civil war were brought before the International Criminal Tribunal for the Former Yugoslavia. They had been surrendered by the Serb and Croat governments, only after considerable economic pressure on the part of Western European countries. Both the political leader of the Bosnian Serbs, Radovan Karadžić, and the commander of their armed forces, Ratko Mladić, were famous for their open public flaunting of the tribunal. As many as fifteen years passed between their indictment and their arrest and extradition to stand trial. As regards the two leaders most responsible, Franjo Tudjman died before he could be indicted. Slobodan Milošević was brought to trial in 2001 and defended himself fiercely, denouncing the court as a tool of imperialism, always insisting that he was protecting the Serb people from the threat of genocide. His sympathizers in Serbia intimidated witnesses against testifying and refused to release potentially incriminating documents to the court. After years of proceedings, Milošević died of a heart attack in 2006, before a verdict could be reached.

In some ways, Milošević had been right about imperialism. Peaceful mediation, diplomatic initiatives, arms embargoes, UN peacekeepers, and international justice—not only had these done little to stop the killings in the former Yugoslavia, they facilitated them. It took imperialist military force, overriding national sovereignty and acting, at times, without UN mandates, to prevent mass murder or to end it. If an international tribunal was able to bring war criminals and mass murderers to justice, it was because they were delivered up as a result of powerful states exerting diplomatic and economic pressure to do so. When those states were unwilling to exert such pressure, as the cases of Karadžić and Mladić show, justice was long denied or delayed.

The killings in Rwanda occurred as the war in the former Yugoslavia was ongoing but were on a completely different scale. There were, by most estimates, fifty times as many victims. Similar conditions to those facilitating mass murder in the Balkans—collapsing governmental authority and a failing state, economic crisis, imagined ethnic and racial differences, politicians' conscious evocation of memories of past killings, and the reluctance of powerful countries to intervene—were also prevalent in central Africa. In contrast to circumstances in Bosnia and, in fact, to most of the mass murders of the Age of Interconnection, the killings in Rwanda were characterized by an unusual degree of popular participation.[21]

Much as in Yugoslavia, the mass murders in Rwanda had their genesis in social tensions dating back to the nineteenth century. The central African region, encompassing what would later be the independent states of Rwanda and Burundi, was characterized by the rule of a pastoral people from the north, the Tutsi. Their subjects were an indigenous, farming population that consisted of a number of tribal groups, among others the Bugoyi, Kinyaga, Nduga, and Rukiga peoples. The collective designation of them as "Hutus" was originally an insult, meaning something like "loutish yokels." Distinctions between these groups were fluid: Tutsi who lost their cattle, the great attribute and wealth of pastoralists, would end up in the farming population, while successful agriculturalists who accumulated wealth and livestock could join the rank of the Tutsis. Clan groups included both farmers and herders; ritual ceremonies they sponsored, such as the *ubuse*, which affirmed the existence of a common, mythical, patrilineal ancestor, or the *kubandwa* worship ritual, in which a ceremonial king and queen were chosen, were designed to emphasizes the coexistence of the two groups.

Two developments made the distinction between herders and farmers more rigid and the social and political superiority of the former more pronounced. One was the rule between 1860 and 1895 of the warrior king Mwami Rawbugiri, who expanded his realm through the campaigns of his Tutsi fighters. He took control of the land from the elders of the farming peoples, and handed pieces of it to his leading warriors. In this procedure, called *ibikingi*, the farmers residing on this land—now all designated as Hutus—were required to perform labor services, two days out of every five, for their new Tutsi overlords. Mwami Rawbugiri transformed a lineage-based society into a seigneurial one, exacerbating the characteristic hostilities of seigneurialism, between lord and peasant. Uprisings of the newly enserfed peasants followed in the mid-1880s.

From the 1897 to 1962, the future Rwanda was under colonial rule, initially by Germany, until Belgian troops conquered the country during the First World War. It was not a tightly administered colony, or one with European settlers; both colonial administrations worked with and through the existing monarchy. An influential political and cultural force under colonialism were the Catholic missionaries, the aptly named White Fathers. Highly successful in propagating the faith, they turned Rwanda into one of the most Christianized countries in Africa. With the spread of Christianity, former "pagan" clan ceremonies that had reinforced the spiritual links between pastoralists and agriculturalists were banned. Missionaries also promoted a different understanding of the distinctions between pastoralists and agriculturalists in both religious and racial terms, perceiving the Tutsis as descendants of Noah's son Ham: tall, slender and of fairer complexion, as such, racially superior to the short, squat, dark Hutus. Creating and controlling the educational system, the missionaries allowed only Tutsis access to higher education, and to potential administrative, professional, and business careers. The sole educational prospect for the Hutus were in the lesser seminaries, training to be parish priests.

After the Second World War, as the European empires entered—in the Belgian case with extreme reluctance—the age of decolonization, politics in Rwanda centered on the clash between Hutus and Tutsis, who increasingly perceived themselves in the racial terms invented by their European colonial rulers. Both Belgian colonial administrators and younger European Catholic priests, embodying the reforming spirit and concern for the poor and oppressed that would characterize the Second Vatican Council and Liberation Theology, supported the nascent Hutu political parties, foremost among them PARMEHUTU, which announced its purpose was to oppose the "hegemony of the invading Tutsi race," calling for a Rwandan republic. Tutsis, by contrast, endorsed the National Union of Ruanda, UNAR, which rejected the plans of their colonial overlords and endorsed the existing royal family. They received support for this position from other African anti-imperialists, such as Patrice Lumumba of the neighboring Belgian Congo. The support of this African socialist and anti-imperialist martyr for a seigneurial monarchy is something his many eulogists and admirers tend to pass over in silence.

Already in the runup to independence, from 1959 to 1961, there were violent clashes between Tutsis and Hutus, leading hundreds of thousands of Tutsis to flee the country, north to Uganda and south to Burundi, helping to orient that latter country's politics on Hutu-Tutsi opposition, which had not been the case in the last years of colonial rule and the initial ones of independence. Just a year after the proclamation of the Rwandan republic, a group of exile Tutsis invaded Rwanda from the south. Their incursion led immediately to anti-Tutsi riots, in which at least ten thousand people were killed. Desperate victims fled for sanctuary in churches, which priests granted and violent crowds respected. The British philosopher, pacifist, and human rights activist Bertrand Russell denounced the mass killings as "the most horrible and systematic massacres we have witnessed since that of the Jews by the Nazis."[22]

In 1973, Minister of Defense, Major-General Juvénal Habyarimana overthrew the Rwandan government in a military coup. Himself a Hutu, although from a tribe in the north of the country and opposed to the southerners who had previously dominated politics, he was one of many authoritarian rulers coming to power in Africa by a military coup in the decade after independence, including Joseph Mobutu in neighboring Zaire. Like Mobutu, Habyarimana's accession to power instituted a quarter century of authoritarian rule. Political parties and competitive elections were banned; only the official, state-sponsored MRND was allowed to engage in political activity. His regime perceived the Tutsi not as invading enemies, but as a national minority within Rwanda. This was a policy with ambiguous outcomes. On the one hand, violence against the Tutsi was not tolerated. On the other, discrimination in higher education and public service was systematized. There was also a bureaucratic racialization of official identities. Individuals, officially classified as Hutus, descendants of Tutsis who had lost their cattle and their status and affluence, were reclassified as Tutsis, following along lines of biological descent.

The earlier period of Habyarimana's rule was relatively prosperous. Economic growth was rapid in the 1970s and early 1980s and Rwanda was regarded at the time as one of the most economically successful African countries. Particularly helpful were rising prices on the world market for Rwanda's two main agricultural exports, coffee and tea.

Habyarimana's regime fell into crisis in the second half of the 1980s. Drought led to food shortages and near famine; a decline in international market prices of the country's leading exports drastically reduced income. GDP fell, a particularly difficult development in a country with a rapid rate of population growth. In a magnified version of Africa's lost decade, Rwanda went from being one of the most economically successful countries of the continent to one of the least. As usual, the World Bank's structural adjustment program, which involved cutting government spending and devaluing the currency, made matters worse, leading to inflation, without any boost to exports.

With the end of the Cold War, the Habyarimana regime, like its counterpart in Zaire, came under pressure from the United States and Western European countries, as well as from its African neighbors, to renounce authoritarianism and to re-establish democracy. New political parties were formed, independent of and in opposition to the government. Also important to the process of democratization were the Tutsi refugees from the violence of the early 1960s in Uganda. Quite a number had worked for the security forces of Uganda's dictator, Idi Amin. After Amin's overthrow, they joined the insurgents opposing his successor, Milton Obote, rising to leading positions within the insurgency. In 1986, the insurgents' leader Yoweri Musevini entered the Ugandan capital of Kampala in triumph. Once in power, he decided it would be best for the stability of his regime if his experienced foreign fighters returned to Rwanda. At the beginning of 1990, the Tutsi exiles, organized into the Rwandan Patriotic Front or RPF, began incursions into

Northern Rwanda. At the same time, they negotiated with the Habyarimana government about a power-sharing agreement, the "Arusha process," named after the site of the talks in Tanzania, one of the negotiation's meditators.

None of the efforts at ending authoritarian rule in Rwanda went as planned. The president did have to appoint members of the opposition parties to cabinet posts and even to the position of prime minister. But he did everything in his power to sabotage their policies and to cripple their actions. For all the negotiations about power sharing with the RPF, there was no actual sharing of power. It was not just the authoritarian president and his followers who were creating a crisis situation in the country, but his opponents as well. The chief opposition party, the Rwandan Democratic Movement or MDR was a revival of PARMEHUTU, a militantly Hutu political party, denouncing the Tutsis as the Hutus' racial enemy. Both official governmental and oppositional Hutu political parties competed to be the most militantly anti-Tutsi. Some parties tried to focus on issues other than older conflicts and hatreds, particularly the Social Democrats (PSD), who asserted that the major problem affecting the country was social and economic inequality. While the PSD members were primarily Hutus, both its leaders and most of its rank and file took a strong stand against the ethnic hatred being promoted by the other Hutu parties. As was the case in the former Yugoslavia, the proponents of a racialized national and ethnic hatred prevailed over their opponents. The assassination of the PSD's courageous and outspoken General Secretary, former Minister of Energy and Public Works Félicien Gatabazi, in February 1994, was a signal that an outbreak of mass violence was imminent.

The process of democratization had led to a paralysis of government, which was reflected in the breakdown of law and order and a wave of individual and collective violence throughout Rwanda between 1991 and 1994. Members of militias and youth groups of the different political parties regularly fought with each other. Even more prevalent were individualized or less formally organized attacks on public order: land occupations, seizure of real and personal property, arson, especially of forestlands, banditry, and street robbery, feuding leading to assaults, brawling, and outright murder were everywhere. Interviewed later in the 1990s, Rwandans asserted that this period of lawlessness, exacerbated by the country's economic difficulties, was a clear predecessor to the killings.

Those killings were brought on by three events. The leaders of the RPF, frustrated, by the lack of progress in the power-sharing talks, launched a full-scale invasion of Rwanda in February 1993, turning the north of the country into a war zone, creating hundreds of thousands of refugees. The second was the assassination of Melchior Ndadaye, the president of neighboring Burundi, in October 1993. The first Hutu to hold that position, and democratically elected to boot, he was overthrown and murdered in a military coup, led by Tutsi army officers. The final straw was the assassination of President Habyarimana, on April 6, 1994. Returning from a one-day regional summit in Tanzania, his presidential aircraft was struck by a surface to air missile, as it was preparing to land at Kigali airport. Just who was responsible for the missile strike remains a mystery to this day: the two main and opposing suspects are the president's violently anti-Tutsi Hutu enemies and members of the invading RPF.

What followed the missile strike was no mystery, namely the murder of almost the entire Tutsi population of Rwanda. What happened often gets presented as a centrally organized exercise of government power. Even before President Habyarimana's assassination, plans for mass murder were underway, including shipments of hundreds of thousands of machetes, ordered by the government. Following the president's assassination, immediately blamed on the RPF, *Radio Milles Collines*, the Kigali radio station under the control of Hutu militants, broadcast repeated calls for the extermination of the *Inyenzi*, or cockroaches, as they derisively described the Tutsi. Government troops, backed by the Interahamwe, the militia of the MDNR, then carried out this mass murder. While this account may have some validity in the war zone of Northern Rwanda, or in the capital city, most of the Tutsi lived in the south of the country, where circumstances were different.

In the south, the war was distant and there were few troops. The area was a stronghold of the MDR, Habyarimana's Hutu opponents. Far from being planned by the government, the killings of the Tutsis were part of a rejection of the government and its authority. Local and regional officials, prefects and burgomasters, often opposed to anti-Tutsi violence, were either intimidated or driven from office by demonstrators, spurred on by the MDR or acting spontaneously. Mobs threatened Tutsis and, especially in rural areas, seized their cattle, slaughtered the cows and, in a festive atmosphere, publicly devoured them, showing how old grievances between herders and farmers could be kept alive by political agitation. These actions quickly segued into violent attacks against Tutsis, who fled to churches, hoping for sanctuary as in the violence of the early 1960s. This time, the crowds no longer respected the sacred premises, and many of the Hutu clergy were only too happy to condone the increasingly murderous assaults, or even to join in them.

Victims trying to flee were found and tracked down by members of the general population, ranging from children to grandparents. Hutu refugees from the Tutsi-dominated government of neighboring Burundi seized Rwandan Tutsis trying to reach safety there. Often neighbors and other personal acquaintances were involved in finding and identifying people fleeing or hiding. Especially when individuals did not look like stereotypical Tutsi, their acquaintances would inform on them. The very existence of such informants was a testimony to the invented nature of "racial" differences between Tutsis and Hutus.

Some 3,500 Tutsis from Gkongo Prefecture engineered a mass escape. Gathering in three large groups, each led and followed by a line of adult men armed with machetes, clubs and bows and arrows, with women, children and livestock in the middle, they marched to the border with Burundi, running down any Hutus in their path. The following day soldiers arrived from the capital, their firearms preventing any further group escapes, facilitating the massacres rather than directly perpetrating them.

At the time of President Habyarimana's assassination, there was a small UN peacekeeping force in Rwanda as part of the Arusha accords. Its commanders were well aware that they could not prevent the incipient mass murders, so the question for the UN was whether to reinforce the peacekeepers or withdraw them; the latter option was the virtually unanimous decision. The government of the United States, which had sponsored the Arusha negotiations, and pressured the Rwandan government to end its authoritarian regime, similarly to the Europeans in the former Yugoslavia, unintentionally created circumstances in which mass murder was possible. And also like the Europeans, they responded to the outbreak of mass murder by doing nothing—a popular policy facilitated by the failure of the American intervention in the Somalian civil war of the previous year. Leftists, who condemned the United States for its previous interventions and would do so for its interventions in Yugoslavia, denounced the United States for not intervening in Rwanda.[23] The French government, with a long history of military interventions in Africa, supported the pro-Hutu regime in Kigali, as a way of maintaining French influence against that of the United States, a piece of post-Cold War power politics. The only country calling for military intervention was the former colonial power, Belgium, a position discredited by the country's past rule in central Africa which had been even by the standards of imperialism, particularly brutal and murderous.

In the end, it was the RPF—armed, outfitted, and supported by Uganda—that overthrew the Rwandan government and ended the three months of killing. Hundreds of thousands of Hutus, fearing retribution, fled to neighboring Congo, where they have remained a permanent element of political and military destabilization. Their fears are understandable, because the Hutus had not left many Tutsis alive. On the order of three-quarters of them had been killed—a thoroughness in mass murder within the dimensions of the Nazis' killing of the Jews of Europe. Overall between eight hundred thousand and one million people (neither the number of victims nor the Tutsi population of Rwanda have been reliably established) were killed in a country of seven million inhabitants. In the post-1945 mass murders, this puts the proportion killed second only to Cambodia. An international criminal tribunal for Rwanda has tried some seventy-five leading perpetrators, and more have come before Rwandan courts, in a country still ruled by the

RPF. But in a mass killing with mass participation, a broader reckoning seems impossible, short of punishing the vast majority of the population.

In spite of the good intentions on display after 1945, the second half of the twentieth century did not mark a break with the killings of the Age of Total War. Murders were perpetrated by both sides in the Cold War and after the Cold War came to an end. If anything, for all their problems, the postwar attempts to bring to justice the perpetrators of mass murder committed by the Second World War's Axis powers were a high point in holding to account individuals responsible for regime criminality. Justice for perpetrators of mass murder in the century's second half has been either nonexistent or has come after lengthy and painful delays.

The mass murders of the 1950s, 1960s, and 1970s showed distinct continuities with the Age of Total War. Killings had a strongly ideological inflection. Some emerged from efforts to create at high speed a communist society—mainly variants on the first mass murders in that direction, carried out under Stalin's rule in the 1930s. Others were anti-communist, a larger-scale and more-violent repetition of efforts to destroy a revolutionary movement first tried out by Italian fascists, German Nazis, and Chinese Nationalists in the 1920s and 1930s. All had substantial elements of central direction and control by the government, the armed forces, and the security services. There was a degree of popular participation, particularly in the anti-communist killings in Indonesia, but the leading role of the government was never in doubt.

The mass murders of the 1990s and their successors in the twenty-first century tended to lack both the strongly ideologized character and the central direction of their predecessors. Carried out by weaker states, they involved a large element of popular participation, whether in the form of militias or hate-filled mobs. The killings of the 1990s were purportedly inspired by strong racial and ethnic differences—albeit ones that had largely been invented and foisted on populations, such as by Serbian intellectuals and politicians or Christian missionaries and colonial administrators.

The fundamental problems of state sovereignty and regime criminality first emerging in the trials of leaders of the Axis powers after 1945 have never been resolved. The only way to stop mass murder has been to use armed force, or, on rare occasions, economic and diplomatic pressure: the outcome of the Second World War; the Indian army helping to liberate Bangladesh from Pakistan; the invasion of Cambodia by Vietnamese troops or of Rwanda by the Ugandan-backed RPF; the US/NATO bombing of the Serbs in the former Yugoslavia. As the examples of the safe havens in Bosnia, or Rwanda demonstrate, UN peacekeepers, lacking great power support, have tended to be worse than nothing. In 1999, when the government of Indonesia very reluctantly agreed to allow its territory of East Timor a referendum on independence, commanders of Indonesian troops and pro-Indonesian militias in the territory, largely leftovers from the regime of the anti-communist generals, openly terrorized the population, killing proponents of independence. The UN peacekeepers stationed there responded to this incipient mass murder by making plans to withdraw; it took the substantial pressure of the great powers, especially an initially very reluctant United States, on the newly democratically elected government of Indonesia to get it to clamp down on these actions and to allow the referendum, which produced a large majority for independence.[24]

As Radhabinod Pal first pointed out in 1947, military actions (or, in rarer cases, economic and diplomatic pressure) to stop mass killings are forms of imperialism—open interference in one state's sovereignty by another, more powerful one. When there was no possibility of military intervention, as was the case with killings in Indonesia and China, there was no possibility of holding anyone to account. The international tribunals for the former Yugoslavia, Cambodia, and Rwanda have only been able to sit in judgment on individuals charged with mass murder because the governments in which those individuals had central roles suffered military defeat and were open to diplomatic and economic pressure.

The early decades of the twenty-first century have been characterized by a continuation of this state of affairs. Large-scale killings and expulsions in the Darfur region of Western Sudan have been discouragingly similar to the mass murders of the 1990s: a weak central government, unable to control an outlying region arming private militias, the *Janjawid*, whose members were made up of pastoralists from the Saheel region south of the Sahara, involved in long-standing conflicts with farmers from Darfur. Supposedly, the militias were Arabs and the farmers Africans. However, these racial and ethnic antagonisms were largely invented by Libya's Colonel Qaddafi and Islamist politicians in the 1980s. The militias engaged in large-scale campaigns of killing and expelling civilians. UN peacekeepers were unable to keep the peace, and one internationally mediated ceasefire followed another. While the UN officially declared the campaigns in Darfur genocide and Sudan's president Omar al-Bashir was indicted by the International Criminal court, he refused to recognize the court's authority and was widely celebrated in Africa and among Islamic countries as an anti-imperialist hero.[25]

Other instances could be cited as well—large-scale murders of civilians and even larger mass expulsions carried out by both the Syrian government, with the assistance of its Iranian and Russian allies and that government's Islamist enemies, following 2011, or the persecution and expulsion of the Rohingya, a Muslim ethnic minority on the part of the government of Myanmar after 2017. The 1990s experience of post-Cold War mass murders, carried out with impunity; the impotence of international organizations and the cynical attitudes of the world's powerful nations, who perhaps could stop the killing but, out of popular indifference and raison d'état, refused to do so; the widespread denunciation of even the feeblest attempts in that direction as imperialism; even the cynical assertion that the victims staged their own killing: all these trends are continuing in force in the new millennium.

13 | Utopias

It had been the greatest war in human history. Fought with terrifying new weapons, ending with the deployment of unparalleled destructive power, characterized by relentless slaughter, within and outside the laws of war, it had left behind tens of millions dead; tens of millions more in flight, social, and economic upheaval across Eurasia; chaotic changes of regime or at least political turmoil, touching virtually every point on the globe. These were apocalyptic circumstances and it is no surprise that the end of the Second World War was accompanied by expectations of the imminent arrival of a new world along with fears of a terrible future, should that new world not come into existence.

These postwar expectations were the first of three waves of worldwide utopian aspirations that characterized the second half of the twentieth century, the other two arriving in the 1960s and the 1990s, respectively. As has been the case with such aspirations throughout human history, the hoped-for—or feared—onset of a fundamentally new era never came to pass. Each wave of utopian expectations ended in disillusion. Yet failed or not, these utopian projects were a crucial part of the three most turbulent years of the Age of Interconnection: 1945, 1968, and 1989. Their legacy, in ideas and institutions, remains perceptible down to the present day.

Apocalypse Denied

> The sun and the stars are all ringing
> With song rising strong from the earth,
> The hope of humanity singing,

A hymn to a new world in birth!

Chorus: United Nations on the march, with flags unfurled,
Together fight for victory
A free new world.

Take heart all you nations swept under
By powers of darkness that ride,
The wrath of the people shall thunder,
Relentless as time and the tide!

As sure as the sun meets the morning
And rivers go down to the sea,
A new day for mankind is dawning,
Our children shall live proud and free!

Written by Harold Rome to music of Dmitri Shostakovich, the "March of the United Nations" was the climax of a 1943 wartime morale-boosting MGM movie musical, *Thousands Cheer*. A version was recorded a year later, by the African American singer Paul Robeson, whose allegiances spanned the United States and Soviet Union, so the song had an endorsement, one might say, from both capitalists and communists. The "March of the United Nations" was sung, among other places, in the United States, the Philippines, and India, throughout the postwar decades, even as late as the 1980s. Originally referring to the Second World War's Allied powers—whose official name was the "United Nations"—the song was quickly transferred to the international organization named after that alliance.[1]

There were three major elements to that postwar "free new world." One was global governance, the great expectations placed in the United Nations. It is hard to remember now just how exciting and popular that new organization and the idea of global cooperation appeared. Six of the largest American cities put in bids to be the site of the UN headquarters, as did quite a number of other places, including municipalities in the Black Hills of South Dakota, Niagara Falls, New York, and the territory of Hawaii. Eighty-one percent of the American public, according to Gallup polling of April 1945, supported joining "a world organization with police power to maintain world peace." A majority even felt that the new organization should have the power to control the armed forces of all nations, including the United States. As late as 1949, when the emerging Cold War was undermining hopes for global governance, the governors of nine states and the mayors of fifty cities proclaimed a "World Government Week," and twenty state legislatures passed resolutions endorsing world government. In June of that year, ninety-one members of the House of Representatives drafted a resolution declaring world government the "fundamental objective" of US foreign policy and stating that the UN should be developed into such a body, with military powers to deter aggression. Sponsors of the resolution included two future presidents, John F. Kennedy and Gerald Ford. The UN was, in fact, originally designed to have just such military powers, since Articles 45–47 of the UN Charta called for the creation of a Military Staff Committee, which would have at its disposal forward air bases for a quick response to armed aggression.[2]

An architect of the United Nations and a veteran of the creation of its predecessor, the League of Nations, was Jan Smuts, the prime minister of South Africa. At the founding conference of the UN, held in San Francisco in the spring of 1945, he inspired the assembled delegates, asserting that "Mankind has arrived at the crisis of its fate . . . of its future as a civilized world." It would take the creation of the United Nations to seal the antifascist victories of the Second World War, to put a "halt to the pilgrimage of death," and to create a world characterized by "faith in justice and the resolve to vindicate the fundamental rights of man." Although an opponent of the Afrikaner advocates of extreme racial segregation, *Apartheid*, Smuts had no doubt that the new postwar world of justice and human rights would include a greater South Africa, extending in a large arc across the south of the continent, whose white population would rule over what he regarded as the racially inferior Africans.[3]

Six months after the assembled delegates met in San Francisco, six thousand miles away in Manchester, the fifth world Pan-African Congress was called to order. Its participants demanded an end to imperialist rule and denounced racism and racial domination. But they, too, were enthusiasts for an unprecedented global governance. The Congress issued a demand "for Black African autonomy and independence, so far and no further than it is possible in this 'One World' for groups and people to rule themselves subject to inevitable world unity and federation." In Asia, anti-imperialist leaders Mohandas Gandhi and Jawaharlal Nehru joined in the chorus of proponents of world government.[4]

The power politics involved in the founding of the UN, the drafting of its Charter, and the formation of its institutions made these hopes seem foolish. There were strong differences of opinion—between the future Cold War antagonists the United States and the USSR threatening to torpedo the whole project; insistence of the British and other colonial powers that their empires be kept far away from any UN jurisdiction; the creation of a powerful Security Council, whose five permanent members had far more influence than any of the other of the world's states; and the widespread reluctance of statesmen and politicians among the powers, great and small, to surrender any of their countries' sovereignty. Yet even contemporaries who recognized the problematic features of the nascent UN did not reject the ideals of global governance. In a polemic he delivered in the fall of 1945,

"Neither Victims nor Executioners," French writer, philosopher, and future Nobel Prize laureate, Albert Camus, made this point. He condemned the UN as a "reinforcement of great power sovereignty at the expense of the sovereignty of smaller nations." His response was nonetheless not to strengthen the latter's sovereignty; rather, he called for a "new order" not either "national or even continental," let alone "Eastern or Western." "It has to be universal." Demanding an elected world parliament, explicitly including representatives of the colonized peoples of Africa and Asia, Camus admitted that his was a utopian proposal. However, he insisted that the choice was between "anachronistic political thinking and utopian thinking."[5]

The polemic appeared in the daily newspaper Camus was editing at the time, *Combat*, originally an underground, resistance periodical in Nazi-occupied France. The venue is significant, because it points to the second element of utopian aspirations at the end of the Second World War, also present in the "March of the United Nations." This was a postwar world of emancipation that would emerge from resistance to the aggression and oppression of the Axis Powers: not only the punishment of the guilty—although that, surely enough—but recognition of the honor of the wartime resistors, and a new social and economic regime of justice and equity. The Charter of the National Council of Resistance, issued in March 1944, when France was still under German occupation, did not simply call for the expulsion of the foreign occupiers, the punishment of traitors and collaborators, the establishment of popular democracy and civil liberties—and not only for metropolitan France but for France's colonial subjects as well. It also demanded a "new republic," in which centers of economic power would be nationalized, cooperatives and trade unions supported, encouraged, and empowered, as well as a regime of expanded and intensive social welfare to ensure all elements of the French nation (and, once again, France's colonial subjects) a just and secure future. In a similar if more exalted vein was the statement of a resistance newspaper in Savoy, in southeastern France, six months later, as the country was in the process of being liberated. The maquisards had sacrificed themselves for a "harmonious wonderful future . . . a free France in a fraternal world."[6]

Certainly florid, as in French rhetorical practice, the statement connects the Second World War struggle against fascism with a radiant future—implicitly, with global governance—in a "fraternal world."

These expectations were widespread in a Europe liberated from Nazi rule. In Northern and Central Italy, anti-fascist resistance groups formed fifteen "partisan republics," where inhabitants of towns and villages practiced direct democracy. In the partisan republic of Val d'Ossola, near Milan, which briefly obtained diplomatic recognition from Switzerland, a woman was appointed as a government minister, a first for a country in which women did not yet have the vote. In hundreds of villages of the country's impoverished south, peasants proclaimed republics, raised the red flag, redistributed the land, formed people's armies and people's courts, and banned crucifixes and pictures of the royal family. Both Pope Pius XII and King Vittorio Emanuele III had been badly compromised by their acquiescence in the fascist policies and failed war of dictator Benito Mussolini. The Nazi regime's grip on its population was considerably tighter. They were able to suppress any forms of political alternatives until their complete military defeat. Nonetheless by May 1945 Saxony was beginning to look like Calabria, as communist activists raised the red flag, collectivized agriculture, and formed soviets. In the town of Pirna, upstream on the Elbe River from Dresden, they moved the weekly day of rest from Sunday to Friday and informed the inhabitants that they were no longer to greet each other with "good day," but with "Red Front." All these actions were local and spontaneous, unsponsored by the occupying Red Army, and rather to its officers' bemusement.[7]

Pirna may have been an extreme case. Still, throughout liberated Europe similar aspirations for an idealized future, one institutionalizing resistance to fascism, were the order of the day. The belief that such a future was connected to the end of capitalism was widespread in the anti-Nazi resistance, and by no means limited to communists. The leader of the Catholic Green Flame partisans in Italy presented anti-capitalism in apocalyptic language, stating that "the age of capitalism that has produced astronomical wealth and led to unspeakable misery is in its death throes . . . burnt itself out in the flames of war." A new era—"infinitely more just, more fraternal and more Christian"—was "being born."[8]

Resistance to and liberation from fascism had been a shot in the arm to a global communist movement badly damaged by fascist persecution and tarnished by the USSR's flirtation with fascism in the wake of the Nazi—Soviet Pact. There were somewhere around one million communists in Europe outside the USSR at the beginning of the Second World War; by war's end their number had multiplied sixfold. Membership growth in Greece and Italy, where communists had played leading roles in resistance to German occupation, were far more pronounced: from 6,000 in 1939 in both countries to 350,000 in the former and 1.8 million in the latter by 1945. In the two Western European countries with the strongest communist parties, France and Italy, this surge in membership during liberation kept the parties going for the next three decades. By war's end, membership of the Chinese Communist Party had grown to over one million. In fact, 1945 marked the first time that communist party members in the USSR were outnumbered by comrades in the rest of the world.[9]

This surge in party membership doubtless had many causes, including admiration for the USSR's role in defeating the Nazis, or the desire to accommodate to potential future rulers (particularly in Eastern Europe, where the Red Army was physically present). However, it was also one of the large-scale manifestations of utopian aspirations after the war. Ironically, it was less connected to the actual policies of the global communist movement itself. Steered by Stalin on a very cautious course, the movement rejected large-scale change and sought political compromise, or, especially in Eastern Europe, counted on the coercive power of the occupying Red Army and the actions of the security apparatus, rather than revolutionary aspirations.[10]

The third of the post-1945 apocalyptic aspirations was the expectation of an imminent end to imperialism and colonial rule. The world's great colonial powers had suffered humiliating military defeats during the war and had emerged from the conflict in a weakened condition, with severe constraints on the financial freedom of action needed to uphold their empires. The prospect of an end to the largest empires in human history was momentous enough. Even more, just as the hopes emerging from the resistance were not limited to an end to foreign occupation, but included the creation of a new society, so, too, did anti-imperialists envisage postcolonial realms as inaugurating a new stage in history Of all the post-1945 aspirations, this one would prove the longest lasting.

As the British Empire in Southeast Asia crumpled under Japanese assault in the initial years of the war, the aspiration for independence in India grew steadily stronger. The anti-imperialist Congress Party responded with its "Quit India" campaign for immediate independence, hoping to rescue India from a collapsing colonial rule before the Japanese army arrived. The officials of the Raj—as British rule was called—responded by arresting Congress leaders. A large, if uncoordinated uprising followed, with strikes, sabotage of war production, disruption of rail and telegraph lines, and attacks on the police; British authority disintegrated in different places for weeks at a time. Ultimately, by shooting thousands of insurgents, Raj authorities were able to reassert their control.

A major figure of the Congress Party in Bengal, Subhas Chandra Bose—little-known in Western countries today, although as important as Nehru, Gandhi, the Muslim League president Muhammad Ali Jinnah or the Dalits' (Untouchables') leader Bhimrao Ambedkar—took the step others were reluctant to do, and explicitly joined the cause of Indian independence to the Axis Powers. Traveling from Berlin to Tokyo via a German U-Boat and Japanese aircraft, he organized the Provisional Government of Azad Hind, or Free India, in Japanese-occupied Singapore and recruited Indians, especially POWs, into an Indian National Army, to advance on Delhi with Japanese troops. Bose's radio broadcasts to an Indian audience proclaimed that liberation from imperialist rule was coming. Not entirely trusting their allies, when the Japanese actually did invade India in the spring of 1944, they allowed just a few INA soldiers to take part in the campaign. The invaders were defeated at the battles of Imphal and Kohima by British troops, mostly Indians fighting for the empire. Bose himself died in a plane crash at the end of the war.

Returning to India after a brief internment, the veterans of the INA received a riotous welcome, with parades, speeches, and garlands, and not just in larger cities, but deep into the countryside. The embarrassed imperial government put three of the army's generals—as it happens, a Hindu, Muslim, and Sikh—on trial in the Red Fort, the fortress in the heart of Delhi. Defended by India's top legal talent, including Congress leader Jawaharlal Nehru, himself just recently released from prison, all three were acquitted. Leaving the courtroom, they were met by a jubilant crowd, carried on their shoulders in a spontaneous parade before hundreds of thousands of spectators. These scenes were repeated in cities across India. In Bose's native city of Calcutta, pro-INA demonstrations took on a particularly sharp edge, including street fighting against British troops. On Indian Independence Day, August 15, 1947, enormous crowds thronged Calcutta's streets chanting the INA slogan, *Jai Hind* ("victory to India"). Hindus and Muslims embraced in public and some two hundred thousand people crowded the Governor's House, taking possession of a symbol of now-vanquished imperial rule— as well as making off with the furnishings. For a few brief moments, the powerful religious hostilities that would shape India's independence were suspended; the transition from opposition to an imperialist past to a glorious, self-determined future seemed secured.[11]

In spite of the hostilities that were building, the hopes connected to a postcolonial future did not entirely fade. During debates in the Indian constituent national assembly, whose very existence was a product of the separation of Indian and Pakistan, S. Radhakrishnan, a prominent Congress Party member and close associate of Nehru, praised him as a "world citizen." The efforts of India's provisional government to assist the Indonesian anti-imperialists in gaining their independence, Radhakrishnan continued, proved that "if India gains freedom [his speech was on August 14, 1947, one day before the formal attainment of independence from British imperial rule] that freedom will be used not merely for the well-being of India but for *Vishva Kalyan*, i.e., world peace, the welfare of mankind." The assembled delegates' applause was thunderous.[12]

The same linkage of liberation from individual imperialist rule to *Vishva Kalyan* was very much a feature of Pan-Africanism and African anti-imperialism. Aimé Césaire, the poet and communist political activist from Martinique, key figure in the formulation of the concept of *Négritude*, a global Pan-Africanist affirmation, declared in his 1950 *Discourse on Colonialism*, that they would join with their "brother slaves," meaning pro-communist workers in Europe, "to create a new society, rich with modern productive power and warm with ancient fraternity."[13]

In 1946, Césaire's fellow proponent of *Négritude* Léopold Senghor, who would become the first president of an independent Senegal, spoke of "a new civilization, whose center will be in Paris, a new humanism . . . on the scale of the universe and of humanity." Continuing on the theme of the transition from anti-fascism to a utopian future, this would require freeing themselves of "all of the seeds of imperialism that, at our invitation, Nazism planted within us." The new world would take the form of an "equal Union of French Socialist Republics." Eight years later, increasingly frustrated by the gap between the rhetoric of transformation and the reality of continued colonial rule, Senghor asserted that "if France continues with this blindness," the result would be apocalyptic. Not just the "fall of France" but "to the destruction of the planet and the end of the hope for man."[14]

Césaire's and Senghor's vision of a post-imperial world involved a practical willingness to compromise with the French government; they were condemned by more militant anti-imperialists. Sékou Touré, first president of an independent Guinea—a country achieving its independence in opposition to the French government rather than in cooperation with it, as was the case in Senegal—and the revolutionary activist Frantz Fanon denounced Senghor as a lackey of imperialism. But for all their political differences, the militants shared with the moderates a utopian view of a post-imperial future. Fanon condemned the idea of modeling independent new states on Europe as a "grotesque and generally obscene emulation." Rather, they had to "make a new start, develop a new way of thinking and endeavor to create a new man."[15]

Anti-imperialists and Pan-Africanists in the Anglophone world were less willing to cooperate than their French-speaking counterparts. But their view of a postcolonial future was no less emphatic. The 1945 Manchester Pan-African Congress declared that freedom from imperialist domination was necessary "to express our thoughts and emotions to adopt and create forms of beauty." The celebration of the independence of Ghana, in March 1957, the first sub-Saharan country to be liberated from imperialist rule—attended by US civil rights leaders Martin Luther King, Jr., and A. Philip Randolph; civil rights leader and diplomat Ralph Bunche; as well as by activists Julius Nyerere and George Padmore; and the prominent development economist from St. Lucia, W. Arthur Lewis—was a moment of realization of English-speaking Pan-Africanists' globalized anti-imperialist aspirations.

Anti-imperialism would involve a transformation of a centuries-old international order of racism, European domination, and slavery. Pan-Africanists led the fight for national self-determination as a basic human right that, at the insistence of the representatives of European imperialists, had not been included in the UN's 1948 Universal Declaration of Human Rights. In 1960, with the passage of UN General Assembly resolution 1514, the Declaration on the Granting of Independence to Colonial Countries and Peoples, which included national self-determination of the colonized as an "inviolable right to complete freedom," they achieved their goal. In all these respects, the aspiration to a post-imperialist and fundamentally new and improved world was the most enduring of the visions circulating at the end of the Second World War.[16]

An apocalypse involves the hope of a transformed, radiant future world, but it also contains the fear of a nightmare future of horror, destruction, and death. Symbolized by the four horsemen of the biblical Book of Revelations, in the post-1945 decades those horsemen had been combined into one overarching, imminent nightmare, itself a result of the Second World War, the prospect of the use of nuclear weapons. The day after the dropping of the atomic bomb on Hiroshima, the Vatican's newspaper, the *Osservatore Romano*, noted, "The last twilight of the war is colored by mortal flames never before seen on the horizons of the universe, from its heavenly dawn to this infernal era. This war gives us a catastrophic conclusion that seems not to put an end to its apocalyptic surprises."[17]

Even in a triumphal United States, the atomic bombings of Japan created a mood of apprehension. *Time* magazine described the end of the war "as the most grimly Pyrrhic of victories." Radio commentator H. V. Kaltenborn argued, "We must assume that with the passage of only a little time, an improved form of the weapon we use today can be turned against us." The *St. Louis Post Dispatch* asserted that science has "signed the mammalian world's death warrant, and deeded an earth in ruins to the ants." Fears that the end of the war was only the overture to nuclear annihilation were widespread. Between 1945 and 1950, newspapers, magazines, pamphlets, bestselling books, even Hollywood films repeatedly depicted America in the ruins of a nuclear war. Fears and hopes overlapped, as it seemed that the only way out of this new, nuclear era was a global government. *One World or None*, the title of a 1946 pamphlet of the Federation of American Scientists, sold more than one hundred thousand copies within weeks of publication.[18]

To a greater or lesser extent, these attitudes were present all around the world other than in the USSR and the newly emergent communist regimes. In 1946, Mao Zedong, called the atomic bomb "a paper tiger which the US reactionaries use to scare people." Whether those living under a communist regime shared that attitude is hard to tell, in view of the regimes' domination of the public sphere, but communist governments exploited fears by launching the 1950 Stockholm Peace Appeal, a Cold War political initiative calling for the prohibition of atomic weapons. The propaganda effect of the initiative tended to be undermined by its proponents' habit of insisting that Soviet atomic weapons were peaceful while American ones were warlike.[19]

Throughout the 1950s, fears of atomic war continued, sometimes simmering beneath the surface, sometimes emerging. These fears found a new focus after fallout from the 1954 US H-bomb test reached the crew of the Japanese fishing boat the *Lucky Dragon*, sending them to the hospital and ultimately killing one of the fishermen. Fear of fallout was an impetus for the "ban the bomb" disarmament campaigns of the later 1950s and early 1960s.

Like the early fears of nuclear war, while prevalent across the world they were centered primarily in English-speaking countries. A new feature was widespread opposition to nuclear weapons in Germany and Japan, leading to large-scale antigovernment demonstrations in a time when both countries were ruled by conservative parties. (Interestingly, concerns about fallout and not the bombing of Hiroshima and Nagasaki sparked opposition to nuclear weapons in Japan.) Official attempts were made to calm fears, by instituting a "civil defense" program. American proponents claimed simple measures, likes the advice to "duck and cover," when a nuclear bomb blast occurred, would make it easy for the country's citizens to survive an attack with nuclear weapons. Behind the scenes, everyone in government admitted that these measures were worthless in case of a thermonuclear war, but they thought it might lead to public support of a policy of nuclear deterrence. In effect, civil defense, was a kind of security theater, playing to a dubious audience.[20]

In the late 1950s and early 1960s, the governments of the United States and the USSR were both conducting hundreds of tests of nuclear weapons. Supposedly, this was all in the service of deterrence, of preventing the use of nuclear weapons by showing the ability to launch a devastating counterattack to a nuclear assault. Actual policies seemed to be moving beyond deterrence toward confrontation, at first in the Berlin Crisis of 1958–61, then fourteen months later during the Cuban Missile Crisis. For ten days in October 1962, an apocalyptic thermonuclear war really did seem imminent.

PROPHETS OF DISILLUSION

Two of the global hopes emerging from the Second World War faded quickly. Global governance gave way to global hostilities. The UN became one of a number of venues for Cold War diplomatic confrontations between the United States and the USSR. As countries in Asia and Africa gained their independence from colonial rule, they used the UN's General Assembly— in which each country had one vote and there was no veto power—to confront their former colonial overlords and countries affiliated with them. The Military Staff Committee retained at best a paper existence, and the veto power of the five permanent members of the Security Council foiled any attempts to use the organization to preserve the peace. The one exception that proves the rule, the UN endorsement of the American intervention in the Korean War, occurred because the USSR was boycotting the Security Council over its refusal to turn over China's seat in it from the anti-communist *Guomindang*, in exile on the island of Taiwan, to the new communist regime in China. It was a mistake the USSR would not repeat.[21]

The immediate postwar hopes for global governance left some traces. As late as 1957, about 40 percent of Americans polled continued to endorse the idea of the UN as a world government with control over every country's armed forces. Generally favorable attitudes toward the UN as an institution continued in American public opinion until the 1970s—admittedly, this was when the United States and its allies lost control of the General Assembly. These favorable attitudes can be found in most countries today.[22]

By contrast, the aspiration toward a new society emerging from the resistance to fascist occupation came to an end much more rapidly and left fewer traces.

One factor was disappointment at attempts to punish traitors and collaborators. It seemed that while small fry were punished, the big fish went free. Condemnation and acquittal were less dependent on actual guilt than on political pressure. Few were brought to account or actually punished, and those convicted were quickly amnestied and released. As was the case with the efforts to punish war criminals and perpetrators of crimes against humanity, the need for reliable allies in the emerging Cold War brought the efforts at justice and retribution to an end, allowing the guilty to return to public life by the 1950s.

Aspirations toward a just society were even more evanescent. The persistence and even expansion of wartime shortages of basic commodities, accompanied by a pervasive black market, made a mockery of them. Standards of living rose during the 1950s, at least in the North Atlantic world. Instead of a new social order, this brought a continuation of the trend toward a consumer society: not transformative change, but more washing machines and TVs. Privatized consumption replaced public participation in a just society.[23]

At least in Western Europe, the post-fascist political scene was characterized by the return of politicians and political institutions from the interwar era, incorporating former fascists, as well as their sympathizers and collaborators. Political movements representing radicalized postwar aspirations were defeated. Sometimes this occurred violently, as was the case in Greece. The communist-led insurgency there, stemming from the wartime resistance, was suppressed by a government whose police and military were well-staffed with former collaborators of the German occupiers, and in receipt of generous US assistance, something the Greek insurgents did not receive from Stalin or Tito. In Italy, the climactic electoral confrontation of 1948 resulted in the defeat of the communists and victory of the Christian Democrats, also supported by the United States and incorporating in their ranks many former adherents of Mussolini. Such Christian Democratic political parties, moderately conservative if modernizing, would play a dominant role in the politics of Western Europe, during the 1950s. In the communist-dominated lands of Eastern Eurasia, there had been a revolution, but the upshot was out of synch with the aspirations: at first a Stalinist dictatorship making preparations for a third world war, and then a bureaucratic-authoritarian regime.[24]

As we've seen, hopes of a post-imperialist new world lasted longer and sometimes segued into the next wave of global utopianism in the 1960s. Even there, Pan-Arabism or Pan-Africanism faded, and independence from colonial rule brought nation-states that were far from being models of a new stage in human history.[25] Recurring apprehensions about the prospect of a thermonuclear war continued through the 1980s. Still, the peaceful outcome of the 1962 Cuban Missile Crisis and the gradual onset of negotiations leading to treaties limiting nuclear testing, the stationing of atomic weapons in outer space, and the deployment of strategically destabilizing forms of nuclear weapons showed that an atomic apocalypse was not inevitable. It was not, as stated in the postwar era, "one world or none." Instead, preventing nuclear war was possible through the process of diplomacy among sovereign states, and did not require a new and fundamentally transformed global order.

So the postwar apocalyptic global transformation was denied, a denial evoked in three books of the era: George Orwell's *1984*; *The New Class*, by Milovan Djilas; and Frantz Fanon's *The Wretched of the Earth*. All three were works impelled by disillusionment, about the failures of the great hopes emerging from the Second World War. Orwell's focused on and showcased disillusionment; Djilas's showed how the seeds of disillusionment were contained in the hopes that created them; and Fanon's clung to a belief that hope would have the last word.

Orwell's *1984* takes place against the backdrop of the great fear of the postwar era—a third world war fought with nuclear weapons, described as the "atomic wars" of the 1950s. Unlike so many fictional works about nuclear warfare, Orwell's atomic wars brought no apocalypse. The London Winston Smith traverses in the novel has no bomb damage, radiation, or signs of reconstruction. People live in "patched up nineteenth century houses," and commute to work on an overcrowded Tube, very much like the 1930s. Instead, the atomic wars have led to social upheaval and civil war, described in the book as "confused street fighting in London itself," and the creation of a revolutionary regime.

At one point in his life, Orwell had believed in a revolutionary change, as reflected in *Homage to Catalonia*, his portrait of anarchist and socialist-dominated Barcelona of the Spanish Civil War. Even during the Second World War, he imagined a fundamentally better postwar world. Written in 1947, *1984* shows how soon those hopes had vanished. Humanity is stuck forever in the Age of Total War, with the three Great Powers, Oceania, Eurasia, and Eastasia, vying for ascendancy. Wartime rationing and wartime shortages are endless; the Ministry of Truth, where Smith works, feeds the public a steady stream of disinformation about the battlefields as well as conditions on the home front. V-2 rockets—with conventional explosives, not atomic ones—rain down at seemingly random intervals. As in the aftermath of the Second World War, war criminals are brought to trial and executed, but aspirations for a new era of justice have been replaced by political cynicism. The great rally, in which it is announced that Oceania is really at war with Eastasia and not Eurasia—a reference to the reversal of alliances brought on by the 1939 Nazi-Soviet Pact—was supposed to end with the public hanging of two thousand Eurasian war criminals. This is called off since Eurasia has become an ally.

1984 is a reckoning with all the victors of the Second World War. The currency of Oceania is the dollar; England has been renamed "Airstrip One," a reference to the way it was overrun with US and Canadian airmen and soldiers, preparing to invade the European continent. The working class reads sensationalist, apolitical tabloid newspapers, shops at market stalls, drinks beer in pubs, and is obsessed with playing the lottery. This is all very British and unlike circumstances in high-Stalinist regimes. Yet Oceania, like all three of *1984*'s Great Powers, is a totalitarian regime, with a single political party, a Stalin-like omnipotent leader, "Big Brother." There are constant purges, show trials with dramatic confessions of the accused, and an endless hunt for political enemies, real, or, mostly, imagined and even manufactured. There is no escape from this world: in an oft-quoted phrase, O'Brien tells Winston Smith as he tortures him, that the future is "a boot stamping on a human face—forever."[26] Written only two years after the war's end, the book is a testament to the rapid termination of the great hopes stemming from the Second World War, even a denial that those hopes had ever been possible.

In *1984*, Orwell condemned all the Second World War's Great Powers, but in his imagined future they had all become regimes with strong Stalinist features. This had the unintended effect of vitiating the book's extreme disillusion. Instead, the work became seen as a denunciation of communism during the Cold War, itself the disappointing outcome of the Second World War but not a world of terminal disillusion. Both hope and disillusionment, come into clearer focus in Milovan Djilas's sociology of communism, *The New Class*.

A close associate of Yugoslav communist leader Josip Broz Tito, Djilas played a leading role in the large and militant communist-led Resistance in Nazi-occupied Yugoslavia during the war and in postwar Yugoslavia served briefly as president of the federal parliament in 1953–54. Already disillusioned with communist rule by that time, he publicly broke with the party, was expelled from it, spent time in jail, and, until his death in 1995, was a political dissident, arguably the first in post-1945 communist regimes. Published abroad in 1957, *The New Class* has become a sociological classic.

The book takes up the idea, first propounded in the 1930s by Stalin's adversary, Leon Trotsky, that after destroying a capitalist class society, communist regimes both created and brought to power a new ruling class—party bureaucrats. In Marxist terms, they controlled the means of production, exploiting and dominating subordinate classes, particularly the workers, in whose name communism claimed to rule. In addition to using past critiques the book anticipates future developments, including the increasing importance of nationalism to communist governments, the way in which the communist economic system would become a regime of chronic scarcity and inadequate supplies of consumer goods, and the transition from a totalitarian state dominated by a single individual to a bureaucratized despotism. The book also includes some ideas typical of the 1950s, such as the potential of atomic energy, or the connection between globalization and the growing role government will play, even in capitalist countries.

What makes the book so powerfully grim is Djilas's description of the moral evolution of communist parties from revolutionary movement to the exercise of power. His description of communist revolutionaries is rhapsodic. Communism grew out of "high moral principles" and the efforts of "devoted, enthusiastic, and clever fighters" who give it their heart and soul, acting with selfish devotion and love for the collective. Women in particular made the necessary sacrifices—"love and motherhood"—for the cause. Passion between men and women had been transformed into something "sexless," and the relationship had become one based on "loyalty, mutual aid, frankness." All this clearly draws on Djilas's own experiences as a partisan commander during the war.[27]

Clearly also drawing on his experiences in communist Yugoslavia, Djilas observes that once the revolutionaries have obtained power, things quickly become very different. Sacrifice to lofty goals becomes "intolerance, incomplete thinking, control of personal life." "The wonderful human characteristics of an isolated movement are slowly transformed into the intolerant and Pharisaical morals of a privileged caste." Once they had attained power, the heroes of the revolutionary movement were transformed into "characterless wretches and stupid defenders of arid formulas."[28] This was all a bitter reckoning with the expectations that a new world would emerge from the defeat of fascism. The comradeship of the partisans seemed already to embody a new social order and a renewed and improved humanity. When the adherents of the glorious new world came to power, the regime they created was not just dictatorial and economically inefficient, it was morally corrupt, a complete betrayal of the principles embodied in the communist-led, anti-Nazi resistance.

Like Djilas, the Martinique native Frantz Fanon played a role in the struggle against Nazism, enlisting in Charles de Gaulle's Free French forces and taking part in the liberation of Alsace in the fall of 1944. Following the Second World War, he studied medicine, becoming a psychiatrist, and, starting in 1953, worked in a hospital in Algiers. Coming into contact with the insurgents of the FLN, who demanded the liberation of Algeria from French rule, he joined their cause, so that he was a participant in both the anti-fascist and anti-imperialist political struggles. He worked for the FLN, editing its newspaper and going on diplomatic missions, until his death from leukemia in 1961. He was just thirty-six years old.

Completed at the end of his life, Fanon's *The Wretched of the Earth*, is perhaps the single most powerful assertion of the hopes connected to anti-imperialism, and also a grudging realization that those hopes might not be realized. The struggle against imperialism in Fanon's work is a process of individual self-transformation and social upheaval. The key word is "violence." Colonial rule is both inherently and explicitly violent, destroying an indigenous social order, cultural traditions, and economic forms, imposed by military conquest, enforced by police action. *The Wretched of the Earth* emphasizes the need for a violent response to imperialist aggression, a response that would bring about both a new social order and new human beings to inhabit it: "For the colonized, life can only surge forth from the decomposing corpse of the colonists." Revolutionary struggle creates a national unity: "a great violent organism rising up as reaction to the initial colonial violence. Groups [of the colonized] recognize each other and the future nation is already indivisible." All of this would, in Fanon's eyes, be psychologically transforming, a literal withdrawal process from the drugged or drunken condition of colonial subjugation. "Violence relieves the colonial subject of his inferiority complex, of his passive and despairing attitudes. It makes him courageous and rehabilitates him in his own eyes." In the process of self-liberation, the "colonized 'thing' becomes a human being."[29]

Violence was also socially transforming. Fanon was skeptical about the revolutionary capabilities of the usual anti-imperialist suspects: political parties, trade unionists, urban workers, teachers, and the urban population more generally, as well as left-wing intellectuals. They were all too willing to compromise with the colonial power, to ask for individual or group privileges. By contrast, peasants and those residing in shanty towns on the outskirts of urban areas, living from casual labor and petty criminality (Fanon described them as the *Lumpenproletariat*, reversing the valuation of an old Marxist term of denigration), would be unrestrained adherents of violent revolution. Only by working closely with these groups and following their lead would ostensible anti-imperialists in Africa be turned into genuine ones.[30]

The transformative and apocalyptic qualities of violent revolutionary activism would be apparent in the newly independent postcolonial regimes. They would, of course, reject taking sides in the Cold War, although Fanon's anti-capitalist and anti-imperialist sentiments do seem to have led him to have a more favorable—or perhaps less negative—view of communist countries. Connecting liberation from imperialism with liberation from fascism, Fanon noted explicitly that the former victims of Nazi rule had demanded reparations from the Germans, so newly independent African countries would insist on reparations from their one-time imperialist overlords, whose rule was no better than that of the fascists.[31]

At the beginning of his book, Fanon describes decolonization in literally apocalyptic terms as "the well-known phrase, 'the last shall be first.'" He notes in the conclusion that colonial liberation is not about reversing existing relations of inequality, placing Africans or Asians on top and Europeans on the bottom. Rather, it involves the rejection of the models of Europe and its own-time settler colonies like the United States, which Fanon regarded as taking European evils to "terrifying dimensions." The inhabitants of the Third World (Fanon's employment of the phrase is an early example of its use in positive, revolutionary terms) would have to create a new and superior stage of human history. "Let us decide not to imitate Europe but aim our brains and muscles in a new direction. Let us attempt to invent the total human being, whose triumph Europe was incapable of bringing about."[32]

The *Wretched of the Earth* begins with an explanation of the personal and social transformation needed to terminate imperialist rule. It ends with an affirmation of a utopian post-imperialist world, in which the emancipatory possibilities created by the end of the Second World War would finally play out in formerly colonized Africa and Asia. In between is an account of the actual governments of liberated Africa that were beginning to emerge as the FLN was still struggling for Algerian independence from France while Fanon, dying of cancer, was writing a book that was his political last will and testament.

This account emphasizes the gap between expectations and realities. Leaders of nominally independent governments, drawn from those social and political groups, whose anti-imperialist vocation Fanon derided, would continue to welcome European capitalist investment, insisting that they get their cut. Their anti-capitalism would consist of nationalizing merchant wholesalers and retailers, businesses often dominated by non-African immigrants, placing these in the hands of the politicians' cronies. Civil service positions and professional occupations would be "Africanized" in a similar fashion, and the new functionaries would continue the contempt their colonial predecessors had shown toward the locals, especially the rural population. Initiatives of industrialization, modernization, and development—Fanon was an advocate of progress and modernization theory—would be lacking. Agriculture would continue in its colonial vein—export-oriented crops like peanuts, cocoa beans, or olives, in a European-dominated global market, although the ownership of plantations might change hands. The peasantry would be neglected, and the Lumpenproletariat, pride of the revolutionary movement, would be "subject to pastimes designed for young people of the capitalist countries: detective novels, small-coin betting machines, obscene photographs, pornographic literature, films banned to those under sixteen, and above all alcohol." Perhaps even worse, professional spectator sports.

Former heroes of anti-imperialism, installed as presidents and prime ministers, would follow an increasingly authoritarian course, relying on their cronies or on the armed forces, politically demobilizing their followers, who had wrested national freedom from imperialist domination. Far from Pan-Africanism or even nationalism inspiring the new regimes, wealthy provinces would attempt secession, workers and small traders would riot against competitors from other African countries, rivalries between different tribal groups would break out, religious conflicts would appear, and hostilities between "Africans" south of the Sahara and "Arabs" north of it would become evident.[33] Like Djilas's critique of communist rule a few years previously, these criticisms of independent African states seem, in retrospect, eerily prescient. *The Wretched of the Earth* can best be understood as an appeal not to give in to disillusionment, to reject the nascent non- or counterrevolutionary post-imperialist regimes, and to hold fast to the utopian aspirations of anti-imperialism.

Of the three prophets of disillusion, only Djilas lived to see the results of his predictions. Orwell died of tuberculosis six months after the publication of *1984*; Fanon, as noted, died in 1961—in Bethesda, Maryland, of all places, given his feelings about the United States; he had been brought there by the CIA for treatment of his leukemia. He just had time to see an advance copy of his great and prophetic polemic right before his death.[34] All three men were deeply committed and politically impassioned, expressive of the hopes and fears arising from the experience of war, but not entirely in synch with the more prosaic, post-apocalyptic postwar era.

Utopianism and Student Unrest

It was the end of the 1960s and students were being unruly. At one university, some were arrested for a common but minor offense. In the past, this police practice had just been shrugged off; this time the students marched through the streets by the thousands in protest. Attempting to disperse the demonstrators, the forces of order brandished nightsticks. Finding them inadequate, they opened fire. One student was killed. Rather than suppress the movement, official violence spurred it on. Sympathy demonstrations followed in many other college towns in the vicinity. Students were joined by secondary school pupils and the unemployed. Violence increased; shop windows were smashed; and businesses were looted. A prominent agitator toured campuses, denouncing government policy and the US war in Vietnam, calling for revolution. He received a rousing reception: red-flag-waving students carried him on their shoulders and thousands of spectators cheered his inflammatory declarations. A month after the initial clash, the protests spread to a more distant, politically turbulent region of the country. Here too, the unemployed and adolescents joined students, and their numbers were reinforced by trade unionists and even some white-collar salaried employees.

The story sounds familiar, perhaps even cliched. That agitator was Tom Hayden, or Rudi Dutschke or Daniel Cohn-Bendit. The demonstrations began at Columbia University, at the Berkeley campus of the University of California, perhaps the Sorbonne or the University of Milan. Affluent young people, preoccupied with their First World problems, propelled by rampaging hormones, broke rules, and clashed with the authorities. Their antics were imitated by less responsible and more violent members of the underclass.

This is a widely circulated image of the turbulence of the Era of Upheaval. There is also a more positive version of the era, in which affluent young people became the partisans of a New Left. Concerned with "post-materialist" issues, such as out-of-control destruction of the environment, a cancerously spreading governmental and corporate bureaucracy, stifling individuals' creativity and life aspirations, senseless, highly mechanized, destructive warfare in Third World countries, or global inequality, they registered their dissent, fundamentally transforming the nature and values of political life. These different views are flip sides of the same coin, placing the upheavals of the 1960s in the social, political, and emotional context of the economically advanced, affluent regions of the world, centered on the North Atlantic.

If this were the case, the story related above would not make much sense. For it occurred in Pakistan. The riots began in November 1968 in Rawalpindi, when students were arrested for bringing goods into the country from neighboring Afghanistan, without paying customs duties. The agitator was Tariq Ali, a young man from a left-wing Pakistani family, whose parents had sent him off to study at Oxford in 1963. Already in the sights of his native country's political police for his antigovernment actions, Ali only multiplied them while residing in the former colonial metropolis. He was elected president of the Oxford Union, in which capacity he sponsored a debate featuring the American Pan-Africanist Malcolm X, and became a leader of the anti-Vietnam War movement in the United Kingdom. His peripatetic activism took him from London to Hanoi, La Paz, and West Berlin. Returning to his homeland as antigovernment demonstrations were peaking, he received a hero's welcome. The protests he both encouraged and epitomized reached their high point in Dhaka, the main city of the eastern half of Pakistan, where thirty thousand demonstrators, only a third of them students, took to the streets as part of a massive, region-wide general strike. The results of the nationwide demonstrations would include the resignation of Pakistan's authoritarian president, Ayub Khan, and the increasing disintegration of Pakistani rule in the eastern half of the country, leading to its secession and emergence in 1971 as an independent Bangladesh.[35]

These events are a particularly dramatic example of what some have begun calling the "global sixties." The designation involves a recognition of the worldwide scale of the upheavals and social and political mass movements of that turbulent decade. It was not just Berkeley, Paris, West Berlin, or New York at the center of things, but also Prague, Warsaw, Mexico City, Montevideo, Dakar, Shanghai, and Dhaka. There were common origins of the turbulence, worldwide, including the coming to adulthood of the large birth cohorts of the immediate post-1945 years, and the public policy of increasing access to secondary and higher education, leading to greater numbers of pupils and students. Global interconnections were also crucial to the era, personal ones, as Tariq Ali's story demonstrates, or those created by the new medium of television.

As might be expected, these worldwide trends played out quite differently in different countries with differing political systems, levels of economic development, cultural traditions, and social structures. Government policy varied from encouragement or even instigation—the China of Mao's Cultural Revolution, or (a much less well-known story) communist East Germany and its leader Walter Ulbricht—to violent repression, occurring in places as varied as Poland, Greece, Mexico, and Ohio, to integration of the new mass movements and the opposition they aroused into existing political conflicts. The scope of the movements themselves depended crucially on whether they could reach a broader base of social support. Such an expansion involved tapping into existing social and political hostilities and resentments—rejection by the Bengalis of East Pakistan of the rule of the Punjabis from the western part of the country, for instance; or the simmering anger of the Peronistas of Argentina against the coup that had overthrown their leader in 1955; or the opposition to bureaucratic factory management on the part of industrial workers in France and Italy. Finally, the goals and aspirations of the movements and upheavals of the period—much more loosely and informally organized than their predecessors of the Age of Total War—varied immensely, ranging from reminiscences of past social struggles, such as the mass movements of the French Popular Front of the 1930s, to distinctly new issues, relating to race, sexuality, or personal self-actualization in a society permeated by the mass media.

Rather than trying to explore every single example of 1960s-era upheaval and the aspirations behind it, or even a large sample of them, which would require a whole book in itself, it might be more helpful to explore the movements of the era in historical and comparative contexts—to consider "diachronic" and "synchronic" elements of the 1960s. Diachronic considerations would include the extent to which the "sixties" represented a break with the past—sudden emergence of movements or greater continuity with previous decades; similarity or difference of aspirations compared to earlier movements, particularly the utopian ones emerging from the Second World War. Complementing these two diachronic lines of investigation, are two synchronic ones: seeing whether aspirations were similar or different in countries with different social structures, levels of economic development, historical trajectories, political institutions, and position in the Cold War—how similar aspirations played out in different circumstances—and the nature of interconnection within mass movements that appeared on a global scale. Just how global were the "global sixties," and if they were global, what forms did that globalization take?[36]

Looking back, it was no surprise that the upheavals of the Second World War led to a wave of revolutionary aspirations. More surprising, given the state of the world in 1945, was that the aspirations led not to transformation but to a postwar era of rapid economic growth, social, and political placidity—the "end of ideology," as American sociologist Daniel Bell declaimed in a widely read book published in 1960. It could be asserted that to understand the postwar era in this way is to project onto the world conditions in the wealthier capitalist countries. The Eastern Bloc was rocked by powerful internal opposition in 1953 and 1956 and by self-inflicted chaos, during the Great Leap Forward. In Africa, Asia, and Latin America, there were episodes of revolution and anti-colonial struggle, among others in Bolivia, Kenya, Vietnam, and Algeria, which were neither particularly peaceful nor evidence of the end of ideology. Yet compared to the Age of Total War, the postwar era was, overall, one of peace and prosperity—an unexpected precursor to a period of widespread upheaval and renewed utopian aspirations.

Often, the transition from placidity to upheaval occurred rapidly, and with a strong sense of sudden rupture: in France, from years of normal labor relations, with the occasional well-organized and limited work stoppage, to the immense nationwide general strike of May 1968. There, as well as in much of the rest of the world, from conformist, and career-oriented university students (contemporary commentators sometimes worried that students were too apolitical), to revolutionaries asserting their will.

Some have pointed to 1960s precursors: discontented Bohemians and an artistic avant-garde; intellectuals analyzing new forms of social oppression and new versions of rebellion, such as the Situationists; or the post-Marxists of the Frankfurt School, especially the future guru of youthful rebellion Herbert Marcuse. (His more sophisticated fellow-thinkers, Theodor Adorno and Max Horkheimer, would prove to be less enthusiastic.) They have pointed to examples of mass movements of the late 1950s and early 1960s, particularly ban-the-bomb demonstrators, opposition to France's colonial war in Algeria, or the demands of African Americans for full rights of citizenship, a mass movement that would be immensely influential around the world. In some countries, particularly the two former Axis powers, Germany and Japan, demonstrations of the late 1950s were much larger than anything occurring during the 1960s.[37]

Another form of continuity can be observed among the activists of the 1960s themselves. As the example of Tariq Ali suggests, and contrary to a long popular tradition of attributing the turbulence of the era to intergenerational rebellion, the student and New Left radicals of the 1960s did not come primarily from conservative households. Rather, their parents were mostly politically left-of-center, ranging from social democrats or liberals in the US New Deal tradition, to outright socialists or communists—whence the British phrase, "red diaper babies"—and the political commitments of youthful activists emerged from values instilled in them at home.[38]

These forms of continuity were not the whole story. While activists may have come from left-wing households, they generally rejected their parents' forms of left-of-center politics, their advocacy of reforms and political gradualism, their anchoring in the issues and sociopolitical world of the Great Depression, in favor of less organized, more aggressive, sometimes violent or coercive forms of political action, often about a new palette of political issues. This viewpoint is summed up in the phrase, coming into common use, of a "New Left." Earlier versions of activism showed continuities with 1950s predecessors. Then, between 1967 and 1974, which literary theorist Frederic Jameson has dubbed the "high 1960s" (the double entendre may not have been intended, but it is certainly appropriate), the physical appearance of political activists, the escalation and radicalization of both forms of political action and the political demands posed, the issues central to that action, and the connections of left-wing politics to an emergent youth culture were very different from the recent past, and marked a distinct break with it.[39]

If the postwar era's aspirations tended to fall into three larger groups—an improved post-fascist order, liberation from imperialism, and global governance—their 1960s counterparts might be placed under two large rubrics: "participation" and Third World inspiration. The first appears in one of the classic documents of the New Left, the June 1962 "Port Huron Statement," of the American radical student group SDS. Aiming its fire at a society of "meaningless work," "depersonalization that reduces human beings to the status of things," "loneliness, estrangement and isolation," the statement called for a new and creative society, work for motives "worthier than money or survival," and a political system of "participatory democracy," in which "decisions would be made by groups in public."[40]

These aspirations, widely shared in Western Europe as well, envisaged an explicitly utopian future of popular participation, self-actualization, and spiritual and psychological self-fulfillment, to be accomplished not by individual actions but through a common, collective purpose. Such motives were not unknown in the mass movements of the Age of Total War and appeared in the political initiatives of a Europe just liberated from fascism. But these were generally in the context of calls for higher popular standards of living. With severe shortages, rapid inflation, the black market, and bread riots all around them, activists would not have stated that there should be worthier motives for work than "money or survival."

At least implicitly, such aspirations were directed against the postwar order. They were an attack on forms of bureaucratic and hierarchical social and political organization in the workplace, schools, and universities. This criticism was extended to politics, even nominally democratic politics, if it was characterized by the competition of professional politicians and organized political parties, without much popular participation beyond the act of voting. Another target was consumerism, which led to isolation and alienation, distinctly lacking in personal self-actualization or self-fulfillment—a point which intellectual critics, connected to the Situationists and the Frankfurt School, had emphasized with vigor and in detail. The consumer society of the mid-1960s was both new and still in fairly nascent form. Yet it seemed self-evident, in view of the unprecedented pace of economic growth, that it was well on its way to encompassing most of the world. Criticism of consumerism was about different ways to organize a prosperity that was taken for granted.

These aspirations also provided a link between political radicalism and the emergent youth culture of the 1960s. Especially in Jameson's high 1960s, as self-fulfillment came to include the sexual realm and opposition to hierarchy and bureaucratic regulations was directed against limitations they placed on students (and young people more generally) in that area, connections between utopian aspirations and the culture of rock music, marijuana smoking, and (much) more casual forms of dress and personal behavior grew closer. The neatly groomed, suited and skirted demonstrators of the first half of the decade gave way to the bearded, hairy (both sexes), jeans-wearing, army-jacketed, and booted crowds of politicized young people in campus occupations, or antiwar and antigovernment demonstrations.

The conjunction of the New Left and the counterculture was never smooth, with some activists deprecating the causes of rock music, marijuana, and sexual liberation as diversions from serious political issues. A particularly poignant example is the contrast in attitude between the Rastafarians, Jamaican counterculturalists, whose immensely popular reggae music emphasized belief in the *Ras Tafari*, the Ethiopian emperor Haile Selassie, as a quasi-divine figure and worldwide symbol of Pan-African solidarity, and Ethiopian student radicals, who perceived that same Haile Selassie as a feudal despot. In a meeting initiated by Ethiopian students in London to denounce the emperor's bungled handling of the 1973 famine, someone had the bright idea of providing entertainment in the form of a Rasta band, which proceeded to sing the praises of the same ruler the students wanted to overthrow.[41]

Interacting with all this was the second element of utopian aspirations, connections with what was coming to be called the Third World: feelings of solidarity with anti-imperialist struggles in Asia, Africa, and Latin America; and, even more, personal identification with those countries and struggles and understanding them as models and inspirations. There are three elements of these forms of connection, what the French called *"tiermondisme,"* "third worldism," which characterized the mass movements of the 1960s.

There was the way that the Third World came to replace previous forms of inspiration, particularly the labor movement and the anti-fascist struggles of the Age of Total War. Neither of the latter totally disappeared. In the later 1960s, Marxist rhetoric flourished, although the many calls for working-class revolution seemed rather disconnected from the actual working class. The heritage of anti-fascism and the Second World War was stronger and appeared in many forms: the crucial role for the New Left in West Germany of the struggle against the "Emergency Laws," passed in 1968, since it was through an earlier form of Emergency Laws that the Nazis first came to power; the readaptation of the two-finger salute of the Second World War Allied powers, their "V for victory," as a symbol of opposition to the Vietnam War. For all these instances, the feeling increasingly developed that a mass movement of younger people needed a different form of inspiration, taken from the struggles of the contemporary world. As early as the Port Huron Statement, which condemned the sterility of older left-wing slogans left over from the 1930s, to the rejection by youthful activists in Spain and Greece, of the anti-fascist struggles of the 1930s Civil War and the communist-led resistance to German occupation as models, the downplaying of older forms of aspiration spread. In countries newly independent from colonial rule, the appeal of the struggles of the Second World War, in which the anti-fascists had been colonial powers or allied to them, had never been that strong in the first place.[42]

The second element of *tiersmondisme* was the identification with the Vietnamese cause in the war in Southeast Asia. Everywhere—literally everywhere in the world—opposition to the US war was central to the mass movements of the 1960s. The precursor to the events of May 1968 in France was neither the relatively modest pre-1968 labor strikes nor university-oriented student activism. It was in the antiwar campaigns of the National Vietnam Committees and the Grass Roots Vietnam Committees (*Comités Vietnam de base*). The high point of the radical student movement in West Germany was the February 1968 Vietnam Congress in Berlin. Even in Latin America, where there were plenty of local examples of counterrevolutionary US intervention, leftists in Argentina, Chile, Uruguay, and Mexico acknowledged the importance of the Vietnam War. Student leftists in Ethiopia, Pakistan, and Zaire, to mention just a few countries, emphasized their solidarity with the Vietnamese and the linking of their struggles. Yassir Arafat's *Fatah* movement, the increasingly dominant Palestinian radical group, rejected previous Pan-Arabist inspirations in favor of the Vietnamese struggle against the United States. By the mid-1960s, ban-the-bomb activists in the United Kingdom, Australia, Japan, Denmark, Sweden, Ireland, the Netherlands, and Austria—among other places—had shifted their focus to opposing the

Vietnam War. Students opposing the early 1970s military dictatorship in Greece saw their struggle against the regime of the colonels, enjoying at least tacit US support, as part of the same conflict as the one in Southeast Asia; their counterparts in Ethiopia, opposing the authoritarian regime of Emperor Haile Selassie, had the exact same attitude.[43]

Vietnam was the leading example of pro-Third World anti-imperialist enthusiasm. However, it was very far from alone. One of the major radicalizing events of the West German student leftists—their organization's acronym SDS the same as that of their American counterparts—was the June 1967 demonstration they sponsored in West Berlin against the visit of the Shah of Iran, in the course of which a student bystander was shot and killed by the police. Of course, the opponents of the Shah with whom the Germans were expressing their solidarity were then leftists rather than Islamists. This conjunction appeared in the major iconic images of youthful radicals around the world—the Cuban revolutionary Che Guevara, traveling the globe to encourage anti-imperialist revolution, launching the slogan, "two, three, many Vietnams," and Mao Zedong, encouraging young people to rise up against CCP bureaucrats. The use of these images of Third World revolution as models appears in a chant, frequently heard at the anti-Vietnam War demonstrations of the late 1960s and early 1970s in the United States: "Mao, Mao, Mao Tse-Tung/Revolution by the young!"[44]

At the time, Mao was steering Chinese foreign policy on an anti-Soviet course, albeit not yet in conjunction with the United States. Identification with Third World anti-imperialism invariably had a distinctly anti-American tinge to it, or at least a strong hostility to its foreign policy. But such a hostility did not imply any particular sympathies for policies of America's Cold War rivals in the USSR. Quite the opposite—and this too marks a distinct break from the Era of Total War—identification with Third World revolutionaries implied a rejection of the USSR and its many Communist Party supporters around the world. Sympathies of New Leftists in the Eastern Bloc, in Hungary, Poland or Czechoslovakia, for the cause of the Vietnamese did not imply any particular enthusiasm for their close allies, the USSR. Students at the University of Warsaw even asserted that American efforts to quash Vietnamese national autonomy and independence were exactly what the USSR was doing in Poland. Taking the Third World as a model and form of identification was a rejection of the two superpowers and the Cold War they were carrying out.[45]

There was a distinctly American variant on Third World inspiration, the interaction between the New Left and the mass movements of African Americans demanding full human rights and civic equality. Initial New Leftists and US student activists were young white people who had volunteered to assist in the campaigns of African Americans and their organizations in southern states against the segregation of public facilities, transportation, and places of business, and for access to the ballot, a right that had been systematically denied African Americans for the previous seven decades. Their experiences of solidarity during these campaigns, particularly in the Mississippi "Freedom Summer" of 1964, became living examples of young leftists' aspirations to a future of solidaristic self-actualization; their experiences of racism, violence and oppression in the South fed into and encouraged a broader criticism of American society; their own campaigns, such as the Free Speech Movement at the University of California, were modeled on their experiences in the South.[46]

The mass movements of African Americans were, from the very beginning, a model and inspiration for the New Left in America, as the Third World would come to be worldwide. From the mid-1960s onward, the two merged. African American political activists began to understand themselves as part of the Third World, to apply Frantz Fanon's *The Wretched of the Earth* to their own situation. They went beyond demanding an equal place in the American political and social system, to demanding a fundamental transformation of that system, a transition symbolized by the emergence of the phrase "Black Power," and the rise of groups such as the Black Panthers. These developments affected white, American New Leftists, one of many features pushing them to radicalize. There emerged a feedback loop as both groups ramped up their demands, radicalized their attitudes, and steered increasingly on a course of confrontation with the government. Given the strongly racist attitudes prevalent among American police, such confrontations would end up with violent and sometimes fatal outcomes among both Black and white activists—though to a far greater extent among the former.[47]

While this identification and self-identification of African American political activists with Algerian, Cuban, Chinese, or Vietnamese revolutionaries may seem, in retrospect, problematic, it was typical of the utopian aspirations of the Era of Upheaval and lived around the world. It could even be used by the political enemies of the activists. One example comes from Poland in March 1968. During large student demonstrations, involving clashes with the police, throughout the country one response of the authorities was to blame it on the Jews. The chairman of the veterans' association Miecesław Moczar condemned the demonstrators as enemies of the nation, in the anti-Semitic traditions of pre-communist Poland. Communist Party leader Władysław Gomułka took a different tack. Referring to the 1967 Arab-Israeli war, which had elicited a fair amount of pro-Israel sentiment in Poland (Israeli military successes understood as a victory over the Arabs' Soviet ally), he denounced "Zionist Jews and Polish citizens" who endorsed "Israel's aggression against the Arab countries," and insisted that "we cannot remain indifferent to people who . . . support the aggressor and destroyer of peace and support its imperialism." It was the regime that was identifying with Third

World revolutionaries, in Gomułka's assertion, while its opponents were actually pro-imperialist.[48]

A similar clash occurred in Zaire in 1969. In one of the largest manifestations of student unrest in Africa, students in the capital Kinshasa launched a mass demonstration against the government, raising the memory of Congolese Pan-Africanist martyr Patrice Lumumba and demanding the Africanization of the Lovanium, the main university in the country, founded by and still largely staffed and administered by Catholic clergy from Belgium. After ordering soldiers to open fire on the demonstrators, killing a hundred of them, President Joseph Mobutu, at the time promoting the memory of Lumumba, announced the university would be Africanized and placed under his control.[49]

While identification with the Third World was a ubiquitous feature of the 1960s, participation, self-actualization, opposition to bureaucratic organization and consumer society, skepticism about formal democracy without much popular participation—all these elements of the era's utopian aspirations, faced a more problematic reception across the world. After all, what meaning did the rejection of a consumer society have in a country where consumerism was marginal or just beginning? How important was self-actualization in a place where famine remained a serious threat? It may have been fine to condemn formal democratic procedures as bureaucratic or lacking popular participation. Still, even formal democracy was preferable to dictatorial rule.

Perhaps surprisingly, these disparities between aspirations and social conditions seem to have been less an obstacle than might be thought. Students everywhere in the world railed at bureaucratic and hierarchical conditions at their universities and demanded more democratic and participatory forms of academic governance—which, admittedly, could take the form of destroying final exams. In poorer countries, criticism of consumerism and calls for self-actualization took a back seat to more economically oriented demands, such as the Ethiopian student radicals' call for "land to the tillers," or the support of Indian Maoists for the land occupations of rural laborers, the "Naxalite" movement. Demands for democracy and opposition to undemocratic regimes were part of student and New Left activism, as the mass movements in Pakistan demonstrated.[50]

There were occasions in which the contrast between local conditions and transnational aspirations became painfully obvious. A dramatic example occurred during the occupation of the Athens Polytechnic in November 1973 by tens of thousands of students opposing Greece's military dictatorship. A group of anarchists, inspired by the events in France of May 1968, started writing graffiti such as "Sexual freedom" or "Long live orgies," "Down with capital," "Down with salary jobs," "Down with the army," or "Patriots are morons." Most of the other students involved in the occupation, even if they were avowed revolutionary Marxist-Leninist Maoists or Trotskyists, were appealing to the general population to bring the military junta to an end, taking on the mantle of Greek patriotism, and imploring ordinary soldiers to join their cause. They therefore either covered up the anarchists' graffiti or, in some accounts of the events, beat them up and expelled them bodily from the occupied university.[51]

More difficult for youthful and student activists was when their aspirations were not shared by members of other social groups. This issue is often framed as a disconnect between mostly affluent students, attracted to ideas about fighting bureaucratic organization and implementing self-actualization, and a working class concentrating on bread-and-butter issues. As shown in Chapter 8, the labor unrest of the era often involved strong opposition to bureaucratic management, so this assertion seems less salient. Another version of this opposition, already formulated at the time, and emphasized even more strongly in subsequent decades, was that the 1960s featured a clash between godless, sex-obsessed, unpatriotic, spoiled young people, and hard-working, God-fearing, chaste, modest, traditionalist patriots. Polemical formulations aside, there really could be a contrast between radicals inspired by the Third World and the powerful political sentiment of nationalism.

One of the famous setbacks of sixties radicalism was the Tlatelolco Massacre. At the beginning of October 1968, Mexican troops, acting on the orders of President Gustavo Diaz, opened fire on demonstrating students in Mexico City opposing authoritarian university administration and an authoritarian central government. Hundreds were killed. The president's office received masses of correspondence praising him for his patriotic deed, directed at the tools of foreign conspirators aiming to destroy Mexico. Public opinion polling found most Mexicans agreeing that "foreign enemies" of the nation were pulling the strings behind the scenes. There was some difference of opinion about who these "foreign enemies" were: some named the communists, others the United States, still others, the Catholic secret society *Opus Dei*. The range cast a revealing light on Mexico's politics. In 1970, seventeen months later, National Guard troops fired on anti-Vietnam War student demonstrators at Kent State University in Ohio, leading to four deaths, far fewer than in Mexico City. Again, however, large segments of public opinion endorsed the shooting, in a similar way, as a patriotic deed.[52] As these examples suggest, Third World political identification and solidarity would garner the most support not in opposition to nationalism but through alignment with it, identifying the enemies of the nation with those of the Third World revolutionaries.

This identification with far-flung revolutionary icons already suggests the globalized nature of the 1960s, but exactly how it did it happen? Often this globalization is seen in terms of personal connections and travel around the world. It is certainly possible to point to individuals who did this: the peripatetic Tariq Ali; the West German exchange student Michael Vester, who helped draft the Port Huron Statement; the summer 1968 journey of American SDS leader Bernadine Dohrn (soon to play a leading role in the terrorist group the Weathermen) to an international meeting of New Leftists in Ljubljana, followed by attending the German SDS conference in Frankfurt. Another example might be the panel discussion hosted by the BBC in June 1968, featuring student leftists from France, West Germany, England (the English representative was Tariq Ali) Czechoslovakia, and Yugoslavia, which ended with all the participants proclaiming their solidarity and intoning the *International*, the revolutionary communist anthem, in their own languages.[53]

All are examples of informal contacts of particular individuals; there is no evidence of either larger-scale personal connections or of any organizational coordination. In this case it was the BBC, a massive media institution, which brought together the student radicals at its London studio. In comparison to past revolutionary movements, or even to ongoing connections of established, old-fashioned left-wing political parties, like the Socialist International, the movements of the 1960s were organized, to the extent they were at all, on a national level. International connections followed closely on regional lines, such as the cooperation of radicals in Uruguay, Chile, and Argentina, which also involved leftists moving across borders to obtain political sanctuary as one country after another was taken over by repressive right-wing dictatorships between 1972 and 1976. Another form of international organization was, paradoxically, national in scope, associations of left-wing students from one country studying abroad, such as Ethiopian students in Europe and in North America.[54]

Overall, international, to say nothing of global, connections of adherents of the Era of Upheaval's aspirations seem to have been relatively feeble. As the example of the BBC panel discussion suggests, connections were formed via the mass media, in line with the description of the US war in Southeast Asia as the first televised war. However, this description ignores the still quite modest global implantation of TV during the 1960s: a relatively new medium, widespread only in Europe and North America, accessible to a minority of households in Latin America, just getting started in Africa, and largely nonexistent in South Asia. For radicals in much of the world, identification with the cause of the Vietnamese was neither the result of personal experience nor of TV viewing but of anti-imperialist sentiments rooted in the previous era of global utopian aspirations, during and after the Second World War, and marks the strongest connection between that era and the 1960s.

On closer examination, globalized connections to the Third World often contained a strong imaginary element. One way to see this is to look at the neglect or misunderstanding of actual Third Worlders. West German activists identified with all manner of Third World causes, from the Congo to Cuba to Iran to Vietnam. The millions of migrant workers from Turkey living in their country, whose ranks were steadily expanding at the time, eluded their solidarity and, mostly, their attention. The events of May 1968 in France began with student demonstrations and unrest at the new campus of the University of Paris in the suburban town of Nanterre. Nanterre was also the site of a *bidonville*, a shanty town of migrant laborers from North and West Africa, many of whom were employed in building the new university. Enormous piles of earth from the construction separated the university from the shanty town, forming two separate universes. A group of French student Maoists tried to overcome this separation by renting a truck and distributing free potatoes to the migrant laborers, an action that puzzled the latter. Like most migrant laborers in Western Europe at the time, they were employed and had money, so little need of free food. What they did need was decent housing, a point missed by the Maoists agitating among the Third World proletariat.[55]

As was the case around the world, Latin American activists modeled themselves on the Cuban Revolution and, especially, its romantic hero Che Guevara. When the Cuban government held its 1966 Tricontinental Congress in Havana, promoting Third World revolution, and celebrating Latin America's adherence to that Third World, it rejected the South American radicals inspired by the Cuban Revolution, inviting, instead, delegations of the official and rather stodgy communist parties, who very much did not identify with Che and his calls for revolution. Activists who rejected both Cold War superpowers and identified with Third World revolution, came up against the fact that some of the Third World revolutionaries with whom they identified, in Cuba and Vietnam, were closely tied to the USSR, and to the Eastern Bloc in the Cold War. While students and other radical leftists in West Berlin were holding their international Vietnam congress to celebrate Third World revolution, most West Berliners, living in a city where the Wall had been built just a half-decade previously, rejected such an identification as rallying to the cause of a Soviet Union and its East German ally that was a visible threat to them.[56]

This difference between the actual and the imagined politics of Third World revolutionaries points to a feature of identification with these revolutionaries: the projection onto that Third World of their own wishes and aspirations. As early as 1964, West Germany's SDS leader Rudi Dutschke proclaimed, "that in the judgement of the character of our era, an era of national liberation in Asia, Africa and Latin America, I am Chinese." The high 1960s brought these attitudes even more into appearance. The more urban guerillas there were, the more self-proclaimed Red Guards and Red Armies made their appearance, the more the Black Panthers sold copies of Mao's little red book and announced that they aspired to be "Black, like Mao," the clearer it became that a lot of the utopian identification with the Third World involved a combination of a real revolution against actual forms of oppression and one that was a fantasy.[57]

QUINTESSENTIAL SIXTIES: THE GPCR AND THE EVENTS OF MAY

In the kaleidoscope of demonstrations, occupations, strikes, riots, clashes with the authorities, and so many other forms of social and political turbulence that characterized the Era of Upheaval, two stand out, for their scope and size, and for their worldwide impact, both at the time and for decades afterward: China's Great Proletarian Cultural Revolution, and the immense wave of strikes and mass demonstrations that engulfed France in May 1968. A closer look at the two, and a comparison of them, brings to light features of the era, including the nature of participation in mass movements with utopian aspirations and the relationship between these mass movements and the government.

The GPCR began with the fears of the aging Mao Zedong about the future of the Chinese communist regime, in particular his suspicion that communist party officials were joining with remnants of pre-communist elites to create a new privileged class. He was determined to mobilize social forces outside the Communist Party to prevent this from happening. Mao was not the only aging figure in the communist world who saw things in this light. East Germany's veteran communist leader Walter Ulbricht—even more of a veteran than Mao, since Ulbricht's work in the socialist labor movement had begun before the First World War—had similar apprehensions about bureaucratization and decline of revolutionary sentiment. His solution was to look to the political activity of young people and to circumvent party channels to mobilize them, using his position as chairman of the Council of State, East Germany's collective government executive. Ulbricht's plans never got very far, largely because he entrusted their implementation to his confidential secretary Erich Honecker, who instead organized other party leaders against them, informed the Soviets of this dangerous deviation from doctrinal orthodoxy, and eventually forced Ulbricht to retire, making himself his successor and terminating his predecessor's plans for anti-bureaucratic upheaval.[58]

Considerably better at political intrigue than his East German counterpart, Mao was able to outmaneuver other communist party leaders and, working outside the regular channels of the state and the party, set up a Central Cultural Revolution Group, staffed by his personal, loyal followers, to implement his vision. Like Ulbricht, central to Mao's plans were young people, and it was among university students, and, even more, secondary school pupils in the capital city that the cultural revolution first got going in the spring of 1966. Organizing themselves into paramilitary groups of Red Guards, the young people publicly denounced and then physically attacked their teachers, party leaders, government officials and other figures of authority, subjecting them to a whole series of humiliations: paraded around wearing dunce caps, coerced into confessions of counterrevolutionary sentiments and actions, and beaten, sometimes with fatal outcomes. These forms of ritual degradation were not inventions of angry young people. They were tactics devised by the communists following their coming to power in 1949 to deal with their political and social enemies, such as landlords, government officials, or prominent members of the communists' political opponents, the *Guomindang*. The Central Cultural Revolution Group made sure that efforts to rein in the Red Guards were foiled, encouraging the young radicals to continue their campaign in Beijing and to travel across China, widely spreading their demands, always describing them as articulating the revolutionary desires of Chairman Mao.[59]

Like youthful activists across the world, these Red Guards were not rejecting their parents; rather, they were themselves the offspring of veteran communists, who had become, after 1949, party leaders, army officers, and state officials. Red Guards were heirs to their parents' revolutionary spirit, directing their fire against a version of their parents' enemies: pre-1949 elites, from, as the regime put it, "black families" including intellectuals who still played a prominent role in secondary and university education. The youthful insurgents described their actions in genealogical, in fact biological terms, as having inherited their revolutionary position from their parents, while their opponents were, in a parallel way, forever condemned by their families' counterrevolutionary past. Red Guards brandished slogans such as "My father is a revolutionary so I inherit the pledge to protect the rivers and mountains by being red/ Your father is a criminal, so don't you fight, or it'll serve you right for having the luck to be born black."[60] Leadership roles and even membership in the Red Guard units at Beijing's high schools and universities were determined by a biologically perceived version of social background: at the top were the children of party leaders, followed at some distance by (the relatively few) offspring of workers and peasants; children of "black" pre-1949 elites were either victims of their fellow pupils and students or, at best, could have, on sufferance, a marginal role as supporters and auxiliaries. This idea of political position and personal virtue as an inherited, biological characteristic sounds perilously close to a racism usually a target of activists inspired by the aspirations of the 1960s.

By late 1966 the Red Guard agitation had spread to Shanghai, then China's largest industrial center, where it gained hundreds of thousands of adherents among the city's workers. As the movement grew, CCP authority dwindled to the point that in February 1967 municipal government was replaced with a Shanghai People's Commune, whose leaders explicitly associated it with the legendary revolutionary government of the Paris Commune of 1871. The founding of the Shanghai Commune appears, at least superficially, as an example of the great effect of sixties aspirations when they spread from students to larger sectors of the population and an attempt at the realization of truly utopian versions of these aspirations.

Very much unlike the well-connected, elite Beijing students and pupils, the Shanghai workers, loosely organized in the very GPCR-sounding Rebel Headquarters of Red Workers were the more marginal elements of the labor force. They included temporary and contract workers whose official residence was in rural areas, had no right to reside permanently in Shanghai, were paid less than their coworkers with permanent residency in the city and also, unlike them, had no guarantees of permanent employment. Another group heavily involved in the agitation were young people who had been sent from Shanghai into the countryside and now demanded that they be allowed to return. In Shanghai's largest factory, the Diesel Works, youthful workers, and older ones who were regarded as politically unreliable, since they had been employed there before 1949 under the government of the *Guomindang*, joined to oppose the authority of the "cadres," factory management consisting largely of army and navy veterans, with "good" class backgrounds, but not necessarily much knowledge of building diesel engines.

The representatives of the Central Cultural Revolution Group sent from Beijing to oversee the insurgency in Shanghai, one of whom, Zhang Chunqiao would later be a member of the "Gang of Four," the radical heirs of Mao, came to decide that all these purportedly revolutionary workers were actually proponents of "economism," narrow, materialistic, counter-revolutionary self-interest, as opposed to the revolutionary devotion to a new socialist way of life demanded by the Cultural Revolution. With the assistance of the army and the official proletarian revolutionary group, the Workers General Headquarters, whose leader Wang Hongwen was yet another future member of the Gang of Four, the rebels were suppressed.

These actions in China's main urban center were a preview of the fate of the Cultural Revolution throughout the country. In the name of Mao's call to destroy the combination of party bureaucracy and remnants of older elites and their forms of thought and cultural affiliations, all manner of social groups, usually starting with young people, and moving on to urban workers and then farmers, organized themselves, gathered weapons, denounced party and government authorities, engaged in public degradation ceremonies of their opponents, and, increasingly, clashed with each other on a steadily larger scale. By the second half of 1967, the chairman moved to reassert centralized authority, sending in the army to disarm the Red Guard militias and to restore order. The youthful radicals who made up the Red Guards and were supposed to be Mao's agents for the revolutionization of China, apparently had the wrong attitudes, and were sent off to the countryside, by the millions, to do agricultural labor and be "re-educated" by the peasants. Large numbers of party cadres were purged, many sent to similar fates as the young radicals in rural areas, while hundreds of thousands were executed.

Neither the aspirations revealed in the movements of the Red Guards nor the plans of Mao to revive revolutionary spirit in China were successful. Following the Chairman's death, the followers who wished to continue his course, the "Gang of Four," were defeated in power struggles and replaced with a new party leadership (it would be fair to say enjoying the support of a populace weary of a decade of upheaval), under Deng Xiaoping, one of the many party leaders purged during the Cultural Revolution. Deng pursued precisely the course Mao had feared, the reintroduction of elements of a capitalist market economy.

At the other end of Eurasia, in a very different country—capitalist, urban, industrial, and affluent rather than socialist, rural, agricultural, and impoverished—with an at least nominally democratic political system (albeit one with distinctly authoritarian tendencies) as opposed to a dictatorship was the other great upheaval of the 1960s, "the events of May 1968" in France. Ideologically, these two instances of the classic sixties were close, each speaking a form of Marxist language, interspersed with praise for Chairman Mao and affirmations of solidarity with the Third World, involving utopian aspirations and attracting worldwide attention, but in the relationship with past forms of social upheaval, in the nature of the social tensions revealed, in the relationship with the state and government and in the ultimate political consequences, the two events were very different.[61]

The upheaval began with clashes between students and university administrators at the Nanterre campus of the University of Paris over questions of personal self-actualization. In a confrontation at the university's swimming pool, the student anarchist Daniel Cohn-Bendit soon to be known as "Danny the Red" (for both his hair color and his politics) demanded of the French Minister of Education students' rights to sexual satisfaction, allowing students in the dorm rooms of those of the opposite sex. The confrontation escalated in the course of March and April, spurred on by small groups of student radicals—in French, *groupuscules*, or "mini-groups"—anarchists, Maoists and Trotskyists, including occupation of the university's administration building and clashes with the police.

In late April and early May, the student strike movement spread across the country, but demonstrations in Toulouse, Montpellier, or St. Étienne had less of an impact than those at the Sorbonne, the original University of Paris campus on the Left Bank. Steadily larger daytime marches through the capital city fed into nighttime protests and clashes with the police in the Latin Quarter, culminating in the evening of May 13–14, the "night of the barricades," when the riot police, the CRS, fought with students, other young people and generally outraged residents. There had been demonstrations of non-student parts of the population and some strikes of blue-collar workers. However, starting on the 14th, the strike movement suddenly became massive: in classic sites of labor disputes, like the auto factories around Paris, or among transport workers, known in France for their long history of labor militancy, and expanding to include the entire country, all larger enterprises, private and public, and all ranks of employees, from unskilled laborers to skilled workers, technicians, and engineers, salaried employees, and even middle management. Not formally called by any of France's three labor federations, the enormous strikes were a spontaneous outburst; in the second half of May the country was paralyzed, with somewhere between seven and ten million people on strike.

Some elements of this upheaval showed clear continuities with past forms of social and political struggle. There had been similar enormous, sudden onset waves of strikes in France in 1936 and 1947. Strikers occupying their workplaces, a very common feature of 1968, had first been tried in France on a large scale in 1936. The two waves of strikes had seen many of the same epicenters of strikes and factory occupations, such as auto manufacturing facilities in the Paris region, and one has to wonder if some of the older, working-class activists in, say, the Renault works in Billancourt in 1968, had been youthful activists there thirty-two years previously. The common cry in the street fighting, denouncing the riot police as Nazis, "CRS-SS!" points to the continuing legacy of the anti-fascist struggles of the Second World War. Another similarity between 1936 and 1968 was the very modest presence of migrant laborers in the 1968 struggles. Far from taking a leading role in the strikes, or even participating in them, migrant workers from Spain and Portugal fled the country. Migrant workers from North Africa were also not well represented among strikers, although they seem to have had a larger role in the street fighting with the police. Unlike the workers of Shanghai during the Cultural Revolution, it was not the most marginal and outcast elements of the French labor force who were front and center in May 1968.

1968 was not simply a rerun of 1936 but contained many distinct new features. One was regional. As is typical in France, the Paris region played a central role. Still, another epicenter of the mass movements of 1968 was Western France. One of the earliest mass demonstrations inspired by the students occurred in eight departments of Brittany on May 8, with over one hundred thousand participants, and such actions as tearing down the American flag in Le Mans and replacing it with a North Vietnamese one. The occupation of the Sud-Aviation factory in the outskirts of Nantes by striking workers was one of the earliest and most vigorous examples of the many factory occupations in the country. In Nantes itself, strikers took over the prefect's office and created a revolutionary commune, directing government and ensuring supplies of food and gasoline.

The west had always been the most conservative part of France, devoutly Catholic and traditionalist. Not only were the events of May a political turnabout, they were characterized by the enthusiastic participation of *"cathos de gauche,"* left-wing Catholics. While both the communist-affiliated union federation the CGT, and the socialist-affiliated FO were distinctly unsympathetic toward the massive outburst of strikes, the former Catholic trade union federation, the only recently secularized CFDT, was much more appreciative and supportive of demands for self-management. Another feature of the mass movements was a petition of 605 Catholic priests in and around Paris calling for the abolition of clerical celibacy. The influence of the Second Vatican Council was eminently perceptible in May 1968.

One of the great slogans of the events was *autogestion*, self-management, and its presence raises the question of the goals and aspirations of the participants in the mass movement. Ideals of self-actualization, contempt for authoritarian bureaucratic hierarchy, and distance from consumerism were very evident among students and high school pupils. The famous street posters put up all over Paris, typically designed by students of the *École des Beaux Arts*, with their slogans, "All power to the imagination," "Be realistic: demand the impossible," "Under the pavement, the beach," point in a surrealist fashion in that direction. It does seem reasonable to ask—and this is a crucial question for the entirety of 1960s mass movements and their aspirations—whether these ideas were largely the province of intellectuals while most strikers were more interested in material demands, oriented toward and not against a consumer society.

Some elements of the strikes do suggest aspirations going beyond the material standbys of wages and hours. When the trade union federations tried to end the strikes in late May by negotiating large wage increases with the employers' federation, the union leaders announcing these results to the strikers were hooted down. Self-management was a slogan spread widely throughout the strikes. By contrast, the demand raised at the Citroën works on the outskirts of Paris, that workers receive from their employer discount auto rentals for their summer vacations, does not exactly suggest a rejection of consumer society. Although the slogan of self-management was widespread, it seems to have been taken most seriously by managers and engineers, by university students and junior faculty, or by journalists of state-run TV and radio, who deeply resented management's orders to report on the events in accordance with the government's wishes (demonstrators, clutching transistor radios, relied on the more objective journalism of Radio Television Luxembourg, privately owned and based just outside of France) and somewhat less so by blue-collar workers. One might say that May 1968, in this respect rather like the GPCR, was an occasion for an enormous outpouring of demands and aspirations by a wide variety of social groups, sometimes aligned, sometimes moving in different directions, sometimes bringing up reminiscences of past struggles, sometimes appearing new and distinctive. Like the GPCR, where everything was articulated in terms of Chairman Mao's plans for creating a new socialist culture, in May 1968, the many aspirations abroad in France did tend to be articulated in the older, Marxist language of the labor movement—and this was true of most of the youthful adherents of the *groupuscules* as well.

If the upheavals of the GPCR had ultimately been repressed by armed force, the same was not true for the events of May. Police responses to the large-scale street disturbances on Paris's Left Bank had been relatively restrained, primarily standing off at a distance and bombarding crowds with tear gas and water cannons. This was very different from the tactics used against the last major demonstrations in Paris, those of Algerian nationalists in 1961–62, when the police had waded into the demonstrators with their nightsticks, assaulting and even killing them, dumping bodies in the Seine. The different tactics in 1968 reflected in part new French riot-control doctrine, but also the difference between the dark-skinned North African demonstrators of the early 1960s, and the distinctly white young French people at the end of the decade.

For their part, the strikes and demonstrations, if largely paralyzing the country, could not be translated into political change—overthrowing the authoritarian rule of French president Charles de Gaulle. Efforts in that direction by a small group of left-of-center politicians foundered, especially on the open hostility of the Communist Party, still the largest group on the left, whose leaders kept their distance from the insurgent students and young people, wanted the strikers back at work with large wage increases, and even had their own antigovernment demonstrations, separate from everyone else's. After two weeks of a nationwide strike, return-to-work sentiment was spreading, perhaps less in Paris, but definitely in France's second and third cities, Marseille and Lyon. In the end, it was nationalism, so often an enemy—as we've seen—of the aspirations of the 1960s, that resolved the situation. Following de Gaulle's dramatic radio address to the nation, an enormous demonstration on the Champs Elysée in Paris on May 31 united conservatives and nationalists of all kinds, former resisters of the Second World War and former supporters of the collaborationist Vichy regime, adherents of de Gaulle's policy of granting independence to Algeria, and opponents of it, who had tried to assassinate the general, and whose auto horns beeping out the three-two rhythm, *Al-gé-rie Fran-çaise* punctuated the march. The immediately following weekend, June 1–3, was the Pentecost holiday, and there was an enormous exodus from Paris for a vacation in the countryside, the highways leading out of the capital completely gridlocked. Bit by bit, over the course of the month of June, strikers returned to work, voluntarily, or with the assistance of the riot police. The triumph of nationalism and consumer society over their enemies was capped off by a victory of the Gaullists in parliamentary elections held in June.

Like the GPCR, the images and slogans of the events of May echoed around the world, but while the very distinct circumstances of Mao's China made a literal recurrence of the Cultural Revolution unlikely, this was not the case with the events of May. A well-known recurrence was just to the southeast in Italy: the *"autonno caldo"* [hot autumn] of 1969, a rolling May 1968, where student strikes and university occupations, industrial workers' strikes and factory occupations, massive street demonstrations and clashes with the police occurred not all at once but in serial fashion across the Italian peninsula. Demands for self-management were widespread, the Italian equivalents of the French ultra-left *groupuscules*, with vaguely Maoist inspiration, such as *Lotta continua* (The Struggle Goes On) and *Potere operai* (Workers Power) were very active and more influential among industrial workers than their French counterparts.[62]

An even more direct echo and imitation of the events of May, much less well known, is a powerful testimony to the global nature of the 1960s. This was in Senegal, a recently independent former French colony in West Africa. Students at the University of Dakar, a cosmopolitan group, including native Senegalese, alongside students from other African countries, as well as from Europe, already angered by the government's plans to cut state scholarships in half, which had resulted in numerous demonstrations, went on strike, May 27, 1968. Very well informed of the events in France and proclaiming their inspirations, like youthful radicals around the world, from Che Guevara, Ho Chi Minh, and Chairman Mao; as well as Pan-Africanists Frantz Fanon, Kwame Nkrumah (whose rule in Ghana had recently been ended by a military coup), and Sékou Touré in Guinea, the students demanded the Africanization of the university, expulsion of foreign administrators and faculty and an end to its links to the French academic system. They denounced the authoritarian government of Senegal's President Leopold Senghor and called for the legalization of opposition political parties.

Senghor's government sent in the riot police to end the demonstrations. This triggered three days of rioting in Senegal's capital Dakar, which spread to other cities, including St. Louis, Thiès, and Kaolack. The Senegalese trade union federation UNTS declared a nationwide general strike. Rather than trying to use the military to crush the mass movement, President Senghor made concessions, agreeing to the students' demands for Africanization and negotiating the first set of collective bargaining wage increases since independence in 1960. His regime, not unlike the one in the former colonial mother country, survived, and further student strikes in 1969 and 1971 were met by drafting strikers into the army. Showing simultaneously the influence of the former colonial ruler and the rejection of its rule, international connections and nation-state specific politics, as well as the ubiquity of the Third World inspirations of the 1960s, the uprising in Senegal provides a worthy pendant to the two quintessential examples of the sixties.⁶³

THE LEGACY OF THE ERA OF UPHEAVAL

If the mass movements embodying utopian aspirations at the end of the Second World War came to an end at least in part as a result of the onset of the placid prosperity of the 1950s, the second wave of global utopianism was terminated by the onset of a period of prolonged economic upheaval, following the first oil price shock of 1973. Even if rejecting consumer society, the 1960s radicals took the prosperity behind it for granted, and its disappearance undermined a crucial presupposition of utopian aspirations of the era. Political repression and military suppression had sometimes played a role in terminating 1945-era utopian aspirations, and this was true for their 1960s counterparts as well: on a small scale in the wealthy lands of the North Atlantic; on a larger one in South America, Czechoslovakia, or China.

So if the High 1960s and their utopian aspirations, along with the mass movements that embodied them, were gone by 1975, what remained of their legacy? One aspect was the incorporation of radical activists into older left-of-center political parties, reinvigorating them and bringing them into power. The unprecedented election victory of the West German Social Democrats in 1972, and the broader regeneration and rejuvenation of the Social Democratic Party were both a result of the mobilization of former New Left activists and young people endorsing their ideas. The attraction of the Social Democrats' charismatic leader and veteran anti-fascist Willy Brandt played a large part in this process; his more pragmatic and technocratic successor, Helmut Schmidt, had a harder time with former New Leftists. While the short-term political impact of the events of May in France had been to strengthen Charles de Gaulle's authoritarian conservative government, over the course of the 1970s, the political left, especially the Socialist Party, gathered strength through gaining support of one-time New Leftists (their communist ally-rivals were singularly unsuccessful at this), culminating in the election of François Mitterrand as president of the Republic in 1981, with a government staffed by former 1960s activists, including the theorist of Third World revolution Régis Debray. There were similar developments in Greece, following the fall of the military dictatorship in 1974, after its disastrous foreign policy adventure and subsequent humiliation by the Turks in Cyprus.⁶⁴

Perhaps the most prominent example of the belated political success of a 1960s radical was in Uruguay. In 2010, José Mujica, a former leader of the urban guerilla group, the *Tupamaros*, famed in the 1960s for their daring bank robberies, and creative propaganda coups, who spent thirteen years in jail, following the crushing of the insurgents by a military regime, was elected president of the Republic, as the candidate of the center-left Broad Front. His five-year term in office included the legalization of marijuana, gay marriage, and abortion, and a strong emphasis on environmentalism. Beyond such reforms, he was known and loved for his ostentatiously modest lifestyle—living in a cottage instead of the presidential palace, donating 90 percent of his salary, driving a twenty-five-year-old VW Bug, instead of being chauffeured in a limousine—a remnant of the quirky propaganda of the 1960s radical group with which he had been affiliated.[65]

These long-term political successes stand against a larger number of setbacks. Particularly in the Anglosphere, former New Leftists have been politically marginalized. The long conservative domination of politics in the age of Reagan and Thatcher was connected with a strong rejection of the radical ideas and mass movements of the 1960s. In 1987, the Labour Party MP Jack Straw told an interviewer that "Going to a Labour Party now is like a throw-back to a National Union of Students [UK New Left student group] in the late 1960s and early 1970s . . ." Of course, this Labour Party of former New Leftists was the same one that was repeatedly humiliated by Margaret Thatcher's Tories. When very modestly center-left governments came to power in the United States and the United Kingdom in the 1990s, they were led by figures such as Bill Clinton and Tony Blair, who, very much unlike José Mujica, or even Willy Brandt, did not embody the spirit of the 1960s. Jack Straw, himself holding a number of prominent positions in Blair's government, including Home Secretary and Foreign Minister, showed little or nothing of his own student radical past in office.[66]

Proponents of China's version of the 1960s, many of whom had already been executed in the late stages of the Cultural Revolution, have clearly not had much effect on Chinese politics, except, perhaps, to reject the Cultural Revolution completely. While some of the 1960s radicals in the Eastern Bloc, such as 1968 University of Warsaw student activist Adam Michnik, would go on to play a significant role in Solidarity and in the events of 1989, the post-communist political scene in the former Eastern Bloc has been dominated by a clash between pro-free-market liberals and authoritarian nationalists, neither of whom can claim to be heirs of the aspirations of the sixties. The same can be said of sixties radicals in Africa or Asia. Perhaps the worst off were those in Ethiopia, who were faced with the choice of either supporting the *Derg*, the vicious, murderous Marxist military dictatorship, and going down with it at the end of the 1980s, or openly opposing it, and becoming its victims.[67]

Another heir of the 1960s were extreme leftist groups around the world, usually one of two versions, "Marxist-Leninists," pro-Chinese Maoists, or revolutionary terrorist organizations. Both emerged, typically in conflict with each other, out of the matrix of the high 1960s replacing earlier aspirations to participation and self-actualization, with a Marxism based on a particularly dogmatic reading of Lenin's and Stalin's writings, while carrying identification with Third World revolution to extremes. The American SDS conference in Chicago in 1969, dominated by the destructive hostility between the future terrorists of the Revolutionary Youth Movement and the Maoist Progressive Labor Party, took the form of a controversy over which group was the authentic vanguard of the proletariat and the genuine ally of Third World revolution, epitomized the split, as much farce as tragedy.[68]

The Marxist-Leninist groups, characterized by extreme hostility to the counterculture, very intrusive monitoring of their adherents' personal lives, rigid, dogmatic versions of an already very dogmatic Leninism, and extreme sectarianism—why West Germany needed four such Maoist political parties, each claiming to uphold the true doctrine, remains a mystery—were not graced with a long life. By the mid-to-late 1970s, they were everywhere—in Senegal and India, as much as in France, the United States, or West Germany—in a state of collapse. The post-Mao policies pursued by Deng Xiaoping and his supporters, meant that the China Maoists once idealized was no longer a communist country.[69]

Although sporting many fewer adherents than the Marxist-Leninists, the terrorists had a considerably greater political impact, through their spectacular airplane hijackings, kidnappings and assassinations, all of which drew immense media attention, in a way that efforts to teach Leninist doctrine to factory workers did not. Terrorists were impelled by powerful feelings of Third World solidarity, coupled with the belief that their own countries' political systems either were already fascistic in nature or about to become so, making a clandestine, violent resistance the only possible course of anti-imperialist action. Not all terrorists were particularly effective. The American Weathermen (later renamed Weather Underground because of the sexist connotations of Weathermen) mostly succeeded in blowing themselves up. Attempts by Ethiopian terrorists to hijack airliners were noticeably unsuccessful. The most effective and active terrorist groups were found in the three former Axis powers—the German and Japanese Red Armies and the Italian Red Brigades—and among the Palestinians. Powerfully symbolic actions, such as the kidnapping and subsequent murder of Italian Christian Democratic politician Aldo Moro and the German business leader Hans-Joachim Schleyer, the kidnapping and murder of Israeli athletes at the 1972 Munich Olympic Games, or taking the participants of the 1975 OPEC conference hostage, convulsed entire countries, sometimes large parts of the world, for weeks at a time.

Far more so than 1960s student radicals or Maoists, the terrorists were very much a globalized movement, with close ties between the Palestinians and other terrorist groups, reversing the usual connections between wealthier and poorer countries, since it was the Palestinians who trained and increasingly directed European and Japanese terrorists, rather than the other way around. In the end, the small size of the terrorist groups and the increasing capabilities of police work told against them. The disastrous reign of the anti-imperialist Khmer Rouge in Cambodia, and the Iranian Revolution of 1979, the beginning of a transition in Third World radicalism from communism to Islamism, were ideological blows similar to that delivered to the Maoists by the policies of Deng Xiaoping.[70]

Former 1960s activists and aspirations also appeared in organizations and political movements emerging in the 1970s devoted to particular single issues, especially environmentalism, feminism, and human rights. The heritage of these aspirations for environmentalist movements was less in the content—apprehensions about the biosphere played a marginal role in sixties radicalism, perhaps more prevalent, in a romanticized way, in the youth culture of the era than in expressly political movements—as it was in the opposition to bureaucracy and hierarchy and calls for self-actualization, which were crucial to the development of environmentalism as mass movement. There were personal interconnections as well, since one-time New Leftist activists and ex-Maoists often turned to environmentalism. Feminists of the 1970s were frequently ex-New Leftists, and their politics continued to reflect 1960s aspirations to self-actualization and Third World inspiration—albeit condemning the way that in the 1960s aspirations to self-actualization either ignored women's aspirations or positively suppressed them. Feminism also involved a pronounced rejection of the macho culture of the radical politics of the high 1960s, with its emphasis on militancy and street fighting, the dominant role of media-savvy male leaders, and the practice, intentional or not, of consigning women to providing refreshments, and secretarial and sexual services.[71]

Another venue for one-time New Leftists was the human rights movement of the 1970s and 1980s, both preexisting but rapidly expanding groups, such as Amnesty International, and new ones emerging at the time, like Doctors without Borders, Helsinki Watch, or Human Rights Watch. These sorts of groups, part of a rapid expansion of international NGOs, whose numbers went from 2,795 in 1972 to 12,686 in 1984, involved a much greater degree of organization and international organization at that, than the casually organized or just disorganized mass movements of the 1960s. In South America, the turn from Third World Revolution to human rights was, frankly, a matter of survival, as military dictatorships sought to eliminate, physically, left-wing opposition.

There was something similar in Eastern Bloc countries, where the human rights movement became a form of expression of political opposition, after mass movements, like the Prague Spring of 1968, or, later, the Solidarity trade union organization of 1980–81, had been suppressed. More broadly, the human rights ideal of holding all governments to a common standard involved a break with 1960s anti-imperialism and Third World inspiration. There were, and still are, proponents of the original 1960s ideals who denounce human rights organizations and human rights theorists as imperialists, imposing their ideas on Third World countries and lacking solidarity with and inspiration from the Third World, at best replacing them with paternalist condescension, at worst using human rights to reimpose colonialism.[72] This clash of opinions is, perhaps, also one form of the heritage of the 1960s.

A Very Different Utopia in the Late-Millennium Era

Both 1968 and 1989 were central years of rapid change on a global scale. Perceptions of change in 1968 were the result of the many instances of uprisings and demonstrations occurring over an entire year, a series of years, actually, and across the world. The barrage of turbulence visible on television was a daily occurrence, but also one that was widely diffused. By contrast, the upheavals of 1989 seemed to be melted down, concentrated, focused on a single night, a single spot, and a single event: the opening of the Berlin Wall in the evening hours of November 9. Recorded live, the event was rebroadcast, rerun and commemorated on television; in still photography, in newspapers, magazines, books, posters, films, music videos, and Coke commercials. Real and fake pieces of the wall were peddled as souvenirs for years afterward. That fateful night might well appear as a world-historical singularity, a global point of inflection. The city out of which the Second World War began and the Age of Total War reached its terrible high point, was the venue for the final, definitive end of that war. In the very same instant, the Second World War was concluded, and the Cold War that emerged from that war was terminated as well. The worldwide confrontations of the two opposing power blocs ceased; the constant, decades-long, background threat of nuclear annihilation vanished with it.

This end of the Cold War marked, or seemed to mark, the victory of one of the contending power blocs, and the political and socioeconomic ideals it embodied. A communist regime, armed to the teeth, with soldiers, paramilitary units, secret police, regular police, and armed volunteers, was defied and defeated by unarmed protestors wanting to burst out of their totalitarian cage, looking for personal freedom and a wealth of consumer goods. Following that November night, a prospect of prosperity, democracy, human rights, free movement, and free markets seemed to stretch far into the future.

In the decade of the 1990s, the sentiments of 1989 took on utopian form: a world of deregulated free-market prosperity, peacefully developing under the benign hegemony of the United States. This third wave of worldwide utopian aspirations was very different from its two predecessors, immediately following the Second World War and in the 1960s. Those had been on the left side of the political spectrum, filled with red flags. Such flags were very much lacking in the mass movements of 1989. While the people pouring into the streets across communist Eurasia may not have had this particular outcome in mind, the utopian aspirations that emerged from their actions were distinctly to the right—Margaret Thatcher's or Milton Friedman's utopia, one might call it. This was a utopia of statesmen, policy makers, and financiers; people in the seats of power, not, as previously the case (with a few exceptions), a utopia of dissidents, insurgents, and the powerless. All three waves of utopian aspirations had their intellectuals, with the first two concentrated among writers, artists, philosophers, and sometimes sociologists; the definers of the utopian aspirations of the Late-Millennium Era were economists, political scientists, journalists, and pundits. If politically different from the first two waves of utopianism, it would share their disappointing fate, although that disillusionment would stretch out into the first two decades of the twenty-first century. Deregulated, privatized free markets would deliver as much economic disruption, impoverishment, and rising inequality as prosperity; the end of communist regimes did unleash freedom, unfortunately not just the freedom to speak and publish or to start businesses, but also the freedom to plunder public property or to attack and murder national enemies. US global hegemony, whether benign or otherwise, called forth increasing opposition, in the form of Islamism, whose consequences would be felt at the very beginning of the new millennium, but also a renascent authoritarian nationalism, whose impact would not become entirely apparent until later in the twenty-first century.

The aspirations of this third wave of utopianism had a long prehistory, going back to the years of the Great Depression. Militant proponents of economic orthodoxy, of policies such as the gold standard, balanced budgets, and a minimal economic presence of the government, particularly clustered in the Vienna Chamber of Commerce, the Institute of International Studies in Geneva, the London School of Economics, and the University of Chicago, but found more broadly among those same economists, journalists, and pundits in Europe and North America, and the businessmen who endorsed their ideas, were increasingly dismayed by policy responses to the persistent economic crisis. Their anathemas extended to a wide variety of measures, including social welfare and public works programs, support of trade unions and collective bargaining agreements, economic planning, tariffs, exchange controls and price supports—all of which, adding to their dismay, were employed by democratic, authoritarian conservative, and fascist regimes, to say nothing of the communists, and their rejection of markets altogether. The experience of the Second World War and the postwar era of utopian aspirations, moving still farther away from economic orthodoxy, led to their organization, the formation in 1947 of an international economics study group and think tank, with the support of Swiss and American businessmen, the Mont Pèlerin Society.[73]

Yet these early opponents of vigorous government economic policies in a crisis situation, or "collectivism," as they called it, were plagued by doubts and hesitations. In the tradition of economics as a dismal science, they openly advocated for declining wages and standards of living along with an increase in economic inequality as a response to the crisis—sometimes as a temporary measure, but often as a permanent condition. Europeans among this group were often skeptical of democracy, seeing it as just allowing the masses, following the lead of demagogues, to interfere in the natural workings of the economy. They proposed various forms of legal and constitutional restrictions on government economic action, whether at the level of individuals states, or via transnational federations and diplomatic agreements, although they were unable to explain how these could come about. Their American counterparts, especially those in the economics department of the University of Chicago during the 1930s, opposed the policies of the New Deal, denouncing government planning, social welfare programs, or encouragement of unionization, but combined their advocacy of unrestricted markets and the primacy of rational self-interest with forms of government action, such as strong antitrust laws or a steep progressive income tax.

These ambiguities appear in the 1944 book of the Austrian economist Friedrich Hayek, *The Road to Serfdom*. In spite of its vigorous attacks on government planning and limitations on "freedom in economic affairs," denouncing them as inevitably leading to totalitarian rule, Hayek did admit that governments could legitimately institute social insurance policies, enforce workplace safety and wages and hours laws, build infrastructure, and institute countercyclical fiscal and monetary policies. These positions may come as a surprise to readers who think of the work as a foundational classic of libertarianism. However, the impact of Hayek's treatise was less through the work itself than via the abridged and rewritten version (none of it done by Hayek himself), which appeared in *Reader's Digest*, leaving out all the qualifications and producing an antigovernment diatribe. Over a million reprints were ordered by corporations and business special-interest groups (twenty-five times the sales of the book); chambers of commerce and bankers' associations gave Hayek a hero's welcome during his 1945 lecture tour of the United States.

This episode showed how the aspirations of the libertarians, radical liberals, or neoliberals as they began calling themselves (exact self-designations varied and were often uncertain) could achieve a maximum public resonance: a uniform, consistent message with no qualifications, amplified in well-funded ways. It would take one of the founding members of the Mont Pèlerin Society, later its dominant figure, to achieve this, the University of Chicago economist Milton Friedman. Perhaps the leading figure of his discipline in the

Age of Interconnection, Friedman's influence stemmed less from his actual economic findings and assertions, many of which, such as the idea that price stability could be obtained by controlling the money supply, or the so-called lifetime income hypothesis, have proven to be incorrect, or, as was the case with his advocacy of floating exchange rates, led to unexpected problems.[74]

Rather, his influence emerged from two other elements of his thought. One was more theoretical, his 1952 essay, "The Methodology of Positive Economics," in which he asserted that it was irrelevant if economic models did not correspond to actual human motivations and reasoning, so long as predictions made from them checked out. With that statement, it became possible to treat people as rational utility maximizers in all aspects of their lives (one of his Chicago colleagues, Gary Becker, would model the decision of couples to have children on the purchase of consumer goods), and to ignore not just any evidence that people were actually not utility maximizers, but also conditions that might interfere with utility maximization, such as externalities, information asymmetries, time horizons, or transaction costs.

The other aspect of Friedman's influence lay in his role as a popularizer: testifying before Congress, giving public lectures, writing bestsellers, such as *Capitalism and Freedom*, and even having his own TV series, *Free to Choose*. In this role as public advocate, Friedman rejected the dour, pessimistic attitudes shown by 1930s neoliberals, or the willingness to compromise Friedrich Hayek had demonstrated in his book. Rather, he followed the *Reader's Digest* version of Hayek's ideas, insisting both that self-interest-oriented market solutions (generally rather extreme versions of them) would not just be successful but would benefit everyone. The poor would benefit from abolishing social welfare, old age pensions, and weakening unions; African Americans would see their inferior position ameliorated, not by civil rights laws, infringing on personal choice, but by rational market incentives to hire and sell to them. If medical care was too expensive, the solution was to abolish medical licensing so there could be more medical providers and eliminating any requirements that drugs be tested for safety and effectiveness. Friedman even rejected government assistance to victims of natural disasters, since it would incentivize them to live in unsafe areas. Both the theory and the public policy betrayed clearly utopian aspirations in the direction of a society designed exclusively around calculations of individualized, purportedly rational self-interest.

In the postwar era of regulated capitalism, these ideas remained politically marginal, although gaining important financial support from business interests.[75] The economic upheavals of the 1970s gave proponents of unregulated and unleashed markets their chance to begin implementing their policies; their influence grew during the 1980s, especially in the governments of conservative icons Ronald Reagan and Margaret Thatcher, both great Friedman admirers, but also in international economic institutions, such as the World Bank, the IMF and OECD, and more broadly in academia and the media. The end of communist regimes, constructed on principles in direct opposition to theirs, was their moment.[76]

An immensely popular account of the post-Cold War world, read and debated throughout Europe and North America, came from political scientist Francis Fukuyama in his 1989 article, expanded into a 1992 book of the same title, *The End of History*. Contrary to his many critics, Fukuyama was not asserting that there would be no more historical events; rather, his point was that the events of 1989 represented the culmination of a long-term trend, resolving the basic questions about the nature of the most desirable economic and political order. The former would, of course, be free-market economies and Fukuyama condemned to the dustbin of history not just communist regimes, but also efforts at import substitution industrialization, the deployment of capital controls, the 1970s idea of a New International Economic Order, and other attempts to limit a globalized capitalism. The triumph of such a capitalism, Fukuyama asserted, was the inevitable result of scientific and technological progress. Capitalism could deploy these for the purposes of consumerism; other economic systems, as history had shown, could not. Twentieth-century history had similarly revealed the one successful political system, "liberal democracy." Here as well, Fukuyama presented the events of 1989 as the culmination of a long trend, including the violent failures of fascist states and the end of military dictatorships during the 1980s in Latin America, Africa, and Asia.

It would be unfair to Fukuyama to describe him, as some critics did, as a simplistic thinker. His picture of a global triumph of the Cold War west came with a number of qualifications and nuances. Unlike Europe, North America, or East Asia, the rest of the world was, in Fukuyama's estimation, not yet completely convinced of the virtues of capitalism and liberal democracy, so history might continue there, while it had ended elsewhere. Among many other things, those countries were often strongholds of nationalist sentiment, which Fukuyama saw as on the wane in his preferred liberal democracies. He was no disciple of the Mont Pèlerin society; his triumphant consumer capitalism included north European social welfare states, as well as Anglo-American Thatcherite and Reaganite ones. Describing the rise of East Asia as an example of the triumph of capitalism, he did have to admit, somewhat uneasily, that East Asian capitalism seemed quite compatible with authoritarian, definitely not liberal-democratic, regimes, and also with a good deal of government economic intervention. A large part of Fukuyama's work, reflecting, perhaps, an overdose of Plato, Hegel, and Nietzsche, dealt with the question of how individuals' psychic need for struggle and accomplishment could be achieved after the end of history. Instead of political conflict, he thought that athletic competition or building business empires (which, in his book, was oddly separated from the free-market capitalism he advocated) might do in its stead.

Fukuyama had strong opinions about the kind of foreign policy required for a post-historical world. Rejecting then fashionable "realist" theories of cynical national self-interest and raison d'état, but also expressing his doubts about the United Nations, where there were far too many countries involved who had not yet recognized the end of history, he recommended instead that the United States cooperate with like-minded countries in organizations such as NATO, the OECD, the G-7, or the General Agreement on Trade and Tariffs (GATT). Since at the time, these were all groups where the United States had a dominant or, at least a leading role, the end of history would have been a world under American dominion.[77]

Fukuyama denied that he was an American triumphalist, claiming that his prototype of the post-historical world was the European Union. While he may have been (at least in the afterword to the 2006 second edition of his book) reluctant to bring out the implications of his ideas, others were not. France's foreign minister Hubert Védrine, memorably described the United States in 1998 as a "hyperpower." President George H. W. Bush, who, as he stated, lacked "the vision thing," nonetheless had no difficulty describing the post-1989 global scene in his 1991 State of the Union address as a "new world order," which could only emerge and become permanent through American leadership.[78] Together, these ideas formed the core of the late twentieth-century utopian aspirations: a world of an increasingly globalized, unregulated, and unlimited capitalist market economy, under the benevolent, multilateralized hegemony of the United States.

The 1990s was a decade of privatization and deregulation, slashing social welfare expenditures, balancing government budgets, and expediting capital flows in the "Washington consensus." It was a period of multilaterally organized American global leadership—apparent in the response to Saddam Hussein's invasion of Kuwait or to the civil wars and mass murders in the former Yugoslavia (conspicuously absent in the mass murders in Rwanda)—that produced decisive results. Features of the era reveal the contours of its utopian aspirations.

One is the strikingly broad consensus in policy-making circles. While many of the measures of deregulation and privatization began under 1980s conservative governments, their center-left 1990s successors, Bill Clinton in the United States, Tony Blair in the United Kingdom, Gerd Schroeder in Germany, or Wim Kok in the Netherlands, continued these policies, sometimes, as was true with Schroeder, in more aggressive fashion than their Milton Friedman-citing predecessors. The most remarkable example of such a political turnabout was India's prime minister from 1991 to 1996, P. V. Narasimha Rao. A one-time radical socialist, as chief minister of the Indian state of Andhra Pradesh in the early 1970s, he had tried to expropriate the landlords and distribute their property to agricultural laborers. A quarter-century later, as India's prime minister, his government devalued the rupee, abolished import quotas and import licenses, slashed subsidies, eliminated controls on foreign exchange and foreign investments (admittedly, one of the foreign investors was the US energy firm Enron, whose fraudulent business practices worked no better in India than in the United States), allowed the formation of private banks, telecommunications companies and airlines, and joined the World Trade Organization. It was a remarkable break with the policies of import substitution industrialization, pursued since India's independence from colonial rule, and a thoroughgoing transformation in the direction of unrestricted markets.[79]

More than anywhere else in the world, the utopian nature of these Late-Millennium Era aspirations appeared in the post-communist countries of Europe. For two decades, governments, political parties, experts, and journalists pursued the unleashing of markets with a bitter determination. Initial policies of "shock therapy," immediate end of administered prices, replaced by market determinations, introduction of convertible currencies and freedom of capital transactions, along with austerity and budget balancing measures, were followed by privatization of government-owned businesses, often by the distribution of vouchers to the general population. By the end of the 1990s, two new policies were developed, long favorites of Friedmanites in Europe and North America, but politically unpalatable there: a flat tax, a non-progressive income tax at the same rate for everyone, thus particularly favorable to members of upper-income groups, and the privatization of old age pensions. Policy makers and almost all political parties of both the left and the right ignored the very different—and quite successful, one might add—policies of gradual transition from planned to market economy carried out in China. They continued their marketization policies with determination, even if the results differed considerably from the promises of their proponents, marching on toward a world of unleashed markets and rationalized individual self-interest until the global economic crisis of 2008.

The new, post-communist governments received reams of advice pointing in this direction from Western consultants and advisers. In the 1970s and '80s, advisers representing these points of view were very distinctly from the Mount Pèlerin wing of economics. The classic example was Milton Friedman's students, *los Chicago Boys*, who advised Augusto Pinochet's military dictatorship in Chile to open markets and to privatize old age pensions. (There was no need to tell the junta to weaken unions; they had already taken care of that, imprisoning and executing union leaders.) This was less the case at the end of the millennium: key advisers to the Russian government, promoting policies of economic shock therapy, such as Jeffrey Sachs or the students of Harvard economics professor Larry Summers, were more Keynesians than Friedman disciples—yet another example of the triumph of utopian free-market aspirations, very much like the deregulatory policies of center-left governments in Europe and North America in that decade.[80]

Besides these individual, freelance advisers, there were the institutional ones, economists from the World Bank, the IMF, the OECD, and the European Bank for Reconstruction and Development, [EBRD] set up by the EU to help finance the transition to capitalism in post-communist Europe. Not just advising, these organizations also created seminars for politicians and government officials to inculcate market principles. They were joined by private foundations devoted to the principles of Mont Pèlerin, such as the American Enterprise Institute, the Adam Smith Institute, or their Swedish counterpart, Timbro. The EBRD even provided a handy yearly scoreboard, its "transition indicators," to show how far along each country was in its march toward a market utopia. Decisions supplemented advice. Privatizing old age insurance was supposed to reduce government spending in the long run, but required, at first, expanded government expenditures, as working age population's payments were diverted from supporting the elderly to investing for their own retirement, meaning that additional funds were required to support those already retired. The World Bank agreed to lend funds for that purpose, and not to count those debts toward the budget deficit, which all advisers agreed had to be reduced.

This advice, and the funds behind them (western countries were generally more generous with advice than with money), was gladly accepted. Vaclav Klaus, the Czech economist/politician who was a leading Eastern European advocate of privatization and shock therapy, famously disparaged the idea of competing policies by stating that the "third way," was the "fastest way to the Third World." Estonian prime minister Matt Laar, who introduced a flat tax in 1994, making his country the first in the entire world to do so, stated that the only thing he knew about economics was from reading the book version of Milton Friedman's TV series *Free to Choose*.[81]

Most remarkable was the attitude of the leaders of Solidarity, the Polish trade union that had defied the communist regime at the beginning of the 1980s and, in retrospect, signaled the beginning of the end of communism in Eastern Europe. As communist rule gave way to a multiparty democracy in Poland around 1989, along with the introduction of basic civil liberties, including freedom to organize and to form associations, the national leaders and local activists of Solidarity made the decision not to rebuild their union. Quite the opposite, they saw unions, labor organization and workers' demands as obstacles on the path to a post-communist Poland, ruled by the imperatives of an unrestricted market. As their preferred policies were put into effect in the first half of the 1990s, under the implacably and extremely market-oriented finance minister, Leszek Balcerowicz, resulting initially in rapid rises in both the unemployment and inflation rates, as well as growing economic inequality, some one-time Solidarity activists, soon to be associated with authoritarian and right-wing populist political parties, began to criticize government policies. The problem was not the rapid transition to capitalism they asserted, but that the transition was not rapid enough; it was being sabotaged by former communist apparatchiks, who needed to be purged from government for capitalism to succeed.[82]

If Eastern Europe of the 1990s was a rich field for the realization of free-market utopian aspirations, it was an equally rich field of disappointments about the results of these aspirations. The promised prosperity and widespread availability of consumer goods—certainly reasonable expectations in view of the decades-long inability of communist regimes to provide them—through the unleashing of rational calculations of self-interest in an unrestrained market failed to happen. Instead, there was inflation, unemployment, severe economic contraction, fraud and pyramid schemes, gangsters bringing violence and extortion to economic exchange, appropriation of formerly public property for private purposes, transfer of assets to Swiss bank accounts and London real estate, fiscal crises, and repudiation of debts. A recounting of examples from Magdeburg to Vladivostok, from the Arctic Circle to the Black Sea, would be a book in itself, but it is possible to make three general observations about the foundering of the utopian aspirations to a world of privatized, unregulated, purportedly rational market incentives.[83]

One was the assumption that incentives were enough: just liberate prices, open up markets and rational, self-interested expectations will assure that everything will arrange itself for the better. Unleashing self-interest without legal institutions to guide it, however, led to problematic results. As newly liberated businesses in Russia tried to collect their accounts receivable and debts owed to them (uncollected debts grew from three trillion rubles in 1994 to forty-nine trillion by 1996), they discovered that the laws were insufficient, the courts were inactive, and bankruptcy proceedings were a farce. Businesses began hiring strong men, *mafiia*, to do this. Of course, once gangsters were in action, they began demanding protection money on a very large scale. Tax collection was notoriously erratic, resulting in businesses keeping two sets of books, one their actual results, the other what they showed the authorities. Once this became a common practice, everyone had to follow, because to report actual business results honestly, would have meant being subject to crippling taxation, as the government, desperate for revenues to balance its budget, would try to collect anything it could. Increasingly, businesses avoided the use of cash and engaged in dubious barter transactions.

Second, and related to this issue of the intersection between self-interest and legal institutions, was a parallel intersection between self-interest and moral institutions. In countries with a long history of market transactions, there is an understanding that some forms of seeking out self-interest are legitimate, while others are morally inappropriate. Under communism, all forms of profit-seeking were described as criminal and immoral; the rapid transition to a regime of self-interest led to a direct turnabout: all forms of self-interest were appropriate. Post-communist Eastern Europe was a playground for fraudsters, for illicit use of connections and personal influence. One example was the prevalence of gigantic pyramid schemes. The Russian MMM firm, purportedly a dealer in commodities and other goods, offered investors returns of 1,000 percent, which it provided by using new investors to pay off the older ones. When the scheme exploded, the firm founder, Sergei Mavrodi, evaded punishment by getting himself elected to the *Duma* and so enjoying the legal immunity of a parliamentary deputy. This Russian scheme—and MMM was just the largest of many—paled before what happened in post-communist Albania. There, the money invested in pyramid schemes, run by shady operators who had been smuggling weapons into war-torn ex-Yugoslavia, came to half the country's GDP and received investments from two-thirds of the population. The explosion of the schemes in 1996–97 led to a small-scale civil war in which over two thousand people died.[84] Of course, pyramid schemes, fraud, capitalizing on illicit influence and the actions of gangsters certainly were and are feature of economic life in countries with a long history of a capitalist market economy. However, nothing before had been seen on the scale of 1990s Eastern Europe.

Finally, there were what might be called the structural conditions in which purportedly rational self-interest was exercised. Privatization of publicly owned businesses by distribution of vouchers to the general population made everyone a property owner. Ideas of restricting sales or transfer of these privatization coupons were rejected by Western economic advisers, since individuals' self-interest would tell them what to do. Only the very difficult economic circumstances prevailing in the 1990s led to most people selling their coupons for a nominal fee—in Russia about the equivalent of four-and-a-half pounds of butter—or "investing" them in holding companies, which were, as it turned out, publicly owned, so that privatization ended up returning firms to public ownership. In these instances, as was typically the case with privatization in the formerly communist countries, regardless of nominal ownership, it was the firm's management that ended up in control of the firm's assets. Abolishing any restrictions on international financial transactions, another key plank of marketization programs, then made it easy for these managers and other well-connected parties to appropriate or the firms' assets (one might call this "looting," but with an inadequate legal framework it was hard to separate legal and illegal activities) and to transfer them abroad.

Initial promises that the unleashing of market-based self-interest would lead to immediate prosperity were quickly replaced with a more dour attitude, one closer to the original embattled free-market enthusiasts of the 1930s, than the cheerful, optimistic version propounded by Milton Friedman: first there would be a period of economic decline, eventually to

TABLE 13.1 The Economic Fate of Post-Communist Eastern Europe

Country	Year permanently exceeding 1989 GDP levels	Maximum GDP Decline
Bulgaria	2007	36%
Czech Republic	2001	14%
Estonia	2000	26%
Hungary	1997	13%
Poland	1993	12%
Romania	1999	14%
Russian Federation	2010	61%
Slovakia	2005	28%
Slovenia	1995	20%

Source: GDP figures from the Maddison Project, https://www.rug.nl/ggdc/historicaldevelopment/maddison/releases/maddison-project-database-2018, Sept. 4, 2020.

be followed by the long-awaited boom, prosperity, and consumerism. Table 13.1 investigates the reality of this claim, showing how long it took in different post-communist countries for per capita GDP to return to 1989 levels and how deep it had fallen before then.

Note that these figures show only when the various countries had regained the level of economic output they had at the end of communism—not a very good place to start, and certainly not a beacon of prosperity. As a statistic, per capita GDP says relatively little about broader standards of living that, in view of increasing income inequality, lagged behind it. Even by these very modest criteria, the results of the 1990s utopian aspirations were disappointing indeed: long periods of economic decline, usually a decade or more, and very steep falls in economic output, ranging from Great Depression level declines of 12 to 15 percent, to the astonishing figures in Russia, the poster child for shock therapy and marketization, of 61 percent. The contrast between these figures and the yearly double-digit increases in the GDP in China, with its gradual and controlled approach to the transition from communism to capitalism speak volumes about the utopian aspirations of the 1990s.

By the end of the 1990s, authoritarian politicians and their political parties became increasingly common in Eastern Europe: Vladimir Putin in Russia, the Kaczynski brothers and their Law and Justice Party in Poland, or Victor Orbán and Fidesz in Hungary. At first, they, like most politicians in Eastern Europe continued the marketization policies. As the newly elected president of the Russian Federation, for instance, Putin both privatized old age pensions and instituted a flat tax. Open rejection of policies of marketization would have to wait for the global economic crisis of 2008. Nonetheless these politicians and their parties all had a strongly authoritarian streak, rejecting democratic, multiparty political systems, civil liberties, and the rule of law, as well as the intellectuals who espoused them. An increasingly aggressive nationalism accompanied the authoritarianism, with a hostility toward international organizations, from the EU to the IMF and World Bank, as well as a skepticism about the political leadership of the United States. What was being rejected were all the promoters of the utopian aspirations to marketization, so, even if their policies were, at first, not expressly contravened, they themselves became enemies, viewed with attitudes ranging from skepticism to hostility.[85]

The growth of an authoritarian nationalism in Eastern Europe, distinctly hostile to both marketization and international institutions, was the beginning of a long-term trend that would extend well into the twenty-first century. Some of these regimes, particularly Vladimir Putin's smarting from the decline and humiliation of the USSR and its successor state the Russian Federation, would follow a course of increasing opposition to a world in which the United States was a hyperpower; others, such as Poland under the Law and Justice Party, would welcome American hegemony. The first and most apparent challenge to the post-1989 American role in the world would come from an unexpected source, the Islamists of Al Qaeda, and their terrorist attack of September 11, 2001.

A shock, certainly to an unprepared US government and general public, but it would be fair to say, to most of the world, the attack elicited a remarkable resonance. There were certainly sympathies, expressed in public demonstrations, moments of silence and statements of diplomatic support, some coming from rather unexpected places, such as the Islamic Republic of Iran, Islamists to be sure, but, as Shi'ites, sworn enemies of the Sunnis of Al Qaeda. There was also another moment that became apparent in the fall of 2001, expressed in the statement of a left-of-center English intellectual, the Cambridge classicist Mary Beard: "however carefully you drew it up, the US had it coming." This was a sentiment widely shared. Perhaps it was not too surprising that it appeared in Arab and Islamic countries, where Palestinians rejoiced in the black eye given the close ally of their Israeli national enemy, a Lebanese newspaper stated, "The arrogance of America punished by an enemy without a name," and passersby on an Istanbul street told reporters, "they [Al Qaeda] have done the right thing." Similar sentiments were expressed in Cairo and Karachi.

The idea that the United States had become too strong, too overbearing, too commanding was articulated around the world in both right- and left-wing circles. The American journalist Peter Hessler, living at the time in China, observed a similar viewpoint, emphasized not by state-run media, but by the one private broadcaster, Phoenix TV—owned in part, oddly enough, by Rupert Murdoch's Fox News. The conservative nationalist French politician Jean Marie Le Pen stated, "One cannot conduct a policy of power which is arrogant and sometimes criminal, without incurring inexpiable hatred." A Brazilian student observed, "I'm not against the American people but the United States got what it deserved." At a left-wing political rally in Rio de Janeiro, banners read, "A minute of silence for America's dead. Fifty-nine minutes for the victims of American policy."[86]

For all the shock of the 9/11 terrorist attack, and the *Schadenfreude* it generated around the world, at the beginning of the new millennium the fate of the utopian aspirations of the 1990s had by no means been decided. Proponents of a world of rationalized self-interest expressed in unlimited free markets, guaranteed by the power of the United States, a very influential group, quite unlike adherents of the two previous waves of worldwide utopian aspirations, continued their attempts to implement their ideals. History was, perhaps, not quite yet at an end, but that end could be perceived on the horizon, and with a little effort, humanity could get there. It would take major developments of the first two decades of the twenty-first century, including the consequences of the 2003 US invasion of Iraq, the global economic crisis of 2008–9, the steady rise of post-communist China to prosperity and worldwide influence, and the spread of authoritarian nationalism well beyond Eastern Europe, to terminate these efforts.[87]

And yet of three waves of utopian aspirations during the Age of Interconnection, it is the final one that seems the most bound by events. For all its many predecessors, stretching back into the 1930s, and its successors, reaching into the twenty-first century, the chronological contours of this wave of utopian aspirations were more sharply defined than those of its predecessors, occupying the period running from the fall of the Berlin Wall to the fall of the Twin Towers, from 11/9 to 9/11.

| Aftermath

THIS BOOK IS A history of the second half of the twentieth century, defined as the years between 1945 and 2001, but readers will have noticed that the first two decades of the twenty-first century keep coming up. When writing about the recent past, it is virtually impossible to avoid the present. Of course, the present is a moving target, changing from year to year, sometimes day to day. The outbreak and spread of the COVID-19 pandemic, as I was finishing the book, is just one recent example. I will confine my observations in this epilogue to the zeros, the years between 2001 and 2010, looking at some selected aspects of those years in the light of what came before and its more immediate legacy. (Inevitably, some more recent developments will slip into the account.) I will focus on three main features: the continuation and acceleration of the economic, social, and demographic trends begun in the 1980s; the rise of China and its rapidly increasing global reach; and the decline of the US-led post-Cold War global order.

Continuing Trends

The global economic interconnections begun in the 1980s set the stage for the next thirty years, as these interconnections increased at an ever more rapid pace. International financial transactions peaked at a daily value of $1.5 trillion in 1998, declined a bit in the 2001 recession, only to rise again in the decade of the zeros to $4 trillion per day by 2010. This rising flood of finance washing across national borders played a large role in the global financial crisis of 2008. That crisis, unlike the more modest downturn of 2001, did nothing to slow the pace of transactions; just the opposite, they rose still more in the years after 2008, and continued to do so in the economic recovery of the following decade. International trade and investment showed a similar pattern, though rates of growth were not quite so pronounced as those of financial transactions.[1]

It was not just goods and capital flowing around the world. The global migrations of the recent past continued unabated. Total migrants in the world (and remember, these official figures are most likely a considerable undercount) went from 174 million in 2000 to 221 million in 2010—and that in spite of the considerable dampening effect on economic conditions of the great recession of 2008–9. The proportion of the world's population who were migrants, according to understated official statistics, went from 2.9 percent in 1990 to 3.2 percent in 2010—and on to 3.5 percent in 2019, involving 272 million people. Trends apparent in the 1980s—trans-Pacific and trans-Caribbean migration to the United States; migration from the countries of the Mediterranean Basin and African lands to the south as well as Asian countries into Europe; and from Asia to the Persian Gulf—continued unabated. In spite of the large numbers of refugees and internally displaced persons, especially in Africa and the Middle East, voluntary migrants continued to make up the largest proportion of individuals crossing the borders of sovereign states. Remittances from migrants, according to the UN, which admits that these official figures understate substantially the actual amounts, rose from $126 billion in 2002 to $698 billion in 2018.[2]

Another feature of global interconnection was the worldwide circulation of information. In 1995, almost at the very end of the millennium, under 1 percent of the world's population were Internet users. Already in 2000, that proportion, growing exponentially, had reached 6.7 percent. In 2010, it was 29 percent and by 2017, roughly half. A World Bank study suggests that by 2020 almost 60 percent of the entire world's population had access to the Internet.[3]

Breaking down these global statistics to individual countries shows an unsurprisingly close connection between affluence and online access. In 2017, the last year for which detailed data are available, in Europe, North America, Japan, South Korea, and Australia, generally over three-quarters of inhabitants were online; in less wealthy countries, such as Brazil, China, or Mexico, some 50 to 60 percent, and falling off from there—about 30 percent in India and Indonesia, down to 5 percent in Chad. Even in Africa, there were states where a steadily growing proportion of the population had obtained online access: a quarter in Nigeria, a third in Ghana, over 40 percent in Côte d'Ivoire. A crucial change occurred in the early 2000s, the introduction of the smartphone, which liberated Internet access from wired networks—whether phone lines, coaxial or fiber optic cable—which were either nonexistent, sparse, or poorly functioning in the world's poorer countries.[4] While cell phones with Internet access had been around since 2000, Apple's introduction of the iPhone in 2007 was the first major commercial success, quickly followed by more affordable versions from Samsung, Huawei, or Xiaomi, among other East Asian firms.

As was the case with telecommunications in the Late-Millennium Era, there is no reason to think that the growing expansion of this worldwide communications network was leading to a homogeneous global information village, of the sort envisaged by Marshall McLuhan in the 1960s, or by techno-enthusiasts, and the journalists who naively agreed with them, three or four decades later. Simple matters, such as differences in connection speeds, or in the size and resolution of screens—these, too, generally a function of income, both between and within individual countries—created very different online experiences. Beyond these income-based differences, there have been a myriad of government policies restricting or channeling Internet access. The best known is the "Great Firewall" of China, begun as the "Golden Shield Project" in 2000, simultaneously with the introduction of Internet access in that country. Over time, online censorship has become increasingly elaborate and extensive in preventing access to websites that do not meet with the government's approval, and steadily more difficult to evade or to circumvent. As China's president Xi Jinping announced at the Second World Internet Conference, held in Wuhan in December 2015, "We should respect the right of individual countries to independently choose their own path of cyber-development," adding that demands for open access to the Internet were foreign interference "in other countries' internal affairs."[5]

There is no need to consider the highly charged topics of censorship and states' sovereign authority to understand the intersection of the global and the local or national in being online. Just consider the differences between purchasing on Amazon versus purchasing on Alibaba, running a web search with Google and running a web search with Baidu, or following EU data security and personal privacy regulations versus following their—generally much laxer—American versions. Another version of the way that global interconnections can reinforce nationalism is the use of worldwide social media platforms to spread nationalist and xenophobic ideas. Similar to many of the experiences of consumerism in 2000 and just after, Internet access may be increasingly global and even, sometimes, mediated by the same corporations across the world, but the experience of it is shaped and distinctly differentiated by local and national circumstances.

In these respects, the first decade of the twenty-first century has reinforced the lessons of the last decades of the twentieth. Growing global interconnection does not imply growing global homogeneity, either simultaneously or sequentially. Globalization can be and often is a force supporting and transforming heterogeneity rather than suppressing it.

An East Asian Decade

Beginning with Japan in the 1960s and 1970s, followed in the 1970s and 1980s by the "four tigers," South Korea, Taiwan, and Hong Kong, it was China's turn during the very last decade of the millennium. In the twenty years on either side of 2000 the country's economic growth was simply astounding. Exact figures differ, in view of technical issues of measurement, but the World Bank's numbers, based on constant 2011 international dollars at purchasing power parity, reveal that China's GDP grew at an average rate of 12.9 percent yearly between 2000 and 2010, faster than the already very impressive 12.7 percent yearly figure for the 1990s. Even the 2008 crisis could not stop the expansion juggernaut. Since this growth rate far outstripped those of the world's wealthier or more populous countries, China's share of the total output of the entire world, about 2.3 percent in 1990, rose to 7.2 percent in 2000 and 13.2 percent in 2010.[6]

While other East Asian countries had managed comparable growth rates in previous decades, their populations were much smaller, so that the sheer material mass of these increases in China's GDP was so much greater. The number of Chinese living in urban areas grew by about two hundred million between 2000 and 2010, an increase greater than the entire population of all but four countries in the world. Electrical generating capacity more than tripled, from three hundred gigawatts in 2000 to almost one thousand, ten years later. By 2008, China was producing more cement than the rest of the world put together. One oft-quoted statistic from the next decade, when Chinese economic growth had actually slowed a bit, was that Chinese cement production between 2011 and 2013 was greater than US cement production in the entire twentieth century. More than infrastructure or output of producers' goods soared; income and consumption were growing rapidly as well. Between 2002 and 2007, peak years of economic growth, per capita incomes of urban households increased at over 11 percent per year; even in the generally poorer rural areas the figure was 7.4 percent annually, both growth rates about twice as fast as in the previous five years.[7]

The consequences of this development—increases in total output occurring at a breakneck speed and massive in scale—spilled across the world. Just the demand for raw materials, from coal to oil to soybeans to so-called rare earths needed for micro- and consumer electronics, had a major economic effect. Between 2005 and 2013, Chinese firms invested $30 billion in Australian minerals deals, and $14 billion in such deals in Latin America. By 2011, China was purchasing 69 percent of Australia's iron ore production and 85 percent of its output of bauxite, aluminum ore. While Chinese purchases and investments were considerable in Australia—one of the world's wealthiest countries—the economic stimulus of the Chinese boom was felt most strongly in Africa and Latin America. In the ten years after 2000, the lost decades of the 1980s and 1990s finally came to an end in Africa, with GDP growth rates above 3 percent every single year, even in 2009, just following the 2008 Crisis. Yearly GDP increases of over 6 percent across the entire African continent in 2002 and between 2004 and 2006 were the fastest rates of economic growth in thirty years.[8]

The global consequences of China's genuine great leap forward—as opposed to Mao's deeply failed version—were apparent not just in demand but in supply. Carrying the policies of export led development to new heights, China's trade surplus soared during the first decade of the twenty-first century. This was a distinct break with much of the Age of Interconnection, when Chinese trade surpluses, along with foreign trade in general, had been at modest levels. Trade surpluses never broke $12 billion yearly, until 1996. From 1997 to 2005, they tripled and quadrupled in size, running between $28 and $51 billion yearly, then soaring upward, going from $125 billion to a peak of $349 billion in 2008. China's total foreign trade, imports plus exports, made up between 40 and 60 percent of its GDP every single year between 2000 and 2010. From toys and clothing to steel and industrial machinery, from consumer electronics to pharmaceuticals, manufactured products, produced in factories belonging both to foreign multinationals and to an increasingly active group of Chinese entrepreneurs, flowed out of China to all the countries of the earth. The sheer physical quantity of Chinese exports going to the United States was so prodigious that freighters, having unloaded in Pacific ports, had nothing they could carry back. Increasingly, they just took on waste material for recycling in China as ballast for the return trip. This exchange—Chinese manufactured goods for American garbage—may have had an economic rationale, since labor costs for recycling were much lower in China than the United States, but the optics of the transaction were degrading for America while demonstrating that the onetime Middle Kingdom had taken over the celebrated sobriquet coined in the nineteenth century for the world's first industrial country, Great Britain, and become the "workshop of the world."[9]

This provision of low-cost goods was a boon to consumerism around the world, especially in lower-income countries, or wealthier ones where growing income inequality was making keeping up consumption more difficult for those lower down the ladder of wealth and income. It also created a severe employment challenge for workers in higher-wage countries trying to produce competing products. One entirely plausible if also dismal estimate is that China's trade surplus was responsible for the loss of some two million jobs in the United States during the zeros, and another 1.7 million in the following decade. Three-fourths of those lost jobs were in manufacturing. Other economists, whose faith in the market is stronger, would dispute these figures or suggest that the lost jobs were replaced with better, more lucrative ones. Whichever side one takes in this argument (I find the dismal case more convincing), the growing presence of China in world markets, along with the increase in international migration, has accelerated the tendency toward a realignment of class structures away from the earlier model of upper, middle, and lower classes, based on occupation and income, toward one in which class structure is determined by individuals' position in a globalized labor market.[10]

In previous decades, individual countries on an economic tear, with GDPs growing much faster than trading partners and the world average, tended to develop balance of payments problems, as they ended up importing more than they exported—the "stop and go" issue of the 1950s and 1960s, or the *bicicleta financeria* of the next three decades, whose consequences, in the East Asian financial crisis of 1997, came painfully close to home for Chinese policy makers. Part of the remarkable nature of the Chinese economy was that it grew faster than anywhere else while simultaneously rolling up an enormous export surplus. The upshot was a gigantic increase in China's foreign exchange reserves, which grew more than tenfold, reaching some $3 trillion by 2010. These assets financed America's balance of trade and government budget deficits; they played a role—admittedly, less than that of funds coming from Western Europe—in financing the real-estate frenzy in the United States and a number of other countries, leading to the 2008–9 global financial crisis.[11]

These funds have made possible increasing Chinese influence in the world: growing investments in Africa, as well as large-scale loans to governments of African countries, generally focused around securing access to raw materials; investments in Eastern and Southern Europe. The purchase of Piraeus, the seaport of Athens, in 2016 by the Chinese shipping firm Cosco, made a particularly strong impression, in view of the storied history of the port, going back to classical antiquity, and its contemporary role as a shipping hub in Southeastern Europe. Standing in the baggage claim area of the Athens airport in the fall of 2019, I could not help noticing all the billboards and electronic signs, in Greek, Chinese, and English, inviting Chinese investments in real estate and a myriad of other economic areas.

Capping off and summing up this entire complex of trade surpluses, securing raw materials, investments, loans, and growing influence was the "New Silk Road," or "Belt and Road" initiative announced in 2013 by Xi Jinping. Proposed spending would exceed one trillion dollars over fifteen years, to fund infrastructure improvements in railroads, highways and ports as well as energy investment projects across Asia and into Europe, via grants, loans to governments and direct investments.

To some observers and a lot of nervous commentators, these all seem to be signs of China's rapid rise toward global domination. Perhaps the successor to the "the American century" will be the East Asian Century. It is not hard to point out ways that stories of China's global reach have been overblown.

The vast amounts of agricultural land Chinese firms had ostensibly bought up in Africa have turned out to be two rubber plantations. The level of Chinse investments in Africa first surpassed those of the United States—and Africa has always been a sideline for US foreign investments—in 2015. The Belt and Road initiative has run into opposition on the part of a number of countries involved; individual projects have been delayed or scaled back, so the ultimate scope of the project remains to be seen.[12]

What can be said is that China's two decades of extremely rapid economic growth, combined with its export surpluses have catapulted the country into a far more influential position throughout the world. China's rise seems even more significant as the years of its most rapid ascent were also those of the decline of the United States, and the post-Cold War global order it dominated. Seemingly unshakable throughout the 1990s, the age of the "end of history," that global order collapsed in the following decade from a combination of long-term structural developments and problematic policy decisions, made under the assumption that American hegemony was unlimited and eternal.

The End of the Post-Cold War Global Order

Characteristic elements of the post-Cold War world were economic policies of deregulation and privatization, expanding the scope of unlimited markets, and a powerful, hegemonic position of the United States around the world, albeit a hegemony generally exercised through multilateral institutions. At times and in particular places, especially post-communist Eastern Europe, these features had appeared in distinctly utopian fashion. The East Asian and Russian financial crises of 1997–98 and Al Qaeda's terrorist attack on the United States in 2001 brought both of these elements into question but had not yet undermined them. The collapse of the post-Cold War global order occurred in the initial decade of the twenty-first century, primarily from two major events: the 2003 US invasion of Iraq, the Third Gulf War; and the 2008 crisis. Paradoxically, the common feature behind these developments leading to the end of the post-1989 global order was the belief in the permanent character of that order and its fundamentally unshakable qualities—its "irreversibility," to use a phrase very popular in referring to the end of communist rule in Eastern Europe.

By far the incomprehensible element of the US government's response to Al Qaeda's terrorist attack on 9/11 was the decision to invade Iraq. Invading Afghanistan, whose Islamist government had supported the terrorists and provided them a safe haven, seemed like a plausible idea and enjoyed the support and endorsement of the United Nations. However, even before the situation in Afghanistan had been stabilized and terrorist leader Osama bin Laden and his chief Afghan ally and patron Mullah Mohammed Omar apprehended, American interest and troop commitments shifted to Iraq. Exactly why overthrowing a secular Pan-Arabist regime, an enemy of the Islamists, was an appropriate response to an Islamist terror campaign seems mysterious, especially in retrospect. The purported reasons offered at the time—that Iraqi leader Saddam Hussein had close ties to bin Laden, and that Hussein was preparing to use weapons of mass destruction against the United States—might have been convincing to a traumatized public opinion, a superficial and corrupt press, and a thoroughly intimidated Democratic political opposition. They were also blatantly false, as those in the know, including substantial numbers of US diplomats, intelligence analysts and high-ranking officers of the armed forces—to say nothing of UN weapons inspectors, and European government officials—understood. The proponents of war with Iraq were highly skilled information manipulators and bureaucratic infighters, as a number of them had shown previously, when they were part of a group rejecting intelligence estimates of the USSR, asserting that the country's military capacity and economic potential was greater than the CIA claimed—an assertion every bit as dubious as the ones they would bring forth about Iraq.

Behind this campaign for war lay the assumptions of the post-1989 world—the era of American hegemony and unleashed markets. The proponents of war had been critics of the more cautious American governments of the 1990s, denouncing them for not using US power more aggressively to reshape the world. Eastern Europe had come first; the Middle East would be next, its countries transformed into pro-American, pro-free-market regimes. "Everyone deserves freedom," President George W. Bush frequently said about Iraq, and the Middle East more generally—by which he meant, an American-style political system, a free-market economy, and freedom of religion—a precursor to his decision to go to war. The aftermath, he felt, would be an Iraq that was "prosperous and free." Paul Wolfowitz, Deputy Secretary of Defense and leading proponent of war with Iraq, saw its future as the "cornerstone of democracy in the Middle East." Bush's National Security Adviser, Condoleezza Rice, among the high officials of the administration perhaps the most skeptical about war with Iraq, exulted when US troops entered Baghdad, "We've done it! . . . It's just like the fall of the Soviet Union!"[13]

Very much unlike the fall of the Soviet Union, which only occurred after four decades of Cold War, was the assumption that, in view of America's dominant role in the world, overthrowing the regime of Saddam Hussein would require very little effort. The number of US troops mustered for the invasion was half of what military planning called for. In contrast to the place of NATO in the Cold War or the pained and strained efforts of the 1990s administrations of George H. W. Bush and Bill Clinton to organize and to sustain large-scale multilateral coalitions to respond to the

Iraqi invasion of Kuwait and to the mass murders in the former Yugoslavia, the US government treated the UN cavalierly, dismissed the objections of its NATO allies, and went to war with a "coalition of the willing," which consisted largely of Great Britain and a scattering of smaller states, mostly from Eastern Europe. Their decisions were in many ways a Cold War hangover, directed against a one-time close ally of the USSR, but did not extend to allowing their soldiers actually to take part in combat. Private military contractors working for the United States outnumbered all the "allied" troops. The American "hyperpower" needed no multilateralism to impress its will on the world.

Planning for a post-Saddam Hussein Iraq was, at best, superficial. The postwar occupation would be brief and would pay for itself via Iraq's oil revenues. The only US government agency that engaged in serious planning for a postwar Iraq was the State Department, also the only agency containing Arabic speakers and people knowledgeable about the region more generally, and, as a result, more skeptical about the ease and brief duration of a postwar occupation. Proponents of war made sure that knowledgeable US diplomats and Middle East experts were excluded from any influence on occupation policy. This was exercised by the "Coalition Political Authority," and its leader L. Paul Bremer, who, after disbanding the entire Iraqi army and prohibiting former members of the dictator's official political party, the pan-Arabist Ba'ath Party, from holding government positions, saw as his main task a "full-scale economic overhaul." He was determined to make "the first genuine free-market economy in the Arab world." Government-owned business would be privatized, following the precedent of post-communist Eastern Europe; Iraq would join the WTO and eliminate tariffs; there would be an ultramodern stock exchange with the most up-to-date electronic stock trading; a revised university system would include "a Western-style graduate business school"; and, inevitably, a flat tax would be introduced. Bremer's staff, none of them with any particular knowledge of the region or the language, largely recruited through the Heritage Foundation, one of the many business-sponsored institutions promoting Mont Pèlerin-style economics, set about the work of turning Iraq into a free-market utopia in the "Green Zone," the former Iraqi dictator's palace complex in the heart of Baghdad on the Tigris River.[14]

The Third Gulf War—the successor to the first, the war between Iraq and Iran in the 1980s, and the second, the response to the Iraqi invasion of Kuwait in 1991—was, in many ways, the quintessence of the utopian aspirations of the 1990s, using America's hegemonic position, no longer fettered by multilateral commitments, to transform a national enemy, and, with it, a whole region, into a model of democratic political institutions and privatized and deregulated markets, based on the principle of rational self-interest.[15] Previous attempts to do so in the much more favorable conditions of post-communist Eastern Europe had enjoyed, at best, a problematic outcome; in Iraq, they were simply a disaster.

The small American army invading was able, with relatively little difficulty, to vanquish the dictator's demoralized armed forces, which melted away rather than fight, but manifestly inadequate to occupy the country: to stop the looting, disorder, and lack of any security of persons and property that followed the end of the dictatorial regime, to secure the occupied country's borders, to restore public services, particularly electricity generation, or even to guard the weapons and ammunition depots of the overthrown tyrant. Disbanding the Iraqi army meant that hundreds of thousands of men with military training and experience were left unemployed and angry. Since holding any responsible position in the professions or public administration in Saddam Hussein's Iraq required joining the Ba'ath Party, the purge of its members left tens of thousands more individuals, trained and knowledgeable, needed for reconstruction, unavailable.

The dreams of an Arab free-market utopia quickly vanished. The electronic stock market lacked electronics, to say nothing of electricity, since it proved impossible to get enough generating capacity even to meet minimal power needs, leading to hours-long power blackouts on a daily basis—which, of course, made any form of economic activity difficult. Taxes, flat or not, could not be collected, in view of the collapse of public administration and public order. Because the state-owned firms were old and dilapidated, no one wanted to buy them—a problem that had already emerged in the 1990s in the former East Germany, when the government of a reunited Germany tried to privatize former state-owned enterprises. If thousands of German bureaucrats, economists, engineers, and lawyers, working in a peaceful and orderly country with a rapidly improving infrastructure, could not carry out this task, how could the handful of Americans in a chaotic, lawless land, with a collapsed infrastructure hope to do so?

Ironically, it was the invasion and the occupation itself which produced the merger of Arab nationalism and Islamism that was the purported reason for the war. Dismissed soldiers and ex-Ba'ath Party members, smarting from the humiliating collapse of their regime, utilizing that regime's unguarded arsenals, joined Islamists pouring into the country across its unguarded borders, to produce, within six months of the end of the war, an increasingly powerful insurrection. Iraq's Shi'ites, oppressed by Saddam Hussein, soon clashed with the US occupation troops, leading to their own insurrection. Badly outnumbered American soldiers resorted to mass roundups of all adult men, as well as torture and degradation of prisoners, which only encouraged still more Iraqis to take up arms. Once these became publicly known, they were deeply toxic to the American position in the world. The worldwide *Schadenfreude*, which had greeted the 9/11 terrorist attacks on the United States was modest compared to what occurred after imperious

Americans had ignored most countries and gone ahead with their imperial adventure. In the end, a commitment of more troops and the expenditure of hundreds of billions of dollars—the very opposite of a cost-free occupation, in both money and human lives—temporarily stabilized the situation. The ultimate result of the Third Gulf War was to increase the strength and influence of both Sunni and Shi'ite forms of Islamism (the latter closely tied to the rising power of Iran) in the Middle East and to destroy America's position in the world, in a way that is only comparable with the Southeast Asian War decades earlier.[16]

If the Third Gulf War had damaged US global hegemony, the multilateral exercise of that hegemony, and the assumption that the hegemony was exercised in a basically benevolent fashion, the 2008 crisis showed that the workings of a globalized deregulated market, based on the calculations of rational, individual self-interest were not automatically self-correcting and did not produce maximal or ideal results. In a sense, this had always been apparent, since the deregulations of the 1980s and 1990s had been accompanied by various forms of reregulation, producing a Second Bretton Woods system framing international economic interaction. A key center of reregulation had been the European Union but the Eurozone economic crisis of 2010–11, an aftershock of the 2008 crisis, showed that reregulated markets could no more deal with globalized financial flows than deregulated ones.[17]

In spite of the political turbulence caused by terrorism and the US invasion of Iraq, the middle years of the 2000s, following the recovery from the 2001 recession, had been a relatively prosperous period. While not reaching the very rapid economic growth rates of the postwar era, they were, worldwide, comparable to the best post-oil price shock periods of economic growth in the Late-Millennium Era. If rates of economic growth across the entire world had been about the same, in the new millennium the results of that growth had been more equitably distributed, since Latin America and Africa, two continents left behind in the last two decades of the twentieth century, enjoyed the best years they had experienced since the 1970s.[18]

As explained earlier in this chapter, these years were a period of rapidly increasing international trade, financial transactions and investments, in other words of an ever-more globalized economy. In the years just before the 2008 crisis there were widespread suspicions that imbalances in this economy might lead to disaster. The United States running an ever-larger trade deficit from the purchase of Chinese manufactured goods and imported oil, as well as a very large government budget deficit, from fighting an expensive war while cutting taxes, had a steadily growing balance of payments deficit, borrowing more and more money from Europe and East Asia. In the world of flexible exchange rates, these sorts of situations resulted in *la bicicleta financiera* that had first plagued Argentina in the 1970s and was behind the international financial crises of the late 1990s. At some point, foreign lenders would become apprehensive about their loans and withdraw their money, leading to simultaneous price spikes and a collapse of economic activity. Such a crisis, occurring in a country that was the center of the global economy, would have immediate, worldwide ramifications.

The 2008 crisis did arise from the place of the United States in a globalized, deregulated capitalism but the feared *bicicleta financeria* never came to pass. In fact, the United States has been able to maintain large balance of trade, balance-of-payments and federal government deficits seemingly indefinitely. Instead, the crisis emerged from the intersection of finance and real estate. As home prices rose and banks and other financial institutions issued mortgages to borrowers, whose incomes made it unlikely they could meet the terms of the loan. The mortgages themselves became the collateral for bonds, or more complex financial products, such as collateralized debt obligations, which were purchased by investors and financial institutions, generally using borrowed money. When the mortgagees defaulted on their loans, as began happening in 2007, the whole pyramid of debt collapsed, slowly at first, and then greatly accelerating during the fall of 2008, in the wake of the bankruptcy of the celebrated Wall Street banking house Lehman Brothers.

The story is complex, with endless details, but there are three large, underlying features that bring it into relationship with trends beginning in the Late-Millennium Era. One is that the whole process was a direct result of the post-1989 utopian aspirations toward a world of rationalized self-interest, mediated by the market. Mortgage lending was deregulated, since the intersection of the rational self-interest of financial institutions and borrowers in an open market would ensure appropriate decisions about lending money. The various financial instruments funding the mortgages were deregulated, especially as the investors in them, banks and high net worth individuals, were sophisticated investors who, policy makers felt, would need no guidance about their self-interest. Those financial instruments were, theoretically, insured against default by "derivatives," the so-called credit default swaps, themselves completely deregulated—quite unlike insurance companies, required by regulators to maintain reserves to cover expected claims. When there were defaults, and very large ones, it turned out that the "counterparties," the issuers of the credit default swaps had no such reserves and could not pay.

The situation reached a critical point following the collapse of Lehman Brothers but the American government refused to step in to rescue the beleaguered financial giant. The argument for inaction was based on yet another of the principles articulated by Milton Friedman and his followers— the idea of moral hazard. If Lehman Brothers were bailed out, this would just encourage others to make risky investments, assuming they, too, would be rescued with taxpayers' funds. This decision came from the same logic as Friedman's assertion that the government should not assist victims of natural disasters, since that would encourage them to live in hazardous areas.

Of course, the enormous financial panic that followed the bankruptcy of the investment bank, its ramifications reaching around the world, attaining all branches of finance, and quickly leading to collapses of production and international trade at a faster rate than after the Wall Street crash of 1929, showed other problems in the situation, which the theorists of rationalized self-interests interacting in unrestrained markets had, apparently, not taken into account.

The second feature of the financial crisis was its globalized nature. While the main real estate bubble was in the United States, there were similar developments—rapidly rising real-estate prices, questionable loans, problematic financial backing—in a number of countries, including the United Kingdom, Ireland, and Spain. The administration of George W. Bush had been particularly adamant in its insistence on the deregulation of financial markets and equally adamant in opposing any attempts to curb questionable financial practices, but similar attitudes prevailed in other countries as well, all examples of the global wave of deregulation beginning in the 1980s, accelerating and accumulating utopian elements in the subsequent decade, and continuing into the new millennium. The financial flows that had made possible the entire enterprise of writing problematic mortgages, using them for collateral on equally problematic financial instruments, to say nothing of the problematic creation of debt to purchase these instruments, were entirely globalized, crossing national and continental boundaries with great rapidity and no legal or regulatory obstacles.

Perhaps more subtly, the origins of the financial crisis reflected the global developments of declining inequality between countries, rising inequality within countries. A major mover of those trends, the fast-rising Chinese export surplus, helped generate the funds that moved around the world and were used to finance the real estate bubble. Loss of jobs and declining income from Chinese competition, particularly in the United States, but in some European countries as well, made it more difficult for a growing segment of the population to afford housing, encouraging the promotion of dubious mortgages, which purported to make real-estate purchases possible for members of middle- or lower-income groups, but really set the mortgagees on the road to default, in doing so pulling out the bottom piece of a whole pyramid of debt.

In the fall of 2008, the decades-long trend toward deregulation and government non-intervention in the market came to a crashing end. Just as there are no atheists in foxholes, there are no unrestrained free-market advocates in major financial crises. Overnight, trillions of dollars, euros, yen, and yuan were mobilized, by central banks and governments, to rescue beleaguered financial markets, and to prevent production and international trade from collapsing, as they were threatening to do. Even in post-communist Europe, which had, for two long decades, resolutely implemented marketization, the crisis brought a turnabout. Flat taxes were repealed and replaced with a progressive system in Slovakia, the Czech Republic, Albania, Ukraine, and Latvia. Privatization of old age pensions was either scaled back or repealed—although the form of repeal, "nationalizing" individual pension balances in Hungary and Russia, or requiring them, as in Poland, to be invested in government bonds, has struck more than a few investors and commentators as a form of theft. The authoritarian nationalist governments that carried out these nationalizations also sometimes nationalized private businesses—the renationalization of energy companies in Vladimir Putin's Russia a particularly good example—opposed the policies of international economic institutions, such as the EU or the World Bank, and generally steered a less globalizing and less market-oriented course.[19]

Eastern European skepticism about EU policies seems not unjustified in view of the results of the sequel to the global financial crisis, the European debt crisis of 2010 and 2011, a function of the large-scale public bailouts of the financial sector. While these expenditures could be managed by leading economies such as the United States, China, or Japan, by the wealthier EU countries, including Germany, France, the Netherlands or Sweden, and even Great Britain, the poorer EU countries, particularly the "PIIGS," Portugal, Ireland, Italy, Greece, and Spain, required loans from the IMF, World Bank, and the EU, to shoulder the burden. The austerity measures the international lending agencies and the EU, especially, required, to ensure that the loans would be repaid, following along the lines of the World Bank's structural adjustment programs and the Washington Consensus of the Late-Millennium Era, greatly intensified the economic downturn resulting from the crisis. A typical response to this situation—a currency devaluation to spur exports and increase economic activity—was impossible, because the poorer countries of Eastern Europe no longer had their own currency but had adopted the joint EU currency, the euro. Fixing the exchange rates of individual EU countries against each other and then merging these currencies into the euro, had been a central element of the Europeans' reregulation response to the wave of deregulations in the international financial system. Now this reregulation was hampering the response to deregulation. Eventually, the crisis was resolved, but at the cost of long years of massive unemployment, continued economic declines and slow and feeble economic recoveries in the countries affected.

By the second decade of the twenty-first century, all the features of the post-1989 global order—American hegemony, multilateralism, globalized, deregulated markets—had come undone. Efforts to reconstruct that order, seen, hesitantly, in the presidency of Barack Obama, proved unavailing. Instead, the authoritarian and nationalist option, pioneered in post-communist Eastern Europe, spread rapidly during the century's second decade, in the China of Xi Jinping, the Russia of Vladimir Putin, the Turkey of Recep Tayyip Erdogan, the governments emerging from the suppression of the mass movements of the Arab Spring, the Great Britain of Brexit, and, of course, the United States of Donald Trump. The post-1989 international order had its problematic features, but what has succeeded it largely seems to have preserved them while eliminating its more positive sides— a discouraging coda to a half-century filled with profound transformations, powerful struggles, and remarkable accomplishments.

| Conclusions

FIVE DECADES AND THE entire world is an impossibly broad canvas on which to paint a picture of general themes underlying major events and significant developments. Inevitably, there will be clashing colors and forms, or features that do not fit, leaving parts of the canvas blank.

Still, it might be possible to sketch in an outline of the portrait, with four main themes, all of which emphasize unprecedented features of the second half of the twentieth century. Of these four themes, two portray a continuity and two involve contrast. One pattern is the age of exponentials, a period of human history in which rapid and accelerating rates of growth occurred in a wide variety of venues. The second is global orders—attempts to organize economic, political, and social, sometimes even intellectual and cultural structures on a worldwide scale. Then there is the contrast between the cosmopolitan and the local, the coexistence—more accurately, the mutual interaction and reinforcement—of a growing network of global interconnections, of movement of goods, capital, people and information across borders of sovereign states, continents, and oceans, with the increasing strength of nationalism, particularism, religious intolerance, and xenophobia. Finally, there is the contrast between great expectations and more prosaic realities.

An Age of Exponentials

The exponential function shown on the next page is used by physical, biological, and social scientists to model a process in which the rate of increase is itself continuously increasing. As the chart shows, this produces a slow start, a curve that, at first, is hard to distinguish from a horizontal straight line. As the process continues, the rate of growth very visibly accelerates, and the

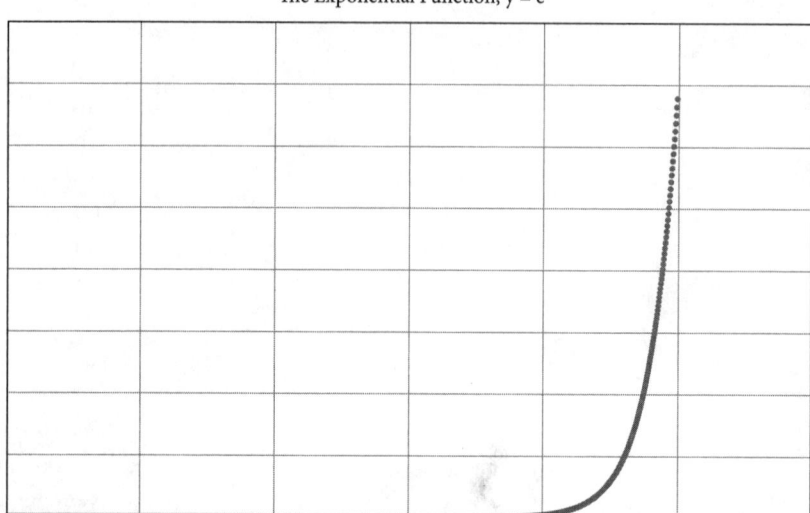

FIGURE C.1 The Exponential Function, $y = e^x$

curve suddenly becomes sharply steeper, heading toward a vertical, soaring straight upward. In the second half of the twentieth century, exponential growth was everywhere, a testimony to economic and technological acceleration, encouraged by favorable political and social organization and global interconnections, reaching breakneck speeds.

This sort of growth could be the culmination of long-term processes, in which the verticality of the curve became ever more noticeable in the Age of Interconnection. A classic example of this evident verticality was human population. It had taken from the very beginning of humanity to 1950, hence hundreds of thousands of years, for the number of people living in the world to go from the few initial human beings to 2.5 billion, but less than forty years to increase another 2.5 billion to 5 billion around 1987. Several other examples, none quite so long term, show the same trend. Total exports in the entire world, valued at constant prices, grew about 2 1/2 times between 1900 and 1950, but then about twenty-two-fold, almost ten times as fast, in the subsequent fifty years. The value of foreign investments has shown a similar trend, with the very rapid increase starting about a decade later. From 1750, the very earliest beginning of human emission of extra greenhouse gases to 1960, over 210 years, carbon dioxide in the atmosphere increased by about 25 parts per million, from 290 to 315, while in the forty years from 1960 to 2000 concentrations went from 315 parts per million to 370, an increase of 55 ppm, more than twice as much in one-fifth the time. To take another example of the emission of toxic gases, some 50 billion cigarettes were consumed across the world in 1900, increasing to 1.67 trillion, 50 years later.

The next increase of 1.5 trillion yearly just took two instead of five decades, with global consumption over 3.1 trillion by 1970.

Exponential growth could make its appearance in the Age of Interconnection more abruptly, without these long periods of preparation. Examples of this sort of (relatively) sudden onset exponential growth would include increases in global oil consumption between 1950 and the early 1970s, the rise in chlorofluorocarbon emissions between 1960 and 1990, growth of international tourist arrivals between 1950 and the initial decades of the twenty-first century, or the growth in the number of households connected to the Internet, from 1990 onward. As these conclusions are being written in late 2021, the rising number of victims of the COVID-19 virus has been a very uncomfortable reminder of the exponential curve's transition from almost horizontal to more and more steeply vertical, in the case of the virus happening in days and weeks, rather than decades and centuries.

In mathematics, the exponential curve extends upward toward infinity, growing faster and faster, getting steeper and steeper. This is impossible in a world of finite human attention and finite material resources; at some point exponential increases have to come to an end. The end to exponential growth of the world's human population came in the Late-Millennium Era: while the globe's population continued to grow, and does so down to the present day, the rate of increase has steadily declined, falling off the ever-steeper slope of the exponential curve. The oil price shocks of the 1970s put an end, apparently once and for all, to exponential rates of growth of petroleum consumption, as did the Montreal Protocol, and its vigorous implementation, for the exponential increases in the emissions of chemicals destroying the ozone layer. It is easy to foresee an end to the growth in the number of households with Internet access, when most or almost all households—or almost all who can afford it—gain access. Something similar will probably happen at some point with tourist arrivals and exports, as already has occurred with global cigarette consumption, which was largely flat between 1990 and 2000. International financial transactions, involving much less interaction with the material world, might continue to grow exponentially for a longer time, although the nature of exponential growth makes it very hard to envisage them increasing at a steadily more rapid pace throughout the entire twenty-first century.

Was there ever a global transition from an, overall, exponential era, to one of a slower pace of growth? The most plausible candidate for such a transition would be the 1970s, the era of oil price shocks, and the Club of Rome's *Limits to Growth*, a decade in which rates of economic and population growth as well as petroleum consumption began a permanent decline, worldwide. It was also a period in which the idea of progress, which had become, at least implicitly, connected to exponential growth, came into question. Such a designation might seem limited, both to the North Atlantic, and to certain, particularly material forms of human interaction with the biosphere. The 1970s marked the beginning of a period of extremely rapid economic growth—admittedly, along with declining rates of population growth—in East Asia, and a transition from a global economy centered around the Atlantic to one focused on the Pacific Rim. It was also a time in which other forms of exponential growth, including financial transactions or consumption in the form of tourist arrivals, really got underway. The arrival of new communications technology in the 1990s enabled yet another outburst of exponential growth in access to the internet and wireless telephone networks (in very recent years, increasingly interrelated), which is still ongoing.

It might be better to say that a question of politics, using political here in the broadest possible sense, has been posed, worldwide, since the 1970s. Is it possible to envisage a post-exponential era? If so, what would it look like? One very large contrast in the contemporary world is between those who continue, at least implicitly, to envisage the continuation of a world of exponentials, and those who admit the possibility of a post-exponential future.

Global Orders

Global orders were a European dream of the Enlightenment. Such orders began to come into focus, although in distinctly Eurocentric fashion, during the nineteenth century, with the creation of world time zones, the first global agencies, such as the International Telegraph Union (today's International Telecommunications Union), or even, in their own exploitative and oppressive way, the worldwide British and French Empires. The League of Nations, more a league of European empires than anything else, was at an attempt—not a very successful one—to create a distinctly global order. In the wake of the Second World War, the idea of global governance, a true global order, seemed like it might have a chance at coming to fruition. The closer the diplomacy of that era is studied, the more that chance seems like a phantasm, or, to put it more positively, a utopian vision.

What the postwar world got instead of global governance was two strongly competing global orders, the age of the Cold War. A clash of self-interested great powers, fully exercising their raison d'état, dragooning or inveighing allies and the undecided to stand behind them, a planned military confrontation, with plans that fortunately never came to fruition, a cultural and consumerist competition, the Cold War was, above all, a contrast between two different visions of global political and socioeconomic orders. It was a contrast felt strongly by contemporaries, from the 1950s to the 1980s, but in retrospect some of the clear lines of division seem more than a little blurred.

Ideological differences were most clearly apparent in economic structures and policies, pitting markets versus planning, private ownership versus public property and acceptance of economic inequality versus an egalitarian ideal. Yet until the 1980s there was a fair amount of planning and public ownership in Western countries, as well as a relatively low level of economic inequality, certainly when compared to earlier and later eras. Communist governments came closer to their economic ideals than Western ones, but there were rather more markets, private ownership and, especially, inequality of life conditions, in communist countries than regimes were willing to admit. In other respects, ideological differences were less clear. Both sides in the Cold War claimed the legacy of the anti-fascist crusade of the Allied Powers in the Second World War and each claimed to embody genuine democracy, while accusing the other of having a fraudulent version of it. If by democracy one means something like competitive multiparty elections, civil liberties, the rule of law, and the independence of civil society from the state, then in the North Atlantic world, as well as in other wealthy countries like Japan or Australia, democracy, admittedly with many flaws, was practiced in more authentic fashion than in communist regimes. In Asia, Africa, and Latin America, both sides in the Cold War, as well as governments claiming to stand aside from that conflict, regularly, and all too often murderously, deviated from democratic ideals and suppressed popular aspirations toward democracy.

Other principles were shared in less controversial fashion on both sides of the Cold War, especially in its initial decades. The idea of progress was widespread across the boundaries of the Cold War; the authority of science and the belief in a great future through the advances of science and technology were very prevalent in both the East and West. There was agreement and even cooperation on the elimination of infectious disease through the use of antibiotics and mass immunizations. Another jointly shared, although in retrospect rather less helpful, relationship to the biosphere was an implicit understanding of it as a resource capable of providing raw materials and diluting toxic emissions to an unlimited extent. Expanding leisure time, and those two ways to fill it, television and tourism, were greeted on both sides of the Cold War divide.

In some ways, the most important feature of the Cold War was that there were two potential global orders in conflict. This produced a search for alternatives, which often took the form of a fetishization of the number three: "third force," "third way," "third world." In the end, two prevailed over three. Efforts at creating an independent global political force centered in the newly independent, postcolonial states of Asia and Africa, with the belated accession of some Latin American countries, from the nonaligned movement to the New International Economic Order, never got traction. The attempts foundered, not just on the hostility of the Cold War powers, but on strong internal divisions among the nonaligned lands themselves. Like both sides in the Cold War, even the adherents of a potential third element in global politics endorsed the idea of progress and the authority of science and technology. There was a pronounced tendency for the nominally nonaligned countries to become aligned with one side of the Cold War, particularly with the communists, although this alignment became more complicated as a result of the growing hostility between the USSR and China. The most successful nonaligned states were those who used their status, not so much to build up a potential new global order, but to tack between the two existing ones.

If the Cold War was a clash of potential global orders, the two sides in it were not symmetrical. The West brought to the contest much larger economic resources, greater military power, and a considerably more attractive popular culture and consumer society; it was much closer to being an actual global order. Economic institutions originally set up as part of the implementation of a global governance in the late phases of the Second World War or its immediate aftermath, the World Bank, the International Monetary Fund, the General Agreement on Trade and Tariffs, became Cold War agencies of worldwide scope. As the basic structures of the global economy were transformed in the 1970s, not only did these institutions change with them, a new acting group for global organization, the G-7, came into existence. Ironically for a form of government based on the idea of economic planning, the world's communist regimes had no comparable internationally shaping and organizing agencies: the COMECON, limited to the western half of Eurasia, and not really all that capable of coordinating between different sovereign states, or the various ad hoc forms of assistance rendered to countries in Asia and Africa by the USSR, China, and even Cuba, lacked the scope, scale, and impact of the institutions of the west.

Even more, the increasing economic globalization of the 1970s and 1980s drew communist states into the global order of their rivals, via globalized oil and financial markets. Yet understanding this process as just one of the two competing Cold War global orders being drawn into the other is not quite correct. The West's own global order was, at the same time, being rapidly transformed, as economic regulations were eliminated, public ownership privatized, and the forces of an increasingly worldwide market economy given ever freer reign. When the Cold War ended, it did seem that the long-held dream of a global order, both institutionally, and in terms of a consensus about the appropriate forms of these political and economic institutions, was present, at least in nascent form. But that global order of the early 1990s was itself was very different from what it had been four decades previously, when it had come into existence.

This one experience with a global order proved short-lived, undermined by the economic collapse of the western half of formerly communist Eurasia, the rise of both Islamism, and nationalism. The former was its own, abortive, and peculiar effort at a global order. The latter was a distinct opponent of the whole idea, increasingly discredited by the dubious military adventures of the United States in the first decade of the twenty-first century, and, of course, the global financial crisis of 2008. Remnants of the post-Cold War global order continue their existence; possible potential alternatives, centered on China, are starting to emerge.

But the situation at the beginning of the third decade of the twenty-first century remains fluid and undetermined. Perhaps there will be no more global orders, just regional ones, although they might not be well suited to an increasingly globalized world. The Cold War era global orders emerged from the world's wealthy and powerful countries centered on the North Atlantic; any future orders will have to be constructed on a larger base, with, at the very least, the cooperation of the countries of East Asia. (Ideally, one would like to see representatives of the entire world involved in the development of a global order, but that notion has been, since the 1940s, a utopian one, if perhaps eminently desirable.) Past global orders have been largely about economic, military, and diplomatic alignments; in view of the increasingly critical relationship between humanity and the biosphere, future global orders might well have to be expanded to include that as well.

The Global and the Particular

In 1848, Karl Marx and Friedrich Engels put an oft-quoted passage in the *Communist Manifesto* about the cultural and political consequences of a globalized economic system:

> Through its exploitation of the world market, the bourgeoisie has shaped the production and consumption of every country in a cosmopolitan direction . . . In place of the old local and national self-sufficiency and isolation there is an . . . all-inclusive mutual dependence of nations. And as in material, so also in intellectual production . . . National one-sidedness and narrow-mindedness become ever more impossible, and from the numerous national and local literatures, a world literature is formed.[1]

Many of Marx's and Engels's contemporaries—admittedly, usually pro-free-trade liberals rather than communists—shared this understanding of parallelism between economic globalization, goods, capital and labor moving across sovereign states, continents and oceans, and intellectual and cultural globalization, an end to nationalism and particularism, a rise in cosmopolitanism. More recently, commentators on globalization have placed the emphasis less on arts and ideas and more on a global consumerism where everyone eats at McDonald's, wears Nikes, texts on a Samsung phone, and drives a Beamer—or at least aspires to do so. Left-wing critics of this viewpoint have admitted the existence of a globalized consumerism but observed that a large proportion of the world's population is excluded from this consumer cornucopia by their poverty (a poverty generally described as resulting from the affluent consumerism of the more fortunate) or that the omnipresence of certain brands, products of global corporations, destroys indigenous cultures, stifles popular self-assertion, and obscures both the environmental damage wrought by consumerism or exclusion from it of the world's poor.

All these assertions sound compelling. An examination of developments suggests that they are not merely incorrect but nearly an inversion of the actual case. Enthusiasm for global governance, hostility to nationalism, and support for transnational ideals, such as those contained in communist, anti-imperialist, and European unity movements, were strongest in the postwar era. Worldwide economic interchange was then at a relatively low level; by a number of measures below the first decade of the twentieth century. In the Late-Millennium Era, the situation was almost completely reversed. Movements of goods, capital, and people had reached unparalleled levels—or, at least, ones not seen since the pre-1914 decades. Nationalism flourished, ever more intransigent, all too frequently less tolerant, with growing xenophobic elements, and ever more particular. Earlier, more encompassing forms of nationalism, such as Pan-Arabism and Pan-Africanism, had fallen by the wayside. Integralist forms of religion, generally, if not always, intolerant of and hostile to other religions, to say nothing of non-believers, were increasingly the public face of faith. The unexpected revival of mass murder in the 1990s, and on into the new millennium, after the ideologically defined killings characteristic of the age of the Cold War had come to an end, along with the Cold War itself, was very closely related to the rise of both intransigent nationalism and integralist religion. The world, c. 2000, was not a particularly hospitable place for cosmopolitanism and this hospitality has declined distinctly in the initial two decades of the twentieth century, while globalization has lurched farther forward.

It is true that from the 1980s onward certain forms of consumerism, in the mass media, in retail, in clothing brands, to name just a few venues, have become steadily more globalized. It is nonetheless important not to exaggerate the extent of global homogeneity. In spite of the vast expansion of TV capacity through the transition from over-the-air broadcast to satellite and cable in the last decade of the twentieth century, most TV content remained domestic rather than imported. Fears of a global Americanization of mass media proved unfounded, as even agencies particularly sensitive to such fears, like UNESCO, admitted. When the same TV programs were broadcast in different countries, they were often interpreted and understood very differently. This was part of a broader pattern of different uses of the same globalized consumer goods or services. The place of fast-food chains as finer dining and community gathering places, in China or African countries at the beginning of the twenty-first century, was evidently extremely different from the use of those same chains in the wealthier countries of Europe or America. Even narrowing the focus to those wealthier lands, the forms of credit and the use of credit for consumerism were noticeably different.

Overall, it might be more appropriate to see the worldwide interchanges of globalization as promoting nationalism and particularism rather than working against them. International sports competition, and their worldwide TV broadcasting have proved to be powerful agencies for a nationalism tied to and promoted by sports—a point made in horrific detail by the enthusiastic participation of Serbian soccer fans in the killing and ethnic cleansing in Bosnia. Evangelical Christianity, Salafism, militant Shiism, militant Hinduism, and Ultra-Orthodox Judaism, to name some of the world's integralist, certainly anti-cosmopolitan and generally rather intolerant religions, have made excellent use of and benefited from global connections (and done so more effectively than their fading, religious modernist competitors), including financial contributions from migrants, seminaries and universities with a worldwide student body and the global deployment of late twentieth-century media technology.

It is not just that global networks of migration, communication, and economic interchange have spread anti-cosmopolitan ideas. Those ideas have all too frequently been a response to global challenges, a refuge from the threatening onset of changes occurring on a worldwide scale. Nations and religions have been sources of certainty and community as worldwide economic changes undermine forms of employment and life expectations, as migration changes the makeup of the population in unsettling terms, or what can be portrayed that way by politicians and the mass media. In the end, the belief that global economic interactions, global reach of communication, and global population movements would foster cosmopolitan outlooks has been one of many forms of utopian thinking.

Expectations and Realities

The Age of Interconnection was an era of great expectations. Just consider some of the more widespread ones. An era of global government, a "fraternal world" was about to appear. The end to the greatest empires of human history would lead to new and better human beings, living in social and political orders superior to any previous one. Atomic energy would create a paradise on earth; space travel would enable humanity to colonize the universe. Antibiotics would eliminate infectious disease. Insurgent young people would overturn existing social and political regimes, shred long-existing traditions, transform everyday life, create a new culture free of alienation and exploitation. A worldwide regime of human rights would guarantee everyone the opportunity to ensure the basic features of their humanity. The looming apocalypse would bring a messianic order to a sinful world. The end of the Cold War would produce a "new world order" of perfectly self-regulating markets under benevolent American hegemony, which would be the "end of history."

Those very same decades were also a time of equally great terrors. Nuclear fission and fusion would produce weapons of immense destructive force whose use would destroy human civilization and perhaps all life on earth. This was, truly, the recurring great fear of the four decades between 1949 and 1989, but there were many others as well. One was the belief that runaway increases in human population would lead to mass starvation and death. Related was the fear that humanity would run out of raw materials—or at least out of petroleum—and face a future of misery and impoverishment. The fear that human activity would destroy the biosphere took on a wide variety of forms: DDT ruthlessly killing off animals; chlorofluorocarbons destroying the ozone layer; allowing solar radiation to wreak havoc; or greenhouse gas emissions making the earth uninhabitable, or at least uninhabitable for the large numbers of people who live on it. These were all science-based fears, but with the growth of integralist religion there were fears of an apocalypse that would bring divine punishment on a sinful humanity.

Some of these hopes and fears go back a long way, to the visions of John of Patmos or to the prophets of ancient Judea. Secularized ideas of human perfectibility and the role of science and technology in bringing about that perfectibility were products of the eighteenth-century Enlightenment and its development across the subsequent hundred years. Malthusian-based gloomy scenarios of the future began as a condemnation of these optimistic hopes and developed alongside them.

Not to reject any of these longer-term origins of great (and terrifying) expectations, but what gave them force and added a whole repertoire of hopes and fears was the Age of Total War. One main reason for this impact was the appalling slaughter of the two world wars, and their global scope, especially the Second World War—both fears arising from this but also hopes of finding ways to bring to an end, once and for all, the conditions that caused it. The massive wave of technological innovation launched in these wars, which included atomic power, rocketry, microelectronics, and antibiotics, provided a basis for both hopes and fears, as did the mass movements emerging from them, such as communism and anti-imperialism. Products of the Age of Total War and integrally linked to it, the great military and diplomatic confrontations of the Age of Interconnection, the Cold War and the global realignment conflict, generated both hopes and—mostly—fears. What was, in effect, the final resolution of the Second World War in 1989–90 seemed to mark the end of both the Cold War and the global realignment conflict. It is certainly true that over the course of the second half of the century, the impact of the Age of Total War on both great hopes and terrible fears began to decline, going from playing a crucial role in the postwar era, to relevant in the Era of Upheaval, although competing with new and different influences, to much less salient in the Late-Millennium Era.

To say that these hopes and fears never became reality is not to underestimate their effects. While there was no global governance, the UN was set up in 1945 and has lasted, along with its many agencies and specialized functions, down to the present day. Countries liberated from fascist rule did not become totally new realms, but revamped their prewar conditions with improved social welfare systems and greater economic security for the working population, as well as a consumer society that drew on these new sources of stability. The greatest colonial empires in human history were dismantled, and former colonial subjects could exercise self-determination, even if the resulting sovereign nation-states were not a new and superior stage in human history. Microelectronics and satellites have changed the way humans work and communicate, although humans have not been working or communicating in outer space or connected to gigantic brains, solving humanity's problems. While antibiotics and mass vaccination campaigns have not eliminated all infectious diseases, they have helped introduce an unprecedented increase in life expectancy at birth, around the world. Radicalization of the 1960s also did not create a totally new human society, free of alienation and oppression, but it did play a role in the development of groups promoting human rights, environmental protection, and feminism (all of these sometimes as much in opposition to the movements of the 1960s as in succession to them), and in the worldwide wave of legislation and administrative action characteristic of the 1970s, improving women's social and political rights, enhancing consumer protection, or protecting the environment.

Fears of a nuclear holocaust played at least a modest role in preventing one from happening, just as fears of population growth outstripping the food supply helped spur on the Green Revolution, which gave the world a new and improved source of basic foodstuffs, and fears of the destruction of the ozone layer led to the Montreal Accords, which really did protect that part of the upper atmosphere. If the new world order of the 1990s proved evanescent, it did play a large role in the economic rise of China and the rescue of a large portion of humanity—by the twenty-first century, not just in China—from conditions of dire poverty, and it did stop an ongoing mass murder in the former Yugoslavia. The apocalypse has not yet arrived, but integralist religions asserting it is on the way have gained hundreds of millions of adherents around the world, with a large variety of political, social, and cultural consequences.

Another way of putting this would be to say that the Age of Interconnection has been an era of the triumph of the prosaic: even the most extreme hopes and fears have not been realized, although the history of the current century is just beginning, and possibilities for hopes, and, especially, fears are still very open. Whatever the current century may bring, the years between 1945 and 2001 marked a sharp change from the Age of Total War, when the prosaic was more the exception than the rule, confined to a few years of relatively peaceful and continuous development between periods of upheaval, or to areas of the world sheltered from the violence of unprecedented military confrontation. It seems reasonable to ask why the prosaic has dominated in the second half of the twentieth century, an age of great hopes and fears, especially after the very turbulent period, 1914–45.

One reason is that a number of the plans for very drastic change in the second half of the century have been dangerously unhinged—the Great Leap Forward, the rule of the Khmer Rouge, the revolutionary regimes in Afghanistan and Ethiopia—collapsing from the weight of their own failure, leaving behind a trail of death. Another plausible reason, from the realm of common sense, would be that after a period of upheaval and turmoil, there is a natural human desire for a respite, for an era of stability and placidity. This might explain the immediate postwar decades, but not the continued domination of the prosaic in view of the many changes and upheavals, starting in the 1970s, that brought the postwar era to an end. Although it might seem counterintuitive, the triumph of the prosaic is likely related to the ongoing process of globalization.

This is the opposite of the way globalization is usually portrayed, as a force of turmoil and disruption: undermining existing industries and ways of doing business, disrupting job and financial markets, reshaping social structures, encouraging migration, bringing new and dangerous ideas to the entire world. None of that is incorrect, but this point of view overlooks the way globalization has created its own worldwide structures, apparent in forms of global markets, new versions of social structures, systems of migration, new ways of interacting with the biosphere, both within and outside the human organism. These globalized structures, to some extent shaped but certainly not controlled even by the world's most powerful political actors—the United States and the other wealthy nations, especially of the North Atlantic, global agencies and institutions, the one-time Eastern Bloc across Eurasia—to say nothing of the less powerful, have an intrinsic stabilizing momentum. There are five particularly consequential examples of the stabilizing, moderating, and repressive features of globalization, largely, although not exclusively, in the later decades of the twentieth century.

More than any other, there was the "Green Revolution," the spread of the most important technological innovation of the second half of the twentieth century, the development of high-yield, hybrid grain crops, from the United

States to Latin America and Asia in the last third of the century, which decisively counteracted the destabilizing—for a while quite scary—consequences of rapid population growth in the three decades following the Second World War. Starting about a decade later, there was the taming of the labor movement at the workplace, on strike and in the political arena. At least in part a consequence of the globalization of industrial production and transport, this taming reduced what had been one of the great forces of disruption, and a reservoir of hopes for fundamental social transformation in the first half of the twentieth century to a depressingly minor factor by the beginning of the twenty-first. A third instance was the inability of the nonaligned countries, following their attainment of independence from colonial rule, to form a powerful and effective bloc in global politics, from the 1970s onward—a result, certainly, of diplomatic pressure and covert action on the part of the United States and other wealthier countries, but above all stemming from the fallout of the oil price shocks of the 1970s, one of the great drivers of globalization in Age of Upheaval.

Following a similar trajectory was the long-term decline and then rapid collapse of the strongest opponent of globalizing tendencies, the communist lands of Eurasia, brought about, at least in part, by the way they became enmeshed in the networks of globalization. The result of both these trends—inability of the poorer countries to form a successful political or economic bloc, and the end of communism—was a globalized market in capital, goods, and labor, leading to revised social structures and to an increase in inequality within individual countries, but a decrease in inequality between countries, both of which seem to have weakened opponents of a globalized capitalist order.

Finally, and certainly related to these proceeding trends, was the spread and development of a consumer society across the world, running over the entire period from the onset of economic recovery from wartime damage to the dramatic rise of China in the world economy during the last decade of the old millennium and the first of the new. It is certainly true, as left-wing critics have observed, that large portions of the world around 2000—most Africans, a large proportion of South Asians, and of inhabitants of Latin America—did not enjoy the fruits of consumerism, but the aspirations to do so were certainly present worldwide, and shaped the desires of the disadvantaged in the direction of participation in consumerism rather than its radical rejection.

None of this is to suggest that these developments occurred automatically. Quite the opposite, they all involved political agency, and the careers of some of the world's prominent political figures from 1960 onward, including Margaret Thatcher, Ronald Reagan, Mikhail Gorbachev, Deng Xiaoping, Gamal 'Abd al-Nasir, or Nelson Mandela, to mention just a few, offer so many examples of decisions and actions that played a substantial role in the advance of globalization in support of the prosaic. Yet political campaigns, diplomatic *démarches*, military and clandestine action, all these instances of agency and initiative, surfed, as it were, on a wave of globalization, in the career of these and so many other leading politicians and government leaders. Often, especially in considering the gap between the long-term successes and the frequently inept instances of US foreign policy in much of the Age of Interconnection, it is hard to avoid the conclusion that the power of the wave was more important than the surfer's skill at riding it.

In the end, this has been the most significant result of the second half of the twentieth century as an Age of Interconnection. The increasing integration of the countries of the world into one globalized system—making the era an age not just of connection but of interconnection—has been a force limiting the possibilities of the great hopes and equally great fears that have been prevalent around the world since the Age of Total War. This coexistence of dramatic aspirations and prosaic realities has been a characteristic feature of the very recent past, shaping our present. It remains to be seen if it can continue into the future.

NOTES

Introduction

1. Jürgen Osterhammel, *The Transformation of the World: A Global History of the Nineteenth Century*, trans. Patrick Camiller (Princeton, NJ: Princeton University Press, 2014).

Chapter 1

1. "What Is the Anthropocene and Are We In It?," accessed June 4, 2015, http://www.smithsonianmag.com/science-nature/what-is-the-anthropocene-and-are-we-in-it-164801414/?no-ist; more generally, J.R. McNeill, *Something New under the Sun: An Environmental History of the Twentieth-Century World* (New York: W.W. Norton, 2000).
2. Many examples in McNeill, *Something New under the Sun*; also, Gerald Markowitz and David Rosner, *Deceit and Denial: The Deadly Politics of Industrial Pollution* (Berkeley: University of California Press, 2002); Sara B. Pritchard, *Confluence: The Nature of Technology and the Remaking of the Rhône* (Cambridge, MA: Harvard University Press, 2011); Brett L. Walker, *Toxic Archipelago: A History of Industrial Disease in Japan* (Seattle: University of Washington Press, 2010).
3. Kate Brown, *Plutopia: Nuclear Families, Atomic Cities and the Great Soviet and American Plutonium Disasters* (Oxford: Oxford University Press, 2013).
4. Lawrence S. Wittner, *The Struggle against the Bomb*. 3 vols. (Stanford, CA: Stanford University Press, 1993–2003), 2:146–48; Steven L. Simon, André Bouville, and Charles E. Land, "Fallout from Nuclear Weapons Tests and Cancer Risks," *American Scientist* 94 (2006): 48–57.
5. David Kinkela, *DDT and the American Century: Global Health, Environmental Politics and the Pesticide That Changed the World* (Chapel Hill: University of North Carolina Press, 2011); Edmund Russell, *War and Nature: Fighting Humans and Insects with Chemicals from World War I to Silent Spring* (Cambridge: Cambridge University Press, 2001), 201, 213–16.

6. Figures on population and economic growth are all from Angus Maddisson, *The World Economy*. 2 vols in 1 (Paris: OECD, 2006).
7. Adam Rome, *The Bulldozer in the Countryside: Suburban Sprawl and the Rise of American Environmentalism* (Cambridge: Cambridge University Press, 2001), 87–118; Franz-Josef Brüggemeier, *Schranken der Natur. Umwelt, Gesellschaft Experimente 1750 bis heute* (Essen: Klartext Verlag, 2014), 241–43.
8. John Soluri, *Banana Cultures: Agriculture, Consumption and Environmental Change in Honduras and the United States* (Austin: University of Texas Press, 2005); Murray Feshbach and Alfred Friendly Jr., *Ecocide in the USSR: Health and Nature under Siege* (New York: Basic Books, 1992), 73–88.
9. Judith Shapiro, *Mao's War against Nature: Politics and the Environment in Revolutionary China* (Cambridge: Cambridge University Press, 2001), 86–89.
10. Frank Uekötter, *The Greenest Nation? A History of German Environmentalism* (Cambridge, MA: MIT Press, 2014), 60–65; Sandra Chaney, *Nature of the Miracle Years: Conservation in West Germany 1945-1975* (New York: Berghahn Books, 2008), 83–108; Pritchard, *Confluence*, 134–59; Markowitz and Rosner, *Deceit and Denial*, 102–3.
11. Walker, *Toxic Archipelago*, 101–7; Douglas R. Weiner, *A Little Corner of Freedom: Russian Nature Protection from Stalin to Gorbachev* (Berkeley: University of California Press, 1999); Michael Bess, *The Light-Green Society: Ecology and Technological Modernity in France 1960—2000* (Chicago: University of Chicago Press, 2003), 67–71; Gary Haq and Alistair Paul, *Environmentalism since 1945* (London: Routledge, 2012), 5–7; Brüggemeier, *Schranken der Natur*, 147–63; Michael L. Lewis, *Inventing Global Ecology: Tracking the Biodiversity Ideal in India, 1947-1997* (Athens: Ohio University Press, 2004).
12. Quoted in Thomas Robertson, *The Malthusian Moment: Global Population Growth and the Birth of American Environmentalism* (New Brunswick, NJ: Rutgers University Press, 2012), 36–37 and chap. 2 more generally.
13. Robert J. Mayhew, *Malthus: The Life and Legacies of an Untimely Prophet* (Cambridge, MA: Belknap Press of Harvard University Press, 2014), chap. 8.
14. Robert Mitchell, Angela Mertig, and Riley Dunlap, "Twenty Years of Environmental Mobilization: Trends among National Environmental Organizations," *Society and Natural Resources* 4 (1991): 219–34; Russell Dalton, "The Greening of the Globe? Cross-national Levels of Environmental Group Membership," *Environmental Politics* 14 (2005): 441–59; Albert Weale, "Great Britain," in *National Environmental Policies: A Comparative Study of Capacity-Building*, ed. Martin Jänicke and Helmut Weidner (Berlin: Springer-Verlag, 1996), 97.
15. Adam Rome, *The Genius of Earth Day; How a 1970 Teach-In Unexpectedly Made the Frist Green Generation* (New York: Hill and Wang, 2013); Uekötter, *The Greenest Nation?*, 81–82; Besse, *Light Green Society*, 85–92.
16. Martin Jänicke and Helmut Weidner, eds., *National Environmental Policies*, Table 1; Uekötter, *Greenest Nation?*, 82–83; Besse, *Light Green Society*, 83.
17. These examples taken from the country studies in Jänicke and Weidner, *National Environmental Policies*; Maria Pilar Garcia, "The Venezuelan Ecology Movement: Symbolic Effectiveness, Social Practices and Political Strategies," in

The Making of Social Movements in Latin America: Identity, Strategy and Democracy, ed. Arturo Escobar and Sonia Alvarez (Boulder, CO: Westview Press, 1992), 150–70.
18. Frank Zelko, *Make It a Green Peace! The Rise of Countercultural Environmentalism* (Oxford: Oxford University Press, 2013).
19. Joanna Burger, *Oil Spills* (New Brunswick, NJ: Rutgers University Press, 1997); Brüggemeier, *Schranken der Natur*, 309–10; Besse, *Light Green Society*, 200 and chap. 3.
20. Ulrich Beck, *Risk Society: Towards A New Modernity*, trans. Mark Ritter (Newbury Park, CA: SAGE Publications, 1992); Charles Perrow, *Normal Accidents*, 2nd ed. (Princeton, NJ: Princeton University Press, 1999).
21. Jonathan Adler, "Fables of the Cuyahoga: Reconstructing a History of Environmental Protection," *Fordham Environmental Law Journal* 89 (2002): 89–146; Walker, *Toxic Archipelago*, 137–75.
22. Brüggemeier, *Schranken der Natur*, 309; McNeil, *Something New under the Sun*, 103.
23. *The Malthusian Moment*, 126, 137, 143, and chap. 6.
24. Mark Hamilton Lytle, *The Gentle Subversive: Rachel Carson, Silent Spring and the Rise of the Environmental Movement* (New York: Oxford University Press, 2007); Jacob Darwin Hamblin, *Arming Mother Nature: The Birth of Catastrophic Environmentalism* (Oxford: Oxford University Press, 2013), 163–65.
25. Besides Lytle, *Gentle Subversive*; also see Priscilla Coit Murphy, *What a Book Can Do: The Publication and Reception of Silent Spring* (Amherst: University of Massachusetts Press, 2005).
26. Christian Albrecht, "'The Atlantic Community in a Global Context': Global Crisis and Atlanticism within the Context of the Club of Rome 1960s to 1970s," *Bulletin of the German Historical Institute* 54, Supplement 10 (2014): 163–82; Donella and Dennis Meadows et al., *The Limits to Growth: A Report for the Club of Rome's Project on the Predicament of Mankind*, 2nd ed. (New York: Universe Books, 1974).
27. Paul Sabin, *The Bet: Paul Ehrlich, Julian Simon, and Our Gamble over Earth's Future* (New Haven, CT: Yale University Press, 2013), chaps. 1–3; Uekötter, *Greenest Nation?*, 107.
28. Vaclav Smil, *Energy in Nature and Society: General Energetics of Complex Systems* (Cambridge, MA: MIT Press, 2008), 337–38.
29. http://www.lead.org.au/Chronology-Making_Leaded_Petrol_History.pdf (accessed June 22, 2015); https://www.unep.org/resources/other-evaluation-reportsdocuments/outcome-and-influence-evaluation-unep-based-partnership (accessed 13 May 2022); McNeil, *Something New*, 54.
30. Jänicke and Weidner, eds., *National Environmental Policies*, Figures 1–7; World Health Organization and United Nations Environment Programme, *Urban Air Pollution in Megacities of the World* (Oxford: Blackwell Publishers, 1992); Mark Cioc, *The Rhine: An Eco-Biography, 1815–2000* (Seattle: University of Washington Press, 2002), chap. 7; "Zander und Lachs schwimmen wieder im Rhein," *Die Welt*, Jan. 9, 2014.
31. "2012 UNEP report on the global environment," p. 45, accessed July 1, 2015, http://www.unep.org/geo/pdfs/geo5/GEO5_report_C2.pdf; World Health Organization, *Urban Air Pollution*, 25, 29, https://www.lung.org/research/sota/city-rankings/most-polluted-cities, accessed May 13, 2022.

32. Smil, *Energy in Nature and Society*, 272.
33. Feshbach and Friendly, *Ecocide*; McNeil, *Something New*, 84–99; Uekötter, *Greenest Nation?*, 128–38; Weiner, *A Little Corner of Freedom*, chaps. 16–19.
34. Feshbach and Friendly, *Ecocide*, 97; Brüggemeier, *Schranken der Natur*, 270–71.
35. Cited in Uekötter, *The Greenest Nation*, 99; cf., Naomi Klein, *This Changes Everything: Capitalism vs. the Climate* (New York: Simon & Schuster, 2014).
36. WHO and UNEP, *Urban Air Pollution*; James David Fahn, *A Land on Fire: The Environmental Consequences of the Southeast Asian Boom* (Boulder, CO: Westview Press, 2003), 26–27; "2012 UNEP report on the global environment," p. 41, accessed July 1, 2015, http://www.unep.org/geo/pdfs/geo5/GEO5_report_C2.pdf.
37. Fahn, *Land on Fire*, 250–54; http://blog.cifor.org/23000/forests-news-update-qa-on-fires-and-haze-in-southeast-asia#.VYwnr-s7_go; "Unspontaneous Combustion," *The Economist*, June 29, 2013, http://www.economist.com/news/asia/21580154-forest-fires-bring-record-levels-air-pollution-and-end-not-sight-unspontaneous, both accessed June 25, 2015. Global overview in Thomas K. Rudel, *Tropical Forests: Regional Paths of Destruction and Regeneration in the Late Twentieth Century* (New York: Columbia University Press, 2005).
38. Rudel, *Tropical Forests*, 401–41, 117–18; Fahn, *A Land on Fire*, chaps 5–6; Peter van der Werff, "Divergent Approaches to the Environment in Kerala," in *Environmental Movements in Asia*, ed. Arne Kalland and Gerard Persoon (Richmond, Surrey: Curzon Press, 1998), 253–69; generally, William F. Laurence, Jeffrey Sayer, and Kenneth G. Cassman, "Agricultural Expansion and Its Impacts on Tropical Nature," *Trends in Ecology and Evolution* 29 (2014): 107–16.
39. Quotes from Hamblin, *Arming Mother Nature*, 197–99; Uekötter, *The Greenest Nation?*, 83.
40. Kalland and Peerson, *Environmental Movements in Asia*; Jeff Haynes, "Power, Politics and Environmental Movements in the Third World," *Environmental Politics* 8 (1999): 222–42; Robert P. Weller, *Discovering Nature: Globalization and Environmental Culture in China and Taiwan* (Cambridge: Cambridge University Press, 2006).
41. Kathryn Hochstetler and Margaret E. Keck, *Greening Brazil: Environmental Activism in State and Society* (Durham, NC: Duke University Press, 2007), 140–85, 191–99. Rudel, *Tropical Forests*, 147–48; Fahn, *A Land on Fire*, chap. 3.
42. A map of these regions as they existed in 2010, according to NASA observations, https://earthobservatory.nasa.gov/images/44677/aquatic-dead-zones, accessed May 13, 2022.
43. Spencer Weart, *The Discovery of Global Warming* (Cambridge, MA: Harvard University Press, 2008).
44. Paul N. Edwards, *A Vast Machine: Computer Models, Climate Data and the Politics of Global Warming* (Cambridge, MA: MIT Press, 2010).
45. Edward A. Parson, *Protecting the Ozone Layer: Science and Strategy* (Oxford: Oxford University Press, 2003).
46. William C. Clark et al., eds., *Learning to Manage Global Environmental Risks: A Comparative History of Social Responses to Climate Change, Ozone Depletion and Acid Rain*. 2 vols. (Cambridge, MA: MIT Press, 2001), 1:27, 67, 74, 100, 102, 116, 171–72, 199, 201, 219, 221, 263 are very interesting graphs of media and

political interest; polling data in Stuart Capstick et al., "International Trends in Public Perception of Climate Change over the Past Quarter Century," *WIREs Climate Change* 6 (2015): 35–61, doi: 10.1002/wcc.321, accessed July 8, 2015.

47. Parson, *Protecting the Ozone Layer*, chaps. 6–8; "2012 UNEP report on the global environment," 51–52, http://www.unep.org/geo/pdfs/geo5/GEO5_report_C2.pdf, accessed July 1, 2015; also, "Scientific Assessment of Ozone Depletion, 2014," https://csl.noaa.gov/assessments/ozone/2014/preface.html, accessed May 13, 2022.

48. Gerald Kutney, *Carbon Politics and the Failure of the Kyoto Protocol* (London: Routledge, 2014).

49. C. Le Quéré et al., "Global Carbon Budget, 2014," *Earth Systems Science Data* 7 (2015): 47–85; cf. also the 2014 global carbon report of the Netherlands Environmental Assessment Agency, http://www.pbl.nl/sites/default/files/cms/publicaties/PBL_2014_Trends_in_global_CO2_emissions_2014_1490_0.pdf, accessed July 2, 2015; most recent figures from the "Global Carbon Project," https://www.globalcarbonproject.org/, accessed May 13, 2022.

50. Figures from https://www.esrl.noaa.gov/gmd/ccgg/trends/mlo.html, accessed June 1, 2020.

51. Naomi Oreskes and Eric Conway, *Merchants of Doubt: How a Handful of Scientists Obscured the Truth on Issues from Tobacco Smoke to Global Warming* (New York: Bloomsbury, 2010).

52. Our World in Data, "Emissions by sector," https://ourworldindata.org/emissions-by-sector, accessed May 13, 2022. A strange coalition of vegans and conservatives making fun of the whole idea of global warming has propounded the notion that cows, by belching and farting, are responsible for a large proportion of greenhouse gas emissions, but all livestock and their manure only emit 5.8 percent of greenhouse gases.

53. Parson, *Protecting the Ozone Layer*, 44, 99, 131.

54. Capstick et al., "International Trends," esp. 54.

55. Parson, *Protecting the Ozone Layer*, 135; Oreskes and Conway, *Merchants of Doubt*, 5–6; Aaron M. McCright and Riley E. Dunlop, "The Politicization of Climate Change and the Polarization in the American Public's View of Global Warming, 2001–2010," *The Sociological Quarterly* 52 (2011): 155–94;, accessed July 9, 2015.

56. Edwards, *A Vast Machine*, 354–55.

57. Deepak K. Ray et al., "Yield Trends Are Insufficient to Double Global Crop Production by 2050," *PLoS One* 8 (6) e66428. doi: 10.1371/journal.pone.0066428, accessed July 8, 2015; Sasha Hafner, "Trends in Maize, Rice and Wheat Yields for 188 Nations over the Past 40 Years: A Prevalence of Linear Growth," *Agriculture, Ecosystems and Environment* 97 (2003): 275–83; Gordon Conway, *One Billion Hungry: Can We Feed the World?* (Ithaca, NY: Cornell University Press, 2012); Vaclav Smil, *Feeding the World: A Challenge for the Twenty-First Century* (Cambridge, MA: MIT Press, 2000).

58. On this point, cf. Sabin, *The Bet*.

59. *The Limits to Growth*, 72–73. The predicted value of 380 ppm carbon dioxide in 2000 was just 3 percent above the actual value of 370 ppm.

Chapter 2

1. Robert Bud, *Penicillin: Triumph and Tragedy* (Oxford: Oxford University Press, 2007), 4–5; also, David Greenwood, *Antimicrobial Drugs: Chronicle of a Twentieth Century Medical Triumph* (Oxford: Oxford University Press, 2008), chaps. 1–2. For what follows, these two books provide most of the details.
2. Bud, *Penicillin*, 98, 102; Iruka K. Okeke and Kayode K. Ogo, "Antimicrobial Use and Resistance in Africa," in *Antimicrobial Resistance in Developing Countries*, ed. Aníbal de J. Sosa et al. (New York: Springer, 2010), 301–14.
3. Cited in Greenwood, *Antimicrobial Drugs*, 112.
4. United Nations Population Division, "World Population Prospects: The 2015 Revision," life-expectancy database, http://esa.un.org/unpd/wpp/Download/Standard/Mortality/, accessed May 9, 2016.
5. James C. Riley, *Low Income Social Growth, and Good Health: A History of Twelve Countries* (Berkeley: University of California Press, 2008); Okeke and Ogo, "Antimicrobial Use and Resistance in Africa," 307; Richard A. Adegbola and Debasish Saha, "Vaccines: A Cost-Effective Strategy to Contain Antimicrobial Resistance," in Sosa et al., *Antimicrobial Resistance*, 477–90; David M. Oshinsky, *Polio: An American Story* (New York: Oxford University Press, 2005); Bud, *Penicillin*, 99–102.
6. Quoted in Scott Podolsky, *The Antibiotic Era: Reform, Resistance and the Pursuit of a Rational Therapeutics* (Baltimore: Johns Hopkins University Press, 2015), 100.
7. Ibid., chap. 5; Bud, *Penicillin*, chap. 7; Greenwood, *Antimicrobial Drugs*, chap. 6.
8. Quoted in Podolsky, *Antibiotic Era*, 143.
9. Ibid., chap. 5; Christian McMillen, *Discovering Tuberculosis: A Global History 1900 to the Present* (New Haven, CT: Yale University Press, 2015), 125–28; other examples in Greenwood, *Antimicrobial Drugs*, 394–98.
10. Brad Spellberg and Bonnie Taylor-Blake, "On the Exoneration of Dr. William H. Stewart: Debunking an Urban Legend," *Infectious Diseases of Poverty* 2 (2013), accessed May 13, 2016, http://www.ncbi.nlm.nih.gov/pmc/articles/PMC3707092, Robert Peckham, *Epidemics in Modern Asia* (Cambridge: Cambridge University Press, 2016), 250–51.
11. Quoted in Ian Glynn and Jennifer Glynn, *The Life and Death of Smallpox* (Cambridge: Cambridge University Press, 2004), 31.
12. Frank Fenner et al., *Smallpox and Its Eradication* (Geneva: World Health Organization, 1988), 174, underestimates of official figures, 174–75, 330 and passim. Cf. also Glynn, *Life and Death of Smallpox* and David Koplow, *Smallpox: The Fight to Eradicate a Global Scourge* (Berkeley: University of California Press, 2003).
13. Sources as in previous note and Donald A. Henderson, *Smallpox: The Death of a Disease* (New York: Prometheus Books, 2009).
14. Richard Carter and Kamini N. Mendis, "Evolutionary and Historical Aspects of the Burden of Malaria," *Clinical Microbiology Reviews* 15 (2002): 564–94, Table 3. More generally, Randall Packard, *The Making of a Tropical Disease: A Short History of Malaria* (Baltimore: Johns Hopkins University Press, 2011);REFC REFO:BKJames Webb Jr., *Humanity's Burden: A Global History of Malaria* (New York: Cambridge University Press, 2009).

15. Frank Snowden, *The Conquest of Malaria: Italy 1900–1962* (New Haven, CT: Yale University Press, 2006), 100, chap. 6 and passim.
16. Leo B. Slater, *War and Disease: Biomedical Research in the Twentieth Century* (New Brunswick, NJ: Rutgers University Press, 2009).
17. David Kinkela, *DDT and the American Century: Global Health, Environmental Politics and the Pesticide That Changed the World* (Chapel Hill: University of North Carolina Press, 2011), 15–32.
18. David Arnold, *Toxic Histories: Poison and Pollution in Modern India* (Cambridge: Cambridge University Press, 2016), 203; McMillen, *Discovering Tuberculosis*, 98.
19. Marcos Cuetos, *Cold War, Deadly Fevers: Malaria Eradication in Mexico, 1955–1975* (Baltimore: Johns Hopkins University Press, 2007).
20. Sources for Figure 2.1: Population from Maddison, *The World Economy*, 612. Malaria cases, 1962–1981 and 1982–97, from "WHO historical documents on Malaria," accessed June 6, 2016. http://www.who.int/malaria/publications/historical_documents/en/ (there are also figures, from the 1950s, which are too incomplete to be useable); 1990–2007 from the WHO "World Malaria Report," 2008, accessed June 16, 2016, http://www.who.int/malaria/publications/atoz/9789241563697/en/. The statistics for 1990–1997 overlap, and the later, more complete ones from the 2008 "World Malaria Report," are 1.49 times the figures in the earlier, 1982–1997, list of cases. I have multiplied all the 1962–1989 figures by 1.49, to account for earlier underreporting—not an ideal solution, but the best possible.
21. Javed Siddiqi, *World Health and World Politics: The World Health Organization and the UN System* (Columbus: University of South Carolina Press, 1995), 126–91; Cueto, *Cold War, Deadly Fevers*, 15–69, 148–66; Webb, *Humanity's Burden*, 166–77; Packard, *Making of a Tropical Disease*, 150–216; Kinkela, *DDT and the American Century*, 90–102, 150, 173–74, 182–86; Snowden, *The Conquest of Malaria*, 194–228; James Webb, "Malaria Control and Eradication Projects in Tropical Africa, 1945–65," in *The Global Challenge of Malaria: Past Lessons and Future Prospects*, ed. Frank Snowden and Richard Bucala (Singapore: World Scientific Publishing Company, 2014), 35–57; Arnold, *Toxic Histories*, 204.
22. Thomas Dormandy, *The White Death: A History of Tuberculosis* (New York: New York University Press, 1999); and Helen Bynum, *Spitting Blood: The History of Tuberculosis* (Oxford: Oxford University Press, 2012).
23. Flurin Condrau, *Lungenheilanstalt und Patientenschicksal* (Göttingen: Vandenhoeck and Ruprecht, 2000), 49–56.
24. K.L. Holloway et al., "Lessons from History of Socioeconomic Improvements: Approach to Treating Multi-Drug-Resistant Tuberculosis," *Journal of Biosocial Science* 46 (2014): 600–20; William Johnson, *The Modern Epidemic: A History of Tuberculosis in Japan* (Cambridge, MA: Harvard University Press, 1995); Condrau, *Lungheilanstalt*, 40; Alan Mitchell, "An Inexact Science: The Statistics of Tuberculosis in Late Nineteenth-Century France," *Social History of Medicine* 3 (1990): 387–403; David Barnes, *The Making of a Social Disease: Tuberculosis in Nineteenth-Century France* (Berkeley: University of California Press, 1995), Tables 1–3; Statistics Finland, "Mortality from tuberculosis, influenza and other

infectious diseases in 1936 to 2010," accessed June 14, 2016, http://www.stat.fi/til/ksyyt/2010/ksyyt_2010_2011-12-16_kat_003_en.html.

25. Condrau, *Lungheilansalt*, passim; Flurin Condrau, "Beyond the Total Institution: Towards a Reinterpretation of the Tuberculosis Sanatorium," in *Tuberculosis Then and Now: Perspectives on the History of an Infectious Disease*, ed. Flurin Condrau and Michael Worboys (Montreal: McGill-Queen's University Press, 2010), 72–99; Linda Bryder, *Below the Magic Mountain: A Social History of Tuberculosis in Twentieth-Century Britain* (Oxford: Clarendon Press, 1988).

26. McMillen, *Discovering Tuberculosis*, 70–118, is very skeptical; Greenwood, *Antimicrobial Drugs*, 142–44, somewhat less so.

27. Greenwood, *Antimicrobial Drugs*, chap. 5; mortality statistics as in n. 24; Alan Yoshioka, "Streptomycin in Postwar Britain: Cultural History of a Miracle Drug," in *Biographies of Remedies: Drugs, Medicines and Contraceptives in Dutch and Anglo-American Healing Cultures*, ed. M. Gijswijt-Hofstra, G.M. Van Heteren, and E.M. Tansey (Amsterdam: Editions, Rodopi B.V., 2002), 203–27; Bryder, *Below the Magic Mountain*, 262–63.

28. Helen Valier, "At Home in the Colonies: The WHO-MRC Trials at the Madras Chemotherapy Centre in the 1950s and 1960s," in Condrau and Worboys, *Tuberculosis Then and Now*, 213–34.

29. Greenwood, *Antimicrobials*, 182–87.

30. Bynum, *Spitting Blood*, 232; Abdel R. Omran, "The Epidemiologic Transition: A Theory of the Epidemiology of Population Change," *Milbank Memorial Fund Quarterly* 49 (1971): 509–38.

31. William Rothstein, *Public Health and the Risk Factor: A History of an Uneven Medical Revolution* (Rochester, NY: University of Rochester Press, 2003).

32. Kirk Jeffrey, *Machines in Our Hearts: The Cardiac Pacemaker, the Implantable Defibrillator and American Health Care* (Baltimore: Johns Hopkins University Press, 2001); David S. Jones, "Visions of a Cure: Visualizations, Clinical Trials and Controversies in Cardiac Therapeutics, 1968–1998," *Isis* 91 (2000): 504–41.

33. Siddhartha Mukherjee, *The Emperor of All Maladies: A Biography of Cancer* (New York: Scribner, 2010).

34. Besides the sources cited in nn. 30 and 32, H.O. Lancaster, *Expectations of Life: A Study in the Demography, Statistics and History of World Mortality* (New York: Springer-Verlag, 1990), 203–22 252–65.

35. WHO, "World Cancer Report 2003," chap. 2, accessed July 11, 2016, http://www.iarc.fr/en/publications/pdfs-online/wcr/2003/; also, Randall E. Harris, *Global Epidemiology of Cancer* (Burlington, MA: Jones and Bartlett, 2016), esp. 29.

36. Richard Peto et al., *Mortality from Smoking in Developed Countries 1950–2000: Indirect Estimates from National Vital Statistics* (Oxford: Oxford University Press, 1994), Table 7. Since women were generally less likely to smoke, smoking only accounted for 10 million of 240 million female deaths in the same countries and the same time.

37. Robert Proctor, *The Nazi War on Cancer* (Princeton, NJ: Princeton University Press, 1999); Allan M. Brandt, *The Cigarette Century: The Rise, Fall and Deadly Persistence of the Product that Defined America* (New York: Basic Books, 2007).

38. Brandt, *The Cigarette Century*, passim; WHO Tobacco Atlas, 2004, accessed July 7, 2016, http://www.who.int/tobacco/statistics/tobacco_atlas/en/print.html.
39. Since all these diseases increase in frequency with age, the death rates are age adjusted, to take changes in the demographic constitution of the population into account. In other words, the decline in the mortality rate of heart disease does not reflect a younger population, less prone to the malady.
40. Rothstein, *Public Health and the Risk Factor*, 185–91; Robert Fogel, *The Escape from Hunger and Premature Death, 1700–2100: Europe, America, and the Third World* (New York: Cambridge University Press, 2004), 99–100; Lancaster, *Expectations of Life*, 258, 455.
41. Rebecca Siegel, Deepa Naishadham, and Ahmedin Jemal, "Cancer Statistics, 2012," *CA: A Cancer Journal for Clinicians* 62 (2012): 10–29. Cancer mortality rates, stabilizing in the 1990s, have fallen by about 30 percent in the initial decades of the twenty-first century, driven by a decline in the frequency of cigarette smoking in previous decades.
42. Kazuo Uemura and Zybněk Piša, "Trends in Cardiovascular Mortality in Industrialized Countries since 1950," *World Health Statistics Quarterly* 41 (1988): 155–67; Statistics Finland, "Mortality from diseases in 1936 to 2010," accessed July 11, 2016, http://www.stat.fi/til/ksyyt/2010/ksyyt_2010_2011-12-16_kat_003_en.html; "Cancer Mortality from Vital Statistics in Japan 1958–2014," http://ganjoho.jp/en/professional/statistics/table_download.html, accessed July 11, 20167; Mukerjhee, *Emperor of all Maladies*, 505; Peto et al., *Mortality from Smoking*, 232–33. The WHO reports on cardiovascular disease and cancer, cited in the following note, also have useful information.
43. World Health Organization, "Global Atlas on Cardiovascular Disease Prevention and Control," 2011, accessed July 11, 2016, http://www.who.int/cardiovascular_diseases/publications/atlas_cvd/en/; Judith A. Finegold, Perviz Asaria, and Darrel P. Francis, "Mortality from Ischaemic Heart Disease by Country, Region and Age: Statistics from World Health Organisation and United Nations," *International Journal of Cardiology* 168 (2013): 934–45; WHO, "World Cancer Report 2003," accessed July 11, 2016, http://www.iarc.fr/en/publications/pdfs-online/wcr/2003/; Rafael Lozano et al, "Global and Regional Mortality from 235 Causes of Death for 20 Age Groups in 1990 and 2010," *Lancet* 380 (2012): 2095–2128.
44. UN life expectancy database, as in n. 4.
45. Rothstein, *Public Health and the Risk Factor*, 339–42.
46. T. Pischen et al., "General Abdominal Adiposity and Risk of Death in Europe," *New England Journal of Medicine* 359 (2008): 2105–20.
47. David B. Allison et al., "Annual Deaths Attributable to Obesity in the United States," *Journal of the American Medical Association* 282 (1999): 1530–38; and Amy Berrington de Gonzalez et al., "Body-Mass Index and Mortality among 1.46 Million White Adults," *The New England Journal of Medicine* 363 (2010): 2211–19.
48. Allison et al., "Annual Deaths," Table 4; and US Vital Statistics for 1991, accessed July 14, 2016, http://www.cdc.gov/nchs/products/vsus/vsus_1980_2003.htm.
49. Fogel, *Escape from Hunger and Premature Death*, 14–16, 25–32.

50. Calculated from K.M. Flegal et al., "Overweight and Obesity in the United States: Prevalence and Trends, 1960–1994," *International Journal of Obesity* 22 (1998): 39–47.
51. Jenny Bua, Lina W. Olsen, and Thorkild I.A. Sørensen, "Secular Trends in Childhood Obesity in Denmark During 50 Years in Relation to Economic Growth," *Obesity* 15 (2007): 977–85; Sara N. Bleich et al., "Why Is the Developed World Obese?," *Annual Review of Public Health* 29 (2008): 273–95; WHO, "World Health Statistics, 2005, Morbidity Table," 16–23, accessed July 15, 2016, http://www.who.int/gho/publications/world_health_statistics/en/.
52. C.A. Monteiro, et al., "Shifting Obesity Trends in Brazil," *European Journal of Clinical Nutrition* 54 (2004): 342–46; C.A. Monteiro et al., "Socioeconomic Status and Obesity in Adult Populations of Developing Countries: A Review," *Bulletin of the World Health Organization* 82 (2004): 940–45; C.A. Monteiro et al., "Obesity and Inequities in Health in the Developing World," *International Journal of Obesity* 28 (2004): 1181–86.
53. Barry Popkin, *The World Is Fat: The Fads, Trends, Policies and Products That Are Fattening the Human Race* (New York: Avery, 2008); S.W. Ng and B.M. Popkin, "Time Use and Physical Activity: A Shift Away from Movement Across the Globe," *Obesity Reviews* 13 (2012): 659–80; Shelley McKenzie, *Getting Physical: The Rise of Fitness Culture in America* (Lawrence: University Press of Kansas, 2013); Bleich et al, "Why Is the Developed World Obese?"; Uri Ladabaum et al., "Obesity, Abdominal Obesity, Physical Activity and Caloric Intake in US Adults: 1988 to 2010," *The American Journal of Medicine* 127 (2014): 717–27.
54. Jonathan Engel, *The Epidemic: A Global History of Aids* (New York: Harper Collins, 2006), chap. 2; David L. Kirp and Ronald Bayer, eds., *AIDS in the Industrialized Democracies: Passions, Politics and Policies* (New Brunswick, NJ: Rutgers University Press, 1992); Peter Baldwin, *Disease and Democracy: The Industrialized World Faces AIDS* (Berkeley: University of California Press, 2005), 205, 267.
55. Cited in Kirp and Bayer, *AIDS in the Industrialized Democracies*, 351; similarly, in China, Peckham, *Epidemics in East Asia*, 274; Baldwin, *Disease and Democracy*, 283–84.
56. Jacques Pepin, *The Origins of AIDS* (Cambridge: Cambridge University Press, 2011); John Iliffe, *The African AIDS Epidemic: A History* (Oxford: James Currey Ltd, 2006); Engel, *The Epidemic*, passim; Peckham, *Epidemics in East Asia*, 264–76.
57. Kirp and Bayer, *AIDS in the Industrialized Democracies*; Engel, *The Epidemic*, chap. 4; Ilifee, *African Aids Epidemic*, 65–66; Baldwin, *Disease and Democracy*, is an extraordinarily perceptive comparative study of policy debates and public health perspectives.
58. Podolsky, *Antibiotic Era*, 161–63.
59. Ibid., chap. 5; McMillen, *Discovering Tuberculosis*, chap. 5; Greenwood, *Antimicrobial Drugs*, chap. 9; Ian M. Gould and Jos W.M. van der Meer, eds., *Antibiotic Policies: Fighting Resistance* (New York: Springer, 2007); Webb, *Humanity's Burden*, 176–77; "Emergence of *Mycobacterium tuberculosis* with Extensive Resistance to Second-Line Drugs—Worldwide, 2000–2004," accessed August 1, 2016, http://www.cdc.gov/mmwr/preview/mmwrhtml/mm5511a2.htm.

60. Paul Farmer, *Infections and Inequalities: The Modern Plagues* (Berkeley: University of California Press, 1999); de J. Sosa et al., *Antimicrobial Resistance in Developing Countries*; McMillen, *Discovering Tuberculosis*, chap. 5.
61. Farmer, *Infections and Inequalities*, 193–200; Bynum, *Spitting Blood*, 245–52; McMillen, *Discovering Tuberculosis*, 206; similarly, Alison Bashford, "The Great White Plague Turns Alien: Tuberculosis and Immigration in Australia, 1901–2001," *Tuberculosis Then and Now*, 100–22.
62. Haidong Wang et al., "Age-Specific and Sex-Specific Mortality in 187 Countries 1970–2010: A Systematic Analysis for the Global Burden of Disease Study 2010," *Lancet* 380 (2010): 2071–94; United Nations Population Division, "World Population Prospects: The 2015 Revision," life-expectancy database, accessed May 9, 2016, http://esa.un.org/unpd/wpp/Download/Standard/Mortality/; Laurie Garrett, *Betrayal of Trust: The Global Collapse of Public Health* (New York: Hyperion, 2000), 602–4, and passim.
63. Engel, *The Epidemic*, chaps. 6, 7, 11, 12; WHO, "World Health Statistics, 2001," 16–22, accessed July 15, 2016, http://www.who.int/gho/publications/world_health_statistics/en/.
64. Cited in McMillen, *Discovering Tuberculosis*, 184; Iliffe, *The African Aids Epidemic*, 38; also, Engel, *The Epidemic*, 224.
65. Iliffe, *The African AIDS Epidemic*, 33; WHO World Health Statistics, 2005, as in n. 51; WHO AIDS database, accessed July 28, 2016, http://www.unaids.org/en/resources/documents/2016/HIV_estimates_with_uncertainty_bounds_1990-2015.
66. Helen Epstein, *The Invisible Cure: Africa, the West and the Fight against AIDS* (New York: Farrar Straus and Giroux, 2007).
67. Ibid.; Iliffe, *The African Aids Epidemic*, 116 and passim; WHO, "World Health Statistics, 2011," 71, accessed July 29, 2016, http://www.who.int/gho/publications/world_health_statistics/en/; Baldwin, *Disease and Democracy*, 29–30.
68. Mortality according to the WHO AIDS database, as in n. 65.
69. Victor D. Rosenthal et al., "Nosocomial Infections in 55 Intensive Care Units of 8 Developing Countries," *Annals of Internal Medicine* 145 (2006): 582–91; Greenwood, *Antimicrobial Drugs*, 398; M. Guzmán-Blanco and R.E. Istúriz, "Antimicrobial Drug Resistance in Latin America and the Caribbean" and Yu-Tsung Huang and Po-Ren Hsueh, "Antimicrobial Drug Resistance in Asia," in de J. Sosa et al., *Antimicrobial Resistance in Developing Countries*, 315–29 and 331–45.
70. McMillen, *Discovering Tuberculosis*, chaps. 10–12; Farmer, *Infections and Inequalities*, chaps. 7–9.
71. Wang et al., "Age- and Sex-Specific Mortality," 2075.
72. Preliminary and still very incomplete findings in Ariel Karlinsky and Dmitry Kobak, "Tracking excess mortality across countries during the COVID-19 pandemic with the World Mortality Dataset," *eLife* 2021;10:e69336, accessed Oct. 21, 2021, https://elifesciences.org/articles/69336.

Chapter 3

1. A salutary skepticism about this whole line of thought in David Edgerton, *The Shock of the Old: Technology and Global History since 1900* (Oxford: Oxford University Press, 2007).
2. Overall figures in Statistical Office of the United Stations, *World Energy Supplies 1956–1959* (New York: United Nations, 1961), 9; regions and individual countries according to Statistical Office of the United Stations, *World Energy Supplies in Selected Years 1929–1950* (New York: United Nations, 1952), 88–90. There are some discrepancies in figures, but not enough to change the basic story.
3. Source of Figure 3.1: UN, *World Energy Supplies*, Nr. 4, 1956–58; UN, *Yearbook of World Energy Statistics* 1975, 1983, 1988–2003. The UN's figures were adjusted in 1990 to increase the extent of "non-combustible" energy sources, so I have revised the pre-1990 figures correspondingly upward.
4. Dick van Lente, ed., *The Nuclear Age in Popular Media: A Transnational History, 1945–1965* (Houndmills, Basingstoke: Palgrave Macmillan, 2012), 31–32, 62–65, 189–90, 206–7 and passim; Spencer Weart, *The Rise of Nuclear Fear* (Cambridge, MA: Harvard University Press, 2012), 85; Paul R. Josephson, *Red Atom: Russia's Nuclear Program from Stalin to Today* (New York: W.H. Freeman and Company, 2000), 118.
5. Josephson, *Red Atom*, 120–34; Boyer, *By the Bomb's Early Light: American Thought and Culture at the Dawn of the Atomic Age* (New York: Pantheon, 1985), chap. 10.
6. Josephson, *Red Atom*., 25–28; Department of International Economic and Social Affairs, *1979 Yearbook of International Energy Statistics* (New York: United Nations, 1981), Table 46. Good international summary in Joachim Radkau, *Aufstieg und Krise der deutschen Atomwirtschaft 1945–1975* (Hamburg: Rowohlt, 1983), 20–26.
7. Radkau, *Aufstieg und Krise*, 25; Lorna Arnold, *Windscale, 1957: Anatomy of a Reactor Accident* (New York: St. Martin's 1992); Gabrielle Hecht, *The Radiance of France: Nuclear Power and National Identity after World War II* (Cambridge, MA: MIT Press, 1998), 310–11.
8. Stephanie Cooke, *In Mortal Hands: A Cautionary History of the Nuclear Age* (New York: Bloomsbury, 2009), 121.
9. Radkau, *Aufstieg und Krise*, 112–23; Hecht, *The Radiance of France*, 110; Robert S. Anderson, *Nucleus and Nation: Scientists, International Networks and Power in India* (Chicago: University of Chicago Press, 2010), 404–11; Abena Dove Osseo-Asare, *Atomic Junction: Nuclear Power in Africa after Independence* (Cambridge: Cambridge University Press, 2019).
10. Radkau, *Aufstieg und* Krise, 78–100; Hecht, *The Radiance of France*, 65–78; Osseo-Asare, *Atomic Junction*, chap. 2; esp. Cooke, *In Mortal Hands*.
11. Yergin, *The Prize*, 328–31, 333, 344, 694–96; Daniel Yergin, *The Quest: Energy, Security and the Remaking of the Modern World* (New York: Penguin Press, 2011), 260.
12. Yergin, *The Quest*, 523–36; "James R. Schlesinger, CIA chief and Cabinet member, dies," *Washington Post*, Mar. 27, 2014.
13. Figures from United Nations *Energy Statistics Yearbooks*, 1983, 1992, and 2000, Table 32 in each case. The actual installed capacity of nuclear power plants increased from 329,000 megawatts in 1990 to 369,000 a decade later, but because

NOTES | 667

overall generating capacity rose more rapidly, the share of atomic power in electrical generation declined.

14. Cooke, *In Mortal Hands*, 133–47; Perrow, *Normal Accidents*, 51–54.
15. Cooke, *In Mortal Hands*, passim; and Michael Besse, *The Light-Green Society: Ecology and Technological Modernity in France, 1960–2000* (Chicago: University of Chicago Press, 2003), 103–4.
16. Charles Seife, *Sun in a Bottle: The Strange History of Fusion and the Science of Wishful Thinking* (New York: Viking, 2008).
17. On the rise of natural gas, Yergin, *The Quest*, 310–41.
18. Per Högselius, *Red Gas: Russia and the Origins of European Energy Dependence* (New York: St. Martin's 2013).
19. Quoted in Joel Wolfe, *Autos and Progress: The Brazilian Search for Modernity* (Oxford: Oxford University Press, 2010), 116; emphasis in original.
20. Lewis H. Siegelbaum, *Cars for Comrades: The Life of the Soviet Automobile* (Ithaca, NY: Cornell University Press, 2008); Christopher Ward, *Brezhnev's Folly: The Building of BAM and Late Soviet Socialism* (Pittsburgh, PA: University of Pittsburgh Press, 2009), 48.
21. Wolfe, *Autos and Progress*, 135–37.
22. Joyce Dargay and Dermot Gately, "Income's Effect on Car and Vehicle Ownership Worldwide: 1960–2015," *Transportation Research* Part A 33 (1999): 101–38; (an updated version is available at http://www.econ.nyu.edu/dept/courses/gately/DGS_Vehicle%20Ownership_2007.pdf, accessed Oct. 10, 2014). Jan Logeman, *Trams or Tailfins? Public and Private Prosperity in Postwar West Germany and the United States* (Chicago: University of Chicago Press, 2012).
23. Erik Eckermann, *World History of the Automobile*. Translated by Peter L. Albrecht. (Warrendale, PA: Society of Automotive Engineers, Inc., 2001), 177; Michael Spivak and Omer Tismhoni, "Fuel Efficiency of Vehicles on US Roads: 1923–2006," *Energy Policy* 37 (2009): 3168–70; McCarthy, *Auto Mania*, 99–147.
24. Bernhard Rieger, *The People's Car: A Global History of the Volkswagen Beetle* (Cambridge, MA: Harvard University Press, 2013).
25. Eckermann, *World History of the Automobile*, 173–75.
26. Figures ibid., 177, plus US light-truck production, according to http://www.epa.gov/fueleconomy/fetrends/1975-2014/420r14023.pdf, accessed Oct. 15, 2014, Table 3.1.
27. Murray Feschbach and Alfred Friendly Jr., *Ecocide in the USSR: Health and Nature under Siege* (New York: Basic Books, 1992), 96.
28. Wolfe, *Autos and Progress*, 116; "The Wabenzi," *New Internationalist*, Sept. 1984, accessed Oct. 21, 2014, http://newint.org/features/1984/09/05/wabenzi/; Lewis H. Siegelbaum, ed., *The Socialist Car: Automobility in the Eastern Bloc* (Ithaca, NY: Cornell University Press, 2011).
29. On these points, McCarthy, *Auto Mania*, 148–252; Eckermann, *World History of the Automobile*, 176, 190–213; David Halberstam, *The Reckoning* (New York: Morrow, 1986); Paul Ingrassia, *Crash Course: The American Automobile Industry's Road from Glory to Disaster* (New York: Random House, 2010).
30. *ICAO Bulletin* 14/6 (1964): 7; 25/10 (Oct. 1970): 11. These figures do not include airplanes in the USSR, which did not become a member of the ICAO until 1970.

31. Automobile ownership according to the sources cited in Table 3.1; air passengers, according to Mitchell, *International Historical Statistics: Europe* Table F6; Mitchell, *International Historical Statistics: Africa* Table F6; Mitchell, *International Historical Statistics: Africa, Asia & Oceania* Table F6 and Mitchell, *International Historical Statistics: The Americas* Table F7. For some countries, figures are only available in passenger kilometers, so I have assumed that the average air voyage was 1,500 km, a figure corresponding to the ICAO's global averages.
32. T.A. Heppenheimer, *Turbulent Skies: The History of Commercial Aviation* (New York: J. Wiley & Sons, 1995), 158–60 and passim; Roger Bilstein, *The American Aerospace Industry: From Workshop to Global Eneterprise* (New York: Twayne Publishers, 1996), 142–45, 175–81; Matthew Lynn, *Birds of Prey: Boeing vs. Airbus: A Battle for the Skies* (New York: Four Walls Eight Windows, 1997); Steven McGuire, *Airbus Industrie: Conflict and Cooperation in US-EC Trade Relations* (Houndmills, Basingstoke: Macmillan, 1997).
33. Bureau of Transportation Statistics, "U.S. Air Carrier Safety Data," accessed Nov. 18, 2021, https://www.bts.gov/content/us-air-carrier-safety-data.
34. Kenneth Owen, *Concorde and the Americans: International Politics of the Supersonic Transport* (Washington, DC: Smithsonian Institution Press, 1997), 5–9 and passim.
35. Particularly informative, and not just about the USSR, is Asif A. Siddiqi, *The Red Rockets Glare: Spaceflight and the Soviet Imagination, 1857–1957* (New York: Cambridge University Press, 2010).
36. Michael J. Neufeld, *The Rocket and the Reich: Peenemünde and the Coming of the Ballistic Missile Era* (Cambridge, MA: Harvard University Press, 1996). American, Soviet, and Japanese forces used rocket weapons during the Second World War, but these were much smaller, solid-fuel missiles.
37. Siddiqi, *Red Rockets Glare*, 196–289; David H. DeVorkin, *Science with a Vengeance: How the Military Created the US Space Sciences after World War II* (New York: Springer-Verlag, 1992); Walter A. McDougall, . . . *the Heavens and the Earth: A Political History of the Space Age* (New York: Basic Books, 1985) is the standard work, now rather outdated.
38. Howard McCurdy, *Space and the American Imagination*, 2nd ed. (Baltimore: Johns Hopkins University Press, 2011), 11–92; Siddiqi, *Red Rockets Glare*, 304–13.
39. Hecht, *Radiance of France*, 113; Anderson, *Nucleus and Nation*, 418.
40. Quote in McCurdy, *Space the American Imagination*, 84; Slava Gerovitch, "The Human Inside the Propaganda Machine: The Public Image and Professional Identity of Soviet Cosmonauts," in *Into the Cosmos: Space Exploration and Soviet Culture*, ed. James Andrew and Asif Siddiqui (Pittsburgh, PA: University of Pittsburgh Press, 2011), 77–106; see also Robert A. Divine, *The Sputnik Challenge: Eisenhower's Response to the Soviet Satellite* (New York: Oxford University Press, 1993).
41. Immensely informative, Asif A. Siddiqi, *Challenge to Apollo: The Soviet Union and the Space Race, 1945–1974* (Washington, DC: NASA History Division, 2000).
42. Anderson, *Nucleus and Nation*, 421, 647 n. 66.
43. McCurdy, *Space and the American Imagination*, 183–206, 225–32

44. Martin Turner, *Rocket and Spacecraft Propulsion: Principles, Practices and New Developments*, 3rd ed. (Berlin: Springer, 2009), 14–16, 99, 323.
45. Divine, *The Sputnik Challenge*, 98; McCurdy, *Space and the American Imagination*, 72–77.
46. Claude Piantadosi, *Mankind beyond Earth: The History, Science and Future of Human Space Exploration* (New York: Columbia University Press, 2012), 137; http://www.ucsua.org/nuclear_weaons_and_global_security/solutions/space-weapons/ucs-satellite-database.html#.VW9MuuyDgo; satellite weight database, accessed June 3, 2015.
47. Konstantin Tsiolkovsky, *Beyond the Planet Earth*, trans. Kenneth Syers (New York: Pergamon Press, 1960) (Russian original published in 1920) 108, 122, 124, 133–34; a later, more sophisticated version is Arthur C. Clarke, "Death and the Senator," in Arthur C. Clarke, *Tales of Ten Worlds* (New York: Dell, 1964), 106–29.
48. Extensive details in Piantadosi, *Mankind beyond Earth*, passim, and Mary Roach, *Packing for Mars: The Curious Science of Life in the Void* (New York: W.W. Norton, 2010); two advocates of manned space exploration who do not downplay its extreme expense and difficulties.
49. Roger D. Launius, "Venus-Earth-Mars: Comparative Climatology and the Search for Life in the Solar System," in *Exploring the Solar System: The History and Science of Planetary Exploration*, ed. Roger Launius (Houndmills, Basingstoke: Macmillan 2013), 223–48.
50. Amy Paige Kaminiski, "Faster, Better, Cheaper: A Sociotechnical Perspective on Programmatic Choice, Success and Failure in NASA's Solar System Exploration Program," in Launius, *Exploring the Solar System*, 77–101; accessed June 4, 2015, http://www.nasa.gov/centers/goddard/news/topstory/2003/1105voyager_facts.html.
51. Andrew K. Johnston, "Exploring Planet Earth: The Development of Satellite Remote Sensing for Earth Science," in Launius, *Exploring the Solar System*, 203–27. Jeffrey T. Richelson, *America's Space Sentinels: DPS Satellites and National Security* (Lawrence: University Press of Kansas, 1999); Erik M. Conway, *Atmospheric Science at NASA: A History* (Baltimore: Johns Hopkins University Press, 2008); Pat Norris, *Spies in the Sky: Surveillance Satellites in War and Peace* (Berlin: Springer Associates, 2008); Richard D. Easton and Eric F. Frazier, *GPS Declassified: From Smart Bombs to Smartphones* (Lincoln, NE: Potomac Books, 2013).
52. Arturo Russo, "Parachuting onto Another World: The European Space Agency's Huygens Mission to Titan," in Launius, *Exploring the Solar* System, 257–321; James Clay Moltz, *Asia's Space Race: National Motivations, Regional Rivalries, and International Risks* (New York: Columbia University Press, 2012); Easton and Frazier, *GPS Declassified*, 178–82.
53. A thoughtful commentary, from 2004, on changing uses of outer space, by someone who knows: James A. Van Allen, "Is Human Space Flight Obsolete?" http://issues.org/20-4/p_van_allen/, accessed Mar. 19, 2015.
54. Chart is from FAO statistics, at faostat3.fao.org/download/Q/Qc/E, accessed Feb. 5, 2014. A helpful regionalized analysis of these statistics is in Hafner, "Trends in Maize, Rice, and Wheat Yields."

55. Noel Kingsbury, *Hybrid: The History and Science of Plant Breeding* (Chicago: University of Chicago Press, 2009).
56. USDA, "Crop Production Historical Track Records," 28–29 (26.6 bushels per acre in the 1870s and 24.24 bushels per acre in the 1930s), accessed Jan. 22, 2015, www.nass.uda.gov/Publication/Todays-Reports/reports/croptr14.pdf.
57. John C. Culver and John Hyde, *American Dreamer: The Life and Times of Henry A. Wallace* (New York: W.W. Norton, 2000).
58. Productivity figures as in n. 54; similar, global figures in Denis J. Murphy, *Plant Breeding and Biotechnology: Societal Context and the Future of Agriculture* (Cambridge: Cambridge University Press, 2007), 220.
59. Warren Belasco, *Meals to Come: A History of the Future of Food* (Berkeley: University of California Press, 2006), 38–51, 201–13.
60. Conway, *One Billion Hungry*, 44.
61. Quoted ibid., 46.
62. Quoted in Murphy, *Plant Breeding and* Biotechnology, 90.
63. Kingsbury, *Hybrid*, 204–11, 254–55; Conway, *One Billion Hungry*, 170–71.
64. A globally renowned example of both red and green criticisms is Vandana Shiva, *The Violence of the Green Revolution* (London: Zed Books, 1991).
65. John H. Perkins, *Geopolitcs and the Green Revolution: Wheat, Genes and the Cold War* (New York: Oxford University Press, 1997).
66. J.L. Anderson, *Industrializing the Corn Belt: Agriculture, Technology and Environment, 1945–1972* (DeKalb: Northern Illinois University Press, 2009); Rita Sharma and Thomas Poleman, *The New Economics of India's Green Revolution* (Ithaca, NY: Cornell University Press, 1993); Mohammad Alauddin and Clement Tisdell, *The "Green Revolution" and Economic Development: The Process and its Impact in Bangladesh* (New York St. Martin's, 1991) or Pamela Matson, ed., *Seeds of Sustainability: Lessons from the Birthplace of the Green Revolution in Agriculture* (Washington, DC: Island Press, 2012).
67. Stephen Brush, *Farmers' Bounty: Locating Crop Diversity in the Contemporary World* (New Haven, CT: Yale University Press, 2004), 17–18, 35, 36, 54, 178 and passim.
68. Conway, *One Billion Hungry*, 260–61.
69. Besides the works of Conway, Murphy, and Kingsbury, Smil, *Feeding the World*, is a very cogent analysis.
70. Eric J. Vettel, *Biotech: The Countercultural Origins of an Industry* (Philadelphia: University of Pennsylvania Press, 2006); Paul F. Lurquin, *The Green Phoenix: A History of Genetically Modified Plants* (New York: Columbia University Press, 2001).
71. Farmers in India have responded to these property claims, not by rejecting GM crops, but by stealing seeds from Monsanto's experimental BT cotton fields and cross-breeding them with local varieties. Kingsbury, *Hybrid*, 417.
72. Conway, *One Billion Hungry*, 174–86, Murphy, *Plant Breeding*, 23–210; and Kingsbury, *Hybrid*, 364–419.
73. Derek Cheung and Eric Brach, *Conquering the Electron: The Geniuses, Visionaries, Egomaniacs and Scoundrels Who Built Our Electronic Age* (Lanham, MD: Rowman & Littlefield, 2014); David L. Morton and Joseph Gabriel, *Electronics: The Life Story*

of a Technology (Baltimore: Johns Hopkins University Press, 2004); and Michael Riordan and Lillian Hoddeson, *Crystal Fire: The Invention of the Transistor and the Birth of the Information Age* (New York: W.W. Norton, 1997); Alfred D. Chandler Jr., *Inventing the Electronic Century: The Epic Story of the Consumer Electronics and Computer Industries* (New York: The Free Press, 2001).

74. Cited in Chandler, *Electronic Century*, 87.
75. Anderson, *Nucleus and Nation*, 340–41.
76. Jack E. Triplett, "The Solow Productivity Paradox: What Do Computers Do to Productivity?," *Canadian Journal of Economics* 32 (1999): 309–34.
77. A wonderful contemporary analysis of this issue: Thomas Landauer, *The Trouble with Computers: Usefulness, Usability and Productivity* (Cambridge, MA: MIT Press, 1995).
78. Jason Dedrick and Kenneth L. Kraemer, *Asia's Computer Challenge* (New York: Oxford University Press, 1998); Chandler, *Electronic Century*, 81, 177–237; Jason Dedrick and Kenneth Kramer, "Globalization of the Personal Conmputer Industry: Trends and Implications," accessed Mar. 4, 2015, http://e.scholarship.org/uc/item/6wq2f4hx.
79. Martin Campbell-Kelly, *From Airline Reservations to Sonic the Hedgehog: A History of the Software Industry* (Cambridge, MA: MIT Press, 2003) 36–49; accessed Nov. 29, 2021, https://www.swift.com/about-us/history.
80. Gunnar Trumbell, *Silicon and the State: French Innovation Policy in the Internet Age* (Washington, DC: Brookings Institution Press, 2002), 66–80. The Minitel service was terminated in 2012: "Minitel, France's precursor to the web to go dark on June 30," *Ars Technica*, accessed Mar. 2, 2015, http://arstechnica.com/gadgets/2012/06/minitel-frances-precursor-to-the-web-to-go-dark-on-june-30/.
81. Janet Abbate, *Inventing the Internet* (Cambridge, MA: MIT Press, 1999).
82. Anderson, *Nucleus and Nation*, 339.
83. Abbate, *Inventing the Internet*, 113–220.
84. "Internet Growth Statistics," http://www.internetworldstats.com/emarketing.htm; US Census Bureau, "Households with a Computer and Internet Use, 1984–2009," http://www.census.gov/hhes/computer/, both accessed Mar. 3, 2015. Internet access in different Western European countries then ranged from 50 percent to 100 percent of US rates. Trumbell, *Silicon and the State*, 69–72.
85. Roger Lowenstein, *Origins of the Crash: The Great Bubble and its Undoing* (New York: Penguin Press, 2004), 101–26, 137–55; John Cassidy, *Dot.con: The Greatest Story Ever Sold* (New York: HarperCollins, 2002), 246 and passim.

Chapter 4

1. Harold James, *International Monetary Cooperation since Bretton Woods* (New York: Oxford University Press, 1996), 53–54; http://www.maynardkeynes.org/john-maynard-keynes-the-war-years.html, accessed May 5, 2010.
2. Paul R. Gregory and Robert C. Stuart, *Russian and Soviet Economic Performance and Structure*, 6th ed. (Reading, MA: Addison-Welsey, 1998), 104–6 and passim.
3. Michael Ellman, *Planning Problems in the USSR: The Contribution of Mathematical Economics to Their Solution 1960–1971* (Cambridge: Cambridge University Press, 1973).

4. Wei Li and Dennis Tao Yang, "The Great Leap Forward: Anatomy of a Planning Disaster," *Journal of Political Economy* 113 (2005): 840–77.
5. Alec Nove, *An Economic History of the USSR 1917–1991*, 3rd ed. (London: Penguin, 1992), 322; LEMO, "Erich Apfel 1917–1965," accessed Sept. 22, 2020, https://www.hdg.de/lemo/biografie/erich-apel.html. There were personal reasons and issues of domestic politics involved in the suicide as well. Jeffrey Kopstein, *The Politics of Economic Decline in East Germany, 1945–1989* (Chapel Hill: University of North Carolina Press, 1997), 57–59.
6. A few examples: Marc Levinson, *The Box: How the Shipping Container Made the World Smaller and the World Economy Bigger* (Princeton, NJ: Princeton University Press, 2006), 39; William R. Childs, *The Texas Railroad Commission: Understanding Regulation in America to the Mid-Twentieth Century* (College Station: Texas A&M University Press, 2005).
7. James Vestal, *Planning for Change: Industrial Policy and Japanese Economic Development 1945–1990* (Oxford: Clarendon Press, 1993), 35–36; Heinrich August Winkler, *MIttelstand, Demokratie und Nationalsozialismus* (Cologne: Kiepenheuer & Witsch, 1972), 184, 188 and passim.
8. Youssef Cassis, *Crises and Opportunities: The Shaping of Modern Finance* (Oxford: Oxford University Press, 2011), 182 n. 61; Janice M. Traflet, *A Nation of Small Shareholders: Marketing Wall Street after World War II* (Baltimore: Johns Hopkins University Press, 2013), 75. By 2000, about half of all US households owned shares of stock or mutual funds.
9. Jelle Visser, "Union Membership Statistics in 24 Countries," *Monthly Labor Review* 129 (2006): 38–49; David Blanchflower, "A Cross-Country Study of Union Membership," *British Journal of Industrial Relations* 45 (2007), 1–28.
10. Thomas Zeiler, *Free Trade, Free World: The Advent of GATT* (Chapel Hill: University of North Carolina Press, 1999); Jeffrey A. Frieden, *Global Capitalism: Its Rise and Fall in the Twentieth Century* (New York: W.W. Norton, 2006), 288.
11. Chalmers Johnson, *MITI and the Japanese Miracle: The Growth of Industrial Policy, 1925–1975* (Stanford, CA: Stanford University Press, 1982), 16, 246–47.
12. "Hippie Express: Loftleider's [sic] Low-Cost Long Haul," *Yesterday's Airlines*, accessed Sept. 22, 2020, https://www.yesterdaysairlines.com/airline-history-blog/hippie-express-loftleidirs-low-cost-long-haul; Anon, "Notes. The Ins and Outs of IATA: Improving the Role of the United States in the Regulation of International Air Fares," *The Yale Law Journal* 81 (1972): 1102–53, esp. n. 105.
13. Daniel Yergin, *The Prize: The Epic Quest for Oil, Money and Power* (New York: Simon & Schuster, 1991), 409–540, 722.
14. Informative, if taking very distinct positions on economic policy, is the official history of the IMF, James, *International Monetary Cooperation since Bretton Woods*.
15. Forrest Capie, *The Bank of England 1950s to 1979* (Cambridge: Cambridge University Press, 2010), 59.
16. Edgar Dosman, *The Life and Times of Raúl Prebisch 1901–1986* (Montreal, Canada: McGill-Queen's University Press, 2008) 276 and passim.
17. An overview of ISI in Frieden, *Global Capitalism*, 309–20.
18. Dosman, *Prebisch*, 248.

19. Jagdish Baghwati, *India in Transition: Freeing the Economy* (Oxford: Clarendon Press, 1993), 2, 10, 15, 17.
20. Vivek Chibber, *Locked in Place: State-Building and Late Industrialization in India* (Princeton, NJ: Princeton University Press, 2003).
21. Angus Maddison, *The World Economy*. 2 vols. in 1 (Paris: OECD, 2006), 640, 643.
22. A.B. Atkinson, "The Distribution of Income in the UK and OECD Countries in the Twentieth Century," *Oxford Review of Economic Policy* 15 (1999): 56–75.
23. Eli Rubin, *Synthetic Socialism: Plastics and Dictatorship in the German Democratic Republic* (Chapel Hill: University of North Carolina Press, 2008).
24. Samuel Baron, *Bloody Saturday in the Soviet Union: Novocherkassk, 1962* (Stanford, CA: Stanford University Press, 2001); more broadly, Robert Hornsby, *Protest, Reform and Repression in Khrushchev's Soviet Union* (Cambridge: Cambridge University Press, 2013), chap. 6.
25. Barry Eichengreen, *Globalizing Capital: A History of the International Monetary System*, 2nd ed. (Princeton, NJ: Princeton University Press, 2008), 107–11; Scott O'Bryan, *The Growth Idea: Purpose and Prosperity in Postwar Japan* (Honolulu: University of Hawai'i Press, 2009), 126–27; Ezra Vogel, *Deng Xiaoping and the Transformation of China* (Cambridge, MA: Harvard University Press, 2011), 428–35, 467–73.
26. Francis J. Gavin, *Gold, Dollars and Power: The Politics of International Monetary Relations, 1958–1971* (Chapel Hill: University of North Carolina. 2004); Barry Eichengreen, *The European Economy since 1945: Coordinated Capitalism and Beyond* (Princeton, NJ: Princeton University Press, 2007), 189.
27. Quoted in Judith Stein, *Pivotal Decade: How the United States Traded Factories for Finance in the Seventies* (New Haven, CT: Yale University Press, 2010), 41.
28. Vestal, *Planning for Change*, 56–57.
29. Sources for Table 4.1: Kofi Annan, "We the People: The Role of the United Nations in the 21st Century," 10, https://www.un.org/en/events/pastevents/pdfs/We_The_Peoples.pdf; Bank for International Settlements, "Triennial Central Bank Survey of Foreign Exchange and over the Counter (OTC) Derivatives Markets in 2019," https://www.bis.org/statistics/rpfx19.htm, both accessed Sept. 22, 2020.
30. Maurice Obstfeld and Alan Taylor, *Global Capital Markets: Integration, Crisis and Growth* (Cambridge: Cambridge University Press, 2004), 52–53.
31. Cassis, *Crises and* Opportunity, 35–36, 103.
32. Klaus Veigel, *Dictatorship, Democracy and Globalization: Argentina and the Cost of Paralysis, 1973–2000* (University Park, PA: Penn State University Press, 2009), 67. Very wonky readers might want to know that in this first instance of the financial bicycle, the value of the Argentine peso actually declined, but domestic prices rose at a slower rate than the peso fell, creating a rise in the real as opposed to the nominal exchange rate.
33. Eiko Maruko Siniawer, "'Toilet Paper Panic': Uncertainty and Insecurity in Early 1970s Japan," *American Historical Review* 126 (2021): 530–54.
34. Emma Rothschild, *Paradise Lost: The End of the Auto-Industrial Age* (New York: Random House, 1973); audio book editions in 1974 and 1977.
35. On American auto manufacturers, see Tom McCarthy, *Auto Mania: Cars, Consumers and the Environment* (New Haven, CT: Yale University Press, 2007), chaps. 9–11.

36. Yergin, *The Prize*, 724–26.
37. On financial deregulation in the United States, see Greta R. Krippner, *Capitalizing on Crisis: The Political Origins of the Rise of Finance* (Cambridge, MA: Harvard University Press, 2011).
38. Chibber, *Locked in Place*, 268–71; Osman Tarek, *Egypt on the Brink from Nasser to the Muslim Brotherhood* (New Haven, CT: Yale University Press, 2013), 55–57, 130–32, 135–38.
39. Abbas Alnaswari, *Arab Nationalism, Oil, and the Political Economy of Dependency* (New York: Greenwood Press, 1991), 102–3, 108.
40. Peter M. Lewis, *Growing Apart: Oil, Politics and Economic Change in Indonesia and Nigeria* (Ann Arbor: University of Michigan Press, 2007); GDP figures from Maddison, *World Economy*, 304, 325.
41. Mitchell Anderson, "The Verdict on Thatcherism Is Clear," *The Tyee*, Mar. 10, 2014, http://thetyee.ca/Opinion/2014/03/10/Thatcherism-Verdict/, accessed May 5, 2020.
42. Frieden, *Global Capitalism*, 370.
43. William Dority Jr. and Bobbie L. Horn, *The Loan Pushers: The Role of Commercial Banks in the International Debt Crisis* (Cambridge, MA: Bollinger Publishers, 1988), 81–82 and passim; Darrell Delamaide, *Debt Shock: The Full Story of the World Credit Crisis* (Garden City, NY: Doubleday, 1984).
44. James, *International Monetary Cooperation*, chaps. 11–12; Victor Bulmer-Thomas, *An Economic History of Latin America since Independence* (Cambridge: Cambridge University Press, 1994), 366–409; Alex E. Fernández Jilberto and André Mommen, "Setting the Neoliberal Development Agenda," in *Liberalization in the Developing World: Institutional and Economic Changes in Latin America, Africa and Asia*, ed. Alex E. Fernández Jilberto, and André Mommen (London: Routledge, 1996), 1–27; James Cronin, *Global Rules: America, Britain and a Disordered World* (New Haven, CT: Yale University Press, 2014), 141–47.
45. Eichengreen, *European Economy*, 297–99; Gregory and Sturat, *Russian and Soviet Economic Performance*, 186–87.
46. Erik Kirschbaum, "East German Hard-Currency Maestro, Alexander Schalck-Golodkowski Dies," *Reuters*, June 22, 2015, https://www.reuters.com/article/us-germany-wall-schalk-golodkowski/east-german-hard-currency-maestro-schalck-golodkowski-dies-idUSKBN0P21Z320150622, accessed June 26, 2020.
47. Immensely informative, Levinson, *The Box*.
48. Robert Fitzgerald, *The Rise of the Global Company: Multinationals and the Making of the Modern World* (Cambridge: Cambridge University Press, 2015), 288 and passim.
49. Levinson, *The Box*, 266; Fitzgerald, *Multinationals*, 423–25, 482–92.
50. Robert C. Feenstra, "Integration of Trade and Disintegration of Production in the Global Economy," *Journal of Economic Perspectives* 12 (1998): 31–50, esp. Table 2.
51. Levinson, *The Box*, 273; Bank for International Settlements, "Triennial Central Bank Survey," March 2002, 15, http://www.bis.org/publ/rpfx02t.pdf, accessed May 23, 2014.

52. Cassis, *Crisis and Opportunity*, 111; Eichengreen, *The European Economy*, 335–56; more generally, Rawi Abdelal, *Capital Rules: The Construction of Global Finance* (Cambridge, MA: Harvard University Press, 2007).
53. Eichengreen, *The European Economy*, 294–334; Nove, *Economic History of the USSR*, 394–419; a brilliant and fierce polemic about the consequences of shock therapy in Joseph Stiglitz, *Globalization and Its Discontents* (New York: W.W. Norton, 2002), chap. 5.
54. David H.D. Truong and Carolyn L. Gates, "Vietnam's Gradualist Economic Reforms," in *Liberalization in the Developing World*, ed. Fernández Jilberto and Mommen, 72–95.
55. John Williamson, "What Washington Means by Policy Reform," accessed Sept. 27, 2014, http://www.iie.com/publications/papers/paper.cfm?researchid=486; examples of the implementation of the consensus in the volume edited by Fernández Jilberto and Mommen in previous note.
56. Shapiro, *Pivotal Decade*, 166–71; James, *International Monetary Cooperation*, 266–70, 277–78, 289–96.
57. Jeffrey Frankel, "The Plaza Accord, 30 Years Later," NBER Working Paper No. 21813, Dec. 2015, https://www.nber.org/papers/w21813, accessed May 5, 2020; Christopher Wood, *The Bubble Economy: Japan's Extraordinary Speculative Bonm of the '80s and the Dramatic Bust of the '90s* (New York: Atlantic Monthly Press, 1992), 50 and passim.
58. Eichengreen, *The European Economy*, 247–50, 282–90, 346–76; Kara Swisher, "Sweden's 'Crazy' 500% Interest Rate," *Washington Post*, Sept. 18, 1992, https://www.washingtonpost.com/archive/politics/1992/09/18/swedens-crazy-500-interest-rate/c3750e89-8fa8-44f4-9028-49f3c0d6c61c/, accessed May 5, 2020.
59. Putting ELI in its long-term historical context: Alice H. Amsden, *The Rise of "The Rest": Challenges to the West from Late-Industrializing Economies* (Oxford: Oxford University Press, 2001).
60. And below that of Angola, Congo, Djibouti, the Ivory Coast, Gabon, Ghana, Liberia, Mozambique, Namibia, Senegal, and the average economist Angus Maddison calculated for forty-two African countries. Maddison, *The World Economy*, 304, 326, 598–603.
61. Alice H. Amsden, *Asia's Next Giant: South Korean and Late Industrialization* (New York: Oxford University Press, 1989); Eun Mee Kim, *Big Business, Strong State: Collusion and Conflict in South Korean Development, 1960–1990* (Albany: State University of New York Press, 1994); Byung-Kook Kim and Ezra Vogel, eds., *The Park Chung Hee Era: The Transformation of South Korea* (Cambridge, MA: Harvard University Press, 2011); Barry Eichengreen, Dwight Perkins, and Kwanho Shin, *From Miracle to Maturity: The Growth of the Korean Economy* (Cambridge, MA: Harvard University Press, 2012).
62. Karl J. Fields, *Enterprise and the State in Korea and Taiwan* (Ithaca, NY: Cornell University Press, 1995); Amsden, *The Rise of the "Rest"*; Johnson, *MITI*, 16; Clyde Prestowitz, *Trading Places: How We Allowed Japan to Take the Lead* (New York: Basic Books, 1988). In the 1980s, it was fashionable to talk about South Korea, Taiwan, Singapore, and Hong Kong as the "four dragons" or the "four tigers" of East Asian economic development. But Singapore and Hong Kong, both city-states whose

economic growth was closely connected to their role as international trade hubs, were unusual places with more free trade-oriented development strategies.
63. The concept of a second or revived Bretton Woods comes from Michael P. Dooley, David Folkerts-Landau, and Peter Garber, "The Revived Bretton Woods System," *The International Journal of Finance and Economics* 9 (2004): 307–13, although used here in a somewhat different way.
64. Steffany Griffith-Jones, Ricardo Gottschalk, and Jacques Cailloux, eds., *International Capital Flows in Calm and Turbulent Times* (Ann Arbor: University of Michigan Press, 2003); Stiglitz, *Globalization*, 89–132, 145–51.
65. Roger Lowenstein, *When Genius Failed: The Rise and Fall of Long-Term Capital Management* (New York: Random House, 2000). Critics have suggested that the dangers to global finance were greatly exaggerated, the fund should have been allowed to fail. Of course, when the Fed followed this advice and refused to bail out Lehman Brothers in the fall of 2008, the results were not entirely encouraging.
66. Chart is taken from Maddison, *The World Economy*, Table 7b.
67. Ibid., 641, 743.
68. Thomas Piketty, *Capital in the Twenty-First Century*, trans. Arthur Goldhammer (Cambridge, MA: Harvard University Press, 2014); cf. the article by A.B. Atkinson, cited in n. 22, written fifteen years previously, and, especially, Branko Milanovic, *Global Inequality: A New Approach for the Age of Industrialization* (Cambridge, MA: Harvard University Press, 2016).
69. Milanovic, *Global Inequality*, chap. 4 and passim.

Chapter 5

1. My estimates from the figures given in Walter Nugent, *Crossings: The Great Transatlantic Migrations, 1870—1914* (Bloomington: Indiana University Press, 1992) Numbers are all very approximate.
2. Marilyn Lake and Henry Reynolds, *Drawing the Global Colour Line: White Men's Countries and the International Challenge of Racial Equality* (Cambridge: Cambridge University Press, 2008).
3. Sunil S. Amrith, *Migration and Diaspora in Modern Asia* (Cambridge: Cambridge University Press, 2011), chaps. 1–2.
4. Christoph Kleßmann, *Polnische Bergarbeiter im Ruhrgebiet* (Göttingen: Vandenhoeck & Ruprecht, 1978), 265 and passim; more generally, Dirk Hoerder, ed., *Labor Migration in the Atlantic Economies: The European and North American Working Class during the Period of Industrialization* (Westport, CT: Greenwood Press, 1985).
5. Amrith, *Migration and Diaspora*, 49–51. Two good global surveys of migration are Adam McKewon, "Global Migration 1846-1940," *Journal of World History* 15 (2004): 155–89 and Dirk Hoerder, "Migrations and Belonging," in *A World Connecting 1870–1945*, ed. Emily S. Rosenberg (Cambridge, MA: Belknap Press, 2012), 435–89.
6. Amrith, *Migration and Diaspora*, 30; Diana Lary, *Chinese Migrations: The Movement of People, Goods, and Ideas over Four Millennia* (Lanham, MD: Rowman and Littlefield, 2012), 106; Nugent, *Crossings*, 35.
7. Lary, *Chinese Migrations*, 95; Steven C. Topik and Allen Wells, "Commodity Chains in a Global Economy," in Rosenberg, *World Connecting*, 706.

8. Nugent, *Crossings*, 30; Lary, *Chinese Migrations*, 93; Amrith, *Migration and Diaspora*, 44–45, 47, 49.
9. Martin Schain, *The Politics of Immigration in France, Great Britain and the United States: A Comparative Study*, 2nd ed. (New York: St. Martin's Press, 2008), 204–6; Stephen Castles and Mark J. Miller, *The Age of Migration: International Population Movements in the Modern World*, 2nd ed. (London: Guilford Press, 1998), 131–32; Andreas Fahrmeir, *Citizenship: The Rise and Fall of a Modern Concept* (New Haven, CT: Yale University Press, 2007), 72–80, 96–106, 144–55.
10. Amrith, *Migration and Diaspora*, 37–38.
11. Peter Gatrell, *The Making of the Modern Refugee* (Oxford: Oxford University Press, 2013), 25–31, 55–72; Maureen Healy, *Vienna and the Fall of the Habsburg Empire: Total War and Everyday Life in World War I* (New York: Cambridge University Press, 2004), 4.
12. Jessica Reinisch and Elizabeth White, eds., *The Disentanglement of Populations: Migration, Expulsion and Displacement in Post-War Europe, 1944–49* (Houndmills, Basingstoke: Palgrave Macmillan, 2011); R.M. Douglas, *Orderly and Humane: The Expulsion of the Germans after the Second World War* (New Haven, CT: Yale University Press, 2012); Gatrell, *Making of the Modern Refugee*, chap. 3.
13. Lary, *Chinese Migrations*, chap. 10; Gatrell, *Modern Refugee*, chap. 6; Yoko Sellek, *Migrant Labour in Japan* (Houndmills, Basingstoke: Palgrave Macmillan, 2001), 17; Mariko Tamanoi, *Memory Maps: The State and Manchuria in Postwar Japan* (Honolulu: University of Hawai'i Press, 2009).
14. https://www.poemhunter.com/poem/partition-2/, accessed Aug. 11, 2017.
15. Ian Talbot and Gurharpal Singh, *The Partition of India* (Cambridge: Cambridge University Press, 2009); Vazira Fazila-Yacoobali Zamindar, *The Long Partition and the Making of Modern South Asia: Refugees, Boundaries, Histories* (New York: Columbia University Press, 2007); Joya Chatterji, *The Spoils of Partition: Bengal and India, 1947–1967* (Cambridge: Cambridge University Press, 2007).
16. Benny Morris, *The Birth of the Palestinian Refugee Problem, 1947–1949* (Cambridge: Cambridge University Press, 1987); Benny Morris, *1948: The First Arab-Israeli War* (New Haven, CT: Yale University Press, 2007).
17. Gatrell, *Modern Refugee*, 3; Gerard Cohen, *In War's Wake: Europe's Displaced Persons in the Postwar Order* (New York: Oxford University Press, 2012), 7.
18. Cohen, *In War's Wake*, chaps. 5–6.
19. Zamindar, *The Long Partition*, chaps. 3–6.
20. Morris, *Palestinian Refugee Problem*, chap. 9; Michael Fischbach, *Records of Dispossession: Palestinian Refugee Property and the Arab-Israeli Conflict* (New York: Columbia University Press, 2003); Michael Fischbach, *Jewish Property Claims against Arab Countries* (New York: Columbia University Press, 2008).
21. Julie Peteet, *Landscapes of Hope and Despair: Palestinian Refugee Camps* (Philadelphia: University of Pennsylvania Press, 2005), 109, 131–33 and passim. Palestinians justified these actions to themselves, by saying that when they returned to Palestine, their houses would be available to Lebanese.
22. Gatrell, *Modern Refugee*, chap. 3; Gil Loescher, *The UNHCR and World Politics: A Perilous Path* (Oxford: Oxford University Press, 2001).

23. Gatrell, *Modern Refugee*, part III; Nicholas Van Hear, *New Diasporas: The Mass Exodus, Dispersal and Regrouping of Migrant Communities* (Seattle: University of Washington Press, 1998); Maria Cristina García, *Seeking Refuge: Central American Migration to Mexico, the United States and Canada* (Berkeley: University of California Press, 2006).
24. Lary, *Chinese Migrations*, chap. 11; Tara Zahra, *The Great Departure: Mass Migrations from Eastern Europe and the Making of the Modern World* (New York: W.W. Norton, 2016), chap. 6; http://www.bpb.de/izpb/48519/der-ausbau-des-neuen-systems-1949-bis-1961?p=all, accessed Aug. 4, 2017. More on the relationship between the two Germanys and the building of the Berlin Wall in the next chapter.
25. Juan Ramon Garcia, *Operation Wetback: The Mass Deportation of Mexican Undocumented Workers in 1954* (Westport, CT: Greenwood Press, 1980); Xioajian Zhao, *Remaking Chinese America: Immigration, Family, and Community, 1940–1965* (New Brunswick, NJ: Rutgers University Press, 2002), chap. 7 and passim; Meredith Oyen, *The Diplomacy of Migration: Transnational Lives and the Making of U.S.-Chinese Relations in the Cold War* (Ithaca, NY: Cornell University Press, 2015), 16–39, 106–27.
26. Frederick Cooper, *Citizenship between Empire and Nation: Recasting France and French Africa, 1945–1960* (Princeton, NJ: Princeton University Press, 2014), 131, 273. More on the efforts at transforming empires during the 1950s in the next chapter.
27. Cohen, *In War's Wake*, 106; Castles and Miller, *Age of Migration*, 73; Edward Pillkington, *Beyond the Mother Country: West Indians and the Notting Hill White Riots* (London: I.B. Tauris, 1988); Mark Olden, "White Riot: The Week Notting Hill Exploded," *The Independent*, Aug. 28, 2008, http://www.independent.co.uk/news/uk/home-news/white-riot-the-week-notting-hill-exploded-912105.html, accessed Aug. 29, 2017.
28. Alec G. Hargreaves, *Multi-Ethnic France: Immigration, Politics, Culture and Society*, 2nd ed. (London: Routledge, 2007), 17–19; Félix F. Germain, *Decolonizing the Republic: African and Caribbean Migrants in Postwar Paris, 1946–1974* (East Lansing: Michigan State University Press, 2016), 24.
29. Two good overviews are John Salt and Hugh Clout, eds., *Migration in Post-War Europe: Geographical Essays* (Oxford: Oxford University Press, 1976); and Russell King, ed., *Mass Migration in Europe: The Legacy and the Future* (Chichester: John Wiley & Sons, 1995).
30. Germain, *Decolonizing the Republic*, xiv, 24, 184.
31. Schain, *Politics of Immigration*, 135–38; Castles and Miller, *Age of Migration*, 73.
32. Carl-Urik Schierup, Peo Hansen, and Stephen Castles, *Migration, Citizenship and the European Welfare State* (Oxford: Oxford University Press, 2006), 28; Ulrich Herbert, *A History of Foreign Labor in Germany, 1880–1980*, trans. William Templer (Ann Arbor: University of Michigan Press, 1990), 203; John Salt, "International Labour Migration: The Geographical Pattern of Demand," in Salt and Clout, *Migration in Post-War Europe*, 82.
33. Amrith, *Migration and Diaspora*, 164–67; Castles and Miller, *Age of Migration*, 116–17, 147; Françoise de Bel-Air, "Demography, Labour Market and Migration in Saudi Arabia," GLMM—EN—No. 1, 2014, Gulf Research Center and European University Institute, http://cadmus.eui.eu/bitstream/handle/1814/32151/GLMM%20ExpNote_01-2014.pdf, accessed Aug. 8, 2017; Prema A. Kurien,

Kaleidoscopic Ethnicity: International Migration and the Reconstruction of Community Identities in India (New Brunswick, NJ: Rutgers University Press, 2002), ix and passim.
34. Salt, "International Labor Migrations," in Salt and Clout, *Migration in Post-War Europe*, 102. Sources cited in nn. 28, 31, and 32, all make these points.
35. A contemporary critical classic on guestworkers in Europe is John Berger and Jean Mohr, *The Seventh Man* (London: Verso, 2010), reprint of the original edition of 1975. Scholarly studies include Rita Chin, *The Guestworker Question in Postwar Germany* (Cambridge: Cambridge University Press, 2007); Germain, *Decolonizing the Republic*. For conditions in the oil states, see the sources cited in n. 33.
36. A.H. Richmond and G.L. Lakshmana, "Recent Developments in Immigration to Canada and Australia: A Comparative Analysis," *International Journal of Comparative Sociology* 17 (1976): 183–205; Bill Ong Hing, *Defining America through Immigration Policy* (Philadelphia: Temple University Press, 2004), 94–95.
37. King, "European International Migration," in King, *Mass Migration*, 19–39; Andrew Geddes, *The Politics of Migration and Immigration in Europe* (London: SAGE, 2003), 118–22; for the United Kingdom, Schain, *The Politics of Immigration*, 128, 144–45.
38. Hargreaves, *Multi-Ethnic France*, 42; Schierup, Hansen, and Castles, *Migration, Citizenship and the European Welfare State*, 98–99; a good case study is Pieter Bevelander, "The Immigration and Integration Experience: The Case of Sweden," in *Immigration Worldwide: Policies, Practices and Trends*, ed. Uma A. Segal, Doreen Elliott, and Naznee Mayadas (Oxford: Oxford University Press, 2010), 286–302.
39. John Wrench, Andrea Rea, and Nouria Oualia, eds., *Migrants, Ethnic Minorities and the Labour Market: Integration and Exclusion in Europe* (New York: St. Martin's, 1999); Robert Leiken, *Europe's Angry Muslims: the Revolt of the Second Generation* (New York: Oxford University Press, 2012), 71–74, 139–40, 244–46 and passim; more optimistic is Marvine Howe, *Al-Andalus Rediscovered: Iberia's New Muslims* (London: Hurst & Company, 2012).
40. Sources as in n. 33.
41. Note 33, and van Hear, *New Diasporas*, 81–93.
42. Rebecca Raijman and Adriana Kemp, "The New Immigration to Israel: Becoming a De Facto Immigration State in the 1990s," in Segal, Elliott, and Mayadas, *Immigration Worldwide*, 227–43.
43. Carmen Teresa Whalen, *From Puerto Rico to Philadelphia: Puerto Rican Workers and Postwar Economies* (Philadelphia: Temple University Press, 2001); Jesse Hoffnung-Garskof, *A Tale of Two Cities: Santo Domingo and New York after 1950* (Princeton, NJ: Princeton University Press, 2008); Cindy Hahamovitch, *No Man's Land: Jamaican Guestworkers in America and the Global History of Deportable Labor* (Princeton, NJ: Princeton University Press, 2011).
44. Geraldo L. Cadava, *Standing on Common Ground: The Making of a Sunbelt Borderland* (Cambridge, MA: Harvard University Press, 2013); Garcia, *Operation Wetback*; Hing, *Defining America*, chap. 7.
45. Schain, *The Politics of Immigration*, 221.
46. Douglas Massey and Jorge Durand, "Why Border Enforcement Backfired," *American Journal of Sociology* 121 (2016): 1557–1600; Schain, *Politics of*

Immigration, 229; Hing, *Defining America*, chaps. 8–10, 12; Maria Cristina García, *Seeking Refuge: Central American Migration to Mexico, the United States and Canada* (Berkeley: University of California Press, 2006).
47. Lary, *Chinese Migrations*, chaps. 13–14; Xiaojian Zhao, *The New Chinese America: Class, Economy and Social Hierarchy* (New Brunswick, NJ: Rutgers University Press, 2010).
48. Uma A. Segal, "United States: The Changing Face of the United States of America," in Segal, Elliott, and Mayadas, *Immigration Worldwide*, 37.
49. Zhao, *The New Chinese America*, 26–28.
50. Figures for the United States from www.dhs.gov/immigration-statistics/yearb ook/2015/table1; for Canada http://epe.lac-bac.gc.ca/100/202/301/immigration _statistics-ef/mp22-1_1996.pdf and http://open.canada.ca/data/en/dataset/ad975 a26-df23-456a-8ada-756191a23695; for Australia, https://www.border.gov.au/ about/reports-publications/research-statistics/statistics/live-in-australia/histori cal-migration-statistics, all accessed Aug. 16, 2017.
51. On late twentieth-century emigrants from Europe, and their differences with and from earlier migrants, Val Colic Preisker, *Migration, Class and Transnational Identities: Croations in Australia and America* (Urbana: University of Illinois Press, 2008); Mary Frances Erdmans, *Opposite Poles: Immigrants and Ethnics in Polish Chicago 1976–1990* (University Park: Pennsylvania State University Press, 1998).
52. Schain, *The Politics of Immigration*, 225; Usha George, "Canada: Immigration to Canada," in Segal, Elliott, and Mayadas, *Immigration Worldwide*, 98; Mel Gray and Kylie Agllias, "Australia: The World in One Place," in Segal, Elliott, and Mayadas, *Immigration Worldwide*, 158–59.
53. Schierup, Hansen, and Castles, *Migration, Citizenship and the European Welfare State*, 98. Libertarian economists assert that these differences are a result of European welfare states discouraging immigrant employment, while America's laissez-faire economy encourages it. Of course, this assertion does not explain low immigrant unemployment in Canada and Australia, two countries with well-developed welfare states.
54. General overviews, Castles and Miller, *Age of Migration*; King, *Mass Migration in Europe*; Segal, Elliott and Mayadas, *Immigration Worldwide*; Amrith, *Migration and Diaspora in Modern Asia*, chap. 5; Hania Zlotnik, "International Migration, 1965– 96: An Overview," *Population and Development Review* 24 (1998): 429–68; also, Howe, *Al-Andalus Rediscovered*; John Chalcraft, *The Invisible Cage: Syrian Migrant Workers in Lebanon* (Stanford, CA: Stanford University Press, 2009); Barbara Ehrenreich and Arlie Hochschild, *Global Women: Nannies, Maids and Sex Workers in the New Economy* (New York: Metropolitan Books, 2002); Eleonora Fayzullaeva, "Labor Migration in Central Asia: Gender Challenges," in *Gender Politics in Post-Communist Eurasia*, ed. Linda Racioppi and Katherine O'Sullivan See (East Lansing: Michigan State University Press, 2009), 237–65.
55. OECD, "International Remittances and their Role in Economic Development," 2006, https://www.oecd.org/els/mig/38840502.pdf; Manuel Orozco, "Worker Remittances in an International Scope," Inter-American Development Bank, 2003, https://publications.iadb.org/bitstream/handle/11319/3771/Worker%20 Remittances%20in%20an%20International%20Scope.pdf?sequence=1;

Mohamed El-Qorchi, "Hawala," *Finance and Development* 39 (2002), http://www.imf.org/external/pubs/ft/fandd/2002/12/elqorchi.htm, all accessed Aug. 17, 2017.
56. Sellek, *Migrant Labour in Japan,* 28–36, 96–97, 108–9, 123 and passim; Wolfgang Herbert, *Foreign Workers and Law Enforcement in Japan* (London: Kegal Paul International, 1996), 54–59, 64–69, 228–40 and passim.
57. Sellek, *Immigrant Labour,* 72–84, 126–29; Takeyuki Tsuda, *Strangers in the Ethnic Homeland: Japanese Brazilian Return Migration in Transnational Perspective* (New York: Columbia University Press, 2003), 98 and passim.
58. Tsuda, *Strangers,* 315–16.
59. Debito Arudou, *Embedded Racism: Japan's Visible Minorities and Racial Discrimination* (Lanham, MD: Lexington Books, 2015); Andrew Lie, *Multiethnic Japan* (Cambridge, MA: Harvard University Press, 2001).
60. Jon Emont, "Japan Prefers Robot Bears to Nurses," *Foreign Policy* Mar. 1, 2017, http://foreignpolicy.com/2017/03/01/japan-prefers-robot-bears-to-foreign-nurses/, accessed Aug. 23, 2017.
61. https://www.theglobalist.com/people-on-the-move/; Pew Research Center, "International Migration: Key Findings from the U.S. Europe and the World," Dec. 15, 2016, http://www.pewresearch.org/fact-tank/2016/12/15/international-migration-key-findings-from-the-u-s-europe-and-the-world/, both accessed Aug. 23, 2017; Zlotnik, "International Migration, 1965–96," esp. 432; similarly, Dorren Elliott, Nazneen S. Mayadas, andREFC REFO:BKCHUma A. Segal, "Immigration Worldwide: Trends and Analysis," in Segal Elliott, and Mayadas, *Immigration Worldwide,* 19.
62. Examples of UN migration statistics: http://www.un.org/en/development/desa/population/migration/data/estimates2/estimates15.shtml; http://www.un.org/en/development/desa/population/migration/publications/migrationreport/docs/MigrationReport2015_Highlights.pdf, both accessed Aug. 23, 2015.
63. Although the practice of referring to such individuals as "undocumented," is politically and morally admirable, it is not very accurate. They often have plenty of documents, just none that grant them the right to reside where they do, according to that country's laws.
64. Zhao, *New Chinese America,* 23–31; Sellek, *Migrant Labour in Japan,* 29, 34; Supang Chantavanich and Ratchada Jayagupta, "Immigration to Thailand: The Case of Migrant Workersfrom Myanmar, Laos, and Cambodia," in Segal, Elliott, and Myadas, *Immigration Worldwide,* 304, 308.
65. "International Migration Report 2015," 21–22; http://www.un.org/en/development/desa/population/migration/publications/migrationreport/docs/MigrationReport2015_Highlights.pdf; UN Department of Economic and Social Affairs t "International Migration Policies: Government Views and Priorities," 2013, chaps. 1, 26, http://www.un.org/en/development/desa/population/publications/pdf/policy/InternationalMigrationPolicies2013/Report%20PDFs/g_Ch_1.pdf both accessed Aug. 23, 2017.
66. Source for Figure 5.2: Immigration Policy Institute, "U.S. Immigrant Population and Share over Time," http://www.migrationpolicy.org/programs/data-hub/charts/immigrant-population-over time, accessed Aug. 23, 2017.

67. Sources for Figure 5.3: http://www.statistikdatabasen.scb.se/pxweb/en/ssd/STA RT__BE__BE0101__BE0101J/Flyttningar/?rxid=84bdbce5-58a8-4829-b49b-58c310697de8 and "Historik statistik för Sverige Del.1 Befolkning," Table 44, http://www.scb.se/Grupp/Hitta_statistik/Historisk_statistik/_Dokument/Histor isk-statistik-for-Sverige-Del-1.pdf, both accessed Aug. 23, 2017.

Chapter 6

1. John Gaddis, *The Long Peace: Inquiries into the History of the Cold War* (New York: Oxford University Press, 1987); a more recent and somewhat different emphasis on the fundamentally peaceful character of the era in Richard Immerman and Petra Goedde, eds., *The Oxford Handbook of the Cold War* (Oxford: Oxford University Press, 2013).
2. Two of the many general histories of the Cold War, Melvyn Leffler, *For the Soul of Mankind: The United States, the Soviet Union and the Cold War* (New York: Hill and Wang, 2007); Odd Westad, *The Cold War: A World History* (New York: Basic Books, 2017).
3. One of many examples, Masuda Hajimu, *Cold War Crucible: The Korean Conflict and the Postwar World* (Cambridge, MA: Harvard University Press, 2015).
4. Jonathan Haslam, *Russia's Cold War: From the October Revolution to the Fall of the Wall* (New Haven, CT: Yale University Press, 2011), 319–27; Vladislav M. Zubok, *A Failed Empire: The Soviet Union in the Cold War from Stalin to Gorbachev* (Chapel Hill: University of North Carolina Press, 2007), 259–64.
5. David Caute, *The Dancer Defects: The Struggle for Cultural Supremacy during the Cold War* (Oxford: Oxford University Press, 2003); Tony Judt, *Past Imperfect: French Intellectuals, 1944–1956* (Berkeley: University of California Press, 1992); Patrick Iber, *Neither Peace nor Freedom: The Cultural Cold War in Latin America* (Cambridge, MA: Harvard University Press, 2015); Stephen Wagg and David L. Andrews, eds., *East Plays West: Sport and the Cold War* (London: Routledge, 2007); Timothy W. Ryback, *Rock Around the Bloc: A History of Rock Music in Eastern Europe and the Soviet Union* (New York: Oxford University Press, 1990); Walter Hixson, *Parting the Curtain: Propaganda, Culture and the Cold War, 1945–1961* (Basingstoke: Macmillan, 1997); György Péteri, ed., *Imagining the West in Eastern Europe and the Soviet Union* (Pittsburgh, PA: University of Pittsburgh Press, 2010).
6. Odd Arne Westad, *The Global Cold War: Third World Interventions and the Making of Our Times* (New York: Cambridge University Press, 2007).
7. Sergey Radchenko, *Unwanted Visionaries: The Soviet Failure in Asia at the End of the Cold War* (Oxford: Oxford University Press, 2014).
8. Jussi M. Hanhimäki, *The Rise and Fall of Détente: American Foreign Policy and the Transformation of the Cold War* (Washington, DC: Potomac Books, 2013), 9.
9. Miroslav Vaněk and Pavel Mücke, eds., *Velvet Revolutions: An Oral History of Czech Society* (Oxford: Oxford University Press, 2016), 27–29; Zubok, *Failed Empire*, 183.
10. This is the main argument of Campbell Craig and Fredrik Logevall, *America's Cold War: The Politics of Insecurity* (Cambridge, MA: Harvard University Press, 2009).
11. Good summary of the diplomacy of the post-1945 diplomacy on Germany, W.R. Smyser, *From Yalta to Berlin: The Cold War Struggle Over Germany* (New York: St. Martin's 1999); Michael Lemke, "'Doppelte Alleinvertretung.' Die nationalen

Wiedervereinigungskonzepte der beiden deutschen Regierungen und die Grundzüge ihrer politischen Realisierung in der DDR (1949-1952/53)," *Zeitschrift für Geschichtswissenschaft* 40 (1992): 531–43.

12. J.H. Brinks, "Political Antifascism in the German Democratic Republic," *Journal of Contemporary History* 32 (1997): 207–17; Catherine J. Plum, *Antifascism after Hitler: East German Youth and Socialist Memory, 1949—1989* (New York: Routledge, 2015); Jonathan Sperber, "17 June 1953: Revisiting a German Revolution," *German History* 22 (2004): 619–43; Norbert Frei, *Adenauer's Germany and the Nazi Past: The Politics of Amnesty and Integration* trans. Joel Golb (New York: Columbia University Press, 2002).

13. William Gray, *Germany's Cold War: The Global Campaign to Isolate East Germany, 1949–1969* (Chapel Hill: University of North Carolina Press, 2003); Young-Sun Hong, *Cold War Germany, the Third World, and the Global Humanitarian Regime* (New York: Cambridge University Press, 2015); Martin H. Geyer, "Der Kampf um nationale Repräsentation: Deutsch-deutsche Sportzbeziehungen und die 'Hallstein-Doktrin,'" *Vierteljahrshefte für Zeitgeschichte 44* (1996): 55–86.

14. William Gray, "Paradoxes of *Ostpolitik*: Revisiting the Moscow and Warsaw Treaties, 1970," *Central European History* 49 (2016): 409–40; Peter Bender, *Die "Neue Ostpolitik" und ihre Folgen: Vom Mauerbau bis zur Wiedervereinigung*, 2nd. ed. (Munich: Deutscher Taschenbuch Verlag, 1995).

15. Diana Lary, *China's Civil War: A Social History, 1945–1949* (Cambridge: Cambridge University Press, 2015); Edwin W. Martin, *Divided Counsel: The Anglo-American Response to Communist Victory in China* (Lexington: University Press of Kentucky, 1986); Yafeng Xia, *Negotiating with the Enemy: U.S-China Talks during the Cold War* (Bloomington? Indiana University Press, 2006); Nicholas Sarantakes, *Dropping the Torch: Jimmy Carter, the Olympic Boycott, and the Cold War* (New York: Cambridge University Press, 2011), 23–25.

16. Seth Michael, *A Concise History of Modern Korea: From the Late Nineteenth Century to the Present* (Lanham, MD: Rowman & Littlefield, 2010), esp. 119; Bruce Cumings, *Korea's Place in the Sun: A Modern History* (New York: Norton, 1997); Jinwung Kim, *A History of Korea: From "Land of the Morning Calm: To States in Conflict* (Bloomington: Indiana University Press, 2010), esp. 367–421; Hong, *Cold War Germany*; Barry Gills, *Korea versus Korea: A Case of Contested Legitimacy* (London: Routledge, 1996), esp. 209; Maddison, *The World Economy*, 562, 566.

17. Seth Jacobs, *Cold War Mandarin: Ngo Dinh Diem and the Origins of America's War in Vietnam, 1950–1963* (Lanham, MD: Rowman & Littlefield, 2006); Jessica M. Chapman, *Cauldron of Resistance: Ngo Dinh Diem, the United States and 1950s Southern Vietnam* (Ithaca, NY: Cornell University Press, 2013).

18. Robert J. MacMahon, *The Limits of Empire: The United States and Southeast Asia since World War II* (New York: Columbia University Press, 1999); Marilyn Young, *The Vietnam Wars, 1945–1990* (New York: HarperCollins, 1991); and Lien-Hang T. Nguyen, *Hanoi's War: An International History of the War for Peace in Vietnam* (Chapel Hill: University of North Carolina Press, 2012.

19. Robert Malley, *The Call from Algeria: Third Worldism, Revolution and the Turn to Islam* (Berkeley: University of California Press, 1996).

20. Cited in Roland Burke, *Decolonization and the Evolution of International Human Rights* (Philadelphia: University of Pennsylvania Press, 2010), 57.
21. Mark Mazower, *No Enchanted Palace: The End of Empire and the Ideological Origins of the United Nations* (Princeton, NJ: Princeton University Press, 2009).
22. W.E.B. DuBois, *The Souls of Black Folk*, e-book, *Project Gutenberg*, pt. 2, accessed May 8, 2020, https://www.gutenberg.org/files/408/408-h/408-h.htm.
23. Quoted in Ronald Hyam, *Britain's Declining Empire: The Road to Decolonisation 1918–1968* (Cambridge: Cambridge University Press, 2006), 368.
24. Vijay Prashad, *The Darker Nations: A People's History of the Third World* (New York: The New Press, 2007).
25. http://www.homme-moderne.org/societe/demo/sauvy/3mondes.html, accessed Dec. 1, 2016.
26. Christoph Kalter, *The Discovery of the Third World: Decolonization and the Rise of the New Left in France, c. 1950–1976*, trans. Thomas Dunlop (Cambridge: Cambridge University Press, 2016); Jeffrey James Byrne, *Mecca of Revolution: Algeria, Decolonization and the Third World Order* (New York: Oxford University Press, 2016); Malley, *The Call from Algeria*.
27. Two impressive descriptions of the immediate postwar world are Ian Buruma, *Year Zero: A History of 1945* (New York: Penguin Books, 2013); and Christopher Bayly and Tim Harper, *Forgotten Wars: Freedom and Revolution in Southeast Asia* (Cambridge, MA: Harvard University Press, 2007).
28. Norman Naimark, *The Russians in Germany: A History of the Soviet Zone of Occupation, 1945–1949* (Cambridge, MA: Harvard University Press, 1995), 205–50; William Rogers Louis, *The British Empire in the Middle East 1945–1951: Arab Nationalism, the United States, and Postwar Imperialism* (New York: Oxford University Press, 1984), 383–571; Arnold Krammer, *The Forgotten Friendship: Israel and the Soviet Bloc, 1947–53* (Urbana: University of Illinois Press, 1974); Lary, *China's Civil War*; Zubok, *Failed Empire*, 79; Haslam, *Russia's Cold War*, 112–16, 151–53.
29. Leffler, *For the Soul of Mankind*, chap. 1.
30. Peter Ruggenthaler, *The Concept of Neutrality in Stalin's Foreign Policy, 1945–1953* (Lanham, MD: Lexington Books, 2015); Kevin McDermott and Matthew Stibbe, eds., *Stalinist Terror in Eastern Europe: Elite Purges and Mass Repression* (Manchester: Manchester University Press, 2010).
31. Marc J. Selverstone, *Constructing the Monolith: The United States, Great Britain and International Communism 1945–1950* (Cambridge, MA: Harvard University Press, 2009), quote, 86, also 38–39, 44, 53, 69, 81–82, 161–62, 200–1 and passim; Vladislav Zubok and Constantine Pleshakov, *Inside the Kremlin's Cold War: From Stalin to Khrushchev* (Cambridge, MA: Harvard University Press, 1996) 76, 114, 122; Anders Stephanson, "Cold War Degree Zero," in *Uncertain Empire: American History and the Idea of the Cold War*, ed. Joel Isaac and Duncan Bell (New York: Oxford University Press, 2012), 19–49; Lawrence Wittner, *The Struggle against the Bomb*. 3 vols. (Stanford, CA: Stanford University Press, 1993–2003), 1, 173, 176.
32. Leffler, *For the Soult of Mankind*, 62–70, 78–69; Michael Hogan, *The Marshall Plan: America, Britain and the Reconstruction of Western Europe, 1947–1952* (New York: Cambridge University Press, 1987).

33. Hiroaki Kuromiya, *The Voices of the Dead: Stalin's Great Terror in the 1930s* (New Haven, CT: Yale University Press, 2007), 2–3 and passim; Zubok, *A Failed Empire*, 78–85; Haslam, *Russia's Cold War*, 120–32; Vojtech Mastny, "Imagining War in Europe: Soviet Strategic Planning," in *War Plans and Alliances in the Cold War: Threat Perception in the East and West*, ed. Vojtech Mastny, Sven Holtsmark, and Andreas Wenger (London: Routledge, 2006), 18–19.
34. William W. Stueck, *The Korean War: An International History* (Princeton, NJ: Princeton University Press, 1995); Nina Tannenwald, *The Nuclear Taboo: The United States and the Non-Use of Nuclear Weapons since 1945* (New York: Cambridge University Press, 2007), chap 4.
35. Jaclyn Stanke, "Stalin's Death and Anglo-American Visions of Ending the Cold War, 1953," in *Visions of the End of the Cold War in Europe*, ed. Frédéric Bozo et al. (New York: Berghahn Books, 2012), 61–73; Campbell Craig, "The Nuclear Revolution: A Product of the Cold War, or Something More"?, in Immerman and Goede, *The Oxford Handbook of the Cold War*, 360–77, esp. 369; Zubok and Pleshakov, *Inside the Kremlin's Cold War*, 192–93; Saki Dockrill, *Eisenhower's New Look: National Security Policy, 1953–61* (New York: St. Martin's 1996).
36. Ronald Hyam, *Britain's Declining Empire*, 104–30; Martin Shipway, *Decolonization and Its Impact: A Comparative Approach to the End of the Colonial Empires* (Oxford: Blackwell, 2008), chaps. 3–5; Jennifer Foray, *Visions of Empire in the Nazi-Occupied Netherlands* (Cambridge: Cambridge University Press, 2012); Bayly and Harper, *Forgotten Wars*; Ian Talbot and Gurharpal Singh, The Partition of India (Cambridge: Cambridge University Press, 2009).
37. Herbert Luethy, *France against Herself,* trans. Eric Mosbacher (New York: Frederick Praeger, 1955), 219 (original French edition 1953); Frederick Cooper, *Citizenship between Empire and Nation: Remaking France and French Africa, 1945–1960* (Princeton, NJ: Princeton University Press, 2014); Hyam, *Britain's Declining Empire*, chaps 2–3.
38. Cooper, *Citizenship*, and Hyam, *Britain's Declining Empire*, as in the previous note, and McMahon, *Limits of Empire*, 31–42.
39. Roham Alvandi, *Nixon, Kissinger and the Shah: The United States and Iran in the Cold War* (New York: Oxford University Press, 2014), 14–17; Hal Brandts, *Latin America's Cold War* (Cambridge, MA: Harvard University Press, 2010), 16–17.
40. James Siekmeier, *The Bolivian Revolution and the United States, 1952 to the Present* (University Park: Pennsylvania State University Press, 2011).
41. Antonia Finnane and Derek McDougall, eds., *Bandung 1955: Little Histories* (Caulfield, Melbourne, Australia: Monash University Press, 2010) (quote on 9); See Sang Tan and Amitav Acharya, *Bandung Revisited: The Legacy of the 1955 Asian-African Conference for International Order* (Singapore: NUS Press, 2008).
42. David Tal, ed., *The 1956 War: Collusion and Rivalry in the Middle East* (Portland, OR: Frank Cass, 2001); Guy Laron, *The Origins of the Suez Crisis: Postwar Development Diplomacy and the Struggle over Third World Industrialization, 1945–1956* (Baltimore: Johns Hopkins University Press, 2013); Louise Richardson, *When Allies Differ: Anglo-American Relations during the Suez and Falklands Crises* (New York: St. Martin's 1996), chaps. 1–2.

43. Shipway, *Decolonization and its Impact*, chap. 8; Hyam, *Britain's Declining Empire*, chap. 4.
44. Daniel Branch, *Defeating Mau Mau, Creating Kenya: Counterinsurgency, Civil War and Decolonization* (Cambridge: Cambridge University Press, 2009); Caroline Elkins, *Imperial Reckoning: The Untold Story of Britain's Gulag in Kenya* (New York: Henry Holt and Co., 2006); Martin Evans, *Algeria: France's Undeclared War* (Oxford: Oxford University Press, 2012); Vincent Crapazano, *The Harkis: The Wound That Never Heals* (Chicago: University of Chicago Press, 2011).; Emanuel Gerard and Bruce Kuklick, *Death in the Congo: Murdering Patrice Lumumba* (Cambridge, MA: Harvard University Press, 2015); Elizabeth Schmidt, *Foreign Interventions in Africa: From the Cold War to the War on Terror* (Cambridge: Cambridge University Press, 2013), esp. chaps. 2–5.
45. Hope Harrison, *Driving the Soviets up the Wall: Soviet-East German Relations, 1953–1961* (Princeton, NJ: Princeton University Press, 2003).
46. Mathias Uhl, "Storming on to Paris: The 1961 Buria Exercise and the Planned Solution of the Berlin Crisis," in Matny, Holtsmark, and Wenger, *War Plans and Alliances*, 46–71.
47. Haslam, *Russia's Cold War*, 199–210; Marc Trachtenberg, *A Constructed Peace: The Making of the European Settlement, 1945–1963* (Princeton, NJ: Princeton University Press, 1999) 253–355; Zubok, *A Failed Empire*, 137–53, has a different emphasis.
48. Aleksandr Fursenko and Timothy Naftali, *"One Hell of a Gamble": Khrushchev, Castro, and Kennedy, 1958-1964* (New York: W.W. Norton, 1997); Sheldon M. Stern, *The Cuban Missile Crisis in American Memory: Myths versus Reality* (Stanford, CA: Stanford University Press, 2012).
49. Garret Martin, *General de Gaulle's Cold War: Challenging American Hegemony 1963–68* (New York: Berghahn Books, 2013); Christian Nuenlist, Anna Locher, and Garret Martin, eds., *Globalizing de Gaulle: International Perspectivers on French Foreign Policies, 1958–1969* (Lanham, MD: Lexington Books, 2010).
50. Lorenz M. Lüthi, *The Sino-Soviet Split: Cold War in the Communist World* (Princeton, NJ: Princeton University Press, 2008); Sergey Radchenko, *Two Suns in the Heavens: The Sino-Soviet Struggle for Supremacy, 1962–1967* (Stanford, CA: Stanford University Press, 2009); Austin Jerrold, *The Sino-Soviet Alliance: An International History* (Chapel Hill: University of North Carolina Press, 2014).
51. Rachenko, *Two Suns in the Heavens*, 82; more generally, Jeremy Friedman, *Shadow Cold War: The Sino-Soviet Competition for the Third World* (Chapel Hill: University of North Carolina Press, 2015).
52. Quotes from Jerrild, *The Sino-Soviet Alliance*, 145; and Lüthy, *The Sino-Soviet Split*, 77; cf. Wittner, *The Struggle against the Bomb*, 2:310–11.
53. Nguyen, *Hanoi's War*, 75–83.
54. Radchenko, *Two Suns*, 174–203.
55. Wittner, *The Struggle against the Bomb*, Vol. 2, chap. 18; Robert Divine, *Blowing on the Wind: The Nuclear Test Ban Debate, 1954–1960* (New York: Oxford University Press, 1978).
56. Michael Morgan, *The Final Act: The Helsinki Accords and the Transformation of the Cold War* (Princeton, NJ: Princeton University Press, 2018).

57. Angela Romano, "The EC Nine's Vision and Attempts at Ending the Cold War," in Bozo et al., *Visions of the End of the Cold War*, 134–46; Joe Renouard, *Human Rights in American Foreign Policy: From the 1960s to the Soviet Collapse* (Philadelphia: University of Pennsylvania Press, 2016), 99–100; Cronin, *Global Rules*, 47–52; Morgan, *The Final Act*, chap. 6.
58. Tanya Harmer, *Allende's Chile and the Inter-American Cold War* (Chapel Hill: University of North Carolina Press, 2011), 118; David Sargent, *A Superpower Transformed: The Remaking of American Foreign Relations in the 1970s* (New York: Oxford University Press, 2015), 50, 63.
59. Robert B. Rakove, *Kennedy, Johnson and the Nonaligned World* (New York: Cambridge University Press, 2013); Philip E. Muehlenbeck, *Betting on the Africans: John F. Kennedy's Courting of African Nationalist Leaders* (New York: Oxford University Press, 2012); Lüthi, *Sino-Soviet Split*, 138–46; Haslam, *Russia's Cold War*, 151–56; Zubok, *Failed Empire*, 110.
60. Westad, *The Global Cold War*, 158–206.
61. Keith Bolander, *Cuba under Siege: American Policy, the Revolution and Its People* (New York: Pagrave Macmillan, 2012); Stephen Rabe, The Killing Zone: The United States Wages Cold War in Latin America (New York: Oxford University Press, 2012), chap. 4; Brandts, *Latin America's Cold War*, 24–38.
62. Friedman, *Shadow Cold War*, 1; Siekmeier, *The Bolivian Revolution*, 102–21; Rabe, *Killing Zone*, 80–84. Many thanks to my colleague Robert Smale for explaining the social and political dynamics of modern Bolivia.
63. Renata Keller, *Mexico's Cold War: Cuba, the United States and the Legacy of the Mexican Revolution* (New York: Cambridge University Press, 2015); 182–90; Malley, *The Call from Algiers*, 89–111; John Graham, "The Non-Aligned Movement after the Havana Summit," *Journal of International Affairs 34* (1980): 163–60; Prashad, *The Darker Nations*, 105–15; Final Document, "Sixth Summit Conference of Heads of State or Government of the Non-Aligned Movement," Havana, Sept. 3–9, 1979, http://cns.miis.edu/nam/documents/Official_Document/6th_Summit_FD_Havana_Declaration_1979_Whole.pdf, accessed Mar. 17, 2017.
64. Hammer, *Allende's Chile*, 240–46 and passim; Elizabeth Schmidt, *Foreign Intervention in Africa*, chaps. 4–6.
65. A recent, if controversial account, Nick Turse, *Kill Anything That Moves: The Real American War in Vietnam* (New York: Henry Holt and Company, 2013).
66. Nguyen, *Hanoi's War*, is very informative on Le Duan and his military and political strategies.
67. McMahon, *Limits of Empire*, 119–24; John Subritzky, *Confronting Sukarno: British, American, Australian and New Zealand Diplomacy in the Malaysian-Indonesian Confrontation, 1961–65* (New York: St. Martin's 2000).
68. Frederik Logevall, *Choosing War: The Lost Chance for Peace and the Escalation of War in Vietnam* (Berkeley: University of California Press, 1999).
69. McMahon, *Limits to Empire*, 106; Fredrik Logevall, "America Isolated: The Western Powers and the Escalation of the War," in *America, the Vietnam War and the World: Comparative and International Perspectives,* ed. Andreas Daum, Lloyd C. Gardner, and Wilfried Mausbach (New York: Cambridge University Press, 2003), 175–96.

70. Quoted in Westad, *The Global Cold War*, 241; more generally, Christopher Andrew and Vasili Mitrokhin, *The World Was Going Our Way: The KGB and the Battle for the Third World* (New York: Basic Books, 2005).
71. Vanessa Ogle, "State Rights against Private Capital: The 'New International Economic Order' and the Struggle over Aid, Trade and Foreign Investment, 1962–1981," Humanity 5 (2014): 211–34; Malley, *Call from Algeria*, 138–46.
72. Guy Laron, *The Six-Day War: The Breaking of the Middle East* (New Haven, CT: Yale University Press, 2017); Michael Oren, *Six Days of War: June 1967 and the Making of the Modern Middle East* (Oxford: Oxford University Press, 2002); Sargeant, *Superpower Transformed*, 150; Haslam, *Moscow's Cold War*, 231–38, 271–76; Zubok, *A Failed Empire*, 238–40.
73. Mark Tessler, *A History of the Israeli-Palestinian Conflict* (Bloomington: Indiana University Press, 1994), Parts IV–V; Haslam, *Russia's Cold War*, 276; Andrew and Mitrokhin, *Going Our Way*, 222–59, and especially Paul Thomas Chamberlin, *The Global Offensive: The United States, the Palestine Liberation Organization and the Making of the Post-Cold War Order* (New York: Oxford University Press, 2012) chap. 6 and passim.
74. Schmidt, *Foreign Intervention in Africa*, chaps. 4–5; Westad, *Global Cold War*, chap. 6; Piero Gleijeses, *Visions of Freedom: Havana, Washington, Pretoria and the Struggle for Southern Africa, 1976–1991* (Chapel Hill: University of North Carolina Press, 1991).
75. Sargent, *A Superpower Transformed*, 53–54 and passim; Alvandi, *Nixon, Kissinger and the Shah*; Harmer, *Allende's Chile*; Srinath Raghavan, *1971: A Global History of the Creation of Bangladesh* (Cambridge, MA: Harvard University Press, 2013).
76. Quote from Haslam, *Russia's Cold War*, 305.
77. Sargent, *Superpower Transformed*, 250–60; Renouard, *Human Rights in American Foreign Policy*, chap. 3; Jim Mann, *Rise of the Vulcans: The History of Bush's War Cabinet* (New York: Viking, 2004), 91–93.
78. Westad, *Global Cold War*, 289–99.
79. Cited in Dominique Avon and Anaïs-Trissa Khatchadourian, trans. Jane Marie Todd. *Hezbollah: A History of the "Party of God."* (Cambridge, MA: Harvard University Press, 2012), 125–26.
80. Ibid., and Augustus Richard Norton, *Hezbollah: A Short History* (Princeton, NJ: Princeton University Press, 2007), which is apologetic but informative.
81. On the very complex domestic and international politics of this issue, Kristina Spohr Readman, "Conflict and Cooperation in Intra-Alliance Nuclear Politics: Western Europe, the United States and the Genesis of NATO's Dual-Track Decision 1977–79," *Journal of Cold War Studies* 13 (2011): 39–89.
82. Sargent, *A Superpower Transformed*, chap. 9.
83. Thomas Barfield, *Afghanistan: A Cultural and Political History* (Princeton, NJ: Princeton University Press, 2010), 210–42; Zewde Bahru, *A History of Modern Ethiopia, 1855–1991,* 2nd ed. (Athens: Ohio University Press, 2001), 228–69 and the very interesting memoirs of Dawit Wolde Giogis, *Red Tears: War, Famine and Revolution in Ethiopia* (Trenton, NJ: Red Sea Press, 1989); Zubok, *A Failed Empire*, 249; Andrew and Mitrokhin, *Going Our Way*, 456–59; Artemy Kalinovsky, *A*

Long Goodbye: The Soviet Withdrawal from Afghanistan (Cambridge MA: Harvard University Press, 2011), chap. 1; Schmidt, *Foreign Intervention in Africa*, 147–54.
84. Sarantakes, *Dropping the Torch*, passim.
85. Robert Scheer, *With Enough Shovels: Regan, Bush and Nuclear War* (New York: Vintage Books, 1983), 18; more generally on Regan and Thatcher, Cronin, *Global Rules*, chaps. 4–5.
86. Richardson, *When Allies Differ*, chaps. 3–4.
87. Immensely informative: Benjamin Fischer, "The Soviet-American War Scare of the 1980s," *International Journal of Intelligence and Counter-Intelligence* 19 (2006): 480–581.
88. Ibid., and Pavel Aksonov, "Stanislaus Petrov: The Man Who May Have Saved the World," BBC News, accessed Apr. 3, 2017, http://www.bbc.com/news/world-europe-24280831.
89. Gleijeses, *Visions of Freedom*, passim; Rabe, *The Killing Zone*, chap. 7; Brandts, *Latin America's Cold War*, chaps. 6–7.
90. Amatzia Baram, *Saddam Husayn and Islam, 1968–2003: Ba'thi Iraq from Secularism to Faith* (Baltimore: Johns Hopkins University Press, 2014), 105. Author's own observation of pro-Iraqi demonstration in New York.
91. Williamson Murray and Kevin M. Woods, *The Iran-Iraq War: A Military and Strategic History* (New York: Cambridge University Press, 2014); quote on 97.
92. Jesse Ferris, *Nasser's Gamble: How Intervention in Yemen Caused the Six-Day War and the Decline of Egyptian Power* (Princeton, NJ: Princeton University Press, 2013).
93. Gilles Kepel, *Jihad: The Trail of Political Islam*, trans. Anthony F. Roberts (Cambridge, MA: Belknap Press of Harvard University Press, 2002), 137, 144–47, chap. 4 and passim; Lawrence Wright, *The Looming Tower: Al-Qaeda and the Road to 9/11* (New York: Knopf, 2006).
94. Panagiotis Dimitrakis, *Secret War in Afghanistan: The Soviet Union, China and Anglo-American Intelligence* (London: I.B. Tauris, 2013).
95. Eckart Conze, Martin Klimke, and Jeremy Varon, eds., *Nuclear Threats, Nuclear Fears and the Cold War of the 1980s* (New York: Cambridge University Press, 2017); Jeffrey Herf, *War by Other Means: Soviet Power, West German Resistance and the Battle of the Euromissiles* (New York: Free Press, 1991); Wittner, *The Struggle against the Bomb*, vol. 3.
96. Anne Cahn, *Killing Détente: The Right Attacks the CIA* (University Park: Penn State University Press, 1998); Mann, *Rise of the Vulcans*, 74–75, 80 and passim; Vogel, *Deng Xiaoping*, 269. Deng's ideas about a northern hemisphere alliance should make it clear that China was never part of a "global South."
97. Quoted in Friedman, *Shadow Cold War*, 220.
98. Chris Miller, *The Struggle to Save the Soviet Economy: Mikhail Gorbachev and the Collapse of the USSR* (Chapel Hill: University of North Carolina Press, 2016).
99. James Graham Wilson, *The Triumph of Improvisation: Gorbachev's Adaptability, Reagan's Engagement, and the End of the Cold War* (Ithaca, NY: Cornell University Press, 2014); David Schmitz, *Bren Scowcroft: Internationalism and Post-Vietnam War American Foreign Policy* (Lanham, MD: Rowman & Littlefield, 2011), chap. 18; Thomas Blanton, "U.S. Policy and the Revolution of 1989," in *Masterpieces of History: The Peaceful End of the Cold War in Europe, 1989*, ed. Svetlana Savranskaya,

Thomas Blanton, and Vladislav Zubok (Budapest: Central European University Press, 2010), 49–98; Serhii Plokhy, *The Last Empire: The Final Days of the Soviet Union* (New York: Basic Books, 2014).

100. Zubok, *Failed Empire*, 267; Michael Szporer, *Solidarity: The Great Workers' Strike of 1980* (Lanham, MD: Lexington Books, 2012).

101. Gail Stokes, *The Walls Came Tumbling Down: The Collapse of Communism in Eastern Europe* (New York: Oxford University Press, 1993); Karsten Timmer, *Vom Aufbruch zum Umbruch. Die Bürgerbewegung in der DDR 1989* (Göttingen: Vandenhoeck & Ruprecht, 2000); Mary Elise Sarotte, *The Collapse: The Accidental Opening of the Berlin Wall* (New York: Basic Books, 2014); Svetlana Savaranskaya, "The Logic of 1989: The Soviet Peaceful Withdrawal from Eastern Europe," in Savaranskaya, Blaanton, and Zubok, *Masterpieces of History*, 1–47.

102. Besides sources cited in the previous note, Cronin, *Global Rules*, 180–207; Schmitz, *Scowcroft*, chap. 22; Mary Elise Sarotte, *1989: The Struggle to Create Post-Cold War Europe* (Princeton, NJ: Princeton University Press, 2009); idem., "Not One Inch Eastward? Bush, Baker, Kohl, Genscher, Gorbachev and the Origin of Russian Resentment toward NATO Enlargement in February 1990," *Diplomatic History* 34 (2010): 119–40.

103. Miller, *Struggle to Save the Soviet Economy*, 1.

104. Mark Kramer, "The Demise of the Soviet Bloc," *Journal of Modern History* 83 (2011): 819–54, esp. 819–26.

105. Vogel, *Deng Xiaoping*, 664–89.

106. Patti Waldmeir, *Anatomy of a Miracle: The End of Apartheid and the Birth of a New South Africa* (New York: W.W. Norton, 1997), esp. 136–39; Andrew and Mitrokhin, *Going Our Way*, 462–70; James Barber, *Mandela's World: The International Dimension of South Africa's Political Revolution 1990–1999* (Athens: Ohio University Press, 2004).

107. Philip Roessler and Harry Verhoeven, *Why Comrades Go to War: Liberation Politics and the Outbreak of Africa's Deadliest Conflict* (Oxford: Oxford University Press, 2016); Jason K. Stearns, *Dancing in the Glory of Monsters: The Collapse of the Congo and the Great War of Africa* (New York: Public Affairs, 2011), 327 and passim.

108. Lawrence Freedman and Efraim Karsh, *The Gulf Conflict, 1990–1991: Diplomacy and War in the New World Order* (Princeton, NJ: Princeton University Press, 1993); Schmitz, *Scowcroft*, 479–84.

109. "To Paris, US Looks Like a 'Hyperpower,'" *New York Times*, Feb. 5, 1999, http://www.nytimes.com/1999/02/05/news/to-paris-us-looks-like-a-hyperpower.html; for Védrine's later reflections on this idea, see his 2008 interview, "What the New Geopolitical World Really Looks Like," http://www.hubertvedrine.net/article-306.html, both accessed Feb. 13, 2017.

110. Mann, *Rise of the Vulcans*, chap. 15; Cronin, *Global Rules*, chap. 9; Melvyn P. Leffler and Jeffrey W. Legro, eds., *In Uncertain Times: American Foreign Policy after the Berlin Wall and 9/11* (Ithaca, NY: Cornell University Pres, 2011); Hal Brands, *From Berlin to Baghdad: America's Search for Purpose in the Post-Cold War World* (Lexington: University Press of Kentucky, 2008).

111. Kepel, *Jihad*; Amatzia Baram, *Saddam Husayn and Islam*.

112. Giles Kepel and Jean-Pierre Milelli, *Al Qaeda in Its Own Words*, trans. Pascale Ghazalen (Cambridge, MA: Harvard University Press, 2008), 47.
113. Wright, *Looming Tower*.

Chapter 7

1. James Ferguson, *Global Shadows: Africa in the Neoliberal World Order* (Durham, NC: Duke University Press, 2006), esp. 184.
2. Colin Crouch, *Social Change in Western Europe* (Oxford: Oxford University Press, 1999), 21–23; Michael B. Katz and Mark J. Stern, *One Nation Divisible: What America Was and What It Is Becoming* (New York: Russell Sage Foundation, 2006), chaps. 1–2; Göran Therborn, *European Modernity and Beyond: The Trajectory of European Societies 1945–2000* (London: SAGE Publications, 1995), 65–80.
3. Joel Andreas, *The Rise of the Red Engineers: The Cultural Revolution and the Origins of China's New Class* (Stanford, CA: Stanford University Press, 2009)REFC REFO:BKJames L. Watson, ed., *Class and Social Stratification in Post-Revolution China* (Cambridge: Cambridge University Press, 1984); Therborn, *European Modernity*, 175–76; Sandrine Kott, *Communism Day-to-Day: State Enterprises in East German Society*, trans. Lisa Godin-Roger (Ann Arbor: University of Michigan Press, 2014), chap. 4.
4. Therborn, *European Modernities*, 66.
5. Gail Kligman and Katherine Verdery, *Peasants under Siege: The Collectivization of Romanian Agriculture, 1949–1962* (Princeton, NJ: Princeton University Press, 2011) is very instructive. Also, Yunxiang Yan, *The Individualization of Chinese Society* (Oxford: Berg, 2009), chap. 1; Li Zhang, *Strangers in the City: Reconfigurations of Space, Power, and Social Networks within China's Floating Population* (Stanford, CA: Stanford University Press, 2001), 25–26; Frank Dikötter, *The Tragedy of Liberation: A History of the Chinese Revolution, 1945–57* (London: Bloomsbury, 2013), chap. 4; Tan Hecheng, *The Killing Wind: A Chinese County's Descent into Madness during the Cultural Revolution*, trans. Stacy Mosher and Guo Jian (Oxford: Oxford University Press, 2017).
6. Kligman and Verdery, *Peasants under Siege*, 414.
7. Brian Owensby, *Intimate Ironies: Modernity and the Making of Middle-Class Lives in Brazil* (Stanford, CA: Stanford University Press, 1999); Rajnarayan Chandavarkar, *History, Culture and the Indian City*, ed. Jennifer Davis, Gordon Johnson, and David Washbrook (Cambridge: Cambridge University Press, 2009); Michael West, *The Rise of an African Middle Class: Colonial Zimbabwe, 1898–1965* (Bloomington: Indiana University Press, 2002); D.S. Parker, *The Idea of the Middle Class: White-Collar Workers and Peruvian Society, 1900–1950* (University Park: Pennsylvania State University Press, 1998).
8. A good example of mid-century seigneurialism in Heidi Tinsman, *Partners in Conflict: The Politics of Gender, Sexuality and Labor in the Chilean Agrarian Reform 1950–1973* (Durham, NC: Duke University Press, 2002), chap. 1; also, Elizabeth Dore, *Myths of Modernity: Peonage and Patriarchy in Nicaragua* (Durham, NC: Duke University Press, 2006).
9. James Ferguson, *Expectations of Modernity: Myths and Meanings of Life in the African Copperbelt* (Berkeley: University of California Press, 1999), esp. chap. 1; on the

practice of both seigneurialism and lineage-based societies in West Africa, Babacar Fall, *Le travail au Sénégal au XXe siècle* (Paris: Éditions Karthala, 2011), chap. 1.

10. Ferguson, *Expectations of Modernity*, 1999, esp. chap. 1; on the practice of both seigneurialism and lineage-based societies in West Africa, Babacar Fall, *Le travail au Sénégal au XXe siècle*, 2011, chap. 1.; Frederick Cooper, *Africa since 1940: The Past of the Present* (Cambridge: Cambridge University Press, 2002), chap. 5.

11. Oliver Zunz, Leonard Schoppa, and Nobuhiro Hiwatari, eds., *Social Contracts under Stress: The Middle Class of America, Europe and Japan at the Turn of the Century* (New York: Russell Sage Foundation, 2002), esp. part 1; Therborn, *European Modernity*, chap. 7.

12. Andrew Gordon, "The Short Happy Life of the Japanese Middle Classes," in Zunz, Schopps and Hawatari, *Social Contracts under Stress*, 109.

13. Hartmut Kaelble, *A Social History of Europe 1945–2000: Recovery and Transformation after Two World Wars*, trans. Liesel Tarquini (New York: Berghahn Books, 2013), 161, 164.

14. An observation this author heard frequently when he was a graduate student in the United States and West Germany during the 1970s.

15. Katz and Stern, *One Nation Divisible*, 96; Mike Savage, *Class Analysis and Social Transformation* (Buckingham: Open University Press, 2000), 60–61. From 1960 onward, the economic situation of college-educated African Americans, both men and women, actually improved vis-à-vis whites without a college education.

16. Michael Bonin, *The Lost Generation: The Rustication of China's Educated Youth (1968–1980)*, trans. Krystyna Horko (Hong Kong: The Chinese University Press, 2013). In areas populated by ethnic minorities, like Western Xinjiang Province, the party leadership refused to let the exiles return home, so their presence would reinforce the position of the Han Chinese.

17. Saskia Sassen, *The Global City: New York, Tokyo, London* (Princeton, NJ: Princeton University Press, 1991); Christopher McKenna, *The World's Newest Profession: Management Consulting in the Twentieth Century* (New York: Cambridge University Press, 2006), 1–5, chap. 7.

18. Andrew Ivaska, *Cultured States: Youth, Gender and Modern Stile in 1960s Dar es Salaam* (Durham, NC: Duke University Press, 2013), 216; Yan, *Individualization of Chinese Society*, chaps. 1–2; Wing-Chung Ho, *The Transition Study of Postsocialist China: An Ethnographic Study of a Modern Community* (Singapore: World Scientific Publishing Co., 2010), esp. 161–68.

19. Avner Offner, "British Manual Workers: From Producers to Consumers, c. 1950–2000," *Contemporary British History* 22 (2008): 537–71; Lutz Raphael, "Life Cycle and Industrial Work: West German and British patterns in Times of Globalization," *German Historical Institute London Bulletin* 38 (2016): 23–45. Edward McClelland, *Nothin' But Blue Skies: The Heyday, Hard Times, and Hopes of America's Industrial Heartland*, (New York: Bloombsbury, 2013); Louis Uchitelle, *The Disposable American: Layoffs and their Consequences* (New York: Knopf, 2006), chap. 1; Jan Breman, *The Labouring Poor in India: Patterns of Exploitation, Subordination and Exclusion* (New Delhi: Oxford University Press, 2003) chap. 7.

20. Mark Erlich and Jeff Grabelsky, "Standing at a Crossroads: The Building Trades in the Twenty-First Century," *Labor History* 46 (2005): 421–45. Guy Standing, *The Precariat: The New Dangerous Class*, 2nd ed. (London: Bloomsbury, 2014), 6–7.
21. Standing, *The Precariat*, esp. 15, 58; Anne Allison, *Precarious Japan* (Durham, NC: Duke University Press, 2013); Jan Breman, *Footlose Labor: Working in India's Informal Economy* (Cambridge: Cambridge University Press, 1996), esp. 3–6.
22. James Ferguson, *Give A Man a Fish: Reflections on the New Politics of Distribution* (Durham, NC: Duke University Press, 2015), 11 and more generally; Nantang Jua, "Body and Soul: Economic Space, Public Morality and Social Integration of Youth in Cameroon," in *How Africa Works: Occupational Change, Identity and Morality*, ed. Deborah Fahy Bryceson (Bourton on Dunsmore: Practical Action Publishing, 2010), chap. 7, esp. 132.
23. J.T. Way, *The Mayan in the Mall: Globalization, Development and the Making of Modern Guatemala* (Durham, NC: Duke University Press, 2012), esp. chap. 6; also ibid., Cooper, *Africa since 1940*, 121–24; Jan Breman, *The Labouring Poor in India*, chap. 4; Bryceson, *How Africa Works*.
24. John Powell, *The Survival of the Fitter: Lives of Some African Engineers* (London: Intermediate Technology Publications, 1995); Kate Meagher, "Social Capital or Social Exclusion? Social Networks and Informal Manufacturing in Nigeria," in Bryceson, *How Africa Works*, 105–26..
25. William van Schendel and Itty Abraham, *Illicit Flows and Criminal Things: States, Borders and the Other Side of Globalization* (Bloomington: Indiana University Press, 2005); Jennifer M. Hazen and Dennis Rodgers, eds., *Global Gangs: Street Violence across the World* (Minneapolis: University of Minnesota Press, 2014); Gary Kynoch, *We Are Fighting the World: A History of the Marashea Gangs in South Africa, 1947–1999* (Athens: Ohio University Press, 2005); AbouMaliq Simone, "Linking Irregular Economies: Remaking Transurban Commercial Networks through New Forms of Social Collaboration," in Bryceson, *How Africa Works*, 87–104, also the essay by Nantan Jua on Cameroon, in the same volume, esp. 136–38; Mary Buckley, "Human Trafficking in the Twenty-First Century: Implications for Russia, Europe and the World," in *Gender Politics in Post-Communist Eurasia*, ed. Linda Racioppi and Katherine O'Sullivan (East Lansing: Michigan State University Press, 2009), 119–45.
26. Cited in McClelland, *Nothin' but Blue Skies*, 198.
27. Figures 7.1–7.3 are all from the data in the UN's "World Population Prospects 2017," accessed Dec. 4, 2017, https://esa.un.org/unpd/wpp/Download/Standard/Population/.
28. A total fertility rate of 2.1, an average of slightly over two children per woman during her natural fertile lifetime, would correspond roughly to a stable population. The figure should be slightly above 2, because not all women live through their entire fertile lifetimes.
29. Detlev Peukert, *Grenzen der Sozialdisziplinierung. Aufstieg und Krise der deutschen Jugendfürsorge von 1878 bis 1932* (Cologne: Bund-Verlag, 1986); Bill Ogersby, *Youth in Britain since 1945* (Oxford: Blackwell, 1998), chap. 2; Juliane Fürst, *Stalin's Lost Generation: Soviet Post-War Youth and the Emergence of Mature Socialism* (Oxford: Oxford University Press, 2010), 7–12; Ibrahim Abdullah,

"'I Am a Rebel': Youth Culture and Violence in Sierra Leone," in *Makers and Breakers: Children and Youth in Postcolonial Africa*, ed. Alcinda Honwana and Filip de Boeck (Oxford: James Currey, 2005), 172–87; Ivaska, *Cultured States*, 124; more generally, on young people in the modern world, Ludivine Bantigny and Ivan Jablonka, eds., *Jeunesse oblige. Histoire des jeunes en France XIXe—XXIe siècle* (Paris: Presses Universitaires de France, 2009).

30. James Gilbert, *A Cycle of Outrage: Americas Reaction to the Juvenile Delinquent in the 1950s* (New York: Oxford University Press, 1986); Ogersby, *Youth in Britain*, 43–47; Uta Poiger, *Jazz Rock and Rebels: Cold War Politics and American Culture in a Divided Germany* (Berkeley: University of California Press, 2000); Valeria Manzano, *The Age of Youth in Argentina: Culture, Politics and Sexuality from Perón to Videla* (Chapel Hill: University of North Carolina Press, 2014), 29–36; Gerd-Rainer Horn, *The Spirit of '68: Rebellion in Western Europe and North America, 1950–1976* (Oxford: Oxford University Press, 2007), 24.

31. National Center for Education Statistics, "120 Years of American Education, A Statistical Protrait," 16–17, 77, accessed Dec. 7, 2017, https://nces.ed.gov/pub s93/93442.pdf; Therborn, *European Modernity*, 259–60; Yossi Shavit and Hans-Peter Blossfeld, eds., *Persistent Inequality: Changing Educational Attainment in Thirteen Countries* (Boulder, CO: Westview Press, 1993); Manzano, *Age of Youth*, 46, 54–55; Elizabeth King and M. Anne Hill, eds., *Women's Education in Developing Countries* (Baltimore: Johns Hopkins University Press, 1993), 5; Ivaska, *Cultured States*, 128–29; Anne Booth, *Economic Change in Modern Indonesia: Colonial and Post-Colonial Comparisons* (Cambridge: Cambridge University Press, 2016), 57–58, 80.

32. Sources cited in n. 29 generally deal with these points.

33. Batigny and Jaablonka, *Jeunesse oblige*, 205.

34. Ibid., 206–8; Manzoan, *Age of Youth*, 88–93; Konrad Dussel, "The Triumph of English-Language Pop Music: West German Radio Programming," in *Between Marx and Coca-Cola: Youth Cultures in Changing European Societies, 1960–1980*, ed. Axel Schildt and Detlef Siegfried (New York: Berghahn Books, 2006) as well as the other essays in this book; Tinsman, *Partners in Conflict*, 234–35.

35. Beth Bailey, *Sex in the Heartland* (Cambridge, MA: Harvard University Press, 1999) is an excellent grassroots study of the counterculture and its enemies; for Tanzania and Uganda, Ivaska, *Cultured States*, esp. chaps. 1–3; Grace Bantebya Kyomuhendo and Marjorie Keniston Mcintosh, *Women, Work and Domestic Virtue in Uganda 1900–2003* (Oxford: James Curry, 2006), 163. For youth culture and its opponents elsewhere in Africa, Abdullah, "'I Am a Rebel,'" 180–82; Thomas, *Politics of the Womb*, 161.

36. Cited in Detlef Siegfried, "Understanding 1968: Youth Rebellion, Generational Change and Postindustrial Society," in Schildt and Siegfried, *Between Marx and Coca-Cola*, 75.

37. Jean Comaroff and John Comaroff, "Reflections on Youth: From the Past to the Postcolony," in Honwana and de Boeck, *Makers and Breakers*, 19–30; Therborn, *European Modernity*, 250–52; Ogersby, *Youth in Britain*, chaps. 7–13.

38. Abram de Swaan, *In Care of the State: Health Care, Education and Welfare in Europe and the USA during the Modern Era* (New York: Oxford University Press, 1988), esp. 194 also, Katz and Stern, *One Nation Divided*, 141–53; World Bank, 1994,

"Averting the Old Age Crisis," accessed Dec. 14, 2017, http://documents.worldbank.org/curated/en/973571468174557899/pdf/multi-page.pdf, esp. 104; Nanna Kildal and Stein Kuhnle, "Old Page Pensions, Poverty and Dignity: Historical Arguments for Universal Pensions," *Global Social Policy* 8 (2008): 208–37.

39. OECD, "Pensions at a Glance, 2017," accessed Dec. 14, 2017, file:///Users/sperberj/Documents/New%20projects/Global%20pdfs/OECD%20Pensions%202017.pdf, chap. 6; International Labour Organization, "Economically Active Population, 1950–2010," accessed Feb. 12, 2018, http://www.ilo.org/public/libdoc/ilo/1997/97B09_301_e_f_s.pdf, 23.

40. Frank Trentmann, *Empire of Things: How We Became a World of Consumers, from the Fifteenth Century to the Twenty-First* (New York: Harper, 2016), 498–519; Therborn, *European Modernity*, 59–60; Michael A. Blazey, "Travel and Retirement Status," *Annals of Tourism Research* 19 (1992): 771–83; Per Gustafson, "Tourism and Seasonal Retirement Migration," *Annals of Tourism Research* 29 (2002): 899–918.

41. The World Bank study of 1994, in n. 37, is a good summary of these questions.

42. OECD "Pensions at a Glance 2017," 102 and 146.

43. World Bank, "Averting the Old Age Crisis," 154; Michael Hiltzik, "Chile's Privatized Social Security System, Beloved by U.S. Conservatives, Is Falling Apart," *Los Angeles Times*, Aug. 12, 2016, accessed Dec. 15, 2017, http://www.latimes.com/business/hiltzik/la-fi-hiltzik-chile-social-security-20160812-snapstory.html; "Over 2 Million Protest Chile's Pinochet-Era Pension System," *Telesur* Mar. 27, 2017, https://www.telesurtv.net/english/news/Thousands-Protest-Chiles-Pinochet-Era-Private-Pension-System-20170326-0009.html, accessed Dec. 15, 2017.

44. Broader demographic overviews: Jay Winter and Michael Teitelbaum, *The Global Spread of Fertility Decline: Population, Fear and Uncertainty* (New Haven, CT: Yale University Press, 2013); James Z. Lee and Wang Feng, *One Quarter of Humanity: Malthusian Mythology and Chinese Realities 1700–2000* (Cambridge, MA: Harvard University Press, 1999).

45. Abigail Haworth, "Why have young people in Japan stopped having sex?," *The Guardian*, Oct. 20, 2013, https://www.theguardian.com/world/2013/oct/20/young-people-japan-stopped-having-sex, accessed Dec. 18, 2017.

46. Kaelble, *Social History of Europe*, 14–19; Elaine Tyler May, *Homeward Bound: American Families in the Cold War Era* (New York: Basic Books, 1988).

47. Rawwida Baksh and Wendy Harcourt, eds., *The Oxford Handbook of Transnational Feminist Movements* (New York: Oxford University Press, 2015), 215–46.

48. Jad Adams, *Women and the Vote: A World History* (Oxford: Oxford University Press, 2014); Sekhar Bandyopadhyay, *Decolonization in South Asia; The Meanings of Freedom in Post-Independence West Bengal, 1947–1952* (London: Routledge, 2009), 172–74.

49. Göran Therborn, *Between Sex and Power: Family in the World, 1900–2000* (London: Routledge 2004), 165, 172; Stephanie J. Ventura, "Changing Patterns of Nonmarital Childbearing in the United States," *NCHS Data Brief* 18, May 2009, https://www.cdc.gov/nchs/data/databriefs/db18.pdf, accessed Feb. 6, 2018; Philip Cutright, "Historical and Contemporary Trends in Illegitimacy," *Archives of Sexual Behavior* 2 (1972): 97–118; United Nations Population Division, "World Fertility Report 2009," Table A.7, http://www.un.org/esa/population/publicati

ons/WFR2009_Web/Data/DataAndSources.html., accessed Feb. 6, 2018. United Nations Population Division, World Fertility Report, 2010, Table A.4, https://www.un.org/en/development/desa/population/publications/dataset/fertility/wfr2012/WFR_2012/Data_and_sources.htm, accessed May 11, 2020.
50. Therborn, *Between Sex and Power*, 163–66.
51. Tinsman, *Partners in Conflict*, 58; Rebecca Davis, *More Perfect Unions: The American Search for Marital Bliss* (Cambridge, MA: Harvard University Press, 2010), 39–40, esp. 168–69; Kate Fisher, *Birth Control, Sex and Marriage in Britain 1918–1960* (Oxford: Oxford University Press, 2006); Wally Seccombe, "Starting to Stop: Working-Class Fertility Decline in Britain," *Past & Present* 126 (1990): 151–88; Angus McLaren, *Twentieth Century Sexuality: A History* (Oxford: Blackwell, 1999), chap. 3; May, *Homeward Bound*, chap. 5; Barbara Ehrenreich, Elizabeth Hess, and Gloria Jacobs, *Re-making Love: The Feminization of Sex* (Garden City, NY: Doubleday, 1986), chap. 2; Elizabeth Heinemann, *Before Porn Was Legal: The Erotica Empire of Beate Uhse* (Chicago: University of Chicago Press, 2011), chap. 2; Marcus Collins, *Modern Love: Personal Relationships in Twentieth-Century Britain* (Newark: University of Delaware Press, 2006), chap. 4.
52. Sources as in previous note and Lara V. Marks, *Sexual Chemistry: A History of the Contraceptive Pill* (New Haven, CT: Yale University Press, 2010), 187–94; Amy Kaler, *Running After Pills: Politics, Gender and Contraception in Colonial Zimbabwe* (Portsmouth, NH: Heinemann, 2006), 82.
53. Cynthia Kreisel, "Happy Motherhood and Lesbian Spaces: Women's Initiative and the Sexual Mores of Postwar Europe," in *Women and Gender in Postwar Europe: From Cold War to European Union*, ed. Joanna Regulska and Bonnie G. Smith (London: Routledge, 2012), 124; Tinsman, *Partners in Conflict*, 157.
54. McLaren, *Twentieth Century Sexuality*, 87–109, 161–63, 187–89; George Chauncey, *Gay New York: Gender, Urban Culture and the Making of the Gay Male World* (New York: Basic Books, 1994); James Green, *Beyond Carnival: Male Homosexuality in Twentieth-Century Brazil* (Chicago: University of Chicago Press, 1999), 6–7; Julian Jackson, *Living in Arcadia: Homosexuality, Politics and Morality in France from the Liberation to AIDS* (Chicago: University of Chicago Press, 2009), Robert G. Moeller, "The Homosexual Man Is a 'Man,' the Homosexual Women Is a 'Woman': Sex, Society, and the Law in Postwar West Germany, in Robert Moeller (ed.), *West Germany under Construction: Politics Society and Culture in the Adenauer Era* (Ann Arbor: University of Michigan Press, 1997), 251–84; Kyle A. Cuorileone, *Manhood and American Political Culture in the Cold War* (New York: Routledge, 2005).
55. Besides the sources cited in the previous four notes, David Ally, *Make Love Not War: The Sexual Revolution: An Unfettered History* (Boston: Little, Brown, 2000) chaps. 1–3; Sybille Steinbacher, *Wie der Sex nach Deutschland kam* (Munich: Siedler Verlag, 2011), chap. 2 and passim; James H. Jones, *Alfred C. Kinsey: A Public/Private Life* (New York: W.W. Norton, 1997).
56. On this point, both generally and with details, Therborn, *Between Sex and Power*, chap. 1, and John C. Caldwell et. al., "The Construction of Adolescence in a Changing World: Implications for Sexuality, Reproduction, and Marriage," *Studies in Family Planning* 29 (1998): 137–53; Patricia Uberoi, *Freedom and Destiny: Gender,*

Family and Popular Culture in India (New Delhi: Oxford University Press, 2006), 29–33, 121–23; Amy Kaler, *Running After Pills*, 147–49 and chap. 5.

57. Thomas F. Fricke, Jui-Shan Chang, and Li-Shou Yang, "Historical and Ethnographic Perspectives on the Chinese Family," in *Social Change and the Family in Taiwan*, ed. Arland Thorton and Hui-shang Lin (Chicago: University of Chicago Press, 1994), 22–48.
58. A classic anthropological study is Jack Goody and S.J. Tambiah, *Bridewealth and Dowry* (Cambridge: Cambridge University Press, 1973).
59. Huang Yingying, "The Rise of Sex and Sexuality Studies in Post-1978 China," in *The Sexual History of the Global South: Sexual Politics in Africa, Asia and Latin America*, ed. Saskiw Wieringa and Horacio Sívori (London: Zed Books, 2013), 22–43.
60. For China, Lee and Wang, *One Quarter of Humanity*, esp. chaps. 4–5.
61. Cf. Uberoi, *Freedom and Destiny*, 123.
62. Ibid., 65–71; Bret L. Billet, *Cultural Relativism in the Face of the West: The Plight of Women and Female Children* (Houndmills, Basingstoke: Palgrave Macmillan, 2007), chaps. 2–3; Lynn M. Thomas, *The Politics of the Womb: Women, Reproduction and the State in Kenya* (Berkeley: University of California Press, 2003). Apologists for female genital mutilation like to refer to it as "female circumcision," and it was and is practiced in areas where it is very common for men to be circumcised. It would be fair to say that both practices are forms of genital mutilation, and neither is harmless, although much worse on women than on men.
63. Chilla Bulbeck, *Re-Orienting Western Feminism: Women's Diversity in a Postcolonial World* (Cambridge: Cambridge University Press, 1998), 148–60; Tom Boellstorff, *The Gay Archipelago: Sexuality and Nation in Indonesia* (Princeton, NJ: Princeton University Press, 2005), 38–39; Marc Epprecht, *Sexuality and Social Justice in Africa: Rethinking Homophobia and Forging Resistance* (London: Zed Books, 2013), 74–76, 113, 115.
64. Leila J. Rupp, *Worlds of Women: The Making of an International Women's Movement* (Princeton, NJ: Princeton University Press, 1997); Kyomuhendo and Mcintosh, *Women, Work and Domestic Virtue*, 97–98.
65. Neil J. Diamant, *Revolutionizing the Family: Politics, Love and Divorce in Urban and Rural China, 1949–1968* (Berkeley: University of California Press, 2000), 341–46.
66. Ibid., 108–9; Donna Harsch, "Sex, Divorce and Women's Waged Work: Private Lives and State Policy in the early German Democratic Republic," in *Gender Politics and Everyday Life in State Socialist Eastern and Central Europe*, ed. Shana Penn and Jill lMassino (Houndmills, Basingstoke: Palgrave Macmillan, 2009), 103.
67. Melissa Feinberg, "Battling for Peace: The Transformation of the Women's Movement in Cold War Czechoslovakia and Eastern Europe," in Regulska and Smith, *Women and Gender in Postwar Europe*, 16–33.
68. It might be objected that the high labor force participation rates of women in their late 20s at the very beginning of communist rule reflected both the death of a large number of men in the Second World War and the prevalence of small-scale agriculture, where being in the household and being in the labor force are hard to tell apart. This is true, but in, say, the poorer lands of capitalist southern Europe,

where these conditions also prevailed, women's labor force participation rates were much lower.
69. ILO labor force statistics, n. 38, and http://www.ilo.org/public/libdoc/ilo/1997/97B09_300_e_f_s.pdf, accessed Feb. 13, 2018.
70. Penn and Massino, *Gender Politics*; Regulska and Smith, *Women and Gender*; Theborn, *European Modernity*, 64; Kott, *Communism Day-to-Day*, chap. 6.
71. Diamant, *Revolutionizing the Family*, chaps. 3–4 and *passim*; Yunxiang Yan, *Private Life under Socialism: Love, Intimacy and Family Change in a Chinese Village 1949–1999* (Stanford, CA: Stanford University Press, 1993), chap. 2 and passim.
72. Marx, *Sexual Chemistry*; also, Elaine Tyler May, *America and the Pill* (New York: Basic Books, 2010); Amy Kaller, *Running After Pills*, chap. 6. Taking birth control pills over a long period of time may increase the (already greater) risk of stroke among women who both smoke cigarettes and have high blood pressure.
73. Winter and Teitelbaum, *Global Spread of Fertility Decline*, 150–66.
74. Lee and Wang, *One Quarter of Humanity*, 92–99; Yan, *Private Life under Socialism*, chap. 8; Yan, *Individualization of Chinese Society*, 38–40; Karen Hardee-Cleaveland and Judith Banister "Fertility Policy and Implementation in China, 1986-88," *Population and Development Review* 14 (1988): 245–86; Susan Greenhalgh, "Controlling Births and Bodies in Village China," *American Ethnologist* 21 (1994): 3–30.
75. Tiana Norgren, *Abortion before Birth Control* (Princeton, NJ: Princeton University Press, 2001).
76. Allyn, *Make Love Not War*; McLaren, *Twentieth Century Sexuality*, chap. 9; Arthur Marwick, *The Sixties: Cultural Revolution in Britain, France, Italy and the United States, c. 1958—1974* (Oxford: Oxford University Press, 1998), chaps. 3–4; Therborn, *Between Sex and Power*, 204–11.
77. Caitrona Clear, *Women's Voice in Ireland: Women's Magazines in the 1950s and 1960s* (London: Bloomsbury Academic, 2016); Heineimann, *Before Porn Was Legal*; similarly, Collins, *Modern Love*, chap. 5.
78. Lawrence B. Finer, "Trends in Premarital Sex in the United States, 1954–2003," *Public Health Reports* 122 (2007): 73–78, Table 1.
79. Therborn, *Between Sex and Power*, 208–10; McLaren, *Twentieth Century Sexuality*, 173–74; Ann K. Blanc and Ann A. Way, "Sexual Behavior and Contraceptive Knowledge and Use among Adolescents in Developing Countries," *Studies in Family Planning* 29 (1998): 106–16, esp. Table 2; Manzona, *Age of Youth in Argentina*.
80. Yan, *Private Life under Socialism*, 52–54.
81. Gretchen Lemke-Santangelo, *Daughters of Aquarius: Women of the Sixties Counterculture* (Lawrence: University Press of Kansas, 2009); Collins, *Modern Life*, 179.
82. Kathleen A. Laughlin and Jacqueline L. Castledine, *Breaking the Wave: Women, Their Organizations, and Feminism, 1945–1985* (New York: Routledge, 2011); Daniel Horowitz, *Betty Friedan and the Making of* The Feminine Mystique: *The American Left, The Cold War and Modern Feminism* (Amherst: University of Massachusetts Press, 1998).

83. On different forms of feminism, Ruth Rosen, *The World Split Open: How the Modern Women's Movement Changed America* (New York: Viking, 2000), chaps. 3–4; internationally, Marwick *The Sixties*, 679–724; Collins, *Modern Love*, 180–96.
84. Judith Ezekiel, *Feminism in the Heartland* (Columbus: Ohio State University Press, 2002), 22; Stephen Brooke, *Sexual Politics: Sexuality, Family Planning and the British Left from the 1880s to the Present Day* (Oxford: Oxford University Press, 2011), 190–91.
85. Marks, *Sexual Chemistry*; May, *America and the Pill*; Norgen, *Abortion before Birth Control*, 65–68, 115–18.
86. Lillian Faderman, *The Gay Revolution: The Story of the Struggle* (New York: Simon & Schuster, 2015); Barry D. Adam, Jan Willem Duyvendak, and André Krouwel, *The Global Emergence of Gay and Lesbian Politics: National Imprints of a Worldwide Movement* (Philadelphia: Temple University Press, 1999); Julian Jackson, *Living in Arcadia*, chap. 7; Green, *Beyond Carnival*, 268–69; Todd Shepherd, *Sex, France and Arab Men, 1962–1979* (Chicago: University of Chicago Press, 2017), chap. 3.
87. Marwick, *The Sixties*, 700–24; McLaren, *Twentieth Century Sexuality*, 182–83; Therborn, *Between Sex and Power*, 100–2; Brooke, *Sexual Politics*, chap. 6; https://www.bpb.de/izpb/10109/sozialliberale-koalition-und-innere-reformen?p=all, accessed Feb. 23, 2018.
88. Josie McLellan, *Love in the Time of Communism: Intimacy and Sexuality in the GDR* (Cambridge: Cambridge University Press, 2011), 46 and passim.
89. Bulbeck, *Reorienting Western Feminism*, 169–70; Raluca Maria Popa, "Translating Equality between Women and Men across Cold War Divides: Women Activists from Hungary and Romania and the Creation of International Women's Year," in Penn and Massino, *Gender Politics and Everyday Life*, 59–74; Peggy Antrobus, *The Global Women's Movement: Origins, Issue and Strategies* (London: Zed Books, 2004), 39.
90. Rawwida Baksh-Soodeen and Wendy Harcourt, eds., *The Oxford Handbook of Transnational Feminist Movements* (New York: Oxford University Press, 2015), esp. 60–61, 68, 159–87, 507–27, 578–600; also, Kyomuhendo and Keniston, *Women Work and Domestic Virtue*, 200–6.
91. International Labour Organization, "Economically Active Population, 1950–2010," accessed Feb. 12, 2018, http://www.ilo.org/public/libdoc/ilo/1997/97Bo9_301_e_f_s.pdf, 27, 29. More recent ILO statistics use a different organizing scheme, not compatible with this one.
92. Crouch, *Social Change*, 75–78; Collins, *Modern Love*, 219; on women and employment, worldwide, in the early twenty-first century, cf. ILO, "Global Employment Trends for Women, March 2009," accessed May 10, 2018, http://www.ilo.org/wcmsp5/groups/public/@dgreports/@dcomm/documents/publication/wcms_103456.pdf.
93. National Center for Education Statistics, "120 Years of American Education, A Statistical Protrait," 76–66, https://nces.ed.gov/pubs93/93442.pdf, accessed Dec. 12, 2017.
94. Kaelble, *Social History of Europe*, 299.
95. OECD, "Higher Education to 2030," Vol. 1, Demography, http://www.keepeek.com/Digital-Asset-Management/oecd/education/higher-education-to-2030-vol

ume-1-demography_9789264040663-en#page2, 269; http://data.uis.unesco.org/download dd033d88-f33d-4deb-9bb0-e705c61cc31d.xls, accessed Feb. 28, 2018; United Nations, "The World's Women 1970–1990: Trends and Statistics," 50–53; https://unstats.un.org/UNSD/demographic/products/Worldswomen/WW1990.pdf. "More Indian women are going to college, but fewer are working," https://scroll.in/article/812591/more-indian-women-are-going-to-college-but-fewer-are-working, all accessed Feb. 28, 2018.

96. http://uis.unesco.org/sites/default/files/datacentre/2017_Educational_attainment_-_Niveau_de_scolarisation.xlsx, accessed Feb. 28, 2018. The countries were chosen because they were among the very few for which data is available over a period of decades.

97. Quoted in Marks, *Sexual Chemistry*, 228.

98. The phrase sexual counterrevolution Ehrenreich, Hess, and Jacobs, *Re-making Love*, chap. 6, although differently from here. Allyn, *Make Love Not War*, chap. 21; Fadermann, *Gay Revolution*, chaps. 19–24; Frédéric Martel, *The Pink and the Black: Homosexuals in France since 1968*, trans. Jane Marie Todd (Stanford, CA: Stanford University Press, 1999), pt. 3; Adam, Duyvendak, and Krouwei, *Global Emergence of Gay and Lesbian Politics*.

99. Ehrenreich, Hess, and Jacobs, *Re-making Love*; Antrobus, *Global Women's Movement*, 97–98; Ruth Dixon-Mueller, *Population Policy and Women's Rights: Transforming Reproductive Choice* (Westport, CT: Praeger, 1993), chap. 7; Thomas, *Politics of the Womb*, 168; Collins, *Modern Love*, 216; Brooke, *Sexual Politics*, chap. 7.

100. As a characteristic example, Sara Salem, "Feminist Critique and Islamic Feminism: The Question of Intersectionality," *The Postcolonialist* 1 (2013), http://postcolonialist.com/civil-discourse/feminist-critique-and-islamic-feminism-the-question-of-intersectionality/, accessed Mar. 21, 2018.

101. Gillian Pascall and Anna Kwak, *Gender Regimes in Transition in Central and Eastern Europe* (Bristol: Policy Press, 2005); Racioppi and See (eds.), *Gender Politics in Post-Communist Eurasia*.

102. Brooke, *Sexual Politics*, 225–68.

103. Figures on women holding political office from Baksh and Harcourt, *Oxford Handbook of Transnational Feminist Movements*, 221–22; Kyomuhendo and Macintosh, *Women, Work and Domestic Virtue*, 191–92.

104. Jane Lewis, *The End of Marriage? Individualism and Intimate Relations* (Cheltenham: E. Elgar, 2001).

105. [United Nations Population Division, "World Fertility Report 2009," Table A.7, http://www.un.org/esa/population/publications/WFR2009_Web/Data/DataAndSources.html., accessed Feb. 6, 2018] United Nations Population Division, World Fertility Report, 2010, Table A.4, https://www.un.org/en/development/desa/population/publications/dataset/fertility/wfr2012/WFR_2012/Data_and_sources.htm, accessed May 11, 2010. Initial figure for Kyrgyzstan is for 1980.

106. Göran, *Between Sex and Power*, 198–207; Abigail Haworth, "Why have young people in Japan stopped having sex?," *The Guardian*, Oct. 20 2013, https://www.theguardian.com/world/2013/oct/20/young-people-japan-stopped-having-sex, accessed Dec. 18, 2017; Allison, *Precarious Japan*, 2–4, 33, 95–96, 99 and passim.

107. Yan, *Individualization*, 72–73 and passim; Yan, *Private Life*; also, Gen Song and Derek Hird, *Men and Masculinities in Contemporary China* (Leiden: Brill, 2014); Pei-Chi Lan, "Among Women: Migrant Domestics and their Taiwanese Employers Across Generations," in Ehrenreich and Hochschild, *Gobal Women*, 169–89.
108. Patricia Uberoi, ed., *Family, Kingship and Marriage in India* (New Delhi: Oxford University Press, 1994), esp. the essay of Ursula Sharma, "Dowry in North India," 341–56; Uberoi, *Freedom and Destiny*, 24–29, 138, 157, 180–263.
109. Caldwell et. al., "The Construction of Adolescence"; Gage and Meekers, "Sexual Activity"; also, Tsitsi B. Masvawure, "Sexual Pleasure and the Premarital Sexual Adventures of Young Women in Zimbabwe," in Wierenga and Sívori, *Sexual History of the Global South*, 344–62; Kyomuhendo and Mcimtosh, *Women, Work and Domestic Virtue*, 239–44; Kaller, *Running After Pills*.
110. Christophe Broqua, "Male Homosexuality in Bamako: A Cross-Cultural and Cross-Historical Perspective," in *Sexual Diversity in Africa: Politics, Theory, Citizenship*, ed. S.N. Nyeck and Marc Epprecht (Montreal, Canada: McGill-Queen's University Press, 2013), 208–14; Rajeev Kumarkamkandath, "Canons of Desire: Male Homosexuality in Twenty-First Century Keralam," in Wieringa and Sívori, *Sexual History of the Global South*, 206–24.
111. Boellstorff, *Gay Archipelago*, 40–41, 62–64, 95–97, 142–43, 162–65, 225 and passim.
112. Sources in n. 109 and Marc Epprecht, "The Making of 'African Sexuality': Early Sources, Current Debates," in Nyeck and Epprecht, *Sexual Diversity in Africa*, 54–66; Stella Nyanzi, "Rhetorical Analysis of President Jammeh's Threats to Behead Homosexuals in the Gambia," in Nyeck and Epprecht, *Sexual Diversity in Africa*, 67–87; Bsile Ndjio, "Sexuality and Nationalist Ideologies in Post-Colonial Cameroon," in Wiering and Sívori, *Sexual History of the Global South*, 120–43; Epprecht, *Sexuality and Social Justice*, 78, 143–47.
113. Ndijio, "Sexuality and Nationalist Ideologies," esp. 128–36; Shari L. Dowrkin, Amanda Lock Swarr, and Cherly Cooky, "The (Mis)Treatment of South African Track star Caster Semenya," in Nyeck and Epprecht, *Sexual Diversity in Africa*, 144–45; Mats Utas, "Agency of Victims: Young Women in the Liberian Civil War," in Honwana and de Boeck, *Makers and Breakers*, 53–79; also, Andrea Cornwall, "To Be A Man Is More Than A Day's Work: Shifting Ideals of Masculinity in Ado-Odo, Southwestern Nigeria," in *Men and Masculinities in Modern Africa*, ed. Lisa Lindsey and Stephan F. Miescher (Portsmouth, NH: Heinemann, 2003), 230–48; Bryceson, *How Africa Works*, chaps. 8–10.

Chapter 8

1. Fall, *Le Travail au Sénégal*, 24–26.
2. Joshua Freeman, *Working Class New York: Life and Labor since World War II* (New York: The New Press 2000), 2–5; Jefferson Cowie, *The Great Exception: The New Deal and the Limits of American Politics* (Princeton, NJ: Princeton University Press, 2016), 157–58; Oliver Dinius, *Brazil's Steel City: Development, Strategic Power, and Industrial Relations in Volta Redonda, 1941–1964* (Stanford, CA: Stanford University Press, 2011), 2; Maurizio Ateni and Pablo Ghigliani, "The Labour Movement in Argentina since 1945: The Limits of Trade Union Reformism," in

Trade Unionism since 1945, 2 vols., ed. Craig Phelan (Bern: Peter Lang, 2009), 2: 224; Norman Caulfield, "Labor Relations in Mexico: Historical Legacies and Some Recent Trends," *Labor History* 45 (2004): 445–67.

3. Herrick Chapman, *State Capitalism and Working-Class Radicalism in the French Aircraft Industry* (Berkeley: University of California Press, 1991), chap. 10; Keith Laybourn, "Trade Unionism in Britain since 1945," in Phelan, *Trade Unionism since 1945*, 1:199–202; László Neumann, "The History of Trade Unionism in Hungary,1945–2002," in ibid., 1: 233 (similarly, the essays in this volume on unions in France, Belgium, and Italy); Jan De Graaf, *Socialism Across the Iron Curtain: Socialist Parties in East and West and the Reconstruction of Europe after 1945* (Cambridge: Cambridge University Press, 2019), 60; Lutz Niethammer, Ulrich Borsdorf, and Peter Brandt, eds., *Arbeiterinitiative 1945* (Wuppertal: Peter Hammer Verlag, 1976); Kaelble *A Social History of Europe*, 227–28.

4. Frederick Cooper, *Decolonization and African Society: The Labour Question in French and British Africa* (Cambridge: Cambridge University Press, 1996), chap. 6; David Hyde, "The East African Railway Strike, 1959–60: Labour's Challenge of Inter-territorialism," *Labor History* 57 (2016): 71–91; Fall, *Le Travail au Sénégal* 140–49; James A. Jones, "The 1947–1948 Railway Strike in French West Africa," in Craig Phelan, *Trade Unions in West Africa: Historical and Contemporary Perspectives* (Bern: Peter Lang, 2011), 45–68.; Kwamina Panford, "Trade Unions, Democratic Transition and Organisational Challenge: The Ghana Trades Union Congress, 1989–2009," in Phelan, *Trade Unions in West Africa*, 145–78.

5. Gerard Griffin, "Australian Trade Unionism since 1945," in Phelan, *Trade Unionism since 1945* 2: 8–10; also, the essays in that volume on India, Korea, Indonesia, and Japan; Andrew Gordon, *The Wages of Affluence: Labor and Management in Postwar Japan* (Cambridge, MA: Harvard University Press, 1998), chaps. 1–2; Rohini Hensman, *Workers, Unions, and Global Capitalism: Lessons from India* (New York: Columbia University Press, 2011), 94–98; Bandyopadhyay, *Decolonization in South Asia*, 40–42.

6. Stephen J. Silva, *Holding the Shop Together: German Industrial Relations in the Postwar Era* (Ithaca, NY: ILR Press, 2013) chaps. 1–2; the relevant essays in Phelan, *Trade Unionism after 1945*; Ulrich Jürgens, Thomas Malsch, and Knuth Dohse, *Breaking from Taylorism: Changing Forms of Work in the Automobile Industry* (Cambridge: Cambridge University Press, 1993) 92–103; Steven Tolliday and Jonathan Zeitlin, "Shop-Floor Bargaining, Contract Unionism and Job Control: An Anglo-American Comparison," in *Between Fordism and Flexibility: The Automobile Industry and its Workers*, ed. Steven Tolliday and Jonathan Zeitlin (Oxford: Berg, 1992), 99–120.

7. Dinius, *Brazil's Steel City,* esp. chaps. 5, 7–8.

8. Cooper, *Decolonization and African Society*, chaps. 7–12; Fall, *Le Travail au Sénégal*,167–253; Hyde, "East African Railway Strike"; Elisabeth Schmidt, "Trade Unions and Nationalism in French Guinea, 1945–1958," in Phelan, *Trade Unions in West Africa*, 69–98.

9. Quote from Paul Kubicek, "Ukrainian Trade Unions since 1945," in Phelan, *Trade Unionism since 1945*, 1: 296. The essays in that volume on unions in Hungary and Poland, as well as those on Eastern Europe in Craig Phelan, ed., *Trade Union*

Revitalisation: Trends and Prospects in 34 Countries (Bern: Peter Lang, 2007) and, especially, Kott, *Communism Day-to-Day*.
10. Rebecca Gumbrell-McCormick and Richard Hyman, *Trade Unions in Western Europe: Hard Times, Hard Choices* (Oxford: Oxford University Press, 2013), 159; Cowrie, *The Great Exception*, 158–63; Freeman, *Working-Class New York*, chaps. 4–5.
11. Gordon, *Wages of Affluence*, chaps. 6–7; Debashish Bhattacherjee, "Trade Unions in India," in Phelan, *Trade Unionism after 1945*, 2: 62–67.
12. Brennan, *Footlose Labor*, 247; Hensman, *Workers, Unionos and Global Capitalism*, 99–101.
13. James P. Brennan, *The Labor Wars in Córdoba, 1955–1976: Ideology, Work and Labor Politics in an Argentine Industrial City* (Cambridge, MA: Harvard University Press, 1994), esp. chap. 5; Philippe Artières and Michelle Zancarini-Fournel, eds., *68 une histoire collective {1962–1981}* (Paris: Éditions La Découverte 2008), esp. pt. II; Sheila Cohen, "The 1968–1974 Labour Upsurge in Britain and America: A Critical History and a Look at what Might Have Been," *Labor History* 4 (2008): 395–416.
14. Cohen, "The 1968–1974 Labour Upsurge," 396; Máximos Algisakis, "Labour Disputes in Western Europe: Typology and Tendencies," *International Labour Review* 136 (1997): 73–94; cf. Therborn, *European Modernities*, 311–12; Freeman, *Working Class New* York, chaps. 11–14; Brennan, *Labor Wars in Cordoba*, chaps. 6–9; Bhattacherjee, "Trade Unions in India," in Phelan, *Trade Unionism after 1945*, 2:68–69.
15. Nicola Pizzolato, "Workers and Revolutionaries at the Twilight of Fordism: The Breakdown of Industrial Relations in the Automobile Plants of Detroit and Turin, 1967–1973," *Labor History* 45 (2004): 419–43; accessed Aug. 13, 2018, https://www.domid.org/de/news/der-ford-streik-%E2%80%93-40-jahre-danach; Cohen, "The 1968–1974 Labour Upsurge," 401; Anders Kjellberg, "The Swedish Model of Industrial Relations: Self-Regulation and Combined Centralisation-Decentralisation," in Phelan, *Trade Unionism since 1945*, 1:173.
16. Bruce E. Kaufman, "Prospects for Union Growth in the United States in the Early 21st Century," in *Unions in the 21st Century: An International Perspective*, ed. Anil Verma and Thomas A. Kochan (Houndmills, Basingstoke: Palgrave Macmillan, 2004), 46; Kjelberg, "The Swedish Model," in Phelan, *Trade Unionism since 1945*, 1:179; Randy Shaw, *Beyond the Fields: Cesar Chavez, the UFW and the Struggle for Justice in the 21st Century* (Berkeley: University of California Press, 2008).
17. Silva, *Holding the Shop Together*, 51–54, 73–75; Kjelberg, "The Swedish Model," as in the previous note; Valeria Pulignano, "An Historical Analysis of Trade Unionism in Italy: Between Pluralism of Ideas and Unity of Action," in Phelan, *Trade Unionism since 1945*, 1:101–11.
18. Silva, *Holding the Shop Together*, 119, 195.
19. Phelan, *Trade Unions in West Africa*; Gérard Kester and Akua O. Britwum, *Trade Unions and Workplace Democracy in Africa* (Aldershot: Ashgate. 2007), chap. 2, 137–38; Hyde, "East African Railway Strike," 86.
20. Caulfield, "Labor Relations in Mexico"; Graciela Bensusán, "Trade Unionism in Mexico: Current Situation and Obstacles to Renewal," in Phelan, *Trade Union Revival*, 76–78; Rainer Dombois, "The New International Division of Labour,

Labour Markets and Automobile Production: The Case of Mexico," in Tolliday and Zeitlin, *Between Fordism and Flexibility*, 244–57.
21. Essays on Japan, Korea, Indonesia, and India, in Phelan, *Trade Unionism since 1945*, vol. 2.
22. Politico, EU, "Economic Impact of Air Traffic Control Strikes in Europe," Sept. 2016, http://www.politico.eu/wp-content/uploads/2016/10/ATCimpactreport A4E.pdf, accessed July 2, 2018.
23. Joseph A. McCartin, *Collision Course: Ronald Reagan, the Air Traffic Controllers and the Strike that Changed America* (New York: Oxford University Press, 2011).
24. Stephen Franklin, *Three Strikes: Labor's Heartland Losses and What They Mean for Working Americans* (New York: The Guilford Press, 2001); Timothy Minchin, "Permanent Replacements and the Breakdown of the 'Social Accord' in Calera, Alabama, 1974–1999," *Labor History* 41 (2001): 371–96; idem., "'Labor's Empty Gun': Permanent Replacements and the International Paper Company Strike of 1987–88," *Labor History* 47 (2006): 21–42; Cowrie, *The Great Exception*, 203–4.
25. H. van Wersch, *The Bombay Textile Strike, 1982–1983* (Bombay: Oxford University Press, 1992); Hensman, *Workers, Unions and Global Capitalism*, 137–42; Saira Menezes, "A Fatal Strike," *The Outlook*, accessed July 9, 2018, https://www.outlo okindia.com/magazine/story/a-fatal-strike/202922.
26. Francis Beckett and David Hencke, *Marching to the Fault Line: The 1984 Miners' Strike and the Death of Industrial Britain* (London: Constable, 2009); Brian Harrison, *Finding a Role? The United Kingdom 1970–1990* (Oxford: Clarendon Press, 2009), 150–75; Peter Ackers, "Gramsci at the Miners' Strike: Remembering the 1984–1985 Eurocommunist Alternative Industrial Relations Strategy," *Labour History* 44 (2014): 151–72; Cohen, "The 1968–1974 Labour Upsurge," 406–7; Jim Phillips, *Collieries, Communities and the Miners' Strike in Scotland, 1984–85* (Manchester: Manchester University Press, 2012).
27. Anthony M. Gould, "The Americanisation of Australian Workplaces," *Labor History* 51 (2010): 363–88; Rice Cooper and Bradon Ellem, "'Less Than Zero': Union Recognition and Bargaining Rights in Australia, 1996–2007," *Labor History* 52 (2011): 49–69.
28. Mark Holstrom, *Industry and Inequality: The Social Anthropology of Indian Labour* (Cambridge: Cambridge University Press, 1984), 173, cf. 174–79.
29. Michael H. Belzer, *Sweatshops on Wheels: Winners and Losers in Trucking Deregulation* (New York: Oxford University Press, 2000); Shane Hamilton, *Trucking Country: The Road to America's Wal-Mart Economy* (Princeton, NJ: Princeton University Press, 2008).
30. Lawrence F. Katz and Alan B. Krueger, "The Rise and Nature of Alternative Work Arrangements in the United States, 1995–2015," National Bureau of Economic Research, accessed July 5, 2018, https://krueger.princeton.edu/sites/default/files/akrueger/files/katz_krueger_cws_-_march_29_20165.pdf; Deborah Goldschmidt and Johannes F. Schmieder, "The Rise of Domestic Outsourcing and the Evolution of the German Wage Structure," National Bureau of Economic Research, accessed July 5, 2018, http://www.nber.org/papers/w21366.pdf. More generally, Danny Vinik, "The Real Future of Work," *Politico*, Jan/Feb. 2018, https://www.politico.com/magazine/story/2018/01/04/future-work-independent-contractors-alternat

ive-work-arrangements-216212, accessed July 5, 2018; Uchitelle, *The Disposable American*.

31. Sources cited in chap. 7, n. 18–20; Eurofund, "Young People and Temporary Employment in Europe," 2013, https://www.eurofound.europa.eu/sites/default/files/ef_files/docs/erm/tn1304017s/tn1304017s.pdf, accessed July 9, 2018; David Karjanen, *The Servant Class City: Urban Revitalization versus the Working Poor in San Diego* (Minneapolis: University of Minnesota Press, 2016).
32. Akua Britwum, "Trade Unions and the Informal Economy in Ghana," in Phelan, *Trade Unions in West Africa*, 200–2; Kester and Britwum, *Trade Unions and Workplace Democracy*, 9–10; similarly, Fall, *Le Travail au Sénégal*, 274–77; Breman, *Footloose Labour*, 3–14.
33. Karjanen, *Servant Class City*, 133; Kester and Britwum, *Trade Unions and Workplace Democracy*, 90–92, 138–41.
34. Rebecca Gumbrell-McCormick and Richard Hyman, *Trade Unions in Western Europe: Hard Times, Hard Choices* (Oxford: Oxford University Press, 2013), 182–84.
35. Visser, "Union Membership Statistics in 24 Countries," Blanchflower, "International Patterns of Union Membership."
36. Sources for Figure 8.1: Gerald Mayer, "Union Membership Trends in the United States,' Cornell University, ILR School, accessed July 10, 2018, https://digitalcommons.ilr.cornell.edu/cgi/viewcontent.cgi?article=1176&context=key_workplace; Gerald Friedman, "U.S. Historical Statistics: New Estimates of Union Membership the United States, 1880–1914," *Historical Methods* 32 (2010): 75–86; Hagen Lesch, "Trade Union Density in International Comparison," accessed July 10, 2018, http://www.cesifo-group.de/DocDL/forum4-04-special-lesch.pdf; Bernhard Ebbinghaus and Jelle Visser, "When Institutions Matter: Union Growth and Decline in Western Europe, 1950–1955," *European Sociological Review* 15 (1999): 135–58; Maurizio Atzeni and Pablo Ghigliani, "The Labour Movement in Argentina since 1945," in Phelan, *Trade Unionism since 1945* 2:333; Josef Mooser, *Arbeiterleben in Deutschland 1900–1970* (Frankfurt: Suhrkamp, 1984), 192; ILO union density statistics, 2014–16, http://www.ilo.org/ilostat/faces/oracle/webcenter/portalapp/pagehierarchy/Page27.jspx?subject=IR&indicator=ILR_TUMT_NOC_RT&datasetCode=A&collectionCode=IR&_afrLoop=346824594105941&_afrWindowMode=0&_afrWindowId=bjl2hebip_1#!%40%40%3Findicator%3DILR_TUMT_NOC_RT%26_afrWindowId%3Dbjl2hebip_1%26subject%3DIR%26_afrLoop%3D346824594105941%26datasetCode%3DA%26collectionCode%3DIR%26_afrWindowMode%3D0%26_adf.ctrl-state%3Dbjl2hebip_45, accessed July 11, 2018. Post-1945 Germany is the Federal Republic; figures do not include the GDR.
37. Union density statistics for over sixty countries, 2004–16 as in the previous note.
38. Essays on the relevant countries in Phelan, *Trade Union Revitalization*; David Ost, *The Defeat of Solidarity: Anger and Politics in Postcommunist Europe* (Ithaca, NY: Cornell University press, 2005).
39. Nelson Lichtenstein, *The Retail Revolution: How Wal-Mart Created a Brave New World of Business* (New York: Henry Holt and Company, 2009), 198–201.
40. Mary Elizabeth Gallagher, *Contagious Capitalism: Globalization and the Politics of Labor in China* (Princeton, NJ: Princeton University Press, 2005), 93 and chap. 4;

cf. Bill Taylor and Qi Li, "China's Creative Approach to 'Union' Organizing," *Labor History* 51 (2010): 411–28.
41. Britwum, "Trade Unions and the Informal Economy," in Phelan, *Trade Unions in West Africa*; Hensman, *Workers, Unions and Global Capitalism*, 205–6.
42. Gay W. Seidman, *Manufacturing Militance: Workers' Movements in Brazil and South Africa* (Berkeley: University of California Press, 1994).
43. Craig Phelan, "Trade Unions, Democratic Waves and Structural Adjustments: The Case of Francophone West Africa," *Labor History* 52 (2011): 461–81; Phelan, *Trade Unions in West Africa*; Kester, *Trade Unions and Workplace Democracy*, chaps. 6–9; essays on unions in India, Japan, Korea, and Indonesia in Phelan, *Trade Union Revitalisation*; Mari Miura, "Labor Politics in Japan during the 'Lost Fifteen Years': From the Politics of Productivity to the Politics of Consumption," *Labor History* 49 (2008): 161–76; Piya Pangsapa, *The Textures of Struggle: The Emergence of Resistance among Garment Workers in Thailand* (Ithaca, NY: ILR Press, 2007).
44. Quote from Timothy Minchin, "Shutting Down 'Big Brown': Reassessing the 1998 UPS Strike and the Fate of American Labor," *Labor History* 53 (2012): 541–60, on 544. On efforts at union revival, Ruth Milkman, *L.A. Story: Immigrant Workers and the Future of the U.S. Labor Movement* (New York: Russell Sage Foundation, 2006); Verma and Kochan, *Unions in the 21st Century*; Gumbrell-McCormick and Hyman, *Trade Unions in Western Europe*; Daniel B. Cornfield and Holly J. McCammon, eds., *Labor Revitalization: Global Perspectives and New Initiatives* (Amsterdam: Elsevier, 2003); Silva, *Holding the Shop Together*, 167–68; Andy Danford, Mike Richardson, and Martin Upchurch, *New Unions, New Workplaces: A Study of Union Resilience in the Restructured Workplace* (London: Routledge, 2003), John Salmon, "Union Organising: The Case of Japan," in Phelan, *Trade Union Revitalization*, 514–17, and other essays in that volume; Timothy Minchin, "'Labor Is back?': The AFL-CIO during the Presidency of J. Sweeney, 1995–2009," *Labor History* 54 (2013): 393–420.
45. Sources for Table 8.2, Lesch, "Trade Union Density," Table 3; *ILO Yearbook of Labour Statistics:* 15 (1955) Tables 4 and 36; 21 (1961): Table 31; 22 (1962): Table 4; 28 (1968): Tables 2 and 27; 35 (1975): Tables 2 and 27.
46. Sources for Table 8.3: *ILO Yearbook of Labour Statistics* 15 (1955): Tables 4 and 36; 21 (1961), Table 31; 22 (1962): Table 4; 28 (1968): Table 27; 35 (1975) Tables 2 and 27; 40 (1980): Table 30; 44 (1984): Table 30; 48 (1988): Table 28; 54 (1994): Table 31; 58 (1998): Table 2A; 2009: 127. Figures for the 1950s in Ghana and Kenya are for 1955–60.
47. L.J. Perry and Patrick J. Wilson, "Trends in Work Stoppages: A Global Perspective," ILO Working Paper No. 47, accessed Aug. 10, 2018, http://www.ilo.org/public/libdoc/ilo/2004/104B09_444_engl.pdf. This paper is also very informative about the quality and availability of national strike statistics.
48. Silva, *Holding the Shop Together*, 142–57; Cowrie, *The Great Exception*, 204–19; Danford, Richardson, and Upchurch, *New Unions, New Workplaces*, 7–8, 144–45.
49. Phelan, "Trade Unions of Francophone West Africa," 468; Blanchflower, "International Patterns of Union Membership" 6; Bhattacherchee, "Trade Unions in India," in Phelan, *Trade Unionism since 1945*, 2:89; Phelan, "Introduction," in ibid., 2:xi.

50. Roland Erne, *European Unions: Labor's Quest for a Transnational Democracy* (Ithaca, NY: ILR Press, 2008); Hensford, *Workers, Unions and Global Capitalism*, 281–319.
51. Sam Davies et al., eds., *Dock Workers: International Explorations in Comparative Labour History, 1790—1970.* 2 vols. (Aldershot: Ashgate, 2000).
52. Levinson, *The Box*; William Finlay, *Work on the Waterfront: Worker Power and Technological Change in a West Coast Port* (Philadelphia: Temple University Press, 1988).
53. William DiFazio, *Longshoremen: Community and Resistance on the Brooklyn Waterfront* (South Hadley, MA: Bergin & Garvey, 1985); Brian Marren, "The Liverpool Dock Strike, 1995–98: A Resurgence of Solidarity in the Age of Globalisation," *Labor History* 57 (2016): 463–81.
54. On the origins and development of this "Fordist" system of auto manufacturing, Zeitlin and Halliday, *Between Fordism and Flexibility*, Part One.
55. John Humphrey, *Capitalist Control and Workers' Struggle in the Brazilian Auto Industry* (Princeton, NJ: Princeton University Press, 1982), 56; Jürgens, Malsch, and Dohse, *Breaking from Taylorism*, 63–82; Laurie Graham, *On the Line at Subaru-Isuzu: The Japanese Model and the American Worker* (Ithaca, NY: ILR Press, 1995), 62–64, 71–76; Ruth Milkman, *Farewell to the Factory: Auto Workers in the Late Twentieth Century* (Berkeley: University of California Press, 1997), chap. 2.
56. Gordon, *Wages of Affluence*, 78–79, 167–73.
57. Jürgens, Malsch, and Dohse, *Breaking from Taylorism*, chaps. 10–11 and passim; Tolliday and Zeitlin, *Between Taylorism and Flexibility*, Part Three; Danford, Richardson, and Upchurch, *New Unions, New Workplaces*, 81–86.
58. Giovannia Contini, "The Rise and Fall of Shop-Floor Bargaining at Fiat 1945–80," in Tolliday and Zeitlin, *Between Fordism and Flexibility*, 144–67.
59. Graham, *On the Line*; Timothy Minchin, "'The Assembly Line and Cars Come First': Labor Relations and the Demise of Nissan Car Manufacturing in Australia," *Labor History* 48 (2007): 327–46; Jürgens, Malsch, and Dohse, *Breaking from Taylorism*, Rieko Okayama, "Industrial Relations in the Japanese Automobile Industry, 1945–1970: The Case of Toyota," in Tolliday and Zeitlin, *Between Fordism and Flexibility*, 168–88.
60. Claas Tatje, "Sein Werk," *Die Zeit*, July 5, 2018, 23–24.
61. Kathleen M. Barry, *Femininity in Flight: A History of Flight Attendants* (Durham, NC: Duke University Press, 2007); Arlie Russell Hochschild, *The Managed Heart: Commercialization of Human Feeling* (Berkeley: University of California Press, 1983), esp. chap. 6; Valerie Vantoch, *The Jet Sex: Airline Stewardesses and the Making of an American Icon* (Philadelphia: University of Pennsylvania Press, 2013).
62. Drew Whitelegg, *Working the Skies: The Fast-Paced, Disorienting World of the Flight Attendants* (New York: New York University Press, 2007), 135–39.
63. Sandra L. Albrecht, "'We Are on Strike!' The Development of Labor Militancy in the Airline Industry," *Labor History* 45 (2004): 101–17; Drew Whitlegg, "Touching Down: Labour Globalisation and the Airline Industry," *Antipode* 35 (2003): 244–63; Barry, *Femininity in Flight*, 215–16; cf. Silva, *Holding the Shop Together*, 164.
64. Whitlegg, *Working the Skies*, is an excellent portrait of the occupation at the beginning of the new millennium.

65. Michael Sean Mahoney, *Histories of Computing*, ed. Thomas Haigh. (Cambridge, MA: Harvard University Press, 2011), 21–117, quote on 103.
66. Mary Lacity and Leslie Willcocks, *Global Information Technology Outsourcing: In Search of Business Advantage* (Chichester: John Wiley & Sons, 2001); Stephen Weiner and Kirsten Meyer, "The Evolution of IT Outsourcing: From its Origins to Current and Future Trends," Arbeitspapiere des Fachbereichs Wirtschafts- und Sozialwissenschaft der Universität Wuppertal, Nr. 202, http://elpub.bib.uni-wuppertal.de/edocs/dokumente/fbb/wirtschaftswissenschaft/arbeitspapiere/202/ab0501.pdf, accessed July 20, 2018.
67. Mary Lacity and Joseph W. Rottman, *Offshore Outsourcing of IT Work: Client and Supplier Perspectives* (Houndmills, Basingstoke: Palgrave Macmillan, 2008).
68. Norman Matloff, "On the Need for Reform of the H-1B Non-Immigrant Work Visa in Computer-Related Occupations," *Michigan Law Review* 36 (2003): 1–99, esp. 29, 65–66, 79–80.
69. Steven Greenhouse, "Temp Workers at Microsoft Win Lawsuit," *New York Times*, Dec. 13, 2000, https://www.nytimes.com/2000/12/13/business/technology-temp-workers-at-microsoft-win-lawsuit.html; Brigid Schulte, "From the Ranks of Microsoft's Permatemps," *Washington Post*, Mar. 28, 2015, https://www.washingtonpost.com/local/from-the-ranks-of-microsofts-permatemps/2015/03/27/64f5c922-cb5d-11e4-8c54-ffb5ba6f2f69_story.html?utm_term=.4c76c07e5c61, both accessed July 20, 2018; Katz and Kruger, "The Rise and Nature of Alternative Work Arrangements," Table 4.

Chapter 9

1. Gershuny, *Changing Times: Work and Leisure in Postindustrial Society* (Oxford: Oxford University Press, 1999).
2. Ibid.; and Mark Aguiar and Eric Hurst, "Measuring Trends in Leisure: The Allocation of Time Over Five Decades," NBER Working Paper 12082, accessed Sept. 24, 2018, http://www.nber.org/papers/w12082.pdf.
3. Valerie Ramey, "Time Spent in Home Production in the Twentieth-Century United States: New Estimates from Old Data," *Journal of Economic History* 69 (2009): 1–47; similar observations for other countries in Gershuny, *Changing Times*, 65–67, 127–28, 130.
4. Alberto Alesina, Eduard Glaeser, and Bruce Sacerdote, "Work and Leisure in the United States and Europe: Why So Different?," *NBER Microeconomics Annual*, 2005, accessed Sept. 25, 2018, http://www.nber.org/papers/w12082.pdf.
5. Gershuny, *Changing Times*, Table 7.10.
6. Gershuny, *Changing Times*, 267–69; Trentmann, *Empire of Things*, 457–58; Avner Offer, *The Challenge of Affluence: Self-Control and Well-Being in the United States and Britain since 1950* (Oxford: Oxford University Press, 2006), 181–84; James Lull, ed., *World Families Watch Television* (Newbury Park, CA: SAGE Publications, 1988).
7. For this and other general assertions about television, Anthony Smith, ed., *Television: An International History* (Oxford: Oxford University Press, 1995); Gary Edgerton et al., *The Columbia History of American Television* (New York: Columbia University Press, 2007); Monique Sauvage, Isabelle Veyrat-Masson, and Géraldine Peols, *Histoire de la télévision française de 1935 à nos jours* (Paris: Nouveau monde

éditions, 2012); Christine E. Evans, *Between Truth and Time: A History of Soviet Central Television* (New Haven, CT: Yale University Press, 2016).
8. Sources cited in previous and Yeidy M. Rivero, *Broadcasting Modernity: Cuban Commercial Television, 1950—1960* (Durham, NC: Duke University Press, 2015).
9. Sources in nn. 7–8, and Rommani Sen Shitak, "Television and Development Communication in India: A Critical Appraisal," *Global Media Journal* 2 (2011): 1–26.
10. Quoted in Simon Partner, *Assembled in Japan: Electrical Goods and the Making of the Japanese Consumer* (Berkeley: University of California Press, 1999), 82 and chap. 3 more generally.
11. Offner, *Challenge of Affluence*, 173–78; Isabelle Gaillard, "Selling Televisions on Credit: The Rise of Consumer Loans in Postwar France," in *The Development of Consumer Credit in Global Perspective*, ed. Jan Logemann (New York: Palgrave McMillan, 2012), 30; Andrew Gordon, "Credit in a Nation of Savers: The Growth of Consumer Borrowing in Japan," idem., 71; Kirstin Roth-Ey, *Moscow Prime Time: How the Soviet Union Built the Media Empire that Lost the Cultural Cold War* (Ithaca: Cornell University Press, 2011), 182–85; Gerard J. Tellis, Stefan Stremersch, and Eden Yin, "The International Takeoff of New Products: The Role of Economics, Culture, and Country Innovativeness," *Marketing Science* 22 (2003): 188–208.
12. Hidetoshi Kato, "Japan," in Smith, *Television*, 290.
13. Laurence Simmons, "Television Then," in *Television in New Zealand: Programming the Nation*, ed. Roger Horrocks and Nicky Perry (Melbourne: Oxford University Press, 2004), 44.
14. Quoted in Suvage, Veyrat-Masson, and Peols, *Histoire de la television française*, 51.
15. Synthesizing this approach, James Shanahan and Michael Morgan, *Television and Its Viewers: Cultivation Theory and Research* (Cambridge: Cambridge University Press, 1999).
16. Eliana La Ferrara, Alberto Chong, and Suzanne Duryea, "Soap Operas and Fertility: Evidence from Brazil," *American Economic Journal: Applied Economics* 4 (2012): 1–31.
17. Edgerton et al., *Columbia History of American Television*, 148–52.
18. Artières and Zancarini-Fournel, 68, 257; Sauvage, Veyrat-Masson, and Poels, *Histoire de la television française*, 89–93.
19. Paulina Bren, *The Greengrocer and His TV: The Culture of Communism after the 1968 Prague Spring* (Ithaca, NY: Cornell University Press, 2010), esp. chap. 6.
20. Marshal McLuhan, *The Gutenberg Galaxy: The Making of Typographic Man* (Toronto, Canada: University of Toronto Press, 1962), 31; Tapio Varis, "The International Flow of Television Programs," UNESCO, 1985, accessed Oct. 8, 2018. http://unesdoc.unesco.org/images/0006/000687/068746eo.pdf.
21. Roth, *Moscow Prime Time*, 183.
22. International Telecommunications Union, "World Telecommunication/ICT Indicators database," 2018, accessed Sept. 20, 2018, https://www.itu.int/en/ITU-D/Statistics/Pages/publications/wtid.aspx.

23. The availability of additional Ultra High Frequency channels potentially increased the number of stations, but special television receivers were needed and the picture quality of UHF broadcasts was poor.
24. For this and the following, besides the sources cited in n. 7, Kenny Segrave, *American Television Abroad: Hollywood's Attempt to Dominate World Television* (Jefferson, NC: McFarland & Company, 1998); Denise Bielby and C. Lee Harrington, *Global TV: Exporting Television and Culture in the World Market* (New York: New York University Press, 2008); Timothy Havens, *Global Television Marketplace* (London: British Film Institute, 2006); Dal Yong Jin, *De-Convergence of Global Media Industries* (London: Routledge, 2013).
25. Timothy Havens, *Black Television Travels: African American Media around the Globe* (New York: New York University Press, 2013), 47–50.
26. John Wigger, *PTL: The Rise and Fall of Jim and Tammy Faye Bakker's Evangelical Empire* (New York: Oxford University Press, 2017), 45–50 and passim.
27. Andrew C. McKevitt, *Consuming Japan: Popular Culture and the Globalizing of 1980s America* (Chapel Hill: The University of North Carolina Press, 2017), chap. 5.
28. Jin, *De-Convergence*, 39 and, more generally, chap. 3.
29. Horrocks, "The History of New Zealand Television: 'An Expensive Medium for a Small Country,'" in *Television in New Zealand*, ed. Horrocks and Perry, chap. 2; Havens, *Global Television Marketplace*, 28, 33–34.
30. Havens, *Global Television Marketplace*, 34–35; Bielby and Harrington, *Global TV*, 50–52.
31. Havens, *Black Television Travels*, 102–9, 128–32.
32. Bielby and Harrington, *Global TV*, 112–15.
33. Preben Sestrup and Anura Goonasekera, "TV Transnationalization: Europe and Asia," UNESCO, "Reports and Papers on Mass Communications," No. 109, 1994, accessed Sept. 6, 2018, http://unesdoc.unesco.org/images/0009/000972/097211eo.pdf, Tables 11 and 49 and passim.
34. Jin, *De-Convergence*, is good on recent media developments.
35. Shanahan and Morgan, *Television and Its Viewers*, 201–19.
36. Graham Dann, "Writing Out the Tourist in Space and Time," *Annals of Tourism Research* 26 (1999): 159–87; Jens Kristian Steen Jacobsen, "Anti-Tourist Attitudes: Mediterranean Charter Tourism." *Annals of Tourism Research* 27 (2000): 284–300.
37. Three sociological/anthropological reflections on tourism and criticisms of tourism are Dean MacCannell, *The Tourist: A New Theory of the Leisure Class*, 2nd ed. (Berkeley: University of California Press, 1999); John Urry, *The Tourist Gaze: Leisure and Travel in Contemporary Societies* (London: SAGE Publications, 1990); Orvar Löfgren, *On Holiday: A History of Vacationing* (Berkeley: University of California Press, 1999).
38. Quoted in John Brohman, "New Directions in Tourist for Third World Development," *Annals of Tourism Research* 23 (1996): 48–70, here on 59 and Urry, *The Tourist Gaze*, unpaginated initial epigraphs.
39. http://www2.unwto.org/content/why-tourism, accessed Nov. 27, 2018; William A. Douglas andREFC REFO:JARTPaulina Raento, "The Tradition of Invention: Conceiving Las Vegas," *Annals of Tourism Research* 31 (2004): 7–23;

Yvette Reisinger and Carol J. Steiner, "Reconceptualizing Object Authenticity," *Annals of Tourism Research* 33 (2006): 65–86.

40. Christopher M. Kopper, "The Breakthrough of the Package Tour in Germany after 1945," *Journal of Tourism History* 1 (2009): 67–92; Victoria De Grazia, *The Culture of Consent: Mass Organization of Leisure in Fascist Italy* (New York: Cambridge University Press, 1981); Diane Koenker, *Club Red: Vacation Travel and the Soviet Dream* (Ithaca, NY: Cornell University Press, 2013), chaps. 1–3; Hal Rothman, *Devil's Bargains: Tourism in the Twentieth-Century American West* (Lawrence: University Press of Kansas, 1998), chap. 6; Susan Rugh, *Are We There Yet? The Gold Age of American Family Vacations* (Lawrence: University Press of Kansas, 2008), esp. chap. 6; Eduardo Elena, *Dignifying Argentina: Peronism, Citizenship and Mass Consumption* (Pittsburgh, PA: University of Pittsburgh Press, 2011), 133–34.
41. Rugh, *Are We There Yet?*; Marty Levenstein, *We Always Have Paris: American Tourists in France since 1930* (Chicago: University of Chicago Press, 2004).
42. Urry, *Tourist Gaze*, 36–37; Löfrgen, *On Holiday*, 244-48; Kopper, "Package Tour"; Ellen Furlough, "Packaging Pleasures: Club Méditerranée and French Consumer Culture, 1950–1968," *French Historical Studies* 18 (1993): 65–81; Rugh, *Are We There Yet?*, 172 and passim.
43. Ellen Furlough and Rosemary Wakeman, "Composing a Landscape: Coastal Mass Tourism and Regional Development in the Languedoc, 1960s–1980s," *International Journal of Maritime History* 9(1997): 187–211; Sina Fabian, *Boom in der Krise. Konsum, Tourismus, Autofahren in Westdeutschland und Großbritannien 1970–1990* (Göttingen: Wallstein Verlag, 2016), chap. 3.
44. Kopper, "Package Tour," 78–82.
45. Ibid., 78–82; Jan Vidar Haukeland, "Non Travelers: The Flip Side of Motivation," *Annals of Tourism Research* 17 (1990): 172–84.
46. Christopher End, *Cold War Holidays: American Tourism in France* (Chapel Hill: University of North Carolina Press, 2004), 135–36.
47. David Wilson, "Paradoxes of Tourism in Goa," *Annals of Tourism Research* 24 (1997): 52–75; Richard Ivan Jobs, *Backpack Ambassadors: How Youth Travel Integrated Europe* (Chicago: University of Chicago Press, 2017).
48. Mark Liechty, *Far Out: Countercultural Seekers and the Tourist Encounter in Nepal* (Chicago: University of Chicago Press, 2017), Parts 1–2.
49. On communist vacations, Koenker, *Club Red*; Christopher Görlich, *Urlaub vom Staat: Tourismus in der DDR* (Cologne: Böhlau, 2012).
50. Koener, *Club Red*, 195–200.
51. Sina, *Boom in der Krise*, 237–46.
52. Koenker, *Club Red*, 186; Raymond Patton, *Punk Crisis: The Global Punk Rock Revolution* (New York: Oxford University Press, 2018), 22–27.
53. See sources cited in n. 49 and Peter J. Buckley and Stephen F. Witt, "Tourism in the Centrally Planned Economies of Europe," *Annals of Tourism Research* 17 (1990): 7–18; Vaněk and Mücke, *Velvet Revolutions*, 161–67.
54. World Tourism Organization, *Tourism Market Trends: Asia and the Pacific* (Madrid: World Tourism Organization, 2002), Part III; David Lehany, "A Political Economy of Asian Sex Tourism," *Annals of Tourism Research* 22 (1995): 367–84;

Hamzzh Muzaini, "Backpacking Southeast Asia: Strategies of 'Looking Local,'" *Annals of Tourism Research* 33 (2006): 144–61.

55. Trevor H.B. Sofield and Fun Mei Sarah Li, "Tourism Development and Cultural Policies in China," *Annals of Tourism Research* 25 (1998): 362–92; Bihu Wu and Liping A. Cai, "Spatial Modeling: Suburban Leisure in Shanghai," *Annals of Tourism Research* 33 (2007): 179–98; Didi Tatlow, "For Many Chinese, Scant Time for Holidays," *New York Times*, Sept. 11, 2015; Sally Peck, "The Truth about Chinese Travelers," *Daily Telegraph*, July 25, 2017, https://www.telegraph.co.uk/travel/destinations/asia/china/how-chinese-tourists-travel-etiquette-and-money/, accessed Dec. 7, 2018.

56. UNTWO, *Tourism Highlights 2017 Edition*, 15, https://www.e-unwto.org/doi/pdf/10.18111/9789284419029, accessed Nov. 28, 2018, and *Tourism Market Trends*, iii.

57. Löfrgen, *On Holiday*, 155–209; Armando Montinari, "The Mediterranean Region: Europe's Summer Leisure Space," in *European Tourism: Regions, Spaces and Restructuring*, ed. Armando Montinari and Allan Williams (Chicester: John Wiley & Sons, 1995), 41–65.

58. Reiner Jackson, "Beyond the Tourist Bubble: Cruiseship Passengers in Port," *Annals of Tourism Research* 31 (2004): 44–60; Adam Weaver, "The McDonaldization Thesis and Cruise Tourism," *Annals of Tourism Research* 32 (2005): 346–66.

59. Lehany, "A Political Economy of Asian Sex Tourism," and, especially, the very informative Erica Lorraine Williams, *Sex Tourism in Bahia: Ambiguous Entanglements* (Urbana: University of Illinois Press, 2013), 68–69 and passim.

60. Edward Herold, Rafael Garcia, and Tony DeMoya, "Female Tourists and Beach Boys: Romance or Sex Tourism?" *Annals of Tourism Research* 28 (2001): 978–97; Williams, *Sex Tourism*, 19–21; similarly Heidi Dahles and Karin Bras, "Entrepreneurs in Romance: Tourism in Indonesia," *Annals of Tourism Research* 26 (1999): 267–93.

61. Glen T. Hvenegaard and Philip Dearden, "Ecotourism versus Tourism in a Thai National Park," *Annals of Tourism Research* 25 (1998): 700–29; David B. Weaver, "Magnitude of Ecotourism in Costa Rica and Kenya," *Annals of Tourism Research* 26 (1999): 792–816.

62. Liechty, *Far Out*, Part Three. Thanks to my colleague Catherine Rymph for an informative account of trekking in Nepal at the very end of the twentieth century.

63. Ibid.; and Barbara Johnson and Ted Edwards, "The Commodification of Mountaineering," *Annals of Tourism Research* 21 (1994): 459–78.

64. On problems of tourist statistics, William F. Theobald, "The Meaning, Scope and Measurement of Travel and Tourism," in *Global Tourism*, 3rd ed., ed. William Theobald (Amsterdam: Elsevier, 2005), 5–24; Buckley and Witt, "Tourism in the Centrally Planned Economies," esp. Table 1. Sources for Figure 9.1 are in Theobald, "Meaning Scope and Measurement," 6 and UNWTO, "Tourism Highlights," 2017 edition, 4, https://www.e-unwto.org/doi/pdf/10.18111/9789284419029, accessed Nov. 28, 2018.

65. Levenstein, *We'll Always Have Paris*, 266; Mitchell Hartman, "The Middle-Class American Vacation: A History," https://www.marketplace.org/2016/07/22/world/

middle-class-american-vacation-history; http://time.com/3892635/vacation-charts/, both accessed Jan. 13, 2019.
66. UNWTO, "European Union Tourism Trends," 33, 74, https://www.e-unwto.org/doi/pdf/10.18111/9789284419470, accessed Jan. 3, 2019.
67. Ibid., 92; Project Time Off, "State of American Vacation, 2018," https://projecttimeoff.com/wp-content/uploads/2018/05/StateofAmericanVacation2018.pdf; Lydia Saad, "Majority of Americans Plan to Vacation this Summer," Gallup, May 31, 2002, https://news.gallup.com/poll/6112/majority-americans-plan-vacation-summer.aspx, both accessed Jan. 4, 2019; "56% of Americans Haven't Taken a Vacation in a Year," *Money*, Aug. 17, 2015, http://time.com/money/4000332/take-a-vacation-now/, accessed Jan. 7, 2019.
68. "The Sad Reason Half of Americans Don't Take All Their Paid Vacation," *Marketwatch*, May 28, 2017, https://www.marketwatch.com/story/55-of-american-workers-dont-take-all-their-paid-vacation-2016-06-15, accessed Jan. 7, 2019.

Chapter 10

1. On critics and proponents of consumerism, Daniel Horowitz, *The Anxieties of Affluence: Critiques of American Consumer Culture, 1939–1979* (Amherst: University of Massachusetts Press, 2004).
2. A recent study of Engel's law in a global context is E.A. Selvanathan and S. Selvanathan, *International Consumption Comparisons: OECD versus LDC* (Singapore: World Scientific Publishing, 2003).
3. On the history of consumerism, more generally, Trentmann, *Empire of Things*, esp. pt. 1; id., "The Modern Genealogy of the Consumer," *Consuming Cultures, Global Perspectives*, ed. John Brewer and Fran Trentmann (Oxford: Berg, 2006), 19–69; Peter Stearns, *Consumerism in World History: The Global Transformation of Desire* (London: Routledge, 2001).
4. Stefan Rinke, *Begegnungen mit dem Yankee: Nordamerikanisierung und soziokultureller Wandel in Chile (1898–1990)* (Cologne: Böhlau Verlag, 2004), 110–19; Frank Dikötter, *Exotic Commodities: Modern Objects and Everyday Life in China* (New York: Columbia University Press, 2006).
5. Victoria de Grazia, *Irresistible Empire: America's Advance through Twentieth-Century Europe* (Cambridge, MA: Harvard University Press, 2005), 78–103.
6. Rebecca Pulju, *Women and Mass Consumer Society in Postwar France* (New York: Cambridge University Press, 2011), 39–49; Lizabeth Cohen, *A Consumers' Republic: The Politics of Mass Consumption in Postwar America* (New York: Alfred A. Knopf, 2003), 100–9.
7. Cohen, *Consumers' Republic*, chaps. 4–6; Alison Clarke, *Tupperware: The Promise of Plastic in 1950s America* (Washington, DC: Smithsonian Institution 1999).
8. Partner, *Assembled in Japan*, 149–77; Pulju, *Women and Mass Consumer Society*, 174–76; Niklaus Jungwith and Gerhard Kromschröder, *Die Pubertät der Republik: Die 50er Jahre der Deutschen* (Frankfurt: Dieter Fricke, 1978), 64.
9. Sperber, "17 June 1953," esp. 634–35, 639.
10. Elena, *Dignifying Argentina*.
11. Clarke, *Tupperware*, 188–92.

12. Pulju, *Women and Mass Consumer Society*, 177; Jennifer Loehlin, *From Rugs to Riches: Housework, Consumption and Modernity in Germany* (Oxford: Berg, 1999), 70; Ralph Jessen and Lydia Langer (eds.), *Transformations of Retailing in Europe after 1945* (Farnham: Ashgate, 2012); Kaelble, *A Social History of Europe*, 62–85; Therborn, *European Modernity*, 139–46; Paulina Bren and Mary Neuburger, eds., *Communism Unwrapped: Consumption in Cold War Eastern Europe* (New York: Oxford University Press, 2012), 3–19 and more generally.
13. De Grazia, *Irresistible Empire*, chap. 5; T.J. Jackson Lears, *Fables of Abundance: A Cultural History of Advertising in America* (New York: Basic Books, 1994); Timothy Burke, *Lifebuoy Men, Lux Women: Commodification, Consumption and Cleanliness in Modern Zimbabwe* (Durham, NC: Duke University Press, 1996)
14. Trentmann, *Empire of Things*, 317–20; Partner, *Assembled in Japan*, 126–32; De Grazia, *Irresistible Empire*, 422–23; http://galbithink.org/cs-ad-dataset.xls, accessed Mar. 25, 2019; Jennifer Loehlin, *From Rugs to Riches: Housework, Consumption and Modernity in Germany* (Oxford: Berg, 1999), chap. 4.
15. Stefan Schwarzkopf, "Managing the Unmanageable: The Professionalization of Market and Consumer Research in Post-War Europe," in Jessen and Langer, *Transformations of Retailing*, 163–78; Horowitz, *Anxieties of Affluence*, chap. 2.
16. Jonathan Sperber, *Property and Civil Society in Southwestern Germany 1820–1914* (Oxford: Oxford University Press, 2005): Margot Finn, *The Character of Credit: Personal Debt in English Culture, 1790–1914* (Cambridge: Cambridge University Press, 2003); Edward Belleisen, *Negotiating Failure: Bankruptcy and Commercial Society in Antebellum America* (Chapel Hill: University of North Carolina Press, 2001); Mischa Suter, "Debt and Its Attachments: Collateral as an Object of Knowledge in Nineteenth-Century Liberalism," *Comparative Studies in Society and History* 59 (2017): 715–42; Robert D. Manning, *Credit Card Nation: The Consequences of America's Addiction to Credit* (New York: Basic Books, 2000), 107–8.
17. De Grazia, *Invisible Empire*, 381–415; Emanuela Scarpellini, "The Long Way to the Supermarket: Entrepreneurial Innovation and Adaptation in 1950s–1960s Italy," in Jessen and Langer, *Transformations of Retailing*, 55–69.
18. Isabelle Gaillard, "Selling Televisions on Credit: The Rise of Consumer Loans in Postwar France," and Rebecca Belvedersi-Kochs, "Moral or Modern Marketing? *Sparkassen* and Consumer Credit in West Germany," both in Logemanm, *The Development of Consumer Credit* 23–40 and 41–81, respectively.
19. Andrew Gordon, "Credit in a Nation of Savers: The Growth of Consumer Borrowing in Japan," in ibid., 63–81; Sean O'Connell, "Business of Working-Class Credit: Subprime Markets in the United Kingdom since 1880," ibid., 85–107; Avram Taylor, *Working Class Credit and Community since 1918* (Houndmills, Basingstoke: Palgrave Macmillan, 2002). Chap. 4; Manning, *Credit Card Nation*, 83, 108.
20. Loehlin, *Rugs to Riches*, 69; Fabian, *Boom in der Krise*, 100.
21. https://www.pgpf.org/chart-archive/0078_Savings-Rate; https://data.worldbank.org/indicator/ny.gds.totl.zs; https://data.oecd.org/hha/household-savings.htm; https://fred.stlouisfed.org/series/PSAVERT, all accessed Mar. 28, 2019. Cf. Trentmann, *Empire of Things*, 417–22.

22. Òscar Jordà, Moritz Schularick, and Alan M. Taylor, "The Great Mortgaging: Housing Finance, Crises, And Business Cycles," NBER Working Paper 20501, 2014, http://www.nber.org/papers/w20501, accessed Jan. 24, 2019.
23. Massimo Florio, *The Great Divestiture: Evaluating the Welfare Impact of the British Privatizations, 1979–1997* (Cambridge, MA: MIT Press, 2004), 36;https://fred.stlouisfed.org/series/FYONGDA188S and https://data.oecd.org/gga/general-government-spending.htm,both accessed Mar. 28, 2019; cf. Trentmann, *Empire of Things*, 536–40; chap. 7, n. 37.
24. Guy Debord, *The Society of the Spectacle* (New York: Zone Books, 1995) [French original, published in 1967]; Herbert Marcuse, *One Dimensional Man: Studies in the Ideology of Advanced Industrial Society* (Boston: Beacon Press, 1964); similar examples from Italy in Emanuela Scarpellini, *Material Nation: A Consumer's History of Modern Italy.* Trans. Daphne Hughes and Andrew Newton (Oxford: Oxford University Press, 2011), 219–21.
25. Timothy Scott Brown, *West Germany and the Global Sixties: The Antiauthoritarian Revolt, 1962—1978* (New York: Cambridge University Press, 2013), 55–56, 79–80; also, Trentmann, *Empire of Things*, 321–22.
26. Quoted in Sabin, *The Bet*, 101; more broadly, 99–102.
27. Trentmann, *Empire of Things*, 323–24; chap. 7 nn. 33–35.
28. Tamas Dombos and Lena Pellandini-Simanyi, "Kids, Cars, or Cashews? Debating and Remembering Consumption in Socialist Hungary," in Bren and Neuberger, *Communism Unwrapped*, 325–50; György Péteri, "Introduction," in Péteri, *Imagining the West*, 9.
29. Partner, *Assembled in Japan*, 141, also, 142; Cohen, *Consumers' Republic*, chap. 8; Matthew Hilton, "Consumer Politics in Post-war Britain," Gunnar Trumbull, "Strategies of Consumer-Group Mobilization: France and Germany in the 1970s," both in Martin Daunton and Matthew Hilton, eds., *The Politics of Consumtion: Material Culture and Citizenship in Europe and America* (Oxford: Berg, 2001), 241–59 and 261–82; Patricia Maclachlan and Frank Trentmann, "Civilizing Markets: Traditions of Consumer Politics in Twentieth-Century Britain, Japan and the United States," in *Markets in Historical Contexts: Ideas and Politics in the Modern World*, ed. Mark Bevir and Frank Trentmannh (Cambridge: Cambridge University Press, 2004), 192; Matthew Hilton, *Consumerism in Twentieth-Century Britain: The Search for a Historical Movement* (Cambridge: Cambridge University Press, 2003), chaps. 6–8; Scarpellini, *Material Nation*, 243.
30. Hilton, *Consumerism*, 304–6.
31. Fabian, *Boom in der Krise*, is a very helpful analysis; also, Scarpellini, *Material Nation*, 225–30.
32. Cohen, *Consumers' Republic*, chap. 7.
33. Phil Wahba, "Can Department Stores Survive?," *Fortune* Feb. 21, 2017, accessed Apr. 22, 2019, http://fortune.com/2017/02/21/department-stores-future-macys-sears/;

   Ralf Banken, "Everything That Exists in Capitalism Can Be Found in the Department Store': The Development of Department Stores in the Federal Republic of Germany, 1949–2000," in Jessen and Langer, *Transformations of Retailing*, 149–51.

34. Manning, *Credit Card Nation*.
35. Trentmann, *Empire of Things*, 423–26; Nita Mathur, "Shopping Malls, Credit Cards and Global Brands: Consumer Culture and Lifestyle of India's New Middle Class," *South Asia Research* 30 (2010): 211–31; Zafar U. Ahmed et al., "Malaysian Consumes' Credit Card Usage Behavior," *Asia Pacific Journal of Marketing and Logistics*, 22 (2010): 528–544. https://www.nerdwallet.com/blog/credit-cards/people-countries-credit-cards-americans/, accessed Apr. 23, 2019.
36. Cohen, *Consumers' Republic*, 390–97; Daniel T. Rodgers, *The Age of Fracture* (Cambridge, MA: Belknap Press, 2011), chap. 2.
37. Lewis, *Growing Apart*, 168–69; Tarek Osman, *Egypt on the Brink: From Nasser to the Muslim Brotherhood* (New Haven, CT: Yale University Press, 2013), 144; more generally, Antonio Estache, Ana Goicoechea, and Lourdes Trujillo, "Utilities Reforms and Corruption in Developing Countries," World Bank Policy Research Working Paper 4081, 2006, http://www-wds.worldbank.org/external/default/WDSContentServer/IW3P/IB/2006/12/06/000016406_20061206151405/Rendered/PDF/wps4081.pdf, accessed May 6, 2019; Florio, *The Great Divestiture*, 222. Over the following quarter-century, water bills more than doubled to £415, https://www.lovemoney.com/news/20775/what-does-average-water-bill-uk-cost, accessed Apr. 24, 2019.
38. Florio, *Great Divestiture*, also n. 22.
39. https://www.investors.com/politics/editorials/airline-deregulation-40th-anniversary/ or https://cei.org/blog/celebrating-40th-anniversary-airline-deregulation https://www.ntu.org/publications/detail/airline-deregulation-at-40, all accessed Apr. 26, 2019.
40. Sources for Figure 10.2: "Historical Statistics of the United States, Millennial Edition," Table Df1112–1125; and Statistical Abstract of the United States, 2002," Table 1035, https://www2.census.gov/library/publications/2002/compendia/statab/122ed/tables/trans.pdf?#, accessed Apr. 26, 2019.
41. An incisive critique in Paul Dempsey and Andrew Goetz, *Airline Deregulation and Laissez-Faire Mythology* (Westport, CT: Quorum Books, 1992), chap. 21.
42. 546AO Report, June 2006, "AIRLINE DEREGULATION: Reregulating the Airline Industry Would Likely Reverse Consumer Benefits and Not Save Airline Pensions," Figure 11, https://www.gao.gov/new.items/d06630.pdf, accessed Apr. 26, 2018; David B. Richards, "Did Passenger Far Savings Occur After Airline Deregulation?," *Journal of the Transportation Research Forum* 46 (2007): 73–93.
43. Anton A. Huurdeman, *The Worldwide History of Telecommunications* (Hoboken, NJ: John Wiley & Sons, 2003), 230; Offer, *Challenge of Affluence*, 191
44. Offer, *Challenge of Affluence*, 191.
45. Florio, *The Great Divestiture*, 299; Huurdeman, *Worldwide History of Telecommunications*, 568.
46. Peter Temin and Louis Galambos, *The Fall of the Bell System: A Study in Prices and Politics* (New York: Cambridge University Press, 1987).
47. Huurdeman, *Worldwide History of Telecommunications*, chap. 33, quote on 548. On the politics of deregulation, Joseph Stiglitz, *The Roaring Nineties: A New History of the World's Most Prosperous Decade* (New York: W.W. Norton, 2003), 96–100; Susan Crawford, *Captive Audience: The Telecom Industry and Monopoly Power in the New*

Gilded Age (New Haven, CT: Yale University Press, 2013); World Bank Policy Research Working Paper 4081, 2006, cited in n. 37.
48. Eric Harwit, *China's Telecommunications Revolution* (Oxford: Oxford University Press, 2008), chap. 3; Florio, *Great Divestiture*, 318–19; Wei Li and Lixin Colin Xu, "The Impact of Privatization and Competition in the Telecommunications Sector around the World," *Journal of Law and Economics* 47 (2004): 395–430.
49. Crawford, *Captive Audience*; Dick Martin, *Tough Calls: AT&T and the Hard Lessons Learned from the Telecom Wars* (New York: AMACOM, 2005); Lisa Endlich, *Optical Illusions: Lucent and the Crash of Telecom* (New York: Simon and Schuster, 2004).
50. Huurdeman, *Worldwide History of Telecommunications*, chap. 32; https://www.statista.com/statistics/274774/forecast-of-mobile-phone-users-worldwide/, accessed May 6, 2019.
51. Ibid., The World Bank, *Africa's ICT Infrastructure: Building on the Communications Revolution* 2011, http://documents.worldbank.org/curated/en/375261468204545149/pdf/632510PUB0ICT000ID0184540BOX361512B.pdf, accessed May 6, 2019; Ravi Agrawal, *India Connected: How the Smartphone Is Transforming the World's Largest Democracy* (New York: Oxford University Press, 2019); Huurdemann, *Worldwide History of Telecommunications*, 527; Scarpellini, *Material Nation*, 247.
52. Emanuele Bacchiocchi, Massimo Florio, and Marco Gambaro, "Telecom Reforms in the EU: Prices and Consumers' Satisfaction," *Telecommunications Policy* 35 (2011): 382–96.
53. Marc Weber Tobias, "How and Why to Buy A Satellite Phone," *Forbes,* Mar. 18, 2013, https://www.forbes.com/sites/marcwebertobias/2013/03/18/how-and-when-to-buy-a-satellite-phone/#2276c7bc647d; https://europa.eu/newsroom/highlights/special-coverage/end-roaming-charges_en; BBC, "EU Roaming Charges Scrapped," June 15, 2017, https://www.bbc.com/news/business-40281013 all accessed May 14, 2019.
54. Hans Peter Hahn, "Consumption Identities, and Agency in Africa: An Overview," in *Decoding Modern Consumer Societies*, ed. Hartmut Berghoff and Uwe Spiekermann (Houndmills, Basingstoke: Palgrave Macmillan, 2012), 72.
55. Chengze Simon Fan, "Economic Development and the Changing Patterns of Consumption in Urban China," in Chua Beng-Huat, *Consumption in Asia: Lifestyles and Identities* (London: Routledge, 2000), 86; Trentmann, *Empire of Things*, 355; Peter Hessler, *Strange Stones: Dispatches from East and West* (New York: Harper Perennial, 2013), 207–24; https://data.worldbank.org/indicator/ny.gds.totl.zs; https://data.oecd.org/hha/household-savings.htm, accessed Mar. 28, 2019.
56. On these points, Beng-Huat, *Consumption in Asia*; Trentmann, *Empire of Things*, chap. 8; Christophe Jaffreiot and Peter van der Veer, *Patterns of Middle Class Consumption in China and India* (New Delhi: SAGE Publications, 2008); Sheldon Garan, "The Transnational Promotion of Saving in Asia," in *The Ambivalent Consumer: Questioning Consumption in East Asia and the West*, ed. Sheldon Garon and Patrician L. Maclachlan (Ithaca, NY: Cornell University Press, 2006), 174–76; chap. 7, nn. 107–8.
57. Paulina Bren, "Tuzex and the Hustler: Living it Up in Czechoslovakia," and Jill Massinio, "From Black Caviar to Blackouts: Gender, Consumption and Lifestyle in Ceaușescu's Romania," in Bren and Neuburger, *Communism Unwrapped*, 27–49,

22–49, as well as the other essays in that book; Jonathan Zaitlin, *The Currency of Socialism: Money and Political Culture in East Germany* (New York: Cambridge University Press, 2009).

58. A.O. Olutayo and O. Akanle, "Fast Food in Ibadan: An Emerging Consumption Pattern," *Africa* 79 (2009): 207–27; Karen Tranberg Hansen, "Filling Up the Wardrobe: Decision Making, Clothing Purchases and Dress Valuation in Lusaka, Zambia," *Consumption in Africa: Anthropological Approaches*, ed. Hans Peter Hahn (Berlin: Lit Verlag, 2008), 79–95; "For Dignity and Development, East Africa Curbs Used Clothes Imports," *New York Times*, Oct. 12, 2017, https://www.nytimes.com/2017/10/12/world/africa/east-africa-rwanda-used-clothing.html; "Dead White People's Clothes," https://www.theroot.com/dead-white-people-s-clothes-1790868999, both accessed May 10, 2019.

59. James L. Watson, "Introduction," in *Golden Arches East: McDonald's in East Asia*, ed. James L. Watson (Stanford, CA: Stanford University Press, 1997), 15; Yong Zhen, *Globalization and the Chinese Retailing Revolution* (Oxford: Chandos Publishing, 2007), 4.

60. Zhen, *Globalization and Chinese Retailing*, 4; Geoff Hiscock, *India's Store Wars* (Singapore: John Wiley & Sons, 2008), 160.

61. Tony Royle, "'Low-road Americanization' and the Global 'McJob': A Longitudinal Analysis of Work, Pay and Unionization in the International Fast-Food Industry," *Labor History* 41 (2010): 249–70; Olutayo and Akanle, "Fast Food in Ibadan"; Watson, *Golden Arches East*; Chua Beng-Huant, "Singaporeans Ingesting McDonald's," in Chua Beng-Huant, *Consumption in Asia*, 183–201; Yan, *Individualization of Chinese Society*, chap. 10.

62. Yong Chen, *Chop Suey, USA: The Story of Chinese Food in America* (New York: Columbia University Press, 2014), 29.

63. Jeffrey M. Pilcker, *Planet Taco: A Global History of Mexican Food* (New York: Oxford University Press, 2012); McKevitt, *Consuming Japan*, esp. chap. 6.

64. Scarpellini, *Material Nation*, 248; Pilcher, *Planet Taco*, 224.

65. Hilton, *British Consumers*, chap. 11; Trentmann, *Empire of Things*, 562–80. Figures given in euros and translated into dollars at the 2007 average exchange rate of 1€ = $1.37.

Chapter 11

1. W. Warren Wagar, *Good Tidings: The Belief in Progress from Darwin to Marcuse* (Bloomington: Indiana University Press, 1972); Sidney Pollard, *The Idea of Progress: History and Society* (Harmondsworth, Middlesex: Penguin Books, 1971); Robert Nisbet, *History of the Idea of Progress* (New York: Basic Books, 1980); Christopher Lasch, *The True and Only Heaven: Progress and Its Critics* (New York: W.W. Norton, 1991); Massimo Salvadori, *Progress: Can We Do without It?*, trans. Patrick Camiller (London: Zed Books, 2008); quote from https://www.un.org/en/sections/un-charter/preamble/index.html, indexed Aug. 20, 2019.

2. Wagar, *Good Tidings*, 241; Michael Latham, *The Right Kind of Revolution: Modernization, Development and U.S. Foreign Policy from the Cold War to the Present* (Ithaca, NY: Cornell University Press, 2011), 126–33; Pulja, *Women and Mass Consumer Society*, 92 n. 120; "General Electric Co.," *Ad-Age Encyclopedia*,

accessed June 17, 2019, https://adage.com/article/adage-encyclopedia/general-electric/98667.
3. Rosario Forlenza, *On the Edge of Democracy: Italy, 1943–1948* (Oxford: Oxford University Press, 2019), 193; Stefan Guth, "One Future Only. The Soviet Union in the Age of the Scientific-Technical Revolution," *Journal of Modern European History* 13 (2015): 355–76; cf. Rubin, *Synthetic Socialism*, chap. 1.
4. Yinghong Cheng, *Creating the "New Man": From Enlightenment Ideals to Socialist Realities* (Honolulu: University of Hawai'i Press, 2009), esp. 134.
5. Cited in Marie-Janine Calic, Dietmar Neutatz, and Julia Obertreis, eds., *The Crisis of Socialist Modernity: The Soviet Union and Yugoslavia in the 1970s* (Göttingen: Vandenhoeck & Ruprecht, 2011), 7; cf. Salvadori, *Progress*, chaps. 2–3; Chap. 6, n. 31.
6. Nils Gilman, *Mandarins of the Future: Modernization Theory in Cold War America* (Baltimore: Johns Hopkins University Press, 2003).
7. Michael Latham, *Right Kind of Revolution*, 10 and passim; Andrei Sakharov, *Progress, Coexistence and Intellectual Freedom*, trans. *New York Times* (New York: W.W. Norton, 1968), esp. 81–85.
8. Gyan Pakrash, *Another Reason: Science and the Imagination of Modern India* (Princeton, NJ: Princeton University Press, 1999), chaps. 3–4; Gilman, *Mandarins of the Future*, 30–31; Christopher Houston, *Kurdistan: Crafting of National Selves* (Oxford: Berg, 2008), 118–22. Atatruk's Iranian nationalist contemporaries held similar views about progress.
9. Jawaharlal Nehru, *The Discovery of India* (New Delhi: Jawaharlal Nehru Memorial Fund, 1982), 54, 288, 508, 517, 509–36 and more generally.
10. Ferguson, *Expectations of Modernity*, 1; Latham, *Right Kind of Revolution*, 65; Heather Hoag, *Developing the Rivers of East and West Africa: An Environmental History* (London: Bloomsbury Academic, 2013), 176–85; Carol Polsgrove, *Ending British Rule in Africa: Writers in a Common Cause* (Manchester: Manchester University Press, 2009), 147; Osseo-Asare, *Atomic Junction*, esp. chap. 4.
11. Nathan Citino, *Envisioning the Arab Future: Modernization in U.S.-Arab Relations, 1945–1967* (Cambridge: Cambridge University Press, 2017), 121 and passim.
12. Gilman, *Mandarins of the Future*, 234–38.
13. The intellectual and political context of J.R.R. Tolkien's work is well discussed in T.A. Shippey, *J.R.R. Tolkien: Author of the Century* (Boston: Houghton Miflin, 2000); and Meredith Veldman, *Fantasy, the Bomb and the Greening of Britain: Romantic Protest 1945–1980* (Cambridge: Cambridge University Press, 1994), 39–111. Tolkien's views on progress, technology, and the Second World War can be followed in Humphrey Carter, ed., *The Letters of J.R.R. Tolkien* (Boston: Houghton Miflin, 1981), 37–38, 63–66, 69, 78, 87–88, 93–94, 111, 115–16, 145–46, 190, 200, 243–44, 246.
14. Quoted in John Calvert, *Sayyid Qutb and the Origins of Radical Islamism* (New York: Columbia University Press, 2010), 89.
15. Sayyid Qutb, "'The America I Have Seen': In the Scale of Human Values," in *America in an Arab Mirror: Images of America in Arabic Travel Literature*, ed. Kamal Abdel-Malek (New York: St. Martin's Press, 2000), 11, 13–14, 20, 22–23.
16. Calvert, *Sayyid Qutb*, 148, 154.

17. Ibid., 232; Fawaz A. Gerges, *Making the Arab World: Nasser, Qutb, and the Clash That Shaped the Middle East* (Princeton, NJ: Princeton University Press, 2018); Citino, *Envisioning the Arab Future* 37–40, 48, 51–53.
18. http://theanarchistlibrary.org/library/dwight-macdonald-the-root-is-man, accessed June 20, 2019.
19. Gregory D. Sumner, *Dwight Macdonald and the Politics Circle: The Challenge of Cosmopolitan Democracy* (Ithaca, NY: Cornell University Press, 1996), 168–72 and passim.
20. Besides the many examples of this given in chaps. 1 and 3, see also Veldman, *Fantasy, the Bomb and the Greening of Britain*, chaps. 10–12.
21. Gilman, *Mandarins of the Future*, chaps. 6–7; Latham, *Right Kind of Revolution*, chaps. 5–6.
22. Citino, *Envisioning the Arab Future*, chap. 7; Paul Chamberlin, *The Global Offensive*; Gerges, *Making the Arab World*, chaps. 11–12.
23. Guth, "One Future Only"; Alfred C. Meyer, "The Idea of Progress in Communist Ideology," in *Progress and its Discontents*, ed. Gabriel Almond, Marvin Chodorow, and Roy Harvey Pearce (Berkeley: University of California Press, 1982), 81.
24. Veldman, *Fantasy, the Bomb and the Greening of Britain*, 152–55; Kyle Miller, "The Bavarian Model? Modernization, Environment and Landscape Planning in the Bavarian Nuclear Power Industry, 1950–1980," PhD diss., University of Missouri, 2009.
25. Jenny Anderson, *The Future of the World: Futurology, Futurists and the Struggle for the Post-Cold War Imagination* (Oxford: Oxford University Press, 2018), esp. chaps. 6–8.
26. Lisa McGirr, *Suburban Warriors: The Origins of the New American Right* (Princeton, NJ: Princeton University Press, 2001), 54, 96; Robertson, *Malthusian Moment*, 209–10.
27. Anselm Doering-Manteuffel and Lutz Raphael, *Nach dem Boom. Perspektiven auf die Zeitgeschichte seit 1970* (Göttingen: Vandenhoeck & Ruprecht, 2008), 67–72, 118–19; General Electric Co.," *Ad-Age Encyclopedia*, accessed June 17, 2019, https://adage.com/article/adage-encyclopedia/general-electric/98667.
28. http://books.google.com/ngrams, accessed June 26, 2019. The graphs are three-year moving averages. Doing graphs of words ignoring capitalization or ones using suffixes ("progressive" as well as "progress") made little difference in results.
29. Mark Mazower, *Governing the World: The History of an Idea* (New York: Penguin Press, 2012), 127–28.
30. Len Scales and Oliver Zimmer, eds., *Power and the Nation in European History* (Cambridge: Cambridge University Press, 2005), is an enlightening confrontation between primordialists and constructivists.
31. On the spread and development of nationalism in the nineteenth century, cf. Paul Gillingham, *Cuauhtémoc's Bones: Forging National Identity in Modern Mexico* (Albuquerque: University of New Mexico Press, 2011); and Timothy Baycroft and Mark Hewitson, eds., *What Is A Nation? Europe 1789–1914* (Oxford: Oxford University Press, 2006).
32. James Leibold, *Reconfiguring Chinese Nationalism: How the Qing Frontier and Its Indigenes Became Chinese* (Houndmills, Basingstoke: Palgrave Macmillan, 2007).

33. Anthony Reid, *Imperial Alchemy: Nationalism and Political Identity in Southeast Asia* (Cambridge: Cambridge University Press, 2010), 45, and chap. 5.
34. Ananya Vajpeyi, *Righteous Republic: The Political Foundations of Modern India* (Cambridge, MA: Harvard University Press, 2012), chap. 4 a.
35. Archie Brown, *The Rise and Fall of Communism* (New York: Ecco, 2009), esp. 112–14.
36. Or Rosenboim, *The Emergence of Globalism: Visions of World Order in Britain and the United States, 1930–1950* (Princeton, NJ: Princeton University Press, 2017), 50 and passim; Glenda Sluga, *Internationalism in the Age of Nationalism* (Philadelphia: University of Pennsylvania Press, 2013), esp. chap. 3; Wittner, *Struggle against the Bomb*, 1: 44–45, 66–71, 113–14.
37. Emilo Gentile, *La Grande Italia: The Myth of the Nation in the 20th Century*, trans. Suzanne Dingee and Jennifer Pudney (Madison: University of Wisconsin Press, 2009), 332–33.
38. Wolfram Kaiser, *Christian Democracy and the Origins of the European Union* (Cambridge: Cambridge University Press, 2007), 189 and more generally; Klaus Dreher, *Helmut Kohl. Leben mit Macht* (Stuttgart: Deutsche-Verlags-Anstalt, 1998), 32.
39. Gilbert, *Surpassing Realism*, 49, chaps. 1–3.
40. Ibid., chaps. 3–5.
41. Benedict Anderson, *Imagined Communities: Reflections on the Origin and Spread of Nationalism* (London: Verso, 2016), 1–2.
42. Max Bergholz, "Sudden Nationhood: The Microdynamics of Intercommunal Relations in Bosnia-Herzegovina after World War II," *American Historical Review* 118 (2013): 679–707.
43. Yitzhak Brudny, *Reinventing Russia: Russian Nationalism and the Soviet State, 1953–1991* (Cambridge, MA: Harvard University Press, 1998); Katherine Verdery, *National Ideology under Socialism: Identity and Cultural Politics in Ceaușescu's Romania* (Berkeley: University of California Press, 1991).
44. Tarik Cyril Amar, *The Paradox of Ukrainian Lviv: A Borderland City between Stalinists, Nazis, and Nationalists* (Ithaca, NY: Cornell University Press, 2015). There was a similar development in the Lithuanian capital, Vilnius, pre-1939 Vilna.
45. Cooper, *Citizenship between Nation and Empire*; also, Adom Getachew, *Worldmaking after Empire: The Rise and Fall of Self-Determination* (Princeton, NJ: Princeton University Press, 2019).
46. Cf. James J. Sheehan, *Where Have All the Soldiers Gone? The Transformation of Modern Europe* (Boston: Houghton Miflin, 2008).
47. James J. Orr, *The Victim as Hero: Ideologies of Peace and National Identity in Postwar Japan* (Honolulu: University of Hawai'i Press, 2001), 1 and passim; Lisa Yoneyama, *Hiroshima Traces: Time, Space and the Dialectics of Memory* (Berkeley: University of California Press, 1999), 1–3; cf. Christian Wicke, *Helmut Kohl's Quest for Normality: His Representation of the German Nation and Himself* (New York: Berghahn Books, 2015); Gentile, *La Grande Italia*, chap. 15.
48. Barbara Keys, *Globalizing Sport: National Rivalry and International Community in the 1930s* (Cambridge, MA: Harvard University Press, 2006).

49. Joshua H. Nadel, *Fútbol! Why Soccer Matters in Latin America* (Gainesville: University Press of Florida, 2014), 44 and more generally.
50. David Rowe, "Sport and the Repudiation of the Global," *International Review for the Sociology of Sport* 30 (2003): 281–94; Vick Duke and Liz Crolley, *Football, Nationality and the State* (Harlow, England: Addison Wesley Longman, 1996); Alan Bairner, *Sport, Nationalism and Globalization: European and North American Perspectives* (Albany: State University of New York Press, 2001).
51. Alison Pargeter, *Libya: The Rise and Fall of Qaddafi* (New Haven, CT: Yale University Press, 2012), 121.
52. Adeed Dawisha, *Arab Nationalism in the Twentieth Century: From Triumph to Despair*, 2nd ed. (Princeton, NJ: Princeton University Press, 2016).
53. Ibid., 147–51; Betty Anderson, *Nationalist Voices in Jordan: The Street and the State* (Austin: University of Texas Press, 2005), 166.
54. Dawisha, *Arab Nationalism*, chaps. 6–7; Pargeter, *Libya*, 44; Anderson, *Nationalist Voices*, chap. 7; Aideed Dawisha, *Iraq: A Political History* (Princeton, NJ: Princeton University Press, 2009), chap. 9; Gerges, *Making the Arab World*, chap. 7; James Jankowski, *Nasser's Egypt, Arab Nationalism, and the United Arab Republic* (Boulder, CO: Lynne Rienner, 2002), chaps. 4–5; Rosie Bsheer, "A Counter-Revolutionary State: Popular Movements and the Making of Saudi Arabia," *Past and Present* 238 (2018): 233–77, esp. 252, 265.
55. Anderson, *Nationalist Voices*, chaps. 8–9; Dawisha, *Arab Nationalism*, chaps. 8–11; Dawisha, *Iraq*, chaps. 9–10; Jankowski, *Nasser's Egypt*, chaps 6–8; Gerges, *Making the Arab World*, chaps. 10–11; Houston, *Kurdistan*, 150–51; Chamberlin, *The Global Offensive*, chap. 1.
56. Dawisha, *Arab Nationalism*, 280, 318–19
57. On Padmore and his circle, Cosgrove, *Ending British Rule in Africa*.
58. Hakim Adi, *Pan-Africanism: A History* (London: Bloomsbury Academic, 2018); Getachew, *Worldmaking after Empire*, 131–38.
59. Thomas Hansen, *The Saffron Wave: Democracy and Hindu Nationalism in Modern India* (Princeton, NJ: Princeton University Press, 1999), 232 and passim; Christophe Jaffrelot and Ingrid Therwarth, "The Global Sangh Privar: A Study of Contemporary Hindusim," in *Religious Internationals in the Modern World: Globalization and Faith Communities since 1750*, ed. Abigail Green and Vincent Viaene (Houndmills, Basingstoke: Palgrave Macmillan, 2012), 343–64. Connections with a global diaspora were also characteristic of Late-Millenial Kurdish, Sri Lankan, and Zionist nationalism.
60. Damien Stankiewicz, *Europe Un-Imagined: Nation and Culture at a French-German Television Channel* (Toronto, Canada: University of Toronto Press, 2017), 17–19; Gilbert, *Surpassing Realism*, chaps. 6–8; Sarah Binzer Hobolt and Sylvain Brouard, "Contesting the European Union? Why the Dutch and the French Rejected the European Constitution," *Political Research Quarterly* 64 (2011): 309–22.
61. Maryon McDonald, *"We Are Not French!" Language, Culture and Identity in Brittany* (London: Routledge, 1989); Duke and Crolley, *Football, Nationality and the State*, 60; more generally, Celia Applegate, "A Europe of Regions: The History and Historiography of Subnational Places in Modern Times," *American Historical Review* 104 (1991): 1157–82.

62. Gerges, *Making the Arab World*, 140, 341, 383; Keppel and Milelli, *Al Qaeda in its Own Words*, 68, 99–100, 117–18, 184–91; Ayesha Jalal, *Partisans of Allah: Jihad in South Asia* (Cambridge, MA: Harvard University Press, 2008), 247; Bernard Rougier, *Everyday Jihad: The Rise of Militant Islam among Palestinians in Lebanon*, trans. Pascale Ghazaleh (Cambridge, MA: Harvard University Press, 2007), 156, 193 and passim.
63. Pargeter, *Libya*, 114–17; Jack Moore, "Isis Rapper Who Married FBI Spy Killed In Syria Strike," *Newsweek*, Jan. 1, 2018, https://www.newsweek.com/isis-rapper-who-married-fbi-spy-killed-syria-strike-785268, accessed Sept. 12, 2019; Beren Cross, "Abdel-Majed Abdel Bary: British Jihadist 'Deserts Isis in Syria and Goes on the Run in Turkey,'" *The Independent*, July 12, 2015, https://www.independent.co.uk/news/uk/home-news/abdel-majed-abdel-bary-british-jihadist-deserted-isis-in-syria-and-is-on-the-run-in-turkey-10384099.html accessed Sept. 12, 2019.
64. Two introductions to secularization theory and its application to the post-1950 era are Benjamin Ziemann, "Säkulaisierung und Neuformierung des Religiösen. Religion und Gesellschaft in der zweiten Hälfte des 20. Jahrhunderts," *Archiv für Sozialgeschichte* 51 (2011): 3–36; and Callum Brown, *Becoming Atheist: Humanism and the Secular West* (London: Bloomsbury Academic, 2017), 1–19.
65. Taylor Branch, *Parting the Waters: America in the King Years 1954–63* (New York: Simon and Schuster, 1988), 81–87; Lillian Calles Berger, *The World Come of Age: An Intellectual History of Liberation Theology* (New York: Oxford University Press, 2018), 140–42.
66. Henri Lauzière, *The Making of Salafism: Islamic Reform in the Twentieth Century* (New York: Columbia University Press, 2016); Natana J. Delong-Bas, *Wahhabi Islam: from Revival and Reform to Global Jihad* (New York: Oxford University Press, 2004); Alexander Thurston, *Salafism in Nigeria: Islam, Preaching and Politics* (Cambridge: Cambridge University Press, 2016), 5–11, 31–63.
67. Generally, Allan Anderson, "The Pentecostal and Charismatic Movements," in *The Cambridge History of Christianity*, Vol. 9, World Christianities, c. 1914 – c. 2000," ed. Hugh McLeod (Cambridge: Cambridge University Press, 2006), 89–106; specific examples in Darren Dochuk, *From Bible Belt to Sun Belt: Plain-Folk Religion, Grassroots Politics and the Rise of Evangelical Conservatism* (New York: W W Norton, 2011); Melissa Wei-Tsing Inouye, *China and the True Jesus: Charisma and Organization in a Chinese Christian Church* (New York: Oxford University Press, 2018); and David Maxwell, *African Gifts of the Spirit: Pentecostalism and the Rise of a Zimbabwean Transnational Religious Movement* (Oxford: James Curry, 2006).
68. Callum Brown, *The Death of Christian Britain: Understanding Secularisation 1800–2000* (London: Routledge, 2001), 156–75; Hugh McLeod, *The Religious Crisis of the 1960s* (Oxford: Oxford University Press, 2007), 1–61; Hugh McLeod and Werner Ustorf, eds., *The Decline of Christendom in Western Europe, 1750–2000* (Cambridge: Cambridge University Press, 2003); Klaus Große Kracht, "Die katholische Welle der 'Stunde Null', Katholische Aktion, missionarische Bewegung und Pastoralmacht in Deutschland, Italien und Frankreich 1945–1960," *Archiv für Sozialgeschichte* 51 (2011): 163–86; Martin Conway, *The Sorrows of Belgium: Liberation and Political Reconstruction 1944–1947* (Oxford: Oxford University Press, 2012), 207–9; Jeffrey Jones, "US Church Membership Down

Sharply in Past Two Decades," accessed Dec. 10, 2019, https://news.gallup.com/poll/248837/church-membership-down-sharply-past-two-decades.aspx.
69. Abdullahi Ibrahim, *Manichean Delirium: Decolonizing the Judiciary and Islamic Renewal in the Sudan, 1898–1985* (Leiden: Brill, 2008); Maxwell, *African Gifts of the Spirit*, 5; Brian Stanley, *Christianity in the Twentieth Century: A World History* (Princeton, NJ: Princeton University Press, 2018), 57–63.
70. Paul Mariani, *Church Militant: Bishop Kung and Catholic Resistance in Communist Shanghai* (Cambridge, MA: Harvard University Press, 2011).
71. David Binder, "On the Trail of Jan Hus," *New York Times*, Nov. 16, 1997, https://www.nytimes.com/1997/11/16/travel/on-the-trail-of-jan-hus.html, accessed Dec. 3, 2019.
72. Markus Anhalt, *Die Macht der Kirchen brechen: Die Mitwirkung der Staatsicherheit bei der Durchsetzung der Jugendweihe in der DDR* (Göttingen: Vandenhoeck & Ruprecht, 2016).
73. Victoria Smolkin, *A Sacred Space Is Never Empty: A History of Soviet Atheism* (Princeton, NJ: Princeton University Press, 2018); Stanley, *Christianity in the Twentieth Century*, 49–55; John Connelly, *Captive University: The Sovietization of East German, Czech and Polish Higher Education, 1945–1956* (Chapel Hill: University of North Carolina Press, 2000); Anahlt, *Macht der Kirchen brechen*, 204–5.
74. Karl Kruse, *One Nation Under God: How Corporate America Invented Christian America* (New York: Basic Books, 2015), 36–38, 95–125 and passim; Roberto Ventresca, *From Fascism to Democracy: Culture and Politics in the Italian Election of 1948* (Toronto, Canada: University of Toronto Press, 2004), chap. 3 and passim; Mariani, *Church Militant*, 21.
75. Gerges, *Making the Arab World*, 85; Lauzière, *The Making of Salafism*, 172, 192; Geoffrey Robinson, *The Killing Season: A History of the Indonesian Massacres, 1965–66* (Princeton, NJ: Princeton University Press, 2018), 171–75.
76. Yves Lambert, "New Christianity, Indifference and Diffused Spirituality," in McLeod and Ustorf, *The Decline of Christendom*, 63–78.
77. Callum Brown, "The People of 'No Religion': The Demographics of Secularisation in the English-Speaking World since c. 1900," *Archiv für Sozialgeschichte* 51 (2011): 37–61; Pew Research Center, "In U.S., Decline of Christianity Continues at Rapid Pace," https://www.pewforum.org/2019/10/17/in-u-s-decline-of-christianity-continues-at-rapid-pace/, accessed Nov. 22, 2019.
78. Best discussion of this is McLeod, *Religious Crisis*.
79. Schnoor, Antje. "Zwischen jenseitiger Erlösung und irdischem Heil. Die Rezeption der Befreiungstheologie in der Gesellschaft Jesu," *Archiv für Sozialgeschichte* 51 (2011): 419–43; James Chappel, *Catholic Modern: The Challenge of Totalitarianism and the Making of the Church* (Cambridge, MA: Harvard University Press, 2018), esp. chap. 6.
80. Sam Brewitt-Taylor, *Christian Radicalism in the Church of England and the Invention of the British Sixties, 1957–70* (Oxford: Oxford University Press, 2018); Stanley, *World History of Christianity*, 209–10.
81. Steven P. Miller, *The Age of Evangelicalism: America's Born-Again Years* (New York: Oxford University Press, 2014); Wigger, *PTL*; Dochuk, *From Bible Belt to Sunbelt*, Parts 3–4. This author, in his first year of university studies, heard

both Daniel Berrigan and Hal Lindsey speak, an experience of deeply different and categorically opposed forms of Christianity, that, in retrospect, deserves the then-current expression, "mind-blowing."

82. David Martin, *Tongues of Fire: The Explosion of Protestantism in Latin America* (Oxford: Blackwell, 1990); R. Andrew Chestnut, *Competitive Spirits: Latin America's New Religious Economy* (Oxford: Oxford University Press, 2003); Maxwell, *African Gifts of the Spirit*; Richard Fox Young, "East Asia," in McLeod, *The Cambridge History of Christianity*, 465.

83. Stéphane Lacroix, *Awakening Islam: The Politics of Religious Dissent in Contemporary Saudi Arabia*, trans. George Holoch (Cambridge, MA: Harvard University Press, 2011); Thurston, *Salafism in Nigeria*, 17–19; quote from Rougier, *Everyday Jihad*, 256.

84. Lauzière, *The Making of Salafism*, 207; Julie Ingersoll, *Building God's Kingdom: Inside the World of Christian Reconstruction* (New York: Oxford University Press, 2015), chap. 6.

85. Maxwell, *African Gifts of the Spirit*, 97, 283–84, 201–7; Marshall, *Political Spiritualities*, 106, 120, 173–74, 197, 199.

86. Jörg Haustein, "Die Pfingstbewegung als Alternative zur Säkularisierung? Zur Wahrnehmung einer global religiösen Bewegung des 20. Jahrhunderts." *Archiv für Sozialgeschichte* 51 (2011): 533–52; Matthew Bowman, *Christian: The Politics of a Word in America* (Cambridge, MA: Harvard University Press, 2018).

87. Wigger, *PTL*, esp. chap. 2; Maxwell, *African Gifts of the Spirit*, 88–94; Lacroix, *Awakening Islam*, 143–44; Darren Dochuk, *Anointed with Oil: How Christianity and Crude Made Modern America* (New York: Basic Books, 2019.), 482–88, 511–13.

88. Philip Jenkins, *The Next Christendom: The Coming of Global Christianity* (New York: Oxford University Press, 2002), 156.

89. Cf. Rougier, *Everyday Jihad*.

90. Lacroix, *Awakening Islam*, 89–100; cf. Philip Jenkins, *Decade of Nightmares: The End of the Sixties and the Making of Eighties America* (New York: Oxford University Press, 2006).

91. Ingersoll, *Building God's Kingdom*, 56–63.

92. Wigger, *PTL*, esp. chap. 4; Maxwell, *African Gifts of the Spirit*, 95–96, 151–61; Marshall, *Political Spiritualities*, chap. 5; Thurston, *Salafism in Nigeria*, chap. 6.

93. John W. O'Malley, *What Happened at Vatican II* (Cambridge, MA: Harvard University Press, 2008).

94. Gerd-Rainer Horn, *The Spirit of Vatican II: Western European Progressive Catholicism in the Long Sixties* (Oxford: Oxford University Press, 2015), 123 and passim.

95. Ibid., and Chappel, *Catholic Modern*, 232–39.

96. Jenkins, *Next Christendom*, 156.

97. John Pollard, "The Papacy," in McLeod, *World Christianities*, 44–49; Edward Cleary, "The Transformation of Latin American Christianity, c. 1950–2000," in ibid., 372–75; Stahley, *Christianity in the Twentieth Century*, 53–55; O'Malley, *What Happened*, 198; R. Scott Appleby, "The Catholic Church as Transnational Actor, 1965–2005," in Green and Viaene, *Religious Internationals*, 319–42; Jenkins, *The Next Christendom*, 146–47.

98. Jenkins, *Next Christendom*, 121, 202–3 and passim; Pew Research Center, "A Changing World: Global Views on Diversity, Gender Equality, Family Life and the Importance of Religion," Chart of Global Attitudes Survey, Q11 and Q95, https://www.pewresearch.org/global/2019/04/22/a-changing-world-global-views-on-diversity-gender-equality-family-life-and-the-importance-of-religion/ accessed Dec. 11, 2019; Frieder Ludwig, "Entsäkularisierung? Religion und Politik im subsaharischen Afrika im Prozess der Dekolonisierung seit den 1960er Jahren," *Archiv für Sozialgeschichte* 51 (2011): 511–31.
99. C. Kirk Hadaway, Penny Long, Marler and Mark Chaves, "What the Polls Don't Show: A Closer Look at U.S. Church Attendance," *American Sociological Review* 58 (1993): 741–52; by the same authors, "Overreporting Church Attendance in America: Evidence That Demands the Same Verdict," *American Sociological Review* 63 (1998): 122–30; Stanley Presser and Linda Stinson, "Data Collection Mode and Social Desirability Bias in Self-Reported Religious Attendance," *American Sociological Review* 63 (1998): 137–45.
100. Detlef Pollack, "Renaissance des Religiösen? Veränderungen auf dem religiösen Feld in ausgewählten Ländern Ost- und Ostmitteleuropas," *Archiv für Sozialgeschichte* 51 (2011): 109–40; Andreas Meier, *Jugendweihe—JugendFEIER. Ein deutsches nostalgisches Fest vor und nach 1990* (Munich: Deutscher Taschenbuchverlag, 1998).
101. Pollack, "Renaissance des Religiösen?"; John Garrard and Carol Garrard, *Russian Orthodoxy Resurgent: Faith and Power in the New Russia* (Princeton, NJ: Princeton University Press, 2008); Dmitry Adamsky, *Russian Nuclear Orthodoxy: Religion, Politics, Strategy* (Stanford, CA: Stanford University Press, 2019).
102. Inouye, *China and the True Jesus*, chaps. 7–9; Mariani, *Church Militant*, 206–27; Stanley, *Christianity in the Twentieth Century*, 146–48.

Chapter 12

1. A helpful overview of mass murder in human history is Donald Bloxham and A. Dirk Moses, eds., *The Oxford Handbook of Genocide Studies* (Oxford: Oxford University Press, 2010).
2. For this and the following, Kim Christian Priemel, *The Betrayal: Nuremberg Trials and German Divergence* (Oxford: Oxford University Press, 2016); Yuma Totani, *The Tokyo War Crimes Trial: The Pursuit of Justice in the Wake of World War II* (Cambridge, MA: Harvard University Press, 2008); Yuma Totani, *Justice in Asia and the Pacific Region, 1945–1952* (New York: Cambridge University Press, 2015); Dan Plesch, *Human Rights after Hitler: The Lost History of Prosecuting Axis War Crimes* (Washington, DC: Georgetown University Press, 2017).
3. Anna Chichopek-Gajraj, *Beyond Violence: Jewish Survivors in Poland and Slovakia, 1944–48* (Cambridge: Cambridge University Press, 2014); Michael Marrus, *Some Measure of Justice: The Holocaust Era Restitution Campaign of the 1990s* (Madison: University of Wisconsin Press, 2009).
4. Totani, *Tokyo War Crimes Trial*, chap. 9; Yoneyama, *Hiroshima Traces*, 16–17.
5. A. Dirk Moses, "Raphael Lemkin, Culture, and the Concept of Genocide," and William A. Schabas, "The Law and Genocide," in *Handbook of Genocide Studies*, ed. Moses and Bloxham, 19–41 and 123–41; Tetani, *Tokyo War Crimes Trial*, 13–142, 253; Prieml, *The Betrayal*, 101–2.

6. Examples of excellent historians' difficulty with the concept include Eric Weitz, *A Century of Genocide: Utopias of Race and Nation* (Princeton, NJ: Princeton University Press, 2003); Ben Kiernan, *The Pol Pot Regime: Race, Power and Genocide in Cambodia under the Khmer Rouge, 1975–79* (New Haven, CT: Yale University Press, 1996); Jess Melvin, *The Army and the Indonesian Genocide: Mechanics of Mass Murder* (London: Routledge, 2018); for the ICTY, cf. Judith Armatta, *Twilight of Impunity: The War Crimes Trial of Slobodan Milosevic* (Durham, NC: Duke University Press, 2010), chap. 11.
7. Shapiro, *Mao's War against Nature*, chaps. 1–2; Andrew Walder, *China under Mao: A Revolution Derailed* (Cambridge MA: Harvard University Press, 2015), esp. chaps. 8–9; Zhou Xun, *Forgotten Voices of Mao's Great Famine, 1958–1962* (New Haven, CT: Yale University Press, 2013); Frank Dikötter, *Mao's Great Famine: The History of China's Most Devastating Catastrophe, 1985–1962* (New York: Walker & Co, 2010); Hecheng, *The Killing Wind*.
8. Walder, *China under Mao*, 277–82; Shapiro, *Mao's War against Nature*, 177–79.
9. Vogel, *Deng Xioaping*, esp. 366–69.
10. Kiernan, *The Pol Pot Regime*
11. Quoted in Kiernan, *The Pol Pot Regime*, 320
12. Seth Mydans, "11 Years, $300 Million and 3 Convictions. Was the Khmer Rouge Tribunal Worth It?," *New York Times*, Apr. 10, 2017, https://www.nytimes.com/2017/04/10/world/asia/cambodia-khmer-rouge-united-nations-tribunal.html
13. On the mass killings in Indonesia, Robinson, *The Killing Season*, Jess Melvin, *The Army and the Indonesian Genocide*; Christian Gerlach, *Extremely Violent Societies: Mass Violence in the Twentieth-Century World* (New York: Cambridge University Press, 2010), chap. 2.
14. John Roosa, *Pretext for Mass Murder: The September 30th Movement and Suharto's Coup d'État in Indonesia* (Madison: University of Wisconsin Press, 2006). Scholarly efforts, particularly by the famous theorist of nationalism, Benedict Anderson, to deny that the communists were planning a coup, are unconvincing.
15. Julia Lovell, *Maoism: A Global History* (New York: Alfred A. Knopf, 2019), 179 and chap. 5.
16. Cf. Gerlach, *Extremely Violent Societies*, 87.
17. For this and what follows, Virginia Garrard-Burnett, *Terror in the Land of the Holy Spirit: Guatemala and General Efraín Montt, 1982–1983* (New York: Oxford University Press, 2010).
18. https://www.ijmonitor.org/efrain-rios-montt-and-mauricio-rodriguez-sanchez-background/, accessed Feb. 20, 2020.
19. This account of events in Yugoslavia relies heavily on Charles Ingrao and Thomas A. Emmert, eds., *Confronting the Yugoslav Controversy: A Scholars' Initiative*, 2nd ed. (West Lafayette, IN: Purdue University Press, 2013); also Armatta, *Twilight of Impunity*, Cathy Carmicheal, "Genocide and Population Displacement in Post-Communist Eastern Europe," in *Oxford Handbook of Genocide Studies*, ed. Bloxham and Moses, 509–28; Philipp Ther, *The Dark Side of Nation-States: Ethnic Cleansing in Modern Europe*, trans. Charlotte Kreutzmüller (New York: Berghahn, 2014); and (with reservations) Paul Mojzes, *Balkan Genocides: Holocaust and Ethnic Cleansing in the Twentieth Century* (Lanham, MD: Rowman & Littlefield, 2015).

20. "Football, Blood and War," *The Guardian*, Jan. 18, 2004, https://www.theguardian.com/observer/osm/story/0,6903,1123137,00.html, accessed Feb. 26, 2020.
21. Mahmood Mamdani, *When Victims Become Killers: Colonialism, Nativism and the Genocide in Rwanda* (Princeton, NJ: Princeton University Press, 2001); Timothy Longman, *Christianity and Genocide in Rwanda* (New York: Cambridge University Press, 2010); and, especially, Jean-Paul Kimonyo, *Rawanda's Popular Genocide: A Perfect Storm*, trans. Wandia Njoya (Boulder, CO: Lynne Rienner Publishers, 2016).
22. Quoted in Kimonyo, *Rwanda's Popular Genocide*, 35. On politics in Burundi, see Aidan Russell, *Politics and Violence in Burundi: The Language of Truth in an Emerging State* (Cambridge: Cambridge University Press, 2019).
23. An academic version of these attacks is Samuel Totten, ed., *Dirty Hands and Vicious Deeds: The US Government's Complicity in Crimes against Humanity and Genocide* (Toronto, Canada: University of Toronto Press, 2018).
24. Geoffrey Robinson, *"If You Leave Us Here We Will Die:" How Genocide Was Stopped in East Timor* (Princeton, NJ: Princeton University Press, 2010), esp. 188–99.
25. M.W. Daly, *Dafur's Sorrow: A History of Destruction and Genocide* (Cambridge: Cambridge University Press, 2007); Gérard Prunier, *Darfur: The Ambiguous Genocide* (Ithaca, NY: Cornell University Press, 2005); accessed Mar. 2, 2020, http://www.coalitionfortheicc.org/cases/omar-albashir.

Chapter 13

1. https://www.bso.org/media/15204/Shosty2.pdf; https://ninacamic.blogspot.com/2004/02/un-on-march.html; "The Screen: 'Thousands Cheer,' Lavish Musical with An All-Star Cast, Makes Its Appearance at War Bond Rally at Astor," *New York Times*, Sept. 14, 1943, https://www.nytimes.com/1943/09/14/archives/the-screen-thousands-cheer-lavish-metro-musical-with-an-allstar.html; https://www.imdb.com/title/tt0036432/; https://www.youtube.com/watch?v=_a9VSvArGpI, all accessed Mar. 27, 2020. Cf. Stephen Hess, *Bit Player: My Life with Presidents and Ideas* (Washington, DC: Brookings Institution Press, 2018), 8; author's personal experiences with the song.
2. Mazower, *Governing the World*, 208, 219; Roper Center, "Seventy Years of U.S. Public Opinion on the United Nations," https://ropercenter.cornell.edu/blog/seventy-years-us-public-opinion-united-nations, accessed Mar. 27, 2020; Paul Kennedy, *The Parliament of Man: The Past, Present and Future of the United Nations* (New York: Random House, 2006), 38, 325–26; Wittner, *Struggle against the Bomb*, 1:70; the volume includes a survey of enthusiasm for global federation around the world.
3. Mazower, *No Enchanted Palace*, 28–29 and chap. 1, more generally.
4. Quote from Getachew, *Worldmaking after Empire*, 73; sources cited in Chap. 11, n. 36; Mazower, *No Enchanted Palace*, chap. 4.
5. Quoted in Gary Wilder, *Freedom Time: Negritude, Decolonization and the Future of the World* (Durham, NC: Duke University Press, 2015), 79–80.
6. Megan Koreman, *The Expectations of Justice: France 1944–1946* (Durham, NC: Duke University Press), 4–5, 189; "Programme du Conseil national de la Résistance," Mar. 15 1944, https://cache.media.eduscol.education.fr/file/droits_homme/19/8/Programme_du_Conseil_national_de_la_Resistance_319198.pdf,

accessed March 30, 2020. The French original of "harmonious, wonderful future," is *les lendemains qui chantent*, the slogan of the left-wing Popular Front of the 1930s.
7. Rosario Forlenza, *On the Edge of Democracy: Italy, 1943–1948* (Oxford: Oxford University Press, 2019), 59–60; Donny Gluckstein, *A People's History of the Second World War: Resistance versus Empire* (London: Pluto Press, 2012), 150; Naimark, *The Russians in Germany*, 254–56; more broadly cf. Niethammer, *Arbeiterinitiative 1945*.
8. Gluckstein, *People's History*, 154.
9. Silvio Pons, *The Global Revolution: A History of International Communism 1917–1991*, trans. Alan Cameron (Oxford: Oxford University Press, 2014), 141–42, 155; Gluckstein, *People's History*, 41; David Kertzer, *Comrades and Christians: Religion and Political Struggle in Communist Italy* (Cambridge: Cambridge University Press, 1980), 53.
10. Pons, *The Global Revolution*, chaps. 3–4.
11. Yasmin Khan, *India at War: The Subcontinent and the Second World War* (Oxford: Oxford University Press, 2015), ix–xi, 118–19, 216–17, 304–5 and passim; David Motadel, "The Global Authoritarian Moment and the Revolt against Empire," *American Historical Review* 124 (2019): 843–77; Bandyopadhyay, *Decolonization in South Asia*, 9–10, 106.
12. Cited in Vajpeyi, *Righteous Republic*, 283–84, n. 26.
13. Wilder, *Freedom Time*, 129 and chap. 5, more generally.
14. Ibid, 143, 154 and, more generally, chap. 6.
15. Ibid., 133–35.
16. Getachew, *Worldmaking after Empire*, 1–2, 92–100.
17. Quoted in Paul Boyer, *By the Bomb's Early Light: American Thought and Culture at the Dawn of the Atomic Age* (New York: Pantheon, 1985), 14.
18. Ibid., 5, 7, chap. 7 and passim.
19. Wittner, *Struggle against the Bomb*, Vol. 1, passim; quote from Alexander C. Cook, "Introduction: The Spiritual Atom Bomb and its Global Fallout," *Mao's Little Red Book: A Global History*, ed. Alexander C. Cook (New York: Cambridge University Press, 2014), 9.
20. Wittner, *The Struggle Against the Bomb*, vol. 2; Guy Oakes, *The Imaginary War: Civil Defense and American Cold War Culture* (New York: Oxford University Press, 1994); Yoneyama, *Hiroshima Traces*; Tracy C. Davis, *Stages of Emergency: Cold War Nuclear Civil Defense* (Durham, NC: Duke University Press, 2007).
21. Mazower, *Governing the World*, chaps. 8–9; Kennedy, *Parliament of Man*, chaps. 2–4.
22. Roper Center, "Seventy Years of U.S. Public Opinion on the United Nations," cited in n. 2; Gallup, "United Nations," https://news.gallup.com/poll/116347/united-nations.aspx; Pew Research Center, "United Nations Gets Mostly Positive Marks from People around the World," https://www.pewresearch.org/fact-tank/2019/09/23/united-nations-gets-mostly-positive-marks-from-people-around-the-world/ both accessed April 3, 202.
23. Koreman, *Expectation of Justice*; István Deak, Jan T. Gross, and Tony Judt, eds., *The Politics of Retribution in Europe: World War II and Its Aftermath* (Princeton, NJ: Princeton University Press, 2000); Sandra Ott, *Living with the Enemy: German Occupation, Collaboration and Justice in the Western Pyrenees*,

1940–1948 (Cambridge: Cambridge University Press, 2017); chap. 10, nn. 8–12; De Graaf, *Socialism across the Iron Curtain*, esp. chaps. 2–3.

24. Essays on Greece Hungary and Czechoslovakia, in Deák, Gross and Judt, *Politics of Retribution*, 212–89; De Graaf, *Socialism across the Iron Curtain*; Forlenza, *On the Edge of Democracy*, chaps. 4–5; Ventresca, *From Fascism to Democracy*; Martin Conway, *The Sorrows of Belgium*. The memoir-history of Ian Buruma, *Year Zero*, is a cynical commentary on great postwar hopes and their quick disappearance.
25. Cf. Getachew, *Worldmaking after Empire*, esp. chap. 5.
26. George Orwell, *1984* (New York: New American Library, 1981), 30–31, 60–62, 64–65, 71–75, 97, 107, 122–23, 148–50, 220.
27. Milovan Djilas, *The New Class: An Analysis of the Communist System* (New York: Frederick A. Praeger, 1957), 153.
28. Ibid., 155.
29. Frantz Fanon, *Les damnés de la terre* (Paris: Gallimard, 1991), 67, 126–27.
30. Ibid., 89–94, 147–70.
31. Ibid., 108–10, 136–41.
32. Ibid., 372–73; see also n. 15.
33. Ibid., 189–248, quote on 238.
34. Thomas Meaney, "Frantz Fanon and the CIA Man," *American Historical Review* 124 (2019): 983–95.
35. Raghavan, *Global History of the Creation of Bangladesh*, 19–23; Tariq Ali, *Street-Fighting Years: An Autobiography of the Sixties*, 2nd ed. (London: Verso, 2005), 320–24.
36. General histories include Marwick, *The Sixties*; Gerd-Rainer Horn, *The Spirit of '68: Rebellion in Western Europe and North America, 1956–1976* (Oxford: Oxford University Press, 2007); Carole Fink, Philipp Gassert, and Detlef Junker, eds., *1968: The World Transformed* (New York: Cambridge University Press, 1997); Todd Gitlin, *The Sixties: Years of Hope Days of Rage* (New York: Bantam Books, 1987). These tend to concentrate on Western Europe and North America, but in addition to several essays in the Fink et. al. volume, which cover other parts of the world, see also Samantha Christiansen and Zachary A. Scarlett, eds., *The Third World in the Global 1960s* (New York: Berghahn Books, 2013).
37. Wesley Sasaki-Uemura, *Organizing the Spontaneous: Citizen Protests in Postwar Japan* (Honolulu: University of Hawai'i Press, 2001).
38. Rebecca Klatch, *A Generation Divided: The New Left, the New Right and the 1960s* (Berkeley: University of California Press, 1999), esp. chap. 2; Robert Gildea, James Mark, and Annette Warring, eds., *Europe's 1968: Voices of Revolt* (Oxford: Oxford University Press, 2013), esp. chap. 2. This author must admit to being such a red diaper baby.
39. Cf. Kostis Kornetis, *Children of the Dictatorship: Student Resistance, Cultural Politics, and the "Long 1960s" in Greece* (New York: Berghahn Books, 2013), 316.
40. Port Huron Statement, from "The Sixties Project," University of Virginia, http://www2.iath.virginia.edu/sixties/HTML_docs/Resources/Primary/Manifestos/SDS_Port_Huron.html, accessed Aug. 4, 2020; for similar ideals in Western Europe, Horn, *Spirit of '68*, chap. 5.

41. Bahru Zewde, *The Quest for a Socialist Utopia: The Ethiopian Student Movement c. 1960–1974* (Woodbridge, Suffolk: James Currey, 2014), 184; James Bradford, "Brother Wally and De Burnin' of Babylon: Walter Rodney's Impact on the Reawakening of Black Power, the Birth of Reggae, and Resistance to Global Imperialism," in Christiansen and Scarlett, *The Third World in the Global 1960s*, 142–56.
42. Gildea et. al., eds., *Europe's 1968* chap. 3; Timothy Scott Brown, *West Germany and the Global Sixties: The Antiauthoritarian Revolt, 1962–1978* (Cambridge: Cambridge University Press, 2013), 90–91; Kornetis, *Children of the Dictatorship*, 21–32.
43. Wittner, *Struggle against the Bomb*, 2:456–62; Aldo Marchesi, *Latin America's Radical Left: Rebellion and Cold War in the Global 1960s*, trans. Laura Perez Carrera (Cambridge: Cambridge University Press, 2018), 75–76, 147; Pensado, *Rebel Mexico*, 176–77, 179; Gildea, Mark, and Warring, *Europe's 1968*, 102–3; Zewde, *Quest for Socialist Utopia*, 20–21, 108, 118, 266–71; Carole Fink, Philipp Gassert, and Detlef Junker, "Introduction," in Fink, Gassert, and Junker, *1968: The World Transformed*, 17–18; Michael Seidman, *The Imaginary Revolution: Parisian Students and Workers in 1968* (New York: Berghahn Books, 2004), 26, 35, 65; Pedro Monaville, "The Destruction of the University: Violence, Political Imagination, and the Student Movement in Congo-Zaire, 1969–1971," in Christiansen and Scarlett, *The Third World in the Global 1960s*, 163; Julia Sloan, "Revolution on the National Stage: Mexico, the PRI, and the Student Movement in 1968," in ibid., 174–75; Chamberlin, *The Global Offensive*, 19–21, 26–27, 185; n. 35.
44. Brown, *West Germany and the Global Sixties*, chap. 1; Jeremy Varon, *Brining the War Home: The Weather Underground, the Red Army Faction and Revolutionary Violence in the Sixties and Seventies* (Berkeley: University of California Press, 2004), chap. 1; Chamberlin, *The Global Offensive*, esp. chap. 1; author's memories of antiwar demonstrations. Good summaries of these attitudes in Lovell, *Maoism*, chap. 8 and Christoph Kalter, "A Shared Space of Imagination, Communication and Action: Perspectives on the History of the 'Third World,'" in Christensen and Scarlett, *The Third World*, 23–38;
45. Gildea, Mark, and Warring, *Europe's 1968*, 101–2.
46. Gitlin, *The Sixties*, 136–70; Hatch, *A Generation Divided*, 74–78; Grace Hale, *A Nation of Outsiders: How the White Middle Class Fell in Love with Rebellion in Postwar America* (New York: Oxford University Press, 2011), chap. 5.
47. Hale, *A Nation of Outsiders*, chap. 6.; Varon, *Bringing the War Home*, 90–91, 155–56 and more generally.
48. Jerzy Eisler, "March 1968 in Poland," in Fink et. al., *1968* 237–51, quote on 240.
49. Monaville, "The Destruction of the University," in Christiansen and Scarlett, *The Third World in the Global 1960s*, 161–70.
50. Avishek Ganguly, "Politics and Periodicals in 1960s: Readings around the 'Naxalite Movement,'" in Christiansen and Scarlett, *The Third World in the Global 1960s*, 57–68; Lovell, *Maoism*, chap. 10; Zewde, *The Quest for Socialist Utopia*, 118–27.
51. Kornetis, *Children of the Dictatorship*, 260–61.
52. Jaime Pensado, *Rebel Mexico: Student Unrest and Authoritarian Political Culture during the Long Sixties* (Stanford, CA: Stanford University Press, 2013),

esp. 16–17, 303; n. 2; Thomas Grace, *Kent State: Death and Dissent in the Long Sixties* (Boston: University of Massachusetts Press, 2016).

53. Martin Klimke, *The Other Alliance: Student Protest in West Germany and the United States in the Global Sixties* (Princeton, NJ: Princeton University Press, 2010), 23, 38–40, 121–22; Christopher R. Hill, *Peace and Power in Cold War Britain: Media, Movements and Democracy, c. 1945–68* (London: Bloomsbury Academic, 2018), 236.

54. Aldo Marchesi, *Latin America's Radical Left*; Zewde, *Quest for a Socialist Utopia*; Talbot Imlay, *The Practice of Socialist Internationalism: European Socialists and International Politics, 1914–1960* (Oxford: Oxford University Press, 2018), esp. Part II.

55. Vincent Lemire, "Nanterre, les bidonvilles et les étudiants," in Artières and Zsancarini-Fournel (eds.), *68 une histoire collective*, 137–43.

56. Marchesi, *Latin America's Radical Left*, 70–71; Brown, *West Germany and the Global Sixties*, 34–35.

57. Lovett, *Maoism*, 271, 278–79; more broadly, chap. 8; Kalter, "A Shared Space of Imagination," in Christiansen and Scarlett, *The Third World*, 32; Richard Wolin, *The Wind from the East: French Intellectuals, the Cultural Revolution, and the Legacy of the 1960s* (Princeton, NJ: Princeton University Press, 2010), chaps. 1–4. Grace Hale, in *A Nation of Outsiders*, identifies this combination of projection and identification very well, but her contention that it was only white, middle-class Americans who engaged in it, seems problematic.

58. Monika Kaiser, *Machtwechsel von Ulbricht zu Honecker. Funktionsmechanismen der SED-Diktatur in Konfliktsituationen 1962 bis 1972* (Berlin: Akadamie Verlag, 1997).

59. Yiching Wu, *The Cultural Revolution at the Margins: Chinese Socialism in Crisis* (Cambridge, MA: Harvard University Press, 2014); and Walder, *China under Mao*, chaps. 9–13.

60. Wu, *Cultural Revolution*, 62.

61. The following account is based on Artières and Zancarini-Fournel, *68 une histoire collective*; and Seidman, *The Imaginary Revolution*.

62. Horn, *The Spirit of '68*, 111–18.

63. Omar Guèye, "May 1968 in Senegal," https://www.versobooks.com/blogs/3880-may-1968-in-senegal, accessed Aug. 13, 2020; Pascal Bianchini, "The 1969 Years: Revolutionary Politics in Senegal," *Review of African Political Economy* 46 (2009): 184–203.

64. Arnulf Baring, *Machtwechsel. Die Ära Brandt-Scheel* (Munich: Deutscher Taschenbuchverlag, 1984); Artières and Zancarini-Fournel, *68, une histoire collective* 671–72, and pt. 4, more generally; Kornetis, *Children of the Dictatorship*, 303.

65. Marchesi, *Latin America's Radical Left*, 215–16, 226–27; Giles Tremlett, "José Mujica: Is This the World's Most Radical President," *The Guardian*, Sept. 18, 2014, https://www.theguardian.com/world/2014/sep/18/-sp-is-this-worlds-most-radical-president-uruguay-jose-mujica, accessed Aug. 14, 2020.

66. Ronald Fraser et al., eds., *1968: A Student Generation in Revolt* (New York: Pantheon Books, 1988), 364; cf. Jenkins, *Decade of Nightmares*.

67. Zewde, *Quest for Socialist Utopia*, 277–79.

68. Gitlin, *The Sixties*, 387–88; Klatch, *A Generation Divided*, 207–11.

69. Lowell, *Maoism*, chaps. 8–10; Klatch, *A Generation Divided*, 143, 240–43, 257–58; Bernard Brillant, Le gauchisme et ses cultures politiques," in Artières and Zancaraini-Fournel, 68, 552–59; Bianchini, "The 1969 Years."
70. Varon, *Bringing the War Home*, is especially insightful; Karrin Hanshew, *Terror and Democracy in West Germany* (New York: Cambridge University Press, 2012); Robin Erica Wagner-Pacifici, *The Moro Morality Play: Terrorism as Social Drama* (Chicago: University of Chicago Press, 1986); Stefan Aust, *Baader-Meinhof: The Inside Story of the R.A.F.*, trans. Anthea Bell (Oxford: Oxford University Press, 2009); Pierre Girarg, "De 1968 au terrorisme: Les Brigades rouges et l'Italie des 'années de plomb,'" in Artières and Zancaraini-Fournel, 68, 462–69; Zewde, *Quest for Socialist Utopia*, 260; Chamberlain, *The Global Offensive*, chap. 5. The Provisional IRA might count as another terrorist group emerging from the sixties, although, as is often the case in Ireland, its ideology was noticeably different from terrorist groups in other countries.
71. Besides sources cited in chap. 1, n. 15, 18 and chap. 7, n. 82–83; Zewde, *Quest for Socialist Utopia*, 221–27; Brown, *West Germany and the Global Sixties*, chap. 7; Klatch, *A Generation Divided*, chap. 6; Florence Rochefort, "L'insurrection féministe," in Artières and Zancarini-Fournel, *68 une histoire collective*, 538–46.
72. Thomas Davies, *NGOs: A New History of Transnational Civil Society* (Oxford; Oxford University Press, 2014), 145; Marchesi, *Latin America's Radical Left*, chap. 5; Samuel Moyn, *The Last Utopia: Human Rights in History* (Cambridge, MA: Harvard University Press, 2010); Wolin, *Wind from the East*, pt. 2; and, above all, Jan Eckel, *The Ambivalence of Good: Human Rights in International Politics since the 1940s*, trans. Rachel Ward (Oxford: Oxford University Press, 2019), esp. chaps. 6, 8–10. Critics of human rights organizations, explicitly citing 1960s attitudes, include Kristin Ross, *May '68 and its Afterlives* (Chicago: University of Chicago Press, 2002), esp. 158–81; Lasse Heerten, *The Biafran War and Postcolonial Humanitarianism: Spectacles of Suffering* (Cambridge: Cambridge University Press, 2017), esp. chap. 9 and 334–41. As noted in the previous chapter, similar arguments were made against US and NATO intervention to stop mass murder during the 1990s.
73. For this and the following, see especially Angus Burgin, *The Great Persuasion: Reinventing Free Markets since the Great Depression* (Cambridge, MA: Harvard University Press, 2012); also, with reservations, Quinn Slobodian, *Globalists: The End of Empire and the Birth of Neoliberalism* (Cambridge, MA: Harvard University Press, 2018).
74. Rodgers, *Age of Fracture*, 54–55; John Campbell and N. Gregory Mankiw, "Permanent Income, Current Income, and Consumption," *Journal of Business and Economic Statistics* 8 (1990): 266–79; Matthew B. Canzoneri, Robert E. Cumby, and Behzad T. Diba, "Euler Equations and Market Interest Rates: A Challenge for Monetary Policy Models," *Journal of Monetary Economics* 54 (2007) 1863–1881; Noah Smith, "Economists Give Up on Milton Friedman's Biggest Idea," https://www.bloomberg.com/opinion/articles/2016-07-26/economists-give-up-on-milton-friedman-s-biggest-idea, accessed Sept. 3, 2020.
75. Kim Philips-Fein, *Invisible Hands: The Businessman's Crusade against the New Deal* (New York: W.W. Norton, 2010).

76. Rodgers, *Age of Fracture*, chap. 2.
77. Francis Fukuyama, "The End of History?," *The National Interest* 16 (1989): 3–18; idem., "A Reply to My Critics," *The National Interest* 18 (1989–90): 21–28; idem., *The End of History and the Last Man*, 2nd ed. (New York: Free Press, 2006); a useful commentary in Rodgers, *Age of Fracture*, 245–47.
78. State of the Union address transcript, *New York Times*, Jan. 30, 1991, https://www.nytimes.com/1991/01/30/us/state-union-transcript-president-s-state-union-message-nation.html; "To Paris, US Looks Like a Hyperpower," *New York Times*, Feb. 5, 1999, https://www.nytimes.com/1999/02/05/news/to-paris-us-looks-like-a-hyperpower.html, both accessed Sept. 4, 2020.
79. Vinay Sitapati, *The Man Who Remade India: A Biography of P.V. Narasimha Rao* (New York: Oxford University Press, 2018).
80. Rodgers, *Age of Fracture*, 247–55.
81. Hilary Appel and Mitchell Orenstein, *From Triumph to Crisis: Neoliberal Economic Reform in Postcommunist Countries* (Cambridge: Cambridge University Press, 2018), quotes on 20 and 105.
82. David Ost, *The Defeat of Solidarity: Anger and Politics in Postcommunist Europe* (Ithaca, NY: Cornell University Press, 2005).
83. Besides the books mentioned in the two notes above, Alena V. Ledeneva, *How Russian Really Works: The Informal Practices that Shaped Post-Soviet Politics and Business* (Ithaca, NY: Cornell University Press, 2006); Lawrence R. Klein and Marshall Pomer, eds., *The New Russia Transition Gone Awry* (Stanford, CA: Stanford University Press, 2001); Jeffrey Hass, *Rethinking the Post-Soviet Experience: Markets, Moral Economies, and Cultural Contradictions of Post-Socialist Russia* (Houndmills, Basingstoke: Palgrave Macmillan, 2012); Vadimn Volkov, *Violent Entrepreneurs: The Use of Force in the Making of Russian Capitalism* (Ithaca, NY: Cornell University Press, 2002); Frederico Varese, *The Russian Mafia: Private Protection in A New Market Economy* (Oxford: Oxford University Press, 2001); Dirk Laabs, *Der deutsche Goldrausch: Die wahre Geschichte der Treuhand* (Munich: Pantheon Verlag, 2012).
84. Christopher Jarvis, "The Rise and Fall of Albania's Pyramid Schemes," *IMF Finance and Development*, Mar. 2000, https://www.imf.org/external/pubs/ft/fandd/2000/03/jarvis.htm, accessed Sept. 9, 2020e.
85. Appel and Orenstein, *From Triumph to Crisis*, 162–69.
86. Richard Crockatt, *America Embattled: September 11, Anti-Americanism and the Global Order* (London: Routledge, 2003), chap. 2; Peter Hessler, *Oracle Bones: A Journey between China's Past and Present* (New York: HarperCollins, 2006), chap. 17. A detailed study of responses to 9/11 remains to be written.
87. For reflections on this process, Jonathan Sperber, "The Failed Promises of 1989 and the Politics of 2016," in *Chaos in the Liberal Order: The Trump Presidency and International Politics in the Twenty-First Century*, ed. Robert Jervis et al. (New York: Columbia University Press, 2018), 172–79, as well as the other essays in the book.

Aftermath

1. https://www.bis.org/statistics/rpfx19.htm; https://ourworldindata.org/trade-and-globalization, both accessed Apr. 24, 2020; Adam Tooze, *Crashed: How a Decade of Financial Crises Changed the World* (New York: Viking, 2018), chap. 3.
2. Detailed statistics, https://www.un.org/en/development/desa/population/migration/data/estimates2/estimates19.asp; a general summary, International Organization for Migration, "World Migration Report," 2020, https://publications.iom.int/system/files/pdf/wmr_2020.pdf both accessed Apr. 27, 2020.
3. Statistics from World Bank Development Indicators, https://datacatalog.worldbank.org/dataset/world-development-indicators; easier summaries in https://ourworldindata.org/internet; more optimistic figures in internetworldstats.com/emarketing.htm, all accessed Apr. 27, 2020.
4. "Taking Stock of the Global Partnership for Development," MDG Gap Task Force Report 2015, 67–69, https://www.un.org/millenniumgoals/pdf/MDG_Gap_2015_E_web.pdf, accessed Apr. 28, 2020.
5. Torfox, "The Great Firewall of China: Background," https://cs.stanford.edu/people/eroberts/cs181/projects/2010-11/FreedomOfInformationChina/the-great-firewall-of-china-background/index.html; Jimmy Wu and Oiwan Lam, "The Evolution of China's Great Firewall: 21 Years of Censorship," Sept. 3, 2017 *Hong Kong Free Press*, https://hongkongfp.com/2017/09/03/evolution-chinas-great-firewall-21-years-censorship/' Elizabeth Economy, "The Great Firewall of China: Xi Jinping's Internet Shutdown," *The Guardian* June 29, 2018, https://www.theguardian.com/news/2018/jun/29/the-great-firewall-of-china-xi-jinpings-internet-shutdown all accessed Apr. 27, 2020.
6. https://data.worldbank.org/indicator/NY.GDP.MKTP.PP.CD?locations=CN;https://www.quandl.com/data/ODA/CHN_PPPSH-China-Share-of-World-GDP-based-on-PPP, both accessed Apr. 28, 2020.
7. https://carboncounter.wordpress.com/2015/06/06/building-china-the-role-of-cement-in-chinas-rapid-development/, accessed Apr. 28, 2020; Ana Swanson, "How China Used more Cement in Three Years Than the US Did in a Century," *Washington Post*, Mar. 24, 2015; Shi Li and Terry Sicular, "The Distribution of Household Income in China: Inequality, Poverty and Policies," *China Quarterly* 217 (2014): 1–41, Tables 1 and 2.
8. Elizabeth Economy and Michael Levi, *By All Means Necessary: How China's Resource Quest Is Changing the World* (New York: Oxford University Press, 2014) 61, 118; https://data.worldbank.org/indicator/NY.GDP.MKTP.KD.ZG?locations=ZG, accessed Apr. 28, 2020.
9. https://www.macrotrends.net/countries/CHN/china/trade-gdp-ratio and https://www.macrotrends.net/countries/CHN/china/trade-gdp-ratio, accessed Apr. 28, 2020; Adam Minter, *Junkyard Planet: Travels in the Billion-Dollar Trash Trade* (New York: Bloomsbury Press, 2013), esp. chap. 5.
10. Economic Policy Institute, "Growing China Trade Deficit Cost 3.7 million American Jobs between 2001 and 2018," https://www.epi.org/files/pdf/181374.pdf, accessed Apr. 29, 2020; Nicholas Bloom, Kyle Handley, Andre Kurman, and Philip Luck, "The Impact of Chinese Trade on U.S. Employment: The Good, The

Bad, and The Debatable," July 2019, https://nbloom.people.stanford.edu/sites/g/files/sbiybj4746/f/bhkl_posted_draft.pdf, accessed June 11, 2020.
11. Tooze, *Crashed*, 31–34, 58, 73–79.
12. Johns Hopkins School of Advanced International Studies, "China-Africa Research Initiative," http://www.sais-cari.org/; Silvia Amaro, "China Bought Most of Greece's Main Port and Now It Wants to Make It the Biggest in Europe," CNBC, Nov. 15, 2019, https://www.cnbc.com/2019/11/15/china-wants-to-turn-greece-piraeus-port-into-europe-biggest.html; Council on Foreign Relations, "China's Massive Belt and Road Initiative," https://www.cfr.org/backgrounder/chinas-massive-belt-and-road-initiative all accessed Apr. 29, 2020; a similar viewpoint in Economy and Levi, *By All Means Necessary*.
13. Quotes from a very informed and revealing journalistic account, Robert Draper, *To Start A War: How the Bush Administration Took America into Iraq* (New York: Penguin Press, 2020), 173, 351, 363, 376.
14. A brilliant contemporary account is Rajiv Chandrasekaran, *Imperial Life in the Emerald City* (New York: Vintage Books, 2006), esp. 70, 107–12, 185, 190.
15. Cf. Rodgers, *Age of Fracture*, 266–68.
16. Besides the books in the two previous notes, particularly helpful for military aspects is Thomas Ricks, *Fiasco: The American Military Adventure in Iraq* (New York: Penguin Press, 2006).
17. Unless otherwise specified, this account of the global economic crisis follows Tooze, *Crashed*.
18. Figures from https://data.worldbank.org/indicator/NY.GDP.MKTP.KD.ZG, accessed Sept. 14, 2020.
19. Appel and Orenstein, *From Triumph to Crisis*, 155–70; Stefan Hedlund, "Russian Pension Reform 'A Threat to Country's Fledgling Financial Markets,'" https://www.gisreportsonline.com/russia-pension-reform-a-threat-to-countrys-fledgling-financial-markets,economy,615.html, accessed Sept. 15, 2020. Chap. 9 of Tooze, *Crashed*, on the crisis in Eastern Europe, is a weaker part of the book.

Conclusions

1. Karl Marx/Friedrich Engels, *Manifest der Kommunistischen Partei*, http://www.mlwerke.de/me/me04/me04_459.htm, accessed Apr. 14, 2020, my translation, which differs slightly from the standard English-language version.

SELECT BIBLIOGRAPHY

Chapter 1: Nature

Brown, Kate. *Plutopia: Nuclear Families, Atomic Cities and the Great Soviet and American Plutonium Disasters.* Oxford: Oxford University Press, 2013.

Brüggemeier, Franz-Josef. *Schranken der Natur. Umwelt, Gesellschaft Experimente 1750 bis heute.* Essen: Klartext Verlag, 2014.

Conway, Gordon. *One Billion Hungry: Can We Feed the World?* Ithaca, NY: Cornell University Press, 2012.

Edwards, Paul N. *A Vast Machine: Computer Models, Climate Data and the Politics of Global Warming.* Cambridge, MA: MIT Press, 2010.

Feschbach, Murray, and Alfred Friendly Jr. *Ecocide in the USSR: Health and Nature under Siege.* New York: Basic Books, 1992.

Hamblin, Jacob Darwin. *Arming Mother Nature: The Birth of Catastrophic Environmentalism.* Oxford: Oxford University Press, 2013.

Hochstetler, Kathryn, and Margaret E. Keck. *Greening Brazil: Environmental Activism in State and Society.* Durham, NC: Duke University Press, 2007.

Jänicke, Martin, and Helmut Weidner, eds. *National Environmental Policies: A Comparative Study of Capacity-Building.* Berlin: Springer–Verlag, 1996.

Kinkela, David. *DDT and the American Century: Global Health, Environmental Politics and the Pesticide That Changed the World.* Chapel Hill: University of North Carolina Press, 2011.

Kutney, Gerald. *Carbon Politics and the Failure of the Kyoto Protocol.* London: Routledge, 2014.

McNeill, J.R. *Something New under the Sun: An Environmental History of the Twentieth-Century World.* New York: W.W. Norton, 2000.

Meadows, Donella, and Dennis Meadows et al. *The Limits to Growth: A Report for the Club of Rome's Project on the Predicament of Mankind*, 2nd ed. New York: Universe Books, 1974.

Oreskes, Naomi, and Eric Conway. *Merchants of Doubt: How a Handful of Scientists Obscured the Truth on Issues from Tobacco Smoke to Global Warming.* New York: Bloomsbury, 2010.
Parson, Edward A. *Protecting the Ozone Layer: Science and Strategy.* Oxford: Oxford University Press, 2003.
Robertson, Thomas. *The Malthusian Moment: Global Population Growth and the Birth of American Environmentalism.* New Brunswick, NJ: Rutgers University Press, 2012.
Rudel, Thomas K. *Tropical Forests: Regional Paths of Destruction and Regeneration in the Late Twentieth Century.* New York: Columbia University Press, 2005.
Sabin, Paul. *The Bet: Paul Ehrlich, Julian Simon, and Our Gamble over Earth's Future.* New Haven, CT: Yale University Press, 2013.
Shapiro, Judith. *Mao's War against Nature: Politics and the Environment in Revolutionary China.* Cambridge: Cambridge University Press, 2001.
Weart, Spencer. *The Discovery of Global Warming.* Cambridge, MA: Harvard University Press, 2008.
Zelko, Frank. *Make It a Green Peace! The Rise of Countercultural Environmentalism.* Oxford: Oxford University Press, 2013.

Chapter 2: Disease

Baldwin, Peter. *Disease and Democracy: The Industrialized World Faces AIDS.* Berkeley: University of California Press, 2005.
Brandt, Allan M. *The Cigarette Century: The Rise, Fall and Deadly Persistence of the Product that Defined America.* New York: Basic Books, 2007.
Bud, Robert. *Penicillin: Triumph and Tragedy.* Oxford: Oxford University Press, 2007.
Bynum, Helen. *Spitting Blood: The History of Tuberculosis.* Oxford: Oxford University Press, 2012.
Engel, Jonathan. *The Epidemic: A Global History of Aids.* New York: Harper Collins, 2006.
Glynn, Jennifer, and Ian Glynn. *The Life and Death of Smallpox.* Cambridge: Cambridge University Press, 2004.
Greenwood, David. *Antimicrobial Drugs: Chronicle of a Twentieth Century Medical Triumph.* Oxford: Oxford University Press, 2008.
Iliffe, John. *The African AIDS Epidemic: A History.* Oxford: James Currey Ltd, 2006.
McMillen, Christian. *Discovering Tuberculosis: A Global History 1900 to the Present.* New Haven, CT: Yale University Press, 2015.
Mukherjee, Siddhartha. *The Emperor of All Maladies: A Biography of Cancer.* New York: Scribner, 2010.
Omran, Abdel R. "The Epidemiologic Transition: A Theory of the Epidemiology of Population Change." *Milbank Memorial Fund Quarterly* 49 (1971): 509–38.
Podolsky, Scott. *The Antibiotic Era: Reform, Resistance and the Pursuit of a Rational Therapeutics.* Baltimore: Johns Hopkins University Press, 2015.
Popkin, Barry. *The World Is Fat: The Fads, Trends, Policies and Products That Are Fattening the Human Race.* New York: Avery, 2008.
Rothstein, William. *Public Health and the Risk Factor: A History of an Uneven Medical Revolution.* Rochester, NY: University of Rochester Press, 2003.

Webb, James Jr. *Humanity's Burden: A Global History of Malaria.* New York: Cambridge University Press, 2009.

Chapter 3: Technologies

Anderson, Robert S. *Nucleus and Nation: Scientists, International Networks and Power in India.* Chicago: University of Chicago Press, 2010.

Campbell-Kelly, Martin. *From Airline Reservations to Sonic the Hedgehog: A History of the Software Industry.* Cambridge, MA: MIT Press, 2003.

Cassidy, John. *Dot.con: The Greatest Story Ever Sold.* New York: HarperCollins, 2002.

Chandler, Alfred D., Jr. *Inventing the Electronic Century: The Epic Story of the Consumer Electronics and Computer Industries.* New York: The Free Press, 2001.

Cooke, Stephanie. *In Mortal Hands: A Cautionary History of the Nuclear Age.* New York: Bloomsbury, 2009.

Easton, Richard, and Eric Frazier. *GPS Declassified: From Smart Bombs to Smartphones.* Lincoln, NE: Potomac Books, 2013.

Eckermann, Erik. *World History of the Automobile.* Translated by Peter L. Albrecht. Warrendale, PA: Society of Automotive Engineers, Inc., 2001.

Edgerton, David. *The Shock of the Old: Technology and Global History since 1900.* Oxford: Oxford University Press, 2007.

Hecht, Gabrielle. *The Radiance of France: Nuclear Power and National Identity after World War II.* Cambridge, MA: MIT Press, 1998.

Heppenheimer, T.A. *Turbulent Skies: The History of Commercial Aviation.* New York: J. Wiley & Sons, 1995.

Josephson, Paul R. *Red Atom: Russia's Nuclear Program from Stalin to Today.* New York: W.H. Freeman and Company, 2000.

Kingsbury, Noel. *Hybrid: The History and Science of Plant Breeding.* Chicago: University of Chicago Press, 2009.

Landauer, Thomas. *The Trouble with Computers: Usefulness, Usability and Productivity.* Cambridge, MA: MIT Press, 1995.

Launius, Roger, ed. *Exploring the Solar System: The History and Science of Planetary Exploration.* Houndmills, Basingstoke: Macmillan 2013.

Lurquin, Paul F. *The Green Phoenix: A History of Genetically Modified Plants.* New York: Columbia University Press, 2001.

McCarthy, Tom. *Auto Mania: Cars, Consumers and the Environment.* New Haven, CT: Yale University Press, 2007.

McCurdy, Howard. *Space and the American Imagination*, 2nd ed. Baltimore: Johns Hopkins University Press, 2011.

McGuire, Steven. *Airbus Industrie: Conflict and Cooperation in US-EC Trade Relations.* Houndmills, Basingstoke: Macmillan, 1997.

Morton, David L., and Joseph Gabriel. *Electronics: The Life Story of a Technology.* Baltimore: Johns Hopkins University Press, 2004.

Murphy, Denis J. *Plant Breeding and Biotechnology: Societal Context and the Future of Agriculture.* Cambridge: Cambridge University Press, 2007.

Osseo-Asare, Abena Dove. *Atomic Junction: Nuclear Power in Africa after Independence.* Cambridge: Cambridge University Press, 2019.

Piantadosi, Claude. *Mankind beyond Earth: The History, Science and Future of Human Space Exploration*. New York: Columbia University Press, 2012.
Rieger, Bernhard. *The People's Car: A Global History of the Volkswagen Beetle*. Cambridge, MA: Harvard University Press, 2013.
Seife, Charles. *Sun in a Bottle: The Strange History of Fusion and the Science of Wishful Thinking*. New York: Viking, 2008.
Siddiqi, Asif A. *Challenge to Apollo: The Soviet Union and the Space Race, 1945–1974*. Washington, DC: NASA History Division, 2000.
Siddiqi, Asif A. *The Red Rockets Glare: Spaceflight and the Soviet Imagination, 1857–1957*. New York: Cambridge University Press, 2010.
Siegelbaum, Lewis H. *Cars for Comrades: The Life of the Soviet Automobile*. Ithaca, NY: Cornell University Press, 2008.
Smil, Vaclav. *Feeding the World: A Challenge for the Twenty-First Century*. Cambridge, MA: MIT Press, 2000.
Triplett, Jack E. "The Solow Productivity Paradox: What Do Computers Do to Productivity?" *Canadian Journal of Economics* 32 (1999): 309–34.
Wolfe, Joel. *Autos and Progress: The Brazilian Search for Modernity*. Oxford: Oxford University Press, 2010.
Yergin, Daniel. *The Prize: The Epic Quest for Oil, Money and Power*. New York: Simon & Schuster, 1991.
Yergin, Daniel. *The Quest: Energy, Security and the Remaking of the Modern World*. New York: Penguin Press, 2011.

Chapter 4: Markets

Abdelal, Rawi. *Capital Rules: The Construction of Global Finance*. Cambridge, MA: Harvard University Press, 2007.
Abdelal, Rawi. *The Rise of "The Rest": Challenges to the West from Late-Industrializing Economies*. Oxford: Oxford University Press, 2001.
Cassis, Youssef. *Crises and Opportunities: The Shaping of Modern Finance*. Oxford: Oxford University Press, 2011.
Chibber, Vivek. *Locked in Place: State-Building and Late Industrialization in India*. Princeton, NJ: Princeton University Press, 2003.
Dosman, Edgar. *The Life and Times of Raúl Prebisch 1901–1986*. Montreal, Canada: McGill-Queen's University Press, 2008.
Eichengreen, Barry. *Globalizing Capital: A History of the International Monetary System*, 2nd ed. Princeton, NJ: Princeton University Press, 2008.
Ellman, Michael. *Planning Problems in the USSR: The Contribution of Mathematical Economics to Their Solution 1960–1971*. Cambridge, MA: Cambridge University Press, 1973.
Feenstra, Robert C. "Integration of Trade and Disintegration of Production in the Global Economy." *Journal of Economic Perspectives* 12 (1998): 31–50.
Fitzgerald, Robert. *The Rise of the Global Company: Multinationals and the Making of the Modern World*. Cambridge: Cambridge University Press, 2015.
Frieden, Jeffrey A. *Global Capitalism: Its Rise and Fall in the Twentieth Century*. New York: W.W. Norton, 2006.

James, Harold. *International Monetary Cooperation since Bretton Woods*. New York: Oxford University Press, 1996.
Krippner Greta R. *Capitalizing on Crisis: The Political Origins of the Rise of Finance*. Cambridge, MA: Harvard University Press, 2011.
Levinson, Marc. *The Box: How the Shipping Container Made the World Smaller and the World Economy Bigger*. Princeton, NJ: Princeton University Press, 2006.
Lewis, Peter M. *Growing Apart: Oil, Politics and Economic Change in Indonesia and Nigeria*. Ann Arbor: University of Michigan Press, 2007.
Maddison, Angus. *The World Economy*. 2 vols. in 1. Paris: OECD, 2006.
Milanovic, Branko. *Global Inequality: A New Approach for the Age of Industrialization*. Cambridge, MA: Harvard University Press, 2016.
Obstfeld, Maurice, and Alan Taylor. *Global Capital Markets: Integration, Crisis and Growth*. Cambridge: Cambridge University Press, 2004.
Piketty, Thomas. *Capital in the Twenty-First Century*. Translated by Arthur Goldhammer. Cambridge, MA: Harvard University Press, 2014.
Stein, Judith. *Pivotal Decade: How the United States Traded Factories for Finance in the Seventies*. New Haven, CT: Yale University Press, 2010.
Stiglitz, Joseph. *Globalization and Its Discontents*. New York: W.W. Norton, 2002.
Vogel, Ezra. *Deng Xiaoping and the Transformation of China*. Cambridge, MA: Harvard University Press, 2011.

Chapter 5: Migrations

Amrith, Sunil S. *Migration and Diaspora in Modern Asia*. Cambridge: Cambridge University Press, 2011.
Castles, Stephen, and Mark J. Miller. *The Age of Migration: International Population Movements in the Modern World*, 2nd ed. London: Guilford Press, 1998.
Cohen, Gerard. *In War's Wake: Europe's Displaced Persons in the Postwar Order*. New York: Oxford University Press, 2012.
Fischbach, Michael. *Records of Dispossession: Palestinian Refugee Property and the Arab-Israeli Conflict*. New York: Columbia University Press, 2003.
García, Maria Cristina. *Seeking Refuge: Central American Migration to Mexico, the United States and Canada*. Berkeley: University of California Press, 2006.
Gatrell, Peter. *The Making of the Modern Refugee*. Oxford: Oxford University Press, 2013.
Hing, Bill Ong. *Defining America through Immigration Policy*. Philadelphia: Temple University Press, 2004.
Kurien, Prema A. *Kaleidoscopic Ethnicity: International Migration and the Reconstruction of Community Identities in India*. New Brunswick, NJ: Rutgers University Press, 2002.
Lary, Diana. *Chinese Migrations: The Movement of People, Goods and Ideas over Four Millennia*. Lanham, MD: Rowman and Littlefield, 2012.
Leiken, Robert. *Europe's Angry Muslims: The Revolt of the Second Generation*. New York: Oxford University Press, 2012.
Loescher, Gil. *The UNHCR and World Politics: A Perilous Path*. Oxford: Oxford University Press, 2001.
Massey, Douglas, and Jorge Durand. "Why Border Enforcement Backfired." *American Journal of Sociology* 121 (2016): 1557–600.

McKewon, Adam. "Global Migration 1846–1940." *Journal of World History* 15 (2004): 155–89.

Morris, Benny. *The Birth of the Palestinian Refugee Problem, 1947–1949.* Cambridge: Cambridge University Press, 1987.

Nugent, Walter. *Crossings: The Great Transatlantic Migrations, 1870–1914.* Bloomington: Indiana University Press, 1992.

Peteet, Julie. *Landscapes of Hope and Despair: Palestinian Refugee Camps.* Philadelphia: University of Pennsylvania Press, 2005.

Salt, John, and Hugh Clout, eds. *Migration in Post-War Europe: Geographical Essays.* Oxford: Oxford University Press, 1976.

Schierup, Carl-Urik, Peo Hansen, and Stephen Castles. *Migration, Citizenship and the European Welfare State.* Oxford: Oxford University Press, 2006.

Segal, Uma A., Doreen Elliott, and Nazneen Mayadas, eds. *Immigration Worldwide: Policies, Practices and Trends.* Oxford: Oxford University Press, 2010.

Sellek, Yoko. *Migrant Labour in Japan.* Houndmills, Basingstoke: Palgrave Macmillan, 2001.

Talbot, Ian, and Gurharpal Singh. *The Partition of India.* Cambridge: Cambridge University Press, 2009.

Tsuda, Takeyuki. *Strangers in the Ethnic Homeland: Japanese Brazilian Return Migration in Transnational Perspective.* New York: Columbia University Press, 2003.

Zamindar, Vazira Fazila-Yacoobali. *The Long Partition and the Making of Modern South Asia: Refugees, Boundaries, Histories.* New York: Columbia University Press, 2007.

Zhao, Xiaojian. *The New Chinese America: Class, Economy and Social Hierarchy.* New Brunswick, NJ: Rutgers University Press, 2010.

Chapter 6: The Powers

Alvandi, Roham. *Nixon, Kissinger and the Shah: The United States and Iran in the Cold War.* New York: Oxford University Press, 2014.

Avon, Dominique, and Anaïs-Trissa Khatchadourian. *Hezbollah: A History of the "Party of God."* Translated by Jane Marie Todd. Cambridge, MA: Harvard University Press, 2012.

Barber, James. *Mandela's World: The International Dimension of South Africa's Political Revolution 1990–99.* Athens: Ohio University Press, 2004.

Bayly, Christopher, and Tim Harper. *Forgotten Wars: Freedom and Revolution in Southeast Asia.* Cambridge, MA: Harvard University Press, 2007.

Bolander, Keith. *Cuba under Siege: American Policy, the Revolution and Its People.* New York: Palgrave Macmillan, 2012.

Brandts, Hal. *Latin America's Cold War.* Cambridge, MA: Harvard University Press, 2010.

Byrne, Jeffrey James. *Mecca of Revolution: Algeria, Decolonization and the Third World Order.* New York: Oxford University Press, 2016.

Cooper, Frederick. *Citizenship between Empire and Nation: Remaking France and French Africa, 1945–1960.* Princeton, NJ: Princeton University Press, 2014.

Fischer, Benjamin. "The Soviet-American War Scare of the 1980s." *International Journal of Intelligence and Counter-Intelligence* 19 (2006): 480–581.

Freedman, Lawrence, and Efraim Karsh. *The Gulf Conflict, 1990–1991: Diplomacy and War in the New World Order.* Princeton, NJ: Princeton University Press, 1993.

Fursenko, Aleksandr, and Timothy Naftali. *"One Hell of a Gamble": Khrushchev, Castro, and Kennedy, 1958–1964.* New York: W.W. Norton, 1997.

Gerard, Emanuel, and Bruce Kuklick. *Death in the Congo: Murdering Patrice Lumumba.* Cambridge, MA: Harvard University Press, 2015.

Gleijeses, Piero. *Visions of Freedom: Havana, Washington, Pretoria and the Struggle for Southern Africa, 1976–1991.* Chapel Hill: University of North Carolina Press, 1991.

Hanhimäki, Jussi M. *The Rise and Fall of Détente: American Foreign Policy and the Transformation of the Cold War.* Washington, DC: Potomac Books, 2013.

Harmer, Tanya. *Allende's Chile and the Inter-American Cold War.* Chapel Hill: University of North Carolina Press, 2011.

Harrison, Hope. *Driving the Soviets Up the Wall: Soviet-East German Relations, 1953–1961.* Princeton, NJ: Princeton University Press, 2003.

Haslam, Jonathan. *Russia's Cold War: From the October Revolution to the Fall of the Wall.* New Haven, CT: Yale University Press, 2011.

Hogan, Michael. *The Marshall Plan: America, Britain and the Reconstruction of Western Europe, 1947–1952.* New York: Cambridge University Press, 1987.

Hong, Young-Sun. *Cold War Germany, the Third World, and the Global Humanitarian Regime.* NY: Cambridge University Press, 2015.

Hyam, Ronald. *Britain's Declining Empire: The Road to Decolonisation 1918–1968.* Cambridge: Cambridge University Press, 2006.

Iber, Patrick. *Neither Peace nor Freedom: The Cultural Cold War in Latin America.* Cambridge, MA: Harvard University Press, 2015.

Kalinovsky, Artemy. *A Long Goodbye: The Soviet Withdrawal from Afghanistan.* Cambridge MA: Harvard University Press, 2011.

Kalter, Christoph. *The Discovery of the Third World: Decolonization and the Rise of the New Left in France, c. 1950–1976.* Translated by Thomas Dunlop. Cambridge: Cambridge University Press, 2016.

Kepel, Gilles. *Jihad: The Trail of Political Islam.* Translated by Anthony F. Roberts. Cambridge, MA: Belknap Press of Harvard University Press, 2002.

Laron, Guy. *The Six-Day War: The Breaking of the Middle East.* New Haven, CT: Yale University Press, 2017.

Leffler, Melvyn. *For the Soul of Mankind: The United States, the Soviet Union and the Cold War.* New York: Hill and Wang, 2007.

Lüthi, Lorenz M. *The Sino-Soviet Split: Cold War in the Communist World.* Princeton, NJ: Princeton University Press, 2008.

MacMahon, Robert J. *The Limits of Empire: The United States and Southeast Asia since World War II.* New York: Columbia University Press, 1999.

Malley, Robert. *The Call from Algeria: Third Worldism, Revolution and the Turn to Islam.* Berkeley: University of California Press, 1996.

Martin, Garret. *General de Gaulle's Cold War: Challenging American Hegemony 1963–68.* New York: Berghahn Books, 2013.

Mastny, Vojtech, Sven Holtsmark, and Andreas Wenger, eds. *War Plans and Alliances in the Cold War: Threat Perception in the East and West.* London: Routledge, 2006.

Morgan, Michael. *The Final Act: The Helsinki Accords and the Transformation of the Cold War*. Princeton, NJ: Princeton University Press, 2018.

Murray, Williamson, and Kevin M. Woods. *The Iran-Iraq War: A Military and Strategic History*. New York: Cambridge University Press, 2014.

Nguyen, Lien-Hang T. *Hanoi's War: An International History of the War for Peace in Vietnam*. Chapel Hill: University of North Carolina Press, 2012.

Ogle, Vanessa. "State Rights against Private Capital: The 'New International Economic Order' and the Struggle over Aid, Trade and Foreign Investment, 1962–1981." *Humanity* 5 (2014): 211–34.

Plokhy, Serhii. *The Last Empire: The Final Days of the Soviet Union*. New York: Basic Books, 2014.

Raghavan, Srinath. *1971: A Global History of the Creation of Bangladesh*. Cambridge, MA: Harvard University Press, 2013.

Readman, Kristina Spohr. "Conflict and Cooperation in Intra-Alliance Nuclear Politics: Western Europe, the United States and the Genesis of NATO's Dual-Track Decision 1977–79." *Journal of Cold War Studies* 13 (2011): 39–89.

Roessler, Philip, and Harry Verhoeven. *Why Comrades Go to War: Liberation Politics and the Outbreak of Africa's Deadliest Conflict*. Oxford: Oxford University Press, 2016.

Sargent, David. *A Superpower Transformed: The Remaking of American Foreign Relations in the 1970s*. New York: Oxford University Press, 2015.

Sarotte, Mary Elise. *1989: The Struggle to Create Post-Cold War Europe*. Princeton, NJ: Princeton University Press, 2009.

Sarotte, Mary Elise. "Not One Inch Eastward? Bush, Baker, Kohl, Genscher, Gorbachev and the Origin of Russian Resentment toward NATO Enlargement in February 1990." *Diplomatic History* 34 (2010): 119–40.

Schmidt, Elizabeth. *Foreign Interventions in Africa: From the Cold War to the War on Terror*. Cambridge: Cambridge University Press, 2013.

Smyser, W. R. *From Yalta to Berlin: The Cold War Struggle over Germany*. New York: St. Martin's, 1999.

Stokes, Gail. *The Walls Came Tumbling Down: The Collapse of Communism in Eastern Europe*. New York: Oxford University Press, 1993.

Timmer, Karsten. *Vom Aufbruch zum Umbruch. Die Bürgerbewegung in der DDR 1989*. Göttingen: Vandenhoeck & Ruprecht, 2000.

Westad, Odd Arne. *The Cold War: A World History*. New York: Basic Books, 2017.

Wilson, James Graham. *The Triumph of Improvisation: Gorbachev's Adaptability, Reagan's Engagement, and the End of the Cold War*. Ithaca, NY: Cornell University Press, 2014.

Wright, Lawrence. *The Looming Tower: Al-Qaeda and the Road to 9/11*. New York: Knopf, 2006.

Zubok, Vladislav M. *A Failed Empire: The Soviet Union in the Cold War from Stalin to Gorbachev*. Chapel Hill: University of North Carolina Press, 2007.

Chapter 7: Societies

Adam, Barry D., Jan Willem Duyvendak, and André Krouwel. *The Global Emergence of Gay and Lesbian Politics: National Imprints of a Worldwide Movement*. Philadelphia: Temple University Press, 1999.

Ally, David. *Make Love Not War: The Sexual Revolution: An Unfettered History*. Boston: Little, Brown, 2000.
Andreas, Joel. *The Rise of the Red Engineers: The Cultural Revolution and the Origins of China's New Class*. Stanford, CA: Stanford University Press, 2009.
Baksh, Rawwida, and Wendy Harcourt, eds. *The Oxford Handbook of Transnational Feminist Movements*. New York: Oxford University Press, 2015.
Boellstorff, Tom. *The Gay Archipelago: Sexuality and Nation in Indonesia*. Princeton, NJ: Princeton University Press, 2005.
Bonin, Michael. *The Lost Generation: The Rustication of China's Educated Youth (1968–1980)*. Translated by Krystyna Horko. Hong Kong: The Chinese University Press, 2013.
Breman, Jan. *The Labouring Poor in India: Patterns of Exploitation, Subordination and Exclusion*. New Delhi: Oxford University Press, 2003.
Bryceson, Deborah Fahy, ed. *How Africa Works: Occupational Change, Identity and Morality*. Bourton on Dunsmore: Practical Action Publishing, 2010.
Collins, Marcus. *Modern Love: Personal Relationships in Twentieth-Century Britain*. Newark: University of Delaware Press, 2006.
Diamant, Neil J. *Revolutionizing the Family: Politics, Love and Divorce in Urban and Rural China, 1949–1968*. Berkeley: University of California Press, 2000.
Ferguson, James. *Global Shadows: Africa in the Neoliberal World Order*. Durham, NC: Duke University Press, 2006.
Green, James. *Beyond Carnival: Male Homosexuality in Twentieth-Century Brazil*. Chicago: University of Chicago Press, 1999.
Honwana, Alcinda, and Filip de Boeck, eds. *Makers and Breakers: Children and Youth in Postcolonial Africa*. Oxford: James Currey, 2005.
Ivaska, Andrew. *Cultured States: Youth, Gender and Modern Style in 1960s Dar es Salaam*. Durham, NC: Duke University Press, 2013.
Kligman, Gail, and Katherine Verdery. *Peasants under Siege: The Collectivization of Romanian Agriculture, 1949–1962*. Princeton, NJ: Princeton University Press, 2011.
Lee, James Z., and Wang Feng. *One Quarter of Humanity: Malthusian Mythology and Chinese Realities 1700–2000*. Cambridge, MA: Harvard University Press, 1999.
Manzano, Valeria. *The Age of Youth in Argentina: Culture, Politics and Sexuality from Perón to Videla*. Chapel Hill: University of North Carolina Press, 2014.
Marks, Lara V. *Sexual Chemistry: A History of the Contraceptive Pill*. New Haven, CT: Yale University Press, 2010.
McLaren, Angus. *Twentieth Century Sexuality: A History*. Oxford: Blackwell, 1999.
Nyeck, S.N., and Marc Epprecht, eds. *Sexual Diversity in Africa: Politics, Theory, Citizenship*. Montreal, Canada: McGill-Queen's University Press, 2013.
Offner, Avner. "British Manual Workers: From Producers to Consumers, c. 1950–2000." *Contemporary British History* 22 (2008): 537–71.
Parker, D.S. *The Idea of the Middle Class: White-Collar Workers and Peruvian Society, 1900–1950*. University Park: Pennsylvania State University Press, 1998.
Pascall, Gillian, and Anna Kwak. *Gender Regimes in Transition in Central and Eastern Europe*. Bristol: Policy Press, 2005.
Rosen, Ruth. *The World Split Open: How the Modern Women's Movement Changed America*. New York: Viking, 2000.

Schendel, William van, and Itty Abraham. Eds. *Illicit Flows and Criminal Things: States, Borders and the Other Side of Globalization.* Bloomington: Indiana University Press, 2005.
Schildt, Axel, and Detlef Siegfried, eds. *Between Marx and Coca-Cola: Youth Cultures in Changing European Societies, 1960–1980.* New York: Berghahn Books, 2006.
Standing, Guy. *The Precariat: The New Dangerous Class*, 2nd ed. London: Bloomsbury, 2014.
Swaan, Abram de. *In Care of the State: Health Care, Education and Welfare in Europe and the USA during the Modern Era.* New York: Oxford University Press, 1988.
Therborn, Göran. *Between Sex and Power: Family in the World, 1900–2000.* London: Routledge 2004.
Therborn, Göran. *European Modernity and Beyond: The Trajectory of European Societies 1945–2000.* London: Sage Publications, 1995.
Tinsman, Heidi. *Partners in Conflict: The Politics of Gender, Sexuality and Labor in the Chilean Agrarian Reform 1950–1973.* Durham, NC: Duke University Press, 2002.
Uberoi, Patricia. *Freedom and Destiny: Gender, Family and Popular Culture in India.* New Delhi: Oxford University Press, 2006.
Wieringa, Saskiw, and Horacio Sívori, eds. *The Sexual History of the Global South: Sexual Politics in Africa, Asia and Latin America.* London: Zed Books, 2013.
Yan, Yunxiang. *The Individualization of Chinese Society.* Oxford: Berg, 2009.
Yan, Yunxiang. *Private Life under Socialism: Love, Intimacy and Family Change in a Chinese Village 1949–1999.* Stanford, CA: Stanford University Press, 1993.

Chapter 8: Labor

Beckett, Francis, and David Hencke. *Marching to the Fault Line: The 1984 Miners' Strike and the Death of Industrial Britain.* London: Constable, 2009.
Breman, Jan. *Footloose Labor: Working in India's Informal Economy.* Cambridge: Cambridge University Press, 1996.
Cooper, Frederick. *Decolonization and African Society: The Labour Question in French and British Africa.* Cambridge: Cambridge University Press, 1996.
Cowie, Jefferson. *The Great Exception: The New Deal and the Limits of American Politics.* Princeton, NJ: Princeton University Press, 2016.
Davies, Sam et al., eds. *Dock Workers: International Explorations in Comparative Labour History, 1790–1970.* 2 vols. Aldershot: Ashgate, 2000.
Dinius, Oliver. *Brazil's Steel City: Development, Strategic Power, and Industrial Relations in Volta Redonda, 1941–1964.* Stanford, CA: Stanford University Press, 2011.
Fall, Babacar. *Le travail au Sénégal au XXe siècle.* Paris: Éditions Karthala, 2011.
Gallagher, Mary Elizabeth. *Contagious Capitalism: Globalization and the Politics of Labor in China.* Princeton, NJ: Princeton University Press, 2005.
Gordon, Andrew. *The Wages of Affluence: Labor and Management in Postwar Japan.* Cambridge, MA: Harvard University Press, 1998.
Gumbrell-McCormick, Rebecca, and Richard Hyman. *Trade Unions in Western Europe: Hard Times, Hard Choices.* Oxford: Oxford University Press, 2013.
Hensman, Rohini. *Workers, Unions and Global Capitalism: Lessons from India.* New York: Columbia University Press, 2011.

Holstrom, Mark. *Industry and Inequality: The Social Anthropology of Indian Labour.* Cambridge: Cambridge University Press, 1984.
Jürgens, Ulrich, Thomas Malsch, and Knuth Dohse. *Breaking from Taylorism: Changing Forms of Work in the Automobile Industry.* Cambridge: Cambridge University Press, 1993.
Lacity, Mary, and Leslie Willcocks. *Global Information Technology Outsourcing: In Search of Business Advantage.* Chichester: John Wiley & Sons, 2001.
Mahoney, Michael Sean. *Histories of Computing,* ed. Thomas Haigh. Cambridge, MA: Harvard University Press, 2011.
McCartin, Joseph A. *Collision Course: Ronald Reagan, the Air Traffic Controllers and the Strike That Changed America.* New York: Oxford University Press, 2011.
Milkman, Ruth. *Farewell to the Factory: Auto Workers in the Late Twentieth Century.* Berkeley: University of California Press, 1997.
Phelan, Craig, ed. *Trade Union Revitalisation: Trends and Prospects in 34 Countries.* Bern: Peter Lang, 2007.
Phelan, Craig, ed. *Trade Unionism since 1945.* 2 vols. Bern: Peter Lang, 2009.
Phelan, Craig, ed. *Trade Unions in West Africa: Historical and Contemporary Perspectives.* Bern: Peter Lang, 2011.
Pizzolato, Nicola. "Workers and Revolutionaries at the Twilight of Fordism: The Breakdown of Industrial Relations in the Automobile Plants of Detroit and Turin, 1967–1973." *Labor History* 45 (2004): 419–43.
Silva, Stephen J. *Holding the Shop Together: German Industrial Relations in the Postwar Era.* Ithaca, NY: ILR Press, 2013.
Vantoch, Valerie. *The Jet Sex: Airline Stewardesses and the Making of an American Icon.* Philadelphia: University of Pennsylvania Press, 2013.
Wersch, H. van. *The Bombay Textile Strike, 1982–1983.* Bombay: Oxford University Press, 1992.

Chapter 9: Leisure

Bren, Paulina. *The Greengrocer and His TV: The Culture of Communism after the 1968 Prague Spring.* Ithaca, NY: Cornell University Press, 2010.
Evans, Christine E. *Between Truth and Time: A History of Soviet Central Television.* New Haven, CT: Yale University Press, 2016.
Fabian, Sina. *Boom in der Krise. Konsum, Tourismus, Autofahren in Westdeutschland und Großbritannien 1970–1990.* Göttingen: Wallstein Verlag, 2016.
Furlough, Ellen. "Packaging Pleasures: Club Méditerranée and French Consumer Culture, 1950–1968." *French Historical Studies* 18 (1993): 65–81.
Gershuny, Jonathan. *Changing Times: Work and Leisure in Postindustrial Society.* Oxford: Oxford University Press, 1999.
Havens, Timothy. *Black Television Travels: African American Media Around the Globe.* New York: NYU Press, 2013.
Havens, Timothy. *Global Television Marketplace.* London: British Film Institute, 2006.
Jin, Dal Yong. *De-convergence of Global Media Industries.* London: Routledge, 2013.
Koenker, Diane. *Club Red: Vacation Travel and the Soviet Dream.* Ithaca, NY: Cornell University Press, 2013.

Levenstein, Marty. *We Always Have Paris: American Tourists in France since 1930*. Chicago: University of Chicago Press, 2004.
Liechty, Mark. *Far Out: Countercultural Seekers and the Tourist Encounter in Nepal*. Chicago: University of Chicago Press, 2017.
Löfgren, Orvar. *On Holiday: A History of Vacationing*. Berkeley: University of California Press, 1999.
Lull, James, ed. *World Families Watch Television*. Newbury Park, CA: SAGE Publications, 1988.
Montinari, Armando, and Allan Williams, eds. *European Tourism: Regions, Spaces and Restructuring*. Chicester: John Wiley & Sons, 1995.
Ramey, Valerie. "Time Spent in Home Production in the Twentieth-Century United States: New Estimates from Old Data." *Journal of Economic History* 69 (2009): 1–47.
Rugh, Susan. *Are We There Yet? The Golden Age of American Family Vacations*. Lawrence: University Press of Kansas, 2008.
Sauvage, Monique, Isabelle Veyrat-Masson, and Géraldine Peols. *Histoire de la télévision française de 1935 à nos jours*. Paris: Nouveau monde éditions, 2012.
Smith, Anthony. Ed. *Television: An International History*. Oxford: Oxford University Press, 1995.
Williams, Erica Lorraine. *Sex Tourism in Bahia: Ambiguous Entanglements*. Urbana: University of Illinois Press, 2013.

Chapter 10: Consumers

Bren, Paulina, and Mary Neuburger, eds. *Communism Unwrapped: Consumption in Cold War Eastern Europe*. New York: Oxford University Press, 2012.
Cohen, Lizabeth. *A Consumers' Republic: The Politics of Mass Consumption in Postwar America*. New York: Alfred A. Knopf, 2003.
Crawford, Susan. *Captive Audience: The Telecom Industry and Monopoly Power in the New Gilded Age*. New Haven, CT: Yale University Press, 2013.
De Grazia, Victoria. *The Culture of Consent: Mass Organization of Leisure in Fascist Italy*. New York: Cambridge University Press, 1981.
Florio, Massimo. *The Great Divestiture: Evaluating the Welfare Impact of the British Privatizations, 1979–1997*. Cambridge, MA: MIT Press, 2004.
Garon, Sheldon, and Patrician L. Maclachlan, eds. *The Ambivalent Consumer: Questioning Consumption in East Asia and the West*. Ithaca, NY: Cornell University Press, 2006.
Hahn, Hans Peter, ed. *Consumption in Africa: Anthropological Approaches*. Berlin: Lit Verlag, 2008.
Hilton, Matthew. *Consumerism in Twentieth-Century Britain: The Search for a Historical Movement*. Cambridge: Cambridge University Press, 2003.
Horowitz, Daniel. *The Anxieties of Affluence: Critiques of American Consumer Culture, 1939–1979*. Amherst: University of Massachusetts Press, 2004.
Huurdeman, Anton A. *The Worldwide History of Telecommunications*. Hoboken, NJ: John Wiley & Sons, 2003.
Jessen, Ralph, and Lydia Langer, eds. *Transformations of Retailing in Europe after 1945*. Farnham: Ashgate, 2012.

Li, Wei, and Lixin Colin Xu. "The Impact of Privatization and Competition in the Telecommunications Sector Around the World." *Journal of Law and Economics* 47 (2004): 395–430.

Logeman, Jan, ed. *The Development of Consumer Credit in Global Perspective*. New York: Palgrave McMillan, 2012.

Manning, Robert D. *Credit Card Nation: The Consequences of America's Addiction to Credit*. New York: Basic Books, 2000.

McKevitt, Andrew C. *Consuming Japan: Popular Culture and the Globalizing of 1980s America*. Chapel Hill: The University of North Carolina Press, 2017.

Partner, Simon. *Assembled in Japan: Electrical Goods and the Making of the Japanese Consumer*. Berkeley: University of California Press, 1999.

Pilcker, Jeffrey M. *Planet Taco: A Global History of Mexican Food*. New York: Oxford University Press, 2012.

Pulju, Rebecca. *Women and Mass Consumer Society in Postwar France*. New York: Cambridge University Press, 2011.

Richards, David B. "Did Passenger Fare Savings Occur after Airline Deregulation?" *Journal of the Transportation Research Forum* 46 (2007): 73–93.

Scarpellini, Emanuela. *Material Nation: A Consumer's History of Modern Italy*. Translated by Daphne Hughes and Andrew Newton. Oxford: Oxford University Press, 2011.

Temin, Peter, and Louis Galambos. *The Fall of the Bell System: A Study in Prices and Politics*. New York: Cambridge University Press, 1987.

Trentmann, Frank. *Empire of Things: How We Became a World of Consumers, from the Fifteenth Century to the Twenty-First*. New York: Harper, 2016.

Watson. James L. *Golden Arches East: McDonald's in East Asia*. Stanford, CA: Stanford University Press, 1997.

Zaitlin, Jonathan. *The Currency of Socialism: Money and Political Culture in East Germany*. New York: Cambridge University Press, 2009.

Chapter 11: Beliefs

Adamsky, Dmitry. *Russian Nuclear Orthodoxy: Religion, Politics, Strategy*. Stanford, CA: Stanford University Press, 2019.

Anderson, Jenny. *The Future of the World: Futurology, Futurists and the Struggle for the Post-Cold War Imagination*. Oxford: Oxford University Press, 2018.

Brewitt-Taylor, Sam. *Christian Radicalism in the Church of England and the Invention of the British Sixties, 1957–70*. Oxford: Oxford University Press, 2018.

Brown, Callum. *The Death of Christian Britain: Understanding Secularisation 1800–2000*. London: Routledge, 2001.

Brown, Callum. "The People of 'No Religion': The Demographics of Secularisation in the English-Speaking World since c. 1900." *Archiv für Sozialgeschichte* 51 (2011): 37–61.

Calvert, John. *Sayyid Qutb and the Origins of Radical Islamism*. New York: Columbia University Press, 2010.

Chappel, James. *Catholic Modern: The Challenge of Totalitarianism and the Making of the Church*. Cambridge, MA: Harvard University Press, 2018.

Cheng, Yinghong. *Creating the "New Man:" From Enlightenment Ideals to Socialist Realities*. Honolulu: University of Hawai'i Press, 2009.

Citino, Nathan. *Envisioning the Arab Future: Modernization in U.S.-Arab Relations, 1945–1967.* Cambridge: Cambridge University Press, 2017.

Dawisha, Adeed. *Arab Nationalism in the Twentieth Century: From Triumph to Despair,* 2nd ed. Princeton, NJ: Princeton University Press, 2016.

Dochuk, Darren. *From Bible Belt to Sun Belt: Plain-Folk Religion, Grassroots Politics and the Rise of Evangelical Conservatism.* New York: W.W. Norton, 2011.

Doering-Manteuffel, Anselm, and Lutz Raphael. *Nach dem Boom. Perspektiven auf die Zeitgeschichte seit 1970.* Göttingen: Vandenhoeck & Ruprecht, 2008.

Gentile, Emilio. *La Grande Italia: The Myth of the Nation in the 20th Century.* Translated by Suzanne Dingee and Jennifer Pudney. Madison: University of Wisconsin Press, 2009.

Gerges, Fawaz A. *Making the Arab World: Nasser, Qutb, and the Clash that Shaped the Middle East.* Princeton, NJ: Princeton University Press, 2018.

Getachew, Adom. *Worldmaking after Empire: The Rise and Fall of Self-Determination.* Princeton, NJ: Princeton University Press, 2019.

Gilman, Nils. *Mandarins of the Future: Modernization Theory in Cold War America.* Baltimore: Johns Hopkins University Press, 2003.

Green, Abigail, and Vincent Viaene, eds. *Religious Internationals in the Modern World: Globalization and Faith Communities since 1750.* Houndmills, Basingstoke: Palgrave Macmillan, 2012.

Guth, Stefan. "One Future Only. The Soviet Union in the Age of the Scientific-Technical Revolution." *Journal of Modern European History* 13 (2015): 355–76.

Hansen, Thomas Blom. *The Saffron Wave: Democracy and Hindu Nationalism in Modern India.* Princeton, NJ: Princeton University Press, 1999.

Ibrahim, Abdullahi. *Manichean Delirium: Decolonizing the Judiciary and Islamic Renewal in the Sudan, 1898–1985.* Leiden: Brill, 2008.

Jenkins, Philip. *The Next Christendom: The Coming of Global Christianity.* New York: Oxford University Press, 2002.

Lacroix, Stéphane. *Awakening Islam: The Politics of Religious Dissent in Contemporary Saudi Arabia.* Translated by George Holoch. Cambridge, MA: Harvard University Press, 2011.

Latham, Michael. *The Right Kind of Revolution: Modernization, Development and U.S. Foreign Policy from the Cold War to the Present.* Ithaca, NY: Cornell University Press, 2011.

Lauzière, Henri. *The Making of Salafism: Islamic Reform in the Twentieth Century.* New York: Columbia University Press, 2016.

Leibold, James. *Reconfiguring Chinese Nationalism: How the Qing Frontier and its Indigenes Became Chinese.* Houndmills, Basingstoke: Palgrave Macmillan, 2007.

Mariani, Paul. *Church Militant: Bishop Kung and Catholic Resistance in Communist Shanghai.* Cambridge, MA: Harvard University Press, 2011.

Martin, David. *Tongues of Fire: The Explosion of Protestantism in Latin America.* Oxford: Blackwell, 1990.

Maxwell, David. *African Gifts of the Spirit: Pentecostalism and the Rise of a Zimbabwean Transnational Religious Movement.* Oxford: James Curry, 2006.

McDonald, Maryon. *"We Are Not French!" Language, Culture and Identity in Brittany.* London: Routledge, 1989.

McLeod, Hugh. *The Religious Crisis of the 1960s.* Oxford: Oxford University Press, 2007.
Miller, Steven P. *The Age of Evangelicalism: America's Born-Again Years.* New York: Oxford University Press, 2014
Nehru, Jawaharlal. *The Discovery of India.* New Delhi: Jawaharlal Nehru Memorial Fund, 1982.
O'Malley, John W. *What Happened at Vatican II.* Cambridge, MA: Harvard University Press, 2008.
Reid, Anthony. *Imperial Alchemy: Nationalism and Political Identity in Southeast Asia.* Cambridge: Cambridge University Press, 2010.
Rougier, Bernard. *Everyday Jihad: The Rise of Militant Islam among Palestinians in Lebanon.* Translated by Pascale Ghazaleh. Cambridge, MA: Harvard University Press, 2007.
Rowe, David. "Sport and the Repudiation of the Global." *International Review for the Sociology of Sport* 30 (2003): 281–94.
Salvadori, Massimo. *Progress: Can We Do without It?* Translated by Patrick Camiller. London: Zed Books, 2008.
Sluga, Glenda., *Internationalism in the Age of Nationalism.* Philadelphia: University of Pennsylvania Press, 2013.
Smolkin, Victoria. *A Sacred Space Is Never Empty: A History of Soviet Atheism.* Princeton, NJ: Princeton University Press, 2018.
Stanley, Brian. *Christianity in the Twentieth Century: A World History.* Princeton, NJ: Princeton University Press, 2018.
Thurston, Alexander. *Salafism in Nigeria: Islam, Preaching and Politics.* Cambridge: Cambridge University Press, 2016.
Vajpeyi, Ananya. *Righteous Republic: The Political Foundations of Modern India.* Cambridge, MA: Harvard University Press, 2012.
Veldman, Meredith. *Fantasy, the Bomb and the Greening of Britain: Romantic Protest 1945–1980.* Cambridge: Cambridge University Press, 1994.
Verdery, Katherine. *National Ideology under Socialism: Identity and Cultural Politics in Ceaușescu's Romania.* Berkeley: University of California Press, 1991.
Wagar, W. Warren. *Good Tidings: The Belief in Progress from Darwin to Marcuse.* Bloomington: Indiana University Press, 1972.
Wigger, John. *PTL: The Rise and Fall of Jim and Tammy Faye Bakker's Evangelical Empire.* New York: Oxford University Press, 2017.

Chapter 12: Mass Murder

Armatta, Judith. *Twilight of Impunity: The War Crimes Trial of Slobodan Milosevic.* Durham, NC: Duke University Press, 2010.
Bloxham, Donald, and A. Dirk Moses, eds. *The Oxford Handbook of Genocide Studies.* Oxford: Oxford University Press, 2010.
Daly. M.W. *Dafur's Sorrow: A History of Destruction and Genocide.* Cambridge: Cambridge University Press, 2007.
Dikötter, Frank. *Mao's Great Famine: The History of China's Most Devastating Catastrophe, 1985–1962.* New York: Walker & Co, 2010.
Garrard-Burnett, Virginia. *Terror in the Land of the Holy Spirit: Guatemala and General Efraín Montt, 1982–1983.* New Yok: Oxford University Press, 2010.

Gerlach, Christian. *Extremely Violent Societies: Mass Violence in the Twentieth-Century World.* New York: Cambridge University Press, 2010.
Ingrao, Charles, and Thomas A. Emmert, eds. *Confronting the Yugoslav Controversy: A Scholars' Initiative*, 2nd ed. West Lafayette, IN: Purdue University Press, 2013.
Kiernan, Ben. *The Pol Pot Regime: Race, Power and Genocide in Cambodia under the Khmer Rouge, 1975–79.* New Haven, CT: Yale University Press, 1996.
Kimonyo, Jean-Paul. *Rawanda's Popular Genocide: A Perfect Storm.* Translated by Wandia Njoya. Boulder, CO: Lynne Rienner Publishers, 2016.
Mamdani, Mahmood. *When Victims Become Killers: Colonialism, Nativism and the Genocide in Rwanda.* Princeton, NJ: Princeton University Press, 2001.
Melvin, Jess. *The Army and the Indonesian Genocide: Mechanics of Mass Murder.* London: Routledge, 2018.
Priemel, Kim Christian. *The Betrayal: Nuremberg Trials and German Divergence.* Oxford: Oxford University Press, 2016.
Prunier, Gérard. *Darfur: The Ambiguous Genocide.* Ithaca NY: Cornell University Press, 2005.
Robinson, Geoffrey. *The Killing Season: A History of the Indonesian Massacres, 1965–66.* Princeton, NJ: Princeton University Press, 2018.
Totani, Yuma. *The Tokyo War Crimes Trial: The Pursuit of Justice in the Wake of World War II.* Cambridge, MA: Harvard University Press, 2008.
Walder, Andrew. *China under Mao: A Revolution Derailed.* Cambridge, MA: Harvard University Press, 2015.

Chapter 13: Utopias

Appel, Hilary, and Mitchell Orenstein. *From Triumph to Crisis: Neoliberal Economic Reform in Postcommunist Countries.* Cambridge: Cambridge University Press, 2018.
Artières, Philippe, and Michelle Zancarini-Fournel, eds. *68 une histoire collective {1962–1981}.* Paris: Éditions La Découverte, 2008.
Burgin, Angus. *The Great Persuasion: Reinventing Free Markets since the Great Depression.* Cambridge, MA: Harvard University Press, 2012.
Chamberlin, Paul Thomas. *The Global Offensive: The United States, the Palestine Liberation Organization and the Making of the Post-Cold War Order.* New York: Oxford University Press, 2012.
Crockatt, Richard. *America Embattled: September 11, Anti-Americanism and the Global Order.* London: Routledge, 2003.
De Graaf, Jan. *Socialism Across the Iron Curtain: Socialist Parties in East and West and the Reconstruction of Europe after 1945.* Cambridge: Cambridge University Press, 2019.
Deak, István, Jan T. Gross, and Tony Judt, eds. *The Politics of Retribution in Europe: World War II and its Aftermath.* Princeton, NJ: Princeton University Press, 2000.
Eckel, Jan. *The Ambivalence of Good: Human Rights in International Politics since the 1940s.* Translated by Rachel Ward. Oxford: Oxford University Press, 2019.
Fanon, Frantz. *Les damnés de la terre.* Paris: Gallimard, 1991.
Fink, Carole, Philipp Gassert, and Detlef Junker, eds. *1968: The World Transformed.* New York: Cambridge University Press, 1997.
Fukuyama, Francis. *The End of History and the Last Man*, 2nd ed. New York: Free Press, 2006.

Getachew, Adom. *Worldmaking after Empire: The Rise and Fall of Self-Determination.* Princeton, NJ: Princeton University Press, 2019.

Horn, Gerd-Rainer. *The Spirit of '68: Rebellion in Western Europe and North America, 1956–1976.* Oxford: Oxford University Press, 2007.

Khan, Yasmin. *India at War: The Subcontinent and the Second World War.* Oxford: Oxford University Press, 2015.

Klein, Lawrence R., and Marshall Pomer, eds. *The New Russia Transition Gone Awry.* Stanford, CA: Stanford University Press, 2001.

Koreman, Megan. *The Expectations of Justice: France 1944– 1946* Durham, NC: Duke University Press, 1999.

Ledeneva, Alena V. *How Russian Really Works: The Informal Practices That Shaped Post-Soviet Politics and Business.* Ithaca, NY: Cornell University Press, 2006.

Marchesi, Aldo. *Latin America's Radical Left: Rebellion and Cold War in the Global 1960s.* Translated by Laura Perez Carrera. Cambridge: Cambridge University Press, 2018.

Mazower, Mark. *Governing the World: The History of an Idea.* New York: Penguin Press, 2012.

Ost, David. *The Defeat of Solidarity: Anger and Politics in Postcommunist Europe.* Ithaca, NY: Cornell University Press, 2005.

Pensado, Jaime. *Rebel Mexico: Student Unrest and Authoritarian Political Culture during the Long Sixties.* Stanford, CA: Stanford University Press, 2013.

Rogers, Daniel. *The Age of Fracture.* Cambridge, MA: Harvard University Press, 2011.

Seidman, Michael. *The Imaginary Revolution: Parisian Students and Workers in 1968.* New York: Berghahn Books, 2004.

Sitapati, Vinay. *The Man Who Remade India: A Biography of P.V. Narasimha Rao.* New York: Oxford University Press, 2018.

Varon, Jeremy. *Bringing the War Home: The Weather Underground, the Red Army Faction and Revolutionary Violence in the Sixties and Seventies.* Berkeley: University of California Press, 2004.

Volkov, Vadim. *Violent Entrepreneurs: The Use of Force in the Making of Russian Capitalism.* Ithaca, NY: Cornell University Press, 2002.

Wittner, Lawrence S. *The Struggle against the Bomb.* 3 vols. Stanford, CA: Stanford University Press, 1993 2003

Wu, Yiching. *The Cultural Revolution at the Margins: Chinese Socialism in Crisis.* Cambridge, MA: Harvard University Press, 2014.

Zewde, Bahru. *The Quest for a Socialist Utopia: The Ethiopian Student Movement c. 1960–1974.* Woodbridge, Suffolk: James Currey, 2014.

INDEX

For the benefit of digital users, indexed terms that span two pages (e.g., 52–53) may, on occasion, appear on only one of those pages.
Figures and Tables are indicated by an italic *f* and *t* following the page number

abortion, 325–27, 335–36, 341–
    42, 347–48
Acheson, Dean, 129
Adenauer, Konrad, 216
Afghanistan
    Cold War and, 209–10, 257, 262, 264–
        65, 267
    communist revolution in, 256–57
    ethnic conflict in, 257
    gender in, 348
    Global Realignment Struggle and, 249
    guerilla warfare in, 262
    Islamism in, 255, 262–63, 275, 348, 509
    refugees in, 179, 262
    Soviet-Afghan war in, 179, 209–11, 256–
        57, 262–63, 273–74, 537
    terrorism in, 276
    transportation in, 24
    US involvement in, 206, 209–10, 262–
        63, 632–33
    Vietnam comparisons to, 262–63
Afkham, Mahnaz, 343
African Americans
    Black Power movement and, 596
    Civil Rights movement and, 591, 595–96
    nationalism and, 496
    neoliberalism and, 616

    New Left and, 595–96
    Pan-Africanism and, 496
    racism against, 595–96
    southern strategy and, 252–53
Age of Interconnection. *See also* Era of
        Upheaval; Late Millennium Era;
        Postwar Era
    as age of exponentials, 641–44
    agriculture and, 112, 115–16
    apocalyptic thinking and, 649–50
    automobiles and, 91
    challenges of writing on, 2–3, 7
    conflict as distinct element of, 206–8, 530
    consumerism and, 436–37
    continuing trends of, 626–40
    disease and, 41, 72–74, 79, 80
    economic development and, 166
    energy and, 91
    environmental impact and, 3, 39
    eras within, 5–6
    expectations and realities of, 649–54
    gender and, 355
    global orders and, 644–47
    globalization and, 1–2, 3, 5–6, 7, 647–49
    historical narrative of, 2–3, 5–6
    human rights and, 649–50
    imagining era of, 3–7

Age of Interconnection (*cont.*)
　importance of, 1–2
　labor movements and, 357–58, 387–88
　leisure and, 400–1, 431, 434, 437
　microelectronics and, 121–22
　migrations and, 205
　nuclear weapons and, 206
　overview of, 1–7, 641–54
　population growth and, 322
　technological development and, 82–83, 100, 115–16, 121–22
　television and, 405, 434
　temporality and, 3
　tourism and, 431
　transportation and, 91, 100
　as triumph of the prosaic, 652
Age of Total War
　Cold War and, 210, 252
　economic development and, 139, 164–65
　energy and, 87
　gender and, 323–24, 355–56
　mass murder and, 530–31, 533, 537–38, 555, 569
　microelectronics and, 125
　migrations and, 169, 180, 181, 183
　nationalism and, 493, 509, 557
　population growth and, 309–10, 314, 355–56
　progress and, 477–78, 482–83, 485, 529
　technological development and, 82–83, 87, 96–97, 125, 333
　transportation and, 94–95, 96–97, 100
　utopian movements and, 583–84, 590, 591, 592, 594
　youth culture and, 314
Age of Upheaval. *See* Era of Upheaval
agriculture, 107–16
　Age of Interconnection and, 112, 115–16
　capitalism and, 108–9, 112, 115
　classes and, 299–301
　Cold War and, 110
　communism and, 110–11, 299–300
　crop yield gains in, 107f, 107–10, 170–71
　economic development and, 110–11, 132
　environmental impact and, 12, 16, 37, 111–13
　fertilizers in, 111, 112, 113
　globalization and, 109–10, 112
　GMO crops in, 113–16, 125
　Green Revolution in, 24, 110, 111–13, 114–15, 651, 652–53

　Late Millennium Era and, 115
　migrations and, 170–71
　modern biological synthesis and, 107, 111
　organic farming in, 113
　population growth and, 24, 107, 113
　technological development and, 12, 107–10, 112, 113–14
　Third World and, 110
Ahmad, Shayk, 519–20
Aidit, D. N., 547, 549
air travel, 4, 96–100, 97f–98, 369–71, 393–96, 421–22, 456–60, 456f, 457f
Al Qaeda, 276, 509, 560–61, 624, 632–33
Albania
　communism in, 560–61, 621–22
　economic development in, 621–22, 638–39
　mass murder and, 557, 560–62
Alexandrov, Anatoli, 85
Algeria
　Arab-Israeli conflict and, 177
　decolonization in, 182–83, 206, 231–32, 235–36, 250, 251–52, 587, 591
　energy in, 91, 149
　Global Realignment Struggle and, 225, 245, 250
　Islamism in, 255, 275
　labor movements in, 367–68
　migrations and, 182–84, 190
　terrorism in, 255
　transportation in, 24–25
　utopian movements in, 591, 596–97, 607
Ali, Tariq, 589–90, 591–92, 598–99
All-China Federation of Trade Unions (ACFTU), 380–81
Allende, Salvador, 210–11, 243, 245, 252–53, 316–17
All-Union Voluntary Society of Auto Enthusiasts, 92–93
Ambedkar, Bhimrao, 577
Amin, Idi, 179–80, 317, 349, 565–66
Amnesty International, 612
Anderson, Benedict, 497
Andrade, Victor, 233–34
Andropov, Yuri, 266, 267
Angola
　civil war in, 252
　Cold War and, 252, 259–60, 264–65
　decolonization in, 206, 251–52

INDEX | 757

Global Realignment Struggle and, 245, 272–73
television in, 406
antibiotics, 41–46, 50, 51, 57, 59–60, 71–72
anti-imperialism. *See* decolonization and anti-imperialism
Antrobus, Peggy, 342–43
apocalyptic thinking
  Age of Interconnection and, 649–50
  decolonization and, 586–87
  disease and, 72–81
  global governance and, 580
  Islamism and, 512, 522
  nuclear weapons and, 206–8, 211, 237, 580, 581, 583
  population growth and, 23
  religion and, 522, 651
  utopian movements and, 576, 577, 580, 583, 586
Arab Spring (2011), 179–80, 504, 639–40
Arab-Israeli conflict
  Camp David peace accords in, 251
  Cold War and, 250–51
  Global Realignment Struggle and, 250–51
  oil embargo resulting from, 147
  refugees in, 176, 178
  terrorism in, 251
  war of 1947 in, 176, 206
  war of 1967 in, 178, 191–92, 206, 250–51, 263, 596–97
  war of 1973 in, 147, 206, 250–51
Arafat, Yassir, 503–4, 594–95
Arbenz, Jacobo, 233, 551–52
d'Arcy, Jean, 407–8, 410
Ardenne, Manfred von, 405
Argentina
  agriculture in, 107–8
  Cold War and, 551
  consumerism in, 441–42, 472–73
  disease in, 78
  economic development in, 136–38, 146–47, 150–51, 152–53, 636–37
  education in, 315–16
  Falklands War in, 258
  gender in, 323–24, 329–30, 340–41
  generational change in, 314, 319
  labor movements in, 358, 360–61, 364–65, 368

  migrations and, 169, 170–72
  nationalism in, 496
  religion in, 513–14
  tourism in, 431
  transportation in, 93–94
  utopian movements in, 599
Arrhenius, Svente, 32
Ataturk, Mustapha Kemal, 480–81
atomic weapons. *See* nuclear weapons
AT&T, 117, 460–64
Auden, W. H., 174–75
Audubon Society, 18
Australia
  agriculture in, 107–8
  consumerism in, 444, 472–73
  disease in, 60, 63
  economic development in, 133–34, 165
  environmental impact in, 15, 25–26
  gender in, 333–34
  internet access in, 627–28
  labor movements in, 360, 375, 384
  leisure in, 402, 404
  migrations and, 169–70, 187–88, 192, 194, 195–97, 195*f*–96
  population growth in, 321
  racism in, 187–88
  refugees in, 177
  religion in, 517–18
  technological development in, 83
  television in, 416–17
  tourism in, 434
  transportation and, 92
Austria
  disease in, 43–44
  migrations and, 183–84
  refugees in, 176, 268
  tourism in, 422
  transportation in, 93
Austro-Hungarian empire, 170, 172–73, 316
automobiles, 4, 12, 24–25, 83, 91–99, 91*t*, 96*f*, 96*t*, 411–12, 411*t*–12
Azzam, Abdullah, 263

Baedeker, Karl, 419–20
Baghwati, Jagdish, 137
Baird, John, 405
Baker, James, 269
Bakker, Jim, 414, 521
Balcerowicz, Leszek, 620–21

Balkan Wars (1911-13), 557
Bandung Conference (1955), 234–35, 240, 243, 245, 247–48, 502, 546
Bangladesh
  agriculture in, 112
  disease in, 66–67
  founding of, 179–80, 252–53, 488, 569–70, 589–90
  Global Realignment Struggle and, 252–53
  mass murders in, 537, 569–70
  migrations and, 185–86, 191, 199–200
  nationalism in, 496
  progress in, 480–81
  refugees in, 179–80
  television in, 412
Bani-Sadr, Abu al-Hasa, 260–61
Bankoff, George, 44
Bardeen, John, 117
Barnard, Christian, 58–59
Barthélémy, René, 405
Baryshnikov, Mikhail, 210
al-Bashir, Omar, 570
Beard, Mary, 624
Beauvoir, Simone de, 341–42
Beck, Ulrich, 20
Becker, Gary, 616
Belgium
  decolonization and, 207–8, 272, 568
  disease in, 78
  gender in, 323–24
  labor movements in, 359, 380
  migrations and, 190
  nationalism in, 508
  population growth in, 297
Bell, Daniel, 591
Bell Labs, 116–17, 460–62, 463–64
Bellamy, Francis, 516
Benin
  communism in, 367
  democratic transition in, 383
  Great Realignment Struggle and, 245
  labor movements in, 367–68, 383
Benjamin, Hilde, 330–31
Berger, Peter, 510
Bergman, Ingrid, 423
Beria, Lavrenty, 231
Berlin Crisis (1961), 210, 236, 581
Berlin Wall, 180–81, 190, 211, 236, 265, 268–69, 272, 276–56, 613, 625

Berners-Lee, Tim, 124
Berrigan, Daniel, 518
Berry, Wendell, 449
Bhabha, Homi, 85
Bhopal chemical disaster (1984), 19–21, 28
Bhutto, Benazir, 349
bin Laden, Osama, 263, 275–76, 632–33
Bismarck, Otto von, 318, 437, 504
Blair, Tony, 610, 618–19
Blitz, Gérard, 421
Blyden, Edward Wilmot, 504–5
Bolivia
  disease in, 78
  gender in, 323–24
  Global Realignment Struggle and, 244–45
  migrations and, 197–98
  revolution in, 233–34, 244–45, 591
Bonhoeffer, Dietrich, 511, 518–19
Bonn summit (1978), 158–59
Borgstrom, Georg, 17
Borlaug, Norman, 109–10, 112–13
Bose, Subhas Chandra, 577–78
Bosnia-Herzegovina
  creation of, 559
  mass murder in, 556, 557–58, 559, 560, 561–62
  nationalism in, 497
Botswana, disease in, 44–45, 74–75
Boumédiène, Henri, 250
Boushey, Homer, 101–2
Boutros-Ghali, Boutros, 559–60
Brandt, Willy, 19, 242, 609, 610
Brazil
  Amazon in, 29–30
  classes in, 300
  Cold War and, 551
  consumerism in, 454–55, 470
  disease in, 51, 67, 68
  economic development in, 29–30, 133–34, 137, 139, 360–61
  education in, 315–16
  environmental impact in, 11, 27–30, 34
  gender in, 323–24, 326, 340–41, 347–48
  generational change in, 319
  Global Realignment Struggle and, 252–53
  human rights in, 253–54
  internet access in, 627–28

labor movements in, 358, 360–61, 365, 368, 382–83
migrations and, 171–72, 200–1
regulation in, 29–30
religion in, 519
sports competitions in, 500–1
television in, 408
tourism in, 428–29
transportation in, 91, 93–94, 97–98
Bremer, L. Paul, 634
Bretton Woods system, 129–30, 135–36, 137–38, 142–43, 145–46, 155, 158–59, 162, 163–64, 222–23, 238–39, 265
Brexit referendum (2016), 508, 644
Brezhnev, Leonid, 249–51, 266, 479, 488
Britain. *See* United Kingdom
British Empire, 226, 227–28, 231–33, 577
Brittain, Walter, 117
Brutents, Karen, 249–50
Bulganin, Nikolai, 478–79
Bulgaria
  communism in, 232–33, 269
  consumerism in, 468
  economic development in, 132
  gender in, 346–47
  nationalism in, 493–94
  tourism in, 433
Bunche, Ralph, 579
Burkina Faso
  disease in, 66–67
  economic development in, 225–26
  television in, 406
Burma. *See* Myanmar
Burundi
  disease in, 46
  mass murder in, 179–80, 563, 567–68
  refugees in, 179–80, 564, 568
Bush, George H. W., 266–67, 269, 273, 274, 558, 618, 633–34
Bush, George W., 274, 633, 638
Butlin, Billy, 421, 423–24, 426–27

Cailliau, Robert, 124
Cambodia
  Cold War and, 210–11
  communism in, 179, 548–49
  mass murder in, 538, 542–45, 554–55, 568–70
  nationalism in, 497
  refugees in, 179, 194
  utopian movements in, 611–12
  Vietnam War and, 210–11, 221, 248–49, 262
Cameroon, television in, 412
Camette, Albert, 56–57
Camp David peace accords (1978), 251
Camus, Albert, 494, 574–75
Canada
  economic development in, 154
  energy in, 85–86
  gender in, 323–24, 326
  generational change in, 319
  migrations and, 171–72, 187–88, 192, 194, 195–96, 195f–96
  population growth in, 24, 321
  racism in, 187–88
  refugees in, 177
  religion in, 517–18
  transportation in, 92, 94
capitalism. *See also* consumerism
  agriculture and, 108–9, 112, 115
  classes and, 298–300
  communism, triumph over, 617–19
  deregulation and, 115, 155, 160, 637
  economic development and, 132, 136–38, 141, 144, 149, 154–55, 160
  environmental impact and, 26–27, 38
  globalization and, 154–55, 617
  Late Millennium Era and, 38, 115, 265, 332
  migrations and, 183
  Postwar Era and, 143–44, 148, 149, 156, 167, 183, 447–48, 495, 616–17
  progress and, 478–80
  regulation and, 143–44, 148, 149, 156, 167, 183, 447–48, 495, 616–17
  Third World and, 27
  utopian movements and, 576, 617–19, 620
cars. *See* automobiles
Carson, Rachel, 21–23, 53–54
Carter, Jimmy, 87, 253–54, 256, 257, 258–59, 370
Castro, Fidel, 225, 237–38, 244–45, 443, 479
Catholic Church
  communism and, 515, 516–17, 523–24
  conservative backlash in, 525
  decline in, 525–26

Catholic Church (*cont.*)
  integralism and, 511, 523–24
  liberation theology and, 521–22, 524, 525
  modernism and, 511, 518, 523–25
  nationalism and, 495
  Vatican II and, 523–25, 551–52, 564, 605–6
Ceauçescu, Elena, 330–31
Ceauçescu, Nicolae, 330–31, 468, 498
Central African Republic (CAR), television in, 412
Central Intelligence Agency (CIA), 233, 244–45, 254, 272, 547, 549–50, 551–52, 632–33
Césaire, Aimé, 578–79
Chad, technological development in, 412, 627–28
Charles, John, 58
Chen Siming, 380–81
Chen Yun, 142
Chenu, Marie-Dominique, 525
Chernobyl nuclear disaster (1986), 19–20, 85–86, 89–90, 488
Chestnut, Andrew, 525
Chiang Kai-Shek (Jiang Jieshi), 218
Chicago School of Economics, 137
Chile
  Cold War and, 210–11, 551
  disease in, 78
  education in, 315–16
  gender in, 324–25, 326, 350–51
  generational change in, 319, 321
  Global Realignment Struggle and, 245
  labor movements in, 362, 365, 368
  migrations and, 169–70
  religion in, 519
  US involvement in, 241, 243
  utopian movements in, 599
  youth culture in, 316–17
China
  agriculture in, 110, 303–4, 338
  civil war in, 217–18, 226–27
  classes in, 299–300, 303–5
  Cold War and, 215, 217–18, 221–22, 229–30, 239–41, 270–71
  consumerism in, 439, 442, 454–55, 466–67, 470–72, 630–31
  Cultural Revolution in, 110–11, 303, 529, 539, 541–42, 543–44, 601–4, 610
  disease in, 43, 52–53, 66–67, 68, 80–81
  economic development in, 15–16, 131–32, 139, 141–42, 156–57, 161–62, 165, 166–67, 218, 335, 539–41, 629–32, 636–37, 638
  environmental impact in, 15–16, 27, 33–34
  gender in, 323–24, 328, 330, 332, 335, 338–39, 346, 351–53
  generational change in, 319
  Global Realignment Struggle and, 234
  Great Leap Forward in, 131–32, 140, 479, 490, 539–42, 543–44, 652
  growing influence of, 631–32
  internet access in, 627–28
  labor movements in, 359, 378–79, 380–81, 387
  market reforms in, 156–57, 218, 271, 332, 463, 604
  mass murder in, 533–34, 538–42, 570
  microelectronics in, 121, 197–98
  migrations and, 169–71, 172, 194–95, 196–97, 306
  nationalism in, 492, 497–98, 506
  one-child policy in, 335
  population growth in, 335
  progress in, 479, 480–81, 490, 544
  Red Guards in, 601–4
  refugees in, 174, 176, 179, 180–81
  religion in, 513–15, 528, 529
  satellites in, 106–7
  Sino-American rapprochement of, 241, 252–53
  Sino-Russian split of, 239–41
  Taiwan and, 218
  telecommunications in, 466
  television in, 411–12, 415–16
  Tiananmen Square demonstrations in, 270–71
  tourism in, 425–26
  transportation in, 93–94, 97–98
Christianity. *See* Catholic Church; Evangelical Protestantism; Pentecostalism
Churchill, Winston, 42, 228, 231, 359, 408–9
CIA (Central Intelligence Agency), 233, 244–45, 254, 272, 547, 549–50, 551–52, 632–33
Civil Rights Act (1964), 341

classes, 298–309
    agriculture and, 299–301
    Baby Boomers and, 302–3
    blurring of lines between, 308
    capitalism and, 298–300
    communism and, 299–300
    economic development and, 301–2, 307–8
    education and, 298–99, 302–3
    Era of Upheaval and, 302–3, 306
    fitters and, 307–8
    gender and, 302–3, 349–50
    globalization and, 304–8, 343–44
    inequality and, 302
    Late Millennium Era and, 303–9
    lineage-based societies and, 301–2
    lower class, 308, 316–17, 403–4, 435, 442, 445, 630–31
    middle class, 87, 93–94, 298–99, 301, 302–3, 341, 445, 501–2
    migrations and, 306–7, 309
    Postwar Era and, 298–99, 302–3
    precariat class and, 306–7
    seigneurialism and, 301–2, 306
    structure of, 298–302, 304–5, 306–7, 308–9
    tourism and, 432–33, 434
    transformation of, 302–9
    upper class, 298–99, 353–54, 402–3, 432–33, 438
    upper-middle class, 352–53, 401–2, 435, 450, 507
    working class, 225, 298–300, 302–3, 314, 341, 446, 631
Clean Air Act (1970), 18–19
Clean Water Act (1970), 18–19, 20
Cleaver, Eldridge, 225, 250
climate change, 30–38, 39–40
Clinton, Bill, 274, 560, 610, 618–19, 633–34
Club Med, 421, 423–24, 427
Club of Rome, 21, 22–23, 39, 40, 449, 486–87, 643–44
CNN, 410, 414–15, 417
Cohen, Lizabeth, 450
Cohn-Bendit, Daniel, 589, 604
Cold War
    Age of Total War and, 210, 252
    agriculture and, 110
    Berlin Crisis in, 210, 236, 581
    Berlin Wall in, 180–81, 190, 211, 216, 236, 265, 268–69, 272, 276–56, 613, 625
    Cuban Missile Crisis in, 210, 211–12, 237–38, 240, 255, 581, 583
    defining features of, 208–9, 210, 266
    détente in, 243, 250–51, 252–54, 256, 258
    development of, 209, 212–16, 227–29
    disease and, 48–49
    economic development and, 136, 143, 156–57, 238–39, 265, 645–46
    end of, 1–2, 207–8, 211, 265–77, 507, 613, 617–18, 632–40, 641–47, 649–51
    environmental impact and, 16, 32
    Era of Upheaval and, 210–11, 238–43
    Euromissiles controversy and, 255–56
    gender and, 355–56
    global orders and, 644–47
    Global Realignment Struggle and, 212, 217, 223–24, 228, 234, 243–54, 256, 261–62, 265, 271–73, 276–77
    human rights and, 242–43, 253–54, 267, 553–54
    Islamism and, 262–63, 265, 275, 276–77
    labor movements and, 363
    Late Millennium Era and, 256–65
    legacy of, 266–77, 632–40, 641–47
    linkage in negotiations during, 243, 248–50
    mass murder and, 538–55
    migrations and, 181
    nationalism and, 494, 497–98, 507
    New Cold War, 257–58, 263–65
    nuclear weapons and, 209, 210, 211, 228, 229, 230–31, 236–37, 241, 243, 258–60, 264, 580–81
    overview of, 1–2, 6, 208–15, 644–47
    progress and, 478–79, 480, 489, 645
    proxy wars and, 209, 210–11, 212, 259–60
    refugees and, 179–80
    religion and, 514, 516
    sports competitions and, 217, 218, 219–20, 257
    Sputnik and, 101–2, 131, 236
    Third World and, 224–26, 260, 645–46
    transportation and, 100, 101–4
    World War II and, 209, 212–15, 227–29, 241–42, 266, 269
    World War III and, 230–31
Combat (newspaper), 575

COMECON, 132, 646
Commonwealth Immigration Act
    (1962), 184
communism
    agriculture and, 110–11, 299–300
    anti-communist mass murder and, 545–
        55, 569
    capitalism's triumph over, 617–19
    central planning and, 130–32, 140–41,
        144, 151–52, 154–55, 167, 645
    classes and, 299–300
    consumerism and, 436, 443, 449–
        50, 468–69
    economic development and, 137, 138–
        39, 140, 154–55, 156–57, 166–67
    end of, 27, 152, 156, 166–67, 197–98,
        275, 378–79
    environmental impact and, 27
    gender and, 330–32, 333, 342–43,
        348, 585
    Islamism and, 275, 517, 611–12
    labor movements and, 369, 378–
        79, 380–81
    mass murder and, 538, 544–45
    nationalism and, 493–94, 497–98,
        506, 584–85
    party bureaucrats in, 584–85
    progress and, 478–80, 482, 488–89
    religion and, 514–17, 521–22, 527–28
    television and, 408–9
    tourism and, 423–24, 434–35
    transition of countries from, 271, 303–4,
        619–23, 622t–23
    utopian movements and, 576–77, 582,
        584–85, 594, 602, 610–11, 619–20
Communist Manifesto (Marx and Engels), 647
computers, 118–22
Comte, August, 477–78, 510
Confederation of South African Trade
    Unions (COSATU), 382
Connally, John, 143
consumerism
    advertising and, 437–38, 440–41, 443–
        44, 448, 450, 478
    Age of Interconnection and, 436–37
    Americanization and, 443–45
    challenges to, 448–51, 467
    communism and, 436, 443, 449–
        50, 468–69
    consumer advocates and, 450, 472
    consumption distinguished from, 437–38
    credit and, 443, 445–47, 453–55
    credit cards, 445, 453–55
    cuisines and, 471
    department stores and, 438, 445, 448–
        49, 453, 472–73
    deregulation and, 439–40, 452, 454,
        455–62, 473
    development of, 438–40, 448–51
    economic development and, 436, 441,
        451, 452, 630–31
    energy and, 436–37, 448, 451
    Engel's law and, 437, 442
    environmental impact and, 448, 449
    Era of Upheaval and, 436–37, 442, 448–
        51, 468
    fair trade movement in, 132, 469–
        70, 472–73
    fast-food restaurants and, 452, 469–
        71, 648–49
    globalization and, 437, 438, 452, 460–
        61, 466–74, 647–49
    identity and, 436, 437–38, 472–73
    inequality and, 452–55, 473, 630–31
    Internet and, 464–65
    Late Millennium Era and, 436–37, 439–
        40, 452–74
    market research and, 443, 444, 452
    myths and realities of, 443–48
    Postwar Era and, 439–48, 452, 472–73
    privatization and, 439–40, 452, 455–
        56, 473
    public spending and, 443, 447–48
    stagnation of, 469–70, 473
    supermarkets and, 442, 445, 451, 452,
        469–70, 472–73
    technological development and, 438
    transportation and, 438–40, 442, 451,
        452–53, 456–60
    utopian movements and, 582, 593, 597
    youth culture and, 316–17, 436–37,
        449, 451
contraception, 333–34, 336, 337,
    340, 341–42
Cook, Thomas, 419–20
Coolidge, Calvin, Jr., 41–42, 72
Cooper, Frederick, 499
Côte d'Ivoire
    internet access in, 627–28
    labor movements in, 367

migrations and, 184, 197–98
television in, 406, 412
COVID-19 pandemic, 4–5, 72–73, 80–81, 434, 626, 643
Cox, Harvey, 510
Croatia
    mass murder in, 111–12, 557–58, 559, 560–62
    migrations and, 183–84, 190
    refugees in, 560–61, 562
    tourism in, 427, 433–34
Crutzen, Paul, 12
Cuba
    Cold War and, 210, 211–12, 237–38, 240, 255, 581
    consumerism in, 442
    disease in, 71
    Global Realignment Struggle and, 225, 244–46
    nationalism in, 506
    refugees in, 179
    revolution in, 244, 600
    television in, 405–6
    utopian movements in, 600
Cuban Missile Crisis (1962), 210, 211–12, 237–38, 240, 255, 581, 583
Cuyahoga River fire (1969), 11, 20
Cyprus, tourism in, 427
Czech Republic
    creation of, 506
    economic development in, 638–39
    gender in, 349f–50
    religion in, 527–28
    television in, 415–16
    transportation in, 917
Czechoslovakia
    Cold War and, 227–28, 269
    consumerism in, 468–69
    disease in, 43–44, 45
    division of, 506
    economic development in, 132, 156–57
    environmental impact in, 25–26
    gender in, 331, 342, 350–51
    human rights in, 612–13
    nationalism in, 498, 557–58
    refugees in, 174
    religion in, 515
    television in, 409

Darfur mass murder, 179–80, 570

Darwin, Charles, 54, 477–78, 479
Davis, Gray, 494
DAWN (Development Alternatives with Women for a New Era), 343
DDT
    disease and, 4–5, 51–55, 71–72, 79, 224–25
    environmental impact and, 11, 14, 15–16, 22, 650
    Global Realignment Struggle and, 224–25
    regulation and, 22
de Gaulle, Charles, 231, 238–39, 251–52, 364–65, 408–9, 496–97, 585–86, 607, 609
Debord, Guy, 448
Debray, Régis, 609
Decline of the West (Spengler), 482
decolonization and anti-imperialism. *See also* Third World
    anti-Americanism and, 595
    apocalyptic thinking and, 586–87
    authoritarianism and, 587–88
    Global Realignment Struggle and, 222–23, 231–34, 235–36, 251–52
    human rights and, 612–13
    inequality and, 587
    Islamism and, 255
    migrations and, 181–84, 197–98
    nationalism and, 495–96, 499, 501–2, 586
    progress and, 481, 488
    refugees and, 174–76, 184
    religion and, 513–14, 518–19
    reparations and, 586
    resistance to, 231–33, 234
    self-determination and, 222–23, 232, 242–43, 491, 506–7, 579–80, 651
    terrorism and, 251
    utopian movements and, 577–80, 583, 586–88, 592, 593–94, 595, 612–13
    violence as necessary for, 586
    youth culture and, 314, 317
DeMars, Nan, 383–84
Demba Waar, Baay, 357
Democratic Republic of Congo (DRC)
    Africa's Great War and, 272–74
    civil war in, 180, 206, 272
    communism in, 244–45
    decolonization in, 70, 235–36, 272

Democratic Republic of Congo (DRC) (*cont.*)
   disease in, 70
   gender in, 354–55
   Global Realignment Struggle and, 244–45, 272–73
   refugees in, 179–80, 568–69
   television in, 406, 412
   utopian movements in, 597
Deneuve, Catherine, 341–42
Deng Xiaoping, 141–42, 156–57, 218, 264–65, 271, 425–26, 542, 604, 611–12
Denmark
   disease in, 66
   economic development in, 154
   gender in, 326, 331
   labor movements in, 359, 380
   nationalism in, 508
   utopian movements in, 594–95
deregulation. *See also* privatization
   capitalism and, 115, 155, 160, 637
   consumerism and, 439–40, 452, 454, 455–62, 473
   economic development and, 144, 148–49, 150, 154–62, 163–64, 166–67, 637–39
   labor movements and, 376–79, 394
   reregulation and, 131, 155, 158, 159, 160, 162–64, 462, 465–66, 636, 644
   telecommunication and, 132–33, 413–14, 456, 460–66, 473
   television and, 413–15
   transportation and, 99, 456–60
   utopian movements and, 613–20, 637–39
Destruction and Protection of Nature (Heim), 17
developing world. *See* Third World
Diaz, Gustavo, 598
Dichter, Ernst, 444
Dietl, Jaroslav, 409
Diop, Cheikh anta, 354
disease
   Age of Interconnection and, 41, 72–74, 79, 80
   antibiotic-resistant bacteria and, 46, 71–75, 78–79
   antibiotics and, 41–46, 50, 51, 57, 59–60, 71–72
   apocalyptic thinking and, 72–81
   biological warfare and, 48–49
   BMI and, 65–66
   cancer, 58, 59, 60, 62–63, 64
   chemotherapy for, 59
   Cold War and, 48–49
   COVID-19 pandemic, 4–5, 72–73, 80–81, 434, 626, 643
   DDT and, 51–55, 71–72, 79
   diet and, 64, 67–68
   economic development and, 56, 66–67
   environmental impact and, 41, 71, 79–80
   future concerns about, 72–81
   gender and, 67
   global obesity epidemic and, 64–68, 65*f*–66, 66*t*, 80
   globalization and, 69–70, 72–73, 80
   heart disease, 58–59, 63, 64–65, 68
   high blood pressure and, 62, 80–81
   HIV/AIDS and, 4–5, 69–79, 80, 311–12, 347
   inequality and, 78–79
   Late Millennium Era and, 64–68, 73
   life expectancy and, 44–45, 63–64, 74–75, 79–80
   low birth weight and, 62, 64, 68, 79
   malaria, 46, 49–55, 53*f*, 57, 72
   mortality rates from infectious disease and, 73*f*, 73–74
   noninfectious diseases, 58–64, 61*f*, 68
   physical activity and, 68
   population growth and, 54
   Postwar Era and, 41, 44–45, 46–57, 79
   public health measures and, 44–45, 46, 50–53, 57, 60–61, 71, 77, 79–80
   regulation and, 45
   religion and, 71
   research on, 63–64, 79
   return of infectious disease and, 69–72, 74–75
   risk factors for, 58–60, 64–68, 75–76
   sexually-transmitted illnesses, 43, 71, 76–77
   smallpox, 46–49, 53–54, 57
   smoking and, 60–61, 61*f*, 62–63, 64–65
   stroke, 61–62, 64
   Third World and, 47–48, 57, 63–64, 66–67, 74–75, 78, 80–81
   transplantation and, 58–59, 62
   tuberculosis, 46, 55–57, 59–60, 72, 74, 78–79, 80

INDEX | 765

vaccines and, 41–42, 44–45, 47, 48, 56–57, 59–60
World War I and, 47, 50–51, 56
World War II and, 43–44, 49, 51–52, 58–59, 79
Djibouti, television in, 406
Djilas, Milovan, 583, 584, 585–86, 587–88
Doctors without Borders, 612
Dohrn, Bernadine, 598–99
Domagk, Gerhard, 42
Dominican Republic
  migrations and, 192–93, 197–98
  tourism in, 429
Dorsey Laboratories, 45
DRC. *See* Democratic Republic of Congo
Dubashi, Jay, 507
DuBois, W. E. B., 223
Dugas, Gaetan, 69
Dulles, John Foster, 243
Duras, Marguerite, 341–42
Durkheim, Emile, 510
Dutschke, Rudi, 589, 600

Earth Day, 18, 21
East Asian economic model, 155, 161–62, 219–20, 393
East Asian financial crisis (1997-98), 146–47, 162–63, 631
EBRD (European Bank for Reconstruction and Development), 620
Ecology of Invasions, The (Elton), 21–22
economic development
  Age of Interconnection and, 166
  Age of Total War and, 139, 164–65
  agriculture and, 110–11, 132
  austerity programs and, 149, 151, 163–64, 305, 445, 639
  bailouts in, 151, 163–64
  bank types and, 133
  bicicleta financeria periods in, 146–47, 158–59, 162–63, 631, 636–37
  Bretton Woods system and, 129–30, 135–36, 137–38, 142–43, 145–46, 155, 158–59, 162, 163–64, 222–23, 238–39, 265
  capitalism and, 132, 136–38, 141, 144, 149, 154–55, 160
  central planning and, 130–32, 140–41, 144, 151–52, 154–55, 167, 645
  classes and, 301–2, 307–8

  Cold War and, 136, 143, 156–57, 238–39, 265, 645–46
  communism and, 137, 138–39, 140, 154–55, 156–57, 166–67
  consumerism and, 436, 441, 451, 452, 630–31
  continuing trends in, 626–28, 636–37
  crisis of 2008 and, 163–64, 167, 197–98, 445, 619–20, 636–39
  crisis of 2010-11 and, 636
  deregulation and, 148–49, 154–62, 163–64, 166–67, 637–39
  disease and, 56, 66–67
  disruptions in, 140–54, 162–67
  East Asian economic model and, 155, 161–62, 219–20, 393
  East Asian financial crisis and, 146–47, 162–63, 631
  energy and, 135, 139–40, 143, 144, 147–51, 185
  environmental impact and, 15, 25–26
  Era of Upheaval and, 140–54, 167
  exchange rates and, 135, 145–47, 155, 159–60
  exponential growth in, 643–44
  Export-Led Industrialization (ELI) and, 160–62
  financial transactions and, 133, 135–36, 144f, 144–45, 154
  floating currency and, 144, 145–46, 159
  foreign investment and, 144f–45, 144–47, 153, 154, 160, 163, 642–43
  GATT and, 134, 618
  gender and, 333, 347–48
  global production and, 164f, 164–65
  Global Realignment Struggle and, 222–23
  global recession and, 149, 158
  globalization and, 27–28, 134–35, 152–53, 154–62, 163–64, 166–67, 626–28, 638, 647–48
  Import Substitution Industrialization (ISI) and, 136–39, 148–49, 160–61, 301–2, 307–8, 360–61, 441, 482
  inequality and, 165–67, 615, 638, 645
  Internet and, 124–25
  labor movements and, 360–61, 367
  Late Millennium Era and, 144, 146–47, 154–67, 321, 636–37
  migrations and, 183–84, 185, 189–90, 198, 627

economic development (*cont.*)
  population growth and, 22–23, 26, 39, 164–65, 321–22
  Postwar Era and, 139, 146–47, 165–66, 167
  privatization and, 144, 162–63, 166–67, 455–56, 645
  progress and, 479–80, 486–88
  regulation and, 132–35, 144, 148–49, 154–62, 167
  religion and, 518
  seniors and, 319–20, 321–22
  shipping containers and, 144, 153–54, 166–67
  speculation and, 144, 145–46
  stagflation and, 143, 448, 486–87
  stop and go periods in, 141–42, 146–47, 158–59, 631
  tariffs and, 134–35
  technological development and, 132, 140, 166
  Third World and, 136–37, 138–39, 150–51
  tourism and, 419, 425–26
  trade deficits and, 141–43, 158–59, 636–37
  transportation and, 94–95
  Washington Consensus in, 157–58, 163–64, 545–46, 618, 639
  World War I and, 143, 154
  World War II and, 129–30, 136
  youth culture and, 316–18
Ecuador, gender in, 323–24
Eden, Anthony, 235
education
  classes and, 298–99, 302–3
  Era of Upheaval and, 316
  gender and, 333, 345–48, 346*f*
  leisure and, 402–4
  population growth and, 315–16
  progress and, 484
  youth culture and, 315–16
Egypt
  economic development in, 137, 148–49
  Global Realignment Struggle and, 234, 244, 251
  Islamism in, 255, 262–63, 275
  nationalism in, 502
  Pan-Arabism in, 502
  privatization in, 455
  progress in, 488

  refugees in, 177, 185
  Suez Crisis in, 234–35, 250–51, 261–62, 502
Ehrlich, Paul, 21, 22, 23, 24
Eichenwald, Heinz, 45
Eisenhower, Dwight, 212, 231, 233–34, 235
El Salvador
  Cold War and, 259–60, 553–54
  gender in, 323–24
  mass murder in, 551–52
ELI (Export-Led Industrialization), 160–62
Elton, Charles, 21–22
Emanuele, Vittorio, III, 575–76
End of History, The (Fukuyama), 617–19
energy, 83–91
  Age of Interconnection and, 91
  Age of Total War and, 87
  consumerism and, 436–37, 448, 451
  economic development and, 135, 139–40, 143, 144, 147–51, 185
  embargos in, 147, 250
  environmental impact and, 12–13, 14, 16, 24, 25, 35, 85–86, 87–90
  exponential growth in, 643–44
  futures in, 144
  gasification and, 87
  global energy production survey, 83*f*–84, 86*f*–87
  Global Realignment Struggle and, 223–24, 249, 250
  natural gas, 90–91, 125, 147–48, 150, 151–52
  nuclear energy, 84–86, 88–90, 488
  oil price shocks in, 35, 39, 86–87, 90, 143, 147–49, 150, 151, 166, 223–24, 430, 436–37, 652–53
  petroleum usage and, 83–85, 86–87, 90, 90*f*
  population growth and, 23, 24
  Postwar Era and, 86–87
  progress and, 488
  recycling of, 88–90
  regulation and, 135
  religion and, 522
  solar power, 87
  technological development and, 83, 87
  Third World, 150–51
Engel, Ernst, 437
Engels, Friedrich, 331, 436, 647–48

England. *See* United Kingdom
Enoki Misako, 340
Environmental Defense Fund, 18
environmental impact
  Age of Interconnection and, 3, 39
  Age of Upheaval and, 17–23
  agriculture and, 12, 16, 37, 111–13
  Anthropocene era of, 12
  biodiversity and, 21–22, 27–28, 39–40, 112–13
  capitalism and, 26–27, 38
  climate change and, 30–38, 39–40
  Cold War and, 16, 32
  communism and, 27
  consumerism and, 448, 449
  DDT and, 11, 14, 15–16, 22
  disasters and, 19–21, 28, 85–86, 89–90, 488
  disease and, 41, 71, 79–80
  economic development and, 15, 25–26
  energy and, 12–13, 14, 16, 24, 25, 35, 85–86, 87–90
  environmental organizations, 18, 19
  Era of Upheaval and, 17–23
  fishing and, 12–13, 16
  globalization and, 15, 27–28
  governmental administrations and, 18–19
  industrialization and, 11–13, 20–21, 27, 28
  insecticides and, 14, 15–16, 21–22
  international recognition of, 18–19, 24, 31
  Late Millennium Era and, 23–40
  lead usage, 16, 24, 26–27
  nature preserves and, 16, 430
  nuclear weapons and, 13–14, 19
  ozone layer and, 24–25, 30–31, 32–34, 36–38
  pollution and, 12, 14, 20–21, 24–26, 30–31
  population growth and, 14–15, 16–17, 21, 22–23, 26, 39–40
  Postwar Era and, 12–17, 39
  radioactivity and, 13–14, 21
  regulation and, 12–13, 18–19, 20, 24–25, 26–27, 33
  taking nature for granted and, 12–17
  Third World and, 27–29, 33
  transportation and, 12, 24–25
  unexpected complexities of, 23–40
  waste disposal and, 15
environmentalism, 16–17, 19–20, 21–22, 26–27, 28–29, 37, 87–88, 449, 486–87, 612
Epprecht, Mark, 353
Era of Upheaval
  classes and, 302–3, 306
  Cold War and, 210–11, 238–43
  consumerism and, 436–37, 442, 448–51, 468
  economic development and, 140–54, 167
  environmental impact and, 17–23
  gender and, 332–43, 355
  labor movements and, 360–69
  leisure and, 402, 435
  migrations and, 180–88
  nationalism and, 497–98
  population growth and, 23, 316, 322
  progress and, 482–83, 486–90, 529
  religion and, 510, 517–23
  seniors and, 319–20
  television and, 435
  tourism and, 421–22, 435
  transportation and, 96
  utopian movements and, 589–91, 596–97, 599, 601, 609–13
eras. *See* Era of Upheaval; Late Millennium Era; Postwar Era
Erdogan, Tayyip, 639–40
Estonia
  economic development in, 620
  nationalism in, 506
  religion in, 527–28
Ethiopia
  Africa's Great War and, 272–73
  agriculture in, 28
  Cold War and, 210–11, 652
  consumerism in, 597
  environmental impact in, 28
  Global Realignment Struggle and, 245, 249, 256–57
  population growth in, 28
  refugees in, 179–80
  revolution in, 257
  terrorism in, 611
  utopian movements in, 594–95, 599, 610
  war with Somalia of, 206, 210–11
Euromissiles controversy, 255–56
European debt crisis of 2010-11, 639

European Economic Community (EEC), 98–99, 155, 156, 496–97, 507
European Space Agency (ESA), 106–7
European Union (EU)
  consumerism and, 472
  creation of, 156, 494–95, 496–97, 507
  economic development and, 2, 156, 639
  end of history and, 618
  human rights and, 558
  labor movements and, 378–79, 387
  nationalism and, 495, 507
  reregulation and, 636
  tourism and, 433
Evangelical Protestantism, 512–13, 519–23, 529
Export-Led Industrialization (ELI), 160–62
Exxon Valdez oil spill (1989), 28

Faisal II, King, 502–3
Falklands War, 258
Fanon, Frantz, 225, 354, 579, 583, 585–88, 596, 608
farming. *See* agriculture
Farnsworth, Philo, 405
Feminine Mystique, The (Friedan), 339
feminism, 329–30, 333, 334–35, 339–41, 342–44, 347–50, 401–2, 612
fertility rates, 311*f*, 311–13, 321, 328, 335, 336, 343–44, 347–48
Feuerbach, Ludwig, 526
Finland
  consumerism in, 444
  disease in, 56
  gender in, 323–24
  generational change in, 319
  labor movements in, 359, 380
  migrations and, 183
  tourism in, 433
Finland, Max, 46
Fleming, Alexander, 42–43, 46
Fleming, Ian, 423
Florio, Massimo, 455–56
Foot, Hugh (Lord Caradon), 223–24
Ford, Gerald, 252–53, 438–39, 573–74
Ford, Henry, 92–93, 94, 390, 438–39
Forrester, Jay, 22
France
  classes in, 299–300, 306–7
  Cold War and, 238–39, 270
  consumerism in, 440–41, 442, 444, 445–46, 454–55
  decolonization and, 182–83, 184, 232
  disease in, 43, 56, 65–66
  economic development in, 141–42, 143, 639
  education in, 315
  energy in, 85–86, 88–90, 91, 135, 147
  environmental impact in, 19–20
  gender in, 323–24, 325–26, 341–42
  labor movements in, 359, 361, 362, 364–65, 386–87, 409, 605, 606–7
  May 1968 protests in, 364–66, 409, 591, 597–98, 599–600, 601, 604–8
  migrations and, 182–84, 185, 190, 306–7
  nationalism in, 494, 508, 607
  nuclear weapons in, 238
  progress in, 478
  Suez Crisis and, 234–35, 250–51, 261–62, 502
  television in, 405–6, 409
  tourism in, 421–22, 426
  transportation in, 97–98, 99–100, 101
  utopian movements in, 575, 591, 594–95, 597–98, 609, 611
  youth culture in, 316–17
Frankfurt School, 444, 591, 593
Free to Choose (TV series), 616, 620
French Popular Front, 590
Friedan, Betty, 339
Friedman, Milton, 137, 144, 615–16, 618–20, 622–23, 637–38
Frommer, Arthur, 422
Fukushima disaster (2011), 19–20, 85–86
Fukuyama, Francis, 617–18

G-7, 155, 158–59, 618, 646
Gaddis, John, 207–8
Gambia, television in, 412
Gandhi, Indira, 28–29, 148–49, 334, 335, 349, 368, 372–73
Gandhi, Mohandas, 52, 481, 494, 506–7, 574, 577
García, Romeo Lucas, 552–53
Gargarin, Yuri, 101–2
Garvey, Marcus, 504–5
Gaud, William, 110
Gauweiler, Peter, 71
gay rights movement, 340–41, 343–44, 347, 348–49
Geigy AG, 51
gender, 322–56

abortion and, 325–27, 335–36, 341–42, 347–48
Age of Interconnection and, 355
Age of Total War and, 323–24, 355–56
arranged marriages and, 327–28, 352
backlash to changes to, 341, 347–48, 354–55
bride-price and, 327–28
censorship and, 326–27, 336–37
classes and, 302–3, 349–50
Cold War and, 355–56
communism and, 330–32, 333, 342–43, 348
companionate marriage and, 323, 343–44, 351–53
contraception and, 325, 326–27, 328, 331–32, 333–34, 336, 337, 340, 341–42, 347–48
cross-dressing and, 328–29, 353–54
discrimination based on, 328, 341, 343–45
disease and, 67
divorce and, 330, 332, 341
dowry and, 327–28
economic development and, 333, 347–48
education and, 333, 345–48, 346f
Era of Upheaval and, 332–43, 355
feminism and, 329–30, 333, 334–35, 339–41, 342–44, 347–50, 401–2, 612
gay rights movement and, 340–41, 343–44, 347, 348–49
gender roles, 323, 327, 328–29, 349–51, 353–54
globalization and, 355–56
illegitimate births and, 349f–50, 349–51
infanticide and, 328
Islamism and, 348
labor movements and, 393–95
Late Millennium Era and, 343–56
leisure and, 400–3, 404
marriage rates and, 324–25, 328
patriarchy and, 329, 335, 354–55
political participation and, 323, 349
population growth and, 321–22, 328, 335, 347–48
Postwar Era and, 323, 332–33
regimes of, 323–24, 327, 328, 329, 332–33, 338, 341, 348–49, 352–53
religion and, 518, 521–22, 526
reproduction and, 324–25, 344f, 344–45

same-sex relations and, 325–27, 328–29, 333, 340–41, 353–55
sexual revolution in, 324–25, 332–33, 336–39, 340–41, 342–43, 348, 429–30, 518, 519, 521–22
single mothers and, 326–27, 349–51
sterilization and, 334–35
Third World and, 342–43
utopian movements and, 612
women's suffrage and, 323–24
youth culture and, 332–33, 336–37, 338–39
General Electric, 118–19, 478, 489–90
generational change. *See* population growth; seniors; youth
Genscher, Hans Dietrich, 26–27
Germany
  Berlin Crisis in, 210, 236, 581
  Berlin Wall in, 180–81, 190, 211, 216, 236, 265, 268–69, 272, 276–56, 613, 625
  Cold War and, 210–11, 215–17, 228–29, 236–37, 241–42, 268–70, 271
  consumerism in, 440–41, 444, 445–47, 448–49, 453, 468–69
  disease in, 43, 51–52, 56, 60, 78
  economic development in, 132–33, 139, 140, 141–43, 152, 154, 156–57, 158–59, 639
  energy in, 85, 87, 91, 147
  environmental impact in, 16, 19, 26–27
  gender in, 323, 326, 330–31, 341, 342–43
  generational change in, 319
  Global Realignment Struggle and, 217
  labor movements in, 359, 362–63, 367, 376–77, 379–80, 387, 389
  migrations and, 170, 183–84, 185, 188–89, 190
  nationalism in, 497–98, 499, 501
  Nazi Germany, 216, 242, 413, 530–32, 575–76
  nuclear weapons and, 580–81
  Nuremberg trial in, 531–32, 533, 536
  partition of, 215–16
  refugees in, 173–74, 177, 180–81
  regulation in, 132–33
  religion in, 515–16, 526, 527–28
  reunification of, 159–60, 270
  sports competitions in, 500–1
  television in, 406–7, 412

Germany (*cont.*)
  terrorism in, 611
  tourism in, 420–22, 423, 424–25
  transportation in, 93, 94, 96–97, 100
  utopian movements in, 591, 594–95, 599–600, 609, 611
  World War II and, 51–52, 87, 94, 96–97, 215–16, 241–42, 269
  youth culture in, 316–17
Gernsbach, Hugo, 100
Gershuny, Jonathan, 403–4
Ghana
  classes in, 307–8
  decolonization in, 359–60, 361, 579
  economic development in, 150–51
  energy in, 84–85, 86
  internet access in, 627–28
  labor movements in, 359–60, 361, 367, 377–78, 381, 384–85
  Pan-Africanism in, 505
  progress in, 481
  television in, 412
Gide, Andre, 494
Giolitti, Giovanni, 50–51
Glass-Steagall Act (1933), 133, 156
Glenn, John, 101–2
global governance, 573–76, 580, 581–82, 592, 648, 649–51
Global Realignment Struggle
  Age of Upheaval and, 238–43
  Bandung Conference and, 234–35, 240, 243, 245, 247–48, 502, 546
  Cold War and, 212, 217, 223–24, 228, 234, 243–54, 256, 261–62, 265, 271–73, 276–77
  DDT and, 224–25
  decolonization and, 222–23, 231–34, 235–36, 251–52
  economic development and, 222–23
  end of, 273, 650–51
  energy and, 223–24, 249, 250
  Islamism and, 223–24, 254–55, 263, 274–77
  New International Information Order in, 249, 250–51
  nuclear weapons and, 240, 252–53
  population growth and, 224–25
  racial conflict and, 223–24, 240
  self-determination and, 222–23, 232, 242–43, 491, 506–7, 579–80, 651
  terrorism and, 251, 255, 276–77
  Third World and, 224–26, 233–34, 240, 245
  World War II and, 231–32
globalization
  Age of Interconnection and, 1–2, 3, 5–6, 7, 647–49
  agriculture and, 109–10, 112
  capitalism and, 154–55, 617
  classes and, 304–8, 343–44
  consumerism and, 437, 438, 452, 460t, 460–61, 466–74, 647–49
  disease and, 69–70, 72–73, 80
  economic development and, 27–28, 134–35, 152–53, 154–62, 163–64, 166–67, 626–28, 638, 647–48
  environmental impact and, 15, 27–28
  gender and, 355–56
  inequality and, 166–67, 653
  labor movements and, 364, 376–79, 386–87
  microelectronics and, 121
  migrations and, 168, 169–80, 192, 205
  nationalism and, 500–1, 648–49
  progress and, 482
  religion and, 509, 521–22, 648–49
  television and, 410–17, 435, 648–49
  terrorism and, 611–12
  Third World and, 27–28
  tourism and, 418–19, 422, 425
  utopian movements and, 598–600, 611–12, 613–14, 617, 648–49
Globke, Hans, 216
Goddard, Robert, 100–1
Gomułka, Władysław, 596–97
Gorbachev, Mikhail, 156–57, 211–12, 266–68, 270–71, 653–54
Gorz, André, 449–50
Gospel of Abundant Life, 489, 522–23
GPS (Global Positioning System), 4, 105–6, 396–97
Gramm-Leach-Billey Act (1999), 156
Grant, Cary, 423
Great Britain. *See* United Kingdom
Great Depression, 107–8, 152–53, 172, 439–40, 464, 623
Great Leap Forward, 131–32, 140, 479, 490, 539–42, 543–44, 652
Greece
  Cold War and, 228
  communism in, 582
  economic development in, 639

gender in, 323–24
migrations and, 183–84
refugees in, 172–73
tourism in, 427
utopian movements in, 594–95, 597–98
Green Revolution, 24, 110, 111–13, 114–15, 651, 652–53
Greenpeace, 18, 19–20
Gromyko, Andrei, 249–50
Grünbaum, Ole, 317–18
Guatemala
classes in, 306, 307
Cold War and, 259–60, 553–54
ethnic conflict in, 552–53
mass murder in, 545–46, 551–55
religion in, 519, 553
US involvement in, 233
Guérin, Camille, 56–57
Guevara, Che, 244–45, 249, 595, 600, 608
Guinea
decolonization in, 579
Global Realignment Struggle and, 240, 245
labor movements in, 359–60, 361, 367, 378
utopian movements in, 608
Guinea-Bissau, Global Realignment Struggle and, 245, 251–52
Gulf War, First (1980-88), 260–62
Gulf War, Second (1990-91), 105–6, 191, 273, 276
Gulf War, Third (2003-11), 264–65, 632–36
Guti, Ezekiel, 521
Gutiérrez, Gustavo, 518

Habyarimana, Juvénal, 564–67, 568
Hadaway, C. Kirk, 526–27
Hagen, Nina, 424–25
Haiti
decolonization in, 209
disease in, 70
migrations and, 193–94, 197–98
Hart-Cellar Act (1965), 187, 192, 193, 196–97
Hayek, Friedrich, 615, 616–17
Heath, Edward, 365
Heim, Roger, 17
Helms, Jesse, 71
Helsinki Conference on Security and Cooperation in Europe (1975), 241–43, 267, 270

Helsinki Watch, 612
Hessler, Peter, 624–25
Hezbollah, 254–55, 276
Hirohito, Emperor, 532, 535–36
Hitler, Adolf, 220, 228, 408–9
HIV/AIDS, 4–5, 69–80, 311–12, 347
Ho Chi Minh, 233, 247, 248–49, 608
Hodel, Donald, 38
the Holocaust, 413, 532
Holstrom, Mark, 376, 398
Homage to Catalonia (Orwell), 583–84
Honecker, Erich, 217, 330–31, 601
Honecker, Margot, 330–31
Honest to God (Robinson), 518–19
Hong Kong
disease in, 46
economic development in, 368, 629
gender in, 351–52
labor movements in, 368, 395
migrations and, 197–98
technological development in, 121
Horáková, Milada, 330–31
Horkheimer, Max, 591
Hulme, Kathryn, 176, 180
human rights
Age of Interconnection and, 649–50
Cold War and, 242–43, 253–54, 267, 553–54
decolonization and, 612–13
migrations and, 189
refugees and, 180
utopian movements and, 612–13, 651
Human Rights Watch, 612
Hungary
authoritarianism in, 623–24
Cold War and, 227–28, 239, 268
consumerism in, 468
economic development in, 156–57, 638–39
gender in, 331, 342–43
labor movements in, 359, 362
refugees in, 174
religion in, 527–28
television in, 415–16
tourism in, 425
Hungry Planet, The (Borgstrom), 17
Hus, Jan, 515
Hussein, King, 502–4
Hussein, Saddam, 191–92, 260, 273, 275, 276, 504, 618, 632–34, 635–36

Huurdeman, Anton, 462
Huxley, Julian, 17

IBM (International Business Machines), 119, 121, 396–97
Ibn Bab, 'Abd al-'Aziz, 520
Iceland
  air travel in, 134–35
  gender in, 331
IG Farben, 42, 51, 57, 210, 532
illness. *See* disease
IMF (International Monetary Fund), 135, 137–38, 141, 151, 163–64, 222–23, 616–17, 620, 623–24, 639
immigration. *See* migrations
Import Substitution Industrialization (ISI), 136–39, 148–49, 160–61, 301–2, 307–8, 360–61, 441, 482
India
  agriculture in, 110, 112
  classes in, 300, 306, 307
  consumerism in, 454–55
  decolonization in, 174–76, 223, 231–33, 495–96, 577–78
  deregulation in, 461
  disease in, 52, 66–67, 68, 74
  economic development in, 133–34, 137, 138, 165
  energy in, 84–85, 86
  environmental impact in, 18, 19–21, 27, 30, 33–34
  gender in, 323–24, 329–30, 334–35, 352, 353
  generational change in, 319
  Global Realignment Struggle and, 234, 244
  internet access in, 627–28
  labor movements in, 360–61, 363–64, 369, 371–75, 376–77, 381, 384–85, 387
  microelectronics in, 123
  migrations and, 169–70, 171, 172, 185–86, 191, 196–97, 306
  nationalism in, 493, 506–7
  partition of, 174–76, 578
  population growth in, 21, 23
  progress in, 480–81, 482, 493
  refugees in, 175–76, 177
  religion in, 513–14, 523
  satellites in, 106–7
  telecommunications in, 466

television in, 406, 412, 416–17
transportation in, 93–94, 97–98, 101
utopian movements in, 578, 611
Indonesia
  Cold War and, 549–50
  decolonization in, 495–96, 546–47, 550
  economic development in, 137, 139, 161–62
  education in, 315–16
  energy in, 149–50
  environmental impact in, 28
  ethnic conflict in, 549
  gender in, 323–24, 328–29, 346, 347–48, 353–54
  Global Realignment Struggle and, 234, 247–48
  human rights in, 253–54
  internet access in, 627–28
  Islamism in, 262–63
  labor movements in, 360, 368, 383
  mass murder in, 545–51, 569–70
  migrations and, 169–70, 191, 201
  nationalism in, 492
  religion in, 549
  telecommunications in, 466
  television in, 412, 415–16
inequality
  classes and, 302
  consumerism and, 452–55, 473, 630–31
  decolonization and, 587
  disease and, 78–79
  economic development and, 165–67, 615, 623, 638, 645
  globalization and, 166–67, 653
  Late Millennium Era and, 403, 452
  population growth and, 165–66
  technological development and, 82, 111
  Third World and, 224
  utopian movements and, 589, 613–14
interconnection. *See* Age of Interconnection
International Air Transport Association (IATA), 134–35
International Confederation of Free Trade Unions, 363
International Council of Women, 329–30
International Criminal Court, 570
International Criminal Tribunal for the Former Yugoslavia, 559–60, 562
International Military Tribunal at Nuremberg, 531–32, 533, 536

INDEX | 773

International Military Tribunal for the Far East, 531–32, 533, 535
International Monetary Fund (IMF), 135, 137–38, 141, 151, 163–64, 222–23, 616–17, 620, 623–24, 639
International Olympic Committee, 218, 500
international relations. *See* Cold War; decolonization and anti-imperialism; Global Realignment Struggle
the Internet
  access to, 123–24, 627–28, 643
  ARPANET precursor to, 122–24
  censorship of, 628
  consumerism and, 464–65
  development of, 121–24
  dot com boom and, 124–25
  economic development and, 124–25
  e-mail and, 123–24
  growth of, 124
  http and, 124
  labor movements and, 396–97
  precursors to, 122–24
  television and, 417
IPCC (Intergovernmental Panel on Climate Change), 34, 36
Iran
  Arab-Israeli conflict and, 251
  Cold War and, 227–28, 261–62
  decolonization in, 233
  disease in, 80–81
  energy in, 147
  gender in, 343
  Global Realignment Struggle and, 234, 252–53, 254, 260–61
  human rights in, 253–54
  Iran-Contra affair, 260–61
  Iran-Iraq war, 260–62
  refugees in, 179
  religion in, 523
  revolution in, 251, 254–55, 257, 611–12
  US involvement in, 233, 252–53, 254–55, 260–61
Iraq
  Cold War and, 261–62
  Global Realignment Struggle and, 244, 251, 260–61, 273
  Iran-Iraq war, 260–62
  Islamism in, 255, 275, 276
  Kuwait invasion by, 191–92, 273, 276, 504, 618, 633–34
  Pan-Arabism and, 502–4
  refugees in, 179–80, 183–84
  US war in, 264–65, 632–36
Ireland
  economic development in, 637–38, 639
  education in, 315
  gender in, 331, 337, 341–42
  mass murder in, 545–46
  migrations and, 182, 183
  nationalism in, 508
  religion in, 517
ISI (Import Substitution Industrialization), 136–39, 148–49, 160–61, 301–2, 307–8, 360–61, 441, 482
Islamism
  apocalyptic thinking and, 512, 522
  Cold War and, 262–63, 265, 275, 276–77
  communism and, 275, 517, 611–12
  decolonization and, 255
  disease and, 76–77
  gender and, 348
  global order and, 646–47
  Global Realignment Struggle and, 223–24, 254–55, 263, 274–77
  integralism in, 514
  jihad in, 190, 263, 484–85, 487
  modernism and, 511–12, 514
  Muslim Brotherhood and, 484–85, 501–4, 517, 519–20
  nationalism and, 508–9
  Pan-Arabism and, 501–2, 635–36
  progress and, 484–85, 488
  rise of, 255
  Salafism and, 512, 513, 519–21, 522–23, 529
  sharia law in, 275, 511–12
  terrorism and, 255, 275–77, 488
  Wahhabism in, 511–12, 519–20
Israel. *See also* Arab-Israeli conflict
  Cold War and, 261–62
  creation of, 250–51
  Global Realignment Struggle and, 249
  Intifada and, 191–92
  migrations and, 191–92
  partition of, 176
  peace process and, 177
  refugees in, 176, 177
  religion in, 523
  Suez Crisis and, 234–35, 250–51, 261–62, 502
  transportation in, 93–94

Italy
  classes in, 299–300, 306
  communism in, 576, 582
  consumerism in, 445
  disease in, 43–44, 50–52
  economic development in, 141–42, 154, 639
  energy in, 85, 91, 135
  environmental impact in, 19–20
  gender in, 323–24, 341, 478–79
  labor movements in, 367, 368, 377, 379, 384, 391–92, 608
  migrations and, 170, 172, 183–84, 188, 197–98, 306
  nationalism in, 494, 499, 501
  progress in, 478–79
  refugees in, 174
  religion in, 516–17
  resistance movement in, 575–76
  terrorism in, 611
  tourism in, 420, 427, 428–29
  transportation in, 391–92
  utopian movements in, 608
  World War II and, 575–76
Ivory Coast. *See* Côte d'Ivoire
Izaak Walton League, 18

Jamaica
  migrations and, 192–93
  religion in, 593
Jameson, Frederic, 592, 593
Jammeh, Yahya, 354
Japan
  classes in, 299–300
  comfort women and, 532
  consumerism in, 440–41, 442, 443–44, 446, 450, 452, 454–55, 464–65, 470, 471–73
  disease in, 43–44, 51, 56, 57, 60, 63, 66, 69
  economic development in, 132–34, 143, 158–59, 161–62, 165, 199–201, 321–22, 629
  energy in, 84–86, 87, 135, 147
  environmental impact in, 18–19, 20, 24, 25–26, 33, 34
  gender in, 323–24, 325–26, 336, 340–41, 346, 350–51
  generational change in, 319, 321–22
  International Military Tribunal for the Far East in, 531–32, 533, 535
  internet access in, 627–28
  labor movements in, 360, 368–69, 377, 383, 384, 386–87, 391–93
  leisure in, 402, 404
  mass murder in, 531–32, 534–35
  microelectronics in, 121
  migrations and, 198–202
  nationalism in, 492, 499
  nuclear weapons and, 580–81
  population growth in, 24, 201, 321–22, 336
  refugees in, 174
  regulation in, 132–33
  satellites in, 106–7
  sports competitions in, 500
  telecommunications in, 466, 467
  television in, 405–7, 412, 416
  terrorism in, 611–12
  tourism in, 425, 427–28, 434, 467
  transportation in, 92, 94, 95–96, 97–98, 100, 391–93
  utopian movements in, 591
  World War II and, 51–52, 198–99, 231
Jenner, Edward, 41–42, 47
Jiang Jieshi (Chiang Kai-Shek), 218
Jiang Qing, 330–31
Jinnah, Muhammad Ali, 577
John Paul II, Pope, 525, 527, 553
John XXIII, Pope, 523–24, 525
Johnson, Lyndon, 248
Johnson-Reed Act (1924), 172, 187, 203–4
Jones, Thomas K., 258
Jordan
  Pan-Arabism and, 501–4
  refugees in, 177, 191

Kabila, Laurent, 272–73
Kaltenborn, H. V., 580
Kanjiro Takayanagi, 405
Kantorovich, Leonid V., 131
Karadžić, Radovan, 562
Kelly, Petra, 258–59
Kennedy, John F., 102, 210, 237, 243, 478, 573–74
Kent State shooting (1970), 598
Kenya
  classes in, 301–2
  decolonization in, 235–36
  disease in, 46
  gender in, 347–48
  labor movements in, 384–85

refugees in, 180
television in, 406
transportation in, 96, 97–98
Kenyatta, Jomo, 504–5
Kérékou, Mathieu, 367
Keynes, John Maynard, 129–30, 136
Khan, Ayub, 589
Khmer Rouge, 542–45, 611–12, 652
Khomeini, Ayatollah, 240–41, 243, 254, 260–61
Khrushchev, Nikita
   agriculture and, 110–11, 131–32
   Cold War and, 234, 236–38
   Cuban Missile Crisis and, 236–38
   Global Realignment Struggle and, 234, 243, 249–50
   religion and, 514
   secret speech of, 239–40, 542
Kim Il-Sung, 219, 229–30, 443
King, Martin Luther, Jr., 511, 518–19, 579
Kinsey, Alfred C., 326–27
Kissinger, Henry, 218, 242–43, 248–49, 252–53, 531–32, 544–45
Klaus, Vaclav, 620
de Klerk, F.W., 272
Koch, Robert, 55, 58
Kohl, Helmut, 257–58, 269–70, 495
Kordashi, George, 416
Korean War (1950-53), 52–53, 96–97, 160–61, 209, 210, 229–31, 442, 581
Kosovo, mass murder in, 275–76, 560–62
Kosygin, Alexi, 249–50
Krupp, Alfred, 423
Kuboyama, Aikichi, 14
Kung Pinmei, Ignatius, 514–15
Kuwait
   energy in, 135, 147
   Global Realignment Struggle and, 273
   Iraqi invasion of, 191–92, 273, 276, 504, 618, 633–34
   migrations and, 185, 191
   transportation in, 92
Kyoto Protocol (1997), 31, 34–35, 36–37

Laar, Matt, 620
labor movements
   Age of Interconnection and, 357–58, 387–88
   automation and, 396–97
   casualization of labor and, 376, 389
   Cold War and, 363
   communism and, 369, 378–79, 380–81
   decline of, 364, 369–79, 384, 386–87, 393
   deregulation and, 376–79, 394
   development of, 358–64
   economic development and, 360–61, 367
   Era of Upheaval and, 360–69
   gender and, 393–95
   globalization and, 364, 376–79, 386–87
   independent contracting and, 376–77, 398
   informal workers and, 377–78, 381, 385
   information technology and, 387–88, 396–99
   Internet and, 396–97
   Late Millennium Era and, 364, 375, 376, 377–99
   manual labor and, 387–90
   migrations and, 182–84, 185–87, 188–90, 192–93, 197–98, 202–3
   militancy in, 360–69, 371, 372, 375, 382, 384
   outsourcing and, 376–77, 386, 397–98
   Postwar Era and, 358–64, 393–94
   quality circles and, 368–69, 391–93
   service-sector jobs and, 387–88
   shipping containers and, 389–90, 391
   strikes and, 357–58, 364–66, 369–75, 383–86, 384f–85
   temporary workers and, 376, 377, 398
   transportation and, 366, 368–71, 382, 390–96
   unions and, 358, 360–64, 365–68, 370, 373, 378–84, 379f, 386–87
   World War I and, 389
Laos, Vietnam War and, 210–11, 221, 225
Late Great Planet Earth, The (Lindsey), 519
Late Millennium Era
   agriculture and, 115
   capitalism and, 38, 115, 265, 332
   classes and, 303–9
   Cold War and, 256–65
   consumerism and, 436–37, 439–40, 452–74
   disease and, 64–68, 73
   economic development and, 144, 146–47, 154–67, 321, 636–37
   environmental impact and, 23–40
   gender and, 343–56
   inequality and, 403, 452

Late Millennium Era (*cont.*)
　labor movements and, 364, 375, 376, 377–99
　leisure and, 400–1, 402–3, 435
　mass murder and, 555–71
　microelectronics and, 122, 125
　migrations and, 188–205
　nationalism and, 505–9
　population growth and, 310, 643
　progress and, 482–83, 488, 489–90
　religion and, 511, 521–23, 526–29
　television and, 410, 413–14, 415, 417
　tourism and, 425–26, 427–28, 429, 430, 431–35
　utopian movements and, 613–25
Latvia
　economic development in, 638–39
　religion in, 527–28
Lazarsfeld, Paul, 444
Le Duan, 247
Le Pen, Jean Marie, 624–25
League of Nations, 83, 178–79, 574, 644
Lebanon
　Global Realignment Struggle and, 234, 254–55
　Islamism in, 275
　Israeli invasion of, 255
　refugees in, 178
　terrorism in, 255
　US involvement in, 255
Lehman Brothers, 637–38
leisure. *See also* television; tourism
　Age of Interconnection and, 400–1, 431, 434, 437
　education and, 402–4
　Era of Upheaval and, 402, 435
　gender and, 400–3, 404
　increases in, 400–4, 434–35
　Late Millennium Era and, 400–1, 402–3, 435
　population growth and, 401
　Postwar Era and, 400–2, 435
　technological development and, 401–2
　time diaries and, 400, 401–2
Lemkin, Raphael, 536–37
Lesotho, disease in, 74–75
Lewis, W. Arthur, 579
Li Jingquan, 540–41
Libya
　energy in, 149
　Global Realignment Struggle and, 245

　nationalism in, 501–2
　Pan-Arabism and, 502
Lieberman, Yuri, 140
Limits to Growth, The (Club of Rome), 21, 22–23, 39, 40, 449, 486–87, 643–44
Lippmann, Walter, 228
Lisbon Treaty (2008), 508
Lloyd-George, David, 491
Long Term Capital Management, 145–46, 163–64
Longworth, Richard, 309
Lucas García, Romeo, 552–53
Lucky Dragon (ship), 14, 580–81
Luethy, Herbert, 232
Lumumba, Patrice, 272–73, 564, 597
Lutz, Bertha, 323
Lysenko, Trofim, 111

Maalin, Ali Maow, 48
Maastricht Accords (1992), 156, 378–79, 507
Macdonald, Dwight, 485–86, 487
Macedonia, mass murder in, 556, 557
MacMillan, Harold, 235
Madagascar, decolonization in, 231–32
Maddison, Angus, 164, 165
Magic Mountain, The (Mann), 56
Mahler, Halfdan, 76, 80–81
Malawi
　disease in, 74–75
　television in, 412
Malaysia
　consumerism in, 454–55, 470
　decolonization in, 232–33
　economic development in, 161–63
　generational change in, 319
　Global Realignment Struggle and, 247–48
　Islamism in, 262–63, 275
　migrations and, 169–70
　stagnation of, 473
　telecommunications in, 466, 467
　television in, 415–16
　tourism in, 425, 434
　transportation in, 93–94
Malcolm X, 504–5, 589
Mali
　gender in, 353
　labor movements in, 383
　migrations and, 184, 190, 197–98
　television in, 412

Malik, Adam, 550
Malthus, Thomas, 16–17, 22–23, 39
Mandela, Nelson, 272, 382, 653–54
Mao Zedong
    Cold War and, 264–65
    consumerism and, 466–67
    Cultural Revolution of, 240–41, 539, 541–42, 601–2
    decolonization and, 595
    environmental impact and, 15–16
    Global Realignment Struggle and, 240
    Great Leap Forward of, 131–32, 479, 490, 539, 544
    migrations and, 194–95
    nuclear weapons and, 580
    progress and, 479, 490
    Sino-Russian split and, 239–41
    tourism and, 425–26
    utopian movements and, 595
"March of Nations" (song), 573
Marcuse, Herbert, 448, 591
markets. *See* economic development
Marshall Plan, 212, 229, 233
Marx, Karl, 225, 298–99, 302–3, 436, 477–78, 510, 542, 647–48
mass movements. *See* utopian movements
mass murder
    Age of Total War and, 530–31, 533, 537–38, 555, 569
    anti-communism as, 545–55, 569
    Cold War and, 538–55
    communism and, 538, 544–45
    criticism of trials for, 532–33, 555
    economic development and, 538–42, 544
    ethnic cleansing and, 559
    failed states and, 555
    genocide and, 530–31, 536–37
    Holocaust and, 532
    human rights and, 554
    individual responsibility for, 534–35
    Late Millennium Era and, 555–71
    legal basis of, 533–36, 569–70
    Nuremberg trials for, 531–32, 533, 536
    Postwar Era and, 531–38
    POW treatment and, 532–33, 535
    social engineering and, 539–40
    sovereignty and, 534–36, 562, 569–70
    Tokyo trials for, 531–32, 535
    war crimes and, 531–32, 533, 536, 561
    World War II and, 530–31, 533–34, 556–57, 569
    Yugoslavia trials for, 559–60, 562
Mauritius, generational change in, 319
Mavrodi, Sergei, 621–22
Mawdudi, Abu Ala, 508–9
May 1968 protests, 364–66, 409, 591, 597–98, 599–600, 601, 604–8
Mazzini, Giuseppe, 314
Mazzolari, Primo, 494
McArthur, Douglas, 230–31
McCarthy, Joseph, 408–9
McCormick, Katherine, 340
McDonald's, 2, 452, 469–70, 471, 473, 647–48
McLuhan, Marshall, 410, 413, 417, 628
medical issues. *See* disease
Meir, Golda, 349
Melvin, Jess, 548
men. *See* gender
Mendel, Gregor, 111
Mendes, Chico, 29–30
Merleau-Ponty, Maurice, 210
Merton, Robert, 163
Mexico
    agriculture in, 112
    consumerism in, 470, 471–72
    disease in, 52–53, 66–67
    economic development in, 133–34, 139
    education in, 315–16
    generational change in, 319, 320–21
    Global Realignment Struggle and, 244
    internet access in, 627–28
    labor movements in, 358, 362, 368
    migrations and, 192–94
    refugees in, 193–94
    religion in, 513–14
    revolution in, 244
    television in, 415–16
    Tlatelolco Massacre in, 598
    transportation in, 93–94
    utopian movements in, 598
Michnik, Adam, 610
microelectronics, 116–25
    Age of Interconnection and, 121–22
    Age of Total War and, 125
    applications of, 117–18
    Cold War and, 121
    computers and, 118–22
    cybernetics and, 95, 119
    development of, 116–17
    globalization and, 121
    Late Millennium Era and, 122, 125

microelectronics (*cont.*)
  miniaturization process and, 120–21, 122
  Moore's Law and, 120–21, 124–25
  networks and, 121–23
  PCs, 121
  Postwar Era and, 119–20
  productivity gains and, 119–20
  semiconductors and, 117
  telecommunication and, 123–24, 125
  transistors and, 117–18
  vacuum tubes and, 116–17
  World War II and, 116–17, 118
Microwave Communications Incorporated (MCI), 462, 463–64
migrations
  Age of Interconnection and, 205
  Age of Total War and, 169, 181, 183
  agriculture and, 170–71
  backlashes to, 182, 186–88, 189–90
  capitalism and, 183
  causes of, 168–69, 178
  changes in, 168–69
  classes and, 306–7, 309
  Cold War and, 181
  decolonization and, 181–84, 197–98
  demographic normalization and, 189–90
  deportations and, 181
  economic development and, 183–84, 185, 189–90, 198, 627
  Era of Upheaval and, 180–88
  family member prioritization in, 195
  frenzy for, 197–205
  globalization and, 168, 169–80, 192, 205
  Great Trans-Mediterranean Migration in, 184–85, 186
  Great Wave of, 169–80, 203–5
  human rights and, 189
  immigrant neighborhoods and, 188, 190
  labor migrations, 182–84, 185–87, 188–90, 192–93, 197–98, 202–3
  Late Millennium Era and, 188–205
  new global order in, 188–205
  permanent settlement and, 171
  population growth and, 182–83, 202–3
  racial conflict and, 187–88
  recasting of, 180–88
  regulation and, 172, 186–88
  remittances and, 198
  undocumented migration, 195, 202–3
  World War I and, 172, 192–93
Milošević, Slobodan, 556, 557, 560–61, 562

Mindszenty, József, 514–15
Mitrany, David, 494
Mitterrand, François, 270, 609
Mladić, Ratko, 562
Mobutu, Joseph, 272–73, 564–65, 597
Moczar, Mieczesław, 596–97
Modern Times (film), 390
Molotov, Vyacheslav, 228
Monnet, Jean, 495
Mont Pèlerin Society, 614–16, 620, 634
Montreal Accords (1988), 31, 33–34, 36–37, 38, 643, 651
Moore, Gordon, 120
Morichika Unpei, 302
Moriyama Yutaka, 336
Moro, Aldo, 611
Morocco
  migrations and, 183–84
  Pan-Arabism and, 502
  refugees in, 177
  tourism in, 427
Morrison, Steven, 457–58
Mossadeq, Mohammed, 233, 254
Mounier, Emmanuel, 220–21
Mozambique
  civil war in, 206
  decolonization in, 251–52
  Global Realignment Struggle and, 245
  labor movements in, 367–68
  television in, 406
Mugabe, Robert, 354
Mujica, José, 609–10
Munich Olympics terrorist attack (1972), 611
Murdoch, Rupert, 375, 415, 624–25
Musevini, Yoweri, 565–66
Muslim Brotherhood, 484–85, 501–4, 517, 519–20
Mussolini, Benito, 50–51, 408–9, 494, 575–76
My Lai massacre (1968), 246–47
Myanmar
  decolonization in, 232–33
  disease in, 51
  mass murder in, 570–71
  migrations and, 179–80, 197–98
  refugees in, 179–80

Naguib, Mohammed, 484–85
Napoleon Bonaparte, 55, 206–7, 209

al-Nasir, Gamal 'Abd
    Cold War and, 235
    economic development and, 482
    Global Realignment Struggle and, 234, 244–45
    Pan-Arabism and, 502, 503–4
    secularization and, 521–22
    Suez crisis and, 234–35
    Vietnam of, 225–26
National Councils of Women, 329–30
National Organization of Women (NOW), 339
nationalism, 491–510. *See also* Pan-Africanism; Pan-Arabism
    Age of Total War and, 493, 509, 557
    challenges to, 493–501, 509
    Cold War and, 494, 497–98, 507
    communism and, 493–94, 497–98, 506
    constructivism in, 491
    decolonization and, 495–96, 499, 501–2, 586
    development of, 491, 492
    Era of Upheaval and, 497–98
    global order and, 646–47
    globalization and, 500–1, 648–49
    hydraulic model of, 497–98
    internationalism and, 494–95
    Islamism and, 508–9
    Late Millennium Era and, 505–9
    militarism and, 499–500
    pacifism and, 499
    Postwar Era and, 494–96, 648
    primordialism in, 491–92, 497–98, 508, 557
    sovereignty and, 491, 506
    sports competitions and, 499–501
    spread of, 491, 529
    world government and, 494–95
    World War I and, 491
NATO (North Atlantic Treaty Organization), 229, 233, 238, 258–59, 269, 561, 569–70, 618, 633–34
nature. *See* agriculture; disease; environmental impact
Nazi Germany, 216, 242, 413, 530–32, 575–76
Ndadaye, Melchior, 566–67
Nehra, Uma, 329–30
Nehru, Jawaharlal, 138, 234, 329–30, 481, 493, 494, 535–36, 577–78

Nelson, Gaylord, 18
Nepal, tourism in, 423, 430–31
Netherlands
    disease in, 43, 60, 78
    economic development in, 133–34, 639
    environmental impact in, 18
    gender in, 331, 333–34, 344–45
    generational change in, 320–21
    labor movements in, 359
    migrations and, 185, 189
    nationalism in, 508
    transportation in, 94
New Class, The (Djilas), 583, 584–85, 587–88
New International Economic Order, 249, 250–51, 617, 645–46
New Left
    Civil Rights movement and, 595–96
    consumerism and, 448, 449, 450
    environmental impact and, 612
    gender and, 339–40
    human rights and, 612
    utopian movements and, 589, 591–92, 593, 594–97, 609–10
New Zealand
    economic development in, 133–34
    gender in, 323–24, 331, 333–34
    labor movements in, 360
    migrations to, 195
    population growth in, 321
    religion in, 517–18
    television in, 407–8, 415
    transportation in, 92, 94
Ngo Dinh Diem, 220–21, 245–46
Nicaragua
    Cold War and, 256–57, 259–60, 264–65, 551–52
    Contra rebels in, 259–61
    Iran-Contra affair, 260–61
    mass murder in, 551–52
    US involvement in, 259–61, 554
Niebuhr, Reinhold, 511
Nielsen, Arthur Charles, 444
Nietzsche, Friedrich Wilhelm, 482, 542, 617–18
Niger
    disease in, 66–67
    television in, 406, 412
Nigeria
    energy in, 149–50

Nigeria (cont.)
  gender in, 353
  internet access in, 627–28
  privatization in, 455
  religion in, 522–23
  television in, 412
  transportation in, 93–94, 96
1984 (Orwell), 583–84
Nixon, Richard
  Arab-Israeli conflict and, 250–51
  Cold War and, 218, 242, 243, 252–54
  doctrine of, 252–53
  economic development and, 143
  environmental impact and, 19
  southern strategy of, 252–53
  Vietnam War and, 248–49
  Watergate affair and, 248–49
Nkrumah, Kwame, 86, 481, 504–5, 608
North Atlantic Treaty Organization
    (NATO), 229, 233, 238, 258–59, 269,
    561, 569–70, 618, 633–34
North Korea
  Cold War and, 215, 218–20, 221–22
  communism in, 154–55
  consumerism in, 442
  economic development in, 219–20
  founding of, 218–19
  nationalism in, 497–98, 506
  sports competition in, 219–20
Norway
  consumerism in, 471–72
  disease in, 60
  energy in, 150
  gender in, 326, 331, 344–45
  generational change in, 319
  labor movements in, 380
Notting Hill race riots (1958), 182
nuclear weapons
  Age of Interconnection and, 206
  apocalyptic thinking and, 206–8, 211,
    237, 580, 581, 583
  Cold War and, 209, 210, 211, 228, 229,
    230–31, 236–37, 241, 243, 258–60,
    264, 580–81
  Cuban Missile Crisis and, 210, 211–12,
    237–38, 240, 255, 581
  development of, 206–7, 580–81
  environmental impact and, 13–14, 19
  Euromissiles controversy and, 255
  Global Realignment Struggle and,
    240, 252–53

Hiroshima and Nagasaki uses of, 580–81
  linkage in negotiations involving,
    243, 248–50
  negotiations on, 241, 255, 256
  opposition to, 580–81
  radioactivity and, 13–14
  rocketry and, 101–2
  SALT and, 241
  SALT II and, 256
  space travel and, 104
  utopian movements and, 583, 594–95
  World War II and, 206–7
  World War III and, 206–7, 651
Nuremberg laws (1935), 216
Nuremberg trial (1945-46), 531–32,
    533, 536
Nureyev, Rudolf, 210
Nyerere, Julius, 222–23, 272–73, 505, 579

Obama, Barack, 639–40
Oberth, Hermann, 100–1
Obote, Milton, 349, 565–66
Obstfeld, Maurice, 144–45
Oh Sadaharu, 200–1
oil price shocks, 35, 39, 86–87, 90, 143,
    147–49, 150, 151, 166, 223–24, 430,
    436–37, 652–53
Oman
  gender in, 346
  migrations and, 185
Omar, Mullah Mohammed, 632–33
On the Waterfront (film), 389
OPEC (Organization of the Petroleum
    Exporting Countries), 135, 147, 148,
    149, 150–51, 250, 611
Operation Wetback (1954), 181, 193
Orbán, Victor, 623–24
Organization of the Petroleum Exporting
    Countries (OPEC), 135, 147, 148,
    149, 150–51, 250, 611
Orwell, George, 57, 228, 583, 588
Osborn, Fairfield, 16–17, 21
Osorio, Carlos Arana, 552
Ossietzky, Carl von, 42
Osterhammel, Jürgen, 2–3
Osterloh, Bernd, 393
Ottoman Empire, 172–73, 323–24, 480–
    81, 501–2, 530
Our Plundered Planet (Osborn), 16–17

Padmore, George, 481, 504–5, 579

Pakistan
    agriculture in, 110
    creation of, 578
    decolonization in, 174–76, 495–96
    gender in, 352
    Global Realignment Struggle and, 249, 252–53
    human rights in, 253–54
    Islamism in, 255, 262–63, 275
    migrations and, 185–86, 191, 196–97
    television in, 406, 412
    utopian movements in, 589–90
Pal, Radhabinod, 535, 555, 570
Palestine
    decolonization in, 174–76, 231–32
    Global Realignment Struggle and, 249
    Intifada in, 191–92
    Islamism in, 275
    migrations and, 191–92
    partition of, 174–75, 176
    refugees in, 177–78
    right of return to, 177
    terrorism and, 611–12
Palestinian Liberation Organization (PLO), 178, 251, 255, 273, 276, 488
Pan-Africanism
    Congress of, 579
    decline of, 583, 648
    decolonization and, 578–80
    nationalism and, 504–6
    Négritude in, 578–79
    Rastafarianism in, 593
    utopian movements and, 578–79
Pan-Arabism
    challenges of, 503–4
    decline of, 583, 648
    decolonization and, 503–4
    development of, 501–2
    Islamism and, 501–2, 635–36
    nationalism and, 501–6, 508–9
    Ottoman Empire and, 502–3
    revival of, 504
    Suez Crisis and, 502
Park Chung Hee, 161, 219
Parker, Janet, 48–49
Pauker, Anna, 330–31
Paul VI, Pope, 347, 525
Pellegrino, Michele, 524
Pentecostalism, 512, 519, 521, 522–23, 553
Perkins, Francis, 323

Perle, Richard, 264–65
Perón, Eva, 442
Perón, Juan, 137–38, 358, 364–65, 441, 472–73, 496
Peru
    classes in, 300
    disease in, 78
    gender in, 329–30
    migrations and, 169–70
    religion in, 519
Petkov, Nikola, 493–94
Petrov, Stansialv, 259
Philip, Prince, 217, 234
Philippines
    agriculture in, 110
    consumerism in, 470
    environmental impact in, 18, 28
    gender in, 353
    migrations and, 169–70, 191–92, 196–98, 199–200, 201
    television in, 415–17
Picasso, Pablo, 210
Piketty, Thomas, 165–66
Pinochet, Augusto, 321, 619–20
Pinto, Lúcio Flávio, 29–30
Pius IX, Pope, 482–83, 524
Pius XII, Pope, 516–17, 523–24, 575–76
Plaza Accords (1985), 158–59
PLO (Palestinian Liberation Organization), 178, 251, 255, 273, 276, 488
Pol Pot, 545
Poland
    authoritarianism in, 623–24
    Cold War and, 227–28, 236–37, 239, 264–65, 267
    consumerism in, 468
    economic development in, 152, 638–39
    gender in, 342, 348
    human rights in, 612–13
    labor movements in, 359, 362, 380, 386–87
    mass murder in, 532–34
    refugees in, 173–74
    Solidarity movement in, 264–65, 267–68, 380, 527, 612–13, 620–21
    transportation in, 96
    utopian movements in, 596–97
Polk, William, 482
Pompidou, George, 19
Population Bomb, The (Ehrlich), 21, 22, 23, 24

population growth
  Age of Interconnection and, 322
  Age of Total War and, 309–10, 314
  agriculture and, 24, 107, 113
  apocalyptic thinking and, 23
  death rates and, 311–12
  disease and, 54
  economic development and, 22–23, 26, 39, 164–65, 321–22
  education and, 315–16
  energy and, 23, 24
  environmental impact and, 14–15, 16–17, 21, 22–23, 26, 39–40
  Era of Upheaval and, 23, 316, 322
  exponential growth in, 643–44
  fertility rates and, 311f, 311–13, 321, 328, 335, 336, 343–44, 347–48
  gender and, 321–22, 328, 335, 347–48
  generational changes and, 309–14, 312f–13
  global growth rates, 309f–10, 309–10
  Global Realignment Struggle and, 224–25
  inequality and, 165–66
  Late Millennium Era and, 310, 643
  leisure and, 401
  Malthusian ideas concerning, 16–17, 22–24, 39–40
  migrations and, 182–83, 202–3
  overpopulation and, 16–17, 21, 22–24, 39
  Postwar Era and, 16–17, 39
  seniors and, 319–20, 321–22
  television and, 408
  Third World and, 28, 311–12
  World War II and, 16–17
  youth culture and, 313, 316
Porsche, Ferdinand, 94–95
Port Huron Statement (1962), 592, 594, 598–99
Portugal
  economic development in, 639
  gender in, 331
  generational change in, 319
  Global Realignment Struggle and, 251–52
  labor movements in, 377
  migrations and, 170, 183–84, 188, 197–98
  television in, 415–16
  tourism in, 433–34
Postwar Era
  capitalism and, 143–44, 148, 149, 156, 167, 183, 447–48, 495, 616–17
  classes and, 298–99, 302–3
  consumerism and, 439–48, 452, 472–73
  disease and, 41, 44–45, 46–57, 79
  economic development and, 139, 146–47, 165–66, 167
  energy and, 86–87
  environmental impact and, 12–17, 39
  gender and, 323, 332–33
  labor movements and, 358–64, 393–94
  leisure and, 400–2, 435
  long peace of, 207–8
  mass murder and, 531–38
  microelectronics and, 119–20
  nationalism and, 494–96, 648
  population growth and, 16–17, 39
  progress and, 479–80, 481, 487, 489
  religion and, 510–17
  television and, 411, 412, 435
  tourism and, 421–22
  transportation and, 92, 94–95, 100–1
  utopian movements and, 591, 592–93, 614–15
Potsdam Conference (1945), 174, 215–16, 242, 269
Poujade, Robert, 18–19
Prebisch, Raúl, 136–38, 148–49
privatization. See also deregulation
  consumerism and, 439–40, 452, 455–56, 473
  economic development and, 144, 162–63, 166–67, 455–56, 645
  religion and, 522
  telecommunication and, 460–64
  television and, 413–15
  transportation and, 455–60
Professional Air Traffic Controllers Organization (PATCO), 369–70
progress, 477–90
  Age of Total War and, 477–78, 482–83, 485, 529
  capitalism and, 478–80
  Cold War and, 478–79, 480, 489, 645
  communism and, 478–80, 482, 488–89
  critics of, 482–86
  decline of, 489f–90, 489–90, 529
  decolonization and, 481, 488

development of, 477–78
economic development and, 479–80, 486–88
education and, 484
energy and, 488
environmentalism and, 486–88
Era of Upheaval and, 482–83, 486–90, 529
evolution and, 477–78, 479
foreign aid and, 480
gender and, 478–79
globalization and, 482
Islamism and, 484–85, 488
Late Millennium Era and, 482–83, 488, 489–90
modernization and, 479–81, 482, 485–86, 487–88
Postwar Era and, 479–80, 481, 487, 489
racial conflict and, 484
technological development and, 484–85, 487, 489
Third World and, 480–81
traditionalism and, 488, 489
Protestant Evangelicalism, 512–13, 519–23, 529
PTL Club, 414–15
Putin, Vladimir, 528, 623–24, 638–40

Qaddafi, Muammar, 501, 570
al-Qahtani, Mohammed, 522
Qutb, Mohammed, 519–20
Qutb, Sayyid, 484–85, 486, 488, 508–9, 519–20

racial conflict, 187–88, 223–24, 240, 425–26, 484, 518–19
Radcliffe, Cyril, 174–75
Radhakrishnan, S., 578
Radio Corporation of America (RCA), 118–19
Radulovich, Milo, 408–9
Ramey, Valerie, 401–2
Randolph, A. Philip, 579
Rao, P. V. Narasimha, 618–19
Rashtriya Mill Mazdoor Sangh (RMMS), 371–72
Ratzinger, Joseph, 525
Rawbugiri, Mwami, 563
Ražnatović, Željko, 558–59
Reagan, Ronald
  Cold War and, 257–58, 259–60, 263–64, 266–67

deregulation and, 265, 455–56, 616–17
economic development and, 158–59, 265
environmental impact and, 37, 87–88
labor movements and, 370–71, 373
mass murder and, 553–54
progress and, 478, 489
utopian movements and, 648
Refugee Convention (1951), 178–79, 180–81, 193–94
refugees
  backlash to, 180–81
  Cold War and, 179–80
  decolonization and, 174–76, 184
  definition of, 178–79, 180–81
  ethnic conflicts and, 179–80
  human rights and, 180
  international agreements on, 178–79, 180–81
  labor migrations and, 184, 188
  non-refoulement principle for, 178–79
  refugee camps, 178
  religion and, 179–80
  return of, 176
  World War I and, 172–73
  World War II and, 173–75, 180
regulation
  capitalism and, 143–44, 148, 149, 156, 167, 183, 447–48, 495, 616–17
  DDT and, 22
  disease and, 45
  economic development and, 132–35, 144, 148–49, 154–62, 167
  energy and, 135
  environmental impact and, 12–13, 18–19, 20, 24–25, 26–27, 33
  migrations and, 172, 186–88
  reregulation and, 131, 155, 158, 159, 160, 162–64, 462, 465–66, 636, 644
religion, 511–29. *See also* Catholic Church; Evangelical Protestantism; Islamism; Pentecostalism
  animism and, 520
  anti-clericalism and, 513–14
  apocalyptic thinking and, 512, 519, 522
  challenges to, 510
  Cold War and, 514, 516
  communism and, 514–17, 521–22, 527–28

religion (*cont.*)
  conversion and, 519
  decline in, 517–18, 525–26, 529
  decolonization and, 513–14, 518–19
  disease and, 71
  economic development and, 518
  energy and, 522
  Era of Upheaval and, 510, 517–23
  gender and, 518, 521–22, 526
  globalization and, 509, 521–22, 648–49
  integralism and, 511, 512, 519–24, 526, 648–49
  Late Millennium Era and, 511, 521–23, 526–29
  liberation theology and, 511, 518, 521, 524, 525
  megachurches and, 519
  missionaries and, 513–14
  modernism and, 511–12, 514, 518–19, 520–21, 523–25, 526, 529
  political dimensions of, 514–15
  Postwar Era and, 510–17
  privatization and, 522
  prosperity Gospel and, 522–23
  racial conflict and, 518–19
  refugees and, 179–80
  revivals of, 519, 521–23, 528, 529
  science and, 520
  secularization and, 510, 511, 513, 518–19, 521–22, 527–28
  technological development and, 521
Republic of Congo, television in, 412
reregulation, 155, 158, 159, 160, 162–64, 462, 465–66, 636, 644
Rice, Condoleezza, 633
rights. *See* human rights
Ríos Montt, Efraim, 552–55
Road to Serfdom, The (Hayek), 615
Road to Survival, The (Vogt), 16–17
Robeson, Paul, 573
Robinson, John, 518–19
Rockefeller, John D., III, 423
Rockefeller, Nelson, 478
rocketry, 100–2, 106–7
Roe v. Wade (1973), 341–42
Rohingyas, 179–80, 570–71
Romania
  classes in, 299–300
  Cold War and, 227–28, 269
  consumerism in, 468
  economic development in, 152
  energy in, 151
  gender in, 330–31, 342
  labor movements in, 378–79, 380
  migrations and, 170, 191–92
  nationalism in, 498, 506
  tourism in, 425
Rome, Harold, 573
Roosevelt, Franklin D., 227–28, 233, 408–9
Roosevelt, Franklin D., Jr., 42
Rostow, Walter, 479–80, 482, 487
Rotermund, Beate, 337
RPF (Rwandan Patriotic Front), 565–67, 568–70
Rugova, Ibrahim, 560–61
Russell, Bertrand, 564
Russia
  authoritarianism in, 623–24
  civil war in, 172–73
  economic development in, 163, 638–39
  labor movements in, 380
  migrations and, 197–98
  refugees in, 172–73
  religion in, 528
  space travel in, 106–7
  television in, 415–16
  transition from USSR in, 274, 621–23
Russian Empire, 170, 172–73
Rwanda
  authoritarian rule in, 564–66
  colonial rule of, 563–64
  coup in, 564–65
  decolonization in, 563–64
  disease in, 46
  economic development in, 565, 566
  environmental impact in, 11
  Global Realignment Struggle and, 272–73
  international criminal tribunal for, 568–69
  mass murder in, 179–80, 273–74, 562–69
  Pan-Africanism and, 237
  refugees in, 179–80, 565–66, 567–68
  religion in, 563–64, 567
  UN involvement in, 568
Rwandan Democratic Movement (MDR), 566, 567

Rwandan Patriotic Front (RPF), 565–67, 568–70

Sachs, Jeffrey, 619–20
Sadat, Anwar, 148–49, 251, 503–4
al-Sa'id, Nuri, 502–3
Sakai Toshihiko, 302
Sakharov, Andrei, 480
Salafism, 512, 513, 519–21, 522–23, 529
SALT (Strategic Arms Limitation Talks) (1972), 241
SALT II (Strategic Arms Limitation Talks) (1972-79), 256
Samant, Datta, 372–73
same-sex relations, 325–27, 328–29, 333, 340–41, 353–55
Sanger, Margaret, 340
Santa Barbara oil spill (1969), 19–20
Sartre, Jean-Paul, 210, 494
satellites, 101–2, 105–7, 236, 414–15, 417
Saud, Muhammad ibn, 511–12
Saudi Arabia
    consumerism in, 470
    energy in, 83, 135
    gender in, 346
    Islamism in, 275, 276, 502–3, 511, 517, 519–20, 521
    migrations and, 185, 191
    Pan-Arabism and, 501–3
Sauvy, Alfred, 224–25
Scargill, Arthur, 373–75
Schalck-Golodkowski, Alexander, 152
Scheer, Robert, 258
Schlesinger, James, 87
Schleyer, Hans-Joachim, 611
Schmidt, Helmut, 256, 609
Scholes, Myron, 163
Schopenhauer, Arthur, 482
Schottky, Walter, 116–17
Schroeder, Gerd, 618–19
Schwarz, Fred, 489
SDS (Students for a Democratic Society), 592, 595, 610–11
secularization, 510, 511, 513, 518–19, 521–22, 527–28
Seitz, Frederick, 38
Selassie, Haile, 593, 594–95
self-actualization, 592–93, 597, 598, 606, 610–11, 612

self-determination, 222–23, 232, 242–43, 491, 506–7, 579–80, 651
Senegal
    decolonization in, 361
    disease in, 77
    migrations and, 184, 197–98
    television in, 412
    utopian movements in, 578–79, 608–9, 611
Senghor, Léopold, 578–79, 608–9
seniors, 318–22
    economic development and, 319–20, 321–22
    Era of Upheaval and, 319–20
    population growth and, 319–20, 321–22
    poverty among, 319–20
    retirement of, 318–19
    social programs for, 318–19, 320–21
    tourism and, 319–20
    World War II and, 318
September 11th attacks
    as blowback for US policies, 209–10, 265, 624–25
    impact of, 624, 632–33
    international support following, 624
    utopian movements and, 624–25
Serbia
    economic development in, 556
    ethnic cleansing in, 559
    Kosovo and, 560–62
    mass murder in, 557, 559, 560–62
    refugees in, 561–62
sexual revolution, 324–25, 332–33, 336–39, 340–41, 342–43, 348, 429–30, 518, 519, 521–22
Shevardnadze, Eduard, 266
Shockley, William, 116–17
Shultz, George, 144
Šik, Ota, 140
Silent Spring (Carson), 21–22, 39–40, 53
Singapore
    environmental impact in, 28
    labor movements in, 368
    microelectronics in, 121
    migrations and, 169–70
    television in, 415–16
    tourism in, 425, 434
Singer, S. Fred, 38
Situationists, 448, 591, 593

Slovakia
  Cold War and, 227–28
  creation of, 506
  economic development in, 638–39
  migrations and, 171
  television in, 415–16
Slovenia, mass murder in, 556, 558, 559
Smuts, Jan, 223, 574
Solow, Robert, 119–20
Somalia
  civil war in, 568
  Cold War and, 210–11
  communist revolution in, 257
  economic development in, 160–61
  Global Realignment Struggle and, 249
  refugees in, 179–80
  US involvement in, 568
Soros, George, 159–60
South Africa
  apartheid regime removed in, 271–72, 574
  classes in, 301–2, 307
  Cold War and, 259–60, 271–72
  consumerism in, 451
  disease in, 74–75
  economic development in, 162–63
  energy in, 87
  Global Realignment Struggle and, 252–53
  human rights in, 253–54
  labor movements in, 359–60, 382–83
  television in, 412
  transportation in, 93–94
South Korea
  Cold War and, 209, 215, 218–20, 221–22
  consumerism in, 467, 470
  economic development in, 139, 160–62, 219–20, 629
  environmental impact in, 18–19, 30
  founding of, 218–19
  gender in, 346
  generational change in, 319
  internet access in, 627–28
  labor movements in, 368, 383
  microelectronics in, 121
  migrations and, 200–1
  refugees in, 179
  religion in, 519
  stagnation of, 473

  television in, 415–17
  tourism in, 425, 428
  transportation in, 93–94, 95–96
South Sudan, refugees in, 179–80
Soviet Union. *See* USSR
space exploration, 4, 102, 103–5, 125
Spain
  anti-fascism in, 594
  economic development in, 639
  gender in, 340–41
  generational change in, 319
  labor movements in, 362, 377, 384
  migrations and, 170, 183–84, 188, 197–98
  nationalism in, 508
  television in, 415–16
  tourism in, 421–22, 427
Spencer, Herbert, 477–78
Spengler, Oswald, 482
sports competitions, 217, 218, 219–20, 257, 500–1, 649
Sputnik satellite (1957), 101–2, 131, 236
Srebrenica mass murder, 560
Stalin, Josef, 140, 226–27, 228, 229–31, 239, 243, 257, 541–42
Stevenson, Adlai, 478
Stewart, William H., 46
Stockholm Peace Appeal (1950), 580
Strauss, Lewis L., 85
Straw, Jack, 610
strikes, 357–58, 364–66, 369–75, 383–86, 384f–85
Students for a Democratic Society (SDS), 592, 595, 610–11
Study of History, A (Toynbee), 482
Sudan
  Darfur region in, 570
  disease in, 46
  gender in, 354–55
  Islamism in, 255, 275
  labor movements in, 359–60
  mass murder in, 570
  refugees in, 179–80
  terrorism in, 276
Suez Crisis (1956), 234–35, 250–51, 261–62, 502
Suharto, Mohamed, 547, 548
Sukarno, 234, 247–48, 546–47, 548, 549, 550
Summers, Larry, 619–20

Sun Yat-Sen, 480–81
Swaminathan, Monkumbu Sambasivan, 112
Sweden
    consumerism in, 444, 460
    disease in, 71
    economic development in, 154, 159–60, 639
    environmental impact in, 18–19
    gender in, 350–51
    labor movements in, 366, 380, 384
    migrations and, 189, 190, 204
Sweeney, John, 383–84
Switzerland
    consumerism in, 444, 447, 472
    disease in, 56, 57
    economic development in, 133–34
    generational change in, 319
    migrations and, 183–84, 185, 186
Sygman Rhee, 219, 220–21
Syria
    civil war in, 528
    Global Realignment Struggle and, 244, 245, 251
    Islamism in, 512, 519–20
    mass murder in, 570–71
    Pan-Arabism and, 502–4
    refugees in, 177, 179–80, 183–84, 191

Taiwan
    Cold War and, 215, 217–18, 221–22
    economic development in, 161–62, 629
    environmental impact in, 30
    gender in, 351–52
    generational change in, 319
    labor movements in, 368
    microelectronics in, 121
    tourism in, 425
    transportation in, 93–94
Takeyuki Tsuda, 200
Tanzania
    decolonization in, 222–23
    education in, 315–16
    gender in, 317
    Global Realignment Struggle and, 245
    labor movements in, 367–68
    Pan-Africanism in, 505
    youth culture in, 317
technological development. See also the Internet; microelectronics; telecommunication; television

Age of Interconnection and, 82–83, 100, 115–16, 121–22
Age of Total War and, 82–83, 87, 96–97, 125, 333
agriculture and, 12, 107–10, 112, 113–14
consumerism and, 438
economic development and, 132, 140, 166
energy and, 83, 87
inequality and, 82, 111
leisure and, 401–2
progress and, 484–85, 487, 489
religion and, 521
television and, 405–6
Third World and, 82
transportation and, 91, 94–96, 105
youth culture and, 316–17
telecommunication
    cell phones, 105–6, 406–7, 452, 464–66, 473, 627–28
    continuing trends in, 627–28
    deregulation and, 132–33, 413–14, 456, 460–66, 473
    GPS in, 4, 105–6, 396–97
    Late-Millennium Era and, 628
    microelectronics and, 123–24, 125
    privatization and, 460–64
    satellites and, 414
    wireless technology in, 464–66
television, 405–17
    Age of Interconnection and, 405, 434
    broadcasts on, 407–8
    cable television, 414–15, 417
    channel options on, 413, 414–15
    communism and, 408–9
    critics of, 408
    deregulation and, 413–15
    Era of Upheaval and, 435
    game shows on, 416
    global village of, 410, 412, 413, 417
    globalization and, 410–17, 435, 648–49
    Internet and, 417
    Late Millennium Era and, 410, 413–14, 415, 417
    mergers and acquisitions in, 415, 417
    miniseries on, 413
    national character of, 416–17
    political influence of, 408–9
    population growth and, 408

television (cont.)
  Postwar Era and, 411, 412, 435
  privatization and, 413–15
  public television, 412
  satellite television and, 414–15, 417
  sitcoms on, 416
  soap operas on, 415–16
  spread of, 406–7, 411–13*t*
  state-run television, 412
  technological development and, 405–6
  transmission of reality and, 407–8
  24-hour cable news on, 414
Tenge Kenzō, 499
Tennessee Valley Authority, 51
terrorism. *See also* September 11th attacks
  decolonization and, 251
  Global Realignment Struggle and, 251, 255, 276–77
  globalization and, 611–12
  Islamism and, 255, 275–77, 488
  Munich Olympics attack, 611
  utopian movements and, 611–12
Thailand
  consumerism in, 470
  disease in, 75–76
  economic development in, 161–63, 202
  labor movements in, 378–79
  migrations and, 169–70, 191–92, 202
  tourism in, 425, 428–29, 434
Thatcher, Margaret
  Cold War and, 257–58, 259–60, 262, 263–64, 266–67, 269–70
  deregulation and, 156, 455–56
  economic development and, 150, 265
  gender and, 349
  labor movements and, 373–75, 389–90
  privatization and, 455–56, 616–17
Therborn, Göran, 324
Third World. *See also* decolonization and anti-imperialism
  agriculture and, 110
  capitalism and, 27
  Cold War and, 224–26, 260, 645–46
  creation of, 224–26
  disease and, 47–48, 57, 63–64, 66–67, 74–75, 78, 80–81
  economic development and, 28, 136–37, 138–39, 150–51
  environmental impact and, 27–29, 33
  gender and, 342–43

  Global Realignment Struggle and, 224–26, 233–34, 240, 245
  globalization and, 27–28
  inequality and, 224
  population growth and, 28, 311–12
  progress and, 480–81
  technological development and, 82
  Third Way and, 136–37, 225, 620, 645–46
  third worldism, 593–95
  tourism and, 433
  transportation and, 93–94
  utopian movements and, 592, 593–98, 599–600, 611–13
Thousands Cheer (film), 573
Three Mile Island (1979), 19–20, 85–86, 89–90
Tibet, Chinese rule in, 179, 423
Tito, Josip, 555–56, 584
Tlatelolco Massacre (1968), 598
Togo, television in, 406
Tokyo military tribunal, 531–32, 535
Tolkien, J. R. R., 483–84, 485, 486, 487
Toronto Conference (1987), 34
Torrey Canyon tanker disaster (1967), 19–20
total war. *See* Age of Total War
Touré, Sékou, 361, 367, 579, 608
tourism, 418–35
  Age of Interconnection and, 431
  authenticity and, 418–19, 432–33
  backpackers in, 422–23
  bargain travelers in, 422
  classes and, 432–33, 434
  communism and, 423–24, 434–35
  criticism of tourists and, 418–19, 432
  development of, 419–20, 421–22
  economic development and, 419, 425–26
  ecotourism, 428, 430
  enclosed experiences and, 427–28
  Era of Upheaval and, 421–22, 435
  frequently and length of, 433–34
  gay sex tourism and, 429
  gender and, 421, 428–29
  globalization and, 418–19, 422, 425
  international tourist arrivals and, 431*f*, 431–33
  Late Millennium Era and, 425–26, 427–28, 429, 430, 431–35
  packages of, 422, 426

political dimensions of, 420
Postwar Era and, 421–22
racial conflict and, 425–26
seniors and, 319–20
sex tourism, 428–30
Third World and, 433
transportation and, 420–22, 425
travel agents and, 427
trekking in, 428, 430
vacation time and, 403–4
World War II and, 420–21
Toynbee, Arnold, 482
transportation, 91–107
Age of Interconnection and, 91, 100
Age of Total War and, 94–95, 96–97, 100
air travel, 4, 96–100, 97f–98, 369–71, 393–96, 421–22, 456–60, 456f, 457f
automobiles, 4, 12, 24–25, 83, 91–99, 91t, 96f, 96t, 411–12, 411t–12
Cold War and, 100, 101–4
consumerism and, 438–40, 442, 451, 452–53, 456–60
economic development and, 94–95
environmental impact and, 12, 24–25
Era of Upheaval and, 96
fuel-efficiency and, 95–96
labor movements and, 366, 368–71, 382, 390–96
Postwar Era and, 92, 94–95, 100–1
privatization and, 455–60
rocketry, 100–2, 106–7
space travel and, 100–6
technological development and, 91, 94–96, 105
Third World and, 93–94
tourism and, 420–22, 425
Tricontinental Congress (1966), 600
Tricontinental Congress (1967), 225, 245
Trotsky, Leon, 584–85
Truman, Harry, 220, 228, 230–31, 480
Tsiolkovsky, Konstantin, 100–1, 103–4
Tudjman, Franjo, 556, 562
Tunisia, tourism in, 427
al-Turabi, Hasan, 276
Turkey
Cold War and, 228, 237
consumerism in, 470
economic development in, 137
environmental impact in, 18

gender in, 323–24
Global Realignment Struggle and, 234
migrations and, 183–84
progress in, 480–81
refugees in, 172–73
tourism in, 427
transportation in, 93–94
Turner, Ted, 414
TV. *See* television

UAE. *See* United Arab Emirates
Uganda
disease in, 77
environmental impact in, 18
gender in, 317, 329–30, 349, 354
Global Realignment Struggle and, 272–73
refugees in, 179–80, 564, 565–66
religion in, 354
television in, 406
Ukraine
Chernobyl nuclear disaster in, 19–20, 85–86, 89–90, 488
Cold War and, 270
creation of, 270
economic development in, 380, 638–39
labor movements in, 361–62, 380
nationalism in, 493–94, 498–99
refugees in, 174
Ulbricht, Walter, 590, 601–2
UNESCO (United Nations Economic, Social and Cultural Organization), 17, 18–19, 346, 416–17, 648–49
UNHCR (United Nations High Commission on Refugees), 178–79
Union of Soviet Socialist Republics. *See* USSR
unions, 358, 360–64, 365–68, 370, 373, 378–84, 379f, 386–87
United Arab Emirates (UAE)
energy in, 147
gender in, 346
migrations and, 185
United Kingdom
Brexit referendum in, 508, 644
classes in, 298–99
consumerism in, 446, 447, 454–55, 472
decolonization and, 182–83, 184, 232
deregulation in, 455–56, 461, 463
disease in, 43, 48–49, 56, 65–66, 68

790 | INDEX

United Kingdom (cont.)
  economic development in, 136, 141–42, 145–46, 154, 159–60, 639
  energy in, 85–86, 147, 150
  environmental impact in, 19
  Falklands War and, 258
  gender in, 323–24, 326, 333–34, 341
  generational change in, 320–21
  labor movements in, 359, 361, 364–66, 369, 373–75, 384, 388, 389–90
  migrations and, 182, 184, 188, 197–98
  nationalism in, 494, 508
  New Commonwealth and, 182, 184, 232
  population growth in, 24
  privatization in, 455–56
  refugees in, 174–75
  religion in, 513, 517–18
  Suez Crisis and, 234–35, 250–51, 261–62, 502
  television in, 405–6, 412, 416
  tourism in, 420
  transportation in, 92, 98–100
  utopian movements in, 610
United Nations (UN)
  Cold War and, 223, 574–75, 581
  decolonization and, 175, 223
  disease and, 44–45, 52–54
  energy and, 83–84, 83f–84
  environmental impact and, 18–19, 34
  founding of, 573–74
  gender and, 342–43, 347–48
  genocide and, 536, 537
  global governance and, 573–75, 581–82, 651
  Global Realignment Struggle and, 223, 249–50
  human rights and, 579–80
  Korean War approval of, 581
  mass murder and, 530, 531–32, 559–60, 570
  migrations and, 202
  New International Information Order and, 249, 250–51
  peacekeeping efforts of, 559–60, 568, 569–70
  progress and, 477–78
  refugees and, 178–79
  sovereignty and, 574–75
  tourism and, 419
  UNESCO of, 17, 18–19, 346, 416–17, 648–49
  UNHCR of, 178–79
  UNRWA of, 178–79
  utopian movements and, 573–74
  war crimes trials and, 531–32
United States. See also Cold War; Vietnam War
  Afghanistan involvement of, 206, 209–10, 262–63, 632–33
  agriculture in, 110–11, 112
  Arab-Israeli conflict involvement of, 251
  Balkans involvement of, 560, 561
  challenges to global order of, 624–25, 632–40, 641–47
  Civil Rights movement in, 595–96
  classes in, 299–300, 303, 305–6
  consumerism in, 439, 440, 443–47, 452, 454–55, 470, 471, 472–73
  decolonization and, 233
  deregulation in, 456, 460–62
  disease in, 43, 44, 51, 56, 60, 63, 65f–66, 65–66, 68, 74, 80–81
  economic development in, 129, 132, 133–34, 136, 142–43, 154, 158–59, 630, 636–38
  education in, 315
  energy in, 84–85, 135
  environmental impact in, 16, 18–19, 25–26, 37
  gender in, 323–24, 325, 331–32, 333–34, 337–38, 341–42, 345, 346–47
  generational change in, 318
  Global Realignment Struggle and, 233–34, 244, 245–46, 249–50, 252–54, 273–75
  human rights and, 253–54, 274, 554
  inequality in, 453
  Iran-Contra affair of, 260–61
  Iraq War of, 264–65, 632–36
  Islamism and, 263, 274–75
  labor movements in, 358, 362–63, 365–66, 369–71, 375, 376–77, 378, 379–80, 383–84, 387, 389–90, 394, 456
  leisure in, 402, 403–4
  Marshall Plan of, 212, 229, 233
  mass murder and, 532–33, 549, 553–54, 560
  McCarthyism in, 208–9
  migrations and, 169–70, 171–72, 181, 187–88, 192–97, 195f–96, 203f, 203–4, 306, 627
  military-industrial complex in, 212

nationalism in, 494, 496, 499
nuclear weapons and, 211–12, 580–81
population growth in, 24, 203f, 203–4, 321
privatization in, 460–64
progress in, 478, 484, 487
racial conflict in, 187–88, 484, 595–96
refugees in, 177, 193–94
regulation in, 18–19, 132, 187
religion in, 511, 513, 516, 517–18, 526–27
Sino-American rapprochement of, 241, 252–53
space exploration and, 106–7
sports competitions and, 500
Strategic Defense Initiative in, 258
telecommunication in, 460–64
television in, 405–6, 410, 412, 415, 416
tourism in, 420–21, 432–34
transportation in, 92, 94, 96, 97–100, 101–2, 456
utopian movements in, 595–96, 610–11, 613–14
Universal Declaration of Human Rights (UN) (1948), 579–80
upheaval. See Era of Upheaval
Uruguay
  economic development in, 319
  education in, 315–16
  gender in, 323–24, 329–30
  generational change in, 319
  television in, 405–6
  utopian movements in, 594–95, 599, 609–10
USSR (Union of Soviet Socialist Republics). See also Cold War
  Afghanistan War of, 179, 209–11, 256–57, 262–63, 273–74
  agriculture in, 110–11, 131–32, 541–42
  Arab-Israeli conflict involvement of, 251
  Berlin Crisis and, 236
  consumerism in, 441, 449–50, 467–68, 470
  de-Stalinization in, 231, 239–40
  disease in, 43, 48–49, 52–53, 60, 74–75
  economic development in, 130–31, 139, 140–41, 151, 152–53, 156–57, 165, 266, 541–42
  ending of, 266–69, 270, 276–77
  energy in, 84–85, 86, 151

environmental impact in, 16, 26
gender in, 331, 342, 345
glasnost in, 266
Global Realignment Struggle and, 243–44, 245, 251
Great Famine in, 140
human rights in, 253
Jewish population of, 251, 253
market reforms in, 156–57
mass murder in, 532–33, 538, 541–42
migrations and, 197–98
nationalism in, 493–94, 497–99, 557–58
nuclear weapons and, 211–12, 580–81
perestroika in, 266
progress in, 478–79, 485
proxy wars and, 209–10
purges in, 229–30
refugees in, 173–74, 179
religion in, 514, 516, 528
Sino-Russian split of, 239–41
space exploration and, 106–7
television in, 405–6, 434–35
tourism in, 420, 423–25
transportation in, 92–93, 96, 98–100, 101–2
utopian movements
  Age of Total War and, 583–84, 590, 591, 592, 594
  anti-Americanism and, 595
  anti-fascism and, 578–79, 592, 594, 605, 645
  apocalyptic thinking and, 576, 577, 580, 583, 586
  capitalism and, 576, 617–19, 620
  Civil Rights movement and, 595–96
  communism and, 576–77, 582, 584–85, 594, 602, 610–11, 619–20
  consumerism and, 582, 593, 597
  decolonization and, 577–80, 583, 586–88, 592, 593–94, 595, 612–13
  democratization and, 575–76, 582
  deregulation and, 613–20, 637–39
  developments in, 591–92
  disillusion with, 581–88
  end of history and, 617–19
  Era of Upheaval and, 589–91, 596–97, 599, 601, 609–13
  gender and, 612

utopian movements (*cont.*)
  global governance and, 573–76, 580, 581–82, 592, 648, 649–51
  global sixties and, 589–92
  globalization and, 598–600, 611–12, 613–14, 617, 648–49
  human rights and, 612–13, 651
  inequality and, 589, 613–14
  influence of, 609–13
  Late Millennium Era and, 613–25
  libertarianism and, 615–16
  neoliberalism and, 615–17
  New Left and, 589, 591–92, 593, 594–97, 609–10
  NGOs and, 612
  nuclear weapons and, 583, 594–95
  participation in, 124, 592–93, 597, 601, 610–11
  Postwar Era and, 591, 592–93, 614–15
  Rastafarianism and, 593
  self-actualization in, 592–93, 597, 598, 606, 610–11, 612
  status quo and, 593
  student unrest and, 588–600
  terrorism and, 611–12
  Third World and, 592, 593–98, 599–600, 611–13
  youth culture and, 592, 593, 612

vacation. *See* tourism
vaccines, 41–42, 44–45, 47, 48, 56–57, 59–60
Védrine, Hubert, 273–74, 618
Venezuela
  energy in, 83, 135, 149
  environmental impact in, 18–19, 30
  generational change in, 319, 321
  migrations and, 172
  transportation in, 93–94
Vester, Michael, 598–99
Vietnam
  decolonization in, 179–80, 206, 233
  economic development in, 142, 156–57, 166–67
  environmental impact in, 18
  Global Realignment Struggle and, 245, 247–49
  labor movements in, 378–79
  migrations and, 169–70
  nationalism in, 497–98, 506
  refugees in, 179
  television in, 415–16
  World War II and, 220–21
Vietnam War
  Age of Total War and, 247, 248–49
  causes of, 247–48
  Cold War and, 207, 209–11, 215, 220–22, 240–41, 247–49
  domino theory and, 247
  ending of, 248–49
  My Lai massacre in, 246–47
  opposition to, 448–49, 588, 591, 594–95, 598, 599–600
  repercussions of, 249–50
  stages of, 246–47
  strategy in, 247
  Third World and, 594–95
Villach Conference (1985), 34
Vine, Jacob, 137
Vo Nguyen Giap, 247
Vogt, William, 16–17, 21
Volksii, Dimitrii, 265
Voyager, 105

Waddilove, Joshua, 446
al-Wahhab, Muhammad Ibn 'Abd, 511–12
Wahhabism, 511–12, 519–20
Waksman, Selman, 57
Walesa, Lech, 268
Wallace, Henry A., 108–9
Wang Hongwen, 603
war crimes, 531–32, 533, 536, 561
Warsaw Pact, 211–12, 222, 231, 236, 258–59, 266–67
Washington Consensus, 157–58, 163–64, 545–46, 618, 639
Watson, Thomas J., Jr., 119
Weathermen, 598–99, 611
Weber, Helene, 323
Weber, Max, 298–99, 510
Wesley, John, 512
White, Harry Dexter, 136
WHO. *See* World Health Organization
Williamson, John, 154–55, 157–58
Wilson, Woodrow, 253, 491
Wim Kok, 618–19
Winston, Clifford, 457–58
Wojtyła, Karol, 525
Wolfowitz, Paul, 264–65, 633
women. *See* gender
World Bank, 36–37, 135, 222–23, 307–8, 377–78, 616–17, 620
World Federation of Trade Unions, 363

World Health Organization (WHO)
    antibiotics and, 44, 71–72
    global obesity epidemic and, 66, 66t
    HIV/AIDS and, 77
    Malaria Eradication Program of, 49, 52, 54–55, 79
    smoking and, 60, 61f
    tuberculosis and, 57
    vaccination campaigns of, 44–45, 48
World Peace Council, 210
World War I
    disease and, 47, 50–51, 56
    economic development and, 143, 154
    labor movements and, 389
    migrations and, 172, 192–93
    nationalism and, 491
    refugees and, 172–73
World War II
    Cold War and, 209, 212–15, 227–29, 241–42, 266, 269
    disease and, 43–44, 49, 51–52, 58–59, 79
    economic development and, 129–30, 136
    Global Realignment Struggle and, 231–32
    legal end of, 242
    mass murder and, 530–31, 533–34, 556–57, 569
    microelectronics and, 116–17, 118
    population growth and, 16–17
    refugees and, 173–75, 180
    seniors and, 318
    tourism and, 420–21
World War III, 206–8, 230–31, 485–86
Wormald, Patrick, 491
Wretched of the Earth, The (Fanon), 583, 586–88, 596

Xi Jinping, 303, 628, 631, 639–40
Xiaojian Zhao, 202

Yalta Conference (1945), 174, 215–16, 242, 269
Yasuhiro Nakasone, 257–58
Yemen
    civil war in, 206
    environmental impact in, 24
    Islamism in, 262–63, 512
    migrations and, 191
    Pan-Arabism and, 503–4
    refugees in, 177
Yom Kippur War (1973), 250–51
Young, Henry, 85–86

youth culture, 314–18
    Age of Total War and, 314
    conservative backlash to, 317
    consumerism and, 316–17, 436–37, 449, 451
    decolonization and, 314, 317
    economic development and, 316–18
    education and, 315–16
    gender and, 317, 332–33, 336–37, 338–39, 344
    juvenile delinquents and, 314
    population growth and, 313, 316
    technological development and, 316–17
    utopian movements and, 592, 593, 612
Yuan Lonping, 110–11
Yugoslavia
    communism in, 584–85
    division of, 506, 556–57
    International Criminal Tribunal for, 559–60, 562
    JNA in, 558–60
    mass murder in, 531–32, 536–37, 555–62
    migrations and, 197–98
    nationalism in, 557–58
    refugees in, 179
    tourism in, 427
    transportation in, 96
    World War II and, 556–57
Yunxiang Yan, 351–52

Zaire. *See* Democratic Republic of Congo (DRC)
Zambia
    consumerism and, 469
    decolonization in, 481
    disease in, 74–75, 76
    education in, 346–47
    gender in, 346–47
    labor movements in, 367–68, 382–83
    progress in, 481
    television in, 406
al-Zawahiri, Ayman, 263, 276
Zhang Chunqiao, 603
Zhdanov, Andrei, 228
Zhou Enlai, 234, 240–41, 541, 549
Zimbabwe
    classes in, 300
    disease in, 74–75
    gender in, 353, 354
    labor movements in, 359–60
    religion in, 521
Zworykin, Vladimir, 405